The Rise and Fall of
Jim Crow

"SICH A GETTING UP STAIRS".

A GENOOINE YANKEE AND PARTIKLAR HANDSOME

SONG

Sung by

Mr T. D. RICE.

Ent. Sta. Hall

Price 1·6

London, Jefferys & Cº 31 Frith Street Soho.

Where may be had the BEST editions

OF JIM CROW, AND "COAL BLACK ROSE."

AND ALSO

THE NEW NIGGER QUADRILLES, 2·6.

The Rise and Fall of Jim Crow

Richard Wormser

St. Martin's Griffin   New York

www.stmartins.com

Book design by James Sinclair

Library of Congress Cataloging-in-Publication Data
Wormser, Richard, 1933–
    The rise and fall of Jim Crow / Richard Wormser.—1st ed.
       p. cm.
    Includes bibliographical references (p. 187) and index (p. 195).
    ISBN 0-312-31324-1 (hc)
    ISBN 0-312-31326-8 (pbk)
    1. African Americas—Segregation—History. 2. African Americans—Segregation—History—Sources. 3. African Americans—Civil rights—History. 4. United States—Race relations. 5. United States—Race relations—Sources. I. Rise and fall of Jim Crow (Television program) II. Title

E185.61 .W935 2003
323.1'96073'009—dc21
                                            2002036876

First St. Martin's Griffin Edition: February 2004

10 9 8 7 6 5 4 3 2 1

To Annie

Pour le bel aujourd'hui

CONTENTS

Acknowledgments   ix

Introduction   xi

Chapter 1   The Promise of Freedom, 1865–1877   1

Chapter 2   Promises Betrayed, 1880–1890   19

Chapter 3   New Roads Taken, 1880–1890   43

Chapter 4   "Jim Crow Comes to Town," 1890–1896   63

Chapter 5   Victories and Defeats, 1897–1900   79

Chapter 6   The Worst of Times, 1900–1917   103

Chapter 7   Prelude to Change: Between Two Wars, 1918–1931   125

Chapter 8   Center Stage for Civil Rights, 1932–1944   145

Chapter 9   The Breakthrough, 1945–1954   165

Epilogue   1954–   183

Bibliography   187

List of Credits   193

Index   195

ACKNOWLEDGMENTS

I would like to thank Dr. Pat Sullivan for reading and critiquing the manuscript; my editor, Diane Reverand, for her support and belief in the project; my agents, Barbara Lowenstein and Madeleine Morel; my colleagues Bill Jersey and Sam Pollard; Ed Breslin for his editing skills; and WNET/Thirteen for helping make the series possible. I am also grateful to all the scholars without whose help the film series upon which this book is based would not have been possible. And especially those men and women I was privileged to interview and who shared with me their stories of tragedy and triumph in the age of Jim Crow.

INTRODUCTION

First on de heel tap, den on the toe
Every time I wheel about I jump Jim Crow
Wheel about, and turn about en do j's so.
And every time I wheel about, I jump Jim Crow.

In 1828, Jim Crow was born. He began his strange career as a minstrel caricature of a black man created by a white man, Thomas "Daddy" Rice, to amuse white audiences. By the 1880s, Jim Crow had become synonymous with a complex system of racial laws and customs in the South that ensured white social, legal, and political domination of blacks. Blacks were segregated, deprived of their right to vote, and subjected to verbal abuse, discrimination, and violence without redress in the courts or support by the white community.

It was in the North that the first Jim Crow laws were passed. Blacks in the North were prohibited from voting in all but five New England states. Schools and public accommodations were segregated. Illinois and Oregon barred blacks from entering the state. Blacks in every Northern city were restricted to ghettoes in the most unsanitary and run-down areas and forced to take menial jobs that white men rejected. White supremacy was as much a part of the Democratic Party in the North as it was in the South.

Northern racial barriers slowly fell after the Civil War. In 1863, California permitted blacks to testify in criminal cases for the first time. Illinois repealed its laws barring blacks from entering, serving on juries, or testifying in court. New York City, San Francisco, Cleveland, and Cincinnati all desegregated their streetcars during the war. Philadelphia followed two years after the war ended. As Northern states repealed some of the more discriminatory legislation against Jim Crow, socially, if not legally, Jim Crow remained in effect. With a few exceptions, blacks for the most part were not allowed to eat in the same restaurants, sleep in the same hotels, or swim at the same beaches as whites. Schools were usually segregated, as were many public events. Most Northern whites shared with Southern whites the belief in the innate superiority of the white "race" over the black.

As punitive and prejudicial as Jim Crow laws were in the North, they never reached the intensity of oppression and degree of violence and sadism that they did in the South. A black person could not swim in the same pool, sit in the same public park, bowl, play pool or, in some states, checkers, drink from the same water fountain or use the same bathroom, marry, be treated in the same hospital, use the same schoolbooks, play baseball with, ride in the same taxicab, sit in the same section of a bus or train, be admitted to any private or public institution, teach in the same school, read in the same library, attend the same theater, or sit in the same area with a white person. Blacks had to address white people as Mr., Mrs., or "Mizz," "Boss," or "Captain" while they, in turn, were called by their first name, or by terms used to indicate social inferiority—"boy," "aunty," or "uncle." Black people, if allowed in a store patronized by whites, had to wait until all white customers were served first. If they attended a movie, they had to sit in the balcony; if they went to a circus, they had to buy tickets at a separate window and sit in a separate section. They had to give way to whites on a sidewalk, remove their hats as a sign of respect when encountering whites, and enter a white person's house by the back door. Whites, on the other hand, could enter a black person's house without knocking, sit without being asked, keep their hats on, and address people in a disrespectful manner. Whites and blacks never ate together, never went to school together, shook hands, or played sports together (except as children). And while the degree of these restrictions often varied from state to state and county to county, white supremacy was the law of the South, and the slightest transgression could be punished by death.

White violence and oppression, however, were only one part of the story of the era of Jim Crow. The other dimension was the ongoing struggle of African Americans for freedom. This struggle took many forms: direct confrontation, subversion, revolt, institution building, and

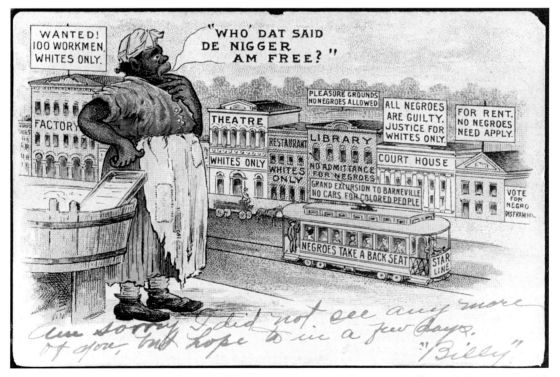

This racist postcard, intended to show blacks in a comic stereotypical manner, actually reveals the extent to which segregation had spread over the South by the early twentieth century.

accommodation. This story was a missing piece of history as far as most Americans were concerned, motivating this book and the film series on which it was based.

* * *

The Rise and Fall of Jim Crow was born out of a four-hour television series with the same name for PBS on the African-American struggle for freedom during the era of Jim Crow. We chose to focus on the South, even though racism was endemic in the North, because it was in the South that racism and white supremacy manifested their most virulent form. The South institutionalized segregation and disfranchisement by law, custom, and violence. From the late 1880s until 1930, it was rare for a white person to speak out publicly against segregation and white supremacy, especially in the South. The South's obsession with racial subordination reinforced the same tendencies that existed throughout the nation. By the end of the nineteenth century, white supremacy, once considered a Southern peculiarity, had become a national ideology.

The series took us seven years to plan, research, write, shoot, and edit, two years longer than it took Ken Burns to make his ten-hour documentary on the Civil War. Without our team of some twenty scholars who guided and corrected us along the way, the films would never have been made. One of the difficulties we encountered was finding images and documents to tell our story in the period between 1880 and World War I. There is not an abundance of material on African-American life in this period because Southern whites, who controlled the image-making process, had little interest in documenting or preserving records of black life prior to the 1930s. The most notable exception to this was lynching. White photographers often capitalized on the atrocity by selling images for postcards or souvenirs of the event.

Our research team, however, was able to uncover a sufficient number of photographs buried in dozens of university and state archives. We also found several outstanding collections of pictures by Southern photographers, such as Henry C. Norman of Natchez, Mississippi. We have selected some of these compelling images for this book, ones that convey the dignity, the struggle, and the character of the people whose lives the programs presented.

One of our major disappointments was the discovery that few, if any, issues survived of the many black newspapers published in the South. Relatively few letters and diaries also survived. There was an abundance of the writings of well-known leaders, who published many of their thoughts and experiences. *The Crisis* magazine, published by the NAACP and edited by W.E.B. Du Bois between 1910 and 1934, was an invaluable source. And there were many letters written by Southern blacks to Northern black newspapers such as the *Chicago Defender, New York Age,* and *Washington Bee.*

Images and documents themselves alone do not tell a story. They lie on the surface of history like floating debris from a shipwreck after the vessel itself has long gone down underneath the waves. Scholars had salvaged much of the material before it reached the "trash bin of history," in order to reconstruct a coherent picture of the past. But for filmmakers, who must weave a story out of the remnants, our primary task was to find the appropriate storytellers.

We divided the series into four parts, each part covering a specific time period: 1865–1895,

1896–1917, 1918–1941, and 1941–1945. Since the last film in the series covered a relatively recent time period, we were able to locate a number of people who either made history or witnessed it. This was the first time that many of them told their story, and it was a great privilege for us to be granted access to their lives. Among those with whom we spoke were men and women from Farmville, Virginia, who as teenagers organized a student strike in 1951. The strike became a lawsuit and one of the five cases that the United States Supreme Court reviewed when it ruled that segregation in education was unconstitutional (*Brown* v. *Board of Education*).

We interviewed civil rights leaders Charles Evers and Reverend Hosea Williams, both of whom had served overseas in World War II and returned to the United States determined to challenge Jim Crow. We tracked down, with a great deal of difficulty, Clinton Adams, a white sharecropper's son, who as a ten-year-old child had inadvertently witnessed a vicious murder of two black men and two pregnant women, and Lamar Howard, who as a teenager was severely beaten because he had seen some of the men who committed the murder gathering near the icehouse where he worked. Then there was Gordon Parks of Georgia, a fanatical member of the Ku Klux Klan, who at the age of nine witnessed his first lynching and chillingly told us the horrifying tale of the murder and of his own brutal life as a child.

We interviewed a number of soldiers who had served in a Jim Crow army during World War II, and had suffered a great deal of racial discrimination. Yet what they remembered was the pride they felt at what they had accomplished. They held no bitterness against those who discriminated against them.

For us, recording the personal testimonies was the most rewarding and fulfilling experience of the project. All of us stood in awe of these men and women who had acted with such courage, took such risks, and yet did not see themselves as particularly heroic. Without their struggles, and the risks taken by the men and women in our film, we might still have legalized segregation in the South today.

As far as presenting the earlier years of Jim Crow, our task was to incorporate the written testimonies of those who did leave behind letters, diaries, and other records. We wanted people to speak with their own voices in the film. Some of these records were fragments; others were rich and full texts. We were fortunate to have the oral history of the life of Ned Cobb, an Alabama sharecropper and tenant farmer who was born when the era of Jim Crow began and died as the civil rights movement ended. His moving life story had been recorded by Ted and Dale Rosengarten, then graduate students at Harvard and Radcliffe. Their work enabled us to build a major sequence around Cobb with the help of his daughter and granddaughter.

There was sufficient material to structure major sequences around pivotal figures during the Jim Crow era, such as W.E.B. Du Bois and Booker T. Washington. These two men were diametrically opposed over the best strategy to fight Jim Crow, and we focused on this conflict. For Isaiah Montgomery, Charlotte Hawkins Brown, Ida B. Wells, and Charles Houston, there was far less first-person material. To tell their stories, we had to combine their own words with those of scholars interviewed on camera. We wanted our scholars to bring these men and women to life by conveying their passion and determination to fight against Jim Crow.

We saw all the stories in the program as being connected to one another, as well as to the overall story we were telling, in the same way that streams merge into other streams until finally they become a river. The individual sequences were our streams, and the river that they formed eventually swept away the legal infrastructure of Jim Crow.

These were the elements we had at our disposal. Making them into a coherent piece was a tedious, frustrating, magical, and, if successful, exhilarating experience. It entailed a good deal of trial and error, false starts, and blind alleys. We also needed the help of others. Film-making is a community effort, and you have to draw upon the insights and suggestions of your colleagues and crew members as well as your own.

The main issue was how to weave the elements we had gathered into a coherent whole. There were individual stories that we wanted to tell, but at the same time we wanted these stories to be part of a larger story. Our goal was not simply to present a journey down the memory lane of history to show a dark period of American life. We chose this subject because we felt that the past has something to say to the present, that this series of programs could use the Jim Crow era to illuminate present-day race relations. We felt that by understanding this era, we might be able to disentangle ourselves from the coils with which Jim Crow continues to ensnare us today. I believe we accomplished what we set out to do. That's what made every hour and every minute of the seven years we worked on this project so rewarding.

The Rise and Fall of
Jim Crow

Chapter I

The Promise of Freedom, 1865–1877

At 4:30 A.M., on the morning of April 12, 1861, Edward Ruffin, a flinty, irascible old man from Virginia who passionately hated the North and who for twenty years had been haranguing the South to secede from the United States, received a singular honor from the Confederate Army: He fired the first shot of the Civil War. Ruffin lit the fuse that hurled a cannonball blazing across the dark sky like a meteor toward Fort Sumter. "Of course I was highly gratified by the compliment and delighted to perform the service," he later boasted. A Union sergeant on the rampart of the fort remembered watching "the burning fuse which marked the course of the shell . . . mounted among the stars."

The Civil War unleashed a tidal wave of patriotic furor that engulfed both sides. Northerners and Southerners alike clamored for what they believed would be a ninety-day bloodless war in which their side would easily emerge victorious. The bloodless ninety days swelled into four blood-filled years. Almost seven hundred thousand men died before the carnage ended.

Both sides insisted at first that the fight was not about slavery. To Southerners, "states' rights" was the catchword; to Northerners, "preserving the Union." Abraham Lincoln made his position clear in a letter to Horace Greeley, publisher of the *New York Tribune*, when he refused demands by Northern abolitionists to end slavery early in the war: "My paramount object in this struggle is to save the Union, and is not either to save or to destroy slavery. If I could save the Union without freeing any slave, I would do it, and if I could save it by freeing all the slaves, I would do it; and if I could save it by freeing some and leaving others alone, I would also do that."

Lincoln was seen by some as not only the Great Emancipator of blacks but of poor Southern whites as well. He was aware that both of them suffered from the same social and economic problems.

But the battle to preserve the Union inevitably became a battle to end slavery. One month later, after the horrific battle of Antietam forced the Southern armies to withdraw from Maryland, Lincoln formally announced the Emancipation Proclamation: "On the first day of January, in the year of our Lord one thousand eight hundred and sixty-three, all persons held as slaves within any State, or designated part of a State, the people whereof shall then be in rebellion against the United States, shall be then, thenceforward, and forever free." Blacks emancipated themselves even before the proclamation. Whenever Union soldiers appeared near where they were enslaved, they fled their plantations. Tens of thousands of freedmen eventually joined the army, helping transform the Union Army into an army of liberation.

Freedom became official on January 31, 1865, when Congress passed the Thirteenth Amendment. For four million African Americans, the "Day of Jubilee" had arrived—the promised time when God would set his people free. As the Union Army swept through the South, at times led by black soldiers, freedmen and freedwomen marched, danced, worshiped, and gave thanks to the Lord and to "Father Abraham." A woman on a plantation in Yorktown, Virginia, ran to a secluded place so her former owner would not see her express her joy. "I jump up and scream 'Glory, glory, hallelujah to Jesus. I's free. I's free. . . . De soul buyers can nebber take my two chillun's lef' me. Nebber can take 'em from me no mo.'"

People created songs to express their newfound freedom:

> Run to do kitchen and shout in de window
> Mammy don't you cook no mo'
> You's free. You's free!
> Run to de hen house and shout:
> Rooster don't you crow no mo'
> You's free! You's free!
> Ol' hen don't you lay no mo' eggs
> You's free! You's free!

Felix Haywood was herding wild horses on the plains of Texas when the news came. "When we learned of our freedom, everybody went wild. We all felt like horses and nobody made us that way but ourselves. We was free. Just like that we was free." When the wife of a black Union soldier asked her husband if she could name their newborn son James Freeman, he replied, "Take good care of our boy because he is born free—free as the bird, free as the wind and free as the sun and his name is Freeman. That just suits me. Thank God! He shall always be a freeman."

Blacks expressed their freedom by organizing parades. They demanded that whites address them as Mr. and Mrs. Women dressed in brightly colored clothes, carried parasols, rode in carriages, refused to give way to whites on the street, and sat with whites on streetcars. Men carried guns and bought dogs and liquor, all of which had been forbidden under slavery. Restricted in their ability to move about during slavery, freedmen and freedwomen exhibited a passion for travel. They organized train excursions to hold picnics and religious meetings in distant places. Whites could not understand why even those who had been well treated left. When one white woman begged her cook to stay on, even offering to pay her twice as much money as she would make elsewhere, the cook refused. Her baffled former mistress asked why she declined such a generous offer. The cook replied, "If I stay here, I'll never know I'm free." One former slave explained, "They seemed to want to get closer to freedom, so they'd know what it was—like it was a place or city."

Even as they enjoyed their freedom, African Americans struggled to define it. Where would they work? What role would they play in the community? Would Southern whites accept them? Where would they live? Would they be able to own land? Would their children receive an education? What political power would they have? To help answer these questions, Congress authorized the Freedmen's Bureau. Administered by the Union Army, the bureau's task was to organize a system of free labor between freedmen and -women and white planters, settle conflicts and disputes between whites and blacks, administer confiscated land, ensure that blacks received justice in the courts, and organize schools. The bureau was also to provide food, fuel, and clothing to the needy of both races on a very limited basis.

Woefully understaffed, the bureau did receive support from other agencies. Hundreds of black and white ministers, missionaries, and teachers flocked to the South with Bibles and spellers to help "uplift the race." Although blacks welcomed Northern assistance, they recognized that the main responsibility for their future lay with themselves. From the very beginning, African Americans began to build their own communities and institutions. They established churches, built schools, and set up benevolent societies to take care of the sick and the elderly, social organizations, including dramatic societies, debating clubs, fire companies, militia groups, and temperance leagues. There was so much activity that one man commented, "We have progressed a century in a year."

Freedmen and freedwomen attempted to restore families destroyed by slavery. Tens of thousands of children and parents, brothers and sisters had been sold away. Newspapers were filled with advertisements from mothers, fathers, children, brothers, and sisters seeking one another.

Sam'l Dove wishes to know the whereabouts of his mother Areno, his sisters Maria, Neziah and Peggy, and his brother Edmond, sold in Richmond.

$200 reward. For our daughter Polly and our son George Washington, carried away as slaves.

Many husbands and wives, brothers and sisters, and aunts and uncles were lost forever to one another. When Henry Spicer discovered, after remarrying, that his beloved first wife, who had been sold away from him and whom he believed dead, was still alive, he wrote her a heartbreaking letter: "I had rather anything happened to me than to have ever been parted from you and the children. I thinks of you and the children every day of my life. My love to you never have failed. Laura, I have got another wife and I am sorry that I am. You feels to me as much as my dear loving wife as you ever did Laura."

The great passion of the freedman became education. Booker T. Washington, who had been born in slavery and whose climb up the educational ladder would become legendary, observed his people's fervent desire for education: "To get inside a schoolhouse would be about the same as getting into heaven. Few people who were not right in the midst of the scenes can form any exact idea of the intense desire which the people of my race showed for education. It was a whole race trying to go to school. Few were too young, and none too old, to make the attempt to learn."

African Americans had a passionate belief in education and went to great lengths to learn how to read and write.

Sidney Andrews, a Northern white journalist sympathetic to black aspirations, noted the same passion as he traveled through the South after the Civil War: "Many of the Negroes . . . common plantation Negroes and day laborers . . . were supporting schools themselves. I had occasion very frequently to notice that porters in stores and laboring men about cotton warehouses and cart drivers in the streets had spelling books with them and were studying them during the time that they were not occupied with their work. Go into the outskirts of any large town . . . and you will see children, and in many instances grown Negroes, sitting in the sun alongside their cabins studying."

By 1866, an estimated five hundred independent schools had sprung up outside the cities and towns. William Channing Gannett, a white missionary from New England, observed that though blacks welcomed white assistance, they did not want white control: "They have a natural praiseworthy pride in keeping their educational institutions in their own hands. There is a jealousy of the superintendence of the white man in this matter. What they desire is assistance without control."

Many white Southerners resented the "Yankees" who had come South to educate blacks. One Southern white woman tried to convince Elizabeth Boutume, a New England schoolteacher, of the futility of her efforts. "I do assure you," the woman said, "you might as well teach your horse or mule to read as these niggers. They can't learn." Boutume replied, "If they can't read, why are you so afraid of school?"

Boutume knew well her students' desire to learn. She told the story of one cook who had ankle chains shackled to her feet by her master so that she would not run away. The woman had still managed to escape, hobbling and dragging herself day and night until she finally reached the school. Her feet were swollen and bloody from the chains biting into her flesh, and she would never walk normally again. When asked why education was so important to her, she answered that, before she died, she wanted to learn at least one thing to show to God when she met him. When a Union general visited Boutume's school and asked the students what message they had for their friends in the North, a child rose up and answered, "Tell them we are rising."

African Americans were as eager to build their own churches as they were to establish their own schools. Churches were the spiritual, educational, and political centers of community life. W. E. B. Du Bois, one of the great black civil rights leaders of the early twentieth century, wrote of the black church:

> The church was the spiritual and social heart of the black community. Various organizations meet here—the church proper, the Sunday school, insurance societies, women's societies, secret societies, and mass meetings of every kind. Entertainments, suppers and lectures are held here besides the five or six weekly services. Employment is found for the idle; strangers are introduced, news is disseminated and charity distributed. At the same time, this social, economic and intellectual center is a religious center of great power . . . the Church often stands as a real conserver of morals, a strengthener of family life, and the final authority on what is Good and Right.

Under slavery, black congregations had been subject to white ministers and churches. Now they either withdrew from white churches or took control, hiring black ministers to replace white ones. In 1867, the black membership of the Methodist church in the South was 40,000. Six years later it had dropped to 653. In 1858, there were 25,000 black Presbyterians. By 1875, the number fell to 1,614. Along with the church, blacks organized benevolent societies, political clubs, fraternal organizations, women's clubs, and labor unions. They raised money for orphanages and soup kitchens for the poor and the aged. Northern black ministers who came South expected to find their congregations completely degraded by slavery and in need of uplift. They learned instead what Thomas Higginbotham had already discovered several years earlier about the Southern black troops he had commanded during the Civil War: "We did not know how the religious temperament of the Negroes had checked the demoralization." James Lynch, a Northern black minister, found freedmen and freedwomen a most responsive audience: "They exhibit a desire to hear and learn that I never imagined. Every word you say while preaching, they drink down and respond to with an earnestness that sets your heart all on fire and you feel that it is indeed God's work to minister to them." When Isaac Brinkerhood, a white Baptist minister from the North, tried to teach blacks to abandon their old black preachers who had conducted secret services during the days of slavery, he discovered that he had a lot to learn himself. Listening to one of these ministers preach, Brinkerhood confessed, "He was an unlearned man who could not read . . . telling of the love of Christ, of Christian faith and duty in a way which I have not yet learned."

As African Americans built their own institutions, they organized conventions to debate and define their future. Men, women, and children attended these conventions, participated in the discussion, and voted. At the Convention of the Colored People of South Carolina in

1865, the delegates requested "that we shall be recognized as men; that the same laws which govern white men shall govern black men; that we have the right of trial by jury of our peers; that no impediments be placed in our way of acquiring homesteads; that, in short, we be dealt with as others are—in equity and in justice."

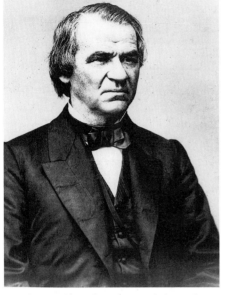

President Andrew Johnson succeeded Lincoln after his assassination. He had promised freedmen he would help them in their freedom, but instead supported those who would restore them to virtual slavery.

For a brief moment, their pleas might have been granted. According to Whitelaw Reid, a Northern reporter touring the South, Southerners seemed to be resigned to the fact that blacks would be major players in a new South. This opportunity was quickly lost. Suddenly and unexpectedly, the South found itself with an ally— the President of the United States, Andrew Johnson.

* * *

Andrew Johnson was described by his contemporaries as quick-tempered, hard-drinking, and mule-headed, a bully whose hatred of slave owners was as intense as his hatred of blacks. Johnson was born and raised in poverty. Through grit and determination he worked his way up in life, becoming governor of Tennessee and a United States senator. Although a slave owner, he favored emancipation. When the South seceded, he remained loyal to the Union. Lincoln rewarded him for his loyalty by choosing him as his vice president in 1864.

During the war, Johnson had taken a hard line regarding the South. "Treason is a crime," he said, "and crime must be punished." Johnson condemned those Southern politicians who had led the South into war. He said that, if he could, "I would arrest them—I would try them—I would convict them—and I would hang them." Many Radical Republicans in Congress—those who supported strong civil and political rights for blacks and harsh punishment of the South—had more hope that Johnson would carry out their policies than they did Lincoln. Some were not at all unhappy that Lincoln had been assassinated. Representative George Julian wrote, "Hostility towards Lincoln's policy of conciliation and contempt for his weakness were undisguised. The universal feeling here among radical men is that his death is a god-send." One senator remarked of Johnson, "I believe that the Almighty continued Mr. Lincoln in office as long as he was useful and then substituted a better man to finish his work."

The Radical Republicans believed that Johnson shared their view of the South. They maintained that the South had forfeited all rights to statehood when it separated itself from the Union. After defeat, it was little better than a conquered nation, barred from representation in Congress and the protection of the Constitution. They wanted to restructure the South to ensure that blacks would receive their rights and whites would be forever loyal to the Union.

Johnson had his own agenda. He did not share the belief that the South had separated itself from the Union. He agreed that the leaders of the South were guilty of treason but, like

Lincoln, Johnson felt that the Union was indissoluble. He wanted to "reconstruct" the South in order to hasten its return to the Union as soon as possible. Moreover, Johnson wanted the South brought back into the Union under white control. While governor of Tennessee, he had promised black people that he would "indeed be your Moses and lead you through the Red Sea of war and bondage to a fairer future of liberty and peace." But Moses became Judas for black people when Johnson became President. For though he had opposed slavery, he did not believe in racial equality. "I believe they [African Americans] have less capacity for governing than any race of people on earth," he said. He opposed extending the vote to blacks and any attempt of the federal government to ensure their civil and political rights.

In May 1865, Johnson issued a proclamation of amnesty and pardon. He generously pardoned all Southerners, except the leaders who supported the Confederacy, as long as they took an oath of loyalty to the Union and accepted emancipation. If Johnson closed the front door to former secessionist leaders, he left the back door wide open. Wealthy white secessionist leaders could be restored to power, and to their property, by individual acts of presidential pardon, which he handed out quite generously.

To ensure that his policies would be carried out, Johnson appointed conservative provisional governors in order to facilitate the return of their states to the Union. These governors had been loyal to the Union until war was declared and then served in the Confederacy. They also echoed Johnson's policies of white supremacy. Governor Benjamin Perry of South Carolina announced, "This is a white man's government and intended for white men only." Governor Benjamin Humphries of Mississippi declared the new order of things: "The Negro is free whether we like it or not. For the purity and progress of both races, they must accept their place in the lower order of things. That place is the cotton fields of the South. Such is the rule of the plantation and the law of God." The *Natchez Courier* editorialized that the two races could not live together as equals: "One must be superior—one must be dominant." If blacks tried to dominate, the *Courier* predicted a race war that would be "a war of extermination."

The South realized that Johnson was their ally. He allowed the states rather than the federal government to determine the future status of blacks. He agreed to the removal of black troops from the South. Contradicting his previous statements to punish traitors, he encouraged the old regime to take political and economic control. In the summer of 1865, whites gathered in political conventions to approve Johnson's demand that they accept the abolishment of slavery, declare secession null and void, and repudiate all state debts incurred during the war. Although all the states eventually did accept his terms, many did so reluctantly and with a great deal of debate. Most representatives the South elected in the fall—even if they had originally been opposed to secession—had supported the Confederacy when war was declared. Having lost the war, the South was determined to win the peace.

* * *

The burning issue for Southern whites was the future of the freedman. Northern journalist Sidney Andrews found Southern whites obsessed by blacks: "Everybody talks about the Negro, all hours of the day and under all circumstances. What would become of him? How would he survive? Where would he work? What could he do? And would he take revenge?"

Whites complained about the way African Americans exercised their freedom. Enraged at the presence of black soldiers guarding their towns, and infuriated by the independence expressed by men and women they once held in bondage, whites often accused blacks of being "disrespectful," "insolent," "insubordinate," and—the worst charge of all—"ungrateful." One planter commented, "The death of slavery is recognized. . . . But we don't believe that because the nigger is free, he ought to be saucy."

Whites claimed that blacks would not work unless forced to. One black freedman challenged this argument: "They say we will not work. He who makes that assertion makes an untruth. We have been working all our lives, not only supporting ourselves, but we have supported our masters, many of them in idleness. White men," he concluded, "didn't know how to work."

George Trowbridge, a New England journalist bitterly opposed to slavery, discovered that it was black labor that was rebuilding the South. "Negroes drove the teams, made the mortar, carried the hods, excavated the old cellars or built new ones. . . . I could not see but that these people worked just as industriously as the white laborers. And yet . . . I was once more informed by a cynical citizen that the Negro, now that he was free, would rob, steal or starve before he would work." And Sidney Andrews added, "It is both absurd and wicked to charge that Negroes as a class are not at work. Their vitality is at least thirty or forty percent greater than that of the average whites. . . . Of course the whites are forever complaining. They demand that all the labor shall be . . . in the hands of the blacks; and all ease and profit . . . in the hands of themselves."

Whites wanted black labor to plant and harvest their crops under some form of strict control. They wanted to determine what to pay their workers, how long they should work, when they should be paid, and how many members of their family should work. To carry out these goals, white legislators in every Southern state enacted a series of laws known as the black codes. Their goal was to restore slavery in substance, if not in name, with the state taking the place of the former "master." While the codes acknowledged that blacks had some rights, including the right to marry, own property, and make contracts, they severely restricted black freedom, forcing blacks to work the white man's land on the white man's terms. If a black man was found to be unemployed, he could be arrested as a vagrant and fined; if he failed to pay his fine, he was turned over to a planter who paid it and then forced him to work off his debt. Anyone who refused to sign a labor contract was imprisoned and forced to work without pay. Blacks who broke contracts could be shipped, fined, and sold into labor for one year. Orphaned children and even children of families could be taken away from their homes, forced to work as apprentices, and even whipped by their employers. Parents had no legal rights to prevent their children from being seized. To ensure that blacks would remain farmers and servants, some codes prohibited them from seeking any employment other than agricultural labor or domestic work without a special license. They could not lease or rent land, nor were they allowed to buy it. Some states denied African Americans the right to vote, hold office, and work and travel where they wanted to. Black people could not live in cities without a special permit. Tax laws were passed that forced blacks to pay poll taxes and occupation taxes that crippled them economically and often

Whites wanted blacks to return to the cotton fields and work for them as they had done in slavery. Blacks wanted to work their own land and be independent of whites. Without land, they felt there could be no freedom.

allowed the state, as a result of nonpayment, to arrest them and send them into forced labor.

The criminal justice system was as harsh as the codes. Blacks had little chance of winning a case in court against a white man or successfully defending themselves against a white man's charge. Sheriffs, judges, and jury members were all white, and most were former Confederate soldiers. Whites were seldom arrested for criminal offenses against blacks and almost never convicted. If plantation owners could no longer legally whip blacks, the state could and did. The state also began to lease blacks for convict labor gangs. Some Southern states also passed the segregation statutes immediately after the Civil War, later to be known as Jim Crow laws. Blacks were segregated on public transportation in Texas, Florida, and Mississippi, and completely banned from access to public institutions.

The codes enraged blacks and many Northerners. "If you call this freedom, what do you call slavery?" one black veteran bitterly asked. The Freedmen's Bureau, which had legal military powers over the conquered South, nullified most of the codes. Although the bureau was willing to overrule the codes, it was also willing to force blacks to work for whites against their will. Many army officers serving as administrators for the bureau worked hand in hand with Southern whites. They helped round up black workers, many of whom had migrated to the cities, and illegally shipped them to plantations. A delegation of African Americans in Richmond complained about their treatment. "In the city of Richmond, the military and police authorities will not allow us to walk the streets day or night, in the regular pursuit of our business or on our way to church, without passes, and passes do not always protect us from arrest, abuse, violence, and imprisonment." Henry McNeal Turner, then a black chaplain in the army, testified, "I have been told over and over by colored persons that they were

Whites launched murderous assaults on blacks at the end of the Civil War. They blamed them for the war and for their defeat and for wanting to be free.

never treated more cruelly than they were by some of the white Yankees. They were subjected to curfews and passes as they had been under slavery. Unemployed men were arrested as vagrants and sent to work on white plantations."

The army encouraged written labor contracts to be drawn up between planters and black workers, which the bureau would enforce. The contracts heavily favored the planters. Since many workers still could not read, the contracts often contained deceptive clauses that cheated them out of their money. Blacks were required to work for a year, and if they left their jobs before then or were fired, they forfeited their pay. The settlements were usually made at the end of the year. This meant that a planter could fire his workers just before they were supposed to be paid and completely avoid paying them. While some contracts allowed for wages, many were based on shares. The workers would receive a certain share of the cotton crop when it was sold, minus expenses for their food, clothes, and medical care. These items were sold on credit during the working season. Since the workers had no cash, they needed credit to survive. The planters and merchants charged exorbitant rates for merchandise and piled on usurious interest. This system later became the basis of sharecropping. Many planters continued to whip and beat their workers as they had during slavery. Whenever they could, planters treated their former slaves brutally, taking out their revenge on them. One worker who escaped complained, "We seen stars in the day time. They treated us dreadful bad. They beat us and they hung us and they starved us. They . . . told us they were going to shoot us and they did hang two of us; and Mr. Pierce, the overseer, knocked one with a fence rail and he died the next day." In South Carolina, when six field workers escaped a white man's farm on which they had been forced to work, the overseer tracked them down, shot one to death, and hanged the other five.

Whites used terror to ensure black subordination. The defeat of the Confederacy had triggered a tidal wave of racial violence against blacks. A former Confederate soldier expressed his hatred of the freedman: "I hope the day will come when we will . . . kill them like dogs. I was never down on a nigger like I am now." Throughout the South, blacks were whipped, beaten, or driven out of their homes or off their land. In Texas, one woman reported that it was a common sight to see the bodies of freedmen floating down a river. In Pine Bluff, Arkansas, twenty-four men, women, and children from a settlement were found "hanging to trees all around the Cabbins."

White men murdered blacks for any reason, or for no reason at all. One murderer explained that the victim "didn't remove his hat." Another said he "wanted to thin out the niggers a little." A third remarked that "he wanted to see a D——d nigger kick." Bodies were mutilated, ears severed, tongues cut out, eyes gouged. Men were beheaded and skinned, the skin then nailed to the barn. In the countryside, night riders whipped and murdered blacks and their white supporters. Black soldiers or former soldiers were often singled out. Whites cut their throats or shot them in the head. One white man walked with his arm around a black soldier and, as they were talking, secretly drew his pistol and shot the soldier in the back. Whites who committed these murders, many of them known to all, went unpunished. Colonel Samuel Thomas of the Freedmen's Bureau reported, "Wherever I go, I hear people talk in such a way as they are unable to conceive of a Negro as having any rights at all. Men

Most blacks wanted to live simply, to raise their own food and a little cotton for cash. In some areas, they had received land grants from the Union Army, but President Johnson rescinded the grants.

will cheat a Negro without feeling a single twinge of conscience. To kill a Negro they do not deem murder. To take property away from a Negro, they do not consider robbery. The reason for all this is simple and manifest. Whites esteem blacks their property by natural right and they treat the colored people just as their profit, caprice or passion may dictate."

Schools were a major target of white wrath. Seeing their former slaves educated was for many Southerners worse than seeing them free. A Southern senator warned, "Keep the spelling book and the land from the possession of the Negro if you hope to control him." Southern planters were furious when blacks forced them to provide schools as part of their work contract. They depended on their tenants' children working in the fields, which school would prevent them from doing. One planter commented, "If you educate the Negro he won't stay where he belongs. They feel the clutch of the iron hand of the white man's unwritten law in their throats." These planters knew that any educated black man would refuse to accept lowly manual labor if he could obtain a better job.

The black schools became targets of white violence. In Alabama, schoolhouses were burned and teachers terrorized. In Louisiana, the walls of a school in one town were covered with obscene language and pictures, and the teacher threatened. In Tennessee, a white teacher was taken at night from his room by a band of disguised men, choked, beaten, and threatened with death if he did not leave town. Local whites refused to rent rooms to Northern white teachers, who then roomed with black families. They were ostracized and sometimes beaten, and many were forced to leave.

For African Americans, perhaps the worst betrayal was President Andrew Johnson's refusal to keep the federal government's promise of land. Land was the foundation on which African Americans planned to build their mansion of freedom. Land would allow them to escape from white domination and achieve economic independence. "Every colored man will be a slave and feel himself a slave until he can raise his own bale of cotton and put his own mark on it and say, 'This is mine,'" Peter Hall, a freedman, explained.

Blacks living along the Georgia and South Carolina coast had good reason to believe that they would be given the lands of those who had enslaved them. Earlier in the year, Secretary of War Edwin Stanton and General William Tecumseh Sherman had met with a delegation of twenty black men from the Savannah area to discuss their freedom. The group's spokesman was Garrison Frazier, an elder in the Baptist ministry. During the meeting, Frazier told Stanton, "The best way we can take care of ourselves is to have land and turn it over by our own labor. . . . We want to be placed on land until we are able to buy it and make it our own."

Black people in the coastal areas of South Carolina and Georgia had already taken over large tracts of land abandoned by their former masters. Sherman legitimized their actions. Several days after the meeting, he issued Field Order Number 15, setting aside more than four hundred thousand acres of abandoned land for forty thousand blacks living on the Georgia and South Carolina Sea Islands and coastal areas. Blacks were allowed to form their own communities and govern themselves without interference from whites, except for military personnel and the federal government. They also chose to plant corn and potatoes rather than cotton—for cotton "had enriched their masters but not themselves."

President Johnson would not allow this to remain. In October 1865, he sent a troubled Union general, Oliver O. Howard, to Edisto Island off the coast of South Carolina. A deeply religious man who hated slavery, Howard was sent to break the bad news to the islanders. When he arrived, he found two thousand angry people gathered to meet him in the Old Episcopal Church. Howard later described the scene in his autobiography: "The auditorium galleries were filled. The rumor preceded my coming had reached the people that I was obliged by the President to restore the land to the old planters, so that evidence of dissatisfaction and sorrow was manifested in every part of the assembly. No progress was made until a sweet-voiced woman began to sing 'Nobody Knows the Trouble I've Seen.'"

Howard addressed the audience: "I have been sent by the President to tell you that your old masters have been pardoned and their plantations are to be given back to them, and that they would hire blacks to work for them. Lay aside your bitter feelings and be reconciled to them." Voices shouted out in protest. "No!" "No suh!" One man rose and addressed Howard directly: "General Howard, why do you take away our lands! You take them from us who are true, always true to the government. You give them to our all-time enemies. The man who gave me 39 lashes, and who stripped and flogged my mother and sister—who keeps land from me well knowing I would not have anything to do with him if I had land of my own— that man I cannot well forgive." All over the South—with few exceptions—blacks were forced, often at bayonet point, to return lands they had occupied.

The Radical Republicans were the moral forces in the Senate. They had supported abolition before the war, pushed for blacks to join the Union army during the war and after the war, and wanted blacks to have full political and civil rights. Thaddeus Stevens (holding cane) was one of the leaders of the group.

Even with the return of their lands, many whites—perhaps hundreds of thousands—were still ruined. Almost every wealthy family had lost its savings. Many were reduced to poverty and had to sell or abandon their homes and plantations, because they could no longer afford to keep them. The South had lost 260,000 men. Almost four million black men and women— once regarded as property and who had done all of the work—were free. "I never did a day's work in my life," one white planter confessed, "and I don't know how to begin." Many formerly wealthy families suffered the fate of a once-proud Virginia family. "The family, one of the oldest and most respectable, once very wealthy and now reduced . . . to large debts, large pride and large wants . . . are now without servants. The young ladies on Wednesdays and Thursdays milked the cows while their father, the general, held the umbrella over them to keep off the rain." White women were terrified of losing servants, because they had to do the housework themselves. To cook dinner, clean house, wash and iron clothes, and carry out similar chores was too hard for many white women. They bitterly complained and longed for the days when their black servants did all the work. Their anger ran deep. One freedwoman reported that her former mistress "hoped that we'd starve to death and she be glad, 'cause it ruin her to lose us." White women rarely recognized that if the work was too hard for them, it was just as hard for black women. One former slave owner, Kate Stone, gradually realized what life was like for her servants: "Even under the best of owners, it was a hard, hard life; to toil six days out of seven, week after week, month after month, year after year as long as life lasted; to be absolutely under control of someone until the last breath was drawn; to win but the bare necessities of life, no hope of more, no matter how hard the work, how long the toil to know that nothing could change your lot. Obedience, revolt, submission, prayers—all were in vain. Waking sometimes in the night as I grow older, I would grow sick with the misery of it all."

Blacks resisted the efforts of whites to control their lives once again. Whenever they could, they insisted that they work shorter hours than they had under slavery, that they be paid for nonfarming jobs like clearing the land, that they be given land to work for themselves, and that they have schools for their children. They wanted their wives and daughters to remain at home rather than work in the fields. At times, they walked off plantations and refused to sign contracts for another year. When some planters resisted all compromise, occasionally their barns or homes were burned down. On plantations and in the cities, black workers went out on strike for better pay. In New Orleans, black and white workers sometimes joined forces to strike for higher wages or better working conditions.

Gradually Southern whites, aided by the Freedmen's Bureau, began to regain control. As one white planter chillingly predicted, "The nigger is going to be made a serf as sure as you live. It won't need any law for that. . . . They're attached to the soil and to their masters as much as ever. I'll stake my life, this is the way it will work." This attitude, found everywhere, revealed to Sidney Andrews that Southern whites were determined to return African Americans to slavery the first chance they got. "If the nation allows the whites to work out the . . . Negro's future in their own way, the condition in three years will be as bad as it was before the war. The viciousness that could not overturn the nation is now mainly engaged in the effort to retain the substance of slavery. What are names if the thing itself remains?"

One reason the South was so confident it could restore slavery in substance was that most white Northerners had no love for blacks, and wanted the South to be brought back into the Union quickly. Industrialists were eagerly eyeing the fortunes to be made by creating a new, modern South on the ruins of the old. Most Republican politicians and party members were willing to go along with President Johnson's policy to leave the fate of African Americans to the South. Although they were willing to allow whites to control blacks, they refused to tolerate injustice and violence. Nor would they allow Southerners to elect political leaders who were once secessionists. The South appeared arrogant to many Northern Republicans, acting as if it had won the war. Republican leaders first tried to work out a compromise with the President.

The driving force of the Republican-controlled Congress was a small group of senators and congressmen collectively known as the Radicals, because they championed full civil and political rights for blacks. While the Radicals were a minority in their own party, they had tremendous influence in the House and Senate. Every major cause they advocated had triumphed—abolition, emancipation, and the arming of black troops during the Civil War. Now they were about to embark on their greatest struggle—to secure the ballot for the black men (women were still not allowed to vote) and full equality in civil rights for all African Americans. They were aware that most Americans opposed black suffrage. When whites in Washington, D.C., voted in referendum on the issue of black suffrage, only 35 were in favor of blacks voting while 6,951 were against.

In 1866, Congress began to eliminate discrimination on the federal and state levels. It repealed a federal law that barred black people from carrying the mail. It allowed African Americans to testify in federal courts and to sit in the visitors' galleries in Congress. The first black lawyer was accredited to the Supreme Court. The Republicans passed a Civil Rights Act, which held that all native-born Americans were entitled to certain basic rights, including the right to sue, to make contracts, to inherit, purchase, and hold land, and to enjoy "full and equal benefit of all laws." The act's goal was to protect blacks against abuse by the state, but it failed to protect them against discrimination by individuals. The Freedmen's Bureau Bill extended the life of the bureau and granted it the power to intervene wherever blacks were denied civil rights enjoyed by whites.

The Republicans expected Johnson to sign the bills. Instead he vetoed both. Politically Johnson felt that by killing the bills, he would win support from Democrats as well as from Republicans. Johnson believed the issue of federal protection of black civil rights would become the political issue he could use to defeat his Republican opponents in the next congressional election. During a rally, someone in the audience asked Johnson, "What does the veto mean?" Before he could answer, a voice from the crowd boomed out, "It is keeping the nigger down."

Johnson had seriously miscalculated. Black civil rights had become a major issue. Congress overrode Johnson's veto of the Civil Rights Act. To ensure that a future Congress would not undo the act, the Republicans also passed the Fourteenth Amendment, which constitutionally guaranteed due process of law to all persons born in the United States. All states were now required to apply civil rights laws equally to blacks and whites. The amendment also disfranchised from national office those who had served in the Confederacy during the war. Before any Southern state could be readmitted into the Union, that state had to ratify the amendment.

If there had been any doubt that federal intervention was needed in the South, it was dispelled in Memphis, in the spring of 1866. A carriage collision between a black and a white taxi driver led to a race riot in which forty-six blacks and two whites were killed, five black women were raped, and hundreds of black-owned buildings were burned to the ground. Three months later, the mayor of New Orleans incited another race riot in which the police shot and killed at least forty blacks and whites attending a political convention. General Philip Sheridan, who was the military commander of the area at the time, described to President Johnson what happened: "As they came out [of the building] the policemen who had formed the circle nearest the building fired upon them, and they were again fired upon by citizens. Many of those wounded and captured . . . were fired upon by their captors. The wounded were stabbed while lying on the ground, and their heads beaten with brickbats." Sheridan concluded in his report: "It was no riot. It was an absolute massacre by the police which was not excelled in murderous cruelty by that of Fort Pillow." (Confederate soldiers had murdered some two hundred blacks at Fort Pillow during the Civil War after they had surrendered.)

The final showdown between Johnson and the Republicans came in the congressional elections of 1866. Before the elections, the President traveled throughout the country bitterly castigating the Republican Congress. Drunk much of the time, Johnson gave rambling and incoherent speeches that helped his enemies. Southerners aided the Northern Republican cause by rejecting the Fourteenth Amendment and electing staunch supporters of the Confederacy to Congress. The Republican victory was overwhelming. The party controlled more than two-thirds of Congress, with enough votes to override any of Johnson's vetoes. Congress refused to seat newly elected representatives from the South, many of whom had been active in the Confederacy. The only exception was Tennessee, which had complied with Congress's wishes and barred former leaders of the Confederacy from holding public office. Reconstruction was now in the hands of the Radical Republicans, and the terms for readmission for the Southern states would be far harsher than the President's had been.

Chapter 2

Promises Betrayed, 1880–1890

The Radical Republicans seized control of Reconstruction with a burning desire to impose their will on the South. In 1867, Congress passed the Reconstruction Act, allowing the federal government to rule the South until the Southern states were readmitted into the Union. The eleven Confederate states of the South were divided into five military districts. Each general in charge of a district was required to prepare the states in his jurisdiction for readmission to the Union. Every state had to amend its constitution to ensure that African Americans would become full citizens of the United States, with their civil and political rights fully protected. Black delegates elected by their communities were to be represented at all of the conventions. A number of men who had supported the Confederacy were denied the right to vote. To be readmitted to the Union, a state had to approve the new provisions guaranteeing civil and political rights for all citizens and had to ratify the Fourteenth Amendment. Congress made it clear that until the Southern states accepted the conditions for Reconstruction, military rule would remain. Senator Richard Yates proclaimed, "The ballot will finish the Negro question. . . . The ballot is the freedman's Moses."

Blacks celebrated the Reconstruction Act as a second emancipation. Union Clubs, formed right after the Civil War as patriotic organizations, immediately became hives of political activity. The clubs held forums and debates, organized parades and demonstrations, built churches and schools, and provided care for the sick and the elderly. They advised farmworkers how to deal with planters who cheated them out of their wages or tricked them into signing long-term contracts that left them in debt. When Congress legalized black suffrage, the Union Clubs became political organizations, supporting candidates for office and explaining to people their political rights and how to vote. The Bible and the Declaration of Independence were always on display at meetings. Armed men guarded the meetings from interference by hostile whites. Some clubs were integrated and provided a political space in which blacks and whites could meet as equals. Many blacks were in favor of breaking down barriers of discrimination. Some small white farmers, struggling to hold on to their land, recognized that both races were in the same ditch and joined with blacks in common cause.

In the fall of 1867, blacks organized constitutional conventions in almost every Southern

In 1867, Congress empowered African Americans with the vote, enabling them to select their own representatives to state and federal government. This political cartoon shows the joyous response of blacks and the unhappy response of Southern whites.

state. Black voters, fully represented for the first time, campaigned with great enthusiasm. In every city and town, politics became their main preoccupation. Planters complained that they had to shut down their farms, because so many of their black workers took off to attend political rallies and conventions. One planter observed, "You never saw a people more excited on the subject of politics than are the Negroes of the South. They are perfectly wild." Black ministers felt that politics was replacing religion. "Politics got in our midst and our revival or religious work for a while began to wane," one minister complained. To deal with this problem, churches turned to politics and ministers preached the Republican Party and the Gospel.

Although women could not vote, they played an active role in politics. One witness said that women were determined that men should vote the Republican ticket: "Women had sticks; no mens were to go to the polls unless their wives were right alongside them; some had hickory sticks; some had nails—four nails drive in the shape of a cross—and dare their husbands to vote any other than the Republican ticket. My sister went with my brother-in-law to the polls and swear to God if he voted the Democratic ticket, she 'will kill him dead in his sleep.' "

On paper, the new state constitutions promised much. They guaranteed blacks equal civil and political rights with whites, and they established schools, prisons, and asylums for the orphaned and insane of both races. They removed many of the discriminations against blacks and outlawed harsh punishments such as whipping. In most states, African Americans were guaranteed the right to sit on juries and testify in court. In South Carolina, it was forbidden to imprison a man or take away his home for debt. Many of the new state constitutions benefited poor whites as well as blacks. As far as equal treatment in public places and on public transportation was concerned, most constitutions avoided these issues because whites bitterly opposed change. Many blacks were willing to accept such separation temporarily as long as they could control their own schools, churches, and social organizations. Their ultimate hope was that, in time, they could create a truly democratic and fully integrated biracial society.

Whites were enraged at being forced to enfranchise blacks. Governor Perry of South Carolina protested to Congress: "The radical Republican Party forgets that this is a white man's government and created for white men only; and that the Supreme Court of the United States has decided that the Negro is not an American citizen under the Federal Constitution. Each and every state of the Union has the unquestionable right of deciding who shall exercise the right of suffrage."

The *Charleston Mercury* warned the victors, "The constitutions and governments will last just as long as the bayonets which ushered them into being shall keep them in existence and not one day longer."

Benjamin Perry was appointed provisional governor of South Carolina by President Johnson. He had been opposed to secession but supported the Confederacy when war started. He was a white supremacist adamantly opposed to black rights.

Although African Americans were now major players in Southern politics, they still were a minority of the population in most states. The great majority of Southern whites supported the Democratic Party, the party of white supremacy. To gain political power, blacks had to join forces with those whites willing to support the Republican Party and black rights. Many were Northern Republicans who had migrated to the South after the war to make their fortunes. Some were confidence men who became notorious for their corruption. Others were bright and capable men who would prove to be good leaders. White Southerners contemptuously lumped them all together under the term "carpetbaggers," a name inspired from the type of luggage they carried. At the same time, a small number of Southern whites supported the Republican Party. Called "scalawags" by most white Southerners, who considered them traitors to the South, many of them were men of property and influence who had been opposed to secession. They felt that the future of the South—as well as their own futures—lay in identifying with Northern interests. The South lacked sufficient capital to recover from the devastation caused by the war and desperately needed Northern financial support. The scalawags were more interested in convincing Northern capitalists to invest in railroads, mines, cotton mills, and machine shops than they were in racial issues.

Even as congressional Reconstruction was making progress, President Johnson remained intent on undermining it. He removed generals who were sympathetic to blacks or willing to

The Radical Republicans took their revenge on President Andrew Johnson by denying him the nomination for President. Instead, they chose Civil War hero Ulysses S. Grant.

carry out Congress's bidding and replaced them with generals hostile to black rights. He removed Secretary of War Edwin Stanton from office despite a congressional law forbidding him to do so. In retaliation, the Radicals attempted to impeach the President but failed by the narrow margin of one vote.

In the summer of 1868, the anti-Johnson faction of the Republican Party got its revenge by denying Johnson their party's nomination for President. Instead, they chose Ulysses S. Grant, an obvious choice. He was a war hero extremely popular with the American people. He had faithfully carried out the Reconstruction policies of Congress, even though he was not particularly sympathetic to African Americans.

Democrats hoped to play the race card to defeat the Republicans. Those Southern states that had changed their constitutions and were readmitted to the Union (Arkansas, Louisiana, Georgia, Florida, Tennessee, North and South Carolina) rallied around the Democratic Party. They used every means to intimidate black voters in order to prevent them from voting: Democratic merchants cut off credit to black Republicans; landlords evicted tenants who dared to vote. And terrorist organizations arose, the most ruthless of which was the Ku Klux Klan.

The Klan was originally organized in 1865 in Pulaski, Tennessee, as a social club by six Confederate veterans. In the beginning, the Klan was a secret fraternity club rather than a terrorist organization. Ku Klux was derived from the Greek word *kuklos,* meaning a band. Klan has no specific meaning but was used for its alliterative sound. The costume adopted by its members was a mask, white robe, and high, conical, pointed hat. According to the founders of the Klan, there was no malicious intent in the beginning. Yet it quickly grew into a terrorist organization. It attracted such former Confederate generals as Nathan Bedford Forrest, the famed cavalry commander whose soldiers murdered captured black troops at Fort Pillow during the Civil War. The Klan spread beyond Tennessee to every state in the South and included mayors, judges, and sheriffs, as well as convicted criminals.

The Klan systematically murdered black politicians and political leaders throughout the South. Since Johnson had appointed federal officers hostile to Reconstruction, they did nothing to prevent the killings or to arrest the killers. Despite the Klan's efforts, blacks voted in large numbers, carrying the South for Grant. One newspaper reporter observed the determination of African Americans to vote: "In defiance of fatigue, hardship, hunger and threats of employers, blacks had come en masse to the polls. Without shoes, [wearing] patched clothing, they stood on line despite a storm waiting for the chance to vote. The hunger to have the same chances as the white men they feel and comprehend."

Rising above the terror, black votes carried enough Southern states for Grant to be elected. Blacks also elected many local Republicans to office. Despite fears by white Democrats of "black domination," whites won most state and local offices. Whites controlled all legislatures except in South Carolina, where blacks gained control of the lower and upper houses. Many blacks refused to run because they did not want to make the Republican Party a black man's party. They felt that, for the sake of racial harmony, it would be better for whites to control the government as long as they were responsive to black political demands. This would change as Reconstruction progressed, and blacks eventually held some six hundred offices, plus hundreds of positions as sheriffs, clerks, policemen, firemen, and aldermen and councilmen.

In 1869, Congress tried to give additional support to black voters by passing the Fifteenth Amendment. On the surface, the amendment prohibited federal and state governments from depriving any citizen of the vote on racial grounds, something that Frederick Douglass, the great spokesman for the black community, had been urging for years. "The South must be opened to the light of law and liberty. . . . The plain common sense way of doing this . . . is simply to establish in the South one law, one government, one administration of justice, one condition to exercise the elective franchise for all men and all colors alike . . . the right of the Negro is the true solution of our national problems."

The amendment, ratified in 1870, contained many loopholes. It failed to make voting requirements universal and protect the rights of blacks to run for office and to sit on juries. Nor did the amendment prohibit literacy tests, poll taxes, and educational testing as requirements for voting. Republicans were fearful that if the amendment were too strong it would infringe on the rights of a state to regulate its own affairs.

* * *

Despite their victories, Southern Republicans remained an alien presence in a hostile land. Most whites refused to accept the Republican Party as legitimate, considering it to have been forced upon them by Northern bayonets. Blacks and whites fought over issues concerning civil rights, patronage, and elected office. White Republican leaders wanted to win the support of Southern whites by appointing influential Democrats to office. Blacks wanted strong civil rights legislation, public schools, orphanages, asylums for the insane, hospitals for both races, and an end to discrimination on public transportation.

The South still lay in ruins with its state treasuries empty. Republicans proposed to revolutionize the region by transforming it into an industrial economy. They tried to woo Northern capital to the South by offering generous financing and land grants to railroad companies. To win these subsidies and favorable laws, railroads and speculators paid substantial bribes to legislators of both parties and both races. By the early 1870s, the railroad boom had ended, leaving many states deeply in debt with nothing to show for it—except higher taxes to pay the bills for the subsidies to the railroads and increased hostility toward the Republicans.

As Republicans struggled to maintain political control, pass civil rights, education, and social welfare laws, modernize the South, and win white support, the Klan unleashed a murderous rampage. Klansmen were filled with passionate intensity to eliminate, eradicate, or exterminate all Republicans, black and white. They beat, whipped, and murdered thousands, and terrorized tens of thousands to prevent them from voting. Blacks often tried to fight back, but they were outnumbered and outgunned. William Coleman, a black farmer in Mississippi, told a congressional investigating committee on Klan activities in 1868 of his own experience with the Klan:

> I grabbed my ax-handle and commenced fighting and they just took me and cut me with their knives. They surrounded me and some had me by the legs and some by the arms and the neck . . . and they took me out to the big road before my gate and whipped me until I couldn't move or holler, but just lay there like a log, and every lick they hit me I grunted like a mule when he is stalled fast and whipped. They left me there for dead, and what it was done for was because I was a radical and I didn't deny my profession . . . and I never will. I will never vote for that conservative ticket if I die.

Plan of the Contemplated Murder of John Campbell.

The Ku Klux Klan was formed as a social club but quickly became a terrorist organization determined to destroy the gains that blacks had made under Reconstruction. White supporters of blacks were also targeted.

Although the main targets of Klan wrath were the political and social leaders of the black community, blacks could be murdered for almost any reason. Men, women, and children, the aged and the crippled, were victims. A 103-year-old woman was whipped, as was a paralyzed man. In Georgia, Abraham Colby, an organizer and leader in the black community, was whipped for hours in front of his wife and children. His little daughter begged the Klansman, "don't take my daddy away." She never recovered from the experience and died soon after. In Mississippi, Jack Dupree's throat was cut and he was disemboweled in front of his wife, who had just given birth to twins. Klansmen burned churches and schools and lynched teachers and educated blacks. Black landowners were driven off their property or murdered if they refused to leave. Blacks were whipped for refusing to work for whites, for having intimate relations with whites, for arguing with whites, for having jobs whites wanted, for reading a newspaper or having a book in their homes—or simply for being black. Klan violence led one black man to write, "We have very dark days here. The colored people are in despair. The rebels boast that the Negroes shall not have as much liberty now as they had under slavery. If things go on thus, our doom is sealed. God knows it is worse than slavery."

A few state governments fought back. In Tennessee and Arkansas, Republicans organized a police force that arrested, tried, and executed Klansmen. In Texas, Governor Edmund Davis organized a crack state police unit; 40 percent of the officers were black. The police made more than six thousand arrests and stopped the Klan. Sometimes blacks and whites fought back. Blacks lynched three whites in Arkansas who murdered a black lawyer. Armed groups of blacks and whites fought or threatened Klansmen in North and South Carolina. The price paid for resistance could be heavy, and many states were helpless against Klan terror. In Colfax, Louisiana, when blacks tried to defend their town against a white mob, 280 were massacred, 50 of whom had surrendered and were unarmed. President Grant condemned the slaughter in a letter to the Senate: "A butchery of citizens was committed at Colfax, which in blood-thirstiness and barbarity is hardly surpassed by any acts of savage warfare. . . . Insuperable obstructions were thrown in the way of punishing these murderers and the so-called conservative papers of the state not only justified the massacre but denounced as federal tyranny and despotism the attempt of the United States officers to bring them to justice."

State governments pleaded for the federal government to send troops. General William Tecumseh Sherman, who had no love for blacks, agreed: "If that is the only alternative I am willing . . . to again appeal to the power of the nation to crush, as we have done once before, this organized civil war."

Between 1870 and 1871, Congress passed a series of Enforcement Acts—criminal codes that protected citizens in their right to vote, to hold office, to serve on juries, and to receive equal protection under the law. If the states failed to act, these codes allowed the federal government to intervene.

President Grant responded by decreeing that "insurgents were in rebellion against the authority of the United States." Federal troops were sent to restore law and order to many areas where violence was raging. In nine counties of South Carolina, martial law was declared, and Klansmen were tried before predominantly black juries. Much of the credit for prosecuting the Klan belonged to Amos Ackerman, Grant's attorney general, who did his best to make the country aware of the extent of Klan violence. Despite his efforts, only a few Klansmen and their sympathizers were tried and sent to jail. Thousands of others fled or were released with fines or warnings. By the time the terror temporarily ended, thousands of blacks and hundreds of whites had been massacred or driven from their homes. For a moment, it seemed that peace and Republican rule were restored. One newspaper predicted what would inevitably happen to blacks when the federal government no longer came to the rescue: "It is impossible that your present power can endure whether you use it for good or ill. Let not your pride nor yet your pretended friends flatter you in the belief that you ever can or ever will, for any length of time, govern the white man of the South. Your present power must surely and soon pass from you. Nothing that it builds will stand, and nothing will remain of it but the prejudices it may create."

* * *

A small but significant number of blacks became quite successful during Reconstruction. John Lynch of Mississippi was elected to Congress between 1873 and 1883. Eventually defeated, he held many posts in the Republican Party and practiced law in Mississippi, Washington, D.C., and Chicago, where he finally lived.

As Klan violence diminished, hope for racial progress was reborn. Signs of racial harmony could be found in many Southern cities. In Columbia, South Carolina, one man noted, "The Negroes are freely admitted to the theater in Columbia, and to other exhibitions, lectures, though whites avoid sitting with them. In Columbia, they are served at bars, soda water fountains, and ice cream saloons." In Virginia, an editorial in the *Virginia Dispatch* noted, "Nobody here objects to sitting in political conventions with Negroes. Nobody here objects to serving on juries with Negroes. No lawyer objects to practicing in court with Negro lawyers present. And in both houses [of the legislature] Negroes are allowed to sit as they have a right to sit." The *Raleigh Standard* admitted that in North Carolina "the two races now sit together, eat at the same table, sit together in the same room, work together, visit and hold debating societies together." Some saloons in Mississippi served whites and blacks at the same bar; some restaurants served whites and blacks in the same room if not at the same table. Albert Morgan, a Northerner who crusaded for education and black political rights in Mississippi, reflected years later, "The period from 1869–1875, was one of substantial, and . . . wonderful progress."

By the early 1870s, blacks had won hundreds of political offices. Some politicians were Northern and Southern free blacks; others were former slaves, some of whom had served in the Union Army. Many could read and write. A few black candidates decided to make politics their career and were elected as congressmen, United States senators, lieutenant governors, state treasurers, superintendents of education, and state legislators. These men included black leaders like Robert Smalls in South Carolina, Blanche Bruce and P.B.S. Pinchback in Louisiana, and John Lynch in Mississippi. For the most part, blacks received such low-level positions as justices of the peace, sheriffs, councilmen, judges, alderman, and members of school boards. Blacks were hired as policemen and firemen in some cities, served on integrated juries, and were appointed or elected magistrates or justices of the peace. A biracial democracy was struggling to take root in precarious soil.

Education remained a high priority. Harriet Beecher Stowe, the author of *Uncle Tom's Cabin,* observed that blacks "cried for the spelling book as bread and pleaded for teachers as a necessity of life." By 1870, black voters had ensured that every Southern state had established a public school system paid for by a state fund, although most schools were segregated. Even in the state institutions for the blind, the races were separated, leading one legislator to remark sardonically, "color was distinguished where no color was seen." In New Orleans, after a bitter fight, black and white students did attend integrated schools. The University of South Carolina was integrated. When white students and the faculty withdrew in protest, other whites took their place and got along well with blacks. In Nashville, and in Washington, D.C., Fisk and Howard universities were established to educate blacks for the professions and for leadership.

Many schools offered the same courses that white children received in the North, including reading, writing, spelling, grammar, diction, history, geography, arithmetic, and music. On the college level, pupils studied Greek, Latin, science, philosophy and, occasionally, a modern language. African Americans saw education as the necessary foundation for improving their lives and preparing them to establish a democratic society in which they would fulfill their responsibilities as citizens.

Some Southerners were startled at the progress blacks made. Edward Allford Pollard, a Virginian, admitted that he "always insisted on regarding the Negro as specifically inferior to the white man—a lower order of human being who was indebted for what he had of civilization to the institution of slavery." Yet Pollard confessed that "his former views of the Negro were wrong." Traveling through the South, he found that African Americans were not the "degraded poor, intellectually helpless people" he had thought they were. Instead he found that "this singularly questionable creature has shown a capacity for education that has astonished . . . his former masters; that he has given proofs of good citizenship . . . that his condition has been on the whole that of progress . . . that so far from being a stationary barbarian, the formerly despised black man promises to become a true follower of the highest civilization and . . . exemplary citizen of the South."

Progress came to the North as well. Legislatures repealed laws that prohibited blacks from voting. Schools and public transportation were integrated in some states. But social and economic discrimination remained. Blacks were still forced to live in ghettoes and work at menial jobs, and were denied access to hotels and restaurants.

Northern interest in the Southern "race question" was eroding. Between 1865 and 1873, Americans were prospering from an economic boom. Railroads crisscrossed the country. Wherever the railroads went, towns and farms followed. The West was opened to the large-scale mining of gold and silver, mass production of lumber and cattle, and commercial agriculture. Factories sprang up in cities. The workforce of the country had changed dramatically as unskilled immigrant factory workers and manual laborers replaced skilled artisans. The country was preoccupied with unions and labor conflicts. Big business began to use its power to organize monopolies, dominating economic and political life. In 1873, the nation's economy collapsed. Millions of workers lost their jobs and wandered the country in search of work.

OCTOBER 31, 1874.]   HARPER'S WEEKLY.   901

"EVERY THING POINTS TO A DEMOCRATIC VICTORY THIS FALL."—SOUTHERN PAPERS.

By 1873, the Democratic Party, which called itself the Party of White Supremacy, had won back most of the Southern states, often using fraud, violence, and intimidation to do so.

The depression was catastrophic for the South. The price of cotton dropped 50 percent, wiping out many small white farmers. Trapped in the quicksand of the South's credit system, unable to pay their mortgages, they lost their farms to the merchants who had extended them credit. By 1880, one-third of white farmers would be tenants or sharecroppers.

The crash destroyed large planters as well. Louis Manigault, a South Carolina planter, sadly witnessed many of his once wealthy neighbors lose everything they had. "Many families who have managed so far to hold out against immediate distress . . . have finally succumbed . . . and I hear of only poverty and misery among those who were the richest and oldest families prior to the war."

Hundreds of thousands of blacks were worse off than they had ever been in their lives. One federal official in Georgia commented, "I thought I had seen poverty in the city, but I never saw anything to compare with the poverty of those Negroes there." The depression also caused the collapse of the Freedman's Bank in 1874. Chartered in 1865, the bank had actively sought deposits from black men and women, churches, and benevolent societies. Tens of thousands of people had entrusted the bank with their life's savings. The directors, who were white, began to speculate during the boom and made large, unsecured loans to railroads and other companies. Frederick Douglass donated ten thousand dollars from his own pocket to help the bank survive. It was too little, too late. The bank collapsed, taking with it the savings—and the hopes—of its depositors.

In 1874, the country revolted against the Republican Party. Democrats swept to victory in Congress, not only overcoming the one-hundred-man Republican majority in the House of Representatives but also winning an additional sixty seats. Republicans still controlled the Senate, but their majority was dramatically reduced.

With the return of the Democrats to power, Reconstruction was now in the hands of its enemies. Even its former supporters had turned against it. Republicans were unwilling to push Reconstruction further. The old guard of Radical Republicans was dying off, and a new generation was emerging. Business, not civil rights, was the main issue of the day. As a final gesture, Republicans passed a watered-down Civil Rights Act just before the Democrats took office. The act outlawed racial discrimination in schools, churches, and cemeteries, and on juries and public transportation—but it was eventually overturned by the Supreme Court. Former abolitionists suddenly declared black suffrage a failure. Even the strongest supporters of emancipation now argued that the best way to protect black rights was to entrust them to the better class of Southern whites. White Republicans in the South abandoned their black supporters and tried to appeal to white Democrats by supporting discriminatory legislation.

Southern Democrats had little interest in cooperating with the Republicans. By 1873, the Democratic Party had "redeemed" Virginia, Tennessee, Georgia, and Texas. In 1874, the Democrats won Arkansas and captured the Florida legislature. In Alabama, where the black and white voting populations were about equal, Democrats won by murdering blacks at the polls on Election Day. The violence was worse in Louisiana. Democrats formed the White League, an organization dedicated to the restoration of white supremacy. Rumors of a coming race war swept through the countryside. The Shreveport *Evening Standard* announced: "White supremacy first, last and all the time, has always been the motto of the white people of Caddo, and they prove their faith by their works. Let the colored man lay aside all political aspirations and allow the united white men to do what it is utter folly for the Negro to resist. The conflict will continue as long as the colored race aspires to the governing power."

Farmers who planned to vote were threatened. One man reported, "The agent of the place I rented said, 'Jim, we are going to carry this thing our own way. You niggers have had things your own way long enough and we white folks are going to have it our own way or kill all you Republican niggers.'"

Blacks persisted in voting despite the violence. E. A. Lever, a plantation owner, was astonished at their perseverance. "Why is it that niggers keep on tryin to raise above their station in life? Some of them are scared to death of night riders visiting their home. Yet even the most scared of them takes an interest in politics and other matters that don't concern him." The situation in Louisiana became so violent that Grant reluctantly sent federal troops into the state to restore order—an act for which he was severely criticized in the North.

Republicans shakily held on to their power in Louisiana as a tidal wave of white supremacy rolled over the South. Mississippi "redeemed" itself from Republican rule by terror and murder in 1875. This strategy, called the Mississippi Plan, was ruthlessly used with great effectiveness throughout the state. Hundreds of black schoolteachers, church leaders, and local Republican organizers were believed murdered. One man bragged that they were shooting blacks "just the same as birds." Governor Adelbert Ames called on President Grant for help. Southern whites were unconcerned. One official commented, "The . . . North satisfied us that if we succeeded winning control of the government of Mississippi, we would be permitted to enjoy it." His observation was correct.

President Grant refused to send troops to help the victims. He complained, "The whole public are tired out with these autumnal outbreaks in the South . . . and are ready now to condemn any interference on the part of the government."

On Election Day, Mississippi's whites either stuffed ballot boxes or destroyed them and drove black voters away from the polls or murdered them. Eighteen-year-old Ann Hedges's husband, Square, was one of the victims.

> They asked where Square was and I did not tell him. Then he said, "If you do not tell, I will shoot your Goddamned brains out." . . . Then they came into the house and turned back the bed and made him come out and called him a damned son of a bitch. They told him to put his shoes on, and I got them and said, I will put them on; and I could not tie them very well; and someone said "Let the God damned shoes be: he don't need any shoes." I put my brother's coat on him and they carried him before them. I never did find him for a week, until the next Saturday. The buzzards had eat his entrails; but the body down here was as natural as ever. His shoes were tied just as I had tied them.

Despite the fact that tens of thousands of blacks, with a few white supporters, tried valiantly to vote, the Democrats won easily. Mississippi was now controlled by white supremacists. Governor Ames, a Republican, commented, "a revolution has taken place—by force of arms—and a race are disfranchised—they are to be returned to a condition of serfdom—an era of second slavery."

By 1876, Democrats had regained control of every Southern state except Louisiana and North and South Carolina. In the state elections of 1876, they were determined to capture all three states. It was also a presidential election year. Both the Democratic candidate Samuel J. Tilden and the Republican candidate Rutherford B. Hayes made it clear that they were opposed to federal interference in Southern affairs.

While the contests in Louisiana and North Carolina would be close, the election in South

Carolina seemed safe for Republicans. Black voters were in the overwhelming majority. South Carolina also had a popular and honest white Republican governor, John Chamberlain, whom many Democrats were willing to support. Chamberlain reduced the state debt and defied black leaders in his party by removing many blacks from office and replacing them with whites. He blocked some political appointments favored by blacks and rooted out corrupt officials. So pleased were white Southerners with his actions that the *Charleston News and Courier* remarked, "If Governor Chamberlain continues to pursue the course he has done for the past twelve months, I think it would be exceedingly unwise and ungrateful for the Democratic Party to oppose his reelection."

Only in Edgefield County was there determined opposition. Whites, led by Martin W. Gary, set out to destroy the Republican Party in the same way that reactionary white Democrats in Mississippi had—by terror and violence. Gary's plan was simple. "Every Democrat should control the vote of one Negro by intimidation . . . argument has no effect on them. They can only be influenced by their fears."

A confrontation occurred on July 4 that gave Gary his opportunity. A black militia group drilling on a public road blocked the passage of two white farmers. A verbal confrontation took place before the whites were allowed to pass. General Matthew Butler, the most powerful political figure in the area, ordered the militia to disband. They refused, and forty of the men, led by their commander, retreated to their armory. Butler led an attack against them. The commander was killed and twenty-five of his men were captured. Five black soldiers were taken into the woods in the early morning and executed in cold blood after they had surrendered. When the Northern press called for the guilty to be brought to justice, Ben Tillman, one of the members of the mob, ordered forty white shirts to be made and stained with wild berries to create the effect of blood. The mob then paraded "waving their bloody shirts" in defiance of the North. No one was convicted for the massacre. Tillman's group became known as the Red Shirts, and the organization spread throughout South Carolina and Georgia.

The murders polarized the state. Democrats who had thought of supporting the popular Republican governor could no longer do so. What turned many Democrats against Chamberlain was his criticism of the role of whites in the killings. Instead, Democrats chose Wade Hampton, once the wealthiest planter in the state and a Civil War hero, as their candidate.

In 1876, Rutherford B. Hayes was declared the winner of a controversial presidential campaign which he had lost in all probability. In order to gain Southern support for his claim, Hayes agreed to officially end Reconstruction.

Chamberlain also antagonized whites by refusing to send in troops to put down a strike in the low country rice plantations. Black workers went out on strike for higher wages and payment in cash rather than in company money that could be used only in company stores. The governor, needing every black vote he could get, refused to interfere, and the strikers won.

Democrats, unconcerned that the federal government would interfere in the election, had a free hand in terrorizing Republicans throughout the state. They formed rifle clubs and threatened to kill any blacks who voted.

On Election Day, Gary told his supporters to vote "early and often." Men from Georgia and North Carolina crossed the border and voted Democratic. Some claimed to have voted eighteen to twenty times despite the presence of federal troops. Violence was commonplace. Although blacks had a twenty-thousand-vote majority in the state, the Democrats declared themselves winners in a close race. Chamberlain refused to accept the results and claimed victory for himself. The same thing happened in Louisiana, where both Democrats and Republicans claimed the office of governor. Both turned to the President of the United States to resolve the dispute. The irony was that there was as much confusion in Washington as to who had been elected president.

A bitter presidential election campaign between Hayes and Tilden ended with Tilden the apparent winner. He was one electoral vote short of the number necessary to win. He had also two hundred thousand more popular votes. The final count of four states—Oregon, Louisiana, South Carolina, and Florida—was in dispute. The Democrats had won most local elections in the Southern states, but the Republicans still controlled the electoral boards. They cast their votes for Hayes, thereby giving him the election. Congressional Democrats threatened to block Hayes from taking office by filibustering in the Senate until Tilden was elected. Newspapers predicted that the country was again on the verge of civil war.

In reality, Southern Democrats were unconcerned about who would be President. Their interest was in home rule, the right to control their states—and blacks—as they saw fit. Needing Democratic support in Congress in order to become President, Hayes offered to end all federal interference in the South. One Republican official wrote, "I think the policy of the new administration will be to conciliate the white men of the South. Carpetbaggers to the rear and niggers take care of yourselves."

A bargain was made between Republicans and Southern Democrats, known as the Compromise of 1877. Enough Democrats agreed not to support a threatened filibuster in the Senate by Tilden's supporters that would have blocked Hayes from becoming President. In return the Republicans agreed to officially end Reconstruction. Hayes became President and recognized the Democratic governors of Louisiana and South Carolina over their Republican opponents.

On April 24, 1877, shortly after his inauguration, Hayes withdrew the last federal troops stationed in New Orleans. As they marched to the Mississippi River to board a steamboat and depart the South forever, Louisiana whites were jubilant. "Bells are chiming," reported one newspaper. "Guns, pistols, crackers and cannons are booming." Northerners were also glad that Reconstruction was put to rest. *The Nation* magazine, once a staunch supporter of black rights, editorialized, "The Negro will disappear from the field of national politics. Henceforth, the nation as a nation, will have nothing more to do with him."

Blacks sadly watched the celebrations. Some openly wept. Charles Harris, a black veteran, wrote, "We obey laws: others make them. We support state educational institutions whose doors are virtually closed to us. We support asylums and hospitals, and our sick, deaf, dumb or blind are met at the door by . . . unjust discriminations. From these and many other oppressions . . . we long to be free." Henry Adams, a black organizer for the Republican Party in Louisiana who had once been enslaved, protested, "The whole South had got into the hands of the very men who held us as slaves." Frederick Douglass cried out in rage against the Republican Party's betrayal of his people: "You have emancipated us. I thank you for it. You have enfranchised us. And I thank you for it. But what is your emancipation—what is your enfranchisement if the black man having been made free by the letter of the law, is unable to exercise that freedom? You have turned us loose to the sky, to the storm, to the whirlwind, and worst of all, you have turned us loose to our infuriated masters. What does it all amount to if the black man after having been freed from the slaveholder's lash is to be subject to the slaveholder's shotgun!"

* * *

In Tennessee, seventy-year-old Benjamin "Pap" Singleton had seen that Reconstruction would fail well before it officially ended. He knew that blacks would not escape the rule of the plantation and the white man's law without their own land. He journeyed to Kansas to see if

One of the main boosters of migration was Benjamin "Pap" Singleton. He organized several groups that migrated to colonies he founded in Kansas, one of which was named after him.

his people could find land there. "We needed land for our children," he later told a congressional committee. "That caused my heart to grieve and sorrow. . . . Pity for my race caused me to work for them. . . . Confidence is perished and faded away. We are going to leave the South." Singleton founded several colonies in Kansas, two of the most successful of which were Dunlap and Singleton's Colony. Another successful black colony, founded by emigrants from Kentucky, was Nicodemus.

To Henry Adams, the Compromise of 1877 signaled the failure of Reconstruction. Adams had risked his life for the Republican Party, successfully recruiting farmers to vote the Republican ticket. After Hayes's betrayal, he organized them to leave the South. He told a congressional committee, "So long as the white men of the South are going to kill us, there was no way that we could better our condition there. We said that the whole South had gotten into the very hands that held us as slaves. We felt we had almost been slaves under these men. Then we said there was no hope for us and we better go."

Adams had hoped to convince blacks to immigrate to Liberia. He did not believe that black people would be accepted in the United States. But Kansas had captured the black imagination. By 1879, Pap Singleton's vision of a mass exodus seemed to be coming true. Kansas had become the Promised Land for tens of thousands of African Americans, a place sacred to them because John Brown struck his first mighty blow against slavery there. God was in Kansas, and black people wanted to go where God was. George Ruby, a black journalist from New Orleans who supported the move, wrote, "The fiat to go forth is irresistible. It is a flight from present sufferings and wrongs to come. The ever present fear which haunts the minds of these our people in the turbulent parishes of the state is that slavery in the horrible form of peonage is approaching." C. P. Hicks in Texas described the anguish of his people in a letter to the governor: "There are no words that can fully express or explain the real condition of my people throughout the South, nor how keenly and deeply they feel the necessity of fleeing from the wrath and long pent-up hatred of their old masters, which they feel assured will ere long burst loose like the pent-up fires of a volcano and crush them if they remain here many years longer."

John Solomon Lewis and his family decided to join the exodus after being threatened by their landlord. "In a fit of madness I one day said to the man, 'It's no use, I works hard and raises big crops and you sells it and keeps the money, and brings me more and more in debt, so I will go somewhere else and try to make headway like white workingmen.' He got very mad and said to me: 'If you try that job, you will get your head shot away.' So I told my wife and she says, 'Let us take to the woods in the night time.' We took to the woods, my wife and four children, and we was three weeks living in the woods."

Although Singleton claimed he was responsible for the movement, in truth there were no leaders. Often people left in small groups, with a minister for spiritual guidance. One migrant said, "Every black man is his own Moses now." Another remarked, "We have found no leader to trust but the God overhead us." The exodusters, as they were called, saw themselves reenacting the exodus of the children of Israel. Whites were considered "Pharoah" and they the "children of Israel." Reaching St. Louis was like crossing over the "Red Sea."

Marching along, yes marching along. To Kansas we are bound.
Surely this must be the Lord that has gone before and opened the way.
Surely this is the time spoken of in history.
Farewell, dear friends, farewell.
Marching along, yes marching along
For Tennessee is a hard slavery state, and we find no friends in that country.
Marching along, yes we are marching along
We want peaceful homes and quiet firesides;
No one to disturb us or turn us out.

Sojourner Truth, who had dedicated her life to fighting slavery, was overjoyed at the exodus. "I have prayed so long that my people would go to Kansas and that God would make straight the way before them. I believe as much in that move as I do in the moving of the children of Egypt going out to Canaan. This colored people is going to be a people. Do you think God has them robbed and scourged all the days of their life for nothing?"

The journey was filled with danger and hardships. Planters, afraid of losing their labor, hunted migrants down and killed many who refused to return. They seized one man who returned to bring out his wife and family, cut off both his hands, and threw them in his wife's lap, saying, "Now go to Kansas and work."

Steamboats passed the exodusters by as they waited patiently along riverbanks for the boats to stop. Their faith that God would ultimately provide for them sustained them. When warned that many might die because they were ill prepared for the journey, one man replied, "In any battle, some soldiers must die."

Those who reached Kansas found that more hardships awaited them. One newspaper reported, "They landed in a cold drizzling rain which soon after turned into a raging storm. Not more than one in fifty had sufficient money to buy medicine with, while the appealing hungry eyes and pinched faces would have turned a heart of stone. Some 245 have died so far. They had expected to be received with open arms and placed immediately in government land, but in place of hospitality, they are met with coldness and distrust."

Although most African Americans supported the exodus, Frederick Douglass was critical: "As a stinging protest against high-handed, greedy and shameless injustice to the defenseless; as a means of opening the blind eye of oppressors to their folly and peril, the Exodus has done invaluable service. As a strategy however, it is a surrender as it would make freedom depend upon migration rather than protection. We cannot but regard the present agitation of an Exodus from the South as ill-timed and hurtful."

The praise for the movement outweighed the criticism. The *New York Times* reported, "It is time to acknowledge that the migration movement among the colored people of the South is one that in its essential spirit and quality must be honored by thoughtful lovers of liberty and progress." In the end, fewer than fifty thousand out of four million blacks living in the South attempted to migrate. And of those who left, many returned. Only a relative few found the promised land in Kansas of which so many dreamed. John Solomon Lewis was one.

"When I landed on the soil, I looked on the ground and I says, this is free ground. Then I looked on the heavens and I said, this is free and beautiful heavens. Then I looked within my heart and I says to myself, I wonder why I was never free before. I asked my wife did she know the grounds we stand on. She said, 'No!' I said it is free ground and she cried like a child for joy."

John Solomon Lewis was one of a fortunate few to gain his own land in Kansas. Most of the four million African Americans who remained in the South would be farmers who worked the white man's land on the white man's terms.

* * *

During Reconstruction, many planters deeply resented the independence shown by black farmers. At first, blacks could often dictate the conditions under which they would work because there was a shortage of workers in many areas, since blacks often migrated to areas where they could make a better living. Republicans passed laws to protect farmworkers from being cheated out of their wages. Planters were required to settle with workers before they could dismiss them. And farm laborers held the first lien on a crop. If a planter defaulted on his debts, his workers would receive the first money before the lenders.

Cotton was still the main crop. Since the South's farm economy was desperately short of money, cotton was the only source of credit. As a result, most farmers were trapped into a one-crop market economy. The self-sufficiency of independent small farmers rapidly disappeared. J. Pope Brown, a cotton farmer, explained, "We were poor, had nothing to go on, had no collateral, and we just had to plant the crop that would bring money right away." As a result, everybody grew cotton, and the overproduction forced the price down.

From this dependency, the sharecropping system evolved. Black (and white) farmers would work the white man's land for a share of the cotton crop. A farmer and his family would contract to grow cotton on a section of land belonging to a landowner. The landowner would supply the sharecropper with a house, animals, tools, and credit at a local store—which he often owned. The sharecropper would use the credit to supply himself and his family during the year with food, clothing, and other necessities. When the crop was sold, the farmer would receive a share of the revenue, from which his debt would be subtracted.

The more a sharecropper could bring to the landlord, the greater his share of the crop. If the farmer offered nothing but his labor, his share would be about a third. If he supplied his own animals or tools, or both, he might receive as much as half to two-thirds.

By the 1870s, variations of sharecropping were the dominant form of labor relations between blacks and whites. The system appeared to be a compromise between black farmers, who wanted to own land, and white planters, who wanted black labor. Black farmers seemed to have gained a certain degree of independence. The family worked their plot of land without daily supervision by their landlord.

But independence was often an illusion, as many sharecroppers became trapped in an endless cycle of debt under the credit system. The landlords and merchants, who were often one and the same, kept the books and charged extremely high prices for their goods. Interest rates could run between 50 and 200 percent. One sharecropper's wife explained, "The furnish man [storekeeper] would put you down in the book for 75 cents for a 50-cent item. Then he would add the interest. Anywhere from 25% to outrageous. So that 50-cent item would end up costing you a dollar or more at least. And that's if the merchant kept an honest book—which of course he didn't."

Some merchants charged sharecroppers for goods they never purchased. After the cotton was sold, many sharecroppers would find that they owed the landlords money for their purchases rather than receive a share of income. As one sharecropper put it, "You'd work all year and come up with five bales of cotton and the landlord would run the books up on you, and you'd come out with nothing." William Holtzclaw of Alabama, a sharecropper's son, remembered how at settlement time their landlord gave them their quarter share of the corn crop. When it came to dividing the five-hundred-pound bales of cotton, then selling at the high price of seventeen cents a pound, every bale went to the landlord. He explained that "they had done ate up their crop that year."

Trouble usually resulted if the tenant or sharecropper challenged the landlord. One farmer reported, "I know we been beat out of money. The landlord said I owe $400 at the beginning of the year. When I said, 'Suh?' he said, 'Don't you dispute my word; the books say so.' When the books say so, you better pay it too, or they will say, 'So, I'm a liar, heh?' You better take to the bushes if you dispute him, for he will string you up for that." One Louisiana farmer reported, "I lived on Joe Williams' place, about two miles southeast of Keachie. I asked Mr. Williams to pay what he owed me on my cotton. He jumped on me and beat me so badly I fear I cannot live. He made me crawl on my knees and call them my God, my master, all because I had asked for a settlement."

When Henry Adams, the Louisiana Republican organizer, tried to get farmers to bring charges against the landlords in court, they were reluctant to do so. "I saw many colored people swindled out of their crops. I led them into the light on how it was done. I told a great many of them to take their contracts to lawyers and get them to force the parties to a settlement, but they told me they were afraid they would get killed. Some few reported to court but were whipped when they went home."

Challenging a landlord could be fatal. Ned Cobb, an Alabama farmer, saw what happened to his neighbor Henry Kirkland and his son Emmet when they dared to question their landlord's accounts. When they presented their set of books to landlord Jasper Clay, "Mr. Clay didn't like that one bit," Cobb recalled. "He flew in a passion—he toted his pistol all the time—over that book business and threwed that pistol on old Uncle Henry and deadened him right there. So he killed the old man on the spot and he threwed his gun on Emmet and shot Emmet through the lung."

William Holtzclaw, son of a black farmer, knew of one black sharecropper who successfully sued. At the trial, the landlord presented his books showing that the sharecropper had received certain items that year. He was confident of victory, because he knew that his sharecropper was illiterate and the jury would be all white. The sharecropper then presented his "books" to the court in the form of a stick that he had bent into the shape of a hexagon. The stick was filled with notches he had cut, organized in such a way that one set represented the purchases that he made and another set the day he purchased it. The jury was so intrigued by his ingenious method that they voted in his favor.

By the end of Reconstruction, blacks were working as sharecroppers on the white man's land, receiving a share of the cotton crop when sold. But most blacks were cheated out of their rightful share and wound up working for nothing.

Since it was dangerous to confront their landlords directly, African Americans protested with humor. In one joke, a black farmer brings in six bales of cotton to a planter and asks for his settlement. The planter examines the books and says, "Well, Josh, looks like you came out dead even again this year." Josh says, "Well, I got two more bales outside still." The landlord angrily throws down his pen. "Damn your ass! Why didn't you say so. Now I got to figure the books all over to make you come out even again." Songs expressed the frustration blacks experienced:

> Our father, who is in heaven
> White man owe me eleven, pay me seven
> Thy kingdom come, thy will be done.
> If I hadn't took that, I woulda had none.

Although it was rare for a black farmer to own land in the rich cotton areas of the South like the Mississippi Delta, thousands of blacks did purchase farms in less desirable areas. Daniel Trotter, a sharecropper in Louisiana, kept an account of how he and his wife saved money penny by penny to buy a farm. His wife would sell dozens of eggs at a time for $5.30 and earn an additional $7.80 from sewing dresses. The family sold four pigs. They earned $70.22 from their share of a cotton crop. He also worked as a repairman, fixing clocks, machinery, and guns. At the end of a year, the family had saved more than $200 and bought a farm. In Texas, Charley and Lucille White purchased a farm for $350. "The house wasn't more than a shack," he later recalled. "Lucille and me always worked hard, both of us. We hadn't ever minded work. But it looks like when we got some land that belonged to us, it just set us on fire. We didn't seem to get half as tired, or if we did we didn't notice it. One day when we was cleaning up the field, Lucille said, 'You know Charley, even the rocks look pretty.'"

The middle ground between sharecropping and owning was tenancy. Blacks would rent farms from year to year, either paying in cash or in bales of cotton. Tenancy was risky, because if the tenant failed to pay his rent, the landlord could take all his possessions. Ned Cobb had seen his father destroyed that way. "They claimed they had a note against him and took all he had. Took his horse and wagon, went into his pen and took his fattened hogs he was raising for his family. They did that because it was out of the knowledge of the colored man exactly how you was subject to the laws. They was a great dark secret to him. Whenever the colored man grew too fast, they'd find a way to cut him down."

Jerry and Addie Holtzclaw began their working lives as sharecroppers. Their son William recalled that their landlord was one of those "gentlemen of the Old South" who had lost most of his wealth during the war, his wealth having consisted mostly of slaves. Since the Holtz-claws had neither tools nor animals, the landlord supplied everything and took three-quarters of the crop. William began working when he was four years old, riding a blind mule while one of his brothers held the plow. He never forgot the "excruciating pain" of hunger he and his brother suffered while his mother worked until midnight as a cook in the landlord's house.

I remember how at night we would often cry for food until falling here and there on the floor we would sob ourselves to sleep. Late at night, sometimes after midnight, mother would return home with . . . a variety of scraps from the white folks' table; waking us all she would place the pan on the floor, or on her knees, and . . . we would eat to our satisfaction. We used our hands and sometimes, in our haste dived head foremost into the pan, very much as pigs after swill. Sometimes our pet pig would come in. We never made any serious objections to dividing with him and I do not recall that he showed any resentment about dividing with us.

Knowing that they could not gain a foothold in life as sharecroppers, in the early 1880s, Jerry Holtzclaw managed to rent forty acres of land around Roanake County, Alabama. On credit he bought a mule, a horse, and a yoke of oxen. His only obligation was to pay his rent (three bales of cotton, worth about $150) at the end of the year and make payments on his debt. Work that had been drudgery to Holtzclaw on their landlord's farm was now a delight on their own land. "I remember when he announced this plan to us children we were so happy at the prospects of owning a wagon and a pair of mules, and of having only a father for boss, that we shouted and leaped for joy."

Life was still hard for the family, even though they had moved up in the world. Perhaps the largest burden fell on Holtzclaw's mother. She had to watch over the children when they were young, prepare all the meals, fetch water from the well or a stream, help feed the animals, work in the fields, take care of the house, and make and mend clothes. Usually she was up before the rest of the family to prepare breakfast and went to bed after everyone else.

Despite the energy and enthusiasm of the Holtzclaw family, disaster plagued them. As Ned Cobb observed, "all God's dangers aren't white men." One of the oxen broke its neck. A mule got a disease called the hooks and died, forcing young William to replace it. He pulled the plow while his sister held the plow handles.

The second year, conditions seemed to improve. By August, the family's corn crop—the source of their profit—was ready for picking. Everyone toiled from dawn to dark Friday and Saturday to pick the ripe, golden ears and pile them on the field to gather on Sunday, but Addie Holtzclaw forbade them to do so. "Sunday is the Lord's day," she said, "and must be kept holy." The corn could wait until Monday.

While the family was in church on Sunday morning, storm clouds suddenly gathered. Thunder roared, lightning flashed, and sheets of torrential rains drowned the fields. Rushing home after the storm ended, the Holtzclaws arrived in time to watch their corn crop swept down a swollen creek.

As the family held on for two more years, tragedies continued. Everyone was stricken by a slow, lingering, mysterious fever. Unable to afford a doctor, they stumbled about as best they could, receiving some help from neighbors. Lola, Holtzclaw's older sister and "the most beloved member of the family," died. After her death, young Holtzclaw saw his grieving father "pray his first prayer before the family altar."

Although the Holtzclaws eventually lost everything and were forced to return to share-cropping, they were determined that their children should escape their fate by getting an education. Jerry and Addie Holtzclaw had already organized their fellow sharecroppers to build a schoolhouse for their children. Building the school was the easy part; getting there was difficult. William Holtzclaw later described how his mother had outfoxed the landlord. "The landlord wanted us to pick cotton. But mother wanted me to remain in school. So she used to outgeneral him by hiding me behind skillets, ovens and pots. Then she would slip me to school the back way, pushing me through the woods and underbrush, until it was safe for me to travel alone. Whereupon she would return to the plantation and try to make up to the landlord for the work of us in the cotton field."

The children suffered physical hardship to go to school. "The schoolhouse was three miles from my home and we walked every day, my little sister carrying me when my legs gave out," William later wrote. "When there was school in the winter, I went with bare feet and scant clothing. My feet cracked and bled freely."

As the children grew older and their labor was needed in the field, the brothers took turns working and going to school. "One day I plowed and he went to school; the next he plowed and I went to school. What he learned during the day, he taught me at night and I did the same for him."

Rural schools were extremely limited. In Holtzclaw's school, "As soon as a pupil could spell 'abasement' in the old blue-back speller, they were made assistant teachers." Eventually they became teachers, with the best of them having advanced only as far as the fourth grade.

Holtzclaw knew that if he stayed with his family, he would lead the dead-end life of a sharecropper. But he could see that his father was broken in spirit and needed his help.

On Christmas Day, 1889, Holtzclaw's father called William to sit with him by an old oak tree in their front yard to give him the greatest Christmas gift he could—his freedom. "Son, you are nearing manhood," he said, "and you have no education. If you remain with me until you are twenty-one, I will not be able to help you. For these reasons, your mother and I have decided to set you free, provided you make one promise—you will educate yourself."

Holtzclaw promised. He left home to find work until he could go to school. Six months later, he came across a little newspaper published by a school called Tuskegee Normal and Industrial Institute, located in the town of Tuskegee, Alabama. In it was the following invitation: "There is an opportunity for a few able-bodied young men to make their way through school, provided they are willing to work. Applications should be made to Booker T. Washington, principal."

Holtzclaw scribbled a note. "Dear Book, I want an ejurcashun, Can I come?" He addressed the envelope to Booker T. Washington with just his name and no town address. Somehow the letter reached its destination. Washington replied. "Come," he said.

Several months later, Holtzclaw arrived. To a young man who had known only a share-cropper's life in the backcountry of Alabama, Tuskegee Institute seemed like paradise. "When I walked out on campus I was startled at what I saw. There before my eyes was a huge pair of mules drawing a machine plow which to me at that time was a mystery. To the rear was a sawmill turning out thousands of feet of lumber daily. There were girls cultivating flowers and boys erecting huge brick buildings. Some were hitching horses and driving carriages while others were milking cows and making cheese. I found some boys studying drawing and others hammering iron, each with an intense earnestness that I had never seen in young men."

Holtzclaw was soon to encounter the man who would become the best-known black man in America—Booker T. Washington.

Chapter 3

New Roads Taken, 1880–1890

In the early 1870s, sixteen-year-old Booker T. Washington, consumed with a passion for education, was determined to study at the then famous school for black youth—Hampton Normal and Agricultural Institute in Hampton, Virginia. Starting out from Malden, West Virginia, he began his five-hundred-mile journey to Hampton, with only part of the route covered by train. When the train reached the end of the line, Washington rode a stagecoach until his money ran out, then began walking and hitching rides on wagons. By the time he reached Richmond, Virginia, he was broke, filthy, and exhausted and still had a hundred miles to go. After crawling underneath an elevated sidewalk, Washington curled up and went to sleep as pedestrians walked above his head. The next day, he found work as a longshore-man. He bought food but continued to sleep under the sidewalk to save money to finish his journey to Hampton.

Hampton Institute was a model for the educational philosophy that would soon dominate Southern education for blacks. Hampton, established by the Freedmen's Bureau in 1869, was run by General Samuel Chapman Armstrong, a Union general with strong Southern attitudes about African Americans. A handsome man with a commanding presence, Armstrong had been one of the youngest Union generals in the Civil War. His self-imposed mission was to train black students to accommodate to Southern whites economically, politically, and socially, and to regard them as their natural superiors. Hampton was a "normal school," something between an intermediate and high school. Its graduates were trained to teach rural children proper work habits and low-level menial skills.

Hampton's teachers were white, and many were Southerners and ex-slaveholders. Segregation was the rule. One black visitor invited to a concert observed, "The rudest and most ignorant white men and women were politely escorted to the platform; respectable and intelligent colored ladies and gentlemen were shown lower seats where they could neither hear nor see the exercises . . . with any pleasure."

Many black students attended Hampton to learn a trade that they hoped would prepare them for the world as teachers and workers. Instead, they found themselves doing menial, often meaningless work, ten hours a day, six days a week. Male students worked on the farm, in the sawmill, and in the kitchens and pantries. They washed dishes, waited tables, and served as houseboys and painters. Women sewed, washed, ironed, cooked, and mended. The objective of these jobs, Armstrong said, "Is not to teach a trade but to get the work done." He wanted his students to love work for its own sake, no matter how demeaning the task. "If you are the right sort of man, you will engage in any sort of labor and dignify it. A man had better work for nothing than spend his time in idling and loafing . . . plow, hoe, ditch; do anything rather than nothing."

Critics like Bishop Henry Turner, an outstanding black clergymen and leader in Georgia, charged that Armstrong's philosophy would teach black youth to excel in the cornfields rather than in the classrooms. One visitor to Hampton observed, "The prime motive of the white men in the South who urge most strongly industrial education of the Negroes is the conviction in their mind that all the Negro needs to know is how to work . . . that the race is doomed to servitude."

In 1881, Booker T. Washington, then in his twenties, arrived in the town of Tuskegee, Alabama, to found a school for black students—and become a legend.

One argument Armstrong offered in defense of his educational philosophy was that there were few skilled jobs for blacks. In the cities, most blacks held unskilled jobs as hotel workers, drivers, porters, construction laborers, servants, and barbers.

As far as Booker T. Washington was concerned, Hampton was paradise and General Armstrong was God. Armstrong became the dominant figure in his life. "I shall always remember that the first time I went into his presence he made the impression upon me of a perfect man. I was made to feel that there was something about him that was superhuman."

Washington maintained his hero worship of Armstrong and his philosophy throughout his life. "At Hampton, I not only learned that it was not a disgrace to labor, but to learn to love labor, not alone for its financial value, but for labor's own sake, and for the independence and self-reliance which the ability to do something the world wants brings."

By 1879, Washington was teaching at Hampton when General Armstrong called him aside after chapel. He said he had received a letter from some "gentlemen in Alabama" asking him to recommend a white principal for a black school they wanted to open there. The letter came from Tuskegee.

Tuskegee was a town of approximately two thousand people located in Macon County. It consisted of plantation houses owned by wealthy landowners, a number of one- and two-story businesses, and a courthouse around which local people, black and white, gathered in racially separate groups. The town was famous for its marathon domino games that lasted from ten-thirty in the morning until six at night.

By the 1880s, whites were fearful that blacks might leave Macon County and join the exodusters. In 1881, the *Tuskegee News,* a local white paper, reported that Macon had lost more population than any other county in the state.

One way whites decided to keep blacks in the community was by agreeing to start a school for black students. A school could also prove an economic boost to a community that was financially hurting. One of the white leaders of the community wrote to General Armstrong at the Hampton Institute, asking him to recommend a white principal for the school. Armstrong replied: "The only man I can suggest is one Booker T. Washington, a graduate of this institution, a very competent, capable mulatto, clear-headed, modest, sensible, polite and a thorough teacher and superior man. The best man we ever had here."

One week later, a telegram arrived, which Armstrong proudly read to the whole school: "Booker T. Washington will suit us. Send him at once."

The campus of Tuskegee consisted of a rundown building and some sheds. From these humble beginnings, Washington created an educational empire.

* * *

When Booker T. Washington first arrived at Tuskegee, he was favorably impressed by the town but somewhat dismayed by the school itself. "Before going to Tuskegee, I had expected to find there a building and all the necessary apparatus ready for me to begin teaching. I found nothing of the kind. I did find, though, hundreds of hungry, earnest souls who wanted to secure knowledge."

The "buildings" consisted of a shanty that was to be used as a classroom and an assembly room provided by a nearby church. The shanty roof was so leaky that a pupil had to hold an umbrella over Washington's head while he taught. His rooming house was no better. On rainy days, the landlady also held an umbrella over his head while he ate breakfast.

To start a school with only a rundown building, a small amount of land, and limited funding was challenge enough. An even greater challenge was winning the confidence of the local white community. Although they had agreed to permit a black school to exist in their midst, Tuskegee's whites were still wary of blacks being educated. They felt that education might bring trouble between the races. Their greatest fear was that once blacks were educated, they would no longer work as sharecroppers on the white man's farm or as domestics in his house. But Washington had a genius for reassuring whites that his method of education for blacks would "not be out of sympathy with agricultural life." The school would benefit the white community by teaching blacks to be better farmers and better domestics. In time, Tuskegee's whites became its staunchest supporters and, as Washington liked to call them, "friends."

On July 4, 1881, Washington officially opened Tuskegee with what he described as thirty "anxious and earnest students," many of whom were already public school teachers. Some were forty years old. Washington was the only teacher. As word of the school spread, other teachers and students began to arrive. All were mature men and women; some were quite elderly. His plan was to train most of his students to be teachers. In turn, they would return to their rural communities and teach the people how to "put new energy and new life into farming," as well as uplift the moral, intellectual, and religious life of the people.

With local white support behind him and his growing ability to secure loans and credit, Washington turned to constructing a new building that would enable him to carry out his goals. He borrowed money to acquire land and mobilized his students, with much grumbling on their part, to clear it. Meanwhile, he recruited local people, black and white, to make donations. Whites donated eating utensils; Hampton Institute sent maps, books, and newspapers; and the students made their own blackboards, chairs, and desks. Blacks contributed labor, supplies, funds, and food. One man who had no money contributed a large hog at a fund-raising meeting. He announced, "Any nigger that's got any love for the race, or respect for himself, will bring a hog to the next meeting."

Washington taught his students how to make bricks, and with those bricks, how to build a building. His emphasis was on teaching vocational skills, but Tuskegee also offered basic academic courses.

Washington had plans to have the students construct the buildings and, by doing this, learn the required construction skills. He envisioned a school that would teach students everything from sewing, cooking, and housekeeping for girls to farming, carpentry, printing, and brickmaking for boys.

Washington thought that once they had a kiln to fire bricks and the right kind of clay, his students could easily learn how to make them. He discovered how wrong he was. Washington and about a hundred students had to wallow in the muck of a mud pit with water and dirt up to their knees in order to scoop out the clay. Several students quit in disgust. The others molded twenty-five thousand bricks with a mixture of clay and sun-dried soil and then fired them in the kiln. But the bricks were not baked at the proper temperature and dissolved into powder and fragments of clay. Washington started over again. When the second and third kilns failed to work properly, many students and teachers were disillusioned and wanted to quit. Washington refused. He was determined to succeed. As far as he was concerned, far more than bricks was at stake. "I knew that we were trying an experiment—that of testing whether or not it was possible for Negroes to build up and control the affairs of a large educational institution. I knew that if we failed it would injure the whole race. I knew that the presumption was against us . . . I felt that people would be surprised if we succeeded. All this made a burden which pressed down upon us, sometimes it seemed, at the rate of a thousand pounds per inch."

Lacking money for a fourth kiln, Washington pawned his cherished gold watch to raise fifteen dollars. The last attempt succeeded and was seen as a sign that the school would succeed.

For Washington, personal hygiene was as important as any book knowl-

In his early years at Tuskegee, Washington worked alongside his students in order to set an example. His goal was to teach them the dignity of labor.

edge. "In all my teaching, I have watched carefully the influence of the toothbrush and I am convinced that there are few single agencies of civilization that are more far-reaching." He knew that he had to change his students' behavior and personal habits as well as educate them. He had traveled around the countryside visiting the homes and schools of local black people and was shocked by the conditions he found. Many families of twelve or more lived in one-room homes. Their main diet was fatback and beans and they had little or no sense of personal hygiene. Washington quickly came to the conclusion that he would have to model Tuskegee on Hampton.

To take the children of such people I had been among for a month and to give them a few hours of book education, I feel would be almost a waste of time. . . . We wanted to teach the students how to bathe; how to care for their teeth and clothing. We wanted to teach them what to eat and how to eat it properly, and how to care for their rooms. Aside from this we wanted to give them such a practical knowledge of some one industry, together with the spirit of thrift, industry and economy, that they would be sure of knowing how to make a living when they left us. We wanted them to study actual things instead of mere books alone.

Washington preached what he called "the gospel of the toothbrush." One student recalled, "If Booker had what the young fellows now call a bug, it was keeping clean. Next to a liar, he hated a dirty man or woman worse than anything else in the world."

Margaret Clifford, Washington's granddaughter, who was born after Washington had died, understood why cleanliness was so important to her grandfather.

Many of the students who came to Tuskegee from homes in rural areas in Macon County, and the South, and elsewhere, wherever they came from, never had the kind of even hygiene teaching that was emphasized in Tuskegee. One student when he went to Hampton, he did not know what to do with two sheets. There were two sheets on the bed, and the first night he slept on top of them, the next night underneath both of them until he noticed that some people were sleeping between the two. And that's how he learned what the two sheets were for. There were students who came there who'd never seen a toothbrush. These were the kinds of character, hygiene, personal things that a parent would teach a child, and this was the way Booker Washington approached students, as a parent would to help his child learn the necessary things of life so that he could find his place in the world among other people.

Another student, William Gregory, was deeply impressed. "Well, that first class was wonderful. We just knew nothin' worth knowin'. All most of us had was strength and we wanted to learn. Booker just overhauled us. I think of how proud we boys were to have one of us, who had been to college, come back to teach us. How our hearts swelled with the feeling that some day we would do likewise. . . ."

Washington's goal was to have Tuskegee train teachers to work in rural areas, teaching children moral values, personal hygiene, self-discipline, and the virtues of work. "My plan was for them to see not only the utility of labor but its beauty and dignity. They would be taught how to lift labor up from drudgery and toil and would learn to love work for its own sake. We wanted them to return to the plantation districts and show people there how to put new energy and new ideas into farming as well as the intellectual and moral and religious life of the people."

Other teachers strongly believed that education of blacks required more than acquiring good habits of hygiene and work. "What we need are race leaders, not followers," said Lucy Laney, an African-American Georgia educator. Her goal was to develop the minds of students rather than their hands.

Mary McLeod Bethune was an outstanding black teacher who encouraged her students to serve their communities. Women teachers played a major role in helping young people overcome the demoralization suffered under Jim Crow.

In 1887, Lucy Laney opened the Haines School in Augusta, Georgia. Students studied English, mathematics, history, chemistry, physics, psychology, sociology, French, and German. Laney's mission was to turn out a generation of women teachers and community leaders who would be the regenerative force in the African-American community and the source of its salvation. "The educated Negro woman, the woman of character and culture, is needed in the schoolroom, not only in the kindergarten and primary school, but in the high school and the college. Not alone in the classroom but as a public lecturer she may give advice and knowledge that will change a whole community and start its people on the upward way."

During the 1880s, an increasing number of black women graduated from schools built and financed by churches. They were motivated by the desire to enter teaching, the only profession then available to them, to help uplift their people. With ten pupils in an abandoned cotton gin house, Emma J. Wilson, a graduate of Scotia College, opened a school in Mayesville, South Carolina. She accepted eggs, chicken, and produce as tuition. After three years of fund-raising, the school had five hundred pupils—and hundreds of chickens and thousands of eggs.

Local people also constructed schools, contributed food, boarded teachers, and gave money when they could. One elderly black woman wrote, "Deer fesser, plese accept this 18 cents it is all i have. i save it out of my washing this week. god will bless you. Send you more next week." A teacher noted in her diary, "Aunt Hester gave a pound of butter and a dime. Grandma Williams a chicken. Effie McCoy, a cake and five cents; Bessie Harvey a dress."

While many rural black students only received a rudimentary education, some teachers and communities made a major effort to give their children the best education they could afford under the circumstances. In the nineteenth century, few children received more than a fourth-grade education.

Teachers had to be imaginative and resourceful to compensate for the lack of supplies. Young women taught students everything from baking cakes and canning peaches to the Declaration of Independence and the Constitution. To the three Rs of reading, 'riting, and 'rithmetic, they added a fourth—race pride. They used ingenuity to compensate for the lack of books, maps, paper, and pencils. One teacher, denied by the local school board an American flag for her classroom, fashioned her own. "We had students draw the National Flag on the blackboard. These flags were assigned a place of honor on the board and became a permanent picture in the room for years. Pupils were careful not to erase the flag when they erased the blackboard."

Many pupils never forgot their teachers. In Promised Land, South Carolina, an all-black community unique in that many families owned their own land, Lizzie Chiles, a legendary teacher, taught them how to survive in a hostile world. Mary Charles, a former student, remembered, "Mrs. Chiles was the best teacher I had. She was a precious lamb, that woman. When she taught you something, it was right. Lizzie Chiles taught the children history and geography. Most important she taught us mathematics so when we dealt with the white man, we wouldn't be cheated. I still remember the way she taught us. If a man was going to plant an acre of corn, and he could plow twenty-five rows to the acre, and have fifty mounds in each row, with three kernels of corn in each mound, how many kernels of corn did he need to plant an acre of land in corn? 3,750!"

In many communities, churches offered Sabbath schools where children were taught on Sundays to read, write, and spell. They ran children's day programs in which such topics as "Does God Favor Education?" and "Who is the True Man and the True Woman?" were discussed as a means of reinforcing values of self-help, race pride, and community solidarity.

Benjamin Mays, a sharecropper's son who was born in a shack in the town of Ninety-Six, South Carolina, and who would go on to become president of Morehouse College and deeply influence Martin Luther King, Jr., recalled how the community supported his desire to learn. When he was nine, he gave a presentation to the congregation in his church's school. "After my recitation, the house went wild. Old women waved their handkerchiefs, old men stomped their feet, and the people applauded long and loud. It was a terrific experience for a nine-year-old boy. There were predictions I would go places in life. The people in the church did not contribute one dime to help me with my education. But they gave me something far more valuable. They gave me encouragement, the thing I most needed. They expressed such confidence in me that I always felt that I could never betray their trust, never let them down."

To help overcome illiteracy, black colleges throughout the South required their students to teach in rural areas during the summer. One Fisk student taught in a Tennessee school before he left to earn his Ph.D. at Harvard. His name was William Edward Burghardt Du Bois. He later recorded his experiences in his book *The Souls of Black Folk.*

The school house was a log hut. There was an entrance where a door once was. Great chinks between the logs served as windows. Furniture was scarce—rough plank benches without backs and at times without legs. There they sat, nearly thirty of them on rough benches, their faces shading from a pale cream to a dark brown, their eyes full of mischief, and the hands grasping Webster's blue-black spelling book. I loved my school and the fine faith the children had in the wisdom of their teacher was truly marvelous. We read and spelled together, wrote a little, picked flowers, sang and listened to stories of the world beyond. There were some whose appetites were whetted by school and their half-wakened thought and weak wings beat against their barriers—barriers of caste, of youth, of life; at last, in dangerous moments, against everything that opposed even a whim.

Although literacy in the black community steadily increased, by the turn of the century only about one-third of the more than two million black children between the age of five and fourteen in the South attended school. There were no school buildings, teachers, or books for them. In 1890, out of 804,000 black children of high school age, 958 were in public high schools and some 20,000 in private schools. In many black schools, there was only one teacher for every ninety-three schoolchildren; white schools averaged one teacher for every fifty-seven students. The average annual expenditure in Mississippi was $14.94 for each white student and $1.86 for each black student.

Alabama tenant farmer Ned Cobb, who never went to school, saw how whites tried to undermine black education. "Weren't no colored schools here worth no count. The white schools would be all floatin' along, runnin' on schedule, colored schools standin' waiting for a class to open. When the colored did start school, we had to supplement the money the state give us with our own money. Some schools wouldn't run over a month or two months, then they'd send word, 'Close the school down! Close the school down! Money's out! Money's out!'"

For many black people, education became a dead end. "Once I was a great believer in Negro education . . . but now I doubt whether it's good or not. You educate your children—then watcha gonna do? You got jobs for them? You got any businesses for them to go into? What's the use of learning to be a bookkeeper if you got no books to keep? Do you think they're going to be content to come back and live in a lil' one-room house wid no electric lights. No! Education changed their tastes; they got to have better things."

Education was a luxury many black men could not afford. To escape the trap of sharecropping, they wandered in search of work in logging and turpentine camps, levees and railroads.

By the 1880s, thousands of men, despairing of earning a living on the land or gaining a meaningful education, were wandering the countryside seeking jobs in work camps and mines scattered throughout the South. They gathered turpentine in Georgia and Mississippi, mined phosphate off the Florida coast, cut timber and sawed lumber in Texas, and built levees alongside women workers in Arkansas and Louisiana. They dug coal in Alabama, Tennessee, and West Virginia and worked on railroads all over the South. There was a crude democracy in some work camps where black and white men worked together. In some industries, they received equal pay. Even though they socialized separately, occasionally interracial bonds developed. Their hard labor and common exploitation united them even as race divided them. They even united to revolt against their exploitation. In the sugarcane parishes of Louisiana, black and white sugarcane cutters went on strike in 1888 for higher wages. Planters broke the strike by massacring more than one hundred black workers in the town of Thibodaux. Black and white miners struck in Tennessee to protest the use of convict labor to replace them in the mines. Twice the state sent in convict labor and twice the miners freed them until the state backed down.

The wandering workers were "masterless men," not attached to the land, or beholden to landlords. Their presence often terrified whites, who feared any strange black man. One white man noted, "In all communities, there are Negroes of whom none knows the coming, going or real names. The Negroes are restive, the whites apprehensive and both are growing more and more suspicious. Such a status is already half hostile even before an overt act is committed."

Whites minimized their fear by maximizing their control. Police arrested unemployed men without cause, charging them as vagrants or falsely accusing them of crimes. Judges passed down extremely harsh sentences. Blacks received far more severe sentences than whites for the same crime. In some states, whites received two years for stealing a cow, blacks five. Whites were sentenced to five years for burglary, blacks twelve to forty.

Most blacks were sent to convict lease camps, which were organized on a deadly combination of racism and profit. Owners of mines, plantations, railroads, and other industries would contract with the state to lease the labor of men sentenced to jail. The prisoners would then be sent to work camps where they would work six to seven days a week from "can't see" to "can't see"—before dawn until after dark. They cleared snake and alligator swamps, dug coal in gas-filled mines, built railroads, and gathered turpentine in hundred-degree heat. Men were worked fourteen hours a day six to seven days a week in conditions that one convict described as "nine kinds of hell." In some camps, men were chained for days in knee-deep pools of muck, their thirst forcing them to drink the water in which they were compelled to deposit their excrement. The men ate and slept on bare ground, without blankets and mattresses and often without clothes. Beatings never ceased. On one plantation farm, a man was given ten lashes for "slow hoeing," five for "sorry planting." Those who tried to escape and were captured were whipped until the blood ran. One guard chillingly commented, "Kill a nigger . . . get another." Another described the punishment that one man received for an infraction of the rules:

Whipcords were fastened around his thumbs, the loose ends flung over a convenient limb and made taut until his toes swung clear of the ground. The scared convicts watched their comrade as he writhed and yelled expecting every moment that the cords would be unfastened and his agony ended. But the captain had determined to make an example and he let the negro hang. The poor wretch's agony was a hideous thing to see. They say his muscles knotted into cramps under the strain. His eyes started from his head and sweat ran down from his body in streams. An hour passed—then two. His shrieks had ceased and his struggles grown feeble, so they let him down and he fell like a log—dead.

Sometimes housed in rolling iron cages like those used for circus animals, fed the worst food, denied medical treatment, men died from malaria, scurvy, frostbite, sunstroke, dysentery, snakebite, shackle poisoning, and murder by violent and sadistic guards. At a time when more than a hundred men a year were lynched, thousands died in convict lease camps. Convict leasing, one former government official said, was a death sentence. George Washington Cable, a Southern writer, investigated several camps and found that though many men had sentences longer than ten years, no one survived a camp more than ten years. Death rates in some camps were as high as 45 percent, seldom below 15. In the North, the death rate was about 1 percent.

Many young children as well as adults were sent to work on convict lease gangs for misdemeanors or simply because their labor was needed. Some children were sentenced to as long as twenty years for a relatively minor crime.

In the convict lease camps, the slightest misdemeanor could be punished with great severity.

One prisoner described his condition: "We leave the cells at 3 o'clock AM and return at 8 PM, going the distance of three miles through rain and snow. We go to cell wet, go to bed wet and arise wet the following morning and every guard knocking beating yelling and every day Some one of us were carried to our last resting place, the grave. Day after day we looked death in the face and was afraid to speak."

Inspection reports often described the horror of the camps. The Mississippi Board of

Health reported, "Most of them have their backs cut in great wales, scars and blisters, some of the skin peeling off as a result of the severe beatings. They were lying there dying, so poor and emaciated that their bones almost came through their skin. We actually saw live vermin crawling over their faces."

Children were not exempt. Twelve-year-old Cy Williams was sentenced to twenty years on a convict lease gang for taking a horse he was too small to ride. Eight-year-old Will Evans received two years for stealing change off a store counter. And Mary Gay was sentenced to thirty days for taking a hat. She was six years old.

By the turn of the century, an estimated twenty thousand to thirty thousand African Americans, one quarter of whom were children, were condemned to hard labor in convict lease camps. Convict leasing had become slavery's replacement. To supply the demand for convict labor, sheriffs arrested blacks for misdemeanors and vagrancy.

For some men in the convict camps, a quick death was better than a slow one. They attempted to escape, knowing they would probably be killed. But they also knew that if they escaped the dogs and the guards, they could count on help from the black community. Many black farmers hid, fed, and clothed escaped convicts, breaking and burying their chains. To help a black man to freedom was a victory over their oppressors.

* * *

Oppression and the imposition of segregation laws did not come all at once to the South. In the 1880s, the situation was still fluid in many areas. While the rural South was noted for its increasingly harsh rule, the cities still offered possibilities for a better life for African Americans. T. McCants Stewart, a black journalist who had left South Carolina to live in Boston, returned for a visit to his native state. He was ready to fight anyone who tried to discriminate against him. "I put a chip on my shoulder and dared any man to knock it off." Stewart was astonished to find that he was accepted wherever he went. He sat wherever he wanted on streetcars and trains. "I entered a dining room as bold as a lion. The whites at the table appeared not to have noted my presence. I can go into saloons and get refreshments even as in New York. I can stop in and drink a glass of soda and be more politely waited on than in New England."

Everywhere Stewart went he saw encouraging signs of racial harmony. The two races worked and lived side by side and debated with one another in debating societies. Working-class blacks and whites often socialized in bars, brothels, gambling dens, and sporting events. He even witnessed a black policeman arrest a white man.

What impressed Stewart in South Carolina was that African Americans voted and were still appointed to minor offices. Public schools for children of both races were functioning. African Americans had their own churches, social clubs, and fraternal organizations. These achievements led Stewart to conclude that the ideals of emancipation were being fulfilled. "If you should ask me, 'watchmen what tell of the night,' I would say, 'The morning light is breaking.'"

As an urban South emerged, bursting with economic and cultural energy, tens of thousands of young black and white people began to migrate to the cities, drawn by their energy. Promoters called it the New South to distinguish it from the South of slavery days. A new breed of Southerner had emerged, ambitious, entrepreneurial, enamored of Northern capital and industrial change. Compared to the North, the South was still in the backwaters of the Industrial Revolution. But the railroads were bringing new ideas, new products, new people, and new opportunities.

Seeing a city for the first time was an experience many rural African Americans like young Henry Proctor never forgot. "When we reached the hill that gave us a full view of the city, such a thrill passed over me as I had never felt before. All at once a vision rose before me. Such a bewilderment of houses, steeples, cupolas; such a commotion of people and vehicles—such a labyrinth of streets."

Many families, like that of Walter Pickens, came to build a better life and to see that their children received an education. In the country, the Pickens children could go to school only six weeks a year. In the town, six months.

The Pickens and the Proctor families were entering into a small but rising urban middle class that embraced Victorian family values: patriarchal authority, feminine modesty, moral rectitude, thrift, hard work, and temperance. Some African Americans hoped, often in vain, that shared values between the "better class" of whites and blacks might mitigate racism. Businessmen played an increasingly important leadership role in the life of the community. They provided a variety of services from construction and catering to barbershops and funeral parlors. The *Richmond Planet* boasted, "Once the black man had no lawyers, doctors, theologians, scientists, authors, editors, druggists, inventors, businessmen, legislators, sheriffs. . . . He has them now."

Women formed missionary societies and benevolent associations and cared for the orphaned young, the poor, the widowed, and the elderly. They formed sewing circles, literary groups, and community-reform groups. They created a cultural world of poetry readings, theater, and classical music concerts. Men joined fraternal organizations and formed military companies, baseball teams, and volunteer fire companies.

As separation between the races began to widen in the 1880s, and blacks were increasingly restricted from participating in the social, political, and civil life of the community, they began to stress self-help and economic development. W.E.B. Du Bois, who would become the foremost scholar of black life by the early twentieth century, later observed this trend: "The colored man wakes in his own house built by colored men, rides to work in a part of a car surrounded by colored people. He reads a colored paper, he is insured by a colored insurance company, he patronizes a colored school with colored teachers, and a colored church with a colored preacher; he is buried by a colored undertaker in a colored graveyard."

The church remained central to the life of the black community, offering spiritual and social services. No man was more influential in the African-American community than the minister and none more valued than a minister who served his congregation well. In his four-year tenure in one church, Winfield Henry Mixon recorded that he attended 193 love feasts and prayer meetings, 42 funerals, 21 weddings, saw 116 sick families, baptized 115 adults and 128 children, delivered 1,152 sermons and lectures, and administered the holy sacrament 14,910 times. He preached a gospel of racial improvement despite the difficulties his congregations faced. "We have been carrying the blaze of Christianity," he wrote in his

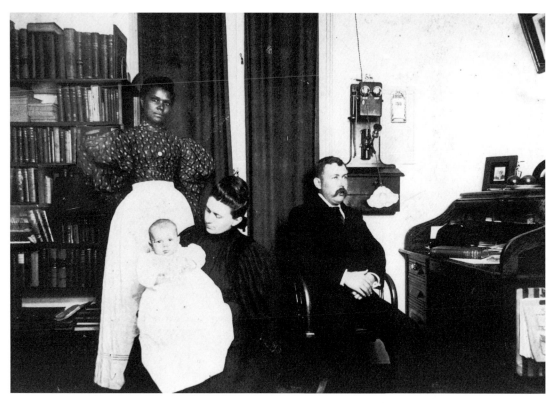

For most black women, the only job available outside the home was that of domestic worker. These women were often exploited by the whites for whom they worked and against whom they sometimes rebelled in sly and subtle ways.

diary. "We have been watching the dancing rays of wealth. We have been driving the shining steel of education through the head of ignorance. We have been teaching our people to have confidence in each other and help each other in business."

Even whites sat up and took notice of the new black middle class. The *Nashville Republican Banner* praised the middle class in one breath and disparaged the working class in another. "The Negro we come in contact with is the thrifty and cleanly barber or dining room servant, and even sometimes the banker and merchant. He is generally improving his opportunity, but unfortunately he cannot be taken as representative of the indolent and shiftless hundreds of thousands whose highest ambition is a drink and a fiddle and a dance."

Yet most of those streaming into the cities were working-class men and women hoping to find jobs and improve their lot in life. For women, work was relatively easy to find. There was a great demand by whites—even by poor whites—for maids, cooks, washerwomen, nannies, and other domestic servants. Since there were so many black women seeking these jobs, they were easily exploited. White men in the household often took sexual advantage of them. White women determined their wages and hours. Cooks were paid anywhere from $4.00 to $10.00 a month and nurses $1.50 to $5.00, depending on their age. If they did not live in, as many didn't because they had their own families, their day began at four in the morning, when they would feed their own children to be at work by five or six. They would work until after dinner, often returning home after their children were asleep. Most worked six days a week and some seven. One domestic worker wrote an anonymous letter describing her condition: "For more than thirty years, or since I was ten years old, I have been a servant in white families. I frequently work from fourteen to sixteen hours a day. I am allowed to go home to my children only once in two weeks. Even then I am not permitted to stay all night. I not only have to nurse a little white child. I have to wash and act as playmate to three other children. And what do I get for this work. The pitiful sum of $10 a month! With this money I'm expected to pay my house rent which is four dollars a month, and to feed and clothe myself and three children."

Behind the masks, there was sorrow. Dorothy Bolden, a maid in Georgia, was interviewed on her working life.

> White folks didn't have no feelin' for you. They pretended they did. They had nannies to give their child comfort. That was my name: "Nanny." They would teach their children they was better than you. You was givin' them all that love and you'd hear them say, "You're not supposed to love nanny. Nanny's a nigger." And they could say it so nasty. Til it would cut your heart out almost and you couldn't say a mumblin' word. A woman knows how to shift the smile when the burden is so heavy. Know how to smile when she want to cry. Smile when sorrow done touched her so deeply. So that's why I feel black women in this field had to pray and had to moan and had to cry. And those prayers were like the waving of an ocean. Like a wave in the ocean you know how it roll over and throw and keep on rolling. Them prayers went a long ways and protected a lot of people. And God wiped away those tears. And the next morning, we had the strength to go on.

Whites often criticized black domestics for being lazy, shiftless, or ignorant when they made mistakes. It didn't occur to them that a cook burning a meal, a washerwoman "accidentally" breaking a button, or a maid leaving without notice was often a deliberate act of rebellion. Behind the smiles, the "yessums," and the masks blacks often wore in the presence of whites was a calculated protest against exploitation. Sometimes this would be expressed in mocking songs:

> Missus in de big house
> Mammy's in the yard
> Missus holdin' her white hands
> Mammy working hard . . .

Sometimes the protest was more direct. In 1881, in Atlanta, black washerwomen went on strike. Working outside people's homes gave them independence, but their pay remained low, sometimes as little as fifty cents a day. The work was grueling. A washerwoman had to draw hundreds of pounds of water from a well to wash, boil, and iron clothes. She had to make her own soap from lye and her own starch from wheat bran, and she had to cut beer barrels in half to make tubs.

The washerwomen formed the Washing Society, a union with more than three thousand members. For more than a month, they resisted the combined pressure of their white patrons and a city government that threatened to charge them high fees for licenses. "We can afford to pay these licenses and will do it before we are defeated, and then we will have full control of the city's washing at our own prices, as the city has control over our husbands' work at their prices. Don't forget this. We mean business." The city used its police power to jail and fine the strikers and break the strike.

For men, finding work was harder. Steady work was rare, and the only way that most could survive was to move from job to job. One man described his working life. "I been factory hand, janitor, porter and butler, and wipin' up engines on the railroad. I worked as a helper for carpenter and layin' brick for masons. I been a driver of teams, a pick and shovel man, and drove steel for a section boss. I was a hand on the Mississippi, and workin' in a steel foundry and seem like I did a hundred mo' jobs."

The influx of thousands of new black people to the cities of the South, the rising of an obviously capable black middle class, and the growing militancy of a generation of young people who were born after slavery deeply troubled whites. They complained about the changes that had been taking place since slavery days. One Southern woman, who once owned slaves, lamented, "They don't sing as they used to. You should have known the old days of the plantation. Every year, it seems that they are losing more and more of their own confessed good humor. I sometimes feel I don't know them anymore. They have grown so glum and serious that I'm free to say I'm scared of them." And a white merchant complained, "The colored race are getting more unreliable. Freedom has ruined them in every way. Only the old timey darkies can be trusted. The young ones are sullen and grow more insolent every day." Blacks agreed. One black youth commented, "Younger Negroes, who are ignorant of the so-called instinctive fear of their fathers, are prone to brood in bitterness and suppressed rage over their wrongs and are more sensitive to injustice and quick to resent it."

As the 1880s progressed, the gulf between the races widened. Many whites felt that more laws were needed to control African Americans. The days of flexible race relations and paternalistic attitudes of whites toward blacks were ending. Whites were demanding new, uniform laws as a means of controlling blacks. From this demand, Jim Crow laws would eventually spread across the South like prairie fire in high wind. Into this darkening period came a diminutive young teacher who would challenge the rising tide of white supremacy and become the foremost agitator of her day. Her name was Ida B. Wells.

Chapter 4

"Jim Crow Comes to Town," 1890–1896

In May 1884, Ida B. Wells, a demure, diminutive, well-dressed young black schoolteacher, was quietly reading in a first-class or "ladies'" car in a train in Tennessee. The white conductor ordered her to move to the "colored" car. Blacks were no longer allowed in the ladies' coach. "I refused," Wells later wrote, "saying the forward car was a smoker, and as I was in the ladies car, I proposed to stay. He tried to drag me out of my seat but the moment he caught hold of my arm, I fastened my teeth on the back of his hand."

Nothing was more offensive to African Americans—especially an African-American woman—than to sit in the Jim Crow car where men of both races drank, smoked, cursed, and spat. W.E.B. Du Bois once described his journey in a segregated car: "The 'Jim-Crow' car is caked with dirt, the floor is gummy and the windows dirty. The conductor gruffly asks for your tickets. Lunch rooms either 'don't serve niggers' or serve them at some dirty and ill-attended hole-in-the-wall. Toilet rooms are often filthy."

The conductor dragged a struggling Wells off the train as white passengers cheered. She sued the railroad and won in the lower courts. The judges agreed that she was indeed a lady, having dressed and acted accordingly, had the appropriate ticket, and deserved to sit in the ladies' coach. A higher court reversed the decision on the grounds that Wells rode the train deliberately to create a disturbance—although there was not the slightest evidence that she did so. The reversal devastated her. "I had firmly believed all along that the law was on our side and would give us justice. I feel shorn of that belief and utterly discouraged. If it were possible, I would gather the race in my arms and fly away with them. God, is there no redress, no peace nor justice for us? Teach us what to do, for I am sorely, bitterly disgusted."

That injustice infuriated Ida Wells was no surprise to those who knew her. Her mother and father had been political activists in Holly Springs, Mississippi, during Reconstruction and had organized blacks to vote the Republican ticket. Both parents, Jim and Lizzie Wells, were great believers in education for their children, and Wells went to college to become a teacher. When her parents died during a yellow fever epidemic in 1878, she accepted a teach-

Ida B. Wells was the first civil rights agitator to emerge after Reconstruction. She traveled throughout the United States and England, crusading, speaking, and writing against lynching for most of her adult life.

ing job in Memphis, the following year. Two years later, Tennessee passed its first Jim Crow laws in public transportation.

Wells felt that unless black people resisted discrimination, they would become demoralized and defeated. "Yes, we'll have to fight, but the fight must be with our own people. So long as the majority are not educated in the points of proper self-respect, so long will our condition be hopeless. What steps shall be taken to unite our people into a real unifying force?"

Wells lived the life of a cultured middle-class black woman in the Victorian world of Memphis. She attended social gatherings at which guests recited Shakespeare, read poetry, and sang German songs—in German. She went to plays and musical events. In 1887, on her twenty-fifth birthday, she noted in her diary, "I have suffered more, learned more, lost more than I ever expect to again. In the last decade, I've only begun to live—to know life as a while with its joys and sorrows. . . . May another ten years find me increased in honesty and purity of purpose and motive!"

Wells found teaching difficult because of the poor conditions of the schools. Black schools received crumbs from the educational table of the city. Wells also discovered that some women teachers had to provide sexual favors to white school board members to get their jobs.

By the mid-1880s, Jim Crow laws were spreading. Public parks had been legislated as off-limits to blacks, and theaters were required to segregate them. In 1888, Tennessee's Democrats, using fraud and intimidation, gained control of the state legislature and immediately introduced legislation to disfranchise blacks. When the Tennessee legislature introduced legislation to eliminate the black vote, Wells counterattacked. Since the end of Reconstruction, blacks in Tennessee had held on to their hard-earned political rights. A shaky coalition of blacks and reluctant whites worked together in the Republican Party to elect candidates. Blacks in Tennessee still maintained some seats in city and state legislative bodies. Whites imposed a poll tax, voter registration laws, and a secret ballot that made selection of candidates far more difficult. Both poor blacks and whites were affected by the law.

Wells began to write and edit several newspapers part-time while she taught, expressing her opposition to segregation. Wells attacked the disfranchisement laws as they were being debated in the Tennessee legislature. "The dailies of our city say that whites must rule this country. But this is an expression without a thought. . . . The old southern voice that made the Negroes jump and run to their holes like rats, is told to shut up, for the Negro of today is not the same as Negroes were thirty years ago. . . . So it is no use to be talking now about Negroes ought to be kept at the bottom where God intended them to stay; the Negro is not expected to stay at the bottom." There was little blacks could do but protest. By 1890, Democrats had cut the black vote by half.

In 1889, Wells became editor and part owner of a newspaper, the *Free Speech and Headlight*. In 1891, she went after the Memphis school board for allowing black schools to remain in such poor condition. She also alluded to the issue of the sexual abuse of black women teachers. The board fired Wells from her teaching job. What Wells found most disturbing was the unwillingness of the parents of her students to protest. "I was saddened by the fact that the parents of the children I was fighting for did not seem to show much interest. One said to me, 'Miss Ida. You ought not to have done it. You might have known they would fire you.'"

Wells was now free to channel her energies into full-time journalism. She traveled through the South selling subscriptions to her newspaper while continuing to write. As blacks lost political power in Tennessee, white violence increased. Wells preached a doctrine of armed self-defense. She carried a gun and was determined to die fighting to protect herself from assaults if it became necessary. She encouraged others to do the same. When blacks in Georgetown, Kentucky, burned down part of the town after several lynchings, Wells approved. "So long as we permit ourselves to be trampled on, so long we will have to endure it. Not until the Negro rises in his might and takes a hand in resenting such cold blooded murders, if he has to burn up whole towns, will a halt be called to wholesale lynching. When the white man knows he runs as great a risk as biting the dust every time his Afro-American victim does, he will have a greater respect for Afro-American life."

THE MOB'S WORK

Done With Guns, Not Ropes

The Three Rioters Shot to Death in an Open Field.

They Were Carried a Mile and a Half Before Killed.

The Bodies Left Where They Fell and the Mob Dispersed.

Calvin McDowell's Face and Head Torn to Shreds.

Will Stewart and Tom Moss Nearly as Badly Riddled.

The Lynchers Left No Clew as to Their Identity.

There Were Between Fifty and Seventy-five in the Party.

They Knew the Ways of the Jail and Gained Easy Access.

They Also Knew the Men They Wanted, But Failed to Find One.

Isaiah Johnson, Alias "Shang" Saved by the Jail Porter.

Nothing Developed at the Inquest by Justice Garvin.

A Sensation Caused by a Reported Uprising.

Judge DuBose Locks Up a Gun Merchant for Selling Arms to Negroes--The Sheriff Patrolling the Suburbs--Resolutions Passed Condemning Barrett the

In 1892, three of Ida B. Wells's friends were murdered by a mob when they defended a grocery store against an attack by men hired by a jealous white competitor to destroy it. This incident launched Wells on her anti-lynching campaign.

In March 1892, violence struck close to Wells. Her close friend Tom Moss, along with two of his friends and their supporters, were arrested for defending themselves against an attack on Moss's store. Moss was a highly respected figure in the black community, a postman as well as the owner of a grocery store. A white competitor, enraged that Moss's store had drawn away his black customers, hired some off-duty deputy sheriffs to destroy it. Moss and his friends, not knowing the men were deputies, resisted. A gun battle broke out, and several deputies were wounded. Late one night, masked vigilantes dragged Moss and his two friends from their cells, took them to a deserted railroad yard, and shot them to death.

Enraged by Moss's death, Wells lashed out at the refusal of Memphis police to arrest the well-known killers. She encouraged blacks to protest with boycotts of white-owned stores and public transportation. Whites were furious. One man indignantly remarked, "I don't see what you niggers are riled up about. You got off light. We first intended to kill off every one of those 100 niggers in jail but concluded to let all go but the leaders."

Blacks composed a song in Moss's honor:

> Tom Moss was an innocent man
> He was at home in bed
> Teacher of a class in Sunday School
> Was shot through the head
> Oh me, oh my, Lord have mercy on me.
> Oh me, oh my, Lord have mercy on me.
> They are roaming the streets with guns
> Looking for us to shoot
> All we can do is pray to the Lord
> There is nothing else we can do.

Wells immediately called for a boycott of the streetcars in order to force prominent whites to pressure the police to arrest the killers. The officials of the line asked her why blacks were boycotting the streetcars. Before replying, she asked them their opinion. One of the officials said he heard that colored people were afraid of electricity. "If that's so," Wells replied, "why did they ride the line for six months before the boycott?" Puzzled, the official then asked Wells for the reason. She quietly pointed out that the boycott started after Tom Moss and the others had been lynched. "But we had nothing to do with the lynching," the officials protested. Wells replied that they also had nothing to do with seeing that the murderers were brought to justice. The boycott would remain.

The lynchings were a turning point in Ida Wells's life. She began to investigate and reveal the real motivations that lay behind lynching. Wells, like many middle-class African Americans, had accepted the myth that only poor blacks were lynched for some heinous crime. Wells was now shocked into recognizing that even innocent middle-class black people could be targets. "I had accepted the idea that although lynching was contrary to law and order, unreasoning anger over the terrible crime of rape led to lynching—and that perhaps the mob was justified in taking his life. But then Thomas Moss, Calvin McDowell and Henry Stewart had been lynched in Memphis and they had committed no crime against a white woman. This is what opened my eyes to what lynching really was—an excuse to get rid of Negroes who were acquiring wealth and property and thus keep the race terrorized and 'keep the niggers down.' "

As Wells investigated the reasons for lynching, she discovered that a number of victims were lynched not for rape, but for having sexual relations with consenting white women. "Nobody in this section of the community believes that old threadbare lie that Negro men rape white women. If Southern men are not careful, a conclusion might be reached which will be very damaging to the moral reputation of their women."

The suggestion that white women would willingly have sexual relations with black men enraged white Memphis. Since Ida Wells did not sign her name to her editorials, the white press assumed that a man had written the article. The *Memphis Scimitar* advocated a violent response: "It will be the duty of those whom he has attacked to tie the wretch to a stake, brand him in the forehead with a hot iron and perform upon him a surgical operation with a pair of shears."

A mob destroyed Ida Wells's newspaper while she was out of town and threatened to kill her on sight should she return. Forced to remain in the North, Wells launched a national—and later international—crusade against lynching that would capture the attention of the nation and Europe.

As Tom Moss lay dying in a Memphis train yard, a reporter who witnessed his murder recorded his last words: "Tell my people to go West. There is no justice here." Ida Wells agreed. "There is nothing we can do about the lynchings now as we are outnumbered and without arms. Therefore, there is only one thing left for us to do—save our money and leave a town which will neither protect our lives and property, nor give us a fair trial in the courts, but takes us out and murders us in cold blood when accused by white persons."

By the late 1880s, the belief of many blacks that racial tensions would eventually work themselves out had been revealed as a false hope. For thousands, the only solution was to move to the all-black towns, where they hoped they could live their lives avoiding contact with whites.

In 1887, a train traveling between Memphis, Tennessee, and Vicksburg, Mississippi, came to an unexpected stop at an isolated spot midway between the two cities. Two men stepped down and entered into a swamp wilderness. One was a white surveyor. The other was an imposing black man in the prime of life. His name was Isaiah Montgomery, a successful businessman who grew up in slavery. His dream was to build a utopia for black people in this inaccessible land of unbroken forest. It was a land where ash and elm trees, pecans and water oaks, walnuts and maples, tangled in a chaos of vines, brush, and cane, grew to enormous heights in ankle-deep water. Little sunlight could penetrate the tangled growth and the region remained in almost perpetual shade. Only deer, bear, and Indians ventured into this jungle. It was here that Montgomery envisioned that black farmers would one day own their own land and black merchants their own businesses. He called his proposed colony Mound Bayou after discovering Indian burial mounds on his property. What he hoped would make Mound Bayou particularly appealing to blacks was that it would be a community without whites. "It's a white man's country," he once said. "Let them run it."

Coming to the conclusion that blacks and whites could no longer live together, Isaiah Montgomery founded the all-black town of Mound Bayou. By the beginning of the twentieth century, the town was a social and economic success.

Montgomery was raised on a Mississippi plantation owned by Joseph Davis, the brother of Confederate president Jefferson Davis. Montgomery's father, Benjamin, had managed the Davis plantation before the Civil War and owned and operated it as a successful all-black enterprise during emancipation. The venture failed when cotton prices collapsed in the 1870s, and the Davis family foreclosed.

Isaiah Montgomery's main problem was finding others willing to risk leaving what little security they had to clear a wilderness and start over again. "It was not easy to find settlers in the early days," he said. "The task of clearing a wild country seemed hopeless to men with so few resources and so little experience." The first settlers cut down trees, drained bayous, built up the land, fought off wild animals and snakes, and lived as frontiersmen. Using axes and dynamite, they transformed the wilderness into farmland. Men built crude log cabins and sold timber for cash crops. Women and children worked for whites on nearby plantations. When the colonists, many of whom had been slaves in Mississippi, complained, Montgomery challenged them. "You have for centuries hewed down forests at the request of a master. Could you not do it for yourselves and your children into successive generations that they may worship and develop under your own vine and fig tree?"

Local whites thought the project was doomed to fail. Ben Green, one of the founders of the colony with Montgomery, encountered a white planter who was pessimistic about the project. "A prominent white planter in conversation with me one day remarked, 'Uncle, I can't see what Montgomery brought you up here for, unless to starve.' I replied, 'Our forefathers wrought in the opening up of the United States for settlement; and with a far greater measure of personal interest we are determined to work out the development of Mound Bayou.'"

The wilderness soon became a frontier. The ragged outline of the forest receded in all directions. People built churches, a post office, and schools. Montgomery insisted that all children of Mound Bayou go to school nine months of the year, almost twice as long as most black children attended school in the rural South. "Do you think that our boys and girls can go to and from our schools daily and not realize the benefit that comes from the industry and thrift they see around them? What chance has the Negro boy or girl who lives in the 'nigger quarters' of the city? They learn to despise their race and to think they can never amount to anything no matter how hard they work or how moral they are and that what they do doesn't count. We are teaching here that the Negro counts."

Booker T. Washington saw towns such as Mound Bayou as a vindication of his philosophy of economic progress for blacks, and urged blacks everywhere to follow its example.

Ben Green, who once was a student there, never forgot the impact the town made on him. "For the children of Mound Bayou, the community was a source of pride. Everything here was Negro, from the symbols of law and authority and the man who ran the bank to the fellow who drove the road scraper. That gave us kids a sense of security and pride that colored kids didn't get elsewhere." Another resident recalled, "My grandmother was eighty-seven. She came here from Virginia, during the time that Montgomery and all of them came to this barren area. She always wanted something for black people. She wanted something other than what she had been doing in slavery, doing what other people telling them what to do. She had in her mind that there must be something else, there must be something better than what she was living under." And a third resident added, "Mound Bayou was special to black people because it was governed by black people. Everything from the bank to the post office was directed by black people. That was something that was unbelievable in this race conscious era where there was so few opportunities other than manual labor for black people."

To keep Mound Bayou a haven for blacks, Montgomery was shrewd enough to remain in the good graces of the powerful white planters. As long as the Mound Bayou citizens did not get involved in state politics, their colony was not harmed. In 1890, whites prepared a massive assault on black political rights by amending the state constitution to exclude them and poor whites as well. And Montgomery would be called upon to play a key role.

In Mississippi, the Lords of the Delta, the white planters who ruled the state, also controlled the votes of black labor that worked for them. The planters were deeply concerned that a new force in Mississippi politics—the small, independent white farmer and merchant—would overthrow their rule. They were represented by such demagogues as James Kimble Vardaman, and deeply resented the planters' control of the state. White planters despised the rising class of white farmers and merchants, and feared them as much as blacks. William Alexander Percy, a Mississippi planter, described them in scathing terms: "They were the sort of people that lynch Negroes, that mistake hoodlumism for wit, and cunning for intelligence, that attend revivals and fights and fornicate in the bushes afterward. They were undiluted Anglo-Saxons. They were the sovereign voter. It was so horrible, it seemed unreal."

Mississippi elections had always been violent, and many courageous blacks and whites who opposed Democratic rule had been murdered. To end this violence, a compromise was reached between the planters and their challengers. Blacks would be constitutionally disfranchised, and corruption and violence at the polls would stop. A constitutional convention was called theoretically to legally disfranchise all illiterate voters. Everyone knew the real purpose. Vardaman, then a rising Mississippi politician, unashamedly confessed the actual motive: "There is no use to equivocate or lie about the matter. Mississippi's constitutional convention was held for no other purpose than to eliminate the nigger from politics; not the ignorant—but the nigger."

Whites warned blacks not to interfere in the change. In spite of the warnings, Marsh Cook, an African American, challenged the Democrats in Jasper County for a seat to the Constitutional Convention as a Republican. He was ambushed on a lonely country road. A local newspaper carried the story of his death: "The *Clarion Ledger* regrets the manner of his killing as assassinations cannot be condoned at any time. Yet the people of Jasper are to be congratulated that they will not be further annoyed by Marsh Cook."

Isaiah Montgomery had been invited to the convention by powerful whites to support disfranchisement, as he was considered "safe." The murder of Marsh Cook had reinforced Montgomery's conviction that blacks and whites should remain separate. When he rose to address the assembly, the hall became quiet.

My mission is to offer an olive branch of peace to bridge a chasm that has been developing and widening for a generation that threatens destruction to you and yours while it promises no enduring prosperity to me and mine. I have stood by, consenting and assisting to strike down the liberties of 123,000 free men. It is a fearful sacrifice laid upon the burning altar of liberty. I only ask that the laws be fairly applied, that the race problem be resolved and that issues be discussed on some other basis than the color line. What answer? Is our sacrifice accepted? Shall the great question be settled?

The Mississippi legislators applauded Montgomery. They then amended the constitution so that blacks had to take a literacy test if they tried to vote. The clause read in part that every voter "shall be able to read any section of the Constitution of this state; or shall be able to understand the same when read to him or give a reasonable interpretation thereof." This gave the registrar the power to accept or reject any potential voter. Since all registrars were white and politically appointed, it was highly unlikely they would allow any black voter to pass the test on his own merits. Whites were also required to take the test, but they were seldom questioned.

Blacks were outraged at Montgomery's speech. They called Montgomery a "traitor" and "Judas" for not challenging disfranchisement. Frederick Douglass flayed him. "His address is a positive disaster to the race. He has been taken in by lying whites. No more flippant fool could have inflicted such a wound in our cause as Mr. Montgomery has." Ida Wells, perhaps recalling that Montgomery had helped her newspaper, softened her criticism. "Montgomery never should have acquiesced but it would have been better to have gone down to defeat still voting against this understanding clause."

If Montgomery was willing to sacrifice black voting rights on the altar of white supremacy, other Mississippi blacks were not. I. W. Mannaway, editor of the *Meridian Fair Play,* called for blacks to resist being denied the right to vote by educating themselves in order to pass the literacy test. He urged every black prayer meeting to serve as a night school and every educator and preacher to teach the illiterate to read. "Do away with the midnight dance and the cheap excursion; stop taking Saturday evening vacations and let every man who can stammer the alphabet consider himself appointed by the Lord to teach one another of his race so much as he knows."

The law was appealed to the Supreme Court. In 1898, in *Williams* v. *Mississippi,* the Court sanctioned disfranchisement. The Court's rationale was that since the law did not, on its surface, discriminate by race, then it was constitutional no matter what its intention was.

Montgomery defended himself by claiming he hadn't surrendered anything that wasn't already lost. As far as he was concerned, the new law promised safety for his people from the violence surrounding them. "Mound Bayou," he said, "was the ship. All else was an open, raging, tempestuous sea."

Whether or not Montgomery made an explicit deal with whites to exchange his vote to protect his town, Mound Bayou prospered in the nineteenth and early twentieth centuries. The town eventually grew to four thousand inhabitants with thirty thousand acres of land owned by the community, producing three thousand bales of cotton and two thousand bushels of corn on six thousand acres. It had a town hall, depot, lighted streets, a half dozen churches, more than forty businesses, a train station, sawmill, three cotton gins, a telephone exchange, schools, a library, and a photographer. It was the self-governing and self-sustaining all-black community that Isaiah Montgomery had envisioned. Mound Bayou received national recognition from Booker T. Washington and Theodore Roosevelt, both of whom visited there and praised it. A reporter who visited the community described it in glowing terms. "The negro colonist of Mound Bayou owns his land or rents it from Negroes. He hauls his cotton to the gins of Mound Bayou, stores it in the warehouses and sells it in the markets of Mound Bayou. He buys his fertilizers, his livestock, and building materials in Mound Bayou. He purchases his calico, jeans, and furniture at the Mound Bayou general emporium. He reads his news in the *Demonstrator*, Mound Bayou's paper. He takes his physical from a negro doctor and gets new teeth from the Mound Bayou dentist. Finally he is buried in Mound Bayou by a negro undertaker."

The racial peace that Isaiah Montgomery hoped disfranchisement would bring to Mississippi was not to be. As blacks lost power, violence against them increased. Prosperous blacks throughout the state were targeted and driven from their communities. "Reverend Buchanan was banished from West Point at a mass meeting of some 100 whites who objected to his prospering, to his elegant horse and buggy, his decent house and his piano. Whites thought his mode of living had a bad effect on the cooks and washerwomen who aspired to do likewise and became less disposed to work for whites. He was ordered to sell his business and remove his family under penalty of death." Montgomery reported that Thomas Harvey, a grocery store owner, was ordered to sell his buggy and walk, and Mr. Meachem was ordered to close his business and don overalls for manual labor. Mr. Cook, who had two taxicab vehicles, would be allowed to run only one and had to sell the other.

Years later Montgomery confided in Booker T. Washington, "I am coming to the conclusion that only federal intervention can bring democracy to America. The dominant race is seeking a retrogression of the Negro back to serfdom and slavery."

* * *

As Mound Bayou prospered around the end of the nineteenth century, a great social upheaval taking place in the farmlands of the Midwest and South seemed to hold some promise for blacks. A political revolt was threatening to become a revolution. By the 1890s, that anger took political form in the Populist movement, or "People's Party" as it was sometimes called. In the South, the target of Populist wrath was the Democratic Party. Cotton prices had dropped from eleven cents a pound down to less than five cents. Below seven cents a pound, farmers lost money and had to mortgage their homes—if they could find a bank that would issue a mortgage. The "big mules," the lords of big business, now controlled the Democratic Party. Southern conservatives, who had for more than a decade ruled unchallenged, now found that they had undermined their own credibility. They had also allied themselves with Northern financial interests at the expense of the farmer.

Most Populists were white supremacists and had refused to allow blacks to join their party. Some, like "Cyclone" Davis, were openly hostile to blacks. "The worst sight of social equality to be seen in this land is the sight of a sweet white girl hoeing cotton in one row and a burly negro in the next. Talk of social equality when your industrial system forces a good woman's Anglo-Saxon girl down on a level with a burly negro in a cotton row. Oh my God! And this in a free America!"

When blacks formed their own organization, the Colored Alliance, both races warily started to cooperate. White farmers were troubled by the question of social equality; black farmers had other, more important concerns. At a Populist meeting one black farmer stated clearly the goal of his people: "We don't want to rule the government; we don't want to come into your family; we don't want to enter your schoolhouse. We want equal rights at the ballot box and equal justice before the law; we want better wages for our labor and better prices for our produce; we want to lift the mortgage from the old cow and mule which they have carried until they are sway-backed; we want to school our child and we want a chance to earn our home."

Black organizers risked their lives to help black farmers free themselves from the domination of white planters. In 1889, Oliver Cromwell of the Colored Alliance traveled to Leflore County, Mississippi, to organize a boycott of local white merchants in order to begin a black farmers' cooperative. Cromwell's life was threatened. When blacks rallied around him to give him support, a local posse suppressed the group in a sea of blood. J. C. Engle, a textile merchant from New York, witnessed the reprisal. "Negroes were shot down like dogs. Members of the posse not only killed people in the swamps but invaded homes and murdered men, women and children. A sixteen-year-old white boy beat the brains out of a little colored girl while a bigger brother with a gun kept the little one's parents off."

While white planters wanted to completely suppress the Colored Alliance, white Populists knew that their political futures depended on the black vote. J. P. Rayner, a black organizer in Texas, warned that they would fail without it. "If you want the Negro to vote the straight People's Party ticket, you must put men on the county tickets whom he likes. Kind words and just treatment go further with the Negro than money and promises."

No one had kinder words and promises for black farmers than Tom Watson, a former Democrat turned Populist. Watson recognized that blacks were not simply the straw men claimed by white supremacy, nor the dependent children of liberal Northerners, but an integral part of the South with a valid place in its political and economic life. He made an unprecedented appeal for the black vote in his campaign against Georgia's Democratic Party. He condemned lynchings, spoke on the same platforms with blacks, and recognized that black and white farmers shared the same hopes. "I pledge you my word and honor that if you stand shoulder to shoulder with us in this fight, you shall have fair play and fair treatment as men and as citizens irrespective of color." Watson organized picnics, barbecues, and camp meetings and formed political clubs for blacks. But political cooperation did not mean socializing. Blacks and whites sat separately when together, yet that did not prevent them from cheering wildly when Watson spoke of their common plight. "You are made to hate each other because on that hatred is rested the keystone of the arch of financial despotism which enslaves you both. You are deceived and blinded because you do not see how this race antagonism perpetuates a monetary system that beggars you both. The colored tenant is in the same boat as the white tenant, the colored laborer with the white laborer and that the accident of color can make no difference in the interests of farmers, croppers and laborers."

Watson's actions seemed to match his words. When H. S. Doyle, a black Populist organizer, received death threats from white Democrats, Watson protected him on his property. He sent word to his supporters for help. Throughout the night armed farmers gathered around Watson's house to protect Doyle. Watson claimed that two thousand people arrived to help. Doyle later recounted that many black farmers were deeply impressed with Watson's gesture. "After that, Mr. Watson was held almost as a savior by the Negroes. They were anxious to touch Mr. Watson's hand, and were often a source of inconvenience to him in their anxiety to see him and shake hands with him, and even touch him."

Watson made it clear that he was not endorsing social equality between the races. When Democrats charged that he had entertained Doyle in his house, Watson called it a lie and stated that when he protected Doyle, he put him in his "nigger house," a separate residence on his property. "They say I am an advocate of social equality between the whites and blacks. THAT IS AN ABSOLUTE FALSEHOOD. I have done no such thing and you colored men know it. It is best that your race and my race dwell apart in our private affairs."

Democrats were enraged at the interracial cooperation between black and white farmers. They accused the Populists of "treason to the white race" and rallied against them under the

Lynchings soared in the 1890s to over one hundred victims a year, with blacks being the primary victims. The killings were marked by an intense degree of sadism that often attracted thousands of spectators.

banner of "preserving white civilization." Although they also allied themselves with blacks opposed to Populism, Democrats accused their opponents of supporting "Negro domination." In the rich cotton areas where planters controlled the black vote, they stuffed the ballot box to offset white votes in Populist counties. In Atlanta, the Democratic candidate for governor offered to increase financial support for black education. The black community was divided. Many felt that white farmers were a far greater threat to black rights than the city Democrats. H. H. Style, an African-American supporter of the Democrats, warned other blacks of the dangers involved. "I am afraid the Populists will eventually ruin my people. They remind them of the wrongs done them and promise to correct them. But they do not tell them that they were in the front ranks when that army of oppression came against the Negro." Harry Lincoln Johnson, a prominent black attorney in Atlanta, echoed the refrain. "The intelligent Negroes of Georgia know that there is far more hate and spleen against the Negroes in the populist camp than in the democratic."

On Election Day, black farmers turned out in record numbers. Although Populists legally won a majority of the offices, Democrats used fraud, manipulation of large numbers of black votes, and violence to steal the elections. At least fifteen blacks and several whites were killed. The African-American vote was split almost evenly in Georgia.

Other states also defeated the Populists by violence and terror. Governor William C. Oates of Alabama confessed that the worst tactics were used in his state. "I told them to go to it, boys. We had to do it. I say it was a necessity. We could not help ourselves."

After the defeat of the Populist movements in several states, violence against blacks intensified. Populists resented the way the black vote had been used to help defeat them. Interracial coalitions began to dissolve. Many whites blamed blacks for their defeat. Whites vowed that never again would the black man be a factor in the white man's politics. States imposed literacy tests giving registrars the discretion to accept or reject blacks' qualification to vote. Poll taxes were passed. Lynchings of blacks soared: 113 in 1891, 161 in 1892, 118 in 1893, 134 in 1894. Until 1905, more than one hundred men and women were lynched every year but one.

The lynchings were often marked by an unprecedented level of sadism. The *Greenwood Observer* sent a reporter to the scene of a lynching of a black man allegedly accused of attacking a white woman. "The mob sliced his body with knives, burned his body with red hot irons, hung him by the neck until he almost choked to death, then revived him and continued the torture. Next they dragged him to the home of the victim's parents where several thousand people were waiting. When they stopped in front of the house, a woman came out and plunged a butcher knife into his heart."

Blacks were enraged but had limited power to express their anger. Minister Winfield Henry Mixon of Alabama wrote in his diary, "Every now and then the wicked, ill-gotten, squint eyed, blood suckers hang, lynch, shoot or burn their superiors—the ebony, pure and most God like in their heart Negro. My pen shall never stand, my voice shall never stop, my tongue shall never cease." Richard Wright would later write of the fear of "white death" that intimidated blacks in his autobiography of growing up in Mississippi and Arkansas. "The white death hung over every male black in the South. A dread of white people came to live permanently in my imagination. I had already grown to feel that there existed men against whom I was powerless, men who could violate my life at will. I felt completely helpless in the face of this threat because there did not exist any possible course of action which could have saved me if I had ever been confronted by a white mob."

In 1895, Booker T. Washington, deeply troubled over the racial fury unleashed in the South, searched for a solution. Invited to speak at the Cotton Exposition in Atlanta, a fair that promoted Southern industry, Washington was encouraged by a display of seeming goodwill on the part of whites. One of the highlights of the fair was the Negro Building containing exhibits demonstrating the scientific, cultural, and mechanical achievements of African Americans.

Many blacks boycotted the exposition. They objected to Atlanta's segregating the audiences at public speeches and on streetcars, to the convict labor used to grade the grounds, and to the fact that the only place blacks could buy refreshments was in the Negro Building. When some out-of-state blacks wrote to a local black newspaper asking if they should attend, the editor bitterly replied, "If they wish to feel that they are inferior to other American citizens, if they want to see on all sides signs that say 'For Whites Only,' or 'No Niggers or Dogs' allowed; if they want to be humiliated and have their man and womanhood crushed out, then come."

For Booker T. Washington, the exposition was an opportunity to promote his agenda rather than protest racism. He had been extremely anxious as he made the trip from Alabama to Atlanta, knowing that one false note in his speech could jeopardize everything he had built at Tuskegee. His audience would be mixed: Southerners, Northerners, white people, and black people. What could he say that would appeal to such a diverse group?

On September 25, the exposition opened. As the white speakers stepped up on the platform, the crowd welcomed them with great enthusiasm. James Creelman, a correspondent for the *New York World,* observed the crowd's reaction to Washington: "When among them a colored man appeared, a sudden chill fell on the whole assemblage. One after another asked, 'What's that nigger doing on the stage?'" But when Washington rose to speak and began by criticizing his people for seeking political and economic power during Reconstruction, the crowd suddenly became very attentive. "Our greatest danger," Washington said, "is that in the great leap from slavery to freedom, we may overlook the fact that the masses of us are to live by the productions of our hands and fail to keep in our mind that we shall prosper as we learn to dignify and glorify common labor. It is at the bottom of life we should begin and not the top." Creelman described what followed: "And when he held his dusky hand high above his head, with the fingers stretched apart, and said to the white people of the South on behalf of his race, 'In all things that are purely social we can be as separate as the finger yet one as the hand in all things essential to mutual progress,' a great sound wave resounded from the walls and the whole audience was on its feet in a delirium of applause." Washington continued: "The wisest of my race understand that the agitation of questions of social equality is the extremest folly and that progress in the enjoyment of all the privileges that will come to us must be the result of severe and constant struggle rather than artificial forcing. The opportunity to earn a dollar in a factory just now is worth infinitely more than to spend a dollar in an opera house."

The *Atlanta Constitution* described his triumph in glowing terms: "When the Negro finished, such an ovation followed as I had never seen before and never expect to see again. Tears ran down the face of many blacks in the audience. Governor Bullock rushed across the platform to seize his hand. White Southern women pulled flowers from the bosom of their dresses and rained them upon the black man on stage."

The white press throughout the nation unanimously acclaimed his speech. Former abolitionists, railroad tycoons, political leaders, and President Grover Cleveland wired their congratulations. The young teacher and scholar W.E.B. Du Bois praised the speech. Many blacks and whites felt that a new era had begun. The race question had been settled. Blacks would forgo their civil rights. They would get justice and economic rights. Booker T. Washington never forgot his triumph that day. "As I sat on the platform with the flower and beauty and culture of the South on either side, and these Southern men and beautiful and cultured Southern women wave their hats and handkerchiefs and clap their hands and shout of approval of what I said, I must have been carried away in a vision and it was hard for me to realize as I spoke that it was not all a beautiful dream, but an actual scene: right here in the heart of the South."

The people who showered praise on him were not the ones who would determine the future of blacks in the South. A new breed of politician was emerging, one who pandered to the racial hatreds of the mob. Among them was James Kimble Vardaman, who would soon be governor of Mississippi. He had his own ideas about Washington's philosophy of accommodation. "The man who says the race problem in the South is settled is just about as capable of judging and understanding such matters as the average nigger is about understanding the philosophy of the Decalogue. I am as opposed to it, I am just as opposed to Booker Washington as a voter, with all his Anglo Saxon refinements, as I am to the coconut-headed, chocolate-colored typical little coon, Andy Dotson, who blacks my shoes every evening." Vardaman made it clear that the compromise Washington offered was unacceptable to him and that the prominent whites who applauded him did not speak for him and his followers.

Nor did Booker T. Washington speak for the whole African-American community. Many blacks angrily rejected Washington's accommodating posture. The fiery, militant Bishop Henry Turner of Atlanta harshly criticized him: "The colored man who will stand up and say in one breath that the Negroid race does not want social equality, and in the next predict a great future in face of all the proscription of which the colored man is a victim, is either an ignoramus or is an advocate of the perpetual servility and degradation of his race."

John Hope, soon to be the first black president of Atlanta University, echoed Turner's criticism: "If we are not striving for equality, in heaven's name for what are we living? I regard it as cowardly and dishonest for any of our colored men to tell white people or colored people we are not striving for equality."

Not far from Tuskegee, tenant farmer Ned Cobb had different thoughts as well.

Booker T. Washington was an important man but he didn't feel for and didn't respect his race of people to go rock bottom for them. He never did get to the root of our troubles. The veil was over our people's eyes and Booker T. Washington didn't try to pull the veil away like he should have done. He should have walked out full faced with all the courage in the world and realized, "I was born to die. What's the use of me to hold everything under the cover if I know it? How come I won't tell it in favor of my people?" Wrong-spirited Booker T. Washington was. He was a man got down with his country in the wrong way.

The year after Booker T. Washington spoke at Atlanta, Homère Plessy, a Creole of Color who legally challenged segregation on common carriers in Louisiana, lost his case. The United States Supreme Court, echoing Booker T. Washington's compromise speech, sanctioned segregation under the fiction of "separate but equal."

Washington's speech earned him a great deal of goodwill but did nothing to help his cause. As racial hatred continued to increase, rumors of impending race war engulfed the South. White voices were heard demanding not only total segregation and disfranchisement but also exclusion and extermination. A Georgia congressman said, "The ultimate extermination of a race is inexpressibly sad, yet if its existence endangers the welfare of mankind, it is fitting that it should be swept away." Black workers in Montgomery, Alabama, prepared to fight back. "We have made up our minds to go down for the race. We expect to carry a goodly number of whites with us. Revenge we will have one way or another. Fires will burn and this town can be sent down to ashes."

As the nineteenth century came to a close, the message sent to African Americans was clear: There was no place for them in white America. Their great hope of emancipation—to earn their livelihoods by their own freely chosen labor, educate their children, enjoy their communities, participate in government, receive justice under law, and become American citizens—had been either denied them or severely restricted. For thirty years, African Americans tried a variety of strategies to deal with the crisis: confrontation, accommodation, resignation, rebellion, separation, and emigration. They met with varying degrees of success. Abandoned by the North, without allies in the South, they would continue their struggle alone, relying on their families, churches, schools, culture, and organizations to sustain them during the virulent onslaught unleashed on them as the twentieth century dawned. Drawing on the great reservoir of faith that lay within the heart of their community, their leaders never let them forget that the promise of emancipation was ordained and would eventually be redeemed.

Chapter 5

Victories and Defeats, 1897–1900

As wave after wave of racial fury inundated the South, a flicker of hope appeared. America declared war on Spain in 1898 and invaded Spain's colonies of Cuba and the Philippines. Black soldiers were needed to fight for their country. Of America's twenty-five-thousand-man standing army, two thousand five hundred were experienced black veterans. They had been fighting America's Indian wars on the deserts and plains of the West for more than twenty years. The Cheyenne called them "Buffalo Soldiers" for their courage in battle and their rough, shaggy appearance.

Black soldiers welcomed the Spanish-American War. Chaplain George Prioleau saw the war as an opportunity for the soldiers to prove themselves. "The men are anxious to go. The country will then hear and know of their bravery. The American Negro is always ready and willing to take up arms to fight and lay down his life in defense of his country's honor." Another soldier viewed the war as a chance to strike a blow against Jim Crow. "We left our homes, wives, mothers, sisters and friends to break down that infernal race prejudice and to have a page in history ascribed to us."

The black press was divided. Not all papers supported the war. The *Washington Bee* editorialized, "The Negro has no reason to fight for Cuba's independence. He is as much in need of independence as Cuba is. His own brothers, fathers, mothers, indeed his children, are shot down as if they were dogs or cattle."

As the soldiers traveled from the North to Florida, intermingled crowds of blacks and whites gathered at stations to welcome them. Chaplain Prioleau never forgot the reception they received. "All the way from Northwest Nebraska this regiment was greeted with cheers. While the Ninth Calvary band played, the people would raise their hats, the heavens resound with cheers. The white hand shaking the black hand. The hearty 'goodbye and God Bless you.'" When the train crossed into the Jim Crow South, the cheering stopped. Reaching Lakeland, Florida, John Lewis of the Tenth Cavalry remarked, "Lakeland is a beautiful little town, . . . but, with all its beauty, it is a hell for the colored people who live here, and they live in dread at all times." Lewis and his fellow soldiers confronted whites when a local druggist refused to sell them a bottle of soda. Abe Collins, a local barber, warned them, "You damn niggers better get out of here," and went to get his pistols. The soldiers stood their ground. Lewis remarked, "I suppose that he was of the opinion that all blacks looked alike to him; but that class of men soon found out they had a different class of colored people to deal with." Collins came out with his pistols and was shot dead.

The soldiers were immediately rushed to the battlefields of Cuba where several soldiers won medals of honor and the regiments were recognized for their bravery and fighting ability. Black troops played a major role in Colonel Theodore Roosevelt's victory at the battle of San Juan Hill. Although Roosevelt acknowledged their contribution at the time, later he would disparage their conduct. Lieutenant John Pershing, who during World War I would command the American army in Europe, was one of many whites who had praise for black soldiers. "White regiments and black regiments representing the young manhood of the North and South fought shoulder to shoulder. It was glorious. For a moment, every thought was forgotten but victory. We officers could have taken our black heroes in our arms."

The era of good feeling passed quickly. White Americans brought Jim Crow to Cuba and the Philippines. They called the people of color of the islands "niggers," and officials denied them their civil and political rights on the grounds that they were racially inferior. John Galloway, a black soldier with the Twenty-Fourth U.S. Infantry, wrote home, "The whites have begun to establish their diabolical race hatred in all its home rancor in Manila, even endeavoring to propagate the phobia among the Spanish and Filipinos." A Filipino boy challenged William Sims, another black soldier: "Why does the American Negro come to fight us when we are a friend to him and have not done anything to him? He is all the same as me—and me is all the same as him. Why don't you fight those people in America who burn Negroes, who make a beast of you?"

A few soldiers did desert to the Filipino cause. Most, Chaplain Prioleau observed, lived bitterly with the contradiction. "Yes, the Negro is loyal to his country's flag. Forgetting that he is ostracized, his race considered dumb as driven cattle, yet, as loyal and true men, he answers his country's call with tears in his eyes and sobs as he goes forth; he sings 'My country tis of thee, Sweet Land of Liberty,' and though the word liberty chokes him, he swallows it and finishes the stanza."

Even as black men fought for their country overseas, 101 were lynched in the South. At the Chicago Exposition of 1898, the usually circumspect Booker T. Washington delivered a sharp speech to an audience that included President William McKinley: "I make no empty statement when I say that we shall have, especially in the Southern part of the country, a cancer growing at the heart of our country, that shall one day prove as dangerous as an attack from an army within or without."

Although Washington almost immediately backed down from his strong words, the cancer he warned about was spreading. In 1898, it reached Wilmington, North Carolina, a city many black residents considered immune from the virulent racial turmoil surrounding them. David Fulton, an African American, found race relations there harmonious. "The best feeling among the races prevailed in Wilmington. The Negro and his white brother walked their beats on the police force; white and black committeemen sat down together in the same

Alex Manly, whose father was a plantation owner, was the African-American editor of the only black daily newspaper in North Carolina, the *Wilmington Daily Record*.

There were many small business owners in North Carolina and other Southern cities. Many of them had originally catered to a white clientele. But by the 1890s, most of their customers were black.

council; white and black teachers taught in the same school. We boast of Wilmington as being ahead of all other Southern cities in the recognition of citizenship among her inhabitants, unstained by such acts of violence that have disgraced other cities." The good feeling that Fulton found in Wilmington seemed to prevail throughout the eastern part of North Carolina. As long as the Democrats ruled, white paternalism gave everything a patina of racial harmony. When a coalition of predominately white Populists and black Republicans defeated the Democrats in 1896 and won political control of the state, Democrats vowed revenge. For many Democrats, black political power, no matter how limited, was intolerable. Julian Carr, one of the most powerful men in Durham, warned that white paternalism had its limits. "If we can wean the Negro from believing that politics is his calling by nature and turn the bent of his mind into the development of manufacturing industries, what will the end be? It is unlimited. But if the Negro is to continue making politics his chief aim, there can be but one ending."

Alex Manly, the fiery black publisher and editor of the *Wilmington Daily Record*, disagreed. Politics was exactly what African Americans needed. "How can the Negro," he asked, "expect to assert his manhood if he denies himself what is his constitutional right to vote and hold office?"

Located in the eastern part of the state, where the Cape Fear River enters into the Atlantic

In 1898, the Democratic Party in North Carolina, determined to drive all blacks out of political office despite the fact that they were a small minority, launched an openly racist campaign based on white supremacy. Blacks were shown in vitriolic cartoons as a threat, especially to white women.

Ocean, Wilmington was a prosperous port town in 1898. Almost two-thirds of its population was black, with a very small but influential middle class. They were teachers, clergymen, lawyers, doctors, businessmen, and journalists, many of whom had attended college. Some had acquired pianos, servants, lace curtains, and expensive carpets. Black businessmen dominated the restaurant and barbershop trade, owned tailor shops and drugstores. Black people held jobs as firemen, policemen, and civil servants. The county had the highest black literacy rate in the state, with more than half the voters able to read and write. Most members of the black community were workingmen and -women, primarily laborers and domestic servants. Wilmington's workers had a reputation for militancy. In the 1890s, the city's whites were shocked when both men and women went out on strike for higher wages.

Alex Manly was one of the leaders of the black community. His father had been a slave owner and former governor of the state, and Manly could easily have passed for white had he wished. He had married into the most prominent and prosperous black family in the city and had started the only black-owned daily newspaper in the state. Though he had a good rapport with whites, many of whom advertised in his newspaper, he believed that the goal of black people was full equality. Throughout the state blacks took pride in their accomplishments and their adoption of white middle-class Victorian values. They felt that by doing so they could establish a bond with whites based on class while separating themselves from the "lower classes." Reverend William C. Smith noted, "Our conduct should teach white people that we are not to be judged as a people by the vulgar rough set that loafs around the street in fifth and idleness." Smith failed to realize that it was not unsuccessful blacks that concerned whites. It was the successful ones.

In 1898, the Democratic Party resolved to take back the state by launching a virulent campaign based on white supremacy. Daniel Schenck, a party leader, warned, "It will be the meanest, vilest, dirtiest campaign since 1876. The slogan of the Democratic Party from the mountains to the sea will be but one word . . . Nigger!" Schenck had also been quoted as saying, "Nothing prevents the white people of the South from annihilating the Negro race, but the military power of the United States government."

The Democrats argued that only they could save the state from what they called "black rule," which, in reality, never existed anywhere. Furnifold Simmons, a Democratic leader, proclaimed, "North Carolina is a WHITE MAN'S STATE and WHITE MEN will rule it, and they will crush the party of Negro domination beneath a majority so overwhelming that no other party will ever dare to attempt to establish Negro rule here."

White terrorist groups like the "Red Shirts"—so-called because they wore red shirts as a symbol that they had killed a black man—mobilized to stop blacks from voting in North Carolina on election day.

The Democrats launched their campaign by appealing to whites' deepest fear—that white women were in danger from black males. Political cartoons exploited that racial myth by showing images of black men or mythical black creatures threatening white women. White women appeared in parades in white dresses holding up signs that said, "Protect Us!" The white newspaper in Wilmington published an inflammatory speech given by Rebecca Felton, a Georgia feminist, a year earlier: "If it requires lynching to protect woman's dearest possession from ravening, drunken human beasts, then I say lynch a thousand negroes a week . . . if it is necessary."

After the election, a white mob in Wilmington began to rampage. They burned down Alex Manly's newspaper offices and opened fire on blacks. A race riot erupted.

The article infuriated Manly. He responded with an editorial sarcastically noting that many of these so-called lynchings for rape were cover-ups for voluntary interracial sexual relations. He pointed out that interracial sex was a two-way street. "Every Negro lynched is called a big burly brute when many had white men as fathers and are not only not black, but are sufficiently attractive to white girls of culture and refinement to fall in love with them. Don't ever think your women will remain pure while you are debauching ours. You sow the seed. The harvest will come in due time."

Manly's editorial fueled raging fires. One white citizen claimed, "This article had made Wilmington seethe with uncontrollable indignation, bitterness and rage. It directly started the overthrow of negro domination and rule in the community." Alfred Waddell, a leader of Wilmington's white militants, declared, "We will not live under these intolerable conditions. We intend to change it if we have to choke the current of Cape Fear River with Negro carcasses." South Carolina's Governor Ben Tillman encouraged members of the Red Shirts, a white terrorist organization whose members wore red shirts to symbolize the blood of black men they had murdered, to take a hand.

Occasionally, a white voice tried to calm the storm. Jane Croly, a local citizen, criticized the Democrats: "The Negroes here are an excellent race and under all the abuse that has been vented on them for months, they have gone quietly on and been polite as if to ward off the persecution they have felt in the air."

Most white women supported Rebecca Cameron, who urged her cousin, Alfred Waddell, to defend white women as violently as necessary. "It has reached the point where blood letting is needed for the health of the commonwealth, and when the depletion occurs, let it be thorough. Solomon says, 'There is a time to kill.' That time seems to have come so get to work. . . . It is time that the shotgun play a part, and an active one, in the current election. We applaud your determination that our old heroic river be choked with bodies of our enemies white and black."

Waddell urged his followers to kill any blacks who tried to vote. "Go to the polls tomorrow," he instructed, "and if you find the Negro out voting, tell him to leave and if he refuses, kill him; shoot him down in his tracks. We shall win tomorrow if we have to do it with guns."

A black women's organization published an advertisement pressuring black men to vote. "Every Negro who refuses to register this next Tuesday in order that he may vote, we shall make it our business to deal with him in a way that shall not be pleasant. He shall be branded as a white-livered coward who would sell his liberty."

Black voters turned out in large numbers, but the Democrats stuffed the ballot boxes and swept to victory. The Republican/Populist coalition was completely routed. Julian Carr telegraphed President McKinley that whites reigned triumphant. "Men with white skins, who drafted the original Magna Carta of American Independence, will rule North Carolina ever hereafter; no need of troops now, praise God!"

In Wilmington, the political victory did not soften white fury. A mob set Manly's newspaper offices on fire and a riot erupted. Whites began to gun down blacks on the streets. Reverend Allen Kirk, a black minister, watched the terror unfold. "Firing began and it seemed like a mighty battle in war time. They went on firing it seemed at every living Negro, poured volleys into fleeing men like sportsmen firing at rabbits in an open field; . . . the shrieks and screams of children, of mothers and wives, caused the blood of the most inhuman person to creep; men lay on the street dead and dying while members of their race walked by unable to do them any good."

Harry Hayden, one of the rioters, stated that many of the mob were not rabble but respectable citizens. "The men who took down their shotguns and cleared the Negroes out of office yesterday were not a mob of plug uglies. They were men of property, intelligence, culture . . . clergyman, lawyers, bankers, merchants. They are not a mob. They are revolutionists asserting a sacred privilege and a right."

Some whites protected blacks. When the mob reached the Sprunt Factory, intending to shoot down the eight hundred workers gathered inside, James Sprunt, the owner, barricaded the doors and pointed guns on the mob from his yacht docked nearby. The mob retreated.

Many blacks took to the woods and swamps to hide. They were followed by Charles Bourke, a journalist from *Collier's* magazine. "In the woods and swamps innocent hundreds of terrified men and women wander about fearful of the vengeance of whites, fearful of death. Without money or food, insufficiently clothed, they fled from civilization and sought refuge in the wilderness. In the night I hear children crying and a voice crooning a mournful song. 'When the battle's over we kin wear a crown in the New Jerusalem.' "

By the next day, the killing ended. Officially, twenty-five blacks had died, but many more may have been killed, their bodies dumped into the river. Hundreds of others were driven out of town, among them Alex Manly, who narrowly escaped a lynch mob. His fair complexion enabled him to pass safely through a white patrol that mistook him for white. One of the mob members even gave him a gun, instructing him, "If you see that nigger Manly, shoot him!" Manly solemnly agreed.

Since a few black and white Republicans still remained in office, Waddell staged a coup

Charlotte Hawkins Brown (right) came to North Carolina to teach as a teenager. By the time she was in her early twenties, she had started her own school with a staff of teachers.

d'état by leading a delegation of Democrats to city hall and the courthouse, and forced the officeholders to resign. Jason Dudley, a local black resident, observed in a letter to Booker T. Washington how well-to-do blacks were targeted: "I met about a thousand soldiers who were drumming four negroes from the city. They were not indolent paupers or drones; they represented between thirty and fifty thousand dollars worth of property . . . It was not the insignificant Negroes that were disturbed, it was the well-to-do and prosperous ones."

Della Johnson, a Wilmington resident, appealed to President McKinley for help. "I, a Negro woman of this city, appeal to you from the depths of my heart to do something in the Negro's behalf. I call upon you as head of the American Nation to help these humble subjects. Are we to die like rats in a trap? Can we call on any other Nation to help? Why do you forsake the Negro? Is this the land of the free and home of the brave? There seems to be no help for us." McKinley did not reply.

As the violence finally ended, David Merrick, a successful black businessman in Durham, stated that Wilmington's blacks had brought the riot upon themselves. "The Negroes have had lots of offices in this state and they have benefited themselves but very little. Nothing compared with what they could have done along business and industrial lines had they given the same time and talent. What difference does it make to us who is elected? Had the Negroes of Wilmington owned half the city, there wouldn't anything happen compared with what did."

George White, the only black congressman from North Carolina, and soon to lose his seat, had another explanation. "This crisis has been brought about by the fact that despite all the oppression that has fallen on our shoulders, we have been rising, steadily rising. This tendency of some of us to rise and assert our manhood is what has brought about this changed condition."

The victory of the Democratic Party led to the disfranchisement of blacks. The black middle class was astounded that they should be included in the new discriminatory legislation. They felt that they had earned the right to be an exception. Reverend L. S. Flag of Asheville wrote, "Surely the men who have befriended us in the past will not, because of the conduct of irresponsible persons, enact a law that will have a tendency to crush the self-respect of those among us who are endeavoring to rise to genteel manhood and true womanhood." The plea fell on deaf ears. The haven that North Carolina had once been for African Americans now became a desert of white supremacy like the rest of the South.

The disastrous election of 1898 did not deter one woman from launching her own fight against Jim Crow in North Carolina. Her name was Charlotte Hawkins Brown, and by the time she was seventeen, she was filled, as she wrote, "with a burning desire to return to the state of my birth and help my people."

Charlotte Hawkins was born in North Carolina but moved with her family to Cambridge, Massachusetts, when she was six. Her parents had named her Lottie Hawkins, but just before graduation from high school, she decided to change her name to Charlotte Eugenia Hawkins. A chance meeting with Alice Freeman Palmer, the wife of a Harvard professor and the first female president of Wellesley College, opened up doors to her that would otherwise have remained closed. Palmer happened to see Hawkins pushing a baby carriage while reading a book of Latin poetry. Palmer took an interest in Hawkins and helped pay her tuition to college. Hawkins had completed one year when she was offered a teaching position at Bethany Institute in rural Sedalia, North Carolina, by the American Missionary Association (AMA). Although only eighteen years old, Hawkins immediately accepted.

In 1901, as Hawkins traveled through North Carolina, the train in which she was riding suddenly stopped in the middle of the woods. The conductor told her that she had arrived at her destination. She warily descended from the train with her suitcases and found herself alone in the forest. She set out and eventually found someone to take her to the school in a horse and wagon. She was shocked at what she saw. "It was unpainted and much weather-beaten. Large, gaping holes showed forth where window panes had once been. The yard was unkempt and grown with stubble. No one seemed to be expecting me. I felt as though I wanted to go back home. I did not then know, as I know do, that God knew what was best for me. I wanted to enter His service but had not thought of entering such a barren field. I said, This is God's way. I must be satisfied."

Hawkins's greatest assets were her own inner strength and fifty pupils eager to learn. Some walked as much as fifteen miles a day to attend school. Most could attend school only during the winter, the harshest time of the year, because their labor was needed on the farm the rest

Religion was central to the life of the black community. It sustained African Americans through the whole era of Jim Crow. Whites would often attend black religious services.

of the year. Organizing her students and their parents, Hawkins cleaned up the school and several adjacent buildings, which she converted into dormitories for girls so they could live there during the school year. Just as the school began to succeed, the AMA withdrew its funding. They offered her another teaching position elsewhere, but the parents of her students begged Hawkins to remain. She agreed. She traveled back to New England on a fund-raising tour, determined to raise enough money to keep the school going for the next year. She visited resorts where wealthy whites gathered. Some hotels allowed her to make a little presentation of music and poetry, give a ten-minute talk about the school, and take up a collection. Her goal was to raise one hundred dollars, which was enough to get her through the first year. She met her goal and became the first black woman to open up a normal school in North Carolina.

Hawkins knew that she had to find patrons in order for her school to survive. Alice Freeman Palmer had indicated that she would give some support, but she died during a trip to Europe. Hawkins named her school the Alice Freeman Palmer Memorial Institute in honor of her friend and set about to raise more funds to keep it going.

During the early years, Hawkins, along with her staff and students, wrote dozens of letters every evening to potential funders.

Dear Mrs. Worth:
I have worried your patience no doubt but I have delivered the message of my soul to you. It is not the message of an individual but the cry of a struggling race.

Please make all checks payable to the treasurer.

Whenever an envelope arrived that contained money, the students and teachers would cheer. When they received a large donation, they would sometimes cry. Whatever the amount, they gave a prayer of thanks. Sometimes the letters they received were patronizing, if not hostile. One woman wrote, "I am sending you ten dollars for your school which I hope will be put to good use. I advise you to instruct your girls to be virtuous, for moral looseness is an unfortunate quality of many young women of your race."

While struggling to keep her school afloat, Hawkins married for a short time and changed her name to Charlotte Hawkins Brown. She continued her campaign to raise money for the school, often using subterfuge. Most white donors would make contributions as long as the school was modeled on the industrial program of Tuskegee Institute. Since Palmer grew its own vegetables and raised livestock, she emphasized these in her fund-raising appeals. As one teacher recalled, "You would pretend to have a vocational school on the outside, and then you'd go in your classroom and teach them French, or Latin and all the things you knew." At one point, Booker T. Washington sent a representative to visit her school. He was critical of the academic program. "All your literary and industrial teaching needs to be made more practical, and especially does the literary teaching need to be correlated with the industrial teaching."

Brown modeled her curriculum based on her own education in Massachusetts. In the

The founders and builders of North Carolina Mutual Life—John Merrick, C. C. Spaulding, and Dr. Aaron Moore—started with a $250 investment and turned it into a multimillion-dollar enterprise.

lower grades, teachers taught spelling, reading, writing, hygiene, and arithmetic; in the upper grades, literature, grammar, geography, history, and agriculture. Foreign languages and civil government were offered to students going to college. Students read books like *Black Beauty, Robinson Crusoe, Silas Marner,* and *Ivanhoe.* They memorized poems and writings of Longfellow, Whittier, Tennyson, and Emerson. Ruth Totton, a former teacher at the school, recalled, "People said she had high falutin' ideas and high aims for her students and she was teaching them the three R's but she was also intent on teaching them leadership qualities."

Brown successfully juggled financial support from the North while cultivating the support and friendship of powerful local whites in nearby Greensboro. Even though racial tensions had cooled in North Carolina after 1898, Jim Crow laws were intensifying. Blacks had been disfranchised in 1900, and Jim Crow signs were proliferating. Brown refused to accept Jim Crow, even though, at times, she had to conform to it. Whenever she had an appointment with her doctor or lawyer, she would phone ahead so that when she arrived, she would be ushered directly into the office rather than wait in the Jim Crow waiting room or into a

Jazz musicians gathered for a picture in New Orleans at the boys' home where Louis Armstrong (seated, front row center) first learned to play music in a band.

vestibule past both the colored and white rooms. She sat in the "ladies' section" of the train. If a conductor forced her to sit in the Jim Crow section, she would sue the railroad. When her students went to town for a concert or movie, she would reserve the theater for them, so they would not be forced to sit in the balcony. Her life was a balancing act between appeasing powerful whites whose support and protection she needed while finding ways to undermine Jim Crow without endangering her school. She tried to instill in her students a refusal to internalize Jim Crow, to go around and above it, to be smart enough and resourceful enough and duplicitous enough not to antagonize white people, and yet to get what they wanted. Elizabeth Meade, one of her early students, recalled, "She taught us that we could do anything that anyone else could do if we wanted to, if we tried to. She always taught us that we could be as good as anybody else regardless of what our color was. And we appreciated that. Cause you go around thinking you can't do this or you will never be nothing or something like that. She told us it wasn't true. We could be anything we wanted to be."

Brown saw herself as part of an ongoing African-American freedom struggle. Later on, she would be one of the leaders in the fight for black woman suffrage. She devoted much of her energies to interracial work with white women's organizations, trying subtly to recruit support for her agenda. She was a member of the National Association of Colored Women, an umbrella organization for state and local women's clubs dedicated to improving the quality of life for African Americans. The NACW was founded in 1896 by the leading African-American women in America, including Ida B. Wells; Mary Church Terrell, its first president; the great abolitionist Harriet Tubman; and May Murray Washington, Booker T. Washington's wife.

Brown's life as a leader in the NACW and as a builder of a school with a reputation for educational excellence often took its toll on her. "Recognizing the need of a cultural approach to life, I have devoted my life to establishing for Negro youth something superior to Jim Crowism. Sometimes the prejudice is so great I feel that I can't stand it a day longer . . . but then I look in the delicate faces of the children and determine to stick it out no matter what the cost."

Many African-American women, like Charlotte Hawkins Brown, dedicated their lives and energies to education. Others, such as Virginia Broughton, focused on church work, using it as a vehicle to improve the lives of women living in poverty. Broughton was a preacher in the Baptist church, who traveled to the deeply rural, semiwild areas of Arkansas and Missouri bringing the word of God. On one journey, she crossed the Mississippi River in a skiff, bailing out water as they crossed from Tennessee to Arkansas, continued her journey in an open-air ox wagon with a stove in the cart to keep warm, and then took a trip on horseback to Cooter, Missouri, a place, she later wrote, referring to herself in the third person, "where few Negro men dared to go to preach and a woman missionary of no race had ever gone." Much of the road was underwater and she was guided on her journey by a minister. "The preacher would ride on ahead and bid Virginia follow him, which she did with much fear and trembling, the water often coming up to her saddle skirts." She not only preached the word of God to men and women but also helped women become literate by reading the Bible.

Some male members of the church adamantly objected to her preaching. One man remarked, "I would rather take a rail and flail the life out of a woman than to hear her speak in church." One minister went to hear her speak in order to verbally destroy her in front of the audience. When she had finished her sermon, the minister rose and addressed the gathering. He confessed his original purpose, adding that after hearing the eloquence of Virginia Broughton's preaching, "I have been washed, rinsed, starched, hung up, dried, sprinkled and ironed, and am now ready to do service; not to destroy but to do all in my power to forward this branch of God's work as zealously as I had determined to oppose it."

* * *

As black men were eliminated from the political life of the community, in some racially moderate communities they were able to gain an economic foothold. In Durham, North Carolina, three black men launched a business enterprise that would become a major force in the life of the city's black community. They were John Merrick; Dr. Aaron Moore, the first black physician in Durham; and C. C. Spaulding.

John Merrick, like Booker T. Washington, had been born in slavery and had worked his way up the economic ladder as a hod carrier, bricklayer, and barber. By 1890, Merrick owned six barbershops and extensive real estate. He cultivated the support of Durham's most powerful whites, including Washington Duke, the tobacco king, and Julian Shakespeare Carr, mill owner and financier. Carr exemplified the disassociated thinking that characterized many paternalistic Southerners. He was genuinely concerned for the well-being of blacks and supported their economic progress. He was also a rabid white supremacist who approved the killing of blacks who stepped out of "their place" by entering politics.

Merrick recognized that as blacks moved into the cities, they had an increasing need for some kind of protection in case of sickness or death of the main family wage earner. In 1898, Merrick formed an insurance company, eventually known as the North Carolina Mutual Life Insurance Company, in partnership with five other local black businessmen. The company's total capital assets were $250 and business prospects seemed so dismal at first that three of his partners dropped out.

While Merrick was the man with economic vision, C. C. Spaulding, his manager and later president of the company, was a dynamic workaholic whose energy and dedication were the driving force behind much of the company's success. Spaulding developed the markets and trained the workforce that would make the company a success. An employee described him as a man who "came to work early in the morning, rolled up his sleeves and did janitor's work, then rolled down his sleeves and worked as an agent. And a little later in the day, he put on his coat and became the general manager."

Spaulding had a number of serious obstacles to overcome. There was a great deal of competition from white insurance companies, many agents of which continually slandered black companies. They charged that black insurance companies were "of little concern and no account and soon bust. They call and call and collect very promptly when you are well but when you are sick, they never come near your house." Spaulding countered these charges with advertisements in the company newspaper stating when, to whom, and how much benefits had been paid.

One problem that infuriated Spaulding was the tendency of black people to buy from whites rather than blacks. He complained that blacks did not support their own people, even when it was cheaper for them to do so. As one of his agents noted, "It is past our understanding why there are colored people who still think that 50 cents in benefits from a white company is as much as $1.00 from a black one."

Spaulding and Merrick's strategy for success was threefold. The company published its own newspaper, the *North Carolina Mutual,* and launched an aggressive advertising campaign that favored the hard sell. One of its ads read, "Death is pursuing you this moment. Don't let your departing words be, 'Good-bye darling. I bequeath you my troubles and my debts.'"

Spaulding also kept premiums low and affordable. Rates started as low as five cents a week. But his strongest asset was well-trained agents. He taught them that the best way to sell policies was to treat customers with respect. "White agents walk into a Negro home without even knocking or taking off their hats. It is up to us to put an end to such discourtesy, and the best way we can do it is to convince them to patronize a colored insurance company of standing. Tell them that every time a Negro takes a policy, its protects him and it employs another Negro."

The company drew well-educated salespeople and office personal. One major attraction of the office was the aristocratic-mannered Susan Gilles, a college graduate who was hired as executive secretary. In an age when very few black women were white-collar workers, Gilles provided a role model for Durham's youth. Impeccably dressed in black skirts, white puffed-sleeved blouses, and whalebone collars, speaking perfect English, and educated with a classical background, Gilles taught stenographic and typing skills to young people. Children visited her office just to see her type. They called her "the girl with the flying fingers who types without even looking at the keys."

Dr. Aaron Moore, the third partner, helped North Carolina Mutual become the driving force of the social and cultural life of the black community. Moore helped establish Lincoln Hospital for blacks as well as a library. He encouraged the company to support a literary society that sponsored reading programs, offered lectures, and held debates, and the Schubert-Shakespeare Club, which offered classical music, plays, and lectures on "social betterment" of the race.

By the early twentieth century, North Carolina Mutual was on its way to becoming a multimillion-dollar corporation. It created hundreds of jobs in the black community and inspired a number of smaller businesses. One of the original agents described its success in a way that would have pleased Booker T. Washington: "The North Carolina Mutual is one of God's ways through which he is reaching our people. His message to us is: 'Lower your buckets where you are.'"

For most black men and women, the comfortable world of the middle class still seemed as remote as the most distant star. The cotton fields and the mule were to be their likely destiny—as it would be their children's and their grandchildren's destiny. Tens of thousands of African Americans rejected farming and headed for the work camps of the South. Wandering black men built levees and laid railroad tracks, dug coal, and gathered turpentine. They were "masterless men" who were not attached to the land or beholden to landlords. The work was hard, the life was brutish, violence was common, and men were exploited. Men sang as they worked. They sang about everything and anything. "Trains, steamboats, steam whistles, sledge hammers, fast women, mean bosses, stubborn mules—all became subjects for their songs," J. C. Handy, the great popularizer of the blues, noted. Singing allowed the workers to blend their physical movements and provided a means of expression and communication. Some were work songs that often poked fun at their white bosses.

> Captain oh Captain you must be cross
> It was six o'clock and you won't knock off.
>
> Captain oh Captain, you must be blind.
> You keep hollerin hurry an I'm darn near flyin.
>
> Cap'n did you heah about all you men going to leave you
> Jes because you make yo' day so long.

In addition to the work songs, a new music was being heard around the turn of the century. The blues had just begun to emerge out of the Delta, and the rich musical tradition of church music, spirituals, work songs, calls and shouts, and African rhythms combined to become a distinct art form. The blues grew out of the hard lives of poor black workers and sharecroppers. Handy pointed out, "the blues did not come from books. Suffering and hard luck were the midwives that birthed these songs. The blues were conceived in aching hearts."

> The first time I met the blues mamma, they come walking through the wood.
> The first time I met the blues baby, they came walking through the woods.
> They stopped at my house first mamma, and done me all the harm they could.
> Now the blues got at me Lord and run me from tree to tree.
> Now the blues got at me Lord and run me from tree to tree.
> You should have heard me begging, Mr. Blues, don't murder me.

One of the early well-known blues singers was Charley Patton. He wandered from town to town, playing in improvised clubs called "juke joints," fighting, drinking, loving women, and free from the control of whites. Patton rambled through western Tennessee, eastern Arkansas, and northeastern Louisiana, entertaining workingmen and -women wherever he went. He was a Saturday night entertainer who sang about troubles with the law:

> When you get into trouble, it's no use screamin and cryin
> When you get into trouble, it's no use screamin and cryin
> Tom Rushend will take you back to the prison house flyin

and about women:

> Baby got a heart like a piece of railroad steel . . .

and about life's sorrows:

> Hard luck is at your front door, blues are in your room
> Hard luck is at your front door, blues are in your room
> Calling at your back door, what is to become of you.

People sang the blues in the fields where they worked, in homes, in prisons, and in clubs. Sidney Bechet, who would become one of the greatest of all the jazz musicians, first heard it in a jailhouse sung by a prisoner protesting his unjust arrest.

> Got me accused of murder, I never harmed a man.
> Got me accused of forgery, can't even write my name.
> Bad luck, bad luck is killin' me
> I just can't stand no more of this third degree.

Bechet noted, "The way he sang it was more than just a man. He was like every man that's been done wrong. Inside of him he's got the memory of all the wrong that's been done to all my people. When the blues is good that kind of memory grow up inside it. The blues, like spirituals, were prayers. One was praying to God and the other was praying to man. They were both the same thing in a way; they were both my people's way of praying to be themselves, praying to be let alone so they could be human."

The blues was carried by drifting men and women into the cities of the South, like New Orleans, where often it blended with other sounds to help create new and vibrant musical forms. At the turn of the century, New Orleans was a lively, exciting world of brass bands and string orchestras, French and Italian opera, Neapolitan music, African drumming, Haitian rhythm, Cuban melody, American spirituals and blues, ragtime and popular music. People sang British folk songs, danced Spanish dances, played French dance and ballet music, and marched to the strains of brass bands based on the Prussian or French models.

New Orleans had two distinct black communities. The oldest was the Creoles of Color, with roots in the French, Spanish, and Caribbean cultures that existed before Louisiana was purchased by America. Creoles of Color were French-speaking Catholics who specialized in

KILLING THE PRISONER.
Angered Citizens Wreak Vengeance on Jackson.

In 1900, Robert Charles, harassed by police, became involved in a shootout with tragic consequences. This drawing from a newspaper article shows the arrest of a friend of Charles, who was not involved but was shot by an enraged white man while in police custody.

such crafts as plastering, carpentry, and tinsmithing. A small number were quite wealthy and educated their children in France. They enjoyed a rich musical tradition, and many were formally trained and could play a variety of music from ragtime to classical. The other black community was English speaking and Protestant, and worked on the docks and in other manual labor jobs. Their musical tradition came from work songs, blues, and the black church.

Around the turn of the century, music in New Orleans was undergoing a transformation. A new sound was being created by musicians like Buddy Bolden, the innovative cornet player famed for his ability to improvise, and Tony Jackson, considered by many "the best pianist they had." One man who helped bring about this musical revolution was Ferdinand La Menthe, a Creole of Color eventually known as "Jelly Roll" Morton. From early childhood, music was a vital part of Morton's family's life. "We always had some kind of musical instruments in the house, including guitar, drums, piano, trombone. We had lots of them, and everybody played for their pleasure." Other rich sources of inspiration that Morton described were the marching bands and the social clubs they represented. "New Orleans was very organization minded. I have never seen such beautiful clubs as they have there. The Broadway Swells, the High Arts, the Bulls and the Bears, the Tramps and the Iroquois. They'd have a great big band. The grand marshal would ride in front with all his aides behind him."

While still a teenager, Morton had been hired to play the piano at Lulu White's bordello in the Storyville section of New Orleans, the most famous red-light district in nineteenth-century America. "In Storyville, lights of all colors were glittering, glaring. Music was pouring into the streets from every house. Women were standing in the doorways, singing or chanting some kind of blues—some very happy, some very sad, some with the desire to end it all with poison, some planning a big outing, a dance or some other kind of enjoyment."

Storyville was a world of prostitution where white and black women were available to white men, and black men were restricted to black women in segregated establishments. Only black musicians were allowed in the whites-only houses. "You could play music there, but you couldn't play there," Morton said. "If a white man even suspected you showed too much interest in one of the ladies, well that could be too bad for you."

In Storyville, Jelly Roll Morton became one of the jazz greats. Jazz was not created in Storyville, but many jazz musicians perfected their own talents by providing musical entertainment for the prostitutes and their customers. Louis Armstrong, who helped make coal deliveries to Storyville as a child, remembered how enthralled he was at hearing the music: "There were all kinds of thrills for me in Storyville. On every corner I could hear music. And such good music. All those glorious trumpets—Joe Oliver, Bunk Johnson—It seemed that all the bands were shooting each other with these hot riffs."

Through their music, musicians could drop their masks and express their deepest feelings. Music provided a rich internal life in a Jim Crow world, which influenced their music but did not determine it. There were tears behind their sounds, but there was joy as well.

Many musicians were workingmen, and music was a part-time profession. Johnny St. Cyr saw work and music as being intimately connected. "To be a jazz musician you had to be a working class of man, out in the open all the time, healthy, strong. See the average working man is very musical. Playing music for him is just relaxing. The more enthusiastic his audience is, the more spirit the working man's got to play."

Black workers in New Orleans were often militant. Dockworkers helped organize one of the few interracial unions in the South, convincing white workers that racial cooperation, not racial conflict, was the only way to higher wages and better working conditions for all. They organized strikes together in the 1890s and won higher wages. One black dockworker commented, "We are tired of being used as an instrument to starve our brother workmen, the white men."

Blacks also fought for civil rights. When the state passed the Railway Separation Act in 1890, segregating public transportation, an organization of Creoles of Color challenged the constitutionality of the law. Rodolphe Desdunes, editor of *The Crusader,* a newspaper for the Creole of Color community, encouraged resistance. "It is more noble and dignified to fight than to show a passive attitude of resignation. Absolute submission augments the oppressor's power and creates doubt about the feelings of the oppressed. . . . No theory of white supremacy, no method of lynching, no class legislation, no undue disqualification of citizenship, no system of enforced ignorance, no privileged classes at the expense of others can be tolerated."

The man who volunteered to make history was Homère Plessy, a Creole of Color who could pass for white. Plessy deliberately seated himself in the white section of a train and then identified himself as "colored." When he refused to move, he was arrested. The case, known as *Plessy* v. *Ferguson,* worked its way up to the United States Supreme Court. In 1896, the Court—which several years earlier had ruled that a state did not have the power to forbid segregation—now decided a state had the power to require it. Segregation was now legal. Justice Henry B. Brown, characterized by one scholar as one of the "dimmer lights" on the Court, wrote in the decision, "If one race is inferior to the other socially, the Constitution of the United States cannot put them on the same level." Two years later, in *Williams* v. *Mississippi,* the Court once again approved white supremacy by allowing states legally to deprive blacks of their right to vote.

As blacks lost political and civil power, white hostility intensified. Whites like John Hearsey, the negrophobic editor and publisher of *The States,* the most influential white newspaper in New Orleans, maliciously stirred up nightmare visions of race war. "Under the dark, seething mass of humanity that surrounds us and is in our midst, all appears peaceful and delightful; we do not know, it seems, what hellish schemes of hate, of arson, of murder, of rape, are being hatched in the dark depths. We are under the regime of the free Negro, in the midst of a dangerous element of a servile uprising. If Negroes listen to the screeds of agitators of the North . . . the result will be a race war and race war means extermination. The Negro problem will be solved and that by extermination."

For Robert Charles, a workingman in New Orleans, the situation had become intolerable. Charles had come to New Orleans from Mississippi in the early 1890s seeking work and entertainment. He worked, as many blacks did, at a variety of jobs, most of which involved manual labor. Although he developed a reputation as a sharp dresser and enjoyed the company of women, he was a man not to be taken lightly, He was over six feet tall, weighed about 190 pounds, and carried a gun. An anonymous friend described him as a serious man. "He was a quiet, fine person, who was always studying and trying to improve himself. He believed that black people should defend themselves against lynching, and he was trying to overcome his anger against whites." That anger began to build as lynchings soared and segregation increased. After one particularly brutal lynching in Georgia, Charles told a friend, "The time has come for every black man to defend himself. It is the duty of every Negro to buy a rifle and keep it ready against the time they may be called upon to act in unison."

As New Orleans became increasingly segregated and opportunities for blacks became more limited, Charles despaired that African Americans would progress in America. He became a supporter of Bishop Henry Turner's back-to-Africa movement and sold Turner's nationalistic newspaper, *Voice of Missions,* in New Orleans. By 1900, Charles was determined to leave America for Liberia. It was not to happen. One evening in July, as Charles and his friend Leonard Price were seated on the steps of a house waiting for their lady friends, two policeman approached and began to question them. A fight broke out. Charles and one of the policeman exchanged shots; both were wounded. Charles fled the scene and returned home. When three policemen came to his home to arrest him, he shot and killed two of them and went into hiding.

Whites in New Orleans went wild. An estimated twenty thousand men searching for Charles were ready to kill any black person, man or woman, they saw. One mayor from a nearby town gave a speech inciting the mob. "I have come down tonight to assist you in teaching the blacks a lesson. I have killed a Negro before and I am willing to kill again. The only way you can teach these niggers a lesson is to go out and lynch a few of them—kill them, string them up, lynch them." Dozens of unsuspecting black men were killed, including the father of jazz, musician Louis "Big Eye" Nelson, who was playing that night. "We heard shooting. All them boys flung themselves out the back. We made it out the window of the gambling house in back, but man, that alley was loaded with folks. We might have been assassinated but we were lucky enough to get to a friend's house. Next day somebody said I better go down to the hospital. Man had been brought in about 2 A.M. in very bad condition and died around sunup. It was my daddy. They had snatched him off his meat-wagon at the French market and killed him."

Four days later, the final shootout took place. Charles was betrayed by an informer, and a mob estimated at twenty thousand gathered outside his hiding place. Jelly Roll Morton described the battle: "The man got into his house and he got his gun and fired from all the windows. Policemen came from all over. There was a mob of them ambushing his house. Every time he raised his rifle and got a policeman in his sights, there'd be another one dead." Before he was shot to death, Charles killed five more men and wounded seventeen. After Charles's death, an admirer wrote a letter to the famous anti-lynching crusader Ida B. Wells. "Dear Mrs. Wells-Barnett: It affords me great pleasure to inform you as far as I know Robert Charles, he has never given trouble to anyone in this city. He was a quiet and peaceful man and too much of a hero to die; few can be found equal to him." "Like many other bad men, Charles had a song originated about him," Jelly Roll Morton later said. "This song was squashed very easily by the police department due to the fact it was a trouble breeder. I once knew the Robert Charles song but I found out it was best for me to forget it and that I did in order to get along with the world on the peaceful side."

Charles had sought freedom and found death. The limits of freedom for musicians in New Orleans were clear. Many would leave the city and travel to the North and West. The sounds of the Delta and New Orleans would produce a new and great music that would enthrall audiences in almost every country in the Western world—and allow its creators to find some degree of the freedom they sought. Sidney Bechet, one of the New Orleans greats, expressed it best of all:

> The music, it was the onliest thing that counted. The music it was having a time for itself. It was moving. It was being free and natural. All the beauty that's ever been. The voice the wind had in Africa and the cries from Congo Square and the fine shouting that came up on Free[dom] Day. The blues and the spirituals and the waiting and the suffering . . . that's all inside the music. And when the music is played right, it does an explaining of all those things. Me, I want to explain myself so bad, I want to have myself understood. And the music, it can do that. The music, it's my whole story.

Chapter 6

The Worst of Times, 1900–1917

There were other sounds of music in the air.

> Coon, coon, coon, I wish my color would fade.
> Coon, coon, coon, I'd like a different shade.
> Coon, coon, coon, from morning, night and noon;
> I wish I was a white man instead of a coon.

As America entered the twentieth century, white Americans sang "coon" songs, the purpose of which was to ridicule and denigrate black people: "All Coons Look Alike to Me," "Coon, Coon, Coon, I Wish My Color Would Fade," "If the Man in the Moon were a Coon," "The Red Headed Coon." White supremacy, once considered a Southern idiosyncrasy, had become a national ideology. A malicious negrophobia—a pathological fear and hatred of blacks—had gripped the country. Respected academics claimed that the Negro was inferior biologically, psychologically, anthropologically, culturally, and historically, despite the fact that there was overwhelming evidence to the contrary. Edward Drinker Cope, a professor of zoology, claimed that black mental growth was permanently arrested at age fourteen. He recommended that blacks should be deported in order to protect from miscegenation "the finest race on earth, the whites of the South." Pseudo-scientific literature joined the cacophony of white supremacy. Their very titles reveal their malicious intent: *The Negro a Beast, The Negro a*

When W.E.B. Du Bois published *The Souls of Black Folk* in 1903, it caused a sensation in the black community. One of the essays in the book took Booker T. Washington to task for his acceptance of a subordinate status for blacks.

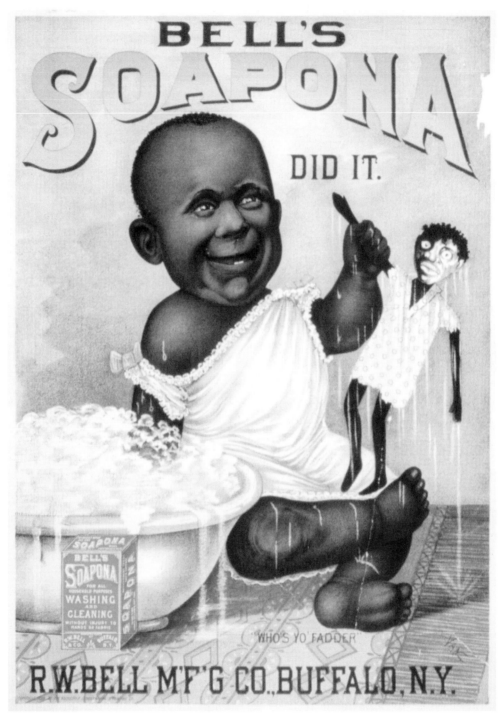

By the turn of the century, white supremacy had become a national ideology and was reinforced by the use of stereotypical images of inferior-looking blacks in advertising.

Menace to Civilization. Popular fiction denigrating blacks flooded the market. Novelist Thomas Dixon portrayed blacks with a racial antipathy in his turn-of-the-century trilogy *The Leopard's Spots: A Romance of the White Man's Burden 1865–1900, The Clansman: A Historical Romance of the Ku Klux Klan,* and *The Traitor: A Story of the Fall of the Invisible Empire.* The novels reviled blacks and glorified the Ku Klux Klan. *The Clansman* was adapted into an extremely popular play, and Dixon often appeared on stage praising the Klan to the exuberant applause of white audiences.

The beginning of the twentieth century witnessed a proliferation of Jim Crow laws in the South. Populists and Democrats, whatever their disputes, were now united in one thing: the total subjugation of blacks and their removal, as far as possible, from the mainstream of Southern life. During the nineteenth century, legal segregation had existed primarily on trains, although social segregation existed in many public places, including restaurants and theaters. Now the South blanketed its cities with Jim Crow laws. The Jim Crow waiting room, seen in only a few Southern states before 1900, was adopted by all. In 1901, North Carolina and Virginia segregated all public transportation, followed by Louisiana in 1902; South Carolina, Arkansas, Tennessee, Maryland, and Mississippi in 1903, and Florida in 1904. Signs proliferated: WHITE, WHITE ONLY, WHITE ONLY SERVED HERE, NO BLACKS ALLOWED, PARK RESERVED FOR WHITES. Separate water fountains and rest rooms were reserved for both races and so indicated. Separate entrances to buildings, separate elevators, separate cashier windows in amusement parks, separate cemeteries for the dead. In Atlanta, blacks and whites who testified as witnesses in court had to swear their oath "to tell the truth" on separate Bibles. Patients were racially separated in hospitals, mental institutions, jails and prisons, and homes for the blind, deaf, elderly, orphans, and the poor. Residential areas were segregated. In Oklahoma, state law required that the phone company install separate booths for the races. North Carolina and Florida required that school textbooks for black and white children be kept separate. In New Orleans, prostitutes were separated by race. Blacks were excluded from parks, swimming pools, beaches, certain neighborhoods, and even towns. Some towns posted signs that read, "Nigger, don't let the sun set on you here."

The proliferation of signs made Pauli Murray glad that her blind grandfather was spared from seeing them. "I saw the things which grandfather could not see—in fact had never seen—the signs which literally screamed at me from every side—on streetcars, over drinking fountains, on doorways: FOR WHITE ONLY, FOR COLORED ONLY, WHITE LADIES, COLORED WOMEN, WHITE, COLORED. If I missed the signs, I had only to follow my nose to the dirtiest, smelliest, most neglected accommodations, or they were pointed out to me by a heavily armed, invariably mountainous red-faced policeman who seemed more to me a signal of calamity than of protection."

The impact of segregation widened a gap within the black community. Middle-class blacks resented that the new laws applied to all black people equally. They could understand why whites would want to restrict "poor" blacks, and some argued that segregation and disfranchisement might be appropriate—even desirable—for them. But for educated, economically successful, and morally upright blacks—the mirror image of the ideal white model for

By the turn of the century, Booker T. Washington was the most influential black man in America. He socialized with rich philanthropists who funded black education and had the power to determine what schools received money.

acceptability in society—the laws were unfair. Their appeal to whites on the basis of their common identity of class interests fell on deaf ears. "Respectable whites" made no distinction between blacks. They would rather identify with poor whites on the basis of race than with successful blacks on the basis of class. What was particularly galling to middle-class blacks was that whites they considered their social inferiors—the bus driver, the elevator operator, the streetcar and train conductor, the theater usher—had power over them. These whites could arbitrarily dictate to blacks as they wished, and if a black person resisted, they had the authority to beat or even kill him.

Consumer products reinforced white supremacy on a national scale. Black stereotypes representing the "happy darky" figure became commonplace. Consumers were greeted by smiling mammies, Aunt Jemima, Uncle Mose, and the Gold Dust Twins on products they bought. These images were incarnations of blacks as Southerners had represented them during slavery days. Stereotypical racial figures appeared on ashtrays, tablecloths, postcards, sheet music, tourist souvenirs, figurines, and a seemingly infinite number of household items. Many images distorted the physical appearance of African Americans; they were never portrayed as real human beings. Images on cigarette packs showed blacks as having large heads, large hands, big lips, and bulging eyes. Some were depicted as playing croquet and hitting themselves instead of the ball. African Americans were represented as an inferior race, people not like white people but totally separate from them. One consequence of these stereotypes was that they helped deaden any national anger against lynching. Many Northerners accepted the Southern view that any black person who did not fit these images of servility was dangerous and probably deserved what he or she received.

At the extreme end of the spectrum of white supremacy were those who preached violence. White radicals rationalized their negrophobia as a response to the so-called regression of blacks toward bestiality. Freedom, they claimed, had made the black a savage creature. The solution was to kill the offender or castrate him and exterminate the race. The radical racists claimed that blacks were lynched because they raped white women, even though rape was not even an issue raised in most lynchings. United States Senator "Pitchfork" Ben Tillman ranted, "So far as I am concerned, he [the Negro] has put himself outside of the law, human and divine. Civilization peels off, any and all of us who are men and we revert to the original savage type whose impulse under any and all circumstances has always been to 'kill, kill, kill.'" Rebecca Felton, Georgia feminist and suffragette, added to the cacophony. "If a rapist was torn to pieces limb by limb and burnt with a slow fire, or hung by the thumbs until the buzzards swarmed around him, he would still be saved some of the revolting torture already inflicted upon a harmless victim. In dealing with such ravenous beasts the best thing to do is rid the earth of such vile and dangerous cattle."

In 1906, negrophobia arrived in Atlanta. For many whites as well as blacks Atlanta seemed to be the least likely place for white racial radicalism. Atlanta was a model city of the new South. The economy was booming. Its population was fast approaching the one-hundred-thousand mark. The number of factories had multiplied by 60 percent since 1900. The number of buildings constructed rose from 230 in 1900 to more than 1,300 by 1906. The Coca-Cola Company had been established. The city was proud of its major department stores, fancy residential areas, 11 major railroad lines, and 160 miles of streetcar lines.

Black businesses were springing up on Auburn Street, soon to be called "Sweet Auburn" because of its economic attractions. Among the successful businessmen were Alonzo Herndon, owner of a barbershop and a life insurance company, who became the richest black man in Georgia, and Moses Amos, the first black pharmacist in the state. There were plenty of jobs for workingmen and -women, although most of those jobs involved menial labor or domestic work at subsistence wages. The city also boasted numerous black publications, the most outstanding of which was the *Voice of the Negro* edited by J. Max Barber. The *Voice of the Negro* published articles by black leaders throughout the South, promoting what it called "higher culture"—literature and the arts. It examined world issues and criticized rabid racists like James Vardaman of Mississippi and "Pitchfork" Ben Tillman of South Carolina while careful not to offend Atlanta's whites.

At the center of its cultural life were the black colleges: Atlanta Baptist College, Gammon

As men were disenfranchised and lost political power, women stepped up their roles through women's clubs. They focused their energies on improving the education, health, and welfare of their communities as well as quietly working to achieve basic rights for all African Americans.

Theological Seminary, Atlanta University, Spelman Seminary, Clark University, and Morris Brown College. The colleges and churches provided much of the intellectual leadership for the black community. The dominating figure was the aristocratic scholar Dr. W. E. B. Du Bois of Atlanta University. Educated at Fisk, Harvard, and the University of Berlin, Du Bois was the first scholar to make the scientific study of African-American life part of the university curriculum. Among Du Bois's peers were John Hope, soon to be the first black president of Atlanta University, Professor J. W. Bowen of Gammon Theological Seminary, Bishop Henry McNeil Turner of the African Methodist Episcopal church and Henry Hugh Proctor, pastor of the Congregationalist church. When whites criticized the black colleges on the grounds that most of their students were enrolled in high school rather than college courses, Du Bois acknowledged that there were weaknesses but pointed out the college's strength. "Above the sneers of the critics stood one crushing rejoinder: in a single generation the colleges put thirty thousand black teachers in the South and wiped out the illiteracy of the majority of black people in the land."

These intellectual and moral leaders of the community, while circumspect in their behavior with Atlanta's whites, were not cut in the conciliatory mold of Booker T. Washington. In 1903, Du Bois had fired his first warning shot at Washington's policy of forgoing black civil and political rights in exchange for economic opportunities and due process of law. Du Bois published *The Souls of Black Folk,* a series of essays, one of which took Washington to task. While praising him from his contributions to the progress of the race, Du Bois criticized Washington for his failures to speak out in its behalf: ". . . so far as Mr. Washington apologizes for injustice, North and South, does not rightly value the privilege and duty of voting, belittles the emasculating effects of caste distinctions, and opposes the higher training and education of our brighter minds—so far as he, the South or the Nation does this—we must unceasingly and firmly oppose them." The following year, Du Bois organized the Niagara Conference at Niagara Falls, at which he invited a number of prominent black leaders to form a civil rights organization to challenge Washington's leadership. The movement ultimately failed but served as a precursor to the National Association for the Advancement of Colored People (NAACP), which was founded five years later. In a statement defining the movement's goals, Du Bois proclaimed, "We claim for ourselves every single right that belongs to a freeborn American, political, civil and social; and until we get these rights we will never cease to protest and assail the ears of America."

Du Bois was not the only voice speaking out. Bishop Henry Turner castigated the United States government when, in his judgment, it committed outrages against black people. After the United States Supreme Court ruled a congressional civil rights law unconstitutional, Turner thundered, "The Supreme Court is an organized mob against the Negro. What can all the people in the United States do when the Court declares that the Negro is a dog? That barbarous decision should be branded, battle-axed, sawed, cut and carved with the most bitter epithets and blistering denunciations that words can express . . . it absolved the allegiance of the Negro to the United States." When Turner said that he preferred ". . . hell to the United States" and called the American flag "a dirty contemptible rag," President Theodore Roosevelt threatened to charge him with treason. Turner retorted that he could prove "forty more times treason against my race under the shadow of the United States flag than they can against me."

Turner, along with Du Bois, Barber, and other leaders, attended a Georgia Equal Rights convention in 1905 that demanded black civil and political rights but carefully avoided the issue of social equality.

African-American women were also quite active in Atlanta. Many joined women's clubs, most of which were affiliated with the National Association of Colored Women, the dominant black women's organization in America. Women took it upon themselves to provide community services to poor blacks and instill in them middle-class standards and values. The race, they maintained, needed uplift by self-help, racial solidarity, temperance, thrift, chastity, social purity, patriarchal authority, and the accumulation of wealth; the instruments by which racial uplift were to be achieved were the churches, fraternal organizations, and, especially, the women's clubs.

The values the women expressed were those of the black middle-class world of the nineteenth century. They shared the belief that if blacks adopted white civilization—and by civilization was meant white middle-class Victorian standards—they would be accepted, or at least escape from the worst outrages of white supremacy.

One outstanding leader was Lugenia Hope, whose background was in social work. Her

Atlanta boasted an intellectual and cultural elite that performed and attended music concerts, plays, and the theater. Much of the intellectual activity was generated from the five black colleges in the city.

husband, John Hope, a severe critic of Booker T. Washington, had been hired to teach classics at Atlanta Baptist College. Lugenia Hope recognized that black women could have enormous influence when they organized. Her vision was to deliver services to every neighborhood in the city through a series of networks built in each community. Hope wandered through the back alleys of the slum areas. The roads were unpaved and full of holes. There were no water mains, and some areas were used as garbage dumps. She proposed that the kindergartens be transformed into community centers that would reach out to all people in the area with a variety of services. She championed such health services as antituberculosis clinics and shelters for the elderly, sewing and literature classes for young women, and playgrounds for children. She felt that women should lobby the city government for better streets, sewerage, and lights, and expose landlords who refused to provide minimum services and shopkeepers who cheated people.

Another activist deeply concerned about bettering her community was Carrie Steele Logan, who worked as a cook and volunteer probation officer for juveniles. Born in slavery, she single-handedly raised money to found the first black orphanage in Atlanta in 1898. "I have seen the hungry, half-clad ignorant children barefooted and crying for bread. I have seen them searching in vain for a place to lay their tired heads; and so I resolved to do something for the children of my race."

While Carrie Steele Logan relied on church groups, many black women worked for community betterment through women's clubs. Organizations like the Sisters of Friendship, Sisters of Love, Daughters of Bethel, and Daughters of Samara—all church related—played an active role in their neighborhoods in community organizations.

Men's organizations and lodges were also active. They provided health benefits for members, gave financial assistance to widows and orphans, worked for civic improvement, offered financial help to students in school, and held parades. Within their own organizations, religious and secular, blacks could run for and hold office, vote, administer the expenditures of moneys, wield power, and gain prestige that was forbidden to them in the white world. The black community had its own ball teams, dramatic societies, and social organizations. This frightened some whites who were afraid that the lodges would breed secret, antiwhite activities. One white state representative, E. H. McMichael, introduced a bill in the Georgia legislature that would have so severely restricted lodges that for all intents and purposes they would have had to shut down. The bill, he said, "would protect the 'good negro' from the wiles and wicked designs of a few scoundrels of his own race who would arouse ambitions that could never be gratified." Blacks rallied against the measure, and it was defeated.

By the turn of the century, Atlanta was becoming the leading black commercial center of the Southeast. Many black businessmen emphasized the importance of blacks patronizing black businesses as a matter of racial pride. As one newspaper noted:

> There is a singular group in Atlanta where a black man may get up in the morning from a mattress made by black men, in a house which a black man built out of lumber which black men cut and planed; he may put on a suit which he bought at a colored haberdashery and socks knit at a colored mill; he may cook victuals from a colored grocery on a stove which black men fashioned; he may earn his living working for colored men, be sick in a colored hospital, and buried from a colored church; and the Negro insurance company will pay his widow to keep his children in a colored school.

Although racial uplift benefited the black community in many ways, it also promoted an elitist philosophy. During emancipation, as blacks struggled for citizenship, material advancement, human rights, education, and democracy, the community as a whole worked together to achieve these ideals. During the Jim Crow years, many middle-class blacks drew class distinctions in which they often blamed the behavior of poor blacks for the "Negro problem." Their task was to uplift these people to middle-class respectability in order to free the race from discrimination. The problem was that the behavior of working and poor people was not the cause of racism. Their condition was the consequence of an oppressive and brutal Jim Crow society. Nor did the middle class always see that working-class people played a dynamic role in community life. They contributed their labor, time, and money to support

A riot had been building for weeks in Atlanta before it exploded. No one knows exactly how many blacks or whites were killed—many bodies were buried secretly. Most of the blacks who were killed had been caught unaware downtown.

schools and other community institutions and helped one another in hard times. Workers sporadically staged strikes and work slowdowns to protest their low wages. On several occasions, washerwomen refused to wash clothes and sanitation workers to clean streets until they were paid a living wage.

Despite the accomplishments of the black community, Atlanta remained one of the most segregated cities in the South. If W.E.B. Du Bois had a meeting with a white lawyer in town,

Walter White (bottom right) was a teenager in Atlanta when the riot took place and was downtown with his postman father, who was making his rounds. What saved his life was that he and his father could pass for white. The riot played a role in White's eventually becoming a civil rights activist.

he would either have to walk up the stairs to his office or take the freight elevator. He could not use the main elevator despite his accomplishments. He would also have to wait for the lawyer in the colored section of his office. If he went shopping in town and wanted to buy a hat in a white store, he could not try it on. If he rode a streetcar or went to a lake for recreation, he would encounter Jim Crow restrictions. As a result, Du Bois walked wherever he went and seldom, if ever, shopped in white Atlanta.

Even with rigid segregation, one historian wrote in 1902, "There has never been a race riot in Atlanta. The white man and the negro have lived together in this city more peacefully and in better spirit than in any other city, in either the north or south." Negrophobia, which was beneath the surface in Atlanta, began to surface in 1905 when Thomas Dixon's play version of his novel *The Clansman* arrived in Atlanta. The play reinforced the image of blacks as either loyal "Sambo"-type servants or vicious "beast-rapists." It glorified the Klan as saving the South from the Negro menace and protecting the honor of white women.

Not all Southerners agreed with Dixon. Joseph Cummings, a former Civil War officer and Klansman, condemned the play. "I regard this reverend gentleman's work in the 'Clansman' as not only nasty—like all his writings—but fiendish and cowardly, because it intends to incite our people to deeds of violence and cruelty towards a defenseless class of people who need our protection and encouragement."

The following year, tensions increased during the political campaign for governor. The candidates were Hoke Smith, a successful and usually racially moderate political leader, and Clark Howell, also a racial moderate, who was editor of the *Atlanta Constitution.* In order to win the election, Smith pandered to the racial hatred of the crowds, invoking the racial massacres in Wilmington. "We can handle them as we did in Wilmington, where the woods were black with their hanging carcasses. Shall it be ballots now or bullets later?" Smith enlisted the support of former Populist leader Tom Watson, who still had great influence over Georgia's white farmers. Watson had abandoned his advocacy of racial cooperation. The price for his support was Smith's promise to disfranchise blacks. Watson unleashed a vituperative campaign against blacks. "The Negro has no comprehension of virtue, honesty, gratitude, truth and principle. It is necessary to lynch him occasionally, and to flog him now and then, to keep him from blaspheming the almighty by his conduct on account of his color and smell."

Bishop Henry Turner struck back. "Disfranchisement is thievery," he said. "Disfranchisement cannot permanently settle the race or suffrage questions, for whatever the barbarism, the negro will climb over it. If the demand is property, we will buy it; if education, we will acquire it. We are determined to vote. Give us liberty, symbolized by the ballot, or give us death."

Even after Smith won, the mood remained tense as the press launched a newspaper war, using alleged assaults by blacks against white women as the ammunition. Although it turned out that most of the so-called crimes were fiction, the articles and editorials were maliciously inflammatory. "To think of the awful crimes being committed against our women is alarming. It seems that men are justified in adopting the most radical punishment for the perpetration of such deeds as can be devised this side of the region of fire and brimstone. Then to Arms Men of Georgia!" Another writer suggested, "Let's continue to kill all negroes who commit the unmentionable crime, and make eunuchs of all male issues before they are 8 days old."

In 1909, W.E.B. Du Bois, critical of Booker T. Washington's philosophy of accommodation, and his domination of funding for black education, exchanged his scholar's life for that of an activist's and joined the National Association for the Advancement of Colored People in New York.

Another target of white outrage was Decatur Street, a world of secondhand stores, pawnshops, cheap foods, pool halls, barber shops, moonshine, clubs and theaters, saloons and dance halls, vaudeville and minstrel shows, blues singers. Here black men and women sought to escape the harshness of the white world and find social dignity and entertainment they could afford. It was also a quarter in which poor whites and blacks drank and gambled together and shared the same prostitutes. The *Atlanta Journal* condemned it: "The whole street stunk. Odors of mullet, of week old beer, of corn and rye whiskey, of frying grease, of barber shops, of humanity rushed pell-mell. . . . Drunken and maudlin negroes, men and women, with the criminal white types, lounged on the sidewalk or staggered through the dense crowds."

Middle-class blacks also railed against Decatur Street. Reverend Proctor condemned the public dance halls as sinful. "The better element does not want them and the worse element should not have them. In the name of Anglo-Saxon civilization, remove these things that are ruining the character of our young men and stealing away the virtue of our young women."

Throughout the third week of September, the *Atlanta Evening News* and the *Atlanta Jour-*

nal, locked in a campaign to attract readers, published a number of special editions with hysterical headlines about black assaults on white women, almost every one of which was false. The headlines intensified the racial hostilities raised by Dixon's play and the political campaign. On Saturday, white crowds along Decatur Street, many of whom were drunk and inflamed by the headlines, began to gather. Men gave speeches about protecting white women from the black menace. Someone shouted, "Kill the niggers," and soon the cry was running along the crowded streets. Some ten thousand men and boys were in the mob. Whenever the whites would see a Negro, someone would cry, "There is one of the black fiends." In a few minutes the black would be dead or beaten unconscious. Men, women, and children were dragged off of streetcars and attacked without mercy. Two Negro barbers working at their chairs made no effort to resist. A brick hit one in the face and shots were fired. Both men fell to the floor. Their clothing was torn from them as souvenirs. Thirteen-year-old Walter White was accompanying his father, a postman, on his mail delivery rounds. They were able to pass through the mob because of their light skin color. White, writing of that night, said they witnessed the mob beat a crippled black man to death. "We saw a lame negro bootblack coming from Herndon's barber shop pathetically trying to outrun a mob of whites. We saw clubs and fists descending to the accompaniment of savage shouting and cursing. Its work done, the mob went after new prey. The body with the withered foot lay dead in a pool of blood in the street."

White and his father returned home, prepared to defend their family and property from the mob that was headed in their direction. With guns in hand, they waited inside the dark house. "We turned out the lights early as did all our neighbors. No one removed his clothes or thought of sleep. Apprehension was tangible. We could almost touch its cold and clammy surface. Toward midnight the unnatural quiet was broken by a roar that grew steady in volume."

When the mob appeared, White wrote that he heard the son of a grocer with whom his family had traded for many years yell, "That's where the nigger mail carrier lives! Let's burn it down. It's too nice for a nigger to live in!" White's father turned to him. "In a voice as quiet as if he was asking me to pass the sugar, he said, 'Son, don't shoot until the first man puts his foot on the lawn and then—don't you miss!' In that instant there opened up in me a great awareness. I knew then who I was. I was a negro . . . a person to be hunted, hanged, abused, discriminated against, kept in poverty and ignorance. It made no difference how intelligent, or talented, my millions of brothers and I were nor how virtuously we lived. A curse like that of Judas was on us."

As the mob advanced toward White's house, blacks in a neighboring house opened fire. The mob hesitated, then retreated. William Crogman, soon to be president of Georgia's Clark College, noted how the riot revealed the irony of racial uplift and its class distinctions. "Here we have worked and prayed and tried to make good men and women out of our colored population, and on our very doorstep the whites kill these good men. But lawless elements in our population, the element we have condemned fights back and it is to these people we owe our lives."

Officially, twenty-five blacks and one white died. Unofficially, more than one hundred may have died. Many were believed to be whites. David Howard, a black mortician, told a friend he had secretly buried a number of whites in the black cemetery. "You have no idea how many white people I had to bury in the Negro cemetery because they didn't want the white people to know who was getting killed by the Negroes in the riots."

The mayor ordered blacks to be searched for firearms. Blacks found ways to circumvent the order. Lugenia Hope, whose husband was guarding the campus of Atlanta Baptist with a rifle, reported, "The Negroes hid their arms and those of their neighbors who were not at home. We had enough to feel secure. It was said they came to the city in coffins. Some were carried in soiled laundry." W.E.B Du Bois, rushing home from Alabama to protect his family, wrote the highly emotional poem "A Litany at Atlanta," which questioned if the riot was not the amusement of a racist white God:

> Bewildered we are, and passion-tost, mad with the madness of a mobbed and mocked and murdered people; straining at the armposts of Thy Throne, we raise our shackled hands and charge Thee, God, by the bones of our stolen fathers, by the tears of our dead mothers, by the very blood of Thy crucified Christ: *What meaneth this?* Tell us the Plan; give us the Sign!
>
> *Keep not Thou silent, O God!*

After the riot, the white business leaders, shocked at what had happened, agreed to meet with black leaders. They were startled to find themselves confronted by one businessman: "If living a sober, industrious, upright life, accumulating property and educating his children is not the standard by which a colored man can live and be protected in the South, what is to become of him? When we aspire to be decent and industrious, we are told we set bad examples to other colored men. Tell us your standards for colored men. What are the requirements under which we may live and be protected?" Whites had no answer.

Booker T. Washington was pleased when whites offered to fire some police officers and arrest some mob leaders. He condemned black rapists along with white rioters and praised the interracial council for its conciliatory efforts. "I would especially urge the colored people in Atlanta not to make the fatal mistake of trying to retaliate. What is needed now is to get the best element of both races together and try to change the deplorable state of affairs. The Atlanta outbreak should not discourage our people but should teach a lesson from which we all can profit." His stance angered many black residents of Atlanta. Some pointed out that they had taken his advice on business and education and did not try to push too hard for their rights. And yet a race riot still happened. Washington's moral authority was shaken.

White conciliation had its limits. The leaders of the city refused to accept responsibility for the riot. When J. Max Barber published an article in a Northern journal blaming whites for the riot, claiming that better-class whites were also members of the mob, he was told either to leave town or face a criminal trial. "Not wanting to be made a slave on a Georgia chain gang, I departed for the North," he said.

Thomas Dixon, whose play *The Clansman* had helped ignite the riots, had no regrets. Race war, he said, was inevitable. "The insolence of the Negro in Atlanta has grown greatly. The outbreak of whites against the Negro was inevitable. There will be many outbreaks as long as the Negro continues to live in the same community as the white man."

The Atlanta riot was followed by disfranchisement, despite black efforts to block it. Du Bois was now determined to give up the scholar's life for that of an activist. In 1909, he traveled to New York to help found the interracial National Association for the Advancement of Colored People. The NAACP would become the foremost champion of black rights in America for the next fifty years.

When World War I began, the black soldiers seen here handcuffed together were sent to Fort Logan, Texas, outside of Houston. Harassed by the police, they struck back, killing sixteen whites.

Du Bois resigned from Atlanta University and became editor of the NAACP's magazine *The Crisis,* which would become the voice of a new generation of black militants. *The Crisis* battled racial discrimination, exposed atrocities and outrages against blacks, supported women's rights, and promoted race pride in the arts and literature. Within four months, the number of subscribers jumped from one thousand to six thousand and eventually soared to more than one hundred thousand.

Du Bois startled his readers in 1912 when he supported Woodrow Wilson for President even though Wilson was a Democrat and a Southerner. Wilson, he said, had promised fairness and justice for blacks, and he seemed a man of his word. In a letter to a black church official, Wilson wrote, "Let me assure my fellow colored citizens the earnest wish to see justice done the colored people in every manner and not merely grudging justice, but justice executed with liberality and cordial good feeling. Should I become President of the United States they may count upon me for absolute fair dealing for everything by which I could assist in advancing their interests of the race." Du Bois had no illusions about Wilson and the Southern Democrats, but he was aware that Northern Republicans had lost interest in supporting black rights. He also perceived that blacks who had migrated to Northern cities were voting and might be willing to vote for Democrats—if Northern Democrats proved sympathetic to demands for their rights.

Du Bois articulated what blacks expected from Wilson: "We want to be treated as men. We want to vote. We want our children to be educated. We want lynching stopped. We want no longer to be herded as cattle on street cars and railroads. We want the right to earn a living and own property. Be not untrue, President Wilson, to the highest ideals of American Democracy."

Du Bois underestimated the political power of the Southern demagogues in the Senate. Mississippi's James Kimble Vardaman and John Sharp Williams, Georgia's Hoke Smith, and South Carolina's Ben Tillman used Wilson's own racial prejudice to their advantage. They persuaded him to dismiss fifteen out of seventeen black supervisors who had been previously appointed to federal jobs and replace them with whites. He also refused to appoint black ambassadors to Haiti and Santo Domingo, posts traditionally awarded to them.

Postmaster General Albert Burelson and Treasury Secretary William McAdoo, both Southerners, issued orders segregating their departments, backed with an executive order from Wilson. They were determined to put blacks "in their place" by forcing them out of positions of competence and authority and into menial jobs. They could be doormen or messengers but not auditor for the navy nor recorder of deeds, two positions that had been held by blacks since Grant was President.

Throughout the country, blacks were segregated or dismissed. In Georgia, the head of the Internal Revenue Division fired all black employees. "There are no government positions for Negroes in the South. A Negro's place is in the corn field," he said. The President's wife, Ellen Wilson, was said to have a hand in expanding the segregation of federal employees in Washington. Black were shunted off into dimly lit and poorly ventilated rooms away from whites, forced out of lunchrooms, and required to use separate toilets. Salaries were reduced, in some cases drastically. W. P. Napper's salary was cut from $1,400 to $720; Julian Ross's was slashed from $1,600 to $600. Experienced clerks were reassigned as messengers and watchmen.

To justify segregation, officials publicized complaints by white women. The standard complaints were made: Women clerks were supposed to be afraid of black men's sexuality and disease. According to one woman, "Several years ago, I was compelled to take dictation from two negro men. I worked for a dark skinned woolly-headed negro. I then felt if a human being would ever be justified in ending her life, I would then for I was a Southern woman, my father a distinguished officer and my mother a woman of greatest refinement." Another woman testified, "The same toilet is used by whites and blacks and some of said blacks have been diseased. That one Negro woman, Alexandria, has been for many years afflicted with a private disease and for dread of using the toilet after her, some of the girls are compelled to suffer physically and mentally."

When a group of black women refused to sit in special lunchrooms reserved for them, they were warned of the consequences by Mrs. Archibald Hopkins, a white woman. "Why do you go where you are not wanted? Do you know that the Democrats are in power? If you people will go along and stay away from places where you are not wanted, we may let you hold your places."

African-American women fought back as best they could. Mary Church Terrell, a member of the highly influential Church family of Memphis and married to one of the few African-American judges in Washington, was one of several women who protested against Jim Crow in the government. "One of the young women came to tell me that an order had been promulgated whereby the colored women clerks in our section would no longer be allowed to enter the lavatory. Then and there I made up my mind I would do everything in my power to prevent that order from being executed." She embarrassed officials by offering a strongly

Despite the intense racial prejudice against them, black soldiers served their country during World War I. Some fought in France alongside French troops, since American generals did not want them serving with white American soldiers. The French people treated them warmly and without prejudice.

worded letter of resignation. In return for moderating her letter and not releasing it publicly, her department agreed to cancel the order.

Despite Wilson's protest that he was under pressure from Southern senators to segregate the government, the President was sympathetic to their demands. "I do approve of the segregation that is being attempted in several of the departments," he wrote to a minister. "It is distinctly to the advantage of the colored people themselves that they should be organized, so far as possible and convenient, in distinct bureaus where they will center their work."

Booker T. Washington, deeply saddened by what was happening, said little publicly. For years he had labored in the vineyards of accommodation, but all it had borne were the bitter fruits of white supremacy. The Wilson administration made him even more despairing. "I have never seen the colored people so discouraged and bitter as they are at the present time. I can't believe President Wilson realizes what harm is being done to both races on account of the recent policy of racial discrimination in the departments." Washington remained publicly silent even though people begged him to speak out. One woman wrote, "We all love and revere you for what you have achieved but we could love and honor you so much more if you would speak out for your people."

Du Bois sharply criticized Wilson in *The Crisis*. "The federal government has set the colored apart as if mere contact with them were contamination. Behind screens and closed doors they now sit as though leprous. How long will it be before the hateful epithets of 'Nigger' and 'Jim Crow' are openly applied?" The NAACP publicly exposed the segregationist policies of the Wilson administration and organized a national campaign of protest. Its efforts checked the spread of Wilson's Jim Crow campaign but did not root out procedures that were already in place.

On the evening of March 21, 1915, President Wilson attended a special screening at the White House of *Birth of a Nation*, a film based on *The Clansman* and directed by D. W. Griffith. The film presented a distorted portrait of the South after the Civil War, glorifying the Ku Klux Klan and denigrating blacks. An enthusiastic Wilson reportedly remarked, "It is like writing history with lightning, and my only regret is that it is all so terribly true." African-American audiences openly wept at its malicious portrayal of blacks while Northern white audiences cheered. Violence erupted in many cities where the film was shown. Gangs of whites roamed city streets attacking blacks. In Lafayette, Indiana, a white man killed a black teenager after seeing the movie. Thomas Dixon reveled in its triumph. "The real purpose of my film," he confessed gleefully, "was to revolutionize Northern audiences that would transform every man into a Southern partisan for life."

As the NAACP fought against the film and tried unsuccessfully to get it banned, the Ku Klux Klan used it to launch a massive recruiting campaign that would bring in millions of members.

In the midst of the battle over *Birth of a Nation*, Booker T. Washington died. Du Bois tactfully praised him for his greatness but also pointed out his weaknesses. "He was the greatest Negro leader since Frederick Douglass and the most distinguished man, white or black, who has come out of the South since the Civil War. Of the good he accomplished there can be no doubt . . . On the other hand, we must lay on the soul of this man, a heavy responsibility for the consummation of Negro disfranchisement, the decline of the Negro college and public school and the firmer establishment of color caste in this land."

Du Bois's battle with Washington was over, but his quarrel with Wilson continued. Although he supported the President when Wilson declared war on Germany in 1917, he did so reluctantly. Black soldiers, he knew, would suffer in America's Jim Crow army.

In 1917, soldiers of the all-black Third Battalion, Twenty-Fourth Infantry were assigned to Fort Logan outside of Houston, Texas. Houston had the largest black community in the state at the time, with a police force that was particularly aggressive toward black people. Clashes developed between the police and the soldiers, many of whom were not Southerners and not used to segregation. Black soldiers suffered beatings and unjustified arrests by the police. When a rumor spread that one of the soldiers, Corporal Charles Baltimore, had been killed by the police, his company prepared to march into town and take revenge. Baltimore had been beaten by the police but not killed, and then returned to camp. But the soldiers had passed their emotional point of no return. They marched into town and opened fire. When the shooting stopped, sixteen whites and four black men were dead. In a rushed and secret court-martial, nineteen men were sentenced to death and forty-three to life imprisonment. The first thirteen to die were not told their sentence or the date of their execution until hours before they were to die. They were denied their right to appeal to the president. The men requested to be shot as soldiers. The army refused their request.

On the night before his execution, on December 11, 1917, Baltimore wrote a farewell letter to his brother.

> I write you for the last time in this world. I am to be executed tomorrow morning. I know this is shocking news but don't worry too much as it is God's will. I was convicted at the general court-martial held here last month; tried for mutiny and murder. It is true that I went downtown with the men who marched out from camp.
> But I am innocent of shedding any blood.
> Goodbye and meet me in heaven.
> Your brother.
> Charles Baltimore

C. E. Butzer, a white soldier, witnessed their deaths:

> The prisoners were sitting in two rows, back to back on folding chairs and the hangman's knots were being adjusted. The men were droning a hymn, very soft and low. All I could make out was "I'm comin home, I'm comin home." Colonel Millard Waltz, the army officer in charge gave the command "Attention!" The prisoners snapped to their feet and stood on trapdoors. Then, as if by preconcerted plan, they broke into a song. It was a dolorous hymn chanted in a nasal monotone. Their last words were addressed to their white guards with whom they had become friendly. And the men of the 24th could be heard to say "Goodbye Boys of Company C."

Du Bois was deeply saddened and angered by the executions. In one of his most powerful editorials, he condemned the system that enabled this tragedy to happen.

Houston was not an ordinary outburst. They were not young recruits; they were not wild and drunkard wastrels. They were disciplined men who said—"This is enough—we'll stand no more." They broke the law. Against their punishment, if it were legal, we cannot protest. But we can protest and we do protest against the shameful treatment which these men and which we, their brothers, receive all our lives, and which our fathers received and which our children await. And above all we raise our clenched hand against the hundreds of thousands of white murderers and rapists and scoundrels who have oppressed, killed, ruined and robbed, and debased their black fellow men and fellow women and yet today walk scot free, unwhipped by justice, and uncondemned by millions of their white fellow citizens and unrebuked by the President of the United States.

While the war reinforced racial prejudice, it also set in motion social forces that would challenge that prejudice. Hundreds of thousands of blacks migrated north to work in factories, while some two hundred thousand African Americans served their country in Europe in a segregated army.

The army went out of its way to discriminate against blacks, especially in France where French citizens were not obsessed with racial distinctions. General John Pershing, commander in chief, sent a directive to the French Military Mission stationed with American troops. It read in part, "We must prevent the rise of any pronounced degree of intimacy between French officers and black officers. . . . We must not eat with them, shake hands with them, seek to talk to them and meet with them outside the requirements of military service. . . . White Americans become very incensed at any particular expression of intimacy between white women and black men."

One all-black regiment, the 369th, fought side by side with French soldiers as equals. The men of the 369th earned an unprecedented number of French military honors: 171 Croix de Guerre, France's highest military medal. African-American soldiers hoped that their patriotic service would earn them recognition, acceptance, and equality in American society on their return. The world war had created a new impetus and a new confidence in those the writer Alain Locke called the "New Negro."

As black soldiers returned home from France, W.E.B. Du Bois summoned them to prepare for what they were about to confront at home. "Make way for democracy. We saved it in France and by the great Jehovah we will save it in the United States or know the reasons why. This country of ours, despite all its better souls have done and dreamed is yet a shameful land. It gloats in lynching, disfranchisement, caste, brutality, and insults. By the gods of heavens we are cowards and jackasses if we do not now marshal every one of our brains and brawn to fight a sterner, longer, more unbending battle against the forces of hell in our own land. We return. We return from fighting. We return fighting."

Chapter 7

Prelude to Change:
Between Two Wars, 1918–1931

It was Walter White's favorite joke. When traveling through the South, he would board the train, seat himself in the "white" section, order a drink, and sometimes have a conversation with his fellow passengers about crops, the weather, the heat—or race. Once, one of his traveling companions expressed anger about "nigruhs" trying to pass for white. "However," the man added confidently, "they can't fool me." Walter White asked how he could tell. "By their fingernails," the man replied. "They're always shaped like half-moons." Looking directly at his traveling companion, his blue eyes calm as lake water, White held up the back of his hand and asked what race he belonged to. The Southerner laughed and said he was definitely a white man. Walter White grinned. He might have burst out laughing, but then he would risk someone discovering that he was a black man. Discovery would get him killed.

Walter White was not playing a practical joke. Nor was he trying to cross the color line for his own advantage. He was on a deadly mission for the NAACP, and his fair complexion was his cover. In 1918, White had become the NAACP's chief investigator of lynching. He would travel to a town where a lynching had occurred, pretend he was a salesman or newspaperman, interview

Lynchings continued in the 1920s. In this image, one of the mob is cutting off the toe of one of the victims to take as a souvenir.

In the 1920s, the NAACP began an extensive anti-lynching campaign in order to get Congress to pass a law making lynching a federal crime. But Southern Senators were able to block the bill from passing.

local whites about the event, gather the names of some of the members of the mob, and then publish the facts in *The Crisis* and other Northern newspapers.

In May, White journeyed to south Georgia to find out why black tenant farmers Hayes and Mary Turner had both been lynched. White casually engaged local people in seemingly unrelated conversations until they freely offered to talk about the Turner lynchings. White discovered that the Turners had worked for a white planter who had been murdered by one of his black tenants. The tenant had fled, and the mob lynched Hayes Turner, accusing him of being an accomplice solely on the grounds that he knew the killer—not a surprising fact since both worked for the same man. Turner's wife, Mary, eight months pregnant, angrily announced that if she ever found out who lynched her husband, she would swear out a warrant for their arrest. The mob went wild and tracked her down. Walter White later reported what happened next.

> Securely they bound her ankles together and, by them, hanged her to a tree. Gasoline and motor oil were thrown upon her dangling clothes; a match wrapped her in sudden flames. Mocking, ribald laughter from her tormentors answered the helpless woman's screams of pain and terror. "Mister you ought to have heard the nigger wench howl," a member of the mob boasted to me a few days later as we stood at the place of Mary Turner's death. The clothes burned from her crisply toasted body, in which, unfortunately life still lingered. A man stepped forward towards the woman and with his knife, ripped open the abdomen in a crude Cæsarean operation. Out tumbled the prematurely born child. Two feeble cries it gave—and received for answer, the heel of a stalwart man, as life was ground out of the tiny form. Under the tree of death was scooped a shallow hole. . . . An empty whisky bottle, quart size, was given for a headstone. Inside its neck was stuck a half-smoked cigar—which had saved the delicate nostrils of one member of the mob from the stench of burning flesh.

The Turner lynchings were a prelude to the racial storms about to sweep across America at the end of World War I. In the summer of 1919, the racial time bomb exploded. Lynchings were brazenly carried out and advertised in newspapers before the event. In Ellisville, Tennessee, local newspapers announced the lynching in advance: "Three Thousand Will Burn Negro," "John Hartfield Will be Lynched by Ellisville Mob at 5 This Afternoon," "Negro Sulky as Burning Nears." Thousands came to watch or participate, jamming trains, bringing their dinners, and turning the event into a festive occasion.

In 1919, twenty-three race riots occurred, in mostly Northern cities. As Chicago sweltered in a blaze of summer's heat, racial temperatures were climbing. On Sunday, July 27, Eugene Williams, a seventeen-year-old black youth, went swimming in Lake Michigan to cool off. Blacks and whites used separate sections of the beach. When Williams mistakenly swam across the color line, screaming white youths hurled rocks at him. Williams frantically tried to swim to safety but drowned before he could make it back to the black section of the beach. The incident triggered a race riot. That night, bands of whites roamed the city streets beating and killing unsuspecting blacks. Blacks fiercely fought back. When the riot finally ended, some fifteen whites and twenty-three blacks were dead.

The Chicago riot was part of a racial frenzy of clashes, massacres, and lynchings throughout the North and the South. All were started by whites. In Washington, D.C., four whites and two blacks were killed. Whites were astonished that blacks dared to fight back. The *New York Times* lamented the new black militancy: "There had been no trouble with the Negro before the war when most admitted the superiority of the white race." A "southern black woman," as she identified herself in a letter to *The Crisis*, praised blacks for fighting back. "The Washington riot gave me a thrill that comes once in a life time . . . at last our men had stood up like men. . . . I stood up alone in my room . . . and exclaimed aloud, 'Oh I thank God, thank God.' The pent up horror, grief and humiliation of a life time—half a century—was being stripped from me."

In October 1919, a race war exploded in Phillips County, Arkansas. On the night of September 30, a small group of black men and women were gathering at a rural church to organize the Progressive Farmers and Household Union of America. They had hired a white lawyer, U. S. Bratton, and were planning to sue their landlords for money owed them for their crops, and for an itemized accounting of their charges at the store. When two white law enforcement officers arrived at the church, one later claiming they were looking for a bootlegger, shots were exchanged. One officer was killed and the other wounded.

As word of the shootings spread throughout the county, the local sheriff sent out a call for men "to hunt Mr. Nigger in his lair." The call went out to Mississippi to come to the aid of white men in Phillips County. Hundreds of armed men jumped into trains, trucks, and cars and crossed into Arkansas, firing out of windows at every black they saw. Some said that if it was black and moving, it was target practice. Frank Moore, one of the farmers at the church, saw the massacre as it unfolded. "The whites sent word that they was comin down here and kill every nigger they found. There were 300 or 400 more white men with guns, shooting and killing women and children."

Farmers were not the only target for the mob. Dr. D.A.E. Johnston, a prominent dentist from Helena, Arkansas, and his three brothers were seized as they returned from a hunting trip. They were chained together in a car and shot to death.

Soldiers from the United States Army eventually restored order, although some claimed they participated in the killings. By the time the shooting ended, twenty-five blacks and five whites were listed as officially dead. Many blacks believed that perhaps as many as two hundred blacks were killed, their bodies dumped in the Mississippi River or left to rot in the canebrake. The stench of the dead could be smelled for miles.

The white establishment charged that blacks had been in a secret conspiracy to rise up and overthrow the white power planters, take their land, and rape their women. No evidence was produced to substantiate the charge. Since five white men were killed during the riot—some probably shot by accident by other whites—more black men had to die. More than seven hundred were arrested. Sixty-seven were sent to prison. Twelve farmers were tried by an all-white jury for the murder of whites. During the trial, a mob surrounded the courthouse, shouting that if the accused black men were not sentenced to death, the mob would lynch them. Prisoners were tortured to confess or to testify against others. Alf Banks, one of the twelve, told his lawyer, "I was frequently whipped and also put in an electric chair and shocked and strangling drugs would be put in my nose to make me tell that others had killed or shot at white people and to force me to testify against them."

The all-white jury debated the charges fewer than eight minutes per man. Each defendant was found guilty. The judge dutifully sentenced all twelve to death. The mob cheered. As far as Arkansas was concerned, the case was closed.

For Walter White the case was far from closed. As far as he was concerned, the trial was a

One reason W.E.B. Du Bois was protective of Fisk was because it was his alma mater. This is his graduation photo in 1887—he is seated at the left.

lynching that wore the mask of law. White traveled to Arkansas posing as a newspaper reporter, first interviewing the governor, who called White "one of the most brilliant newspapermen he had ever met," and then traveling to Phillips County, the scene of the massacre. During his investigation, a black man approached White and warned him that a lynching party was being prepared for him. His identity had been discovered. White immediately boarded the first train out of Helena. As he anxiously waited for the train to leave the station, the conductor approached him. "You're leaving just before the fun is about to start. There's a damned yellow nigger down here passing for white and the boys are gonna get him. . . . When they get through with him, he won't pass for white no more." White later wrote, "No matter what the distance, I shall never take a train ride as long as that one. Later in Memphis, I learned that news had been circulated there that I had been lynched in Arkansas that afternoon."

White published the real story behind the massacre that challenged Arkansas's version of the events. He wrote that the attempt of blacks to form a union to control their own labor angered whites who were determined to destroy it by any means.

The NAACP hired local lawyers to appeal the death sentence of the twelve convicted farmers. Among them was Scipio Africanus Jones, a black lawyer from Little Rock born in slavery, who argued that the presence of the mob outside the courthouse during the trial made it impossible for the defendants to receive a fair trial. After several years of fighting to have the twelve men freed, the United States Supreme Court agreed to hear the case. On February 19, 1923, in a landmark decision (*Moore* v. *Dempsey*) that became a major step in defending the rights of black defendants, Justice Oliver Wendell Holmes wrote, "If the whole case is a mask—that counsel, jury and judge were swept to the fatal end by an irresistible tide of public passion—and the state courts refuse to correct the wrong, then nothing can prevent this court from securing to the petitioners their constitutional rights."

More and greater violence was yet to come. In 1921, the worst race riot in America occurred in Tulsa, Oklahoma, a city that boasted one of the most prosperous African-American communities in the country. The city had three black millionaires and numerous prosperous black businessmen. When a young woman elevator operator charged a black youth with assault—it seemed that he accidentally stepped on her toe—the youth was arrested. Seventy-five armed blacks went to the jail to protect him from a mob, but no mob had gathered. As the men were about to leave, a white man tried to take away the gun of a black man. The confrontation suddenly escalated into a gun battle. Several whites were killed and injured and two blacks were killed. Mobs of enraged white men roamed the black section of Greenwood, breaking into houses, gunning down blacks in their beds, and setting fire to houses and businesses. By the next morning, the black section of Greenwood lay in ashes. Thirty-five city blocks had been burned to the ground. Six thousand blacks had been rounded up by the mob, and more than eight hundred were wounded. Anywhere between seventy-five to three hundred African Americans might have been killed. Not a single white was ever prosecuted.

The NAACP urgently tried to stem the violence by focusing national attention on what was happening in the South and lobbying for federal anti-lynching laws. Supported by Congressmen L. C. Dyer of Missouri, the NAACP pushed to make lynching a federal crime, emphasizing that more than 50 percent of those people lynched were already in the custody of law enforcement officials. The NAACP charged that a good many sheriffs had arranged for their prisoners to be handed over to the mob.

* * *

For W.E.B. Du Bois, there were other battles to be fought in addition to lynching. The training grounds for what he called "the talented tenth," that 10 percent of the race that he believed would lead the fight against Jim Crow, were the liberal arts black colleges like his beloved alma mater Fisk University in Nashville. In the mid-1920s, Du Bois saw that the liberal arts tradition in general, and Fisk University in particular, was threatened. Using *The Crisis* as his platform, Du Bois clashed with some of the most powerful and influential men in America.

Du Bois had graduated from Fisk in the 1880s, and he cherished the university that had intellectually nourished him. He considered Fisk the crown jewel of the black colleges. It had an integrated faculty and more than six hundred students, many of whom came from the elite families of the black middle class. "Fisk is the college—the shrine of my young years of high idealism and infinite faith," he wrote. "I have known it in the great days of its leaders—Cravath, Spence, Morgan—firm, splendid souls to whom compromise with evil was death. They were men radical in their belief in Negro equality."

The churches that had once financially supported Fisk and other black colleges had run out of money. In their place emerged a new breed of philanthropists who no longer believed in black equality. They were businessmen of great wealth—men like Andrew Carnegie, John D. Rockefeller, George Foster Peabody, and Julius Rosenwald—whose foundations supported black and white schools in the rural South. They did not want to transform the South but to make it run more efficiently. Black education for them was primarily a means to socialize black children to accept a subordinate status, not a means of improving their lives.

The most powerful of the philanthropic foundations was the General Education Board, founded by John D. Rockefeller. Its first president, William Baldwin, perfectly incarnated its philosophy. Baldwin, the son of a former abolitionist who fought to end slavery, despised abolitionism. He was described as a nervous, impatient man, intolerant of dissent and convinced that African Americans were innately inferior. He hated black intellectuals, "especially those who have been educated at Harvard," pointedly referring to the Harvard-educated Du Bois. He charged, "Their problem was that it was purely an attempt on their part to be white people." He believed that blacks could not be educated much beyond the three R's, that they were a child race two hundred years behind the Anglo-Saxon in development.

In the 1890s, Baldwin paid a surprise visit to Tuskegee and became a disciple of industrial education. He enthusiastically embraced Booker T. Washington's plan to train black teachers to instruct their students to accept Jim Crow and Southern whites as "their best friends." Aware that Southerners were suspicious of Northern white support for black schools, Baldwin reassured them that the General Education Board intended to reinforce the Southern way of life, not challenge it. He told one audience, "Time has proven that the Negro is best fitted to perform the heavy labor of the South. The Negro and the mule is the only combination to grow cotton. He will willingly fill the more menial positions and do the heavy work at less wages than the white man."

Baldwin issued a warning to black educators. "Avoid social questions; leave politics alone; continue to be patient; live moral lives; learn to work; and know that is a crime for any teacher, white or black, to educate the negro for positions that are not open to him." These remarks led Du Bois to reply, "There are those rich and intelligent people who masquerade as the Negro's friend in order to educate a race of scullions and then complain of their lack of proven ability."

Baldwin and his fellow philanthropists wanted to dismantle liberal arts instruction in African-American schools and colleges. Their goal was to bring social harmony and industrial progress to the South by making black schools vocational institutions like Tuskegee and Hampton. They felt that vocational training would be good for blacks, good for the South, and good for business, as it would keep labor unions out. Fisk was on their list. They agreed with Robert L. Jones, Tennessee's superintendent of education, who commented, "I would have his academic education limited, for I am inclined to think that the negro can best be utilized on the farms, in the shops and, in fact, in all lines of trade."

In 1915, the trustees of Fisk hired Fayette McKenzie, a white educator, as president of the university. Du Bois welcomed him at first. "I saw in him a new type of young, scientific philanthropist come to help and re-establish training among Negroes."

McKenzie's motto was, "Let Us Dare to Be a University. . . . A Negro is . . . capable of the highest scholarship . . . and a Negro college . . . can measure up at every point with the standard colleges of the land." Part of McKenzie's plan was to raise a million-dollar endowment from Northern foundations in order to upgrade the quality of education at Fisk and make it free from financial worries. Although there was some concern among board members about liberalism at Fisk, some recognized that a few black colleges were needed to train the ministers, doctors, and lawyers who would serve the black community. The board wanted to see that McKenzie had the support of Nashville's white community and that the school produced students who would accommodate the realities of white supremacy and accept "complete separation" of the races.

The board soon discovered that McKenzie was their kind of educator. Convinced that black adolescents were extremely sensual beings who had to be controlled, McKenzie imposed strict rules of behavior on men and women, regulating almost every moment of their lives. He banned dating and most contact between men and women. He imposed a strict dress code for women. They were required to wear high-necked gingham dresses with long sleeves, white between April and November, blue the rest of the year. "The skirt could be gathered but could have no more than three tucks or ruffles. No lace or embroidery trimming was allowed. . . . Chiffon, georgette, organdy or other thin waists were proscribed."

Smoking was not allowed. Jazz playing was forbidden on the piano. He ended intercollegiate baseball and track, barred fraternities and the NAACP from campus. McKenzie abolished student government and the student literary magazine, *The Herald.* He even censored Du Bois's magazine, *The Crisis.* He monitored all student oration and debates, expelled students without due process, and fired faculty members he felt were disloyal. He encouraged snitching, preferred docile students, and ignored Nashville's black community. To McKenzie and his supporters, the spirit of Fisk University was incarnated in its famous choir, which for fifty years had entertained white audiences around the world with mournful spirituals rooted in slavery days.

In the 1920s, jazz, not spirituals, was the soul of black music. Jazz was the voice of rebellious youth demanding new freedoms from old ways. On the Fisk campus, the irresistible forces of the new jazz age collided with the immovable resistance of the old ways. At Vanderbilt University across town, white students dressed in the styles of the day, drank from hip flasks, petted in the back of cars, smoked, danced, and listened to jazz music. Fisk's black students complained to Du Bois. Some expressed serious concerns about censorship and paternalism. Others were more troubled by the limits on their personal freedom. One coed wrote, "The girls of the student body might have been able to get along with the orders forbidding them to talk to boys. They may have been peaceful with the orders which forbade dancing, but when they keep wearing cotton stockings and gingham dresses, it is too much."

The white citizens of Nashville, impressed with McKenzie's rule, pledged fifty thousand dollars to the endowment fund, the first time a Southern community had done so for a black college.

In 1923, Julius Rosenwald visited Fisk. The founder of Sears Roebuck had contributed millions of dollars for black elementary and secondary schools throughout the South. Known as Rosenwald schools, they were built mostly by local people who contributed their labor and often raised part of the money. Rosenwald and the state contributed the rest. Thousands of Rosenwald schools were constructed in the 1920s and 1930s, and they provided much of the education for black children. In 1927, Tennessee spent $21.02 for every white child and only $11.88 for every black child.

Rosenwald was far more liberal and sympathetic than other philantropists to black aspirations, yet Fisk's students troubled him. "There seems to be an air of superiority among them and a desire to take on the spirit of a white university rather than the spirit which has always impressed me at Tuskegee."

Despite the concern, the board agreed to the endowment. They felt that McKenzie would see to it that Fisk students accepted the Southern way of life rather than challenged it. They expected Fisk not to produce any more Du Boises. To Du Bois, the issue was the soul of the university. "Suppose we lose Fisk; suppose we lose every cent that the entrenched millionaires have set aside to buy our freedom. They have the power, they have the wealth but Glory be to God, we still have our own souls and led by young men as these let us neither flinch nor falter, but fight and fight and fight again." Du Bois saw that McKenzie was accommodating to the South and had accepted white supremacy in exchange for an endowment. Instead of producing the "New Negro," a militant youth who would insist on his full rights as an American and be a race leader, Fisk was in danger of producing Booker T. Washingtons who would accept Jim Crow. This betrayed the ideals of democracy and equality of the abolitionist founders of Fisk.

At the end of May 1924, a deeply troubled Du Bois boarded a train to visit Fisk in Nashville. His daughter Yolande was graduating and he had been invited by McKenzie to address the alumni the following day. On June 2, with the president of the university, the trustees, students, and alumni packing Cravath Memorial Chapel and no doubt expecting a eulogy of McKenzie, Du Bois lowered the boom on him. *"Duiturni Silenti,"* he began, quoting "To My Long Continued Silence," Cicero's great oration before the Roman Senate almost two thousand years earlier. The smiling faces of McKenzie and his supporters turned to startled ones as Du Bois lashed McKenzie with fierce words of criticism. "I have never known an institution whose alumni are more bitter and disgusted with the present situation in this university. In Fisk today, discipline is choking freedom, threats are replacing inspiration, iron clad rules, suspicion, tale bearing are almost universal." Expecting to hear his praises sung by the man whom many considered the voice of black America, McKenzie was scolded like a naughty child in front of the whole world. Du Bois blasted him for his tyrannical rule, for selling out Fisk's birthright to wealthy philanthropists, and for subjecting female students to Jim Crow humiliations. "I am told the president of Fisk University took fifteen girls from the glee club, girls from some of the best Negro families in the United States, carried them down town at night to a white men's club, took them down an alley and admitted them through a servant's entrance, and had them sing in a basement while these white men smoked and laughed. If Erastus Cravath, one of our founders knew that a thing like that happened at Fisk

University, he would rise from the grave and protest against this disgrace and sacrilege." The students and some teachers broke out in thunderous applause. McKenzie spied one young lady furiously clapping from a seat in front of the chapel. Shortly afterward, she was charged with cheating and suspended.

Du Bois's speech added fuel to the fires of protest that had been burning on campus. George Streator, a returned World War I veteran, and one of the student leaders, kept Du Bois informed by mail of what was happening. In one letter, he reported how a teacher was using the classroom as a forum to support McKenzie. "Miss Chasin, a professor in English, assigned a 5000 word essay on the subject 'Why Dr. McKenzie should be retained at Fisk.' You know the predicament of the students. Say 'no' they'll flunk. Say 'yes' they'll surely get a good grade."

In November 1924, the board trustees arrived on campus and were immediately greeted by students chanting anti-McKenzie and pro–Du Bois statements: "Away with the Tsar" and "Down with the Tyrant." Streator presented a list of grievances to the trustees. The trustees recommended to McKenzie that he make a few minor concessions. McKenzie seemed to have agreed. Then, during a chapel service in February 1925, he revealed that the conciliatory hand masked an iron fist. He told the students, "A complete ignoring of the charges made against the university will be the policy of the board of trustees of Fisk University. The policy is unchanged. Those who don't like it can go." The battle escalated. Students responded with a brief but noisy demonstration. The students overturned chapel seats and broke windows, all the while keeping up a steady shouting of "Du Bois, Du Bois" and singing "Before I'll be a slave, I'll be buried in my grave."

McKenzie immediately retaliated by summoning the feared Nashville police to campus. Nashville blacks had continually suffered at the hands of the local police. A black minister had recently been killed by them, and a black youth was dragged out of his hospital bed and lynched without police interference. Two black women had been beaten by whites and a black merchant gunned down by a white saloon owner.

Eighty policemen armed with riot guns broke down the doors to the men's dormitory, smashed windows, and beat and arrested six of the seven students whom McKenzie had claimed were the ringleaders of the demonstration. The students were charged with a felony, a crime for which they could be sent to prison. McKenzie confessed that he lacked proof that the arrested men were guilty of any of the charges he made. "These men have spoken against my policies all throughout the year," he weakly explained. "While I had no proof these were the disturbers, I felt that they might be behind it." The charges against the students were dropped and after they were released, they left the school.

In response to the arrests, the students called a strike that polarized the Nashville community. Du Bois cheered them on. "I thank God that the younger generation of black students have the guts to yell and fight when their noses are rubbed in the mud." The white community completely supported McKenzie; the black community, the students. McKenzie mobilized Nashville's white civic clubs, which honored him with a luncheon. "When I was introduced, everybody in the room rose to his feet and a great many yelled as well as a great many cheered. I feel that never before in the United States has a white man in our work had such a hold on the city as I have in Nashville." He implied that should he not

The Great Depression hit the rural South with all the force of an economic tornado, destroying the lives and dreams of many sharecroppers and their children.

receive unconditional support from the black community and the trustees, "Not only will the white citizens and money of Nashville be turned into other directions, but the same will perhaps be true of a considerable part of the North."

The students struck, with Du Bois's blessing and moral support and with the alumni and the local black community behind them. They held fast for eight weeks despite pressure. Local white banks and the post office no longer would cash their checks. The black community stepped in to the rescue. They housed and fed them, advanced money, and were unwavering in their support. Coeds showed their rebellion by wearing flapper dresses, silk stockings, and high heels.

Du Bois now tried to rally the black community in support of his war against McKenzie and the General Education Board. To Du Bois's disgust, McKenzie received support from hundreds of parents of students. "We are heartily in accord with you and denounce this unbridled uprising among the students," wrote Mr. and Mrs. Alpha O. Young. "I hope you will continue strict rules and regulations for by such we feel our boys and girls are safe there," James T. Wright, a father of a student, wrote. "Get more machine guns and stay on the job. We need you and the sacrifices you are making for our people," W.L.B. Johnson agreed. Du Bois would later respond,

> "There were parents and alumna who insisted that even if the school authorities are wrong, it was the business of black boys and girls to submit. When students are willing to jeopardize their whole lives in an appeal for justice, the business of parents is to encourage and uphold their protesting children instead of cowing and disgracing them."

Despite having the trustees' support, McKenzie's rule was finished. Two months later, he resigned.

The victory had repercussions on other black campuses. At Howard University, a confrontation between the white president and the black faculty and student body led to the president's resignation and the appointment of the school's first black president. At Hampton, the battle was between the students and a white autocratic president supported by a condescending white faculty. Hampton was little more than a technical high school. Philanthropists lavished a great deal of money on the school because it was the embodiment of their ideal of black education. Du Bois sarcastically remarked that it had everything money could buy—except racial integrity. The strike was defeated, but it forced changes in the curriculum.

For many students, graduation from college was no guarantee of a good job in the South. Many of the best and brightest joined the mass migration that had begun before World War I and continued throughout the 1920s. The *Chicago Defender* continued its campaign to encourage blacks to leave. For millions of blacks, the paper kept alive the vision of the North as the land of freedom, a dream that had been in the hearts of black men and women since slavery time. Young Richard Wright, who became a nationally acclaimed writer, remembered how the North kept hope alive during the dark days of his childhood in the Deep South. "The North symbolized to me all that I had not felt or seen; it had no relation to what actually

The Scottsboro Boys were nine black youths who were riding a freight train when they were arrested for fighting with whites. When two women hoboes were discovered on the train, the boys were charged with rape and sentenced to death, although no rape had occurred. Their lives were saved by the legal campaign of the Communist Party.

existed. Yet by imagining a place where everything is possible, it kept hope alive inside of me."

The newspaper was banned in certain towns and counties of the South because whites feared its articles would cause their black laborers to leave for Chicago. Whites burned any copies of the paper they found. Blacks caught reading the newspaper could be flogged. Those bringing it in could be killed. Despite the censorship, blacks smuggled or sold the paper in almost every Southern city and town. Preachers read it to their congregations, barbers to their customers, the literate to the illiterate. One man commented, "My people grab it like a mule grabs a mouthful of fine fodder." Memphis Slim, a blues musician, recalled, "I was in a place called Marigold, Mississippi. They had a restaurant there and in the back, they had a peephole. And can you imagine what they were doing? They were reading the *Chicago Defender* and they had a lookout man at the door with a peephole. If a white man came into the restaurant, they'd stick the *Defender* into the stove and start playing checkers."

Blacks saw the exodus as a fulfillment of God's promise. A Birmingham minister offered the following prayer to his congregation: "We feel and believe that this great Exodus is God's hand and plan. In a mysterious way God is moving upon the hearts of our people to go where He has prepared for them."

Among those who migrated were the most creative people in the South. Jazz musicians came from New Orleans to play in Chicago, Kansas City, and New York. Blues players came from the Delta. The New York–based NAACP welcomed writer Zora Neale Hurston, poets Langston Hughes and Countee Cullen, and sculptor Augusta Savage. They, along with other black artists, created a cultural florescence known as the Harlem Renaissance.

The Harlem Renaissance was part of the Roaring Twenties, an age of sexual liberation, bootleg liquor, mobsters, and speakeasies. The country was swept up in a frenzy as stock prices reached astronomical figures.

In 1929, hard times came to America with the Great Depression. No group of people was hit harder than rural blacks. The price of cotton spiraled downward from eighteen to six cents a pound. Two-thirds of some two million black farmers made no money or went into debt. Those who could find work might do so for fifteen cents a day worth of credit at a landlord's store. There was no money to pay teachers. Black maids were fired by the thousands. Hundreds of thousands left the land for the cities, abandoning their fields and homes. Even traditional "Negro jobs"—busboys, elevator operators, garbage men, porters, maids, and cooks—were sought by desperate unemployed whites. In Atlanta, a Klan-like group called the Black Shirts paraded, carrying signs that read, "No jobs for niggers until every white man has a job." In other cities, people shouted, "Niggers back to the cotton fields. City jobs are for white men." In Mississippi, where blacks traditionally held certain jobs on trains, unemployed white men, seeking their jobs, ambushed and killed them as the train passed by their hiding places.

On March 2, 1931, as the Depression deepened, a number of unemployed white and black youths seeking work were riding separately on a freight train passing through Alabama. When a white man stepped on the hand of a black rider, the incident escalated into a fight. The whites were thrown off the train and immediately notified a local sheriff, who telegraphed ahead to the town of Paint Rock to stop the train and arrest all blacks on it.

An angry sheriff's posse met the train an hour later and seized nine black youths, some of whom had never seen each other until that moment. One of the youths was nineteen-year-old Clarence Norris. "They made all us boys come out of the train and line up. There was these men with guns, I don't know what they are—policemen, firemen. They had uniforms. All I remember was they had brass buttons. Some are yellin, 'let's take these niggers to a tree. Let's take these niggers and hang them.'"

As the sheriff's deputies continued to search the train, they discovered what seemed to be two white youths who turned out to be two young women, Ruby Bates and Victoria Price, dressed in boys' clothing. Suddenly the assault charge escalated into a rape case, although Clarence Norris swore that none of the youths had seen the women on the train. "And we didn't see no womens until they brought them to the jailhouse. And then one of the police asked—Victoria Price—which ones had you? And she pointed out five of the boys and said, 'this one-this one-this one-this one and that one.' Then they asked Ruby Bates. And she didn't say nothin. Then one of the white men's say, 'no need of askin her nothin'. The other four must of had her.' And that's the way a rape charge was framed against us. I never will forget it."

Bates and Price were mill workers and semiprostitutes, who were also riding the train seeking work. They had dressed as boys for protection, although the night before they had slept with some white men who were also riding trains.

The sheriff encouraged the women to bring rape charges against the nine black youths. Both women agreed. The nine youths were quickly tried and convicted of rape in the town of Scottsboro, Alabama. Eight of the nine were sentenced to death, the other to life imprisonment because he was only twelve years old. Immediately after their sentences, the American Communist Party burst on the scene, announcing it would fight to free all the boys.

The Communist Party USA was the only political organization in America before 1930 that championed black rights and full political, social, and civil equality. Their slogan, "self-determination in the black belt," meant that blacks should have their own "nation" in the South because this was where the greatest number of them lived. This idea came as a directive to the American party from Stalin and the Soviet Union. The Soviet Union had regarded American blacks as an oppressed colonial people rather than as an oppressed minority. Many American Communists simply ignored the directive or considered it a long-range goal.

The party had arrived in Alabama in 1930 and organized workers in the steel industry and coal mines around Birmingham. The dramatic entrance of the Communists into Alabama electrified blacks. They were amazed that the party advocated and practiced complete racial equality. When Communists formed a sharecroppers' union, they were surprised to receive thousands of responses from black tenant farmers.

The union then made a major effort to involve the local black community. Organizers visited churches and spoke—often over the objections of conservative ministers—about the party's vigorous defense of the Scottsboro defendants. Union organizers often preached to their audiences in biblical terms, or they combined the teachings of Marx and Lenin with the Gospels of John and Paul. They began and concluded their speeches with a prayer and saw no contradiction between being a Baptist and a Communist. For them, Jesus, Marx, and Lenin were fellow revolutionaries. The Communist organizers gave old songs new verses. "Give Me That Old Time Religion" became a vehicle for a Scottsboro Boys song.

> The Scottsboro Verdict
> The Scottsboro Verdict
> The Scottsboro Verdict
> Is not good enough for me.
>
> It's good for the big fat bosses
> For the workers' double crossers
> For low down slaves and hosses
> But it ain't good enough for me.

Ned Cobb was an Alabama tenant farmer who had managed to succeed despite the Jim Crow world in which he lived. In 1931, he joined the Sharecroppers Union to fight for the rights of all sharecroppers and farmers. He was involved in a shootout, was wounded, and was imprisoned for thirteen years, leaving his wife and children to run the farm.

Under the guise of sewing circles, the union organized farmers' wives. They met and discussed political and economic issues, read the Communist *Daily Worker* and *Working Women,* carried out union correspondence, and wrote letters to newspapers to encourage others. The union tried to organize white farmers as well. Lemon Johnson, an organizer and colleague of Ned Cobb, discovered that though many were sympathetic to the union, few dared risk crossing the racial divide. J. C. Davis, a white sharecropper, was lynched for his sympathies to the union.

Organizing was highly dangerous work. Union members were frequently murdered, their bodies dumped into the swamp. Some union leaders hid in the woods at night. Posses scoured the countryside for Albert Jackson, a Northern secretary of the union. He wrote of the constant fear he and his fellow union members had of being caught: "The terror drive continues. As I write, there is a lookout to warn me of the approach of lynchers. Constant vigil is kept at all times. Sleep is tortured with nightmares of lynching, terror and murder. Food settles with lumps in your stomach. But the struggle must go on!"

In Camp Hill, Alabama, a shootout had occurred between a black union leader, Ralph Gray, and a sheriff. Gray was standing guard while union members were meeting in a vacant house nearby. When the sheriff came to break up the meeting and make arrests, Gray intercepted him, and the two men confronted each other. An angry quarrel escalated into a shootout in which both men were wounded, the sheriff in the stomach and Gray in the legs. Gray was taken to his home and decided to remain there. His brother Tom later said that when the posse arrived, one member "tore the furniture all apart, broke the butter churn, spilt the milk out and even burned the mattresses." One of the posse "poked a pistol into Brother Ralph's mouth and shot down his throat." Gray's wife and children were in the room. The mob then burned down his house and dumped his body on the steps of the Dadeville courthouse where groups of angry whites shot and kicked the lifeless body. "Other blacks were arrested and mobs attacked sections of the black community, beating and killing farmers and terrorizing their families. Many fled into the woods for safety."

Despite the dangers, others continued to join the sharecroppers' union. Among them was Ned Cobb, a black farmer in Tallapoosa County, and a number of his friends and neighbors. Cobb was drawn to communism not because Marxism-Leninism appealed to him but because he regarded the Communists as the descendants of the Northern abolitionists who once brought Reconstruction to the South but failed to carry it through. Cobb remembered that his grandmother had predicted their return. "My Grandam Cealy used to say what used to be will come again. Colored people once knowed what it was like to live in freedom before they came to this country and they would know it again. I heard them words when I was a boy. It was instilled in me many a time, 'The bottom rail will be on the top. The poor will banish away their toils and snares.'"

Ned Cobb was a relatively prosperous tenant farmer who had successfully navigated the treacherous waters of race relations in rural Alabama. He was also deeply aware of the injustices of the South. "Ever since I've been in God's world, I've never had no rights, no voice in nothing that the white man didn't want me to have—even been cut out of book learning.

They'd give you a good name if you is obedient to them and didn't question them. You begin to cry about your rights and the mistreatin' of you and they'd murder you."

One of Cobb's major activities was persuading others to join the union. "I talked it over with folks. I told them it was a good thing in favor of the colored race. I told them that the organization would back you up and fight your battles with you. Some of them was too scared to join and some of them was too scared not to join; they didn't want to be left alone when push comes to shove."

In December 1932, Cobb received word that the sheriff was coming to foreclose on the property of his friend and fellow union member Clifford James. Cobb, putting his pistol in his pocket, decided to intervene. "I thought an organization is an organization and if I don't mean anything by joinin', I ought to keep my ass out of it. I had swore to stand up for poor black farmers—and poor white farmers if they'd taken a notion to join."

When Cobb arrived at the farm with several other union members, the foreclosure was just beginning. He politely asked the deputy to delay the process and give James a little time to pay his debt. The deputy refused. "I got orders to take it and I'll be damned if I ain't going to take it," Cobb quoted him as saying. Cobb replied that the only way he would allow him to take it was over his dead body. As Cobb later said, he was ready to start "a shooting frolic" if the foreclosure continued. The deputy left to gather reinforcements. Cobb, Clifford James, and several other union members remained. When the sheriff returned with a group of officers, Cobb stayed outside for a few moments while the posse spread out. As Cobb slowly walked back to the house, a deputy named Platt raised his shotgun. "I started in the house. Took one or two steps—BOOM—Mr. Platt threw his gun on me. BOOM BOOM. Shot me two more times before I could get in the door. He filled my hind end up from the bend of my legs to my hips with shot. My feet is just sloshing with blood. I snatched out my .32 Smith and Wesson and I commenced shooting at Platt. Good God, he jumped behind a tree, soon as that pistol fired. Every one of them officers run like the devil away from there. That Smith and Wesson is barking too much for them to stand."

When the shooting stopped, one union man was dead and several others were wounded, including Clifford James and Milo Bentley. Cobb escaped, and his family rushed him to the hospital at Tuskegee. James walked seventeen miles to the hospital, where he was treated for gunshot wounds. His doctor turned him in to the police. Cobb was not kept at the hospital, because the staff feared what might happen if whites discovered his presence there.

Vigilantes began to terrorize the black community, breaking into homes and beating and shooting people. One of the reported victims pistol-whipped was an elderly, blind black woman who was close to a hundred years old.

Cobb and the others were captured. The police threw the wounded James and Bentley into a damp jail cell and refused them medical treatment. They died of their wounds and pneumonia.

Ned Cobb was tried and found guilty. He was offered a lighter sentence if he supplied the names of other union members. He refused and was sent to prison for thirteen years. "Something done in your behalf, you've got to risk," he said. "You take such work as this. I see more good of it than I can really explain."

Despite the violence, union organizing continued. In 1933, the political landscape dramatically changed with the election of Franklin Delano Roosevelt. A new era in civil rights was about to begin that would radically transform America.

Chapter 8

Center Stage for Civil Rights, 1932–1944

In 1932, Franklin Delano Roosevelt was elected President of the United States by an over-whelming majority—of white votes. While more than 60 percent of the white community supported him, more than 60 percent of the black community voted against him. Although Roosevelt was a Northerner, his sympathies seemed to lie with the white supremacist South. As assistant secretary of the navy under Woodrow Wilson, Roosevelt had helped segregate his department. As governor of New York, he neither supported black civil rights nor appointed blacks to office. He boasted of his Southern roots and considered himself an honorary citizen of Georgia, where he owned property. During the election campaign, when the NAACP sent him a questionnaire about his position on civil rights for blacks, he did not respond. Expect-ing no consideration from Roosevelt or the Democratic Party, most blacks voted for Herbert Hoover, even though Hoover had supported a lily-white policy within his party, appointed few blacks to office, and refused to be photographed with any black leaders. African Ameri-cans voted Republican not because they had any illusions about Hoover but because they felt that the Republicans would do less damage to their few rights than the Democrats.

In the early years of Roosevelt's first term, their suspicions seemed justified. The President had no intention of angering the Southerners who controlled Congress by challenging estab-lished racial policies. His first priority was to end the Depression, and he needed the support of the Southern politicians who had the power to block his efforts. Federal agencies took their cue from the President during the early years of his first term. Many of them were run by men who held deep prejudices against blacks. When relief efforts got under way, blacks had to wait at the end of the line and received less money than whites. They received fewer jobs, less access to federal programs, and less relief money for equal work. When Congress passed the National Recovery Act, mandating that all workers be paid equally for the same work, Southern employers, used to paying blacks less, fired them and hired white workers to replace them. In 1933, the Agricultural Adjustment Administration was established. One of its purposes was to revive the dying cotton economy. Planters were paid to reduce the

At the beginning of his first term, President Franklin Delano Roosevelt did not give any consideration to the problems blacks were suffering as a result of the Depression. However, his wife, Eleanor, an advocate for black rights, convinced the President to include African Americans in the New Deal programs.

amount of land on which they would grow cotton. Part of that subsidy was supposed to be paid to their sharecroppers, though few sharecroppers received any benefits, and no action was taken against the planters. Having reduced their acreage, landlords then proceeded to evict their tenants from the land, adding to their misery. The Civilian Conservation Corps, established the same year, was designed to provide training and employment for youths. Out of the first two hundred fifty thousand recruits, only seven thousand five hundred were black despite the fact that twice as many black youths were out of work as white. As historian Harvard Sitkoff pointed out, white America was receiving a New Deal, while blacks were getting the same old raw deal.

Eleanor Roosevelt was one of the few who championed their cause in the White House. Mrs. Roosevelt had become increasingly aware of the injustices suffered by African Americans. She began to speak out publicly against race prejudice. She supported anti-lynching campaigns and anti–poll tax measures. She attended conferences with black speakers and spoke out urging justice and greater equality for blacks. She became a go-between between civil rights activists and the President, despite opposition to her efforts by many of Roosevelt's pro-Southern White House staff. The President began to respond to his wife's pleas for his administration to take action on behalf of blacks. His motives were not altogether altruistic. Roosevelt had noticed that the black vote in a number of key cities in the North had become significant, and could make the difference in a close election.

The President allowed black leaders access and became the first Democratic President to have his picture taken with them. He spoke out against lynching and called it murder. He appointed William Hastie as the first black federal judge and consulted with black leaders. He promised fair treatment of blacks by the federal government. And while his powers were limited by a Congress that was virtually held hostage by segregationist senators, Roosevelt gave hope and encouragement to black people everywhere.

As the President and Mrs. Roosevelt publicly addressed black concerns, the federal agencies followed suit. The Works Progress Administration, under the leadership of Harry Hopkins, and the Public Works Administration, led by Harold Ickes, swung into action. Both Hopkins and Ickes were, like Mrs. Roosevelt, pro–civil rights. They had hired many highly qualified young men and women on the basis of their professional abilities. Ickes and Hopkins wanted to bring not only blacks but also poor whites and workingmen and -women into the mainstream of American life. They built schools and libraries for blacks, and created federally subsidized housing.

Having received the green light to translate their beliefs into action, the New Dealers set out to incorporate blacks into federal programs. The government opened tens of thousands of jobs to blacks on public works projects and in the federal government at the same salaries as whites. Although most blacks filled unskilled positions, many black professionals were hired, from librarians to lawyers, economists to engineers. The Federal Theater Project hired black actors, directors, and stagehands. Tens of thousands of black youth were admitted into training programs including the Civilian Conservation Corps. Unemployed and disabled blacks became eligible for federal relief. The Farm Security Administration, led by Henry Wallace, distributed benefits to Southern black farmers, although still far short of that received by whites. As a result of the New Deal's policies, blacks received better health care, better education, better jobs, and increased benefits.

Many federal programs were directed by coalitions of blacks and liberal Southern whites. Outstanding black administrators like Robert Weaver worked with liberal Southerners, including Aubrey Williams, Virginia and Clifford Durr, Clark Foreman, and Will Alexander. Other young white Southerners, like Joseph Gelders and Palmer Weber, lobbied for legislation providing for federal protection of voting rights. For black and liberal whites, what the South needed was a second Reconstruction—one that would complete the first.

For some whites, the journey to liberalism began with a personal journey to overcome their own prejudices. Virginia Durr, who came from a prominent Alabama family, recalled that her moment of truth began when she was at Wellesley College in Massachusetts. She went to the dining room the first night she was there, and a black student was sitting at her table. She got up, marched out of the room, went upstairs, and waited for the head of the house. She told her she couldn't possibly eat at the table with a Negro girl. The house supervisor replied, "Wellesley College has rules. If you can't obey the rules, then you can withdraw." Durr said that if her father heard of her eating at the same table with a black person, he would be furious. She had been taught that to eat at the table of a Negro would be committing a terrible sin against society. This was the first time she became aware that her attitude was considered foolish by some people. It undermined her faith, her solid conviction of what she had been raised to believe. From that night on, she sat at the table without further complaint. It was the first small step on her long march supporting integration.

Perhaps the single most influential person in Washington on behalf of black civil rights was Mary McLeod Bethune. Bethune began life as a sharecropper's daughter, educated herself before attending Moody Bible Institute in Chicago, became a teacher, and founded one of the outstanding black schools for girls in the South (Daytona Normal and Industrial Institute for Negro Girls, now Bethune-Cookman College). She told her students, "You enter to learn and depart to serve." She then became a leader in the women's club movement. Bethune played a major role in helping develop the deep humanism of the President's wife and focusing it on the African-American struggle for freedom. Bethune became the unofficial leader of Roosevelt's "kitchen cabinet," a group composed of high-ranking black officials who sought to coordinate government policy regarding African Americans.

Bethune did not tolerate racial slurs. According to legend, she was walking across the lawn of the White House on her way to meet with the president and Mrs. Roosevelt when a white gardener from the South called out, "Aunty, where do you think you're going?" Bethune stopped, whirled about, fiercely looked the gardener dead in the eye, and then suddenly smiled. "Oh," she said. "I'm sorry I didn't recognize you. Which of my sister's children are you?"

The push for social change in race relations came from below as well as above. Civil rights activists organized boycotts against segregated facilities and demonstrations against white store owners in Northern cities who refused to hire blacks. Their slogan was, "Don't buy where you can't work."

The leading radical group of the era was the Communist Party. Its emphasis on interracial unity, the visibility of black leaders in the struggle, and its willingness to confront the police and politicians transformed the civil rights movement. The party's militant defense of the Scottsboro Boys inspired the respect and admiration of the black community. African Americans enthusiastically welcomed black and white Communists battling the police for black rights, leading hunger marches, and demonstrating for relief for the needy, an end to evictions, and jobs for the unemployed.

The agitation even won the support of members of the black establishment. Mordecai Johnson, the first African-American president of Howard University, publicly stated, "I don't mind being called a Communist. The day will come when being a Communist will be the highest honor that can be made to any individual." The *Chicago Defender* editorialized, "How can we go to war with the Communist Party? We may not agree with its entire program but there is one item we do agree with, and that is the zealousness with which it guards the rights of the race." Charles Houston, then dean of the Howard University Law School, saw the consequence of the Communist Party's militancy. "Communists are offering Negroes full and complete brotherhood without condition of race, creed or previous condition of servitude.

They are the first to fire the masses with a sense of their raw potential power and the first to openly preach the doctrine of mass resistance and mass struggle. . . . The Communists have made it impossible for any aspirant to Negro leadership to advocate anything less than full economic, social and political equality."

The Communists were not the only organization that preached and practiced integration. During the 1930s, in Arkansas, the Southern Tenant Farmers Union brought black and white sharecroppers and tenant farmers together in a struggle to get money owed them by their landlords. The United Mine Workers, the Steel Workers Organizing Committee, and the Mine, Mill and Smelter Workers sent organizers to Birmingham to form unions in their respective industries. Mine workers had had interracial unions since the turn of the century.

W.E.B. Du Bois, long an advocate of integration, suddenly shifted gears. In 1934, Du Bois, responding to the deep entrenchment of Jim Crow in the North, proposed that African Americans voluntarily segregate themselves, build their own businesses, and run their own schools. He was not suggesting segregation as a permanent move but as a tactic that would help the black community to gain parity with whites. "I know that this article will forthwith be interpreted by certain illiterate nitwits as a plea for segregated Negro schools. It is not. It is saying in plain English that a separate Negro school where children are treated like human beings, trained by teachers of their own race, who know what it means to be black, is infi-nitely better than making our boys and girls doormats to be spit and trampled upon and lied to by ignorant social climbers whose sole claim to superiority is the ability to kick niggers when they are down."

The article sent shock waves through the NAACP leadership. The organization's mission had always been to achieve full integration of blacks in every aspect of American life. What Du Bois was suggesting was heresy. The NAACP board confronted Du Bois and told him that integration was the organization's goal and he had to accept it.

For twenty-four years, Du Bois, as editor of *The Crisis,* was the militant voice of the NAACP. His control over *The Crisis* had been challenged, but he had always prevailed. In 1929, when Walter White was appointed to succeed James Weldon Johnson as head of the organization, a conflict between the two strong-willed men seemed inevitable. White was not concerned with the broader issues that sometimes preoccupied Du Bois. He wanted *The Crisis* to cover what the NAACP

In the 1930s, Walter White became the head of the National Association for the Advancement of Colored People. Under his leadership, the NAACP launched a campaign to have Congress pass a federal anti-lynching law and attack segregation in the courts.

The leader of the NAACP's legal strategy to challenge the constitutionality of segregation in the federal courts was Charles Houston, seated at right. Standing is his protégé, Thurgood Marshall. They are arguing that their client, Donald Gaines Murray, seated between them, was illegally denied entrance to the University of Maryland law school because of his race. The Maryland court agreed.

was doing. White made a play to gain control of *The Crisis,* a move that angered Du Bois. He withstood the challenge. But now he was told either to retract his position or step down. Du Bois chose to resign.

As Du Bois left the NAACP, Charles Hamilton Houston, a black lawyer from Washington, D.C., and dean of Howard's Law School, arrived to help lead the fight against Jim Crow. Houston had dedicated his life to fighting race prejudice. During World War I, he had witnessed hundreds of black soldiers unjustly prosecuted by the military establishment without cause. "I made up my mind that if I ever got through this war, I would study law and use my time fighting for men who could not strike back."

Setting up a law practice with his father in Washington, D.C., Houston was one of approximately one thousand black lawyers, less than 1 percent of the total number of lawyers practicing in America. He was determined to help remedy this situation. Appointed dean of Howard University Law School in 1929, Houston transformed the school into a first-rate institution. He trained a cadre of young lawyers in civil rights laws, a course seldom if ever offered in law schools anywhere. His students included Thurgood Marshall, Spottiswood

Robinson, and Oliver Hill, all of whom would play major roles in challenging Jim Crow in the courts. Hill recalled that Houston was so tough as a teacher that his students, among themselves, called him " 'Iron Shoes' and 'Cement Pants' . . . and a few other names that don't bear repeating. He was harder on himself than he was on us. But he had to be. He was preparing us for war. He had a soldier's faith that every battle must be fought until it is won and without pause to take account of those stricken in the fray—even if it meant himself."

Houston felt that if black people were ever to achieve equal justice under law, they would have to act in their own behalf. He had watched with growing optimism as the Supreme Court began to make decisions favorable to black rights regarding criminal procedures, especially in the Scottsboro case. When Roosevelt began to appoint liberal judges to the Court, Houston felt the time had come to challenge segregation itself.

Houston was convinced that the battle for civil rights had to be won in the schools but fought in the courts. He understood that judges were not going to make decisions that would overturn rulings having to do with constitutional interpretation unless absolutely necessary. He felt that if he confronted the "separate but equal" doctrine laid down in *Plessy* v. *Ferguson* in 1898, the court would most likely reject the challenge. If, however, he insisted that *Plessy* be enforced—that is, if the NAACP sued a state to make its schools for black children equal to those for whites—then he could chip away segregation. The states would either have to build new schools for blacks, which they could not afford, or admit blacks into white schools. If the courts agreed with his argument, he could prepare to challenge the legal basis of segregation itself.

Houston decided that the NAACP had to carefully select cases that stood a good chance of winning. Those cases would establish a precedent that "would make plain the inequality that existed in educational opportunities of blacks and whites. And would make true equality too expensive for states to maintain." The ultimate goal was always integration. As Houston told one audience, "The NAACP will never compromise with segregation. It is not a question of wanting to sit in class with white students. It is a question of vindicating one's citizenship."

In 1934, Houston traveled to South Carolina county by county with a movie camera and filmed the profound inequality between black and white schools. He documented the abysmal conditions that young black children experienced and made notes. "Moore's Pond School. The nearest drinking water is across the highway at an abandoned gasoline station. The children sit inside on crowded benches. No desks, no chairs, one old piece of blackboard. The cracks in the floor are so wide that pencils often roll through to the ground when dropped. No pit. No lime. Just ashes from the stove to cover the [human] waste."

Houston also spoke at black colleges, churches, and union halls, met with teachers' groups, consulted with black lawyers, and addressed local NAACP chapters. His message was the same: Black people must lead their own struggle for civil rights and not wait for the white man to do it for them. "I have confidence in the capacity within the black community and the Negro race to bring about change. The struggle is always greater when it springs from the soil than when it is a foreign growth." He felt that black lawyers should take the lead in securing the full rights of citizenship guaranteed to African Americans by the Reconstruction amendments.

Houston also discovered that local leaders like Modjeska Simkins were organizing voters in an effort to breach the walls of the all-white primary. Simkins had used Roosevelt's popularity with black voters. "Roosevelt took the jug by the handle," she said. "He tried to give the people who were shot down and had nothing, something. It was a shot in the arm for Negroes." Her strategy was get people to pay their poll tax and register to vote in the general election first before tackling the primary. "Voting in the general election was a way of getting people's feet wet. . . . But we knew that nothing would come of this until we could vote in the primary, which was the only real election." Ralph Bunche, while working as a chief investigator for the Myrdal-Carnegie monumental study of the Negro (which formed the basis for Gunnar Myrdal's *An American Dilemma*), visited South Carolina and was favorably impressed. "Despite the hardships frequently imposed by registrars, increasing numbers of Negroes in the South are demonstrating an amazing amount of patience, perseverance and determination, and keep returning after rejections until they get their name on the registration books." In a number of Southern cities, blacks held mock elections with posters and meetings to elect a "bronze" mayor, that is, an unofficial mayor of the black community.

As voter registration drives slowly moved forward in the South, Houston prepared his challenge to segregation in the courts. There were major changes taking place in the Supreme Court concerning due process of law. The Court asserted its power to supervise administration of justice by examining evidence of discrimination for itself. The Court overturned convictions in which black defendants had been mentally and physically tortured to extract confessions or had been denied competent attorneys. The Court also ruled that if black citizens were deliberately excluded from jury rolls by a county, subsequent convictions were invalid. Other rulings struck down restrictive covenants that made it illegal to sell a house to blacks and peonage laws forcing blacks to work as virtual slave labor in order to pay off debts. The Court also mandated that black and white teachers be paid equal salaries.

Houston felt that his strongest case of inequality in education would be at the graduate school level. Most Southern states did not provide graduate studies for blacks and did not allow them into white graduate schools. He found the case he wanted in Missouri. Lloyd Gaines, a college graduate, had been denied entrance to the law school at the University of Missouri because of race. Houston argued that the state was obligated either to build a law school for blacks equal to that of whites or admit Gaines to the University of Missouri. The Supreme Court agreed. The Gaines decision breached the walls of segregation. It meant that every state must either build a separate graduate school for blacks or integrate. And if this were true for graduate schools, then why not high schools? And elementary schools?

Walter White supported Houston's strategy in the courts, but he had his own agenda. Throughout his career with the NAACP, he had been determined to see Congress pass a federal anti-lynching law. Lynching, he charged, was still a part of Southern culture and would not be eradicated without a federal law. He noted that the number of lynchings had risen during the Depression from a low of 7 in 1929, to 21 in 1930, to a high of 28 in 1933.

Despite the growing public revulsion against lynching, Roosevelt would not fight for an anti-lynching bill. He admitted to White that he was personally in favor of it, and he let that be known to Congress. He would not, however, challenge the Southern bloc of senators, who could defeat his programs for economic recovery. White met with the President on several occasions to discuss his support. White later revealed that the Roosevelt was unwilling to challenge the Southern leadership. "I did not choose the tools with which I must work," he reportedly told White. "If I come out for the anti-lynching bill they will block every bill I ask Congress to pass. I just can't take that risk."

To pressure Congress, White and the NAACP launched a major publicity campaign to organize grass-roots support for the bill. They published an account of the horrific lynching of Claude Neal by a mob from Alabama that seized Neal from a jail in Florida—with the cooperation of local law enforcement officials. The NAACP official filed a report describing how Neal was killed.

An eye witness told the NAACP investigator that parts of Neal's body [i.e., his genitals] were cut off and he was made to eat them. Then they sliced his sides and stomachs with knives and every now and then somebody would cut off a finger or toe. Red hot irons were used on the 'nigger' from top to bottom. From time to time during the torture, a rope would be tied around Neal's neck and he was pulled up over a limb and held there until he was almost choked to death when he would be let down and the torture begin again. After several hours of this unspeakable torture, "they just decided to kill him."

Churches and synagogues sent letters to congressmen urging them to pass the bill. Whatever the national feelings on black civil rights might have been, a consensus against lynching was developing in the South as well as the North. Southern newspapers editorialized against lynching. Southern churches condemned it. Scholars published studies exposing that rape—the Southern rationale for lynching—was seldom involved in most lynchings. A widely circulated brochure of the NAACP reminded the nation of the potential damage to all children. "Do not look at the Negro, look at the white children," it said. "What havoc is being wrought in their minds?"

In 1936, a bill was introduced in the House of Representatives allowing the federal government to intervene in lynchings, if local officials failed to act. As debate began, Governor Henry Lamar White of Mississippi publicly boasted that there was no need for a federal anti-lynching bill as Mississippi had not had a lynching in fifteen months. The following day, during a debate on the bill, Representative Arthur Mitchell of Illinois rose and read to his fellow congressmen an article from a Southern newspaper published the day after the governor's statement, describing what happened to two young black men in Duck Hill, Mississippi. They were taken from the custody of the sheriff, tied to trees, horsewhipped, their bodies mutilated with blowtorches, castrated, and shot to death. Their bodies were burned to ashes. The House listened to the report in total silence and then voted two to one in favor of the bill. Only one representative from a Southern state, Maury Maverick, a liberal congressmen from Texas, voted for the bill.

Even though the bill sailed through the House, it still had to pass formidable opposition in the Senate. Every attempt made to pass such a law foundered on the reefs of a filibuster by Southern senators, who prevented the issue from coming to a vote. Although a majority of

Women played a major role in the anti-lynching and voter registration drives in the 1940s and 1950s.

senators were in favor of the bill, and the president had made it clear he would sign it if passed, Southern senators were determined to kill it. In 1938, the bill finally reached the Senate floor. As Walter White sat in the gallery, Southern senators rallied around the battle flag of states' rights for seven weeks. Senator Allen Ellender proclaimed his allegiance to white supremacy on the floor of the United States Senate. "I believe in white supremacy and as long as I am in the Senate, I expect to vote for it. We have fought to subjugate the Negro in the South. It was costly; it was bitter; but how sweet the victory." With Republican help, Southern Democrats defeated all efforts to bring the bill to a vote. In the end, the filibuster could not be stopped. The bill was withdrawn.

Despite the defeat, there were victories. The NAACP emerged with its reputation enhanced. The fight had gathered national support and brought thousands of new members into the civil rights movement. The number of lynchings dropped to a low of two by 1939.

The Southern states began to pass local anti-lynching laws, although no one was immediately prosecuted. And Southern whites themselves joined the fight.

Jesse Daniel Ames, a white Texan and an activist, had long worked for interracial cooperation if not integration. For Ames, lynching was an insult to white women as well as an outrage on black men. She debunked the myth fostered by Southern white males that lynching was necessary to protect white women. White women did not need protection from black men, because relatively few black men raped white women.

In the early 1930s, Ames formed an organization of Southern white women to campaign against lynching. Called the Association of Southern Women for the Prevention of Lynching (ASWPL), the organization's mission was to get community leaders and law enforcement officials to sign pledges that they would do everything they could to prevent lynchings of prisoners in their communities. The pledge read in part, "We declare lynching an indefensible crime, destructive of all principles of government, hostile to every ideal of religion and humanity, degrading and debasing to every person involved. We pledge ourselves to create a new public opinion in the South which will not condone for any reason whatever acts of the mob or lynchers."

The women recruited local churches, social clubs, politicians, and law enforcement officials to sign pledges condemning lynching. They held lectures, published anti-lynching pamphlets, and talked at colleges and fraternal organizations. One woman wrote, "I got me as many officers of the law as I could to sign it. I felt they are the ones to enforce this pledge. They said . . . that they would do their part." Women made it clear to local officials that they had the vote and would use it accordingly. One ASWPL mailing to its members reminded them of their voting power: "If it is an election year, have you talked with your candidates for sheriff? Have you asked each candidate what he will do to prevent lynchings if elected? The voters will decide for or against elections this year."

When a suspect for a crime was taken into custody, the local ASWPL might send a telegram requesting the local sheriff to take whatever steps were necessary to prevent mob violence. The organization encouraged local people to call them if they heard rumors that a lynching might take place. One report read,

> On Friday, Mr. Glen Rainey heard someone boast that there would be a "dead nigger" at Decatur because he had raped a woman. Mr. Rainey came to the office and made a report. Mrs. Tilly called the sheriff Jake Hall. As he was not in she talked with Mrs. Hall who assured her there would be no killing. Mrs. Tilly then got in touch with the Methodist women in Decatur. These in turn called other people and asked them to also call the sheriff, the mayor, the chief of police and the county police. Early in the afternoon, the prisoner was removed from the Dekalb county jail for safe-keeping.

ASWPL women often ran into resistance. Jesse Daniel Ames reported, "Women went into communities where there had been a lynching. Many of the people were surly, belligerent. Women were by no means safe. They knew of the constant dangers and didn't forget to pray. Many were threatened. I know women who wouldn't tell their husbands the threat because they feared their families would make them quit work." She herself received letters condemning her. One anonymous letter came from Florida after the lynching of Claude Neal: "If you are that much of a Negro lover, you better go to the North where you can mingle with them. I am a free born Southerner and am glad to say I wish that they would have some more lynchings, just as they did this one."

Holland's, a Southern magazine, described the conditions under which some women worked: "These dauntless women have gone, times without number, to peace officers in charge of prisoners who might become victims of lynchings and pleaded for preventative action. They have gone into situations so tense few men would intrude. They have faced threats of all kinds from truculent individuals and even organizations in the South. They have been ridiculed. They have been ordered by municipal officials not to speak. They have gone into community after community, where lynchings have occurred and patiently searched out the facts of the case for their records."

Ames was against lynching, but she was also against federal intervention in lynching. She felt that it was up to the states themselves—pressured by Southern women—to pass and enforce their own anti-lynching laws.

As the decade came to an end, civil rights was now becoming a national issue, and blacks had good reason to hope. Paul Robeson returned to the United States in 1939 after being away for four years. He could see that after a decade of struggle, most blacks still labored as menials, too many were still unemployed, most were segregated in the North, and white supremacy still reigned in the South. When asked about his impressions, Robeson replied, "Conditions are far from ideal. They are not so much changed in fact as they appear to be in the hopes of liberals and Negro leaders. Change is in the air and this is the best sign of all."

Change *was* in the air. A tremor was felt throughout the South from deep in the piney woods to the lush cotton fields of the Delta, from sleepy towns and hamlets to the slowly growing urban centers. Change was shaking the seemingly impregnable bastion of Jim Crow. Whites and blacks, Southerners and Northerners, politicians and clergymen, ordinary citizens and civil rights leaders were calling for an end to some of the worst aspects of segregation lynching, the poll tax, and the white primary. They advocated better schools and better jobs for blacks. If most Southerners dared not call for integration, it was clear that the country was headed in that direction. Only a few Southerners had the courage to say what had to happen—the dismantling of all forms of segregation.

The high point of the liberal attempt to reform the South came at the convocation of the Southern Conference for Human Welfare, held in Birmingham in 1938. Southern liberal politicians, black activists, government officials, college professors, radical and mainstream labor organizations, grass-roots organizers, newspaper editors, and clergymen gathered to discuss modernizing the South. They raised a number of major issues, from ending lynching and abolishing the poll tax to making plans for Southern economic development and interracial cooperation. Eleanor Roosevelt attended with the president's blessing. The first two sessions were integrated despite a Birmingham law forbidding such gatherings to take place. When the Birmingham police ordered the convention to segregate its seating, Mrs. Roosevelt placed her chair on the dividing line between the races as an act of defiance. Virginia Durr recalled the atmosphere of the convention. "Oh, it was a love feast. There must have been 1,500 or more people there from all over the South, black and white, labor union people and New Dealers. Southern meetings always include a lot of preaching and praying and hymn singing, and this was no exception. The whole meeting was just full of love and hope. The whole South was coming together to make a new day. It was the New Deal come South!"

In the summer of 1941, as war began in Europe, defense industries began to boom in the United States, producing weapons for America and her ally, Great Britain. Though jobs were plentiful for hundreds of thousands of whites, they were almost nonexistent for blacks. Only a few thousand were hired—and most of these were jobs as porters and janitors. In the aerospace industry alone, out of its 107,000 workers, only 300 blacks were employed. Over 50 percent of defense employers said they would not hire black workers no matter how skilled they were.

Black leaders called a meeting in Chicago to devise a plan to force industry to open up more jobs for blacks. As one suggestion was made after another, one exasperated woman stood up. "Mr. Chairman," she reportedly called out, "we ought to throw fifty thousand Negroes . . . bring them from all over the country, any way they can get there and throw them around the White House until we get some action."

A. Philip Randolph, head of the Brotherhood of Sleeping Car Porters, seized upon the suggestion. He called for a massive demonstration of blacks in the nation's capital on July 1. Several days later he announced the March on Washington. He said that ten thousand people would demonstrate for jobs and fair treatment. "The whole National Defense System reeks with race prejudice, hatred, discrimination. It is time to wake up Washington as it has never been shocked before. . . . We would rather die on our feet fighting for Negro rights than to live on our knees as halfmen, begging for a pittance."

The announcement electrified the black community. Grass-roots support for the march sprang up everywhere. Church congregations raised money to rent buses. Schoolchildren saved their allowances. Almost every black organization agreed to participate. Whites began to panic. When blacks were accused by the press of being unpatriotic, one black youth replied, "The army Jim Crows us. The Navy only lets us serve as mess men. The Red Cross refuses our blood. Employers and labor unions shut us out. Lynchings continue. We are disfranchised, jim-crowed, spat upon. What more can Hitler do than that?"

President Roosevelt feared that a race riot would break out if the march took place. He asked his wife and several white civil rights leaders to intervene. Randolph held fast. Unless the President acted, the march would take place on schedule. Mrs. Roosevelt told Randolph that she felt the march would harm the cause for which Randolph was fighting. He replied that it had already done some good, "for if you were not concerned, you wouldn't be here." As the deadline approached, the press predicted that more than one hundred thousand people would march on Washington. Asked by reporters where the marchers would eat and sleep, Randolph, aware that Washington was a highly segregated city, replied that they would frequent white hotels and restaurants. The very thought that blacks would march into their hotels and restaurants, sleep on their sheets, and eat off the same plates terrified whites.

Roosevelt finally agreed to meet with Randolph and NAACP head Walter White. He used

Although most black soldiers were used in work details, some saw combat and distinguished themselves in battle. They served in the infantry, tank corps, and air force.

his considerable personal charm to dissuade them from the march. They refused. He asked how many would march. They replied that one hundred thousand would, an inflated number, but it impressed the President. He asked what they wanted. They told him they wanted him to integrate the army and forbid discrimination in defense industries. Roosevelt compromised. He said he could not integrate the army, but he would ban racial discrimination in industry. He issued Executive Order Number 8802, establishing a Committee on Fair Employment Practices with the authority to investigate and end discrimination in defense industries, government, and unions. Randolph called off the march. The order had limited effect in the defense industry, but it set an important civil rights precedent. For the first time, blacks had demanded their rights from the federal government rather than asked for them. And they had gained a partial victory.

When America entered World War II, the drive for black civil rights stalled. The primary objective of the nation was to win the war, just as a decade earlier it had been to end the Depression. Black leaders and celebrities pledged their full support for the war effort, including militants A. Philip Randolph and W.E.B. Du Bois, writers Langston Hughes and Richard Wright, world heavyweight champion Joe Louis, actress Hattie McDaniel, and singer Josh

White. The Communist Party, the strongest advocate for black rights and employment in the 1930s, now focused on Hitler as he invaded Russia and threatened the center of world communism. Although the *Pittsburgh Courier* launched a "Double V" campaign—victory over fascism in Europe and Jim Crow at home—in reality there was no systematic fight against Jim Crow during the war. Grievances were rarely harped on. Organizations considered militant received little support from the black community. Occasional demonstrations organized for civil rights were poorly attended. Contributions slowed to a trickle. The NAACP took a conservative course and increased its membership. There were race riots in the South caused by whites, and lynchings began to rise again. Thirteen men were lynched in 1940–1941, including two black teenagers, Charles Lang and Ernest Green, who were supposedly kidding around with a young white girl they were friendly with. A white passerby in a car interpreted the horseplay as an attempted assault and a mob hanged them from a bridge.

Many black soldiers suffered from racial discrimination. Jim Crow was practiced in Northern bases as well as Southern. Men and women in the army ate at segregated tables, slept in segregated barracks, and rode in segregated buses. Thousands wrote letters of racial protest to federal officials. Private Charles Wilson asked for an executive order "whereby Negro soldiers would be integrated . . . as fighting men, instead of . . . as housekeepers." Major Samuel Ransom, after pointing out how blacks were called "niggers" by whites regardless of their rank and were separated in barracks and mess halls, reported that the men felt that "they just might as well die in the guardhouse as in this slave camp." A soldier who signed himself as "a disgusted negro trooper" wrote, "This place is a living hell and we feel that we can't tolerate these conditions much longer." Others reported how they were beaten or their comrades were killed. Private Latrophe Jenkins wrote, "If this war is won by America who's going to help us win ours?"

Black women who joined the Women's Army Corps were also discriminated against. They were segregated from whites in many camps, and certain hotels and restaurants in non-Southern cities were declared off limits. Occasionally they suffered from police brutality. Four WACs who had been trained as orderlies were told by their white commanding officer, "I don't want any black WACS as medical technicians around this hospital. I want them to scrub and do dirty work." The WACs went on strike; they were court-martialed and sentenced to a year of hard labor. The case was reviewed, the verdict overturned, the nurses restored, and their commanding officer reprimanded.

Black soldiers sometimes fought and won their own battles. When a group of black soldiers who were carrying out a maneuver in rural Louisiana tried to buy some ice cream at a country store, the door was locked on them and a "gun totin' cracker" stood ready at the back door. The men returned to the carrier and pulled back a canvas to reveal a 50-mm machine gun.

The team that operated the gun pulled a belt of ammunition out of its box and slapped it into place, and the triggerman swung the gun around to cover the doorway of the ice cream parlor. "The only sound was of the activities of the men, no words . . . I stepped back into the carrier, picked up my rifle. All of our clips being slapped into place at the same time sounded like a cannon going off. None of us had any illusions as to what would happen when that fifty caliber opened up on the ice cream shack. It would cut it and everybody inside in half. We knew every white regiment and division in the state, plus the police at every level would be called down on our heads. Without a word we had decided to make our stand. Fortunately for all concerned, the crackers inside realized that this was for real, these were not 'niggers' playing soldier, these were black men who planned to kill and die for that right."

The door was unlocked and the men were served.

Yet despite the surge of racism, many blacks still hoped that by following a pattern of racial uplift, legal redress of grievances in the courts, and cooperation with the "better class" of whites, they would eventually achieve their goals. They pointed out that jobs were opening up, especially in the federal government. Many argued that persuasion, reason, and good behavior would eventually overcome race prejudice. They appealed to the conciliatory philosophy of Booker T. Washington, rather than directly confronting Jim Crow and the color line. They hoped that things would get better after the war. The question still remained: Who would risk making them better? To try could be lethal. When Elbert Williams, head of the NAACP in Brownsville, Tennessee, tried to organize a voter registration drive, he was lynched.

Yet there were countercurrents. In Winston-Salem, black workers, who were racially segregated in the factory, spontaneously went on strike in the 1940s to protest working conditions. They joined the CIO and forced the company to recognize them.

In Columbia, South Carolina, blacks organized a campaign to register to vote. At that time the registration books were kept in places of white-owned business. When a group of blacks wanting to register entered, the books suddenly disappeared from sight. When whites entered to register, the books mysteriously appeared again.

In one ward, blacks were standing outside a candy store where a white woman registrar had denied that she had the books, although they had seen whites registering. George Elmore, a light-skinned black man, entered the store for a Coke. Mistaking him for white, she encouraged him to register. As he did so she said to him, "Them damn niggers out there tried to get their names in our books but I didn't let them." When Elmore finished, the registrar checked the book to make sure he had signed in properly. When she saw that his address was in the black section of town, she screamed, "You're a damned nigger!" Elmore replied, "Yes ma'm." "Well," she said, defeated, "tell them other niggers they can come in here an' enroll if they want to." Elmore's name was later stricken from the books, but he challenged it in court and won.

Osceola McKaine, an NAACP organizer in Columbia, noted, "We are living in the midst perhaps of the greatest revolution within human experience. No nation will be as it was before peace comes." The war's end brought new jobs into the region and gave a vital boost of energy to a dying agricultural economy. Jim Crow had, in part, been sustained by the fact that most of the South was rural. Black and white relations were often defined by the cotton economy of landlord and tenant farmers. The war hastened the death of this relationship and brought a new consciousness in the minds of many blacks and some whites that things could no longer remain the same. Tens of thousands joined the NAACP to prepare for this change.

Hundreds of thousands of Southern blacks left the South for jobs in the North or joined the army. Most of the black soldiers in the army served in segregated units. The marines and the air force refused to take blacks into their service until later in the war. Most black soldiers were used in noncombat military jobs.

More than a million black civilians left the South as agriculture continued to decline and machines replaced human labor. For many black Southerners, the war enabled them to discover new experiences in large Northern cities. One of the biggest changes had to do with white women. James Nix, a veteran, remembered the taboos on white women imposed on him as a child. "We was on a bus and a little white girl got on with a long, pretty ponytail. And I told my father 'that girl has some pretty hair.' And my father told me to shut up. And when he got home, he gave me some hell. 'Don't you know stuff life like that will get you killed . . . get you hung!?' " Roscoe Pickett recalled that his mother used to warn him about white girls. "She told me over and over again, when you go to town with your daddy, don't you be looking at no white girls. And it never dawned on me to ask her why." When Pickett was stationed in Chicago by the army during the war, he was startled to discover that white girls thought nothing of sitting next to him on a bus. He also discovered that when he went to a movie, he could sit wherever he wanted in the theater. In Mississippi, he could sit only in the colored section of the balcony. These experiences helped him realize an important fact about himself—that he didn't have to accept the way of life that the white South wanted to impose on him. "I knew then that I wasn't going to go back on the farm. I knew that I was going to go to college somewhere. That's the thing that changed my life. I knew that a black man could do things other than mess around plowing with an ox, messing around cutting cross ties. That's the thing that changed me."

For James Jones, who served in the 761st Tank Battalion and saw action in Europe, it was the French who made a profound difference in his life. "The French had a certain kind of openness and warmth that they exhibited towards minorities that was just unexplainable. You wouldn't know you were black when you were in their company." One soldier recalled that when he was invited to dinner at the home of an English family, they put a pillow on his seat. Later the wife explained the pillow was put there so he wouldn't have to sit on his tail. "Whites," she said, "had told us that you had this tail and you were monkeys."

Relationships between black and white soldiers were mixed. Some white outfits were openly hostile toward black soldiers. The hostility would sometimes break into violence, and white soldiers would attack, beat, and even kill blacks. Some black and white soldiers formed friendships when serving together—especially men who fought together on the front lines. When they returned home, the color line once again reappeared.

One source of irritation to black soldiers was the way German prisoners of war were treated in the South. Despite the fact that the Germans incarcerated in the South had fought against America, and may have even killed American soldiers, they were allowed to take bus trips downtown and sit with other whites in the front of the bus, eat in restaurants, and enjoy other public facilities, all of which were denied to blacks.

The war changed many black attitudes about Jim Crow. Luella Newsome, who served as a

As the war came to an end, whites were determined to maintain segregation no matter what the cost. Returning soldiers once more returned to the back of the bus when they reached the South.

WAC, said, "It had to change, because we're not going to have it this way anymore." Many came back with a militant attitude ready to fight. Many black soldiers realized that Jim Crow was not inevitable, and the South didn't have to be that way. "We thought it was the way it was supposed to be," one soldier remarked. "We was dumb to the facts and didn't know." But when black soldiers were treated as human beings by other whites in different countries, "it opened up my eyes to the racial problems." Reverend Hosea Williams remembered how his attitude had changed, "I realized that hell, if I got to fight and we got to fight and die for America, why should we be treated like slaves in America? If we've got to fight and die for America just like the white boys, why can't we enjoy the same rights as white boys?"

In 1944, the United States Supreme Court, in a decision that would have profound repercussions in the postwar years, ruled in *Smith* v. *Allright* that the all-white primary—which had been the most effective tool for barring blacks from political participation in the South—was illegal. When the state of South Carolina refused to abide by the Court's decision, John McCray, publisher of the *Columbia Lighthouse and Informer,* along with Osceola McKaine, Modjeska Simkins, and Reverend James Hinton, organized the South Carolina Progressive Democratic Party (PDP) as an alternative to the regular Democratic Party. The quartet had been fighting for black rights throughout the 1930s and 1940s, organizing NAACP chapters, speaking and writing on behalf of black voting rights and equal pay for teachers. The PDP sent a delegation to the 1944 Democratic convention to challenge the seating of the regular delegation. The challenge was unsuccessful, but the PDP ran its own candidate, Osceola McKaine, for the U.S. Senate, the first black man to run for a statewide office since Reconstruction. Over the next five years, largely due to the PDP's statewide organizing efforts, the number of registered black voters in South Carolina increased from three thousand five hundred to fifty thousand.

As the war ended, Charles Houston, whose health was failing, was pleased. The court was headed in the direction he had anticipated, the NAACP was growing in number, civil rights was now a national issue, and black voter registration was starting to climb. Even though he was no longer working for the NAACP, Houston's strategy had transformed the legal culture within this country. But he knew that there was still a long way to go before the walls of Jim Crow would come tumbling down. The admonition he had issued a few years earlier still held true: "So far so good," but the fight had just begun. "Maybe the next generation will be able to take time out to rest, but we have too far to go and too much work to do. Shout if you want but don't shout too soon."

By the end of World War II, the legal walls of segregation were about to come tumbling down. The all-white primary had been struck down by the United States Supreme Court, to be followed in 1946 by segregation in interstate busing.

Chapter 9

The Breakthrough, 1945–1954

Boom times came to America. Americans had survived the Great Depression and a world war, and now they were rewarded with an abundance of consumer goods: Baggies and television sets, prefabricated homes and refrigerators, air-conditioning and automobiles.

In the postwar years, America was heading for a showdown over race relations. The minstrel stereotypes of black performers like Butterfly McQueen, Amos and Andy, and Step-and-Fetchit were fading out, while black heroes like Jackie Robinson, Sidney Poitier, and Ralph Bunche faded in. Blacks and progressive whites were assaulting Jim Crow at every opportunity. The United States Supreme Court was breaking down the barriers. By 1946, It had ordered several graduate schools to integrate their student body and declared the all-white primary and segregation on interstate buses unconstitutional. Some Southern liberals—many of whom were journalists—wanted both races to enjoy equal benefits but remain separated. They had not yet seen that equality was impossible as long as one race was segregated.

Despite the liberal trends, the old reactionary South still reigned supreme. If the South was no longer a land that time forgot, it was still a land rooted in the past. When it came to educating its children, providing a living wage for most of its people, offering decent housing, healthy diets, and reasonable medical care, the eleven states that had formed the Confederacy were still at the end of the line behind the thirty-seven other states. Collectively the Southern states spent half as much as non-Southern states educating white children and even less for their black children. One out of four Southern children of both races stopped school by the fifth grade. The South had the fewest doctors per capita and the highest death rate of mothers and babies at birth. Of the thirty-six million people living in the region, one quarter of whom were black, one out of three earned less than $250 a year. Most adults did not vote. In Virginia, less than 15 percent of the eligible voters went to the polls. For Southern farmers, mules still outnumbered tractors, thirteen to one. The lords of the South—the old-time politicians and "big mules" of industry—planned to keep the South just the way it was. It preferred the region to be poor (except for themselves and their cronies), undemocratic, and as separate from the North as possible. Most of all, they were determined to keep race rela-

Clinton Adams was ten years old when he witnessed a quadruple murder committed in Walton County, Georgia, in 1946. Threatened with death, he kept quiet about what he had seen until the 1990s.

tions frozen. White supremacy remained the foundation upon which the South had constructed its edifice, and any violation could end in death.

When blacks came home after the war, whites were prepared to "put them back in their place." Henry Murphy said that when he returned and called his father in Mississippi, his father warned him not to come home with his uniform on. "He said that the police was beating black soldiers and searching them. If they had a picture of a white woman in his wallet, they'd kill him." Murphy returned home dressed as a sharecropper in overalls and a jumper. Dabney Hammer, who came back to Mississippi wearing medals, encountered a white man in his hometown of Clarksdale. "Oweee, look at them spangles on your chest. Glad you back. Let me tell you one thing don't you forget . . . you're still a nigger." The homecoming of Reverend Hosea Williams, who was later to become Martin Luther King's right-hand man, was more traumatic:

And we got to Americus, Georgia, the hometown of ex-president Jimmy Carter. And I had to change buses there. Blacks could not go in the bus station. There was no place in the station for blacks. And if you wanted to purchase anything from the snack bar, it was a window, and you would peck on that window and this lady would open this window and sell you if she wanted to. And I tried to get her to give me a glass of water. She would never give me, she just ignored me. I looked through that window up at the front there, and there was a water fountain. And I didn't go in but I tried to lean inside and get me a cup of water, and those white people beat me till I was unconscious. They thought I was dead. Now, I had all these medals on. That's one thing you'd thought they might would have respected. And they beat me until they thought I was dead, and called a black undertaker who picked me up and found I had a pulse and still breathing, and carried me there to a hospital there in Thomasville, Georgia. And I laid there crying eight weeks wishing Adolf Hitler had won the war.

In Birmingham, Alabama, the police department, under the command of Eugene "Bull" Conner, unleashed its own private war against black veterans. Policemen were reported to have killed as many as five ex-soldiers in six weeks. In South Carolina, a policeman rammed the butt of his club into the eyes of Isaac Woodard, blinding him, because he had got into a shouting match with a bus driver. In Tennessee, black veterans and police had a shootout in which several police were wounded and two blacks were shot to death while in police custody. In Georgia, Maceo Snipes was shot to death for voting, and eight convicts were shot to death by the warden, who claimed they were trying to escape. John Jones was blowtorched in Louisiana because he had refused to part with a war souvenir and had criticized whites for cheating his grandfather.

One of the worst episodes of racial violence in Georgia occurred in Walton County. It began when a fight broke out between Roger Malcolm, a black farmer, and his white landlord, Barney Hester. Some said Hester was trying to break up a fight between Malcolm and his wife. Others said that he had shown a sexual interest in her. Whatever the cause, Malcolm stabbed Hester and seriously wounded him. Malcolm was arrested and Hester hospitalized. By stabbing a white man in rural Georgia, Malcolm had broken one of the most inviolable racial taboos. Rumors that a lynching was imminent raced around the county.

George Dorsey, a returned veteran and Dorothy Malcolm's brother, asked his landlord, Loy Harrison, to intervene on behalf of his brother-in-law. Harrison, a cotton planter and bootlegger, could have been a poster boy for a Southern redneck. He was over six feet tall and weighed 250 pounds, with a large gut and a scar running down the side of his face. He resented the fact that Dorsey had shown a good deal of independence since his return home from the army. Ten-year-old Clinton Adams, a white sharecropper's son whose family also

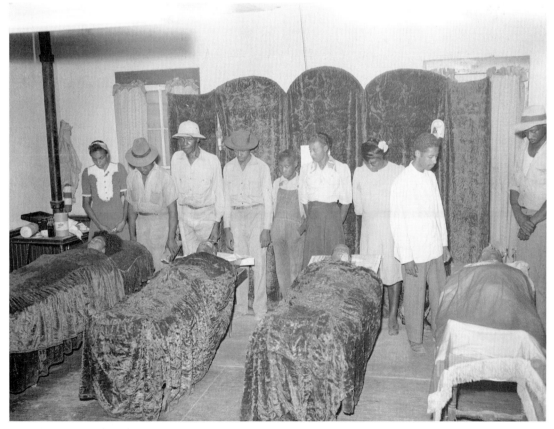

Four men and women were murdered because they had violated the racial code of the South. Roger Malcolm, one of the victims, had wounded a white man in a fight. Malcolm's wife, sister, and brother-in-law tried to help him avoid being lynched and were also killed.

worked for Harrison, was fond of his neighbor Dorsey. Dorsey had helped his family many times doing chores around the house when his father was sick.

Adams remembered Dorsey's return from the war and how his attitude had changed. "George came home from the army in 1945 and I met him down the road down there and walked him all the way home. And he was telling me about being in the army. He was real proud of that. And he had some medals on. He felt he was as good as any white man and if you was black in this county, you didn't cross a white man."

Dorsey asked Harrison if he would save his brother-in-law from a lynching by bailing him out of jail and putting him to work on his property until the trial. He knew that if Malcolm stayed on Harrison's land, nobody would bother him. Harrison first refused, then unexpectedly changed his mind. On July 25, Harrison, along with Dorsey, his common-law wife May Murray, and Dorothy Malcolm, bailed Malcolm out of jail. Inexplicably, the paperwork took all afternoon and bail was extremely low. As sundown approached, Harrison loaded the two couples into his car and headed toward his farm. Instead of using the main road, Harrison turned off onto a dirt back road that led past Dorsey's farm to Moore Ford's Bridge, which spanned the Apalachee River, and eventually to Harrison's farm.

Clinton Adams and a friend were playing by the river next to the bridge. They were curious when they saw Harrison's car go by, for cars seldom used that road. When Harrison reached the bridge, he found the road blocked by a car. Another car suddenly pulled up behind Harrison's. About fifteen or twenty men with guns came out of the woods and pulled the two men out of the car and tied them up. Dorothy Malcolm recognized one of the men, Harrison later claimed, and called out to him. "Please don't kill them," she said. The others immediately dragged the two pleading women out of the car and tied them up alongside the men.

Meanwhile, Clinton Adams and his friend, hearing the shouts and screams, ran over to the scene and lay down in the grass to watch.

And we seen it was Klan 'cause we knew some of them. And we said they're going to whoop [whip] them. Well, that's what the Klan was doing, whoop people, you know. And it didn't matter if you was black or white, if they had a notion to whip your butt, you were going to get one. And they pushed and shoved them and knocked them around. And all at once, these four guys, they just come up there and pull guns—and bang. And everything went into slow motion for me. And they started shooting people, standing up over them, shooting down on them. People was shooting in the trees, every which way. I was shaking so bad. And when they left, everything went silent. And I stood up, and when I stood up it was like right there. And George, I knew him because he was my good buddy. And you could see the smoke and air bubbling out. And their faces was just a mess, I mean literally shot to pieces.

The massacre at Moore's Ford Bridge caused a national cry of outrage. The governor of Georgia posted a ten-thousand-dollar reward for information about the killers. Journalists and ministers in Georgia condemned the killings. President Truman ordered the FBI to investigate the case. The local sheriff investigated the crime but found no suspects. The Georgia Bureau of Investigation, the state attorney general, and other law enforcement agencies also investigated. But no one would testify, least of all young Adams who, at first, was willing to tell what he had seen—until the local sheriff visited his family's farm. "Two or three days later the sheriff was asking momma questions and I was just sitting on the porch. I told them right quick who done it. Big-mouth me. And he said, 'Come here boy.' So I went over to him. 'I want to tell you something.' He said, 'I can put some of these people in jail but I can't put all of them. And if they found out you know what you know, it could come back on you, your momma, your sister, or your brother.' And he said the best thing you can ever do is never mention this again."

Adams kept quiet. So did the rest of the county. Lamar Howard, a black teenager, was severely beaten because white mob members knew he had seen some of them gather at a local icehouse where he worked, and suspected he had talked to the police. Louis Hutchison, one of the FBI agents assigned to the case, stated, "We received no help from the sheriff's department." Many local whites seemed unconcerned about the killings and more interested in finding souvenirs. One resident walked over to the crime scene, spotted a tooth from one of the victims, picked it up, and gave it to his girlfriend to wear on her charm bracelet.

The chief suspect in the killings was Loy Harrison. Harrison claimed that a member of the mob held him at gunpoint and he was helpless to do anything about what happened. He said he did not recognize any members of the mob. The FBI did not believe his story but was unable to break it.

Clinton Adams eventually left the state. Some years later, when he was an adult, he returned for a visit and spoke to Harrison about the killings. "I asked Mr. Loy. I said, 'Why did you and them people kill George and Doris?' He said, 'Well, before George went into the army he was a pretty good nigger, but after he got out he thought he was as good as any white man.'"

Not all Southern officials condoned violence. Georgia's governor, Ellis Arnell, offered a major reward for information leading to the arrest of the killers. Arnell and his assistant attorney general, Daniel Duke, prosecuted the Klan. Stetson Kennedy, a labor journalist who infiltrated the Klan and a neo-Nazi group, the Columbians, was able to gather evidence to convict several members. In the overwhelming majority of murder cases, no one was ever arrested. No suspects identified. No one prosecuted and no one convicted. The killers all had the same name as far as most grand juries were concerned: "death by parties unknown." A few courageous Southern attorneys managed to get an occasional indictment, but no jury would ever convict the killers, no matter how strong the evidence against them.

In spite of—and sometimes because of—the reign of terror, blacks relentlessly moved forward. In 1946, they mobilized to take advantage of *Smith* v. *Allright,* the Supreme Court decision that struck down the white primary. Voter registration drives were organized in every Southern state. In South Carolina, the NAACP began to register black voters. In Alabama, black veterans staged a march in support of black voting rights. In Mississippi, Medgar and Charles Evers decided that they would vote in the state election of 1946. They wanted to cast their ballots against Senator Theodore Bilbo, one of the most racist demagogues to hold office in Mississippi. One writer described him as "short—jug eared, pot bellied—a 'runt' by his own description," who reveled in racial spleen. Bilbo was running for reelection and there seemed little chance of defeating him. Yet thousands of blacks, many of them veterans like the Evers brothers, wanted to cast their protest vote against him. As Charles Evers recalled,

We had five of us and we went to vote that day. All those whites I had known all my life. I couldn't believe it. I just looked at them. They had the room blocked off. They had guns, shotguns and rifles. And I walked up to them and I said, "Get out of the way," just like that. And Medgar said, "No Charlie." I said "I'm going to register." And a little old white lady, I'll never forget that, came out and said, "Charles, not now. Your day will come." I said, "No, ma'am, I want to register. I want to vote today." And old Andy May said, "If you'll vote you'll be a dead nigger." I said, "Well, kill me now, then, you SOB." And she said, "No, Charles. Please. Not now." And Medgar was right behind me. He said, "Come on, Charlie, let's get out of here. We'll come back." He grabbed me by the arm. "You know what Dad said. Look a peckerwood in the eye and he can't do a thing." And you could hear a rat piss on cotton. And we just backed out and went on down the street.

In 1946, two years after the United States Supreme Court declared the all-white primary illegal, blacks began to register to vote. In Atlanta, Georgia, the black vote won the election for a white moderate Congresswoman over her conservative opponent.

Eugene Talmadge, the Georgia demagogue running for governor in 1946, promised that blacks would not vote in the Georgia primary. But African Americans continued to register despite Talmadge's opposition.

Bilbo was reelected, and many blacks who tried to vote were beaten. After the election, Mississippi whites were shocked when hundreds of black veterans who had been denied their right to vote challenged the results in court and at a special Senate committee hearing. The Republican-controlled Senate, which considered Bilbo a disgrace, voted not to seat him. The reason had more to do with politics than morality. Bilbo was alleged to have accepted kickbacks from contractors he helped win bids, and the Republicans were fed up with him. In order to avoid a standoff with Southern Democrats, the Republicans agreed to compromise. Bilbo, who needed an operation, would temporarily yield his seat. The issue would be resolved after the operation. Bilbo never returned. The man who had vituperated blacks all his political life died of throat and mouth cancer.

Blacks flexed their political muscle all over the South. In Atlanta, John Wesley Dobbs, head of the black Masons in Georgia, took the lead. For decades, Dobbs had preached his gospel of success as "the Buck, the Book, and the Ballot." "When ten thousand Negroes get registered," he said, "the signal light of opportunity will automatically change from red to green." In 1946, the light changed.

In 1947, Harry Truman became the first President of the United States to address the National Association for the Advancement of Colored People. He did so on the steps of the Lincoln Memorial.

The Masons and other organizations began to register black voters throughout Georgia. In Atlanta, Grace Hamilton of the All-Citizens Registration Committee helped women voters to register with the aid of teachers' groups. Mary McLeod Bethune encouraged them: "We women will ring doorbells, make house-to-house canvasses, work with the ministers and the churches, the good times clubs and the civics groups, the labor unions and the professional organizations of both races and all creeds."

In Atlanta, a close political contest had developed between the liberal and conservative congressional candidates in a special primary election. The liberal candidate, Helen Douglas Mankin, needed the black vote to win but couldn't openly court it because of the backlash it might trigger in the white community. On the night before the election, after the last edition of the evening newspaper had been published, the word went out to the black community: "Vote for the woman!" The next day, as the votes were counted, Mankin was slightly trailing her opponent. But the black wards were counted last. When their votes came in, Mankin was declared the winner.

There were other signs of progress. Black policemen and firemen were slowly being hired; a few black politicians were elected. Despite the fact that some 750,000 blacks were now voting in the South, compared to 50,000 in 1932 (a jump from 1 percent of the voting-age population to 15 percent), victories over the old guard were still few and far between. In Georgia, race-baiting Eugene Talmadge—whom Hosea Williams characterized as "the political Adolf Hitler of Georgia"—won the primary for governor. His campaign slogan was to keep blacks from voting in the primary. For the most part, die-hard segregationists continued to rule.

As the Cold War with the Soviet Union intensified, and the nation was becoming increasingly anti-Communist and intolerant, Harry Truman astonished everyone by suddenly turning his attention to civil rights. Truman had been outraged at the murder of dozens of black veterans. Although he once held strong racial biases—he had used the word *nigger* freely in his speech—he decided to make civil rights a national issue in 1947. He authorized a fifteen-man committee on civil rights to recommend new legislation to protect people from discrimination. On the steps of the Lincoln Memorial, he became the first President of the United States to address the NAACP. He promised that the federal government would act now to end discrimination, violence, and race prejudice in American life. Shortly afterward, his panel issued its report, confirming that segregation, lynching, and discrimination at the polls had to be put to an end.

In the election year of 1948, Truman continued to push for civil rights. While he felt that it was the right thing to do, he also was aware that he had to win the black vote in order to be elected. He was also being pressured by Henry Wallace, who was running for President on the Progressive ticket and had made civil rights a major issue of the campaign.

Although most political analysts predicted a Republican landslide, Truman believed that the election would depend on a handful of cities in the North. The balance of power would be held by the black vote. Senator Hubert Humphrey, who was deeply committed to civil rights, had successfully maneuvered the Democratic Party to support a strong civil rights plank—much stronger than Truman wanted—in its platform. Southerners charged that the civil rights program was Communist inspired. Strom Thurmond, governor of South Carolina, and a group of Southern delegates stormed out of the Democratic convention when the civil rights platform passed and formed their own States' Rights party based on segregation. A reporter asked Thurmond why he abandoned the Democrats when Truman wasn't doing anything different from Franklin Roosevelt. Thurmond replied, "Yes—but Truman really means it."

After the convention, Truman continued on course. He ordered the army integrated, a move brought about, in part, by the intense pressure of civil rights leader A. Philip Randolph. Randolph threatened to organize a boycott of the armed services by blacks if Truman failed to act. Truman's order mandated nondiscrimination in federal employment and equality of treatment and opportunity in the armed services. Truman's civil rights stance won him the black vote in 1948 and, with it, the presidential election.

Truman's victory overwhelmed Thurmond and the States' Rights Party. Not only did Thurmond lose seven out of the eleven Southern states, but Truman gathered many more white votes than Thurmond in the South. Southern blacks and liberals hoped that the President's victory would be a death blow to white supremacy and that liberal reform would move forward. But the forces of reaction quickly regrouped. The Congress that Truman faced in 1948 was dominated by reactionaries of both parties, all of whom were opposed to federal civil rights legislation. Taking advantage of the Cold War and the anti-Communist hysteria sweeping the country, the Southern old guard launched a vicious propaganda campaign linking black civil rights with communism. Anyone who was for the former was obviously a member of the latter.

The resistance of Southern politicians to change resonated throughout the South, especially in school districts where blacks were fighting for better education for their children. When Reverend Joseph De Laine and James Gibson asked R. W. Elliot, the chairman of the Clarendon County, South Carolina, school board, if the board would pay for a bus for black children—there were thirty buses for white children and none for blacks—Elliot unsurprisingly replied, "We ain't got no money for buses for your nigger children." The answer was what De Laine had expected—even hoped for—even though he knew it might cost him his life.

Clarendon County was a cotton county of about four thousand farms, 85 percent of which were owned by whites. Most blacks earned less than one thousand dollars a year and had a fourth-grade education. Blacks who violated the code of white supremacy immediately felt the pressure. They could lose their jobs, homes, and possibly their lives.

Schools for black children consisted of dilapidated shacks, underpaid teachers, overcrowded classes, and lack of supplies. Clarendon spent $179 for each white child and $43 for each black child. In some areas, pupils had to walk ten or more miles to get to school each day.

De Laine and his wife were both teachers and had grown up in the county. He was also a minister, like his father before him. Inwardly seething at the injustice that surrounded him, De Laine remained outwardly compliant. One day he attended a summer session at Allen University in Columbia, South Carolina, where Reverend James Hinton of the NAACP gave a lecture. De Laine's life was never the same afterward.

Reverend Hinton was one of a coalition of freedom fighters in Columbia that included Modjeska Simkins, Osceola McKaine, and James McCray—all members of the NAACP. After the war, they had been instrumental in organizing voter registration drives in South Carolina that shook up the white establishment. Black schools in the state were atrocious, Hinton said. The conditions needed to be challenged in the courts. A good place to start was with the inequality of transportation. Not only had the school district failed to provide a bus, but when the parents bought their own bus, the school board even refused to pay for gas.

De Laine met with Thurgood Marshall, the chief legal strategist for the NAACP, for advice. Marshall told him that to bring a suit he needed at least twenty names on the petition to go to court. In Clarendon County, it was a formidable task. Almost every black man was beholden to whites. And there was always the Klan.

De Laine's first task was to get rid of a corrupt principal the whites had appointed to run one of the black schools. He had stolen money, bullied his teachers, and cheated his students. De Laine gathered the local people together and told them that in order to get the white school board to move, they had to jointly sign a petition. They were willing to do it, but they wanted De Laine to lead them. He declined. Twice more they insisted and finally he accepted, but on one condition: The fight they were about to begin had to be carried all the way to the state education board if necessary and, if that failed, then into the courts. They agreed. Two days later, De Laine was fired, as he had expected.

The state education board put pressure on the local board to resolve the matter. The board reluctantly complied. The principal was fired. The white superintendent then offered the job to De Laine—in return for which he would call off the protest. De Laine refused. The superintendent appointed his wife as acting principal. De Laine still refused to yield. Eight months later, he got the twenty names Marshall had requested. Since the names were listed in alphabetical order, the case was identified by the first name on the petition; it became known as *Briggs* v *Elliot*. After Briggs signed, he was asked by his boss at the gas station where he worked if he knew what he was doing. Briggs replied that he was doing it for his children. The day after Christmas, he was fired. Shortly afterward, his wife was fired from her job as a chambermaid and his credit was cut off at the bank.

De Laine continued his fight. He was sent death threats by the Klan, his wife and nieces were fired from school, a twenty-thousand-dollar lawsuit was filed against him by the crooked principal. The situation become so intolerable that De Laine's denomination transferred him to another church away from the community. De Laine was gone, but the case now had a life of its own.

As the Briggs case began its slow-motion journey through the courts, another sleeping giant was waking in Farmville, Virginia. This giant was a sixteen-year-old girl by the name of Barbara Johns.

Farmville was located in Prince Edward County, the tobacco-growing region of south-central Virginia. Farmville's population was under five thousand in 1950. Both Robert E. Lee and U. S. Grant had stopped at Farmville during the Civil War, a few days apart.

Farmville was not the virulent Deep South of Mississippi but the seemingly benign Upper South of Virginia. Kennell Jackson, a black resident, did not think of the town as a "racially oppressive place." Farmville, he said, was "not only a good community and a supportive community for blacks, but an ambitious community." If the Klan was around, few people knew and nobody advertised it. Most farmers, black and white, were small, independent landholders. Black and white relationships were cordial. But blacks still drank from the colored water fountain, used the colored public bathroom, did not try to eat at the white drugstore or restaurant, and sat in the "roost" of the movie theater. Hodges Brown, a high school student, said that he was once told that the reason blacks had to sit upstairs was that in case of a fire, the whites downstairs would be able to get out first. John Stokes remembered that the first time he became aware of segregation was when he was seven or eight years old. "I was down there at J. J. Newberry's and started to the water fountain and momma said, 'no you can't go there.' And I said, 'why?' And momma said, 'that's because it's for whites only.' And I knew then that we were living in a world that had differences due to color." Reverend Samuel Williams experienced the separation at an early age. "You are there and we are here. We worked for you and that is all. We don't worship together. We don't play together. This is a white school over here. This is a black school over there with lesser facilities. You go your way as white people and we go our way as black people."

Traditionally, Farmville—like the rest of Virginia—had not been enthusiastic about education for any of its children. A high school for white children was not built until the 1920s. Farmville's whites did not see a need for black education. What would they do with it? Most would do only menial work they could learn on the job. One white resident later explained, "If the Negroes wanted a library or swimming pool, we'd help them get it. But they're not interested. They want pool rooms and dance halls. They're more interested in drinking and carousing than in reading and swimming. We have a saying around here. 'Be a Negro on Saturday night and you'll never want to be a white man again.'"

Farmville's black parents wanted a high school for their children, but they ran into white resistance. They had to put a great deal of pressure on the white school board even to get it to expand their elementary school to the eleventh grade. In 1939, the board, with federal money, finally capitulated to black demands and built the Robert Russa Moton high school, after a black Virginian who had succeeded Booker T. Washington at Tuskegee.

The high school accommodated 180 pupils. On opening day, 165 students registered. The following year, 219. By 1951, the school population was 477 and still climbing. Hodges Brown recalled classes being held on the stage of the auditorium and even on a school bus. Many of the supplies that the students received were hand-me-downs from the white school. Writing scribbled in books by the previous users was erased.

The parents of Moton children had formed a PTA and brought pressure on the board to build a new and better high school for black students. John Lancaster and Reverend Leslie Francis Griffin were two of the members of the PTA. Griffin was a sophisticated, well-educated minister who had studied the works of two outstanding theologians, Paul Tillich and Reinhold Niebuhr. Born and raised in Farmville, he had returned home after serving in a tank corps under General George Patton during World War II. Griffin took over the First Baptist Church after his father died. He believed that Christianity demanded social action, and he felt that his mission was to inspire his congregation to question the way things were in

Farmville. As part of his program, he recruited the required fifty people needed to form a chapter of the NAACP.

Edna Allen loved to hear his sermons: "He was bright. He was articulate. He was well read. He had an agenda. His sermons were totally different. You usually left his church a little disturbed. He made me want to read and find out more things." Reverend Griffin felt that most black people in Farmville were docile. The conservative black leaders whom whites consulted when they wanted to know anything about the black community were cut in the mold of Booker T. Washington. They believed that by staying on the good side of whites, never protesting or causing trouble, they could ask favors of whites and in that way make some progress. Griffin wanted to shake up this way of thinking, but he knew that he had his work cut out for him. Too many blacks were dependent on whites for their livelihood.

Griffin and Lancaster, along with other PTA members, attended the school meetings over a period of several years, urging them to build a new high school for black students. The board was willing in principle but extremely slow in practice. A new school would require floating a bond issue, which Farmville's white residents would have to support. Most voters would be reluctant to support it, as they did not believe blacks needed much of an education.

Lancaster knew that the board was deliberately dragging its feet. "1944, 45, 46, 47, 48, we were going through this process. We even went so far as to go to the board with a three-point plan. And I remember very specifically one board member looked at it and said if we build a school like that, every Tom, Dick, and Harry will be going to school. And that was the first time it dawned on me that there wasn't any intention for us to go to school."

But if the physical plant of the school was poor, the teaching staff was excellent. Kennell Jackson maintains that Moton "was a great engine of achievement and ambition on the part of the students . . . and the teachers. They were surpassing the limitations that the school system had imposed on us and were doing a great job of educating the people." John Watson recalled, "I didn't need an integrated student body to get a good education. Our teachers were on us all the time to do our best. It wasn't about sitting beside a given person. It was about a quality education and we could no longer get a quality education in this building."

The school board offered an interim compromise. Until they could raise the money to build a new school, they would put up temporary buildings to relieve the overcrowding. The board built shacks made of wood with tarpaper roofs. Students called them "chicken coops." Edna Allen recalled how the shacks compared to the white school. "They had an atrium in the center of the school where you could walk out of the cafeteria and kind of sit in a garden and eat. Damn we didn't even have a cafeteria. The building was beautiful. And I couldn't believe that this was what they had for a building and I'm sitting in those shacks with an umbrella up on rainy days so the ink wouldn't run on my paper."

Carl Allen recalled the potbelly stove used to heat the rooms. The students who sat by it in the winter would get red hot while those by the door turned blue with cold. They had to keep their coats on in class. Sometimes, the gym teacher would hold boxing matches in the shacks. "You were in trouble if you got too near those stoves."

For Farmville blacks, the shacks were another example of white contempt. And none felt it more keenly than Barbara Rose Johns.

Barbara Johns was sixteen years old when she organized the students at the Robert Russa Moton High School in Farmville, Virginia, to go on strike to protest their inferior school facilities. The strike led to a lawsuit that became one of the five cases the United States Supreme Court reviewed when it overturned segregation.

Although she was born in New York City in 1935, where her family had migrated to find work, Barbara Johns's family was rooted in Prince Edward County. Her parents and grandparents had been born there. During World War II, Barbara Johns lived on a tobacco farm with her maternal grandmother, Mary Croner. Barbara's younger sister, Joan Johns Cobbs, says that Croner was "the backbone of the family. Kept us all in line and kept us together."

Barbara Johns helped care for and pick tobacco in her free time and worked in the country store owned by her uncle, Vernon Johns, who was also a strong influence on her life. Vernon Johns was a minister and a legend in Prince Edward County and elsewhere in the South. Well educated, a dynamic speaker, a believer in the church as an agent of change, he sought to shake up his congregations by exhorting and chastising them for their complacency and docility. He would also stand up to whites. Joan Johns Cobbs remembers how Uncle Vernon would constantly test them. "He was the type of person who always questioned us about history or some current affair. So a lot of times we'd try and avoid him because we didn't know if we knew the answer to some of his questions. I mean he felt that we should know our history. And if we couldn't give an answer he'd say, you should know this because it's part of your history. He was constantly challenging our minds."

Barbara Johns's grandmothers were both strong women who were not afraid of whites. Joan Johns Cobbs remembers that Barbara was of the same mold. "She used to get angry that white customers would come into the store and call her family relatives by their first name or use "uncle" or "auntie" when addressing them. She was especially upset about everyone calling my mother and father Violet and Robert, and we had to address them as mister or missus. And so she asked a white man one day why did he call our mother by her first name? And he called my father 'uncle Robert.' And she said, 'He's not your uncle, so why do you call him uncle Robert?' She would often say things like that to white people."

Barbara Johns keenly felt the difference between her school and the white school. "I remember thinking how unfair it was," she once said. "I kept thinking about it all the way home. I thought about it a lot while I was in bed and I was still thinking about it the next day."

Other students were also aware of the difference between the two schools. Hodges Brown envied the white school's baseball team. "I used to go over to their ballgames. You couldn't go inside, you had to stand at the fence, you know, and look through. They had beautiful uniforms, big band. . . . And that's the kind of thing I always wanted you know if I were to go to high school. But it wasn't that way. Those things happened down South." Carl Allen remembered the hand-me-down football uniforms they received. And John Watson recalled the used textbooks. What infuriated one student was the movies they showed the students.

Every movie we saw in this auditorium had all white actors and actresses. You might see a black actor playing a subservient role. But the one film that they had that featured an all black cast with only one white actor was a film they had on personal hygiene. And it was about the pitfalls of gonorrhea and syphilis. And all the people who had gonorrhea and syphilis were blacks. The only white person in that film was the doctor. And in my head, all the white kids that would see that film and then look at me, they would see the worst that society had to offer. Because how do you know that this young man here doesn't have syphilis. Because we saw it in the movie and when you see it in a movie, it's true.

Barbara Johns decided to act. She called a meeting on a football field with five students she could trust. John Stokes was one. "Barbara came up with the idea. She said, 'we'll go on strike.' I was churning inside because I knew that we were skating on thin ice. We were really playing with something that we didn't know had that much power. We were scared at the time. But we knew we had to pull it off."

The major obstacle was the presence of the principal M. Boyd Jones. "Jones was a strong man," John Watson recalled. "We knew that if he was on campus, there was not going to be a strike."

Watson and the others formulated a plan to get Jones off campus on the day of the meeting. "We pretended we were businessmen calling to tell him that his students were downtown making disturbances and would he please come down and take care of it. As I think back on it, I don't think we fooled him. I think he just played along."

Barbara's sister was in class when an announcement was made to go to the assembly, something that seemed perfectly normal. When she arrived in the auditorium, she was astonished to see that the students had asked the teachers to leave. They all complied, although some were reluctant. "Barbara came in and walked onto the stage. And I remember saying to myself 'What is going on? Why is she up there?' And she started to talk and tell us how very bad conditions were in the school and how she needed everyone's cooperation. And that in order to effect change, we had to go out on strike. And I remember sitting in my seat and sort of cowering down because she was talking so forcefully and without any fear. And I remember the first reaction I had was fear. I thought 'Oh my goodness what's going to happen to us now?' Later she chastised me for my fear. I was crying at one point, because I was afraid that our family would be torn apart in some fashion. But she said, nothing's going to happen."

One student was electrified by her speech. "She put into words what I had been feeling, words I didn't know how to say, perhaps afraid to say them because of the repercussions. But she put it all into words and it was so simple—that we have a right to these things. We have a right to decent books. We have a right to good teachers. We have a right to have a school equal to the white kids. She didn't talk about integration. She talked about equality."

Some students were scared. "A lot of people were scared," Stokes remembered. "Some of Barbara's closest friends were scared to death for her. They said why did you do that. She said, we have to make a change and I mean right now. You know Barbara was very dynamic when she wasn't quiet. And then you'd look over there and you see this docile person and you would say, she isn't anything like that. Oh yes she was. And that is why she made such a good leader. We could not have selected a better leader."

The students made signs and marched into town. They met with T. J. McIlwaine, superintendent of schools, who believed that the strike was not the students' idea but that they were being manipulated by adults. He ordered them to return to their classes. John Stokes was at the meeting. "He said, 'You are upstarts. And you need to go back to school before all your parents are in jail.' And that's what frightened us when he said our parents were going to jail. And when a member of my family said, 'How big is the Farmville jail?' from that point on there was no stopping us." The students escalated the conflict. They asked the NAACP to help them.

The NAACP in Virginia, led by attorneys Oliver Hill and Spottiswood Robinson, had launched dozens of legal assaults on the Virginia schools in the courts. Their strategy had been to force the state to make black schools equal to white schools. If schools had to be separate, then according to *Plessy,* Hill said that they "damned well" better be equal. Hill and Robinson won a major victory when the courts authorized that black teachers had to receive the same pay as white teachers. They had other victories, such as requiring school districts to provide equal transportation. Even a few country districts were willing to provide equal schools. Many school districts balked at fulfilling the court's mandates, even though board members were personally fined by the courts for dragging their feet. The NAACP was being worn down by having to bring hundreds, maybe even thousands of cases to force each school district to provide equal facilities. When school boards complained they didn't have the money to upgrade the black schools, Hill suggested an easier solution: integrate them. The cost would be minimal. One enraged school board member threatened, "The first little black son of a bitch that comes down the road to set foot in that school, I'll take my shotgun and blow his brains out." But despite the threats, Thurgood Marshall was resolved the time had come for David to take on Goliath. No more piecemeal attacks on segregation. It was time to throw out the whole system.

The NAACP attorneys met with the parents and students at the First Baptist Church in Farmville to ask them whether they would support a lawsuit for integrating the schools. The striking students were in favor, but the question was whether their parents would support them. When a former principal, J. B. Pervall, rose to criticize that step, Barbara Johns stood and shouted out, "Don't let Mr. Charlie, Mr. Tommy, or Mr. Pervall stop you from backing us. We are depending upon you." Reverend Griffin seconded her remarks. "Anyone who would not back these children after they stepped out on a limb is not a man. Anyone who will not fight against racial prejudice is not a man." The parents cheered. They would back their children. John Stokes never forgot that moment.

> That night at the Baptist Church was one that I shall remember as long as I live. I mean it was just like watching Jackie Robinson in Ebbets field. It was the most beautiful sight I've ever seen. And they [the parents] came in there and they were truly behind us. Really and truly behind us. The NAACP was astounded to find that people who had been dormant and quiet for so long quiescent for so long were ready to back their children. And he [Griffin] said, if you are really ready to back them, then you have to sign this petition. And that's how we found out we could separate the wheat from the chaff. Because some of the blacks didn't sign. My mother and father signed.

The case entered the court as *Davis* v. *County School Board of Prince Edward County.* Whites believed that Reverend Griffin, John Lancaster, and M. Boyd Jones were somehow behind the strike and that they and the NAACP had manipulated the children. They retaliated, and black families suffered. Kennell Jackson's mother and aunt were fired from their teaching jobs. His father lost his business. "It was like the town had been hit by a neutron bomb," Jackson said. "Everything was standing but nothing was going on. The whole economic, educational infrastructure was sort of vacuumed out of the town. For all intents and purposes, black Farmville died during this time." Whites stopped buying vegetables from John Stokes's family. Some stopped speaking to them. Edna Allen's parents lost their jobs. Some parents received anonymous threatening phone calls, and Barbara Johns was threatened with death and sent to live with her uncle Vernon in Alabama. Most students were concerned that their actions might cause M. Boyd Jones to lose his job. Stokes said that he had told him in front of his parents, "You all have to do what you have to do. I'll find a job. I'll find a job. Because this is bigger than any of us." He was fired.

Like streams flowing into a river, the Farmville case merged with the Briggs case from South Carolina and three other cases and flowed past the federal district courts—where the suit was rejected—to the United States Supreme Court. In 1954, the Court, in a unanimous decision, achieved with great effort by Chief Justice Earl Warren, ruled that segregation in the field of education was inherently unequal. John Stokes was overjoyed: "When I heard of the historic decision I said, thank God. Thank God. At last someone has listened to us. And those were my very words. Someone has listened to us. Hopefully we shall see a change."

In 1954, the United States Supreme Court acknowledged the seventy-year fight of African Americans to have Jim Crow declared unconstitutional. The Court ruled that segregation in education is inherently unequal. This opened the door to overturning legal segregation in other areas of public life.

In 1954, eighty-nine years after the end of the Civil War, the death knell of legal Jim Crow tolled. The United States Supreme Court ruled segregation in education unconstitutional, destroying the legal rationale for Jim Crow. In some ways, America was already on the road to integration by the 1950s. Black and white athletes played together on the same professional teams. White and black teenagers danced to the same music. Blacks became more visible in public life. National television and radio programs were reaching Southern audiences, communicating new ideas and the changing times. Many hoped that after the initial shock of the *Brown* decision, the South would accept reality and adapt itself accordingly.

But many Southern whites were filled with passionate intensity to preserve segregation. In 1956, 101 congressmen from the South issued a Southern Manifesto that rejected the Court's decision and pledged "to use all lawful means to bring about a reversal of this decision." Southern school districts began to devise strategies that would circumvent the Court's decision. In some areas, parents were allowed to send their children to whatever school they wanted, even if it was out of their community. Few black parents wanted to risk sending their children to an all-white school where they would be harassed and possibly beaten. District courts with judges often sympathetic to segregation granted extensive delays.

President Dwight D. Eisenhower waffled on the issue. He refused to provide the leadership so badly needed at that time. Many believed that he was opposed to the decision and regretted the fact that he had appointed Earl Warren as chief justice of the Court. He acknowledged that the Court decision was now the law of the land, but at the same time he admitted that it would be hard, perhaps impossible, to change people's thinking in the matter. When federal court orders to integrate the University of Alabama and a high school in Mansfield, Texas, were ignored Eisenhower did nothing. In 1957, as some citizens of Arkansas were trying to work out a means to integrate the schools as ordered by a federal court, Governor Orval Faubus ordered the Arkansas national guard to block black students from entering. A reluctant Eisenhower was finally forced to send paratroopers into the community to restore order and integrate the schools. His moral weakness encouraged further white resistance. Antisegregationist White Citizen's Councils, its members middle-class whites, sprang up all over the South. The Ku Klux Klan jumped into action. Blacks who supported integrating the schools were fired, lost their financial credit and bank loans, and sometimes were beaten and murdered. For a brief moment, it seemed that the South would successfully resist integration. But the walls of the fortress of segregation had been irrevocably breached, and through them would pour the armies of the civil rights movement.

Black people once again would make their own history. In February 1960, four black college students from North Carolina Agricultural and Technical College entered a Woolworth's in Greensboro, sat at the white-only lunch counter, ordered coffee, and were refused service. An hour later they left, but they returned the next day. On Thursday, white students from the University of North Carolina's women's college sat with them. The act of defiance caught the imagination of black and white students throughout the country. By the end of the year, some fifty thousand students had staged sit-ins throughout the South, and the civil rights movement was launched.

White Southerners suddenly found themselves trapped between the hammer and the anvil. As civil rights activists, led by Dr. Martin Luther King, Jr., and student leaders shook the foundations of segregation with protests, demonstrations, and sit-ins, the federal government hammered them with civil rights laws and court decisions. Whites sometimes responded with violence, murder, and beatings, but despite their resistance, the victory had been secured. Black and white students gradually went to school with each other. Blacks sat downstairs in movie theaters, ate at once segregated lunch counters, shopped in stores previously closed to them, and worked at jobs that had been denied them.

But if the battle was won, the war against racial prejudice continued. By the 1970s, a counterreaction began to set in as Northern as well as Southern whites resisted black gains. Conservative Supreme Court justices began to circumscribe black rights. Parents sent their children to all-white private schools as public schools became increasingly black. The Republican Party in the South became identified as the champion of white interests and gained political power in almost every Southern state.

All of this would not have been surprising to Ned Cobb, the Alabama sharecropper who recounted his life to two Harvard graduate students in the 1970s. Cobb had been born in the 1880s and had lived through the worst years of Jim Crow between 1890 and 1970. He had stood up against the system in 1931 when he supported a union drive to organize black farmworkers and went to prison for thirteen years as a result. By the end of his life in 1972, he had lived long enough to watch with joy as the school bus passed his house every morning carrying black and white children to the same school. But he knew that the great victory he had helped bring about was far from won.

How many people is it today that it needs and it required to carry out this movement? . . . It's taken time, and it will take more time before it's finished. Who's to do it. It's the best people in the United States to do it, in defense of the uneducated, the unknowledged ones that's livin' here in this country. They're goin' to win! They're goin' to win! But it's going to take a great effort. It won't come easy . . . it's going to take thousands and millions of words, thousands and millions of steps to complete this business. I'd love to know that the black race has finally shed the veil from their eyes and the shackles from their feet.

The veil has been lifted, but the shackles remain. Though Jim Crow is no longer codified in the laws, and the racial climate has decidedly improved, white supremacy is still a vital part of the American psyche. Racial violence toward blacks, though no longer rampant, explodes periodically. Schools have slipped back into a pattern of segregation. The doors of business, once closed to blacks, are only barely open. Race prejudice still has its appeal to millions of Americans. Civil rights activists charge that the United States Supreme Court once again supports the opponents of racial equality and justice.

To continue the battle against racial prejudice in the future requires strengths borrowed from the past. Those who struggle today can draw inspiration from the men and women who stood up and said no in the time of Jim Crow.

BIBLIOGRAPHY

Anderson, James. *The Education of Blacks in the South, 1860–1935.* Chapel Hill: University of North Carolina Press, 1988.

Andrews, Sidney. *The South Since the War.* New York: Arno Press, 1969.

Apthker, Herbert. *A Documentary History of the Negro People in the United States, 1910–1932, Vol. 3.* New York: Carol Publishing Group, 1933.

Ayers, Edward. *The Promise of the New South: Life After Reconstruction.* New York: Oxford University Press, 1992.

Baker, Ray Stannard. *Following the Color Line: American Negro Citizenship in the Progressive Era.* New York: Harper & Row, 1964.

Barnett, Ida Wells. *On Lynching: (Southern Horror: A Red Record: Mob Rule in New Orleans).* New York: Arno Press, 1969.

Bauerlein, Mark. *Negrophobia, A Race Riot in Atlanta, 1906.* San Francisco: Encounter Books, 2001.

Bechet, Sidney. *Treat It Gentle: An Autobiography.* New York: De Capo Press, 1978.

Bethel, Elizabeth Rauh. *Promiseland.* Philadelphia: Temple University Press, 1981.

Broughton, Virgina W. *Twenty Years Experience as a Missionary:* Chicago: The Pony Press, 1907.

Brundage, Fitzhugh W. *Lynching in the New South: Georgia and Virginia, 1880–1930.* Urbana: University of Illinois Press, 1993.

Cobb, James C., and Michael V. Namorato, eds. *The New Deal and the South.* Jackson: University Press of Mississippi, 1984.

Cortner, Richard C. *A Mob Intent on Death, the NAACP and the Arkansas Riot Cases.* Middletown: Wesleyan University Press, 1988.

Daniel, Pete. *The Shadow of Slavery: Peonage in the South, 1901–1969.* Urbana: University of Illinois Press, 1972.

Davis, Elizabeth. *Lifting as They Climb: The National Association of Colored Women.* Washington, D.C.: National Association of Colored Women, 1933.

Dittmer, John. *Black Georgia in the Progressive Era, 1900–1920.* Urbana: University of Illinois Press, 1977.

Du Bois, W.E.B. *The Autobiography of W.E.B. Du Bois.* New York: International Publishers, 1958.

———. *The Souls of Black Folk.* New York: Avon, 1965.

Duster, Alfreda. *Crusade for Justice: The Autobiography of Ida B. Wells.* Chicago: University of Chicago Press, 1970.

Edmonds, Helen. *The Negro and Fusion Politics in North Carolina, 1894–1901.* Chapel Hill: University of North Carolina Press, 1955.

Egerton, John. *Speak Now Against the Day.* Chapel Hill: University of North Carolina Press, 1995.

Engs, Robert Francis. *Educating the Disfranchised and the Disinherited: Samuel Chapman Armstrong and Hampton Institute 1839–1893.* Knoxville: University of Tennessee Press, 1999.

Foner, Eric. *Reconstruction: America's Unfinished Revolution 1863–1877.* New York: Harper & Row, 1988.

Foner, Philip. *Organized Labor and the Black Worker.* New York: International Publishers, 1974.

Fredrickson, George M. *The Black Image in the White Mind.* New York: Harper & Row, 1971.

Friedman, Lawrence. *The White Savage: Racial Fantasies in the Post-Bellum South.* Englewood Cliffs, NJ: Prentice Hall, 1970.

Gaines, Kevin. *Uplifting the Race: Black Leadership, Politics and Culture in the Twentieth Century.* Chapel Hill: University of North Carolina Press, 1996.

Gaither, Gerald. *Blacks and the Populist Revolt: Ballots and Bigotry in the New South.* Tuscaloosa: University of Alabama Press, 1975.

Gatewood, Willard. *Black Americans and the White Man's Burden, 1898–1903.* Urbana: University of Illinois Press, 1975.

———. *"Smoke Yankees" and the Struggle for Empire: Letters from Negro Soldiers, 1898–1902.* Urbana: University of Illinois Press, 1971.

Giddings, Paul. *Where and When I Enter: The Impact of Black Women on Race and Sex in America.* New York: William Morrow, 1984.

Gilmore, Glenda. *Gender and Jim Crow: Women and the Politics of White Supremacy in North Carolina, 1896–1920.* Chapel Hill: University of North Carolina Press, 1996.

Gossett, Thomas. *Race: The History of an Idea in America.* New York: Schocken Books, 1965.

Greenwood, Janet. *Bittersweet Legacy: The Black and White Better Classes in Charlotte, 1850–1910.* Chapel Hill: University of North Carolina Press, 1994.

Hair, William Ivy. *Bourbonism and Agrarian Protest: Louisiana Politics, 1877–1900.* Baton Rouge: Louisiana State University Press, 1969.

———. *Carnival of Fury: Robert Charles and the New Orleans Race Riot of 1900.* Baton Rouge: Louisiana State University Press, 1976.

Harlan, Louis. *Booker T. Washington, the Making of a Black Leader.* New York: Oxford University Press, 1972.

———. *Booker T. Washington, the Wizard of Tuskegee, 1901–1915.* New York: Oxford University Press, 1983.

Harlan, Louis R., et al., eds. *The Booker T. Washington Papers.* 14 vols. Urbana: University of Illinois Press, 1972–1989.

Hayden, Henry. *The Story of the Wilmington Rebellion* (booklet). Wilmington, NC, 1936.

Haynes, Robert V. *A Night of Violence, The Houston Riot of 1917.* Baton Rouge: Louisiana State University Press, 1976.

Hermann, Janet Sharp. *The Pursuit of a Dream.* Jackson: University Press of Mississippi, 1999.

Higginbotham, Evelyn Brooks. *Righteous Discontent: The Women's Movement in the Black Baptist Church, 1880–1920.* Cambridge: Harvard University Press, 1993.

Holmes, William. *The White Chief: James Kimble Vardaman.* Baton Rouge: Louisiana State University Press, 1970.

Holtzclaw, William Henry. *The Black Man's Burden.* New York: Neale Publishers, 1915.

Howard, O. O. *Autobiography of Oliver Otis Howard, Major General, United States Army.* New York: Baker and Taylor, 1907.

Hunter, Tera. "Household Laborers and Work in the Making: Afro-American Women and Work in the Urban South, 1861–1920." Manuscript.

Jones, Jacqueline. *Labor of Love, Labor of Sorrow: Black Women, Work and Family from Slavery to the Present.* New York: Basic Books, 1985.

Kelley, Robin. *Hammer and Hoe: Alabama Communists During the Great Depression.* Chapel Hill: University of North Carolina Press, 1990.

———. *Race Rebels: Culture, Politics and the Black Working Class.* New York: Free Press, 1994.

Key, V. O., Jr. *Southern Politics in State and Nation.* Knoxville: University of Tennessee Press, 1996.

Kirk, Allen, J. "A Statement of Facts Concerning the Bloody Riot in Wilmington, North Carolina, Thursday, November 10, 1898." Durham, NC: Duke University Library.

Kirwan, Albert. *Revolt of the Rednecks: Mississippi Politics, 1876–1925.* New York: Harper & Row, 1951.

Kluger, Richard. *Simple Justice.* New York: Vintage Books, 1977.

Kousser, J. Morgan. *The Shaping of Southern Politics: Suffrage Restriction and the Establishment of the One-Party South 1880–1910.* New Haven: Yale University Press, 1973.

Lawson, Steven F. *Black Ballots, Voting Rights in the South, 1944–1969.* New York: Columbia University Press, 1976.

Levine, Lawrence. *Black Culture and Black Consciousness: Afro American Folk Thought from Slavery to Freedom.* New York: Oxford University Press, 1977.

————. *The Unpredictable Past.* New York: Oxford University Press, 1993.

Lewis, David Levering. *W.E.B. Du Bois: The Biography of a Race, 1865–1919.* New York: Holt, 1993.

————. *W.E.B. Du Bois: The Fight for Equality and the American Century, 1919–1963.* New York: Holt, 2000.

Lincoln, Eric. *The Black Church in the African American Experience.* Durham: Duke University Press, 1991.

Litwack, Leon. *Been in the Storm So Long: The Aftermath of Slavery.* New York: Alfred A. Knopf, 1979.

————. *Trouble in Mind: Black Southerners in the Age of Jim Crow.* New York: Alfred A. Knopf, 1998.

Logan, Rayford. *The Betrayal of the Negro: From Rutherford B. Hayes to Woodrow Wilson.* New York: Collier, 1965.

Lomax, Alan. *Mister Jelly Roll.* New York: Pantheon, 1965.

Mays, Benjamin. *Born to Rebel: An Autobiography.* Athens: University of Georgia Press, 1971.

McMillen, Neil. *Dark Journey: Black Mississippians in the Age of Jim Crow.* Urbana: University of Illinois Press, 1990.

Meier, August. *Negro Thought in America 1880–1915: Racial Ideologies in the Age of Booker T. Washington.* Ann Arbor: University of Michigan Press, 1966.

Oshinsky, David. *Worse Than Slavery: Parchment and the Ordeal of Jim Crow Justice.* New York: Free Press, 1996.

Painter, Nell Irvin. *Exodusters: Black Migration to Kansas after Reconstruction.* New York: W. W. Norton, 1976.

Pickens, William. *Bursting Bonds.* Boston: Jordan and More, 1923.

Proctor, Henry Hugh. *Between Black and White: Autobiographical Sketches.* Boston: Pilgrim Press, 1925.

Rabinowitz, Howard. *Race Relations in the Urban South, 1865–1890.* New York: Oxford University Press, 1978.

Raper, Arthur. *The Tragedy of Lynching.* New York: Negro Press, 1969.

Reddick J. L. "The Negro and the Populist Movement in Georgia." Master's thesis, Atlanta University, 1937.

Redding, Saunders. *Lonesome Road.* New York: Doubleday, 1958.

Redkey, Edwin. *Black Exodus: Black Nationalist and Back-to-Africa Movements, 1890–1910.* New Haven: Yale University Press, 1969.

Reid, Whitelaw. *After the War, A Southern Tour.* New York: Harper & Row, 1965.

Rosengarten, Theodore. *All God's Dangers: The Life of Nate Shaw.* New York: Alfred A. Knopf, 1975.

Rouse, Jacqueline Anne. *Lugenia Burns Hope, Black Southern Reformer.* Athens: University of Georgia Press, 1989.

Shapiro, Herbert. *White Violence and Black Response from Reconstruction to Montgomery.* Amherst: University of Massachusetts Press, 1988.

Simkins, Francis Butler. *Pitchfork Ben Tillman.* Baton Rouge: Louisiana State University Press, 1944.

Sitkoff, Harvard. *A New Deal For Blacks.* New York: Oxford University Press, 1978.

Smith, Robert. *They Closed Their Schools, Prince Edward County, Virginia, 1951–1964.* Farmville: Martha E. Forrester Council of Women, 1996.

Stampp, Kenneth M. *The Era of Reconstruction, 1865–1877.* New York: Alfred A. Knopf, 1965.

Sterling, Dorothy, ed. *We Are Your Sisters.* New York: W. W. Norton, 1984.

Sullivan, Patricia. *Days of Hope, Race and Democracy in the New Deal Era.* Chapel Hill: University of North Carolina Press, 1996.

Thorne, Jack. *Hanover, or, The Persecution of the Lowly: A Story of the Wilmington Massacre.* New York: Arno Press, 1969.

Tindall, George. *The Emergence of the New South, 1913–1945.* Baton Rouge: Louisiana State University Press, 1967.

Trelease, Allen W. *White Terror: The Ku Klux Klan Conspiracy and Southern Reconstruction.* New York: Harper & Row, 1971.

Trowbridge, J. T. *The Desolate South 1865–1866: A Picture of the Battlefields and of the Devastated Confederacy.* New York: Duell, Sloane and Pearce, 1956.

Wadelington, Charles and Richard F. Knapp. *Charlotte Hawkins Brown and Palmer Memorial Institute.* Chapel Hill: University of North Carolina Press, 1999.

Washington, Booker T. *The Negro in Business.* New York: Johnson Reprint Co., 1970.

———. "A Town Owned by Negroes." *World's Work* 18, no. 3 (July 1907).

———. *Up from Slavery.* New York: Avon, 1965.

Washington, Booker T., and W.E.B. Du Bois. *The Negro in the South.* New York: Citadel, 1970.

Wells-Barnett, Ida. *On Lynchings: Southern Horrors, A Red Record, Mob Rule in New Orleans.* New York: Arno Press, 1969.

———. *Southern Horrors and Other Writings.* Boston: Bedford Books, 1997.

White, C. C. *No Quittin' Sense.* Austin: University of Texas Press, 1969.

White, Walter. *A Man Called White.* Athens: University of Georgia Press, 1995.

Williamson, Joel. *The Crucible of Race: Black-White Relationships in the American South Since Emancipation.* New York: Oxford University Press, 1984.

———. *Rage for Order.* New York: Oxford University Press, 1986.

Woodward, C. Vann. *Origins of the New South, 1877–1913.* Baton Rouge: Louisiana State University Press, 1987.

———. *The Strange Career of Jim Crow.* New York: Oxford University Press, 1974.

———. *Tom Watson: Agrarian Rebel.* New York: Oxford University Press, 1937.

Harvard Theater Collection, Houghton Library: frontispiece

Duke University, Rare Book, Manuscripts and Special Collections Library: xii

Valentine Richmond History Center: xvi, 50

New-York Historical Society: 1, 4, 10

Library of Congress: 6, 9, 12, 14, 20, 21, 22, 24, 28, 31, 38, 42, 45, 46, 47, 55, 65, 68, 74, 82, 85, 104, 108, 110, 125, 126, 149, 150

Collection of Joan W. and Thomas H. Gandy: 18, 26, 52-53, 62, 89

Kansas State Historical Society: 33

Photographs and Prints Division, Schomburg Center for Research and Black Culture, New York Public Library: 44, 129, 158, 162

From the Collection of the Florida State Archives: 49

Syracuse University Library, Department of Special Collections: 56

North Carolina Room, Durham County Library: 59

University of Chicago Library, Special Collections Research Center: 64

Xavier University Archives and Special Collections: 69, 106

H. W. Parlee, Erik Overbey Collection, University of South Alabama Archives: 78

Cape Fear Museum: 81

North Carolina Collection, University of North Carolina Libraries at Chapel Hill: 83, 91

North Carolina Office of History and Archives: 84

North Carolina Department of Cultural Resources, Office of Archives and History: 87

Hogan Jazz Archive, Tulane University: 92

New Orleans Public Library: 97

Holsinger Studio Collection, Albert H. Small Special Collections Library, University of Virginia: 104

Special Collections and Archives, W.E.B. Du Bois Library, University of Massachusetts at Amherst: 103, 115

Atlanta History Center: 112

Yale Collection of Literature, Beinecke Rare Book and Manuscript Library: 113

Fort Sam Houston Museum: 118

National Archives: 120

Doris Ulmann Photographic Collection, University Archives, University of Oregon Library: 126 (PH.3499), 135 (PH.5301)

Morgan County Archives: 137

Private Collection, Ted and Dale Rosengarten: 140

Museum of Natural History: 144

Denver Public Library: 146

Bettmann/Corbis: 154, 167, 182

Washington, D.C., Public Library: 164

Courtesy of Clinton Adams: 166

Special Collections Department, Georgia State University: 170

Hargrett Rare Book and Manuscript Library/University of Georgia: 171

Harry S. Truman Library: 172

Courtesy of Joan Johns Cobb: 178

INDEX

Ackerman, Amos, 25
Adams, Clinton, xiv, 166p, 167–68
    Malcolm, Roger and, 167–68
Adams, Henry, 33, 37
    Liberia and, 33
Alexander, Will, 147
All-Citizens Registration Committee, 173
    Bethune, Mary McLeod and, 173
    Hamilton, Grace and, 173
Allen, Edna, 177
Alonzo, Herndon, 107
AMA. See American Missionary Association (AMA)
American Communist Party, 138–40, 148
    black civil rights and, 138–40, 148–49
    Scottsboro Boys and, 138, 140
American Dilemma, An (Bunche), 152
American Missionary Association (AMA), 89–90
Ames, Adelbert, 30
Ames, Jesse Daniel, 155
Amos and Andy, 165
Andrews, Sidney, 4, 7–8, 15
Armstrong, Louis, 92p
    jazz and, 98
Armstrong, Samuel Chapman, 43–44
    Tuskegee Institute and, 43–44, 45
Arnell, Ellis, 169
Association of Southern Women for the Prevention
        of Lynching, 155–56
    Ames, Jesse Daniel and, 155–56
Atlanta
    black urban migration to, 107
    economic disparity in, 107, 113–15
    importance of black colleges in, 107–8
    population statistics for, 107
    race riots and, 112, 115–16
Atlanta Constitution, The, 76

Atlanta Evening News, 115
Atlanta Journal, 115
"Aunt Jemima," 106

Baldwin, William, 131
Baltimore, Charles, 122
Barber, J. Max, 107, 117–18
Bates, Ruby, 138–39
    Scottsboro Boys and, 138–39
Bechet, Sidney, 96–97, 101
Bentley, Milo, 142
Bethany Institute, 89
    educational guidelines at, 90–91
    Hawkins Brown, Charlotte and, 89–90
    Jim Crow laws and, 92
    Palmer, Alice, 90
Bethune, Mary McLeod, 49p, 148
    All-Citizens Registration Committee and, 148
    early days of, 148
    Roosevelt, Franklin Delano and, 148
Bethune-Bookman College, 148
Bilbo, Theodore, 169–70
Birth of a Nation, 121
    Clansman, The, and, 121
    Griffith, D. W. and, 121
    Ku Klux Klan and, 121–22
    NAACP (National Association for the Advance-
        ment of Colored People) and, 121
    violence as a result of, 121
black churches
    Brinkerhood, Isaac and, 5
    Broughton, Virginia and, 93
    community importance of, 5, 58, 89p
    educational role of, 50
    Lynch, James and, 5
    Mixon, William Henry and, 58

"black codes," 8
  early segregation and, 9
  legal rights as part of, 9
  sharecropping as a result of, 11
  stipulations of, 8
black education
  Armstrong, Samuel Chapman and, 44
  Baldwin, William and, 131
  Bethune, Mary McLeod and, 49, 148
  Boutume, Elizabeth and, 4–5
  costs spent for, 51, 133
  De Laine, James and, 44
  Elliot, R.W. and, 174
  enrollment rates in, 51
  Freedmen's Bureau and, 3
  Gibson, James and, 174
  independent schools and, 4
  Jones, Robert L. and, 131–32
  Mississippi Plan and, 30
  Pollard, Edward Allford and, 27–28
  segregation in, 27–28
  Stowe, Harriet Beecher and, 27
  Washington, Booker T. and, 3–4
  Wilson, Emma J. and, 49
  women's role in, 48–50
black land ownership, 37
  Mound Bayou and, 67, 69–72
  Promised Land and, 50
  Trotter, Daniel and, 37–38
black social organizations
  community importance of, 110
  creation of, 3
  Daughters of Bethel and, 111
  Daughters of Samara and, 111
  Lugenia Hope and, 109–10
  McMichael, E. H. and, 111
  Sisters of Friendship and, 111
  Sisters of Love and, 111
  women's role in, 58–59, 109
blues, the
  Bechet, Sidney and, 96–97
  Handy, J. C. , and, 95–96
  New Orleans and, 97–98
  origins of, 96
  Patton, Charley and, 96
  sample lyrics for, 95–96
Bolden, Buddy, 98
Bolden, Dorothy, 60
Boutume, Elizabeth, 4
Bratton, U.S., 128
Briggs v. *Elliot,* 175
Brinkerhood, Isaac, 5
Brotherhood of the Sleeping Car Porters, 157

  Randolph, A Philip and, 157
Broughton, Virginia, 93
Brown, Hodges, 176, 179
Brown, J. Pope, 36
Brown, John, 34
Brown v. *Board of Education,* xiv
Bruce, Blanche, 27
"Buffalo Soldiers," 79
Bunche, Ralph, 152, 165
  American Dilemma, An and, 152
Butler, Matthew, 31
Butzer, C. E., 122

Cable, George Washington, 55
Carnegie, Andrew, 131
"carpetbaggers," 21
Carr, Julian, 82
Chamberlain, John, 31
charitable organizations
  creation of, 5
Charles, Mary, 50
Charles, Robert, 97*p*, 99–100
Charleston Mercury, 21
Charleston News and Courier, 31
Chicago
  urban migration to, 137–38
Chicago Defender, The, xiii, 136–37, 148
Chiles, Lizzie, 50
Church Terrell, Mary, 93
civil rights
  Bethune, Mary McLeod and, 148
  Eisenhower, Dwight D. and, 183
  Eleanor Roosevelt and, 146
  Fourteenth Amendment and, 20
  Humphrey, Hubert and, 173
  Humphries, Benjamin and, 7
  Johnson, Andrew and, 7
  NAACP (National Association for the Advance-
    ment of Colored People) and, 118
  Natchez Courier, The, and, 7
  Perry, Benjamin and, 7
  Truman, Harry S. and, 173
Civil Rights Act of 1865, 16
Civil War
  Lincoln and, 1
  loss of life during, 1, 15
  Ruffin, Edward and, 1
Civilian Conservation Corps, 146
  black acceptance in, 146–47
Clansman, The, 114, 118
Clark University, 108
Clay, Jasper, 37
Cleveland, Grover, 76

Clifford, Margaret, 48
Cobb, Ned, xiv, 37–38, 51, 140*p*, 141, 184
    Bentley, Milo and, 142
    James, Clifford and, 142
    Rosengarten, Dale and, xiv
    Rosengarten, Ted and, xiv
Colby, Abraham, 25
Coleman, William, 24
Collins, Abe, 79
Colored Alliance, 72
    Cromwell, Oliver and, 72
    Watson, Tom and, 73
Committee on Fair Employment Practices, 158
Compromise of 1877, 32–34
Connor, Eugene "Bull," 166
convict lease camps, 54–56, 55*p*, 56*p*
    children in, 56
    death rates in, 55
    violence in, 54–57
Cook, Marsh, 70
Cope, Edward Drinker, 104
Cotton Exposition, 75–76
    segregation at, 75
    Washington, Booker T. at, 75–76
Creelman, James, 75
Creoles of Color, 97–98
    Plessy, Homère and, 99
    Railway Separation Act and, 99
Crisis, The, xiii, 118, 120, 127, 130, 149–50
    Du Bois, W.E.B. and, xiii, 118
    NAACP (National Association for the Advance-
        ment of Colored People) and, xiii
Croly, Jane, 85
Cromwell, Oliver, 72
Cullen, Countee, 138
Cyr, Johnny St., 98

Davis v. *County School Board of Prince Edward
    County,* 181
"Day of Jubilee," 2
De Laine, Joseph, 174
Democratic Party, 28*p*, 83*p*
    Populist Movement and, 72–74, 82
    Reconstruction and, 29
    Southern states' support of, 21–22
    white supremacy and, 84–86
Demonstrator, The, 71
Depression of 1873, 28–29
    effect on the South of, 28–29
    Freedman's Bank and, 29
Dixon, Thomas, 105
    Atlanta race riots and, 118
    Clansman, The, 114

Dobbs, John Wesley, 171
domestic work
    Washing Society and, 60
Dorsey, George, 167
Douglass, Frederick, 23, 29, 33, 35, 71
    Freedman's Bank and, 29
    Kansas migration and, 35–36
Doyle, H.S., 73
    Watson, Tom and, 73
Du Bois, W.E.B., xiv, 5, 51, 58, 63, 76, 115*p*, 123
    Atlanta race riots and, 116–17
    Atlanta University and, 108
    Fisk University and, 51, 129*p*
    McKenzie, Fayette and, 133–34
    NAACP (National Association for the Advance-
        ment of Colored People) and, 118
    Niagara Conference at Niagara Falls, 109
    Souls of Black Folk, The, and, 51, 109
    "talented tenth" and, 130
    Wilson, Woodrow and, 118–21
Dudley, Jason, 88
Duke, Daniel, 169
Dunlap Colony, 34
Dupree, Jack, 25
Durr, Virginia, 147
    early days of, 147–48

Edisto Island, 13–14
    Howard, Oliver O. and, 13–14
Eisenhower, Dwight D., 183
    civil rights and, 183
Ellender, Allen, 154
Elliot, R. W., 174
Elmore, George, 160
Emancipation Proclamation, 2
Enforcement Acts, 25
Engle, J. C., 72–73
Evans, Will, 57
Evening Standard, 29
Evers, Charles, xiv

Farmville
    Johns, Barbara Rose and, 177–81
    Rose Moton High School and, 177–79
Felton, Rebecca, 84, 107
Field Order 15, 13
Fifteenth Amendment, 20*p*, 23
Fisk University, 27
    Du Bois, W.E.B. and, 51, 129*p*
    General Education Board and, 131
    McKenzie, Fayette and, 132
    Rosenwald, Julius and, 133
Foreman, Clark, 147

Forrest, Nathan Bedford, 22
Fort Pillow, 17
Fourteenth Amendment, 16–17
Frazier, Garrison, 13
Free Speech and Headlight,The, 65
Freedman's Bank, 29
    African-American investment in, 29
    collapse of, 29
Freedmen's Bureau, 3, 9, 11, 15, 43
    assistance for, 3
    "black codes" and, 9
    Hampton Normal and Agricultural Institute
        and, 43
    Turner, Samuel and, 3, 11
Freeman, James, 2
Fulton, David, 80

Gaines, Lloyd, 152
Galloway, John, 80
Gammon Theological Seminary Atlanta University,
    108
Gannett, William Channing, 4
Gary, Martin W., 31–32
Gay, Mary, 57
General Education Board, 131, 136
    Du Bois, W.E.B. and, 136
    Rockefeller, John D. and, 131
Gibson, James, 174
Gilles, Susan, 95
"Give Me That Old Time Religion," 139
"Gold Dust Twins,The," 106
Grant, Ulysses S., 22, 22*p*
    Ku Klux Klan and, 25–26
Great Depression, 138
    Agricultural Adjustment Administration and, 145
    Civilian Conservation Corps, 146
    lynching during, 162
    National Recovery Act and, 145
    Roosevelt, Franklin Delano and, 145
    the South affected by, 135*p*, 138–39
Greeley, Horace, 1
Green, Ben, 68
Green, Ernest, 159
Greenwood Observer,The, 74
Gregory, William, 48
Griffith, D. W., 121

Haines School, 49
Hall, Peter, 13
Hamilton, Grace, 173
    All-Citizens Registration Committee and, 173
Hammer, Dabney, 166
Hampton Institute, 43, 45–46

Freedman's Bureau and, 43
    segregation at, 43
    Washington, Booker T. and, 43, 46–48
Hampton, Wade, 31
Handy, J. C., 95
Harlem Renaissance, 138
    Cullen, Countee and, 138
    Hughes, Langston and, 138
    Hurston, Zora Neale and, 138
    Savage, Augusta and, 138
Harris, Charles, 33
Hawkins Brown, Charlotte, xiv, 87*p*, 88–93
    American Missionary Association (AMA) and, 89
    Bethany Institute and, 89–92
    early days of, 88–89
    Palmer, Alice and, 88
Hayden, Harry, 86
Hayes, Rutherford B., 30–31, 30*p*
    Compromise of 1877 and, 32
Haywood, Felix, 2
    Freeman, James and, 2
Hearsey, John, 99
Hedges, Ann, 30
Hedges, Square, 30
Herald,The, 132
Hicks, C. P., 34
Higgenbotham, Thomas, 5
Hill, Oliver, 151, 180
Hinton, James, 163, 174
    South Carolina Progressive Democratic Party
        and, 163
Holland's, 156
Holtzclaw, Addie, 39–41
Holtzclaw, Jerry, 39–41
Holtzclaw, William, 39–41
    Tuskegee Institute, 41
Hope, John, 77, 108
Hopkins, Archibald, 120
Hopkins, Harold, 147
Houston, Charles, xiv, 148, 150*p*, 163
    Gaines, Lloyd and, 152
    Howard University, 150
    Marshall, Thurgood and, 150–51
    NAACP (National Association for the Advance-
        ment of Colored People), 150
Howard, Lamar, xiv, 169
Howard, Oliver O., 13
Howard University, 27, 136
    Johnson, Mordecai and, 148
Howell, Clark, 114
Hughes, Langston, 138
Humphrey, Hubert, 172
Hurston, Zora Neale, 138

Ickes, Harold, 147

Jackson, Albert, 141
Jackson, Kennel, 175
Jackson, Tony, 98
James, Clifford, 142
jazz, 99, 132
    Armstrong, Louis and, 98
    New Orleans and, 99
Jim Crow laws, 164p
    armed services and, 122
    federal government and, 119–20
    public parks and, 64
    public transportation and, 64
    rail travel under, 63
    Southern acceptance of, 105
    Tennessee and, 64–65
    theaters and, 64
    voting rights under, 64–65
    World War II effect on, 161
Johns, Barbara Rose, 177–81, 178p
    early days of, 178–79
    Farmville and, 177–81, 178p
    Pervall, J. B. and, 180
    Rose Moton High School and, 177–79
Johnson, Andrew, 6–7, 6p
    Civil Rights Act of 1865 and, 16
    Edisto Island and, 13
    Ku Klux Klan and, 22–23
    land claims and, 13–14
    Lincoln, Abraham and, 6
Johnson, James Weldon, 149
Johnson, Mordecai, 148
Jones, Robert L., 132–32
Jones, Scipio Africanus, 130
    NAACP (National Association for the Advance-
        ment of Colored People) and, 130
Jones, John, 167
Julian, George, 6

Kansas migration, 33–35
    Lewis, John Solomon, 35–36
    Ruby, George and, 34
    Singleton, Benjamin "Paps" and, 33–34
    Truth, Sojourner and, 35
Kennedy, Stetson, 169
King, Martin Luther, Jr. 50, 184
Kirk, Allen, 86
Kirkland, Henry, 37
Ku Klux Klan, xiv, 22–26, 24p
    Ackerman, Amos and, 25–26
    Birth of a Nation and, 121–22
    Colby, Abraham and, 25

Coleman, William and, 24
Davis, Edmund and, xiv, 22, 25
Dixon,Thomas and, 105
Kennedy, Stetson and, 169
Malcolm, Roger and, 168–69
origins of, 22
Parks, Gordon and, xiv
Reconstruction and, 22

La Menthe, Ferdinand. *See also* Morton, "Jelly Roll,"
    98, 100–101
    jazz and, 98
labor rights, 8–13, 9p
    armed services and, 10
    "black codes" effect on, 8
    labor contracts as part of, 8
    sharecropping as a result of, 11
land claims
    Edisto Island, 13–14
    Field Order 15 and, 13
    Frazier, Garrison and, 13
    Hall, Peter and, 13
    Sherman, William Tecumseh, 13
    Stanton, Edwin and, 13
Laney, Lucy, 48–49
    Haines School and, 49
Lang, Charles, 159
Lever, E.A., 30
Lewis, John, *79*
Lewis, John Solomon, 34–36
Lincoln, Abraham, 1p, 6–7
    Emancipation Proclamation and, 2
    Greeley, Horace and, 1
    Johnson, Andrew and, 6
    "Radical Republicans" and, 6–7
    Southern secession and, 6–7
Logan, Carrie Steele, 110–11
Lords of the Delta, 69–70
    Vardaman, James Kimble and, 70
Louis, Joe, 158
Lynch, James, 5
Lynch, John, 26, 26p
lynching, 65–67, 74p, 125p, 154p
    Ames, Jesse Daniel and, 155
    Green, Ernest and, 159
    increases in, 74
    Lang, Charles, 159
    NAACP (National Association for the Advance-
        ment of Colored People) and, 130
    Neal, Claude and, 153
    Roosevelt, Franklin Delano and, 147, 152
    White, Henry Lamar, 153

Malcolm, Roger, 167, 167p
Manigault, Louis, 28
Manly, Alex, 81p, 82–88
    Wilmington Daily Record and, 85p, 88
Mannaway, I. W., 71
    Meridian Fair Play and, 71
Marshall, Thurgood, 150p, 175
Mays, Benjamin, 50
    Morehouse College and, 50
McDaniel, Hattie, 158
McDowell, Calvin, 66
McIlwaine, T. J., 180
McKaine, Osceola, 160, 163, 175
Mckenzie, Fayette, 132
    Fisk University and, 132
McKray, James, 175
McMichael, E.H., 111
McQueen, Butterfly, 165
Meade, Elizabeth, 92
Meridian Fair Play, 71
Merrick, David, 88
Merrick, John, 91p, 93–94
    Duke, Washington and, 94
    early days of, 93–94
    North Carolina Mutual Life and, 95–96
Methodist church
    black membership in, 5
Mine, Mill and Smelter Workers, The, 149
Mississippi Plan, 30
    Grant, Ulysses S. and, 30
Mixon, Winfield Henry, 58, 75
Montgomery, Isaiah, xiv, 67–72, 68p
    early days of, 68
    Green, Ben and, 68
    Mound Bayou and, 67, 69–72
Moore, Aaron, 91p, 93–94
    North Carolina Mutual Life and, 93–95
Moore, Frank, 128
Morehouse College, 50
Morris Brown College, 108
Morton, "Jelly Roll." *See also* La Menthe, Ferdinand,
    98, 100–101
    jazz and, 98
Moses, Amos, 107
Moss, Thomas, 66–67
Mound Bayou, 67, 69–72
    creation of, 67–68
    Green, Ben and, 68–69
    Montgomery, Isaiah and, 67, 69–72
    Roosevelt, Theodore and, 71
    social impact of, 68–69
    Washington, Booker T. and, 71
Murphy, Henry, 166

Murray, Donald Gaines, 150

NAACP (National Association for the Advancement
    of Colored People), xiii, 118, 126p, 149p
    Birth of a Nation and, 121
    Crisis, The, xiii, 118, 120
    Du Bois, W.E.B. and, 118
    Dyer, L. C. and, 130
    Houston, Charles and, 149–51
    Jones, Scipio Africanus and, 130
    Marshall, Thurgood and, 175
    origins of, 118
    Roosevelt, Franklin Delano, 145
    Truman, Harry S. and, 172
    voter registration and, 169
    Williams, Elbert and, 160
NACW. *See* National Association of Colored
    Women
Nashville Republican Banner, The, 59
Natchez Courier, The, 7
National Association of Colored Women (NACW), 93
    Church Terrell, Mary and, 93
    Hawkins Brown, Charlotte and, 93
    Tubman, Harriet and, 93
    Wells, Ida B. and, 93
National Recovery Act, 145
Nation, The, 32–33
Neal, Claude, 153
New Deal, 146
    blacks and, 147
New York Age, xiii
New York Times, The, 35, 127
New York Tribune
    Lincoln, Abraham and, 1
New York World, 75
Newsome, Louella, 161
Niagara Conference at Niagara Falls, 109
    NAACP (National Association for the Advance-
    ment of Colored people) and, 109
Nicodemus Colony, 34
Niebuhr, Reinhold, 176
Nix, James, 161
Norman, Henry C.
    photography of, xiii
Norris, Clarence, 138–39
    Scottsboro Boys and, 138–39
North Carolina Mutual Life, 91p, 94–95
    beginnings of, 94
    Merrick, John and, 93–95
    Moore, Aaron and, 93–95
    Spaulding, C. C. and, 93–95

Oates, William C., 74

Palmer, Alice, 88
Parks, Gordon, xiv
Patton, Charley, 96
Peabody, George Foster, 131
Percy, William Alexander, 70
Perry, Benjamin, 7, 21*p*
Pershing, John, 80, 123
Pervall, J. B., 180
    Johns, Barbara Rose and, 180
Pickens, Walter, 58
Picket, Roscoe, 161
Pinchback, P.B.S., 27
Pittsburgh Courier, 159
Plessy, Homère, 77, 99
    Plessy v. *Ferguson* and, 99
Poitier, Sidney, 165
political organizations, 5–6, 19–20
    Convention of the Colored People of South Car-
        olina and, 6
    creation of, 5
    Union Clubs, 19
    women's role in, 20
"poll taxes," 74
Pollard, Edward Allford, 27–28
Populist Movement, 72–74
    Colored Alliance and, 73
    Democratic Party and, 72
    Doyle, H. S. and, 73
    Oates, William C., 74
    Watson, Tom and, 114
Presbyterian church
    black membership in, 5
Price, Leonard, 100
Price, Victoria, 138–39
    Scottboro Boys and, 138–39
Prioleau, George, 79–80
Proctor, Henry, 57, 108
Progressive Farmers and Household Union of
    America, 128
    Bratton, U. S. and, 128
Promised Land, 50
    Chiles, Lizzie and, 50

"Radical Republicans," 6, 14*p*, 16–17
    abolition and, 16
    African-American civil rights and, 16–17
    African-American voting rights and, 16
    Civil Rights Act of 1865 and, 16–17
    Fourteenth Amendment and, 16–17, 19
    Johnson, Andrew and, 16–17
    Stevens, Thaddeus and, 14*p*
Railway Separation Act, 99
    Creoles of Color and, 99

Raleigh Standard,The, 26
Randolph, A. Philip, 157, 174
Rayner, J. P., 73
Reconstruction
    Compromise of 1877 and, 32
    Democratic Party and, 29
    Johnson, Andrew and, 21–22
    Northern states and, 16
Reconstruction Act of 1867, 19
    Fourteenth Amendment and, 19
    Yates, Richard and, 19
Red Shirts, 31, 84*p*, 85
    origins of, 31
Reid, Whitlaw, 6
Republican Party
    Compromise of 1877 and, 32
    Gary, Martin W. and, 31
    Grant, Ulysses S. and, 22
    Mississippi and, 30
    "scalawags" as part of, 21
Rice, Thomas "Daddy," xi
Richmond Planet,The, 57
Rise and Fall of Jim Crow,The
    Adams, Clinton and, xiv
    Brown, Charlotte Hawkins and, xiv
    Chicago Defender and, xiii
    Cobb, Ned and, xiv
    Du Bois, W.E.B. and, xiv
    Evers, Charles and, xiv
    Houston, Charles and, xiv
    Howard, Lamar and, xiv
    Montgomery, Isaiah and, xiv
    New York Age and, xiii
    Parks, Gordon and, xiv
    PBS (Public Broadcasting System) and, xiii
    research difficulties for, xiii
    time of completion for, xiii
    Washington Bee and, xiii
    Washington, Booker T. and, xiv
    Wells, Ida B. and, xiv
    Williams, Hosea and, xiv
Robeson, Paul, 156, *156*
Robinson, Jackie, 165
Robinson, Spottiswood, 180
Rockefeller, John D., 131
Roosevelt, Eleanor, 146*p*
Roosevelt, Franklin Delano, 143, 146*p*
    Bethune, Mary McLeod, 148
    Eleanor Roosevelt and, 146
    presidency of, 145
    Southern support of, 146
    White, Ralph and, 157–58
Roosevelt, Theodore, 71, 80

"Buffalo Soldiers" and, 80
Rosenwald, Julius, 131, 133
    Fisk University and, 133
Ruby, George, 34
Ruffin, Edward, 1

Savage, Augusta, 138
"scalawags," 21
Schenck, Daniel, 84
Scimitar Memphis,The, 67
Scottsboro Boys,The, 137*p,* 151
    American Communist Party and, 139
    Bates, Ruby and, 139
    "Give Me That Old Time Religion" and, 139
    Norris, Clarence and, 138–39
    Price, Victoria and, 138
"separate but equal," 77
    Du Bois, W.E.B. and, 149
sharecropping, 38*p*
    abuses in, 36–37
    Adams, Henry and, 37
    Holtzclaw, William and, 39–41
    origins of, 11, 36
    profiteering in, 36
    Southern Tenant Farmers Union and, 149
Sheridan, Philip, 16
Sherman, William Tecumseh, 13, 25
    Field Order 15 and, 13
Simkins, Modjeska, 152, 163, 175
Sims, William, 80
Singleton, Benjamin "Pap"
    Kansas and, 33–34
Singleton's Colony, 34
sit-ins, 184
    North Carolina Agricultural and Technical College and, 184
Sitkoff, Harvard, 146
Smalls, Robert, 27
Smith, Hoke, 114, 119
Smith v. *Allright,* 163, 169
Smith, William C., 83–84
Snipes, Maceo, 166
South Carolina Progressive Democratic Party, 163
    Hinton, James and, 163
Southern Conference for Human Welfare, 156
    Roosevelt, Eleanor and, 156
Southern secession
    Johnson, Andrew and, 6–7
    "Radical Republicans" and, 6–7
Southern Tenant Farmers Union, 149
Spanish-American War, 79
    "Buffalo Soldiers" and, 79
Spaulding, C. C., 91*p,* 93–94

North Carolina Mutual Life and, 93–95
Spelman Seminary, 108
Spicer, Henry, 3
Stanton, Edwin, 13, 22
States' Rights Party, 174
    Thurmond, Strom and, 174
States,The, 99
Steel Workers Organizing Committee, 149
Step-and-Fetchit, 165
Stevens, Thaddeus, 14*p*
Stewart, T. McCants, 57
Stewart,Henry, 66
Stone, Kate, 15
Style, H. H., 74
suffrage movement
    black women's role in, 92–93
    National Association of Colored Women and, 93

"talented tenth," 130
Talmadge, Eugene, 171*p,* 173
tax laws, 8
    poll taxes and, 8
Terrell, Mary Church, 120
Thirteenth Amendment, 2
    "Day of Jubilee" and, 2
    passage of, 2
Thomas, Samuel, 11
Thurmond, Strom, 173
    States' Rights Party, 173
Tilden, Samuel J., 30–32
Tillman, Ben, 31, 85, 106
    Red Shirts and, 31
Totton, Ruth, 91
Trotter, Daniel, 38–39
Trowbridge, George, 8
Truman, Harry S., 172*p*
    NAACP (National Association for the Advancement of Colored People) and, 172
Truth, Sojourner, 35
Tubman, Harriet, 93
Turner, Henry McNeal, 9–10, 44, 76, 100, 108
Tuskegee Institute, 41, 44–48, 45*p,* 46*p,* 99
    Armstrong, Samuel Chapman and, 43–44
    Bethany Institute and, 99
    construction of, 47
    early days of, 46–48
    General Education Board and, 131
    Gregory, William and, 48
    Holtzclaw, William and, 41
    location of, 45
    Washington, Booker T. and, 41
Tuskegee News, 45

"Uncle Mose," 106
Union Army
    Freedmen's Bureau and, 3
Union Clubs, 19
United Mine Workers, 149
urban migration, 57–58
    effect of World War II on, 161
    employment opportunities in, 60
    Pickens, Walter and, 58
    Proctor, Henry and, 58

Vardaman, James Kimble, 70, 76, 107, 119
Virginia Dispatch, 26
Voice of the Negro, 107
voter registration, 152, 160, 163, 169, 171–73
    Dobbs, John Wesley and, 171
    NAACP (National Association for the Advance-
        ment of Colored People) and, 169
voting rights, 7, 16, 32
    abuses of, 29–32, 70
    Fifteenth Amendment and, 23
    Johnson, Andrew and, 7
    Ku Klux Klan and, 23–25
    "literacy" tests and, 70, 74
    Mound Bayou and, 70–71
    "Radical Republicans" and, 15–17
    Simkins, Modjeska and, 152
    White League and, 29
    Williams v. *Mississippi* and, 71

Waddell, Alfred, 85
Warren, Earl, 181, 183
Washing Society, 60
Washington Bee, xiii, 79
    Spanish-American War and, 79
Washington, Booker T., xiv, 3, 40–41, 43, 44*p,* 69*p,*
        106*p*
    Atlanta race riots and, 117
    Chapman, Samuel Armstrong and, 43
    Cotton Exposition and, 75–76
    early days of, 43
    Hampton Institute and, 45
    Mound Bayou and, 69
    Tuskegee Institute and, 40–41
Washington, Mae Murray, 93
Watson, Tom, 73, 114
Weaver, Robert, 147
Wells, Ida B., xiv, 61, 62*p,* 63–67, 64*p*
    early days of, 64
    Free Speech and Headlight, The, 65–67
    Moss, Thomas and, 66–67
Wells, Jim, 63

Wells, Lizzie, 63
White, Charley, 39
White Citizen's Councils, 183
White, Henry Lamar, 153
White, Josh, 158
White League, 29
White, Lucille, 39
White, Walter
    Atlanta race riots and, 113*p,* 116–17
    NAACP (National Advancement for the
        Advancement of Colored people) and,
        125, 128–29, 149*p,* 150*p,* 153
Williams, Aubrey, 147
Williams, Cy, 57
Williams, Elbert, 160
Williams, Eugene, 127
Williams, Hosea, xiv, 162, 166
    King, Martin Luther, Jr., xiv, 162, 166
Williams, John Sharp, 119
Williams v. *Mississippi,* 71, 99
Wilmington Daily Record, 82
    Manly, Alex and, 82, 85
Wilson, Emma J., 49
Wilson, Woodrow, 118–21
Women's Army Corps, 159
    black women and, 159
Woodard, Isaac, 166
Works Progress Administration, 147
World War I, 120*p*
World War II
    black support for, 158
    blacks soldiers during, 158*p*
    Jones, James and, 161
    lynchings during, 159
Wright, Richard, 75, 136–37, 158

Yates, Richard, 20

W9-AKP-035

Introduction to Global Politics

SIXTH EDITION

Steven L. Lamy,
John S. Masker,
John Baylis,
Steve Smith,
Patricia Owens

Your personal
redemption code is:

MYPDJMRG64WQPY2QTFYU

Introduction to Global Politics comes with a wealth of digital learning materials. These can be unlocked by using your personal redemption code to complete two simple one-time registration processes outlined below.

Follow these directions to access your resources:

Oxford Insight Study Guide

Optimize your learning—and your grades—with this powerful tool that provides personal practice tailored to your own needs.

› Visit oup.com/he/lamy6e

› Click the link to Oxford Insight Study Guide

› Click "Create a new account" and follow the on-screen prompts

› On the Your Courses screen, select "Add a Course"

› Enter the course key provided by your instructor

› Enter the access code on this card when prompted on the payment screen.

Additional Digital Course Materials

Access a wealth of core activities and resources designed to enrich your learning experience.

If your instructor has integrated the resources from your text into your school's Learning Management System (LMS)—Blackboard, Canvas, Brightspace, Moodle, or other

› Log in to your instructor's course within your school's LMS

› When you click a link to a resource that is access-protected, you will be prompted to register

› Follow the on-screen instructions

If your instructor has instructed you to enroll in an Oxford Learning Cloud course

› Visit the course invitation URL provided by your instructor

› If you already have an oup. instructure.com account you will be added to the course automatically; if not, create an account by providing your name and email

› When you click a link to a resource that is access-protected, you will be prompted to register

› Follow the on-screen instructions

If you are using the resources for self-study only

› Visit oup.com/he/lamy6e

› Select the edition you are using, then select student resources for that edition

› Click the link to upgrade your access to the student resources

› Follow the on-screen instructions

OXFORD
UNIVERSITY PRESS

INTRODUCTION TO
Global Politics

SIXTH EDITION

STEVEN L. LAMY
University of Southern California

JOHN S. MASKER
Temple University

JOHN BAYLIS
Swansea University

STEVE SMITH
University of Exeter

PATRICIA OWENS
University of Oxford

New York   Oxford
OXFORD UNIVERSITY PRESS

Oxford University Press is a department of the University of Oxford.
It furthers the University's objective of excellence in research, scholarship,
and education by publishing worldwide. Oxford is a registered trade mark of
Oxford University Press in the UK and certain other countries.

Published in the United States of America by Oxford University Press
198 Madison Avenue, New York, NY 10016, United States of America.

Library of Congress Cataloging-in-Publication Data

Names: Lamy, Steven L., author. | Masker, John Scott, author. | Baylis,
    John, author. | Smith, Steve, author. | Owens, Patricia, author.
Title: Introduction to global politics / Steven L. Lamy, University of
    Southern California, John S. Masker, Temple University, John Baylis,
    Swansea University, Steve Smith, University of Exeter, Patricia Owens,
    University of Sussex.
Description: Sixth edition. | New York : Oxford University Press, [2021] |
    Includes bibliographical references and index.
Identifiers: LCCN 2020013872 (print) | LCCN 2020013873 (ebook) | ISBN
    9780197527719 (paperback) | ISBN 9780197527726 (epub)
Subjects: LCSH: Geopolitics. | World politics. | International relations.
Classification: LCC JC319 .I66 2021 (print) | LCC JC319 (ebook) | DDC
    327—dc23
LC record available at https://lccn.loc.gov/2020013872
LC ebook record available at https://lccn.loc.gov/2020013873

Printing Number: 9 8 7 6 5 4 3 2 1
Printed by Quad/Graphics, Inc., Mexico

BRIEF CONTENTS

About the Authors ix
Maps of the World xiii
Preface xxii

PART I: FOUNDATIONS OF GLOBAL POLITICS

CHAPTER 1 Introduction to Global Politics 2
CHAPTER 2 The Evolution of Global Politics 32
CHAPTER 3 Realism, Liberalism, and Critical Theories 76

PART II: GLOBAL ACTORS

CHAPTER 4 Making Foreign Policy 122
CHAPTER 5 Global and Regional Governance 166

PART III: GLOBAL ISSUES

CHAPTER 6 Global Security, Military Power, and Terrorism 218
CHAPTER 7 Human Rights and Human Security 268
CHAPTER 8 Global Trade and Finance 306
CHAPTER 9 Poverty, Development, and Hunger 342
CHAPTER 10 Environmental Issues 372

Glossary 410
References 425
Credits 435
Index 437

CONTENTS

About the Authors ix
Maps of the World xiii
Preface xxii

PART I: FOUNDATIONS OF GLOBAL POLITICS

CHAPTER 1 Introduction to Global Politics 2

John Baylis, Anthony McGrew, Steve Smith, Steven L. Lamy, and John Masker

Introduction 8
International Relations and Global Politics 11
    Global Actors 12
    Global Issues 14
Theories of Global Politics 15
    What Are Theories? 15
    Theoretical Traditions in International
        Relations 16
    The Rise of Realism 17
    Rival Theories 18
Research Approaches: Historical, Social Scientific, and
    Constructivist 20
    The Historical Approach 20
    The Social Scientific Approach: Levels of Analysis 20
    The Constructivist Approach 22
Dimensions of Globalization 23
Conclusion 28

FEATURES
    CASE STUDY Global Production and the iPhone 26
    WHAT'S TRENDING? The End of Liberal Dreams? 29
    THINKING ABOUT GLOBAL POLITICS Why Should I Care? 31

CHAPTER 2 The Evolution of Global Politics 32

David Armstrong, Michael Cox, Len Scott, Steven L. Lamy, and John Masker

Introduction 35
The Significance of the Peace of Westphalia 36
Revolutionary Wars 37
World Wars: Modern and Total 39
Legacies and Consequences of European Colonialism 43
Cold War 46
    Onset of the Cold War 47
    Conflict, Confrontation, and Compromise 49
    The Rise and Fall of Détente 51
    From Détente to a Second Cold War 52
From the End of the Cold War to the War on Terrorism 54
Globalization: Challenging the International Order? 56
    From Superpower to Hyperpower: US Primacy 57
    Europe in the New World System 59
    Russia: From Yeltsin to Putin 62
    East Asia: Primed for Rivalry? 64
    Latin America: Becoming Global Players 67
The War on Terrorism: From 9/11 to Iraq, Afghanistan,
    and Syria 69
Conclusion 73

FEATURES
    THEORY IN PRACTICE Perception, Continuity, and Change
      After January 20, 2009 60
    CASE STUDY The War That Never Ends 72
    WHAT'S TRENDING? The End of Peace? 73
    THINKING ABOUT GLOBAL POLITICS Understanding and
      Resolving International Conflicts 75

CHAPTER 3 Realism, Liberalism, and Critical Theories 76

Tim Dunne, Brian C. Schmidt, Stephen Hobden, Richard Wyn Jones, Steve Smith, Steven L. Lamy, and John Masker

Introduction 79
What Is Realism? 80
   The Essential Realism 81
      Statism 81
      Survival 82
      Self-Help 83
   One Realism or Many? 85
      Classical Realism 86
      Structural Realism, or Neorealism 87
      Contemporary Realist Challenges to Structural Realism 88
What Is Liberalism? 89
   Defining Liberalism 92
   The Essential Liberalism 93
   Neoliberalism 98
   Liberalism in Practice 99
Critical Theories 104
   The Essential Marxism 105
   Third World Socialists 108
   Feminist Theory 110
   Constructivism 114
Conclusion 118

FEATURES
   CASE STUDY The Power of Ideas: Politics and Neoliberalism 101
   THEORY IN PRACTICE What Makes a Theory "Alternative" or Critical? 109
   THEORY IN PRACTICE Jane Addams and the Women's International League for Peace and Freedom 116
   WHAT'S TRENDING? Will Capitalism Survive? 118
   THINKING ABOUT GLOBAL POLITICS The Melian Dialogue: Realism and the Preparation for War 120

PART II: GLOBAL ACTORS

CHAPTER 4 Making Foreign Policy 122

Steven L. Lamy and John Masker

Introduction 125
What Is Foreign Policy? 126
   States, Nationalism, and National Interests 126
   Foreign Policy from Different Perspectives 130
   Who Makes Foreign Policy? 134
What Do We Expect From Foreign Policy? 135
Levels of Analysis in Foreign Policy 136
   Individual Factors, or the Human Dimension 137
   National Factors, or Domestic Attributes 137
   Systemic Factors, or the Nature of the International System 139
   Global Factors 140
The Foreign Policy Process 141
   Phase One: Initiation or Articulation 142
   Phase Two: The Formulation of Foreign Policy 144
   Phase Three: Foreign Policy Implementation 145
   Phase Four: Foreign Policy Evaluation 145
Foreign Policy Strategies and Tools 147
   Sticks: Military and Economic Tools 148
   Carrots: Foreign Assistance 150
   Sermons: Diplomatic Messaging and the Use of the Media 153
   Soft and Hard Power in Foreign Policy 154
Foreign Policy Styles and Traditions 156
   Great-Power Foreign Policy 157
   Middle-Power Foreign Policy 159
   Small-State Foreign Policy 160
Conclusion 162

FEATURES
   CASE STUDY Refugees 131
   THEORY IN PRACTICE Central America: A Perpetual Pursuit of Union? 146
   THEORY IN PRACTICE The Impact of Globalization on Different Kinds of States 158
   WHAT'S TRENDING? Women Do Matter 162
   THINKING ABOUT GLOBAL POLITICS Designing a New World Order 164

CHAPTER 5 Global and Regional Governance 166

Devon Curtis, Christian Reus-Smit, Paul Taylor, Steven L. Lamy, and John Masker

Introduction 169
International Law 171
   International Order and Institutions 171
   Criticisms of International Law 174
   From International to Supranational Law? 175
The United Nations 176
   A Brief History of the United Nations 177
   The UN's Principal Organs 178
      The Security Council 178
      The General Assembly 180
      The Secretariat 181
      The Economic and Social Council 181
      The Trusteeship Council 182
      The International Court of Justice 182
Maintenance of International
   Peace and Security 183
   Increased Attention to Conditions Within
      States 185
   Intervention Within States 187
   Economic and Social Questions 190
The Reform Process of the United Nations 190
   Country Level 191
   Headquarters Level 191
The European Union and Other
   Regional Organizations 193
   The Process of European Integration 193
   Other Regional Actors: The African
      Union and the Organization of
      American States 197
   China as a Leader of Global
      Institutions 198
The Growth of Global Civil Society 198
Multinational Corporations 200
INGOs as Global Political Actors 203
   Sources of INGO Power 205
   Forms of INGO Power 206
      Information Politics 206
      Symbolic Politics 207
      Leverage Politics 207
      Accountability Politics 208
      Global Campaign Politics 208
Celebrity Diplomacy 208
Foundations and Think Tanks 211
Criminal and Terrorist Networks as Global
   Actors 212
Conclusion 213
FEATURES
   THEORY IN PRACTICE Neoconservatives and the
     United Nations 188
   CASE STUDY A Global Campaign: The Baby Milk Advocacy
     Network 204

   THEORY IN PRACTICE NGOs and Protecting the Rights of
     Children 209
   WHAT'S TRENDING? A World Order Without Arms? 215
   THINKING ABOUT GLOBAL POLITICS Who Could Help
     Tomorrow? Twenty Global Problems and Global Issues
     Networks 216

PART III: GLOBAL ISSUES

CHAPTER 6 Global Security, Military Power, and Terrorism 218

John Baylis, Darryl Howlett, James D. Kiras, Steven L. Lamy, and John Masker

Introduction 221
What Is "Security"? 222
Mainstream and Critical Approaches to Security 224
   Realist and Neorealist Views on Global Security 225
   Liberal Institutionalist Views on Global Security 226
   The Constructivist Approach to Global Security 227
   The Feminist Approach to Global Security 228
   Marxist and Radical Liberal or Utopian Approaches to
     Security 230
The Changing Character of War 230
   The Nature of War 231
   The Revolution in Military Affairs 233
   Hybrid Warfare 236
   Postmodern War 236
   Globalization and New Wars 237
   New Roles for NATO? 239
Nuclear Proliferation and Nonproliferation 240
   Proliferation Optimism and Pessimism 241
   Nuclear Weapons Effects 243
   The Current Nuclear Age 245
   Nuclear Motivations 246
   Nuclear Capabilities and Intentions 247

Terrorism and Extremism 248
Terrorism: From Domestic to Global Phenomenon 251
The Impact of Globalization on Terrorism 253
    Cultural Explanations 253
    Economic Explanations 256
    Religion and "New" Terrorism 257
    The Current Challenge: The Persistence of the Islamic
       State 258
Globalization, Technology, and Terrorism 261
    Proselytizing 261
    Security of Terrorist Organizations 262
    Mobility 262
Combating Terrorism 263
    Counterterrorism Activities 263
Conclusion 265
FEATURES
    `CASE STUDY` US Drone Warfare: A Robotic Revolution in
      Modern Combat 238
    `THEORY IN PRACTICE` The Realist-Theory Perspective and
      the War on Terrorism 250
    `THEORY IN PRACTICE` The Shanghai Cooperation
      Organization: Fighting Terrorism in the Former
      Communist Bloc 255
    `WHAT'S TRENDING?` New Strategies and Tools
      of War 266
    `THINKING ABOUT GLOBAL POLITICS` Perspectives on the Arms
      Race 267

CHAPTER 7 Human Rights and Human
Security 268

Amitav Acharya, Alex J. Bellamy, Chris Brown, Nicholas J.
Wheeler, Steven L. Lamy, and John Masker

Introduction 270
What Are Human Rights? 272
    The Liberal Account of Rights 273
    Human Rights and State Sovereignty 274
International Human Rights Legislation 275
    The Universal Declaration of Human Rights 276
    Subsequent UN Legislation 277
    Enforcement of Human Rights Legislation 278
What Is Human Security? 279
    Origin of the Concept 279
    Human Security and Development 280
    Human Security and Refugees 280
    Common Security 282
History of Humanitarian Activism and
    Intervention 283

Contemporary Cases of Intervention and
    Nonintervention 284
    Universalism Challenged 286
Humanitarian Dimensions 291
    Political and Economic Rights and Security 291
    Human Rights and Human Security During
      Conflict 293
    Gender, Identity, and Human Security 296
The Role of the International Community 299
    Responsibility to Protect, Prevent, and Rebuild 301
    Basic Principles 302
Conclusion 303
FEATURES
    `CASE STUDY` A Failed Intervention 288
    `THEORY IN PRACTICE` Asian Values 289
    `THEORY IN PRACTICE` Gendered Perspective on Human
      Rights 298
    `WHAT'S TRENDING?` The Human Rights Network 303
    `THINKING ABOUT GLOBAL POLITICS` What Should Be Done?
      National Interests Versus Human Interests 305

CHAPTER 8 Global Trade and
Finance 306

Steven L. Lamy and John Masker

Introduction 310
The Emergence of a Global Trade and Monetary
    System 312
Global Trade and Finance Actors in a Globalizing
    Economy 317
    Cross-Border Transactions 319
    Open-Border Transactions 321
    Transborder Transactions 324
Global Trade 325
    Transborder Production 326
    Transborder Products 327
Global Finance 329
    Global Money 330
    Global Banking 331
    Global Securities 332
    Global Derivatives 334
Continuity and Change in Economic Globalization 335
    Irregular Incidence 335
    The Persistence of Territory 336
    The Survival of the State 337
    The Continuance of Nationalism and Cultural
      Diversity 338
Conclusion 339

FEATURES

> `THEORY IN PRACTICE` Contending Views of
> Capitalism 315
>
> `THEORY IN PRACTICE` Globalization and "America
> First" 322
>
> `CASE STUDY` Southern Debt in Global Finance 333
>
> `WHAT'S TRENDING?` Managing Global Political Risks 340
>
> `THINKING ABOUT GLOBAL POLITICS` Globalization: Productive,
> Predatory, or Inconsequential? 341

`CHAPTER 9` Poverty, Development,
and Hunger 342

Caroline Thomas, Steven L. Lamy, and John Masker

Introduction 344

Poverty 346

Development 348

> Post-1945 International Economic Liberalism and the
> Orthodox Development Model 350
>
> The Post-1945 International Economic Order: Results 351
>
> Economic Development: Orthodox and Alternative
> Evaluations 352
>
> A Critical Alternative View of Development 354
>
> Democracy, Empowerment, and Development 355
>
> The Orthodoxy Incorporates Criticisms 356
>
> An Appraisal of the Responses of the Orthodox
> Approach to Its Critics 358

Hunger 362

> The Orthodox, Nature-Focused Explanation of
> Hunger 362
>
> The Entitlement, Society-Focused Explanation of
> Hunger 364
>
> Globalization and Hunger 366

Conclusion 369

FEATURES

> `THEORY IN PRACTICE` The Terms of Development 357
>
> `CASE STUDY` Life in Zimbabwe: Poverty, Hunger,
> Development, and Politics 360

> `WHAT'S TRENDING?` Saving a Life 368
>
> `THINKING ABOUT GLOBAL POLITICS` Development Assistance
> as Foreign Policy Statecraft 370

`CHAPTER 10` Environmental Issues 372

John Vogler, Steven L. Lamy, and John Masker

Introduction 375

Environmental Issues on the International Agenda:
> A Brief History 376
>
> The Paris Climate Summit 2015 and 2016 381
>
> From Bonn 2017 to Madrid 2019 384

The Environment and International Relations Theory 385

The Functions of International Environmental
> Cooperation 390
>
> Transboundary Trade and Pollution Control 391
>
> Norm Creation 393
>
> Aid and Capacity Building 394
>
> Scientific Understanding 395
>
> Governing the Commons 396
>
> Environmental Regimes 397

Climate Change 399

Conclusion 405

FEATURES

> `GLOBAL PERSPECTIVE` The "Doomsday" Seed Vault 388
>
> `THEORY IN PRACTICE` Regime Theory and the Montreal
> Protocol 389
>
> `CASE STUDY` Common But Differentiated
> Responsibilities? 404
>
> `WHAT'S TRENDING?` Is the Human Game Coming to an
> End? 406
>
> `THINKING ABOUT GLOBAL POLITICS` The Environment: Images
> and Options 407

Glossary 410

References 425

Credits 435

Index 437

Amitav Acharya

Amitav Acharya is the UNESCO Chair in Transnational Challenges and Governance and Professor of International Relations at American University, Washington, DC. His recent books include *The End of American World Order* (Polity 2013), *Rethinking Power, Institutions, and Ideas in World Politics: Whose IR?* (Routledge 2013); *Why Govern? Rethinking Demand and Progress in Global Governance*, editor (Cambridge 2017) and *Human Security: From Concept to Practice*, co-editor (World Scientific 2011). His articles on international relations theory, norm diffusion, comparative regionalism, and Asian security have appeared in *International Organization*, *World Politics*, *International Security*, *Journal of Peace Research*, and *International Studies Quarterly*.

David Armstrong

David Armstrong is Emeritus Professor of International Relations at the University of Exeter. His books include *Revolutionary Diplomacy* (California University Press 1977), *The Rise of the International Organization* (Macmillan 1981), *Revolution and World Order* (Clarendon Press 1993), *International Law and International Relations* (co-authored with Theo Farrell and Hélène Lambert; Cambridge 2007), and *Routledge Handbook of International Law* (editor; Routledge 2009).

John Baylis

John Baylis is Emeritus Professor at Swansea University. Until his retirement in 2008 he was Professor of Politics and International Relations and Pro-Vice-Chancellor at the university. His PhD and DLitt are from the University of Wales. He is the author of more than twenty books, the most recent of which are *The Globalization of World Politics: An Introduction to International Relations* (8th ed. with Steve Smith and Patricia Owens; Oxford 2019), *Strategy in the Contemporary World: An Introduction to Strategic Studies* (6th ed. with James Wirtz and Colin S. Gray; Oxford 2018), *The British Nuclear Experience: The Role of Beliefs, Culture, and Identity* (with Kristan Stoddart; Oxford 2015), and *Wales and the Bomb: The Role of Welsh Scientists and Engineers in the British Nuclear Programme* (University of Wales Press 2019).

Alex J. Bellamy

Alex J. Bellamy is Professor of Peace and Conflict Studies and Director of the Asia Pacific Centre for the Responsibility to Protect at the University of Queensland, Australia. He is Fellow of the Academy of Social Sciences in Australia and has been a Visiting Fellow at the University of Oxford. Recent books include *Massacres and Morality: Mass Atrocities in an Age of Non-Combatant Immunity* (Oxford 2012), *East Asia's Other Miracle: Explaining the Decline of Mass Atrocities* (Oxford 2017), and *World Peace (And How We Can Achieve It)* (Oxford 2020).

Chris Brown

Chris Brown is Emeritus Professor of International Relations at the London School of Economics and Political Science and the author of *International Relations Theory: New Normative Approaches* (Columbia 1992), *Understanding International Relations* (Palgrave Macmillan 1997; 4th ed. 2009), *Sovereignty, Rights and Justice* (Polity 2002), *Practical Judgement in International Political Theory* (Routledge 2010), and *International Society, Global Polity* (Sage 2015), as well as numerous book chapters and journal articles in the field of international political theory. He edited *Political Restructuring in Europe: Ethical Perspectives* (Routledge 1994) and co-edited (with Terry Nardin and N. J. Rengger) *International Relations in Political Thought: Texts from the Greeks to the First World War* (Cambridge 2002) and (with Robyn Eckersley) *The Oxford Handbook of International*

Political Theory (2018). A former Chair of the British International Studies Association (1998–1999), he was Head of the Department of International Relations at the London School of Economics from 2004 to 2007.

Michael Cox

Michael Cox is Emeritus Professor of International Relations at the London School of Economics and Political Science, and Director of LSE IDEAS, the number one university affiliated think tank in the world. He is the author, editor, and co-editor of several books, including *Soft Power and US Foreign Policy* (Routledge 2010), *The Global 1989* (Cambridge 2010), *US Foreign Policy* (Oxford 2008; 3rd edition 2018), *Twentieth Century International Relations* (eight volumes; Sage 2006), *E. H. Carr: A Critical Appraisal* (Palgrave 2000), *A Farewell to Arms: Beyond the Good Friday Agreement* (2nd ed., Manchester University Press 2006), *American Democracy Promotion* (Oxford 2000), *US Foreign Policy After the Cold War: Superpower Without a Mission?* (Pinter 1995), and *The Interregnum: Controversies in World Politics, 1989–1999* (Cambridge 1999). His most recent books include a collection of his essays *The Post-Cold War Order* (Routledge 2018); a new edition of E. H. Carr's *The Twenty Years' Crisis* (Palgrave 2016); and a centennial edition of John Maynard Keynes's *The Economic Consequences of the Peace* (Macmillan 2019). He is currently working on a new history of the London School of Economics titled *The School: The LSE and the Making of the Modern World*.

Devon Curtis

Devon E. A. Curtis is Senior Lecturer in the Department of Politics and International Studies at the University of Cambridge and a Fellow of Emmanuel College. Her main research interests and publications deal with power sharing and governance arrangements following conflict; UN peace building; the "transformation" of rebel movements to political parties in Africa; and critical perspectives on conflict, peace building, and development.

Tim Dunne

Tim Dunne is Pro-Vice-Chancellor and Professor of International Relations at The University of Queensland. Recent publications include *The Oxford Handbook of the Responsibility to Protect* (co-edited with Alex J. Bellamy, 2016), *The Globalization of International Society* (co-edited with Christian Reus-Smit in 2017), and a new edition (with Ian Hall) of Herbert Butterfield and Martin Wight (eds.), *Diplomatic Investigations: Essays in the Theory of International Politics* (2019). He is a Fellow of the Academy of Social Sciences Australia.

Stephen Hobden

Stephen Hobden is Reader in International Relations at the University of East London, where he teaches courses on international relations theory. He is currently working on a research project, together with his colleague Erika Cudworth, on complexity theory and international relations. This has resulted in the publication of a number of articles, together with the books *Posthuman International Relations: Complexity, Ecology and Global Politics* (Zed 2011) and *The Emancipatory Project of Posthumanism* (Routledge 2017).

Darryl Howlett

Darryl Howlett is Senior Lecturer in the Division of Politics and International Relations at the University of Southampton. His most recent publications include *NPT Briefing Book* (2015 edition with John Simpson, Hassan Elbahtimy, and Isabelle Anstey; Centre for Science and Security Studies, King's College London, UK, in association with the James Martin Center for Nonproliferation Studies at the Middlebury Institute of International Studies at Monterey [US]); (with Jeffrey S. Lantis) "Strategic Culture," in *Strategy in the Contemporary World* (John Baylis, James Wirtz, Colin S. Gray, editors; 5th ed., Oxford 2016); and "Cyber Security and the Critical National Infrastructure," in *Homeland Security in the UK* (Paul Wilkinson, editor; Routledge 2007).

Richard Wyn Jones

Richard Wyn Jones is Professor of Welsh Politics and Director of the Wales Governance Centre at Cardiff University. He has written extensively on Welsh politics, devolution, and nationalism, while his book *Security, Strategy and Critical Theory* (Rienner 1999) is regarded as one of the founding statements of Critical Security Studies. His most recent book, *Englishness: Understanding the Political Force Transforming British*

Politics (written with Ailsa Henderson) will be published by Oxford University Press in 2021.

James D. Kiras

James D. Kiras is Professor at the School of Advanced Air and Space Studies, Maxwell Air Force Base, Alabama, where he has directed the School's course of instruction on irregular warfare for over a dozen years. He is a Senior Fellow of the Joint Special Operations University, Tampa, Florida; a Fellow of Irregular Warfare Studies at the US Air Force Special Operations School, Hurlburt Field, FL; and a founding member of the Special Operations Research Association and its peer-reviewed publication, the *Special Operations Journal*. He worked for a number of years in the defense policy and consulting, counterterrorism, and special operations, and publishes and lectures regularly on these subjects. His most recent book, co-authored with other contributors, is in its revised second edition: *Understanding Modern Warfare* (Cambridge 2016). Dr. Kiras's first book was entitled *Special Operations and Strategy: From World War II to the War on Terrorism* (Routledge 2006).

Steven L. Lamy

Steven L. Lamy is Professor of International Relations, Environmental Studies and Spatial Sciences in the School of International Relations at the University of Southern California. He is also the Director of the Global Policy Institute at USC. His current research focuses on theoretical narratives and the shaping of foreign policy choices.

John S. Masker

John S. Masker is Associate Professor of Political Science at Temple University, where he teaches international relations and political theory. In 2019 he was Visiting Scholar in Politics at the University of Otago in Dunedin, New Zealand. Masker has written about nuclear nonproliferation, Russian foreign policy, and US foreign policy.

Anthony McGrew

Anthony McGrew is Distinguished Professor of Global Public Policy, College of Liberal Arts, Shanghai University, Shanghai.

Patricia Owens

Patricia Owens is Professor of International Relations and Fellow of Somerville College at the University of Oxford. She was a Visiting Professor at UCLA and the University of Sydney, and has held research fellowships at Harvard, Oxford, Princeton, UC–Berkeley, and the University of Southern California. She is author of *Between War and Politics* (Oxford 2007), *Economy of Force* (Cambridge 2015), which won the Susan Strange Prize, and she directs the Leverhulme Research Project on Women and the History of International Thought.

Christian Reus-Smit

Christian Reus-Smit is a Fellow of the Academy of the Social Sciences in Australia, and Professor of International Relations at the University of Queensland. He is author of *Individual Rights and the Making of the International System* (Cambridge 2013), *American Power and World Order* (Polity Press 2004), and *The Moral Purpose of the State* (Princeton University Press 1999); co-author of *Special Responsibilities: Global Problems and American Power* (Cambridge 2012); editor of *The Politics of International Law* (Cambridge 2004); and co-editor of *The Oxford Handbook of International Relations* (Oxford 2008), *Resolving International Crises of Legitimacy* (special issue, International Politics 2007), and *Between Sovereignty and Global Governance* (Macmillan 1998).

Brian C. Schmidt

Brian C. Schmidt is Associate Professor of Political Science at Carleton University, Ottawa, Canada. He is the author of *The Political Discourse of Anarchy: A Disciplinary History of International Relations* (SUNY 1998), *Imperialism and Internationalism in the Discipline of International Relations*, co-edited with David Long (SUNY 2005), *International Relations and the First Great Debate* (Routledge 2012) and *Historiographical Investigations in International Relations*, edited by Brian C. Schmidt and Nicolas Guilhot (Palgrave Macmillan 2019).

Len Scott

Len Scott is Emeritus Professor of International History and Intelligence Studies at Aberystwyth University. His

publications include *The Cuban Missile Crisis: A Critical Reappraisal* (Routledge 2015), co-edited with R. Gerald Hughes; *An International History of the Cuban Missile Crisis: A 50-Year Retrospective* (Routledge 2014), co-edited with David Gioe and Christopher Andrew; *Intelligence and International Security: New Perspectives and Agendas* (Routledge, 2011), co-edited with R. Gerald Hughes and Martin Alexander; and *The Cuban Missile Crisis and the Threat of Nuclear War: Lessons from History* (Continuum Books, 2007).

Steve Smith

Sir Steve Smith is Vice Chancellor and Professor of International Relations at the University of Exeter. He has held Professorships of International Relations at the University of Wales, Aberystwyth, and the University of East Anglia and has also taught at the State University of New York (Albany) and Huddersfield Polytechnic. He was President of the International Studies Association for 2003–2004 and was elected to be an Academician of the Social Sciences in 2000. He was the editor of the prestigious Cambridge University Press/British International Studies Association series from 1986 to 2005. In 1999 he received the Susan Strange Award of the International Studies Association for the person who has most challenged the received wisdom in the profession. He is the author or editor of fifteen books, including (with the late Professor Martin Hollis) *Explaining and Understanding International Relations* (Oxford 1989) and (co-edited with Ken Booth and Marysia Zalewski) *International Theory: Positivism and Beyond* (Cambridge 1995), and some one hundred academic papers and chapters in major journals and edited collections. From 2009 to 2011 he was President of Universities UK.

Paul Taylor

Paul Taylor is Emeritus Professor of International Relations and, until July 2004, was the Director of the European Institute at the London School of Economics, where he specialized in international organization within the European Union and the United Nations system. Most recently he has published *The End of European Integration: Anti-Europeanism Examined* (Routledge 2008), *International Organization in the Age of Globalization* (Continuum 2003; paperback version June 2005), and *The Careless State* (Bloomsbury 2010). He is a graduate of the University College of Wales, Aberystwyth, and the London School of Economics.

John Vogler

John Vogler is Professor of International Relations in the School of Politics, International Relations and Environment (SPIRE) at Keele University, UK. He is a member of the ESRC Centre for Climate Change Economics and Policy. His books include *The Global Commons: Environmental and Technological Governance* (John Wiley 2000) and, with Charlotte Bretherton, *The European Union as a Global Actor* (Routledge 2006). He has also edited, with Mark Imber, *The Environment and International Relations* (Routledge 1996) and, with Alan Russell, *The International Politics of Biotechnology* (Manchester University Press 2000). His latest book is *Climate Change in World Politics* (Palgrave/Macmillan 2016).

Nicholas J. Wheeler

Nicholas J. Wheeler is Professor of International Relations in the Department of Political Science and International Studies at the University of Birmingham. His publications include: *Trusting Enemies: Interpersonal Relationships in International Conflict* (2018); (with Ken Booth) *The Security Dilemma: Fear, Cooperation, and Trust in World Politics* (2008) and *Saving Strangers: Humanitarian Intervention in International Society* (2000). He is co-editor with Professors Christian Reus-Smit and Evelyn Goh of the Cambridge Series in International Relations, Associate Editor of the *Journal of Trust Research*, and a Fellow of the Academy of Social Sciences.

Maps of the World

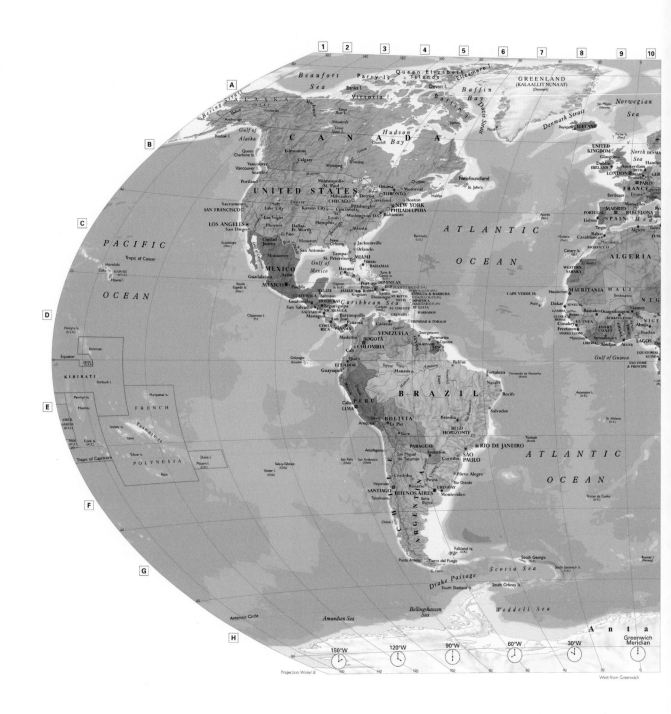

Projection: Winkel III

West from Greenwich

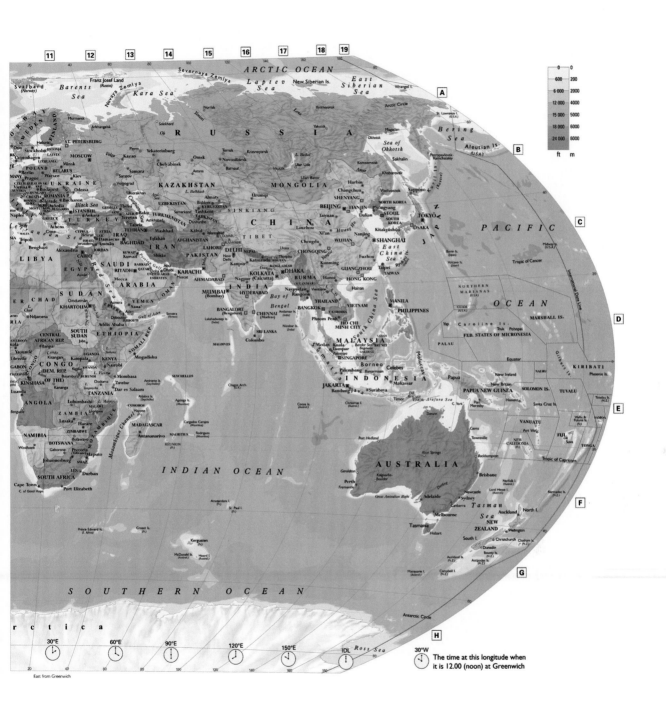

ARCTIC OCEAN

Svalbard *(Norway)* · Barents Sea · Franz Josef Land *(Russia)* · Novaya Zemlya · Kara Sea · Severnaya Zemlya · Laptev Sea · New Siberian Is. · East Siberian Sea · Wrangel I. · **A**

Arctic Circle · St. Lawrence I. *(USA)* · Bering Sea · **B**

NORWAY · SWEDEN · FINLAND · Oslo · Helsinki · ST. PETERSBURG · Murmansk · Arkhangelsk · Ob' · Salekhard · Noril'sk · Lena · Verkhoyansk · Yakutsk · Okhotsk · Magadan · Sea of Okhotsk · Petropavlovsk-Kamchatsky · Aleutian Is. *(USA)*

Stockholm · ESTONIA · LATVIA · MOSCOW · Volga · Perm · Yekaterinburg · Tomsk · Krasnoyarsk · Irkutsk · Sakhalin · Khabarovsk

Copenhagen · LITHUANIA · Minsk · Kazan · Chelyabinsk · Omsk · Novosibirsk · Barnaul · L. Baikal · Ulan Ude · Amur · Vladivostok · Sapporo · JAPAN

DENMARK · Berlin · POLAND · Warsaw · BELARUS · Kiev · RUSSIA · Samara · Volgograd · Astana · KAZAKHSTAN · L. Balkhash · Almaty · Ürümqi · MONGOLIA · Ulan Bator · Harbin · SHENYANG · NORTH KOREA · Pyongyang · SEOUL · SOUTH KOREA · TOKYO · OSAKA · Kitakyushu

Prague · CZECH REPUBLIC · Vienna · SLOVAKIA · HUNGARY · UKRAINE · Odessa · Black Sea · Rostov · Astrakhan · Aral Sea · UZBEKISTAN · Bishkek · KYRGYZSTAN · Tashkent · Samarkand · TAJIKISTAN · SINKIANG · BEIJING · TIANJIN · Taiyuan · DALIAN · PACIFIC

AUSTRIA · CROATIA · ROMANIA · Bucharest · BOSNIA · SERBIA · BULGARIA · Sofia · GEORGIA · Tbilisi · ARM. · AZER. · Baku · TURKMENISTAN · Ashkhabad · Dushanbe · CHINA · Lanzhou · Xi'an · Hwang · Nanjing · SHANGHAI · East China Sea · **C**

ITALY · Naples · MONT. · ALB. · GREECE · Athens · Izmir · TURKEY · Ankara · SYRIA · Tabriz · Mashhad · AFGHANISTAN · Kabul · Islamabad · Kashmir · TIBET · Lhasa · Chengdu · WUHAN · CHONGQING · Fuzhou · JAPAN

Sicily · Malta · Crete · CYPRUS · Aleppo · Damascus · Beirut · IRAQ · BAGHDAD · Esfahan · IRAN · Shiraz · LAHORE · DELHI · NEPAL · Katmandu · BANGLADESH · Kunming · GUANGZHOU · Taipei · TAIWAN · East China Sea

Tripoli · Benghazi · Alexandria · CAIRO · ISRAEL · JORDAN · KUWAIT · Kuwait · BAHRAIN · QATAR · PAKISTAN · Kanpur · Ganges · KOLKATA (Calcutta) · DHAKA · BURMA (MYANMAR) · Hanoi · HONG KONG

LIBYA · EGYPT · Aswan · SAUDI · RIYADH · Abu Dhabi · UNITED ARAB EMIRATES · Muscat · KARACHI · AHMADABAD · Nagpur · Rangoon · Hainan

CHAD · SUDAN · KHARTOUM · Mecca · ARABIA · OMAN · MUMBAI (Bombay) · INDIA · HYDERABAD · Bay of Bengal · THAILAND · BANGKOK · VIETNAM · MANILA · PHILIPPINES · NORTHERN MARIANAS · GUAM *(USA)* · MARSHALL IS. · **D**

Omdurman · L. Chad · N'djamena · ERITREA · Sana'a · YEMEN · Gulf of Aden · Socotra *(Yemen)* · Laccadive Is. *(India)* · BANGALORE (Bengaluru) · CHENNAI (Madras) · Andaman Is. *(India)* · CAMBODIA · Phnom Penh · HO CHI MINH CITY · Caroline Is. · Yap · Truk · Pohnpei · FED. STATES OF MICRONESIA

CENTRAL AFRICAN REP. · SOUTH SUDAN · ETHIOPIA · Addis Ababa · Djibouti · SOMALILAND · Nicobar Is. *(India)* · SRI LANKA · Colombo · MALDIVES · MALAYSIA · PALAU

CAMEROON · Yaoundé · UGANDA · KENYA · Nairobi · Mogadishu · Medan · Kuala Lumpur · Bandar Seri Begawan · BRUNEI · SARAWAK · Equator · NAURU

GABON · CONGO · DEM. REP. OF THE CONGO · RWANDA · BURUNDI · TANZANIA · Dodoma · Dar es Salaam · SINGAPORE · Borneo · Celebes · Moluccas · Papua · KIRIBATI · Gilbert Is. · Phoenix Is.

Libreville · Brazzaville · KINSHASA · Kananga · Lubumbashi · Mombasa · SEYCHELLES · Aldabra Is. *(Seychelles)* · JAKARTA · Java · Surabaya · INDONESIA · PAPUA NEW GUINEA · New Ireland · New Britain · Port Moresby · SOLOMON IS. · TUVALU

Luanda · ANGOLA · ZAMBIA · Lusaka · MALAWI · Lilongwe · COMOROS · Agalega Is. *(Mauritius)* · Palembang · Banjarmasin · Makassar · Timor · Arafura Sea · C. York · Santa Cruz Is. · **E**

Benguela · ZIMBABWE · Harare · MOZAMBIQUE · MADAGASCAR · Antananarivo · MAURITIUS · Rodrigues *(Mauritius)* · Cargados Carajos · Cocos Is. *(Austral.)* · Christmas I. *(Austral.)* · Darwin · Cairns · NEW CALEDONIA · VANUATU · Port Vila · FIJI · Suva · SAMOA · Wallis & Futuna Is. *(Fr.)* · TONGA

NAMIBIA · Windhoek · BOTSWANA · Gaborone · Pretoria · SWAZ. · Townsville · Rockhampton · Tropic of Capricorn

Cape Town · C. of Good Hope · SOUTH AFRICA · LES. · Johannesburg · Maputo · Durban · Port Elizabeth · INDIAN OCEAN · Port Hedland · Alice Springs · AUSTRALIA · Brisbane · Norfolk I. *(Austral.)* · Lord Howe I. *(Austral.)* · Kermadec Is. *(N.Z.)*

Prince Edward Is. *(S. Africa)* · Crozet Is. *(Fr.)* · Amsterdam I. *(Fr.)* · St. Paul I. *(Fr.)* · Geraldton · Kalgoorlie-Boulder · Great Australian Bight · Perth · Fremantle · Adelaide · Darling · Newcastle · Sydney · Canberra · Tasman Sea · Auckland · North I. · **F**

Kerguelen *(Fr.)* · Melbourne · NEW ZEALAND · Wellington · Chatham Is. *(N.Z.)*

McDonald Is. *(Austral.)* · Heard I. *(Austral.)* · Tasmania · Hobart · South I. · Christchurch · Dunedin · Bounty Is. *(N.Z.)* · Antipodes Is. *(N.Z.)*

SOUTHERN OCEAN · Macquarie I. *(Austral.)* · Campbell I. *(N.Z.)* · **G**

Antarctic Circle · **H**

Antarctica · Ross Sea

30°E · 60°E · 90°E · 120°E · 150°E · IDL · 30°W

East from Greenwich

The time at this longitude when it is 12.00 (noon) at Greenwich

ft · m
0 · 0
600 · 200
6 000 · 2000
12 000 · 4000
15 000 · 5000
18 000 · 6000
24 000 · 8000

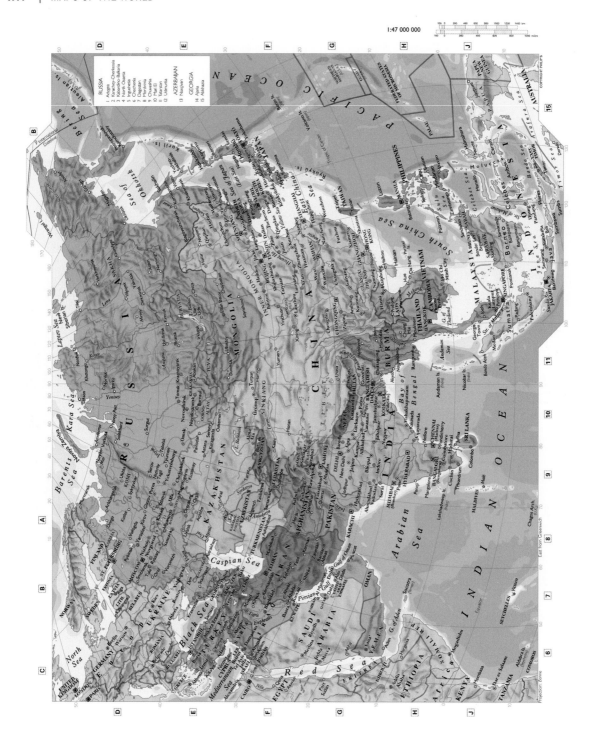

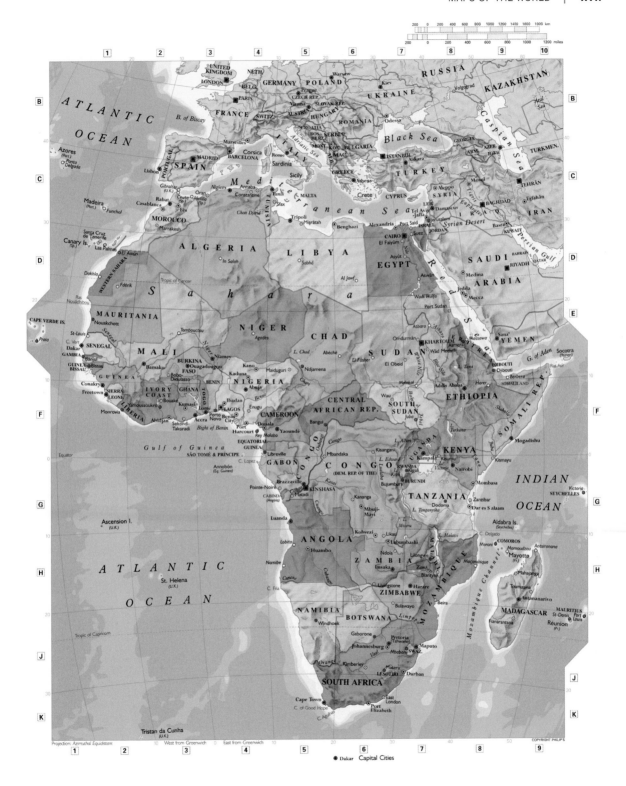

Projection: Azimuthal Equidistant   West from Greenwich   East from Greenwich   COPYRIGHT PHILIPS

● Dakar Capital Cities

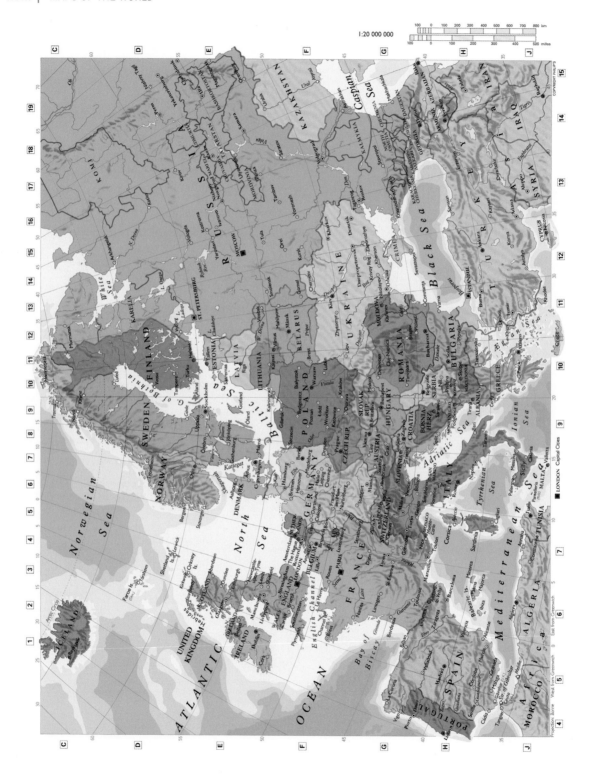

1:35 000 000

Projection: Lambert's Azimuthal Equal Area

◼ LIMA Capital Cities

COPYRIGHT PHILIP'S

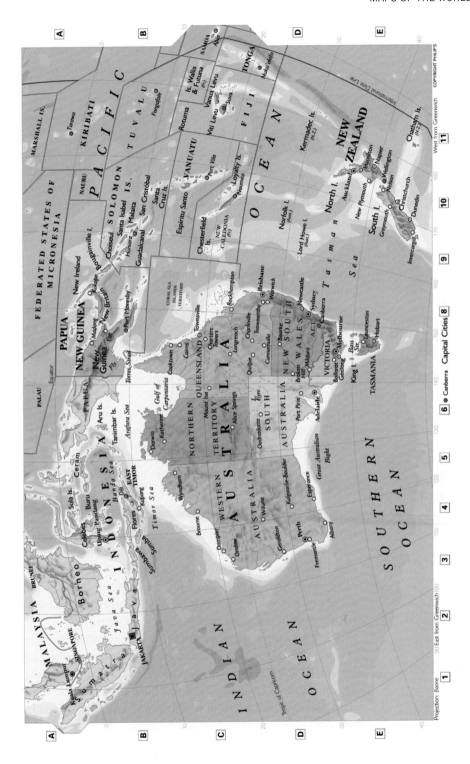

PREFACE

We have written this edition of *Introduction to Global Politics* with an increasingly interdependent world in mind. Perhaps the word "globalization" has become so overplayed that it has not retained much of its original force. Certainly, recent elections in the United States, the Brexit vote in Great Britain, and elections across Europe suggest that many citizens fear globalization and have reacted by demanding more nationalist and protectionist policies. In some cases this nationalism has become both militant and violent, and the victims are the "other"—the refugee, the immigrant, and the minority. At the same time, there is no unifying topic more important than globalization, no political trend of the same magnitude. Even our everyday decisions—those as seemingly trivial and isolated as what food to eat, what clothes to wear, what books to read, or what movies to see—affect the quality of life of everyone around us and of billions of people in distant countries. Meanwhile, decisions made around the world affect our daily lives. Not only is the world changing, becoming more complex and interconnected than ever before, but also the nature of this course is evolving. No matter what it is called—international relations, world politics, or global politics—the course has transformed in recent years, asking us to examine not only relations among countries but also a broader context of global events and issues. In this book, we therefore take a global approach that fosters an awareness of and appreciation for a variety of worldviews. To quote the French writer Marcel Proust, we believe that "the real voyage of discovery consists not in seeking new landscapes but in having new eyes."

A Global Approach

So what does it mean to take a "global" view of world politics? By this, we mean two things. First, this textbook brings together academics from around the world, drawing from a diversity of thought unmatched by other textbooks. Despite the range of views represented here, all of the contributors teach international relations courses, and we agree on emphasizing the challenges we all face as members of a global community. This book thus introduces students not only to the diversity of thinking in our field but also to its common elements.

Second, we discuss in some detail the various critical actors in global politics. We explore the role of individual nation-states, as well as international institutions such as the United Nations and the European Union, and critically important economic institutions, including the World Bank Group and the World Trade Organization. We carefully assess how different groups and individuals have shaped these global institutions, holding different views on how best to govern this world of nearly two hundred independent nation-states. We also explore the growing number and significance of nongovernmental actors, both multinational corporations, such as Nike and Starbucks, and nongovernmental organizations, such as Oxfam and Doctors Without Borders. The entire world saw how important these actors were as we experienced several significant events early in the twenty-first century: the 2008 global economic crisis; the 2011 earthquake, tsunami, and nuclear crisis in Japan, estimated to be the most expensive disaster in history; the 2015 terror attacks in Paris, which demonstrated that the Islamic State is more than just a regional threat; the 2015 Paris Climate Change Conference; and the current migrant and refugee crisis fueled by the ongoing conflicts and violence in Syria, Iraq, Afghanistan, and parts of Africa. The field is changing as the world changes. With this sixth edition of *Introduction to Global Politics*, we hope to improve on the standard conversation, to bring the introductory course more in line with today's research, and to ask (and try to answer) the kinds of questions most relevant for students of world politics today.

This textbook will introduce students to the mainstream theoretical traditions of realism and liberalism and to critical approaches that are often left out of other texts, including constructivism, Marxism, feminism, and utopianism (Chapter 3). Our goal is to introduce students to all relevant voices so they can make an informed choice about how best to both explain and understand our world. We clearly lay out important theories so that they illuminate the actors and issues we discuss, rather than cloud them in further mystery. In short, we hope these pages will help each student develop a more informed worldview.

Learning Goals

An important assumption of this text is that theory matters. Every individual sees the world through theories and uses them to organize, evaluate, and critically review contending positions in controversial policy areas. Unfortunately, many people take positions that lack supporting evidence; they accept a statement or position as true or valid because it fits with their beliefs or reinforces what they believe to be true. After completing a course using this text, students will know more about the global system, the most important global actors, and the issues that shape the priorities and behavior of states and other actors in that system. This text encourages students to approach global politics in an informed, well-reasoned, and theoretically grounded manner. Overall, the chapters in this edition focus on four core learning objectives:

1. To develop a comprehensive understanding of the various theoretical traditions in global politics and the roles they play.
2. To understand the relationship between theory and policymaking or problem solving in global politics.
3. To appreciate the diversity of worldviews and theoretical assumptions that may inform political situations.
4. To develop an understanding of the global system and thereby increase the capacity to act or participate at various levels within it.

At the beginning of each chapter, we identify specific learning objectives that stem from these overarching goals. The review questions at the end of the chapter check that students have met the learning objectives.

After reading and discussing this chapter, you should be able to:

Describe key global actors and their role in addressing global issues.

Understand the importance of theories and resulting narratives used by scholars and policymakers in the field of international relations.

Explain the concept of levels of analysis.

Define the term *globalization*.

Explain academic disagreements about the character and the effects of globalization.

REVIEW QUESTIONS

1. Is globalization a new phenomenon in world politics?
2. In what ways are you linked to globalization?
3. How do ideas about globalization shape our understanding of the trend?
4. How can different levels of analysis lead to different explanations of the impact of globalization on global politics?
5. Why do theories matter?
6. International relations began as a problem-solving discipline in response to World War I. What are the global problems that now define our field of study?

Organization

This edition of *Introduction to Global Politics* includes ten chapters and is divided into three parts:

FOUNDATIONS OF GLOBAL POLITICS

Covers the basic concepts, history, and theories of global politics.

GLOBAL ACTORS

Introduces the main actors on the world stage—from states to intergovernmental organizations to transnational actors and nongovernmental agencies.

GLOBAL ISSUES

Focuses on issues of crucial importance to the security and prosperity of the people in the world.

In the last section of the book, we discuss war, terrorism, human rights, and human security. We also focus on global trade and finance and the environment, with an emphasis on development and environmental sustainability. Each chapter provides essential information about the issue area and presents case studies and worldview questions that encourage students to think about these issues from contending perspectives.

Pedagogical Features

To aid students in the development of their own, more well-informed worldview, we supply several active-learning features, outside the main text, within every chapter. These boxed essays and other elements provide discussion questions and bring into sharp relief some of the unique themes of this book:

- **Theory in Practice** These features examine real-world scenarios through a variety of theoretical lenses, demonstrating the explanatory power of theories in global politics.
- **Case Studies** For a more in-depth analysis of a subject, students can turn to these essays that delve into world events.

- **What's Your Worldview?** These short, critical-thinking questions in every chapter challenge students to develop their own, more well-informed ideas about global actors and issues.
- **Thinking About Global Politics** This feature at the end of each chapter presents in-class activities dealing with real-world political issues. These activities give students the opportunity to develop their critical-thinking skills and apply what they have learned. Each activity includes follow-up questions or writing prompts.
- **Engaging With the World** These short boxes in the margin highlight opportunities to get involved with organizations working for positive change in the world.
- **What's Trending?** This a new feature that introduces students to an interesting argument in global politics presented by a well-known author in our field of study.

Every part of this textbook has been developed with today's college student in mind. The book includes a number of integrated study aids—such as chapter opening learning objectives, a running glossary, lists of key terms, and review questions—all of which help students read and retain important information while extending their learning experience. Two opposing quotations open every chapter, setting up two sides of one possible debate for students to consider while reading. At the end of every chapter, rather than

---

THEORY IN PRACTICE

Neoconservatives and the United Nations

THE CHALLENGE

For analysts from the realist school of thought, states exist in an anarchic, self-help world, looking to their own power resources for national security. This was the perspective of the neoconservatives who dominated the administration of US president George W. Bush. They subscribed to a strain of realist thinking that is best called hegemonist; that is, they believed the United States should use its power solely to secure its interests in the world. They were realists with idealistic tendencies, seeking to remake the world through promoting, by force if necessary, freedom, democracy, and free enterprise.

Paul Wolfowitz, an important voice in the neoconservative camp, wrote that global leadership was all about "demonstrating that your friends will be protected and taken care of, that your enemies will be punished, and those who refuse to support you will live to regret having done so."* Although it would be wrong to assume that all realist thinkers and policymakers are opposed to international organizations such as the United Nations, most are wary of any organizations that prevent them from securing their national interests. The belief is that alliances should be only short-term events because allies might desert you in a crisis.

For some realists, such as the Bush neoconservatives, committing security to a collective security organization is even worse than an alliance because, in a worst-case situation, the alliance might gang up on your country. Even in the best-case situation, it would be a bad idea to submit your military forces to foreign leadership.

OPTIONS

In its early years, before the wave of decolonization in Africa and Asia, the United Nations' US-based realist critics did not have the ear of the country's political leadership. Presidents Truman and Eisenhower both found a way around the USSR's Security Council veto by working through the General Assembly, a body that at the time was very friendly to the United States and its goals. However, with the end of European control of Africa and Asia, the General Assembly changed. The body frequently passed resolutions condemning the United States and its allies. One result was a growing movement to end US involvement in the United Nations, especially among the key foreign policy advisers to President Reagan.

APPLICATION

In the 1980s, political realists saw no tangible benefit for the United States to remain active in the United Nations once the leaders in Washington could no longer count on a UN rubber stamp for US policies. For a number of years, the United States did not pay its dues to the United Nations.

This rejection of UN-style multilateralism revived with the George W. Bush presidency, beginning in 2001. In a controversial recess appointment, Bush chose John Bolton to be the US ambassador to the United Nations in 2005. This appointment came as a surprise because Bolton was a staunch opponent of multilateral organizations such as the United Nations. The Bush foreign policy advisers were against the peacekeeping operation in the former Yugoslavia. In her criticism of Clinton administration foreign policy, then national security adviser Condoleezza Rice said the United States would not send its troops to countries for nation building. More important, the Bush administration did not want to have its hands tied when dealing with Iraq and its alleged store of nuclear, chemical, and biological weapons. President Bush and his top advisers believed that sanctions—an important weapon in the United Nations' moral-suasion arsenal—would never force Iraq to disarm and that only force could do so. The irony is that, after the 2003 invasion, the United States' own weapons inspectors could find no evidence that Iraq had any of the banned weapons.

*Paul Wolfowitz, "Remembering the Future," *National Interest* 59 (Spring 2000): 41.

For Discussion

1. What might be a Marxist criticism of the United Nations and its operations?
2. Is there any way to overcome realists' beliefs about international anarchy and the impossibility of global governance?
3. Some utopians believe that a world government would end war and provide answers to other global challenges. Do you agree? Why or why not?
4. Do the five permanent members of the Security Council have too much power over the operations of the organization? Why or why not?

WHAT'S YOUR WORLDVIEW?

Scholars continue to study the reasons that states go to war. What do you think are some of the causes for past wars like World Wars I and II? What about the causes of wars today? Can we make any generalizations about why wars happen?

WHAT'S TRENDING?

The End of Peace?

In Michael Mandelbaum's latest book, *The Rise and Fall of Peace on Earth* (2019), he makes a very compelling argument that the liberal international order—the global political and economic system established by the United States and its allies after 1945—is seriously weakened if not on the way to ending. The liberal order is being eroded by the actions of three authoritarian nation-states: Iran, Russia, and China.

The United States has provided security and systems of governance that provided order and stability and that has helped the global economy prosper.

Mandelbaum's core argument is that since the fall of the Berlin Wall, the world has experienced twenty-five years of great-power peace. This is not to say that there have been no conflicts and violence across the world. The civil wars in Yugoslavia, Syria, and Yemen and the continuing wars in Afghanistan and Iraq have killed thousands of people. But since the end of the Cold War, China, Russia, and the United States have not fought a major war.

A vibrant global economy and US military dominance kept the peace, but now "autocracy" has destroyed the peace. Mandelbaum's argument is that this post–Cold War peace ended because Iran, China, and Russia "adopted foreign policies of aggressive nationalism" that reignited the security competition in the world. Leaders of each of these nation-states sought to enhance their standing with their domestic populations by presenting themselves as defenders of the country against expansionary nationalism like the United States and ideas and norms that challenge the dominant beliefs and traditions of their state. In Russia, China, and Iran, nationalism has become their source of power, and by "wrapping themselves in the flag" the leaders gain legitimacy at home. Thus, aggressive nationalism and not having a successful economic or political system keep these leaders in power.

simply summarizing the contents for students, we provide a conclusion that requires students to analyze the various topics and themes of the chapter a bit more critically, placing everything they have learned into a broader context across chapters. Students need to acquire strong critical-thinking skills; they need to learn how to make connections among real-world events they hear about in the news and the ideas they learn about in class—and so it is with these goals in mind that the authors and editors have developed this edition.

One last point with regard to pedagogical features: The art program has been carefully selected to support critical thinking as well. Not only do we present a number of maps that offer unique global perspectives on historical events and modern world trends, but also we have incorporated data graphics and compelling photographs to engage students visually. The captions of many of these images include questions for further thought—once again connecting the reader back to the core content of the course, with an interesting prompt or relevant point.

New to This Edition

We have thoroughly updated this edition of *Introduction to Global Politics* in light of recent trends and events that are shaping our world, such as the trade war between the United States and China and the rise of populism and nationalism around the world. In addition, we have streamlined each chapter, revised for more balanced coverage, and strengthened our focus on active learning. In making these revisions, we have taken into account the helpful comments from reviewers, as well as our own experience using the previous editions in our classes.

Revision Highlights

The first three editions of *Introduction to Global Politics* were published in two formats, a fourteen-chapter edition and a brief ten-chapter edition. Like the fourth and fifth editions, this sixth edition is a ten-chapter hybrid edition, which contains balanced coverage of the major theoretical perspectives of international relations, a thorough examination of global actors, and an engaging introduction to global issues such as global trade and finance and the environment. This briefer text encourages students to examine the world by applying foundational concepts to historical and contemporary events, issues, and headlines. We have combined essential concepts with classic and current research, learning aids, and contemporary examples.

In addition, adopters of *Introduction to Global Politics* will find:

- We have threaded critical international relations theories throughout the text more evenly.
- Revised case studies offer updated and further analysis on topics such as global production and the failed intervention to stop genocide in Darfur.
- Throughout the textbook, figures, tables, maps, and graphs have been added, replaced, or updated with the latest and most accurate statistics and information.

- The new feature "What's Trending?" in each chapter presents an influential book on that chapter's subject.
- We have updated the "Engaging With the World" features.
- We have significantly updated our photo program, replacing more than half of the photos in the text to coincide with textual updates and keep pace with current events.

Chapter-by-Chapter Improvements

Chapter 1: Introduction to Global Politics
- Expanded theoretical coverage introduces students to the three theoretical traditions in international relations theory: Machiavellian, Grotian, and Kantian.
- We have presented the concept of narratives as a tool to understand global politics.

Chapter 2: The Evolution of Global Politics
- The revised chapter-opening vignette addresses the goals of nation-states for survival and influence in the global system and how critical trends, such as the diffusion of power and increasing demands for vital resources, influence such goals.
- Expanded coverage of relations between the United States and Cuba addresses the restoration of diplomatic ties.
- Further examination of the war on terrorism includes the completion of NATO's International Security Assistance Force mission in Afghanistan and its subsequent transition to the ongoing Resolute Support Mission.
- We have revised coverage of the origins of the 2003 Iraq War.
- The Theory in Practice feature "Perception, Continuity, and Change After January 20, 2009" has been updated to address the course of the Arab Spring.
- Updated statistics and graphics include "Wars Since 1945" and "Estimated Global Nuclear Warheads as of 2019."

Chapter 3: Realism, Liberalism, and Critical Theories
- Overlapping content between Chapter 3 and the first two introductory chapters has been eliminated, effectively streamlining the chapter and bringing into clearer focus its objectives of defining and describing the origins of international relations theories, as well as explaining the relation among the levels of analysis and the different variations of the five schools of thought.
- The latest on the most pertinent international relations matters is discussed, including how world leaders should deal with nationalism and extremist networks like the Islamic State.

Chapter 4: Making Foreign Policy
- The revised opening discusses ongoing international efforts to end the Yemen conflict.
- Updated coverage and analysis of the UN Framework Convention on Climate Change have been provided.

- Discussion of foreign policy evaluation has been expanded to include criticism of the CIA's detention and treatment of prisoners taken in the wars in Iraq and Afghanistan.
- Additional examples of NGO influence on human rights have been provided—for example, Human Rights Watch pressuring the Chinese government to abolish its system of re-education through labor detention.
- Updated statistics and graphics include "Failed or Fragile State Index," "Top Ten Foreign Aid Donors," and "Share of World Military Expenditures of the Fifteen States With the Highest Expenditure" to reflect the most recent publicly available data.

Chapter 5: Global and Regional Governance

- The revised chapter-opening vignette addresses the impact of the apparent rapprochement between North Korea and the United States.
- Coverage of the European Union has been updated to reflect the departure of the United Kingdom.
- New content discusses China's role in global institutions.
- The case study "A Global Campaign: The Baby Milk Advocacy Network" has been updated to include recent statistics from the World Health Organization.
- Updated statistics and graphics include "UN Peacekeeping Operations as of August 31, 2019," "INGO Growth Continues," and "Distribution of Think Tanks in the World."

Chapter 6: Global Security, Military Power, and Terrorism

- Updated information on conflicts includes the Syrian civil war, the rise of the Islamic State and its goal to establish an Islamic caliphate, and the UN peacekeeping mission in the Central African Republic to prevent civil wars and sectarian conflicts.
- Discussion has been added about hybrid warfare and "gray zone" tactics.
- Discussion has been added about the relevance of NATO in a post–Cold War era.
- Examples of the importance of collective action and reliance on international/regional organizations have been included—for example, in the case of the 2015 Iran nuclear deal and the resistance to President Trump's efforts to kill this deal.
- Expanded discussion has been provided on the effects of nuclear weapons and the idea that the international community is experiencing a new nuclear age in which weapons of mass destruction are used to secure a strategic advantage.
- There is a new discussion of cyberwarfare.
- The case study "US Drone Warfare: A Robotic Revolution in Modern Combat" has been updated to include recent statistics on drone strikes.
- Updated information has been included on the spread of jihadists, Al Qaeda, and ISIS and the geographical extent to which the Obama administration (and future administrations) will have to go to find them.
- Updated statistics and graphics include revisions to "Arms Deliveries Worldwide" and "Arms Transfer Agreements Worldwide"; "Top Locations of

Islamic State Twitter Users" and "Thirteen Years of Terror in Western Europe"; the addition of a new map, "Where ISIS Has Directed and Inspired Attacks"; and the table detailing the interactor relationship of those involved in the Syrian civil war.

Chapter 7: Human Rights and Human Security
- Information on the latest human rights crises has been provided—for example, the refugee crisis, the Syrian civil war, and South Sudan.
- Discussion of the Millennium Development Goals has been expanded.
- Discussion of human rights effects of civil wars has been expanded.
- The revised case study "A Failed Intervention" discusses the genocide in Darfur.
- Updated statistics have been provided on current UN peacekeeping operations and conflicts.
- Discussion of gender and human rights has been added.

Chapter 8: Global Trade and Finance
- Updated analysis has been provided on the current status of global economic interconnection—for example, the role that governmental intervention has in the economy of nation-states (free markets included), the impact of the slowdown of China's economy, and the effects of increasing global foreign direct investment.
- Discussion of the effects of revived economic nationalism has been added.
- Updated discussion has been included on the Trans-Pacific Partnership and its subsequent implications as the largest regional trade agreement in history, and the United States' exit from the agreement.
- The Theory in Practice feature "Contending Views of Capitalism" has been updated to reflect recent changes in the Chinese economy and the cyberwarfare tactics China uses against the United States.
- Updated statistics and graphics include "Main Trading Nations," "Public Global Governance Agencies for Trade and Finance," "Real GDP Growth," and "Holdings of US Treasury Securities."

Chapter 9: Poverty, Development, and Hunger
- Updated discussion has been included on the results of the Millennium Development Goals process (including an updated "Progress Chart for UN Millennium Development Goals") and the UN's subsequent adoption of the new 2030 Agenda for Sustainable Development (illustrated by "Sustainable Development Goals").
- Updated discussions have been provided of world population statistics and estimated population growth projections, including new graphics "Projected World Population" and "Fastest-Growing Populations."
- Statistics were updated where relevant throughout the chapter.
- The case study on Zimbabwe was updated.
- There is a new world hunger map.

Chapter 10: Environmental Issues

- Updated discussions include the latest environmental issues, such as the rising number of carbon emissions, the effects climate change and environmental degradation are having as causes of major violence in regard to specific ethnic communities that compete for scarce resources, and how each succeeding year has been "the hottest year in recorded history."
- Discussion has been included on how climate change is the greatest challenge to economic and political stability across the world.
- Discussion of the global grassroots "climate strikes" has been added.
- Discussion of the so-called war on science has been added.
- The revised discussion of the latest Intergovernmental Panel on Climate Change report addresses the rise of global surface temperatures, the continued shrinking of sea ice, and how human influence correlates to climate change and increasing levels of greenhouse gas emissions in the atmosphere.
- Information and analysis have been added about the 2015 Paris Climate Change Conference, its outcomes, the results of the 2019 Madrid summit, and the importance of adhering to pledges to curb emissions and keep global temperature rises under 2°C. New concluding thoughts and analysis are added as well.
- The table detailing "Recent Global Environmental Actions" has been revised to focus on events and actions of the past thirty years.
- Updated statistics and graphics include "Global Greenhouse Gas Emissions by Type of Gas" and two new graphics: "Number of Oil Spills Between 1970 and 2015" and "Largest Producers of CO_2 Emissions Worldwide."
- A discussion of "eco-feminism" has been added.
- The "Doomsday" Seed Vault feature has been revised to reflect recent flooding events.

▶ Teaching and Learning Tools

Oxford University Press offers instructors and students a comprehensive ancillary package for qualified adopters of *Introduction to Global Politics*.

Ancillary Resource Center (ARC)

This convenient, instructor-focused website provides access to all of the up-to-date teaching resources for this text—at any time—while guaranteeing the security of grade-significant resources. In addition, it allows OUP to keep instructors informed when new content becomes available. Register for access and create your individual user account by clicking on the Instructor's Resources link at **www.oup.com/he/lamy6e**. Available on the ARC:

- **Instructor's Manual:** The Instructor's Resource Manual includes chapter objectives, a detailed chapter outline, lecture suggestions and activities, discussion questions, video resources, and web resources.

- **Test Item File:** This resource includes nearly 1,000 test items, including multiple-choice, short answer, and essay questions. Questions are identified as factual, conceptual, or applied, and correct answers are keyed to the text pages where the concepts are presented.
- **Computerized Test Bank:** The computerized test bank that accompanies this text is designed for both novice and advanced users. It enables instructors to create and edit questions, create randomized quizzes and tests with an easy-to-use drag-and-drop tool, publish quizzes and tests to online courses, and print quizzes and tests for paper-based assessments.
- **PowerPoint Presentations:** Each chapter's slide deck includes a succinct chapter outline and incorporates relevant chapter graphics.

Digital Learning Tools at www.oup.com/he/lamy6e

Introduction to Global Politics comes with an extensive array of digital learning tools to ensure your students get the most out of your course. Several assignment types provide your students with various activities that teach core concepts, allow students to develop data literacy around important contemporary topics and issues, and to role play as decision makers to engage with problems that simulate real world political challenges. The activities are optimized to work on any mobile device or computer. For users of learning management systems, results can be recorded to the gradebooks in one of several currently supported systems. Access to these activities are provided free with purchase of a new print or electronic textbook. These and additional study tools are available at www.oup.com/he/lamy6e, through links embedded in the enhanced ebook, and within course cartridges. Each activity type is described below:

- **Interactive Media Activities** are simulations of real world events, problems, and challenges developed to connect text and classroom topics to everyday life.
- **Media Tutorials:** These animated videos are designed to teach key concepts from the course, as well as address important contemporary issues.
- **Issue Navigators:** These *new* features offer students an interactive way to explore data related to major issues in American politics today, and allow students to reflect on the sources of their own views and opinions.

E-Book

Oxford's Enhanced eBooks combine high quality text content with multimedia and self-assessment activities to deliver a more engaging and interactive learning experience. The Enhanced eBook version of Introduction to Global Politics is available via RedShelf, VitalSource, and other leading higher education eBook vendors.

Optimize Student Learning with the Oxford Insight Study Guide

All new print and digital copies of **Introduction to Global Politics, 6e** include access to the *Oxford Insight Study Guide*, a powerful, data-driven, and personalized digital learning tool that reinforces key concepts from the text and encourages effective reading and study habits. Developed with a learning-science-based design,

Oxford Insight Study Guide engages students in an active and highly dynamic review of chapter content, empowering them to critically assess their own understanding of course material. Real-time, actionable data generated by student activity in the tool helps instructors ensure that each student is best supported along their unique learning path.

Learning Management System Integration

OUP offers the ability to integrate OUP content into currently supported version of Canvas, D2L, or Blackboard. Please contact your Oxford University Press sales representative at (800) 280-0208.

Packaging Options

Adopters of *Introduction to Global Politics* can package **ANY** Oxford University Press book with the text for a 20 percent savings off the total package price. See our many trade and scholarly offerings at www.oup.com/us, then contact your local Oxford University Press sales representative to request a package ISBN.

In addition, the following items can be packaged with the text for FREE:

- *Oxford Pocket World Atlas,* Sixth Edition: This full-color atlas is a handy reference for international relations and global politics students.
- **Very Short Introduction Series:** These very brief texts offer succinct introductions to a variety of topics. Titles include *Terrorism* by Townshend, *Globalization*, Second Edition, by Steger, and *Global Warming* by Maslin, among others.
- *The Student Research and Writing Guide for Political Science:* This brief guide provides students with the information and tools necessary to conduct research and write research paper. The guide explains how to get started writing a research paper, describes the parts of a research paper, and presents the citation formats found in academic writing.

Acknowledgments

The authors wish to thank all members of Oxford University Press, including Jennifer Carpenter, Executive Editor; Ishan Desai-Geller, Editorial Assistant; William Murray, Senior Production Editor; Patricia Berube, Project Manager; Michele Laseau, Art Director; Adeline Colebaugh, Marketing Assistant; and Tony Mathias, Marketing Manager.

Beyond the individual authors and editors of this edition, Steve Lamy would like to thank his research assistants Aram Dommerholt, Erin Pineda, Stefan Catana, Elizabeth Shepherd, Bennett Rine, Helen Williams, and Olivia Sanchez and his students in the School of International Relations at USC. John Masker thanks Mark Pollack and Janine Heywood.

Likewise, there are many others who are unaffiliated with the authors and editors, who contributed to this new edition's shape and success as well.

We owe a debt of gratitude to the following people, who reviewed the previous four editions and have provided invaluable insight into putting together the past and future editions of this book:

Supplements Author

John Masker, Temple University (first through fifth editions)
Michael Pfonner, University of Southern California (sixth edition)

First Edition Reviewers

Ali R. Abootalebi
University of Wisconsin, Eau Claire

Linda S. Adams
Baylor University

Klint Alexander
Vanderbilt University

Youngshik D. Bong
American University

Marijke Breuning
University of North Texas

Alison Brysk
University of California, Irvine

Jeanie Bukowski
Bradley University

Manochehr Dorraj
Texas Christian University

John S. Duffield
Georgia State University

Michelle Frasher-Rae
Ohio University

Brian Frederking
McKendree University

Matthew Fuhrmann
University of South Carolina

David M. Goldberg
College of DuPage

Jeannie Grussendorf
Georgia State University

James R. Hedtke
Cabrini College

Jeanne Hey
Miami University

Jeneen Hobby
Cleveland State University

Arend A. Holtslag
University of Massachusetts, Lowell

Christopher Housenick
American University

Aida A. Hozic
University of Florida

Maorong Jiang
Creighton University

Michael D. Kanner
University of Colorado at Boulder

Aaron Karp
Old Dominion University

Joyce P. Kaufman
Whittier College

Bernd Kaussler
James Madison University

Howard Lehman
University of Utah

Steven Lobell
University of Utah

Domenic Maffei
Caldwell College

Mary K. Meyer McAleese
Eckerd College

Mark J. Mullenbach
University of Central Arkansas

William W. Newmann
Virginia Commonwealth University

Miroslav Nincic
University of California, Davis

Michael Nojeim
Prairie View A&M University

Richard Nolan
University of Florida

Asli Peker
New York University

Meg Rincker
Purdue University Calumet

Brigitte H. Schulz
Trinity College

Shalendra D. Sharma
University of San Francisco

David Skidmore
Drake University

Michael Struett
North Carolina State University

James Larry Taulbee
Emory University

Faedah Totah
Virginia Commonwealth University

John Tuman
University of Nevada, Las Vegas

Brian R. Urlacher
University of North Dakota

Thomas J. Vogly
University of Arizona

Kimberly Weir
Northern Kentucky University

Yi Yang
James Madison University

Brief First Edition Reviewers

Ali R. Abootalebi
University of Wisconsin, Eau Claire

Daniel Chong
Rollins College

Michaelene Cox
Illinois State University

Roberto Dominguez
Suffolk University

Joseph J. Foy
University of Wisconsin, Waukesha

Daniel K. Gibran
Tennessee State University

James Michael Greig
University of North Texas

Steven W. Hook
Kent State University

Jeffrey Lewis
Cleveland State University

Nicole Burtchett
Washington State University

Fredline M'Cormack-Hale
Seton Hall University

Jessica Peet
University of Florida

Amanda M. Rosen
Webster University

James C. Ross
University of Northern Colorado

Donald H. Roy
Ferris State University

Barbara Salera
Washington State University

Noha Shawki
Illinois State University

M. Scott Solomon
University of South Florida

Donovan C. Chau
California State University, San Bernardino

Jelena Subotic
Georgia State University

Milind Thakar
University of Indianapolis

Glenn Dale Thomas III
University of Memphis

Kimberly Weir
Northern Kentucky University

Min Ye
Coastal Carolina University

Second Edition Reviewers

Michael R. Baysdell
Saginaw Valley State University

Pamela Blackmon
Pennsylvania State University

Richard P. Farkas
DePaul University

Stefan Fritsch
Bowling Green State University

Robert F. Gorman
Texas State University, San Marcos

Jeannie Grussendorf
Georgia State University

Clinton G. Hewan
Northern Kentucky University

Carrie Humphreys
The University of Utah

Michael G. Jackson
Stonehill College

Michael D. Kanner
University of Colorado at Boulder

Lisa Kissopoulos
Northern Kentucky University

Greg Knehans
University of North Carolina at Greensboro

Cecelia Lynch
University of California, Irvine

Domenic Maffei
Caldwell College

Eduardo Magalhães III
Simpson College

Lawrence P. Markowitz
Rowan University

Emily Rodio
Saint Joseph's University

Anna M. Rulska
North Georgia College & State University

Maria Sampanis
California State University, Sacramento

Edwin A. Taylor III
Missouri Western State University

Alana Tiemessen
University of Massachusetts Amherst

Robert E. Williams
Pepperdine University

Brief Second Edition Reviewers

Leah Michelle Graham
University of North Alabama

Eric A. Heinze
University of Oklahoma

Courtney Hillebrecht
University of Nebraska, Lincoln

Paul E. Lenze Jr.
Northern Arizona University

Andrea Malji
University of Kentucky

Timothy Schorn
University of South Dakota

Jacob Shively
Indiana University

Jelena Subotic
Georgia State University

Richard Tanksley
North Idaho College

Scott Wallace
Indiana University Purdue University Indianapolis

Third Edition Reviewers

Jennifer Bloxom
Colorado State University

Kevin J. S. Duska Jr.
The Ohio State University

John J. Jablowski Jr.
Penn State University

Paul A. Mego
University of Memphis, Lambuth

Alexei Shevchenko
California State University Fullerton

Veronica Ward
Utah State University

Winn W. Wasson
University of Wisconsin, Washington County

Fourth Edition Reviewers

Richard W. Coughlin
Florida Gulf Coast University

Mariam Dekanozishvili
Coastal Carolina University

Ryan Gibb
Baker University

Michael Huelshoff
University of New Orleans

Michael D. Kanner
University of Colorado at Boulder

Paul A. Mego
University of Memphis, Lambuth

Sara Moats
Florida International University

Jason J. Morrissette
Marshall University

Amit Ron
Arizona State University

Elton Skendaj
University of Miami

Stacy B. Taninchev
Gonzaga University

Daniel Tirone
Louisiana State University

Krista Tuomi
American University

Robert E. Williams Jr.
Pepperdine University

Fifth Edition Reviewers

Pamela Blockman
Pennsylvania State University, Altoona

Rachel Ellett
Beloit College

Ewan Harrison
Rutgers University, New Brunswick

Daniel Kinderman
University of Delaware

Nerses Kopalyan
University of Nevada, Las Vegas

Robert Weiner
University of Massachusetts Boston

Sixth Edition Reviewers

Oana Armeanu
University of Southern Indiana

Bill Bannister
University of Colorado–Colorado Springs

Melissa Buehler
Miami Dade College

Alexandru Grigorescu
Loyola University Chicago

Jeffrey Kaplow
College of William & Mary

Karthika Sasikumar
San Jose State University

Jacob Shively
University of West Florida

Mark Souva
Florida State University

Stacy Taninchev
Gonzaga University

Daniel Tirone
Louisiana State University

The book would not have been the same without the assistance and insight from these outstanding scholars and teachers. Meanwhile, any errors you may find in the book remain our own. We welcome your feedback and thank you for your support.

Steven L. Lamy
John S. Masker
John Baylis
Steve Smith

INTRODUCTION TO
Global Politics

1 Introduction to Global Politics

World leaders representing the leading global economic and political actors met in Osaka, Japan, in late June 2019 for the G20 meetings. Here French president Macron discusses the world economy with German chancellor Angela Merkel and Canadian prime minister Justin Trudeau. As the United States withdraws from its leadership role, other leaders like these three will need to promote and protect the liberal economic system. Who do you think will lead in this new world order?

The real voyage of discovery consists not in seeking new landscapes but in having new eyes.

—MARCEL PROUST

Globalization is the inexorable integration of markets, nation-states and technologies to a degree never witnessed before, in a way enabling individuals, corporations and nation-states to reach around the world farther, faster, deeper and cheaper than ever before.

—THOMAS FRIEDMAN

Who will lead the world in this century, in this era of globalization? Will American leadership come to an end because of a dysfunctional polarized political system and presidential administration that is taking on positions that might be called economic nationalist or neo-mercantilist? Will great-power political competition return with the United States, Russia, and China arguing over system rules, competing for resources and markets and how best to respond to global challenges? With Brexit and the United States turning inward, the Western alliance created after World War II is under siege. So which countries will assume the mantle of leadership, and will this new global leader be willing to set aside national interests for the good of the global system? Russia is an authoritarian state with a formidable military but significant internal problems and little regard for the rights of its citizens and the sovereign rights of its neighbors. Great Britain is politically divided and its withdrawal from the European Union suggests that it may also become more of an economic nationalist state. Germany is clearly emerging as Europe's economic, political, and some would say moral leader due to its refugee asylum policies; however, its history and its current identity make global leadership less likely. India and China are emerging as major economic players, both have millions of citizens mired in poverty, and both have significant domestic challenges that may preclude an activist role in global politics. We need to remember that the United States and its allies created a global system after World War II that provided opportunities for most countries to prosper. This is not to say, however, that the current system does not struggle with significant global challenges, such as how to help the "bottom billion," the poorest billion people in the world. But will the new great powers take responsibility for

CHAPTER OUTLINE

Introduction 8

International Relations and Global Politics 11

Theories of Global Politics 15

Research Approaches: Historical, Social Scientific, and Constructivist 20

Dimensions of Globalization 23

Conclusion 28

FEATURES

CASE STUDY Global Production and the iPhone 26

WHAT'S TRENDING? The End of Liberal Dreams? 29

THINKING ABOUT GLOBAL POLITICS Why Should I Care? 31

After reading and discussing this chapter, you should be able to:

Describe key global actors and their role in addressing global issues.

Understand the importance of theories and resulting narratives used by scholars and policymakers in the field of international relations.

Explain the concept of levels of analysis.

Define the term *globalization*.

Explain academic disagreements about the character and the effects of globalization.

Globalization A historical process involving a fundamental shift or transformation in the spatial scale of human social organization that links distant communities and expands the reach of power relations across regions and continents.

providing the material resources needed to manage global problems? Maybe as important, what set of ideas and norms will guide the actions of these new leaders? Will the liberal internationalists' ideas that "won" the Cold War serve as the ruling narrative for leaders today or will a non-Western authoritarian set of rules become the ruling narrative?

Henry Kissinger, in his 2014 book *World Order*, suggests that we are living in a world of increasingly contradictory realities that challenge the sovereignty and autonomy of the nation-state and threaten the stability created by a balance-of-power system. Kissinger emphasizes several challenges that every student of international relations should consider and explore in detail. These include:

- Internal and external forces are challenging the independence and authority of the nation-state. Some states are paralyzed by ineffective political leadership, and others face separatist movements that seek to create their own nation-state. All states are constrained by the forces of globalization that may limit their ability to provide security and economic prosperity.
- The political and economic institutions and structures are "at variance." The economic system and the cyberworld are global, and the political structure is still based on the nation-state. Cold War–era institutions such as the World Bank and even the United Nations may be inadequate to manage the forces of globalization and respond to global challenges such as environmental degradation and global extremism.

Kissinger and many others have suggested that reconstruction of the international system may be the ultimate challenge of our time.

The world is changing, and that change is not only about terrorist networks or the end of the Cold War. Globalization—especially economic globalization—has dramatically reshuffled global power arrangements and created new alliances and coalitions with the power to shape our future security and well-being. By **globalization**, we mean *the process of increasing interconnectedness among societies such that events in one part of the world more and more have effects on peoples and societies far away.* This is still a world without a central government or common power, but we all depend on the willingness of some states to provide order, enforce the rule of law, and lead and manage the institutions essential to controlling the processes of globalization. At the same time, we expect our governments to provide security and opportunities for economic growth, and that is not easily done in this era. Who will lead is one question, and who can afford to lead is maybe an even more important question. Still, the global war on extremism and terrorism, with tremendous costs in terms of blood and treasure, continues to shape the foreign policies of many states. And we know that all nation-states were dramatically affected by the global economic crisis that pinched the wealthy and crushed those without the natural and human resources necessary to compete.

Like past societies, citizens across this world face more challenges than just economic ones. The world is facing a major refugee crisis caused by wars in Africa, the Middle East, and other failed or fragile states, such as Syria, Sudan, Yemen, Venezuela, and Myanmar. The US interventions in both Afghanistan and Iraq did not result in the creation of stable multiethnic democratic states. Communal or ethnic violence continues to destabilize both nation-states, which has caused many Afghan and Iraqi citizens to flee. The conflict in Syria continues. It has raged for more than eight years and is considered the deadliest conflict in the twenty-first century, with over 500,000 deaths. Additionally, 5.7 million Syrians have fled the war and 6.1 million Syrians have been internally displaced. More concerning is the involvement of so many outside actors in this civil war. The United States is supporting several anti-Assad groups and is battling what is left of the Islamic State with its Kurdish allies. Russia is supporting Assad and, by its actions, risking conflict with the United States and its allies. Turkey is also fighting the Islamic State but is concerned that the Kurds might gain territory for an independent state on the Turkish border with Syria. Iran and Saudi Arabia are also indirectly involved, and the European Union has been fighting the Islamic State but has been overwhelmed by refugees from Syria and other conflicts in the Middle East and Africa.

Syria and now Yemen represents what many believe is the biggest challenge that the world faces: ungoverned regions of the world. This is where we find failed or fragile states that often act as incubators of terrorism and fail to provide for their citizens. Further, areas of conflict create tremendous humanitarian crises. The lack of economic security or poverty is often a reason that people seek radical change or simply leave their homelands.

One definitional element of globalization is the interdependence of national economies. Recently, Europe battled its own debt crisis, which threatened the entire global financial system. This crisis started in 2009 with Greece's inability to stabilize its finances. The euro area continues to face economic issues, which are heightened by the influx of refugees from conflict regions around the world. Germany is taking the lead to stabilize the euro, prevent the collapse of Greece, and contain the crisis. Germany has also taken the lead in accepting refugees and promoting humanitarian responses to this human tragedy. One should note that by taking this humanitarian position toward refugees, Angela Merkel's ruling party lost support in recent elections. This raises an important issue: the rising tide of populism and nationalism that has contributed to many right-wing political party victories across Europe and the United States.

How we react to momentous global challenges like the "four famines" humanitarian crises created by war and violence in Yemen, South Sudan, Nigeria, and Somalia and the increasingly destructive effects of global climate change and weather weirding is linked to how we identify ourselves and the narrative that guides our policy choices. Are we nationalists or internationalists? Do we embrace globalization and work to manage it to our advantage, or do we become economic nationalists and work to withdraw from the global economy? We have seen the rise of antiglobalization movements across the world. The Brexit vote in the United Kingdom and the economic nationalism message that helped elect Donald Trump have seriously eroded the liberal economic system established by the United States and its allies after World War II. But is it even possible to withdraw from a global economy that provides goods and services for most of the world? You might be surprised to know how connected you are to the world. Look at the labels in your clothing. The tag says "Made in someplace," but have you ever wondered how the pieces of your sneakers, for example, got to the factory where they were assembled? Or how the shoes traveled from that factory in Asia to the store in California, Kansas, Texas, or Vermont where you purchased them? Have you ever asked yourself who made your sneakers? How does that person live? How do others in the world view the United States or other wealthy and powerful states where people buy these sneakers? How you are connected goes beyond looking at the goods and services you purchase in a given day. Do you have a passport and have you traveled internationally? Do you have a web-capable cellphone and are you constantly plugged in to internet applications like Facebook? Are you on Skype talking to friends you met while on a study-abroad program? Have you signed up for news alerts from news agencies? Do you also read the international news from foreign sources such as the BBC or Al Jazeera? Do you belong to a global nongovernmental organization

(NGO) like Human Rights Watch, Oxfam, or Greenpeace, which are all dedicated to resolving global problems?

All of us have connections to the world that we are not aware of. Other connections we make, like joining a political group or student club on campus, are more personal and immediate. Yet both types of connections—known and unknown—help shape our identities as individuals in the wider world. The purpose of this book is to help you understand the world of politics that provides those connections. Along the way, you will see how interdependent we all are and how our way of life is shaped by forces of globalization.

We need to remember that globalization is a multidimensional process. Economic or market globalization involves processes of trade, production, and finance that are pushed by communications, technology, and the networking of national markets into a global economy (Hebron and Stack 2011). Political globalization is the spread of political ideas, values, norms, practices, and policies. Those who study globalization also look at its impact on the state and the ability of the state to do what is expected by its citizens. There are two positions here: (1) *hyperglobalists*, who see the state losing authority and sharing power with other actors, and (2) *skeptics*, who believe that states can use globalization to enhance their power and authority.

Perhaps as important as economic globalization is cultural globalization. This involves the spread of popular culture, in areas such as music, film, literature, and consumerism, and the global diffusion of more traditional cultural ideas found in religious and ethnic communities. Globalization is a powerful force that may challenge or at times enhance the authority of both state and nonstate actors in a variety of policy sectors. In many nation-states, most notably the United States with the election of Donald Trump with his America First message, the UK vote to leave the European Union, or Brexit, or the Five Star Movement in Italy, there appears to be a fear of globalization and an unrealistic view that countries can withdraw from this global system. Leaders need to remember that in the world today, economic interdependence, not independence, is the reality.

This chapter presents an overview of the textbook—the main actors and topics that we will examine. It also introduces the theories that will guide us in our study of global politics. You will learn more about globalization, and you will begin that important journey of discovery by developing new eyes. You will begin to see how different theories construct our world.

▶ Introduction

In its 2017 publication, *Global Trends: Paradox of Progress*, the US National Intelligence Council presents a future scenario that suggests that we are "living in a paradox": a world that is more prosperous and possibly more dangerous than ever before. Very few countries have escaped extremist movements and terrorist attacks. The "global war on terrorism" began in 2001 and continues today. The US wars in Afghanistan and Iraq are the two longest in US history, and they are likely to go on for a very long time. Yet, there are other challenges that will shape global politics for many years ahead. If this era of globalization means the end of US dominance, it may not mean the end of the liberal international order in which capitalism, democratic values, and the rule of law guide the behavior of societies and states. But to survive and prevent a new world disorder, leaders and citizens must address the following six challenges:

- The challenge of providing global economic and political order and system stability
- The challenge of achieving human security and addressing global poverty
- The challenge of maintaining the authority and sovereignty of the nation-state
- The challenge of protecting and promoting human rights
- The challenge presented by excessive nationalism and extremism
- The challenge of addressing environmental degradation and the fate of the natural world

Many young citizens took to the streets to protest the election of Boris Johnson as prime minister. Johnson was a leading supporter of the British withdrawal from the European Union or Brexit. Many believe that the fear of globalization and its economic, political, and cultural consequences, especially among older voters, was the primary reason for the narrow rejection of membership in the EU. Should we be concerned that nationalism is on the rise and that a multilateral experiment like the EU is under siege?

These six challenges define the agenda for any student of international relations and will be directly addressed in the issue chapters in this text.

Extremism and terrorist activities across the world in the last nineteen years underscore the seriousness of those who want a war against Western culture and its political and economic dominance. In Kissinger's terms, this may be the most serious threat to world order.

Currently, the ISIS network, once an affiliate of Al-Qaeda, has lost its territorial caliphate but still operates in Iraq and Syria and smaller territories in Libya, Nigeria, and Afghanistan. It has claimed responsibility for attacks in Paris, Brussels, Manchester, and other cities throughout Europe. The attacks were coordinated by using some of the most powerful technologies of the globalized world—namely, mobile phones, international bank accounts, and the internet.

Moreover, the key personnel traveled regularly among continents, using yet another symbol of globalization, mass air travel. More recently, countries must deal with home-grown terrorists. There are two distinctive varieties of these domestic terrorists. First, there are young citizens who may be immigrants or the sons and daughters of immigrants who are radicalized by religious narratives that emphasize the evils of Western popular culture and undermine the norms and values of liberty, freedom of expression, and equality of individuals in every society. A second group of domestic terrorists are the nationalists who see their culture being overwhelmed by immigrants and people of color. Both these groups embrace narratives or stories that inspire hate and violence and create a Manichean view (i.e., us vs. them) of the world. In addition, these narratives are promoted and disseminated across the globe through social media. The white supremacist terrorist in El Paso was inspired by the manifesto posted on the web by the New Zealand extremist who killed fifty-one worshippers at a mosque and an Islamic center.

Still, globalization can also be seen as one of the causes of these attacks. In many parts of the world dominated by traditional cultures and religious communities, fundamentalists see globalization as a Western process bringing popular culture and Western ideas that undermine their core values and beliefs. This "Westoxification" pushed and promoted by globalization is the enemy, and the United States is the leader of this noxious process. In a similar vein, nationalists want to stop the movement of people and the mixing of cultures. They see multiculturalism as a threat to who they are and the traditions and values that define their state. We are all experiencing the "globalization of nationalism," and with that comes violence, intolerance, and a weakening of governance across the world.

We know that extremist movements representing various ethnic and nationalist communities are using technology and communication tools to promote their positions and even to organize their activities that democratic states have difficulty controlling. Many states and even some of the extremists are trying to control, manage, and, if possible, stop the process of globalization. This is possible in totalitarian societies, but it is becoming more difficult as the internet and global communications spread around the world. The upheavals in North Africa and the Middle East—the so-called Arab Spring—were organized using social networks like Facebook and messaging services like Twitter. Change agents across the globe are certainly aided by new communication technologies, and these are transboundary tools that states cannot effectively contain.

Although there are many indicators that the world has become increasingly globalized over the last thirty-five years, in many ways, the 9/11 attack on the United States, the numerous attacks on European cities, the 2008 economic crisis, and the ongoing conflicts in the Middle East and Africa are the clearest symbols of how distant events reverberate around the world. Other wicked global problems, such as climate change and global poverty, demand a global response, and the 2015 Paris Agreement on climate change and the recently announced UN Sustainable Development Goals suggest that some nation-states are willing to cooperate to respond to these global challenges. These successes do not always last. The euphoria created by the Paris Agreement on climate was short-lived after the Trump administration stated that it would withdraw from this agreement—a clear example of how domestic politics shapes foreign policy.

Generally, people care most about what is going on at home or in their local communities. We usually elect people to office who promise to provide jobs, fix roads, offer loans for housing, build good schools, and provide quality health care. These promises may get candidates votes, but people in office soon learn that many of the promises cannot be fulfilled without considering the dynamics of the global economy and the impact of major global events. Leaders are now realizing that to provide for their citizens they must manage the processes of globalization, and this is not a task one country can do alone. We all became aware of the breadth and depth of globalization with the economic crisis that began in 2008 and still has continuing effects in 2020. The costs of this global financial crisis were unemployment, home foreclosures, bank failures, a collapse in the stock markets around the world, and a general anger and dissatisfaction with political leaders for failing to anticipate these problems and respond before the near collapse. Continuing discontent with the economy led to the successful Brexit vote, the election of Emmanuel Macron in France, the election of Donald Trump, and changes in political leadership around the world.

G20, or Group of Twenty An assembly of governments and leaders from twenty of the world's largest economies: Argentina, Australia, Brazil, Canada, China, France, Germany, India, Indonesia, Italy, Japan, Mexico, Republic of Korea, Russian Federation, Saudi Arabia, South Africa, Turkey, United Kingdom, United States, and the European Union.

Governments, leaders of global institutions such as the International Monetary Fund (IMF) and the World Bank, and regional organizations like the European Union must prove they can regulate global finance and manage the processes of globalization. World leaders and corporate executives are concerned about the trade war between China and the United States and the resulting economic slowdown in China. Although China's 6.2 percent growth is the envy of most countries, any slowdown might have a major negative impact on trade in areas of global commodities like iron ore and other minerals. At the 2019 **G20, or Group of Twenty**, meetings in Osaka, Japan, the Japanese prime minister, Shinzo Abe, presented an agenda that was to deal with multilateral trade, global health, climate change, women's empowerment, and global data governance. Unfortunately, the outcomes of these meetings are dramatically shaped by domestic politics. US opposition to a strong position on "battling protectionism" and addressing climate change led to a weaker final declaration. The final document did include two new areas for cooperation: a commitment to facilitate the "free flow of data" and an agreement to embrace the Osaka Blue Ocean Vision that addresses marine plastic waste.

Models of Chinese high-speed trains are on display at a major trade fair in Mostar, Bosnia. Chinese investments in Eastern and Central Europe are booming and the European Union leadership is very concerned. Whereas any EU funding comes with conditionality, the Chinese investments have few requirements. The EU uses its loans and investments to promote democracy, human rights, and sustainable development. China's loans are made entirely for economic reasons. How will Chinese loan and infrastructure programs influence the distribution of global power?

Probably the two most important issues—trade rules and climate change—were not seriously addressed due to US opposition, and this may be the cost of trying to find consensus at these major global conferences and meetings. It is also a recurring theme in global politics: The national interests of major powers usually triumph over the more general interests of the global community.

Again, the aim of this book is to provide an overview of global politics in this globalized world. Let us start, though, with a few words about the title. It is not accidental. First, we want to introduce you to global politics as distinct from international politics or international relations (a distinction we will explain shortly). Second, many think the contemporary, post–Cold War world is markedly different from previous periods because of the effects of globalization. We think it is especially difficult to explain global politics in such an era because globalization is a particularly controversial term. There is considerable dispute over just what it means to talk of this being an era of globalization and whether it means the main features of global politics are any different from those of previous eras. In this introduction, we explain how we propose to deal with the concept of globalization, and we offer you some arguments for and against seeing it as an important new development in global politics.

Before turning to globalization, we want to set the scene for the chapters that follow. We will first discuss the various terms used to describe international relations, world politics, and global politics, and then we will spend some time looking at the main ways global politics has been explained.

◢ International Relations and Global Politics

Why does the title of this book refer to **global politics** rather than to international politics or **international relations**? These are the traditional names used to describe the kinds of interactions and processes that are the concern of this text. Our reason for choosing the phrase *global politics* is that it is more inclusive than either of the alternative terms. With this phrase, we mean to highlight our interest in the politics and political patterns in the world, and not only those among nation-states (as the term *international politics* implies). We are interested in relations among organizations that may or may not be states—for example, multinational companies, terrorist groups, or international **nongovernmental organizations (NGOs)**; these are all known as **transnational actors**. Although the term *international relations* does represent a widening of concern from simply the political relations among nation-states, it still restricts focus to *inter-national* relations. We think relations among cities or provinces and other **governments** or international organizations can be equally important. Therefore, we prefer to characterize the relations we are interested in as those of world politics—or more specifically, given the powerful influences of globalization, global politics.

However, we do not want such fine distinctions regarding word choice to force you to define politics too narrowly. You will see this issue arising repeatedly

Global politics The politics of global social relations in which the pursuit of power, interests, order, and justice transcends regions and continents.

International relations The study of the interactions of states (countries) and other actors in the international system.

Nongovernmental organization (NGO) An organization, usually a grassroots one, that has policy goals but is not governmental in its makeup. An NGO is any group of people relating to each other regularly in some formal manner and engaging in collective action, provided the activities are noncommercial and nonviolent and are not conducted on behalf of a government.

Transnational actor Any nongovernmental actor, such as a multinational corporation or a global religious humanitarian organization, that has dealings with any actor from another country or with an international organization.

Government The people and agencies that have the power and legitimate authority to determine who gets what, when, where, and how within a given territory.

in the chapters that follow because many academics want to define politics very widely. One obvious example concerns the relationship between politics and economics; there is clearly an overlap, and a lot of bargaining power goes to the person who can persuade others that the existing distribution of resources is simply economic rather than political. So we want you to think about politics very broadly for the time being. Several features of the contemporary world that you may not have previously thought of as political will be described as such in the chapters that follow. Our focus is on the patterns of political relations, defined broadly, that characterize the contemporary world.

Global Actors

After reviewing the foundational and theoretical aspects of global politics in Chapters 2 and 3, we will take a close look at a number of important actors on the world stage. Nation-states (countries) are the most important actors in global politics because they are the actors that engage in diplomatic relations, sign the treaties that create the legal foundation for world politics, and go to war.

Increasingly, however, **nonstate actors** are playing important roles in global politics. These can be international or regional organizations that are composed of states. The United Nations (discussed further in Chapter 5) is the most famous actor in this category; others include the European Union, the Organization of American States (OAS), the Shanghai Cooperation Organization, and the African Union. **Multinational corporations (MNCs)** have also become important players in world politics. These large business organizations can have their headquarters in one country, their design staff in another, and their production facilities in several other countries. MNCs are important in many ways but perhaps most significantly because a factory can provide vital jobs in a developing country. Nike may be the iconic example of a global multinational for many in the world, but China's global communication technology company Huawei and the British-Dutch Unilever consumer products company are well known around the world. These MNCs shape both economics and politics.

In Chapter 5, we will provide an in-depth look at these and other nonstate actors, including a discussion of NGOs, which have increased in numbers and influence in global politics. NGOs like the International Rescue Committee or World Vision provide expertise for policymakers and provide programs and resources to address global problems like the global refugee crisis and global health issues. To clarify the difference, some authors call MNCs for-profit nonstate actors and NGOs not-for-profit nonstate actors. We will also look at foundations and research think tanks that are playing more important roles in global politics. Finally, we will explore the role played by individuals, including celebrities, who become involved in diplomacy. To lay the groundwork for that future discussion, let's take a moment now to look more closely at the definitions—and debates—involving states and nation-states, as well as to consider the problems of the traditional state-centered approach to studying global politics.

Nonstate actor Any participant in global politics that is neither acting in the name of government nor created and served by government. Nongovernmental organizations, terrorist networks, global crime syndicates, and multinational corporations are examples.

Multinational corporation or enterprise (MNC/MNE) A business or firm with administration, production, distribution, and marketing located in countries around the world. Such a business moves money, goods, services, and technology around the world depending on where the firm can make the most profit.

Nation A community of people who share a common sense of identity, which may be derived from language, culture, or ethnicity; this community may be a minority within a single country or live in more than one country.

State A legal territorial entity composed of a stable population and a government; it possesses a monopoly over the legitimate use of force; its sovereignty is recognized by other states in the international system.

Nation-state A political community in which the state claims legitimacy on the grounds that it represents all citizens, including those who may identify as a separate community or nation.

Like many of the terms used in the study of global politics, the terms *state* and *nation-state* can be somewhat confusing. The two parts of the term *nation-state* derive from different sources. **Nation** derives from the idea that a group of people sharing the same geographic space, the same language, the same culture, and the same history also share a common identity. As most political scientists use the term, *nation* conveys a group identity that is bigger than a family group or tribal unit. **State** has its origins in Latin and in the legal system of the Roman Empire. In political science, *state* is a particularly divisive term because, as we will see in Chapter 3, academics disagree about what the term means. At a minimum, political scientists agree that the state is the highest-level political structure that makes authoritative decisions within a territorially based political unit. What makes the term confusing for many students in the United States is that the country comprises subunits called "states." When nation and state are combined in the pair nation-state, we have a term that describes a political unit within which people share an identity. It is important to note that *the state is not always coincidental with a nation*. While the state for many political scientists is a set of governing institutions, *nation* refers to the people who share a history, language, religion, or other cultural attributes. The Flemish in Belgium, the Welsh in the United Kingdom, and the Iroquois of the United States and Canada are examples of nations found within states. Most states, even when called nation-states, actually comprise several nations. As we will see in this book, many problems in the modern international system result from nations with historical rivalry that are forced to live within the borders of one state.

The concepts of state and sovereignty are critical to understand if you are a student of international relations, a diplomat, or a political leader. The **nation-state**—sometimes called "country" or simply "state"—is the primary unit of analysis in the study of international relations. As we will discuss in Chapter 2, the treaties that resulted in the Peace of Westphalia (which ended the Thirty Years' War in 1648) recognized the state as supreme and the sovereign power within its boundaries. The Westphalian ideal of sovereignty emphasizes the principle of the inviolability of the borders of a state. Furthermore, all states agreed with the idea that it was not acceptable to intervene in the internal affairs of other states. **Sovereignty** is a complex and contested concept in international relations; essentially, it suggests that within a given territory the leaders of a state have absolute and final political authority. However, sociologist Manuel Castells (2005) has suggested that the modern nation-state might be adversely affected by

Globalization and partisan political battles have contributed to the importance of subnational actors and nongovernmental actors in the policymaking process. A global process such as climate change affects all actors at all levels. Here Anne Hidalgo, mayor of Paris and president of C40, meets with former California governor Arnold Schwarzenegger, who now leads R20, a coalition of subnational governments and other actors with a focus on green infrastructure projects. C40 is a network of some ninety cities that are promoting climate action around the world. With some national governments dismissing the Paris Agreement and refusing to recognize the effects of climate change, do you think these coalitions provide a way forward for reform and problem solving?

Sovereignty The condition of a state having control and authority over its own territory and being free from any higher legal authority. It is related to, but distinct from, the condition of a government being free from any external political constraints.

The crisis of equity is felt all over the world. Women are often denied access to their fair share of resources, opportunities, and decision-making power within societies. Here, women protest in Lausanne, Switzerland, demanding fair pay, equal rights, and an end to sexual harassment and violence against women. How effective are these global movements for social justice, and what factors work against these efforts?

globalization in four ways; indeed, all our political institutions are facing the same four crises:

1. States cannot effectively manage global problems unilaterally and thus suffer a *crisis of efficiency.*
2. Policymakers are not always representative of their citizens' interests, and as policymaking becomes more global, decisions are made further away from citizens. This is a *crisis of legitimacy.*
3. Citizens are being pulled toward their cultural identity and toward identity and affiliation with NGOs and other civil-society actors. A variety of forces pull them away from citizen identity and have created a *crisis of identity.*
4. Globalization has increased inequality in many states and created a *crisis of equity.*

Castells argues that nation-states must create collaborative networks with NGOs and other nonstate actors to respond effectively to these crises. The nation-state will survive, but states might be forced to share sovereignty with other global actors to provide for their citizens, meet their obligations, and combat world issues. It will not be easy to convince nationalists that sharing sovereignty with nonstate actors is a good strategy.

Global Issues

In Chapters 6 through 10, we will turn to global issues, demonstrating the connections among state and nonstate actors in the international system, and consider how these global issues are inextricably linked. First, we consider global security and military power—that is, the traditional responsibility of countries to provide for the physical security of the state's territory. We also examine terrorism, including the various groups that use this method and the ways that countries have responded to both global and domestic threats. Chapter 7 discusses an emerging issue area of global politics: human rights and human security. The last three chapters examine the intersections of trade, finance, poverty, development, and environmental issues. Each of these topics overlaps with the others, and it's important not to read these chapters merely in a straightforward fashion but also to review the information from previous chapters as you progress through your coursework.

WHAT'S YOUR WORLDVIEW?

Identity is a major issue in most societies. Do you identify with a particular ethnic community or a nation? Are you an active member of an NGO, like Amnesty International or Greenpeace International? How do these identities affect your responsibilities as a citizen of a nation-state?

The International Forum on Globalization

Formed in 1994, this is a research, advocacy, and action organization focused on the impacts of dominant economic and geopolitical policies. It is led by an international board of scholars and citizen-movement leaders from ten countries. IFG collaborates with environmental, social justice, and antimilitarism activists, seeking secure models of democracy and sustainability, locally and globally.

IFG convenes private strategic seminars, large public education events, and "teach-ins" and publishes books and reports. It has also generated effective public protest actions, as in Seattle in 1999 against the WTO. Current campaigns focus on the rapidly growing inequities and "plutocratic controls" of global economic policies and practices. This research organization offers a variety of unpaid internships. If you are concerned about issues of social justice and environmental justice, this may be an organization that you might want to work with in the future. You might develop some real political economy research skills.

Theory A proposed explanation of an event or behavior of an actor in the real world. Definitions range from "an unproven assumption" to "a working hypothesis that proposes an explanation for an action or behavior." In international relations, we have intuitive theories, empirical theories, and normative theories.

Theories of Global Politics

The basic problem facing anyone who tries to understand contemporary global politics is that there's so much material to look at that it's difficult to know which things matter and which do not. Where would you start if you wanted to explain the most important global political processes? How, for example, would you explain the US decision to use military force to support rebels in Syria? Why did Russia counter with its own military force to support the current Syrian government? How will the world respond to the challenges created by climate change? What impact will the trade war between the United States and China have on the global economy? Why are the number of extremist groups and the use of violence on the rise? Is this violence the result of failed states or a failure of leadership? Questions such as these seem impossible to answer definitively. Whether we are aware of it or not, whenever we are faced with such questions, we have to resort to **theories** to understand them and to develop effective responses.

Mexico made a deal with the US government to reduce the flow of migrants to the United States. If they refused to act, the United States threatened to impose tariffs on all Mexican exports. Migrants line up every day to find a way to live and work in the United States. A Kantian would support the free flow of people, goods, services, and ideas, and thus, the movement of people would not be illegal. What do you think?

What Are Theories?

A theory is not some grand formal model with hypotheses and assumptions. Rather, *a theory is*

Tradition In international relations, a way of thinking that describes the nature of international politics. Such traditions include Machiavellian, Grotian, Kantian, and Marxism as a critical theory.

Machiavellian tradition A tradition in international relations theory named for Niccolò Machiavelli that characterizes the international system as anarchic; states are constantly in conflict and pursue their own interests as they see fit.

Grotian tradition A liberal tradition in international relations theory named for Hugo Grotius that emphasizes the rule of law and multilateral cooperation. Grotians believe the international system is not anarchic, but interdependent: A society of states is created in part by international law, treaties, alliances, and diplomacy, which states are bound by and ought to uphold.

Kantian tradition A revolutionary tradition in international relations theory named for Immanuel Kant that emphasizes human interests over state interests.

Prescription Recommendations for state survival in the international system based on international relations traditions.

Idealism Referred to by realists as utopianism since it underestimates the logic of power politics and the constraints this imposes on political action. Idealism as a substantive theory of international relations is generally associated with the claim that it is possible to create a world of peace based on the rule of law.

a kind of simplifying device that allows you to decide which facts matter and which do not. A good analogy is sunglasses with different-colored lenses. Put on a red pair and the world looks red; put on a yellow pair and it looks yellow. The world is not any different; it just looks different. So it is with theories. In the sections that follow we will briefly mention the main theoretical views that have dominated the study of global politics to give you an idea of the colors they paint the world. But before we do, please note that we do not think of theory as merely an option. It is not as if you can avoid theory and instead look directly at the facts. This is impossible because the only way you can decide which of the millions of possible facts to look at is by adhering to some theory that tells you which ones matter the most.

You may not even be aware of your theory. It may just be the view of the world you have inherited from family, a group of friends, or the media. It may just seem to be common sense to you and not anything complicated like a theory. But your theoretical assumptions are implicit (implied though not plainly expressed) rather than explicit (stated clearly and in detail), and we prefer to be as explicit as possible when it comes to thinking about global politics.

Theoretical Traditions in International Relations

Martin Wight (1913–1972), one of the founding scholars in the English School of international relations, introduced his students to three **traditions** in international relations theory: **Machiavellian** (named for the Italian Renaissance politician, philosopher, and writer Niccolò Machiavelli), **Grotian** (after Dutch jurist Hugo Grotius), and **Kantian** (named for German philosopher Immanuel Kant). We might also add Marxism, which falls under a critical tradition, meaning it is a theory that advocates a transformation of the existing system. Each tradition describes the "nature of international politics," according to its adherents, which informs policy **prescriptions** for state survival in the international system. For Machiavellians, the international system is anarchic and states are constantly in conflict: States pursue their own interests as they see fit and systems of law and diplomacy cannot prevent future wars. The Machiavellian tradition describes the most pessimistic shade of realism, which is discussed in the following section. It is important to note that not all realists embrace such a negative view of human relations or accept the best description of international politics as a "war of all against all."

The Grotian tradition focuses on law and order. For Grotians, the international system is not anarchic. Instead, political and economic exchanges result in an interdependent society of states, created in part by international law, treaties, alliances, and diplomacy. Grotians recognize that no central authority governs international society, and that conflict and cooperation can both occur. Nevertheless, states are bound by legal and moral constraints they themselves intentionally embed in the international institutions they create. Since all states benefit from the order provided by this rule-based society, they are morally obligated to uphold it.

Kantians, on the other hand, argue that human, not state, interactions properly define international relations; therefore, the latter should promote individual well-being and protect the community of humankind. For many modern-day Kantians, the state system preferred by Machiavellians and Grotians actually causes most global problems, conflict, and violence.

The Marxist tradition is a transformational view that recognizes that the structure of the international system as it exists today creates structural violence. What this means is that the structure of the system prevents full participation by all citizens and actually denies these citizens access to resources and opportunities. To Marxists, globalization is a "race to the bottom" or the constant search for cheap labor and minimal rules that protect people and the environment. Marxist seek a system change that is emancipatory, providing economic and political rights to all and responding to what Professor Castells called the crisis of equity.

Wight recognized that his traditions were ideal types and that there were many "subdivisions" in each. As students of international relations, we must recognize that most leaders borrow their ideas for policy from several traditions, but Machiavellian realism and Grotian liberalism are the dominant perspectives among world leaders.

Normative theory The systematic analyses of the ethical, moral, and political principles that either govern or ought to govern the organization or conduct of global politics; the belief that theories should be concerned with what ought to be rather than merely diagnosing what is.

The Rise of Realism

People have tried to make sense of world politics for centuries, especially since the separate academic discipline of international politics was formed in 1919, when the Department of International Politics was set up at the University of Wales, Aberystwyth. The man who established that department, a Welsh industrialist named David Davies, saw its purpose as to help prevent war. By studying international politics scientifically, many scholars believed they could find the causes of the world's main political problems and put forward solutions to help politicians solve them. After the end of World War I, the discipline was marked by this commitment to changing the world, and a number of antiwar organizations embraced this **idealism**. We call such a position **normative**, as its proponents concerned themselves with what *ought to be*.

Realism A theoretical approach that analyzes all international relations as the relation of states engaged in the pursuit of power. Realists see the international system as anarchic, or without a common power, and they believe conflict is endemic in the international system.

Opponents of this normative position characterized it as overly idealistic in that it focused on means of preventing war and even making war and violence obsolete. They adopted a theory they called **realism**, which emphasized seeing the world as it really is rather than how we would like it to be. The world as seen by realists is not a very pleasant place; human beings are at best oriented toward their own self-interest and probably much worse. To them, notions such as the perfectibility of human beings and the possibility of an improvement of world politics seem

Chinese and Pakistani soldiers admire Russian military hardware at the Chebarkul training center in Russia's Chelyabinsk Region. These soldiers were participating in the final stage of the joint counterterrorism exercise Peace Mission 2018 involving member-states of the Shanghai Cooperation Organization. Both Russia and China are increasing their military strength and asserting themselves around the world. Do you see this as a challenge to the liberal world order supported by the US military?

Liberalism A theoretical approach that argues for human rights, parliamentary democracy, and free trade—while also maintaining that all such goals must begin *within a state*.

Marxism A theory critical of the status quo, or dominant capitalist paradigm. It is a critique of the capitalist political economy from the view of the revolutionary proletariat, or workers. Marxists' ideal is a stateless and classless society.

Constructivism An approach to international politics that concerns itself with the centrality of ideas and human consciousness. As constructivists have examined global politics, they have been broadly interested in how the structure constructs the actors' identities and interests, how their interactions are organized and constrained by that structure, and how their very interaction serves to either reproduce or transform that structure.

Feminism A political project to understand and to end women's inequality and oppression. Feminist theories tend to be critical of the biases of the discipline. Many feminists focus their research on the areas where women are excluded from the analysis of major international issues and concerns.

Interparadigm debate The debate between the main theoretical approaches in the field of global politics.

far-fetched. This debate between idealism and realism has continued to the present day, but it is fair to say that realism has tended to have the upper hand. It appears to accord more with common sense than does idealism, especially when the media bombard us daily with images of how awful humans can be to one another.

Having said this, we would like you to think about whether such a realist view is as neutral as it may seem commonsensical. After all, if we teach global politics to generations of students and tell them that people are selfish, then doesn't that become common sense? And don't they simply repeat what they have been taught when they go off into the media, when they go to work for the government or the military, or when they talk to their children at the dinner table and, if in positions of power, act accordingly? This may be why political leaders find it so important to control the story that gives a situation meaning. We will leave you to think about this. For now, we would like to keep the issue open and point out that we are not convinced that realism is as objective or nonnormative as it is often portrayed.

Rival Theories

Although realism has been the dominant way of explaining global politics in the last nearly one hundred years, it is not the only way. In Chapter 3, we will examine not only realism but also its main rival, **liberalism**, which is a broad category that actually includes Grotian and Kantian traditions and critical approaches such as **Marxism**, **constructivism**, **feminist theory**, and utopian views. Both realism and liberalism are considered mainstream or traditional theories. We use the word *critical* to identify theories or approaches that critique traditional theories—that advocate transforming the present global system and creating an alternative system.

In the 1980s, it became common to talk of an **interparadigm debate** among realism, liberalism, and Marxism; that is, these three major theories (designated **paradigms** by influential philosopher of natural science Thomas Kuhn) were in competition, and the truth about global politics lay in the debate among them. At first glance, each seems to be particularly good at explaining certain aspects of global politics, and an obvious temptation is to try to combine them into some overall account. But this is not the easy option it may seem. These three theories, along with the more recently influential constructivism, are not so much different views of the same world as *four views of different worlds*.

Let us examine this claim more closely. It is clear that each of these four broad theoretical traditions focuses on different aspects of global politics (realism on the power relations among states, liberalism on a much wider set of interactions among states and nonstate actors, Marxist theory on the patterns of the world economy, and constructivism on the ways ideas and values shape our image of the world). However, each is saying more than this. Each view claims that it is picking out the most important features of global politics and that it offers a better account than the rival theories. Thus, the four approaches are really in competition with one another, and while you can certainly choose among them, it is not so easy to add bits from one to the others. For example, if you are a Marxist theorist, you think state behavior is ultimately determined by class forces—forces that the realist does not think affect state behavior. Similarly, constructivism suggests that actors do not face a world that is fixed but rather one that they can in principle change—in direct contrast to the core beliefs of realists and Marxists alike. That is, these four theories are really versions of what global politics is like rather than partial pictures of it. They do not agree on what global politics is fundamentally all about.

We should note that most scholars view constructivism, which has become increasingly influential since the 1990s, as a critical *approach* to studying international relations rather than a *theory*. Nick Onuf, a key constructivist scholar, has stated that constructivism is not a theory but a way of studying social relations. We like the way Michael Barnett (2011) compares constructivism with rational choice theory. Rational choice theory is a social theory suggesting that all actors act with fixed preferences, which are to always maximize benefits and minimize costs (see Table 1.1). Constructivism is also a social theory that is concerned with the relationship between agents and structures and the importance of ideas. From Barnett's view, constructivism is not a substantive theory; that is, it does not have common views about states, the international system, and human behavior, as realism and liberalism do.

We do not think any one of these theoretical perspectives has all the answers when it comes to explaining world politics in an era of globalization. In fact, each sees globalization differently. We do not want to tell you which theory

Research approaches help us explain the Obama administration's decision to pursue and eventually kill Osama bin Laden. How would historians, social scientists, and constructivists explain and describe this decision? Which makes more sense to you?

Paradigm A model or example. In the case of international relations theory, the term is a rough synonym for "academic perspective." A paradigm provides the basis for a theory, describing what is real and significant in a given area so that we can select appropriate research questions.

TABLE 1.1	**Decision Makers: Rationality and Politics**

Rational choice: An economic principle that assumes that individuals always make prudent and logical decisions that provide them with the greatest benefit or satisfaction and that are in their highest self-interest.

Bounded rationality: Decision makers do not always have the ability and information to make a rational decision or one that is optimal. Instead, they first simplify the list of choices available and then apply rationality. Thus, instead of value maximizing, the decision maker is value satisficing. Herbert Simon, who proposed this model, suggested that people are only partly rational and emotions, values, and previous experiences may help shape the decision.

Prospect theory: Involves risk aversion and risk acceptance. Decision makers in an environment of gain will avoid risky options and those in an environment of losses will accept risky options.

Poliheuristic theory: A two-stage analysis in which decision makers first eliminate choices based on cognitive shortcuts and then subject the remaining choices to rational processing.

seems best, since the purpose of this book is to give you a variety of conceptual lenses. By the end of the book, we hope you will work out which of these theories (if any) best explains globalization and other elements of global politics. However, we want to reinforce here our earlier comment that theories do not portray "the" truth. The theories see globalization differently because they presume what is most important in global politics. There is no answer as to which theory has the "truest" or "most correct" view of globalization or any other aspect of global politics.

▶ Research Approaches: Historical, Social Scientific, and Constructivist

As curious individuals, we are all interested in understanding the nature of global politics and the behavior of different actors in this global society. Two of the more traditional ways of doing research are the historical and social scientific approaches. A less traditional method of understanding the world is the constructivist approach. These three research approaches, in combination with theories, help us explain and understand decisions and events in global politics.

The Historical Approach

Historians arrive at an understanding of why states take certain actions, or why events happen, after careful review of public documents, memoirs, and interviews with key actors. Their goal is to understand a particular decision or event and create a thorough description or narrative that helps us understand decisions that key actors made. The goal is not to understand all wars or all actions by states but to create a history of a particular war or a very thorough description of a country's decision to take a certain policy position.

The Social Scientific Approach: Levels of Analysis

The intellectual interests of social scientists are slightly different. Social scientists want to bring the precision and certainty of the natural sciences to the social world. Uncomfortable with the subjectivity and ambiguity of many historical accounts, social scientists develop hypotheses based on dependent (Y) and independent (X) variables (e.g., "if X, then Y"); they then test and confirm these hypotheses or revise and refine them until they are accurate. They seek to explain international relations behavior, predict what others may do in similar situations, and develop a list of policy options or prescriptions for relevant policymakers. Research, then, is the search for the independent variable. For example, how do we explain a nation-state's allocation of development assistance or foreign aid? We know the amount of development assistance (dependent variable), but we now must find the independent variable that might explain this allocation. Many social scientists are focusing on big data and are using very sophisticated computer languages and analytical tools to understand how these data can be used to explain human behavior.

Independent variables reside in one of four **levels of analysis** (which we will discuss in greater depth in Chapter 4):

- **Individual/Human Dimension**: This level explores the range of variables that can affect leaders' policy choices and implementation strategies. Current research reveals that individuals matter, particularly in the midst of crises, when decisions require secrecy and/or involve only a few actors, or when time is of the essence. The influence of individuals increases when they have a great deal of latitude to make decisions and when they have expertise and a keen interest in foreign policy.
- **Domestic Sources or National Attributes**: Factors at this level include a state's history, traditions, and political, economic, cultural, and social structures, as well as military power, economic wealth, and demographics, and more permanent elements like geographic location and resource base.
- **Systemic Factors**: To most realists, the anarchic nature of international relations may be the most important factor at this level. However, the individual and collective actions states have taken to cope with anarchy via treaties, alliances, and trade conventions—formal contracts created by states in an attempt to provide order—also constitute significant systemic factors. More informal constraints based on traditions, common goals, and shared norms shape state behavior as well. For example, most states respect the sovereignty of all states and follow the rule of international law because they expect others to do the same. This notion of reciprocity is the primary incentive for states to support a rule-based international system. Finally, distribution of power in the system (e.g., bipolar, multipolar) and the nature of order (e.g., balance of power, collective security) are also important systemic factors. Remember, the international system is created by the interaction of states and other powerful actors like international and regional organizations.
- **Global Factors**: Often confused with system-level factors, global-level variables challenge notions of boundaries and sovereignty. The processes that define globalization are multidimensional and originate from multiple levels. Globalization and its economic, political, cultural, and social dimensions derive from decisions made or actions taken by individuals, states, and international and regional organizations or other nonstate actors, but they are seldom traceable to the actions of any one state or even a group of states. A technological innovation (e.g., the internet and the information revolution) that diffuses through the system affecting everyone but that does not belong to any single actor is an obvious example. The movement of capital by multinational banks, the broadcasts of CNN, and the revolutionary ideas of religious fundamentalists all represent global factors that shape policy behavior. Natural conditions such as environmental degradation, pandemics (AIDS, severe acute respiratory syndrome [SARS], and the flu), and weather patterns also affect foreign policy. Consider, for example, how global climate change and resulting changes in weather patterns might result in excessive rain or

Individual/human dimension This level of analysis explores the range of variables that can affect leaders' policy choices and implementation strategies. Belief systems, personality factors, and other psychological factors often influence decision-making.

Domestic sources or national attributes Factors at this level include a state's history, traditions, and political, economic, cultural, and social structures, as well as military power, economic wealth, and demographics, and more permanent elements like geographic location and resource base.

Systemic factors To most realists, the anarchic nature of international relations may be the most important factor at this level. However, the individual and collective actions states have taken to cope with anarchy via treaties, alliances, and trade conventions—formal contracts created by states in an attempt to provide order— also constitute significant systemic factors.

Global factors Often confused with system-level factors, global-level variables challenge notions of boundaries and sovereignty. The processes that define globalization are multidimensional and originate from multiple levels. Globalization and its economic, political, cultural, and social dimensions derive from decisions made or actions taken by individuals, states, and international and regional organizations or other nonstate actors, but they are seldom traceable to the actions of any one state or even a group of states.

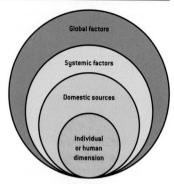

Levels of Analysis.

In the study of global politics, there are four levels of analysis. Some scholars would say there are only three levels, but the authors of this book make a distinction between *systemic* (or international) factors and *global* factors. What is the argument for this distinction?

the opposite, a drought. Might these conditions influence a country's trade policies? Will a country now need to import food and establish trade relations with other food-producing states? Climate is a global factor that may have an impact on the globalization process.

What is exciting about research in our field is that there is always disagreement about which variables explain the most. The strength of any one argument is based on the quality of the empirical evidence collected to support the hypothesis being tested. Since we are not lab scientists, we cannot conduct experiments with control groups to test our propositions. Instead, we look to the work of historians, public-policy records, government documents, interviews, budgets, and journalists' accounts to gather evidence to confirm or reject hypotheses.

The level chosen as a source for an independent variable depends on the situation you wish to examine, the availability of data or evidence, your research skills and interests, and, finally, your creativity and imagination. Each level is like a drawer in a toolbox; the analytic approaches or variables at each level are the tools that the researcher uses to develop and explore the explanatory power of three kinds of hypotheses: (1) causal hypotheses: if it rains, it will flood; (2) relational hypotheses: if it rains, flooding in certain geologic and geographic areas will worsen; and (3) impact hypotheses: if it rains more than *n* amount, the flooding will be particularly severe.

None of this is new. Both the ancient Greek historian Thucydides and the Enlightenment philosopher Immanuel Kant indirectly discussed levels of analysis in their efforts to explain state behavior. Thucydides focused on the explanatory potential of power capabilities and even suggested that the distribution of power in the international system influenced a state's behavior. Kant referred to the first three levels of analysis when he suggested that nation-states could avoid war by eliminating standing armies, managing the self-interests of rival leaders, and finding ways to provide order in the international system.

The Constructivist Approach

Constructivists question the underlying assumptions supporting historical and social scientific approaches to understanding international relations. Instead, these scholars postulate that there is no single historical narrative. Rather, the interests of specific actors shape the story, and it is their control of that story that gives them power. No perspective offers the truth because words, meanings, symbols, and identities are subjective and are used by individuals, groups, and society to gain and maintain power.

Further, constructivists argue that all of us interpret events and global conditions according to our beliefs, interests, values, and goals. We are not free to do anything we want in any given situation; instead, we are handed a menu reflective of the dominant interests and goals of powerful groups within a state or in the international system. There are a number of studies that try to explain and understand the behavior of nation-states by looking at the beliefs and meanings held by political elites who make foreign policy.

▶ Dimensions of Globalization

As we have said, our goal in this book is to offer an overview of world politics in a globalized era. A globalized world is one in which political, economic, cultural, and social events become more and more interconnected and also one in which they have more impact. That is, societies are affected more extensively and more deeply by events of other societies. These events can conveniently be divided into three types: social, economic, and political. In each case, the world seems to be shrinking, and people are increasingly aware of this. The internet and the vast variety of social media outlets, including the Dark Web, is the most graphic example, since it allows you to sit at home and have instant communication with websites around the world. E-mail has also transformed communications in a way that the authors of this book would not have envisaged twenty years ago.

But these are only the most obvious examples. Others include worldwide television communications, podcasts, global newspapers, global production of goods, global franchises such as Apple computers and phones and Facebook, and risks such as climate change and nuclear proliferation. It is this pattern of events that seems to have changed the nature of world politics from what it was just a few years ago. The important point is not only that the world has changed but also that the changes are qualitative and not merely quantitative; a strong case can be made that a new world political system has emerged as a result of globalization.

Having noted this, we want to point out that globalization is not some entirely new phenomenon in world history. Indeed, as we will examine later on, many argue that it is merely a new name for a long-term feature. We leave it to you to judge whether in its current manifestation it represents a new phase in world history or merely a continuation of processes that have been around for a long time, but we do want to note that there have been several precursors to globalization. Hence, looking beyond this quick history of globalization that follows, in Chapter 2 we will also present more detailed examples of previous international orders.

Our final task in this introductory chapter is to offer a summary of the main arguments for and against globalization as a distinct new phase in world politics. We do not expect you to decide where you stand on the issue at this stage, but keep this information in mind as you read the rest of this book. The main arguments in favor of globalization representing a new era of world politics are the following:

1. *The pace of economic transformation is so great that it has created a new world of politics.* States are no longer closed units; they cannot fully control their own economies. The global economy is more interdependent than ever, with trade and finances ever expanding.

Global polity The collective structures and processes by which "interests are articulated and aggregated, decisions are made, values allocated and policies conducted through international or transnational political processes" (Ougaard 2004, 5).

Cosmopolitan culture A pattern of relations within which people share the same goals and aspirations, generally to improve that culture for all members.

Risk culture A pattern of relations within which people share the same perils.

2. *Social media and communications have fundamentally revolutionized the way we deal with the rest of the world.* Now events on one side of the world can be immediately observed on the other side. Electronic communications are also converging and thus altering our notions of the social groups we work with and live in. For example, consider how the Arab Spring events in Tunisia and Egypt and the revolution in Libya were influenced by social networking tools. One might also consider how the image of the United States in the world is influenced by President Trump's use of his Twitter account to communicate with the world.

3. *There is now, more than ever before, a global culture* such that most urban areas resemble one another. The urban world shares a common culture, much of it emanating from Hollywood and shaped by a global consumer culture.

4. *The world is becoming more homogeneous in some material and ideational areas.* Differences in political and economic thinking among people are diminishing. The desire for democracy is still mostly universal, and capitalism is still a dominant economic strategy, but currently nationalism and even authoritarianism are on the rise in many states.

5. *Time and space seem to be collapsing.* Our old ideas of geography and chronology are undermined by the speed of modern communications and media.

6. *A* **global polity** *is emerging*, with transnational social and political movements and the beginnings of a transfer of allegiance from the state to substate, transnational, and international bodies. Global governance has become an important part of managing globalization.

7. *A* **cosmopolitan culture** *is developing.* People are beginning to "think globally and act locally."

8. *A* **risk culture** *is emerging.* People realize both that the main risks that face them are global (e.g., climate change and pandemics) and that states are unable to deal with the problems without some form of cooperation and the creation of multilateral processes of decision making.

Local citizens pray at a makeshift memorial for the victims of the August 2019 mass shooting at a shopping complex in El Paso, Texas. The El Paso massacre is the latest attack in which the gunman praised the March shootings in Christchurch, New Zealand, where an Australian white supremacist is charged with killing fifty-one worshippers at two mosques. Hatred and ignorance are easily spread by various social media outlets. Is the speed by which information—good and bad—flows around the world a good or bad thing? Should it be managed by states or other actors in the system? If not controlled, how might it influence global politics?

However, just as there are powerful reasons for seeing globalization as a new stage in world politics, often allied to the view that globalization is progressive—that is, it improves the lives of people—there are also arguments that suggest the opposite. Some of the main ones are as follows:

1. One obvious objection to the globalization thesis is that it is *merely a buzzword to denote the latest phase of capitalism.* In a very powerful

critique of globalization theory, Hirst and Thompson (1996) argue that one effect of the globalization thesis is that it makes it appear as if national governments are powerless in the face of global trends. This ends up paralyzing governmental attempts to subject global economic forces to control and regulation. Believing that most globalization theory lacks historical depth, they point out that it paints the current situation as *more special than it is* and also as more firmly entrenched than it might in fact be. Current trends may be reversible. They conclude that the more extreme versions of globalization are "a myth," and they support this claim with five main conclusions from their study of the contemporary world economy (1996, 2–3). First, the present internationalized economy is not unique in history. In some respects, they say, it is less open than the international economy was between 1870 and 1914. Second, they find that genuinely transnational companies are relatively rare; most are national companies trading internationally. There is no trend toward the development of international companies. Third, there is no shift of finance and capital from the developed to the underdeveloped worlds. Direct investment is highly concentrated among the countries of the developed world. Fourth, the world economy is not global; rather, trade, investment, and financial flows are concentrated in and among three blocs—Europe, North America, and Asia. Finally, they argue that this group of three blocs could, if they coordinated policies, regulate global economic markets and forces. Note that Hirst and Thompson are looking only at economic theories of globalization, and many of the main accounts deal with factors such as communications and culture more than economics. Nonetheless, theirs is a very powerful critique of one of the main planks of the more extreme globalization thesis, with their central criticism that seeing the global economy as something beyond our control both misleads us and prevents us from developing policies to control the national economy.

2. Another obvious objection is that globalization is very *uneven in its effects*. At times, it sounds very much like a Western theory applicable only to a small part of humankind. To pretend that even a small minority of the world's population can connect to the World Wide Web is clearly an exaggeration, when in reality most people on the planet have probably never made a telephone call in their lives. Thus, certain aspects of globalization apply primarily to the developed world. We are in danger of overestimating globalization's extent and depth.

3. A related objection is that globalization may be *the latest stage of Western imperialism*. It is the old modernization theory (a controversial theory that suggests nation-states move naturally from traditional societies that are rural and agricultural to modern societies that are complex, urban, and industrial) in a new guise. The forces that are being globalized are conveniently those found in the Western world. What about non-Western values? Where do they fit in to this emerging global world? The worry is that they do not fit in at all, and what is celebrated in globalization is the triumph of a Western worldview at the expense of the worldviews of other cultures.

4. Critics have also noted that there are *people who have much to lose* as the world becomes more globalized. This is because globalization represents the

Global Production and the iPhone

BACKGROUND

Apple uses several different global manufacturers to build the iPhone. Take a closer look at any of its components and you will see just how global the iPhone manufacturing process truly is. In the iPhone 6s and 6s Plus, the central A series microchip, which makes the smartphone run, is made by two suppliers: the Taiwan Semiconductor Manufacturing Company and Samsung, a South Korean multinational company. InvenSense, a San Jose, California–based company, designed the iPhone's gyroscope, which makes the screen rotate between portrait and landscape mode. Japanese multinational corporation Sony supplies the image sensor for the front and back cameras, and another Japanese company, Toshiba, supplies storage, as does SK Hynix of South Korea. These components and more come together in factories in mainland China where the iPhone is assembled.

THE CASE

Relative to Western standards, in China working conditions are poor and wages are low: Workers typically live in dormitories and work up to twelve hours a day. Nevertheless, such factories help to reduce rural poverty by employing large numbers of workers. Apple executives argue that outsourcing to countries such as China and Taiwan is crucial to the development of the company and its innovation. Not only is labor cheaper but also "the vast scale of overseas factories as well as the flexibility, diligence and industrial skills of foreign workers have so outpaced their American counterparts that 'Made in the U.S.A.' is no longer a viable option for most Apple products." The assembly of iPhones in China continues during the trade war with China. There are some concerns that prices may increase because of tariffs and that Apple's sales may decrease in the United States and even in China. The trade war represents an economic nationalist battle between the United States and China. It may also indicate a battle between state capitalism practiced by China and the liberal free trade system created by the US that has operated successfully for over seventy years. Neo-mercantilism involves protecting national industries and constraining the free flow of goods and services that a free-trade system promotes. In the past, protectionist policies have contributed to major conflicts, including the two world wars. We may not be headed for a major war, but any conflict between two major powers like China and the United States is never a good thing.

OUTCOME

Trade wars may continue, but Apple seems to have been only slightly hurt. Since the first iPhone launched in 2007, it has become a major revenue driver for Apple, which is the largest public company in the world: As of 2018, it is a trillion-dollar company. In the first quarter of 2019, Apple's income was $84.3 billion. Those who own shares in Apple have benefited immensely from the globalization of the iPhone.

For Discussion

1. Many people are what we call economic nationalists—they support policies and practices that help keep jobs in their home country. How much more would you be willing to pay for your iPhone if it were made in your country? Is where it's manufactured at all important to you? Why or why not?

2. Some critics of globalization suggest that it allows companies to search for the lowest common denominator, meaning low wages, no labor or safety laws, and no environmental standards. Without these constraints, profits can be quite high. Should consumers consider these factors before buying products? Should there be global standards for wages, worker safety, and protection of the environment? Why or why not?

3. Most global production takes advantage of each country's comparative strengths or assets, and the result is a great product at a good price. Is this not how capitalism should work? Explain.

SOURCES

Charles Duhigg and Keith Bradsher, "How the U.S. Lost Out on iPhone Work," *New York Times*, January 21, 2012, http://www.nytimes.com/2012/01/22/business/apple-america-and-a-squeezed-middle-class.html?hp.

Compare Camp, "How & Where iPhone Is Made: Comparison of Apple's Manufacturing Process," September 17, 2014, http://comparecamp.com/how-where-iphone-is-made-comparison-of-apples-manufacturing-process/.

CASE STUDY *continued*

Grace Huang, "Sony to Spend 45 Billion Yen to Boost Sensor Capacity," *Bloomberg Business*, April 7, 2015, http://www.bloomberg.com/news/articles/2015-04-07/sony-to-spend-45-billion-yen-to-boost-sensor-capacity.

Jordan Golson, "Apple's iPhone Chips Aren't as Different as Some Have Reported," October 13, 2015, http://www.techrepublic.com/article/apples-iphone-chips-arent-as-different-as-some-have-reported/.

Rupert Neate, "Apple Calls 2015 'Most Successful Year Ever' After Making Reported $234bn," *The Guardian*, October 27, 2015, http://www.theguardian.com/technology/2015/oct/27/apple-2015-revenue-iphone-sales.

World Bank, *Global Economic Prospects 2007: Managing the Next Wave of Globalization* (Washington, D.C.: World Bank, 2006), 118.

success of liberal capitalism in an economically divided world. Perhaps one outcome is that globalization allows the more efficient exploitation of less well-off states, and all in the name of openness. The technologies accompanying globalization are technologies that automatically benefit the richest economies in the world and allow their interests to override local economies. So not only is globalization imperialist, but also it is exploitative.

5. We also need to make the straightforward point that *not all globalized forces are necessarily good ones.* Globalization makes it easier for drug cartels and terrorists to operate, and the World Wide Web's anarchy raises crucial questions of censorship and preventing access to certain kinds of material. For example, globalization may also spread ideas that encourage violence, intolerance, and hate. Extremists share racist ideas in manifestos they share on the internet, and these words inspire others to use violence.

6. Turning to the so-called **global governance** aspects of globalization, the main worry here is about *responsibility.* To whom are the transnational social movements responsible and democratically accountable? If Microsoft or Shell becomes more and more powerful in the world, does this not raise the issue of how accountable it is to democratic control? David Held has made a strong case for the development of what he calls **cosmopolitan democracy** (1995), but this cosmopolitan democracy has clearly defined legal and democratic features. The concern is precisely that most of the emerging powerful actors in a globalized world are not accountable. This argument also applies to seemingly good global actors such as Oxfam and the World Wildlife Fund.

7. Finally, *there seems to be a* **paradox** *at the heart of the globalization thesis.* On the one hand, globalization is usually portrayed as the triumph of Western, market-led values. But how do we then explain the tremendous economic success that some national economies have had in the globalized world? Consider the economic success of China and India and the so-called Tigers of Asia, countries such as Singapore, Taiwan, Malaysia, and South Korea. These countries have enjoyed some of the highest growth rates in the international economy but subscribe to

Global governance The regulation and coordination of transnational issue areas by nation-states, international and regional organizations, and private agencies through the establishment of international regimes. These regimes may focus on problem solving or the simple enforcement of rules and regulations.

Cosmopolitan democracy A condition in which international organizations, transnational corporations, and global markets are accountable to the peoples of the world.

Paradox A seemingly absurd or self-contradictory statement that, when investigated or explained, may prove to be well founded or true.

Germany's Ursula von der Leyen, left, delivers her speech at the European Parliament in Strasbourg, eastern France, on July 16, 2019. von der Leyen outlined her vision and plans as the new EU Commission president. We do not have a global government, but regional organizations like the European Union do provide regional governance that promotes common interests and promotes democratic values and the rule of law. Is regional governance the way forward as we try to manage the processes of globalization?

very different views of the role of the state in managing the economy and the place of individual rights, privileges, political rights, and freedoms. The paradox, then, will be if these countries can continue to modernize so successfully without adopting many Western values. If they can, what does this do to one of the main themes of globalization—namely, the argument that globalization represents the spreading across the globe of a set of values? If these countries do continue to follow their own roads toward economic and social modernization, then we must anticipate future disputes between Western and non-Western values over issues like human rights, gender, and religion. The challenges to the liberal order are multiplying and are supported by Russia, China, India, and many leaders within Europe and even the United States.

We hope these arguments for and against the dominant way of representing globalization will cause you to think deeply about the utility of the concept in explaining contemporary world politics. The chapters that follow do not take a common stance *for* or *against* globalization. We will end by posing some questions that we would like you to keep in mind as you read the remaining chapters:

- Is globalization a *new* phenomenon in world politics?
- Which theory best explains the effects of globalization?
- Is globalization a positive or a negative development?
- Does globalization make the state obsolete?
- Does globalization make the world more or less democratic?
- Is globalization merely Western imperialism in a new guise?
- Does globalization make armed conflicts more or less likely?
- Last but not least, what will *your* role be in world politics? How will you choose to identify yourself and participate locally, nationally, and globally? Has globalization increased your opportunities to engage with the world?

Conclusion

We hope this introduction and the chapters that follow help you answer these questions. We also hope this book as a whole provides you with a good overview of the politics of the contemporary world.

We think it important to conclude this chapter by stressing that globalization clearly is a very complex phenomenon that is contradictory and difficult to comprehend. Just as the internet is a liberating force, it is also how those groups who seek to spread violence and hate communicate. Similarly, various media outlets can bring us live stories so that we understand more about the world. But global media provides a means of communicating very specific messages about the vulnerability of the countries targeted by extremists and ultimately a way of constructing the categories within which we reacted. Finally, maybe the most fundamental lesson of all this violence is that not all people in the world share a view of globalization as a progressive force in world politics. Those who attack our societies, including the 9/11 attack on the United States and the almost daily attacks in many developing countries, are rejecting, in part, the globalization-as-Westernization project. *Globalization is therefore not one thing.*

How we think about it will reflect not merely the theories we accept but also our own positions in this globalized world. In this sense, the ultimate paradox of these acts of violence

One of the biggest challenges world leaders face is ungoverned territory or failed states. Neighboring states or extremist movements often support competing factions. This fighter is from a militia known as the Security Belt, which is funded and armed by the United Arab Emirates. Yemen's civil war has been deadlocked for months, with neither side making major gains. At one of the most active front lines, militiamen backed by the Saudi-led coalition are dug in, exchanging shelling every night with Iranian-allied Houthi rebels only a few hundred meters away. Why should you or anyone interested in global politics care about this distant conflict?

The End of Liberal Dreams?

In an important new book, *The Great Delusion: Liberal Dreams and International Realities* (2018), University of Chicago professor John Mearsheimer makes a convincing argument that the liberal international order established by the United States after World War II has not worked. Mearsheimer states that what he calls "liberal hegemony" was "destined to fail." The goal of this liberal hegemony was to promote democracy and capitalism and to build and support international institutions that encourage multilateralism and are guided by international law. Professor Mearsheimer argues that any great power must be concerned with other great powers and cannot ignore realism and realist thinking and its focus on balance of power, security, and survival.

Liberalism is also challenged by nationalism and its emphasis on self-determination and the importance of maintaining sovereignty. Nationalists argue that foreign policy should be about securing national interests and limiting global activism.

Much of international relations is a battle of narratives or stories that tell us how to look at the world and are often the basis of policy decisions. Professor Mearsheimer makes the critical point that theory is "indispensable for understanding how the world works." We think that theories like realism and liberalism shape narratives and, in an interactive dance, narratives or stories may influence theory development and revisions. We all need to keep in mind that some of the narratives that are embraced by citizens and leaders are not based on evidence or experience. The reality they embrace may actually misuse theories and narratives to secure political or economic advantages.

With the United States withdrawing from many of its global commitments, including the support of the liberal order the United States established, and the rise of two authoritarian nationalist states in Russia and China, is the world looking at the end of liberal hegemony? What kind of system do the leaders of the great powers want to create and support?

and extremism is that the answers to questions such as what it was, what it meant, and how to respond to it may themselves ultimately depend on the social, cultural, economic, and political spaces we occupy in a globalized world. That is, world politics suddenly becomes very personal: How does your economic position, your ethnicity, your gender, your culture, or your religion determine what globalization means to you?

CONTRIBUTORS TO CHAPTER 1: *John Baylis, Anthony McGrew, Steve Smith, Steven L. Lamy, and John Masker*

KEY TERMS

Constructivism, p. 18
Cosmopolitan culture, p.24
Cosmopolitan
   democracy, p. 27
Domestic sources or
   national attributes, p. 21
Feminist theory, p. 18
G20, or Group of
   Twenty, p. 10
Global factors, p. 21
Global governance, p. 27
Globalization, p. 4

Global politics, p. 11
Global polity, p. 24
Governments, p. 11
Grotian, p. 16
Idealism, p. 17
Individual/human
   dimension, p. 21
International relations, p. 11
Interparadigm debate, p. 18
Kantian, p. 16
Levels of analysis, p. 21
Liberalism, p. 18

Machiavellian, p. 16
Marxism, p. 18
Multinational corporations
   (MNCs), p. 12
Nation, p. 13
Nation-state, p. 13
Nongovernmental
   organizations
   (NGOs), p. 11
Nonstate actors, p. 12
Normative, p. 17
Paradigms, p. 18

Paradox, p. 27
Prescriptions, p. 16
Realism, p. 17
Risk culture, p. 24
Sovereignty, p. 13
State, p. 13
Systemic factors, p. 21
Theories, p. 15
Traditions, p. 16
Transnational actors, p. 11

REVIEW QUESTIONS

1. Is globalization a new phenomenon in world politics?

2. In what ways are you linked to globalization?

3. How do ideas about globalization shape our understanding of the trend?

4. How can different levels of analysis lead to different explanations of the impact of globalization on global politics?

5. Why do theories matter?

6. International relations began as a problem-solving discipline in response to World War I. What are the global problems that now define our field of study?

Learn more with this chapter's digital tools, including the Oxford Insight Study Guide, at **www.oup.com/he/lamy6e**.

Why Should I Care?

In this chapter, we have discussed how forces of globalization shape all of our lives. We know that these forces of globalization influence nation-states, but how do they shape your life and the activities of your family and friends? How is your quality of life shaped by global factors that have created a global economy and a global consumer culture? How are your personal choices influenced by the actions of distant actors and economic, political, and cultural conditions pushed by globalization?

PART ONE: YOU AS A GLOBAL CONSUMER

Consider the following questions in small groups, with a focus on how you are linked in a web of interdependence that may shape the choices you make. Also understand that you are making choices in different sectors of global society. It is like playing chess on three or four different chessboards. You are making choices in the economic sector, political sector, and cultural sector. In turn, these choices affect social relations and have profound implications for the natural world, or the environmental sector.

1. With the iPhone case in mind, consider how many items in your daily commodity basket (the sum total of goods and services purchased in a given time frame) are not local and are imported from a foreign country.
2. Do you think dependency on foreign goods and services matters? How might your choices influence people in your community and people in distant lands?
3. Individuals, like countries, need to avoid situations where their choices create an unhealthy dependency on foreign goods and services. For example, a country's dependency on oil makes it vulnerable to corporations and countries that supply it. It is okay to depend on products, but you hope this dependency has low political and economic costs. For example, our dependency on oil makes us vulnerable because it is too hard to find a substitute. This is called *vulnerability interdependence*. But our dependency on good French wine can be replaced by a dependency on good Chilean or Australian wine. The cost of finding an alternative is low; thus, this is called *sensitivity interdependence*. These sensitivity situations are unavoidable in a global economy. Again, considering your lifestyle, are you in the vulnerability or sensitivity category? Is it easy to stay in the sensitivity category?

PART TWO: ASSESSING YOUR POLITICAL CONNECTIONS

1. The entire world changed with the terrorist attacks against the United States, Spain, the United Kingdom, and, recently, Paris and Beirut. How has global politics changed, and how have these changes affected you and your family?
2. Identify four international events that have occurred in the last six months that have had a direct impact on political life in your country. Be specific about how these events have changed the game of domestic politics.
3. What about leadership in this world of global politics? When you consider the impact of globalization and the complex issues we all face as citizens in rich and poor states, what skills and competencies do you think leaders need to be successful in securing the interests of their citizens and providing for world order?

WRITING ASSIGNMENT: MORAL INTERDEPENDENCY

We have become so interdependent economically and politically, but do we recognize our moral responsibility to people who are not our citizens? Do we have any responsibility for the impact of our foreign policy decisions on other countries? For example, in the pursuit of wealth and prosperity, we may trade for oil with authoritarian regimes that oppress their citizens. Are we also culpable? By providing that regime with financial resources, are we contributing to its reign of terror?

2 The Evolution of Global Politics

With the world divided among three great powers—China, Russia, and the United States—organizations like the G20 may become more important venues for discussion among great powers. The G20 is made up of nineteen countries plus the European Union. Saudi Arabia assumes the leadership of this organization as chair of its next summit in November 2020.

> *History repeats itself, first as tragedy, second as farce.*
>
> **—KARL MARX**

> *If history repeats itself, and the unexpected always happens, how incapable must Man be of learning from experience.*
>
> **—GEORGE BERNARD SHAW**

> *History never really says goodbye. History says, "See you later."*
>
> **—EDUARDO GALEANO**

All nation-states have goals that may be unstated but are essential for survival and influence in the global system. These goals include the following:

1. Maintain and protect the state's sovereignty.
2. Protect autonomy, which allows for both independence and flexibility.
3. Maintain existing levels of power and influence and work to increase both relative to other policy actors.
4. Secure representation in global and regional institutions and gain a voice in global policy formulation.

Most nation-states have think tanks or special task forces that explore possible future world scenarios. This is how states prepare for the uncertainty of global politics. In the United States, the National Intelligence Council publishes reports that provide a framework for thinking about the future by focusing on "critical trends and possible discontinuities," such as those in the areas of globalization, demography, and the environment. In one of their recent publications, *Global Trends 2030: Alternative Worlds* (2012), the authors discuss megatrends, game changers, and potential future worlds.

Among the megatrends is the *diffusion of power,* meaning that there will be no dominant world power and that power will shift to networks and coalitions of public and private actors. Another critical megatrend will be *increasing demands for food, water, and energy.* With climate change, scarcity may increase the competition for these resources. Thus, regional organizations, especially those covering a specific region or with specific functions like the Arctic Council, could prosper.

CHAPTER OUTLINE

Introduction 35

The Significance of the Peace of Westphalia 36

Revolutionary Wars 37

World Wars: Modern and Total 39

Legacies and Consequences of European Colonialism 43

Cold War 46

From the End of the Cold War to the War on Terrorism 54

Globalization: Challenging the International Order? 56

The War on Terrorism: From 9/11 to Iraq, Afghanistan, and Syria 69

Conclusion 73

FEATURES

THEORY IN PRACTICE Perception, Continuity, and Change After January 20, 2009 60

CASE STUDY The War That Never Ends 72

WHAT'S TRENDING? The End of Peace? 73

THINKING ABOUT GLOBAL POLITICS Understanding and Resolving International Conflicts 75

LEARNING OBJECTIVES

After reading and discussing this chapter, you should be able to:

Identify the European great powers of the eighteenth century, and list the defining characteristics of international politics in that era.

Outline the major changes in world politics resulting from the French Revolution and Napoleonic Wars.

Define the major developments in international relations during the nineteenth century, and identify the major powers of that period.

Compare and contrast the contending explanations for World Wars I and II.

Explain how the end of European colonization in Africa and Asia changed world politics.

Outline the effects of the end of the Cold War on global and regional politics.

Unfortunately, many policy efforts promoting multilateralism and sharing sovereignty are being challenged by nationalist leaders across the world.

Another trend is the increasing number of disputes among players in the *global economy* that threaten economic and political stability. Economic nationalism is on the rise, and global economic institutions created after World War II may need reform. The leaders of nation-states have worked for years to find ways to encourage cooperation and multilateralism and discourage economic nationalism and trade disputes. These disputes over trade rules or the control over scarce but vital resources have shaped diplomatic practices and, at times, military actions. States have used their power unilaterally to secure resources or protect their material interests. Other times, they have participated with other states to create multilateral systems of governance to manage trade and provide stability in all markets. These disputes and their resolution have shaped global politics for centuries. But, with the acceleration of technology, the increasing importance of social media and the significance of new challenges to the sovereignty and autonomy of nation-states make governing at any level more complex and difficult.

Sometimes, it's difficult to imagine how things might ever improve; other times, it's easy to get caught up in the moment, when something significant or strange occurs on the world stage. Yet each of the current global challenges discussed here and in Chapter 1 stems from a deeper world history, and knowing about these histories takes us a step closer to understanding global politics—past, present, and future.

Perhaps, despite the concerns about the future fueled by current crises, the international system has actually moved in a positive direction. After all, countries that were enemies in World War II and the Cold War—including France, Germany, and many of the former Soviet Union's allies in Eastern Europe—are today working together to bring economic prosperity to the world as members of the European Union. The accumulation of human history—political change, economic progress, medical breakthroughs, the lives of ordinary people—is part of the fabric of struggle and cooperation, strife and comity.

Our goal in this chapter is to demonstrate, briefly, how the international system, and in some ways the global society, has evolved during the last four hundred years. It is, of course, not possible to cover all of international political history in one chapter. Therefore, our attention here will be primarily on significant political events; in other chapters, we will discuss social and economic trends.

▶ Introduction

The history of international relations did not begin in 1648, but as we'll explain, it's a good place to begin our story. Kingdoms, empires, city-states, and nation-states have for centuries interacted in the same kinds of patterns that emerged after the end of the Thirty Years' War (1618–1648).

In China, Africa, India, and ancient Greece, political units of various sizes had engaged in economic relations, exchanged ambassadors, and fought wars for centuries prior. And globalization is not a new phenomenon; it dates back to the premodern era, when the Silk Road constituted one of the first overland and transcontinental trade routes, connecting eastern, southern, and western Asia with the Mediterranean and European world. Similarly, early maritime trade routes, particularly the Indian Ocean trade route, played an important part in east-to-west exchanges of culture, language, and goods, all the way from the Roman period to the seventeenth century.

But we choose to begin with 1648 because an event during that year represents a major dividing line in history: The Peace of Westphalia, which ended the Thirty Years' War, established the principle of sovereignty. Crucial in delimiting the political rights and authority of monarchs, it added significantly to the developing template for the international system, now referred to as the "globalized system," that is a theme of this book: arrangements for governance, human rights, and economics that form the basis of the contemporary world.

In this chapter, we will discuss wars and political upheavals. It is a sweeping tale, covering the American and French Revolutions, two world wars, the end of European colonization of Africa and Asia, the Cold War and the changes in the international political system that followed its end, and the terrorist attacks of the early and mid-2000s. Our goal is to provide some background, or context, for you to understand how states make foreign policy and how they organize to govern the global system (Chapter 4 and 5), as well as the topics that we will examine in depth in Chapters 6 through 10.

After reading and discussing this chapter, you should have a better understanding of the origins of the modern international system. This is primarily a Western, Eurocentric system—one that spread even as former empires tried to contain European expansion. You will also have a better understanding of the Cold War and its effects on the world. Some have called the Cold War "World War III," as it was a global ideological battle for the hearts and minds of all peoples. If it was a war about two contending rule books—one being the US or Western view of capitalism and democratic governance and the other being the Soviet brand of socialism and authoritarian government—is the post–Cold War crisis about how to apply the Western rules? Some authorities have suggested that the current global war on terrorism is actually World War IV. This chapter encourages you to explore various dimensions of the US-led war on terrorism that is now centered on Afghanistan, Pakistan, Syria, Iraq, Yemen, and Libya and in several other African countries. These are not just wars on terrorism but they represent the

Protestant Reformation
A social and political movement begun in 1517 in reaction to the widespread perception that the Catholic Church had become corrupt and had lost its moral compass.

Thirty Years' War (1618–1648)
The last of the great wars in Europe fought nominally for religion.

Peace of Westphalia (1648) A series of treaties that ended the Thirty Years' War and was crucial in delimiting the political rights and authority of European monarchs.

Sovereign equality The idea that all countries have the same rights, including the right of noninterference in their internal affairs.

Society of states An association of sovereign states based on their common interests, values, and norms.

Balance of power In the international system, a state of affairs in which there is parity and stability among competing forces, and no one state is sufficiently strong to dominate all the others. Realists believe that a balance of power among great powers is the only way to provide global stability.

Peace of Utrecht (1713) The agreement that ended the War of the Spanish Succession and helped to consolidate the link between sovereign authority and territorial boundaries in Europe. This treaty refined the territorial scope of sovereign rights of states.

challenge faced in trying to find stability in ungoverned territories. In most of these regions, the Western idea of the nation-state has failed.

Most important, you'll gain a sense that history matters because it shapes political institutions and influences how leaders make decisions. Leaders in situations of uncertainty often refer to lessons from historical events. Analogical reasoning, or learning from history, is an important element of decision making in our complex international environment.

▶ The Significance of the Peace of Westphalia

When Martin Luther nailed his Ninety-Five Theses to the door of the cathedral in Wittenberg, Germany, in 1517, he launched more than the **Protestant Reformation**. For the next century, monarchs across Europe found in religion a justification to begin wars that were actually about politics and economics. The **Thirty Years' War** (1618–1648) was the last of these religious conflicts in Europe and ostensibly began over a disagreement about the right of political leaders to choose a state religion. The opponents—including at various times Denmark, France, Austria, Sweden, Spain, and the principalities of the Holy Roman Empire—conducted most of their operations in Germany, killing tens of thousands of soldiers and civilians and devastating cities and farmland.

The **Peace of Westphalia** in 1648 not only ended this catastrophic conflict but also ushered in the contemporary international system by establishing the principle of sovereignty (a state's control and authority over its own territory). Political leaders, aware that the fighting had solved nothing and brought only widespread destruction, codified in the accord the right of the more than three hundred German states that constituted the Holy Roman Empire to conduct their own diplomatic relations—a very clear acknowledgment of their sovereignty. They were also to enjoy "an exact and reciprocal Equality": the first formal acceptance of **sovereign equality** (the idea that countries have the same right to sovereignty) for a significant number of states.

More generally, the peace may be seen as encapsulating the very idea of a **society of states**, an association of sovereign states based on their common interests, values, and norms. The participants of the conference, representing no fewer than 194 states, including ambassadors from the Netherlands, Spain, Sweden, France, Austria, and several of the larger German principalities, very clearly and explicitly took over from the papacy the right to confer international legitimacy on individual rulers and states and to insist that states observe religious toleration in their internal policies (Armstrong 1993, 30–38). The **balance of power**—parity and stability among competing powers—was formally incorporated in the **Peace of Utrecht**, which ended the War of the Spanish Succession (1701–1714), when a "just equilibrium of power" was formally declared to be the "best and most solid basis of mutual friendship and durable harmony."

The period from 1648 to 1776 saw the international system that had been taking shape over the previous two hundred years come to fruition. Wars were frequent, if lacking the ideological intensity that religion brought to the Thirty Years' War. Some states, notably the Ottoman Empire, slowly declined; others, such as Britain and Russia, rose. Hundreds of ministates still existed, but it was the interaction among no more than ten key players that determined the course of events.

Yet despite constant change and many wars, Europe in its entirety constituted a kind of republic, as eighteenth- and nineteenth-century European writers argued. Some pointed to religious and cultural similarities in seeking to explain this phenomenon, but the central elements that all agreed on were a determination by all states to preserve their freedom, a mutual recognition of one another's right to an independent existence, and, above all, a reliance on the balance of power. Diplomacy and international law were seen as the other two key institutions of international society, as long as the latter was based clearly on state consent. As Torbjørn Knutsen (1997) points out, the Peace of Westphalia supported a new view of international law among states: They moved from seeing it as divinely inspired to seeing it as a set of customs, conventions, and rules of conduct created and enforced by states and their leaders.

▶ Revolutionary Wars

Against this background of a polite, nominally rule-based European international society, the American and French Revolutions (1776 and 1789, respectively) had profound consequences. In the case of the United States, one consequence was its eventual emergence as a global superpower in the twentieth century; the consequences of the French Revolution were more immediate. First, the revolutionary insistence that sovereignty was vested in the nation rather than in the rulers gave a crucial impetus to the idea of **national self-determination**. This principle would increasingly dominate international politics in the nineteenth and twentieth centuries and endanger imperial systems that were seen as denying the rights of nations (people connected by linguistic, ethnic, and cultural bonds) to become sovereign states themselves.

National self-determination The right or desire of distinct national groups to become states and to rule themselves.

The second consequence of the French Revolution stemmed from the response of the main European powers. After the defeat of the French emperor Napoleon in 1815, the leading states increasingly set themselves apart from the smaller ones as a kind of great powers' club. This system, known as the **Concert of Europe**, lasted until World War I. Its aims were to maintain the European balance of power drawn up at the end of the Napoleonic Wars and reach decisions on potentially divisive issues. The leading dynastic powers, Austria and Russia, wanted the concert to give itself the formal right to intervene against any revolution. Britain, which was the least threatened by revolution, strongly resisted this proposition on the grounds that such a move would violate the key principle of nonintervention. However, the concert unquestionably marked a shift away from the free-for-all and highly decentralized system of eighteenth-century international society toward a more managed, hierarchical system. This shift affected all

Concert of Europe An informal institution created in 1815 by the five great powers of Europe (Austria, Britain, France, Prussia, and Russia), whereby they agreed on controlling revolutionary forces, managing the balance of power, and accepting interventions to keep current leaders in power. This system kept the peace in Europe from 1815 until World War I.

The Congress of Vienna (1814–1815) was led by Austria, Russia, Prussia, and Britain. France played a greater role later in the Congress. The main purpose was to re-establish order and create a balance-of-power system after the Napoleonic wars. The participants were reasonably successful and the great powers emerged as the rule makers. Do we need another Congress of Vienna to determine the nature of our new world order and decide on the new rules of order?

Congress of Vienna A meeting of major European leaders (1814–1815) that redrew the political map of Europe after the Napoleonic Wars. The congress was an attempt to restore a conservative political order in the continent.

three of the key institutional underpinnings of the Westphalian international society: the balance of power, diplomacy, and international law.

In 1814, the powers had already formally declared their intention to create a "system of real and permanent balance of power in Europe," and in 1815, during the **Congress of Vienna**, they carefully redrew the map of Europe to implement this system. The main diplomatic development was the greatly increased use of conferences to consider and sometimes settle matters of general interest. In a few technical areas, such as international postal services, telegraphy, and sanitation, permanent international organizations were set up. In international law, the powers sought to draft "a procedure of international legitimation of change" (Clark 1980, 91), especially in the area of territorial change.

Developments external and internal to the European concert system brought about its demise. Externally, after the American Civil War, the United States began to become a world power. Two events indicate this changing status. First, President Theodore ("Teddy") Roosevelt brokered the Treaty of Portsmouth, New Hampshire, that ended the Russo-Japanese War in 1905. Second, Roosevelt sent the new American battle fleet, called the Great White Fleet for its paint scheme, around the world in a cruise that lasted from December 1907 to February 1909.

Meanwhile, a critical internal change to the European concert system was the hardening of the great powers, as they were called, into two rival blocs after the Franco-Prussian War of 1870–1871. Previously, the balance-of-power mentality had meant that the major countries would realign themselves as necessary to keep any one power from becoming dominant. Prussian statesman and first chancellor of Germany Otto von Bismarck's creation of the German Empire in 1871 caused a major imbalance in the concert system. His alliance system was flexible and complex, and it maintained order among European states, but with Bismarck out of power since 1890, less skilled leaders let the alliance rules and protocols lapse. France focused more on Europe and less on Africa, and the German kaiser let the Russians ally with Great Britain. One result of these developments was the carnage of World War I.

World Wars: Modern and Total

Wars on a global scale shocked international society. Although separated by twenty years, World Wars I and II have some similarities beyond mere geography (see Map 2.1). Changes in military technology shaped the ways combatants fought: Machine guns, airplanes, and submarines all influenced operations. Both wars also featured controversies over the treatment of civilians. Indiscriminate bombing of cities occurred during both wars and reached its lowest point with the British and American firebomb air raids on Germany and Japan. Yet one major distinction between the two world wars is this: The Nazi death camps were at the time without parallel in human history. Unfortunately, genocide and ethnic cleansing have since continued to plague the world.

For the victorious Allies, the question of how World War I began became a question of how far the Germans and their allies should be held responsible. In 1919, at the Versailles Palace outside Paris, the victors imposed a statement of German war guilt in Article 231 of the final settlement, primarily to justify the reparations they demanded. Debates among historians about the war's origins have focused on political, military, and systemic factors. Some have suggested that responsibility for the war was diffuse, as its origins lay in complex dynamics of the respective alliances and their military imperatives. One of the more influential postwar interpretations, however, came from West German historian Fritz Fischer, who, in his 1967 book *Germany's Aims in the First World War*, argued that German aggression, motivated by the internal political needs of an autocratic elite, was responsible for the war.

However complex or contested the origins of the war are in retrospect, the motivations of those who fought are more explicable. The masses of the belligerent states shared nationalist beliefs and patriotic values. As they marched off to fight, most

WHAT'S YOUR WORLDVIEW?

Scholars continue to study the reasons that states go to war. What do you think are some of the causes for past wars like World Wars I and II? What about the causes of wars today? Can we make any generalizations about why wars happen?

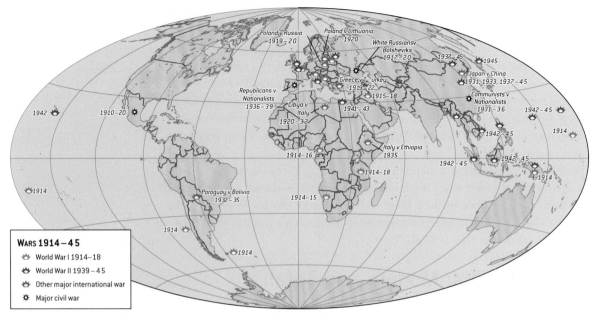

Map 2.1 **Wars 1914–1945.**

The two world wars were responsible for perhaps more than eighty million deaths. World War I was essentially a European territorial dispute, which, because of extensive European empires, spread as far afield as Africa and Southeast Asia. World War II also started as a European conflict but spread to the Pacific when Japan seized territory. In the interwar period, disputes broke out over territory in South America and East Asia, but elsewhere, the reluctance of the colonial powers to become embroiled in territorial disputes maintained an uneasy peace.

World War I was one of the bloodiest wars in history. Over sixty-five million people served in the various armies and over ten million were killed. When the war ended, the global community demanded some form of global governance to prevent war and provide world order. The League of Nations was created and a global peace movement made up of religious and secular groups was born.

thought the war would be short, victorious, and, in many cases, glorious. The reality of the European battlefield and the advent of **trench warfare** determined otherwise. Defensive military technologies, symbolized by the machine gun, triumphed over the tactics and strategy of attrition, though by November 1918 the Allied offensive finally achieved the rapid advances that helped bring an end to the fighting. It was total war in the sense that whole societies and economies were mobilized: Men were conscripted into armies, and women went to work in factories. The western and eastern fronts remained the crucibles of the fighting, although conflict spread to various parts of the globe. Japan, for example, went to war in 1914 as an ally of Britain.

In response to German aggression on the high seas and domestic public opinion that supported the Allies, the United States entered the war in 1917 under President Woodrow Wilson.

His vision of international society and world order, articulated in his **Fourteen Points**, would drive the agenda of the Paris Peace Conference in 1919. The overthrow of the Russian czar in February 1917 by what became known as the Provisional Government, and the seizure of power by the Bolsheviks in November 1917, soon led Russia's new leaders to negotiate withdrawal from the war. Germany no longer fought on two fronts but faced a new threat as the United States mobilized resources. With the failure of Germany's last great military offensive in the west in 1918 and with an increasingly effective British naval blockade, Germany agreed to an **armistice** (ceasefire).

The **Treaty of Versailles**, which formally ended the war, established the **League of Nations** and specified the rights and obligations of the victorious and defeated powers (including the notorious regime of reparations on Germany). It failed, however, to tackle what was for some the central problem of European security after 1870: a united and frustrated Germany. The treaty precipitated German revenge by creating new states out of former German and Austrian territories and devising contested borders. The League of Nations failed because the major powers—namely, France, Great Britain, and the United States—were not able to set aside their national interests for the good of a collective global interest. France sought to punish Germany, Great Britain was focused on its empire, and the United States failed to join the League, wanting nothing to do with settling European conflicts.

For some scholars, 1914–1945 represents two acts in a single play, or a thirty-year war. The British international relations theorist E. H. Carr, for example, saw the period from 1919 to 1939 as a twenty-year crisis, which he believed resulted from an unrealistic and utopian peace treaty that did not address the real causes of the war. Economic factors were also crucial contributors to the outbreak of World War II. World War I boosted production levels for Japan and the United States, but it devastated production facilities in Europe. Britain and France demanded reparations from Germany to pay for their reconstruction.

The Great Depression of the 1930s, though not caused by World War I, also contributed to the outbreak of World War II. It crippled not only the US economy but also the global economy. The damage it caused lowered the prestige of **liberal democracy** (a representative form of democracy), thereby strengthening extremist forces. Long-term consequences of the Great Depression included widespread unemployment and economic stagnation. Global trade and financial transactions increased, but this growing interdependence of national economies did not result in free trade; instead, protectionist policies (e.g., tariffs to protect domestic interests) increased. The resulting change in the international political system helped bring about the collapse of the trade, finance, and economic management systems.

The effect on German society was particularly significant. All modernized states suffered mass unemployment, but in Germany, inflation was acute. Economic and political instability provided the ground in which support for the Nazis took root. By 1933, Adolf Hitler had achieved power, and the transformation of the German state began. There remain debates about how far Hitler's ambitions were carefully thought through and how much he seized opportunities. A. J. P. Taylor

Trench warfare Combat in which armies dug elaborate defensive fortifications in the ground, as both sides did in World War I. Because of the power of weapons like machine guns and rapid-fire cannons, trenches often gave the advantage in battle to the defenders.

Fourteen Points President Woodrow Wilson's vision of international society, first articulated in January 1918, included the principle of self-determination, the conduct of diplomacy on an open (not secret) basis, and the establishment of an association of nation-states to provide guarantees of independence and territorial integrity (League of Nations).

Armistice A cease-fire agreement between enemies in wartime. In the case of World War I, the armistice began at 11 a.m. on November 11, 1918.

Treaty of Versailles, 1919 The agreement that formally ended World War I (1914–1918).

League of Nations The first permanent collective international security organization aimed at preventing future wars and resolving global problems. The League failed due to the unwillingness of the United States to join and the inability of its members to commit to a real international community.

Treasury. A $75,000 wheelbarrow of mutilated money on way to vaults. Employee in picture has wheeled barrow 50 years. Neg. No. 48/

Going grocery shopping? In the early 1920s, the German Weimar Republic that was created as a democratic experiment suffered hyperinflation and other issues related to stability. The currency was worthless, and a viable means of exchange is critical for stability. The economic collapse led to political unrest and the rise of the Nazi party.

provided a controversial analysis in his 1961 book *Origins of the Second World War*, in which he argued that Hitler was no different from other German political leaders. What was different about Germany this time was the particular philosophy of Nazism and ideas of racial supremacy and imperial expansion.

British and French attempts to negotiate with Hitler culminated in the **Munich Agreement of 1938**. In an effort to appease Germany, Britain and France acquiesced to Hitler's territorial claims over the Sudetenland in Czechoslovakia, but within months, Germany had seized the rest of Czechoslovakia and was preparing for war on Poland. Since then, **appeasement** has generally been seen as synonymous with a craven collapse before the demands of dictators—encouraging, not disarming, their aggressive designs. Recent debates about appeasement have focused on whether there were realistic alternatives to negotiation, given the lack of military preparedness to confront Hitler.

Liberal democracy A state with democratic or representative government and a capitalist economy that promotes multilateralism and free trade. Domestic interests, values, and institutions shape foreign policy. Liberal democracies champion freedom of the individual, constitutional civil and political rights, and laissez-faire economic arrangements.

Munich Agreement of 1938 An agreement negotiated after a conference held in Munich between Germany and the United Kingdom and other major powers of Europe along with Czechoslovakia. It permitted Nazi Germany's annexation of Czechoslovakia's Sudetenland, an area along the Czech border that was inhabited primarily by ethnic Germans.

By 1939, the defensive military technologies of World War I gave way to armored warfare and air power, as the German **blitzkrieg** brought speedy victories over Poland and in the west. Hitler was also drawn into the Balkans and North Africa in support of his Italian ally, Mussolini. The invasion of the Soviet Union in June 1941 plainly demonstrated the scale of fighting and scope of Hitler's aims. Although Germany had massive early victories on the eastern front, winter saw a stalemate and the mobilization of Soviet peoples and armies. German treatment of civilian populations and Soviet prisoners of war reflected Nazi ideas of racial supremacy and resulted in the deaths of millions. German anti-Semitism and the development of concentration camps gained new momentum after a decision on the "Final Solution of the Jewish Question" in 1942. The term **Holocaust** entered the political lexicon of the twentieth century, as the Nazis attempted the **genocide** of the Jewish people and other minorities, such as the Roma, in Europe.

By 1941, German submarines and American warships were in an undeclared war. The imposition of American economic sanctions on Japan precipitated Japanese military preparations for a surprise attack on the US fleet at Pearl Harbor on December 7, 1941. When Germany and Italy declared war on America in support of their Japanese ally, President Franklin Roosevelt decided to assign priority to the European over the Pacific theater of war. After a combined strategic bombing offensive with the British against German cities, the Allies launched a second front in France, which the Soviets had pressed for.

Defeat of Germany in May 1945 came before the atomic bomb was ready. In an effort to shorten the war, avoid an invasion of Japan, and push the Japanese government to surrender, the United States dropped the first atomic bomb on Hiroshima on August 6, 1945, and the second on Nagasaki on August 9, 1945. The United States was the first and is still the only state to use these weapons of mass destruction in war. The destruction of the two Japanese cities remains enormously controversial. Aside from voicing moral objections to bombing civilian populations, historians have engaged in fierce debate about why the bombs were dropped.

When World War II ended, the United States and the Soviet Union remained as the two dominant countries in world politics. For some people in the United States, their homeland largely untouched by the destruction of the war, the country seemed poised to take its proper position as world leader. For the leaders of the Soviet Union, the world looked ready for the expansion of the Soviet style of rule. In the next section, we examine the process of decolonization of Western European holdings. This process provided both countries, soon to be called **superpowers**, with many opportunities to expand their influence. The United States was willing to commit resources to stabilize the world economy and build global political structures to manage trade, development, and financial affairs.

Adding new technology that the enemy does not have often leads to victory. Making sure the world knows about your new weapons is part of propaganda. This photo shows a tank of the German Wehrmacht as they prepared for the invasion of Poland on September 1, 1939. The Nazis overwhelmed Europe and almost won the war by using their superior weapons and well-trained soldiers.

Legacies and Consequences of European Colonialism

The effects of World War II helped cause the demise of European imperialism in the twentieth century (see Maps 2.2 and 2.3). More than marking an end of Western European dominance in world politics, the end of imperialism seemed to be the death knell for the European style of managing international relations. This change took place against the background of the Cold War, which we will discuss in the next section. But it's important first to appreciate the context of decolonization because it reflected and contributed to the decreasing importance of Europe as the arbiter of world affairs.

The belief that national self-determination should be a guiding principle in international politics marked a transformation of attitudes and values; during the age of imperialism, political status accrued to imperial powers. However, after 1945, imperialism became a term of disgrace. Colonialism of the past and the new UN Charter (which established the United Nations) were increasingly recognized as incompatible, though independence was often slow and sometimes marked by prolonged and armed struggle, especially in many African and Asian states. The Cold War also complicated and hindered the transition to independence. Various factors influenced the process of decolonization: the attitude of the colonial power,

Appeasement A policy of making concessions to a territorially acquisitive state in the hope that settlement of more modest claims will assuage that state's expansionist appetites.

Blitzkrieg The German term for "lightning war." This was an offensive strategy that used the combination of mechanized forces—especially tanks—and aircraft as mobile artillery to exploit breaches in an enemy's front line.

Holocaust The attempts by the Nazis to murder the Jewish population of Europe. Some 6 million Jewish people were killed in concentration camps, along with a further million that included Soviet prisoners, Roma, Poles, communists, homosexuals, and the physically or mentally disabled.

Genocide The deliberate and systematic extermination of an ethnic, national, tribal, or religious group.

Superpower A state with a dominant position in the international system. It has the will and the means to influence the actions of other states in favor of its own interests, and it projects its power on a global scale to secure its national interests.

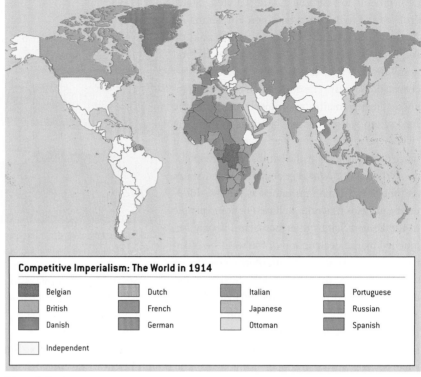

Competitive Imperialism: The World in 1914

▨ Belgian	▨ Dutch	▨ Italian	▨ Portuguese
▨ British	▨ French	▨ Japanese	▨ Russian
▨ Danish	▨ German	▨ Ottoman	▨ Spanish
▨ Independent		

Map 2.2 **Former Colonial Territories.**

Decolonization did not happen all at once. One of the final symbols of colonization racism and repression was South African apartheid. In this photo, citizens of Ghana conduct a war dance against apartheid during demonstrations in Accra, Ghana, on August 1, 1960. A leading intellectual voice for self-determination and self-reliance was Ghana's prime minister, Kwame Nkrumah. He led Ghana's total boycott against the union of South Africa and most other African states followed his lead.

the ideology and strategy of the anti-imperialist forces, and the role of external powers. Political, economic, and military factors played various roles in shaping the transfer of power. Different imperial powers and newly emerging independent states had different experiences of withdrawal from empire.

There was no one pattern of decolonization in Africa and Asia, and the paths to independence reflected attitudes of colonial powers, the nature of local nationalist or revolutionary movements, ethnic and racial factors, and, in some cases, the involvement of external states, including the Cold War protagonists. How far these divisions were created or exacerbated by the imperial powers is an important question in examining the political stability of the newly independent states. Equally important is how capable the new political leaderships in these societies were in tackling their political and economic problems.

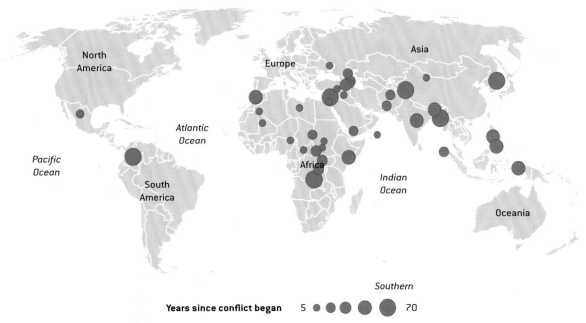

Years since conflict began 5 ● ● ● ● ⬤ 70

Map 2.3 **Wars Since 1945.**

As European colonial control was largely destroyed between 1945 and 1970, new nation-states were created. One result was an increase in localized wars, mainly arising from boundary disputes, and in civil wars caused by conflicts between different ethnic groups or between those with conflicting religious or political beliefs. Note that many of these wars directly or indirectly involved the United States and Soviet Union. An estimated twenty-five to thirty million people died in these wars, two-thirds of whom were civilians.

The decolonization process in Africa was complicated by the number of European states involved in formal empire and the different national interests of these colonizing states. The economic crises created by the war forced the British, French, and Belgians to exploit the riches of their colonies. Portugal saw its colonies Angola, Mozambique, and Portuguese Guinea as essential elements in its economic and political survival. Belgium held on to its colonies in Central Africa until 1960, and France worked to assimilate its colonies into a French imperial order. The British strategy was to devolve more authority to local elites and create a more informal empire.

The 1960s was a period of accelerated decolonization and the beginning of many internal conflicts in Africa. Many of these new states failed because they did not have adequate political or economic structures, lacked experienced and educated leaders, and were culturally diverse, with little or no loyalty toward any newly created nation-state. Each was still dependent on its former colonial masters. This dependency still shapes the domestic and foreign policies of these states today.

In Asia, the relationship between nationalism and revolutionary Marxism was a potent force. In Malaya (now part of Malaysia), the British defeated a communist insurgent movement (1948–1960). In Indochina, a peninsula in Southeast Asia consisting of Burma (Myanmar), Thailand, Malaya, Laos, Cambodia, and Vietnam, the French failed to do likewise (1946–1954). For the Vietnamese, resentment over centuries of foreign oppression—by the Chinese, Japanese, and French—soon focused on a new imperialist adversary, the United States. Early American reluctance to support European imperialism gave way to incremental and covert commitments, and then, from 1965, to open military and political support of the newly created state of South Vietnam.

American leaders and a very influential anticommunist interest community spoke of a domino theory, in which if one state fell to communism, the next would be at risk. Chinese and Soviet support provided additional Cold War contexts. Washington failed, however, to coordinate limited war objectives with an effective political strategy and, once victory was no longer possible, sought to disengage from Vietnam through "peace with honor." The Tet (Vietnamese New Year) offensive of the Vietcong guerrillas in 1968 marked a decisive moment, convincing many Americans that the war would not be won, though it was not until 1973 that American forces finally withdrew, two years before South Vietnam was defeated. Many wars in Asia and Africa started as colonial wars and quickly became proxy wars in the Cold War struggle between the superpowers.

The global trend toward decolonization was a key development in the twentieth century, though one frequently offset by local circumstances. Yet while imperialism withered, other forms of domination, or **hegemony**, took shape. Simply stated, hegemony means a state has the capacity and the will to shape and govern the international system. Both the United States and the Soviet Union were vying for global hegemony during the Cold War. The notion of hegemony has been used to criticize the behavior of the superpowers, most notably with Soviet hegemony in Eastern Europe and American hegemony in Central America. For both countries, this struggle for dominance, regardless of the term used, was the central element of the period we discuss in the next section, the Cold War.

◤ Cold War

The rise of the United States as a global power after 1945 was of paramount importance in international politics. Its conflict with the Soviet Union provided one of the crucial dynamics in world affairs—one that affected, directly or indirectly, every part of the world. In the West, historians have debated with vigor and acrimony which country was responsible for the collapse of the wartime alliance between Moscow and Washington. The rise of the USSR as a global power after 1945 is equally crucial in this period. Relations between Moscow and its Eastern European "allies," with the People's Republic of China (PRC), and with revolutionary forces in the third world have been vital issues in world politics, as well as key factors in Soviet-American affairs. If one feature of the **Cold War** was its **bipolar** structure, another was its highly divided character, born out of profoundly opposing views about the best way of organizing society: the Western system of market **capitalism** or the Eastern bloc's centrally planned economies.

Hegemony A system regulated by a dominant leader, or political (and/or economic) domination of a region. It also means power and control exercised by a leading state over other states.

Cold War The period from 1946 to 1991 defined by ideological conflict and rivalry between the United States and the Soviet Union. This was a global struggle for the hearts and minds of citizens around the world that was characterized by political conflict, military competition, proxy wars, and economic competition.

Bipolar An international political order in which two states dominate all others. It is often used to describe the nature of the international system when the two superpowers, the Soviet Union and the United States, were dominant powers during the Cold War.

Capitalism A system of production in which human labor and its products are commodities that are bought and sold in the marketplace.

Yet for all its intensity, the Cold War was very much a managed conflict in which both sides recognized the limits of what they could do. Certainly, policymakers in the East and the West appeared to accept in private—if not in public—that their rival had legitimate security concerns. The Cold War was thus fought within a framework of informal rules. This framework helps explain why the conflict remained "cold"—at least in terms of general war between the United States and the Soviet Union, since millions of people died during the period of 1945 to 1990 in what have been called "brushfire" or "proxy" wars in Africa and Asia.

Indeed, how and why the Cold War remained cold have been subjects of much academic debate. Few, however, would dispute the fact that whatever else may have divided the two superpowers—ideology, economics, and the struggle for global influence—they were in full agreement about one thing: the overriding need to prevent a nuclear war that neither could win without destroying the world and themselves. In the end, this is why the superpowers acted with such caution for the greater part of the Cold War era. In fact, given the very real fear of outright nuclear war, the shared aim of the two superpowers was not to destroy the other—though a few on both sides occasionally talked in such terms—but rather to contain the other's ambitions while avoiding anything that might lead to dangerous escalation (only once, in 1962, with the Cuban Missile Crisis, did the two superpowers come close to a nuclear exchange). This situation in turn helps explain another important feature of the Cold War: its stalemated and hence seemingly permanent character.

Some historians date the origins of the Cold War to the Russian Revolution of 1917, but most focus on events between 1945 and 1950. Whether the Cold War was inevitable, whether it was the consequence of mistakes and misperceptions, and whether it reflected the response of Western leaders to aggressive Soviet intent are central questions in debates about the origins and dynamics of the Cold War. Until 1989, these debates drew only from Western archives and sources and reflected Western assumptions and perceptions. With the end of the Cold War, greater evidence has emerged of Soviet and US motivations and understanding.

Onset of the Cold War

The start of the Cold War in Europe reflected a failure to implement the principles agreed on at the 1945 wartime conferences of Yalta and Potsdam. The futures of Germany and various Central and Eastern European countries, notably Poland, were issues of growing tension between the former wartime allies. Reconciling principles of national self-determination with national security was a formidable task. In the West, there was growing feeling that Soviet policy toward Eastern Europe was guided not by historical concern with security but by ideological expansion. In March 1947, the Truman administration sought to justify limited aid to Turkey and Greece with rhetoric

WHAT'S YOUR WORLDVIEW?

The United States and the USSR fought many proxy wars across the globe. One writer lists some fifty-eight wars from 1945 to 1989 (Holsti 1991). Roughly 52 percent of the current armed conflicts began during the Cold War. Given these statistics, is it correct to call the period 1945–1989 a "Cold War," or was it a series of hot proxy wars or maybe World War III?

Truman Doctrine A statement made by President Harry Truman in March 1947 that it "must be the policy of the United States to support free people who are resisting attempted subjugation by armed minorities or by outside pressures."

Containment An American political strategy for resisting perceived Soviet expansion.

Marshall Plan Officially known as the European Recovery Program, it was a program of financial and other economic aid for Europe after World War II. Proposed by Secretary of State George Marshall in 1948, it was offered to all European states, including the Soviet Union.

designed to arouse awareness of Soviet ambitions and a declaration that America would support those threatened by Soviet subversion or expansion. The **Truman Doctrine** and the associated policy of **containment** expressed the self-image of the United States as inherently defensive. These were underpinned by the **Marshall Plan** for European economic recovery, proclaimed in June 1947, which was essential to the economic rebuilding of Western Europe. In Eastern Europe, democratic socialist and other anticommunist forces were undermined and eliminated as Marxist-Leninist regimes, loyal to Moscow, were installed. The only exception was in Yugoslavia, where the Marxist leader Marshal Tito consolidated his position while maintaining independence from Moscow.

The first major confrontation of the Cold War took place over Berlin beginning in 1948 (see Table 2.1). During the Yalta and Potsdam Conferences, Germany was divided among the four victorious powers: the United States, the Soviet Union, Great Britain, and France. Its former capital, Berlin, although positioned deep in the heart of the Soviet zone of occupation, was also divided into four sectors, with the result that the Western zones of the city were surrounded by Soviet-controlled territory. In June 1948, Stalin sought to resolve Berlin's status by severing road and rail communications to the three Western-controlled sectors of the city. West Berlin's population and political autonomy were kept alive by a massive US airlift, and Stalin ended the blockade in May 1949. The crisis saw the deployment of American long-range bombers in Britain, officially described as "atomic capable," though none was armed with nuclear weapons. US military deployment was followed by political commitment enshrined in the **North Atlantic Treaty Organization (NATO)** treaty signed in April 1949. The key article of the treaty—that an attack on one member would be treated as an attack on all—accorded with the principle of collective self-defense enshrined in Article 51 of the UN Charter. In practice, the cornerstone of the alliance was the commitment of the United States to defend Western Europe. In reality, this soon meant the willingness of the United States to use nuclear weapons to deter Soviet aggression. For the Soviet Union, political encirclement soon entailed a growing military, and specifically nuclear, threat.

Although the origins of the Cold War were in Europe, events and conflicts in Asia and elsewhere were also crucial. In 1949, the thirty-year Chinese civil war ended in victory for the communists under Mao Zedong. This had a major impact on Asian affairs and on perceptions in both Moscow and Washington. In June 1950, the North Korean attack on South Korea was interpreted as part of a general communist

To counter a possible Soviet threat to Europe, the United States and its allies created a collective defense organization in 1949. In this photo, Secretary of State Dean Acheson signs the Atlantic defense treaty for the United States. Vice President Alben W. Barkley, left, and President Harry Truman watch the signing process.

TABLE 2.1	**Cold War Crises and Proxy Wars**

Years	Crisis	Key Actors
1948–1949	Berlin Soviet Blockade	USSR/US/UK
1950–1953	Korean Conflict	North Korea/South Korea/US/PRC
1954–1955	Taiwan Strait	US/PRC
1961	Berlin	USSR/US/NATO
1962	Cuba	USSR/US/Cuba
1965–1973	Vietnam War	US/North Korea/Russia/China
1970	Cambodia Secret Bombing	US/North Vietnam/Russia/China
1973	Arab-Israeli War	Egypt/Israel/Syria/Jordan/US/USSR
1975–2002	Angola	US/USSR/Cuba/China/South Africa
1979–1992	Afghanistan	USSR/US/Saudi Arabia/Pakistan
1979–1990	Nicaragua–El Salvador	US/USSR/Cuba

strategy and as a test case for American resolve and the will of the UN to withstand aggression. The resulting American and UN commitment, followed in October 1950 by Chinese involvement, led to a war lasting three years in which more than three million people died before prewar borders were restored. North and South Korea themselves remained locked in seemingly perpetual hostility, even after the Cold War (See Table 2.1).

Conflict, Confrontation, and Compromise

One consequence of the Korean War was the buildup of American forces in Western Europe, lest communist aggression in Asia distract from the American-perceived real intent in Europe. The idea that communism was a monolithic political entity controlled from Moscow became an enduring American fixation not shared in London and elsewhere. Western Europeans nevertheless depended on the United States for military security, and this dependency deepened as the Cold War confrontation in Europe was consolidated. The rearmament of the Federal Republic of Germany (West Germany) in 1954 precipitated the creation of the **Warsaw Pact** in 1955, an agreement of mutual defense and military aid signed by communist European states of Eastern Europe under Soviet influence. The military buildup continued apace, with unprecedented concentrations of conventional and, moreover, nuclear forces. By the 1960s, there were some seven thousand nuclear weapons in Western Europe alone. NATO deployed nuclear weapons to offset Soviet conventional superiority, and Soviet short-range, or "theater nuclear," forces in Europe compensated for overall American nuclear superiority.

North Atlantic Treaty Organization (NATO) Organization established by treaty in April 1949 including twelve (later sixteen) countries from Western Europe and North America. The most important aspect of the NATO alliance was the US commitment to defend Western Europe. Today NATO has twenty-eight member states.

Warsaw Pact An agreement of mutual defense and military aid signed in May 1955 in response to West Germany's rearmament and entry into NATO. It comprised the USSR and seven communist states (though Albania withdrew support in 1961). The pact was officially dissolved in July 1991.

The death of Stalin in March 1953 portended significant consequences for the USSR at home and abroad. Stalin's eventual successor, Nikita Khrushchev, strove to modernize Soviet society, and in the process he helped unleash reformist forces in Eastern Europe. While Poland was controlled, the situation in Hungary threatened Soviet hegemony, and in 1956, the intervention of the Red Army brought bloodshed to the streets of Budapest and international condemnation on Moscow. Soviet intervention coincided with an attack on Egypt by Britain, France, and Israel, precipitated by Colonel Nasser's nationalization of the Suez Canal in a manner that displeased Britain, the former colonial occupier. The French took part in the attack because Nasser's government was providing support to anti-French rebels in Algeria. The British government's actions provoked fierce domestic and international criticism and the most serious rift in the "special relationship" between Britain and the United States. President Dwight Eisenhower was strongly opposed to the actions of the US allies, and in the face of what were effectively US economic sanctions (a threat to cut off American oil exports to Britain), the British abandoned the operation, as well as their support for the French and Israelis.

Khrushchev's policy toward the West mixed a search for political coexistence with the pursuit of ideological confrontation. Soviet support for movements of national liberation aroused fears in the West of a global communist challenge. American commitment to liberal democracy and national self-determination was often subordinated to Cold War perspectives, as well as to US economic and political interests. The Cold War saw the growth of large permanent intelligence organizations, whose roles ranged from estimating intentions and capabilities of adversaries to covert intervention in the affairs of other states. Crises over Berlin in 1961 and Cuba in 1962 marked the most dangerous moments of the Cold War. In both, there was a risk of direct military confrontation and, certainly in October 1962, the possibility of nuclear war. How close the world came to Armageddon during the Cuban Missile Crisis and exactly why peace was preserved remain matters of debate among historians and surviving officials.

The events of 1962 were followed by a more stable period of coexistence and competition. Nuclear arsenals, nevertheless, continued to grow. Whether this is best characterized as an **arms race** or whether internal political and bureaucratic pressures drove the growth of nuclear arsenals is open to interpretation. For Washington, commitments to NATO allies also provided pressures and opportunities to develop and deploy their own shorter-range (tactical and theater) nuclear weapons. The global nuclear dimension increased with the emergence of other nuclear-weapon states: Britain in 1952, France in 1960, and China in 1964. Growing concern at the spread, or proliferation, of nuclear weapons led to the negotiation of the Nuclear Nonproliferation Treaty (NPT) in 1968, wherein states that had nuclear weapons committed themselves to halt the arms race, and those that did not possess them promised not to develop them. Despite successes of the NPT, by 1990, several states had developed or were developing nuclear weapons, notably Israel, India, Pakistan, and apartheid South Africa. (Libya and South

Arms race A central concept in realist thought. As states build up their military to address real or perceived threats to their national security, they may create insecurity in other states. These states in turn develop their military capacities and thus begin an arms race. This never-ending pursuit of security creates the condition we know as a security dilemma.

Africa later gave up their nuclear weapons programs and remain the only states to have done so.)

The Rise and Fall of Détente

At the same time that America's commitment in Vietnam was deepening, Soviet-Chinese relations were deteriorating. Indeed, by 1969, the PRC and the Soviet Union had fought a minor border war over a territorial dispute. Despite (or because of) these tensions, the foundations for what became known as **détente** were laid between the Soviet Union and the United States and for what became known as **rapprochement** between China and the United States. Both terms, long a part of the language of diplomacy, refer to the processes by which countries seek to improve their relations. Détente in Europe had its origins in the **Ostpolitik** of German chancellor Willy Brandt and resulted in agreements that recognized the peculiar status of Berlin and the sovereignty of East Germany. For his efforts, which finally bore fruit with the end of the Cold War in 1989, Brandt won the Nobel Peace Prize. Soviet-American détente had its roots in mutual recognition of the need to avoid nuclear crises and in the economic and military incentives in avoiding an unconstrained arms race. Both Washington and Moscow also looked toward Beijing when making their bilateral calculations.

In the West, détente was associated with the political leadership of President Richard Nixon and his adviser Henry Kissinger, who were also instrumental in Sino-American rapprochement. This new phase in Soviet-American relations did not mark an end to political conflict, as each side pursued political goals, some of which were increasingly incompatible with the aspirations of the other superpower. Both sides supported friendly regimes and movements and subverted adversaries. All this came as various political upheavals were taking place in the third world. The question of how far the superpowers could control their friends, and how far they were entangled by their commitments, was underlined in 1973 when the Arab-Israeli War embroiled both the United States and the Soviet Union in what became a potentially dangerous confrontation. Getting the superpowers involved in the war—whether by design or serendipity—helped create the political conditions for Egyptian-Israeli rapprochement. Diplomatic and strategic relations were transformed as Egypt switched its allegiance from Moscow to Washington. In the short term, Egypt was isolated in the Arab world. For Israel, fear of a war of annihilation fought on two fronts was lifted. Yet continuing political violence, terrorism, and the enduring enmity

Détente The relaxation of tension between East and West; Soviet-American détente lasted from the late 1960s to the late 1970s and was characterized by negotiations and nuclear arms control agreements.

Rapprochement The re-establishment of more friendly relations between the People's Republic of China and the United States in the early 1970s.

Ostpolitik The West German government's "Eastern Policy" of the mid- to late 1960s, designed to develop relations between West Germany and members of the Warsaw Pact.

Two critically important Cold War decision-makers for the United States are pictured here. President Richard Nixon, right, offers his congratulations to Secretary of State Henry A. Kissinger after the secretary won the 1973 Nobel Peace Prize. Kissinger shared the prize with North Vietnamese diplomat Le Duc Tho for their efforts to end the Vietnam War. Nixon and Kissinger also opened relations with China and shifted the balance of power toward the United States over the Soviet Union.

between Israel and other Arab states proved insurmountable obstacles to a more permanent regional settlement.

In Washington, Soviet support for revolutionary movements in the third world was seen as evidence of duplicity. Some American politicians and academics claim that Moscow's support for revolutionary forces in Ethiopia in 1975 killed détente. Others cite the Soviet role in Angola in 1978. Furthermore, the perception that the USSR was using arms control agreements to gain military advantage was linked to Soviet behavior in the third world. Growing Soviet military superiority was reflected in growing Soviet influence, it was argued. Critics claimed the Strategic Arms Limitation Talks (SALT) process enabled the Soviets to deploy multiple independently targetable warheads on their large **intercontinental ballistic missiles (ICBMs)**, threatening key American forces. America faced a "window of vulnerability," critics of détente claimed. The view from Moscow was different, reflecting different assumptions about the scope and purpose of détente and the nature of nuclear deterrence. Other events were also seen to weaken American influence. The overthrow of the shah of Iran in 1979 resulted in the loss of an important Western ally in the region, though the ensuing militant Islamic government was hostile to both superpowers.

December 1979 marked a point of transition in East-West affairs. NATO agreed to deploy land-based Cruise and Pershing II missiles in Europe if negotiations with the Soviets did not reduce what NATO saw as a serious imbalance. Later in the month, Soviet armed forces intervened in Afghanistan to support their revolutionary allies. The USSR was bitterly condemned in the West and in the third world for its actions and soon became committed to a protracted and bloody struggle that many compared to the American war in Vietnam. In Washington, President Jimmy Carter, who had sought to control arms and reduce tensions with the USSR, hardened his view of the Soviet Union. The first reaction was the Carter Doctrine, which clearly stated that any Soviet attack on countries in the Persian Gulf would be seen as a direct attack on US vital interests. Another result was the Carter administration's decision to boycott the 1980 Summer Olympics in Moscow. Nevertheless, Republicans increasingly used foreign and defense policy to attack the Carter presidency. Perceptions of American weakness abroad permeated domestic politics, and in 1980 Ronald Reagan was elected president. He was committed to a more confrontational approach with the Soviets on arms control, third world conflicts, and East-West relations in general.

From Détente to a Second Cold War

In the West, critics of détente and arms control, some of whom would later advise the George W. Bush presidential administration, argued in the 1970s and 1980s that the Soviets were acquiring nuclear superiority. Some suggested that the United States should pursue policies and strategies based on the idea that victory in nuclear war was possible. The election of Ronald Reagan in 1980 was a watershed in Soviet-American relations. Reagan had made it clear during the election campaign that the United States would take a tough stance in its relations with the Soviet

Intercontinental ballistic missiles (ICBMs) Weapons system the United States and Soviet Union developed to threaten each other with destruction. The thirty- to forty-minute flight times of the missiles created a situation that is sometimes called "mutually assured destruction" (MAD) or "the balance of terror."

Union. In two monumental speeches delivered in March 1983, Reagan stated that the Soviet Union was the "focus of evil in the modern world," and he coined the phrase "evil empire" to describe the USSR. In the second speech, he outlined his idea for a strategic defense against Soviet missiles. One issue that Reagan inherited, and that loomed large in the breakdown of relations between East and West, was nuclear missiles in Europe. NATO's decision to deploy land-based missiles capable of striking Soviet territory precipitated a period of great tension in relations between NATO and the USSR and political friction within NATO.

Reagan's own incautious public remarks reinforced perceptions that he was as ill informed as he was dangerous in matters nuclear, though key arms policies were consistent with those of his predecessor, Jimmy Carter. On arms control, Reagan was not interested in agreements that would freeze the status quo for the sake of getting agreement, and Soviet and American negotiators proved unable to make progress in talks on long-range and intermediate-range weapons. One particular idea had significant consequences for arms control and for Washington's relations with its allies and its adversaries. The **Strategic Defense Initiative (SDI)**, quickly dubbed "Star Wars" after the movie, was a research program designed to explore the feasibility of space-based defenses against ballistic missiles. The Soviets appeared to take SDI very seriously and claimed that Reagan's real purpose was to regain the nuclear monopoly of the 1950s. The technological advances claimed by SDI proponents did not materialize, however, and the program was eventually reduced and marginalized, although never fully eliminated from the US defense budget.

The resulting period of tension and confrontation between the superpowers has been described as the second cold war or the end of détente and compared to the early period of confrontation and tension from 1946 to 1953. In Western Europe and the Soviet Union, there was real fear of nuclear war. Much of this fear was a reaction to the rhetoric and policies of the Reagan administration. The world viewed American statements on nuclear weapons, military intervention in Grenada in 1983, and an air raid against Libya in 1986 as evidence of a new belligerence. Reagan's policy toward Central America and his support for the rebel Contras in Nicaragua were sources of controversy within the United States and internationally. The International Court of Justice (ICJ), a judicial court of the United Nations (which we'll discuss in Chapter 5), found the United States guilty of violating international law in 1986 for sowing sea mines in Nicaraguan harbors. The Reagan administration ignored this ruling, claiming the ICJ lacked jurisdiction in this situation.

The Reagan administration's use of military power was nonetheless limited: Rhetoric and perception were at variance with reality. Nevertheless, there is evidence that the Soviet leadership took very seriously the words (and deeds) of the Reagan administration, and there were some who believed that Washington was planning a nuclear first strike. In 1983, Soviet air defenses shot down a South Korean civilian airliner in Soviet airspace. The American reaction and the imminent deployment of US nuclear missiles in Europe created a climate of great tension in East-West relations.

Strategic Defense Initiative (SDI) A controversial strategic policy advocated by the Reagan administration and nuclear physicists such as Edward Teller, who helped create the hydrogen bomb. The plan, which was often derisively nicknamed "Star Wars," called for a defensive missile shield that would make Soviet offensive missiles ineffective by destroying them in flight.

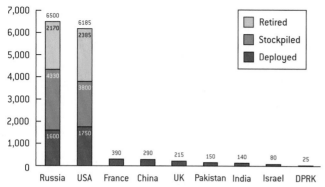

Figure 2.1 Estimated Global Nuclear Warheads in 2019.
The world's nuclear-armed states possess a combined total of approximately fourteen thousand nuclear warheads in 2019. In 1986, during the Cold War, there were over seventy thousand nuclear warheads.

Glasnost A policy of greater openness pursued by Soviet leader Mikhail Gorbachev from 1985, involving more toleration of internal dissent and criticism.

Perestroika Gorbachev's policy of restructuring, pursued in tandem with glasnost and intended to modernize the Soviet political and economic system.

Strategic Arms Reductions Treaty (START) Negotiations between the United States and Soviet Union over limiting nuclear arsenals began in 1982 and progressed at a very slow pace over eight years. The eventual treaty in 1991 broke new ground because it called for a reduction of nuclear arms rather than just a limit on the growth of these weapons.

Throughout the early 1980s, the ill health of a series of Soviet leaders (Brezhnev, Andropov, and Chernenko) inhibited Soviet responses to the American challenge and the American threat. In 1985, however, Mikhail Gorbachev became general secretary of the Soviet Communist Party. Gorbachev's "new thinking" in foreign policy and his domestic reforms created a revolution both in the USSR's foreign relations and within Soviet society. At home, **glasnost** (or openness) and **perestroika** (or restructuring) unleashed nationalist and other forces that, to Gorbachev's dismay, were to destroy the USSR.

Gorbachev paved the way for agreements on nuclear and conventional forces that helped ease the tensions of the early 1980s. In 1987, he traveled to Washington to sign the Intermediate Nuclear Forces (INF) Treaty, banning intermediate-range nuclear missiles, including Cruise and Pershing II. This agreement was heralded as a triumph for the Soviet leader, but NATO leaders, including Reagan and British prime minister Margaret Thatcher, argued that it was vindication of the policies pursued by NATO since 1979. The INF Treaty was concluded more quickly than a new agreement on cutting strategic nuclear weapons, in part because of continuing Soviet opposition to SDI. And it was Reagan's successor, George H. W. Bush, who concluded a **Strategic Arms Reduction Treaty (START)** agreement that reduced long-range nuclear weapons (though only back to the level they had been in the early 1980s). Gorbachev used agreements on nuclear weapons as a means of building trust and demonstrated the serious and radical nature of his purpose. However, despite similar radical agreements on conventional forces in Europe (culminating in the Paris agreement of 1990), the end of the Cold War marked success in nuclear arms control rather than nuclear disarmament. The histories of the Cold War and of the atomic bomb are very closely connected, but although the Cold War is now over, nuclear weapons are still very much in existence. We will discuss the issues surrounding nuclear weapons in Chapter 6 (See Figure 2.1).

▶ From the End of the Cold War to the War on Terrorism

The first major global conflict after the Cold War ended was the 1990 Iraqi invasion of neighboring Kuwait. The United States led a comprehensive multilateral diplomatic and military effort to punish the former president of Iraq, Saddam Hussein, for his actions and to signal to the world that this kind of violation of international law would not stand. The war to liberate Kuwait lasted only forty-two days, and an international coalition of diplomats and military forces helped define the "New World Order" espoused by President George H. W. Bush. The United States wisely included the Soviet Union in its plans and effectively used the UN Security Council to pass more than twelve resolutions condemning the actions of Iraq. What the first President Bush created was a US-led global coalition that was supported by all five permanent members of the Security Council (China, France, the Russian Federation, the United Kingdom, and the United States)—a first since the establishment of the United Nations. The invasion of Kuwait was illegal under international law, and the major powers were willing to work together to protect and promote a "rule-based system."

WHAT'S YOUR WORLDVIEW?

After the Cold War, leaders and citizens alike thought we would have a peace dividend—less money spent on arms and more money for social programs. Yet, for a variety of reasons, arms spending has not declined much. The war on terrorism has certainly increased the need for spending, but are there other reasons?

The world in 1990 was full of promise (especially for the victors of the Cold War) but full of risk as well. It was also replete with the sources of further conflict. This New World Order, as the first President Bush called it, existed briefly between two eras: one defined by an ongoing struggle between two competing secular ideologies and another shaped by an emerging clash between two conceptions of civilization itself.

The Cold War divided the world for more than forty years, threatened humanity with near destruction, and led to the death of at least twenty-five million people, mostly in the highly contested zone that came to be referred to as the "third world" during the Cold War. Yet despite these dangers and costs, the Cold War in its core areas still managed to create a degree of stability that the world had not experienced since the early part of the twentieth century. For this reason, many came to view the bipolar order after 1947 as something that was not merely the expression of a given international reality but also desirable and defensible. As we will see in Chapter 3, some realists seemed to celebrate the superpower relationship on the grounds that a world with two balancing powers, each limiting the actions of the other, was likely to be a far more stable world than one with several competing states.

What happened in Eastern Europe in 1989, of course, produced enormous shock waves. Many people hoped that Gorbachev's reforms would make the world a safer and more humane place. Hardly anybody, though, seriously anticipated the collapse of communism and the destruction of the Berlin Wall. Moreover, few believed that this revolutionary process could be achieved peacefully. It was all rather surprising for those who had thought this superpower rivalry would never end without some type of nuclear confrontation. Now world leaders had to remake the world and find ways to integrate former enemies back into the West.

The tasks they confronted certainly seemed very great, ranging from the institutional one of devising new tasks for bodies such as NATO, the UN, and the European Union (created in 1992) to the more economic challenge of facilitating the transition in countries that had little experience running **market democracies**.

Market democracies See *liberal democracy.*

Many questioned the need for high military spending, arguing that if the world was now becoming a safer and more integrated place, what then was the purpose of spending billions on weapons?

Globalization: Challenging the International Order?

If the Cold War period was marked by a clear and sharp divide between opposing socioeconomic systems operating by radically different standards, then the post–Cold War order could readily be characterized as one in which many states were compelled to play by a single set of rules within an increasingly competitive world economy. The term most frequently used to describe this new system of international relations was *globalization*.

Globalization, however, meant different things to different theorists. For one school, the hyperglobalists, it was assumed to be undermining borders and states—quite literally abolishing the Westphalian system. Journalist and author Thomas Friedman (2005) argued that globalization has changed world politics forever, giving individuals more tools to influence markets and governments and create networks that challenge the power of states. Skeptics agreed that globalization provided a different context within which international relations were now being played out, but rejected the notion that it was doing away with the state or destroying the underlying logic of **anarchy**. As we discussed in Chapter 1, some writers were even skeptical of whether there was anything especially novel about globalization. Such skepticism, however, did not prevent globalization's critics and defenders from engaging in an extended debate about its impact on global inequality, climate change, and the more general distribution of power in the international system. Globalization was a fact of economic life and there was no escaping its logic. The only thing one could do (using the oft-repeated words of President Bill Clinton) was to "compete not retreat." Moreover, if one did not do so, the future for one's own people, and by implication one's state, was bleak.

If there was little meeting of minds among politicians and academics, there was little doubt about the impact globalization was having on the world economy, in particular in North America, Europe, and East Asia. Here, at least, the theoretical debate about the novelty, existence, and meaning of the phenomenon was being resolved, as this triad of economic power (over 80 percent of the world's total) experienced reasonable growth, increased economic interdependence, and massive wealth creation.

There was also something distinctly unethical about an apparently unregulated economic process that made billions for the few (especially those in the financial sector) while generating insecurity for the many. Globalization's defenders inferred that this was a price worth paying if there was to be any semblance of economic progress. In a world where extreme competition ruled and money moved at the flick of a switch, there was only one thing worse than being part of this runaway system—and that was not being part of it.

Anarchy A system operating in the absence of any central government. It does not imply chaos but, in realist theory, the absence of political authority.

From Superpower to Hyperpower: US Primacy

If a one-world economy operating under the same set of highly competitive rules was at least one consequence of the end of the Cold War, another was a major resurgence of American self-confidence in a new international system where it seemed to have no serious rival. This was not only a development that few had foretold (in the 1970s and 1980s, many analysts believed that the United States was in decline) but also one that many had thought impossible (most realists in fact believed that after the Cold War the world would become genuinely multipolar). It was also a situation many feared on the grounds that an America with no obvious peer competitor would act more assertively and with less restraint. That aside, all of the most obvious indicators by the late 1990s—military, economic, and cultural—seemed to point to only one conclusion: As a result of the Soviet collapse, followed in short order by an economic crisis in Japan and Europe's failure to manage two ethnic wars in the former Yugoslavia, the United States had been transformed from a mere superpower to what the French foreign minister Hubert Vedrine in 1998 termed a **hyperpower**. Former secretary of state Madeleine Albright may have also agreed, in her own way, with this assessment, although she used more diplomatic language; she called the United States "the indispensable power" in global politics. To many inside and outside the United States, it was a unipolar moment with US liberal internationalism guiding the behavior of states.

This claim to unilateral privilege was linked to a particularly bleak view of the world shared by many, though not all, US policymakers. The Cold War may have been over, they agreed: America may have emerged triumphant. But this was no reason to be complacent. To repeat a phrase often used at the time, although the "dragon" in the form of the USSR had been slain, there were still many "vipers and snakes" lurking in the tall grass. Among the five most dangerous and pernicious of these were various rogue or pariah states (Iran, Iraq, North Korea, Libya, and Cuba), the constant threat of nuclear proliferation (made all the more likely by the disintegration of the USSR and the unfolding nuclear arms race between Pakistan and India), and the threat of religious fundamentalists and ideological extremists (all the more virulent now because of the fallout from the last great battlefield of the Cold War in Afghanistan). Indeed, long before 9/11, the dangers posed by radical Islamism were very well known to US intelligence, beginning with the bombing of the US Marine barracks in Beirut, Lebanon, in October 1983 that caused the deaths of almost three hundred American personnel. The devastating bombing of the World Trade Center in 1993 and of the US embassies in Tanzania and Kenya five years later, as well as the audacious attack on the USS *Cole* in 2000, all pointed to a new form of **terrorism** that could be neither deterred nor easily defeated by conventional means.

Yet despite these threats, there was no clear indication that the United States was eager during the 1990s to project its power with any serious purpose. The United States may have possessed vast capabilities, but there appeared to be no real desire in a post–Cold War environment to expend American blood and treasure in

Hyperpower The situation of the United States after the Cold War ended. With the Soviet Union's military might greatly diminished and China having primarily only regional power-projecting capability, the United States was unchallenged in the world.

Terrorism The use of violence by nonstate groups or, in some cases, states to inspire fear by attacking civilians and/or symbolic targets and eliminating opposition groups. This is done for purposes such as drawing widespread attention to a grievance, provoking a severe response, or wearing down an opponent's moral resolve to effect political change.

Attacks on US and Western interests have been on the rise in the last few years. This photo shows an oil tanker on fire in the Sea of Oman. Two other oil tankers near the strategic Strait of Hormuz were reportedly attacked. This is an assault on a key industry that supports the global economic system. The US Navy moved ships into the region and the US government and its allies blamed Iran for the confrontation.

foreign adventures. The desire sank even further following the debacle in Somalia in 1993: the death of eighteen US soldiers there created its own kind of syndrome that made any more US forays abroad extremely unlikely. The United States after the Cold War was thus a most curious hegemon. On the one hand, its power seemed to be unrivaled (and was); on the other, it seemed to have very little idea about how to use this power other than to bomb the occasional rogue state when deemed necessary, while supporting diplomatic solutions to most problems when need be (as in the cases of the Middle East and North Korea). The end of the Cold War and the disappearance of the Soviet threat may have rendered the international system more secure and the United States more powerful, but it also made the United States a very reluctant warrior. In a very important sense, the United States during the 1990s remained a superpower without a mission.

President George H. W. Bush sought a new world order shaped by Wilsonian ideas: spreading democratic ideas and practices; promoting capitalism through trade, investment, and economic development; and supporting the rule of law through systems of regional and global governance. President Clinton continued that strategy but found himself dealing with state-building issues within the former Soviet bloc (e.g., Yugoslavia) and with failed states in Africa (e.g., Somalia). It was during the Clinton administration that some global actors began to reject some of the aforementioned Wilsonian ideas and other Western values and practices that were being projected on the world by the powerful cultural and economic forces of globalization. Many extremist movements sought to protect their cultures and openly resisted outsiders and those who sought to "modernize" their societies. Competitors for political and economic power also rose up against what they perceived as a global system of rules and practices created and controlled by the United States. Calls for reforming global institutions like the UN, the World Bank, the International Monetary Fund (IMF), and the World Trade Organization increased dramatically, and some states went farther by creating new trade organizations and creating new treaties to contain the actions of the great powers. The terrorist attacks on September 11, 2001, changed all of that. The United States launched the global war on terrorism, and new enemies and new competitors emerged. Although the second Bush administration was entangled in wars in Iraq and Afghanistan, the rest of the world moved on. China emerged as a major economic player, and Russia made it clear that it was not prepared to surrender its Cold War status as one of the world's major powers with its own sphere of influence and its own ideas about how to manage the world.

Europe in the New World System

If the most pressing post–Cold War problem for the United States was how to develop a coherent global policy in a world where there was no single major threat to its interests, then for Europe, the main issue was how to manage the new enlarged space that had been created as a result of the events in 1989. Indeed, while more triumphant Americans would continue to proclaim that it was they who had won the Cold War in Europe, it was Europeans who were the real beneficiaries. A continent that had once been divided was now whole again. Germany had been peacefully united. The states of Eastern Europe had achieved the right of self-determination. The threat of war with potentially devastating consequences for Europe had been eliminated. Naturally, the transition from one order to another was not going to happen without certain costs, borne most notably by those who would now have to face up to life under competitive capitalism. And the collapse of communism in some countries was not an entirely bloodless affair, as ethnic conflict in former Yugoslavia (1990–1999) revealed only too tragically. With that said, a post–Cold War Europe still had much to look forward to.

Although many in Europe debated the region's future, policymakers were confronted with the more concrete issue of how to bring the East back into the West, a process that went under the general heading of enlargement. In terms of policy outcome, the strategy scored some notable successes. By 2007, the European Union had grown to twenty-seven members, and NATO was one fewer at twenty-six, with most of the new members coming from the former Soviet bloc. In 2019 the European Union has 28 members, including the United Kingdom; when the UK leaves, it will be 27. NATO has 28 members with the addition of Montenegro in 2017, and it has four candidate or aspiring members. The two bodies also changed their club-like character in the process, much to the consternation of some people in the original member states, who found the entrants from the former Soviet bloc to be as much trouble as asset. According to critics, enlargement had proceeded so rapidly that the essential core meaning of both organizations had been lost. The European Union, some argued, had been so keen to enlarge that it had lost the will to integrate. NATO meanwhile could no longer be regarded as a serious military organization with an integrated command structure. One significant aspect of this was the "out of area" problem that limited NATO activities to Europe itself. This would change after 9/11. Still, it was difficult not to be impressed by the capacity of NATO and the European Union in their new roles. These institutions had helped shape part of Europe during the Cold War and were now being employed to help manage the relatively successful (though never easy) transition from one kind of European order to another. For those who had earlier disparaged the part institutions might play in preventing anarchy in Europe, the important roles played by the European Union and NATO seemed to prove that institutions were essential.

Europe, it was generally recognized, remained what it had effectively been since the end of World War II: a work in progress. The problem was that nobody could quite

Perception, Continuity, and Change After January 20, 2009

The study of global politics depends to a great extent on perception and the importance of belief systems that lead to the construction of those perceptions. How we think about the world often determines what we think is important. This habit of mind helps explain how political leaders and opinion makers in the United States were unprepared for two key events of the late twentieth century: the collapse of the Soviet Union and the rise of militant Islamic fundamentalism. The signs of the two events were in plain sight if you knew what to look for.

ISIS extremists slaughter nonbelievers in Iraq. As the new face of terrorism, ISIS is seen as more dangerous and more intolerant than other extremist terrorist movements. A global coalition is fighting ISIS in Iraq and Syria, and the Russians have joined the fight supporting the Syrian government. Instability in the region is increasing and the chance to control the process of change is disappearing quickly.

In the case of Islamic fundamentalism, certainly if you lived in a country with a large Muslim population, you would have been aware of the growing appeal of fundamentalist strains of Islam. The Wahabi sect in Saudi Arabia, for instance, forms the basis for society there. Egypt has had problems with violence linked to the Muslim Brotherhood since the time of British colonization. Indeed, the Brotherhood is often blamed for the assassination of President Anwar Sadat. In Afghanistan, the United States itself helped arm Islamic fundamentalists in their war against the Soviet invasion during the 1980s. The trend was visible every day in public as people rejected European styles of dress: More men grew beards, and more women adopted the clothing styles the fundamentalists preferred.

If North American and European leaders were not ready for the impact of Islamic fundamentalism, how unprepared are people in the rest of the world for trends resulting from the Arab Spring, the killing of Osama bin Laden, the end of

the war in Iraq and Afghanistan, and the rise of the Islamic State, or ISIS? Politics and society remain the same in most of the other Arab states, but the civil wars in Syria and Yemen have increased instability in these areas. The administration of President Barack Obama abandoned the unilateral strategies of the Bush years in favor of the multilateralism that framed the intervention in Libya and shaped the decision to lift sanctions on Iran after it agreed to halt its production of nuclear weapons. If we start with the global war on terrorism, we can see that some things now are the same, and some are not. For example, in the early months of 2009, the newly elected Obama administration continued to use Predator drone aircraft to attack suspected Islamic militants in tribal areas in Pakistan along the Afghanistan border. Operation Geronimo, which resulted in the bin Laden's death, was launched without the permission of Pakistani leaders. Pakistani officials objected to drone attacks during the Bush years, but President Obama decided that the raids must continue, and it is likely that these kinds of attacks will continue with or without the support of Pakistan. The Trump administration initially increased the role of the military in Afghanistan and is now withdrawing troops. The US is currently involved in cease fire and peace talks with the Taliban. The administration is working with a tentative peace treaty that will reduce the number of US troops but the US cannot convince the government of Afghanistan to meet with the Taliban. Further, violence continues in Afghanistan as ISIS is now part of the conflict and it is targeting the government of Afghanistan and remaining US forces. Withdrawing from Afghanistan does not mean the end of US military intervention in this region. Tbe decision by the Trump administration to recognize Jerusalem as the capital of Israel created significant opposition to US policy in the region. Iran and its ally, Hezbollah, are countering US actions in Lebanon, Iraq, and Yemen.

Change does not always occur in a direction that can be controlled. One result of the Arab Spring is the move away from autocratic regimes toward democratic systems. Unfortunately, only one nation-state involved in the Arab Spring movement has remained democratic. A moderate Islamic party won more than 40 percent of the vote in the 2011 elections in Tunisia. The Muslim Brotherhood's Freedom and Justice Party and the ultraconservative Salafis together won more than 70 percent of the seats in the new Egyptian parliament in early 2012. However, in 2013, the Egyptian military overthrew the legally elected government led by President Mohammed Morsi. The United States and its allies in the West and in the Middle East are in a political bind: Should they support religious parties that represent extremist views or nondemocratic forces like the Egyptian military that overthrew an elected government?

For people outside the United States, it is difficult to assess the meaning of apparent continuity or change in US foreign policy. One source of this difficulty is the perception popular in the developing world that the United States is the global hegemonic oppressor. People have been socialized by family members, schools, and religious and political leaders to blame the United States for their suffering. This perception may not be based on fact, and it could be as incorrect as the perception that all Muslims are terrorists or that Islamic fundamentalism poses a threat to Europe and the United States. However, perceptions and images are often more powerful than reality.

For Discussion

1. Images die a slow death. Many people in the West still distrust Russians because of the Cold War, which has been over since the late 1980s. How do we overcome the misperceptions that shape our views of other cultures?

2. Do you think countries like the United States and other major powers need an enemy? Does having foes serve political or economic interests? Explain.

3. Do you think the United States and the West will be able to work with the Islamist parties in Egypt, Tunisia, Iraq, and Afghanistan? Why or why not?

agree when, if ever, this work would be completed and where, if anywhere, the European Union would end. Some analysts remained remarkably upbeat. The European Union's capacity for dealing with the consequences of the end of the Cold War, its successful introduction of a single currency (the euro, in January 2002), and its ability to bring in new members all pointed to one obvious conclusion: Its future was ensured. Many, however, were more skeptical. After a decade-long period of expansion and experimentation, Europe, they believed, had reached a dead end. It was more divided than united over basic constitutional ends, and it faced several challenges—economic, cultural, and political—to which there seemed to be no easy answers. Indeed, according to some commentators, European leaders not only confronted older issues that remained unsolved but also faced a host of new ones (e.g., the euro crisis with a debt-ridden Greece and refugees arriving from conflict regions in the Middle East and Africa) to which they had no ready-made solutions.

The latest challenge to the European Union is the decision by the citizens of the United Kingdom to exit the European Union. British exit, or Brexit, became final on 31 January 2020 and for the next year or so the UK government will be negotiating new trade agreements and extricating from a significant number of EU rules and regulations. The UK may also chose to renegotiate its relations with many of the 27 members of the EU. It is too early to tell what that will do to the British economy or the European Union. The decision to leave was not overwhelmingly popular in the United Kingdom. The vote was close: 51.9 percent sought to leave and 48.1 percent wanted to stay. Wales and England voted to exit and Scotland and Northern Ireland voted to stay. A significant number of young and university-educated citizens believed that the economic future of the United Kingdom depended on being an active member of the European Union, and they voted to stay in large numbers. Economic nationalists and many who had lost their jobs due to the forces of economic globalization and the introduction of new technologies that made some jobs obsolete saw the European Union as a major threat. Of course, there were complaints of excessive rules and bureaucratic inefficiency, but much of the discontent had to do with what was presented by many supporters of Brexit as a loss of autonomy and sovereignty. The majority of citizens in the United Kingdom were against the shifting of decision-making authority away from London to Brussels. Another factor was the open-border policy of the European Union. It is fair to say that many citizens of other EU member states had sought jobs and a better life in the United Kingdom. To those British citizens without work, these outsiders were seen as a threat not only to their well-being but also to the dominant culture.

A good capitalist would say that in theory, capitalism means the free flow of goods, services, people, and ideas. Globalization certainly pushes those ideas, but economic nationalists—like those who supported Brexit—seek to block rather than manage the forces of globalization. Institutions of governance like the European Union are needed to manage globalization so it benefits all members of the union. It should be noted that economic nationalism was one of the factors in the United States that helped to elect Donald Trump to the presidency and keeps him popular with his supporters.

Europe may have been well aware of where it was coming from, but it had no blueprint for where it wanted to go.

Russia: From Yeltsin to Putin

One of the many problems facing the new Europe after the Cold War was how to define its relationship with postcommunist Russia, a country confronting several degrees of stress after 1991 as it began to transform itself from a Marxist superpower with a planned economy to a democratic country that was liberal and market oriented. As even the most confident of Europeans accepted, none of this was going to be easy for a state that had experienced the same system for nearly three-quarters of a century. And so it proved during the 1990s, an especially painful decade during which Russia lost its ability to effectively challenge the United States and was instead a declining power with diminishing economic and ideological assets. Furthermore, there was not much in the way of economic compensation. On the contrary, as a result of its speedy adoption of Western-style privatization, Russia underwent something close to a 1930s-style economic depression, with industrial production plummeting, living standards sinking, and whole regions once devoted to Cold War military production experiencing a free fall.

President Boris Yeltsin's foreign policy, meanwhile, did little to reassure many Russians. Indeed, his decision to get close to Russia's old capitalist enemies gave the distinct impression that he was selling out to the West. This made him a hero to many outside Russia. However, to many ordinary Russians, it seemed as if he (like his predecessor Gorbachev) was conceding everything and getting very little in return. Nationalists and old communists, still present in significant numbers, were especially scathing. Yeltsin and his team, they argued, not only had given away Russia's assets at "discount prices" to a new class of **oligarchs** but also were trying to turn Russia into a Western dependency. In short, he was not standing up for Russia's national interests.

Whether his successor Vladimir Putin, a former official in the KGB, had a clear vision for Russia when he took over the presidency matters less than the fact that, having assumed office, he began to stake out very different positions. These included greater authoritarianism and nationalism at home, a much clearer recognition that the interests of Russia and those of the West would not always be one and the same, and what turned into a persistent drive to bring the Russian economy—and Russia's huge natural resources—back under state control. This did not lead to turning back the clock to Soviet times. What it did mean, though, was that the West's leaders could no longer regard the country as a potential strategic partner. Certainly, Western governments could not assume that Russia would forever be in a state of decline. The West must instead confront a state with almost unlimited supplies of oil and gas and with a leadership determined to defend Russia's interests and to restore Russia to a position of global leadership.

In 1984, both Prime Minister Margaret Thatcher and President Ronald Reagan were dedicated to increasing tensions during the Cold War. The two of them were working to outspend the Soviet Union and to out-muscle the Soviets around the world. Thatcher and Reagan were both Machiavellian realists who wanted to defeat the Soviet Union and promote democracy and capitalism around the world.

Still, the West had less to fear now than during the Cold War. Economic reform had made Russia dependent on the West (though some Western countries, like Germany, depended on Russia for their energy requirements). Furthermore, the official political ideology did not in any way challenge Western institutions or values. Nor was Russia the military power it had once been during Soviet times. Indeed, not only was it unable to prevent some of its former republics from either membership in former enemy institutions like NATO or moving more openly into the Western camp but also, by 2007, it was effectively encircled by the three Baltic republics to the northwest, an increasingly pro-Western Ukraine to the south, and Georgia in the Caucasus. Adding to its potential woes was the fact that many of its more loyal, regional allies ran highly repressive and potentially unstable governments: Belarus, Turkmenistan, and Azerbaijan, for example.

Meanwhile, in Chechnya, Russia faced an insurgency beginning in 1994 that not only revealed deep weaknesses in the Russian military but also brought down Western outrage on its head—perhaps not to the point of causing a rupture but certainly enough to sour relations. Many in the United States and a few in Europe were compelled to conclude that while Russia may have changed in several positive ways since the collapse of the USSR, it still maintained an authoritarian outlook, a disregard for human rights, a willingness to use military force, and an inclination toward empire.

President Trump came to power suggesting that President Putin was someone that we could work with, but several areas of conflict are preventing a warming of great-power relations.

WHAT'S YOUR WORLDVIEW?

President Putin has taken many positions that challenge the interests of the United States and the West, including supporting the government of Syria with military forces and using cyberwarfare to disrupt US and European elections. Is Russia trying to re-establish its role as a major superpower by challenging Western views of liberal democracy and presenting an illiberal authoritarian governing option?

International Service for Human Rights (ISHR)

The International Service for Human Rights is an independent, nongovernmental organization (NGO) dedicated to promoting and protecting human rights. ISHR memebers achieve this by supporting human rights defenders, strengthening human rights systems, and leading and participating in coalitions for human rights change.

ISHR's internship program provides a wide range of opportunities for students and recent graduates who intend to work in an NGO and in the field of human rights. ISHR recruits all year long and interns participate in ISHR's work in both Geneva and New York. An ISHR internship offers a unique opportunity to learn about the workings of the international human rights system and the functioning of a human rights NGO. An internship will increase your understanding of current human rights issues at the international, regional, and national levels. It will also enable you to develop your skills and competencies for future employment in the human rights sector.

For more information go to https://www.ishr.ch.

First is the controversy over Russian involvement in the US presidential election. A second area of controversy involves NATO. There have been several complaints from Lithuania and other Baltic states that Russian intelligence is responsible for recent cyberattacks and is interested in regaining influence over the Baltic region. Another NATO issue is the ongoing expansion of the Western alliance. Recently, the Balkan nation-state of Montenegro became the twenty-ninth member of NATO. The Russians saw this as a hostile move raising questions about the US intent. Obviously, a third area of concern is the fact that the United States and Russia support opposite sides in the Syrian civil war. These differences are significant, but there are critical policy issues that will not be resolved without US-Russian cooperation. Will we be able to address climate change without US-Russian cooperation? Is it possible to contain North Korea without great-power cooperation including Russia, China, and the United States? Someone needs to lead, and the current US administration seems to be withdrawing from several critical areas of global governance, so we may need a new great-power concert to address critical global challenges.

East Asia: Primed for Rivalry?

If perceived lessons from history continue to play a crucial role in shaping modern Western images of post-Soviet Russia, then the past also plays a part in defining the international relations of East Asia—and a most bloody past it has been. The time following World War II was punctuated by several devastating wars (in China, Korea, and Vietnam), revolutionary insurgencies (in the Philippines,

Russian president Vladimir Putin speaks to the media after the G20 summit in Osaka, Japan. Putin sees the West as the enemy of Russia and he has aggressively pursued a policy aimed at challenging the West and its allies. Russian military interventions in Ukraine and Syria and Russian cyberinterference in US and European elections are part of this aggressive strategy.

Malaya, and Indonesia), authoritarian rule (nearly everywhere), and revolutionary extremism (most tragically in Cambodia). The contrast with the postwar European experience could not have been more pronounced. Scholars of international relations point out that whereas Europe managed to form a new liberal security community during the Cold War, East Asia did not. In part, this was the result of the formation of the European Union and the creation of NATO (organizations that had no equivalents in Asia). But it was also because Germany managed to effect a serious reconciliation with its immediate neighbors while Japan (for largely internal reasons) did not. The end of the Cold War in Europe transformed the continent dramatically, but this was much less true in East Asia, where powerful communist parties continued to rule in China, North Korea, and Vietnam. Additionally, several territorial disputes, one between Japan and Russia and another between China and its neighbors over islands and navigation rights in the South China Sea, threatened the security of the region.

For all these reasons, East Asia, far from being primed for peace, was still ripe for new rivalries. Europe's very bloody past between 1914 and 1945, went the argument, could easily turn into Asia's future. This was not a view shared by every commentator, however. In fact, as events unfolded, this uncompromisingly tough-minded realist perspective came under sustained criticism. Critics did not deny the possibility of future disturbances: How could they, given Korean division, North Korea's nuclear weapons program, and China's claim to Taiwan? But several factors did suggest that the region was not quite the powder keg some thought it to be.

The first and most important factor was the great economic success experienced by the region itself. The sources of this have been much debated, with some people suggesting that the underlying reasons were cultural and others that they were directly economic (cheap labor plus plentiful capital); a few believed they were the by-product of the application of a nonliberal model of development employing the strong state to drive through rapid economic development from above. Some have also argued that the United States played a crucial role by opening its market to East Asian goods while providing the region with critical security on the cheap. Whatever the cause or combination of causes, the fact remains that by the end of the twentieth century, East Asia had become the third-largest powerhouse in the global economy, accounting for nearly 25 percent of world **gross domestic product (GDP)**.

Second, although many states in East Asia may have had powerful memories of past conflicts, these were beginning to be overridden in the 1990s by a growth in regional trade and investment. Economic pressures and material self-interest appeared to be driving countries in the region together rather than apart. The process of East Asian economic integration was not quick—the **Association of Southeast Asian Nations (ASEAN)** was only formed in 1967. Nor was integration accompanied by the formation of anything like the European Union. However, once regionalism began to take off during the 1990s, it showed no signs of slowing down.

A third reason for optimism lay with Japan. Here, despite an apparent inability to unambiguously apologize for past misdeeds and atrocities—a failure that cost it dearly in terms of **soft power** (see Chapter 4) influence in the region—its policies could hardly be characterized as disturbing. On the contrary, having adopted its famous peace constitution in the 1950s and renounced the possibility of ever acquiring nuclear weapons (Japan was one of the strongest upholders of the original 1968 Nonproliferation Treaty), Japan demonstrated no interest in upsetting its neighbors by acting in anything other than a benign manner. Furthermore, by spreading its considerable largesse in the form of aid and large-scale investment, it went some of the way toward fostering better international relations in the region. Even its old rival China was a significant beneficiary, and by 2003, more than five thousand Japanese companies were operating on the Chinese mainland. However, in a move that perhaps reflects concern for aggressive behavior by China and North Korea, the Japanese parliament approved legislation that allows for the Japanese self-defense forces to engage in foreign conflicts.

This leads us to China. Much has been written about "rising China," especially by analysts who argue—in classical realist fashion—that when new powerful states emerge onto the international stage, they are bound to disturb the existing balance of power. China looks benign now, they agree. It will look different in a few years' time—once it has risen. However, there may be more cause for guarded optimism than pessimism, largely because China has adopted policies (both economic and military) whose purpose clearly is to reassure its neighbors that it can rise peacefully and thus effectively prove the realists wrong. It has also translated policy into action by supporting regional integration, exporting its considerable capital to other countries in East Asia, and working as a responsible party rather than a spoiler inside regional multilateral institutions. Such policies are beginning to bear fruit, with greater numbers of once-skeptical neighbors viewing China as a benevolent instrument of development rather than a threat.

Gross domestic product (GDP) The sum of all economic activity that takes place within a country.

Association of Southeast Asian Nations (ASEAN) A geopolitical and economic organization of several countries located in Southeast Asia. Initially formed as a display of solidarity against communism, it has since redefined and broadened its aims to include the acceleration of economic growth and the promotion of regional peace.

Soft power The influence and authority deriving from the attraction that a country's political, social, and economic ideas, beliefs, and practices have for people living in other countries.

However, recent Chinese moves to build artificial islands to extend its territorial waters and, thus, its control of strategic waterways seem to have adversely affected some of the more positive feelings about this rising power.

In the end, however, all strategic roads in China (and in East Asia as a whole) lead to the one state whose presence in the region remains critical: the United States. Though theoretically opposed to a unipolar world in which there is only one significant global player, the new Chinese leadership has pursued a most cautious policy toward the United States. No doubt some Americans will continue to be wary of a state run by the Communist Party, whose human rights record can hardly be described as exemplary. However, as long as China continues to act in a cooperative fashion, there is a good chance that relations will continue to prosper. There is no guaranteeing the long-term outcome. With growth rates around 10 percent per year, with its apparently insatiable demand for overseas raw materials, and with enormous dollar reserves at its disposal, China has already changed the terms of the debate about the future of international politics. Of course, it remains to be seen what effects the global economic collapse that began in 2008 will have on China; in 2015, China devalued its currency, which caused world financial markets to suspect a potential weakening of its economy. China may be overly dependent on foreign investment and militarily light years behind the United States, but even so, it presents a set of challenges that did not exist in the much simpler days of the Cold War. Indeed, one of the great ironies of international history may be that China as a rising capitalist power playing by the rules of the market may turn out to be more of a problem for the West than China the communist power of the past.

India is a nuclear state and its neighbors China and Pakistan also have nuclear weapons. India and Pakistan are always fighting over Kashmir and both are increasing military spending. China is watching both countries carefully and is concerned with India's growing military power. Is this a new arms race in Asia, with China, India, and Pakistan seeking military supremacy?

Latin America: Becoming Global Players

Early in the nineteenth century, a patron–client relationship developed between the United States and Latin America. The Monroe Doctrine (1823) stated that any European country attempting to intervene in the Americas would be seen as an aggressor, and the United States would respond in kind. President Theodore Roosevelt added his corollary in 1904 that proclaimed the US right to intervene in cases of "flagrant wrongdoing" by a Latin American government, which usually meant a country was acting against US interests.

In the great ideological struggle between the United States and the Soviet Union, Latin American countries were expected to be client states of the United States and to take pro-US positions in disputes with the Soviet Union. Cuba was the pariah state because of its alliance with the USSR and its communist government. Any government that strayed from the US orbit was usually replaced in a covert coup or overthrown by local forces loyal to the United States for the sake of its own economic and strategic interests. The United States tried to overthrow the regimes in Cuba and Nicaragua, and it was successful in removing procommunist leaders in Guatemala, Chile, and Grenada. Unfortunately for the United States, its image in Latin America today has been tarnished due to the fact that many of the authoritarian military leaders in Latin America were supported by the United States.

Since 9/11, the United States has not prioritized relations with Latin America, and other countries, such as China, have become more influential in the region. This may change as the United States has backed a new leader for Venezuela and Jair Bolsonaro, a conservative nationalist recently elected in Brazil, is said to be a Trump-like leader who has already taken controversial positions on the 2019 Amazon fires promoting economic development over the environment. Meanwhile, Brazil, Venezuela, and Chile have become important global and regional players. Brazil, owing in part to its energy and manufacturing industries, has become an important member of the newly emerging Brazil, Russia, India, China, and South Africa (BRICS) powers, and its soft power diplomacy campaigns have landed it the 2014 World Cup and the 2016 Summer Olympics. Chile has become a major player in global trade and in regional and global institutions such as the Organization of American States and the UN. As a very stable social democratic state, Chile is emerging as an active middle power in global politics. Venezuela under the late president Hugo Chávez and his successor Nicolas Maduro presented a challenge to US leadership, if not hegemonic practices in Latin America. He increased trade and investment with China, conducted military exercises with Russia, and created an alternative economic development program that allocates five times more aid than the United States in Latin America.

Recent history, including the war on terrorism and the Bush administration's emphasis on unilateralism and preemptive war, has hurt the image of the United States in the region. The European Union is now the largest investor in Latin America, and trade with China is increasing. For decades, the US policy of not recognizing and boycotting Cuba was considered obsolete, but in December 2014 President Obama announced the restoration of full diplomatic relations with the island nation. Although the US trade embargo remained in effect, the United States planned to ease restrictions on remittances, travel, and banking, marking a dramatic turning point in US-Cuban relations and, more broadly, US-Latin American relations. Most, if not all, of these reforms have been overturned by the current administration. Reminding us all of the language of the Cold War, the Trump administration levied new sanctions on Cuba, Venezuela, and Nicaragua with the stated goal of preventing the spread of socialism and communism and preventing human rights abuses in these countries.

Furthermore, the Trump administration overhauled the North American Free Trade Agreement (NAFTA), creating a new trade agreement that the Trump administration claims is better for US workers, farmers, and manufacturers. The US, Mexico and Canada Agreement (USMCA) has been labeled as NAFTA 2.0 but it does include some important changes, including new labor laws and wage rules, intellectual property rules, and more open agricultural markets. As of the summer of 2019, only Mexico has ratified the agreement.

▶ The War on Terrorism: From 9/11 to Iraq, Afghanistan, and Syria

The end of the Cold War marked one of the great turning points of the late twentieth century, but 9/11 was a reminder that the international order that had come into being as a result was not one that found ready acceptance everywhere. Osama bin Laden was no doubt motivated by far more than a dislike of globalization and American primacy. As many analysts have pointed out, bin Laden's vision was one that pointed back to a golden age of Islam rather than forward to something modern. That said, his chosen method of attacking the United States using four planes, his use of video to communicate with followers, his employment of the global financial system to fund operations, and his primary goal of driving the United States out of the Middle East could hardly be described as medieval. He represented a very modern threat, one that could not be dealt with by traditional means. Old strategies, such as containment and deterrence, were no longer relevant. If this was the beginning of a "new global war on terrorism," as some argued at the time, then it was unlikely to be fought using policies and methods learned between 1947 and 1989.

This new nonstate network threat, led by a man whose various pronouncements owed more to holy texts than anything else, made it difficult for some in the West to understand the true character of radical Islamic movements and their use of terrorist tactics. As the controversial war on terrorism unfolded—first in Afghanistan and then in Iraq, Iran, and Pakistan—some began to view the United States as the imperial source of most of the world's growing problems.

The new threat environment provided the United States with a fixed point of reference around which to organize its international affairs. It built close relations with many states—Russia, India, Pakistan, and China perhaps being the most important—that were now prepared to join it in waging a global war against terror. After the 9/11 attacks, Bush administration officials felt compelled to act in a far more assertive fashion abroad. Indeed, some of Bush's more conservative supporters believed that one of the reasons for the attack on the United States in the first place was that it had not been assertive enough in the 1990s. Finally, policymakers in the Bush administration seemed to abandon the defense of the status quo in the Middle East. The events of 9/11, they argued, had changed the original formula whereby the United States turned a blind eye to autocratic regimes that existed in the region in exchange for cheap oil and stability. US dependency on these two commodities was no longer enough to justify making deals with states like Saudi Arabia that produced the dangerous ideologies that inspired terrorism.

This sort of thinking paved the way for the war against Iraq in 2003. However, Iraq had not been involved in 9/11; the regime itself was secular and it shared the same goal as the United States in seeking to contain the geopolitical ambitions of Islamic Iran. For these reasons, different analysts have identified different factors to explain the war, including the ideological influence exercised by the neoconservatives on President Bush, America's close relationship with Israel, and America's desire to control Iraq's oil. This leaves us with more questions than answers, with possibly the most credible answer being the less conspiratorial one: The United States went to war partly because it thought it would win fairly easily, partly because it got its intelligence wrong, and partly because some political leaders thought—rather unwisely—that building a new regime in Iraq would be just as easy as getting rid of the old one.

Regardless of the motive, it was clear by 2009 that the Iraq War was a strategic blunder that neither delivered stable democracy to Iraq nor inspired others in the region to undertake serious political reform. It also had the doubly dangerous consequence of disturbing the whole of the Middle East, while making it possible for Iran to gain even greater influence in the region than it had before. In fact, by undermining the old regime in Iraq, the United States effectively created a vacuum into which an increasingly self-confident Iranian regime has marched. Finally, as a result of their action in Iraq, the United States and its allies provided radical Islamists around the world with a rallying point that they appear to have exploited with some skill, as is illustrated by the rise of the Islamic State.

After the 9/11 attacks, Al-Qaeda was given sanctuary by the Taliban government in Afghanistan. The United States immediately demanded that the leaders of this terrorist network be turned over to the United States for trial. The Taliban refused, and on October 7, 2001, the US military invaded Afghanistan, destroyed Al-Qaeda's terrorist training camps, and overthrew the Taliban-controlled government. NATO members invoked Article 5 and came to the aid of the United States.

NATO took command of the International Security Assistance Force (ISAF) in 2003. Since 2009, the United States has moved away from a counterinsurgency policy that put an emphasis on protecting civilians, providing services, and nation building toward more direct military action: increasing airstrikes in both Afghanistan and Pakistan, the use of drones for surveillance and attacks on suspected terrorist leaders, a dramatic increase in covert operations, and the use of special-forces surprise attacks on terrorist camps in the tribal regions that extend into Pakistan.

The Trump administration has made fighting the Islamic State or ISIS in the Middle East and parts of Africa one of his top priorities. In Iraq and Syria, President Trump has removed many of the constraints imposed by the Obama administration. These rules restricted airstrikes and tactical raids in places like Somalia. Early on in the Trump administration, the then Secretary of Defense Jim Mattis had the authority to raise troop levels in Iraq, Afghanistan, and Syria. With many changes in the Trump administration's defense and foreign policy team, it appears that the military is running the US war on terrorism.

The Trump administration has been vague about its goals in the Syrian civil war. Trump has said that he is open to an alliance with Russia to defeat the Islamic State. In Afghanistan, the

The credibility of the United States and key officials like Secretary of State Colin Powell was significantly undermined by the decision to go to war with Iraq and remove the Iraqi leadership from power. This may be attributed to the power of Vice President Dick Cheney and his neoconservative colleagues, who sought to recreate the world based on US values and interests.

Trump administration has made it clear that the goal is winning and not state building. Trump clearly stated that no military forces would be used to construct a democratic state in Afghanistan.

The Trump administration has also announced a new South Asia policy that links Afghanistan, Pakistan, and India. Pakistan harbors many of the terrorist groups—providing a safe haven and a staging ground for the Taliban and other extremist groups. The United States has threatened to cut off aid to Pakistan if they refuse to help. To convince India to help, the United States intends to leverage India's dependence on trade with the United States.

The nineteen-year war in Afghanistan continues; the Syrian civil war continues as an humanitarian disaster; the war in Yemen threatens to expand to a war between Saudi Arabia and Iran; and, finally, backsliding in Iraq means more US troops and military resources will be sent to that region of the world. Meanwhile, the number of US troops and military installations are on the rise. The United States now has a military presence in thirteen African countries.

With the successful covert operation that resulted in the killing of Osama bin Laden in 2011, many citizens in NATO countries were wondering why their men and women continued to fight and die for a corrupt and ineffective government in Afghanistan. Suicide bombers continued to kill civilians who cooperated with the United States and the Afghan government, and the Taliban resurged, taking refuge in Pakistan. One of the most dangerous terrorist groups, the Haqqani network, is based in Pakistan and funded by the Pakistani intelligence agency, the Inter-Services Intelligence directorate (ISI). The Afghanistan government claims that the ISI has supported a fivefold increase in insurgent attacks since 2006.

Meanwhile, the NATO ISAF mission was completed in 2014, and in January 2015, NATO began to train, advise, and assist Afghanistan's security forces in noncombat roles under the Resolute Support Mission. However, renewed Taliban military activities, including the taking of Kunduz, a major northern Afghan city, suggest that the Afghan government might have trouble containing insurgent forces.

The United States and Pakistan are allies, but they have different interests in Afghanistan. The United States hopes that when it withdraws, Afghanistan will be a relatively stable, prosperous, and democratic state that is no longer an incubator for terrorists. Pakistan does not want a strong Afghanistan that might be governed by ethnic Tajiks, who are traditionally allies of India. We must remember that India and Pakistan are rivals in this region and both have nuclear weapons. When the United States and NATO withdraw completely, peace and stability in this region may not yet be achieved.

With or without the war in Afghanistan, however, the West would still likely be confronted by the challenge of violent radical Islam. This is a movement that not only feeds off Western blunders and policies (especially American ones in the Middle East and South Asia) but also is based on a set of cultural values, state practices, and historical grievances that make it almost impossible to deal with effectively—without compromising what it means to be part of the West. Herein, though, lies another problem: how precisely to define this conflict.

It was fashionable to characterize it as one between two different "civilizations" (a term originally made popular by American writer Samuel Huntington

The War That Never Ends

Background

International relations, as a field, has always been concerned with the origins of wars. Long-term changes in the balance of power, fear of encirclement, imperial ambition—not to mention misperception and ideology—have all been employed at one time or another to explain why states engage in military action. The Iraq War presents a useful, and possibly difficult, test case for various theories of war origins. Several competing explanations have been advanced so far to explain the US decision to go to war against Iraq in 2003. These include, among others, the official argument that Iraq represented a serious and potentially rising threat to a critically important region; the more materialist thesis that the United States was determined to secure direct control of Iraq's massive reserves of oil; and the popular claim that the war was the product of pressures arising from within the United States itself—here identified as the Israel lobby, the ideologically inclined neoconservatives, and their various supporters on the Christian right. This coalition was joined by a few liberals who wanted a regime change and wanted Saddam Hussein punished as a brutal dictator.

The Case

The student of world politics, however, is still left with a number of unanswered questions. First, would the war have happened without the quite unexpected election of George W. Bush in late 2000? That is, did the president make a huge difference to the decision taken? Second, could Bush have then led the United States into war without the profound shock created by the equally unexpected attack of 9/11? Considered this way, wasn't the war largely the by-product of fear and insecurity? Third, what role did British Prime Minister Tony Blair play? Indeed, was this a war made possible by an alliance with one of the major powers and a permanent member of the UN Security Council? Fourth, would it have been feasible at all if various American writers and policymakers had not thought the United States so powerful that it could more or less do anything in the world? That is, to what extent did the notion of the "unipolar moment" contribute to the final decision to go to war? Furthermore, were the intellectual grounds for the war not also laid by

those during the post–Cold War period who thought it wise to promote democracy and encouraged others to intervene in the internal affairs of sovereign states for humanitarian purposes? Finally, to what extent could one argue that the Iraq War was in the US national interest—and if it was, then why did so many realists oppose the war?

Outcome

The year 2013 was the tenth anniversary of British participation in the invasion of Iraq and the opposition to that decision is still very strong among the UK population. In July 2016, the Chilcot Report on the Iraq War concluded that the British decision to go to war was based on flawed intelligence. The former prime minister claimed he made the decision in good faith based on the information that he was provided by the United States. The debate in reaction to the Chilcot Report in the United Kingdom clearly serves as a reminder to all leaders to be more cautious about sending troops to war based on incomplete information and to be careful about trusting an ally.

For Discussion

1. The debates about the role of think tanks like the Project for a New American Century and individuals like William Kristol, Richard Perle, and Paul Wolfowitz in shaping the decisions of the Bush administration will continue for years. How important are policy advisers like these, and when do they have the most influence?
2. Did the ideas of George W. Bush, Dick Cheney, and Colin Powell matter in shaping US policy? Were their advisers just as important? Explain.
3. Some experts have suggested that the Bush administration was very Wilsonian in that it aimed to rebuild the Middle East based on American values of liberal democracy. Is there anything new about a country wanting to project its values? Could this have been done without the preemptive use of force? Explain.
4. Although American troops remain in Iraq, the Iraq War is now officially over. Was it worth the human and financial costs? Why or why not?

in 1993). Nevertheless, there was something distinctly uncompromising about a conflict between those on the one side who supported democracy, **pluralism**, individualism, and a separation between state and church and those on the other who preached intolerance and supported **theocracy** while calling for armed struggle and **jihad** against the unbeliever. Not that these views were shared by all Muslims; indeed, these radical views were roundly condemned by the overwhelming majority of Muslim clerics and followers of Islam. Still, as the antagonism unfolded, there seemed to be enough disaffected people in enough societies—including Western ones—to make this aggressive ideology an occasional but potent threat. The way the world in general and the West in particular deal with it will likely determine the shape of international relations for many years to come.

Conclusion

In this chapter, we have seen some of the trends and events that created the contemporary globalized system. War (both "hot" and "cold"), revolutions, and colonization and its collapse each had a role in the evolution of international society. The irony might be found in this fact: Religion played a role in both 1648 and 2001. The signatories of the Peace of Westphalia wanted to remove religion from European international politics. Members of Al-Qaeda and now the Islamic State and its allies want to bring religion back into global politics.

The Peace of Westphalia in the seventeenth century created an international system in Europe that many people at the time believed would make for more orderly politics on the continent. In the same way, the end of the Cold War in the twentieth century seemed to promise a more peaceful world. But as we have seen in this chapter, these hopes went unfulfilled. The effects of revolutions, wars, and European imperialism have revealed the hollow nature of the European international system. Moreover, during the Cold War—while much of the attention of politicians and academics in the

Pluralism A political theory holding that political power and influence in society do not belong just to the citizens nor only to elite groups in various sectors of society but are distributed among a wide number of groups in the society. It can also mean a recognition of ethnic, racial, and cultural diversity.

Theocracy A state based on religion.

Jihad In Arabic, *jihad* means "struggle." Jihad can refer to a purely internal struggle to be a better Muslim or a struggle to make society more closely align with the teachings of the Koran.

WHAT'S TRENDING?

The End of Peace?

In Michael Mandelbaum's latest book, *The Rise and Fall of Peace on Earth* (2019), he makes a very compelling argument that the liberal international order—the global political and economic system established by the United States and its allies after 1945—is seriously weakened if not on the way to ending. The liberal order is being eroded by the actions of three authoritarian nation-states: Iran, Russia, and China.

The United States has provided security and systems of governance that provided order and stability and that has helped the global economy prosper.

Mandelbaum's core argument is that since the fall of the Berlin Wall, the world has experienced twenty-five years of great-power peace. This is not to say that there have been no conflicts and violence across the world. The civil wars in Yugoslavia, Syria, and Yemen and the continuing wars in Afghanistan and Iraq have killed thousands of people. But since the end of the Cold War, China, Russia, and the United States have not fought a major war.

A vibrant global economy and US military dominance kept the peace, but now "autocracy" has destroyed the peace. Mandelbaum's argument is that this post–Cold War peace ended because Iran, China, and Russia "adopted foreign policies of aggressive nationalism" that reignited the security competition in the world. Leaders of each of these nation-states sought to enhance their standing with their domestic populations by presenting themselves as defenders of the country against expansionary predators like the United States and ideas and norms that challenge the dominant beliefs and traditions of their state. In Russia, China, and Iran, nationalism has become their source of power, and by "wrapping themselves in the flag" the leaders gain legitimacy at home. Thus, aggressive nationalism and not having a successful economic or political system keep these leaders in power.

developed world was focused on the US-USSR confrontation—other wars, economic trends, and social movements around the world were too often ignored. As a result, the euphoria in Western Europe and the United States that followed the end of the Soviet Union soon gave way to a new set of challenges and threats.

The United States and its allies created a liberal world order that resulted in a relatively stable system that allowed many nation-states to prosper. We must now contend with changes in that liberal order and the rise of nationalist movements and major authoritarian powers. (See *What Is Trending* in this chapter.) The critical question is this: Who will lead the global system now that the United States has abandoned its leadership role?

CONTRIBUTORS TO CHAPTER 2: *David Armstrong, Michael Cox, Len Scott, Steven L. Lamy, and John Masker*

KEY TERMS

Anarchy, p. 56
Appeasement, p. 43
Armistice, p. 41
Arms race, p. 50
Association of Southeast Asian Nations (ASEAN), p. 66
Balance of power, p. 36
Bipolar, p. 46
Blitzkrieg, p.43
Capitalism, p. 46
Cold War, p. 46
Concert of Europe, p. 37
Congress of Vienna, p. 38
Containment, p. 48
Détente, p. 51

Fourteen Points, p. 41
Genocide, p. 44
Glasnost, p. 54
Gross domestic product (GDP), p. 66
Hegemony, p. 46
Holocaust, p. 43
Hyperpower, p. 57
Intercontinental ballistic missiles (ICBMs), p. 52
Jihad, p. 73
League of Nations, p. 41
Liberal democracy, p. 42
Market democracies, p. 55
Marshall Plan, p. 48

Munich Agreement of 1938, p. 42
National self-determination, p. 37
North Atlantic Treaty Organization (NATO), p. 49
Oligarchs, p. 51
Ostpolitik, p. 36
Peace of Utrecht (1713), p. 36
Peace of Westphalia (1648), p. 36
Perestroika, p. 54
Pluralism, p. 73
Protestant Reformation, p. 36
Rapprochement, p. 51
Society of states, p. 36

Soft power, p. 66
Sovereign equality, p. 36
Strategic Arms Reduction Treaty (START), p. 54
Strategic Defense Initiative (SDI), p. 53
Superpower, p. 44
Terrorism, p. 57
Theocracy, p. 73
Thirty Years' War (1618–1648), p. 36
Treaty of Versailles, 1919, p.41
Trench warfare, p. 41
Truman Doctrine, p.48
Warsaw Pact, p. 49

REVIEW QUESTIONS

1. Was the international system of nineteenth-century Europ merely a means of legitimizing imperialism? Explain.

2. How did the method by which European colonies in Africa and Asia gained their independence determine their postindependence internal politics?

3. Why did the United States become involved in wars in Asia after 1950? Illustrate your answer by reference to either the Korean War or the Vietnam War.

4. How have scholars of international relations attempted to explain the end of the Cold War?

5. Why did liberal theorists predict that the world would become a more stable place after the end of the Cold War, and why did realists disagree with them?

6. If the United States won the Cold War, why did it have such problems defining a grand strategy for itself after 1989 and before 9/11?

7. How has globalization since the Cold War changed the basic character of world politics?

8. How successfully has Europe adapted to the challenges facing it since the end of the Cold War?

9. How has the war on terrorism changed global politics?

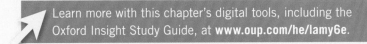

Learn more with this chapter's digital tools, including the Oxford Insight Study Guide, at **www.oup.com/he/lamy6e**.

THINKING ABOUT GLOBAL POLITICS

Understanding and Resolving International Conflicts

INTRODUCTION

In this exercise, you will be asked to analyze several conflict situations from the perspective of different state and non-state actors or players directly or indirectly involved in a given conflict. First, we ask you to explore the causes of this conflict, and second, we ask you to consider possible ways of managing or resolving the conflict. You might have to do some research to find answers to our questions. This is a great opportunity to explore the wide variety of sources on the web and in your university or college library.

PROCEDURE

This is a cooperative learning exercise. In groups of three or four, begin by reviewing the Cold War conflicts in this chapter and the conflicts in Chapter 6.

1. Review the Cold War conflicts and identify those that might still be going on. For those that have ended, how did they end? What were the reasons these conflicts were resolved?
2. Now look at the conflicts from 1946 to 2009. Pay particular attention to conflicts that began after the Cold War and respond to the following questions:
   a. Who is involved in this conflict? Primary actors? Secondary actors?
   b. What do these actors claim are the causes of the conflict?
   c. What other factors serve to accentuate the conflict and increase its lethality?
3. In Chapters 1 and 4, we introduce you to levels of analysis: tools for explaining decision making and the behavior of states in the international system. Since war and conflict are a constant in the international system, we can use levels to explain why wars begin and how they might end. With your cooperative learning team, come up with plausible explanations for the start of each conflict. Was it caused by the leader's desire for power (level 1), the state's need for oil (level 2), or the fear of a neighbor's military buildup or the security dilemma (level 3)? Now share your list of plausible explanations with the rest of the class. See if you can reach agreement on the most frequent reasons that countries go to war. Are there any patterns that develop? You might also check your ideas with the work of historians or official records on the war. If we know why countries go to war, can we anticipate and even prevent future wars?
4. Now, with some understanding of why wars begin, let's review several examples of peacemaking efforts. There are many examples of conflicts that have ended peacefully. Select at least two of these conflicts and identify the factors that helped all the parties reach an acceptable peace. For example, was one party defeated and forced to accept a peace agreement, like Japan and Germany in World War II, or was peace achieved because a third party offered mediation and assistance, as Norway did to help reach a peace agreement in Sri Lanka?

WRITING ASSIGNMENT

What has this exercise taught you about the difficulties of preventing future wars and the problems associated with peacemaking? Do you think peace, defined as an absence of war, is a utopian dream? Must we live in a world where all we can hope to do is manage conflict and prevent systemic war?

3 Realism, Liberalism, and Critical Theories

US soldiers train during Cyber Quest, a simulation of combat missions where they were introduced to advanced cyber, electronic warfare, and signal equipment. The future of warfare is likely hybrid warfare or "gray zone" tactics that include cyberattacks, the use of fake news, propaganda, economic sanctions and blackmail, proxy wars, and military maneuvers and expansion. Are our security institutions prepared for this form of warfare?

All philosophies tend to elevate their truths into suppositions of absolute validity, based upon the authority of reason and claiming what the modern age calls science.

—**HANS MORGENTHAU**

Theory is always for some one, and for some purpose.

—**ROBERT W. COX**

Most leaders must deal with the possibility of war and conflict. Since the time of Thucydides, states have had to deal with an anarchic international system, which means the absence of a common power or agreed-upon rules that govern the international system. Most leaders of nation-states have embraced a realist view of the international system, and that means these leaders are focused on their own national interests and are skeptical about chances for cooperation. It is obvious that both the first and second world wars encouraged world leaders to reach agreements to end all future wars. Many leaders were encouraged by liberal thinking that suggested that democratic states are less likely to go to war and that international law and open markets also contribute to peace. The battle between liberal internationalists and realists intensified at this point in time.

We know that every nation-state must provide security for its citizens, and since the end of World War II, leaders have come together to create regional and global institutions that promote collective military action to respond to security challenges and to protect their interests. Today, these institutions focus on extremist organizations that use terrorism or states that use aggressive behavior in an attempt to challenge order and stability in the global system. War is a constant, and it is a contest of beliefs and the desire for more territory or power. Today, new areas of geopolitical conflict and technology are changing the nature of war and increasing the difficulty of providing security for people in rich and poor states.

We may also be in a new era of great power conflict. Both Russia and China have rejected the liberal order that the United States has promoted since the end of World War II. This liberal internationalism was the foundation of American leadership during the Cold War and was the basis of US leadership in the twenty-five years after the Cold War. Nationalism and realism appear to be

CHAPTER OUTLINE

Introduction 79

What Is Realism? 80

What Is Liberalism? 89

Critical Theories 104

Conclusion 118

FEATURES

CASE STUDY The Power of Ideas: Politics and Neoliberalism 101

THEORY IN PRACTICE What Makes a Theory "Alternative" or Critical? 109

THEORY IN PRACTICE Jane Addams and the Women's International League for Peace and Freedom 116

WHAT'S TRENDING? Will Capitalism Survive? 118

THINKING ABOUT GLOBAL POLITICS The Melian Dialogue: Realism and the Preparation for War 120

on the rise. Russia and China are authoritarian states and are using their military resources to defend their spheres of influence and protect their sovereignty. Russia has annexed the Crimea and continues to challenge the stability of Ukraine, and China is building artificial islands as military bases in the South China Sea. A great power war is unlikely, but the chances for miscalculation may be on the rise. For example, all three great powers may be concerned that one of the other two will develop sophisticated technologies that will make their nuclear or conventional weapons systems inoperable.

The entire world seems to be in an arena of uncertainty, if not conflict, about how best to organize and govern the global system. We are convinced that theories, traditions, and narratives matter, and the conflict between different ways of seeing the world and organizing our political systems has returned. We simply cannot understand how things are without understanding the theoretical traditions in international relations.

From the realist perspective, negotiations and diplomacy have both costs and benefits. Realists believe one must always negotiate from strength and be prepared to act with force or the threat of force when dealing with rogue states or terrorist networks that have no intention of following international rules. On the other hand, liberal internationalists believe that international institutions and diplomatic efforts can reduce the power and influence of radical networks and rogue states. For example, in the area of nuclear weapons, the power, prestige, and influence of the United States and liberal institutions like the International Atomic Energy Agency (IAEA) are being undermined by North Korea and Iran. Realists argue that the basic flaw of liberal thinking is that a rogue state can be talked out of developing nuclear weapons. Instead, realists believe the major powers must put pressure on North Korea by choking off its ability to export and import weapons and military equipment, cutting off all access to financial resources, and pressuring China to rein in its North Korean ally. Similarly, realists argue that all states must respond collectively to defeat ISIS. Liberal thinkers still hold out hope for arms control talks and successful coercive diplomacy efforts aimed at persuading North Korean leaders to end their intransigence and join the international community of nation-states and containing or ending the extremist strategies of ISIS and other radical networks.

◤ Introduction

Theory is used to make sense of what is going on in this complex world. Theory both shapes and is shaped by traditions, beliefs, values, and experiences. From these we develop stories or narratives that reflect our beliefs and the theories about the world that we embrace. As scholars, we are always asking why people explain things in a particular way or why they accept a certain description of a problem or global issue. Why do they see the issue differently than you do? Why do they make that argument? These are questions we must constantly ask if we are committed to seeing the world as critical thinkers.

A simple story about human security follows that illustrates the way theories and narratives determine how we see global issues and how we may react to these issues.

Family planning and the health of women and children are critical elements of any human security agenda. In early 2017, Lilianne Ploumen, the former minister of foreign trade and development cooperation for the Netherlands, decided to respond to the Trump administration's decision to restore the global gag rule—first introduced by the Reagan administration in 1984—that bans non-US organizations from receiving any US funds if they give information about and referrals for abortion or if they provide safe abortions. Minister Ploumen created *She Decides*, a global movement aimed at supporting the rights of both girls and women to decide freely about their health and about family planning. Over fifty governments attended its first conference, and the organization raised 80 million euros to replace the funds eliminated by the Trump administration.

The countries that led this effort, the Netherlands, Belgium, and Sweden, are social democratic states that believe that government has a responsibility to protect and promote human security. This could be described as a Kantian narrative that embraces a *radical liberal theory*, which we explore in this chapter. The Trump administration and the Reagan administration back in 1984 embrace a more conservative narrative that puts national interest over the interests of citizens of other states. This position also supports a critical assumption of *realist theory* that emphasizes sovereignty and noninterference in the domestic affairs of other states.

Whether the issue is about women's rights or the bellicose rhetoric emanating from both President Trump and Kim Jong Un over North Korea's nuclear weapons program, there are always many positions that are based on competing narratives and theories. Regarding North Korea, the Trump administration seems to be willing to use force, whereas our European allies suggest that diplomacy is the only way out of the crisis. Neither side wants North Korea to develop its nuclear missile program, but they take different positions based on how they see the world.

Theories are essential in your development as an informed critical thinker and an effective decision maker. One of the basic skills of citizenship in this era of globalization is to be able to *describe, explain, predict, and prescribe* (DEPP) from these different theoretical positions. For example, how do realists describe the war in Syria? How do they explain its origins? What do they think is likely to

Theory A proposed explanation of an event or behavior of an actor in the real world. Definitions range from "an unproven assumption" to "a working hypothesis that proposes an explanation for an action or behavior." In international relations, we have intuitive theories, empirical theories, and normative theories.

happen in the next few months, and what should be done about it? These analytic skills are essential for you as a scholar in this field. They also will help determine your level and form of *participation* in the global system. Thus, after you finish reading and discussing this chapter, you should know how realists, liberals, and critical thinkers *describe, explain, predict, prescribe, and eventually participate* (DEPPP) in global politics and frame global issues.

What Is Realism?

Realism A theoretical approach that analyzes all international relations as the relation of states engaged in the pursuit of power. Realists see the international system as anarchic, or without a common power, and they believe conflict is endemic in the international system.

Power This is a contested concept. Many political scientists believe that power is the capacity to do things and, in social and political situations, to affect others to get the outcome one wants. Sources of power include material or tangible resources and control over meaning or ideas.

Over the centuries, various world leaders have sought to create international rules to make life more stable and predictable by decreasing outbreaks of violent aggression. As you will recall from Chapter 2, the Peace of Westphalia (1648) established a principle that still governs international relations: sovereignty. The key European nations who signed the peace treaties agreed that only a legitimate government could exercise control over its citizens and territory, could act independently and flexibly in its relations with other states, and could craft its own strategies and policies aimed at securing perceived national interests. By inference, no state could interfere in the domestic affairs of any other state. Of course, the principle of sovereignty applied more to the continent of Europe and less to societies anywhere else on Earth; nevertheless, sovereignty was—and still is today—a critically important concept.

By declaring some regions of the world sovereign and agreeing that sovereign states could not legally interfere with the internal business of other sovereign states, political leaders *thought* they had solved the problem of foreign wars. However, this attempt to eliminate war failed early and often: Within a year of the Peace of Westphalia, England invaded Ireland; within four years, the English and the Dutch were at war; within six years, Russia and Poland were at war; and so it went.

With this reality in mind, it is relatively easy to understand why the earliest perspective on international relations, referred to as **realism**, is based on the following three assumptions:

1. States are the only actors in international relations that matter.
2. A policymaker's primary responsibility is to create, maintain, and increase national **power**—the means available to a state to secure its national interests—at all costs.
3. No central authority stands above the state. The anarchic nature of the international system is an essential assumption for realist thinkers and, in fact, for most liberal thinkers and even some critical-approach thinkers.

The Chinese Belt and Road Initiative is aimed at building a new "silk road" to advance Chinese economic interests. The government in Sri Lanka agreed to lease a southern seaport to a Chinese joint venture in exchange for loans to build the port. These protestors representing farmers and Marxist party members were concerned about giving up sovereignty to Chinese interests. In this case the Sri Lankan government was not able to keep up the payments and China took over the port. Is this a new form of imperialism?

The world perceived by realists is lawless, competitive, and uncertain. In fact, one influential philosopher who helped define realism, Thomas Hobbes, published this pessimistic observation about life in his political treatise *Leviathan*: "The life of man is solitary, poor, nasty, brutish and short." The only way to avoid misery and anarchy, according to Hobbes (1651), was to have a strong ruler of a strong state impose order and provide protection from external attack.

The Essential Realism

In later sections, we will see how realism can be regarded as a broad theoretical umbrella covering a variety of perspectives, each with its own leading authors and texts. Despite the numerous denominations, keep in mind that, essentially, all realists subscribe to the following three Ss: *statism*, *survival*, and *self-help*. Let's discuss these three essential elements in more detail and also examine some of realism's shortcomings.

Statism

For realists, the state is the main actor, and sovereignty is its distinguishing trait. The meaning of the sovereign state is inextricably bound up with the use of force. In terms of its internal dimension, to illustrate this relationship between violence and the state, we need to look no further than Max Weber's famous definition of the state as "the monopoly of the legitimate use of physical force within a given territory" (M. J. Smith 1986, 23). Within this territorial space, **sovereignty** means that the state has supreme authority to make and enforce laws. This is the basis of the unwritten contract between individuals and the state. According to Hobbes, for example, we trade our liberty in return for a guarantee of security (safety and protection of a way of life). Once security has been established, **civil society** can begin—a society of individuals and groups not acting as participants in any government institutions or in the interests of commercial companies. But in the absence of security, people are in the state of nature where there can be no business, no art, no culture, no society. The first move for the realist, then, is to organize power domestically. Only after power has been organized can community begin.

Realist international theory assumes that, domestically, the problem of order and security is solved. However, in the real world—in the relations among independent sovereign states—insecurities, dangers, and threats to the very existence of the state loom large. Realists primarily explain this on the basis that the very condition for order and security—namely, the existence of a sovereign world government—is missing from the international realm. Realists claim that in this condition of anarchy, states compete with other states for power and security.

The nature of the competition is viewed in zero–sum terms: More for one state means less for another. This competitive logic of power politics makes agreement on universal principles difficult, apart from the principle of nonintervention in the internal affairs of other sovereign states. But realists suspend even this

Sovereignty The condition of a state having control and authority over its own territory and being free from any higher legal authority. It is related to, but distinct from, the condition of a government being free from any external political constraints.

Civil society The totality of all individuals and groups in a society who are not acting as participants in any government institutions or acting in the interests of commercial companies.

principle—as we saw in the previous chapter, designed in seventeenth-century Europe to facilitate coexistence—and argue that in practice, nonintervention does not apply in relations between great powers and their regional neighbors. As evidenced by the most recent behavior of the United States in Afghanistan and Iraq, modern hegemonic (dominant) states are able to influence events far beyond their borders, overturning the nonintervention principle on the grounds of national security and international order.

Given that the first move of the state is to organize power domestically and maintain law and order, and the second is to accumulate power internationally, it is important to consider in more depth what realists mean by power. The classical realist Hans Morgenthau offers the following definition of power: "Man's control over the minds and actions of other men" (1948/1955, 26). There are two important points that realists make about the elusive concept of power. First, power is a relational concept; one does not exercise power in a vacuum but in relation to another entity. Second, power is a relative concept; calculations need to be made not only about one's own power capabilities but also about the power that other states possess. Yet the task of accurately assessing the power of states is infinitely complex. Too often, power calculations are reduced to counting the number of troops, tanks, aircraft, and naval ships a country possesses in the mistaken belief that this translates into the ability to get other actors to do something they would not otherwise do.

Survival

The second principle that unites realists is the assertion that in international politics the preeminent goal is survival. Although realists disagree as to whether the accumulation of power is an end in itself, one would think there is no dissenting from the argument that security is states' ultimate concern. Survival is held to be a precondition for attaining all other goals, whether these involve conquest or merely independence. According to Kenneth Waltz, "beyond the survival motive, the aims of states may be endlessly varied" (1979, 91).

Niccolò Machiavelli tried to make a science out of his reflections on state survival. His book *The Prince* codifies a set of maxims that would enable leaders to maintain their hold on power. In important respects, we find two related Machiavellian themes recurring in the writings of modern realists; both derive from the idea that international politics requires different moral and political rules from those of domestic politics. The first is the task of understanding what realists believe to be the true nature of international politics; the second is the need to protect the state at all costs (even if this means the sacrifice of one's own citizens). These concerns place a heavy burden on the shoulders of state leaders. In the words of Henry Kissinger, the academic realist who became secretary of state during the Nixon presidency, "a nation's survival is its first and ultimate responsibility; it cannot be compromised or put to risk" (1977, 204). Their guide must be an **ethic of responsibility**: the careful weighing of consequences and the realization that individual immoral acts might need to be carried out for the greater good.

Ethic of responsibility For realists, it represents the limits of ethics in international politics; it involves the weighing up of consequences and the realization that positive outcomes may result from amoral actions.

An ethic of responsibility is frequently used as a justification for breaking the laws of war, as in the case of the British nighttime firebombing raids on Nazi Germany, or the Bush administration's decision to alter its obligations on the issue of torture as it concerned suspected terrorists held at Guantánamo Bay. The principal difficulty with the realist formulation of an ethic of responsibility is that, while instructing leaders to consider the consequences of their actions, it does not provide a guide for how state leaders should weigh the consequences (M. J. Smith 1986, 51).

Not only does realism provide an alternative moral code for state leaders, proponents claim, but also it suggests a wider objection to the whole enterprise of bringing **ethics** into international politics. (Morality is what is good, right, and proper, and ethics is the examination, justification, and analysis of morality as custom or practice.) Starting from the assumption that each state has its own particular values and beliefs, realists argue that the state is the supreme good and there can be no community beyond borders. This moral relativism has generated a substantial body of criticism, particularly from some liberal theorists who endorse the notion of universal human rights.

Self-Help

Kenneth Waltz's *Theory of International Politics* (1979) brought to the realist tradition a deeper understanding of the international system itself. Unlike many other realists, Waltz argued that international politics is not unique due to the regularity of war and conflict because this is also familiar in domestic politics. The key difference between domestic and international orders lies in their structure. In the domestic polity, citizens usually do not need to defend themselves. In the international system, there is no higher authority, no global police officer, to prevent and counter the use of force. Security can therefore be realized only through **self-help**. In an anarchic structure, "self-help is necessarily the principle of action" (Waltz 1979, 111). But in the course of providing for one's own security, the state in question will automatically be fueling the insecurity of other states.

The term given to this spiral of insecurity is the **security dilemma**. According to Nick Wheeler and Ken Booth, security dilemmas exist "when the military preparations of one state create an irresolvable uncertainty in the mind of another as to whether those preparations are for 'defensive' purposes only (to enhance its security in an uncertain world) or whether they are for offensive purposes (to change the status quo to its advantage)" (1992, 30). This scenario suggests that one state's quest for security is often another state's

Ethics Ethical studies in international relations and foreign policy include the identification, illumination, and application of relevant moral norms to the conduct of foreign policy and assessing the moral architecture of the international system.

Self-help In realist theory, in an anarchic system, states cannot assume other states will come to their defense even if they are allies. Each state must take care of itself.

Security dilemma In an anarchic international system (one with no common central power), when one state seeks to improve its security, it creates insecurity in other states.

This Russian S-400 missile system has recently been purchased by Turkey and India. This has caused a number of problems for the United States and the North Atlantic Treaty Organization (NATO). Turkey is a member of NATO, and buying Russian weapons challenges the goals of the security community. In the case of India, the US is concerned that their reliance on Russian military equipment might give Russia more influence over the Indian government. Are we in a new global battle for allies and spheres of influence?

Multipolar system

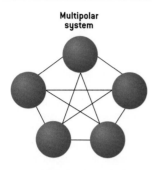

Bipolar

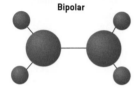

Unipolar (Hegemony)

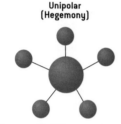

Power, Politics, and Polarity.

Which of these power arrangements best represents the world today? What about the world of the early twentieth century? Nineteenth century? How does theory help us understand these global power dynamics?

Anarchic system A realist description of the international system that suggests there is no common power or central governing structure.

source of insecurity. States find it very difficult to trust one another and often view the intentions of others in a negative light. Thus, the military preparations of one state are likely to be matched by neighboring states. The irony is that at the end of the day, states often feel no more secure than before they undertook measures to enhance their own security.

In a self-help system, structural realists argue that the balance of power, or parity and stability among competing powers, will emerge even in the absence of a conscious policy to maintain it (i.e., prudent statecraft). Waltz argues that balances of power result irrespective of the intentions of any particular state. In an **anarchic system** populated by states with leaders who seek to perpetuate themselves, alliances will be formed that seek to check and balance the power against threatening states. Classical realists, however, are more likely to emphasize the crucial role state leaders and diplomats play in maintaining the balance of power. That is, the balance of power is not natural or inevitable; the leaders of states construct it.

However, various kinds of realists debate the stability of a balance-of-power system. (See Figure 3.1) Many argue that the balance of power has been replaced by an unbalanced unipolar order. It is questionable whether other countries will actively attempt to balance against the United States as structural realism might predict. But whether it is the contrived balance of the Concert of Europe in the early nineteenth century or the more fortuitous balance of the Cold War, balances of power are broken—through either war or peaceful change—and new balances emerge. What the perennial collapsing of the balance of power demonstrates is that states are at best able to mitigate the worst consequences of the security dilemma but are not able to escape it due to the absence of trust in international relations.

Historically, realists have illustrated the lack of trust among states by reference to Enlightenment thinker Jean-Jacques Rousseau's parable of the stag hunt. In *Man, the State and War*, Kenneth Waltz revisits the parable:

> *Assume that five men who have acquired a rudimentary ability to speak and to understand each other happen to come together at a time when all of them suffer from hunger. The hunger of each will be satisfied by the fifth part of a stag, so they "agree" to cooperate in a project to trap one. But also the hunger of any one of them will be satisfied by a hare, so, as a hare comes within reach, one of them grabs it. The defector obtains the means of satisfying his hunger but in doing so permits the stag to escape. His immediate interest prevails over consideration for his fellows. (1959, 167–168)*

Waltz argues that the metaphor of the stag hunt provides a basis for understanding the problem of coordinating the interests of the individual versus the interests of the common good and the payoff between short-term interests and long-term interests. In the self-help system of international politics, the logic of self-interest mitigates against the provision of collective goods, such as "security" or "free trade." In the case of the latter, according to the theory of **comparative advantage**, all states would be wealthier in a world that allowed freedom of goods and services across borders. But individual states, or groups of states like the European Union, can increase their wealth by pursuing **protectionist** policies, such as tariffs on foreign goods, as long as other states do not respond in kind.

Of course, the logical outcome is for the remaining states to become protectionist, international trade to collapse, and a subsequent world recession to reduce the wealth of each state. Thus, the question is not whether all will be better off through cooperation but rather who will likely gain more than another. It is because of this concern with relative-gains issues that realists argue that cooperation is difficult to achieve in a self-help system.

One Realism or Many?

So far in this chapter, we have treated the realist lens as if it were a unified set of beliefs and propositions. It is, however, not at all that way, as both the model's supporters and critics have pointed out. The belief that there is not one realism but many leads logically to a delineation of different types of realism. Next, we will outline key differences between classical realism and structural realism, or neorealism. A summary of the varieties of realism outlined appears in Table 3.1.

Comparative advantage A theory developed by David Ricardo stating that two countries will both gain from trade if, in the absence of trade, they have different relative costs for producing the same goods. Even if one country is more efficient in the production of all goods than the other (absolute advantage), both countries will still gain by trading with each other as long as they have different relative efficiencies.

TABLE 3.1	**A Taxonomy of Realisms**			
Type of Realism	**Key Thinkers**	**Key Texts**	**Big Idea**	
Classical Realism (Human Nature)	Thucydides (ca. 430–406 BCE)	*The Peloponnesian War*	International politics is driven by an endless struggle for power that has its roots in human nature. Justice, law, and society either have no place or are circumscribed.	
	Machiavelli (1532)	*The Prince*	Political realism recognizes that principles are subordinated to policies; the ultimate skill of the state leader is to accept, and adapt to, the changing power-political configurations in global politics.	
	Morgenthau (1948)	*Politics Among Nations*	Politics is governed by laws that are created by human nature. The mechanism we use to understand international politics is the concept of interests defined in terms of power.	
Structural Realism (International System)	Rousseau (c. 1750)	*The State of War*	It is not human nature but the anarchical system that fosters fear, jealousy, suspicion, and insecurity.	
	Waltz (1979)	*Theory of International Politics*	Anarchy causes logic of self-help, in which states seek to maximize their security. The most stable distribution of power in the system is bipolarity.	
	Mearsheimer (2001)	*Tragedy of Great Power Politics*	The anarchic, self-help system compels states to maximize their relative power position.	
Neoclassical Realism	Zakaria (1998)	*From Wealth to Power*	The systemic account of world politics provided by structural realism is incomplete. It needs to be supplemented with better accounts of unit-level variables such as how power is perceived and how leadership is exercised.	

Protectionist An economic policy of restraining trade between states through methods such as tariffs on imported goods, restrictive quotas, and a variety of other government regulations designed to allow "fair competition" among imports and goods and services produced domestically.

Classical realism The belief that it is fundamentally the nature of people and the state to act in a way that places interests over ideologies. The drive for power and the will to dominate are held to be fundamental aspects of human nature.

Classical Realism

The lineage of **classical realism** begins with Thucydides' representation of power politics as a law of human behavior. The classical realists argued that the drive for power and the will to dominate are the fundamental aspects of human nature. The behavior of the state as a self-seeking egoist is understood to be merely a reflection of the characteristics of the people that make up the state. Therefore, it is human nature that explains why international politics is necessarily power politics. This reduction of realism to a condition of human nature is one that frequently reappears in the leading works of the doctrine, most famously in the work of Hans Morgenthau. The important point for Morgenthau is, first, to recognize that these laws exist and, second, to devise the most appropriate policies that are consistent with the basic fact that human beings are flawed creatures.

Another distinguishing characteristic of classical realism is its adherents' belief in the primordial character of power and ethics. Classical realism is fundamentally about the struggle for belonging, a struggle that is often violent. Patriotic virtue is required for communities to survive in this historic battle between good and evil, a virtue that long predates the emergence of sovereignty-based notions of community in the mid-seventeenth century. Classical realists therefore differ from contemporary realists in the sense that they engaged with moral philosophy and sought to reconstruct an understanding of virtue in light of practice and historical circumstance.

Thucydides was the historian of the Peloponnesian War, a conflict between two great powers in the ancient Greek world, Athens and Sparta. Though he was a disgraced general on the losing side, Thucydides' work has been admired by subsequent generations of realists for its insights into many of the perennial issues of international politics. One of the significant episodes of the war between Athens and Sparta is known as the "Melian dialogue" and provides a fascinating illustration of a number of key realist principles. At the end of this chapter, the "Thinking About Global Politics" feature reconstructs Thucydides' version of the dialogue between the Melians and the Athenian leaders who arrived on the island of Melos to assert their right of conquest over the islanders. In short, what the Athenians are asserting over the Melians is the logic of power politics and the duty of a hegemon to maintain order. Because of their vastly superior military force, they are able to present a fait accompli to the Melians: either submit peacefully or be exterminated. Citing their neutrality in the war, the Melians for their part try to buck the logic of power politics, appealing in turn with arguments grounded in justice, God, and their lack of support for the Spartans. As the dialogue makes clear, although at a military disadvantage and bound to lose, the Melians chose to fight. Their defeat became the basis for a maxim of realism: "The strong do what they have the power to do and the weak accept what they have to accept."

How is a leader supposed to act in a world animated by such malevolent forces? The answer given by Machiavelli is that all obligations and treaties with other states must be disregarded if the security of the community is under threat. Moreover, imperial expansion is legitimate, as it is a means of gaining greater security. Other classical realists, however, advocate a more temperate understanding of moral conduct. Mid-twentieth-century realists such as Butterfield, Carr, Morgenthau, and Wolfers believed that wise leadership and the pursuit of the national interest in ways that are compatible with international order could mitigate anarchy. Taking their lead from Thucydides, they recognized that acting purely on the basis of power and self-interest without any consideration of moral and ethical principles frequently results in self-defeating policies.

Structural Realism, or Neorealism

Structural realists, sometimes called neorealists, concur that international politics is essentially a struggle for power, but they do not endorse the classical-realist assumption that this is a result of human nature. Instead, structural realists attribute security competition and interstate conflict to the lack of an overarching authority above states and the relative distribution of power in the international system.

> **Structural realism (neorealism)** A theory of realism that maintains that the international system and the condition of anarchy or no common power push states and individuals to act in a way that places interests over ideologies. This condition creates a self-help system. The international system is seen as a structure acting on the state with individuals below the level of the state acting as agency on the state as a whole.

Kenneth Waltz, the best-known structural realist, defines the structure of the international system in terms of three elements—organizing principle, differentiation of units, and distribution of capabilities, or power. He identifies two different organizing principles: anarchy, the decentralized realm of international politics, and hierarchy, the basis of domestic order. He argues that the units of the international system are functionally similar sovereign states; hence, unit-level variation is irrelevant in explaining international outcomes. It is the third tier, the distribution of capabilities across units, that is, according to Waltz, the key independent variable to understanding important international outcomes such as war and peace, alliance politics, and the balance of power. Many structural realists are interested in providing a rank ordering of states so as to differentiate and count the number of great powers that exist at any particular point in time. The number of great powers in turn determines the structure of the international system.

How does the international distribution of power impact the behavior of states, particularly their power-seeking behavior? In the most general sense, Waltz argues that states, especially the great powers, must be sensitive to the capabilities of other states. The possibility that any state may use force to advance its interests results in all states being worried about their survival. According to Waltz, power is a means to the end of security: "Because power is a possibly useful means, sensible statesmen try to have an appropriate amount of it." He adds, "In crucial situations, however, the ultimate concern of states is not for power but for security" (1989, 40). In other words, rather than being power maximizers, states, according to Waltz, are *security* maximizers. He argues that power maximization often proves to be dysfunctional because it triggers a counterbalancing coalition of states.

A different account of the power dynamics that operate in the anarchic system is provided by John Mearsheimer's theory of **offensive realism**, another variant of structural realism. While sharing many of the basic assumptions of

> **Offensive realism** A structural theory of realism that views states as power maximizers.

Defensive realism A structural theory of realism that views states as security maximizers—more concerned with absolute power as opposed to relative power. According to this view, it is unwise for states to try to maximize their share of power and seek hegemony.

Waltz's structural-realist theory, frequently termed **defensive realism**, Mearsheimer differs from Waltz when it comes to describing the behavior of states. Most fundamentally, "offensive realism parts company with defensive realism over the question of how much power states want" (Mearsheimer 2001, 21). According to Mearsheimer, the structure of the international system compels states to maximize their relative power position. Under anarchy, he agrees that self-help is the basic principle of action. Yet he also argues that while all states possess some offensive military capability, there is a great deal of uncertainty about the intentions of other states. Consequently, Mearsheimer concludes that there are no satisfied or status quo states; rather, all states are continuously searching for opportunities to gain power at the expense of other states. Contrary to Waltz, Mearsheimer argues that states recognize that the best path to peace is to accumulate more power than anyone else. The ideal position is to be the global hegemon of the international system; however, Mearsheimer believes that global hegemony is impossible and therefore concludes that the world is condemned to perpetual great-power competition.

Contemporary Realist Challenges to Structural Realism

Although offensive realism makes an important contribution to realism, some contemporary realists are skeptical of the notion that the international distribution of power alone can explain the behavior of states. **Neoclassical-realist** scholars have attempted to build a bridge between international structural factors and unit-level factors, such as the perceptions of state leaders, state–society relationships, and the motivations of states (we will learn more about the various levels of analysis—*individual, national, systemic,* and *global*—in Chapter 4). According to Stephen Walt, the causal logic of neoclassical realism "places domestic politics as an intervening variable between the distribution of power and foreign policy behavior" (2002, 211).

Neoclassical realism A version of realism that combines both structural factors such as the distribution of power and unit-level factors such as the interests of states.

One important intervening variable is leaders themselves—namely, how they perceive the international distribution of power, given that there is no objective, independent reading of the distribution of power. Structural realists assume that all states have a similar set of interests, but neoclassical realists such as Randall Schweller (1996) argue that historically this is not the case. He argues, with respect to Waltz, that the assumption that all states have an interest in security results in neorealism exhibiting a profoundly status quo bias. Not only do states differ in terms of their interests, but also they differ in terms of state strength, or the ability to extract and direct

This photo shows a military exercise in Lithuania organized by the US Army in Europe involving thirteen NATO member countries and six thousand troops. Most of the Baltic states are NATO members and they are increasing spending due to the threat of Russian military activities and greater spending on new and improved weapon systems. Russia's battle against the West and its desire to retain its spheres of influence may lead to more security tensions in future years.

resources at their disposal in the pursuit of particular interests. Neoclassical realists argue that different types of states possess different capacities to translate the various elements of national power into state power. Thus, contrary to Waltz, all states cannot be treated as "like units" with similar goals, interests, and values.

Given the varieties of realism that exist, it is perhaps a mistake to understand traditions as a single stream of thought, handed down in a neatly wrapped package from one generation of realists to another. Instead, it is preferable to think of living traditions like realism as the embodiment of both continuities and conflicts. Despite the different strands running through the tradition, there is a sense in which all realists share a common set of propositions.

In the next section, we will examine liberalism, another tradition within the field of international relations theory. We will see that realism and liberalism share certain assumptions about the international system but disagree strongly about others.

◢ What Is Liberalism?

After World War I, the leaders of the victorious states—the United States, the United Kingdom, and France—adapted the underlying principles of political and economic **liberalism** they had been practicing domestically since the seventeenth and eighteenth centuries to international relations in an attempt to avoid a second devastating war. Liberal thought is grounded in the notion that human nature is good, not evil; that states can thrive best in a world governed by morality and law; and that reason and rationality will compel states to cooperate to achieve mutually held goals in peace (see Table 3.2 for a list of noteworthy liberal thinkers). Envisioning a world where compliance with the principles of liberalism would facilitate more harmonious relationships among global actors, the United States, the United Kingdom, and France sought to recast the rules of international relations as they drafted the 1919 Treaty of Versailles and the charter for the League of Nations.

Liberalism A theoretical approach that argues for human rights, parliamentary democracy, and free trade—while also maintaining that all such goals must begin *within a state*.

Just as realism derives from the observations and interpretations of political situations, so does liberalism. The seeds of a liberal perspective had been sown in the wake of the fifteenth century's so-called Age of Discovery, which fostered the rampant expansion of global commerce as states, explorer entrepreneurs, and trading companies became involved in the business of exchanging goods and services. Commerce across political and cultural boundaries was never just a simple matter of private individuals swapping one commodity for another (otherwise known as *barter*) or for money. To engage in commerce, these pioneer global traders had to negotiate the terms of trade—that is, how much of one commodity was worth how much of another, or how much money; they had to abide by new and different cultural norms and legal systems; and they had to bargain with political leaders to gain and maintain market access. Trade formed linkages that transcended political, social, cultural, and economic boundaries.

As trade expanded to include the exchange of a wider variety of commodities from all over the world, so did the linkages. Over time, a complex web of

TABLE 3.2	**Taxonomy of Liberalism**	
Classical Liberals		
Hugo Grotius	*On the Law of War and Peace* (1625)	Natural law gives way to international law where contracts, oaths, and a system of just war exist and must be abided.
John Locke	*Two Treatises of Government* (1689)	The State of Nature provides for the equality and freedom of every man before the law, as well as the right to own property.
Immanuel Kant	*Perpetual Peace* (1795)	Peace is to be secured by the abolition of standing armies, the proliferation of democratic states, and respect for state sovereignty.
Richard Cobden	*England, Ireland and America, by a Manchester Manufacturer* (1835)	Free trade would create a more peaceful world order and lead to increased individual liberty, prosperity, and interdependency.
Contemporary Liberals		
Woodrow Wilson	*Fourteen Points* (1918)	A liberal internationalists, he sought transparency among states, the proliferation of free trade, the reduction of arms, and the creation of a multinational institution to ensure the implementation of mutual agreements—considered by many to be idealism.
David Mitrany	*The Functional Theory of Politics* (1975)	Interstate trade and cooperation in common sectors are mutually beneficial and will spill over to include other sectors—functionalism.
Hedley Bull	*The Anarchical Society* (1977)	The state has control over its people and a certain territory and advocates a "society of states" bound by common rules and interests—pluralism.

connections evolved along with the multitude of formal and informal agreements needed to facilitate commerce. As economic and social interactions crossed political boundaries with increasing frequency, trade and immigration patterns rendered realist guidelines decreasingly useful to policymakers. It was no longer so easy to engage in unilateral actions without experiencing economic repercussions, as World War I had emphatically demonstrated.

Realism, however, prevailed. Its logic, combined with the realities of the world, led to its continued domination of global and foreign policymaking. The major world powers of the twentieth century were not willing to abandon unilateralism. The United States never ratified the treaty creating the League of Nations (due to concerns about future entanglements in European wars), France sought revenge over Germany, and the United Kingdom sought to limit the power of the League. Then, one by one, Germany, Japan, and Italy violated Versailles Treaty covenants and sought to regain lost power by acquiring resources and invading other states.

The world was soon consumed by World War II, which, like its predecessor, committed combatant and noncombatant alike to the national cause of winning. In a desperate effort to end the war and to signal to others evidence of its military might, the United States dropped atomic bombs on Hiroshima and Nagasaki, Japan, triggering a profound and fundamental change in international and human relations.

As World War II came to an end, key decision makers in the United States recognized that the United States needed to be an active player on the world scene; they also saw that the United States had the financial and military power to enforce a new world order based on its political and economic visions. Moreover, they realized that, in a world where sovereignty remained the reigning principle, decisions affecting two or more states required the participation of all affected stakeholders and the backing of the rule of law. Embedded in this **multilateralist** approach to global governance is a principle of political liberalism—namely, that the "governed" (in this case, states) should have a say in the development of those rules, norms, and principles by which they will be governed. The political leaders of the United States and its allies created a host of international governmental organizations (IGOs), such as the United Nations and the Bretton Woods economic institutions, to manage global relations in key political and economic arenas. The mandates of these IGOs were informed by **liberal internationalism**, a combination of

Multilateralism The process by which states work together to solve a common problem.

Liberal internationalism A perspective that seeks to transform international relations to emphasize peace, individual freedom, and prosperity and to replicate domestic models of liberal democracy at the international level.

ENGAGING WITH THE WORLD

Environmental Defense Fund

This is one of the world's largest environmental organizations, with more than two million members and a staff of seven hundred scientists, economists, policy experts, and other professionals around the world. The EDF believes that prosperity and environmental stewardship must go hand in hand. EDF staff are optimists, because they have seen smart ideas make a huge difference. EDF is building strong partnerships across interests to ensure lasting success. EDF is addressing today's most urgent environmental challenges by working in partnership with others.

EDF offers internships and fellowships for students and recent graduates in a variety of programs and departments throughout the organization. By joining EDF as an intern, you too can be part of a vibrant workplace that welcomes diverse perspectives, talents, and contributions, where innovation and a focus on results are a way of life. EDF's Internship Program welcomes intellectually hungry leaders to join us, advance our work, and cultivate the skills and relationships needed for a successful career working for the environment. For more information on how to apply for an internship, check out https://www.edf.org/jobs/internships-fellowships.

- democratic values (political liberalism),
- free trade markets (economic liberalism),
- multilateral cooperation (multilateralism), and
- a rule-based international society that respects sovereignty and human rights.

We will discuss these principles further as we define the boundaries of liberal thinking and begin to understand how neoliberalism and radical liberalism have since evolved their own set of arguments from the liberal tradition.

Defining Liberalism

In essence, liberalism argues for human rights, parliamentary democracy, and free trade—while also maintaining that all such goals must begin *within a state*. The early European liberals thought that reforms within one's own country would be the first step in a long process that could eventually extend to world affairs. Although the belief in the possibility of progress is one identifier of a liberal approach to politics (Clark 1989, 49–66), there are other general propositions that define the broad tradition of liberalism.

Perhaps the appropriate way to begin this discussion is with a four-dimensional definition (Doyle 1997, 207). First, all citizens are equal before the law and possess certain basic rights to education, access to a free press, and religious toleration. Second, the legislative assembly of the state possesses only the authority invested in it by the people, whose basic rights it may not abuse. Third, a key dimension of the liberty of the individual is the right to own property, including productive forces. Fourth, liberalism contends that the most effective system of economic exchange is one that is largely market driven and not one that is subordinate to bureaucratic regulation and control, either domestically or internationally. When these propositions are taken together, we see a stark contrast between liberal values of individualism, tolerance, freedom, and constitutionalism and realism's conservatism, which places a higher value on order and authority and is willing to sacrifice the liberty of the individual for the stability of the community.

Although in the past many writers have tended to view liberalism as a theory of domestic government, what is becoming more apparent is the explicit connection between liberalism as a *domestic* political and economic theory and liberalism as an *international* theory. Properly conceived, liberal thought on a global scale embodies a domestic political and economic system *operating at the international level*. Like individuals, states have different characteristics; some are bellicose and war prone, whereas others are tolerant and peaceful. In short, the identity of the state determines its outward orientation. Liberals see a further parallel between individuals and sovereign states. Although the character of states may differ, all states in a global society are accorded certain "natural" rights, such as the generalized right to nonintervention in their domestic affairs. We see this in the "one state, one vote" principle in the UN General Assembly (see Chapter 6 for more on the United Nations).

On another level, the domestic analogy refers to the extension of ideas that originated inside liberal states to the international realm, such as the coordinating role played by institutions and the centrality of the rule of law to the idea of a just order. Historically, liberals have agreed with realists that war is a recurring feature of the anarchic states system. But unlike realists, they do not identify **anarchy** as the cause of war. Certain strands of liberalism see the causes of war located in **imperialism**, others in the failure of the balance of power, and still others in the problem of undemocratic regimes. And can we prevent war through collective security, commerce, or world government? While it can be productive to think about the various strands of liberal thought and their differing prescriptions (Doyle 1997, 205–300), given the limited space permitted to deal with a broad and complex tradition, the emphasis here is on the core concepts of international liberalism and the way these relate to the goals of order and justice on a global scale.

Unlike what we learned about realism, liberalism is at its heart a doctrine of change and belief in progress. Liberalism pulls in two directions: Its commitment to freedom in the economic and social spheres leans in the direction of a minimalist role for governing institutions, while the democratic political culture required for basic freedoms to be safeguarded requires robust and interventionist institutions. This has variously been interpreted as a tension between different liberal goals and more broadly as a sign of rival and incompatible conceptions of liberalism. Should a liberal polity—no matter what the size or scale—preserve the right of individuals to retain property and privilege, or should liberalism elevate equality over liberty so that resources are redistributed from the strong to the weak? When we look at politics on a global scale, it is clear that inequalities are far greater while at the same time our institutional capacity to do something about them is that much less. As writers on globalization remind us, the intensification of global flows in trade, resources, and people has weakened the state's capacity to govern.

The Essential Liberalism

Immanuel Kant and Jeremy Bentham were two of the leading liberals of the **Enlightenment**. Both were reacting to the barbarity of international relations, what Kant described as "the lawless state of savagery," at a time when domestic politics was at the cusp of a new age of rights, citizenship, and constitutionalism. Their abhorrence of the lawless savagery led them individually to elaborate plans for "perpetual peace." Although written more than two centuries ago, these manifestos contain the seeds of core liberal ideas, in particular the belief that reason could deliver freedom and justice in international relations. For Kant, the imperative to achieve perpetual peace required the transformation of individual consciousness, republican constitutionalism, and a federal contract between states to abolish war (rather than to regulate it, as earlier international lawyers had argued). This federation was likened to a permanent peace treaty rather than a "super-state" actor or world government.

WHAT'S YOUR WORLDVIEW?

Liberal internationalism emerged as a dominant perspective after the two world wars. After these conflicts, most states wanted to return to a rule-based system that promotes democracy and free trade. Different elements of liberalism competed with realist thinking throughout the Cold War. The end of the Cold War meant the triumph of liberal internationalism, but now many are seeing a rise of nationalism, authoritarianism, and realist thinking. Do you think we are headed to a conflict among major powers in critical regions of the world?

Anarchy A system operating in the absence of any central government. It does not imply chaos but, in realist theory, the absence of political authority.

Imperialism The practice of foreign conquest and rule in the context of global relations of hierarchy and subordination. It can lead to the establishment of an empire.

Enlightenment A movement associated with rationalist thinkers of the eighteenth century. Key ideas (which some would argue remain mottoes for our age) include secularism, progress, reason, science, knowledge, and freedom. The motto of the Enlightenment is *"Sapere aude!"* (Have courage to know!) (Kant 1991, 54).

One the best examples of how liberal ideas can contribute to peace and a cooperative community of nation-states is the European Union. In this photo, British prime minister Boris Johnson shakes hands with European Commission president Jean-Claude Juncker during a press conference at EU headquarters in Brussels. Britain and the European Union reached a new tentative Brexit deal. The United Kingdom is leaving this community, but the remaining twenty-seven members will continue to cooperate and maintain a peace in Europe. Nationalism may undermine future efforts at cooperation not only in Europe.

Democratic peace thesis A central plank of liberal-internationalist thought, the democratic peace thesis makes two claims: first, liberal polities exhibit restraint in their relations with other liberal polities (the so-called separate peace), but second, they are imprudent in relations with authoritarian states. The validity of the democratic peace thesis has been fiercely debated in the international relations literature.

Kant's claim that liberal states are peaceful in their international relations with other liberal states was revived in the 1980s. In a much-cited article, Michael Doyle argued that liberal states have created a "separate peace" (1986, 1151). According to Doyle, there are two elements to the Kantian legacy: restraint among liberal states and "international imprudence" in relations with nonliberal states.

Although empirical evidence seems to support the **democratic peace thesis**, it is important to bear in mind the limitations of the argument. For the theory to be compelling, believers in the thesis need to provide an explanation of why war has become unthinkable between liberal states. Kant argued that if the decision to use force was taken by the people rather than by the prince, then the frequency of conflicts would be drastically reduced. Democratic or liberal states tend not to go to war with other liberal or democratic states, but they *will* go to war with nonliberal or undemocratic states. Historical evidence supports this point. Thus, Kant's idea that democratic states will not go to war cannot be supported.

An alternative explanation for the democratic peace thesis might be that liberal states tend to be wealthy and therefore have less to gain—and more to lose—by engaging in conflicts than poorer, authoritarian states. Perhaps the most convincing explanation of all is the simple fact that liberal states tend to be in relations of amity with other liberal states. War between Canada and the United States is unthinkable, perhaps not because of their liberal democratic constitutions but because they are friends with a high degree of convergence in economic and political matters (Wendt 1999, 298–299). Indeed, war between states with contrasting political and economic systems may also be unthinkable because they have a history of friendly relations. An example here is Mexico and Cuba, which maintain close bilateral relations despite their history of divergent economic ideologies.

Two centuries after Kant first called for a "pacific federation," the validity of the idea that democracies are more pacific continues to attract a great deal of scholarly interest. The claim has also found its way into the public discourse of Western states' foreign policy, appearing in speeches made by US presidents as diverse as Ronald Reagan, Bill Clinton, George W. Bush, and Barack Obama. Less crusading voices within the liberal tradition believe that a legal and institutional framework must be established that includes states with different cultures and traditions. At the end of the eighteenth century, Jeremy Bentham advocated such a belief in the power of law to solve the problem of war. "Establish a common tribunal" and "the necessity for war no longer follows from a difference of opinion" (Luard 1992, 416). Like many liberal thinkers after him, Bentham showed that federal states such as the German Diet, the American Confederation, and the Swiss League were able to transform their identity from one based on conflicting interests to a more peaceful federation.

Because liberal politics and capitalism are intimately linked, many writers believe, with Adam Smith, that the elimination of tariffs, duties, and other restrictions on imports would be a vital step in dissemination of liberalism's program. For example, the belief of Richard Cobden, a British politician and public intellectual, that **free trade** would create a more peaceful world order is a core idea of nineteenth-century liberalism. Trade brings mutual gains to all the players irrespective of their size or the nature of their economies. It is perhaps not surprising that this argument found its most vocal supporters in Britain; the supposed universal value of free trade brought disproportionate gains to the hegemonic power. There was never an admission that free trade among countries at different stages of development would lead to relations of dominance and subservience.

> **Free trade** An essential element of capitalism that argues for no barriers or minimal barriers to the exchange of goods, services, and investments among states.

Like free trade, the idea of a "natural harmony of interests" in international political and economic relations came under challenge in the early part of the twentieth century. The fact that Britain and Germany had highly interdependent economies before World War I seemed to confirm the fatal flaw in the association of economic interdependence with peace. From the turn of the century, the contradictions within European civilization, of progress and exemplarism on the one hand and the harnessing of industrial power for military purposes on the other, could no longer be contained. Europe stumbled into a horrific war, resulting in the deaths of 15 million people. Not only did the war end three **empires**, but also it was a contributing factor to the Russian Revolution of 1917.

> **Empire** A distinct type of political entity, which may or may not be a state, possessing both a home territory and foreign territories. This may include conquered nations and colonies.

World War I shifted liberal thinking toward a recognition that peace is not a natural condition but one that must be constructed. Perhaps the most famous advocate of an international authority for the management of international relations was Woodrow Wilson. According to this US president, peace could only be secured with the creation of an international organization to regulate the international anarchy. Security could not be left to secret bilateral diplomatic deals and a blind faith in the balance of power. Just as peace had to be enforced in domestic society, the international domain needed a system of regulation for coping with disputes and an international force that could be mobilized if nonviolent conflict resolution failed. In this sense, more than any other strand of liberalism, idealism rests on the idea that we can replicate the liberalism we know domestically at the international level (Suganami 1989, 94–113).

Along with calls for free trade and self-determination, in his famous "Fourteen Points" speech to Congress in January 1918, Wilson argued that "a general association of nations must be formed" to preserve the coming peace; the League of Nations was to be that general association. For the League to be effective, it needed to have the military power to deter aggression and, when necessary, to use

Collective security An arrangement where "each state in the system accepts that the security of one is the concern of all, and agrees to join in a collective response to aggression" (Roberts and Kingsbury 1993, 30).

a preponderance of power to enforce its will. This was the idea behind the **collective security** system that was central to the League of Nations. Collective security refers to an arrangement where "each state in the system accepts that the security of one is the concern of all, and agrees to join in a collective response to aggression" (Roberts and Kingsbury 1993, 30). It can be contrasted with an alliance system of security, where a number of states join together, usually as a response to a specific external threat (sometimes known as "collective defense"). In the case of the League of Nations, its charter noted the obligation that, in the event of war, all member states must cease normal relations with the offending state, impose sanctions, and, if necessary, commit their armed forces to the disposal of the League Council should the use of force be required to restore the status quo. The League's constitution also called for the self-determination of all nation-states, another founding characteristic of liberal-idealist thinking on international relations.

Unfortunately, the overall experience of the League of Nations as a peacekeeper was a failure. While the moral rhetoric at the creation of the League was decidedly liberal and idealist, in practice states remained imprisoned by self-interest in the style of realism. There is no better example of this than the US decision not to join the institution it had created. With the Soviet Union initially outside the system for ideological reasons, the League of Nations quickly became a debating society for the member states. Hitler's decision in March 1936 to reoccupy the Rhineland, a designated demilitarized zone according to the terms of the Treaty of Versailles, effectively ended the League.

The Treaty of Versailles ended World War I and may have created new problems. The leaders pictured here had different interests. The United States convinced them to support the League of Nations, a liberal internationalist idea, in an attempt to create a collective security organization and prevent future wars. Then, the United States abandoned this organization. How did this decision influence the creation of the United Nations?

According to the realist's version of the history of the discipline of international relations, the collapse of the League of Nations dealt a near-fatal blow to liberal idealism. There is no doubt that the language of liberalism after 1945 was more pragmatic; how could anyone living in the shadow of the Holocaust be optimistic? Yet familiar core ideas of liberalism—belief in the benefits of progress, free trade, and respect for human rights—remained. Key political leaders in Europe and North America recognized the need to replace the League with another international institution with responsibility for international peace and security. Only this time, in the case of the United Nations, there was an awareness of the need for a consensus between the great powers for enforcement action to be taken. The framers of the UN Charter therefore included a provision (Article 27) allowing any of the five permanent members of the Security Council the power of veto. This revision constituted an important modification to the classical model of collective security (A. Roberts 1996, 315). The framers of the UN Charter also acknowledged that security was more than guns and thus created the Economic and Social Council (see Chapter 5) to build what became known as *human security*, which we will examine in Chapter 7. With the ideological polarity of the Cold War, the UN procedures for collective security were ineffectual (as either of the superpowers and their allies would veto any action proposed by the other). It was not until the end of the Cold War that a collective security system was put into operation, following the invasion of Kuwait by Iraq on August 2, 1990.

An important argument advanced by liberals in the early postwar period concerned the state's inability to cope with modernization. David Mitrany (1943), a pioneer **integration** theorist, argued that transnational cooperation was required to resolve common problems. His core concept was **functionalism**, meaning the likelihood that cooperation in one sector would lead governments to extend the range of collaboration across other sectors, known as *spillover*. As states become more embedded in an integration process, the benefits of cooperation and the costs of withdrawing from cooperative ventures increase. The history of the European Union supports Mitrany's assertion.

Academic interest in the benefits of transnational cooperation informed a new generation of scholars whose argument was not simply about the mutual gains from trade but that other **transnational nonstate actors** were beginning to challenge the dominance of sovereign states. Global politics, according to pluralists, was no longer an exclusive arena for states. The inability of the United States to win the Vietnam War provided the impetus to this research because that conflict seemed to challenge realism's central claims about power determining outcomes in international politics. In one of the central texts of this genre, Robert Keohane and Joseph Nye (1972) argued that the centrality of other actors, such as interest groups, transnational corporations (e.g., Shell Oil or AIG), and nongovernmental organizations (NGOs) like Oxfam or Human Rights Watch, had to be taken into consideration. They also asserted that military power had a declining utility in international politics. The overriding image of international relations is one of a cobweb of diverse actors linked through multiple channels of interaction.

Although the phenomenon of transnationalism was an important addition to the international relations theorists' vocabulary, it remained underdeveloped as a theoretical concept. Perhaps the most important contribution of **pluralism** was its elaboration of **interdependence**. Due to the expansion of capitalism and the emergence of a global culture, pluralists recognized a growing interconnectedness in which "changes in one part of the system have direct and indirect consequences for the rest of the system" (Little 1996, 77). Absolute state autonomy, so keenly entrenched in the minds of state leaders, was being circumscribed by interdependence. Such a development brought with it enhanced potential for cooperation, as well as increased levels of vulnerability.

In the course of their engagement with other neorealists, early pluralists modified their position. Neoliberals, as they came to be known, conceded that the

Integration A process of ever-closer union between states in a regional or international context. The process often begins with cooperation to solve technical problems.

Functionalism An idea formulated by early proponents of European integration that suggests cooperation should begin with efforts aimed at resolving specific regional or transnational problems. It is assumed that resolution of these problems will lead to cooperation, or spillover, in other policy areas.

Transnational nonstate actor Any nonstate or nongovernmental actor from one country that has relations with any actor from another country or with an international organization.

Pluralism A political theory holding that political power and influence in society do not belong just to the citizens nor only to elite groups in various sectors of society but are distributed among a wide number of groups in the society. It can also mean a recognition of ethnic, racial, and cultural diversity.

Interdependence A condition where states (or peoples) are affected by decisions taken by others. Interdependence can be symmetric (i.e., both sets of actors are affected equally) or asymmetric (i.e., the impact varies between actors).

core assumptions of neorealism were indeed correct: the anarchic international structure, the centrality of states, and a rationalist approach to social scientific inquiry. Where they differed was in the argument that anarchy does not mean durable patterns of cooperation are impossible; the creation of international regimes matters here, as they facilitate cooperation by sharing information, reinforcing reciprocity, and making defection from norms easier to punish. Moreover, neoliberals argued that actors would enter into cooperative agreements if the gains were evenly shared. Neorealists disputed this hypothesis, saying that what matters is a question not so much of mutual gains as of **relative gains**: A neorealist (or structural-realist) state needs to be sure that it has more to gain than its rivals from a particular bargain or regime.

Relative gains One of the factors that realists argue constrain the willingness of states to cooperate. States are less concerned about whether everyone benefits (absolute gains) and more concerned about whether someone may benefit more than someone else.

Neoliberalism

There are two important arguments that set **neoliberalism** apart from democratic peace liberalism and the liberal idealism of the interwar period. First, academic inquiry should be guided by a commitment to a scientific approach to theory building. Whatever deeply held personal values scholars maintain, their task must be to observe regularities, formulate hypotheses as to why that relationship holds, and subject these to critical scrutiny. This separation of fact and value puts neoliberals on the positivist or social scientific research side of the methodological divide. Second, writers such as Keohane are critical of the naive assumption of nineteenth-century liberals that commerce breeds peace. A free trade system, according to Keohane, provides incentives for cooperation but does not guarantee it.

Neoliberalism Theory shaped by the ideas of commercial, republican, sociological, and institutional liberalism. Neoliberals see the international system as anarchic but believe relations can be managed by the establishment of international regimes and institutions. Neoliberals think actors with common interests will try to maximize absolute gains.

Neoliberal institutionalism (or institutional theory) shares many of the assumptions of neorealism; however, its adherents claim that neorealists focus excessively on conflict and competition and minimize the chances for cooperation even in an anarchic international system. Neoliberal-institutional organizations such as the Bank for International Settlements, the International Monetary Fund (IMF), and the World Bank are both the mediators and the means to achieve cooperation among actors in the system. Currently, neoliberal institutionalists are focusing their research on issues of global governance and the creation and maintenance of institutions associated with managing the processes of globalization.

For neoliberal institutionalists, the focus on mutual interests extends beyond trade and development issues. With the end of the Cold War, states were forced to address new security concerns like the threat of terrorism, the proliferation of nuclear weapons, and an increasing number of internal conflicts that threatened regional and global security. Graham Allison (2000) states that one of the consequences of the globalization of security concerns like terrorism, drug trafficking, and COVID-19 is the realization that threats to any country's security cannot be addressed unilaterally. Successful responses to security threats require the creation of regional and global regimes that promote cooperation among states and the coordination of policy responses to these new security threats.

Robert Keohane (2002a) suggests that one result of the 9/11 terrorist attacks on the United States was the creation of a very broad coalition against terrorism involving a large number of states and key global and regional institutions. Neoliberals support cooperative multilateralism and are generally critical of the preemptive and unilateral use of force as is condoned in the 2002 Bush Doctrine. Most neoliberals would believe that the US-led war with Iraq undermined the legitimacy and influence of global and regional security institutions that operated so successfully in the first Gulf War (1990–1991) and continue to work effectively in Afghanistan.

President Trump has not been a supporter of multilateralism and other liberal ideas. He killed the Iran nuclear deal, a multilateral agreement involving most of the major powers. He recently made the decision to withdraw from the Intermediate-Range Nuclear Forces (INF) Treaty with Russia. One must wonder if many of the treaties and agreements that have kept us safe and encouraged cooperation among nation-states will survive this period of nationalism.

The neoliberal-institutional perspective is more relevant in issue areas where states have mutual interests. For example, most world leaders believe that we will all benefit from an open trade system, and many support trade rules that protect the environment. Institutions have been created to manage international behavior in both areas. The neoliberal view may have less relevance in areas in which states have no mutual interests. Thus, cooperation in military or national security areas, where someone's gain is perceived as someone else's loss (a zero–sum perspective), may be more difficult to achieve.

Liberalism in Practice

When applying liberal ideas to international relations today, we find two clusters of responses to the problems and possibilities posed by globalization. Before outlining these responses, let us quickly recall the definition of liberalism, the four components being *juridical equality*, *democracy*, *liberty*, and the *free market*. As we will see, these same values can be pursued by very different political strategies.

The first response we will address is that of the **liberalism of privilege** (Richardson 1997, 18). According to this perspective, the problems of globalization need to be addressed by a combination of strong democratic states in the core of the international system, robust regimes, and open markets and institutions. For an example of the strategy in practice, we need look no further than the success of the liberal hegemony of the post-1945 era. In the aftermath of World War II, the United States took the opportunity to embed certain fundamental liberal principles into the rules and institutions of international society. Contrary to realist thinking, US leaders chose to forfeit short-run gains in return for a durable settlement that benefited all the world's states.

Liberalism of privilege The perspective that developed democratic states have a responsibility to spread liberal values for the benefit of all peoples of Earth.

According to US writer G. John Ikenberry, a defender of the liberal order, the United States signaled the cooperative basis of its power in a number of ways. First, the United States was an example to other members of international society insofar as its political system is open and allows different voices

WHAT'S YOUR WORLDVIEW?

A recent book by Thomas Piketty, Capital in the Twenty-first Century, *claims that income inequality has increased sharply since the late 1970s. Do the wealthy states have a responsibility to assist the poor states?*

Radical liberalism The utopian side of liberalism best exemplified by the academic community called the World Order Models Project. These scholars advocate a world in which states promote values like social justice, economic well-being, peace, and ecological balance. The scholars see the liberal order as predatory and clearly in need of transformation.

Liberalism and multilateralism aimed at responding and solving global problems is still embraced by some world leaders. Here, former British prime minister Gordon Brown speaks about the new multilateralism with his colleague, the former secretary of state Madeleine Albright. Brown has recently been working with the United Nations on the Sustainable Development Goals. Can we respond to global challenges without cooperation?

to be heard. Second, the United States advocated a global free trade regime in accordance with the idea that free trade brings benefits to all participants. Third, the United States appeared, to its allies at least, as a reluctant hegemon that would not seek to exploit its significant power-political advantage. Fourth, the United States created and participated in a range of important international institutions that constrained the country's actions (see Chapters 2 and 8 for discussions of such institutions as the Bretton Woods system, the World Trade Organization, and NATO).

Let us accept for a moment that the neoliberal argument is basically correct: The post-1945 international order has been successful and durable because US hegemony has been liberal. The logic of this position is one of institutional conservatism, meaning that to respond effectively to global economic and security problems, there is no alternative to working within the existing institutional structure. At the other end of the spectrum, critics see the current liberal international order as highly unresponsive to the needs of weaker states and peoples. According to the IMF, income inequality has increased in both advanced and developing economies in recent decades. The UN Development Programme's 2015 Human Development Report states that nearly 830 million people around the world are classified as working poor and live on less than $2.00 a day; according to the Multidimensional Poverty Index (MPI), the ten poorest countries are in sub-Saharan Africa.

Given that liberalism has produced such unequal gains for the West and the rest, it is not surprising that the United States as a hegemonic power has become obsessed with the question of preserving and extending its control of institutions, markets, and resources, just as realists predicted it would. When this hegemonic liberal order comes under challenge, as it did on 9/11, the response is uncompromising. It is notable, in this respect, that President George W. Bush mobilized the language of liberalism against Al Qaeda, the Taliban, and Iraq. He referred to the 2003 war against Iraq as "freedom's war," and defenders of Operation Iraqi Freedom frequently use the term *liberation*.

This strategy of preserving and extending liberal institutions is open to a number of criticisms. For the sake of simplicity, we will gather these under the umbrella of **radical liberalism**, which sees liberalism as benefiting only a few states and individuals. Table 3.3 summarizes the core assumptions of realism, liberalism, and radical liberalism/utopianism. Proponents of radical liberalism object to the understanding of liberalism embodied in the neoliberal defense of contemporary international institutions. The liberal character of those institutions is assumed rather than subjected to critical scrutiny. As a result, the incoherence of the

The Power of Ideas: Politics and Neoliberalism

BACKGROUND

A very good example of the hegemonic power of the United States, many Marxists would argue, is the success that it has had in getting neoliberal policies accepted as the norm throughout the world.

THE CASE

The set of policies most closely associated with the neoliberal project (in particular, reduction of state spending, currency devaluation, privatization, and the promotion of free markets) is known as the Washington Consensus. Many would argue that these are commonsense policies and that third world countries that have adopted them have merely realized that such economic policies best reflect their interests. However, Marxists would argue that an analysis of the self-interest of the hegemon and the use of coercive power provides a more convincing explanation of why such policies have been adopted.

The adoption of neoliberal policies by third world countries has had a number of implications. Spending on health and education has been reduced, they have been forced to rely more on the export of raw materials, and their markets have been saturated with manufactured goods from the industrialized world. It does not take a conspiracy theorist to suggest that these neoliberal policies are in the interests of capitalists in the developed world. There are three main areas where the adoption of neoliberal policies in the third world is in the direct interest of the developed world. First, there is the area of free trade. We need not enter into arguments about the benefits of free trade, but it is clear that it will always be in the interest of the hegemon to promote free trade; this is because, assuming it is the most efficient producer, its goods will be the cheapest anywhere in the world. It is only if countries put up barriers to trade to protect their own production that the hegemon's products will be more expensive than theirs. Second, there is the area of raw materials. If third world countries are going to compete in a free trade situation, the usual result is that they become more reliant on the export of raw materials (because their industrial products cannot compete in a free trade situation with those of the developed world). Again, this is in the interest of the hegemon, as increases in the supply of raw material exports mean that the price falls. Additionally, where third world countries have devalued their currency as part of a neoliberal package, the price of their exported raw materials goes down. Finally, when third world governments have privatized industries, investors from North America and Europe have frequently been able to snap up airlines, telecommunications companies, and oil industries at bargain prices.

If neoliberal policies appear to have such negative results for third world countries, why have they been so widely adopted? This is where the coercive element comes in. Through the 1970s and 1980s and continuing to today, there has been a major debt crisis between the third world and the West. This debt crisis came about primarily as a result of excessive and unwise lending by Western banks. Third world countries were unable to pay off the interest on these debts, let alone the debts themselves. As a result, they turned to the major global financial institutions, such as the IMF, for assistance. Although the IMF is a part of the UN system, it is heavily controlled by Western countries, in particular the United States. For example, the United States has 22.64 percent of the votes, while Mozambique has only 0.06 percent. In total, the ten most industrialized countries have more than 50 percent of the votes.

OUTCOME

For third world countries, the price of getting assistance was that they would implement neoliberal policies. Only once these were implemented, and only on the condition that the policies were maintained, would the IMF agree to provide aid to continue with debt repayment.

Hence, Marxists would argue that a deeper analysis of the adoption of neoliberal policies is required. Such an analysis would suggest that the global acceptance of neoliberalism is very much in the interests of the developed world and has involved a large degree of coercion. That such policies seem "natural" and "common sense" is an indication of the hegemonic power of the United States.

For Discussion

1. China's economic policies are based on state control of the economy. All capitalist activities serve the interests of the nation-state. This system, called the Beijing Consensus, is seen as a challenge to the dominance of the neoliberal Washington Consensus. Will China's economic success encourage other nation-states to take more control over their economies?

2. The recent Brexit vote in the United Kingdom and the trade policies of the Trump administration suggest that the idea of free trade is being undermined by protectionism or economic nationalism. Does this suggest the end of the liberal international order or the Washington Consensus?

| TABLE 3.3 | Realism, Liberalism, and Radical Liberalism/Utopianism: A Review of Core Assumptions |

	Realism	Liberalism	Radical Liberalism/ Utopianism
Main Actors	States	States, NGOs, and groups	States, NGOs, groups, and individuals
Central Concern	Relative power	Welfare and security	Peace, social justice, and human security
Typical Behavior	Self-help	Cooperation	Promotion of ideas
Basis for Power	Tangible resources (military/economic)	Issue specific, both hard and soft power	Political legitimacy and value of ideas
Nature of Interstate Relations	Unregulated competition and limited alliances	Interest-based regimes, coordination and collaboration among states	Norm-based regimes
Ideal State of the World	Stability through balance of power	Equitable system managed by regional organizations/ international organizations	World community

purposes underpinning these institutions is often overlooked. The kind of economic liberalization advocated by Western financial institutions, particularly in economically impoverished countries, frequently comes into conflict with the norms of democracy and human rights. Three examples illustrate this dilemma.

First, the more the West becomes involved in the organization of developing states' political and economic infrastructure, the less those states can be accountable to their domestic constituencies. The critical democratic link between the government and the people, which is central to modern liberal forms of representative democracy, is therefore broken (Hurrell and Woods 1995, 463). Second, to qualify for Western aid and loans, states are often required to meet harsh economic criteria requiring cuts in many welfare programs. The example of the poorest children in parts of Africa having to pay for primary school education (Booth and Dunne 1999, 310)—which is their right according to the Universal Declaration of Human Rights—is a stark reminder that economic liberty and political equality are frequently opposed. Third, the inflexible response of the IMF, the World Bank, and other international financial institutions to various crises in the world economy has contributed to a backlash against liberalism. Richard Falk puts this dilemma starkly: There is, he argues, a tension between "the ethical imperatives of the global neighborhood and the dynamics of economic globalization" (1995a, 573). Radical liberals argue that the hegemonic institutional order has fallen prey to the neoliberal consensus, which minimizes the role of the public sector in providing for welfare and elevates the market as the appropriate mechanism for allocating resources, investment, and employment opportunities.

If we take the area of political economy, the power exerted by the West and its international financial institutions perpetuates structural inequality. A good example here is the issue of free trade, which the West has pushed in areas where it gains from an open policy (e.g., in manufactured goods and financial services) but resisted in areas where it stands to lose (e.g., agriculture and textiles). At a deeper level, radical liberals worry that *all* statist models of governance are undemocratic, as elites are notoriously self-serving.

A second critique that radical liberals pursue focuses on the illiberal nature of the regimes and institutions. There is a massive **democratic deficit** at the global level; policy decisions are not subject to review by citizens. Only the fifteen members of the UN Security Council can determine issues of international peace and

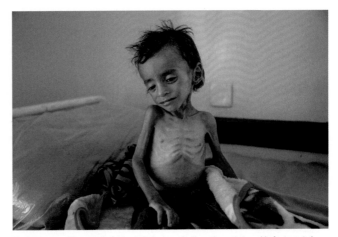

Human security needs to be the focus of all nation-states. Unfortunately, humanitarian crises such as the one in Yemen continue to create conditions of malnutrition and diseases that kill the young and the innocent. Radical liberals or Kantian liberals see these situations as the most important security challenge the world will face. Wars like this are clear indications that the liberal international order has failed many nation-states. Can any one economic and political system prevent wars and humanitarian disasters?

security, and only the five permanent members (the United States, the United Kingdom, France, China, and Russia) can exercise veto power. Thus, it is hypothetically possible for up to two hundred states in the world to believe that military action ought to be taken, but such an action would contravene the UN Charter if one of the permanent members were to cast a veto.

In place of the Westphalian and UN models, David Held outlines a **cosmopolitan democracy**. This requires, in the first instance, the creation of regional parliaments and the extension of the authority of such regional bodies (e.g., the European Union) that already exist. Second, human rights conventions must be entrenched in national parliaments and monitored by a new International Court of Human Rights. Third, reform of the United Nations, or its replacement with a genuinely democratic and accountable global parliament, "is necessary." Held espouses that if democracy is to thrive, it must penetrate the institutions and regimes that manage global politics.

Radical liberals place great importance on the civilizing capacity of global society. While the rule of law and the democratization of international institutions are core components of the liberal project, it is also vital that citizens' networks are broadened and deepened to monitor and cajole these institutions. These groups form a linkage among individuals, states, and global institutions. It is easy to portray radical-liberal thinking as utopian, but we should not forget the many achievements of global civil society so far. The evolution of international humanitarian law and the extent to which these laws find compliance are largely due to the millions of individuals who are active supporters of human rights

Democratic deficit Leaders have created many policymaking institutions at the global, regional, and national levels with policymaking power led by individuals who are appointed and not elected. Thus, policy decisions are not subject to review by citizens.

Cosmopolitan democracy A condition in which international organizations, transnational corporations, and global markets are accountable to the peoples of the world.

groups like Amnesty International and Human Rights Watch (Falk 1995b, 164). Similarly, global protest movements have been responsible for the heightened sensitivity to environmental degradation everywhere.

Critical Theories

As we have seen, realism and liberalism offer valuable insights into the interplay of states; however, they have certain shortcomings. With the exception of Marxism, the critical theories or perspectives we examine in this latter part of the chapter have recently become part of the international relations discourse, in part as a response to these shortcomings but also in reaction to a different set of stimuli. Indeed, Marxism, feminist theory, and constructivism can each provide important tools to understand trends and events in global politics and globalization in ways that realism and liberalism cannot. Many might ask: Why spend time on Marxism since the Soviet Union collapsed? Most socialists or Marxists have two very convincing answers. First, the Soviet Union never provided a model of the ideal socialist or Marxist society. Michael Harrington (1989, 79), an American socialist, describes Soviet socialism as follows:

> [Soviet] Socialism was a bureaucratically controlled and planned economy that carried out the function of primitive accumulation and thus achieved rapid modernization. The state owned the means of production, which made some people think it must be socialist; but the party and the bureaucracy owned the state by virtue of a dictatorial monopoly of political power.

Harrington calleds the Soviet system a moral disaster for socialism. It was a totalitarian state and not an ideal expression of Marxism.

A second reason is globalization. Karl Marx and Friedrich Engels, the founders of Marxist theory (1848), described how increasing interdependence will inevitably create a single global market and a global consumer culture:

> The need for a constantly expanding market for its products chases the bourgeoisie over the surface of the globe. In place of wants, satisfied by the production of country, we find new wants, requiring for their satisfaction the products of distant lands and climes.

A global economy shifts the key elements of Marxist thought from the domestic level to the global level.

We have emphasized the point that theory matters because we all embrace theories that help us understand the world and explain how and why things happen. After reading and discussing this chapter, you will have a better understanding of critical voices—those that question the assumptions of the dominant theories and paradigms (see Table 3.4 for an overview of these alternative theories). Marxists ask us to look at the world from the perspective of workers and not the owners; feminists ask us to look at the lives of women; and constructivists ask us to consider how ideas, images, and values shape our worldview and our construction of reality.

TABLE 3.4	Alternative International Relations Theories at the Beginning of the Twenty-First Century

	Central Idea	View of International System	Key Authors
Marxism	Global capitalist system eliminates harmony of interestszof workers.	Core–periphery relationship. Unfair terms of international trade. Underdevelopment in periphery.	Prebisch, Frank, Cardoso, O'Donnell
Constructivism	Seeks to understand change. Ideas are social creations. Relationships result from historical processes. Ideas can evolve, replace older ways of thinking.	A process. Result of hegemonic ideas. Can change as a result of evolving ideas.	Onuf, Walker, Wendt
Liberal Feminism	Change women's subordinate position in existing political systems.	Improve women's representation in INGOs. End gender bias in INGOs and NGOs.	Caprioli, Enloe, Elshtain, Tickner, Tobias

The Essential Marxism

We turn our attention first to **Marxism**, the oldest of the challengers. Marxist ideas inspired many political movements in the developing world in the period of decolonization through the 1970s and 1980s. Although the Communist Party state of the Soviet Union is gone and never reached the goal of a pure expression of Marxism, and the authoritarian Chinese Communist Party permits a form of capitalism in China, the central ideas of Marxism can still help us understand the inequality that characterizes the globalized economy.

A Marxist interpretation of world politics has been influential since the mid-1800s. In his inaugural address to the Working Men's International Association in London in 1864, Karl Marx told his audience that history had "taught the working classes the duty to master [for] themselves the mysteries of international politics." However, despite the fact that Marx himself wrote copiously about international affairs, most of this writing was journalistic in character. He did not incorporate the international dimension into his theoretical description of capitalism. This omission should perhaps not surprise us. The sheer scale of the theoretical enterprise in which he was engaged, as well as the nature of his own methodology, inevitably meant that Marx's work would remain contingent and unfinished.

Marx was an enormously prolific writer whose ideas developed and changed over time. The *Collected Works* produced by Progress Publishers in Moscow, for instance, contains fifty volumes of very thick books. Hence, it is not surprising that his legacy has been open to numerous interpretations. In addition, real-world developments have led to the revision of his ideas in light of experience. A variety of schools of thought have emerged that claim Marx as a direct inspiration or whose work can be linked to Marx's legacy.

Marxism A theory critical of the status quo, or dominant capitalist paradigm. It is a critique of the capitalist political economy from the view of the revolutionary proletariat, or workers. Marxists' ideal is a stateless and classless society.

Four strands of contemporary Marxist thought have made major contributions to thinking about global politics. Before we discuss what is distinctive about these approaches, it is important that we examine their essential commonalities.

First, all the theorists discussed in this section share with Marx the view that the social, political, and economic world should be analyzed as a totality. The academic division of the social world into different areas of inquiry—history, philosophy, economics, political science, sociology, international relations, and so on—is both arbitrary and unhelpful. None can be understood without knowledge of the others: The social world has to be studied as a whole. Regardless of the scale and complexity of the social world, for Marxist theorists, the disciplinary boundaries that characterize the contemporary social sciences need to be transcended if we are to generate a proper understanding of the dynamics of global politics.

Another key element of Marxist thought, which underlines this concern with interconnection and context, is the materialist conception of history. The central contention here is that economic development is effectively the motor of history. The central dynamic that Marx identifies is tension between the means of production (e.g., labor, tools, technology) and relations of production (technical and institutional relationships) that together form the **economic base** of a given society. As the means of production develop—for example, through technological advancement—previous relations of production become outmoded, limiting effective utilization of the new productive capacity. This limitation in turn leads to a process of social change that transforms relations of production to better accommodate the new configuration of means. For example, computer-driven machines for manufacturing might replace auto-factory workers, or the workers' jobs might be moved to a country where labor and production costs are lower. Workers are still needed, but fewer, and most of those must be retrained to repair computers or develop software and no longer make car doors. The recent crisis in the US auto industry is still having profound negative effects in industrial cities like Detroit and Cleveland, forever changing the political, economic, and social landscape. In other words, developments in the economic base act as a catalyst for the broader transformation of society as a whole. This is because, as Marx argues in the preface to his *Contribution to the Critique of Political Economy*, "the mode of production of material life conditions the social, political and intellectual life process in general." Thus, the legal, political, and cultural institutions and practices of a given society reflect and reinforce—in a more or less mediated form—the pattern of power and control in the economy. It follows logically, therefore, that change in the economic base ultimately leads to change in the "legal and political **superstructure**."

Class plays a key role in Marxist analysis. Marx defines class as "social relations between the producers, and the conditions under which they exchange their activities and share in the total act of production" (Marx 1867). For most Americans, class is simply a way of designating an individual's position within the income distribution of a society. Upper, middle, and lower income classes represent income groups in our society. For Marxists, however, your income does not

Economic base For Marxists, the substructure of the society is the relationship between owners and workers. Capitalists own the means of production and control technology and resources. The workers are employed by the capitalists, and they are alienated, exploited, and estranged from their work and their society.

Superstructure The government or political structure that is controlled by those who own the means of production.

Class A social group that in Marxism is identified by its relationship with the means of production and the distribution of societal resources. Thus, we have the bourgeoisie (the owners or upper classes) and the proletariat (the workers).

determine your class. Instead, your class is defined by your position within the hierarchy of production. In contrast to liberals, who believe that there is an essential harmony of interest between various social groups, Marxists hold that society is systemically prone to class conflict. *The Communist Manifesto*, which Marx coauthored with Friedrich Engels, argues that "the history of all hitherto existing societies is the history of class struggle" (Marx and Engels 1848). In capitalist society, says Marx, the main axis of conflict is between the bourgeoisie (the capitalists) and the proletariat (the workers).

The Marxist perspective on globalization seeks to describe the ways inequality affects the lives of millions of people. Marx and Engels predicted that capitalism would spread around the world, and only then would the proletariat become aware of their exploitation as workers, alienation from their government, and estrangement from society ruled by the bourgeoisie. In this situation, globalization might be the catalyst for awareness and eventual transformation.

Despite his commitment to rigorous scholarship, Marx did not think it either possible or desirable for the analyst to remain a detached or neutral observer of this great clash between capital and labor. He argued that "philosophers have only interpreted the world in various ways; the point, however, is to change it" (Marx 1888). Marx was committed to the cause of emancipation. He was not interested in developing an understanding of the dynamics of capitalist society simply for the sake of it. Rather, he expected such an understanding to make it easier to overthrow the prevailing order and replace it with a communist society—a society in which wage labor and private property are abolished and social relations transformed.

It is important to emphasize that the essential elements of Marxist thought are also contested. There is disagreement as to how these ideas and concepts should be interpreted and how they should be put into operation. Analysts also differ over which elements of Marxist thought are most relevant, which have been proven to be mistaken, and which should now be considered as outmoded or in need of radical overhaul. Moreover, there are substantial differences between them in terms of their attitudes toward the legacy of Marx's ideas. The work of the more contemporary Marxists, for example, draws far more directly on Marx's original ideas than does the work of the critical theorists. Indeed, the critical theorists would probably be more comfortable being viewed as post-Marxists than as straightforward Marxists. But even for them, as the very term *post-Marxism* suggests, the ideas of Marx remain a basic point of departure.

WHAT'S YOUR WORLDVIEW?

Has globalization increased worker exploitation and therefore the likelihood of revolution according to Marxist political thought? How would liberals respond to Marxist accusations?

Marx was a socialist, but not the first. Marxism is a critical theory—critical of the neoliberal capitalist system—and seeks radical transformation of the global power structure. The Soviet Union was Marxist in name only, so Marxism is not dead and still inspires many who seek radical change. Capitalism has not worked for everyone.

International relations theorist Robert W. Cox provides a transition from contemporary Marxism to more recent theoretical developments. In his 1981 article "Social Forces, States, and World Orders: Beyond International Relations Theory," Cox analyzes the state of international relations theory as a whole and one of its major subfields, international political economy. This article became an important wedge in the process of toppling realism's dominance in international relations. The sentence that has become one of the most often-quoted lines in all of contemporary international relations theory reads as follows: "Theory is always *for* some one, and *for* some purpose" (1981, 128). This quote expresses a worldview that follows logically from a broad Marxist position that has been explored in this section. If ideas and values are (ultimately) a reflection of a particular set of social relations and are transformed as those relations are themselves transformed, then this suggests that all knowledge of political relations must reflect a certain context, a certain time, a certain space. Thus, politics cannot be objective and timeless in the way some traditional realists and contemporary structural realists, for example, would like to claim.

One key implication is that there can be no simple separation between facts and values. Whether consciously or not, all theorists inevitably bring their values to bear on their analysis. Cox suggests that we need to look closely at each theory, each idea, and each analysis that claims to be objective or value-free and ask who or what it is for and what purpose it serves. He subjects realism, and in particular its contemporary variant structural realism, to an extended criticism on these grounds.

According to Cox, these theories serve the interests of those who prosper under the prevailing order—that is, the inhabitants of the developed states and, in particular, the ruling elites. Their purpose, again whether consciously or not, is to reinforce and legitimate the status quo. They do this by making the current configuration of international relations appear natural and immutable. When realists (falsely, according to Cox and many other analysts) claim to be describing the world as it is, as it has been, and as it always will be, what they are in fact doing is reinforcing the ruling hegemony in the current world order. In the same way, according to a contemporary neoliberal argument, blindly accepting globalization as a beneficial process reinforces the hegemony of the countries, corporations, and their stockholders. Cox extends his argument by contrasting **problem-solving theory** with **critical theory**. Problem-solving theory accepts the parameters of the present order while attempting to fix its problems and thus helps legitimate an unjust and deeply iniquitous system.

Third World Socialists

Following World War II, many former European colonies declared independence. To build sovereign states, they rejected prevailing economic theories of the day—especially Soviet-style socialism and Western capitalism—in favor of political-economic development strategies based on autarchy (economic self-sufficiency), which were sensitive to the history, values, experience, resources, and specific attributes of each region. They recognized that, for most developing states,

Problem-solving theory Realism and liberalism are problem-solving theories that address issues and questions within the dominant paradigm or the present system. How can we fix capitalism? How can we make a society more democratic? These are problem-solving questions that assume nothing is wrong with the core elements of the system.

Critical theory Theories that are critical of the status quo and reject the idea that things can be fixed under the present system. These theories challenge core assumptions of the dominant paradigm and argue for transformation and not just reform.

What Makes a Theory "Alternative" or Critical?

If you grew up in the United States, you have probably internalized a combination of the liberal and realist perspectives. To keep with our simile that theories are like eyeglasses, you are in essence wearing bifocals, combining both liberal and realist visions of different worlds. You probably think that you live in a mostly peaceful and law-abiding society with a free market economic system in which anyone can become rich. This is the rough outline of the liberal model. While you have this view of the domestic situation, you most likely look at international events quite differently. Here, the realist model describes what you see: If countries are not at war, then they are constantly seeking some kind of an advantage, such as in trade negotiations, for example. Individuals and states are oriented toward their own self-interest, and international politics is a constant struggle for power and material resources.

However, for someone who grew up in the former Eastern bloc of communist countries, the view of your society could be quite different, especially if you were a child of a member of the ruling Communist Party. For that person, Marxism, not capitalism, is the dominant political-economic model. In fact, in some ways, the theory of Marxism in the USSR was like a religion: It had an explanation for history, it described how to live properly, and it offered a utopian workers' paradise as a reward for living correctly.

A Marxist could look at life in the United States and see exploitation everywhere. Workers in factories are alienated from the products they make. Without an employee discount, for instance, an assembly line worker at a General Motors factory could never afford to own the car that went by on the conveyor belt. Schools are designed to create good future workers by teaching the benefits of arriving on time, being polite to the teacher, and submitting perfect homework. The income gap between rich and poor is wide and getting wider.

For this imagined child of the Communist Party in the USSR, life is good and not based on exploitation. There are special shops for party members, where shortages of meat are rare and you can purchase white bread, not the rough rye loaves found in other stores. You would probably also attend school with other children like yourself and have science labs with the latest equipment. If you catch the flu in the winter, you will not have to wait in long lines to see a doctor.

The Marxist perspective on international affairs would sound a bit like realism but with a socialist spin. Where realism sees constant struggles for power, the Marxist doctrine of the USSR saw capitalist encirclement of the Soviet Union and the exploitation of the developing world. The doctrine preached class warfare on a global scale, and the USSR extended foreign aid in "fraternal cooperation" with its socialist friends.

Imagine still that you were a student born in the USSR: In your classes on foreign relations, you would learn that the "correlation of forces" was beginning to turn in the direction of the socialist world. You would also learn that your country was peace loving and had pledged to never use nuclear weapons first in a war with the capitalist NATO countries.

Although this is a stylized reality we have asked you to imagine, it does prove a point: What is "alternative" depends on your perspective. An alternative perspective can also be critical of the status quo. In all likelihood, you, this hypothetical student in the USSR, would know that you had a privileged status in society. You might be uncomfortable with it because you could see the exploitation of people in the "workers' paradise": tiny apartments with a shared bathroom down the hall; food shortages; drab clothing selections; a yearlong wait to purchase a car, and then no choice of color. In the workplace, people seem like the assembly line workers in the capitalist West: bored and underpaid. A popular joke in the 1970s Soviet Union was "we pretend to work, and the state pretends to pay us."

However, for all its shortcomings, it would be *your* Marxist perspective, and you might feel good about it. Meanwhile, you would consider the liberal capitalist model perilous until perhaps 1989, when you would learn what it meant to see things from the other perspective.

For Discussion

1. We suggest in the text that the Soviet Union was an authoritarian/totalitarian state capitalist system and not truly a communist or Marxist society. Its authoritarianism made it an alternative to democracy. What examples are there, if any, of Marxist societies? Is Marxism at all relevant today?

2. Does realism help us understand Russian society better than Marxism? Why or why not? What about utopian societies?

3. What examples do we have, if any, of experiments in utopian societies? Would you say a real Marxist society was utopian?

the major resources are people and land, so states must intervene to replace exploitation with citizen access to economic resources and opportunities. Finally, they stressed the importance of producing for local consumption, presciently fearing that development strategies requiring rapid industrialization or reliance on export-driven industries would increase dependency levels.

Although defined by different experiences and contexts, Julius Nyerere, the first president of Tanzania; Kwame Nkrumah, the first prime minister and president of Ghana; Mohandas Gandhi, leader of the Indian independence movement; and Mao Zedong, former chairman of the Chinese Communist Party, led socialist and populist revolutions against former colonial powers. Subsequently, they battled new "colonizing" economic forces that increased their countries' dependency on the North, thereby reducing their power and independence in the international system. Each of these third world socialist movements shared five critical elements:

1. Intensely nationalistic, they targeted all forms of colonialism and foreign economic domination.
2. As radical movements, they rejected exploitation and injustice and were willing to use force to initiate change.
3. Capitalism was identified with imperialism, an immoral system, wherein wealth accumulation came at the expense of others.
4. Their inspiration was the masses—city workers and rural peasants—whose needs should have been served by the political and economic systems that govern them.
5. They were socialist, meaning the state owned much of the core industries.

Feminist Theory

Feminism A political project to understand and to end women's inequality and oppression. Feminist theories tend to be critical of the biases of the discipline. Many feminists focus their research on the areas where women are excluded from the analysis of major international issues and concerns.

Often misunderstood as an attack on men, **feminist theory** provides useful tools with which to analyze a range of political events and policy decisions. The title of this section, "Feminist Theory," is both deliberate and misleading. It is deliberate in that it focuses on the socially constructed roles that women occupy in world politics. It is misleading because this question must be understood in the context of the construction of differences between women and men and contingent understandings of masculinity and femininity. In other words, the focus could more accurately be on gender than on women because the very categories of women and men, and the concepts of masculinity and femininity, are highly contested in much feminist research. Similarly, distinctions such as liberal and socialist are slightly misleading because these categories do not exactly correspond to the diverse thinking of feminist scholars, especially in contemporary work, in which elements from each type are often integrated. The fundamental point is that if we look through gendered lenses, we will get a different view of global politics (See Table 3.5).

TABLE 3.5	J. Ann Tickner's Reformulation of Hans Morgenthau's Principles of Political Realism

Morgenthau's Six Principles	Tickner's Six Principles
Politics, like society in general, is governed by objective laws that have their roots in human nature. which is unchanging; therefore, it is possible to develop a rational theory that reflects these objective laws.	A feminist perspective believes that objectivity, as it is culturally defined, is associated with masculinity. Therefore, supposedly "objective" laws of human nature are based on a partial masculine view of human nature. Human nature is both masculine and feminine: It contains elements of social reproduction and development as well as political domination. Dynamic objectivity offers us a more connected view of objectivity with less potential for domination.
The main signpost of political realism is the concept of interest defined in terms of power which infuses rational order into the subject matter of politics, and thus makes the theoretical understanding of politics possible. Political realism stresses the rational, objective, and unemotional.	A feminist perspective believes that the national interest is multidimensional and contextually contingent. Therefore, it cannot be defined solely in terms of power. In the contemporary world the national interest demands cooperative rather than zero-sum solutions to a set of interdependent global problems which include nuclear war, economic well-being, and environmental degradation.
Realism assumes that interest defined as power is an objective category which is universally valid but not with a meaning that is fixed once and for all. Power is the control of man over man.	Power cannot be infused with meaning that is universally valid. Power as domination and control privileges masculinity and ignores the possibility of collective empowerment, another aspect of power often associated with femininity.
Political realism is aware of the moral significance of political action. It is also aware of the tension between the moral command and the requirements of successful political action.	A feminist perspective rejects the possibility of separating moral command from political action. All political action has moral significance. The realist agenda for maximizing order through power and control prioritizes the moral command of order over those of justice and the satisfaction of basic needs necessary to ensure social reproduction.
Political realism refuses to identify the moral aspirations of a particular nation with the moral laws that govern the universe. It is the concept of interest defined in terms of power that saves us from moral excess and political folly.	While recognizing that the moral aspirations of particular nations cannot be equated with universal moral principles, a feminist perspective seeks to find common moral elements in human aspirations that could become the basis for de-escalating international conflict and building international community.
The political realist maintains the autonomy of the political sphere. He asks, "How does this policy affect the power of the nation?" Political realism is based on a pluralistic conception of human nature. A man who is nothing but "political man" would be a beast, for he would be completely lacking in moral restraints. But, in order to develop an autonomous theory of political behavior, "political man" must be abstracted from other aspects of nature.	A feminist perspective denies the validity of the autonomy of the political. Since autonomy is associated with masculinity in Western culture, disciplinary efforts to construct a worldview that does not rest on a pluralistic conception of human nature are partial and masculine. Building boundaries around a narrowly defined political realm defines political in a way that excludes the concerns and contributions of women.

Source: Tickner (1988: 430–431, 437–438).

The term *gender* usually refers to the social construction of the difference between men and women. Although it is a complex concept, here is one way to think of it: Biology determines your sex; a mix of social and cultural norms, as well as your own sense of identity, determines your gender. Some theories assume natural and biological (e.g., sex) differences between men and women; some do not. What all of the most interesting work in this field does, however, is analyze how gender both *affects* global politics and *is an effect of* global politics. That is, feminist theorists examine how different concepts (e.g., the state or sovereignty) are "gendered" and in turn how this gendering of concepts can have differential consequences for men and women (Steans 1998). Feminists have always been interested in how understandings of gender affect the lives of men and women (Brittan 1989; Seidler 1989; Connell 1995; Carver 1996; Zalewski and Parpart 1998). As with all theoretical traditions, there are different shades of feminism that combine with some of the more traditional theoretical ideas in global politics.

Feminist theory in international relations originally grew from work on the politics of development and peace research. By the late 1980s, a first wave of feminism, **liberal feminism**, was more forcefully posing the question of "where are the women in global politics?" The meaning of liberal in this context is decidedly *not* the same as the meaning we discussed earlier in the chapter. This definition is more in line with traditional views of liberalism that put equal and nondiscriminatory liberty at the center of the international debate.

Liberal feminism A position that advocates equal rights for women but also supports a more progressive policy agenda, including social justice, peace, economic well-being, and ecological balance.

In the context of feminism, the term *liberal* starts from the notion that the key units of society are individuals, that these individuals are biologically determined as either men or women, and that these individuals possess specific rights and are equal. One strong argument of liberal feminism is that all rights should be granted to women equally with men. Here we can see how the state is gendered insofar as rights, such as voting rights and the right to possess property, have been predicated solely on the experiences and expectations of men—and, typically, a certain ethnic or racial class of men. Thus, taking women seriously made a difference to the standard view of global politics. Liberal feminists look at the ways women are excluded from power and prevented from playing a full part in political activity. They examine how women have been restricted to roles critically important for the functioning of things but not usually deemed important for theories of global politics. To give you an example of political discrepancies by gender, Table 3.6 shows the percentage of women in national parliaments by region in 2017.

To ask "where are the women?" was at the time quite a radical political act, precisely because women were absent from the standard texts of international relations, and thus they appeared invisible. Writers such as Cynthia Enloe (1989, 1993, 2000) began from the premise that if we simply started to ask "where are the women?" we would be able to see their presence in and importance to global politics, as well as the ways their exclusion from global politics was presumed a "natural" consequence of their biological or natural roles. After all, it was not that women were actually absent from global politics. Indeed, they played central roles either as cheap factory labor, as prostitutes around military bases, or as hotel maids.

TABLE 3.6	**Percentage of Women in National Parliaments by Region**		
	Regional Averages		
	Single House or Lower House	**Upper House or Senate**	**Both Houses Combined**
Nordic countries	42.5%	—	—
Americas	30.6%	31.4%	30.7%
Europe—OSCE member countries (including Nordic countries)	28.6%	28.0%	28.5%
Europe—OSCE member countries (excluding Nordic countries)	27.2%	28.0%	27.4%
Sub-Saharan Africa	23.9%	22.2%	23.7%
Middle East and North Africa	19.0%	12.5%	18.1%
Asia	19.8%	17.4%	19.5%
Pacific	16.3%	36.0%	18.4%

Source: Inter-Parliamentary Union (percentages as of December 1, 2018), http://ipu.org/wmn-e/world.htm.

The point is that traditional international theory either ignored these contributions or, if it recognized them at all, designated them as less important than the actions of states*men*. Enloe demonstrated just how critically important were the activities of women—for example, as wives of diplomats and soldiers or as models of correct European behavior—to the functioning of the international economic and political systems both during the era of European colonialism and afterward. She illustrated exactly how crucial women and the conventional arrangements of "women's and men's work" were to the continued functioning of international politics.

Most specifically, Enloe documented how the concept and practice of militarization influenced the lives and choices of men and women around the world. "Militarization," she writes, "is a step-by-step process by which a person or a thing gradually comes to be controlled by the military or comes to depend for its well-being on militaristic ideas" (2000, 3; also see Elshtain 1987; Elshtain and Tobias 1990). Enloe is an example of a scholar who begins from a liberal premise—that women and men should have equal rights and responsibilities in global politics—but draws on socialist feminism to analyze the role of economic structures and on standpoint feminism to highlight the unique and particular contributions of women.

There are a number of waves of feminism, and the descriptions of the focus in each wave seem to vary according to who you read. The current fourth wave of feminist research and activism has been described as a movement that combines politics, psychology, and spirituality with a goal of societal change. Social media

Intersectionality A way of understanding and analyzing the complexity in the world, in people, and in human experiences. The events and conditions of social and political life and the self can seldom be understood as shaped by one factor. They are generally shaped by many factors in diverse and mutually influencing ways.

Constructivism An approach to international politics that concerns itself with the centrality of ideas and human consciousness. As constructivists have examined global politics, they have been broadly interested in how the structure constructs the actors' identities and interests, how their interactions are organized and constrained by that structure, and how their very interaction serves to either reproduce or transform that structure.

plays an important role in this wave, with an emphasis on gender equality and social justice. There has been an increased focus on **intersectionality** with a focus on how multiple oppressions intersect. The intersectionality framework focuses on how class, race, age, ability, sexuality, gender, and other issues combine to shape the experience of women in our societies. Patricia Hill Collins and Sirma Bilge (2016) suggest that intersectionality is the overriding principle for feminists today and offer a useful definition:

> *Intersectionality is a way of understanding and analyzing the complexity in the world, in people, and in human experiences. The events and conditions of social and political life and the self can seldom be understood as shaped by one factor. They are generally shaped by many factors in diverse and mutually influencing ways.*

Many feminist scholars point out that when women are added to any study, researchers will ask questions that are not normally part of the dominant research agenda. Early feminists studying global politics or foreign policy sought to include women's experiences and perspectives to improve our ability to understand and explain global phenomena.

Constructivism

Most writers who call themselves **constructivists** argue that our actions and words make society, and society in turn shapes our actions and words. Ideas, beliefs, and values are important because they influence the identities and interests of states and the eventual selection of policies and strategies that transform our world. As part of this process, we construct rules that first identify for us the key players (i.e., who has agency) in a given situation, recognizing that no one actor in the international system is an agent in all policy situations; then those rules instruct, direct, and commit actors to take certain actions. For example, realist rules during the Cold War dictated that all states were subservient to and would follow the lead of the United States or the Soviet Union. However, actual practice does not always comply with the rules: Frequently, states found areas where these superpowers had little interest—such as development or peacekeeping—and established a niche to serve their interests. The George W. Bush administration tried to assert a similar pattern of hegemonic rules after the attacks of September 11, 2001, with phrases like "coalition of the willing" and "you are either with us or you are with the terrorists."

Several thousand people wearing the color purple marched in the streets of Lyon, France, following the call of the Nous Toutes collective. The demonstrators were denouncing gender-based and sexual violence against women. This march was part of a national movement to mark the International Day for the Elimination of Violence Against Women in 2018. As many have suggested, women's rights are human rights.

Over time, rules and practices can form a stable pattern that serves the interests of key agents. These patterns become "institutions." The Cold War was a twentieth-century institution, and the global economy is a good example of a twenty-first-century institution. Its rules and practices are based on neoliberal free market capitalism that best serves the interests of corporations, global economic institutions, and the wealthy states. The wealthy states' power in the system is based on both material factors (e.g., control of resources) and discursive power (based on knowledge and the control of language and ideas within a society).

A leading constructivist, Alexander Wendt, seeks to understand "how global politics is socially constructed" (1995, 71). Wendt claimed that "anarchy is what states make of it" (1992, 391), arguing that anarchy in the international system does not have to result in competition, security dilemmas, arms races, or conflict. States have plenty of options; they are only limited by rules, practices, and institutions that they themselves have created. How a country reacts to anarchy reflects its particular understanding of that condition.

Constructivists argue that the international system is defined by socially constructed realities, and therefore, to understand the system, one must focus on shared rules, practices, meanings, identities, and norms. These factors define the interests, identities, preferences, and actions of each state in the system. By emphasizing the social construction of reality, we also are questioning what is frequently taken for granted. This raises several issues. One is a concern with the origins of social constructs that now appear to us as natural and are part of our social vocabulary. After all, the notion of sovereignty did not always exist; it was a product of historical forces and human interactions, which generated new distinctions regarding where political authority resided. Although individuals have been forced to flee their homes throughout the course of human history, the political and legal category of refugees is only a century old. To understand the origins of these concepts requires attention to the interplay between existing ideas and institutions, the political calculations by leaders who had ulterior motives, and morally minded actors who were attempting to improve humanity.

Also of concern to constructivists are alternative pathways. Although world history can be seen as patterned and somewhat predictable, there are contingencies—historical accidents and human intervention can force history to change course. The events of 9/11 and the response by the Bush administration arguably transformed the direction of global politics. Would the world be different today if Al Gore had been elected president instead? This interest in possible and counterfactual worlds works against historical determinism. Wendt's (1992) claim that "anarchy is what states make of it" calls attention to how different beliefs and practices will generate divergent patterns and organization of global politics. A world of nonviolent activists like Mahatma Gandhi would be very different from a world of violent extremists like Osama bin Laden.

Constructivists also examine how actors make their activities meaningful. Following Max Weber's insight that "we are cultural beings with the capacity and the will to take a deliberate attitude toward the world and to lend it *significance*" (1949, 81), constructivists attempt to recover the meanings that actors give to

Jane Addams and the Women's International League for Peace and Freedom

There are many political and religious groups that oppose war. Some are pacifists and others are proponents of just war or negotiations short of war. The Women's Peace Party (WPP), led by activist Jane Addams (1860–1935), was one of the first groups to protest against World War I. On January 10, 1915, more than three thousand people met in Washington, D.C., and endorsed a platform that inspired President Wilson's Fourteen Points for peace; their planks included the following (Addams 1922/2002, 6–7):

1. Convene a meeting of neutral nations to promote peace.
2. Limit arms production and nationalize the arms industries.
3. Oppose militarism in the United States.
4. Promote peace through education.
5. Insist on democratic control over foreign policy.
6. Extend suffrage to women, thereby humanizing governments.
7. Replace the "balance of power" system with a "concert of nations" system.
8. Develop a global governance system based on the rule of law, not coercion.
9. Deploy nonforce options to control rivals.
10. Work to eliminate the causes of war, like poverty.
11. Appoint a commission of experts to promote international peace.

Addams and her colleagues strongly believed that if an international organization had been in place when dialogue among European powers failed, it could have mediated the dispute before it exploded into a major war.

The WPP became the American section of the pacifist Women's International League for Peace and Freedom (WILPF), which was established in the Netherlands in spring 1915 as a federation of women organized in twenty-one countries. Participants argued that the choice "between violence and passive acceptance of unjust conditions" was a false one. As true Kantians, they believed that "courage, determination, moral power, generous indignation, active good-will, and education can be used to secure goals rather than violence" (Addams 1922/2002, 145–146). Delegates of the WILPF visited fourteen countries, both belligerent and neutral, and urged leaders to end the war and to address the causes of violence in the international system. Repeatedly, they confronted the dominance of realist thinking:

> We heard the same opinion expressed by these men of the governments responsible for the promotion of the war; each one said that his country would be ready to stop the war immediately if some honorable method of securing peace were provided; each one disclaimed responsibility for the continuance of war; each one predicted European bankruptcy if the war were prolonged, and each one grew pale and distressed as he spoke of the loss of his gallant young countrymen. (Addams 1922/2002, 11)

Considered by many to be the "most dangerous woman in America" for her opposition to the US entry into World War I and her challenges of the world's leaders and their vested interests, Addams was awarded the Nobel Peace Prize in 1935 for her efforts aimed at ending the war and providing relief for the victims of war.

For Discussion

1. What organizations are promoting both a pacifist and feminist agenda in today's global politics debates?
2. How important were pacifist groups in the period between World War I and World War II?
3. Women like Jane Addams played an important role in both American and international politics. Why do students of international relations never hear about her?
4. Why does the study of global politics often neglect the contributions of individual people? How do their contributions matter?

their practices and to the objects they create. Constructivists argue that culture, rather than private belief, informs the meanings people give to their action. Sometimes, constructivists have presumed that such meanings derive from a hardened culture. However, because culture is fractured and society has different interpretations of what is meaningful activity, scholars must consider these cultural fault lines. To pinpoint or fix any precise meaning is largely a political and temporary accomplishment; it is not to discover some transcendent truth.

Some of the most important debates in global politics are about how to define particular activities. Development, human rights, security, humanitarian intervention, sovereignty—topics that we discuss in later chapters—are important orienting concepts that can have any number of meanings. States and nonstate actors have rival interpretations of the meanings of these concepts and will fight to try to have their preferred meaning collectively accepted.

The fact that these meanings are fixed through politics, and that once these meanings are fixed they have consequences for the ability of people to determine their fates, suggests an alternative way of thinking about power. Most international relations theorists treat power as the ability of one state to compel another state to do what it otherwise would not and tend to focus on the material technologies, such as military firepower and economic statecraft, that have this persuasive effect. Constructivists have offered two important additions to this view of power. The forces of power go beyond **material**: They also can be **ideational** or discursive. Ideational power is more than control over meaning; it is also the acceptance of ideas or a way of life. The notion that *your* way of thinking is the norm is but one example of ideational power.

Consider the issue of **legitimacy**. States, including great powers, crave legitimacy—the belief that they are acting according to and pursuing the values of the broader international community. There is a direct relationship between state legitimacy and the costs associated with a course of action. The greater the legitimacy, the easier time state leaders will have convincing others to cooperate with their policies. The lesser the legitimacy, the more costly the action is. This means that even great powers will frequently feel the need to alter their policies to be viewed as legitimate—or bear the consequences. Further evidence of the constraining power of legitimacy is offered by the tactic of "naming and shaming" by human rights activists. For example, human rights advocates led by Mia Farrow used the threat of a boycott of the 2008 Olympics to persuade China to stop jailing dissidents and persecuting religious and ethnic minorities. China did allow for some changes, but because of its economic and political power, it was able to ignore calls for major reforms. If states did not care about their legitimacy—about their reputation and the perception that they were acting in a manner consistent with prevailing international standards—then such a tactic would have little visible impact.

Material Things we can see, measure, consume, and use, such as military forces, oil, and currency.

Ideational/ideal interest The psychological, moral, and ethical goals of a state as it sets foreign and domestic policy.

Legitimacy An authority that is respected and recognized by those it rules and by rulers or leaders of other states. The source of legitimacy can be laws or a constitution and the support of the society.

One important theoretical perspective that we should not ignore is the ecotopian tradition. These can vary from the deep green critical ecotopians to the more reformist Green parties throughout Europe and much of the Western world. In this photo, Green party members from Germany at their party council meetings may be celebrating the fact that in the European parliamentary elections the party finished second. How do you explain the success of the Greens in Europe?

▶ Conclusion

In this chapter, we learned that for realists, global politics is an endless struggle for dominance and power. Power can be control over something tangible, like resources and territory, or it can be a struggle for something intangible, like prestige. However, because of its pessimistic opinion about human nature, realist doctrine tends to see enemies or competitors everywhere and assumes that all states are constantly on the verge of war. Although it shares some of realism's ideas about international systemic anarchy, liberalism offers a less violent explanation for global politics. Many proponents of the liberal perspective believe that long-term international cooperation is possible and will lead to human material and spiritual progress. Both realism and liberalism are valuable theories because they can help us understand some of the various interactions, events, and behaviors of global politics.

However, in recent history, the dominance of the theories of realism and liberalism have been challenged within mainstream scholarly thinking, which has led to growing intellectual appeal of a range of new approaches developed to understand world politics in ways that realism and liberalism cannot. The theories that we call "critical" suggest other ways of interpreting global events.

Although proponents of the critical theories presented in this chapter seek to challenge the conventionally dominant theories of international relations, their work does more than that. In addition to offering new critical ways to view the field, these critical theories, if combined with aspects of realism and liberalism,

WHAT'S TRENDING?

Will Capitalism Survive?

Paul Collier, an Oxford economist, wrote *The Bottom Billion* (2007), an important book about morality, ethics, and the development of capitalism and the global capitalist system. Collier raises several questions about morality and the kind of capitalism we are experiencing today. He also discusses the possible futures created by different capitalist narratives and practices. The concept of narratives is critical to his argument. People are repeatedly exposed to narratives and stories that help them develop a "sense of belonging to a group and a place." Collier goes on to argue that we develop this identity before we develop the capacity to make rational choices. Narratives create our identity. These narratives tell us about who we are, what we ought to do, and the norms that govern the behavior of our group. Narratives have a third function, and that is telling us how the world works.

Collier introduces three types of narratives: obligation, belonging, and causality. Narratives of obligation instill fairness and loyalty and tell us how important reciprocity is in human relations. Narratives of belonging tell us who is taking part and who is part of our community, and narratives of causality suggest why the decisions we are obliged to take are purposive. In combination these narratives create a belief system and help build a community and move the system from the selfishness of humans to obligation persons who recognize that they are part of a larger community. An ideal capitalist system is based on communities and reciprocity and values such as loyalty, fairness, and liberty. Capitalism must be ethical as well as prosperous, and the ethics of community must be restored. Collier's view of good capitalism is based on his experience growing up in Northern England, where members of the community took care of each other. The idea of a social democracy in which the purpose of government is to ensure that no one is unfairly advantaged or disadvantaged is the kind of capitalism that Collier seems to favor. It may be the only way to close the gap between rich and poor and address the divisions within our societies.

give us a richer understanding of international processes. We can see, for example, that war might result not only from countries' struggle for material power but also from the power of ideas or constructed notions of a proper masculine role in society. A student of international relations who aims to become a critical thinker must consider all theoretical perspectives in attempting to understand our world.

As you continue reading, think of the various theories as eyeglasses to help you see the central problem of each issue. You should be open to multiple interpretations of events and remember that no one theory can explain everything because, by accepting a single theory as your basis for understanding and explaining global politics, you are excluding other perspectives that might also be valid.

CONTRIBUTORS TO CHAPTER 3: *Tim Dunne, Brian C. Schmidt, Stephen Hobden, Richard Wyn Jones, Steve Smith, Steven L. Lamy, and John Masker*

KEY TERMS

Anarchic system, p. 84
Anarchy, p. 93
Civil society, p. 81
Class, p. 106
Classical realism, p. 86
Collective security, p. 96
Comparative advantage, p. 85
Constructivists, p. 114
Cosmopolitan democracy, p. 103
Critical theory, p. 108
Defensive realism, p. 88
Democratic deficit, p. 103
Democratic peace thesis, p. 94

Economic base, p. 106
Empires, p. 95
Enlightenment, p. 93
Ethic of responsibility, p. 82
Ethics, p. 83
Feminist theory, p. 82
Free trade, p. 95
Functionalism, p. 97
Ideational, p. 117
Imperialism, p. 93
Integration, p. 97
Interdependence, p. 97
Intersectionality, p. 114
Legitimacy, p. 117

Liberal feminism, p. 117
Liberal internationalism, p. 91
Liberalism, p. 89
Liberalism of privilege, p. 99
Marxism, p. 105
Material, p. 117
Multilateralist, p. 91
Neoclassical-realist, p. 88
Neoliberalism, p. 98
Offensive realism, p. 87
Pluralism, p. 97
Power, p. 80

Problem-solving theory, p. 108
Protectionist, p. 86
Radical liberalism, p. 100
Realism, p. 80
Relative gains, p. 98
Security dilemma, p. 83
Self-help, p. 83
Sovereignty, p. 81
Structural realists, p. 87
Superstructure, p. 106
Theory, p. 79
Transnational nonstate actors, p. 97

REVIEW QUESTIONS

1. Is realism anything more than the ideology of powerful, satisfied states?
2. How would a realist explain the origins of the war on terrorism?
3. How might realists explain the impact globalization has on world politics?
4. Should liberal states promote their values abroad? Is force a legitimate instrument in securing this goal?
5. Whose strategy of dealing with globalization do you find more convincing: those who believe that states and institutions should maintain the current order or those who

believe in reform driven by international or regional organizations or global civil society?
6. Why have critical theoretical approaches become more popular in recent years?
7. How would you explain the continuing vitality of Marxist thought in a post–Cold War world?
8. Feminists define gender as a social construction. What does this mean? What kinds of questions does international relations feminism try to answer using gender as a category of analysis?

9. Women's participation at the highest levels of international and national policymaking has been extremely limited. Do you think this is important for understanding global politics?

10. What is the core concept of constructivism?

11. What do you think are the core issues for the study of global change, and how does

constructivism help you address those issues? Alternatively, how does a constructivist framework help you identify new issues that you had not previously considered?

12. Which of the three critical approaches discussed in this chapter do you think offers the best account of global politics? Why?

Learn more with this chapter's digital tools, including the Oxford Insight Study Guide, at **www.oup.com/he/lamy6e**.

THINKING ABOUT GLOBAL POLITICS

The Melian Dialogue: Realism and the Preparation for War

BACKGROUND

Thucydides, the former Athenian general and historian, wrote that the history of the Peloponnesian War was "not an essay which is to win applause of the moment, but a possession of all time." Most realists find references to all of their core beliefs in this important document. The Melians were citizens of the Isle of Melos, which was a colony of Sparta. The Melians would not submit to the Athenians as many of the other islands had. Athens was a dominant sea power, and Sparta was more of a land power. At first, Melos tried neutrality, but Athens attacked and plundered the territory and then sent envoys to negotiate. A short excerpt from the dialogue appears next (Thucydides 1954/1972, 401–407). Note that the symbol [. . .] indicates one or more line breaks from the original text.

THE DIALOGUE

ATHENIANS: THEN WE ON OUR SIDE WILL USE NO FINE PHRASES SAYING, FOR EXAMPLE, THAT WE HAVE A RIGHT TO OUR EMPIRE BECAUSE WE DEFEATED THE PERSIANS. [. . .] You know as well as we do that, when these matters are discussed by practical people, the standard of justice depends on the equality of power to compel and that in fact the strong do what they have the power to do and the weak accept what they have to accept.

MELIANS: . . . You should not destroy a principle that is to the general good of all men—namely, that in the case of all who fall into danger there should be such a thing as fair play and just dealing. . . .

ATHENIANS: THIS IS NO FAIR FIGHT, WITH HONOR ON ONE SIDE AND SHAME ON THE OTHER. It is rather a question of saving your lives and not resisting those who are far too strong for you.

MELIANS: IT IS DIFFICULT . . . for us to oppose your power and fortune. . . . Nevertheless we trust that the gods will give us fortune as good as yours. . . .

ATHENIANS: OUR OPINION OF THE GODS AND OUR KNOWLEDGE OF MEN LEAD US TO CONCLUDE THAT IT IS A GENERAL AND NECESSARY LAW OF NATURE TO RULE WHATEVER ONE CAN. This is not a law that we made ourselves, nor were we the first to act upon it when it was made. We found it already in existence, and we

continued

shall leave it to exist forever among those who come after us. We are merely acting in accordance with it, and we know that you or anybody else with the same power as ours would be acting in precisely the same way. [. . .] You seem to forget that if one follows one's self-interest one wants to be safe, whereas the path of justice and honor involves one in danger. [. . .] This is the safe rule—to stand up to one's equals, to behave with deference to one's superiors, and to treat one's inferiors with moderation.

MELIANS: OUR DECISION, ATHENIANS, IS JUST THE SAME AS IT WAS AT FIRST. We are not prepared to give up in a short moment the liberty which our city has enjoyed from its foundation for seven hundred years.

ATHENIANS: . . . You seem to us . . . to see uncertainties as realities, simply because you would like them to be so.

For Discussion

1. As you think of all the assumptions of realism discussed in this chapter, how many of these do you see articulated in this brief dialogue?
2. Later in this dialogue, the Athenians tell the Melians that "the strong do what they will and the weak do what they must." Do you think this phrase is still relevant today?
3. Melos was an ally of the great military power, Sparta. What should Sparta do once it finds out what Athens has done? What theory informed your strategy?

4 Making Foreign Policy

UN Secretary-General Antonio Guterres and the Swedish Minister for International Development Cooperation and Climate and Deputy Prime Minister Isabella Loevin after the High-Level Pledging Event for the Humanitarian Crisis in Yemen, at the European headquarters of the United Nations in Geneva, Switzerland. There is never enough money to adequately address humanitarian crises, and Yemen presents more serious problems because of the involvement of Iran, the United States, Saudi Arabia, and other Middle East states. Do you think all of the wealthy states should have an obligation to address such issues? Why or why not?

Only in the post–Cold War period did the internal affairs of other countries become the primary focus. This is what made the period distinctive. What had been a hobby became a full-time job.

—MICHAEL MANDELBAUM

Foreign policy has, for decades, provided an outward manifestation of American domestic ambitions, urges, and fears. In our time, it has increasingly become an expression of domestic dysfunction—an attempt to manage or defer coming to terms with contradictions besetting the way of life.

—ANDREW BACEVICH

Middle powers like Norway, Finland, Denmark, and Sweden see themselves as global problem solvers and often work with other states and international organizations to find solutions to major global problems. Middle powers often lead major global policy debates; examples include Canada and Norway as leaders in the area of human security and the establishment of the International Criminal Court. Global factors affect all states, however, and therefore play a role in shaping the foreign policy of all states. In the opening photo, the Secretary-General of the United Nations, Antonio Guterres, is leading an effort to find funds to address the humanitarian crisis in Yemen that has been the result of their civil war. The fighting in Yemen between the government of Yemen and the Houthi rebels began in 2015; some 70,000 people have been killed, and over 20 million Yemenis are lacking enough food and other supplies to survive. In the photo, the Swedish Minister for Development Cooperation is standing with the Secretary-General as one of the leaders of these humanitarian efforts. The Swedish government is one of the sponsors of the mediation that resulted in the Stockholm Agreement, which provided a ceasefire in several key cities and included the redeployment of troops from both sides. It also included a call for the opening of humanitarian corridors to allow for the flow of assistance and prisoner swaps.

Sweden is a problem-solving "middle power" and has developed a foreign policy that emphasizes humanitarian issues and international human rights law. In addition to the UN and the International Committee on the Red Cross, most international sponsors were concerned about international

CHAPTER OUTLINE

Introduction 125

What Is Foreign Policy? 126

What Do We Expect From Foreign Policy? 135

Levels of Analysis in Foreign Policy 136

The Foreign Policy Process 141

Foreign Policy Strategies and Tools 147

Foreign Policy Styles and Traditions 156

Conclusion 162

FEATURES

CASE STUDY Refugees 131

THEORY IN PRACTICE Central America: A Perpetual Pursuit of Union? 146

THEORY IN PRACTICE The Impact of Globalization on Different Kinds of States 158

WHAT'S TRENDING? Women Do Matter 162

THINKING ABOUT GLOBAL POLITICS Designing a New World Order 164 crimes and human rights abuses perpetrated by both sides in this conflict. The efforts of those states and nonstate actors promoting human rights were up against the geopolitical interests of the United States, Saudi Arabia, and Iran, who back opposite sides in this civil war.

Such conflicts between national interests are played out in foreign policy every day.

Climate change, a global phenomenon, is shaping the foreign policy priorities of many small developing states like the Philippines and Vietnam, as well as Asian middle powers like Japan and South Korea, and even European middle powers like Sweden, Norway, and Denmark. In 2007, the Pacific Small Island Developing States was established as an informal group of eleven island countries. They list their first challenge as climate change and use the forums of the United Nations to promote their national and regional interests. Ambassador Marlene Moses of Nauru suggested that these eleven states share vulnerabilities such as their size and remoteness and the fact that their "low-lying nature exposes them to adverse effects of climate change," which has a major impact on national security. Since 2009, the UN General Assembly has recognized the link between climate change and global security. Recently in his encyclical *Laudato Si: On Care for Our Common Home*, Pope Francis made a convincing argument that climate change is linked to poverty and social justice. To Pope Francis and many others, this is the critical issue of today and the future. The pope and the Ecumenical Patriarch Bartholomew (the Green Patriarch) issued a statement in 2017 calling the planet God's creation, and they made the argument that it is our moral duty to respect the natural world and it is wrong for people to treat it like a personal possession rather than a gift from God for the use of all people.

Most states put military and economic security over environmental policies that might address the causes of climate change. The small states of the Pacific and Japan, the European members of the Arctic Council, and the participants of the 2013 African Climate Conference are working to convince the rest of the world that global consumerism is altering Earth's climate and threatening human survival, especially in vulnerable states. Yet, the current US administration withdrew the United States from the Paris Accords and refuses to recognize the connection between human activity and increasing emissions that contributes to climate change. More recently, the US Secretary of State, Mike Pompeo, refused to approve a joint statement from the Arctic Council because it mentioned climate change and the Paris Climate Accords. This was the first time that the Arctic Council did not release a joint statement at the end of the two-year chairmanship of one of its eight member states. Finland passed the chair position to Iceland and the remaining seven members all supported aggressive policies to address climate change.

As we will see in this chapter, there may be both concrete and abstract limits to what one person can accomplish in foreign policy. We will discuss the methods that political leaders around the world use in pursuit of their foreign policy goals, including promoting and securing what they see as the national interests of their countries. All countries in the post–Cold War world—rich and poor, large and small, democratic and authoritarian— operate within the same set of limits and possibilities in the domestic and international arenas.

Introduction

Each of the theories we examined in Chapter 3 describes the behavior of an actor called the state. As you will recall from Chapter 1, there is a lot of disagreement in international relations theory about what we mean by "the state." But for this chapter, we need to begin by accepting that the state *exists* and that it is the most important actor in the contemporary globalized international system so that we can better understand the relationship among nations and states, nationalism and national interests, and globalization and global politics. (As a review, we define *state* as a legal territorial entity, *nation* as a community of people who share a common sense of identity, and *nation-state* as a political community in which the state claims legitimacy on the grounds that it represents the nation.) Only by accepting that the state exists will we be able to discuss the process by which the system of states interacts. We call this process **foreign policy**.

We begin this chapter with a definition of foreign policy and explore the questions of who makes foreign policy and what we expect from it. We then present a brief overview of levels of analysis and the study of foreign policy behavior. Here we show you how to explain *why* states make certain choices over others. In the next section of the chapter, we offer an analytic framework of the foreign policy process, providing an overview of how most states make foreign policy. We go on to explore **statecraft**, the methods and tools that governmental leaders use to secure and promote their national interests. We also consider the growing importance of *soft power* in the post–Cold War era, which is defined more by globalization and global challenges. We will see how, in global politics, foreign policy actors often pursue different goals simultaneously because foreign policy connects domestic politics and international relations. For example, a leader might advocate human rights policy to satisfy domestic interest groups but maintain trade relations with an authoritarian

Foreign policy style Often shaped by a state's political culture, history, and traditions, this describes how a country deals with other states and how it approaches any decision-making situation. For example, does it act unilaterally or multilaterally? Does it seek consensus on an agreement or does it go with majority rule?

Statecraft The methods and tools that national leaders use to achieve the national interests of a state.

state to satisfy a need for natural resources. In the final section of the chapter, we look at foreign policy styles and traditions across great, middle, and small states around the world.

After reading and discussing this chapter, you will have a sense of how most states make foreign policy and the factors that shape it—how citizens and their leaders articulate, promote, and eventually secure their national interests. You will have a deeper understanding of levels of analysis, categories of analytic tools that students and scholars in our field use to explain the foreign policy of all states. You will also be introduced to some of the strategies, tools, and approaches that nation-states use to secure their interests and promote their ideas and values in our global system.

▶ What Is Foreign Policy?

National interest The material and ideational goals of a nation-state.

Material interest The physical goals of state officials as they set foreign and domestic policy.

Ideational/ideal interest The psychological, moral, and ethical goals of a state as it sets foreign and domestic policy.

Foreign policy is the articulation of **national interests** (the goals of a nation-state) and the means chosen to secure those interests, both material and ideational, in the international arena. **Material interests** may be trade agreements, energy resources, and even control over strategic territory. **Ideational interests** include the promotion of values, norms, and policy ideas that enhance the security and prosperity of a nation-state. Individuals (especially political leaders or elites), interest groups, geographic position, traditions, norms, and values all shape the national interests of any state. International events, global factors such as the internet and climate change, and the actions of both friends and enemies can also influence a country's national interests.

States, Nationalism, and National Interests

Since foreign policy aims to secure a country's national interests and promote its values, it is critical to understand the relationship among states, nationalism, and national interests. To do so, we must keep in mind the following points:

1. From about the mid-seventeenth century, an order of sovereign, territorial states known as the Westphalian system (discussed in Chapter 2) developed in Europe.
2. The rise of nationalism from the late eighteenth century rationalized this state order, later extending beyond Europe until the whole world was organized as a series of nation-states. International relations were, and to many still are, primarily relations among nation-states.
3. Globalization may undermine this political order by eroding sovereign territorial power and by creating competing identities and multiple loyalties.

With these points in mind, we will first outline key concepts and debates concerning nationalism and nation-states, which will inform our discussion of foreign policy.

Nationalism is the idea that the world is divided into nations, and these nations provide the overriding focus of political identity and loyalty that in turn demands **national self-determination**. Nationalism can be considered as ideology, as politics, and as sentiments. Definitions of nationalism usually frame it as ideology, a political worldview. **Civic nationalism** is defined by a common citizenship regardless of ethnicity, race, religion, gender, or language. All citizens are united in their loyalty toward and identity with a nation-state. They also embrace a set of political practices, traditions, and values that we call a political culture. Civic nationalism and **ethnonationalism** differ in the fact that civic nationalism maintains loyalty to the state and lacks a racial or ethnic element, whereas ethnonationalism is defined by loyalty toward a specific ethnic community such as a language or religious community. Ethnic nationalists generally seek to create their own sovereign nation-state separate from the state in which they reside.

However, we might ignore nationalist ideology unless it becomes significant. This can happen if nationalism shapes people's sense of identity: nationalism as sentiments. The Brexit movement in Great Britain was a nationalist reaction to European Union regionalism and globalization. The Trump election was also a nationalist movement. His America First campaign continues and is a reaction to the global economy and the global movement of people, goods, services, and ideas. In 2019, there has been a significant increase in nationalist or populist political movements in several European states like Hungary and Italy, and recently Hindu nationalism in India has influenced national elections. It can also happen if nationalism is taken up by movements able to form nation-states: nationalism as politics empowered via self-determination. Nationalism is an important element of any country's foreign policy and the formation of national interests.

As defined by Goldstein and Keohane (1993), ideas as beliefs held by individuals matter (1) when they provide road maps for decision makers who are formulating and implementing policy and (2) when they become embedded in institutions that are part of the foreign policy process. Ideas and interests help us explain the actions of all states. In the case of the United States, many Americans believe that it is a nation unlike any other, and that other states should emulate its values and traditions; this is often called "American exceptionalism." Many of the original settlers to the United States, especially in the New England colonies, brought with them an idea that they had a covenant with God to create a new nation that would lead humanity to greatness. This notion of exceptionalism has often translated into a foreign policy that promotes US values and traditions across the world and frames all US actions as blessed by a higher power. Presidents from Washington to Obama have sought to promote US democracy and free market values around the world.

Of course, this idea of exceptionalism and national purpose is not unique to the United States. In Russia, after the fall of the Soviet Union, some argued for Russian exceptionalism based on a more humanitarian, postcapitalist, Russian spiritualism. Certainly, Putin's policy of undermining the Ukrainian government and taking over Crimea, his support for the ruthless Syrian regime, and his

Nationalism The idea that the world is divided into nations that provide the overriding focus of political identity and loyalty, which in turn should be the basis for defining the population of states. Nationalism also can refer to this idea in the form of a strong sense of identity (*sentiment*) or organizations and movements seeking to realize this idea (*politics*).

National self-determination The right or desire of distinct national groups to become states and to rule themselves.

Civic nationalism The idea that an association of people can identify themselves as belonging to the nation and have equal and shared political rights and allegiance to similar political procedures.

Ethnonationalism A strain of nationalism marked by the desire of an ethnic community to have absolute authority over its own political, economic, and social affairs. Loyalty and identity shift from the state to an ethnic community that seeks to create its own state.

Nationalism seems to be taking over all of Europe, but those who believe in sharing sovereignty and working together in a community of states are still attempting to build a stronger European Union. This pro-EU demonstrator in Berlin, Germany, marches at an event called "A Europe for All—Your Voice Against Nationalism."

Premodern state A state within which the primary identity of citizens or subjects is to national, religious, or ethnic communities.

Failed or collapsed state A state that fails to provide basic services for its citizens. Such a state cannot protect its boundaries, provide a system of law and order, or maintain a functioning marketplace and means of exchange.

Fragile state A state that has not yet failed but whose leaders lack the will or capacity to perform core state functions.

Modern state A political unit within which citizens identify with the state and see the state as legitimate. This state has a monopoly over the use of force and is able to provide citizens with key services.

Postmodern state A political unit within which citizens are less nationalistic and more cosmopolitan in their outlook on both domestic and foreign policy.

efforts to create a coalition of authoritarian states suggest that he wants to restore Russia's exceptional "great power" status. Every state has a vision about how the world should be ordered, but only a few have the means to follow through with their beliefs about order, security, and justice. In short, this is how nationalism can shape foreign policy as a sentiment and political ideology.

Robert Cooper (2000) provides an interesting view of the evolution of the nation-state and the role of nationalism in a global age. Cooper suggests that the world can be divided into three types of states: premodern, modern, and postmodern states. In **premodern states**, individuals are more loyal to subnational, religious, and ethnic communities. People do not always identify as citizens of these very weak states, which are essentially what we call **failed (collapsed)** or **fragile states**. Afghanistan, Zimbabwe, Somalia, North Korea, and Iraq are examples (see Table 4.1). These states lack complete control over their own territory and their key governing institutions are unstable and ineffective. They are also incapable of executing meaningful agreements with other countries and do not have the capacity to provide even basic services for their citizens. These are states that have minimal or nonexistent foreign policies except for the relationships they have with states that provide them with aid and essential services. In most cases, their allies supply weapons and police and military equipment.

Modern states are traditional nation-states with control over their territory and the ability to protect their citizens and provide services that allow for the accumulation of wealth. China, India, and Brazil are examples of modern states. Their foreign policies tend to focus on economic interests and a desire to become a major power in their region. In these states, citizens identify with the state, and nationalism tends to be very high. For example, the 2008 Summer Olympics in China gave world viewers an indication of the strength of Chinese nationalism. We all saw the same form of nationalism during the 2014 World Cup in Brazil and again during the 2016 Summer Olympics. India's acquisition of nuclear weapons, its rise as a leader of the G20 economic group, and the favorable nationalist reaction within India serve as another example of the relationship between nationalism and foreign policy in a modern state.

Postmodern states include the states that make up the liberal Western world, such as the United States and the European states. Postmodern states are linked with other states in both formal and informal arrangements at the regional and global levels. Citizens are less nationalistic and more cosmopolitan in their outlook on both domestic and foreign policy. Indeed, in most postmodern states, the

TABLE 4.1	**Listing of Failed or Fragile States**	
Rank	**State**	**Factors Contributing to the State's Fragility**
1	Yemen	Jihadist terrorism, human rights abuses, external interference, poverty, disease, lack of food and clean water
2	Somalia	Jihadist terrorism, piracy, poverty, food insecurity
3	South Sudan	Poverty, corruption, food shortages, armed conflict, human rights abuses
4	Syria	Civil war, religious conflicts, economic issues, political instability, human flight, authoritarian rule
5	Congo,	Civil war, massive human rights abuses, disease, mass rape and torture
6	Democratic Republic of the Central African Republic	Natural disasters, inadequate infrastructure, terrorism, violent protests, governmental coups
7	Chad	Poverty, influx of refugees, radicalized youth population, tribal/religious conflicts
8	Sudan	Civil war, authoritarian government, terrorism, poverty, overdependence on oil
9	Afghanistan	Violent protests, assassinations by Taliban, external interference, drug trade
10	Zimbabwe	Corruption, economic issues, failing infrastructure
11	Haiti	Corruption, forced evictions, poverty, crime, continued inability to cope with effects of natural disasters
12	Guinea	Economic issues, humans rights abuses, political instability and corruption

Source: Fund for Peace, Fragile States Index 2019 https://fundforpeace.org/2019/04/10/fragile-states-index-2019/

distinction between domestic and foreign policies is virtually nonexistent. Policymaking authority is shared among a variety of actors at the local, national, regional, and international levels. For example, the European Union now develops common foreign policy positions, and most postmodern states depend on the North Atlantic Treaty Organization (NATO) for their external security. Postmodern states share, trade, and borrow sovereignty with other public and private actors.

While modern states are consumed with economic growth and building up their power and authority at home and abroad, postmodern states are multilateralists, busy building regional and global regimes to deal with the security challenges presented by modern and premodern states. Premodern states can

WHAT'S YOUR WORLDVIEW?

Is nationalism essential for a state to be strong and to take on any leadership position in the global system, or does it simply give national leaders confidence or political support for elections? Do you think the recent spate of nationalism diminishes efforts toward multilateralism and cooperative problem solving? Think about how countries failed to cooperate in addressing COVID-19.

In this photo, President Putin meets with President Xi Jinping at a Belt and Road Forum in 2019. These two authoritarian leaders are working together to undermine the Western liberal order to restore their power in their respective regions. China is using the Belt and Road program to enhance its global influence. How does their attempt to gain global leadership impact the foreign policy of other states great or small?

become incubators for terrorism, drug sales, human trafficking, arms trading, and even piracy. Many are also kleptocracies, or states ruled by corrupt leaders who steal the state's resources and use its police and security forces to repress dissidents. In a kleptocracy, corrupt leaders often benefit if the state is failed or fragile, as there are no institutions of government to punish them for their crimes. A revolution is often the only way to get rid of these corrupt leaders. The Arab Spring that began in late 2010 led to the end of three kleptocracies: Egypt, Tunisia, and Libya. Unfortunately, only Tunisia survives as a democratic state.

Foreign policy decisions result from premodern, modern, and postmodern political circumstances. It should be noted that even in undemocratic or authoritarian states, domestic interests such as those favored by military leaders, government bureaucrats, and business leaders shape both domestic and foreign policy. Citizens might not have as much to say about what their leaders decide to do in the international system, but bureaucratic agencies and elites do have a voice. Consider how the Chinese business community has worked to open up the communist regime in that country. As we will see later in this chapter, the foreign policy process is essentially a balancing act between domestic and international factors.

Foreign Policy from Different Perspectives

So which interests are *national*? Why these interests over others? Who determines these interests? In broad terms, a state's national interests fall into the following categories:

1. Security: the survival of the society, maintaining independence, and protecting territory.
2. Economic welfare: economic well-being and market stability.
3. Prestige: status, image, and level of respect and trust.
4. Promoting values and political ideology: making the world like you.
5. Expanding territory or control over vital resources: increasing power or resources.
6. Seeking peace and stability: playing a role in maintaining world order and being a rule maker.

As we have seen so far in this book, however, different theoretical views provide different perspectives on both issues and policies. Neoclassical realists, for example, believe that domestic political interests play a role in shaping foreign policy, and thus, a state's priorities may change. For classical realists, however, national interests are relatively unchangeable over time. Hans Morgenthau argued that a state's national interest is the pursuit of power and that power, once

Refugees

BACKGROUND
Who is a refugee? As refugees, can they be called citizens of any country? Why does this category matter and how has it changed? How do refugee issues challenge those making foreign policy? Do we have a responsibility people who leave their homes, including migrants, temporary workers, displaced peoples, and refugees.

THE CASE
Prior to the twentieth century, "refugee" as a legal category did not exist, and it was not until World War I that states recognized people as refugees and gave them rights. Who was a refugee? Although World War I displaced many people, Western states limited their compassion to Russians who were fleeing the Bolsheviks (it was easier to accuse a rival state of persecuting its people); only they were entitled to assistance from states. However, High Commissioner Fridtjof Nansen applied it to others in Europe who also had fled their country and needed assistance. Although states frequently permitted him to expand into other regions and provide more assistance, states also pushed back and refused to give international recognition or assistance to many in need—most notably, when Jews were fleeing Nazi Germany. After World War II, and because of mass displacement, states re-examined who could be called a refugee and what assistance they could receive. Because Western states were worried about having obligations to millions of people around the world, they defined a refugee as an individual "outside the country of his origin owing to a well-founded fear of persecution" as a consequence of events that occurred in Europe before 1951. This definition excluded those outside Europe who were displaced because of war or natural disasters arising from events after 1951. Objecting to this arbitrary definition that excluded so many, the UN High Commissioner for Refugees, working with aid agencies and permissive states, seized on events outside Europe and argued that there was no principled reason to deny to others what was given to Europeans. Over time, the political meaning of *refugee* came to include anyone who was forced to flee his or her home and crossed an international border. Eventually, states

changed the international legal meaning to reflect the new political realities.

In the contemporary era of Rwanda, Darfur, Bosnia after the Cold War, and now Syria, Afghanistan, Iraq, and Myanmar, we are likely to call someone a refugee if he or she is forced to flee his or her home because of circumstances caused by others, without having to cross an international border. To capture the idea of those who flee but are still in their homeland, we use the term *internally displaced persons*. Indeed, the concept of refugees has expanded impressively over the last hundred years, resulting in millions of people who are now entitled to forms of assistance that are a matter of life and death. Watching this world tragedy unfold has led many states to support the human security movement and the UN resolution on the responsibility to protect (see Chapters 5 and 7).

OUTCOME
One reason states wanted to differentiate "statutory" refugees from internally displaced persons is that they have little interest in extending their international legal obligations to

Turkey's president, Recep Tayyip Erdogan, arrives to talk at a ceremony in Ankara, Turkey, to condemn a Kurdish attack on Turkish citizens. Kurdish fighters detonated an explosive device on a road in southeast Turkey, killing at least seven soldiers. Erdogan condemned the attack and said Turkey would not be deterred from its fight against the rebels. This fight continues today on the Syrian border.

Refugees *continued*

millions of people and do not want to become too involved in the domestic affairs of states. For example, in the early 1990s, refugees fleeing the civil war in the former Yugoslavia flooded into Germany. However, the German government was already paying for the reunification with East Germany and could not afford to support more refugees at the time. Therefore, because of domestic political reasons, the German government had to look to other states for a solution to a foreign policy problem. The German government chose to lobby for intervention by the European Union, NATO, and the United Nations. Today, Germany is also in the middle of political turmoil due to its policy of accepting many refugees over the last two years. Germany accepted some 890,000 refugees in 2015 and about 280,000 in 2016. The government led by Chancellor Merkel lost the majority in the parliament because of its decision to take in so many refugees. A more nationalist, antirefugee party, the Alternative for Germany, or AfD, got enough votes to be the primary opposition party. Most refugees to Germany are fleeing war and poverty. The top five countries of origin of those applying for asylum in Germany are Syria, Afghanistan, Iraq, Iran, and Eritrea.

The wealthy and more powerful states will need to address the problem of failed or fragile states if they are going to better manage refugee flows and deal with the challenges of human security in these regions.

In the near future, the most likely source of refugees will be climate refugees, or people fleeing severe environmental degradation. This problem is about not only the future of island states but also crop failures and famine caused by drought in many African states. The severity of the storms that hit Houston and Puerto Rico suggest that even wealthy states are not immune from their own refugee crises.

For Discussion

1. Do states have a responsibility to accept all refugees?
2. Should states intervene in other states to alleviate the conditions that cause people to leave their home countries?
3. Should domestic political considerations—such as electoral politics—shape the refugee policy of a state?

acquired, is used to secure material aims, protect social and physical quality of life, and promote specific ideological or normative goals. As we saw in Chapter 3, classical realists like Morgenthau believe in a state-centric international system in which states act as a single coherent actor that pursues national interests in a rational manner. Here, "rational" means selecting a policy path that maximizes benefits for the state and minimizes risks. Morgenthau and his disciples considered "national interest as the pursuit of power" the essence of politics.

For realists, the principal national interest is national security, or maintaining the integrity of a country's territory and its economic, political, and cultural institutions. Power is essential for national security, and most realists define power in military terms. Morgenthau argued that to understand foreign policy, one needs to understand the "political and cultural context within which foreign policy is formulated" and that interests and ideas shape foreign policy actions and priorities. He quotes the noted scholar Max Weber to make his point: "Interests (material and ideal), not ideas, dominate directly the actions of men. Yet the 'images of the world' created by these ideas have very often served as switches determining the tracks on which the dynamism of interests kept actions moving" (1960, 9).

Robert Pastor (1999) argues that a state's leaders rank their foreign policy goals from *vital* or *essential* to *desirable*. From his realist view, Pastor ranks national interests as follows:

1. National security that includes the defense of borders and the prevention of external influence over domestic affairs.
2. The pursuit of economic interests and securing vital resources.
3. The defense of a country's traditions and values, and the promotion of its ideals in the international system.
4. The implicit and explicit effort to make the world more like itself.

The objectives of foreign policy, according to many realists, must be defined in terms of material national interests and must be supported by adequate power. Military power is dominant in the realm of realism; however, in this era of globalization, the tools of statecraft have changed in both their utility and efficacy. All major states today, for instance, have substantial armed forces, yet all states face the potential of attacks by terrorist groups, and a strong military is not always an effective deterrent. With Russian interference in the US elections and numerous other hacking violations, it is clear that states will now have to prepare for cyberwarfare.

As we discussed in Chapter 3, proponents of the liberal perspective on international relations believe that a state's power is not measured by force alone. Liberals seek power not only in terms of military power; power and influence in the international system may also depend on diplomacy and skills of persuasion. For Grotian liberals, a state may be able to secure its national interests by (1) maintaining rule of law in the international system and (2) empowering international institutions and regimes that promote global governance in policy areas such as economic development and global finance. Liberal internationalists like former Canadian foreign minister Lloyd Axworthy (2003, 5) have taken bold steps to reform the international system and shift foreign policy priorities from narrow national interests to a much more universal focus on human security and human interests. Axworthy described a goal that many liberal middle powers have embraced:

> We propose a way of seeing the world and tackling global issues that derives from serving individual human needs, not just those of the nation-state or powerful economic interests.

Liberal internationalism in this case has evolved to embrace a more Kantian or normative view of national priorities and interests.

Constructivists, meanwhile, believe that state interests and foreign policy goals are "defined in the context of internationally held norms and understandings about what is good and appropriate" (Finnemore 1996b, 2). Awareness that this normative context changes over time helps us understand shifts in foreign policy behavior. For example, the more internationalist context that came with the end of the Cold War supported a shift from ideological conflict to engagement and cooperation, and as a result, many states returned to their own traditions and values as guideposts for foreign policy.

Marxists, on the other hand, believe that foreign policy is generally controlled by economic and political elites who also control power at home. National interests are determined by the wealthy and powerful, not the average citizen. This belief leads to the conclusions that wars are fought primarily for economic reasons and the goals of a country's development-assistance programs are to make poor countries dependent on the donor state, thus keeping them in the position of providing cheap labor, cheap resources, and a welcome place for foreign investors. Utopians such as the academics who made up the World Order Models Project (WOMP) advocate a foreign policy that shifts national interests to more global or human interests such as peace, social justice, economic well-being, and ecological balance.

Who Makes Foreign Policy?

We need to remind ourselves that human beings have agency in foreign policy. It is not the state that decides; it is individuals representing the state. Leaders, bureaucrats, members of parliament, and ministers make decisions, and these decisions are shaped by a variety of factors, such as past events, national attributes, dominant values or the narrative that defines a country's political culture, policy decisions made by both internal and external actors, and the nature of global politics. The values and beliefs of the individual clearly shape the final decisions. We discuss the various factors that shape foreign policy decision making later in this chapter when we discuss levels of analysis.

When exploring the question of who makes foreign policy, we are interested in those who make decisions on behalf of states or organizations within a state. Both public and private actors may shape foreign policy. At each phase of the foreign policy process, different actors will become involved and attempt to shape policy. Thus, it is important to understand the dominant narrative in each society. This narrative is based on beliefs, traditions, and practices and is formulated and promoted by the elites within a society. This narrative or national story is used to interpret the world and it shapes the actions of states.

It is important to start with individuals in formal government positions: foreign ministers, a secretary of state in the United States, or a key minister of trade or defense. Generally, members of the executive branch or the prime minister's cabinet are the ones who *initiate* foreign policy, and they work through the legislature and parliament to *formulate* the policy. Government agencies generally work with the private sector or other governments to *implement* policy decisions. Private actors such as banks, transnational enterprises, nongovernmental organizations (NGOs), universities, and think tanks may play a role in any part of the foreign policy process. Other governments and regional and international organizations may also be involved in helping formulate and implement foreign policy. NGOs and corporations do not directly make policy, but they can have a profound influence on public officials who do make the final policy decisions.

WHAT'S YOUR WORLDVIEW?

Who do you think determines a country's foreign policy priorities? Many scholars suggest that elites determine foreign policy actions because citizens care more about domestic policy issues. Do you agree with that position or have things changed because of globalization and the abundance of information available through social media?

What Do We Expect From Foreign Policy?

National interests are usually related to what we, as citizens, expect from our governments. At the basic level, we want the state to protect our borders, provide internal security and a system of law and order, and support and maintain a means of exchange or a marketplace. This is the point at which domestic and international policy distinctions begin to blur. Foreign policy and domestic policies are clearly interdependent in this global age. Most foreign policy experts believe that citizens expect their state's foreign policy to deliver in seven areas (Hill 2003, 44–45):

1. Protecting citizens living or traveling in a foreign country.
2. Projecting an image or identity in the international system that enhances a state's prestige and makes that state's values, beliefs, and traditions attractive to other states in the international system.
3. Maintaining the "status quo" in terms of providing stability and protecting citizens against external threats.
4. Advancing prosperity and providing the ways and means for accumulating wealth.
5. Assisting leaders in making decisions about whether to intervene in a global crisis or get involved in an alliance or international institution.
6. Providing support for international negotiations aimed at creating and maintaining a stable world order.
7. Working toward protecting the global commons (e.g., oceans) and providing global public goods (e.g., clean air).

A variety of internal and external actors and structures influence and shape these foreign policy goals. Globalization has pushed domestic and foreign policy processes into a complex and interconnected relationship. Domestic societies are more exposed to external or international developments, and foreign policies both shape and are shaped by domestic developments. In capitals across the world, foreign policy leaders talk about policy issues that are transnational in nature, like migration, poverty, environmental challenges, and trade. In crafting government policies to slow climate change, for example, political leaders must contend with the demands of business and industry groups and those of concerned citizens at home—not to mention demands that leaders, corporations, and citizens of other states bring to negotiations. These leaders also understand how domestic interests often prevent the realization of foreign policy goals. One of the most difficult issues for foreign policy leaders is how to make bold foreign policy decisions without alienating a powerful domestic group that might influence the next election. For example, the leaders of the world knew that genocide was taking place in Darfur, and yet few states were willing to intervene in the area to stop the killing. Humanitarian intervention presents a difficult policy choice for most leaders because it is hard to convince domestic groups to sacrifice blood and treasure for people from distant lands. "Where are our national interests?" often becomes a familiar question in political circles around the world.

Now that we have covered some foundational aspects of what foreign policy is, who makes it, and what we expect from it, we revisit levels of analysis (introduced in Chapter 1) to look at *why* states make the foreign policy decisions they do.

Levels of Analysis in Foreign Policy

As a student of foreign policy, you might be interested in finding answers to puzzles or unexpected actions by a state. For example, why did North Korea's leaders decide to develop nuclear weapons? Why do Nordic governments give so much development assistance? These are complex issues, but some explanations are better than others. Foreign policy analysis is the search for factors or variables that explain the most about a state's behavior. Scholars doing research in this area are interested in questions like the following: Why do states behave in a certain way? What factors explain a state's behavior? Why do leaders pick one option over another? If a state spends a significant amount of money on its military, what factors explain that choice? Although there are always questions about "agency," or which actors actually make foreign policy, foreign policy analysis offers plausible explanations for foreign policy behavior. We say "plausible explanations" because this is not an exact science: The social scientist trying to explain foreign policy puzzles can never replicate the certainty of the natural scientist working in the lab and controlling all the variables. Yet if the social scientist can identify factors that shape foreign policy, it might help us better understand the foreign policy process and even predict how states might behave in similar situations. In this section, we will discuss one such approach to the agency question: levels of analysis. As the British scholar Barry Buzan has written,

> Levels provide a framework within which one can theorize; they are not theories themselves. They enable one to locate the sources of explanation and outcomes of theories that have been composed.

In Chapter 1, we discussed how some researchers in international relations attempt to replicate the research methods and assumptions of the natural sciences. The idea here is that one can develop theories, test them by gathering evidence, and find useful explanations for the decisions made by leaders. Foreign policy analysis, a subfield of international relations, puts the individual at the center of decision making. Most studies of decision making begin with the assumption that all decision makers act rationally or always act to maximize benefits and minimize costs. In his classic study of decision making in a crisis situation, *Essence of Decision*, Graham Allison (1971) introduces three models, or analytic tools, for explaining decision making. The first, the rational-actor model, or RAM, provides a useful example of using rationality. The other two models, organizational behavior and bureaucratic politics, are second-level or domestic-level tools. Unfortunately, some foreign policy decision makers cannot meet the requirements of rationality. For example, it may not be possible for policymakers to know all of their options and assign values to those options. They may lack access to information essential to selecting policies that result in value maximization. Thus, other factors, like a decision maker's belief system, the political structure of a state, or the distribution of power in the international system, may influence the range of choices and the eventual policy choice.

Most texts suggest that there are three levels of analysis: *individual*, or the human dimension; *national* attributes, or the domestic factors; and *systemic* conditions, or the nature of the international system. A number of scholars have added a fourth level that focuses on *global* conditions or factors (see Table 4.2). Discussions about the importance of globalization and technological innovations, like the internet, suggest that these factors potentially influence decisions made by national leaders.

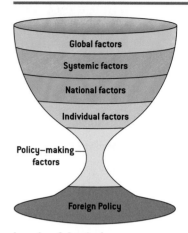

Levels of Analysis in Foreign Policy.
Many factors influence foreign policy. As a scholar, one must consider each level when trying to explain the behavior of nation-states.

Individual Factors, or the Human Dimension

We assume that all leaders are rational actors (i.e., always selecting a policy path that maximizes benefits and minimizes costs), but other factors like beliefs, personality, attributes, images, and perceptions also shape decision making. Foreign policy research suggests that these other factors are most important in a crisis situation, a decision requiring secrecy and thus involving few actors, or a decision demanding a quick response. This level is also important when a leader is given a great deal of latitude to make a decision and when the decision maker has an interest or expertise in foreign policy.

To act rationally, leaders must be able to know all of their options, be capable of assigning values to these options, and have enough information to select the higher-valued options. Those who use these other idiosyncratic factors like *belief systems* or *personality types* to explain behavior do not believe any decision maker can be rational all of the time. Most decision makers operate in an environment of uncertainty with imperfect information. Many leaders talk about "going with their gut" when they are making decisions in crises, but they are usually relying on previous experience (e.g., analogical reasoning) or their worldview (e.g., realism, liberalism, Marxism, feminism, constructivism). Leaders filter information through their worldviews, which include both principled and causal beliefs, and generally seek programs that fit with these beliefs. For example, former British prime minister Margaret Thatcher, with a strong realist belief system, convinced George H. W. Bush to take the 1990 Iraqi invasion of Kuwait seriously and respond militarily. She also decided to use force rather than diplomacy to take back the Falkland Islands after the Argentine invasion in 1982.

National Factors, or Domestic Attributes

At the domestic or national level, researchers look at a country's history and traditions and at its political, economic, cultural, and social structures. Regime

TABLE 4.2	Levels of Analysis: Explaining the Behavior of Global Actors
Level of Analysis	**Analytical Tools Used to Explain the Foreign Policy Actions of States**
Individual	• Bounded rationality • Biological explanations • Motivation/personality • Perception/images • Belief systems/information processing/operational code
Domestic Factors	• Power capabilities • Domestic politics • Decision-making styles and structures: bureaucratic politics and organizational behavior • Size and resource base • Geographic factors/geopolitics • Political structure and political culture • Economic system • Narratives
Systemic	• Level of anarchy or order • Distribution of power • Obligations, treaties, alliances • Regimes or governing arrangements
Global Man-Made and Natural Conditions	• Global social movements • Environmental conditions and challenges • Social media and traditional media and popular cultural forces • Global networks both for good and for ill • Ideas, values, and norms that transcend culture and time

type—such as whether a state is a parliamentary democracy or authoritarian with unelected leaders and a strong single-party bureaucracy—shapes the choice of foreign policy strategies. The role of political parties and interest groups or NGOs within a society is also an important variable at the domestic level.

An area of study that crosses over to some of the constructivist research in foreign policy is the focus on cultural values and national traditions and ruling narratives. Valerie Hudson (2007) suggests that national identity and cultural variables may be more important today than systemic factors like balance of power in shaping foreign policy. Citizens in social democratic states with political cultures that promote social justice and economic well-being expect their foreign policy programs to advance these same values. Makers of foreign policy have belief systems about how the world works, and this combines with national traditions and dominant or ruling narratives to create a menu from which leaders make their choices. Related to the concept of national or group belief systems is the role of narratives. Narratives are stories that we hear very often that give us a sense of belonging to a group or a place. We discussed the importance of narratives about capitalism in the *What Is Trending?* section in Chapter 3. In foreign policy, narratives shape what a country will do, and they serve to create a niche or grand strategy. The United States and Russia make choices based on a great-power narrative, whereas Chile and Norway make choices that reflect a middle power narrative.

Changing elements that shape policy include military power, economic wealth, and demographic factors. More permanent elements like geographic location and resource base also matter. A powerful variable in many democratic societies is domestic politics, or electoral calculations. Politicians often find that they are unable to achieve their desired goals because of the demands of the election cycle. A further complication is the role of bureaucracies in the policy process. Unelected civil servants can influence outcomes that politicians want. Academic work includes many such examples, notably Graham Allison's study of the Cuban missile crisis, *Essence of Decision*. In his exploration of crisis decision making within the Kennedy administration, Allison found that **standard operating procedures (SOPs)**, or the way things are usually done in an organization, are major determinants of foreign policy behavior. Large organizations employ SOPs to respond to a range of events. For instance, when a natural disaster like a hurricane or earthquake happens, agencies have plans ready to provide the correct kind of assistance. Normally, a state's agencies of all kinds—military, intelligence, foreign affairs—have SOPs ready for every foreseeable eventuality. Bureaucratic politics, Allison's third model, suggests that within every government, bureaucratic agencies compete with one another for control over resources and policy. The eventual result of this competition is the policy.

> **Standard operating procedures (SOPs)** The prepared-response patterns that organizations create to react to general categories of events, crises, and actions.

Systemic Factors, or the Nature of the International System

The anarchic nature of the international system—its lack of a central authority—may be the most important factor at the systemic level. However, countries take individual and collective actions to cope with this lack of a global central authority. Thus, treaties, alliances, and trade conventions, which states agree to abide by, are seen as systemic constraints.

A country's behavior is also shaped by more informal systemic constraints based on traditions, common goals, and shared norms. For example, most states respect the sovereignty of all states, and most follow the rule of international law. These laws cannot be enforced, but states abide by them because they expect others to do the same. This notion of **reciprocity** is the primary incentive for states to support a rule-based international system. The distribution of power in the system (e.g., unipolar, bipolar, multipolar, nonpolar) and the nature of order (e.g., balance of power, collective security) are also important system-level factors. Neorealists believe that the lack of a common power or a central government at the global level is the defining element of international relations, and a state's foreign policy is aimed primarily at survival in this anarchic system. Kenneth Waltz describes this anarchic condition of the system (1959, 238):

> Each state pursues its own interests, however defined, in ways it judges best. Force is a means of achieving the external ends of states because there exists no consistent, reliable process of reconciling the conflicts of interest that inevitably arise among similar units in a condition of anarchy.

Liberals, on the other hand, believe that anarchy forces states to create rules and develop regimes or governing arrangements aimed at encouraging cooperation and multilateralism. Today, many liberals focus on more effective global governance across policy areas. As the world has learned with the very recent global economic crisis, rules and regulations that govern all markets are indeed essential.

Global Factors

Global factors are often confused with system-level factors. Simply stated, the difference is that global factors are not necessarily created by states, whereas systemic factors are. Global-level variables can be the outcome of decisions or technology made by individuals, interest groups, states, or nonstate actors. For example, the internet and social media, created and used by private actors, have played a major role in organizing opposition forces in the Arab Spring countries of Egypt, Tunisia, Libya, and most recently Syria. Both radical and humanitarian groups use these resources to rally support for their causes and to challenge the power of key states. For example, ISIS has mastered the use of social media for recruiting young Muslims to join their extremist movement, and this has prompted the United States, the United Kingdom, and other countries to develop social media programs to counter jihadist messaging. No one state owns the internet or the various social media outlets, and yet these can be valuable tools aimed at shaping foreign policy.

Global factors may also be the results of natural conditions. These factors cannot be traced to the actions of any one state or even group of states. In fact, they usually challenge the ideas of boundaries and sovereignty. The internet and resulting information revolution, the movement of capital by multinational banks, CNN or BBC broadcasts, and the revolutionary ideas of religious fundamentalists all represent global factors that might shape policy behavior. The process of globalization promotes such factors. Environmental conditions such as pollution, pandemics, climate change, and resulting drought or severe storms can also have a global impact on foreign policy; for example, they may lead to new alliances for resolving the crisis at hand or to conflicts over the control of critical resources, such as clean water.

Social scientists may combine variables to reach an explanation of a particular foreign policy decision. But social science researchers want to isolate key variables or factors that explain the decision made. They are guided by the goals of precision and parsimony. Advocates of the scientific approach, or **positivists**, want to be able to say that US policy toward Iraq, for example, can best be explained by looking at the personality of George W. Bush or the power of the Defense Department and the office of the vice president in shaping policy. Each of these bureaucratic organizations made the case for war. What is exciting about research in our field is that there is always disagreement about which variables explain the most. Thus, someone could say with equal certainty that US economic interests—namely, our dependency on oil—offer a better explanation for the decisions to launch a "war of choice," something we will discuss more in Chapter 6. The strength of anyone's argument is based on the quality of the empirical evidence that one collects to support the hypothesis being tested. We use the work of historians, public-policy records, government documents, interviews, budgets, and journalists' accounts to gather evidence to confirm or reject our hypotheses.

There are various ways to understand and explain foreign policy. Some are positivist and others are postpositivist. However, by utilizing the different levels of analysis to explain foreign policy, we might be able to predict what states would do in a given situation. Likewise, we can use previous decisions as analogs and make suggestions or prescriptions for future foreign policy. Next, we will discuss how foreign policy is accomplished by examining the strategies and tools that states might use to secure their goals and meet their priorities in the international system.

The Foreign Policy Process

So far we have examined the explanations and influences of foreign policy, answering questions of why and what for; in this section, we get down to the nuts and bolts and look at the process of how foreign policy comes about. You may be surprised to learn that the apparatus used to make foreign policy in most democratic countries is basically the same. Political systems tend to divide the responsibility for decision making between members of the executive branch, which carries out the policies, and the deliberative or legislative branch, which sets spending priorities and guidelines for the executive to follow. Deliberative bodies often have a responsibility to oversee the actions of the executive branch. Both branches of government might subdivide responsibility further into geographic regions, economic sectors, or military affairs. In addition to the governmental actors with legal authority, there are also any number of individuals and groups outside the government structure that might seek to influence the policy process. The actors that make up this informal sector vary by issue area, but they can include business groups, NGOs, religious groups, news media, and private citizens.

As we suggested earlier in the chapter, even authoritarian or totalitarian states have decision-making processes in which government ministries debate issues and work with private interests to promote specific policy positions. Leaders rarely act alone and create a foreign policy that adheres specifically to their own interests. For example, military leaders and various bureaucrats within North Korea support the intransigence of the state in its defiance of the United States and the international community to build nuclear weapons.

The study of foreign policy making assumes that governmental officials with the legal authority to act do so in a logical manner. Political scientists call this the "rational-actor model" of foreign policy making. Proponents of this model assert that a government's foreign policy officials are able to (1) define a problem, (2) develop responses to the problem, (3) act upon one or more of the responses, and then (4) evaluate the effectiveness of the policy. In the following sections, we discuss these four phases in more depth.

Phase One: Initiation or Articulation

Issues are often first articulated or otherwise promoted by media and interest groups who are attempting to influence the policymaking process. Information about a foreign policy issue is disseminated, and as public awareness of an issue increases, the informed public may pressure elected officials to either act on the issue or, in some cases, stay clear of the problem.

Both internal (formal) and external (informal) actors may push a certain position and pressure leaders to take action. For example, in the case of the conflict and genocide in Darfur, NGOs using the internet provided the public with information about the atrocities. These same NGOs initiated further global-awareness campaigns with celebrities and notable public leaders that attracted the attention of major media outlets and many elected officials who recognized the importance of the issue for either moral reasons or pragmatic electoral calculations.

Individuals and research institutes (often called "think tanks"; see Table 4.3) can initiate a debate about a foreign policy issue. A natural disaster, unexpected tragedy, or crisis might also inspire some official reaction from governments. For example, in general, the American public is not supportive of increasing foreign aid, but if a flood or earthquake devastates an area outside the country, US citizens generally support some form of emergency aid and expect that the government will respond. Social media and the increasing number of NGOs and global social movements act as a catalyst for action by government officials.

Technology and social media may contribute to the democratization of foreign policy. Today, citizens in industrialized states have an opportunity to be better informed than ever before, and they are presented with a variety of options to become actively involved in a particular issue area. Citizen involvement also now transcends borders: Global or transnational social movements have mobilized citizens to work to end hunger, forgive debt, and end the use of certain weapons. These campaigns have been successful in their efforts to persuade governments to use official foreign policy tools to address their concerns. For example, in 2017, the celebrity George Clooney, representing the Global Emergency Response Coalition, asked the American public to help feed some 20 million people in African and Middle Eastern countries facing starvation. The countries include Nigeria, Yemen, South Sudan, and Somalia. He made the point that a child dies every ten minutes in many of these poor states. The United Nations requested $6.1 billion in food aid to address the famine. Only about 36 percent of the goal has been pledged and the NGO or citizen sector is working to build support and to encourage states to act.

| **TABLE 4.3** | **Some U.S. Foreign Policy Think Tanks** |

Brookings Institution is a highly authoritative nonprofit public-policy organization whose mission is to conduct high-quality independent research and provide innovative, practical recommendations that strengthen American democracy; foster the economic and social welfare, security, and opportunity of all Americans; and secure a more open, safe, prosperous, and cooperative international system.

Council on Foreign Relations is an independent, nonpartisan membership organization, think tank, and publisher dedicated to being a resource for its members, government officials, business executives, journalists, educators and students, civic and religious leaders, and other interested citizens to help them better understand the world and the foreign policy choices facing the United States and other countries. The council publishes *Foreign Policy*, a leading journal of international affairs and US foreign policy.

Heritage Foundation is a conservative-leaning think tank committed to building an America where freedom, opportunity, prosperity, and civil society flourish.

Carnegie Endowment for International Peace (CEIP) is one of America's leading institutions for researching and analyzing international affairs and making recommendations for US foreign policy. The CEIP, with over a hundred employees, is headquartered in Washington, D.C., with offices in four other countries.

RAND Corporation is a nonprofit think tank formed to offer research and analysis to the US armed forces. The organization has since expanded to work with other governments, private foundations, international organizations, and commercial organizations on a host of nondefense issues.

American Enterprise Institute (AEI) is a conservative think tank founded in 1943. Its mission is "to defend the principles and improve the institutions of American freedom and democratic capitalism—limited government, private enterprise, individual liberty and responsibility, vigilant and effective defense and foreign policies, political accountability, and open debate."

Center for American Progress is a liberal political-policy research and advocacy organization. Its website describes it as "a nonpartisan research and educational institute dedicated to promoting a strong, just and free America that ensures opportunity for all."

New America is dedicated to the renewal of American politics, prosperity, and purpose in the digital age through big ideas, technological innovation, next-generation politics, and creative engagement with broad audiences.

Hudson Institute is an independent research organization promoting new ideas for the advancement of global security, prosperity, and freedom. Founded in 1961 by strategist Herman Kahn, Hudson Institute challenges conventional thinking and helps manage strategic transitions to the future through interdisciplinary studies in defense, international relations, economics, health care, technology, culture, and law.

Berggruen Institute's mission is to sponsor research and programs to develop foundational ideas and, through them, shape political, economic, and social institutions for the twenty-first century. Globalization and technology challenges many of our traditions and political and economic institutions. With new social movements emerging, Berggruen Institute seeks to encourage reflection and analysis of our most fundamental beliefs and the systems founded on them.

Global and domestic actors also have an impact on policymakers in authoritarian or nondemocratic states. China continues to be a favorite target for human rights groups, and they have had some impact on Chinese domestic policies. For example, with the help of pressure from groups like Human Rights Watch, in

Reciprocity A form of statecraft that employs a retaliatory strategy, cooperating only if others do likewise.

Positivists Analysts who use the scientific method to structure their research.

2013, the Chinese government announced that it would abolish the detention system known as re-education through labor whereby people who had committed crimes, as well as political and religious dissidents, were detained. Tragically, many of these NGOs have had no impact on policymakers in fragile states like Zimbabwe or Syria. In many authoritarian states like Russia and China, they have become targets of government agencies seeking to control their activities.

Phase Two: The Formulation of Foreign Policy

The formulation phase of policymaking involves the creation of an official government policy. Internal and external actors—individuals, interest groups, corporations, and foreign governments—initiate policy debates and put pressure on policymakers to act. Parliaments, executive offices, ministries, and bureaucratic agencies must then work to develop an effective foreign policy. The legislative branches of most governments hold hearings with expert witnesses to learn more about global issues and to learn ways to address these issues. The recent debates in the US Congress about Russian interference in the US elections included testimony from leading social media corporations such as Facebook and Twitter. One can only hope that this expertise has an influence on public policy.

Specialists who work inside and outside government typically provide essential information for policymakers. Often, in the policymaking process, the original intention of the policy is loaded with other priorities that might help the politician get re-elected or that might help a bureaucracy gain more power and resources. In noncrisis situations, foreign policy is formulated much like domestic policy. It is a complex process involving legislatures, executive agencies, ministries and departments, and a wide variety of internal and external interest communities.

In crisis situations, foreign policy is made by a smaller group of individuals and agencies. Since the end of World War I, in the United States and many other Western democracies, the executive branch or cabinet has taken over the foreign policy process. Foreign ministries, defense departments, and special advisers to the prime minister or president are usually charged with responding to a crisis. In the administration of George W. Bush, decisions about the war in Iraq were made by a group of advisers comprising members of the National Security Council, the vice president's office, and the Defense Department; the State Department was often left out or its ideas were dismissed by the president's inner circle.

Although in most democracies elected members of legislatures serve on committees with foreign policy oversight, most of these committees react to policy plans formulated by the head of government and that person's advisers. Most legislative bodies do have budget responsibilities and can use this power to support or change foreign policy priorities. However, shrewd leaders who appeal to the public for support of their foreign policy actions can neutralize the legislature's power of the purse. For example, few members of the US Congress challenge funding for military actions or aid programs for an important ally, for fear of being called anti-military or unpatriotic. Generally, when dealing in areas of foreign policy, the old adage applies: "Partisanship ends at the water's edge." After 9/11, it was very easy for the Bush administration to get congressional support for any program that could be framed as part of the global war on terrorism. More recently, in 2014, the US Congress displayed bipartisan support and approved the Obama administration's plan to train and arm Syrian rebels in the fight against Islamic State militants. Things seem to be changing in the United States and among many of our allies. Certainly, many in Washington, D.C., do not support the actions of the Trump administration with the North American Free Trade Agreement (NAFTA), Russia, North Korea, the Middle East, and the ongoing wars in Afghanistan and Iraq. Foreign policy consensus in the United States does not exist. In Great Britain, the country is divided over the decision to leave the European Union, and in Germany, the ruling party lost seats in the most recent election over its policy of accepting refugees. Many states, especially democratic ones, seem to be turning inward, and this will have an impact on foreign policy strategies.

Phase Three: Foreign Policy Implementation

Once a policy is decided in a legislature, department, or ministry, it is usually assigned to policy actors in a ministry or department and other affiliated actors in the field, who are expected to implement the policy. For example, if Congress passes a bill allocating funds for development assistance or foreign aid, the money is sent to the most appropriate agency: in this case, the US Agency for International Development (USAID), which receives the funds and distributes them to its various field offices. The money is then given to development projects that may have been organized by local governments, NGOs, and development agencies from other countries. It is not unusual for countries to form coalitions with local communities, NGOs, and other aid agencies. However, funds are not always spent on intended projects, and they are often not spent at all. Corruption, project delays, new priorities, and leadership changes often get in the way of intended consequences. US agencies intending to reduce poverty in developing countries must deal with a variety of factors that might delay a program or prevent it from reaching its goals.

Phase Four: Foreign Policy Evaluation

Policy evaluation, the final step in the policymaking process, is often neglected or overlooked. Although a review provision might be built into a given program, the administrators of the policy might have a personal interest in keeping the program active. The media may focus their attention on the policy outcomes if the policy program was a success or a failure. All interested parties will have a position and will try to influence future decisions in this policy area. Often, the very public and private actors involved in the previous phases of the policy process will be involved in the evaluation of policy outcomes.

Most legislatures conduct public hearings related to major foreign policy expenditures. These hearings can become particularly important if a policy program has failed or had a major impact on a society. Consider, for instance, the Iraq Study Group's hearings on the Iraq War or congressional committee

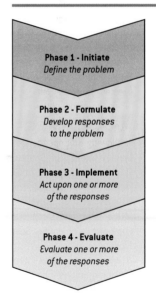

A Typical Decision-Making Process.

What do we mean by *rational actor?* What about this model suggests rationality? Of course, this graphic is a simplification. Can you draw a more complex process model, or flow chart, based on what you have read so far? What other steps or loops would your model depict?

Central America: A Perpetual Pursuit of Union?

THE ISSUE

The theory of functionalism suggests that states may come together to address common problems or cooperate to meet common needs. The European Union started as a community of states sharing resources and expertise to produce coal and steel. This sort of functional cooperation can still happen in many regions of the world. The foreign policies of Central American states can seem to present a paradox. The outside observer sees a number of small countries with a common history, a relatively high degree of common identity, and apparently everything to gain from integration. So why have these states not integrated? This is a case of particularistic domestic goals undermining what seems to some outside observers a logical regional option.

BACKGROUND

Following independence, the Captaincy-General of Guatemala became the Federal Republic of Central America (1823–1839) before splitting into Guatemala, El Salvador, Honduras, Nicaragua, and Costa Rica. Restoration of this union has been a constant theme in integrationist discourse. Yet Central America was more a collection of communities than a clearly defined overarching entity. Non-Guatemalan elites resisted leadership by Guatemala, and Costa Rica early on showed a tendency toward isolationism. Nationalism grew, conflict undermined unionism, and outside involvement was often unhelpful. Various sources of division thus coexisted with a powerful mythology of union.

In 1907, a Central American Peace Conference was convened in Washington to help end local conflicts and led to a short-lived Central American Court of Justice (1908–1918). The Organization

of Central American States (ODECA) was created in 1951 with the goal of recreating regional unity. The first organizations of functional cooperation emerged around this time. Some twenty-five such bodies now exist, covering everything from water to electrical energy and creating a complex web of regional interactions. Formal economic integration began in 1960 with the Central American Common Market (CACM). Intraregional trade grew, but the system entered crisis at the end of the 1960s. Efforts at reform in the 1970s were overtaken by political crises and conflicts. In the 1980s, integration became associated with the Central American peace process. In this context of confidence building, a Central American Parliament was created as a forum for regional dialogue. In 1991, with conflicts in El Salvador and Nicaragua ended, the Cold War over, and a new wave of regional integration across the world, a new period began with the creation of the Central American Integration System (SICA). This system aimed to provide a global approach to integration, with four subsystems—political, economic, social, and cultural.

RECENT HISTORY

Although the Central American Parliament is directly elected, it has no powers and it does not include Costa Rica. As of 2015, only Guatemala, El Salvador, Honduras, and Nicaragua participated in the Central American Court of Justice. There have been repeated discussions of institutional reform, however. In 2005, intraregional trade represented around 27 percent of exports and 12 percent of imports. Most goods originating in Central American countries enjoy free circulation. The same levels of external tariff were applied for 95 percent of goods;

thus, general negotiations for a Central American customs union began in 2004. International agreements are also shaping the future of Central America. The Central American countries signed a free trade agreement with the United States in 2004 modeled on NAFTA. In 2006, they also began to negotiate an association agreement with the European Union, including a free trade agreement.

SICA has advanced efforts aimed at encouraging more integration by providing a legal framework for dispute resolution and helping member states avoid war. SICA membership includes the seven nation-states of Central America (Belize, Costa Rica, El Salvador, Guatemala, Honduras, Nicaragua, and Panama) plus the Dominican Republic. In 2008, SICA announced an agreement to begin pursuit of a common currency and common passport for citizens of the member states. However, as of February 2016, none of these goals has been realized. While the pursuit of union continues at the international level, it is hindered by goals and motivations found at the individual and domestic levels.

For Discussion

1. Does it make sense for Central America to have its own political and economic union, or should it be part of a larger Latin American union?

2. Globalization may force countries into creating larger common markets. In what other policy areas would a union make sense?

3. What would the United States and Mexico think about such a union?

4. What are the internal and external factors working either for a union or against more cooperation?

hearings on the future of NATO or US trade policy toward China. Congress tends to use every opportunity to evaluate the foreign policy activities of a particular administration. In some political systems, like that of the United Kingdom and Canada, the prime minister must face the parliamentary opposition during a legislative session called "question time." This form of evaluation generally attracts a great deal of public attention and comments from opposition politicians.

Another form of evaluation that usually triggers policy actions is comprehensive studies done by universities, think tanks, research institutions, and NGOs. Human Rights Watch, Greenpeace, the International Crisis Group, the International Committee of the Red Cross, and hundreds of other interest groups provide policymakers with comprehensive studies on nearly every foreign policy issue. To illustrate, in 2014, the US Senate Select Committee on Intelligence, chaired by Senator Dianne Feinstein, released a 6,700-page report criticizing the CIA's detention and treatment of prisoners taken in the wars in Iraq and Afghanistan. This report may have a major impact on future decisions about how to treat individuals taken prisoner in the war on terrorism; it may also damage the image of the United States among friends and foes alike. This is one reason that some states avoid public hearings and comprehensive reviews of policy programs.

Foreign Policy Strategies and Tools

The organized statements of goals and beliefs that political leaders formulate and the methods they intend to employ to achieve those goals are called foreign policy strategies or **doctrine**. For the political leaders of a state, a foreign policy doctrine acts as a kind of GPS for charting policy strategies and determining national priorities. The doctrine guides decisions such as where to invest critical resources to secure long- and short-term goals.

Doctrine A stated principle of government policy, mainly in foreign or military affairs, or the set of beliefs held and taught by an individual or political group.

Most states have coherent foreign policy strategies to attain both material and ideational goals. For example, after emerging from apartheid and exclusive white rule in the late 1980s, South Africa developed a foreign policy that promotes human rights across the world and supports an African Renaissance. Similarly, after years of rule by military dictators, Chile decided on an activist foreign policy based on the theme of "diplomacy for development." The hope is that this policy will help Chile overcome its structural constraints of size and geographic location and allow it to develop a niche as a regional leader and an honest broker in international affairs.

All countries have three kinds of foreign policy tools to choose from: sticks, carrots, and sermons. "Sticks" refer to threats, "carrots" to inducements, and "sermons" to what diplomats might call moral suasion. We could also add the power that comes with having a positive image or reputation in the international system. Being an honest broker, or a moral leader seeking to help resolve regional conflicts, can also become a source of power in the international world. Leaders from Norway, for example, took the lead to resolve the Middle East conflict with the Oslo Accords in 1993 and to mediate the ethnic conflict in Sri Lanka in 2002 and are currently working to resolve the conflict in Venezuela. Norwegian leaders are supported in these endeavors because Norwegian citizens see it as their responsibility to the global community. Norwegian nationalism includes a strong sense of internationalism. It is important to remember that, because of differences in resources, population, and level of economic development, some countries might not be able to use some or any of the options we discuss in the following sections.

Sticks: Military and Economic Tools

In the international system of the realist perspective that influences many political leaders, states must secure their interests by military power. Since there is no common power or central government and no agreement on rules governing the system, some countries use force or the threat of force to secure their interests and gain more power and influence in the international system. Other military tools include military aid or assistance, sharing intelligence, alliances, military research, and technological innovations.

Sometimes, the decision to deploy a weapon system can be a stick for diplomats to use. The George W. Bush administration supported the development and deployment of a ballistic missile defense system in Eastern Europe to defend Europe against missiles from Iran or terrorist groups in the Middle East. Perhaps fearing growing US power and influence in the region, the Russian government saw the installation of such a defense system as a menace to Russia's security needs. In response, the Obama administration offered the Russians a carrot by declining to build the missile defense system. Now Russian support of rebels in Ukraine and the annexation of Crimea have caused some concerns among Baltic nation-states, and the United States has responded with guarantees of military support from NATO.

Unfortunately, spending scarce national resources on military equipment does not guarantee safety. For instance, the United States enjoys military hegemony in the world today and spends more on its military than any other nation-state (see Figure 4.1). Yet the sale of weapons by private actors and even many states has created real security challenges for the entire world. New security challenges presented by global terrorism networks have resulted in a number of new security arrangements and the sharing of both technical resources and military personnel. NATO, for example, has expanded its mandate to address the wars in Afghanistan, Iraq, and Syria. A new form of warfare (discussed in Chapter 6) is hybrid warfare, which draws from a variety of instruments, including terrorism, insurgency, criminality, conventional operations, and information operations (Freedman 2017, 222–229). Russia used this form of warfare in its conflict with Ukraine.

There are times when military strength and sanctions are not at all effective in shaping the actions of others. The United States has recently used the threat of force and ever-increasing sanctions to persuade North Korea to give up its nuclear program. To date, diplomacy has failed and so have the "sticks"—both sanctions and the threat of force. It appears that the North Korean regime is not at all moved by the suffering of the North Korean people. The people of North Korea are malnourished and have few of the benefits that most people enjoy.

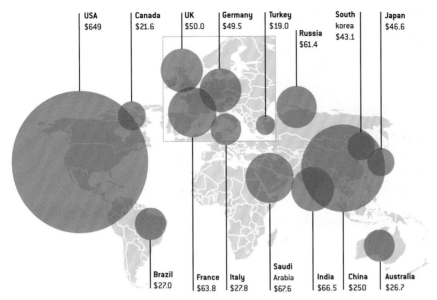

Figure 4.1 Share of World Military Expenditure of the Fifteen States with the Highest Expenditure in 2018.
Source: SIPRI Military Expenditure Database.

The use of foreign policy sticks is not limited to leaders who have adopted the realist perspective on global politics. Liberals also recognize the importance of military tools of statecraft. Woodrow Wilson did not shy away from using America's military resources to help end World War I. However, he called for a collective security arrangement with the League of Nations. Today, progressive-liberal states such as Canada, the Netherlands, and Denmark are active members of NATO who have willingly deployed their armed forces in Iraq and Afghanistan. Many middle and small powers are active participants in peacekeeping forces in conflict regions around the world. Collective humanitarian interventions and peacekeeping are military tools that are becoming more important in areas where states have failed to provide basic security or are disintegrating (see Chapter 7 for more information on peacekeeping operations).

A new form of warfare may present major challenges for both liberals and realists. Cyberwarfare, or an attack on a country's computer and information systems, could cause an economic collapse. Russia used cyberattacks to influence the US presidential election, and they have used cyber tools in Estonia and Georgia to weaken confidence in these governments and make their citizens and leaders feel vulnerable to outside forces. With our ever-increasing dependency on technology, this form of warfare is likely to increase. China has used cyberwarfare to attack computer systems in the United States, and Israel used a computer worm, Stuxnet, to disrupt Iran's nuclear program. Military resources are not much help here. Most states are not well prepared for such an attack, and the perpetrators could be states, terrorist networks, or a single computer expert.

North Korean leader Kim Jong Un and U.S. president Donald Trump take a walk after their first meeting in Hanoi, Vietnam. The North Korean leader has been trying to end the US-led trade sanctions that have hurt North Korea's already-struggling economy. The United States is using these sanctions to persuade North Korea to give up its nuclear weapons and to stop developing and testing them.

Economic sanctions A tool of statecraft that seeks to get a state to behave by coercion of a monetary kind—for example, freezing banking assets, cutting aid programs, or banning trade.

Arms embargo Similar to economic sanctions, an arms embargo stops the flow of arms from one country to another.

In addition to military inducements, states can employ economic sticks. This type of influence can include **economic sanctions**, boycotts, **arms embargoes**, and punitive tariffs. Sanctions are used to both alter domestic politics and influence the foreign policy behavior of a target state. In the war on terrorism, the United States froze bank and investment assets from Afghanistan and Iraq, as well as several Islamic charity organizations. Blocking access to multilateral lending institutions such as the World Bank and investment restrictions have become major tools in attempts to influence state behavior at home and abroad. Economic sanctions can also involve the buying and selling of large quantities of a target state's currency to manipulate its exchange rate and create an economic crisis. Additionally, restrictions on travel and business are often used to force change in a society.

An example of an effective sanction effort was the global cultural, political, and economic boycott of South Africa during its apartheid regime. Currently, members of the UN Security Council are using sanctions to punish North Korea for its production and testing of nuclear weapons and Russia is being sanctioned for its invasion of Ukraine. Prior to the 2015 Iran nuclear deal, sanctions were imposed on Iran for pursuing nuclear weapons as well. The United States and the European Union have also imposed sanctions on the Syrian government for its use of chemical weapons and its behavior in the ongoing civil war. Russia has also been sanctioned for its conflict with Ukraine.

The Trump administration has also used sanctions against Turkey and Iran, and it has added tariffs in his trade war with China and the European Union. Usually, consumers on all sides pay for these actions as prices rise and trading comes to a halt. Trade wars have in the past led to violence and war, but the current US administration sees this as a way of gaining leverage and influence with target countries.

Economic tools need not be all negative, however. States often use the promise of material assistance to reach a desired goal.

Carrots: Foreign Assistance

Most of the wealthy states in the international system are donor states, or states that give a significant amount of development assistance or aid to less wealthy or poor states. For donor states, development assistance is a means of pursuing foreign policy objectives. There are at least five forms of foreign assistance:

1. *Project aid* provides a grant or loan to a country or an NGO for a specific project.

2. *Program aid* is given to a government to create certain policy conditions in the recipient country, such as opening a market or supporting balance of payments.

3. *Technical assistance* provides a country with equipment or technicians in a given policy area.

4. *Humanitarian* or *disaster assistance* provides states funds for food, materials, medicine, and other basic supplies.

5. *Military* or *security aid* is often given to allies or partners in programs like the war on terrorism or to those participating in UN peacekeeping activities.

As we will discuss more fully in Chapter 9, states give aid for a variety of purposes, but most states tie their aid to national interests such as security, economic growth, or prestige. Food aid helps the hungry, but it also helps farmers in the donor state who sell their crops and cattle to the government. Even the most generous states use this economic tool to serve some of their own domestic interests. Assistance programs include the sharing of expertise and technology. Giving humanitarian assistance may also enhance a state's prestige and its image in the international system. Christine Ingebritsen (2006, 283) argues that the small countries of Scandinavia, consistently major donors, have played a pivotal role in promoting global social justice and strengthening norms of ethical behavior (see Chapter 7). These small and middle powers have used carrots such as development assistance, trade agreements, and other nonforce resources to encourage peaceful resolution of conflict, promote multilateralism, and work toward a more equitable distribution of global wealth. A typical Nordic aid program might include funding for public health and education, environmental protection, promotion of human rights and democracy, and family planning. The Nordic countries also give a high percentage of their aid to multilateral organizations and NGOs working in developing regions of the world (see Figure 4.2). About 40 percent of UNICEF's budget comes from Nordic countries, and organizations like Oxfam and Save the Children receive funds from Nordic governments.

Development assistance and aid programs in the United States are administered by USAID. Under the Clinton administration, the number of USAID goals was trimmed from thirty to five. These reflected the neoliberal

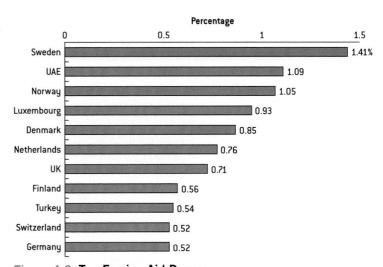

Figure 4.2 Top Foreign Aid Donors.
Do you see a pattern among the countries on this list? What motivates these states to give such large amounts of aid?
Source: OECD.

Many government aid agencies are working with nonstate actors to create effective aid programs. These trisector alliances involve corporations, foundations, NGOs, and governments. This photo shows Bono, from the Irish rock band U2; French fashion designer Olivier Rousteing; French president Emmanuel Macron; and Bill Gates, founder of Microsoft and co-chairman of the Bill & Melinda Gates Foundation, during the funding conference of Global Fund to Fight AIDS, Tuberculosis and Malaria. This group opened a drive to raise $14 billion to fight global epidemics but faces an uphill battle due to donor fatigue.

goals of the administration for the enlargement of democratic and capitalist states:

1. Provision of human relief.
2. Stabilization of population growth.
3. Promotion of democracy.
4. Environmental protection.
5. Economic growth.

These goals changed slightly with the George W. Bush administration. Namely, a focus was placed on preventing HIV/AIDS, and family-planning programs were no longer supported.

Other economic tools include trade agreements, the provision of loans, and the sharing of development or trade experts. Countries give economic resources in two main methods: directly to another country, in what are called "bilateral agreements," or indirectly through global institutions like the World Bank, the International Monetary Fund (IMF), and a variety of regional development banks like the Asian Development Bank. World Bank aid in the developing world can finance a range of projects, such as rural electrification or creating an export-driven agricultural market.

Center for Strategic and International Studies

Established in Washington, D.C., over fifty years ago, the Center for Strategic and International Studies (CSIS) is a bipartisan, nonprofit policy research organization dedicated to providing strategic insights and policy solutions to help decision makers chart a course toward a better world. CSIS is one of the world's preeminent international policy institutions focused on defense and security; regional study; and transnational challenges ranging from energy and trade to global development and economic integration. CSIS is regularly called upon by Congress, the executive branch, the media, and others to explain the day's events and offer recommendations to improve US strategy. CSIS offers full-time and part-time internships for undergraduates, advanced students, and recent graduates who are interested in gaining practical experience in public policy. Interns participate in a variety of activities that support individual programs, including research, writing, and project development.

For more information and how to apply, go to https://www.csis.org/programs/about-us/careers-and-internships/internships.

Sermons: Diplomatic Messaging and the Use of the Media

Military and economic sticks address material interests. "Sermons" address ideal interests. These might include *demarches*, or simple warnings, directives, or position statements sent to governments as a form of moral suasion. A charismatic leader giving a speech to the world can be a powerful diplomatic tool. President Obama's speech on June 4, 2009, given in Cairo, Egypt, addressed a global audience and was a clear attempt to convince the Muslim world that the US policy toward Islam was going to change. Minutes after its completion, the US government had it on the internet in several languages. This is a kind of public diplomacy; it represents an effective use of modern media and global communications to serve political purposes.

President Trump's use of Twitter has brought a new dimension to diplomacy that many traditional diplomats have trouble accepting. Rather than a deliberative and careful assessment of a given situation followed by an official statement, policy decisions are being made with a 140- or 280-character tweet, often without advice from policy experts. Calling world leaders names may be seen as a favorable move by partisan supporters, but it does not help in global efforts to create a stable, rule-based society that respects the sovereignty and autonomy of each nation-state. Thoughtful deliberation should also rule out firing key diplomats without an explanation and without any consideration for the future viability of their offices. Constant turnover of critical officials does not help the image of the US in global affairs.

Diplomacy plays a critical role in the preservation of peace and world order. Many experts consider it a lost art undermined by advanced communications, summit meetings, the increasing importance of international and regional organizations, and the demands of a global media industry that is persistently looking for information and often exposing secret agreements. Traditional diplomatic historians assert that diplomacy performs four important functions:

Diplomacy The process by which international actors communicate as they seek to resolve conflicts without going to war and find solutions to complex global problems.

1. Communication among actors.
2. Negotiation.
3. Participation in regional and international organizations.
4. Promotion of trade and other economic interests.

Diplomats today must deal with a host of new global challenges that require cooperation among state and nonstate actors. Diplomatic meetings aimed at addressing global challenges like climate change, terrorism, organized crime, human rights, and international investments are becoming major sources of power for countries with basic knowledge, scientific expertise, and the means to implement the policies. The role states play in the development of global regimes is an important source of power in this era of globalization. Small and middle powers tend to value the role of diplomacy and use some of their most qualified foreign policy experts in diplomatic roles.

Sports are very much a part of soft power and diplomacy. In this photo, French president Emmanuel Macron celebrates the first goal for France with his wife Brigitte Macron and many political and football officials during the 2019 FIFA Women's World Cup in France. During international men's and women's competitions, countries seem to come together and battle on the athletic pitch and not on the battlefield.

Public diplomacy The use of media, the internet, and other cultural outlets to communicate the message of a state.

Coercive diplomacy The use of diplomatic and military methods that force a state to concede to another state. These methods may include the threat of force and the mobilization of the military to gradually "turn the screw" but exclude the actual use of force. The implication is that war is the next step if diplomacy fails.

Hard power The material threats and inducements leaders employ to achieve the goals of their state.

Public diplomacy is fast becoming an important foreign policy tool. In the past, this form of diplomacy might have been called propaganda, but today, it involves telling the world about the positive characteristics of your society. These educational, cultural, and informational programs are also an important source of power. Countries can provide funds for educational exchanges of students, faculty, and diplomats. The US Fulbright Program, for example, sends students and scholars from the United States around the world and brings foreign scholars to the United States. International foundations can also provide this type of funding. One example is the Aga Khan International Scholarship Foundation, which provides scholarships each year for postgraduate studies to outstanding students from developing countries. Concerts, book tours, movies, and art exhibits are all part of a country's efforts to promote its values and cultural attributes. During the Cold War, the US Information Agency sponsored tours of jazz bands to the Soviet Union and other communist countries. Media sources are also ways to promote a state's interests and make a state attractive to others. For example, the BBC and the Voice of America provide global radio programs that attract listeners and learners across the world.

Finally, in a world of nuclear weapons and internal wars that kill both civilians and soldiers, **coercive diplomacy** has become a valuable foreign policy tool because "it seeks to persuade an opponent to cease his aggression" rather than go to war (George 1991, 5). In 1990, the George H. W. Bush administration used a strategy of coercive diplomacy in an attempt to get Saddam Hussein to leave Kuwait. The Bush administration made a clear demand, or *ultimatum*, that the Iraqi government ignored. The administration then took a variety of steps that involved the buildup of forces, economic sanctions, and diplomatic maneuvers in the United Nations. This strategy of gradually turning the screw was aimed at getting Iraq to see how costly a war with the United States and a coalition of forces representing some thirty-six countries would be. In this case, coercive diplomacy failed because Iraq did not back down, and the US-led coalition destroyed the Iraqi military with the blessings of the United Nations and most of the world community.

Soft and Hard Power in Foreign Policy

One way to understand the methods in which foreign policy is made is to think of both carrots and sticks as **hard-power** tools. However, these inducements and threats are only part of the diplomatic process in the international system. Harvard professor and former Clinton administration official Joseph Nye introduced the concept of **soft power**, or the ability to "shape the preferences of others"(2004, 5–15). Soft power, as Nye presented the concept, tries to coopt people and countries rather than threaten or coerce them. Political leaders can use soft power to encourage cooperation and to shape what other states want in the international system. A country's culture and ideology are important sources of soft power.

Nye asserts that the soft power of any country is based on three sources: (1) its culture, (2) its political values, and (3) its foreign policy. If a country's culture is attractive to others, it can be a source of power. Similarly, if a country's political values—like democracy and respect for human rights—are attractive to other citizens and other states, then that country can gain power and influence in the international system. Finally, a country with a moral foreign policy can also have power and influence in the international system.

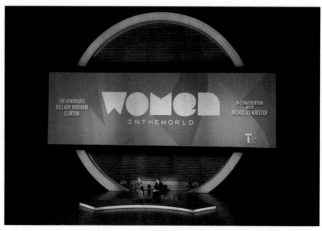

There are many sources of soft power, including global conferences dealing with critical global issues and informing the world about these issues. In this photo, former Secretary of State Hillary Clinton speaks to the *New York Times* columnist and global activist Nicholas Kristof during the Women in the World Summit at Lincoln Center in New York in 2017. Women's issues are a critical part of the human security agenda, and governments are often pushed by nonstate actors and influential individuals.

From this view, we see that the United States may have lost its international standing because of its use of torture and prisoner abuse in Iraq and secret prisons around the world; when the United States lost moral credibility, its foreign policy activities were more likely to be seen as unethical by most of the global community. Nye suggests that if a country promotes values that other states want, leadership will cost less.

Soft power is not merely the same as influence. After all, influence can also rest on the hard power of threats or payments. Soft power is more than just persuasion, or the ability to move people by arguments, though that is an important part of it. It is also the ability to attract, and attraction often leads to acquiescence. Simply put, in behavioral terms, soft power is *attractive power*.

Both hard- and soft-power tools are an important part of any leader's foreign policy doctrine and policy agenda. In this **nonpolar world** (Haass 2008), where no one state or group of states controls all power and authority, and where power and influence are distributed among a variety of state and nonstate actors, it will be harder to control these actors and even harder to build multilateral alliances to respond to global challenges. With no clear concentration of power in many policy areas, the number of threats and vulnerabilities is likely to increase, and states will need to work harder to maintain order and stability. Most experts predict that all states and transnational actors will need to combine resources to address the most significant global problems the world faces. The entire global effort aimed at addressing climate change, for example, will require major collective action. Globalization may not have changed enduring national interests such as security and prosperity, but it has certainly changed how states pursue these interests.

Soft power The influence and authority deriving from the attraction that a country's political, social, and economic ideas, beliefs, and practices have for people living in other countries.

Nonpolar world A world in which there are many power centers, and many of them are not nation-states. Power is diffused and in many hands in many policy areas.

▶ Foreign Policy Styles and Traditions

No examination of how foreign policy works would be complete without a discussion of various styles and traditions, as well as the various ways great powers, middle powers, and weak states may differ in their approaches. Analysts of foreign policy behavior often assert that factors such as the geographic size of a country, its resource base, and its population can determine the kind of foreign policy—or style—a country will undertake. A **foreign policy style** is often the result of how a country deals with other members of the international community. When this style continues over a long period of time, we call it a **foreign policy tradition**. The foreign policy style and tradition include a common set of public assumptions about the role of the state in the international system. A tradition includes national beliefs about how the world works and what leaders must do to secure their national interests. Styles and traditions promote different foreign policy strategies, and each suggests different sets of policy priorities. In this section, we discuss some aspects of foreign policy style and foreign policy tradition.

The foreign policy of all states is aimed at securing national interests and responding to the needs, values, and interests of their citizens. All states seek a role, or *niche*, in the international system. James Rosenau (1981) suggested that all states develop a strategy for adapting to the conditions created by the international system. Smaller states with limited resources and little capacity to influence other powers by unilateral actions are likely to select an **acquiescent strategy**. This strategy suggests they will adapt their interests to fit with the interests of larger and more powerful regional or global leaders. Consider, for example, the role of "client states" and alliances during the Cold War. These states followed the lead of the United States or Soviet Union and were rewarded with the promise of security and prosperity in the form of aid, military assistance, and trade agreements.

States that were once global leaders and even hegemonic powers at times seek policies aimed at preserving their power and status in the international system. This **preservative strategy** has been employed by countries like the United Kingdom and France. Preservative policies include taking a leadership role in international and regional organizations, identifying issues that need attention, and taking the lead in responding to these challenges. The United Kingdom's efforts to lead the debt relief campaign and France's role in the recent Paris climate talks (or COP21) are examples of this behavior.

The most powerful states seek to retain and possibly increase their power and authority by adapting a **promotive foreign policy**. The United States and the Soviet Union promoted their views, values, and interests after World War II as they competed for the hearts and minds of citizens around the globe. Each superpower created an alliance structure that divided the world into two armed camps with the capacity to destroy the world as we know it. After the Cold War, US leaders talked about establishing a new world order that served the interests of the United States and its allies. Some experts talked

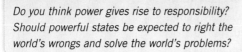

about the unipolar moment, a time when the United States could promote its values, traditions, and interests to create a peaceful and prosperous world.

There are always states that believe the existing international system is unfair, oppressive, violent, and alienating. These states seek to transform the international system by promoting an **intransigent foreign policy**. They do not accept the rules of the game and mobilize their resources to challenge the great powers in the international system. During the 1960s and 1970s, leaders of the Nonaligned Movement (NAM)—namely, Cuba, Pakistan, India, and Indonesia—pushed intransigent policy programs that challenged the dominant rules of the international system. Today, North Korea and Iran are challenging great-power rules—namely, the rules that restrict the number of states with nuclear weapons.

Intransigent foreign policy A foreign policy that challenges the rules established by the great powers or rule-making states.

To a certain extent, these four **adaptation strategies** describe the foreign policies of states today. States adapt to circumstances and events and the structure of the system. Some international relations theorists propose that the choice from among these strategies is linked to a given country's size or influence in the international system. This assertion has been, at times, the center of a significant debate among academics. Although it is clear that countries choose a foreign policy strategy because of their resources and needs, it is not always the case that size determines a particular policy option. A brief overview of what we might expect from great, middle, and small powers follows. States are constantly adapting to changes in the international system and to the domestic factors that might limit a state's ability to act in the system or, conversely, provide opportunities for more active participation.

Adaptation strategies Changes in foreign policy behavior in reaction to changes in the international system or international events and adjusting national goals to conform to the effects of events external to that state.

Great-Power Foreign Policy

Most of the research about **great-power** politics and foreign policy is shaped by traditional realist assumptions about world politics and as a result tends to ignore cases that contradict the academic goal of a parsimonious theory. It is also, as we learned in Chapter 3, an arguably bleak perspective because it sees enemies everywhere. For example, John Mearsheimer (2001, 29–32), an influential realist scholar, contends that great powers always seek to maximize their share of world power, and all great powers seek hegemony in the international system.

Great power A state that has the political, economic, and military resources to shape the world beyond its borders. In most cases, such a state has the will and capacity to define the rules of the international system.

For all great powers, survival is the primary goal. These states all think strategically about how to survive in a system where all states are potential threats. More specifically, the goals of great powers include advancing the economic and political interests of their people and maintaining the rules and institutions in the international system that serve their interests. The United States and its allies created the primary institutions of global governance after World War II. The only significant challenge to that system was advanced by the Soviet Union. Some have called the Cold War a war about whose rule book would be followed. With the end of the Cold War, there is now only one rule book, and the battle is over which rules to apply and how to apply them. Countries invited to the G8 and G20 meetings are all great global and regional powers. They meet once a year to debate best ways to respond

The Impact of Globalization on Different Kinds of States

The Asian economic crisis of 1997, which was triggered by the weakness of Asian financial systems, highlighted states' different capacities for responding to globalization. Even though all states in the region were affected by the crisis, their responses suggested that some enjoyed more choice or sovereignty than others. Indonesia, Thailand, and the Republic of Korea turned to the IMF for assistance, which was conditional on several policies mostly defined by the IMF itself in Washington, D.C. Malaysia, meanwhile, formulated its own strategy for adjustment and imposed policies such as capital controls, which Washington greatly disapproved of. Although globalists and skeptics alike treat all states as equal in their arguments about globalization, we should question whether this equality is true. (Globalists think that globalization is changing the world and undermining the authority of states, whereas skeptics still see the state as the primary actor in global politics and believe the state can and will manage the processes of globalization.)

One way to think about the impact of globalization is to distinguish between strong states and weak states. At the extreme end, strong states shape the rules and institutions that have made a global economy possible. We have already seen the way US policies shaped the creation, implementation, and breakdown of the Bretton Woods system. A more general description of strong states is that they can control—to some degree—the nature and speed of their integration into the world economy. Into this category, we might place not only relatively strong industrialized countries but also developing countries such as Brazil, Malaysia, China, and India. In all of these cases, globalization is having a powerful effect, as evidenced by the restructuring of national and private industries in industrialized countries and the past decade of economic liberalization in Brazil and China. Yet, at the same time, in each of these countries, there are high protective barriers in important sectors of the economy and serious debates about capital controls and the regulation of international capital. The capacity of these countries to control their integration into the world economy is doubtless related to their size, resources, geostrategic advantages, and economic strength. However, interestingly, it also seems related to their national ideology and the domestic power of the state. One characteristic that all strong states have in common is that they guard with equal ferocity their independence in economic policy, foreign policy, human rights, and security issues.

Weak states, by contrast, suffer from a lack of choice in their international economic relations. They have little or no influence in the creation and enforcement of rules in the system, and they have exercised little control over their own integration into the world economy. For example, in the aftermath of the debt crisis of the 1980s, many weak states opened up their economies, liberalized, and deregulated, more as a result of coercive liberalization than of a democratic policy choice. In the 1990s, this continued with what an international economist called "forced harmonization," whereby, for instance, in the case of trade negotiations on intellectual property, developing countries were coerced into an agreement that transferred "billions of dollars' worth of monopoly profits from poor countries to rich countries under the guise of protecting the property rights of inventors" (Rodrik 1999).

Supporters of Venezuela's opposition leader and self-proclaimed interim president, Juan Guaidó, cheer for him during a rally where he spoke in 2019. Representatives of the Venezuelan government and the opposition have returned to Norway for a mediation effort aimed at resolving the political crisis, after months of escalating tension between Venezuelan president Nicolás Maduro and Guaidó, the US-backed opposition leader.

to economic crises, humanitarian challenges, and security issues, and what they decide in these areas affects the entire world.

Mistrust and uncertainty force states to act always in accordance with their own self-interest. Mearsheimer (2001, 33) suggests that great powers act "selfishly in a self-help world." This means the foreign policies of great powers are focused on gaining power and authority in the military world and beyond. Great powers seek to lead in all policy sectors, but the dominant currency is military power, and all great powers must respond to the **security dilemma**. Without any form of central authority in the international system, states must seek security through military power and security alliances.

Middle-Power Foreign Policy

Relying again on realist assumptions and definitions, a scholar might focus on national attributes such as land area, resource base, population, and military capabilities to distinguish **middle powers** from small or weak states and great powers. However, in a world where power and influence are no longer solely defined in terms of physical attributes and military strength, a state's behavior or experience in various policy situations may provide better insights into how that state sees itself and how others see its role in the international system. Most middle powers are liberal states with social democratic political systems and economies based on trade. This means their survival and prosperity depend on global stability and order. These states seek incremental reform by extending a liberal world order, which they see as the most effective way to achieve both human and national security. Canada, Australia, and the Nordic countries are great examples of active middle powers.

In describing the importance of a "behavioral" measure of middle powers, Cooper, Higgott, and Nossal (1993) describe their attributes as follows:

A. *Catalysts*: States that provide resources and expertise to take leadership roles in global initiatives.
B. *Facilitators*: States that play active roles in setting agendas in global policy discussions and building coalitions for collaborative responses.
C. *Managers*: Middle powers that support institution building at the international level and encourage support for existing international organizations and multinational activities.

The same authors quote Gareth Evans, a former Australian minister for foreign affairs and trade, in describing a concept called **niche diplomacy**. This form

Italian Filippo Grandi, UN High Commissioner for Refugees, speaks to the press about the launch of the UN's 2018 joint response plan for the Rohingya humanitarian crisis at the European headquarters of the United Nations in Geneva, Switzerland. Middle and small powers are strong supporters of international and regional organizations. They have faith in their abilities to manage and address global problems. Why do you think it is so difficult to adequately address issues like genocide and violence against innocent civilians?

Security dilemma In an anarchic international system (one with no common central power), when one state seeks to improve its security, it creates insecurity in other states.

Middle powers These states, because of their position and past roles in international affairs, have very distinctive interests in world order. Middle powers are activists in international and regional forums, and they are confirmed multilateralists in most issue areas.

Niche diplomacy Every state has its national interests and its areas of comparative advantage over other international actors. This is its area of expertise and where it has the greatest interest. Hence, this is where the state concentrates its foreign policy resources.

of middle-power activism "involves concentrating resources in specific areas best able to generate returns worth having, rather than trying to cover the field" (Cooper et al. 1993, 25–26).

The middle powers, because of their position and past roles in international affairs, have very distinctive interests in the future order. Middle powers are activists in international and regional forums, and they are confirmed multilateralists in most issue areas. They actively support an equitable and pluralistic rule-based system. They are, for the most part, trading states and thus favor a relatively open and stable world market. Since stability is so important to them, most middle powers see themselves as global problem solvers, mediators, and moderators in international disputes (Holbraad 1984; Wood 1998). Middle powers usually play a leadership role in regional organizations (e.g., the European Union) and in functionally specific institutions such as the World Health Organization (WHO) and the Development Assistance Committee (DAC) of the Organisation of Economic Co-operation and Development (OECD).

A third view of middle powers places an emphasis on the **normative orientation** of this group of states. Although subject to much criticism, the image of middle powers as potentially wiser and more virtuous than other states is usually promoted by national leaders and progressive interest groups to gain domestic support for international activism and to enhance the reputation of their states in the international community. This image of global moral leaders, bridging the gap between rich and poor communities, fits well with the egalitarian social democratic values of most Western middle powers. Robert Cox (1989, 834–835) argues that the traditional normative aims of middle powers—namely, greater social equity and a call for more diffusion of power in the system—might give them more leverage as principled problem solvers in continuing economic and political challenges faced by all states in the system today.

The middle powers may play a critical role as the catalysts of problem-solving initiatives or the managers of regimes initiated by greater powers with less interest for internationalism and little domestic support for egalitarian goals and values.

Normative orientation In foreign policy, promoting certain norms and values and being prescriptive in one's foreign policy goals.

Small-State Foreign Policy

Researchers agree that small states are defined by a small land mass, gross national product (or GNP), and population. In addition, they usually do not have large military forces or the resources to have a significant impact on global politics. However, if they act in concert with other states, it is possible for small states to have an impact on the international system. For example, the like-minded states that played a pivotal role in the formation of the International Criminal Court (ICC) included a coalition of small and middle powers.

Small states can also identify a niche and develop expertise in a given policy area. Most wealthy small states, like Belgium or New Zealand, often focus their foreign policy on trade and economic issues. They will also participate in regional organizations and at times take leadership roles in crisis situations. New Zealand, along with Australia and the island state of Vanuatu, took the lead to create a nuclear-free zone in the Pacific in 1985. The Reagan administration's response to this action demonstrates the limits to small-state actions: When the New Zealand Labour government banned nuclear-capable US Navy ships from its harbors, the United States terminated security cooperation with the country. Belgium is one of the most active members of the European Union, NATO, and every other regional and international organization. Because of its colonial past, it has worked with many African states in development and peacekeeping activities.

It should be stated that with the end of the Cold War and the intensity of forces of globalization, there has been a change in the valuation of states' capacities and their potential influence in the international system. After all, military power may not be as important as policy expertise or technology in this new world where new security challenges include climate change, pandemics, poverty, and cyberwarfare. Foreign policy in a nonpolar world (i.e., power is diffused and held by a variety of state and nonstate actors) is less constrained by the structure of the system and allows for more flexibility and independence. Globalization has also increased the number of opportunities for citizen participation, and technology like the internet makes it much easier to organize for a specific cause or policy position and to promote a small state's national interest in the global community.

Some small states have taken on the role of norm entrepreneurs in the international system. Christine Ingebritsen et al. (2006, 275) describe this role:

> Thus, Scandinavia, a group of militarily weak, economically dependent small states, pursues "social power" by acting as a norm entrepreneur in the international community. In three policy areas (the environment, international security, and global welfare), Scandinavia has acted to promote a particular view of the good society.

Other attributes of small-state foreign policy include the following (Henderson et al. 1980, 3–5):

- Most small states have limited financial and human resources and thus have to decide carefully when and where to participate. Generally, this means a limited global role and a focus on their geographic region and the interests of their own citizens.
- With limited resources (their citizens), most small states focus on economic and trade issues.
- Small states generally take an active role in regional and international organizations.

Sweden, although a small country, is providing global leadership in the struggle for gender equality. It recently joined Denmark, Finland, Belgium, the Netherlands, and Luxembourg to pledge to raise $600 million to replace money withdrawn by US president Donald Trump when he signed the global gag rule, which banned funding for groups that support abortion. Domestic politics in the United States has shifted and the world must expect a significant change from previous policy positions.

Multilateralism is a preferred strategy, and small states consider it the best way to secure their interests.

- Small states can play critical roles in alliances and in global policy regimes. Many of these states have resources and expertise, and they seek roles as global problem solvers in policy areas of importance to their domestic population.

As the space between domestic and foreign policy sectors blurs or even disappears, domestic politics and the interests of citizens play a greater role in shaping foreign policy. In both small and middle powers, what citizens expect from states at home has a significant influence on how these states behave internationally.

Conclusion

In this chapter, we provided an overview of the primary issues and actors in the foreign policy process. We saw that many variables shape the world of diplomacy in the contemporary international system: material needs, ideas, and people themselves. The rational-actor model offers one way to understand the policy-making process. We also considered different styles and traditions in foreign policy. In the following chapters, we will turn to specific topics that make up the critical challenges in the international system; for example, we will see how globalization is undermining the autonomy of the nation-state. International and regional organizations like the United Nations and the European Union, NGOs, and multinational corporations are each eroding the nation-state's power; they influence some of the core policy areas that were once the sole responsibility of nation-states. This trend is an important factor shaping relations in the contemporary world.

WHAT'S TRENDING?

Women Do Matter

Foreign policy doctrines are often seen as road maps or sextants that guide the direction of a country's foreign policy. Most Americans remember the Monroe Doctrine from high school social studies. It told the world that the Western Hemisphere was our domain and other countries should stay out of the region. Others might remember the Reagan Doctrine, developed by Jeanne Kirkpatrick, which outlined a strategy of confronting communism around the world and accepting alliances with nasty authoritarian regimes because they were our allies in the fight against communism. This justified our support of the government in South Africa that practiced the heinous racist system of apartheid, which denied human rights to all black citizens of the country. There were many other similar regimes that we embraced.

In the very first pages of their book *The Hillary Doctrine, Sex and American Foreign Policy* (2015), Valerie M. Hudson and Patricia Leidl give us some sense of what Hillary Clinton's foreign policy doctrine was all about. In contrast to many other US foreign policy doctrines, the

WHAT'S TRENDING? *continued*

"Hillary Doctrine" states that empowering women and girls is a cornerstone of US foreign policy not because it may be a moral or humanitarian issue but because it is a security and prosperity issue. Ultimately, it is a peace issue. Secretary Clinton was not the first to make a strong case for human rights or women's rights, but under President Obama, she made women's issues central to US foreign policy. The Hillary Doctrine made a strong case that the subjugation of women is a threat to security and stability. She made the argument that in areas where women are denied rights and where they are dehumanized and oppressed, one is likely to find extremism and authoritarian rule that presents a security threat to the entire world. Further, peace and prosperity depends on giving rights and privileges to women and girls in every society.

While the US First Lady, the US Senator from New York, and US Secretary of State, Hillary Clinton promoted programs that addressed violence against women and girls and worked to formulate and implement policies aimed at education, health, and social services for women and their families. In the 2010 review of US State Department programs, the Quadrennial Diplomacy and Development Review (QDDR), the US State Department and the US Agency for International Development set an agenda to focus on six policy areas, including sustainable economic growth, food security, global health, and climate change. The document made numerous references to empowering women and girls and investing in programs that would prepare them to lead so they can help solve the global challenges that threaten our world today.

The world may have first heard about Clinton's commitment to women's rights when she addressed the 1995 Fourth World Conference on Women in Bejing, China. It was then that she stated, "Women's rights are human rights and human rights are women's rights." The goal of those who support this view is to have the core ideas in the Hillary Doctrine become SOPs for the US foreign policy community. The authors make a case for change as their final point: "*seeing women as integral to national and international security will have become as natural and unremarkable as not seeing them once was*" (p. 334).

CONTRIBUTORS TO CHAPTER 4: *Steven L. Lamy and John Masker*

KEY TERMS

Acquiescent strategy, p. 156
Adaptation strategies, p. 157
Arms embargo, p. 150
Civic nationalism, p. 127
Coercive diplomacy, p. 154
Diplomacy, p. 153
Doctrine, p. 153
Economic sanctions, p. 150
Ethnonationalism, p. 127
Failed or collapsed state, p. 128
Foreign policy, p. 125

Foreign policy style, p. 156
Foreign policy tradition, p. 128
Fragile state, p. 128
Great power, p. 157
Hard power, p. 154
Ideational interest, p. 126
Intransigent foreign policy, p. 157
Material interest, p. 126
Middle powers, p.159
Modern state, p. 128

National interest, p.126
National self-determination, p. 127
Nationalism, p. 127
Niche diplomacy, p. 159
Nonpolar world, p. 155
Nonpolar world, p. 155
Normative orientation, p. 160
Positivists, p. 144
Postmodern state, p.128
Premodern state, p. 128

Preservative strategy, p. 156
Promotive foreign policy, p. 156
Public diplomacy, p. 154
Reciprocity, p. 144
Security dilemma, p. 159
Soft power, p. 155
Standard operating procedures (SOPs), p. 139
Statecraft, p.125

REVIEW QUESTIONS

1. Why has nationalism spread across the world in the last two centuries?

2. How has the rise of the modern state shaped the development of nationalism?

3. In what ways do personal characteristics affect outcomes in the rational-actor model?

4. What are the four levels of analysis? How are they used to explain the behavior of states?

5. How do bureaucracies influence the foreign policy process?

6. Do small states have any power and influence in the international system?

7. "Contemporary globalization erodes nation-state sovereignty but does *not* undermine nationalism." Discuss.

8. Who are the actors in creating foreign policy? What are the phases?

9. What is a foreign policy doctrine?

10. Do you think the foreign policy process is shifting away from the state?

 Learn more with this chapter's digital tools, including the Oxford Insight Study Guide, at **www.oup.com/he/lamy6e**.

THINKING ABOUT GLOBAL POLITICS

Designing a New World Order

BACKGROUND

The significant changes in the political and economic land-scape in Europe and the former Soviet Union, the unprec-edented collective response to Iraqi aggression in Kuwait, and the puzzling failure of the major powers to respond effectively to aggression in Somalia, Rwanda, and the former Yugoslavia suggest that it may be time for the rule-making actors in the international system to establish a new set of standards and rules of behavior for the new world order. This new system of explicit and implicit rules and structures will replace the East-West Cold War "bipo-larity," or the "balance of nuclear terror." Many leaders, including former presidents George H. W. Bush and Bill Clinton, have frequently invoked the concept of "new world order" as a justification for foreign policy decisions. How-ever, there does not seem to be any consensus in the United States or in other nation-states about the structure of this new world order. Some world leaders have called for a series of discussions about the future of world politics in an effort to prevent US hegemony and avoid drifting toward a new era of competition and anarchy. They want to know their role in this new system. Who will be the new rule makers? How will order be maintained? What are the rules? What are the new security challenges? These are some of the questions leaders are asking.

EXPECTATIONS

In this small-group discussion exercise, you will explore various world-order models, review how changes in the structure of the system might influence or shape foreign policies of states, and then make a case for a new US global strategy and a new world order.

PROCEDURE

1. Review the options presented in the "World-Order Models" section that follows. You may want to review historical periods when these systems were in opera-tion (not all systems of order presented on this sheet have been implemented).

2. With reference to a traditional realist's three system-level challenges and constraints—order, anarchy, and the security dilemma—which world-order system would you find most effective for US interests? What about the interests of other major powers (e.g.,

continued

Japan, Germany, Russia, and Great Britain)? What about the concerns of developing states or the Global South?

3. Discuss the nature of foreign policy under each system structure. For example, how would the foreign policy of major, middle, and small powers be influenced if the system moved from bipolarity to hegemony? Review each possible system structure and its influence on foreign policy.

WORLD-ORDER MODELS

One-Country Rule: One country governs the rest of the world, controlling all resources, industry, and trade. The superpower determines the national interest of all other nations and the interest of the world; all are defined in terms of the superpower's interests.

Bipolar: Two superpowers have divided the world. Each controls a large group of countries and controls the resources, industry, and trade within its bloc. Relations between the two blocs are determined by the superpowers to serve their own interests.

Polycentrism: Each country has its own government and controls its own resources, industry, and trade. There are no international organizations or alliances; every country operates in its own interest.

Regionalism: Countries located in the same part of the world have formed regional governments that control resources, industry, and trade within each region. Relations between regions are governed by regional interests.

World Law: All nations of the world have established a world authority that makes laws against international violence and has agencies to enforce these laws, keep the peace, and resolve conflicts. Individual nations control their own resources, industry, internal security, and trade. The world authority acts only to prevent the use of violence in relations between nations.

Some Other Order: Draw your own model of an international system. Specify how international relations, trade, and security are handled in your model. Why is your model better than any of the other models?

DISCUSSION AND FOLLOW-UP

If time permits, in small groups, discuss what you think will be the major issues facing the world's leaders in the next ten years. Then try to reach consensus on a system structure (i.e., world-order model) that you feel will create an international environment that will enable states to constructively and effectively respond to these issues.

5 Global and Regional Governance

Vassily Nebenzia, Permanent Representative of the Russian Federation to the United Nations and President of the Security Council for the month of September 2019, leads a UN Security Council discussion on peacekeeping operations. There are thirteen active peacekeeping operations, and the United States and China provide the most funding for these operations.

Any international order presupposes a substantial measure of general consent. We shall, indeed, condemn ourselves to disappointment if we exaggerate the role which morality is likely to play. The fatal dualism of politics will always keep considerations of morality entangled with considerations of power.

—E. H. CARR

This is an age of contradiction. The world's colossus does not, and cannot, have the imperial ambitions of past hegemons. The nature of modern reality is such that no power completely controls its own fate, and self-sufficiency is more of a mirage than ever. The requisites of daily life, and the solutions to most of the problems states face, require international cooperation.

—ARTHUR A. STEIN

CHAPTER OUTLINE

Introduction 169

International Law 171

The United Nations 176

Maintenance of International Peace and Security 183

The Reform Process of the United Nations 190

The European Union and Other Regional Organizations 193

The Growth of Global Civil Society 198

Multinational Corporations 200

INGOs as Global Political Actors 203

Celebrity Diplomacy 208

Foundations and Think Tanks 211

Criminal and Terrorist Networks as Global Actors 212

Conclusion 213

FEATURES

THEORY IN PRACTICE Neoconservatives and the United Nations 188

CASE STUDY A Global Campaign: The Baby Milk Advocacy Network 204

GLOBAL PERSPECTIVE NGOs and Protecting the Rights of Children 209

WHAT'S TRENDING? A World Order Without Arms? 215

THINKING ABOUT GLOBAL POLITICS Who Could Help Tomorrow? Twenty Global Problems and Global Issues Networks 216

The search for order and the quest for a global community in which members promote prosperity, democracy, and a rule-based global order is an ongoing quest that requires leadership and the commitment of all of the key players in the international system. Global and regional institutions play a key role in providing order and stability. Most of the global institutions that we rely on were created at the end of World War II and reflect Cold War realities. Leaders across the world must ask if it is time to reform institutions like the United Nations and the financial and economic institutions like the World Bank, the International Monetary Fund (IMF), and even the World Trade Organization (WTO). Do you think the global community faces challenges that require new institutions and new decision-making procedures?

Countries cannot respond effectively to most of the challenges that threaten peace and stability, human rights, and economic well-being by acting alone. Cooperation, partnerships, and multilateralism are practices that are essential for responding to these crises and maintaining a rule-based global system. Further, global and regional organizations are critical players in any strategy to solve the persistent and newly emerging challenges that we face.

Various agencies of the United Nations with state and nonstate actors as partners are taking the lead in responding to many major crisis situations. For example, the United Nations High Commissioner for Refugees is dealing with the Syrian refugee crisis (over 13.1 million people have fled the war and 13.1 million are in need of some assistance), as well as refugee crises in Sudan and Central America and the Rohingya refugee crisis in Bangladesh. The World Health Organization (WHO) and the World Food Programme are trying to feed and provide medicine for 12 million people per month in Yemen, which has been devastated by a war between forces loyal to the internationally recognized government and forces that are part of the Houthi rebel movement.

One of the biggest issues facing the UN Security Council is the North Korean nuclear program. US officials have stated that North Korea is the greatest threat to the world today. Nikki Haley, the former US ambassador to the United Nations, clearly stated that the world will never accept a nuclear-armed North Korea. The world watched in 2018 as North and South Korean leaders met and talked about finally ending the Korean War. For the first time, North Korean dictator Kim Jong Un expressed willingness to discuss denuclearization, if and when he met with President Trump. Kim Jong Un and President Trump met in Singapore in June 2018 and released a joint statement agreeing to security guarantees for North Korea and to begin negotiations on denuclearization. A second meeting in 2019 in Hanoi abruptly ended with no agreement because of differing views on when to end US sanctions on North Korea. Later in June 2019, Trump met Kim Jong Un at the DMZ in North Korea and agreed to restart talks. These are bilateral talks—with some input from South Korea—that do not involve the rest of the global community. Why would the United States risk its reputation on negotiations that seem to be going in a negative direction? Why not use the UN as the place for negotiations? The United Nations has passed eight rounds of sanctions since North Korea's first nuclear test. The most recent sanctions include the following:

- Halt or cap North Korea's oil imports.
- Ban textile imports.
- End overseas labor contracts.
- Suppress all smuggling efforts.
- Stop all joint ventures.
- Sanction designated North Korean government individuals and entities.

North Korea is one of many crises that will have an impact on global stability. Most experts believe that North Korea has no interest in giving up its weapons. John Bolton, the former Trump national security advisor, opposed the talks with North Korea and clearly stated that he thought North Korea would never give up its weapons. It is always possible that we may stumble into a nuclear war that both sides really do not want. Scott Sagan (2017), a leading expert on nuclear proliferation, suggests that North Korea no longer poses a nonproliferation problem; instead, it is now a nuclear deterrence problem. So who will monitor North Korea's nuclear activities? Yes, the United States and other major powers must act here, but a strong United Nations and its related agencies and more effective regional organizations are essential for the creation and maintenance of a **multilateral** rules-based order. This chapter explores the institutions that might provide the only path toward resolving or managing the existential crises that threaten our survival.

Multilateralism The process by which states work together to solve a common problem.

Introduction

Leaders in all countries face the challenge of managing the processes of globalization. States seek to create international institutions and laws that enable them to secure their national interests in a more globalized society. **Global governance** describes the formal and informal processes and institutions that guide and control the activities of both state and nonstate actors in the international system; global governance does not mean the creation of a world government. After all, this governance is not always led by states, nor is it always led by international organizations that are created by states.

Indeed, multinational corporations (MNCs) and even nongovernmental organizations (NGOs) create rules and regulations to govern behavior in some policy areas. For example, banks will set up informal rules for exchanging currencies, and NGOs have set up ethical rules for fundraising and intervention in crisis regions. As demonstrated by the work of Elinor Ostrom, the 2009 Nobel Prize winner in economics, sometimes private, nongovernmental groups can do a better job of creating rules for governing a shared resource. In this case, the state is the primary actor but not the only one in global governance.

In this complex and increasingly global system, states are working with international and regional organizations like the United Nations and the European Union and **nonstate actors** like Oxfam, Save the Children, and Amnesty International through diplomacy, international law, and regimes or international governing arrangements to solve common regional and global problems. Cary Coglianese (2000, 299–301) suggests that international organizations and international law are critical in responding to three types of problems:

Global governance The regulation and coordination of transnational issue areas by nation-states, international and regional organizations, and private agencies through the establishment of international regimes. These regimes may focus on problem solving or the simple enforcement of rules and regulations.

Nonstate actor Any participant in global politics that is neither acting in the name of government nor created and served by government. Nongovernmental organizations, terrorist networks, global crime syndicates, and multinational corporations are examples.

1. Coordinating global linkages: In this area, rules and laws are critical for managing the exchanges of information, products, services, money, and finance and even for managing collective responses to criminal activity.

2. Responding to common problems: The global community faces common problems like climate change, poverty, human rights abuses, refugees, and pandemics, all of which require some form of coordination and collective policy response.
3. Protecting core values: Institutions and laws are essential for protecting and promoting core values like equality, liberty, democracy, and justice across the world.

The problems listed here and others increase with globalization. States will undoubtedly become more dependent on international and regional institutions like the United Nations or the African Union to promote international and regional cooperation in these critical areas. The global system has institutions capable of coordinating responses to global crises, but successful responses depend on voluntary compliance by both state and nonstate actors. If global actors consider the laws, regimes, and institutions to be fair and legitimate, they will be more likely to comply. Here we mean international laws, or the body of legal standards, procedures, and institutions that govern the interactions of sovereign states. A **regime** is a governing arrangement that guides states and transnational actors and institutions (described in detail in the next section); it is a set of rules, norms, and practices that shape the behavior of all actors in a given issue area. **International law** is an international institution.

Regionalism has become a pervasive feature of international affairs. According to the WTO, all of its members are party to one or more regional trade agreements, and as of January 2019 nearly 467 notifications of such agreements were received, 291 of which are in force. Regional peacekeeping forces have become active in some parts of the world. In past decades, regionalism has become one of the forces challenging the traditional centrality of states in international relations.

That challenge comes from two directions. The word *region* and its derivatives denote one distinguishable part of some larger geographical area. Yet they are used in different ways. On the one hand, regions are territories within a state, occasionally crossing state borders. On the other hand, regions are particular areas of the world, covering a number of different sovereign states. We focus on this latter description of regionalism in our discussion.

In this chapter, we discuss four linked topics:

- First, we introduce the basics of international law that provide a framework for the interactions of states, international and regional actors, and nonstate actors in global politics.
- Next, we turn to the United Nations, the largest international organization with a mandate to prevent future world wars and protect human rights.
- We then discuss the concept of regional integration, with a focus on the European Union, the most successful and comprehensive regional organization.
- In the final section, we explore the wide variety of nonstate actors and the increasingly important role these actors are playing in global politics.

Regime A set of implicit or explicit principles, norms, rules, and decision-making procedures around which actors' expectations converge in a given area of international relations. Often simply defined as a governing arrangement in a regional or global policy area.

International law The formal rules of conduct that states acknowledge or contract between themselves.

International Law

In this section, we consider the practice of modern international law and the debates surrounding its nature and efficacy. For our purposes, there is one central question: What is the relationship between international law and international politics? If the power and interests of states are what matters, as we discussed in Chapter 4, then international law is either a servant of the powerful or an irrelevant curiosity. And yet, if international law does *not* matter, then why do states and other actors devote so much effort to negotiating new legal regimes and augmenting existing ones? Why does so much international debate revolve around the legality of state behavior, the applicability of legal rules, and the legal obligations incumbent on states? Moreover, why is compliance with international law so high, even by domestic standards?

International law is best understood as a core international institution—a set of norms, rules, and practices created by states and other actors to facilitate diverse social goals, from order and coexistence to justice and human development. It is an institution with distinctive historical roots, and understanding these roots is essential to grasping its unique institutional features.

International Order and Institutions

Realists portray international relations as a struggle for power, a realm in which states are "continuously preparing for, actively involved in, or recovering from organized violence in the form of war" (Morgenthau 1985, 52). Although war has certainly been a recurrent feature of international life, it is a crude and deeply dysfunctional way for states to ensure their security or realize their interests. Because of this, states have devoted as much, if not more, effort to liberating themselves from the condition of war than to embroiling themselves in violent conflict. Creating some modicum of international order has been an abiding common interest of most states most of the time (Bull 1977, 8).

To achieve international order, states have created international institutions. People often confuse institutions and organizations, incorrectly using the two terms interchangeably. **International institutions** are commonly defined as complexes of norms, rules, and practices that "prescribe behavioral roles, constrain activity, and shape expectations" (Keohane 1989a, 3; see Table 5.1). **International organizations**, like the United Nations, are physical entities that have staffs, head offices, and letterheads. International

International institutions Complexes of norms, rules, and practices that prescribe behavioral roles, constrain activity, and shape expectations.

International organization Any institution with formal procedures and formal membership from three or more countries. The minimum number of countries is set at three, rather than two, because multilateral relationships have significantly greater complexity than bilateral relationships.

Russian engineers practice mine clearing in the Arctic region of Russia. The Ottawa Treaty, which bans the use of landmines, went into effect in 1999. It has been ratified by 164 nation-states, but 33 countries have not signed it, including China, Russia, and the United States. The euphoria associated with the campaign to ban landmines may be overwhelmed by great-power involvement in conflict situations. For example, do you think Russian troops have used mines in Syria?

institutions can exist without any organizational structure—the 1997 Ottawa Convention banning land mines is an institution, but there is no head office. Many institutions have organizational dimensions, however. The WTO (formerly the General Agreement on Tariffs and Trade) is an institution with a very strong organizational structure. Whereas institutions can exist without an organizational dimension, international organizations cannot exist without an institutional framework. Their very existence presupposes a set of norms, rules, and principles that empower them to act and that they are charged to uphold. If states had never negotiated the Charter of the United Nations, the organization could not exist, let alone function.

In modern international society, states have created three levels of institutions:

- There are deep constitutional institutions, such as the principle of sovereignty, which define the terms of legitimate statehood.
- States have also created fundamental institutions, like international law and multilateralism, which provide the basic rules and practices that shape how states solve cooperation and coordination problems. These are the institutional norms, techniques, and structures that states and other actors invoke and employ when they have common ends they want to achieve or clashing interests they want to contain.
- Last, states have developed issue-specific institutions or regimes, such as the Treaty on the Nonproliferation of Nuclear Weapons, which enact fundamental institutional practices in particular realms of interstate relations. The treaty is a concrete expression of the practices of international law and multilateralism in the field of arms control.

We are concerned here with the middle-level, fundamental institutions. These are "the elementary rules of practice that states formulate to solve the coordination and collaboration problems associated with coexistence under anarchy" (Reus-Smit 1999, 14). In modern international society, a range of such institutions exist, including international law, multilateralism, bilateralism, diplomacy, and management by the great powers. Since the middle of the nineteenth century, however, the first two (international law and multilateralism) have provided the basic framework for international cooperation and the pursuit of order.

How do states develop international law? Why do states follow international law if there is no international government to enforce these laws? Why is international law not given a higher priority in the study of international relations? These are important questions that might help us understand the development of international law as an international institution.

Multilateral diplomacy
Cooperation among three or more states based on, or with a view to formulating, reciprocally binding rules of conduct.

The principal mechanism modern states employ to legislate international law is **multilateral diplomacy**, commonly defined as cooperation among three or more states based on, or with a view to formulating, reciprocally binding rules of conduct. It is a norm of the modern international legal system that states are

| TABLE 5.1 | Levels of International Institutions |

Institution	Description
Constitutional	Constitutional institutions consist of the primary rules and norms of international society without which society among sovereign states could not exist. The most commonly recognized of these is the norm of sovereignty, which holds that within the state, power and authority are centralized and hierarchical, and outside the state no higher authority exists. The norm of sovereignty is supported by a range of auxiliary norms, such as the right to self-determination and the norm of nonintervention.
Fundamental	Fundamental institutions rest on the foundation provided by constitutional institutions. They represent the basic norms and practices that sovereign states employ to facilitate coexistence and cooperation under conditions of international anarchy. They are the rudimentary practices states reach for when seeking to collaborate or coordinate their behavior. Fundamental institutions have varied from one historical system of states to another, but in the modern international system, contractual international law and multilateralism have been the most important.
Issue Specific, or Regimes	Issue-specific institutions, or *regimes*, are the most visible or palpable of all international institutions. They are the sets of rules, norms, and decision-making procedures that states formulate to define legitimate actors and action in a given domain of international life. Examples of regimes are the Framework Convention on Climate Change and the International Covenant on Civil and Political Rights. Importantly, issue-specific institutions or regimes are concrete enactments of fundamental institutional practices such as international law and multilateralism.

obliged to observe legal rules because they have consented to those rules. A state that has not consented to the rules of a particular legal treaty is not bound by those rules. The only exception to this concerns rules of customary international law, and even then, implied or tacit consent plays an important role in the determination of which rules have customary status.

In many historical periods, and in many social and cultural settings, the political and legal realms are entwined. For instance, the absolutist conception of sovereignty bound the two realms together in the figure of the sovereign. In the modern era, by contrast, the political and legal realms are thought to be radically different, with their own logics and institutional settings. Domestically, this view informs ideas about the constitutional separation of powers; internationally, it has encouraged the view that international politics and law are separate spheres of social action. This has affected not only how the academic disciplines of international relations and law have evolved but also how state practice has evolved.

Realists generally believe that international law should serve the interests of the powerful states. This perspective has led to criticisms of international law and of international organizations like the United Nations, which protects the interests of major powers by focusing decision-making power in the Security Council. As we will discuss, some non-Western states argue that many of these laws do not account for their interests, traditions, and values.

Criticisms of International Law

From one perspective, international law is easily cast as a Western, even imperial, institution. As we have seen, its roots lie in the European intellectual movements of the sixteenth and seventeenth centuries. Ideas propagated at that time drew a clear distinction between international laws that were appropriate among Christian peoples and those that should govern how Christians related to peoples in the Muslim world, the Americas, and, later, Asia. The former were based on assumptions of the inherent equality of Christian peoples and the latter on the inherent superiority of Christians over non-Christians.

Further evidence of this Western bias can be found in the "standard of civilization" that European powers codified in international law during the nineteenth century (Gong 1984). According to this standard, non-Western polities were granted sovereign recognition only if they exhibited certain domestic political characteristics and only if they were willing and able to participate in the prevailing diplomatic practices. The standard was heavily biased toward Western political and legal institutions as the accepted model. Based on this standard, European powers divided the world's peoples into "civilized," "barbarian," and "savage" societies, divisions they used to justify various degrees of Western authority.

Many claim that Western bias still characterizes the international legal order. Critics point to the Anglo-European dominance of major legal institutions, most notably the UN Security Council, and international human rights law, which they argue imposes a set of Western values about the rights of the individual on non-Western societies where such ideas are alien. Another indication of this bias is the recent challenge to the 1998 Rome statute that created the International Criminal Court (ICC). In October 2016, Burundi and South Africa voted to withdraw from the ICC, claiming anti-African bias in their pursuit of potential world criminals. Both Kenya and Namibia are also considering withdrawing.

According to this argument, Western powers use their privileged position on the Security Council to intervene in the domestic politics of weak, developing countries. There is truth in these criticisms. However, the nature and role of international law in contemporary world politics are more complex than they appear. At the heart of the modern international legal system lies a set of customary norms that uphold the legal equality of all sovereign states, as well as their rights to self-determination and nonintervention. Non-Western states have been the most vigorous proponents and defenders of these cardinal legal norms. In addition, non-Western peoples were more centrally involved in the development of the international human rights regime than is commonly acknowledged. The Universal Declaration of Human Rights (1948) was the product of a deliberate and systematic process of intercultural dialogue, involving representatives of all of the world's major cultures (Glendon 2002). The International Covenant on Civil and Political Rights (1966), often portrayed as a reflection of Western values, was shaped in critical ways by newly independent postcolonial states (Reus-Smit 2001).

What's more, international human rights law has been an important resource in the struggles of many subject peoples against repressive governments and against institutions such as colonialism.

From International to Supranational Law?

So long as international law was designed primarily to facilitate international order—to protect the negative liberties (i.e., freedom from outside interference) of sovereign states—it remained a limited, if essential, institution. In recent decades, however, states have sought to move beyond the simple pursuit of international order toward the objective of global governance, and international law has begun to change in fascinating ways.

First, although states are "still at the heart of the international legal system" (Higgins 1994, 39), individuals, groups, and organizations are increasingly recognized as subjects of international law. An expansive body of international human rights law has developed, supported by evolving mechanisms of enforcement. Examples of enforcement include the war crimes tribunals (discussed later in this chapter) for Rwanda and the former Yugoslavia, the creation of the ICC, and the twenty-three cases the ICC is pursuing against war criminals.

Second, nonstate actors are becoming important *agents* in the international legal process. Although such actors cannot formally enact international law and their practices do not contribute to the development of customary international law, they often play a crucial role in the following:

- Shaping the normative environment in which states codify specific legal rules.
- Providing information to national governments that encourages the redefinition of state interests and the convergence of policies across states.
- Drafting international treaties and conventions (the first of which was the 1864 Geneva Convention, drafted by the International Committee of the Red Cross; Finnemore 1996a, 1996b).

Third, the rules, norms, and principles of international law are no longer confined to maintaining international order, narrowly defined. Recent decisions by the UN Security Council have treated gross violations of human rights by sovereign states as threats to global peace and security, thus legitimating action under Chapter VII of the UN Charter. (Examples include the authorization of measures to protect civilians in Libya in 2011 and more recent UN interventions in Liberia, the Central African Republic, and the Democratic Republic of Congo.) In doing so, the Security Council implies that international order is dependent on the maintenance of at least minimum standards of global justice.

Because of these changes, international law might be gradually transforming into a system of supranational law. States are no longer the only subjects and agents of international law, and it has expanded into global regulation, with a scope encompassing issues of both justice and order.

This desire to promote a rule-based global society that would protect human rights and prevent war led world leaders to create the United Nations in 1945. We now take a step back in time and turn to a discussion of this important international institution.

United Nations Founded in 1945 following World War II, it is an international organization composed of 193 member states dedicated to addressing issues related to peace and security, development, human rights, humanitarian affairs, and international law.

Supranational global organization An authoritative international organization that operates above the nation-state.

State sovereignty The concept that all countries are equal under international law and that they are protected from outside interference; this is the basis on which the United Nations and other international and regional organizations operate.

The United Nations

The **United Nations** has the unique status of being the largest international organization, what some call a **supranational global organization**, and the only one that has a universal focus. Other supranational organizations with more specific responsibilities include the World Bank, the IMF, and the WTO. The states that make up the United Nations created a group of international institutions, which include the central system located in New York; the Specialized Agencies, such as the WHO and the International Labor Organization; and the Programmes and Funds, such as the United Nations Children's Fund (UNICEF) and the United Nations Development Programme. When it was created in the aftermath of World War II, the United Nations reflected the hope for a just and peaceful global community.

The United Nations is the only global institution with legitimacy that derives from universal membership and a mandate that encompasses security, economic and social development, and the protection of human rights and the environment. Yet the United Nations was created by states for states, and questions about the meaning of **state sovereignty** and the limits of UN action remain key issues.

Since its founding, UN activities have expanded to address political, economic, and social conditions within states. Threats to global security addressed by the United Nations now include interstate conflict and threats by nonstate actors. In 2005, the United Nations established the **Responsibility to Protect Resolution (R2P)**, asserting the moral obligation for states to intervene in other states that violate human rights. It was reaffirmed by the UN Security Council in 2006, and in 2009, Ban Ki-moon, who was then UN secretary-general, issued a report on implementing R2P for discussion in the UN General Assembly.

Despite the expanding scope of UN activities, there are some questions about the relevance and effectiveness of the United Nations. The failure of the United States and the United Kingdom to get clear UN Security Council authorization for the war in Iraq in 2003 led to well-publicized criticism of the United Nations and a crisis in international relations. Yet the

In 2019, motorcyclists ride through a market that is closed due to a strike in Rawalpindi, Pakistan. Traders have largely kept their businesses shut across the country to protest a new sales tax regime that was imposed in response to an IMF mandate, part of a $6 billion bailout package. International financial institutions are often criticized by governments and citizens for their drastic economic measures.

troubled aftermath of the invasion and persistent questions about the legitimacy of a war that was not sanctioned by the United Nations show that it has acquired important moral status in international society.

After describing the history and main organs of the United Nations, this section looks at its changing role in addressing matters of peace and security and economic and social development. We also focus on how the United Nations' role has evolved in response to changes in the global political context and on some of the problems that it still faces.

A Brief History of the United Nations

The United Nations was established on October 24, 1945, by fifty-one countries as a result of initiatives taken by the governments of the states that had led the war against Italy, Germany, and Japan. As early as 1939, American and British diplomats were discussing the need for a more effective international organization like the United Nations. It was intended to be a **collective security** organization, an arrangement where "each state in the system accepts that the security of one is the concern of all, and agrees to join in a collective response to aggression" (A. Roberts and Kingsbury 1993, 30). Unfortunately, as we will see later in this chapter, the Cold War bipolar international system undermined the UN's effectiveness in security affairs.

There are 193 member states of the United Nations—nearly every state in the world. Notable exceptions include Western Sahara and Kosovo (neither of which is recognized as a self-governing territory), Taiwan (which is not recognized as a separate territory from China), and Palestine and Vatican City (both of which enjoy nonmember observer status). Member states agree to accept the obligations of the **United Nations Charter**, an international treaty that sets out basic principles of international relations. According to the Charter, the United Nations has four purposes: to maintain international peace and security, to develop friendly relations among nations, to cooperate in solving international problems and in promoting respect for human rights, and to be a center for harmonizing the actions of nations. At the United Nations, all the member states—large and small, rich and poor, with differing political views and social systems—have a voice and a vote in this process. Interestingly, although the United Nations was clearly created as a grouping of states, the Charter refers to the needs and interests of peoples, as well as those of states (see Table 5.2).

In many ways, the United Nations was set up to correct the problems of its predecessor, the **League of Nations**. The League of Nations was established after World War I and was intended to make future wars impossible, but it lacked effective power. There was no clear division of responsibility between the main executive committee (the League Council) and the League Assembly, which included all member states. Both the League Assembly and the League Council could only make recommendations, not binding resolutions, and these recommendations had to be approved unanimously. Any government was free to reject any recommendation. Furthermore, there was no mechanism for coordinating military or

Responsibility to Protect Resolution (R2P) Resolution supported by the United Nations in 2005 to determine the international community's responsibility in preventing mass atrocities, reacting to crises, protecting citizens, rebuilding, and preventing future problems.

Collective security An arrangement where "each state in the system accepts that the security of one is the concern of all, and agrees to join in a collective response to aggression" (Roberts and Kingsbury 1993, 30).

United Nations General Assembly Often referred to as a "parliament of nations," it is composed of all member states, which meet to consider the world's most pressing problems. Each state has one vote, and a two-thirds majority in the General Assembly is required for decisions on key issues. Decisions reached by the General Assembly only have the status of recommendations and are not binding.

League of Nations The first permanent collective international security organization aimed at preventing future wars and resolving global problems. The League failed due to the unwillingness of the United States to join and the inability of its members to commit to a real international community.

TABLE 5.2	The UN Charter Contains References to Both the Rights of States and the Rights of People

Type of Right	Supporting Excerpt from the Charter
People	**The Preamble** of the UN Charter asserts that "We the peoples of the United Nations [are] determined [. . .] to reaffirm faith in fundamental human rights, in the dignity and worth of the human person, in the equal rights of men and women and of nations large and small."
People	**Article 1(2)** states that the purpose of the United Nations is to develop "friendly relations among nations based on respect for the principle of equal rights and self-determination of peoples and to take other appropriate measures to strengthen universal peace."
State	**Article 2(7)** states that "Nothing contained in the present Charter shall authorize the United Nations to intervene in matters which are essentially within the domestic jurisdiction of any state."
State	**Chapter VI** deals with the "Pacific Settlement of Disputes."
State	**Article 33** states that "The parties to any dispute, the continuance of which is likely to endanger the maintenance of international peace and security, shall, first of all, seek a solution by negotiation, enquiry, mediation, conciliation, arbitration, judicial settlement, resort to regional agencies or arrangements, or other peaceful means of their own choice."
State	**Chapter VII** deals with "Action With Respect to Threats to the Peace, Breaches of the Peace, and Acts of Aggression."
State	**Article 42** states that the Security Council "may take such action by air, sea, or land forces as may be necessary to maintain or restore international peace and security." The Security Council has sometimes authorized member states to use "all necessary means," and this has been accepted as a legitimate application of Chapter VII powers.
State	**Article 99** authorizes the secretary-general to "bring to the attention of the Security Council any matter which in his opinion may threaten the maintenance of international peace and security."

economic actions against miscreant states. Key states, such as the United States, were not members of the League. By World War II, the League had failed to address a number of acts of aggression.

The UN's Principal Organs

The structure of the United Nations was intended to avoid some of the problems faced by the League of Nations. The United Nations has six main organs: the Security Council, the General Assembly, the Secretariat, the Economic and Social Council, the Trusteeship Council, and the International Court of Justice (see Figure 5.1).

The Security Council

United Nations Security Council The council made up of five permanent member states (sometimes called the P5)—namely, Great Britain, China, France, Russia, and the United States—and ten nonpermanent members. The P5 all have a veto power over all Security Council decisions.

The **United Nations Security Council** was given the main responsibility for maintaining international peace and security. It is made up of fifteen member states, ten nonpermanent members and five permanent members (sometimes called the P5): the United States, Britain, France, Russia (previously the Soviet Union)—the victors in

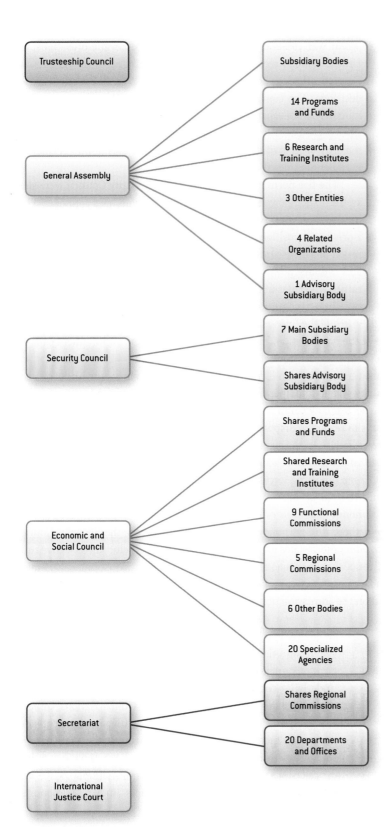

Figure 5.1 **The Structure of the United Nations.**

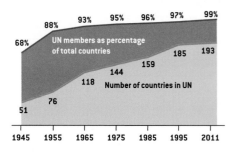

Growth in UN Membership.

Of the 196 countries in the world, 193 are UN members. The most recent member to join was South Sudan, in 2011. With more tensions among the great powers (the United States, China, and Russia), will the UN Security Council be able to act on any major global issue?

Veto power The right of the five permanent members of the Security Council (United States, Russia, China, France, and Great Britain) to forbid any action by the United Nations.

Economic sanctions A tool of statecraft that seeks to get a state to behave by coercion of a monetary kind—for example, freezing banking assets, cutting aid programs, or banning trade.

World War II—and China. In contrast to the League of Nations, the United Nations recognized great-power prerogatives in the Security Council, offering each of the P5 a **veto power** over all Security Council decisions. The convention emerged that abstention by a permanent member is not regarded as a veto. Unlike with the League, the decisions of the Security Council are binding and must be passed by only a majority of nine of the fifteen members. However, if one permanent member dissents, the resolution does not pass.

The five permanent members of the Security Council were seen as the major powers when the United Nations was founded. They were granted a veto on the view that if the great powers were not given a privileged position, the United Nations would not work. This recognition of a state's influence being proportional to its size and political and military power stems from the realist notion that power determines who rules in the international system. Indeed, this tension between the recognition of power politics through the Security Council veto and the universal ideals underlying the United Nations is a defining feature of the organization. There have been widespread and frequent calls for the reform of the Security Council, but this is very difficult. In both theoretical and policy terms, the inability to reform the Security Council shows the limits of a collective security system and liberal thinking that suggests all states are equal.

When the Security Council considers a threat to international peace, it first explores ways to settle the dispute peacefully. It might suggest principles for a settlement or mediation. In the event of fighting, the Security Council tries to secure a ceasefire. It might send a peacekeeping mission to help the parties maintain the truce and to keep opposing forces apart. The Security Council can also take measures to enforce its decisions under Chapter VII of the Charter, for instance, by imposing **economic sanctions** or ordering an arms embargo. (See Chapter 4 for a discussion of these foreign policy tools.) On rare occasions, the Security Council has authorized member states to use all necessary means, including collective military action, to see that its decisions are carried out. The Security Council also makes recommendations to the General Assembly on the appointment of a new secretary-general and on the admission of new members to the United Nations.

The General Assembly

The recognition of power politics through veto power in the Security Council can be contrasted with the universal principles underlying the other organs of the United Nations. All UN member states are represented in the **United Nations General Assembly**—a "parliament of nations"—which meets to consider the world's most pressing problems. Each member state has one vote. A two-thirds majority in the General Assembly is required for decisions on key issues such as international peace and security, the admission of new members, and the UN budget.

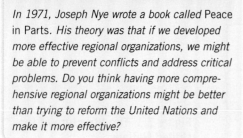

WHAT'S YOUR WORLDVIEW?

In 1971, Joseph Nye wrote a book called Peace in Parts. *His theory was that if we developed more effective regional organizations, we might be able to prevent conflicts and address critical problems. Do you think having more comprehensive regional organizations might be better than trying to reform the United Nations and make it more effective?*

A simple majority is required for other matters. However, the decisions reached by the General Assembly only have the status of recommendations, rather than binding decisions. One of the few exceptions is the General Assembly's Fifth Committee, which makes decisions on the budget that are binding on members.

The General Assembly can consider any matter within the scope of the UN Charter. Recent topics discussed by the General Assembly include the impact of globalization on societies, the role of diamonds in fueling conflict, international cooperation in the peaceful uses of outer space, peacekeeping operations, sustainable development, and international migration. Because General Assembly resolutions are nonbinding, they cannot force action by any state, but the Assembly's recommendations are important indications of world opinion and represent the moral authority of the community of nation-states.

The Secretariat

The **United Nations Secretariat** carries out the substantive and administrative work of the United Nations as directed by the General Assembly, the Security Council, and the other organs. It is led by the secretary-general, who provides overall administrative guidance. In January 2017, Antonio Guterres from Portugal was sworn in as the ninth secretary-general.

On the recommendation of the other bodies, the Secretariat also carries out a number of research functions and some quasi-management functions. Yet the role of the Secretariat remains primarily bureaucratic, and it lacks the political power of, for instance, the Commission of the European Union. The one exception to this is the power of the secretary-general, under Article 99 of the Charter, to bring situations that are likely to lead to a breakdown of international peace and security to the attention of the Security Council. This article was the legal basis for the remarkable expansion of the diplomatic role of the secretary-general. The secretary-general is empowered to become involved in a large range of areas that can be loosely interpreted as threats to peace, including economic and social problems and humanitarian crises.

The Economic and Social Council

The **United Nations Economic and Social Council (ECOSOC)**, under the overall authority of the General Assembly, is intended to coordinate the economic and social work of the United Nations and the UN family of organizations. It also consults with NGOs, thereby maintaining a vital link between the United Nations and civil society. ECOSOC's subsidiary bodies include functional commissions, such as the Commission on the Status of Women, and regional commissions, such as the Economic Commission for Africa.

The UN Charter established ECOSOC to oversee economic and social institutions. ECOSOC does not have necessary management powers, however; it can only issue recommendations and receive reports. In consequence, the United Nations' economic and social organizations have continually searched for better ways of achieving effective management.

United Nations Secretariat The Secretariat carries out the administrative work of the United Nations as directed by the General Assembly, Security Council, and other organs. The Secretariat is led by the secretary-general, who provides overall administrative guidance.

United Nations Charter (1945) The legal regime that created the United Nations. The charter defines the structure of the United Nations, the powers of its constitutive agencies, and the rights and obligations of sovereign states party to the charter.

United Nations Economic and Social Council (ECOSOC) This council is intended to coordinate the economic and social work of the United Nations and the UN family organizations. The ECOSOC has a direct link to civil society through communications with nongovernmental organizations.

UNICEF-USA

UNICEF focuses its programs on saving and protecting the most vulnerable children in areas suffering from humanitarian crises such as Yemen, Syria, and the Sudan. UNICEF dedicates 89 percent of every dollar donated to children in need. A limited number of unpaid internship opportunities are available in our New York City National Headquarters and regional offices for current university students. Interns support the U.S. Fund in a variety of areas, including fundraising, marketing, and communications as well as general research and administration. Contact:https://www.unicefusa.org.

The Trusteeship Council

United Nations Trusteeship Council Upon creation of the United Nations, this council was established to provide international supervision for eleven Trust Territories administered by seven member states in an effort to prepare them for self-government or independence. By 1994, all Trust Territories had attained self-government or independence, and the council now meets on an ad hoc basis.

When the United Nations was created, the **United Nations Trusteeship Council** was established to provide international supervision for eleven Trust Territories administered by seven member states and to ensure that adequate steps were taken to prepare the territories for self-government or independence. By 1994, all Trust Territories had attained self-government or independence, either as separate states or by joining neighboring independent countries. The last to do so was the Trust Territory of the Pacific Islands, Palau, which had been previously administered by the United States under special rules with the United Nations called a strategic trust. With its work completed, the Trusteeship Council now consists of the five permanent members of the Security Council. It has amended its rules of procedure to allow it to meet when necessary.

The International Court of Justice

International Court of Justice (ICJ) The main judicial organ of the United Nations consisting of fifteen judges elected jointly by the General Assembly and Security Council. The ICJ handles disputes between states, not individuals and states, and although a state does not have to participate in a case, if it elects to do so it must obey the decision.

The **International Court of Justice (ICJ)** is the main judicial organ of the United Nations. Consisting of fifteen judges elected jointly by the General Assembly and the Security Council, the ICJ decides disputes between countries. Participation by states in a proceeding is voluntary, but if a state agrees to participate, it is obligated to comply with the ICJ's decision. The ICJ also provides advisory opinions to other UN organs and specialized agencies on request. Only states may bring cases before the ICJ. If people who live in one state want to bring a suit against another state, they must get their home state to file the suit.

Three factors reduce the effectiveness of the ICJ:

- First, the competence, or jurisdiction, of the ICJ is limited, as already noted, to cases that states bring against states. The ICJ's statutory jurisdiction extends to anything related to a state's undertakings by signing the UN Charter and any matter related to a ratified treaty. If a state is not a signatory, there can be no recourse to the ICJ. In addition, if the United Nations itself is a party to the case, at least one state party of the ICJ must be an applicant as well.

- Second is the question of compulsory jurisdiction. States that are party to the ICJ statute are not bound by compulsory jurisdiction unless they agree to it; this is the "option clause" problem. For example, in the *Aerial Incident of July 27, 1955 (Israel v. Bulgaria)*, the ICJ found that Bulgaria was not liable for damages because its compulsory jurisdiction option had expired.
- A third factor—the state reservations—follows from the option-clause problems: Not only may a state let its compulsory jurisdiction lapse but also it can refuse to accept the ICJ jurisdiction if the state claims that its own existing national law covers the issue before the courts. This occurred in a 1957 case in which Norway sued France over a debt owed to Norwegian investors. France claimed that its domestic legal system had jurisdiction in the matter, and Norway lost.

In Chapter 7, we discuss the ICC, an independent international organization that is not part of the United Nations.

Maintenance of International Peace and Security

Political context has shaped the performance of the United Nations in questions of peace and security. Clearly, changes in international society since the United Nations was founded in 1945 have had an impact on the UN system. The Cold War hampered the functioning of the UN Security Council, because the veto could be used whenever the major interests of the United States or Soviet Union were threatened. From 1945 to 1990, 193 substantive vetoes were invoked in the Security Council, compared with only thirty-one substantive vetoes from 1990 to 2015. Furthermore, although the UN Charter provided for a standing army to be set up by agreement between the Security Council and consenting states, the East–West Cold War rivalry made this impossible to implement. The result was that the UN Security Council could not function in the way the UN founders had expected.

Because member states could not agree on the arrangements laid out in Chapter VII of the Charter, a series of improvisations followed to address matters of peace and security:

- First, the United Nations established a procedure under which the Security Council agreed to a mandate for an agent to act on its behalf. This occurred in the Korean conflict in 1950 and the Gulf War in 1990, when the United States and its allies took principal action.
- Second, the United Nations has engaged in classical peacekeeping, which involves establishing a UN force under UN command to be placed between disputing parties after a ceasefire. Such a force uses its weapons only in

self-defense, is established with the consent of the host state, and does not include forces from the major powers. The first instance of this was in 1956, when a UN force was sent to Egypt to facilitate the exodus of the British and French forces from the Suez Canal area and then to stand between Egyptian and Israeli forces. Since the Suez crisis, there have been a number of classical peacekeeping missions—for instance, at the Green Line in Cyprus, in the Golan Heights, and after the decade-long Iraq–Iran War. The primary drawback to this kind of peacekeeping operation is that it is not effective if the warring parties do not want peace. Such operations can also be difficult to conclude.

Peace enforcement An action designed to bring hostile parties to agreement; it may occur without the consent of the parties.

- Third, a new kind of peacekeeping, sometimes called multidimensional peacekeeping or **peace enforcement**, emerged after the Cold War. These missions are more likely to use force for humanitarian ends when order has collapsed within states (see Chapter 7 for more information). A key problem has been that peacekeepers have found it increasingly difficult to maintain a neutral position and have been targeted by belligerents. Examples include the intervention in Somalia in the early 1990s and intervention in the former Yugoslavia in the mid-1990s. In both cases, until the European Union, the North Atlantic Treaty Organization (NATO), or the United States was directly involved in the operations, peace was elusive.

After the end of the Cold War, the UN agenda for peace and security expanded quickly. Boutros Boutros-Ghali, who was then secretary-general, outlined a more ambitious role for the United Nations in his seminal report, *An Agenda for Peace* (1992). The report described interconnected roles for the United Nations to maintain peace and security in the post–Cold War context. These included four main kinds of activities:

1. **Preventive diplomacy**, which involves confidence-building measures, fact finding, and preventive deployment of UN authorized forces.
2. **Peacemaking**, designed to bring hostile parties to agreement, essentially through peaceful means.
3. **Peacekeeping**, the deployment of a UN presence in the field with the consent of all parties (classical peacekeeping).
4. **Postconflict peacebuilding**, which ideally will develop the social, political, and economic infrastructure to prevent further violence and to consolidate peace.

However, when all peaceful means have failed, peace enforcement authorized under Chapter VII of the Charter might be necessary, and it may occur without the consent of the parties in conflict.

In 2019, the total number of peacekeeping personnel (troops, military observers, police, civilian personnel, and UN volunteers) in the United Nations' thirteen ongoing peacekeeping operations was just over 110,000 (UN 2019).

Since 1948, over 5,000 UN peacekeeping forces have been killed; in current operations, 1,516 UN personnel were killed (see Table 5.3).

One might assume that UN peacekeepers cause little or no problems in countries where the peacekeepers operate. One major problem is sexual violence against women and children. Twenty years ago, peacekeepers in Cambodia sexually abused women and girls, but little was done about these assaults. Recently, reports of sexual violence against young children have involved peacekeepers from France, Georgia, Burundi, and Gabon in the Central African Republic. There were 145 reported cases in 2016. The UN secretary-general Antonio Gutierres announced new measures to put "the rights and the dignity of victims first" and to focus efforts on "ending the impunity" of those peacekeepers found guilty of crimes and abuses. Many social media outlets and human rights organizations like Code Blue have focused on "ending impunity for sexual exploitation and abuse" by UN peacekeeping personnel. UN Resolution 2272, passed in March 2016, focuses on preventing sexual exploitation and abuse was passed.

WHAT'S YOUR WORLDVIEW?

Why would a country decide to participate in a UN peacekeeping operation? What factors would motivate it to participate in such a collective action? Is this part of a country's dominant or strategic narrative?

Increased Attention to Conditions Within States

The new peacekeeping was the product of a greater preparedness to intervene within states. An increasing number of people believed that the international community, working through the United Nations, should address individual political and civil rights, as well as the right to basic provisions like food, water, health care, and accommodation. Under this view, violations of individuals' rights

TABLE 5.3	Thirteen UN Peacekeeping Operations (as of August 31, 2019)		
Location	**Origin of Operation**	**Location**	**Origin of Operation**
Middle East (UNTSO)	1948	Darfur	2007
India and Pakistan	1949	Congo, Democratic Republic of	2010
Cyprus	1964	South Sudan	2011
Syria	1974	Sudan	2011
Lebanon	1978	Mali	2013
Western Sahara	1991	Central African Republic	2014
Kosovo	1999		

Source: Copyright © United Nations 2019. United Nations Peacekeeping Fact Sheet: http://www.un.org/en/peacekeeping/resources/statistics/factsheet.shtml

UN peacekeepers hold their flag as they observe Israeli excavators working near the southern border village of Mays al-Jabal, Lebanon. As Israeli excavators dig into the rocky ground, Lebanese across the frontier gather to watch what Israel calls the Northern Shield operation aimed at destroying attack tunnels built by Hezbollah. The tension in this region cannot be overestimated. What is being done to end this conflict?

Human security The security of people, including their physical safety, their economic and social well-being, respect for their dignity, and the protection of their human rights.

were a major cause of disturbances in relations between states: A lack of internal justice risked international disorder. The United Nations reinforced this new perception that pursuing justice for individuals, or ensuring **human security**, was an aspect of national interest. (We discuss human security in Chapter 7.)

In some states, contributions to activities such as peacekeeping were defended in terms of national interest. States such as Canada and Norway could justify their contributions to peacekeeping as a "moral" course of action, but these contributions also served their national interests by enhancing their status in the international community. The Japanese also responded to moral pressure founded in national interest when they contributed substantially to defraying the cost of British involvement in the 1990–1991 Gulf War. This act can be explained in terms of the synthesis of morality and interest. For some states, a good reputation in the United Nations had become an important national goal.

In the past, the United Nations had helped to promote the traditional view of the primacy of international order between states over justice for individuals, so the new focus on individual rights was a significant change. What accounts for this change? We offer two reasons:

- First, the international environment had changed. The Cold War standoff between the East and the West meant that member states did not want to question the conditions of the sovereignty of states.
- Second, some analysts made strong arguments that challenged the privileging of statehood over justice during the process of decolonization. Charles Beitz was one of the first, concluding that statehood should not be unconditional and that the situation of individuals after independence demanded attention (Beitz 1979). Michael Walzer (1977) and Terry Nardin (1983) came to similar conclusions: States were conditional entities in that their right to exist should be dependent on a criterion of performance. Such writings helped alter the moral content of diplomacy.

The new relationship between order and justice was, therefore, a product of particular circumstances. After the Cold War, the international community began to sense that threats to international peace and security did not emanate only from aggression between states. Rather, global peace was also threatened by civil conflict (including refugee flows and regional instability), humanitarian emergencies, violations of global standards of human rights, and other conditions such as poverty and inequality.

More recently, other types of nonstate-based threats, such as terrorism and the proliferation of small arms and weapons of mass destruction, have had an increasingly prominent place on the UN security agenda. Partly in response to the terrorist attacks in the United States in 2001, as well as the impasse reached in the UN Security Council over Iraq in 2003, Kofi Annan, then the UN secretary-general, named a high-level panel to examine the major threats and challenges to global peace. The final report, *A More Secure World: Our Shared Responsibility* (UN 2004), emphasized the interconnected nature of security threats and presented development, security, and human rights as mutually reinforcing. Although many of the report's recommendations were not implemented, it led to the establishment of a new UN Peacebuilding Commission.

The UN Peacebuilding Commission was established in December 2005 as an advisory subsidiary body of the General Assembly and the Security Council. The secretary-general's High-Level Panel on Threats, Challenges, and Change argued that existing UN mechanisms were insufficient in responding to the particular needs of states emerging from conflict. Many countries, such as Liberia, Haiti, and Somalia in the 1990s, had signed peace agreements and hosted UN peacekeeping missions but reverted to violent conflict. The Peacebuilding Commission aims to provide targeted support to countries in the volatile postconflict phase to prevent the recurrence of conflict. It proposes integrated strategies and priorities for postconflict recovery to improve coordination among the myriad actors involved in postconflict activities. The establishment of the Peacebuilding Commission is indicative of a growing trend at the United Nations to coordinate security and development programming.

Intervention Within States

As the international community more clearly understood issues of peace and security to include human security and justice, it expected the United Nations to take on a stronger role in maintaining standards for individuals within states. One difficulty in carrying out this new task was that it seemed to run against the doctrine of nonintervention. **Intervention** was traditionally defined as a deliberate incursion into a state, without its consent, by some outside agency to change the functioning, policies, and goals of its government and achieve effects that favor the intervening agency (Vincent 1974).

The founders of the United Nations viewed sovereignty as central to the system of states. States were equal members of international society and were equal with regard to international law. Sovereignty also implied that states recognized no higher authority than themselves and no superior jurisdiction. Intervention in the traditional sense was in opposition to the principles of international society, and it could be tolerated only as an exception to the rule.

By the 1990s, some believed that there should be a return to an earlier period when intervention was justified, but that a wider range of instruments should be

Intervention The direct involvement within a state by an outside actor to achieve an outcome preferred by the intervening agency without the consent of the host state.

THEORY IN PRACTICE

Neoconservatives and the United Nations

THE CHALLENGE

For analysts from the realist school of thought, states exist in an anarchic, self-help world, looking to their own power resources for national security. This was the perspective of the neoconservatives who dominated the administration of US president George W. Bush. They subscribed to a strain of realist thinking that is best called hegemonist; that is, they believed the United States should use its power solely to secure its interests in the world. They were realists with idealistic tendencies, seeking to remake the world through promoting, by force if necessary, freedom, democracy, and free enterprise.

Paul Wolfowitz, an important voice in the neoconservative camp, wrote that global leadership was all about "demonstrating that your friends will be protected and taken care of, that your enemies will be punished, and those who refuse to support you will live to regret having done so."* Although it would be wrong to assume that all realist thinkers and policymakers are opposed to international organizations such as the United Nations, most are wary of any organizations that prevent them from securing their national interests. The belief is that alliances should be only short-term events because allies might desert you in a crisis.

For some realists, such as the Bush neoconservatives, committing security to a collective security organization is even worse than an alliance because, in a worst-case situation, the alliance might gang up on your country. Even in the best-case situation, it would be a bad idea to submit your military forces to foreign leadership.

OPTIONS

In its early years, before the wave of decolonization in Africa and Asia, the United Nations' US-based realist critics did not have the ear of the country's political leadership. Presidents Truman and Eisenhower both found a way around the USSR's Security Council veto by working through the General Assembly, a body that at the time was very friendly to the United States and its goals. However, with the end of European control of Africa and Asia, the General Assembly changed. The body frequently passed resolutions condemning the United States and its allies. One result was a growing movement to end US involvement in the United Nations, especially among the key foreign policy advisers to President Reagan.

APPLICATION

In the 1980s, political realists saw no tangible benefit for the United States to remain active in the United Nations once the leaders in Washington could no longer count on a UN rubber stamp for US policies. For a number of years, the United States did not pay its dues to the United Nations.

This rejection of UN-style multilateralism revived with the George W. Bush presidency, beginning in 2001. In a controversial recess appointment, Bush chose John Bolton to be the US ambassador to the United Nations in 2005. This appointment came as a surprise because Bolton was a staunch opponent of multilateral organizations such as the United Nations. The Bush foreign policy advisers were against the peacekeeping operation in the former Yugoslavia. In her criticism of Clinton administration foreign policy, then national security adviser Condoleezza Rice said the United States would not send its troops to countries for nation building. More important, the Bush administration did not want to have its hands tied when dealing with Iraq and its alleged store of nuclear, chemical, and biological weapons. President Bush and his top advisers believed that sanctions—an important weapon in the United Nations' moral-suasion arsenal—would never force Iraq to disarm and that only force could do so. The irony is that, after the 2003 invasion, the United States' own weapons inspectors could find no evidence that Iraq had any of the banned weapons.

*Paul Wolfowitz, "Remembering the Future," *National Interest* 59 (Spring 2000): 41.

For Discussion

1. What might be a Marxist criticism of the United Nations and its operations?
2. Is there any way to overcome realists' beliefs about international anarchy and the impossibility of global governance?
3. Some utopians believe that a world government would end war and provide answers to other global challenges. Do you agree? Why or why not?
4. Do the five permanent members of the Security Council have too much power over the operations of the organization? Why or why not?

used. Supporters of this idea insisted on a key role for the United Nations in granting a license to intervene. They pointed out that the UN Charter did not assert merely the rights of states, but also the rights of peoples: Statehood could be interpreted as being conditional on respect for such rights. There was ample evidence in the UN Charter to justify the view that extreme transgressions of human rights could be a justification for intervention by the international community.

Yet there have been only a few occasions where a UN resolution justified intervention because of gross infringements of human rights. The justification of NATO's intervention in Kosovo in 1999 represented a break from the past in that it included a clear humanitarian element. Kosovo was arguably the first occasion in which international forces were used in defiance of a sovereign state to protect humanitarian standards. NATO launched an air campaign in March 1999 in Kosovo against the Republic of Yugoslavia without a mandate from the Security Council because Russia had declared that it would veto such action. Nonetheless, NATO states noted that by intervening to stop ethnic cleansing and crimes against humanity in Kosovo, they were acting in accordance with the principles of the UN Charter. The US action against Afghanistan in 2001 is an exceptional case in which the UN Security Council acknowledged the right of a state that had been attacked—referring to the events of 9/11—to respond in its own defense.

The difficulty in relaxing the principle of nonintervention should not be underestimated. For instance, the United Nations was reluctant to send troops to Rwanda, Bosnia, Kosovo, and Sudan to respond to acts of ethnic cleansing and genocide. More recently, the United Nations took several weeks to decide to intervene to protect civilians in Libya in 2011, and the UN launched a short-lived observer mission to Syria in 2012 but failed to initiate any mission to protect Syrian civilians. Some fear a slippery slope whereby a relaxation of the nonintervention principle by the United Nations will lead to military action by individual states without UN approval. There are significant numbers of non-UN actors, including regional organizations, involved in peace operations, and several states are suspicious of what appears to be the granting of a license to intervene in their affairs.

An increasing readiness by the United Nations to intervene within states to promote internal justice for individuals would indicate a movement toward global governance and away from unconditional sovereignty. There have been some signs of movement in this direction, but principles of state sovereignty and nonintervention remain important. There is no clear consensus on these points. There is still some support for the view that Article 2(7) of the UN Charter should be interpreted strictly: There can be no intervention within a state without the express consent of the government of that state. Others believe that intervention within a country to promote human rights is justifiable only on the basis of a threat to international peace and security. Evidence of a threat to international peace and security could be the appearance of significant numbers of refugees or the judgment that other states might intervene militarily. Some liberal internationalists argue that this condition is flexible enough to justify intervention to defend human rights whenever possible.

WHAT'S YOUR WORLDVIEW?

Much was written about the need to invoke the Responsibility to Protect (R2P) doctrine to help the citizens of Libya. NATO members cited R2P to justify intervention. The UN and the Arab League estimate that over 400,000 have died in the Syrian civil war. Why has the world done so little about this civil war and the death of innocents?

Overall, the United Nations' record on the maintenance of international peace and security has been mixed. There has been a stronger assertion of the responsibility of international society, represented by the United Nations, for gross offenses against populations. However, the practice has been patchy.

Economic and Social Questions

As we have discussed, conditions within states, including human rights, justice, development, and equality, have a bearing on global peace. The more integrated global context has meant that economic and social problems in one part of the world might affect other areas. Furthermore, promoting social and economic development is an important UN goal.

The number of institutions within the UN system that address economic and social issues has increased significantly since the founding of the United Nations. Nonetheless, the main contributor states have been giving less and less to economic and social institutions. In 2000, the United Nations convened a Millennium Summit, where heads of state committed themselves to a series of measurable goals and targets, known as the Millennium Development Goals (MDGs), discussed in detail in Chapter 9. Although these eight goals were not completely achieved by 2015, UN efforts lifted more than 1 billion people out of extreme poverty and provided access to education and health care to a significant number of people on the margins of their societies. There is still much more to do, which is why the member states of the United Nations agreed to the 2030 Sustainable Development Agenda that includes seventeen sustainable development goals and 169 targets. These build on the MDGs and seek to "free the human race from the tyranny of poverty" and focus development on sustainable economic, social, and environmental goals.

◤ The Reform Process of the United Nations

In his important book *The Parliament of Man* (2006), Paul Kennedy suggests that any reform of the United Nations will need to be partial, gradual, and carefully executed. He argues that the need to make the United Nations more effective, representative, and accountable to its members is greater today than it was in the past because of a number of global developments, including the following:

1. The emergence of new great powers like India and Brazil and older powers like Japan and Germany who have been left out of the Security Council. Are the current members of the Security Council willing to add new members or even change the decision-making structure?
2. The presence of truly global issues that threaten the world as we know it. These include environmental degradation, terrorism, the proliferation

of weapons of all kinds, and the persistence of global poverty. Is the United Nations interested in or capable of responding to these issues?

In the mid- to late 1990s, alongside growing UN involvement in development issues, the UN economic and social arrangements underwent reform at two levels: first, reforms concerned with operations at the country (field) level, and second, reforms at the general, or headquarters, level.

San Francisco was the scene of the signing of the UN Charter in 1945. Has the time come to revise the document and reform the United Nations?

Country Level

The continuing complaints of NGOs about poor UN performance in the field served as a powerful stimulus for reform. A key feature of the reforms at the country level was the adoption of Country Strategy Notes. These were statements about the overall development process tailored to the specific needs of individual countries. They were written on the basis of discussions among the Specialized Agencies, Programmes and Funds, donors, and the host country. The merit of the Country Strategy Notes is that they clearly set out targets, roles, and priorities.

Other reforms at the country level included the strengthening of the resident coordinator's role and enhanced authority for field-level officers. There was also an effort to introduce improved communication facilities and information sharing. The activities of the various UN organizations were brought together in single locations, or "UN houses," which facilitated interagency communication and collegiality. The adoption of the MDG framework and subsequent Sustainable Development Goals has also helped country field staff achieve a more coherent approach to development.

Headquarters Level

If the UN's role in economic and social affairs at the country level was to be effective, reform was also required at the headquarters level. Because the Security Council is the main executive body within the United Nations, it is not surprising that many discussions of UN reform have focused on it.

The founders of the United Nations deliberately established a universal General Assembly and a restricted Security Council that required unanimity among the great powers. Granting permanent seats and the right to a veto to the great powers of the time was an essential feature of the deal.

The composition and decision-making procedures of the Security Council were increasingly challenged as membership in the United Nations grew, particularly after decolonization. Yet the only significant reform of the Security Council occurred in 1965, when it was enlarged from eleven to fifteen members and the required majority grew from seven to nine votes. The veto power of the permanent five members was left intact.

The Security Council does not reflect today's distribution of military or economic power, and it does not reflect a geographic balance. Germany and Japan have made strong cases for permanent membership. Developing countries have demanded more representation on the Security Council, particularly South Africa, India, Egypt, Brazil, and Nigeria. Should the European Union be represented instead of Great Britain, France, and Germany individually? How would Pakistan feel about India's candidacy? How would South Africa feel about a Nigerian seat? What about representation by an Islamic country? These issues are not easy to resolve. Likewise, it is very unlikely that the P5 states will relinquish their veto. Although large-scale reform has proved impossible thus far, changes in Security Council working procedures have made it more transparent and accountable to the member states.

Reform efforts in the 1990s focused on the reorganization and rationalization of the ECOSOC, the UN family of economic and social organizations. These efforts allowed ECOSOC to become more assertive and to take a leading role in the coordination of the UN system. They also aimed to eliminate duplication and overlap in the work of the functional commissions.

Overall, economic and social reorganization meant that the two poles of the system were better coordinated: the pole where intentions are defined through global conferences and agendas and the pole where programs are implemented. Programs at the field level were better integrated, and field officers were given enhanced discretion. The reform of ECOSOC sharpened its capacity to shape broad agreements into cross-sectoral programs with well-defined objectives.

The United Kingdom is in the process of leaving the European Union. The country is politically divided and polarized over the Brexit issue. This photo shows pro-EU demonstrators with a banner during the "No to Boris. Yes to Europe" march in central London.

At the same time, ECOSOC acquired greater capacity to act as a conduit through which the results of field-level monitoring could be conveyed upward to the functional commissions. These new processes had the effect of strengthening the norms, values, and goals of a multilateral system.

▶ The European Union and Other Regional Organizations

Regionalism can be seen as one of the few instruments states can use to try to manage the effects of globalization. We define it as the use of regional rather than central systems of administration or economic, cultural, or political affiliation. If individual states no longer have the effective capacity to regulate, regionalism might be a means to regain some control over global market forces—and to counter the more negative social consequences of globalization.

The Process of European Integration

In Europe, regionalism after 1945 took the form of a gradual process of integration leading to the emergence of the **European Union (EU)**. It was initially a purely West European creation among the "original six" member states, born out of the desire for reconciliation between France and Germany in a context of ambitious federalist plans for a united Europe. Yet the process has taken the form of a progressive construction of an institutional architecture, a legal framework, and a wide range of policies, which in 2016 encompassed twenty-eight European states.

The European Coal and Steel Community was created in 1951 (in force in 1952), followed by the European Economic Community and the European Atomic Energy Community in 1957 (in force in 1958). These treaties involved a conferral of Community competence, or standards, in various areas—the supranational management of coal and steel, the creation and regulation of an internal market, and common policies in trade, competition, agriculture, and transport. Since then, powers have been extended to include new legislative competences in some fields such as the environment. Since the 1992 Treaty on European Union (the Maastricht Treaty, in force in 1993), the integration process has also involved the adoption of stronger forms of unification, notably monetary union, as well as cooperation in economic and employment policy, and more intergovernmental cooperation in foreign and security policy.

From very limited beginnings, in terms of both membership and scope, the European Union has gradually developed to become an important political and economic actor whose presence has a significant impact internationally and domestically. This gradual process of European integration has taken place at various levels. The first is the signature and reform of the basic treaties. These are the result of intergovernmental conferences, where representatives of national governments negotiate the legal framework within which the EU institutions operate. Such treaty changes require ratification in each country.

European Union (EU) The union formally created in 1992 following the signing of the Maastricht Treaty. The origins of the European Union can be traced back to 1951 and the creation of the European Coal and Steel Community, followed in 1957 with a broader customs union (the Treaty of Rome, 1958). Originally a grouping of six countries in 1957, "Europe" grew by adding new members in 1973, 1981, and 1986. Since the fall of the planned economies in Eastern Europe in 1989, Europe has grown and now includes twenty-eight member states.

Within this framework, the institutions have considerable powers to adopt decisions and manage policies (Table 5.4), although the dynamics of decision making differ significantly across arenas. There are important differences between the more integrated areas of economic regulation and the more intergovernmental pillars of foreign policy and police or judicial cooperation in criminal matters. In some areas, a country might have to accept decisions imposed on it by the (qualified) majority of member states. In other areas, it might be able to block decisions.

To understand the integration process, one needs to take account of the role played by both member states *and* supranational institutions. Member states are not just represented by national governments, as a host of state, nonstate, and transnational actors participate in the processes of domestic preference formation and direct representation of interests in the key EU institutions. The relative openness of the European policy process means that political groups and economic interests will try to influence EU decision making if they feel that their position is not sufficiently represented by national governments. That is one reason the European Union is increasingly seen as a system of multilevel governance, involving a plurality of actors on different territorial levels: supranational, national, and local.

TABLE 5.4 Institutions of the European Union

EU Institution	Responsibilities	Location
European Commission	Initiating, administering, and overseeing the implementation of EU policies and legislation	Brussels and Luxembourg
European Parliament (EP)	Acting as directly elected representatives of EU citizens, scrutinizing the operation of the other institutions, and, in certain areas, sharing the power to legislate	Strasbourg, Brussels, and Luxembourg
Council of Ministers	Representing the views of national governments and determining, in many areas jointly with the EP, the ultimate shape of EU legislation	Brussels (some meetings in Luxembourg)
European Council	Holding regular summits of the heads of state or government and the president of the commission, setting the EU's broad agenda, and acting as a forum of last resort to find agreement on divisive issues (Note: different from the Council of Europe)	Brussels
European Court of Justice	Acting as the EU's highest court (supported by a Court of First Instance)	Luxembourg
European Central Bank	Setting interest rates and controlling the money supply of the single European currency, the euro	Frankfurt
Court of Auditors	Auditing the revenues and the expenditure under the EU budget	Luxembourg

The complexity of the EU institutional machinery, together with continuous change over time, has spawned a lively debate among integration theorists (Rosamond 2000; Wiener and Diez 2004). Some scholars regard the European Union as sui generis—in a category of its own—and therefore in need of the development of dedicated theories of integration. The most prominent among these has been neofunctionalism, which sought to explain the evolution of integration in terms of "spillover" from one policy sector to another as resources and loyalties of elites were transferred to the European level. As aspects of EU politics have come to resemble the domestic politics of states, scholars have turned to approaches drawn from comparative politics or the study of governance in different states.

Japanese prime minister Shinzo Abe (third from right) and business leaders meet German chancellor Angela Merkel (third from left) at the prime minister's office in Tokyo in 2019. With the United States withdrawing from trade agreements and being critical of global institutions, the US allies are acting on their own. Japan and Germany confirmed that the two countries would contribute to the global economy and further deepen bilateral cooperation. These two countries seem to believe in the liberal international order.

However, the exchange between "supranational" and "intergovernmental" approaches has had the greatest impact on the study of European integration. Supranational approaches regard the emergence of supranational institutions in Europe as a distinct feature and turn these into the main object of analysis. Here, the politics above the level of states is regarded as the most significant, and consequently the political actors and institutions at the European level receive the most attention.

Intergovernmental approaches, on the other hand, continue to regard states as the most important aspect of the integration process. Consequently, they concentrate on the study of politics *between* and *within* states. But most scholars would agree that no analysis of the European Union is complete without studying both the operation and evolution of the central institutions and the input from political actors in the member states.

The prospect of an ever *wider* European Union has raised serious questions about the nature and direction of the integration process. The 2004 enlargement, when ten additional states joined the European Union, was seen as a qualitative leap. Concerns that the enlarged European Union, if not reformed substantially, would find it difficult to make decisions and maintain a reliable legal framework led to several attempts to reform the treaties. The most wide-ranging proposals, and the most significant change in the language of integration, came with the treaty establishing a constitution for Europe that EU governments signed in 2004. The very fact that the European Union should discuss something referred to in the media as a European Constitution is a sign of how far it has developed from its modest beginnings. However, the Constitutional Treaty was rejected in referendums in France and the Netherlands, raising serious doubts not only about this attempt at institutional reform but also about ambitions for a formal constitutional process more generally.

After years of debate, the European Union's reform treaty came into force on December 1, 2009. EU leaders believe the now-ratified Lisbon Treaty will rejuvenate the decision-making apparatus of all of the EU institutions, making the functioning of the twenty-eight-member European Union more efficient and democratic.

During the recent global economic crisis, Germany emerged as the clear leader of the Eurozone and the European Union. Some in Germany are talking about a remaking of the European Union that would include more financial union, including some control over the members' budgets and spending; creating a eurobonds program; renegotiating many of the treaties that bind the EU members together; and even going so far as to create a federal Europe. Many EU optimists thought a major crisis might serve as a catalyst for greater European integration. Those supporting further EU integration were dealt a significant setback when the British voted to leave the European Union in June 2016. Negotiations to leave began in earnest in 2018 and the UK formally left the EU on January 31, 2020. The primary goal of the UK is to create a policy environment that respects the autonomy of each actor. The UK seeks control over its own laws and no longer accepts any EU jurisdiction. The entire Brexit movement was a UK first, nationalist movement. The bargaining process between the EU and the UK began deliberations in February 2020 and the process is scheduled to end 31 December 2020. The fight between the "remainers" and "leavers" is likely to continue for a long time in the future. This entire process has helped to create a politically polarized British society. All the effects of this process are unknown, but we may soon see another referendum on Scottish independence since Scotland voted in favor of staying in the European Union. The United Kingdom will not maintain all the benefits of membership, but they are hoping for a deal on trade, regulatory coordination, and cooperation on external and domestic security. The European Union is moving on and working to develop a comprehensive strategy that addresses political and economic security issues. The European Union is the world's largest economy and it is a major player in global trade. It will remain so once the British leave the union. Unlike the current US administration, the European Union plans on pursuing more comprehensive free trade agreements, and its leadership will work to maintain an open global economic system.

So why did 52 percent of UK citizens decide to leave the European Union? Experts have various opinions, but it is obvious that nationalism and a concern with the effects of globalization played a key role. Much like the anti-elite and nationalist movement that elected Donald Trump in the United States, British

Boris Johnson arrives at 10 Downing Street to make his first speech as prime minister. Johnson said he would rather "die in a ditch" than stop the Brexit process. The European Union's leaders have been incredibly patient with the unpredictable British political situation.

voters believed that the European Union and globalization pushed immigrants into the United Kingdom and that these immigrants were overtaxing the British social systems. This was more than a fear of losing sovereignty and giving up control to an overly bureaucratic European government. On a personal level, British citizens were afraid that the open borders required by the European Union would overburden schools, hospitals, and social services. A touch of Islamophobia may have also influenced this decision to leave this successful integrated community and key global player.

Other Regional Actors: The African Union and the Organization of American States

The **African Union (AU)** is the most important intergovernmental organization in Africa. It replaced the **Organization of African Unity (OAU)** in July 2002. The AU is made up of fifty-five African states. The OAU was established in 1963 to provide a collective voice for Africa and to work to end all forms of colonization. It also sought to promote economic development and human rights and to improve the quality of life for all Africans. However, the OAU's record was not good, especially considering that nineteen of the twenty-three poorest countries in the world are in Africa. A number of major conflicts are creating almost insurmountable human security problems across the continent. Despite its general ineffectiveness, the OAU did succeed in encouraging its members to cooperate as a voting bloc in international organizations like the United Nations.

The AU still must deal with many of the same challenges as it attempts to fulfill its vision of creating "an integrated, prosperous and peaceful Africa, driven by its own citizens and representing a dynamic force in the global arena." The AU has a long way to go to be considered a successful regional organization. Achieving this success might be even more difficult as major powers like China, India, the United States, and European states all compete for access to African resources and turn a blind eye to abuses of governance in many states.

Turning to the Americas, the **Organization of American States (OAS)** is the world's oldest regional organization, founded in 1890. Known at the time as the International Union of American Republics, it changed its name to the Organization of American States in 1948. Its charter states that the goals of the organization are to create "an order of peace and justice, to promote their solidarity, to strengthen their collaboration, and to defend their sovereignty, their territorial integrity, and their independence." During the Cold War, the US obsession with communism drove the OAS to intervene in the affairs of states and at times use extralegal activities to make certain that friendly governments stayed in power. The main pillars of the OAS are democracy, human rights, regional security, and economic development. In the thirty-five-member organization, the United States remains the dominant power, but with rising powers like Brazil, Chile, and Argentina and the intransigent Venezuela, the OAS could become a very effective regional organization and a major player in global politics.

African Union (AU) Created in 2002 and consisting of fifty-five member states, this union was formed as a successor to the Organization of African Unity. It maintains fourteen goals primarily centered on African unity and security, human rights, peace security and stability, economy, sustainable development, and equality.

Organization of African Unity (OAU) A regional organization founded in 1963 as a way to foster solidarity among African countries, promote African independence, and throw off the vestiges of colonial rule. The OAU had a policy of noninterference in member states, and it had no means for intervening in conflicts; as a result, this organization could be only a passive bystander in many violent conflicts.

Organization of American States (OAS) A regional international organization composed of thirty-five member states. It is the world's oldest regional organization, founded in 1890 as the International Union of American Republics; in 1948 it changed its name to the OAS. Its goals are to create "an order of peace and justice, to promote their solidarity, to strengthen their collaboration, and to defend their sovereignty, their territorial integrity, and their independence."

A man holds up the Spanish message: "The final battle will be in Miraflores," referring to the Presidential Palace in Venezuela. The United States and other OAS members recognize the opposition leader, Juan Guaidó, as Venezuela's interim president. Should the OAS play a more active role promoting democracy and economic stability in the Americas?

China as a Leader of Global Institutions

China, like any great power, is trying to shape global institutions or create new global institutions that could challenge or undermine the institutions created by the US-led global order. A 2017 study by John Ikenberry and Darren Lim at the Brookings Institute suggested that China was "building a network of counter-hegemonic institutions" that serve Chinese interests and may increase its influence and power. The New Development Bank, sometimes called the BRICS (Brazil, Russia, India, China, and South Africa) bank, focuses on infrastructure and sustainable development projects. The New Development Bank has a $100 billion fund that is seen as an alternative to the Western liberal institutions like the World Bank and the IMF.

Another new institution is the Asian Infrastructure Investment Bank, which was started by China with some ninety-three member states—but not Japan and the United States. This bank has thirty-four projects, and 60 percent are co-financed with other multilateral development banks and the World Bank.

The Brookings study suggests that China may be trying to reform existing institutions and to increase its influence and authority in existing institutions or create a rival economic and political order.

Global and regional state organizations are but one piece of the emerging pattern of global governance. We turn now to nongovernmental actors and examine their role in international life.

▶ The Growth of Global Civil Society

International nongovernmental organization (INGO) A formal nongovernmental organization with members from at least three countries.

Civil society The totality of all individuals and groups in a society who are not acting as participants in any government institutions or acting in the interests of commercial companies.

The world of global activism is led by a number of nonstate actors: **international nongovernmental organizations** or **INGOs** (NGOs with members from at least three countries); philanthropic foundations that give money to global social movements; and powerful, wealthy, or famous individuals (e.g., Bill Gates, Bono, George Soros, and the Dalai Lama) who use their expertise and resources to influence the formulation and implementation of public policy. All of these actors together make up what is known as a global or transnational **civil society**. Anheier, Glasius, and Kaldor (2004) define global civil society as

> *a supranational sphere of social and political participation in which citizen groups, social movements and individuals engage in dialogue, debate, confrontation and negotiation with each other, with governments, international and regional governmental organizations and with multinational corporations.*

Global civil society occupies the space between the state and the market; it is not constrained by national boundaries. Religious organizations, schools and other educational institutions, trade unions, and service organizations like Rotary International make up a traditional list of civil-society actors. Scholars in this area (e.g., Keck and Sikkink 1998) have added to this list INGOs, research groups or epistemic communities, foundations, and media organizations. Global civil society also includes social movements and advocacy networks. A **social movement** is defined as a mode of collective action that challenges ways of life, thinking, dominant norms, and moral codes; seeks answers to global problems; and promotes reform or transformation in political and economic institutions. Transnational social movement organizations (TSMOs), often made up of NGOs and like-minded governments and international organizations, have led many successful global campaigns to address issues such as famine in Africa, landmines, and corporate social responsibility in developing countries.

Transnational advocacy networks (TANs) are "networks of activists, distinguishable largely by the centrality of principled ideas or values in motivating their formation" (Keck and Sikkink 1998, 1). The advocates or activists in these networks "promote normative positions, lobby for policy reforms, and play an important role in policy debates over a wide variety of social issues" (Keck and Sikkink 1998, 8–9). Both INGOs and governments can play a central role in these networks. TANs and TSMOs have taken advantage of the forces of globalization to increase the political effectiveness of their various campaigns, and the ease of communicating online has contributed to their rise. These movements and networks, which target governments at all levels, in some cases provide critical resources for political change and innovation. Making connections with other actors across the world is much easier with social media, global media outlets, greater financial resources, and INGO links to governments, academic institutions, and even global corporations.

Although not, strictly speaking, part of the global civil society, MNCs have formed their own INGOs and pro-business networks to lobby for their own interests and to counter the increasingly effective efforts of more progressive INGOs and TANs. Most global corporations support trade-and-aid policies, which encourage open markets and provide stability and protection for their investments. These corporations and their INGOs are up against numerous public campaigns to make corporations more accountable to the public and to force them to address environmental concerns, human rights, and social justice issues.

Some scholars have suggested that power and authority have shifted from states and public authorities toward actors in the global civil society. Although it is true that INGOs do provide services and resources in areas where states have failed to provide for their citizens, filling those gaps is only part of what these actors do for the world. In many situations, INGOs, think tanks, foundations, and even MNCs act as innovators and catalysts for change. Understanding the complexities of the global economy requires understanding more than states and intergovernmental organizations (IGOs). This is the world of global politics, not simply international relations, and we need to understand the specific roles played by the many types of nonstate actors.

Social movement A mode of collective action that challenges ways of life, thinking, dominant norms, and moral codes; seeks answers to global problems; and promotes reform or transformation in political and economic institutions.

Transnational advocacy network (TAN) A network of activists—often, a coalition of nongovernmental organizations—distinguishable largely by the centrality of principled ideas or values in motivating its formation.

In the next sections of this chapter, we will introduce you to the major non-state actors that play important roles in the development of policy at the local, national, and global levels. In some cases, actors such as think tanks and research institutes provide expertise in the *formulation* of policy options. In other cases, actors such as NGOs may partner with states to *implement* policy decisions. We will explore who these actors are and what kind of power and influence they have.

Multinational Corporations

Multinational corporations or enterprises (MNCs/MNEs) are firms with subsidiaries that extend the production and marketing of the firm beyond the boundaries of any one country. The foreign subsidiaries of an MNC are directly owned by the parent corporation. MNCs are not included under the umbrella of civil society because they are for profit. Some experts use the terms *MNC* and *transnational corporation* interchangeably; however, Andrew Hines, an expert for BNET (now CBS Money Watch), makes a clear distinction between four types of international businesses:

1. *International companies* are simply importers and exporters with no investments or operations outside the home countries.
2. *Multinational companies* have investments around the world, but they adjust their products and services to local markets.
3. *Global companies* have investments and a presence in many countries, and they use the same brand and image in all markets.
4. *Transnational companies* are complex organizations that invest in foreign operations, and although they have a central corporate office, they allow foreign markets to make decisions about marketing and research and development.

To simplify our analysis, we will focus on MNCs and assume that transnational corporations are similar in the role they play as global actors. Most MNCs have their origins in developed countries, and they invest throughout the world. The number of MNCs increased exponentially after World War II. Most MNCs at the time were from the United States, the United Kingdom, Japan, Germany, and France. Recently, China, India, Russia, Brazil, and Korea have added MNCs to the market. Indeed, because of their interests in global markets and their interests in selling to the world, the nationality of MNCs may be irrelevant. As consumers, we look for the best products at the best price, and we usually make little noise about purchasing a product made by a foreign corporation. National leaders do not seem to be concerned when multinationals build factories in their country or when they purchase critically important industries. MNCs are global because they seek markets for investments, cheap but skilled labor, and access to resources essential for making their products. MNCs have power because they control scarce and critically important economic resources, they have the ability to move resources around the world, and they have advantages in areas of marketing and consumer loyalty.

Generally, MNCs get a bad review as representatives of Western capitalist culture, guilty of exploiting labor and crowding out local businesses. Many MNCs are seen as enemies of the people, supporting oppressive governments and contributing to pollution, poverty, and corruption. This view may be both outdated in some cases and limited, however, and views of MNCs vary according to one's theoretical perspective. Liberals see MNCs as a positive force, spreading technology, efficiency, and wealth. Economic nationalists, or neomercantilists, argue that MNCs threaten national sovereignty and dilute national wealth. Finally, Marxists see MNCs as representatives of the core-capitalist states, creating dependencies in countries where they invest and helping create and maintain a core-periphery global economic structure. According to this view, MNCs participate in predatory globalization, or the search for investment opportunities in countries where labor is cheap and where laws aimed at protecting the welfare of workers and the environment are either not enforced or nonexistent. Essentially, Marxists argue that MNCs put profits above all else.

However, many NGOs work with MNCs to create opportunities for work in developing countries and to respond to human needs such as clean water, basic education, and health care. MNCs also give many small local businesses access to markets, financial credit, and technological infrastructure. The view of MNCs is changing because these corporations realize that they need a positive image to attract customers. Their ability to attract customers and make profits depends in part on providing resources, expertise, and training to local populations, thus becoming partners in development. Many governments now compete for investments from MNCs. Not only do they provide jobs and help build infrastructure, but also MNCs are often engines of change and reform in corrupt and mismanaged governments.

Why do companies invest abroad? The decision to become a multinational firm is not only about access to markets but also about finding competitive advantages for the firm. These might be technological innovations and efficient production costs, for example, which make manufacturing more profitable at a foreign location.

We have made the claim that MNCs are playing a more positive role in many developing countries. To address the argument that MNCs are only interested in profits, we will consider the case of India's economy, which is predicted to be as big as China's in ten to fifteen years. The 1.37 billion people living in India are becoming more affluent, more educated, and more politically active, and they are demanding more from both the public and private sectors. At the same time, MNCs are more concerned about attracting customers, and that means providing a good product and being good citizens in this market.

However, India has had its share of problems with MNCs more interested in profit than the well-being of its workers and neighbors. A prime example is the

1984 tragedy at a Union Carbide factory in Bhopal, where a toxic gas leak killed 3,800 people and left several thousand with permanent disabilities. Union Carbide, a US-based MNC, was one of the first US companies to invest in India, and it produced pesticides for India's agricultural sector. In the final settlement, Union Carbide paid out close to $500 million to victims and to build clinics and other facilities in the region.

Another MNC with a more than one-hundred-year history in India is Nestlé. This corporation has had to deal with charges of malpractice, corruption, and generally putting profits ahead of the needs and interests of its consumers. (See the Case Study in this chapter.) Nestlé India has eight factories that produce milk, which Indians drink in great quantities. One small factory in the Punjab region depends on about 180 farmers for its supply of milk, and those farmers were having problems with their animals. Nestlé brought in agronomists, veterinarians, and agricultural education experts to work with the local farmers to help maintain healthier herds that produced more milk. Nestlé clearly benefited, but so did the local farmers.

MNCs are also involved in a number of partnership projects with governments and INGOs. Since 2002, the US Agency for International Development (USAID) has been working with Albanian farmers and Land O'Lakes, a food-producing MNC, to increase the quality of dairy products and to provide jobs for twelve thousand farmers and dairy processors. In several Latin American countries, the Nature Conservancy, a US-based NGO, has been working with an MNC, FEMSA (along with the Inter-American Development Bank and the Global Environment Facility), to establish a social investment foundation that supports education, science, and technology. FEMSA is the world's largest Coca-Cola bottling company and a major beer distributor in Latin America. More than 50 million people will benefit from this partnership, which will work to restore forests and grasslands where clean water originates. In Colombia, the conservation trust fund is aimed at protecting rivers and watersheds that provide clean drinking water for people in Bogotá.

Saudi leaders sponsored the Future Investment Initiative forum in October 2019. The government is planning a stock offering of a small part of state-run oil giant Saudi Aramco, the sixth largest corporation in the world. Saudi Arabia is involved in a controversial war in Yemen and the Crown Prince has been implicated in the killing of a journalist critical of the regime. Yet, Aramco's stock sale will likely attract investors around the world. Do investors ever consider moral challenges before they invest?

Several factors make these public and private partnerships more likely in the future. Governments have fewer financial resources for global projects. Citizens are becoming more aware of vital global challenges and more critical of bad behavior by both public and private actors, and IGOs and INGOs are providing expertise and other resources to facilitate global responses to address these challenges.

INGOs as Global Political Actors

Nongovernmental organizations (NGOs) are autonomous organizations that are not instruments of any government, are not for profit, and are formal legal entities. These exist within societies as domestic NGOs, like the Sierra Club in the United States, or as INGOs. They campaign for certain causes (e.g., Amnesty International for human rights), represent the interests of specific professionals (e.g., international trade unions), and include charitable organizations (e.g., CARE and Oxfam).

As long as nation-states have fought wars or famine has plagued societies, civil-society organizations have played a role in trying to find solutions to these problems. In 1874, there were thirty-two registered INGOs; in 1914, there were more than a thousand. One of the best-known INGOs is the International Red Cross, which was founded by Jean Henri Dunant in 1859 after the Battle of Solferino, and was awarded the Nobel Peace Prize in 1917, 1944, and 1963. The Red Cross directed the implementation of the first Geneva Convention on the humane treatment of wounded soldiers and prisoners of war. Another INGO, Save the Children, was formed after World War I, and Médecins Sans Frontières (Doctors Without Borders) was started after the Biafran civil war in Nigeria in the late 1960s. INGOs have been willing to work in crisis situations when governments are reluctant to become involved. In the 1990s, INGOs began to work more closely with each other and with governments and IGOs like the World Bank and the United Nations.

NGOs often act collectively in pursuit of their interests or values, and some scholars believe that they are shifting political power away from the state. NGOs work with states and regional and international organizations, but most global politics scholars believe that the state no longer monopolizes the political world. Most of the NGOs working in what some have called the most idealist and "imagined" global communities are progressive organizations working to reform or transform the current global system. They aim to do so by making decision-making arenas more democratic, transparent, equitable, and environmentally friendly. As Rischard (2002) argues in his book on global problems, NGOs tend to work in three broad areas:

- *Sharing our planet*—issues such as climate change, ocean pollution, and biodiversity.
- *Sharing our humanity*—issues that focus on global health, education, human rights, war, violence, and repression.
- Governance, or *sharing our rule book*—issues that involve international laws and institutions.

Private Sector Actors: The Ten Largest Global Corporations.

Walmart
Sinopec Group
Royal Dutch Shell
China National Petroleum
State Grid
Saudi Aramco
British Petroleum
Exxon Mobil
Volkswagen
Toyota Motor

The Spanish NGO Proactiva Open Arms rescues a baby in the Mediterranean Sea 45 miles (72 kilometers) from Libya. Proactiva was involved in a tense high-seas standoff last year when the crew refused to hand over 218 migrants rescued at sea to the Libyan coast guard. A judge dropped the charges and Proactiva stated that it has always operated according to international rules. NGOs often represent human interests, and that may challenge more narrow national interests.

A Global Campaign: The Baby Milk Advocacy Network

BACKGROUND

The prototype for global campaigning by NGOs has been the International Baby Food Action Network (IBFAN), which challenges the marketing of dried milk powder by the major food and pharmaceutical transnational corporations (TNCs). In the early 1970s, medical staff in developing countries gradually became aware that the death rate for babies was rising because of decreased breastfeeding. If the family was poor and used insufficient milk powder, the baby was undernourished. If the water or the bottle was not sterile, the baby developed gastric diseases. Bottle feeding today causes around 1.5 million deaths a year.

THE CASE

The question was first taken up by the *New Internationalist* magazine and War on Want (WoW) in Britain in 1973–1974. A Swiss NGO, the Third World Action Group (AgDW), then published a revised translation of WoW's report under the title "Nestlé Kills Babies." When Nestlé sued for libel, AgDW mobilized groups from around the world to supply evidence for their defense. The Swiss court found AgDW guilty in December 1976 on one of Nestlé's four original counts, on the technical basis that Nestlé was only indirectly responsible for the deaths.

The question moved to the United States, when religious groups involved in Latin America fought another court case against pharmaceutical company Bristol-Myers Squibb. Increased awareness led to organization by a new group, the Infant Formula Action Coalition, of a boycott of Nestlé's products, which spread to many countries. In the hope of diffusing the increasing pressure, the International Council of Infant Food Industries accepted a proposal by the late senator Edward Kennedy for the WHO and UNICEF to hold a meeting on infant feeding in October 1979. Rather than seeing the issue depoliticized, the companies found they were facing demands to limit their marketing. The meeting also taught a group of NGOs how much they could benefit from working together with a common political strategy. They decided to continue to cooperate by forming IBFAN as a global advocacy network.

The new network was able to mobilize a diverse coalition of medical professionals, religious groups, development activists, women's groups, community organizations, consumer lobbies, and the boycott campaigners. Against intense opposition from the TNCs and the US administration, IBFAN succeeded in achieving the adoption of an International Code of Marketing of Breast-Milk Substitutes, by WHO's assembly, in May 1981. The key provisions of the code were that "there should be no advertising or other form of promotion to the general public" nor any provision of free samples to mothers.

OUTCOME

According to WHO, as of 2011, 37 out of 199 countries reporting had passed laws reflecting all of the recommendations of the code; another 69 countries fully prohibit advertising of breast-milk substitutes. Many countries, however, still have weak legal provisions or voluntary policies. IBFAN's work continues along two tracks: It monitors and reports violations of the code by companies, including in countries where marketing is now illegal, and it seeks to upgrade the law in countries that are only partially implementing the code.

Sources: This account is based on A. Chetley (1986), *The Politics of Baby Foods* (London: Pinter); information at http://www.ibfan.org, the IBFAN website; and WHO (2013, revised), *Country Implementation of the International Code of Marketing of Breast-milk Substitutes: Status Report 2011* (Geneva: World Health Organization).

For Discussion

1. The global campaign against Nestlé led to this action network. Is this an effective way to shape national policy?
2. When and where do global campaigns work?
3. What is the "boomerang pattern," and what role did it play in the Nestlé campaign?

Thus, trade and investment rules promoted by neoliberal institutions like the WTO and the World Bank have become the target of concern for many global activists.

In 2020, there are 72,500 INGOs. They are generally seen as independent, altruistic, idealistic, and progressive; however, not all INGOs support progressive changes. Some represent the status quo, and some support authoritarian or racist preferred futures (e.g., there are many neo-Nazi INGOs). Transnational or multinational corporations sponsor NGOs and advocacy networks that are also a part of this global civil society. There are a variety of INGOs, differentiated by their purpose, organization, and sponsorship. These include the following:

- *BINGOs*: business and industry INGOs like the World Economic Forum, the World Business Council for Sustainable Development, and the Global Business Council on HIV and AIDS.
- *GRINGOs*: government-regulated and -initiated INGOs; many authoritarian states sponsor these to keep watch on dissidents and the activities of foreign interests.
- *QUANGOs*: sometimes called quasi-INGOs because they receive most of their funds from public sources although they are still independent.
- *RINGOs*: INGOs that are sponsored by religious groups and often promote religious norms and values; World Vision, Caritas, and Norwegian Church Fund are examples.

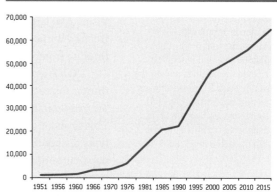

INGO Growth Continues.
What impact does the growth of INGOs have on nationstates and other global actors?

What kind of power do these INGOs have? How can they counter the economic and political power of global corporations? Do they have any influence over nation-states?

Sources of INGO Power

A critical question is how much power INGOs and other transnational actors have to implement their own strategic plans and affect the policy of governments and intergovernmental organizations. We know that MNCs can use their money and the promise of jobs, investment, and access to new technologies to influence governments, but what about religious organizations like World Vision or think tanks like the Brookings Institution? Let us look at INGOs to assess their sources of influence.

In many societies, especially the pluralist social democratic states (e.g., Sweden, Denmark, the Netherlands), domestic NGOs and INGOs play an important role as partners in the policy process. Some NGOs are not as independent from public agencies as they claim to be. These so-called QUANGOs are often supported by governments to carry out policy programs that governments cannot or will not implement.

To illustrate, INGOs have played a critical role in implementing development-assistance programs throughout the world. The International Red Cross claims the INGOs working in the development and human security areas give out more money than the World Bank. Most of this money comes from governments

Multinational corporation or enterprise (MNC/MNE) A business or firm with administration, production, distribution, and marketing located in countries around the world. Such a business moves money, goods, services, and technology around the world depending on where the firm can make the most profit.

and public agencies. Organizations like Oxfam in the United Kingdom, World Vision (the largest privately funded Christian relief-and-development NGO), and Doctors Without Borders receive anywhere from 25 percent to 50 percent of their funding from various government sources.

INGOs are also supported by private sources like corporations and philanthropic foundations. In December 2011, Google announced that it would provide $11.5 million in grants to ten organizations working to end the practice of slavery. This is about 25 percent of what Google was giving away to charitable organizations during the holiday season. The grant was to be used by a coalition on international antitrafficking organizations. The International Justice Mission (IJM) was the lead organization in this effort. More specifically, the IJM in India, one of the fourteen field offices, led intervention and rescue missions. The IJM is a human rights agency that rescues victims of slavery, sexual exploitation, and other forms of violent oppression. Prior to this gift, most of IJM's funding came from private sources, and less than 1 percent of its funding had come from major corporations or corporate foundations. Another important member of this coalition is CNN and its CNN Freedom project, which started in March 2011. CNN, a global media superpower, has broadcast more than two hundred stories about human trafficking and modern-day slavery. This kind of exposure educates citizens and their leaders and pressures them to act.

Obviously, government funding increases the ability of INGOs to assist people in need and to help governments carry out some of their foreign policy goals. As governments are forced to cut back their workforce, many duties are being picked up by INGOs. Not only do INGO employees deliver services to the poor and protect citizens in conflict areas, but also INGOs like Amnesty International and Human Rights Watch provide policymakers and interested citizens with valuable information and research reports that can be used to develop new laws and policy programs. Their research expertise gives them access to policymakers, and often their ideas and interests become part of public policy.

Forms of INGO Power

Forms of INGO power discussed by Keck and Sikkink (1998) include information politics, symbolic politics, leverage politics, accountability politics, and global campaign politics. We will briefly discuss each of these.

Information Politics

INGOs and other civil-society actors use a variety of social media outlets, newsletters, and websites to keep their followers informed, solicit donations, and mobilize citizens to take positions supporting their causes. During antiglobalization demonstrations at WTO or G8 talks, many activists use digital cameras and audio streams to share the day-to-day events with other activists in distant lands. This builds support and a stronger sense of community among INGOs and other activist groups.

Another part of information politics is the research and studies that many INGOs provide media reporters and government officials. Because of their expertise and their access to critical players in crisis situations, NGOs can also provide important technical and strategic information, which can be used to influence policymakers and inform other activists.

Symbolic Politics

Activist leaders of INGOs identify a critical issue or event and provide explanations that frame the issue so it becomes a catalyst for growth of the movement. The shelling of a café in Sarajevo by Bosnian Serb forces during the civil war in Yugoslavia was used as a symbolic event by human rights INGOs who were demanding US intervention to stop the ethnic cleansing in Bosnia.

INGOs use their position in society and their role in crises as a way of increasing awareness and expanding support for their cause. When the Red Cross, Doctors Without Borders, and the International Campaign to Ban Landmines were awarded the Nobel Peace Prize, this called attention to their cause and gave the groups more legitimacy throughout the world. INGOs and the transnational social movements they participate in often use big stories to gain public attention, more members, financial contributions, and the attention of those with political power. In the 1980s, Irish rock star Bob Geldof (who played Wall in the Pink Floyd–inspired movie) turned the world's attention to famine in western Africa. His activism led musicians in the United Kingdom, the United States, and Canada to each produce their own "We Are the World" records and sponsor a series of globally televised concerts to raise public awareness and collect funds for famine relief.

Some of these big stories that are picked up by the media are based on false or incomplete information. A good example is the 1995 Brent Spar incident. Greenpeace launched an attack on an obsolete oil rig, called the Brent Spar, in the North Sea to protest the decision by Shell to sink it. Greenpeace claimed that the environmental damage would be worse by sinking the rig than by towing it to shore and dismantling it there. Yet independent environmental studies clearly showed that the environmental damage would be greater if the rig were towed to shore and dismantled. Still, Greenpeace continued with its campaign and forced the government of Germany and Shell Oil to dismantle the rig on land. Both traditional and social media sources can be used to turn the facts about natural disasters and the aftermath of war and violence into human stories.

Leverage Politics

INGOs often use material leverage (e.g., money or goods) or moral leverage to persuade governments to act in certain ways or to encourage other INGOs to support their position on an issue. They often shame governments into acting in a certain way. They are adept at using the media to expose hypocritical behaviors and to make certain the public is aware of unpopular practices by governments, transnational corporations, and other actors. With greater access to media and information technology, INGOs have access to larger audiences. These INGOs demand more accountability and have increasing power and influence, which helps them to shape the domestic and foreign policy process.

Accountability Politics

INGOs are able to use a number of information and media sources to act as watchdogs and force governments and political leaders to follow up on their public promises. Unfortunately, this pressure does not always work. Both George H. W. Bush and Bill Clinton promised to push China to improve its human rights record before they would support new trade relations. Once elected, both presidents caved in to trade interests and failed to address human rights concerns. Although INGOs are not always successful, they continue to use their resources to pressure governments to close the gap between promises and performances.

Global Campaign Politics

A relatively new tool for NGOs, civil-society actors, and like-minded governments is a global campaign that uses the media, local activist networks, and, if necessary, product boycotts like the one described in the Nestlé case study. The use of social networking sites and the proliferation of NGOs across the world have made it easier to establish and maintain such campaigns. The One Campaign aimed at addressing global poverty and campaigns seeking to provide assistance to victims of natural disasters have also benefited from what we know as celebrity diplomacy (discussed in the next section). We are all familiar with the roles played by Bono, Radiohead, and Wyclef Jean in mobilizing public support for their humanitarian causes. Many of these global campaigns play on our love for music, film, and other forms of entertainment. With the internet and social media, it is relatively easy to identify a global issue, build an organization, promote a particular set of values and actions, and raise both financial and volunteer support for your cause. It is even easier if you can link your cause to a major event or to the popularity of a certain artist or sports hero.

Nongovernmental organization (NGO) An organization, usually a grassroots one, that has policy goals but is not governmental in its makeup. An NGO is any group of people relating to each other regularly in some formal manner and engaging in collective action, provided the activities are noncommercial and nonviolent and are not conducted on behalf of a government.

▶ Celebrity Diplomacy

In 2005, *Time* magazine named Bono and Bill and Melinda Gates persons of the year for their contributions to the global community. Bono, lead singer in the Irish rock group U2, has been described by James Traub of the *New York Times* as a "one-man state who fills his treasury with the global currency of fame." He has used this fame to lead major global campaigns to end global poverty. Andrew Cooper suggests that global activism by well-known celebrities is part of a more open and robust process of diplomacy that is the opposite of the insulated and secretive world of traditional diplomacy (2008). Cooper suggests this new form of diplomacy may be eroding the authority and legitimacy of more traditional forms of diplomatic activity. Many celebrities have used their status and resources to achieve goals that reflect their own values. The International Campaign to Ban Landmines became headline news when the late Princess Diana became its international spokesperson. Angelina Jolie and Brad Pitt have become spokespersons for a variety of causes related to children and refugees and created a charitable foundation to aid humanitarian causes around the world. The Jolie/Pitt Foundation gave away $2 million—$1 million to Global Action for Children (now defunct) and $1 million to Doctors Without Borders—to help families affected by HIV/AIDS and extreme poverty.

NGOs and Protecting the Rights of Children

Do NGOs matter? People on one side of this academic dispute believe that NGOs are important actors that influence a range of behaviors in international relations. This is especially true for both liberal thinkers and many who embrace critical theories and ideas. On the other side are many realists who believe that governments are the most important actors—some believe the only actors that matter—in the study of the discipline. Somewhere in the middle are analysts who think that, by combining the study of states and NGOs, we can begin to understand the complexities of international relations. This dispute is primarily a disagreement of the kind you learned about in Chapter 3: What is the proper unit of analysis in the study of globalization and international relations?

For children around the world, these academic exercises miss the point: NGOs matter. Without the work of NGOs to supply food, provide education, and promote awareness, the lives of children would be much worse. In countries around the world each day, children are forced to be soldiers in civil wars, they starve, they lack basic health services, they are forced to work in factories for less pay than adults, and they are physically abused and forced into sex slavery.

Each day, hundreds of local and transnational NGOs strive to improve living conditions for millions of people under the age of eighteen by attempting to implement the UN Millennium Development Goals and subsequent Sustainable Development Goals. NGOs also hold each country accountable for its ratification of the 1989 Convention on the Rights of the Child. Because the United Nations is an organization of sovereign and nominally equal countries, it is sometimes unable to do as much as some governments would like. NGOs, because they are not responsible to national governments, can apply moral suasion through public-awareness campaigns to help people in need.

Two of the more famous NGOs working to help children are Oxfam and Human Rights Watch, which focus on three main areas of children's rights: basic needs such as food, clothing, shelter, and health care; education; and security, including juvenile justice and ending war. Although these are also problems in industrialized countries, they represent greater challenges in the developing world, where governments lack the resources to provide for these needs. For example, Oxfam International's seventeen member groups work in more than one hundred countries helping people to help themselves by providing the tools and seeds for them to grow their own food. Oxfam also works in the area of arms control, seeking to encourage governments to stop expensive weapons sales and to redirect the money to basic human needs in developing countries.

Human Rights Watch has programs aimed at ending abuses of people regardless of age; however, the organization believes that children are at risk because of their vulnerable status in many societies. The group raises awareness about the horrible conditions that children face around the world: being detained in "social protection centers" in Vietnam, where they are forced to work long hours for much less than the prevailing local wage scale; being forced to fight in civil wars in Africa and Asia; or being used as sex workers in some countries, where they are then denied access to medical care, including HIV/AIDS medicines. The Children's Rights Division of Human Rights Watch has worked with the ICC to try to end the use of child soldiers and sexual trafficking in children.

Academic analysts of international politics might disagree about the worth of NGOs in the study of international society, but NGOs clearly have a positive effect daily on the lives of millions of people who are most at risk. NGOs are able to assume tasks that governments are unable or unwilling to do themselves.

For Discussion
1. If states fail to protect children, is there not a place for NGO intervention?
2. Children and their rights are hardly the focus of most international relations discussions. How do NGOs bring these concerns to our attention?
3. As the agenda of international relations shifts to human security issues, or freedom from fear and freedom from want, how important will nonstate actors be in the future?

As we face many global problems that do not belong to any one nation-state, celebrities often become advocates for global action. A major voice for environmental issues, Leonardo DiCaprio joins Michael Douglas, Jane Goodall, and Stevie Wonder at the UN ahead of International Day of Peace. Their books, movies, songs, and actions inspire many citizens to act.

Not all celebrities promote progressive or cosmopolitan causes like global governance, social justice, human security, and protecting the environment. Some celebrities represent more conservative political causes and movements, like the late Charlton Heston, president of the National Rifle Association. This is not a new phenomenon; countries have always used movie stars and entertainers to sell war bonds and promote public campaigns.

Celebrities, like any of us, use social media to communicate their messages, but they can also use their celebrity status to sell more than just movies and music. They sell ideas and normative values and positions to their adoring fans and use technology and global media to convince political leaders to embrace their positions. Traditional diplomats are very critical of these celebrity actions and suggest that they lack the expertise and dedication to the real goals of traditional diplomacy. Critics say it is okay for celebrities to raise funds for humanitarian issues, but they are not representatives of states and they need to be careful not to interfere with any official diplomatic agenda.

A new group of celebrities are entrepreneurs who have made billions and have created foundations and philanthropic organizations to promote and fund their special causes. Mark Zuckerberg, the cofounder and chief executive of Facebook, is at the top of the list of the new rich doing something for the world. In 2015, he announced that he and his wife would give 99 percent of their Facebook shares, holdings currently worth more than $45 billion, to charitable purposes over the course of their lives. Their organization, the Chan Zuckerberg Initiative, will focus on education, curing disease, connecting people, and building strong communities. This is a very effective practice called **venture philanthropy**, and it is having an especially large impact in the developing world. British aviation magnate Richard Branson has focused his wealth on global social and environmental problems. He has established a green-energy carbon war room and a fund to reward scientists for finding new ways to control climate change and remove carbon from the environment.

As governments cut social programs at home and development-assistance programs, and failed or fragile states are unable or unwilling to provide basic services for their citizens, foundations and individual philanthropists are willing to step up and support innovative programs that encourage local business development and efforts to solve persistent societal challenges.

Venture philanthropy The practice of supporting philanthropists or social entrepreneurs by providing them with networking and leveraging opportunities.

Foundations and Think Tanks

A foundation is a nonstate actor that is established as a charitable trust or a non-profit INGO with the purpose of making grants to other institutions or to individuals for a variety of purposes. Many world leaders establish foundations when they leave office to continue to make a difference in global affairs. For example, the Nelson Mandela Foundation was established in 1999 to continue the work of this great leader, especially in the areas of reconciliation in divided societies and social justice. Another example is the William J. Clinton Foundation, which sponsors global initiatives that allow governments to respond to major global challenges such as the need for education, safe drinking water, and clean air.

Foundations do not simply step in and provide funding where the state has left a vacuum. Rather, foundations want to be change agents and encourage reform and innovation in societies across the globe. Some of the more successful and enduring foundations are in the United States, but many wealthy individuals in Europe and Asia have established foundations to help their countries and their neighbors. For example, the Bharti Foundation, founded by telecom billionaire Sunil Mittal, has opened more than two hundred schools to address the problem of illiteracy and has funded teacher training programs and libraries. Foundations play a major role in funding research institutes and communities of scholars and experts who are essential sources of information for those who formulate, implement, and eventually evaluate policy decisions and processes.

Other notable philanthropic foundations that have had a major impact on global politics include the Bill and Melinda Gates Foundation, the Rockefeller Foundation, the Open Society Foundations, the MacArthur Foundation, the Ford Foundation, and the Aga Khan Foundation. Many of these foundations fund research institutes, universities, and think tanks.

Think tanks (also known as research institutes) vary in size, resource base, policy orientation, and political influence in either national or global politics. Some are scholarly and focus on nonpartisan research, whereas others represent a particular political position or ideology. Many focus on ideas like free market capitalism, socialism, or civic engagement.

Think tanks have increased in number and influence as critical players in global politics, and their increasing importance is the result of a variety of factors. One obvious reason has to do with the complexity of issues now facing policymakers. Most of the officials we elect or appoint to handle these issues are not experts. They depend on the communities of experts often found within think tanks and research institutes. Another reason for the growth of these actors is that although we are flooded with information, it is very hard to decide what information is reliable. Think tanks and research institutes with a long history of producing reliable information based on sound research offer public officials information they can

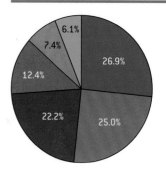

	Europe 2219
	NA 2058
	Asia 1829
	South & Central America 1023
	Sub-saharan Africa 612
	Sub-saharan Africa 612

Distribution of Think Tanks in the World.

Who shapes the policy agenda when European and North American research institutes dominate policy research?

use with confidence. These think tanks play a critical role by providing the following services:

- Disseminating research reports and other briefing documents.
- Promoting specific policy strategies and ideas.
- Providing essential information to political parties, public officials, policy bureaucracies, the media, and the general public.
- Evaluating policy programs and decision-making processes.

◤ Criminal and Terrorist Networks as Global Actors

Globalization has provided a number of opportunities for the spread of positive ideas and opportunities, as well as trade, travel, and communications. There is, of course, a dark side to globalization, and that is the opportunities it provides for criminal networks to expand their activities and increase their profits and the number of victims. A variety of informal organizations and criminal gangs engage in violent or criminal behavior across the globe. We can make a distinction between activity that is considered criminal around the world—such as theft, fraud, personal violence, piracy, or drug trafficking—and activity that is claimed by those undertaking it to have legitimate political motives. In reality, the distinction becomes blurred when criminals claim political motives or political groups are responsible for acts such as terrorism, torture, or involving children in violence. For all governments, neither criminal activity nor political violence can be legitimate within their own jurisdiction, nor is it generally legitimate in other countries.

Politically, the most important criminal industries are illicit trading in arms, drugs, and people. In a 2003 article in *Foreign Policy*, Moises Naim argues that the war on terrorism has obscured the importance of five other global wars that we are losing, those on

- drug interdiction,
- the illegal arms trade,
- the protection of intellectual property and the prevention of piracy and counterfeiting of products,
- human trafficking, and
- money laundering and the smuggling of money, gold coins, and other valuables.

Even when governments are strong and reasonably effective, a range of factors can hinder their ability to respond to the threats presented by global criminal networks. These include inadequate laws, bureaucratic jurisdictional disputes, and enforcement strategies that work well at home but not in a more complex global environment.

While it is possible to win these wars against powerful criminal networks, governments will not win without some serious thinking about how we organize states and how we think about the international system. World leaders must begin to share or even trade sovereignty. They must open their systems to global institutions sponsoring multilateral enforcement activities. States must find ways to regulate transboundary activities and to reach some agreement on a set of regulations that will be enforced in every market across the globe. Successful efforts to end these wars might also depend on a change in our attitudes about community and the individual. If we continue to promote the goal of individual advancement over peace and stability in our communities, these wars could continue for a long time.

We discuss terrorism and terrorist networks in depth in Chapter 6, so for now we merely want to emphasize that terrorist organizations are nonstate actors that have an impact on all actors in the international system. Terrorism is very difficult to eliminate because groups using terrorism are usually part of larger, decentralized global networks. President George W. Bush described the battle against it as "fourth-generation warfare," which involves nation-states in wars with nonstate global networks.

Terrorist networks are global networks composed of many different groups that might or might not share an ideological position. These groups are usually united only in their desire to overthrow a government or a regional or global system of governance or replace a way of life or a hegemonic ideology. This *new terrorism* is characterized by its global reach, decentralized structure, a seemingly wide-open targeting strategy with no regard for civilians, and more obscure and extreme goals and objectives. Radical groups who are likely to use terrorism are often linked to NGOs and foundations that are supported by sympathetic states or by states seeking to keep extremists out of their lands.

We should not forget that some states also support terrorist activities, and in some cases, their military or police forces are the terrorists. In the pursuit of national interests, states might not always follow the rules.

Conclusion

International law, international and regional organizations, and INGOs collectively play an important role in the governance of our global

WHAT'S YOUR WORLDVIEW?

With globalization becoming a more important factor in shaping our quality of life, should we be more open to collective multilateralism, global governance, and problem-solving alliances of public and private actors?

Human trafficking is one of the major challenges that national officials have not been able to contain. In this photo Suzanne Beck, of the Victims Resource Center, pours red sand into the grooves of a brick in a park in Wilkes-Barre, Pennsylvania, as a symbol of those who have fallen victim to human trafficking. The event was hosted by the Victims Resource Center for World Trafficking Day.

society. These institutions provide the infrastructure of a truly global system in which it is possible to think about a global common good and a world where human interests trump national interests. There are three pillars of global governance (Muldoon 2004):

1. A political pillar that includes diplomacy, international law, and global and regional organizations like the United Nations, the WTO, and the European Union.
2. An economic pillar that includes MNCs, international banking and industry associations, global labor movements, and global economic movements.
3. A social pillar that includes actors within the global civil society, such as INGOs, and global social movements.

International and regional organizations play a critical role in governing the policy areas that transcend the nation-state. The effectiveness and perhaps the fairness of global policy will often depend on the efficacy of international law. Thus, all these institutions play a role in the governance of this global society.

The capacity of the United Nations in its economic and social work, its development work, and its management of peacekeeping and postconflict reconstruction has expanded since the 1990s. Nonetheless, further changes and adaptations within the UN system are necessary.

With regard to regional organizations, the European Union is the best example of how far the integration process can go and how much sovereignty states are willing to share or surrender. However, the prospect of an ever-wider European Union has raised serious questions about the nature and direction of the integration process.

Nongovernmental actors can also play an important role in making international society work. NGOs can hold governments accountable for their international commitments in a number of ways. Using modern communications methods, transnational social movements can call attention to a problem, recruit members to help, and bring needed relief, often faster than states are able to mobilize. However, nongovernmental actors do not have the stability that most states do, and their effectiveness can vary dramatically from year to year, from region to region, because their support and structure are entirely member dependent.

For all the reasons we have outlined in this chapter, international law, international organizations, and INGOs remain important elements in our discussions about the future of international politics. Nation-states are not the only actors, and NGOs, MNCs, and criminal networks play an increasingly important role in shaping the foreign policy of nation-states. These nonstate actors are shaping the international agenda and forcing states to pay attention to their actions.

A World Order Without Arms?

Much of what we write about in international relations is inspired by or a reaction to realist thinking. Realism and power politics tend to be the coin of the realm, In fact, the well-known realist Henry Kissinger, in his book *World Order* (2014), states clearly that "a reconstruction of the international system is the ultimate challenge in our time." Kissinger tells us that every international order is challenged by any shift in the balance of power and the legitimacy of the state itself. It may not help that global economy and processes of globalization may undermine the power and authority of the state. Richard Falk, one of the founding members of the World Order Models Project, is a modern-day Kantian who advocates for a new global order and a humanitarian foreign policy in his book *Power Shift: On the New Global Order* (2016).

Falk's humanitarian foreign policy differs from a traditional realist foreign policy in many ways. It seeks to focus on human interests, not just national interests, and seeks a global order different than balance of power. Falk supports opening up the foreign policy process to all interests and actors. Foreign policy should not be controlled exclusively by elites. Youth, women, and marginalized groups need to be brought into the process. The present system and the foreign policy process cannot effectively address issues of war, peace, and human security. What is needed is a transformative movement and a new geopolitics that replaces the "present logic of world order" that secures structures of authority based on realist ideas and practices, including sovereignty, hierarchy, inequality, and the exploitation of the weak and the powerless (111).

As a Kantian, Falk is a believer in democratic principles and universal or cosmopolitan rights that require "insurgent reason" and developing and practicing "normative knowledge." The World Order Models Project promoted foreign policies based on peace, social justice, economic well-being, and environmental sustainability. To achieve these goals, the world needs to think beyond incremental change and focus on transformation. His book ends with a quote attributed to St. Francis: *Start by doing what is necessary, then what is possible and suddenly you are doing the impossible* (128).

CONTRIBUTORS TO CHAPTER 5: *Devon Curtis, Christian Reus-Smit, Paul Taylor, Steven L. Lamy, and John Masker*

KEY TERMS

African Union (AU), p. 197
Civil society, p. 198
Collective security, p. 177
Economic sanctions, p. 180
European Union (EU), p. 193
Global governance, p. 169
Human security, p. 186
International Court of Justice (ICJ), p. 182
International institution, p. 171
International law, p. 170

International nongovernmental organization (INGO), p. 198
International organization, p. 171
Intervention, p. 187
League of Nations, p. 177
Multilateral diplomacy, p. 172
Multilateralism, p. 169

Multinational corporation or enterprise (MNC/MNE), p. 200
Nongovernmental organization (NGO), p. 203
Nonstate actor, p. 169
Organization of African Unity (OAU), p. 197
Organization of American States (OAS), p. 197
Peace enforcement, p. 184

Peacekeeping, p. 184
Peacemaking, p. 184
Postconflict peacebuilding, p. 184
Preventive diplomacy, p. 184
Regime, p. 170
Responsibility to Protect Resolution (R2P), p. 176
Social movement, p. 199
State sovereignty, p. 176
Supranational global organization, p. 176

Transnational advocacy
    network (TAN), p. 199
United Nations, p. 176
United Nations Charter,
    p. 177

United Nations Economic
    and Social Council
    (ECOSOC), p. 181
United Nations General
    Assembly, p. 189

United Nations Secretariat,
    p. 181
United Nations Security
    Council, p. 178

United Nations Trusteeship
    Council, p. 182
Venture philanthropy,
    p. 210
Veto power, p. 180

REVIEW QUESTIONS

1. Can you think of other factors, in addition to the ones listed in the chapter, that contributed to the rise of modern international law in the past two centuries?

2. Do you find the argument that states create institutions to sustain international order persuasive?

3. What do you think are the strengths and weaknesses of the international legal system?

4. What have been the driving forces behind processes of regional integration and cooperation?

5. What impact have processes of regional integration had on the state?

6. Compare and contrast European integration with regional cooperation in other areas of the world.

7. How does the United Nations try to maintain world order?

8. How has UN peacekeeping evolved?

Learn more with this chapter's digital tools, including the Oxford Insight Study Guide, at **www.oup.com/he/lamy6e**.

THINKING ABOUT GLOBAL POLITICS

Who Could Help Tomorrow? Twenty Global Problems and Global Issues Networks

This is a *problem-based* exercise that simply asks you to consider which public, private, and civil-society actors should pool their resources and effectively respond to global problems. The idea for this comes from a book by J. F. Rischard, *High Noon: Twenty Global Problems, Twenty Years to Solve Them* (2002). He is a former vice president of the World Bank, and his book has been at the center of discussion at several major global conferences. Now, it is your turn to think about these issues and possible solutions. Rischard believes that two major stresses present unprecedented problems and opportunities. These two stresses are demographic changes, including population growth and income distribution, and the new global economy, which includes a technological revolution and the globalization of production, trade, and investment. These stress factors contribute to a number of global issues or challenges that require the attention

of all citizens of the world. Here are the three issue areas and some specific challenges in each category:

- Sharing our planet: Issues involving the global commons—**global warming, biodiversity and ecosystem losses, fisheries depletion, deforestation, water deficits, and maritime safety and pollution.**

- Sharing our humanity: Issues requiring a global commitment—**poverty, peacekeeping, conflict prevention, counterterrorism, education for all, global infectious diseases, the digital divide, and natural-disaster prevention and mitigation.**

- Sharing our rulebook: Issues needing a global regulatory approach—**reinventing taxation for the twenty-first century; biotechnology rules; global financial architecture; illegal drugs; trade, investment, and competition rules; intellectual property rights; e-commerce rules; and international labor laws and migration rules.**

continued

Who can help to solve or manage these problems? How about a coalition of public, private, and civil-society actors? According to Rischard, partnerships like these are the only way forward. Global coalitions or global information networks (GINs) are similar in purpose to TANs and TSMOs. Each GIN enlists members from governments, international civil-society organizations, and businesses to address the issues that challenge global stability and often create real human-security problems.

In small groups of three or four, identify one of the problems or challenges in the three preceding categories. In your group, discuss the nature of the problem and identify actors who you think could help respond to it. You need at least two actors in each of the three categories (six total actors): two governments, two NGOs, and two businesses.

This is your problem-solving coalition, or GIN. Why did you select these actors? What resources or expertise do they bring to the problem-solving activities? How will each actor participate in the situation? How will each solve or manage the problem?

For example, if water pollution is the issue, maybe you should involve Canada and Saudi Arabia. Canada has large supplies of clean water, and Saudi Arabia has money to pay for the program and a need for water. NGOs might include the Global Water Campaign and Oxfam; businesses that sell water, like Nestlé and Coca-Cola, might also have skills, interests, and resources.

Your assignment is to put together the most effective coalition to respond to the potential crisis and tell us how it will work.

6 Global Security, Military Power, and Terrorism

The Middle East remains a region of conflict and war, and the United States maintains a military presence in several areas. Here the aircraft carrier USS *Abraham Lincoln* transits the Suez Canal in Egypt. The United States sent naval vessels to the region to protect oil tankers from being attacked by Iranian forces. US military dominance in this region is being challenged by new technologies and a new round of great-power competition.

Only the dead have seen the end of war.

—PLATO

War exposes the capacity for evil that lurks not far below the surface within all of us. And this is why for many, war is so hard to discuss once it is over.

—CHRIS HEDGES

Wars in the twenty-first century have been and continue to be conflicts within failed or fragile states. About 39 percent of these conflicts are in Africa, another 39 percent are in Asia, and most of the rest are in the Middle East. The current civil war in Syria, which began in 2011, is both an ideological and ethnic conflict that has global implications. The December 2015 attacks in San Bernardino, California, were blamed on the Islamic State and, like the attacks in Paris in November 2015, were in retaliation for US and French participation in the Syrian civil war. A recent study by the Institute for Economics and Peace states that conflicts killed 180,000 in 2014, and the total costs of these conflicts equaled 13.4 percent of the world's gross domestic product (GDP); the deadliest wars were in Syria and Iraq. More recent figures suggest that global violence costs 12.4 percent of global GDP, or $1,988 per person. The Islamic State seized territory in several Middle East countries and slaughtered their rivals and civilians they labeled as nonbelievers. Radical or extremist Islamist groups like the Taliban in Afghanistan and Pakistan, Boko Haram in Nigeria, and Al-Shabaab in other African states are engaged in violent attacks undermining the power and authority of very weak states. Although the Islamic State may have lost their territory or their caliphate, their followers are still fighting in several countries around the region pushing their extremist positions. The US withdrawal of troops in this region actually allowed many ISIS fighters to escape prisons and return to the battlefield.

Consider the war in the Democratic Republic of the Congo, which is the world's most lethal conflict since World War II. It has lasted more than sixteen years—although several rebel groups agreed to a ceasefire in late 2013—and taken the lives of over 5.4 million people,

CHAPTER OUTLINE

Introduction 221

What Is "Security"? 222

Mainstream and Critical Approaches to Security 224

The Changing Character of War 230

Nuclear Proliferation and Nonproliferation 240

Terrorism and Extremism 248

Terrorism: From Domestic to Global Phenomenon 251

The Impact of Globalization on Terrorism 253

Globalization, Technology, and Terrorism 261

Combating Terrorism 263

Conclusion 265

FEATURES

CASE STUDY US Drone Warfare: A Robotic Revolution in Modern Combat 238

THEORY IN PRACTICE The Realist-Theory Perspective and the War on Terrorism 250

THEORY IN PRACTICE The Shanghai Cooperation Organization: Fighting Terrorism in the Former Communist Bloc 255

WHAT'S TRENDING? New Strategies and Tools of War 266

THINKING ABOUT GLOBAL POLITICS Perspectives on the Arms Race 267

LEARNING OBJECTIVES

After reading and discussing this chapter, you should be able to:

Define and explain different theoretical views of security.

Explain the changes in warfare in recent years, sometimes called the "revolution in military affairs."

Define hybrid warfare and learn about other new war-fighting strategies.

Discuss the threat that nuclear weapon proliferation poses to international peace.

Define terrorism, including the role of perception in defining which groups are "terrorists" and which are legitimate groups that use unconventional methods.

Define the law-enforcement and war-on-terrorism approaches to fighting terrorists.

including an estimated 2.7 million children. Some twenty rebel groups and armies from nine nation-states are fighting in a territory as large as all of Western Europe, often committing acts of sexual violence in their assaults. Ethnic or tribal disputes, poverty, and the lust for power and treasure all contribute to this war. Fundamentally, there is no government to respond, and even twenty thousand UN peacekeepers have been unable to contain the conflict. In December 2013, the eighth UN peacekeeping mission in Africa began operations in the Central African Republic. The primary goal of the mission was to stop the sectarian violence where Muslim and Christian groups preyed on each other, creating what UN officials called "pregenocidal" conditions. Human Rights Watch reports that since September 2015, at least one hundred people have died in this ongoing ethnic violence, and efforts aimed at creating peace and stability are undermined by violence between Muslim Seleka rebels and the "anti-balaka" Christian militia. Civil wars and sectarian conflicts like those in the Democratic Republic of the Congo and the Central African Republic present the biggest security challenges to those who seek global order. Even some of the more stable states in this region of Africa are now facing human rights abuses and violence. Cameroon is dealing with secessionist movements in the English-speaking region and is under attacks by another Islamic militant group, Boko Haram. Over 600,000 citizens of Cameroon have been displaced and several hundred have been killed in this region since 2017. Internal violence, extremist groups, and civil wars are changing the nature of warfare and forcing nation-states to adapt new strategies for fighting wars.

Ungoverned territory in Africa, the Middle East, and Asia will present the world with the greatest number of security challenges. However, pariah states like North Korea and Iran that challenge the nuclear nonproliferation regime present more existential challenges. The entire world will suffer if the ruling states cannot cooperate to control weapons of mass destruction.

We have entered a period where the shape of war is changing. Nation-states are now unlikely to engage in wars of choice. The era of deploying large armies to fight large land wars might be over, replaced by precision strikes and drone raids and hybrid warfare that includes cyberattacks, social media propaganda, economic sabotage, and proxy wars. The new type of warfare lasts for years, is financially draining, costs thousands or even millions of lives, and poses extraordinary defensive challenges.

Although we seem to have become complacent over nuclear proliferation and the chances of a nuclear confrontation, the chances of a nuclear confrontation are still very real. Authoritarian states like North Korea and Iran are seeking to defend their interests in what they perceive as hostile environments, and nuclear powers like India and Pakistan are at each other's throats because of longstanding disputes over Kashmir. We must not forget that there are radicals always in the market for weapons of mass destruction, and Russia, China, and Iran are using what are called *gray zone* tactics to undermine political stability in the United States and other Western countries. For example, social media outlets are being used to promote populist groups and widen divisions within societies to weaken Western political systems.

Our material interests and lifestyle choices, if not our moral responsibilities, draw us all into these conflicts. For whatever reason, war has been a feature of life for most of recorded history. In this chapter, we examine national security, international or global security, terrorism, and conflict from a number of academic perspectives. We will try to determine whether the arena of human conflict has changed in an age of globalization.

▶ Introduction

Is global security, meaning a world without war and extremist violence, possible to achieve? For much of the intellectual history of the world, a debate has raged about the causes of war. For some writers, especially historians, the causes of war are unique to each case. Other writers believe that it is possible to provide a wider, more generalized explanation. Some analysts, for example, see the causes lying in human nature, others in the outcome of the internal organization of states, and yet others in international anarchy.

The end of the Cold War reshaped the debate. Some liberal theorists—including Grotian and Kantian versions of liberal thinking (discussed in Chapter 3)—claimed to see the dawn of a new world order. For other analysts, however, realism or neorealism remained the best approach to thinking about international security. In their view, very little of substance had changed as a result of the events of 1989. The end of the Cold War initially brought into existence a new, more cooperative era between the superpowers. However, this more harmonious phase was only temporary, because countries still interacted in an anarchic international system. For the thousands of people who have died, events seemed to support the realist and neorealist worldviews. With the first Gulf War (1990–1991), the ongoing civil wars in Africa and Asia, the 9/11 attacks, and the wars in Afghanistan, Iraq, Syria, and now Yemen, it became increasingly clear that states and nonstate actors (including international

Security The measures taken by states to ensure the safety of their citizens, the protection of their way of life, and the survival of their nation-state. Security can also mean the ownership of property that gives an individual the ability to secure the enjoyment or enforcement of a right or a basic human need.

National security A fundamental value in the foreign policy of states secured by a variety of tools of statecraft, including military actions, diplomacy, economic resources, and international agreements and alliances. It also depends on a stable and productive domestic society.

Widening school of international security Sometimes called the Copenhagen school, these are authors who extend the definition of security to include economic, political, societal, and environmental policy areas.

terrorist groups or networks) continued to view the use of force and violence as an effective way to achieve their objectives.

We begin with a look at the basic definitions and disagreements central to the field, including what is meant by *security*, and we explore the relationship between national and global security. Then we examine the traditional ways of thinking about national security, and the influence these ideas about national security have had on contemporary thinking. We follow this examination with a survey of alternative ideas and approaches that have emerged in the literature in recent years. Next we turn to the pressing question of nuclear weapons proliferation, including a brief overview of these weapons and a discussion of attempts to prevent their spread in the years after the Cold War. Finally, we discuss a transnational trend—terrorism—that has changed the nature of global conflict and security.

What Is "Security"?

Most writers agree that **security** is a contested concept. There is a consensus that it implies freedom from threats to core values (for both individuals and groups), but there is a major disagreement about whether the main focus of inquiry should be on *individual*, *national*, or *international* security. During the Cold War period, most writing on the subject was dominated by the idea of **national security** and the realist model that asserts states should develop military capabilities to deal with the threats they confront. More recently, however, a number of contemporary writers have argued for an expanded conception of security outward from the limits of parochial national security to include a range of other considerations and avoid ethnocentrism. This conception is known as the **widening school of international security** because of proponents' desire to widen the definition to include economic, political, social, and even environmental issues as part of a global security agenda.

Further, not all who study security issues focus on the tension between national and international security (see Table 6.1). Some argue that such an emphasis ignores the fundamental changes that have been taking place in world politics. Others argue that much more attention should be given to "societal security," the idea that growing regional integration is undermining the classical political order based on nation-states, leaving states exposed within larger political frameworks. We see this development in the European Union, and plans for an expanded and more effective African Union might indicate a similar trend in the Western Hemisphere. At the same time, the fragmentation of various

Innocent civilians are often the target of extremist groups. In this photo, schoolgirls abducted by Boko Haram are being released. Nigerian security forces have not been very effective in stopping such criminal acts by extremists. How do armed forces protect citizens in ungoverned territories?

TABLE 6.1	**Comparing Worldviews**

View of National Security as a Policy Issue

Realist	Liberal (Grotian)	Global Humanist (Kantian Liberals)	Marxist
• Military power is essential in supporting the primary objective of a state's national interest: survival. • In an anarchic, state-centric system, war is inevitable. • Self-help: no other state or institution can be relied on to guarantee your survival.	• Nations should practice collective security as a means of cooperation and assured protection of national interest, sharing the use of resources. • Nations have shared responsibility for foreign policy successes and failures. • Wars undertaken for purposes of expediency are unjust. Defense of life and defense of property are just causes, but if the cause of war is unjust, all acts arising from it are immoral.* • Anticipatory self-defense is forbidden. • Complete security is impossible.	• Arms reduction is a desirable step toward disarmament. • The international norm against the use of nuclear weapons should be strengthened. • Security policy should be guided by a sense of human solidarity that transcends the nation rather than by a desire to maximize national military power. • Human interest should take priority over national interest.	• National security is the protection of those who own the means of production. • There is no need for a large, oppressive military force if people are not oppressed and exploited by a small and powerful group of capitalist elites. • Inequality is the main security threat in the global system.

Murphy, Cornelius F., Jr. "The Grotian Vision of World Order." American Journal of International Law *Jul. 76.3 (1982): 477–498. JSTOR. Web. Sept. 31, 2011. 481. http://www.jstor.org/stable/2200783.*

states, like the Soviet Union and Yugoslavia, has created new problems of boundaries, minorities, and organizing ideologies that are causing increasing regional instability (Weaver et al. 1993, 196). These dual processes of integration and fragmentation have led to the argument that ethnonationalist groups, rather than states, should become the center of attention for security analysts.

Disagreements about definitions of security matter, because these academic arguments often influence the policy decisions that political leaders make. If political leaders believe their primary responsibility is national security, then building a safe international system for all countries is of secondary importance. Barry Buzan (1991) concisely describes the security challenge:

> In the case of security, the discussion is about the pursuit of freedom from threat. When this discussion is in the context of the international system, security is about the ability of states and societies to maintain their independent identity and their functional integrity.

Today, many security specialists suggest that the most important contemporary trend is the broad process of **globalization** that is taking place. Globalization challenges what we expect a nation-state to provide its citizens. It might hinder the ability of leaders to protect boundaries, provide order at home, and maintain and promote a productive economic system. We learned in Chapter 1 that the process of globalization challenges a state's legitimacy, efficiency, and identity, which brings

Globalization A historical process involving a fundamental shift or transformation in the spatial scale of human social organization that links distant communities and expands the reach of power relations across regions and continents.

Terrorism The use of violence by nonstate groups or, in some cases, states to inspire fear by attacking civilians and/or symbolic targets and eliminating opposition groups. This is done for purposes such as drawing widespread attention to a grievance, provoking a severe response, or wearing down an opponent's moral resolve to effect political change.

Community A human association in which members share common symbols and wish to cooperate to realize common objectives.

new risks and dangers. These include the increase in radical or extremist groups who are willing to use **terrorism** across the world, global climate change, a breakdown of the global monetary system, and the proliferation of weapons of mass destruction. These threats to security, on a global level, are viewed as being largely outside the control of a single state or groups of nation-states. Theorists believe only the development of a global security **community** can deal with such threats adequately.

In the aftermath of 9/11, Jonathan Friedman (2003, ix) argued that we are living in a world

> *where polarization, both vertical and horizontal, both class and ethnic, has become rampant, and where violence has become more globalized and fragmented at the same time, and is no longer a question of wars between states but of sub-state conflicts, globally networked and financed, in which states have become one actor, increasingly privatized, amongst others.*

Many feel that the post-9/11 era is a new and extremely dangerous period in world history. However, whether the world today is so different from the past is a matter of much contemporary discussion. To consider the current meaning of security, we need to look at the way security has been traditionally conceived.

Mainstream and Critical Approaches to Security

As we discussed in Chapter 2, from the Peace of Westphalia onward, states have been regarded as the only legitimate, and by far the most powerful, actors in the international system. They have been the universal standard of political legitimacy, with no higher authority to regulate their interactions with one another. States have therefore taken the view that there is no alternative but to seek their own protection in what has been described as a self-help world. For most modern political leaders and academics, realism has been the analytic lens best suited to understanding war and security; other lenses that we discuss in the chapter must all respond to realism.

We also saw in Chapter 3 that many academics have developed theories attempting to explain international politics as something other than a struggle among power-seeking countries. These alternatives to both realism and some strains of liberalism have become vibrant intellectual challenges to those mainstream ideas about the causes of war and peace.

Failed or fragile states present many security challenges. In this photo, UN peacekeepers in Kinshasa, Democratic Republic of Congo, patrol during an election campaign with a campaign poster for Joseph Kabila in the background. The government of the Democratic Republic of Congo is corrupt and is failing to provide most of its citizens with economic, political, or human security.

Realist and Neorealist Views on Global Security

The historical debate about how best to achieve national security tends to paint a rather pessimistic picture of the implications of state sovereignty. Realists viewed the international system as a brutal arena in which states would seek to achieve their own security at the expense of their neighbors. According to this view, permanent peace was unlikely to be achieved. All that states could do was try to balance the power of other states to prevent any one state from achieving overall hegemony.

Structural realism, a permutation of realism, argues that states tend to act aggressively toward one another because of the following:

- The international system is anarchic, which implies that there is no central authority capable of controlling state behavior.
- States claiming sovereignty will inevitably develop offensive military capabilities to defend themselves and extend their power. Hence, they are potentially dangerous to one another.
- Uncertainty, leading to a lack of trust, is inherent in the international system. States can never be sure of the intentions of their neighbors, and therefore, they must always be on their guard.
- States will want to maintain their independence and sovereignty, and as a result, survival will be the most basic driving force influencing their behavior.
- Although states are rational, they will often make miscalculations. In a world of imperfect information, potential antagonists will always have an incentive to misrepresent their own capabilities to keep their opponents guessing. This may lead to mistakes about real national interests.

According to this view, national security (or insecurity) is largely the result of the anarchic structure of the international system. The implication is that international politics in the future is likely to be as violent as international politics in the past. In a 1990 article entitled "Back to the Future," John Mearsheimer argued that the end of the Cold War was likely to usher in a return to the traditional multilateral, balance-of-power politics of the past. Mearsheimer viewed the Cold War as a period of peace and stability brought about by the bipolar structure of power that prevailed. With the collapse of this system, he argued that extreme nationalism and ethnic rivalries would lead to widespread instability and conflict, reflective of the kind of great-power rivalries that had blighted international relations since the seventeenth century.

Indeed, most contemporary neorealists or structural-realist writers see little prospect of a significant improvement in security in the post–Cold War world. The 1991 Gulf War; the violent disintegration of the former Yugoslavia and parts of the former Soviet Union; continuing violence in the Middle East, especially in Syria and Yemen; and the wars in Afghanistan and Iraq after the 2003 invasion all support the notion that we continue to live in a world of mistrust and constant security competition. They suggest there are two main factors that continue to make cooperation difficult. The first is the prospect of cheating; the second is the concern states have regarding relative gains.

Neorealists do not deny that states often cooperate or that in the post–Cold War era there are even greater opportunities than in the past for states to work together. They argue, however, that there are distinct limits to this cooperation because the people who lead states have always been and remain fearful that others will attempt to gain advantages by cheating on any agreements reached. This risk is regarded as particularly important given the nature of modern military technology, which can bring about very rapid shifts in the balance of power between states. "Such a development," Mearsheimer has argued, "could create a window of opportunity for the cheating side to inflict a decisive defeat on the victim state" (1994–1995, 20). States realize that this is the case, and although they join alliances and sign arms control agreements, they remain cautious and aware of the need to provide for their own national security in the last resort.

Cooperation is also inhibited, according to many neorealist writers, because states tend to be concerned with **relative gains** rather than **absolute gains**. Instead of being interested in cooperation because it will benefit both partners, states always need to be aware of how much they are gaining compared with the cooperating state. Because all states will attempt to maximize their gains in a competitive, mistrustful, and uncertain international environment, the thinking goes, cooperation will always be very difficult to achieve and hard to maintain.

Liberal Institutionalist Views on Global Security

One of the main characteristics of the neorealist approach to global security is the belief that international institutions do not play a very important role in the prevention of war. Institutions are seen as the product of state interests and the constraints imposed by the international system. According to this view, interests and constraints shape decisions on whether to cooperate or compete, not the institutions.

Political leaders and international relations specialists have challenged such views. British foreign secretary Douglas Hurd, for example, made the case in June 1992 that institutions had played, and continued to play, a crucial role in enhancing security, particularly in Europe. He argued that the West had developed "a set of international institutions which have proved their worth for one set of problems" (Hurd, quoted in Mearsheimer 1994–1995). He argued that the great challenge of the post–Cold War era was to adapt these institutions to deal with the new circumstances that prevailed.

Hurd and other Western leaders believed that a framework of complementary, mutually reinforcing institutions—such as the European Union (EU), the **North Atlantic Treaty Organization (NATO)**, the Western European Union, and the Organization for Security and Co-operation in Europe—could be developed to promote a more durable and stable European security system for the post–Cold War era. Although the past may have been characterized by frequent wars and conflict, they see important changes taking place in international relations that may relax the

Relative gains One of the factors that realists argue constrain the willingness of states to cooperate. States are less concerned about whether everyone benefits (absolute gains) and more concerned about whether someone may benefit more than someone else.

Absolute gains The notion that all states seek to have more power and influence in the system to secure their national interests. Offensive neorealists are also concerned with increasing power relative to other states. One must have enough power to secure interests and more power than any other state in the system—friend or foe.

North Atlantic Treaty Organization (NATO) Organization established by treaty in April 1949 including twelve (later sixteen) countries from Western Europe and North America. The most important aspect of the NATO alliance was the US commitment to defend Western Europe. Today NATO has twenty-eight member states.

traditional security competition among states. This approach, known as liberal institutionalism, argues that international institutions are much more important in helping achieve global cooperation and stability than structural realists realize (see Chapter 3 and 5). Certainly, the fact that there has not been a war in Western Europe in more than seventy years supports this perspective. Supporters also point to the developments within the European Union and NATO in the post–Cold War era and claim that, by investing major resources, states clearly demonstrate their belief in the importance of institutions. The creation of the Eurozone of shared currency and NATO's deployment of troops outside Europe also provide evidence of this trend.

Russia has used "gray zone" tactics in its war with Ukraine. Such tactics include cyberattacks, sabotage, subversion, sponsoring proxy wars, and even military interventions. In this photo Ukrainian soldiers dig trenches as they fight Russian proxy troops.

As such, the liberal-institutionalist approach suggests that international institutions operating on the basis of reciprocity will be a component of any lasting peace. Although international institutions themselves are unlikely to eradicate war from the international system, they can play a part in helping achieve greater cooperation among states.

One question liberal institutionalists might examine is why war is absent in some parts of the contemporary world. The North Atlantic region, for example, has been described as a **security community**, a group of states for whom war has disappeared as a means of resolving disputes with one another, although they may continue to use war against opponents outside the security community. One common characteristic of these states is that they are all democracies, and it has been suggested that although democracies will go to war, they are not prepared to fight against another democracy. As we discussed in Chapter 3, the **democratic peace thesis** argues that where groups of democracies inhabit a region, war will become extinct in that region, and as democracy spreads throughout the world, war will decline. However, we must keep in mind the danger that wars will occur as democracies attempt to overthrow nondemocratic regimes in attempts to spread democracy. When the Bush administration invaded Iraq in 2003, they argued that a democratic Iraq would become the seed from which democracy and therefore peace would grow in the Middle East. In cases like this, war ends up being fought in the name of peace.

The Constructivist Approach to Global Security

Constructivists often assert that international relations are affected not only by power politics but also by ideas. This assertion places most constructivist thinkers in the liberal tradition. According to this view, the fundamental structures of international politics are **social** rather than strictly **material**. Constructivists therefore argue that changes in the nature of social interaction between states can bring a fundamental shift toward greater international security.

Security community A regional group of countries that have the same guiding philosophical ideals—usually liberal-democratic principles, norms, values, and traditions—and tend to have the same style of political systems.

Democratic peace thesis A central plank of liberal-internationalist thought, the democratic peace thesis makes two claims: first, liberal polities exhibit restraint in their relations with other liberal polities (the so-called separate peace), but second, they are imprudent in relations with authoritarian states. The validity of the democratic peace thesis has been fiercely debated in the international relations literature.

Social movement A mode of collective action that challenges ways of life, thinking, dominant norms, and moral codes; seeks answers to global problems; and promotes reform or transformation in political and economic institutions.

Material Things we can see, measure, consume, and use, such as military forces, oil, and currency.

Constructivists think about international politics very differently than neo-realists. The latter tend to view structure as made up only of a distribution of material capabilities. Constructivists, on the other hand, view structure as the product of social relationships. Social structures are made possible by shared knowledge, material resources, and practices. According to this perspective, the security dilemma is a social structure in which leaders of states are so distrustful that they make worst-case assumptions about one another's intentions. As a result, they define their interests in "self-help" terms. In contrast, a security community is a social structure composed of shared knowledge in which states trust one another to resolve disputes without war.

The emphasis on the structure of shared knowledge is important in constructivist thinking. Social structures include material things, like tanks and economic resources, but these acquire meaning only through the shared knowledge in which they are embedded. The idea of power politics, or **realpolitik**, has meaning to the extent that states accept the idea as a basic rule of international politics. According to social-constructivist writers, power politics is an idea that does affect the way states behave, but it does not describe all interstate behavior. States are also influenced by other ideas and **norms**, such as the rule of law and the importance of institutional cooperation and restraint.

Realpolitik First used to describe the foreign policy of Bismarck in Prussia, it describes the practice of diplomacy based on the assessment of power, territory, and material interests, with little concern for ethical realities.

Norms These specify general standards of behavior and identify the rights and obligations of states. Together, norms and principles define the essential character of a regime, and these cannot be changed without transforming the nature of the regime.

Although constructivists argue that security dilemmas are not ruled by fate—or any higher autonomous power—they differ over whether they can be escaped. For some, the fact that structures are socially constructed does not necessarily mean that they can be changed. Many constructivists, however, are more optimistic. They point to the changes in ideas represented by perestroika and glasnost. These concepts, which Soviet Communist Party general secretary Mikhail Gorbachev introduced in the USSR during the second half of the 1980s, led to a shared knowledge about the end of the Cold War. Once both sides accepted that the Cold War was over, it really was over. According to this view, understanding the crucial role of social structure is important in developing policies and processes of interaction that will lead toward cooperation rather than conflict. If there are opportunities for promoting social change, most constructivists believe it would be irresponsible not to pursue such policies.

The Feminist Approach to Global Security

Although constructivists and realists disagree about the relationship between ideas and material factors, they tend to agree on the central role of the state in debates about international security. Other theorists, however, believe that the state has been given too much prominence. Keith Krause and Michael C. Williams (1997, 34) have defined critical security studies in the following terms:

> *Contemporary debates over the nature of security often float on a sea of unvoiced assumptions and deeper theoretical issues concerning to what and to whom the term security refers.... What most contributions to the debate thus share are two inter-related concerns: what security is and how we study it.*

What they also share is a wish to de-emphasize the role of the state and to reconceptualize security. For critical-security theorists, states should not be the center of analysis, because not only are they extremely diverse in character but also they are often part of the problem of insecurity in the international system. While they can be providers of security, they can also be a source of threat to their own people. Therefore, attention should be focused on the individual rather than the state. Although a number of different approaches make up critical security studies, the feminist approach is one that challenges the traditional emphasis on the central role of the state in studies of international security. Although there are significant differences among feminist theorists, all share the view that books and articles on international politics in general, and international security in particular, have been written from a "masculine" point of view. In her work, Ann Tickner (1992, 191) argues that women have "seldom been recognized by the security literature" despite the fact that conflicts affect women as much as, if not more than, men. The vast majority of casualties and refugees in war are women and children, and the rape of women is often used as a tool of war (see Chapter 7).

Feminist writers argue that if gender is brought more explicitly into the study of security, not only will new issues and critical perspectives be added to the security agenda but also the result will be a fundamentally different view of the nature of international security. If we look at the language used to describe war, we can see one way security is gendered. As Carol Cohn wrote in her essay "Sex and Death in the Rational World of Defense Intellectuals" (1987), the world of defense policymaking tends to be dominated by men who employ sexual and other euphemisms to describe their work. These include "servicing the target" instead of "bombing it"; "collateral damage" instead of "dead civilians"; "patting the missile" instead of "getting a tour of a Trident missile–carrying submarine." Cohn and others write that this is the result of war being "man's work."

Contemporary conflicts like those in Bosnia and Sudan pose a critical problem for the international community of whether to intervene in the domestic affairs of sovereign states to safeguard minority and individual human rights (see Chapter 7). This dilemma reflects the historic transformation of human society that is taking place at the beginning of the twenty-first century. Many global theorists, especially feminist scholars and practitioners, argue that it is now increasingly necessary to think of the security of individuals and of groups within the emergent global society. Although states remain an important factor in the international system,

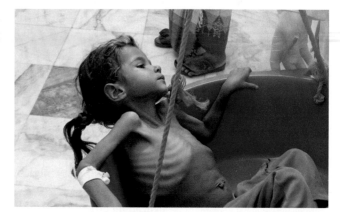

Feminist views on security strive to transfer the focus of war and conflict from states and sovereignty to the individuals affected by these wars and to human security. In this photo, a severely malnourished girl is weighed at the Aslam Health Center in Yemen. She is one of the millions dying of starvation in a civil war that involves Saudi Arabia, Iran, and indirectly the United States. Rivals in these wars often block any form of international aid.

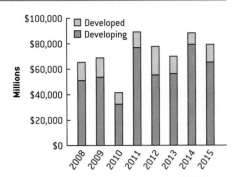

Arms Deliveries Worldwide (in Millions of Dollars).

Which region accounts for the most arms delivery—the North or the South? Based on what you have studied so far in this course, how would you explain the trends you see in this graph?

they are being transformed as they struggle to deal with the range of new challenges—including those of security—that face them.

Marxist and Radical Liberal or Utopian Approaches to Security

Marxists believe that capitalism is the source of most of the world's security problems. Workers are exploited, alienated, and estranged from their societies. Thus, workers in poor states are prime targets for radical leaders planning to challenge the rich and the powerful by overthrowing governments that repress the voices of those on the margins. In a global economy, Marxists represent workers around the world and support a transformation of the current economic and political system—or, as some might say, a global revolution. Globalization has spread capitalist ideas, as well as the ideas of those who see capitalism as a source of conflict and inequality. Marxist ideas have inspired many secular radicals who seek to create systems of governance that provide for basic human needs and address the inequalities within most societies. Although there are no states that are openly supporting Marxist revolutions, there are anarchist and Marxist terrorist networks and cells that present a security challenge to all states. For these groups, the source of insecurity is poverty and the denial of access to societal resources.

For radical liberals or utopians, the major security concern may be the **military-industrial complex**, a term coined by President Dwight D. Eisenhower as he warned the American public of the power and influence of the defense industries and their special relationship with the military. Part of this concern is over a strategic culture that emphasizes national security over human security. Current military budgets distract from efforts aimed at eliminating global poverty and providing for economic well-being and social justice. More than that, current military spending exacerbates the problems of environmental degradation and allows repressive elites to deny citizens basic human rights. Thus, for radical liberals, in a worldview that puts national interests over human interests, realist thinking is the source of insecurity.

▶ The Changing Character of War

Postmodernity An international system where domestic and international affairs are intertwined, national borders are permeable, and states have rejected the use of force for resolving conflict. The European Union is an example of the evolution of the state-centric system (Cooper 2003).

In the contemporary world, powerful pressures are significantly changing national economies and societies. Some of these pressures reflect the impact of globalization; others are the result of the broader effects of **postmodernity**, an international system where domestic and international affairs are intertwined. The cumulative effect has been to change perceptions of external threats. These changed perceptions have in turn influenced beliefs regarding the utility of force as an instrument of policy and the forms and functions of war. In the past two centuries, the modern era of history, some states have used war as a brutal form of politics (typified by the two world wars). In the post–Cold War period, however, the kinds of threats that have driven the accumulation of military power in the developed world have not taken the form of traditional state-to-state military rivalry. Instead, they have been more amorphous and less predictable threats such as terrorism, insurgencies, and internal crises in other countries.

Further, the battlefield has become battlespace and hybrid wars have become the norm. The Marine general Charles Krulak, quoted in Lawrence Freedman's book *The Future of War* (2017, 223), discusses the "three block war" as the requirements of the modern battlefield. What this means is that in the same day, all within three blocks, troops need to provide humanitarian assistance; engage in peacekeeping by keeping warring factions apart; and engage in a highly lethal battle. Other military leaders, like former secretary of defense General Mattis, talked about a four block war that included psychological and information operations.

In an era of unprecedented communications technologies, new fields of warfare have emerged. The tangible capacity for war making has also been developing. Military technology with enormous destructive capacity is becoming available to more and more states. This is important not just because the technology to produce and deliver **weapons of mass destruction (WMDs)** is spreading, but also because highly advanced conventional military technology is becoming more widely available. One of the effects of the end of the Cold War was that there was a massive process of disarmament by the former Cold War enemies. This surplus weaponry, much of it highly advanced equipment, flooded the global arms market and was sold off comparatively cheaply.

Weapons of mass destruction (WMDs) A category defined by the United Nations in 1948 to include "atomic explosive weapons, radioactive material weapons, lethal chemical and biological weapons, and any weapons developed in the future which have characteristics comparable in destructive effects to those of the atomic bomb or other weapons mentioned above."

The Nature of War

Wars are fought for reasons. The Western understanding of war, following the ideas of the Prussian military thinker and soldier Carl von Clausewitz, is that it is instrumental, a means to an end. Wars in this perspective are not random violence; they reflect a conscious decision to engage in them for a rational political purpose. Writing in the early 1800s, Clausewitz defined war as an act of violence intended to compel one's opponent to fulfill one's will. Often, people who initiate wars rationalize them by appealing to common belief and value systems. There are wide varieties of factors that can contribute to the outbreak of war, such as nationalism, class conflict, human nature, and so on. These are the main drivers of change rather than war itself. War is not something that is imposed by an outside force. The willingness to go to war comes from within states and societies.

One of Clausewitz's central arguments is that war is a form of social and political behavior. If we operate with a broad and flexible understanding of what constitutes politics, this remains true today. As our understanding of politics, and of the forms it can take, has evolved in the postmodern era, we should expect the same to be true of the character of war because that is itself a form of politics.

The political nature of war has been evolving in recent decades under the impact of globalization, which has increasingly eroded the economic, political,

Cooperative security can help keep the costs of war down and may even deter some aggressive states. NATO members provide security for Iceland. This photo shows a Czech JAS-39 Gripen fighter at the air base in Keflavik, Iceland. The Czech mission is to protect the Icelandic airspace since Iceland has no military but provides an excellent space for watching Russian military activities.

and cultural autonomy of the state. Contemporary warfare takes place in a local context, but it is also played out in wider fields and is influenced by nongovernmental organizations, intergovernmental organizations, regional and global media, and internet users. In many ways, contemporary wars are fought partly on television, and the media therefore have a powerful role in providing a framework of understanding for the viewers of the conflict. Reaching beyond the effect of 24/7 television news channels, Al Qaeda and ISIS, for instance, use the internet to disseminate propaganda. The award-winning documentary *Control Room* showed how the 2003 invasion of Iraq became an exercise in the US government trying to restrict the images a globalized audience saw on its televisions. One effect of the constant coverage of international violence by the global media may be to gradually weaken the legal, moral, and political constraints against the use of force by making it appear routine. The advent of such "war fatigue" might make recourse to war appear a normal feature of international relations.

Nevertheless, war, in terms of both preparation and its actual conduct, may be a powerful catalyst for change, but technological or even political modernization does not necessarily imply moral progress. Evolution in war, including its contemporary forms, may involve change that is morally problematic, as is the case with the forces of globalization more generally. War is a profound agent of historical change, but it is not the fundamental driving force of history. For many analysts, war's nature as the use of organized violence in pursuit of political goals always remains the same and is unaltered even by radical changes in political forms or in the motives leading to conflict, or by technological advances (Gray 1999, 169).

For Clausewitz and Gray, there is an important distinction between the *nature* and the *character* of war. The former refers to the constant, universal, and inherent qualities that ultimately define war throughout the ages, such as violence, chance, and uncertainty. The latter relates to the impermanent, circumstantial, and adaptive features that war develops and that account for the different periods of warfare throughout history, each displaying attributes determined by sociopolitical and historical preconditions while also influencing those conditions.

Revolution in military affairs (RMA) The effect generated by the marriage of advanced communications and information processing with state-of-the-art weapons and delivery systems. It is a means of overcoming the uncertainty and confusion that are part of any battle in war.

Tactics The conduct and management of military capabilities in or near the battle area.

A number of questions follow from this survey of war in relation to its contemporary and future forms. Does the current era have a dominant form of war, and if so, what is it? In what ways are the processes associated with globalization changing contemporary warfare? In what ways are the characteristics of postmodernity reflected in contemporary modes of warfare?

The Revolution in Military Affairs

Although many observers have suggested that the character of war is changing significantly, their reasons for coming to this conclusion are often quite different. One school of thought focuses on the concept of the **revolution in military affairs (RMA)**. This concept became popular after the American victory in the 1991 Gulf War. The manner in which superior technology and doctrine appeared to give the United States an almost effortless victory, if the Iraqi war deaths are ignored, suggested that future conflicts would be decided by the possession of technological advantages such as advanced guided weapons and space satellites. However, the subsequent popularity of the RMA concept has not produced a clear consensus on what exactly it is or what its implications might be. Although analysts agree that RMA involves a radical change or some form of discontinuity in the history of warfare, there is disagreement regarding how and when these changes or discontinuities take place or what their causes are.

Proponents of RMA argue that recent breakthroughs and likely future advances in military technology mean that military operations will be conducted with such speed, precision, and selective destruction that the whole character of war will change and this will profoundly affect the way military and political affairs are conducted. Most of the RMA literature focuses on the implications of developments in technology. In the conflicts in Kuwait (1991), Serbia (1999), and Iraq (2003), American technology proved vastly superior to that of the opponent. In particular, computing and space technology allowed the US forces to acquire information about the enemy to a degree never before seen in warfare and allowed precision targeting of weapon systems to destroy vital objectives without inflicting unnecessary casualties on civilians (although absolute precision and reliability proved impossible to achieve). Advanced communications allowed generals to exercise detailed and instant control over the developing battle and to respond quickly. Opponents lacking counters to these technologies found themselves helpless in the face of overwhelming American superiority. However, the RMA emphasis on military technology and **tactics** risks producing an oversimplified picture of what is an extremely complex phenomenon in which non-technological factors can play a crucial part in the outcome.

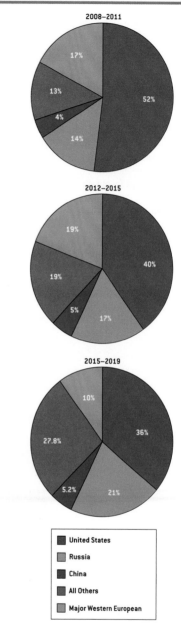

Arms Transfer Agreements Worldwide.

The conventional arms suppliers here are shown as percentages. Do you notice a shift between the two date ranges compared here? Is it significant? How would you explain the relative stability of conventional arms suppliers worldwide?

Asymmetric conflicts In symmetric warfare, armies with comparable weapons, tactics, and organizational structures do battle. Wars are fought on near-equal terms. When stakes are high and those actors in conflict are not equal in terms of weapons and technology, the weaker side adopts asymmetric tactics such as guerrilla warfare, roadside bombs, attacks on civilians, and other terrorist tactics.

Most of the literature and debate on RMA is based on a particularly Western concept of fighting in war and tends to take for granted the dominance conferred by technological superiority. The current RMA may be useful only in certain well-defined situations. For example, there is little discussion of what might happen if the United States were to fight a country with similar capabilities or that is able to deploy countermeasures. There has been far less discussion of how a state might use unconventional or asymmetric responses to fight effectively against a more technologically sophisticated opponent. Asymmetry works both ways. **Asymmetric conflicts** since 1990 have been fought by US-led coalitions against Iraq (in 1991 and again in 2003), Yugoslavia, Afghanistan, and Syria. Because of the extreme superiority in combat power of the coalition, the battle phases of these asymmetric conflicts have been fairly brief and have produced relatively few combat deaths compared with the Cold War period. However, in the postconventional insurgency phases in Iraq and Afghanistan, asymmetry has produced guerrilla-style conflict against the technological superiority of the coalition forces.

The conflicts in Iraq and Afghanistan (see the case study in this chapter) raised major questions about the pattern of warfare likely after RMA. US military supremacy across the combat spectrum does not translate well in wars against networks of radical terrorists. In Afghanistan, the United States has tried a counterinsurgency (COIN) strategy with mixed results. A COIN policy involves fighting the enemy and stabilizing the country by helping develop an effective government. A COIN strategy might include

TV screens showing a photo of North Korea's weapon systems and a meeting between South Korea's foreign minister, Kang Kyung-wha, and the US special representative for North Korea, Stephen Biegun. The US and South Korean militaries evaluated the two projectiles North Korea flew Thursday as short-range missiles. All the talks of peace and halting nuclear weapons development in North Korea appear to have resulted in no positive results. What about the US efforts to create peace in the region?

1. providing security for the local population and preventing attacks against civilians,
2. protecting infrastructure and providing safe regions for civilians,
3. helping local government provide basic services for citizens, and
4. helping shift loyalties from insurgents to local authorities.

COIN is expensive, and it requires patience and a commitment on the part of occupation forces (and the public who pay for it) to stay for a long time.

The Obama administration's drawdown in troop strength and the reluctance of some NATO allies to continue sending troops to combat regions in Afghanistan forced a shift from a more costly and time-consuming COIN policy to a more direct counterterrorism policy. Counterterrorism is more about direct military actions. It refers to the identification, tracking, and elimination of terrorist networks. This may be the future of warfare in asymmetric situations. A counterterrorism strategy includes

1. using technology to hunt and track the enemy,
2. sharing intelligence with other states, and
3. targeting insurgent leadership with unmanned drones and covert operations.

Counterterrorism is an aggressive way to fight wars, but it requires fewer troops than COIN and does not require a long-term commitment to state building.

In 2013, the Obama administration's rules of engagement stated that individuals must be a threat to American troops and any assault must leave civilians unharmed. The Trump administration has moved decision making on tactical issues from the White House to commanders in the field. The military has more freedom to make tactical decisions. Airstrikes were increased in the first six months of 2017, and the UN announced that civilian deaths were up by 70 percent. International relations scholar and former military officer Andrew Bacevich (2017) suggested that the current policy in both Iraq and Afghanistan is based on two assumptions that may result in an even larger and longer war. These assumptions are that:

1. sustained US military action is the only way of defeating terrorism, and
2. the physical presence of US troops in fragile and vulnerable Muslim-majority states makes them less hospitable to terrorist networks.

This means the United States and its remaining allies in Afghanistan and Iraq may continue to be involved in the nation-building

The global war on terrorism has created a great need for counterterrorism exercises by police and members of the military. In this photo German armed forces are standing during an exercise with police in the military training area in Brandenburg, Germany. These kinds of cooperative projects are happening across the world as terrorists are seen as both a law enforcement and national security problem.

process in countries where corruption, civil conflict, and ethnic rivalries may prevent any resolution and reconciliation by external forces.

Hybrid Warfare

Hybrid war was described in a recent *Economist* (2018) report on the future of war as the use of *gray zone* tactics that include cyberattacks, propaganda, subversion, economic blackmail, sabotage, sponsorship of proxy wars, and at times aggressive military expansion. Several nation-states, including Russia, China, and Iran, employ gray zone tactics to secure their interests. Russia's hybrid war strategy is to undermine the United States and the West and to encourage divisions within Western societies. Russia has supported the radical right populist movements and political parties throughout Europe. However, the best example of how these gray zone tactics or hybrid warfare works is how Russia used this strategy against Ukraine. Russia used propaganda to create opposition to the government; used cyberattacks on public utilities; engaged in covert operations; trained and provided military equipment to pro-Russian forces; and disrupted economic activities. A hybrid war strategy allows nation-states to overcome the military superiority of greater powers, including the United States. Key players in the cyberwar game are listed in Table 6.2.

Data breaches and malware attacks are a threat to governments, businesses, and private citizens. As our reliance on technology increases, so does the chance that our personal security and our national security may be at risk. Figure 6.1 shows significant cyber incidents.

Postmodern War

Global society is moving from the modern to the postmodern age. This process has been under way for several decades and is the result of a wide range of economic, cultural, social, and political changes that are altering the meaning of the "state" and the "nation." It has been marked by a shift from production to information as a core output of advanced economies. As this happens, it will affect the character of war.

In some parts of the world, the state is deliberately transferring functions, including military functions, to private authorities and businesses. Over the past decade, the "outsourcing" of war has become an increasing trend, as more and more states have contracted out key military services to privatized military firms (PMFs) like Academi (formerly known as Xe Services LLC, or Blackwater). These companies sell a wide range of war-related services to states, overwhelmingly in the logistical and security roles rather than direct combat. The growth of

TABLE 6.2	**Key Players in the Cyberwar Game**
North Korea	Bureau 121
China	PLA Unit 61398 (People's Liberation Army)
United States	DCLeaks
Russia	CyberVor, Fancy Bear, Shadow Brokers (suspected)
Iran	Iranian Cyber Army
Israel	NSO, Unit 8200
Unaffiliated	Anonymous, Lizard Squad, Ourmine, LulzSec, Hacking Team

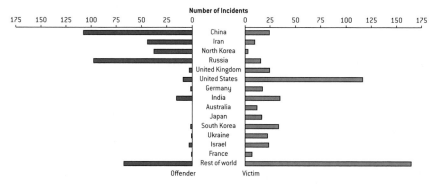

Figure 6.1 Significant Cyber Incidents.
Source: https://www.csis.org/programs/cybersecurity-and-governance/technology-policy-program/other-projects-cybersecurity.

PMFs reflects a broader global trend toward the privatization of public assets. By providing training and equipment, PMFs have influenced the outcomes of several recent wars, including those in Angola, Croatia, Ethiopia, and Sierra Leone. PMFs played a significant role in the 2003 US-led invasion of Iraq. They have also become the targets of criticism and lawsuits for wrongful death, as with the case of the Blackwater guards who in 2007 killed several unarmed Iraqi civilians.

In other areas, political actors have seized previously state-held functions. For example, many of the world's armies are relying more on child soldiers, paramilitary forces, and private armies. At the same time, globalization has weakened the national forms of identity that have dominated international relations in the past two centuries, and it has reinvigorated earlier forms of political identity and organization, such as religious, ethnic, and clan loyalties.

The greatly increased role of the media is another feature of this evolution. As we discussed earlier in the chapter, live broadcasts make media far more important in terms of shaping or even constructing understandings of particular wars by making war more transparent. Journalists have effectively been transformed from observers into active participants, facing most of the same dangers as soldiers and helping shape the course of the war through their reporting. Just as modernity and its wars were based on the mode of production, so postmodernity and its wars reflect the mode of information.

Globalization and New Wars

Mary Kaldor (1999) has suggested that a category of **new wars** has emerged since the mid-1980s. Just as earlier wars were linked to the emergence and creation of states, new wars are related to the disintegration and collapse of states, and much of the pressure on such states has come from the effects of globalization. In the past decade, 95 percent of armed conflicts have taken place within states rather than between them. The new wars occur in situations where the economy of the state is performing extremely poorly, or even collapsing, so that the tax revenues and power of the state decline dramatically, producing an increase in corruption

New wars Wars of identity between different ethnic communities or nations, and wars that are caused by the collapse of states or the fragmentation of multiethnic states. Most of these new wars are internal or civil wars.

Congress, suspect that Iran will ignore the terms of the deal and that this arrangement will ultimately allow them to develop a nuclear weapon. In October 2017, the Trump administration announced that it will not certify the Iran nuclear deal, known as the Joint Comprehensive Plan of Action. Trump has proclaimed that this agreement was a bad deal for the United States and its allies. In May 2018, the Trump administration announced it was pulling out of the Iran treaty and reinstating sanctions against Iran. The other parties—the permanent members of the UN Security Council plus Germany (or the P5 plus 1)—to the Iran nuclear deal have indicated that the deal would remain even if the United States pulls out. The European Union played a major role in the negotiations as well, and with the withdrawal of the United States as the leader in areas like the Iran deal and the Paris climate accord, the European Union will likely become the next diplomatic leader.

In return for the lifting of sanctions, Iran will shut down some twelve thousand nuclear centrifuges and will ship 98 percent of its enriched fuel to outside countries in a fuel swap. They will also destroy their core plutonium reactor, and inspectors from the International Atomic Energy Agency will monitor the entire process.

Unfortunately, this same sort of global diplomacy has not been replicated in East Asia as the region tries to deal with North Korean nuclear proliferation. North Korean leaders see these weapons as a guarantee of its security in a hostile region. The United States has taken an aggressive position, even threatening a preemptive strike if North Korea continues to test nuclear devices and missile delivery systems. South Korea has the most to lose if war breaks out, and their leaders have been exploring diplomatic solutions, including meeting North Korean leaders at the recent Winter Olympic Games. Japan is also using the North Korean bellicosity to explore changing its security grand strategy that has remained constant since the end of World War II. Both states are looking toward the United States for a solution.

President Trump and the North Korean leader, Kim Jong Un, have met several times, with the president claiming that he can persuade the North Koreans to give up their nuclear program and become a member of the global community of states. To date, there has been no progress. China and Russia seem to support the talks, but both these countries are unwilling or incapable of containing North Korean nuclear proliferation. The key question for the United States and its East Asian allies might be whether it will need to pursue deterrence rather than denuclearization.

While John Bolton was President Trump's national security advisor he was an opponent of the president's North Korea policy, but he did persuade the president to take a hard line on Iran. With Bolton's departure from office, is it possible that the United States will rejoin the Iran nuclear deal?

The Current Nuclear Age

In Prague on April 5, 2009, President Obama talked about ridding the world of nuclear weapons:

> *The existence of thousands of nuclear weapons is the most dangerous legacy of the Cold War. No nuclear war was fought between the United States and the Soviet Union, but generations lived with the knowledge that their world could be erased in a single flash of light. Cities like Prague that existed for centuries, that embodied the beauty and the talent of so much of humanity, would have ceased to exist.*
>
> *Today, the Cold War has disappeared but thousands of those weapons have not. In a strange turn of history, the threat of global nuclear war has gone down, but the risk of a nuclear attack has gone up. More nations have acquired these weapons. Testing has continued. Black market trade in nuclear secrets and nuclear materials abounds. The technology to build a bomb has spread. Terrorists are determined to buy, build or steal one. Our efforts to contain these dangers are centered on a global nonproliferation regime, but as more people and nations break the rules, we could reach the point where the center cannot hold.*

Prior to this speech by Obama, the Global Zero movement was launched in 2008. Led by two hundred global leaders and thousands of citizens, the goal of the movement is to work toward the elimination of all nuclear weapons. The leadership of Global Zero announced a two-phase plan aimed at stopping the spread of nuclear weapons: securing all existing weapons, and then eliminating them. For the first phase of the project, the group asked the United States and Russia to cut their weapons stock down to a thousand warheads and other nuclear states to freeze their arsenals. While this is one possible scenario for the future, a 2015 article in *The Economist* suggests we have entered a new nuclear age, one that is more dangerous than the Cold War given the existence of rogue regimes and new rivalries among the major nuclear powers.

During the Cold War, most had faith in the idea that neither side would risk mutually assured destruction (MAD) and launch a nuclear weapon. However, this new age is one where states might use nuclear weapons to secure a strategic advantage. In 2015, President Obama budgeted for $350 billion to modernize the US nuclear arsenal. Russia also increased its defense budget, one-third of which is devoted to nuclear weapons. China is also adding to its nuclear stocks and is investing in submarines and mobile missiles. The actions of both India and Pakistan are unknown.

Both Russia and the United States are still modernizing their nuclear weapons systems. One factor complicating the idea of MAD as deterrence is the risk that cyberattacks with sophisticated technology could undermine command and control systems that keep nuclear powers from going to war. Another problem for the future is that the Trump administration has a disdain for any treaty that limits US options. First, the Trump administration pulled the United States out of the Intermediate-Range Nuclear Forces Agreement. This 1987 treaty, signed by former president Ronald Reagan, prohibited land-based short-range ballistic or cruise missiles. These missiles can be destabilizing because those targeted by these missiles have little time to launch countermeasures. Currently, the Trump administration wants to let the 2011 New Start treaty with Russia expire. This treaty limits strategic arsenals. President Trump wants the treaty to include other states like China, but their leaders are not interested in being part of this treaty. The Russians claim that negotiations need to begin early in 2020 if the Russia and the United States are to reach agreement by the 2021 expiration date.

What is the best response to this era of uncertainty and potential global nuclear violence? The NPT, if enforced, creates a rule-based system that will control the spread of nuclear weapons. The *security dilemma* is mitigated by a vigorous arms control regime supported by the major powers and the international community.

Nuclear Motivations

Given the economic cost of creating a nuclear weapons program, an obvious question is this: Why would a state in the developing world choose to divert scarce resources to a program of questionable value? It is necessary to consider a range of factors that might influence nuclear weapons acquisition. These could include militarism and traditional technological factors that influence the availability of nuclear technology, as well as having a cadre of trained nuclear scientists. Another factor is domestic politics, including imperatives within a political party, or a domestic political situation that might propel a state toward nuclear weapons. Matters of diplomacy also influence the acquisition of nuclear weapons. Through diplomatic bargaining, the acquisition of a nuclear capability can be used to influence or bargain with both perceived allies and enemies. Ultimately, acquiring a nuclear capability deters other states from intervening in one's affairs.

Sagan (2004, 45–46) argues that beyond the *realist/neorealist* argument for building nuclear weapons—states develop these weapons when they face a significant threat—one must consider the influence of domestic interest groups and bureaucratic agencies that benefit from the production of nuclear weapons, missile systems, and other related technologies. In addition, one must consider the value of these weapons in domestic political debates about security and their normative value as symbols of power and modernity. What does it mean to be a major power? Nuclear weapons serve an important symbolic function and help to shape a state's identity (Sagan 2004, 64). In our current international system, the possession of nuclear weapons identifies a country as a major player, and thus some countries want to be seen as a member of this exclusive club.

Nuclear terrorism The use of or threat to use nuclear weapons or nuclear materials to achieve the goals of rogue states or revolutionary or radical organizations.

Studies conducted during the 1970s and 1980s on **nuclear terrorism** indicated that there were risks associated with particular groups acquiring a nuclear device or threatening to attack nuclear installations. One study by the International Task Force on Prevention of Nuclear Terrorism concluded that it was possible for a terrorist group to build a crude nuclear device provided it had sufficient quantities of chemical high explosives and weapons-usable fissile materials. More significant, it was felt that such a group would be more interested in generating social disruption by making a credible nuclear threat rather than actually detonating a nuclear device and causing mass killing and destruction (Leventhal and Alexander 1987). More recent occurrences have served to alter this latter judgment.

Events in the mid-1990s, such as the first bombing of the World Trade Center in New York in 1993 and the attack against the US government building in Oklahoma in April 1995, revealed the extent of damage and loss of life that could be caused. Although both instances involved traditional methods of inflicting damage, the use of nerve agents (chemical weapons) in an underground train network in central Tokyo in March 1995 to cause both death and widespread panic has been viewed as representing a quantum change in methods. These concerns have intensified since the tragic events of September 11, 2001, when the World Trade Center was destroyed by a coordinated attack using civilian aircraft loaded with aviation fuel as the method of destruction. The attacks changed the assumption about terrorist use of CBRN capabilities (Wilkinson 2003).

Nuclear Capabilities and Intentions

The past and present nuclear programs in Iraq, India, Iran, Pakistan, and North Korea have raised important issues concerning capabilities and intentions. These instances reveal the difficulties in obtaining consensus in international forums on how to respond to **noncompliance** and the problems associated with verifying treaty compliance in situations where special inspection or nuclear development arrangements are agreed upon. In the case of Iraq, an inspection arrangement known as a UN Special Committee was established following the 1991 Gulf War to oversee the dismantlement of the WMDs program that had come to light as a result of the conflict. By the late 1990s, problems were encountered over access to particular sites, and UN Special Committee inspectors were withdrawn. Disagreements also surfaced among the five permanent members of the UN Security Council concerning how to implement the UN resolutions that had been passed in connection with Iraq since 1991. These had not been resolved at the time of the 2003 intervention in Iraq, and subsequent inspections in that country were unable to find evidence of significant undeclared WMDs.

The complexity associated with compliance is evident in the ongoing case of Iran. The country became the subject of attention from the International Atomic Energy Agency (IAEA) over delays in signing a protocol, added to Iran's safeguards agreement, requiring increased transparency by NNWS. Although Iran later signed the protocol, the discovery by the IAEA of undeclared facilities capable of enriching uranium fueled speculation. In an effort to find a solution, a dialogue between Iran, France, Germany, and the United Kingdom began in October 2003. Although an agreement was reached in November 2004, the situation was not resolved, and by 2006, the UN Security Council passed resolutions, under Chapter VII of the UN Charter, requiring Iran to comply with its international obligations. During the administration of former president of Iran Mahmoud Ahmadinejad, the IAEA had difficulty getting Iran to agree to verification

Noncompliance The failure of states or other actors to abide by treaties or rules supported by international regimes.

mechanisms, which complicated an already dangerous Middle East security picture. Since the 2015 Iran nuclear deal was reached, which calls for Iran to cease its nuclear weapons program, the international community hopes that a compliant Iran will no longer pose a nuclear threat to regional—and global—politics. Now that the Trump administration has abandoned the nuclear deal and reimposed sanctions, there is a greater chance of renewed tensions in the region. Iran's involvement in the civil war in Yemen and its continuing support for Hezbollah and insurgent groups in Iraq was one reason why the Trump administration suggested the Iran nuclear deal was inadequate.

Decisions regarding war and purchasing weapons needed to fight a war are state actions. However, increasingly since the end of the Cold War, states are facing security threats from nonstate actors. During the Cold War, the bipolar regime dominated a range of issues, reducing ethnonationalism or religious fundamentalism to secondary status. As a result of globalization, the declining centrality of the state has created space for groups with subnational or pan-national agendas to act. The subject of the next section—terrorism—is the preferred method of intervention for many of these nonstate groups.

Terrorism and Extremism

Terrorism and globalization share at least one quality—both are complex phenomena open to subjective interpretation. RAND researcher Brian Michael Jenkins (2016) recently described the phenomenon of terrorism:

> *Terrorist attacks are designed to be dramatic events, calculated to capture attention and create alarm and cause people to exaggerate the strength of terrorists and the threat they pose.*

Definitions of terrorism vary widely, but all depart from a common point. Terrorism is characterized, first and foremost, by the use of violence. This tactic of violence takes many forms and often indiscriminately targets noncombatants. The purpose for which violence is used, and its root causes, is where most of the disagreements about terrorism begin.

Historically, the term *terrorism* described state violence against citizens—for example, during the French Revolution or the Stalinist era of the Soviet Union. Over the past half-century, however, the definition of terrorism has evolved to mean the use of violence by nonstate groups or networks to achieve political change. Terrorism differs from criminal violence in its degree of political legitimacy. Those sympathetic to terrorist causes suggest that violence, including the death of innocent people, is the only remaining option that can draw attention to the plight of the aggrieved. Such causes have included ideological, ethnic, and religious exclusion or persecution.

Defining terrorism can be difficult because groups often advocate multiple grievances and compete with one another for resources and support. In addition, the relative importance of these grievances within groups can change over time.

Those targeted by terrorists are less inclined to see any justification, much less legitimacy, behind attacks that are designed to spread fear by killing and maiming civilians. As a result, the term *terrorist* has a pejorative value that is useful in delegitimizing those who commit such acts.

Audrey Kurth Cronin, an academic authority on terrorism, has outlined different types of terrorist groups and their historical importance in the following way:

WHAT'S YOUR WORLDVIEW?

Who is winning the global war on terrorism? Experts suggest that any progress is difficult to assess. What factors tell us who is winning? Are we safer now than we were when this global battle started?

> There are four types of terrorist organizations currently operating around the world, categorized mainly by their source of motivation: left-wing terrorists, right-wing terrorists, ethnonationalist/separatist terrorists, and religious or "sacred" terrorists. All four types have enjoyed periods of relative prominence in the modern era, with left-wing terrorism intertwined with the Communist movement and currently practiced by Maoists in Peru and Nepal, right-wing terrorism employed by Neo-Nazi skinheads in several European countries drawing its inspiration from Fascism, and the bulk of ethnonationalist/separatist terrorism accompanying the wave of decolonization especially in the immediate post–World War II years and in places like Northern Ireland and Spain. Currently, "sacred" terrorism is becoming more significant. Of course, these categories are not perfect, as many groups have a mix of motivating ideologies—some ethnonationalist groups, for example, have religious characteristics or agendas—but usually one ideology or motivation dominates. (Cronin 2002/3, 39)

Even with the use of violence by states, there is disagreement on what constitutes the legitimate application of armed force. For example, during the 1980s, Libya sponsored terrorist acts as an indirect method of attacking the United States, France, and the United Kingdom. Those states, in turn, condemned Libyan sponsorship as contravening international norms and responded with the customary methods of global politics: sanctions, international court cases, and occasional uses of force. Disagreement associated with the invasion of Iraq in 2003 relates to interpretations over whether the conditions for "just war" were met before military operations commenced. Some suggest that the conditions were not met and that actions by the coalition should be considered an "act of terrorism" conducted by states. Leaders in the United States and the United Kingdom dismiss the charge on the basis that a greater evil was removed. Violating international norms in the pursuit of terrorists runs the risk of playing into perceptions that the state itself is a terrorist threat.

A military officer patrols outside the bombed St. Anthony's Church in Colombo, Sri Lanka, one month after Islamist militants killed more than 250 people in a suicide terror attack. The church is now under reconstruction. Terrorist attacks continue across the world and authorities seem to be unable to anticipate or prevent them. What are some reasons this extremism continues?

The Realist-Theory Perspective and the War on Terrorism

THE CHALLENGE

Debates about political theories have had an important role in government debates about how secular Western democracies can best fight terrorism. The realist tradition asserts that countries are the most important actors—in fact, sometimes the only actors that matter—in international politics. Many political scientists in the realist tradition also maintain that questions of morality should not restrain the actions of a country that is under threat of an attack.

OPTIONS

These components of realism can explain why the Bush administration was seemingly surprised by the September 11, 2001, attacks and why the government reacted the way it did. For example, on August 6, 2001, national security adviser Condoleezza Rice gave President Bush a briefing that included a memo titled "Bin Laden Determined to Strike in US," which documented plans of the Al Qaeda organization (*The 9/11 Commission Report*, New York: Norton; p. 261). This was the most recent of a series of warnings about possible terrorist attacks on the United States or on American interests around the world.

Realist theory helps us to understand why the Bush administration did not act aggressively on these reports: The theory asserts that *states* are the primary threat to other *states*. Despite the previous successful Al Qaeda attacks on the US embassies in Kenya and Tanzania, and the near sinking of the destroyer USS *Cole*, members of the Bush administration might have believed that a small nonstate group was not able to launch another attack. In addition, the Bush administration was preoccupied with North Korea's nuclear weapons program and an incident in which a Chinese fighter aircraft had damaged a US Navy maritime surveillance aircraft, forcing it to land in China. Logically for President Bush and his advisers, North Korea and China presented a more pressing threat to the United States.

Realist international relations theory also provides an explanation for the Bush administration's actions after September 11, 2001. If, as the memo said, Osama bin Laden was determined to attack the United States, President Bush was equally determined that it would not happen again. Therefore, the United States soon attacked Afghanistan, seeking to depose the Taliban government that had offered sanctuary to bin Laden and other members of the Al Qaeda leadership. More telling, however, was the Bush administration's decision to label as "unlawful combatants" anyone whom US military personnel captured and detain them at the US Navy base at Guantánamo, Cuba, or in secret prisons around the world. The increasingly unpopular practice of "extraordinary rendition" was another component of the policy. Extraordinary rendition was the capture and transfer of suspected terrorists to unspecified foreign sites for purposes of detention and often torture. Some nongovernmental human rights organizations called the actions violations of international law, but the Bush administration, echoing a key aspect of the realist perspective, called the decisions morally necessary to protect the United States.

For Discussion

The terrorist challenge facing nation-states raises the enduring question of international relations: When is it appropriate for national leaders to violate international law and moral codes of conduct to protect their citizens? Is torture acceptable if it protects a nation-state?

As with other forms of irregular, or asymmetric, warfare, terrorism is designed to achieve political change for the purpose of obtaining power to right a perceived wrong. However, according to some analysts, terrorism is the weakest form of irregular warfare with which to alter the political landscape. The reason for this weakness is that terrorist groups rarely possess the broader support of the population that characterizes insurgency and revolution, and the methods of terrorists often alienate potential supporters of the cause. Terrorist groups often lack support for their objectives because the changes they seek are based on radical ideas that do not have widespread appeal. To effect change, terrorists must provoke drastic responses that act as a catalyst for change or weaken their opponent's moral resolve.

As with definitions of terrorism, there is general agreement on at least one aspect of globalization. Technologies allow the transfer of goods, services, and information almost anywhere quickly and efficiently. In the case of information, the transfer can be secure and is nearly instantaneous. The extent of social, cultural, and political change brought on by globalization, including increasing interconnectedness and homogeneity in the international system, remains the subject of much disagreement and debate. These disagreements, in turn, influence discussion of the extent to which globalization has contributed to the rise of modern terrorism. There is little doubt that the technologies associated with globalization have been used to improve the effectiveness and reach of terrorist groups. For example, social media outlets have played an important role in helping groups like the Islamic State recruit young people to their cause. The relationship between globalization and terrorism is best understood as the next step in the evolution of political violence since terrorism became a transnational phenomenon in the 1960s. To understand the changes perceived in terrorism globally, it is useful to understand the evolution of terrorism from a primarily domestic political event to a global phenomenon.

▶ Terrorism: From Domestic to Global Phenomenon

Historically, nonstate terrorist groups have used readily available means to permit small numbers of individuals to spread fear as widely as possible. In the late nineteenth and early twentieth centuries, anarchists relied on railroads for travel and killed with revolvers and dynamite. Yet terrorists and acts of terrorism rarely had an impact beyond national borders, in part because the activists often sought political change within a specific country. Three factors led to the birth of transnational terrorism in 1968: (1) the expansion of commercial air travel, (2) the availability of televised news coverage, and (3) broad political and ideological interests among extremists that converged on a common cause. As a result, terrorism grew from a local to a transnational threat. Air travel gave terrorists unprecedented mobility.

For example, the Japanese Red Army trained in one country and attacked in another, as with the 1972 Lod Airport massacre in Israel. In the United States, some radicals forced airplanes to go to Cuba. Air travel appealed to terrorists because airport security measures, including passport control, were less stringent when terrorists began hijacking airlines, referred to as **skyjackings**. States also acquiesced to terrorist demands, frequently for money, which encouraged further incidents. The success of this tactic spurred other terrorist groups, as well as criminals and political refugees, to follow suit. Incidents of hijacking increased dramatically from five in 1966 to ninety-four in 1969. Shared political ideologies stimulated cooperation and some exchanges between groups as diverse as the

Skyjackings The takeover of a commercial airplane for the purpose of taking hostages and using them to bargain for a particular political or economic goal.

With the death of Abu Bakr al-Baghdadi, the leader of ISIS, and the group's defeat in Syria, will their terrorist activities likely subside in the Middle East or will another extremist group simply assume their activities?

Irish Republican Army (IRA) and the Basque separatist organization Euzkadi Ta Askatasuna (ETA). Besides sharing techniques and technical experience, groups demanded the release of imprisoned "fellow revolutionaries" in different countries, giving the impression of a coordinated global terrorist network. The reality was that groups formed short-term relationships of convenience, based around weapons, capabilities, and money, to advance local political objectives. For example, members of the IRA did not launch attacks in Spain to help the ETA, but they did share resources.

Televised news coverage and the internet also played a role in expanding the audience, who could witness the theater of terrorism in their own homes. People who had never heard of "the plight of the Palestinians" became more aware of the issue after live coverage of incidents such as the hostage taking conducted by Black September during the 1972 Munich Olympics. Although some considered media coverage "the oxygen that sustains terrorism," terrorists discovered that reporters and audiences lost interest in repeat performances over time. To sustain viewer interest and compete for coverage, terrorist groups undertook increasingly

Are We Safer Now? Brian Jenkins on the War on Terrorism

As the global war on terror continues, here is one expert's views on the positive and negative effects of this war.

THE POSITIVES

- Worse-case scenarios have not been realized.
- A world war has not broken out and the operational capabilities of the major terrorist groups remain limited.
- A major terrorist network has not developed.
- ISIS has been defeated in its attempt to build a caliphate in Syria and Iraq.
- Various attacks have not resulted in major political gains.
- Cooperation among security officials aimed at thwarting terrorist attacks is increasing across the world.

THE NEGATIVES

- The terrorist enemies persist and have survived US and other Western efforts at stopping them.
- The extremists seem determined to continue their attacks.
- Jihadis have a powerful ideological message that is attractive and convincing to many individuals on the margins.
- Although defeated in one area, many extremist groups are resilient and continue to harm innocent civilians and simply do not quit.
- Fragile states or ungoverned territories act as incubators of terrorist activities and recruitment.
- Citizens remain fearful and limit their travel and participation in society, although governments have been very successful at containing terrorists.

Source: Jenkins, Brian Michael. "Fifteen Years On, Where Are We in the 'War on Terror'?" RAND, http://www.rand.org/2016/09

spectacular attacks, such as the seizure of Organization of Petroleum Exporting Countries delegates by "Carlos the Jackal," whose real name was Ilich Ramírez Sánchez, in Austria in December 1975. Terrorism experts speculated that terrorist leaders understood that horrific, mass-casualty attacks might cross a threshold of violence. This might explain why few terrorist groups attempted to acquire or use WMDs, including nuclear, chemical, and biological weapons (see Figure 6.1).

The Impact of Globalization on Terrorism

Al Qaeda, "The Base" or "The Foundation," received global recognition as a result of its attacks conducted in New York and Washington, D.C., on September 11, 2001. Since then, and even after the death of Osama bin Laden in 2011, experts have debated what Al Qaeda is, what it represents, and the actual threat it poses (see Table 6.3 for a list of its affiliates and extent of its reach). In early 2006, the Office of the Chairman of the Joint Chiefs of Staff in the Pentagon released the *National Military Strategic Plan for the War on Terrorism*, which sought to characterize the fluid nature of militant Islamic terrorism:

> *There is no monolithic enemy network with a single set of goals and objectives. The nature of the threat is more complicated. In the GWOT [global war on terrorism], the primary enemy is a transnational movement of extremist organizations, networks, and individuals—and their state and nonstate supporters—which have in common that they exploit Islam and use terrorism for ideological ends. The Al Qaeda Associated Movement (AQAM), comprised of Al Qaeda and affiliated radical groups, is the most dangerous present manifestation of such extremism. The [Al Qaeda network's] adaptation or evolution resulted in the creation of an extremist "movement," referred to by intelligence analysts as AQAM, extending extremism and terrorist tactics well beyond the original organization. This adaptation has resulted in decentralizing control in the network and franchising its extremist efforts within the movement. (National Military Strategic Plan for the War on Terrorism [Unclassified], 13)*

Efforts to explain the vitality of global terrorism in general—and Al Qaeda in particular—focus on three areas linked to aspects of globalization: culture, economics, and religion.

Cultural Explanations

Culture is one way to explain why militant Islam's call for armed struggle has been successful in underdeveloped countries. Culture also explains many of the ethnic conflicts, and violence between religious and language groups, across the world. The 1990s were a period of unprecedented ethnic violence and terrorism that included the genocide in Rwanda and the ethnic cleansing in the former Yugoslavia. Many fundamentalist groups believe that violence is the only method to preserve traditions and values against a cultural tsunami of Western products and **materialism**. Once sought after as an entry method to economic prosperity,

Al Qaeda Most commonly associated with Osama bin Laden, "The Base" (its meaning in Arabic) is a religious-based group whose fighters swear an oath of fealty to the leadership that succeeded bin Laden.

Materialism In this context, it is the spreading of a global consumer culture and popular-culture artifacts like music, books, and movies. Christopher Lasch called this the "ceaseless translation of luxuries into necessities." These elements are seen as undermining traditional cultural values and norms.

| TABLE 6.3 | **Al Qaeda and Its Extremist Affiliates** |

Group Name	Description
Al Qaeda in the Arabian Peninsula (AQAP)	Originally a Saudi-based organization set up by bin Laden after 9/11. In 2009, AQAP joined with a group in Yemen where it focuses its terrorism; AQAP also has a focus on the United States as a target.
Al Qaeda in the Islamic Maghreb (AQIM)	Founded in 2003 as a successor to the 1990s Algerian jihad, it emerged from the Salafist Group for Preaching and Combat. Their targets are the French and American crusaders. This group has extended its terrorism to Libya, Mali, Mauritania, and Niger.
Al Shabaab	Founded in 2012 with loyalty toward Al Qaeda, Al Shabaab means "young men" in Arabic. These are Somali militants taking advantage of a failed state and attacking the United States and UN peacekeepers. They are best known for their attack on a shopping mall in Kenya.
Boko Haram	This Salafist Islamist sect emerged in Northeast Nigeria in 2003 and clashes with government authorities. In Hausa, their name means "Western education is forbidden." In 2014, this group abducted 276 young schoolgirls.
Jemaah Islamiyah	This militant Islamist group seeks to establish an Islamic state across Southeast Asia. The group has targeted US and Western interests in Indonesia, Singapore, and the Philippines and attacked tourist areas in Bali in 2002 and 2005.
Nusra Front	Known as the Front for the Defense of the Syrian People, the Nusra Front began operating in Syria in 2011. Their favorite strategy is suicide bombing. They have pledged allegiance to Al Qaeda and they seek an Islamic state in Syria.
Hamas	The largest of several Palestinian militant Islamist groups. Hamas is an Arabic acronym for the Islamic Resistance Movement. Committed to the destruction of Israel, the group originated in 1987 following the first intifada, or Palestinian uprising, against Israel's occupation of the West Bank and Gaza Strip. Since 2005, Hamas has also engaged in the Palestinian political process.
Society of the Muslim Brothers	A transnational Sunni Islamist organization founded in Egypt. The Brotherhood's stated goal is to instill the Koran and the Sunnah, or the traditional part of Islamic law that is based on the words and deeds of the Prophet Muhamad, as the "sole reference point for guiding the everyday life of any Muslim family, individual, community, and the nation-state."
Al Qaeda in the Indian Subcontinent	AQIS is an Islamist militant group that opposes the governments of Afghanistan, Pakistan, India, Myanmar, Bhutan, Nepal, and several other south Asian countries. Their goal is to establish Islamic states in the region.
Lashkar-e-Taiba	Founded in 1987, Lashkar-e-Taiba is defined as the *Army of the Good*. It is one of the largest and most active Islamic militant organizations in South Asia, operating primarily from Pakistan. It has been accused by India of launching many attacks in their country.

Source: Daniel Byman, Al Qaeda, The Islamic State and the Global Jihadist Movement *(Oxford: 2015).*

Western secular, materialist values are increasingly rejected by those seeking to regain or preserve their own unique cultural identity. The phenomenon of rejecting the West is not new; one could argue that it began almost two hundred years ago as the strength of the Ottoman Empire waned. Since then, the social changes

The Shanghai Cooperation Organization: Fighting Terrorism in the Former Communist Bloc

Although often missing from the headlines of North American media, terrorism is a threat to countries not directly involved in the global war on terrorism. Liberal theories, especially those that emphasize democracy and fundamental rights, dominate discussions in the United States and Western Europe. Liberals also discuss the proper methods to stop attacks, and their debates center on matters of ethics and morality. To put it briefly, what *should* Western-style democracies do to confront terrorist groups, especially those with Islamist links that seek to destroy open societies based on tolerance? *Can* democracy and inclusive institutions survive if Western governments must occasionally bend their own laws to safeguard society?

Such questions of appropriate methods to combat terrorism tend not to restrain the governments of China and the former Soviet republics Russia, Kazakhstan, Kyrgyzstan, Tajikistan, and Uzbekistan, which together created the Shanghai Cooperation Organization (SCO) in June 2001. None of these countries are paragons of democratic virtue. According to the annual survey of the human rights organization Freedom House, Kyrgyzstan ranks the highest of the six SCO countries, and it is only partly free.

Government officials in all of the countries regularly suppress and occasionally murder independent journalists who criticize those who hold political power. Opposition political parties find their offices closed, their assets seized, their telephones tapped, and their members harassed and arrested. Religious minorities are often jailed if they practice their rituals in public. All of this sounds like the description of terror: a state repressing its own subjects or citizens.

Yet from the time of its founding, the SCO called itself an antiterror institution, and its greatest threat is Islamist radical groups. Certainly, given the role that Taliban fighters played in defeating the Soviet invasion of Afghanistan in the 1980s and the Islamic aspect to the Russian war in Chechnya, it made sense that Russia would see an Islamic threat. However, media organizations in the United States miss the effect that separatist groups have in Chinese politics—for example, the Muslim Uighurs who live in the Sinkiang region in the west of the country. According to the CIA's *World Factbook*, Islam is the primary religious identification for the majority of people in Kyrgyzstan (75 percent), Tajikistan (90 percent), and Uzbekistan (88 percent). Each member state of the SCO must, therefore, take a different approach to its own Muslim problem. The leaders of the most Islamic states fear that a Taliban style of Sunni Islam might become popular and challenge the legitimacy of the secular governments. Both Russia and China fear that Islamic radicals might push for independence.

Thus, for SCO member states, the greatest threat is not external attack but internal collapse. As a result, terrorism and separatism are linked in the Shanghai Convention on Combating Terrorism, Separatism, and Extremism signed in June 2001. The SCO held its first joint antiterror war games in August 2003 in Kazakhstan. There was perhaps a message in the choice of host country for the exercise. Kazakhstan's population is about 24 percent Russian and has, after China and Russia, the fewest number of people who self-identify as Muslims: about 70 percent. In Kazakhstan, Russians have the most to fear from Islamic radicals, yet at the same time, the exercises might offend the fewest number of Muslims.

Despite the antiterrorist stand of the SCO, some US government officials have been wary of the motives of the group. Some feared that China and Russia might apply pressure to the Central Asian states to have them force the United States to leave the bases it had in Kyrgyzstan in support of its war against the Taliban in Afghanistan. Neoconservatives in the United States who advocated the spread of democracy also expressed concerns that China and Russia might form an alliance similar to the Holy Alliance that Russia, Prussia, and Austria-Hungary created after the Napoleonic wars. The early-1800s alliance was strongly antidemocratic, repressing political and civil liberties. Some analysts believe that by seeking to slow an inevitable process of liberalism, the Holy Alliance brought about the destruction that it wanted to avoid.

Since its founding, the SCO has expanded its mandate to include joint security and economic development programs. In July 2015, India and Pakistan began the accession process to become SCO members, but at the

THEORY IN PRACTICE *continued*

time of this writing, their membership has not been finalized; a number of other states serve as observer states and dialogue partners. However, the organization's regional influence is limited due to underfunding and the limited power capabilities of members to make collective decisions. More often than not, member states are preoccupied by their own independent agendas, which weaken cohesion and breed mistrust.

For Discussion

1. Do you find it strange that authoritarian states want to fight terrorism? Might they respond to terrorism differently?

2. Could this coalition of authoritarian states actually work against the spread of democracy and the ending of global terrorism?

3. All the states in this coalition have significant Muslim populations. Are their concerns about internal order or global terrorism?

---

associated with globalization and the spread of free market capitalism appear to be overwhelming the identity or values of groups who perceive themselves as the losers in the new international system. In an attempt to preserve their threatened identity and values, groups actively distinguish themselves from despised "others." At the local level, this cultural friction could translate into conflicts divided along religious or ethnic lines to safeguard **identity**.

Economic Explanations

Not everyone agrees that defense of cultural identity is the primary motivation for globalized terrorist violence. Others see economic aspects as the crucial motivating factor in the use of violence to effect political change. Although globalization provides access to a world market for goods and services, the net result has also been perceived as a form of Western economic **imperialism**. The United States and the postindustrial states of Western Europe form the global North or economic core that dominates international economic institutions, sets exchange rates, and determines fiscal policies. The actions and policies can be unfavorable to the underdeveloped countries, or global South, that make up the periphery or gap. Political decisions by the leaders of underdeveloped countries to deregulate or privatize industries to be competitive globally could lead to significant social and economic upheaval. The citizenry might shift loyalties to illegal activities such as terrorism if the state breaks its social contract (Junaid 2005, 143–144).

Wealth is also linked to personal security and violence. With little opportunity to obtain wealth locally, individuals will leave to pursue opportunities in other countries. The result is emigration and the rapid growth of burgeoning urban centers that act as regional hubs for the flow of global resources. Movement, however, is no guarantee that individual aspirations will be realized. In cases where they are not, individuals might turn to violence for reasons that are criminal (e.g., personal gain) or political (e.g., to change the existing political system through insurgency or terrorism). Paradoxically, rising standards of living and greater access to educational opportunities associated with globalization could lead to increased expectations. If those expectations are unmet, individuals

Identity The understanding of the self in relationship to an "other." Identities are social and thus always formed in relationship to others. Constructivists generally hold that identities shape interests; we cannot know what we want unless we know who we are. But because identities are social and produced through interactions, identities can change.

Imperialism The practice of foreign conquest and rule in the context of global relations of hierarchy and subordination. It can lead to the establishment of an empire.

may turn to extreme political views and action against "the system" that denies them the opportunity to realize their ambitions.

However, the explanation that recent terrorist violence is a reaction to economic globalization could be flawed for a number of reasons, including the personal wealth and social upbringing of a number of members of global terrorist groups, as well as trends in regional patterns of terrorist recruitment. Many former leaders and members of transnational terrorist groups, including the German Red Army Faction and the Italian Red Brigades, came from respectable middle- and upper-class families. The same holds true for a number of modern-day antiglobalization anarchists. Within militant Islamic groups, most of their leaders and senior operatives attended graduate schools around the globe in fields as diverse as engineering and theology and were neither poor nor downtrodden (Sageman 2004, 73–74).

Anti-government political forces in Afghanistan protest the US government after the military tested a massive new weapon—"the mother of all bombs"—on an empty village in eastern Afghanistan. To many in this country, the United States is the terrorist, not the Taliban.

Religion and "New" Terrorism

In the decade prior to 9/11, a number of scholars and experts perceived that fundamental changes were taking place in the character of terrorism. The use of violence for political purposes, to change state ideology or the representation of ethnic minority groups, had failed in its purpose and a new trend was emerging. **Postmodern** or **"new" terrorism** was conducted for different reasons altogether and seemed to be driven by the power of ideas of the kind that constructivist international relations theory describes. Motivated by promises of rewards in the afterlife, some terrorists are driven by religious reasons to kill as many of the nonbelievers and unfaithful as possible (Laqueur 1996, 32–33). Although suicide tactics had been observed in Lebanon as early as 1983, militant Islam had previously been viewed as a state-sponsored, regional phenomenon (Wright 1986, 19–21).

New terrorism is seen as a reaction to the perceived oppression of Muslims worldwide and the spiritual bankruptcy of the West. As globalization spreads and societies become increasingly interconnected, Muslims have a choice: accept Western beliefs to better integrate, or preserve their spiritual purity by rebelling. Believers in the global **jihad** view the rulers of countries such as Pakistan, Saudi Arabia, or Iraq as apostates who have compromised their values in the pursuit and maintenance of secular, state-based power. The only possible response is to fight against such influences through jihad. Jihad is understood by most Islamic scholars and imams to mean the internal struggle for purity spiritually, although it has also been interpreted historically as a method to establish the basis for just

WHAT'S YOUR WORLDVIEW?

Poverty might not be a direct cause of terrorist activities, but do you think it contributes to attitudes that make people susceptible to recruitment by radical groups?

Postmodern or "new" terrorism Groups and individuals subscribing to millennial and apocalyptic ideologies and system-level goals. Most value destruction for its own sake, unlike most terrorists in the past, who had specific goals, usually tied to a territory.

"New" terrorism See Postmodern or "new" terrorism.

Jihad In Arabic, *jihad* means "struggle." Jihad can refer to a purely internal struggle to be a better Muslim or a struggle to make society more closely align with the teachings of the Koran.

war. Extremists who espouse militant Islam understand jihad in a different way: For the jihadi terrorist, there can be no compromise with either infidels or apostates.

The difference in value structures between secular and religious terrorists makes the responses to the latter difficult. Religious terrorists will kill themselves and others because they believe that they will receive rewards in the afterlife. Differences in value structures make the deterrence of religious terrorism difficult, if not impossible, as secular states cannot credibly threaten materially the ideas that terrorists value spiritually. Secular terrorism has had as its goal the pursuit of power to correct flaws within society but retain the overarching system. Religious terrorism, by contrast, does not seek to modify but rather to replace the normative structure of society (Cronin 2002/3, 41).

The use of religion, as a reaction to and an explanation for the phenomenon of global terrorism, contains some of the same incongruities as those focused on cultural and economic aspects. For Western observers, religious reasons appear to explain how individual terrorists are persuaded to take their own lives and kill others. Personal motivations can include promises of financial rewards for family members, gaining fame within a community, taking revenge for some grievance, or simply achieving a form of self-actualization. Yet few religious terrorist leaders, planners, and coordinators martyr themselves. Religion provides terrorist groups with a crucial advantage: the mandate and sanction of the divine to commit otherwise illegal or immoral acts. There is a substantial difference between religious motivation as the single driving factor to commit acts of terrorism and the ultimate purpose for which violence is being used.

The Current Challenge: The Persistence of the Islamic State

The Islamic State (ISIS) is part of the Al Qaeda family, but they have different goals and do not agree on all targets and strategies. Estimates vary when accounting for the size of its forces. ISIS did control an area the size of Indiana, including the Iraqi city of Mosul, the country's second-largest city, as well as areas in Syria, but its forces were driven out of most of Iraq and Syria. Russian and Syrian government forces and rebel forces, including those supported by the United States, drove ISIS out of Syria in 2017. The territorial caliphate no longer exists, but the organization and its strategy persist. At the time of its ascendancy, the Islamic State was earning millions of dollars a day on the black market selling oil, but it also sells spoils of war and sponsors a variety of illegal activities, such as smuggling antiquities and human trafficking. With the loss of territory, the sources of funds may diminish significantly. However, many experts suggest that ISIS is a bigger threat than Al Qaeda because it is attracting recruits from around the world. When it controlled territory and proclaimed a caliphate, it acted like a regular state—providing basic services, taxing the people, and providing law and order. Unfortunately, it was a cruel state for those under its rule who did not believe in its conservative Sunni Islamic views, and sharia law governed the actions of all of its citizens. These rules and practices still apply to any territory ISIS may control.

Although ISIS was set back by recent losses, its goal is to erase the colonial boundaries imposed by Western powers and create an Islamic empire that stretches from Spain to South and Southeast Asia. Those standing in the way of this new Islamic caliphate are the nonbelievers and those who believe in the Western liberal ideas that promote democracy and individual freedoms, which contradict elements of Islamic thought and sharia law. The Islamic State followed the seven-stage strategy developed by Al Qaeda in 2005 in its pursuit of an Islamic caliphate (Hoffman 2016):

- **Stage I: The Awakening Stage, 2000–2003** The September 11, 2001, attacks occurred, and this attack on the West and the United States reawakened the caliphate.
- **Stage II: The Eye-Opening Stage, 2003–2006** With the US invasion of Iraq, the war with the enemy began, and a prolonged war will weaken the United States and the West.
- **Stage III: The Rising Up and Standing on the Feet Stage, 2007–2010** Extremism and terror tactics to new venues across Africa and globally are expanded.
- **Stage IV: The Recovery Stage, 2010–2013** After the death of bin Laden, ISIS regroups and takes advantage of the changes promoted by the Arab Spring to topple apostate regimes like Syria.
- **Stage V: Declaration of the Caliphate Stage, 2013–2016** ISIS moves ahead of Al Qaeda by establishing rule over a large area and acting like a state.
- **Stage VI: The Total Confrontation, 2016–2020** The caliphate is created, and in turn the leaders create an Islamic army to fight the holy war between believers and nonbelievers.
- **Stage VII: The Definitive Stage, 2020–2022** The caliphate triumphs over the entire world.

Analysts suggested that the Islamic State was in Stage V and trying to pull the United States and the West into a major confrontation. They hope to regain their territory so their apocalyptic prophecies that suggest this will be the final battle and they will defeat the nonbelievers will become reality. All their victories to date suggest that the prophecies are true and act as great recruiting tools for young Muslims looking to fulfill personal religious goals.

Additionally, another concern for the West is the return of battle-tested Islamic State fighters to their homelands to carry out attacks. Extremists who were trained and then fought for the Islamic State caliphate in Syria and Iraq carried out the Paris attacks, which resulted in the deaths of more than one hundred people, and inspired the attack in San Bernardino, California, which left fourteen

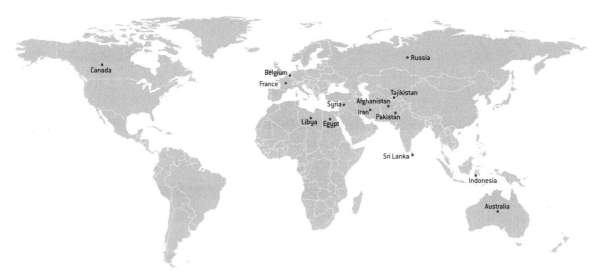

Map 6.2 **Where ISIS Has Directed and Inspired Attacks.**

Can a nation-state respond to networks like this without global cooperation?

people dead. This is what political analyst Bruce Hoffman calls the "boomerang effect" and may be how the Islamic State takes its extremist violence to countries across the world and brings the West into the "total confrontation" (see Map 6.2). The Syrian civil war may ultimately be the conflict that triggers this event (see Table 6.4).

TABLE 6.4 **Interactor Relationship Guide to the Syrian War**

LEGEND : Allies | It's Complicated | Enemies

	Syrian Government	Syrian Rebels	ISIS	Jabhat al-Nusra	Kurds	US and Allies	Iraq	Iran and Hezbollah	Russia	Saudi Arabia/ Gulf States	Turkey
Syrian Government											
Syrian Rebels											
ISIS											
Jabhat al-Nusra											
Kurds											
US and Allies											
Iraq											
Iran and Hezbollah											
Russia											
Saudi Arabia/ Gulf States											
Turkey											

Sources: Almukhtar, Sarah, K. K. Rebecca Lai, and Sergio Pecanha. "Untangling the Overlapping Conflicts in the Syrian War."
New York Times, *Oct. 18, 2015, International section: 14.*
Kirk, Joshua. *"The Middle East Friendship Chart." Slate.com. July 17, 2015. accessed Oct. 22, 2015.*

▶ Globalization, Technology, and Terrorism

Few challenge the point that terrorism has become much more pervasive worldwide as a result of the processes and technologies of globalization. The technological advances associated with globalization have improved the capabilities of terrorist groups to plan and conduct operations with far more devastation and coordination than their predecessors could have imagined. In particular, technologies have improved the capability of groups and cells to carry out attacks on a wider and more lethal scale.

Proselytizing

States traditionally have had an advantage in their ability to control information flows and use their resources to win the battle of hearts and minds against terrorist groups. Terrorist leaders understand how the internet has changed this dynamic: "We [know that we] are in a battle, and that more than half of this battle is taking place in the battlefield of the media. And that we are in a media battle in a race for the hearts and minds of our Umma" (Office of the Director of National Intelligence 2005, 10).

The continued expansion of the number of internet service providers, especially in states with relaxed or ambivalent content policies or laws, combined with capable and cheap computers, software, peripherals, and wireless technologies, has empowered individuals and groups to post tracts on or send messages throughout the World Wide Web. One form of empowerment is the virtual presence that individuals have. Although prominent jihadi terrorists' physical presence can be removed through imprisonment or death, their virtual presence and influence are immortalized on the Web.

Another form of empowerment for terrorist groups, brought on by globalization, is the volume, range, and sophistication of propaganda materials. Terrorist groups were once limited to mimeographed manifestos and typed communiqués. Terrorist supporters and sympathizers now build their own websites. An early example was a website sympathetic to the Peruvian Tupac Amaru Revolutionary Movement. This website posted the group's communiqués and videos during the seizure of the Japanese embassy in Lima in 1996. Webmasters sympathetic to terrorist groups also control the content and connotation of the material posted on their websites. The website of the Sri Lankan group Liberation Tigers of Tamil Eelam, for example, posts items that cast the group as an internationally accepted organization committed to conflict resolution. Messages, files, and polemics can be dispatched to almost anywhere on the globe via the internet or text messaging, almost instantaneously.

Terrorist groups in Chechnya and the Middle East have also made increasing use of video cameras to record the preparations for attacks, and their results, including successful roadside bombings and the downing of helicopters. With the right software and a little knowledge, individuals or small groups can download or obtain digital footage and music and produce videos that appeal to specific groups. Video footage is useful in inspiring potential recruits and seeking donations from support elements within the organization. For example, terrorist recruiters distributed videos of sniper and other attacks against coalition forces in

WHAT'S YOUR WORLDVIEW?

Would you be willing to live with fewer personal freedoms if it meant better security? For example, would you accept rules that would allow governments to monitor your communications and your computer activity?

Iraq, produced by the Al Qaeda media-production group As-Sahab. The competition among global news outlets like CNN, MSNBC, and Al Jazeera ensures that the images of successful or dramatic attacks reach the widest audience possible.

Security of Terrorist Organizations

Terrorist cells without adequate security precautions are vulnerable to discovery and detection. Translations of captured Al Qaeda manuals, for example, demonstrate the high value their writers place on security, including surveillance and countersurveillance techniques. The technological enablers of globalization assist terrorist cells and leaders in preserving security in a number of ways, including distributing elements in a coordinated network, remaining mobile, and utilizing clandestine or encrypted communications.

The security of terrorist organizations has historically been preserved by limiting communication and information exchanges between cells. This ensures that if one cell is compromised, its members only know each other's identities and not those of other cells. Thus, the damage done to the organization is minimized. Security is even more important to **clandestine** or **"sleeper" cells** operating on their own without central direction. The use of specific codes and ciphers, known only to a few individuals, is one way of preserving the security of an organization. Although codes and ciphers inevitably have been broken and information has been obtained through interrogation, such activities take time. During that time, terrorist groups adjust their location and operating methods in an attempt to stay ahead of counterterrorist forces. Technological advancements, including faster processing speeds and software developments, now mean that those sympathetic to terrorist causes can contribute virtually through servers located hundreds or thousands of miles away.

Clandestine or "sleeper" cell Usually, a group of people sent by an intelligence organization or terrorist network that remains dormant in a target country until activated by a message to carry out a mission, which could include prearranged attacks.

Mobility

The reduced size and increased capabilities of personal electronics also give terrorists mobility advantages. Mobility has always been a crucial consideration for terrorists and insurgents alike, given the superior resources that states have been able to bring to bear against them. In open societies that have well-developed infrastructures, terrorists have been able to move rapidly within and between borders, and this complicates efforts to track them because they exploit the very societal values they seek to destroy.

The globalization of commerce has also improved terrorist mobility. The volume of air travel and goods that pass through ports has increased exponentially through globalization. Between states, measures have been taken to ease the flow of goods, services, and ideas; to improve efficiency; and to reduce costs. One example is the European Schengen Agreement, in which border security measures between EU member states have been relaxed to speed deliveries. Market demands for efficiencies of supply, manufacture, delivery, and cost have complicated states' efforts to prevent members of terrorist groups from exploiting gaps in security measures. Additional mobility also allows terrorist groups to transfer expertise, as demonstrated by the arrest of three members of the IRA suspected of training counterparts in the Fuerzas Armadas Revolucionarias de Colombia in Bogotá in August 2001.

Terrorists' use of transportation is not necessarily overt, as the volume of goods transported in support of a globalized economy is staggering and difficult to monitor effectively. For example, customs officials cannot inspect all of the vehicles or containers passing through border points or ports. To illustrate the scale of the problem, the United States receives 10 million containers per year, and one port, Los Angeles, processes the equivalent of 12,000 twenty-foot containers daily. Western government officials fear that terrorist groups will use containers as a convenient and cheap means to ship WMDs.

Combating Terrorism

States plagued by transnational terrorism responded individually and collectively to combat the phenomenon during the Cold War. These responses ranged in scope and effectiveness and included passing antiterrorism laws, taking preventive security measures at airports, and creating special-operations counterterrorism forces such as the West German Grenzschutzgruppe-9 (GSG-9). Successful rescues in Entebbe (1976), Mogadishu (1977), and Prince's Gate, London (1980) demonstrated that national counterterrorism forces could respond effectively both domestically and abroad. A normative approach to tackling the problem, founded on the principles of international law and collective action, was less successful. Attempts by the United Nations to define and proscribe transnational terrorism bogged down in the General Assembly over semantics (i.e., deciding on the definition of a terrorist), but other cooperative initiatives were successfully implemented. These included the conventions adopted through the International Civil Aviation Organization to improve information sharing and legal cooperation, such as The Hague Convention for the Suppression of Unlawful Seizure of Aircraft (1970). Another collective response to improve information sharing and collaborative action was the creation of the Public Safety and Terrorism Sub-Directorate within Interpol in 1985. However, most initiatives and responses throughout this decade were unilateral, regional, or ad hoc in nature.

Counterterrorism Activities

Paul Pillar (2001, 29–39), a former high-level CIA official, suggests that counterterrorist policies must address at least four important issue areas:

- Develop a thorough *understanding* of the variety of economic, political, and sociocultural issues and conditions that contribute to decisions by individuals or groups to use terrorist tactics. Know that some people who become terrorists will not give up that role no matter what is done to correct unacceptable conditions.
- Completely assess the *capabilities* of terrorist groups and design programs that reduce their ability to attack.

- Review and understand the *intentions* of terrorists and make certain not to reward any of their activities with concessions.
- Create a *defense* based on counterterrorist measures that would convince terrorists that it is not worth an attack (deterrence).

There are a number of policy instruments available to those trying to prevent further terrorist attacks (Pillar 2001; Purdy 2004–2005). The first counterterrorist instrument that states might use is *diplomacy*. Leaders might use persuasion and various incentives to encourage foreign governments to suppress certain group activities and to abide by rules and procedures that might prevent terrorist activities. Global policies are welcome, but usually bilateral diplomatic agreements are more effective. It is easier to reward or punish a single state for its compliance or noncompliance with a bilateral or regional agreement than try to monitor the activities of some two hundred nation-states.

A second counterterrorism strategy is the *mobilization of nongovernmental organizations* to promote international law and educate the world about the causes of terrorism, the importance of the rule of law, and the human costs of violence and terrorism.

A third counterterrorist activity is *law enforcement*. Terrorist activities are illegal—violating both national and international law. New laws, special courts, prisons, and new penalties are all part of the war on terrorism. Police forces across the world are now cooperating to identify, arrest, and punish terrorist groups. Stricter law enforcement and increased surveillance, however, have caused some concerns related to the loss of certain civil liberties. The most controversial aspects of the global war on terrorism have been the long-term imprisonment of terrorists, the use of torture and other punitive forms of interrogation, and the illegal transferring of prisoners to nondemocratic states where torture is regularly used.

A fourth counterterrorism strategy involves the use of *financial controls* that track, freeze, and seize financial resources that support terrorist activities. The 1999 International Convention for the Suppression of the Financing of Terrorism criminalizes the collection of funds for any terrorist activity. Unfortunately, because of numerous offshore accounts, internet banking, and a global banking and financial system that makes it easy to hide and transfer funds, controlling this financial process is extremely difficult and will require both private- and public-sector collaboration.

A fifth counterterrorist strategy is the *use of military force*. The use of military force against states that support terrorism is a just cause and is supported by international law. Problems arise when the enemy is a nonstate actor, a network of terrorist organizations operating in a variety of states. How do you justify retaliating strikes against sovereign states that might not support terrorists within their boundaries?

The strategic use of force might be the only way to respond to groups willing to use force to achieve their goals. If supported by the international community and international law, force can be an effective tool. The multilateral effort to end Taliban rule in Afghanistan, and the continuing NATO operation, provides an example of a just multilateral effort to close terrorist training camps, arrest leaders of Al Qaeda, and build an effective state that is capable of providing for its citizens.

The final counterterrorist tool is *intelligence and covert action*. This involves both the use of technical intelligence, such as the monitoring of phone calls and emails, and human intelligence, and information collected by spies. The collection of information is not easy, because extremists and others willing to use terrorism are difficult to locate. Pillar (2001, 110) also points out that analysis is as difficult as collecting information. He suggests that there might just be too much information, and it is difficult to decide what is relevant and what is simply useless chatter.

To deal with transnational terrorism, the global community must address its most problematic modern aspect: the appeal of messages

Most global sports and cultural events are potential targets for terrorists, and governments spend a great deal of money trying to prevent these attacks. In this photo, Japanese security officials practice responding to chemical attacks that might disrupt the 2019 Rugby World Cup.

that inspire terrorists to commit horrific acts of violence. Killing or capturing individuals does little to halt the spread of extremist viewpoints that occur under the guise of discussion and education. In the case of Islam, for example, radical mullahs and imams twist the tenets of the religion into a doctrine of action and hatred, where spiritual achievement occurs through destruction rather than personal enlightenment. In other words, suicide attacks offer the promise of private goods (spiritual reward) rather than public goods (positive contributions to the community over a lifetime). Precisely how the processes and technologies of globalization can assist in delegitimizing the pedagogy that incites terrorists will remain one of the most vexing challenges for the global community for years to come.

Conclusion

Questions of war and peace are central to the existence of every country. In this chapter, we have examined the many ways academics analyze security affairs and how these ideas influence the decisions political leaders make on war and weapons procurement, especially nuclear weapons and nuclear proliferation. We also discussed the growing importance of technology and its use as part of hybrid warfare and cyberattacks. We are all potential victims of malware and threats to the institutions and services that we depend on in our everyday lives. Terrorism, another salient issue in global security, remains a complex phenomenon in which violence is used to obtain political power to redress grievances that might have become more acute through the process of globalization. The challenge for the global community will be in utilizing its advantages to win the war of ideas that motivates and sustains those responsible for the current wave of violence in all of its forms.

New Strategies and Tools of War

In this chapter we shared ideas and factual information about wars past, present, and future. In the final chapter of his book *The Future of War: A History* (2017), Lawrence Freedman discusses how and why the ideas about the nature of war are changing. He states that the classical model of war was all about the enemies fighting; one side lost and the other won. The international system may have changed because of the war, or it may have stayed the same. Disputes ended but were often not resolved. Freedman makes the point that both sides in a war sought a *knockout blow* so as to avoid a long struggle. Delivering the knockout blow is made more difficult by each side's misperceptions about the enemy's strength, capacity, and intentions as well as an inability to completely understand how things will work out on the battlefield. No one can match the US fighting forces, yet the war in Afghanistan has lasted over eighteen years, and there are no winners in Iraq. The author makes a convincing case that superior technology and new weapons systems do not guarantee a quick and decisive victory. One cannot "neglect war's political and human dimensions" and the uncertainty of war (279).

Professor Freedman makes a convincing case that the discovery and use of nuclear weapons was the innovation that transformed our thinking about war. Although a nonproliferation regime exists and the major nuclear powers have used these weapons for deterrence, we still could have a nuclear war. He argues that countries lacking conventional strength may use nuclear weapons to level the playing field. Russian moves in the Middle East and its actions in the Ukraine, or India and Pakistan's feud over Kashmir, could result in a nuclear confrontation.

Freedman warns us that civil wars and conflicts in ungoverned regions are likely to increase. He argues that Islamist extremism is and will remain a global challenge now and in the future. These extremist groups are "networked, ruthless, and capable," and the world must respond (284). Given the US track record in places like Syria and Libya, a robust response may not be forthcoming.

Finally, Freedman refers to a 2013 article in *Foreign Policy* by David Rothkopf that introduces the concept of *cool war.* This describes *gray zone* conflicts located between war and peace but shaped so as to avoid major wars. Why is cool war seen as an alternative to actual warfare? Freedman suggests that states are becoming less willing to commit forces to armed conflicts, so they look for other ways to attack their enemies. Subverting elections, engaging in cyberwarfare, and imposing economic sanctions are all tools used frequently by states and even some nonstate actors to achieve their goals.

CONTRIBUTORS TO CHAPTER 6: *John Baylis, Darryl Howlett, James D. Kiras, Steven L. Lamy, and John Masker*

KEY TERMS

Absolute gains, p. 226
Al Qaeda, p. 253
Asymmetric conflicts, p. 234
Clandestine or "sleeper" cell, p. 262
Community, p. 224
Democratic peace thesis, p. 227
Failed states, p. 239
Globalization, p. 223
Identity, p. 256
Imperialism, p. 256

Jihad, p. 257
Material structure, p. 227
Materialism, p. 253
Military-industrial complex, p. 230
National security, p. 222
"New" terrorism, p. 257
New wars, p. 237
Noncompliance, p. 247
Non–nuclear weapon states (NNWSs), p. 242
Norms, p. 228

North Atlantic Treaty Organization (NATO), p. 226
Nuclear deterrence, p. 241
Nuclear terrorism, p. 246
Postmodern or "new" terrorism, p. 257
Postmodernity, p. 230
Realpolitik, p. 228
Relative gains, p. 226
Revolution in military affairs (RMA), p. 233

Security, p. 222
Security community, p. 227
Skyjackings, p. 251
Social structure, p. 227
Tactics, p. 233
Terrorism, p. 224
Weapons of mass destruction (WMDs), p. 231
Widening school of international security, p. 222

REVIEW QUESTIONS

1. Why is security a "contested concept"? How do academic disagreements about the term reflect the theory perspectives we studied in Chapter 3?
2. According to realists, why do states find it difficult to cooperate? How do constructivists explain cooperation?
3. Is the tension between national and global security resolvable?
4. Has international security changed since the United States began its global war on terrorism? How?
5. What are the main arguments for and against the proliferation of nuclear weapons? To what extent might these arguments be the result of a person's theory-based worldview?
6. How might nonstate actors represent a new nuclear-proliferation challenge?
7. Why do some authors believe that war between the current great powers is highly unlikely?
8. What are the major cyberthreats faced by all nation-states?
9. What is "asymmetric warfare"?
10. What is hybrid war and how might it shape future relations among great powers?
11. When and how did terrorism become a truly global phenomenon?
12. Of all the factors that motivate terrorists, is any one more important than others, and if so, why?
13. What role does technology play in terrorism, and will it change how terrorists operate in the future? If so, how?
14. What is the primary challenge that individual states and the global community as a whole face in confronting terrorism?
15. How can globalization be useful in diminishing the underlying causes of terrorism?

 Learn more with this chapter's digital tools, including the Oxford Insight Study Guide, at **www.oup.com/he/lamy6e**.

THINKING ABOUT GLOBAL POLITICS

Perspectives on the Arms Race

OBJECTIVE

The goal of this exercise is difficult to reach: consensus on a national security policy or national strategy for the United States with regard to nuclear weapons. After doing some research online and in your library, you will explore with your classmates the importance of worldviews in determining national interests. Your professor might put you into groups.

PROCEDURE

This is not a debate but a discussion. You should try to consider the assumptions of national security from three significant groups participating in arms debates within the United States. These are the major groups:

- Arms advocates (realists)
- Arms control advocates (liberals)
- Disarmament advocates (select an Alternative Theory; see Chapter 3)

1. Review with your classmates the basic worldview positions and corresponding policy priorities of each group (reread Chapters 2 and 3).
2. Divide your class into three groups representing these views.
3. Explore these general questions in your discussion:
   a. What does the United States want its nuclear weapons to do?
   b. What should our nuclear strategy be?
   c. How can the United States use nuclear weapons to achieve its foreign policy and national security goals?

FOLLOW-UP

Take time to review your readings from the semester so far (both in this textbook and in whatever supplemental readings your professor has assigned). Make a list of statements made in these materials that support your position, which you will use in your next class. During class, your professor might choose to have you (or a group leader) write these statements on the board and ask others in the class to respond to your selections.

7 Human Rights and Human Security

The world faces more humanitarian challenges because of the rise of failed states and civil wars like the one in Yemen. This results in more refugees and internally displaced people, including children who have little food, no health care, and no chance to go to school. What is being done and why are the UN High Commissioner for Refugees (UNHCR) and other humanitarian actors unable to meet the growing needs in this crisis?

Where you are born should not dictate your potential as a human being.

—ROMEO DALLAIRE

If a tyrant should inflict upon his subject such treatment that no one is warranted in inflicting, other states may exercise a right of humanitarian intervention.

—HUGO GROTIUS

Men and women die and suffer very differently in war. In 2002, for example, 90 percent of direct war deaths were men (University of British Columbia, Human Security Center 2005). Women die in war, but they are also victims of sexual violence and predatory behavior by combatants, and at times are victimized by those who have come to help. Sexual violence is a devastating tactic of war in many fragile states and ungoverned territories where extremists challenge authority. Since the early 2000s, there have been a number of cases of aid workers and peacekeepers coercing women and girls into providing sexual services in exchange for protection assistance and support for children and other family members. In March 2016, the United Nations adopted the first resolution that holds peacekeepers accountable for committing sexual violence. Resolution 2272 will attempt to address the gaps in past reforms that have not stopped sexual abuse. This resolution gives the UN secretary-general the authority to remove a national contingent from peacekeeping operations and replace it if there is evidence of sexual exploitation and abuse by the group. This resolution also requires that UN members investigate and report allegations of exploitation and abuse. These new rules make sense, and one might ask why it has taken so long for world leaders to act. These are rules that cover crimes already covered in both domestic and international law. Unfortunately, this failure to demand accountability and allowing crimes against humanity to continue suggest a failure to accept the priority of human rights over national interests. We must be concerned as violence against women and children in conflict regions increases and the perpetrators are often those who are supposed to be the protectors.

In this chapter, we will examine the linked concepts of human rights and human security, both of which emerged

CHAPTER OUTLINE

Introduction 270

What Are Human Rights? 272

International Human Rights Legislation 275

What Is Human Security? 279

History of Humanitarian Activism and Intervention 283

Humanitarian Dimensions 291

The Role of the International Community 299

Conclusion 303

FEATURES

CASE STUDY A Failed Intervention 288

THEORY IN PRACTICE Asian Values 289

THEORY IN PRACTICE Gendered Perspective on Human Rights 298

WHAT'S TRENDING? The Human Rights Network 303

THINKING ABOUT GLOBAL POLITICS What Should Be Done? National Interests Versus Human Interests 305 from the effects of World War II. We will see that there are many reasons to hope that the world community one day will be able to stop human rights abuses and provide security to all people. But because the successful promotion of both human rights and human security depends on the international community, there may be as many reasons to be pessimistic about the prospects for a better world. After all, protecting the rights of individuals can infringe on the prerogatives of governments and thus on the notion of sovereign equality of countries. As we have seen elsewhere in this book, however, globalization is changing many traditions in world affairs.

This tension between the rights of the *individual* and the rights of *society* is a significant barrier to the creation of human security. As we will see in the first section of this chapter, there were intellectual disagreements in the nineteenth and early twentieth centuries about answers to basic questions: What is a human right? What rights should be protected? And by whom? Must these rights be universal? We are still looking for answers to these questions. How can we discuss such a broad issue as global security on a smaller, human scale? What should it look like and why is it important? What opportunities still exist for political and military leaders to circumvent, undermine, and exploit international and domestic laws?

Introduction

As in other areas of the study of global politics, there are disagreements about human rights and human security. Like the debates in other areas, the splits tend to be down the same lines as the international relations theories we discussed in Chapter 3 (see Table 7.1). However, the fundamental question is a simple one: *Do countries have an obligation to improve the living conditions and protect the rights of people who live in other countries?*

Furthermore, if there is such an obligation, what are its legal foundations? And who would define the terms of human rights? Clearly, such rights would rest within a legal system. But whose? And what kind? Some of the contemporary disagreement about the obligation to promote human rights and human security stems from a history of colonialism. For example, the modern concept of individual human rights originally developed in Europe. Yet, as many European countries colonized other regions of the world (and even other parts of Europe), these rights were often not extended to other peoples who were seen as not human. Today, for many people who live in Africa and Asia, these human rights may appear to derive from their problematic colonial heritage. Why should it necessarily mean something different to be human in Africa than in Europe?

TABLE 7.1	**Comparing Worldviews on Aspects of Human Rights**			
	Realist	**Liberal**	**Utopian**	**Marxist**
Impact on National Security	• Corporate and governmental leaders want international governments that support them, even if establishing these governments causes violence and repression.	• Citizens should have the right to self-determination and open governments that are responsive to public opinion. • Those holding sovereign power need to act responsibly. • An individual should submit to an established authority unless this authority violates an individual's conscience: disobedience is a lesser evil than the slaughter of the innocent.	• Self-determination increases the likelihood of long-term peace by facilitating the participation of all groups in the determination of their own affairs.	• The biggest security threat is global poverty and a capitalist system that rewards the rich and fails to provide employment and quality of life for those on the margins.
Economic Consequences	• Government activities should not advocate radical change, even if this change is designed to help abolish poverty for the lower classes.	• Through the reciprocity of mutual needs a great society of states develops, characterized by common norms and customs. These norms and customs are embodied in the law of nations and in natural law and are binding on all nations. States abide by these rules out of long-term, enlightened self-interest.	• Self-determination facilitates a more equitable sharing of the economic resources of the globe. • Collective responsibility and human equality apply both internally within a society and externally between societies.	
Human Rights Implications	• There should be no radical socioeconomic changes aimed at achieving human rights for the dispossessed.	• Humans are endowed equally with the right to do what is necessary for self-preservation, and to be the sole arbiters of what is necessary to expand their own liberty.	• Human rights are profoundly important guidelines for policymaking. • Self-determination is a fundamental human right that contributes to spiritual and psychological well-being and should therefore be universally nurtured.	• A global capitalist class will allow for some human rights but none that would challenge its power and economic interests. The right to quality of life and access to societal resources or an equitable distribution of societal resources is not part of a capitalist system.

TABLE 7.1	*continued*			
	Realist	**Liberal**	**Utopian**	**Marxist**
Environment	• Corporations focus resources and productive capacity on maximizing profit rather than fulfilling human needs.	• Rights involve protection of quality of life, and that includes clean air and water, and a healthy lifestyle. The rule of law can be used to protect the environment, and actions need to be taken collectively.	• If the rights of other societies are respected, productivity will eventually conform to meeting universal human needs. • Existing productive capacity for unessential goods should be converted into production of food and other essential items, leading to the better disposal of pollutants and conservation of resources.	• The environment is not a resource to be abused and exploited for the good of a few. It must serve the interests of all, and all should have access to environmental resources to create a high quality of life.

What Are Human Rights?

Human rights The inalienable rights such as life, liberty, and the pursuit of happiness that one is entitled to because one is human.

Natural law The idea that humans have an essential nature, which dictates that certain kinds of human goods are always and everywhere desired; because of this, there are common moral standards that govern all human relations, and these common standards can be discerned by the application of reason to human affairs.

Charter rights Civil liberties guaranteed in a written document such as a constitution.

The theory of **human rights** developed in Europe during the Middle Ages, and it rested on the idea of **natural law**—that humans have an essential nature. Natural law theorists differed on many issues, but they agreed on the following: (1) there are universal moral standards that support individual rights; (2) there is a general duty to adhere to these standards; and (3) the application of these standards is not limited to any particular legal system, community, state, race, religion, or civilization (Finnis 1980). These central propositions are the origin of modern rhetoric on *universal* human rights.

Natural law provided the theory, but in the rougher world of medieval political practice, rights had different connotations. During this time, rights were concessions extracted from a superior, usually by force. The Magna Carta (1215) is a case in point. In it, the barons of England obliged King John to grant to them and their heirs in perpetuity a series of liberties that are, for the most part, very specific and related to particular grievances. The Magna Carta is based on the important principle that the subjects of the king owe him duty only if he meets their claims. Thus, the Magna Carta is a political contract.

Although rights as part of natural law and those established by political contract are not inherently incompatible, these two kinds of rights are based on opposing principles. Whereas rights based on natural law are derived from the notion of human flourishing and are universal, **charter rights** are the result of a political contract and, by definition, are limited to the parties to the contract and thus restricted in time and space.

The Liberal Account of Rights

The complex language of medieval thinking on rights carried over into the modern period. Political philosophers such as Hugo Grotius, Thomas Hobbes, and John Locke continued to use notions of natural law, albeit in radically different ways from their predecessors. Gradually, a synthesis of the concepts of natural rights and charter rights emerged. Known as the **liberal account of rights**, this position is made up of two basic components:

> **Liberal account of rights** The belief that humans have inherent rights that the state has a responsibility to protect.

1. Human beings possess rights to life, liberty, the secure possession of property, the exercise of freedom of speech, and so on, which are inalienable—cannot be traded away—and unconditional. The only acceptable reason for constraining any one individual is to protect the rights of another.
2. The primary function of government is to protect these rights. Political institutions are to be judged on their performance of this function, and political obligation rests on their success in this. In short, political life is based on a kind of implicit or explicit contract between people and government.

From a philosophical and conceptual point of view, this position is easy to denigrate as a mishmash of half-digested medieval ideas. It assumes that individuals and their rights predate society—and yet how could they exist without being part of a society? For philosopher Jeremy Bentham, the function of government was to promote the general good (which he called utility), and the idea that individuals might have the right to undermine this seemed to him madness, especially since no one could tell him where these rights came from. Karl Marx, on the other hand, and many subsequent radicals pointed out that the liberal position stresses property rights to the advantage of the rich and powerful. All these points raise compelling questions, but they underestimate the powerful rhetorical appeal of the liberal position. Most people are less likely to be worried about the philosophical inadequacies associated with the liberal position on human rights than they are to be attracted by the obvious benefits of living in a political system based on or influenced by it.

One of the uncertain features of the liberal position is the extent to which the rights it describes are universal. For example, the fundamental document of the French Revolution, the Declaration of the Rights of Man and of the Citizen, is by its very title intended to be of universal scope. However, the universalism of Article 1,

After previous genocides, world leaders promised "never again"—and yet we are now holding candlelight vigils in Rwanda marking the 25th anniversary of their genocide and we continue to hold memorials to honor the genocide and mass killings in Bosnia, Myanmar, Sudan, and other regions where ethnic cleansing is ravaging minority populations. Why does the global community fail to prevent genocides after making the promise of "never again"?

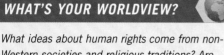

What ideas about human rights come from non-Western societies and religious traditions? Are Western ideals and non-Western ideals about human rights in opposition? In what ways, if any, are such rights and practices viewed differently?

"Men are born and remain free and equal in respect of rights," is then followed by Article 3, "The nation is essentially the source of all sovereignty." When revolutionary and Napoleonic France moved to bring the Rights of Man to the rest of Europe, the end result looked to most contemporaries remarkably like a French empire. The liberal position, while universal in principle, is particular in application, and it more or less takes state boundaries for granted.

The humanitarianism and international standard setting of the nineteenth and twentieth centuries brought these issues to the foreground. The Congress of Vienna of 1815 saw the great powers accept an obligation to end the slave trade, which was finally abolished by the Brussels Convention of 1890, while slavery itself was formally outlawed by the Slavery Convention of 1926. The Hague Conventions of 1907 and the Geneva Conventions of 1926 were designed to introduce humanitarian considerations into the conduct of war. The International Labor Office, formed in 1901, and its successor, the International Labor Organization, attempted to set standards in the workplace via measures such as the Convention Concerning Forced or Compulsory Labor of 1930.

In short, for Western European proponents of the liberal account of rights, human rights were intended to be protections for individuals against oppressive rulers, whether unelected monarchs or the choice of democratic majorities. The English and French colonizers of Asia and Africa took that notion of individual rights with them, and many believed it could take root in other cultures. As we will see, our modern notion of human rights is tied to the colonial experience, and over the centuries, this notion has evolved and been the subject of many disagreements.

Human Rights and State Sovereignty

Humanitarian measures taken together may provide a framework for some kind of global governance, but in many states, it is difficult to override a policy of **nonintervention**—not intervening in the affairs of other states—which is related to the notion of sovereignty. For example, abolishing the slave trade, which involved international transactions, was much easier than abolishing slavery, which concerns what states do to their own people; indeed, pockets of slavery survive to this day in parts of Africa, Asia, and the Middle East.

When it comes to humanitarian impulses, the difficulty in realizing them is that a basic principle of international society is the sovereignty of states, which requires respect toward and noninterference with the institutions of member states. In nineteenth-century England, radical liberals, such as statesmen John Bright and Richard Cobden, were bitterly critical of traditional diplomacy but supported the norm of nonintervention. They argued that their opponents, who claimed moral reasons in support of interventions, were in fact motivated by power politics.

Cobden was a consistent anti-interventionist and anti-imperialist; other liberals were more selective. Prime Minister of Great Britain William Gladstone's

Nonintervention The principle that external powers should not intervene in the domestic affairs of sovereign states.

1870s campaign to throw the Ottoman Empire out of Europe was based on the more common view that different standards applied to "civilized" and "uncivilized" peoples. In Gladstone's view, the Ottoman Empire—although a full member of international society since 1856—could not claim the rights of a sovereign state because its institutions did not meet the requisite standards. Indeed, this latter position was briefly established in international law in the notion of **standards of civilization**, a nineteenth-century, European discourse about what made a country civilized or uncivilized. In the twenty-first century, this notion may disturb and unsettle us, yet current conventional thinking on human rights is based on very similar ideas.

The willingness of liberals to extend their thinking on human rights toward direct intervention characterized the second half of the twentieth century. The horrors of World War I stimulated attempts to create a peace system based on a form of international government, and although the League of Nations Covenant of 1919 had no explicit human rights provision, the underlying assumption was that its members would be states governed by the rule of law and respecting individual rights. The UN Charter of 1945, in the wake of World War II, does have some explicit reference to human rights—a tribute to the impact of the horrors of that war and, in particular, the murder of millions of Jews, Roma people, and Slavs in the extermination camps of National Socialist Germany. In this context, the need to assert a universal position was deeply felt, and the scene was set for the burst of international human rights legislation during the postwar era.

> **Standards of civilization** A nineteenth-century, European discourse about which values and norms made a country civilized or barbaric and uncivilized. The conclusion was that civilized countries should colonize barbaric regions for the latter's benefit.

International Human Rights Legislation

The post–World War II humanitarian impulse led to a flurry of lawmaking and standard setting, which gave rise to what are known as *generations* of rights. First-generation rights focus on individual rights such as free speech, freedom of religion, and voting rights—rights that protect the individual from the potential abuses of the state. Second-generation rights include social, economic, and cultural rights. This group of rights includes the right to employment, housing, health care, and education. First- and second-generation rights are covered by the Universal Declaration of Human Rights and the European Union's Charter of Fundamental Rights. Third-generation rights are more focused on collective or group rights and have not been adopted by most states. These include the right to natural resources, the right to self-determination, the right to clean air, and the right to communicate. Many of these rights emerge from major global conferences that focus on transboundary issues such as the environment, racism, information and communications, and the rights of minorities and women. The current UN Sustainable Development Goals (SDGs) fall into the third-generation rights, and that might explain why some nation-states are not as supportive as they could be in helping to secure these goals—another case of national interests trumping wider global and human interests.

The Universal Declaration of Human Rights

In 1948, the UN General Assembly established a baseline of human rights for its member states to follow. The **Universal Declaration of Human Rights** set out thirty basic political, civil, economic, and social rights that sought to define which specific rights all people share as humans. In the words of the Preamble to the declaration, "the peoples of the United Nations reaffirmed their faith in fundamental human rights, in the dignity and worth of the human person and of the equal rights of men and women." The enumerated entitlements included freedom from torture, freedom of opinion, equal treatment before the law, freedom of movement within a country, the right to own property, the right to education, and the right to work.

There were two shortcomings in the Universal Declaration. First, it was nonbinding on the member states of the United Nations. Countries' leaders could pledge to support the goals of the document but then point to a range of political or economic problems that stopped them from full implementation. Article 29 bolstered their rationale for nonintervention: "Everyone has duties to the community in which alone the free and full development of his personality is possible." A second difficulty was the European origins of these rights. As the wave of decolonization swept Asia and Africa, newly independent countries eagerly embraced the tenets of human rights law. Unfortunately, as civil strife threatened to split some of these countries, some leaders blamed it on the pattern of oppression that the colonizers had created, and they used the provisions of Article 29 as the political justification for postcolonial repression.

Despite its shortcomings, the Universal Declaration of Human Rights is, symbolically, a central piece of legislation. This was the first time in history that the international community had attempted to define a comprehensive code for the internal government of its members. During the late 1940s, the West dominated the United Nations, and the contents of the declaration represented this fact, with its emphasis on political freedom. The voting was forty-eight for and none against. Eight states abstained, for interestingly different reasons.

South Africa abstained. The white-dominated regime in South Africa denied political rights to the majority of its people and clearly could not accept that "all are born free and equal in dignity and rights" (Article 1), claiming it violated the protection of the domestic jurisdiction of states guaranteed by Article 2(7) of the UN

Under the 1993 Chemical Weapons Convention, there is a worldwide ban on the production, stockpiling, and use of chemical weapons. The use of chemical weapons is a violation of international law and a gross violation of human rights. Syria's leaders are using chemical weapons on their own citizens, but world leaders have not taken collective action to punish Syria. In this photo, British foreign secretary Boris Johnson and French foreign affairs minister Jean-Yves Le Drian shake hands after the 2018 meeting on the International Partnership against Impunity for the Use of Chemical Weapons, in Paris. Why do you think these international organizations are so ineffective?

Charter. This is a clear and uncomplicated case of a first-generation (political) rights issue.

The Soviet Union and five Soviet-bloc countries abstained. Although Stalin's USSR was clearly a tyranny, the Soviet government did not officially object to the political freedoms set forth in the declaration. Instead, the Soviet objection was to the absence of sufficient attention to social and economic rights by comparison to the detailed elaboration of "bourgeois" freedoms and property rights. The Soviets saw the declaration as a Cold War document designed to stigmatize socialist regimes—a not wholly inaccurate description of the motives of its promulgators.

Saudi Arabia abstained. It was one of the few non-Western members of the United Nations in 1948 and just about the only one whose system of government was not, in principle, based on some Western model. Saudi Arabia objected to the dec-

Pakistani human rights activist Malala Yousafzai, center, raises her hands in triumph with some of the schoolgirls who escaped from their Boko Haram kidnappers in Nigeria. Extremists may present one of the most significant challenges to human rights, and many governments can do very little to stop these violations. If governments cannot protect their citizens, who will?

laration on religious grounds, explicitly objecting to Article 18, which specifies the freedom to change and practice the religion of one's choice. These provisions did not merely contravene specific Saudi laws, which, for example, forbade (and still forbid) the practice of the Christian religion in Saudi Arabia, but they also contravened the tenets of Islam, which does not recognize a right of apostasy, or the renunciation of a religious belief. Here, to complete the picture, we have an assertion of third-generation rights and a denial of the universalism of the declaration. These themes emerged at the beginning of the universal human rights regime and would characterize the politics of human rights for the next sixty years.

Subsequent UN Legislation

Building on the promise of the Universal Declaration, the United Nations took the lead in creating major legally binding international conventions that define the rights of specific groups, including women, children, and migrant workers, and that aim to eliminate torture and racial discrimination. There are ten core human rights instruments, each of which has a committee of experts that monitor the implementation and enforcement of these treaties. Some of the more important conventions or covenants that have attracted attention recently due to global challenges and events include the following:

- International Covenant on Civil and Political Rights (1966): challenged by authoritarian rule in many states, including Egypt, China, Russia, Turkey, and Pakistan.
- Convention on the Elimination of All Forms of Discrimination Against Women (1979): challenged by governments in Saudi Arabia, Pakistan,

Sudan, Afghanistan, and Iraq. Islamist extremist groups in the Middle East, Africa, and Asia also pose a significant challenge to the convention.

- Convention Against Torture and Other Cruel, Inhuman, or Degrading Treatment or Punishment (1984): challenged by many authoritarian states and the United States in its war on terrorism. The George W. Bush administration used the law to its advantage and changed the definitions of torture to circumvent the prohibitions against torture and cruel and inhumane activities when dealing with suspected terrorists.

These conventions and others provide the intellectual and legal basis for the concept of human security, which we examine later in the chapter.

Enforcement of Human Rights Legislation

A significant number of states, global civil society actors, parliamentarians, lawyers, trade unions, and global social movements have embraced the Universal Declaration of Human Rights, and each promotes these rights and uses them as guidelines in its professional and personal activities. The UN Commission on Human Rights has the power to monitor, report, and advise, but the United Nations lacks the resources and authority to enforce these rights. Member states may, however, publicly criticize or shame states guilty of violating the rights of their citizens. Some states, such as the social democratic countries of Europe, have placed conditions on aid and trade agreements, demanding that states follow the rights articulated in all UN legal conventions. With the 2005 Responsibility to Protect (R2P) agreement, states have the obligation to prevent abuse and to protect citizens from governments that abuse the rights of their citizens.

ENGAGING WITH THE WORLD

Global March

The Global March Against Child Labor is a global network of various groups including trade unions, educators, and nongovernmental organizations (NGOs) that work toward eliminating and preventing all forms of child labor, human trafficking, and slavery. Two prominent goals are promoting the UN SDGs and the ratification and implementation of the International Labor Organization (ILO)'s labor standards. Global March has a three-pronged strategy, what they call the *triangular paradigm*, that focuses on preventing child labor, promoting basic education and literacy, and eliminating poverty. The organization has plenty of opportunities for volunteers all around the world. Contact them at https://globalmarch.org/.

▶ What Is Human Security?

Like the doctrines of human rights, the concept of **human security** represents a powerful but controversial attempt by sections of the academic and policy community to redefine and broaden the meaning of security. Traditionally, security meant protection of the sovereignty and territorial integrity of states from external military threats. This was the essence of the concept of national security, which dominated security analysis and policymaking during the Cold War period. In the 1970s and 1980s, academic literature on security, responding to the Middle East oil crisis and the growing awareness of worldwide environmental degradation, began to describe security in broader, nonmilitary terms. Yet the state remained the object of security, or the entity to be protected.

The concept of human security challenges the state-centric notion of security by focusing on the individual. Human security is about security for the people rather than for states or governments. Hence, it has generated much debate. Critics wonder whether such an approach would widen the boundaries of security studies too much and whether "securitizing" the individual is the best way to address the challenges facing the international community from the forces of globalization. On the other side, advocates of human security find that the concept effectively highlights the dangers to human safety and survival posed by poverty, disease, environmental stress, and human rights abuses, as well as armed conflict. These disagreements notwithstanding, the concept of human security captures a growing realization that, in an era of rapid globalization, security must encompass a broader range of concerns and challenges than simply defending the state from external military attack.

> **Human security** The security of people, including their physical safety, their economic and social well-being, respect for their dignity, and the protection of their human rights.

Origin of the Concept

The origin of the concept of human security can be traced to the publication of the *Human Development Report* of 1994, issued by the UN Development Programme. The report defined the scope of human security to include seven areas:

- *Economic security*—ensuring basic income for all people, usually from productive and remunerative work or, as the last resort, from some publicly financed safety net.
- *Food security*—ensuring that all people at all times have both physical and economic access to basic food.
- *Health security*—guaranteeing a minimum of protection from diseases and unhealthy lifestyles.
- *Environmental security*—protecting people from the short- and long-term ravages of nature, human threats in nature, and deterioration of the natural environment.
- *Personal security*—protecting people from physical violence, whether from the state or external states, from violent individuals and substate factors, from domestic abuse, or from predatory adults.

- *Community security*—protecting people from the loss of traditional relationships and values and from sectarian and ethnic violence.
- *Political security*—ensuring that people live in a society that honors their basic human rights, and ensuring the freedom of individuals and groups from government attempts to exercise control over ideas and information.

The seven areas appear to describe the basic purpose of every country; and yet, as with other UN programs, the *Human Development Report* has had numerous critics. The primary complaint has been that the report has issued an unfunded mandate: It could be used to admonish countries that did not reach the standards, yet the report provided little or no funding to reach them. As you will see in the next section, this tension between standard setting in human rights and human security and assessing country performance has been a consistent strain since 1945. The leaders of many governments resent what they perceive as interference in the sovereign affairs of their countries.

Human Security and Development

Unlike many other efforts to redefine security, where political scientists played a major role, human security was the handiwork of a group of development economists, such as the late Pakistani economist Mahbub ul Haq, who conceptualized the UN Development Programme's *Human Development Report*. They were increasingly dissatisfied with the orthodox notion of development, which viewed it as a function of economic growth. Instead, they proposed a concept of **human development** that focuses on building human capabilities to confront and overcome poverty, illiteracy, diseases, discrimination, restrictions on political freedom, and the threat of violent conflict: "Individual freedoms and rights matter a great deal, but people are restricted in what they can do with that freedom if they are poor, ill, illiterate, discriminated against, threatened by violent conflict or denied a political voice" (UN Development Programme 2011, 18–19).

Closely related to the attempt to create a broader paradigm for development was the growing concern about the negative impact of defense spending on development, or the "guns versus butter" dilemma. As a global study headed by Inga Thorsson of Sweden concluded, "the arms race and development are in a competitive relationship" (Roche 1986, 8). Drawing on this study, a UN-sponsored International Conference on the Relationship Between Disarmament and Development, in 1986 in Paris, sought "to enlarge world understanding that human security demands more resources for development and fewer for arms."

Human Security and Refugees

One of the most disturbing trends in recent years is the number of refugees fleeing conflicts across the world. The numbers are staggering and their presence has raised some very interesting questions about the responsibility we all have to those in need. According to the Office of the United Nations High Commissioner for Refugees (UNHCR), there are about 21 million refugees and over 40 million

Human development The notion that it is possible to improve the lives of people. Basically, it is about increasing the number of choices people have. These may include living a long and healthy life, access to education, and a better standard of living.

people displaced in their own land. The countries where these refugees have landed do not have the resources to provide adequate housing, food, health care, education, and security for them. What is needed is more humanitarian assistance that addresses poverty in crisis regions, as well as resources to provide for all who arrive in foreign lands.

In 1950, the UNHCR was established to help people who were left without homes after World War II. Until recently, half of the refugees of concern to the UNHCR were in Asia, and about 28 percent were in African countries. The UNHCR has been successful in its attempt to emphasize three policy strategies: repatriation, or returning people to their homelands; integrating refugees into a place of residence; or resettling the refugees in a country sympathetic to their plight. By the end of 2017, close to 70 million individuals were forcibly displaced across the globe, including 25 million refugees, 40 million internally displaced individuals, and over 3 million asylum seekers. Over two-thirds of the refugees come from Syria, Afghanistan, South Sudan, Myanmar, and Somalia. At this time, the most serious flashpoints for refugees and human security may be in Syria, where a civil war has been going on since 2011. The civil war in Yemen has created a humanitarian emergency, with over 20 million people in need of assistance. Cholera alone is killing over a million, and over 15 million are near starvation.

The number of refugees fleeing the Syrian conflict to neighboring countries, such as Lebanon and several European states, has exceeded 4 million, which confirms that the Syrian crisis is the world's single largest refugee crisis in almost a quarter of a century under the UNHCR's mandate. Not all refugees fleeing to Europe are from Syria, however; Germany expects to take in about 800,000 refugees from Syria, Iraq, Afghanistan, Ukraine, and other conflict-affected regions. Germany has received the most migrants, with over 362,000 asylum applications filed as of November 2015. As of January 2016, European Union countries have received over 942,000 claims for asylum from refugees.

Since the war began, over 12 million Syrians have been displaced by the civil war. The United Nations estimates that 6.6 million people are internally displaced, meaning that they have been forced to leave their homes but that they still reside within the borders of Syria, and over 470,000 have been killed in the conflict. The Syrian civil war and refugee crisis has caused the international community to reassess migration policies and look for solutions that meet the needs of both national and human security. Unfortunately, questions remain regarding how to best respond to the crisis and what roles host countries should play in terms of providing relief and fostering integration.

A new refugee crisis has developed on the US border. New rules in the United States have limited immigration from Mexico and Central America. In this photo, migrants wait outside the offices of the Mexican Commission for Refugee Assistance for documents permitting them to be in the country.

A rather new crisis is taking place in Bangladesh: 671,000 Rohingya refugees have fled to Bangladesh from Myanmar, where they are being targeted by government forces. The UN High Commissioner for Human Rights has called this crisis a textbook example of ethnic cleansing. The Rohingya ethnic community has been in Myanmar since the twelfth century. They are Muslims living in a majority Buddhist country, and because they were stripped of their citizenship in 1982, they are the largest stateless minority living in the Rakhine state of Myanmar. They have no rights and are seen by the Myanmar government as immigrants from Bangladesh. Human rights observers and journalists have documented numerous cases of the Myanmar army burning villages and unleashing a campaign of violence aimed at men, women, and children. Many of the refugee situations around the world today are the result of one dominant ethnic community expelling or attempting to eliminate other minority communities. By denying the Rohingya citizenship, they can be denied social services and the protections afforded citizens. This is not a new story for our human community. We have often treated "outsiders" as if they are illegal criminals or worse. As an international community, we have not accepted the simple fact that everyone has some rights simply because they are human beings.

A refugee crisis is fast developing in the Western Hemisphere. The economic and political crisis in Venezuela has created more than 4 million refugees, and political unrest in Bolivia and Chile raises serious human rights concerns.

Common Security

The move toward human security was also advanced by the work of several international commissions. They offered a broader view of security that looked beyond the Cold War emphasis on East–West military competition. Foremost among them was the Palme Commission of 1982, which proposed the doctrine of **common security**, emphasizing noncompetitive, cooperative approaches to achieving human security for all. Its report stressed that "in the Third World countries, as in all our countries, security requires economic progress as well as freedom from military fear" (Palme Commission 1982, xii). In 1987, the report of the World Commission on Environment and Development (also known as the Brundtland Commission) highlighted the linkage between environmental degradation and conflict: "The real sources of insecurity encompass unsustainable development, and its effects can become intertwined with traditional forms of conflict in a manner that can extend and deepen the latter" (Brundtland et al. 1987, 230).

Common security At times called "cooperative security," it stresses noncompetitive approaches and cooperative approaches through which states—both friends and foes—can achieve security. It is the belief that no one is secure until all people are secure from threats of war.

More recently, Pope Francis has added his voice to the conversation about climate change and human security. In his papal encyclical *Laudato Si, On Care for Our Common Home*, the pope suggests that the first victims of climate change will be the poor. This is not a new message, but it points to the need to address our economic priorities and understand that the changing climate will create a new group of refugees who will be pushed out of their homes by nature or by the rich and powerful seeking a place to survive or resources to consume.

History of Humanitarian Activism and Intervention

As the concepts of human rights and human security have developed, many opinion leaders and politicians in democratic societies have become increasingly aware that the state must take action in the face of challenges to human lives and dignity. In effect, many politicians have come to believe that the state should do more than defend borders and that cooperative and purposeful international action might be necessary to safeguard people.

One reason human security has become a more salient issue in recent decades is that civil wars and intrastate conflicts are more frequent. These have entailed huge losses of life, ethnic cleansing, displacement of people within and across borders, and disease outbreaks. Traditional national security approaches have not been sufficiently sensitive toward conflicts that arise over cultural, ethnic, and religious differences, as happened in Eastern Europe, Africa, and Central Asia in the post–Cold War era (Tow and Trood 2000).

Another reason for greater humanitarian awareness is the spread of democratization (see Map 7.1), which has been accompanied by more emphasis on human rights and **humanitarian intervention**. Proponents of interventions take the position that the international community is justified in intervening in the internal affairs of states accused of gross violation of human rights. This has led to the realization that while the concept of national security has not been rendered irrelevant, it no longer sufficiently accounts for the kinds of danger that threaten societies, states, and the international community.

The notion of human security has also been brought front and center by crises induced by accelerating globalization. For example, the widespread poverty, unemployment, and social dislocation caused by the Asian financial crisis of 1997 underscored people's vulnerability to the effects of economic globalization (Acharya 2004). This vulnerability played a major role in the 2010–2011 **Arab Spring** revolutionary uprisings, which began in Tunisia and spread across Egypt, Libya, Syria, Yemen, Bahrain, Saudi Arabia, and Jordan. At the heart of these protests was a desire for more democratic and transparent political systems and more open and equitable economic systems. Citizens across the Arab world demanded an end to authoritarian rule and sought greater access to resources and wealth that were held by very few in their countries. During the recent global

Humanitarian intervention The use of military force by external actors to end a threat to people within a sovereign state.

Arab Spring Protests and revolutionary uprisings that began in Tunisia in 2010 and spread across Egypt, Libya, Syria, Yemen, Bahrain, Saudi Arabia, and Jordan in 2011. At their core was a desire for more democratic and transparent political systems and more open and equitable economic systems.

Antigovernment protests in Chile erupted because of harsh economic policies that increase the gap between rich and poor. Most citizens in this Latin American country cannot afford basic human needs such as medical care, housing, and education. Similar street demonstrations are happening in Bolivia because the government has not been able to provide human security: freedom from fear, freedom from want, and the rule of law. As more states fail, will conflicts such as these spread across the globe?

economic recession, however, international aid agencies saw a sharp decline in donations for countries and individuals, thus undermining their ability to meet basic needs.

Contemporary Cases of Intervention and Nonintervention

It has become common to describe the immediate post–Cold War period as something of a golden era for humanitarian activism and intervention. Thomas Weiss (2004, 136) argues that "the notion that human beings matter more than sovereignty radiated brightly, albeit briefly, across the international political horizon of the 1990s." This was symbolized for many by the North Atlantic Treaty Organization (NATO)'s intervention to halt Serb atrocities in Kosovo in March 1999 and the Australian-led intervention to end mass atrocities in East Timor. But the 1990s also saw the world stand aside during the genocides in Rwanda and Srebrenica. To make sense of these developments, let's focus on international interventions in northern Iraq, Somalia, Rwanda, and Kosovo and divide our discussion into three parts: the place of humanitarian impulses in decisions to intervene; the legality and legitimacy of the interventions; and the effectiveness of these military interventions.

In the cases of northern Iraq in April 1991 and Somalia in December 1992, domestic public opinion played an important role in pressuring policymakers

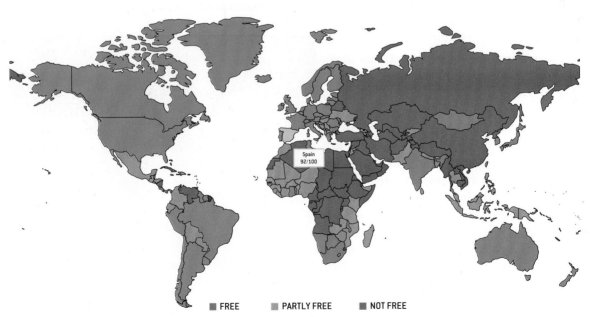

■ FREE   ■ PARTLY FREE   ■ NOT FREE

Map 7.1 **Democracy in the World, 2019.**

This map from Freedom House represents a specifically American view of democracy. In many countries, democracy is only tenuously established, and human rights abuses continue.

Source: Freedom in the World 2018, Democracy in Crisis https://freedomhouse.org/report/freedom-world/freedom-world-2019

into using force for humanitarian purposes. In the face of a massive refugee crisis caused by Saddam Hussein's oppression of the Kurds in the aftermath of the 1991 Gulf War, US, British, French, and Dutch military forces intervened to create protected "safe havens" for the Kurdish people. Similarly, the US military intervention in Somalia in December 1992 was a response to sentiments of compassion on the part of US citizens. This sense of solidarity disappeared, however, once the United States began sustaining casualties.

WHAT'S YOUR WORLDVIEW?

Why is the idea of humanitarian intervention so controversial? Why are states so unwilling to intervene to save people in danger? Consider the ongoing humanitarian disasters in Myanmar, Syria, Yemen, and Sudan. Why does the world simply sit back and watch people die?

The fact that the White House pulled the plug on its Somali intervention after the loss of eighteen US Rangers in a firefight in October 1993 indicates how capricious public opinion is. Television pictures of starving and dying Somalis had persuaded the outgoing George H. W. Bush administration to launch a humanitarian rescue mission, but once the US public saw dead Americans dragged through the streets of Mogadishu, the Clinton administration announced a timetable for withdrawal. What the Somalia case demonstrates is that the "CNN effect" is a double-edged sword: It can pressure governments into humanitarian intervention yet with equal speed produce public disillusionment and calls for withdrawal. These cases also suggest that even if there are no vital national interests at stake, liberal states might launch humanitarian rescue missions if sufficient public pressure is mobilized. Certainly, there is no evidence in either of these cases to support the realist claim that states cloak power-political motives behind the guise of humanitarianism.

By contrast, the French intervention in Rwanda in July 1994 seems to be an example of abuse. France had propped up the one-party Hutu state for twenty years, even providing troops when the Rwandan Patriotic Front (RPF), consisting largely of members of the rival Tutsi population and operating out of neighboring Uganda, threatened to overrun the country in 1990 and 1993. French President François Mitterrand was reportedly eager to restore waning French influence in Africa and was fearful that an RPF victory in French-speaking Rwanda would bring the country under the influence of Anglophones. France therefore did not intervene until the latter stages of the genocide against the Tutsis, which was ended primarily by the RPF's military victory. Thus, it seems that French behavior accorded with the realist premise that states will risk their soldiers only in defense of the national interest. French leaders may have been partly motivated by humanitarian sentiments, but this seems to be a case of a state abusing the concept of humanitarian intervention because the primary purpose of the intervention was to protect French national interests.

The moral question raised by French intervention is why international society failed to intervene when the genocide began in early April 1994. French intervention may have saved some lives, but it came far too late to halt the genocide. Some 800,000 people were killed in a mere hundred days. The failure of international society to stop the genocide indicates that state leaders remain gripped by the mindset of national interests trumping human interests. There was no intervention for the simple reason that those with the military capability to stop the genocide were unwilling to sacrifice troops and treasure to protect Rwandans. International solidarity in the face of genocide was limited to moral outrage and the provision of humanitarian aid.

If the French intervention in Rwanda can be criticized for being too little too late, NATO's intervention in Kosovo in 1999 was criticized for being too much too soon. At the beginning of the war, NATO said it was intervening to prevent a humanitarian catastrophe. To do this, NATO aircraft were given two objectives: reduce Serbia's military capacity and coerce Slobodan Milošević, president of the Federal Republic of Yugoslavia, into accepting a peace agreement with the Albanian majority population of Kosovo. (Kosovo was an autonomous province within Serbia, which lay within the greater Yugoslavia.) NATO claimed that the resort to force was justifiable for the following reasons. First, it was argued that Serbian actions in Kosovo had created a humanitarian emergency and breached a range of international legal commitments. Second, NATO governments argued that the Serbs were committing crimes against humanity, possibly including genocide. Third, it was contended that the Milošević regime's use of force against the Kosovar Albanians challenged global norms of common humanity.

Closer analysis of the justifications articulated by Western leaders suggests that while humanitarianism may have provided the primary impulse for action, it was by no means the exclusive impulse, and the complexity of the motives of the interveners colored the character of the intervention. Indeed, NATO was propelled into action by a mixture of humanitarian concern and self-interest gathered around three sets of issues. The first might be called the "Srebrenica syndrome"—a fear that, left unchecked, Milošević's henchmen would replicate the carnage of Bosnia. The second is related directly to self-interest and was a concern that protracted conflict in the southern Balkans would create a massive refugee crisis in Europe. Finally, NATO governments were worried that if they failed to contain the crisis, it would spread to several neighboring states, especially Macedonia, Albania, and Bulgaria (Bellamy 2002, 3). This suggests that humanitarian intervention might be prompted by mixed motives. It only becomes a problem if the nonhumanitarian motives undermine the chances of achieving the humanitarian purposes.

Universalism Challenged

Paradoxically, the success of the global human rights regime caused a growing backlash to the development of international norms of behavior. If taken seriously and at face value, human rights laws after 1945 would create a situation where all states would be obliged to conform to a quite rigid template that dictated most aspects of their political, social, and economic structures and policies. And so, from 1945, opponents of both the human rights and the human security regimes objected that (1) the norms were an unwarranted intrusion in the affairs of sovereign states and (2) these norms also sought to overturn existing assumptions about the role of the state and its jurisdiction.

Conventional defenders of human rights and human security argue that universalism would be a good thing; the spread of best practice in these matters is in the interest of all people. Others disagree. Does post-1945 law constitute best practice? The feminist critique of universal human rights is particularly appropriate here. The universal documents all, in varying degrees, privilege a patriarchal view of the family as the basic unit of society. Even such documents as the Convention on the Elimination of All Forms of Discrimination Against Women (CEDAW) of 1979 do no more than extend to women the standard liberal package of rights, and modern feminists debate whether this constitutes a genuine advance (Peters and Wolper 1995).

More fundamentally, is the very idea of "best practice" sound? We have already met one objection to the idea in the Saudi abstention of 1948. The argument is simple: Universalism is destructive not only to undesirable differences between societies but also to desirable and desired differences. The human rights movement stresses the *common* humanity of the peoples of the world, but for many, the qualities that distinguish us from one another are as important as the characteristics that unify us. For example, the Declaration of Principles of Indigenous Rights adopted in Panama in 1984 by a nongovernmental group, the World Council of Indigenous Peoples, lays out positions that are designed to preserve the traditions, customs, institutions, and practices of indigenous peoples (many of which, it need hardly be said, contradict contemporary liberal norms). As with feminist critiques, the argument here is that the present international human rights regime rests too heavily on the experiences of one part of humanity, in this case, Western Europe, Canada, and the United States. Of course, in practice, the cultural critique and the feminist critique may lead in different directions.

CASE STUDY

A Failed Intervention

Background

The Darfur Genocide refers to the current mass slaughter of civilians in Western Sudan, which has claimed the lives of more than 300,000 people and displaced nearly 2.5 million others. The killings began in the early 2000s and continue today. The genocide is being carried out by a group of government-armed and -funded Arab militias known as the Janjaweed, which translates to "devils on horseback." The Janjaweed are destroying Darfurians by burning villages and raping and torturing civilians.

The Case

US Secretary of State Colin Powell declared the ongoing conflict in Darfur a genocide on September 4, 2004, and on February 18, 2006, President George W. Bush called for the number of international troops in Darfur to be doubled. On September 17, 2006, British prime minister Tony Blair wrote an open letter to the members of the European Union calling for a unified response to the crisis. In supporting the United Nations Security Council Resolution in 2007 to authorize the deployment of up to 26,000 peacekeepers to try to stop the violence in Darfur, British prime minister Gordon Brown said in a speech before the UN General Assembly that the Darfur crisis was "the greatest humanitarian disaster the world faces today." The British government also endorsed the International Criminal Court (ICC)'s indictment against Sudanese president Omar al-Bashir for committing crimes against humanity, war crimes, and genocide and urged the Sudanese government to cooperate with the ICC.

Unfortunately, the world seems to have forgotten about Darfur, but the killing and human rights violations have continued. The government of Sudan has been able to contain the flow of information by closing the UN

A Failed Intervention *continued*

Women and children living in the ZamZam camp for displaced people in northern Darfur. The Sudanese government is trying to convince the United Nations that things are stable, citizens are protected, and the peacekeeping forces should leave, yet several NGOs claim that atrocities continue and the world must return its attention to this region. Why do you think the world seems to have moved on and forgotten these victims of violence?

Human Rights Office in the capital of Khartoum and convincing peacekeepers to leave regions they deem stable. Once the peacekeepers leave, the atrocities begin again. In 2014, the Satellite Sentinel Project, an organization dedicated to ending genocide and crimes against humanity, was able to confirm that the Sudanese government had burned and bombed some six villages in Darfur's eastern Jebel Marra region.

The government of Sudan has used aid money from Qatar to build model villages for those displaced by the continuing violence. However, Human Rights Watch recently uncovered an incident of mass rape in one of these model villages. In October 2014 in the village of Tabit, soldiers from the Sudanese army raped over two hundred women in a thirty-six-hour period. Human rights courts have ruled that rape by police or soldiers is an act of torture because it is used as an instrument of terror and is a tactic of social control and ethnic domination.

Outcome

The crimes against humanity continue today with only NGOs demanding action. The international community has imposed some sanctions, but enforcement is uneven. The United States and its European allies have no stomach for another intervention after Afghanistan, Iraq, Libya, and Syria. A major constraint is the fact that both China and Russia have worked to block many UN resolutions in attempts to appease the Sudanese government. From its seat on the UN Security Council, China has been Sudan's chief diplomatic ally. China invests heavily in Sudanese oil (Sudan is China's largest overseas oil provider), and China supplies Sudan's military with helicopters, tanks, and fighter planes. For decades, Russia and China have maintained a strong economic and politically strategic partnership and have opposed the presence of UN peacekeeping troops in Sudan. Russia strongly supports Sudan's territorial integrity and opposes the creation of an independent Darfur state. Russia is also Sudan's strongest investment partner and considers Sudan an important global ally in Africa.

For Discussion

1. Genocide continues and states have often not responded despite the fact that many states have signed international agreements requiring a collective response to this criminal behavior. Why do you think states have failed to act collectively to stop genocide and other crimes against humanity?
2. Do some research to find out what kinds of sanctions have been imposed on Sudan by the international community. Why do you think these have failed to stop the genocide? Would different types of sanctions be more effective?

This philosophical point took on a political form in the 1990s. In the immediate post–Cold War world, and especially after the election of President Bill Clinton in 1992, there was some talk of the United States adopting active policies of democracy promotion. A number of East Asian governments and intellectuals

Asian Values

More research in global politics is focusing on the importance of beliefs, traditions, and values and the resulting narratives or stories that may guide the actions of individuals, groups, and even nation-states. The fact that Western states, intergovernmental organizations, and NGOs have sometimes taken it upon themselves to promote human rights has often been resented as hypocritical in the non-Western world, where the imperialist record of the West over the last four centuries has not been forgotten. In the 1990s, this resentment led a number of the leaders of the quasi-authoritarian newly industrializing nations of Southeast Asia to assert the existence of Asian values that could be counterposed to the (allegedly) Western values associated with the international human rights regime.

Such thinking was partially reflected in the Bangkok Declaration of 1993, made by Asian ministers in the run-up to the Vienna Conference of that year (for texts, see Tang 1994). Western notions of human rights were seen as excessively individualistic, as opposed to Asian societies' stress on the family, and insufficiently supportive of (if not downright hostile to) religion. Further, some regarded the West as morally decadent because of the growth of gay rights and the relative success of the women's movement in combating gender discrimination. Some have argued that such positions are simply intended to legitimate authoritarian rule, although it should be noted that "Asian values" can perform this task only if the argument strikes a chord with ordinary people.

More to the point, are the conservative positions expressed by proponents of Asian values actually Asian in any genuine sense? Many Western conservatives and fundamentalists share their critique of the West, while progressive Asian human rights activists are critical. Notions such as "the West" or "Asia" are unacceptably essentialist. All cultures and civilizations contain different and often conflicting tendencies; the world of Islam or of "Confucian capitalism" is no more monolithic than is Christianity or Western secularism. The Asian values argument petered out at the end of the 1990s, but the problems it illustrated remain.

For Discussion

1. Is this really a debate between Asian and Western values, or is it a debate between universal views on rights versus more limited views on rights? Why?
2. Will the world ever come to agreement on a universal view of rights that applies to all? Why or why not?

asserted in response the notion that there were specifically "Asian values" that required defending from this development. The argument was that human rights boil down to no more than a set of particular social choices that need not be considered binding by those whose values (and, hence, social choices) are differently formed—for example, by Islam or Confucianism rather than by an increasingly secularized Christianity. The wording of the Vienna Declaration on Human Rights of 1993, which refers to the need to bear in mind "the significance of national and regional particularities and various historical, cultural and religious backgrounds" when considering human rights, partially reflects this viewpoint—and has been criticized for this by some human rights activists.

Returning to the history of rights, it is here that the distinction between rights grounded in natural law and rights grounded in a contract becomes crucial. As noted earlier, it is only if rights are grounded in some account of human progress and reason that they may be regarded as genuinely universal in scope. But is this position, as its adherents insist, free of cultural bias, a set of ideas that all rational beings must accept? It seems not, at least insofar as many apparently rational Muslims, Hindus, Buddhists, atheists, utilitarians, and so on clearly do not accept its doctrines. It seems that either the standards derived from natural law (or a similar doctrine) are cast in such general terms that virtually any continuing social system will exemplify them or, if the standards are cast more specifically, they are not in fact universally desired.

Of course, we are under no obligation to accept all critiques of universalism at face value. Human rights may have first emerged in the West, but this does not in itself make rights thinking Western. Perhaps an apparently principled rejection of universalism is, in fact, no more than a rationalization of tyranny. How do we know that the inhabitants of Saudi Arabia, say, prefer not to live in a democratic system with Western liberal rights, as their government asserts? There is an obvious dilemma here: If we insist that we will only accept democratically validated regimes, we will be imposing an alien test of legitimacy on these societies. Yet what other form of validation is available?

In any event, the body of legal acts for the protection of universal human rights applies, does it not, even if rights are essentially convenient fictions? Again, defenders of difference will argue that international law is itself a Western, universalist notion, and they rightly note that the Western record of adherence to universal norms does not justify any claim to moral superiority. They point to the many crimes of the age of imperialism, as well as to contemporary issues such as the treatment of asylum seekers and refugees and, of course, the byproducts of the global war on terrorism such as torture and imprisonment without trial.

There is no neutral language for discussing human rights. Whatever way the question is posed reflects a particular viewpoint, and this is no accident: It is built into the nature of the discourse. Is there any way the notion of universal rights can be saved from its critics? Two modern approaches seem fruitful. Even if we find it difficult to specify human *rights*, it may still be possible to talk of human *wrongs*. Similarly, some have argued that it is easier to specify what is *unjust* than what is *just* (see Booth 1999). To use Michael Walzer's terminology (1994), there may be no thick moral code that is universally acceptable, to which all local codes conform, but there may be a thin code that at least can be used to delegitimize some actions. Thus, for example, the Genocide Convention of 1948 seems a plausible example of a piece of international legislation that outlaws an obvious wrong, and while some local variations in the rights associated with gender may be unavoidable, it is still possible to say that practices that severely restrict human capabilities, such as female genital mutilation, are simply wrong. Any code that did not condemn such suffering would be unworthy of respect.

This may not take us as far as some would wish. Essential to this approach is the notion that there are some practices that many would condemn but that must be tolerated, but it may be the most appropriate response to contemporary pluralism. An alternative approach involves recognizing that human rights are based on a particular culture—Richard Rorty (1993) calls this the "human rights culture"—and it requires defending them in these terms rather than by reference to some cross-cultural code. This approach would involve abandoning the idea that human rights exist. Instead, it involves proselytizing on behalf of the sort of culture in which rights are deemed to exist. The essential point is that human life is safer, pleasanter, and more dignified when rights are acknowledged than when they are not.

▶ Humanitarian Dimensions

Both human rights and human security have become part of an international discourse about proper norms of behavior and the best methods to promote these norms. The disagreements that exist today tend to be questions about the responsibilities of governments to live up to these standards. In this section, we discuss some dimensions of this discourse, with particular emphasis on political and economic rights and security, human rights and human security during times of conflict, rights to and security of natural resources, and women's rights.

Political and Economic Rights and Security

"No one shall be subjected to torture or to cruel, inhuman or degrading treatment or punishment" (UN Declaration, Article 5, Covenant on Civil and Political Rights, Article 7, Convention on Torture, etc.). Although this immunity is well established, what does this mean in practice for someone faced with the prospect of such treatment? If the person is fortunate enough to live in a country governed by the rule of law, domestic courts may uphold his or her immunity, and the international side of things will come into play only on the margins. A European who is dissatisfied with treatment at home may be able to take a legal dispute over a particular practice beyond his or her national courts to the European Commission on Human Rights and the European Court of Human Rights. In non-European countries governed by the rule of law, no such direct remedy is available, but the notion of universal rights at least reinforces the rhetorical case for rights that are established elsewhere.

The more interesting case emerges if potential victims do not live in such a law-governed society—that is, if their government and courts are the problem and not the source of a possible solution. What assistance should they expect from the international community? What consequences will flow from their government's failure to live up to its obligations? The problem is that even in cases where violations are quite blatant, it may be difficult to see what other states are able to do, even supposing they are willing to act.

During the Cold War, the West regularly issued verbal condemnations of human rights violations by the Soviet Union and its associates but rarely acted on these condemnations. The power of the Soviet Union made direct intervention imprudent, and even relatively minor sanctions would be adopted only if the general state of East–West relations suggested this would be appropriate. Similar considerations apply today to relations between Western countries and China. Conversely, violations by countries associated with the West are routinely

The ongoing political and economic crisis in Venezuela has resulted in a significant movement of Venezuelan citizens into Colombia to find a way to survive. This is a crisis that is likely to get worse rather than better as long as the political and economic problems in Venezuela continue. Why do you think regional organizations like the Organization of American States (OAS) have failed to intervene?

overlooked or, in some cases, even justified; the global war on terrorism provides contemporary examples.

All told, it seems unlikely that individuals who are ill treated by authoritarian regimes will find any real support from the international community unless their persecutors are weak, of no strategic significance, and commercially unimportant. Even then, it is unlikely that effective action will be taken unless one additional factor is present—namely, the force of public opinion. The growth of humanitarian NGOs has produced a context in which the force of public opinion can sometimes make itself felt, not necessarily in the oppressing regime, but in the policy-formation processes of the potential providers of aid. This in turn may goad states into action.

The situation with respect to second-generation rights is more complicated. Consider, for example, "the right of everyone to an adequate standard of living for himself and his family, including adequate food, clothing and housing, and to the continuous improvement of living conditions" (Covenant on Economic, Social and Cultural Rights, Article 11.1) or the "right of everyone to be free from hunger" (Article 11.2). It has been argued that such rights are, or should be, central.

The covenant makes the realization of these rights an obligation on its signatories, but this is arguably a different kind of obligation from the obligation to refrain from, for example, "cruel or degrading" punishments. In the latter case, as with other basically political rights, the remedy is clearly in the hands of national governments. The way to end torture is, simply, for states to stop torturing. The right not to be tortured is associated with a duty not to torture. The right to be free from hunger, on the other hand, is not a matter of a duty on the part of one's own and other states not to pursue policies that lead to starvation. It also involves a duty to act to "ensure an equitable distribution of world food supplies in relation to need" (Covenant on Economic, Social and Cultural Rights, Article 11.2[b]). The distinction here is sometimes seen as that between "negative" and "positive" rights, although this is not entirely satisfactory, because negative (political) rights often require positive action if they are to be protected effectively. In any event, there are problems with the notion of economic rights.

First, it is by no means clear that, even assuming goodwill, these social and economic goals could always be met, and to think in terms of having a right to something that could not be achieved is to misuse language. In such circumstances, a right simply means "a generally desirable state of affairs," and this weakening of the concept may have the effect of undermining more precise claims to rights that actually can be achieved (e.g., the right not to be tortured).

Second, some states may seek to use economic and social rights more directly to undermine political rights. Dictatorial regimes in poor countries quite frequently justify the curtailment of political rights in the name of promoting economic growth or economic equality. In fact, there is no reason to accept the general validity of this argument—Amartya Sen argues cogently that development and freedom go together (Sen 1999)—but it will still be made and not always in bad faith.

WHAT'S YOUR WORLDVIEW?

In this time, when many states are failing to adequately care for their citizens, is the international community responsible for providing the human security for their citizens?

Finally, if it is accepted that all states have a positive duty to promote economic well-being and freedom from hunger everywhere, then the consequences go beyond the requirement of the rich to share with the poor. Virtually all national social and economic policies become a matter for international regulation. Rich states would have a duty to make economic and social policy with a view to its consequences on the poor, but so would poor states. The poor's right to assistance creates a duty on the rich to assist, but this in turn creates a right of the rich to insist that the poor have a duty not to worsen their plight—for example, by failing to restrict population growth or by inappropriate economic policies. Aid programs promoted by the Commonwealth and World Bank, and the structural-adjustment programs of the International Monetary Fund, regularly include conditions of this kind. They are, however, widely resented because they contradict another widely supported economic and social right: "All peoples have the right of self-determination. By virtue of that right they freely determine their political status and freely pursue their economic, social and cultural development" (Covenant on Economic, Social and Cultural Rights, Article 1.1). Even when applied in a well-meaning and consistent way, external pressures to change policy are rarely popular, even with those they are intended to benefit.

On the other hand, it is certainly true that people suffering from brutal poverty and severe malnourishment are unlikely to be able to exercise any rights at all unless their condition is attended to. It may be true that the transfers required to raise living standards to an acceptable level across the world are sufficiently modest and that they would not raise the problems we have outlined. Still, most economic and social rights are best seen as collectively agreed-on aspirations rather than as rights as the term has conventionally been used.

Human Rights and Human Security During Conflict

What is the reason for the continued importance of national security over human rights and human security? For developing countries, state sovereignty and territorial integrity take precedence over the security of the individual. Many countries in the developing world are artificial nation-states whose boundaries were drawn arbitrarily by the colonial powers in the nineteenth century without regard for the ethnic composition or historical linkages among peoples. State responses to ethnic separatist movements (now conflated with terrorism), which are partly rooted in people's rejection of colonial-imposed boundaries, have been accompanied by the most egregious violations of human security by governments. Moreover, many third world states, as well as China, remain under authoritarian rule.

Human security is stymied by the lack of political space for alternatives to state ideologies and by restrictions on civil liberties imposed by authoritarian regimes to ensure their own survival.

In both the developed and the developing world, one of the most powerful challenges to human rights and human security has come from the war on terrorism led by the United States. The terrorist attacks of 9/11 revived the traditional emphasis of states on national security (Suhrke 2004, 365). Although terrorists target innocent civilians and thus threaten human security, governments have used the war on terrorism to restrict and violate civil liberties. The US decision to put Saddam Hussein on trial in an Iraqi court rather than the ICC illustrated the continued US defiance of a key policy instrument of human security, even though it focused on the more Western-oriented conception of "freedom from fear." The US questioning of the applicability of the Geneva Conventions, and the abandoning of its commitments on the issue of torture in the context of war in Iraq, further undermined the agenda of human security. So did Russia's flouting of a wide range of its international commitments—including the laws of war, Conference on Security and Co-operation in Europe (CSCE) and Organization for Security and Co-operation in Europe (OSCE) commitments, and international and regional conventions on torture—in the context of its war in Chechnya and its current support of insurgents in Ukraine.

A pioneering report released by the Human Security Center, formerly affiliated with the University of British Columbia, in 2005 points to several significant trends in armed conflicts around the world, most notably an overall downward trend (see Figure 7.1). What explains this trend in armed conflicts? The report lists several factors:

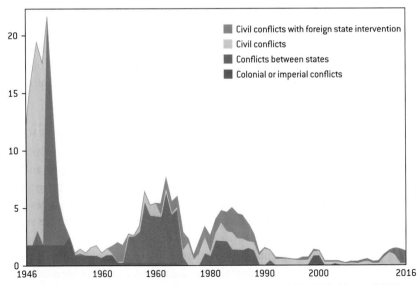

Figure 7.1 State-Based Battle-Related Deaths per 100,000 Since 1946.
Source: UCDP/PRIO

- Growing democratization (the underlying assumption here being that democracies tend to be better at peaceful resolution of conflicts).
- Rising economic interdependence (which increases the costs of conflict).
- The declining economic utility of war, owing to the fact that resources can be more easily bought in the international marketplace than acquired through force.
- The growth in the number of international institutions that can mediate in conflicts.
- The impact of international norms against violence such as human sacrifice, witch burning, slavery, dueling, war crimes, and genocide.
- The end of colonialism and the end of the Cold War.

Another specific reason for the downward trend identified by the report is the dramatic increase in the role of the United Nations in areas such as preventive diplomacy, peacemaking activities, and postconflict peacebuilding. The willingness of the UN Security Council to use military action to enforce peace agreements, the deterrent effects of war crime trials by the ICC and other tribunals, and the greater resort to reconciliation and addressing the root causes of conflict have all contributed to a general decrease in armed conflicts since the early 1990s.

The optimism created by the report did not last long, however. The 2009/2010 Human Security Report found a 25 percent increase in armed conflicts between 2003 and 2008, a large percentage of which were related to Islamist political violence. While the war on terrorism played an important part in the increasing number and the deadliness of conflicts, viewed from a longer-term perspective, the level of conflict in the Islamic world is lower than two decades earlier. Yet the possibility of increasing violence remains given the failure of the Arab Spring, the rise of ISIS and the ongoing Syrian civil war, and general instability in transitional societies.

Moreover, there are some horrific costs associated with these conflicts. For example, deaths directly or indirectly attributed to the conflict in the Democratic Republic of Congo since 1998 have surpassed casualties sustained by Britain in World Wars I and II combined. In Iraq, a team of American and Iraqi epidemiologists estimated that Iraq's mortality rate more than doubled following the US invasion, from 5.5 deaths per 1,000 people in the year before the invasion to 13.3 deaths per 1,000 people per year in the postinvasion period. Violence continues even though the war officially ended in December 2011. As of June 2019, the Iraq Body Count Project estimates that between 183,000 and 206,000 Iraqi civilians have been killed since the US invasion in March 2003 (http://www.iraqbodycount.org).

The share of civilian casualties in armed conflict has increased since World War II. Civilians accounted for 10 percent of the victims during World War I and 50 percent of the victims during World War II. In recent wars, civilians constitute between 80 and 85 percent of the victims. Many of these victims are children, women, the sick, and the elderly (*Gendering Human Security* 2001, 18).

International terrorist incidents and related fatalities have also increased in recent years. According to the National Consortium for the Study of Terrorism and Responses to Terrorism at the University of Maryland, the number of terrorist attacks resulting in the deaths of more than 100 civilians averaged about 4.2 per year between 1978 and 2013. In 2014, that number increased dramatically to 26 per year. Although that number decreased to 14 per year in 2015, it is still too high a number and reflects the lack of security in many areas of the world.

Furthermore, some of the most serious issues of human security in armed conflicts still need to be overcome, such as the recruitment of child soldiers and the use of landmines. Although exact figures are unknown, the United Nations estimates that there are some 300,000 child soldiers involved in more than thirty conflicts in the world today. According to the International Campaign to Ban Landmines, landmines and unexploded ordinances caused over 7,239 casualties in 2017. Progress has been made, but there are still sixty countries around the world contaminated by landmines. Despite the justified optimism generated by the Ottawa Treaty (formally known as the Convention on the Prohibition of the Use, Stockpiling, Production, and Transfer of Anti-Personnel Mines and on Their Destruction), there are still thirty-five states that have not signed the treaty, and most of them have stockpiles of landmines and reserve the right to use them. Collectively, these states have about 50 million mines, and China, Russia, the United States, India, and Pakistan maintain the largest stockpiles.

Finally, the decline in armed conflicts around the world is not necessarily irreversible. Some of the factors contributing to the decline of conflicts, such as democratization and the peace-operations role of the United Nations, can suffer setbacks due to lack of support from major powers and the international community. And there remain serious possible threats to international peace and security that can cause widespread casualties, such as a conflict in the Korean Peninsula and ongoing conflicts in the Middle East.

It is worth noting that battle deaths themselves are not an adequate indicator of threats to human security posed by armed conflict. Many armed conflicts have indirect consequences on human life and well-being. Wars are a major source of economic disruption, disease, and ecological destruction, which in turn undermine human development and thus create a vicious cycle of conflict and underdevelopment. As the *Human Development Report* (UN Development Programme 2005, 12) put it: "Conflict undermines nutrition and public health, destroys education systems, devastates livelihoods and retards prospects for economic growth." Those who take a broad definition of human security must look at threats to the survival and safety of the individual not only from violent conflict but also from nonviolent factors such as disease, environmental degradation, and natural disasters.

Gender, Identity, and Human Security

The relationship between gender and human security has multiple dimensions. The UN Inter-Agency Committee on Women and Gender Equality notes five aspects: (1) violence against women and girls; (2) gender inequalities in control over resources; (3) gender inequalities in power and decision making; (4) women's human rights; and (5) women (and men) as actors, not victims (United Nations Inter-Agency Committee on Women and Gender Equality 1999, 1). Recent conflicts have shown women as victims of rape, torture, and sexual slavery. For example, between 250,000 and 500,000 women were raped during the 1994 genocide in Rwanda. Such atrocities against women are now recognized as a crime against humanity (Rehn and Sirleaf 2002, 9).

As of May 2019, forty-two countries have extended the right to marry or form a civil partnership to same-sex couples. However, some sixty-eight countries have laws that criminalize same-sex relations, and in eleven states the penalty for sexual relations is death. Rights groups routinely report on homosexuals and lesbians being imprisoned or killed.

War-affected areas often see a sharp increase in domestic violence directed at women and a growth in the number of women trafficked to become forced laborers or sex workers. According to the US State Department, 600,000 to 800,000 people are trafficked across international borders every year; 80 percent are female and 50 percent are children. Human trafficking is the third largest criminal industry, behind drugs and illegal arms sales. It has been noted that women become targets of rape and sexual violence because they serve as a social and cultural symbol. Hence, violence against them may be undertaken as a deliberate strategy to undermine the social fabric of an opponent. According to the UNHCR, women and girls make up approximately half of any refugee or internally displaced population.

Another important aspect of the gender dimension of human security is the role of women as actors in conflicts. This involves considering the participation of women in combat. In the Eritrean war of independence, women made up 25 to 30 percent of combatants. A similar proportion of women were fighting along with the Tamil Tigers. And although the Islamic State is generally oppressive toward women, approximately 10 percent of its Western recruits are female. Women play an even larger role in support functions, such as logistics, staff, and intelligence services, in a conflict. Securing women's participation in combat may be motivated by a desire, among the parties to a conflict, to increase the legitimacy of their cause. It signifies "a broad social consensus and solidarity, both to their own population and to the outside world" (*Gendering Human Security* 2001, 18).

In recent years, there has been a growing awareness of the need to secure the greater participation of women in international peace operations. The UN Department of Peacekeeping Operations noted in a 2000 report:

> *Women's presence [in peacekeeping missions] improves access and support for local women; it makes male peacekeepers more reflective and responsible; and it broadens the repertoire of skills and styles available within the mission, often with the effect of reducing conflict and confrontation. Gender mainstreaming is not just fair, it is beneficial.* (Cited in Rehn and Sirleaf 2002, 63)

In 2000, UN Security Council Resolution 1325 was passed, which mandated a review of the impact of armed conflict on women and the role of women in peace operations and conflict resolution. The review, *Women, Peace and Security,* was released in 2002. In his introduction to the report, then UN secretary-general Kofi Annan noted that "women still form a minority of those who participate in peace and security negotiations, and receive less attention than men in post-conflict agreements, disarmament and reconstruction" (United Nations 2002, ix). There is still a long way to go before the international community can fully realize the benefits of greater participation by women in UN peace operations and conflict-resolution activities.

Gendered Perspective on Human Rights

THE CHALLENGE

Before the emergence of a global feminist movement, it was conventional for human rights treaties to be cast in language that assumes that the rights bearer is a man and the head of a household. Many feminists argue that this convention reflects more than an old-fashioned turn of phrase. The classic political and civil rights (freedom of speech, of association, from arbitrary arrest, etc.) assume that the rights bearer will be living, or would wish to live, a life of active citizenship, but until very recently, such a life was denied to nearly all women in nearly all cultures. Instead of this public life, women were limited to the private sphere and subjected to the arbitrary and capricious power of the male head of the household. Only recently in Western liberal democracies have women been able to vote, to stand for office, or to own property in their own name, and issues such as the criminalization of rape in marriage and the effective prevention of domestic violence against women are still controversial. The situation is even worse in some non-Western polities. It may be that a genuinely gender-neutral account of human rights is possible, but some radical feminists argue that an altogether different kind of thinking is required (see Mackinnon 1993).

OPTIONS

Both cultural critics and feminists argue, convincingly, that the model of a rights bearer inherent in the contemporary international human rights regime is based on the experiences of Western men. Agreement collapses, however, when the implications of this common position are explored. Liberal feminists wish to see the rights of men extended to women, whereas radical feminists wish to promote a new model of what it is to be human that privileges neither men nor women. Most cultural critics, on the other hand, wish to preserve inherited status and power differences based on gender.

APPLICATION

The contradictions here are sharpest when it comes to relations between the world of Islam and the human rights regime, largely because relations between Islam and the West are so fraught on

A global press and the internet have made local and national decisions the concern of communities across the globe. Here Indonesian Muslim students protest the French decision to ban Muslim headscarves and other religious clothing in public schools.

other grounds that all differences are magnified. Radical or traditional Islamists argue for conventional gender roles, support quite severe restrictions on the freedom of women, and promote the compulsory wearing of restrictive clothing such as the niqab or the burqa. Many of these petty restrictions have no basis in the Koran or the sayings of the Prophet Muhammad and can simply be understood as methods of preserving male dominance—although it should be said that they are often accepted by Muslim women as ways of asserting their identity. More serious for the human rights regime are those verses of the Koran that unambiguously deny gender equality. It is often (and truly) said that the Koran's attitude toward the status of women was in advance of much contemporary seventh-century thought—including Christian and Jewish thought of the age. However, it remains the case that, for example, in a sharia court, the evidence of a woman is worth less than that of a man, and sexual intercourse outside marriage is punishable for a woman even in the case of rape. The other Abrahamic religions continue to preserve misogynist vestiges, but mainstream Christian and Jewish theologians have reinterpreted those aspects of their traditions that radically disadvantage women. Given the importance attached to the literal text of the Koran, this reinterpretation will prove more difficult for Muslims, though many Islamic thinkers discuss women's rights. The role of women under Islam will be a continuing problem for the international human rights regime as it attempts to divest itself of its Western Judeo-Christian heritage and adopt a more inclusive framework. Of course, it will be an even bigger problem for women who live in oppressive Muslim regimes.

For Discussion

1. Should local cultural standards outweigh externally derived norms?
2. The rights of women all over the world, including in many Organisation for Economic Co-operation and Development (OECD) countries, are at risk. To what extent is the focus on women in Islamic societies justified?
3. Are certain human rights not universal?

We introduced the darker side of UN peacekeeping and the abuse of women and children at the beginning of the chapter. These issues will need to be addressed by every member of the UN, but the inability of fragile or failed states to protect their citizens in times of turmoil is likely to increase and the world community must decide whether to intervene and with what resources.

Globalization has made it more difficult for leaders of countries to assert that national cultural norms are more important than global standards of behavior. Transnational corporations, the globalized entertainment industry, and the United Nations itself all penetrate national borders and erode traditional values. As we will see in the next section, the international community of countries is actively involved in this process.

The Role of the International Community

Because of the broad and contested nature of the idea of human security, it is difficult to evaluate policies undertaken by the international community that can be specifically regarded as human security measures. But the most important multilateral actions include the creation of the ICC, the signing of the Ottawa Treaty, and the 2005 R2P document adopted by the United Nations, which (as discussed in Chapter 5) asserted the moral obligations for states to intervene against human rights violations in other states.

The ICC was established on July 1, 2002, with its headquarters in The Hague, Netherlands, although its proceedings may take place anywhere. It is a permanent institution with "the power to exercise its jurisdiction over persons for the most serious crimes of international concern" (Rome Statute, Article 1). These crimes include genocide, crimes against humanity, war crimes, and the crime of aggression, although the court would not exercise its jurisdiction over the crime of aggression until such time as the state parties agree on a definition of the crime and set out the conditions under which it may be prosecuted. The ICC is a "court of last resort." It is "complementary to national criminal jurisdictions," meaning that it can only exercise its jurisdiction when national courts are unwilling or unable to investigate or prosecute such crimes (Rome Statute, Article 1). The court can only prosecute crimes that were committed on or after July 1, 2002, the date its founding treaty entered into force. Since its establishment, the ICC has opened investigations in several countries, including Uganda, the Democratic Republic of Congo, Sudan, the Central African Republic, Kenya, Libya, and Mali.

The Convention on the Prohibition of the Use, Stockpiling, Production, and Transfer of Anti-Personnel Mines and on Their Destruction, signed in Ottawa on December 3–4, 1997, bans the development, production, acquisition, stockpiling, transfer, and use of antipersonnel mines (Ottawa Treaty, Article 1, General Obligations, 1997). It also obliges signatories to destroy existing stockpiles. Among the countries that have yet to sign the treaty are the People's Republic of China, the Russian Federation, and the United States.

The surge in UN peacekeeping and peacebuilding operations has contributed to the decline in conflict and enhanced prospects for human security. There have been seventy-one UN peacekeeping operations since 1948, and sixteen are under way. In 2006, a UN Peace-building Commission was inaugurated, whose goal is to assist in postconflict recovery and reconstruction, including institution building and sustainable development, in countries emerging from conflict. The United Nations has also been at center stage in promoting the idea of humanitarian intervention, a central policy element of human security. The concept of humanitarian intervention was endorsed by the report of the UN Secretary-General's High-Level Panel on Threats, Challenges and Change, *A More Secure World* (2004, 66, 106); by a subsequent report entitled *In Larger Freedom* (United Nations 2005); and, finally, by the UN General Assembly in September 2005.

One way to get the world to care about a human rights issue is to use celebrities to champion the issue. In this photo, human rights lawyer Amal Clooney and Nobel Peace prize laureate Nadia Murad speak to the UN Security Council about sexual violence in war and the need to reclassify rape as a weapon of war.

United Nations specialized agencies play a crucial role in promoting human security. For example, the UN Development Programme and the World Health Organization (WHO)

have been at the forefront of fighting poverty and disease, respectively. Other UN agencies, such as the UN High Commissioner for Refugees (UNHCR), UN Children's Fund (UNICEF), and UN Development Fund for Women (UNIFEM), have played a central role in getting particular issues, such as refugees and the rights of children and women, onto the agenda for discussion and in providing a platform for advocacy and action (MacFarlane and Khong 2006).

NGOs contribute to human security in a number of ways: giving information and early warning about conflicts, providing a channel for relief operations (often being the first to do so in areas of conflict or natural disaster), and supporting government- or UN-sponsored peacebuilding and rehabilitation missions. NGOs also play a central role in promoting sustainable development. A leading NGO with a human security mission is the International Committee of the Red Cross (ICRC). Established in Geneva, it has a unique authority based on the international humanitarian law of the Geneva Conventions to protect the lives and dignity of victims of war and internal violence, including the war-wounded, prisoners, refugees, civilians, and other noncombatants, and to provide them with assistance. Other NGOs include Médicins Sans Frontières (Doctors Without Borders; emergency medical assistance), Save the Children (protection of children), and Amnesty International (human rights).

At times, these agencies overlap in the services they provide or the issue for which they advocate. As you will see, this tends to be the case in international relations. However, given the complex nature of international human rights law and the demands of providing for human security, each organization can play a part in helping advance the international agenda.

WHAT'S YOUR WORLDVIEW?

The failure of the international community to respond to crises in Africa and the Middle East raises questions about who will or should act to protect citizens. Do you think the United Nations should have its own independent military force for humanitarian intervention, peacemaking, and even state building? Is this the only way to ensure that something is done about these crimes against humanity?

Responsibility to Protect, Prevent, and Rebuild

At the UN Millennium Assembly in 2000, former Canadian prime minister Jean Chrétien announced that Canada would sponsor an International Commission on Intervention and State Sovereignty (ICISS). The government invited Gareth Evans, a former Australian foreign minister and current head of the International Crisis Group, and Mohamed Sahnoun, a former Algerian diplomat and an experienced UN adviser, to serve as co-chairs. At the behest of Canadian foreign minister Lloyd Axworthy, the commission was charged with finding "new ways of reconciling seemingly irreconcilable notions of intervention and state sovereignty" (International

Ethnic violence in Kenya erupted after allegations of a rigged election in 2007. This conflict was resolved after mediation by the UN. This was considered an R2P situation by UN and African Union leaders.

Commission on Intervention and Sovereignty 2001, 81). This was a very careful review of the right of humanitarian intervention. The key question the commission explored is whether it is appropriate for states to take coercive military action in another state for the purposes of protecting citizens at risk in that other state.

Basic Principles

The basic principles (International Commission on Intervention and Sovereignty 2001, xi) of the report fit nicely with many of the universal goals of religious NGOs:

1. State sovereignty implies responsibility, and the primary responsibility for the protection of its people lies within the state itself.
2. Where a population is suffering serious harm, as a result of internal war, insurgency, repression, or state failure, and the state in question is unwilling or unable to halt or avert it, the principle of nonintervention yields to the international Responsibility to Protect, whose elements, or specific responsibilities, include the following:
   1. The Responsibility to Prevent: This means addressing the causes of conflict and other crises that put populations at risk.
   2. The Responsibility to React: This refers to the necessity to respond to situations that put individuals at risk with appropriate measures, which might include various forms of intervention.
   3. The Responsibility to Rebuild: After a natural disaster or military intervention, the international community must provide assistance for recovery and reconstruction. In addition, the international community should assist with reconciliation efforts aimed at addressing the causes of conflict and violence.
   4. The Responsibility to Protect (R2P): Documents and resulting strategies all emphasize the importance of prevention. Clearly stated, that means addressing fundamental *human security* issues: freedom from fear, freedom from want, and the need for the rule of law to provide for a just and peaceful society.

R2P is limited in its scope. To get by the opponents of this document, those supporting this document were forced to limit the crimes that would trigger intervention by the global community. The four crimes are genocide, war crimes, ethnic cleansing, and crimes against humanity. Thus, R2P as a justification for intervention does not apply to threats to human life caused by natural disasters, pandemics, authoritarian regimes, armed conflict, and human rights abuses. As early as the 1990s, then UN secretary-general Kofi Annan argued that the sovereignty-intervention debate was all about two kinds of sovereignty: *national sovereignty had to be weighed and balanced against individual sovereignty as recognized in international human rights instruments* (Evans 2008, 37). The R2P document was approved by the UN World Summit in 2005. It was reaffirmed by the members of the UN Security Council in April 2006 as they adopted a resolution on the Protection of Civilians in Armed Conflict (Evans 2008, 51). The UN General

Assembly talked about invoking the R2P policy in Darfur in 2006, but the first application was said to be the successful mediation led by Kofi Annan after ethnic violence in Kenya led to over a thousand deaths.

The 2011 situation in Libya presented the most recent test of the R2P principle. In March 2011, the UN Security Council authorized an intervention to protect the citizens of Libya from attacks by pro-Qaddafi forces. World leaders most likely sought to avoid another 1995 Srebrenica massacre, and once again, NATO used its superior air power and surveillance resources to protect citizens, prevent more conflict, and rebuild Libya as a democratic state. The United Nations has not been able to authorize an intervention in Syria to protect the citizens and slow the flow of refugees because both China and Russia, as permanent members of the UN Security Council, will veto any application of R2P. This may raise questions about the decision-making processes of the United Nations that favor great-power interests over human interests.

Conclusion

For more than sixty years, leaders and citizens of countries have worked to develop the paired concepts of human rights and human security. Although governments around the world—including some in Europe and North America,

---

WHAT'S TRENDING?

The Human Rights Network

The human rights movement today is being promoted by a number of global civil-society actors, including NGOs, think tanks, foundations, and many citizens as individuals or in informal groups. Some of these actors are cooperating with governments and the business community to promote human rights. These groups form networks that operate in a world without borders and take advantage of network connections that provide efficient and reliable information and adapt to changes in the system much better than a more hierarchical state system. Anne-Marie Slaughter challenges the traditional view of how international relations works in her 2017 book, *The Chess Board and the Web: Strategies of Connection in a Networked World.* She cites a variety of scholars who make the case that all world politics has been redefined by globalization. A web of global economic, political, cultural, and social relations shapes the lives of individuals and the actions of public agencies, corporations, and nonstate actors. The traditional view of international relations suggests the game is played on three separate chess boards: military, economic, and the social or civil-society board. In the new networked world, an actor's position and connectedness will give that actor bargaining power and social power

that may offset the need for greater military power. This gives middle and small powers more influence in the global system, and those are the states that tend to lead efforts to promote human rights and all humanitarian efforts.

Slaughter suggests that the increasing importance of networks with a combination of critical public and private actors has opened up efforts for political reform and a rethinking of some of the rules and norms that define the traditional international system. For example, in the early 2000s two middle powers, Canada and Norway, led efforts to end the use of antipersonnel landmines, initiated the human security movement, and created a commission that designed the R2P document. In all of these efforts, coalitions of actors worked to formulate and implement these policy programs. One of the best examples of how these networks work was on display in the creation of the ICC. The great powers or the P5 were opposed to the ICC, but a network of middle powers, developing states, and the NGO community provided expertise and political support that defeated the great powers. This might illustrate the author's prediction that future problem solvers will need strategies of connection.

the intellectual homelands of the concepts—from time to time violate the very freedoms they endorsed when they ratified the various human rights treaties, it is understood that these are transgressions of longstanding norms of behavior. Certainly, more can be done to promote freedom from fear and freedom from want.

Perhaps the greatest challenge today in the issue area of human rights and human security is the need to change the ways government officials and citizens see the role of the state. Does it exist solely to defend the country along the lines suggested in the Westphalian model of an independent and sovereign state? Or do we have an obligation as humans to help other humans in need? Until this is resolved, debates about human rights and human security will continue.

CONTRIBUTORS TO CHAPTER 7: *Amitav Acharya, Alex J. Bellamy, Chris Brown, Nicholas J. Wheeler, Steven L. Lamy, and John Masker*

KEY TERMS

Arab Spring, p. 283
Charter rights, p. 272
Common security, p. 282
Human development, p. 280

Human rights, p. 272
Human security, p. 279
Humanitarian
  intervention, p.283

Liberal account of
  rights, p. 273
Natural law, p. 272
Nonintervention, p. 274

Standards of civilization,
  p. 275
Universal Declaration of
  Human Rights, p. 276

REVIEW QUESTIONS

1. What is the relationship between rights and duties?

2. Why is the promotion of human rights so rarely seen as an appropriate foreign policy goal of states?

3. What are the problems involved in assigning rights to peoples as opposed to individuals?

4. In what ways can gender bias be identified in the modern human rights regime?

5. What is the relationship between democracy and human rights? Is it always the case that democracies are more likely to respect human rights than authoritarian regimes?

6. Can the compromising of human rights in the face of the threat of terrorism ever be justified as the lesser of two evils?

7. What is human security? How is it different from the concept of national security?

8. Describe the main difference between the two conceptions of human security: freedom from fear and freedom from want. Are the two understandings irreconcilable?

9. How do you link poverty and health with human security?

10. What are the main areas of progress in the promotion of human security by the international community?

11. What are the obstacles to human security promotion by the international community?

12. Why do we need to give special consideration to the suffering of women in conflict zones?

 Learn more with this chapter's digital tools, including the Oxford Insight Study Guide, at **www.oup.com/he/lamy6e**.

What Should Be Done? National Interests Versus Human Interests

BACKGROUND

Takastand is a new nation-state that once was part of a large authoritarian empire. It is resource-rich and is located in a strategic region that is important to many of the major powers, including China, India, Russia, and the United States. It is a multiethnic state with five major ethnocultural communities. Although it professes to be a democratic state, one political party controls the government. This political party also represents the dominant ethnic community, and it openly discriminates against the other ethnic communities. The police and the military have led secret raids against ethnic minorities, and international human rights organizations have found mass graves. The Takastand government denies any connections to the human rights abuses and blames international criminal networks or fundamentalist religious groups that are attempting to overthrow the government. The government also believes that stability is more important than rights at this stage of the country's development. Furthermore, the government's claim that it is being attacked by fundamentalist Islamic forces backed by Al Qaeda has led to significant security assistance from the US government and its NATO partners.

Most of the opposition groups claim that they stand for individual rights and freedoms and democracy, and they all claim that they will implement a true democracy that protects the rights and freedoms of all citizens. They also claim that they will end the country's dependency on the West and that they will challenge the hegemony of the United States and its allies.

Although this is a very poor country, it has significant energy reserves, but most of the profits end up in the hands of the political and military elites. Close to 85 percent of the wealth is controlled by 13 percent of the population. A number of European governments and NGOs have established effective development programs focusing on the UN's Sustainable Development Goals. More women and children in rural areas are now receiving health care, food, and education. The government representatives in these regions control the programs and usually demand payments to allow them to continue. Recently, they have arrested NGO workers and local activists who challenged their authority. Four NGO project leaders were arrested, prosecuted before a military court, and sentenced to death.

ASSIGNMENT

This action has prompted an international conference to address the human security problems and the repression in Takastand. The conference is modeled after similar conferences held to decide how to help Rwanda, Iraq, and Afghanistan. Your assignment is to describe how the world should respond. Take a look at other international-assistance conferences and use those models for your work. Is this a military, political, economic, or human rights issue? Then follow these three steps in planning your conference. This can be a group activity.

Step One

What issues should the conference address? Consider economic, political, military, and human rights and security issues.

Step Two

Consider who should be involved. Should this be an action of the United Nations, or should the great powers take care of this crisis? What role should NGOs play in this human security crisis?

Step Three
Answer these questions:

- Is stability in this region more important than human rights? Why or why not?
- Is it more important to provide access to economic opportunities or to provide cultural and political freedoms? Why?
- Should citizens of some countries be forced to give up rights and freedoms so that others may have access to material goods and resources that help them enjoy the good life? Why?

8 Global Trade and Finance

Russian president Vladimir Putin, front left, Chinese president Xi Jinping, center, and Egyptian president Abdel-Fattah El-Sisi arrive at the Belt and Road Forum in Beijing in early 2019. Russia and China are working together to develop energy resources in the Arctic region and are participating in joint military exercises. Both China and Russia are seeking to extend their influence in the Middle East, and Egypt is a key player.

A global economy is characterized not only by the free movement of goods and services but more importantly the free movement of ideas and of capital.

—GEORGE SOROS

My guiding principle is that prosperity can be shared. We create wealth together. The global economy is not a zero–sum game.

—JULIA GILLARD

In a global economy, all actors have different interests and different goals. The *Pax Americana* that the United States created after World War II established a liberal economic world order that allowed for various forms of capitalism and a wide variety of trade policies, meaning some states were more protectionist than others. Usually a country's trade policies reflected the national interest and ideological views of the dominant political interests. The United States led this system and kept it open for all possible players, but now the United States appears to be giving the lead to other states. The liberal economic system created and promoted by the United States is now challenged by economic nationalist and the state capitalism of China. As we explore a significant part of the global economy in this chapter, we will begin with three current perspectives and policy strategies on the future of global trade and investment. We compare Chinese, US, and EU views on trade, prosperity, and economic security. We should also mention both Russia and India. Although a major military power, Russia is not a major economic power, but as it develops its oil and gas resources its influence, especially over Europe, may grow. India has the possibility to become a major economic player competing with China in many Asian markets.

In 2013, China launched Belt and Road, a new global investment project in which the Chinese government will underwrite billions of dollars of infrastructure investment in countries along the old Silk Road that centuries ago linked China with Europe. China will spend $150 billion a year in some sixty-eight countries that have signed on to this project. This is a way for China to invest some of its significant foreign reserves to create new markets for Chinese companies, such as its high-speed rail companies and its building materials and construction enterprises. Investments will also protect and improve Chinese trade routes in

CHAPTER OUTLINE

Introduction 310

The Emergence of a Global Trade and Monetary System 312

Global Trade and Finance Actors in a Globalizing Economy 317

Global Trade 325

Global Finance 329

Continuity and Change in Economic Globalization 335

Conclusion 339

FEATURES

THEORY IN PRACTICE Contending Views of Capitalism 315

THEORY IN PRACTICE Globalization and "America First" 322

CASE STUDY Southern Debt in Global Finance 333

WHAT'S TRENDING? Managing Global Political Risks 340

THINKING ABOUT GLOBAL POLITICS Globalization: Productive, Predatory, or Inconsequential? 341

Foreign direct investment (FDI) The capital speculation by citizens or organizations of one country into markets or industries in another country.

many developing regions in Asia, Africa, and parts of Europe. China uses aid, trade, and **foreign direct investment (FDI)** to build goodwill, expand its political influence, secure markets, and guarantee access to strategic minerals and energy resources. China now lends more money to developing countries than the World Bank. China is emerging as a big foreign investor in the global economy, with 12 percent global outward investment. According to the United Nations Conference on Trade and Development (UNCTAD), in 2016, Chinese outward FDIs were higher than inward investments ($183 billion vs. $133 billion, respectively).

It should be noted that China is also the largest investor in countries run by dictators who care little for human rights, environmental standards, and the rights of workers. Countries working with China include Zimbabwe, North Korea, Niger, Angola, and Myanmar. China envisions a vast global network of trade, investment, and infrastructure development that offers an alternative to the Western liberal international economic order. China 2025, the global strategy announced in 2015, seeks to make China the global leader in innovation and manufacturing. For example, the battle for 5G supremacy between the United States and China is not unlike the arms race of the past between the Soviet Union and the United States.

In early 2017, President Donald Trump announced that the United States would abandon its efforts to build a twelve-nation Trans-Pacific Partnership (TPP) that would have tied the United States to East Asian economies and would have created a trade bulwark against a rising Chinese trading behemoth.

The president also declared the end of multinational trade agreements, thereby abandoning a free trade strategy practiced by both Republican and Democratic administrations since the beginning of the Cold War. Both China and the Association of South East Asian Nations have led the creation of a multilateral trade association to fill the space left when the United States abandoned the TPP. The Regional Comprehensive Economic Partnership includes sixteen Asian countries, including China, Japan, South Korea, Australia, New Zealand, and India. This trade association represents 30 percent of the global economy and 30 percent of the world's population.

In the 2017 National Security Strategy, the Trump administration stated that the United States would target unfair trading practices, address persistent trade imbalances, and break down trade barriers to increase US exports. China was the primary target for the Trump administration's sanctions, aimed at decreasing the trade deficit with China and protecting intellectual property rights. The trade war with China continues and is influencing trade and investment patterns globally. In October 2019, the International Monetary Fund (IMF) estimated that this trade war between the United States and China would cost the world economy some $700 billion by 2020.

The United States will increase bilateral trade and investment agreements with countries committed to fair and reciprocal trade. It will use its power and influence to counter unfair trade practices and work to end foreign corruption, and will partner with countries to build their export markets, promote free trade, and encourage private-sector growth. The Trump administration has decided to embrace an energy dominance strategy as a consumer, producer, and energy innovator. The national strategy suggests that US leadership is "indispensable to countering an anti-growth energy agenda that is detrimental to US economic and energy security interests." The America First strategy accuses Russia and China of trying to make economies less free and less fair and labels them as "revisionist powers" trying to rewrite global rules to serve their interests.

The EU global strategy, "Shared Vision, Common Action: A Stronger Europe," seeks to promote the security and prosperity of its citizens, safeguard their democratic members, and manage interdependence by engaging with the world. The European Union will promote a rules-based global order with multilateralism as its key principle. The European Union believes that economic prosperity must be shared and will require that states work to achieve the UN's Sustainable Development Goals. The European Union supports an open and fair global economic system and will partner with other states, regional organizations, and global institutions.

These three perspectives on our global economy suggest different views of capitalism and how best to organize global markets.

The global economy creates great opportunities for citizens around the world, but it also increases the linkages among various actors and can increase the chances that vulnerabilities will spread among actors in the global system.

Nobel Prize–winning economist Joseph Stiglitz stated in 2010 that one of the legacies of the last economic crisis will be a new debate on which kind of economic system "is most likely to deliver the greatest benefit." Communism is out of the debate, but what about Asian capitalism with its emphasis on an economy that enriches the state, or the Nordic social democratic strategy that is creating economic stability and growth in Sweden? Time will tell whether the future of capitalism will include more or less government intervention in the market and whether states will continue to provide their citizens with a wide variety of social services.

The economic collapse of 2008–2009 involved more than bad personal finances and massive government bailouts for banks and corporations. Indeed, in early 2009, Dennis Blair, then the director of national intelligence for the United States, warned members of the Senate that the global economic crisis was the most serious security challenge facing the United States and the world. Blair stated that 25 percent of the countries in the world have experienced low-level instability attributed to unemployment and poor economic conditions. Economic refugees might topple weak governments, and failed states might never get off the bottom. Even wealthy states have been adversely affected by the global economic crisis; after all, working and effective global trade and financial systems are also critical elements of global security.

▶ Introduction

The globalization of world politics involves, among other things, a globalization of economics. As we discussed in previous chapters, politics and economics are inseparable within social relations. Economics does not explain everything, but no account of world politics (and, hence, no analysis of globalization as a key issue of contemporary world history) is adequate if it does not explore the economic dimension of global politics and the global marketplace. This global market is built on the assumptions of *economic liberalism*—described by Adam Smith (1723–1790) as a system of natural liberty in which government intervention is minimal and individuals are encouraged to invent, develop businesses, and meet their basic human needs. Liberal economic thinking has emerged as the dominant economic belief system, and, since the end of the USSR and its state capitalism, some would argue the only game in town. However, *mercantilist* and *socialist* belief systems still influence economic decision making in some states. For example, state capitalism best describes the Chinese economy and socialist ideas shape the economies of many Nordic countries.

Great Depression The global economic collapse that ensued following the Wall Street stock market crash in October 1929. Economic shock waves rippled around a world already densely interconnected by webs of trade and foreign direct investment.

When the **Great Depression** struck in 1929, international trade measures such as increased tariffs exacerbated the preexisting domestic market distortions. International trade, however, did not lend itself to solutions like the IMF and World Bank of the Bretton Woods system. John Maynard Keynes, Harry Dexter White, and the other economists and political leaders who met in New Hampshire in July 1944 planned a third part of the system, the International Trade Organization. Unfortunately, largely because of opposition in the US Senate, the Havana Charter of the International Trade Organization never entered into force. In its place, the General Agreement on Tariffs and Trade (GATT) secretariat—which was intended to oversee trade on a temporary basis—took on the task of organizing global trade negotiations.

Most of global politics is about peaceful practices and transactions among nation-states. Economic decisions related to trade and economic development make up most of the foreign policy activities of nation-states, regardless of their size and wealth. The current global market was created by political agreements made by national leaders at the regional and global level. Thus, to understand political economy, students of international relations need to focus on the interaction of states and markets. Political economy is the study of how states and other political actors intervene in the economy to serve the interests of their state and nonstate actors, like private corporations that employ their citizens. The extent of political intervention in the market has been a fixture of global politics for centuries, but since the end of World War II, the creation of regimes or governing arrangements to manage the global economy has increased significantly. Some might argue that as the processes of globalization have increased, so have the efforts of states to manage it.

In his book *The Imperious Economy* (1982), David Calleo argued that the United States used its power, imagination, and energy to shape the global economy and the institutions of global governance. The United States created a "Western liberal dream" or a "Pax Americana," described as follows:

> *A closely-knit world system of vigorously prosperous democracies, enjoying security from military aggression, permitting the free movement of goods, money, and enterprise among themselves, and promoting the rapid development and integration of those nations whom liberal progress has left behind.*

This US-led liberal order helped finance and provide essential political and military support for the European Common Market and other regional organizations.

With the end of the Cold War, the liberal international economic order faced several challenges. For example, the major global economic institutions created during the Cold War needed to be reformed to include the nation-states of the former Soviet bloc and to address the persistent income gap between the more developed North and the developing South. Further, the global economic system had to deal with the emergence of China and other Asian states as economic players. However, the most significant challenge was the rapid pace of economic globalization. The critical question facing policymakers and scholars alike was whether the global political and economic institutions created in the aftermath of World War II could successfully manage economic globalization. Would the United Nations and its agencies like the World Health Organization and the UN Development Programme have the financial resources and expertise to address issues of poverty that hinder poor states from participating in the global economy? Would the IMF have the resources and political support to prevent financial instability as national economies declined due to job loss? Would the **World Trade Organization (WTO)** be able to prevent trade disputes as protectionist

World Trade Organization (WTO) A permanent institution established in 1995 to replace the provisional General Agreement on Tariffs and Trade (GATT). It has greater powers of enforcement and a wider agenda, covering services, intellectual property, and investment issues, as well as merchandise trade.

policies aimed at preventing job loss disrupted trade deals? As we will see in this chapter, much of political economy is all about the creation of regimes aimed at managing globalization and creating peaceful strategies for managing complex interdependence.

Bretton Woods system A system of economic and financial accords that created the International Monetary Fund, the World Bank, and the General Agreement on Tariffs and Trade/World Trade Organization following World War II. It is named after the hamlet in northern New Hampshire where leaders from forty-four countries met in 1944.

World Bank Group (WBG) A collection of five agencies, the first established in 1945, with head offices in Washington, DC. The WBG promotes development in medium- and low-income countries with project loans, structural-adjustment programs, and various advisory services.

Special Drawing Right (SDR) Members of the International Monetary Fund (IMF) have the right to borrow this asset from the organization up to the amount that the country has invested in the IMF. The SDR is based on the value of a "basket" of the world's leading currencies: British pound, euro, Japanese yen, and US dollar.

Marshall Plan Officially known as the European Recovery Program, it was a program of financial and other economic aid for Europe after World War II. Proposed by Secretary of State George Marshall in 1948, it was offered to all European states, including the Soviet Union.

The Emergence of a Global Trade and Monetary System

The post–World War II period was the high point of US political, economic, and military power. The US dollar replaced the British pound sterling as the chief reserve currency and was considered as good as gold by countries rebuilding after the war or those emerging from a colonial past. An ounce of gold cost $35, and this provided economic stability for all currencies that used the dollar as a reserve currency. However, this monetary aspect of pegging the dollar to gold eventually ended because of US balance-of-payment issues and the decline of the value of the dollar. Most economists agree that letting the value of the dollar float marked the end of the **Bretton Woods system**, which was established in 1944 at a resort in rural New Hampshire. There, the United States and its allies created a number of financial institutions aimed at managing the global economy, referred to as the Bretton Woods institutions: the IMF, the **World Bank Group (WBG)**, and the WTO. The institutions created at the time survive to this day and continue to play a major role in shaping the global economy. In the following paragraphs, to develop a more complete understanding of the economic world, we will discuss the key actors that have the power to determine access to global economic resources.

The IMF was formed when representatives from forty-four nation-states signed articles of agreement in 1944. It began operations in 1947. Its goal was to secure international monetary cooperation, stabilize currency exchange rates, and work to expand international currency liquidity to promote trade and job creation. The IMF uses tools like **Special Drawing Rights (SDRs)** to transfer funds from the IMF to national banks to address balance-of-payment problems.

The International Bank for Reconstruction and Development, now known as the World Bank, was originally established to give loans to economically stable countries that could afford to repay them. This strict requirement for loans was first challenged by the **Marshall Plan** and the Dodge Line, which provided grants to European states and Japan for reconstruction. In 1947, the World Bank shifted its goals from reconstruction to development, emphasizing economic liberalization as the ruling narrative for dealing with global economic problems, especially in the developing world, and promoted this strategy through its loans and programs. The World Bank consists of the International Bank for Reconstruction and Development and the International Development Association, which was founded in 1960 to provide "soft" or interest-free loans or credits and grants to the poorest developing countries.

The WBG also includes three additional organizations. The International Finance Corporation was established in 1956 to provide funds for private-sector institutions to encourage the development of local investment markets and to stimulate the international flow of capital into developing markets. To promote FDI into developing countries, the Multilateral Investment Guarantee Agency was established in 1988. This agency provides political risk insurance to investors and lending institutions. With any financial transaction, there is a chance that disagreements and disputes will arise, and these disputes could potentially prevent the completion of important development activities. The International Centre for Settlement of Investment Disputes provides the essential services for resolving such disputes.

How did the Bretton Woods conference of 1944 set up a political and economic system that clearly benefited the United States and its allies?

Another important set of actors that play an important role in promoting trade and finance in the global economy are regional development banks. These multilateral financial institutions provide low-interest loans and grants for a variety of programs, including infrastructure development, health, education, and environmental and natural resource management. There are four major regional development banks:

- African Development Bank
- Asian Development Bank
- European Bank for Reconstruction and Development
- Inter-American Development Bank

The United States is a member of each of these banks and is involved in providing financial assistance in the form of soft or hard loans. Soft loans have low interest rates and a long period for repayment; hard loans have higher interest rates and are usually asset based. The funding for these regional banks comes from financial markets and donor states.

As was noted in Chapter 5, China has been instrumental in creating two financial institutions that are focused on infrastructure and sustainable development. In 2015, China and its BRICS partners (Brazil, Russia, India, China, and South Africa) created the New Development Bank as an alternative to the World Bank and the IMF. The Asian Infrastructure Investment Bank, with ninety-three members, was established in 2016. The United States and Japan are the only major economies that are not members.

Many scholars and policymakers believe that protectionist trade policies or *beggar thy neighbor* trade policies may have contributed to the start of both world wars. Negotiations to eliminate or reduce tariffs began in the late 1940s, and by 1947 the GATT, a system of treaties among more than one hundred nation-states, established rules for the conduct of international trade. The GATT reflected a postwar consensus on free trade that was promoted by and served US national

New International Economic Order (NIEO) A declaration adopted by the UN General Assembly calling for a restructuring of the international order toward greater equity for developing countries, particularly in reference to a wide range of issues related to trade, finance, commodities, and debt.

Free market A market ruled by the forces of supply and demand, where all buying and selling is not constrained by government regulations or interventions.

interests. The GATT and the WTO provided a transparent and predictable rule-based trading system, and today the WTO also provides members with a dispute settlement process that serves to resolve conflicts of interest.

In addition to the WTO procedures and rules, states have established both bilateral and multilateral trade agreements. Free trade areas are established to eliminate tariffs on most trade deals, and some agreements also include the reduction of restrictions on investments and services. Critics have suggested that most free trade agreements favor large corporations and encourage companies to move jobs overseas. Although expanded trade produces cheap goods and services, it may also lead to lower domestic wages. Economic globalization is often associated with wage stagnation and growth in inequality within and between states.

It is also worth noting that the global economy is influenced by the actions of multinational or transnational corporations. Some critics of globalization argue that global corporations, transnational banks, consulting firms, and financial institutions are controlling the world's resources and deciding which countries get rich and which remain poor. Many critics see the globalization process as uneven or even predatory. Investors and transnational corporations are in search of the *lowest common denominator*—namely, cheap labor, fewer rules and regulations, low-cost commodities, and safe and stable areas in which to invest or build their production facilities.

Developing states began criticizing the liberal economic order at the Summit of Non-Aligned Nations in Algiers in 1973. During this time, the Organization of the Petroleum Exporting Countries (OPEC) challenged the global pricing of oil and shifted wealth to oil-producing countries at the expense of large multinational corporations. The success of OPEC inspired other commodity-producing countries to think about establishing cartels to increase the prices of coffee, tin, rubber, and other exports from developing states. At about the same time, economic and political scholars in the developing world were promoting dependency theory as an explanation for the persistence of global **poverty**. This theory suggested that dependence is a situation in which the economy of state A is dependent on the growth in state B. Political elites in both states work to maintain the economic system that benefits them.

In April 1974, the United Nations adopted the Declaration on the Establishment of a **New International Economic Order**. The New International Economic Order demands were aimed at addressing the persistence of poverty and the slow pace of economic development in the global South. The document called for actions such as indexing the prices of commodities by linking them to the costs of manufactured goods, increasing the amount of official development assistance, and lowering tariffs on manufactured goods from developing countries. As the developing world challenged the equity of the liberal economic order, it became clear that the world was clearly divided about the efficacy of the system.

Contending Views of Capitalism

Ever since Deng Xiaoping introduced **free market** reforms in 1978 and opened China to the outside world, China's economy grew at a rate of about 10 percent per year, although in 2015 it slipped to approximately 7 percent. China quickly became the industrial workshop for the world and is currently the world's second-largest economy. The concern among many is whether China will use its economic wealth and influence to extend its power in a nationalistic or mercantilist way. China is a successful state capitalist system, and because of its economic strength, it was able to avoid most of the economic crisis from 2008 to the present. However, in 2015, China devalued its currency, which caused world financial markets to suspect a potential weakening of its economy. There are many in Washington and in European capitals who see China as an economic and potentially a military or security threat. Many people are asking if the future will be a peaceful one with the great powers, including China, Russia, and India, working together to find solutions to the global economic crisis, or if instead there will be a new scramble for resources and markets that increases the tensions and conflicts among the major powers. Many free market capitalists have complained about China's monetary policies and its use of subsidies to support certain industries. One reason for the concern is a misunderstanding or lack of knowledge about the differences between the Anglo-American form of capitalism, known as the *Washington Consensus*, with its emphasis on minimal government and free market solutions, and the Asian form of capitalism,

the *Beijing Consensus*, with its emphasis on the economy serving the interests of the state.

Writer and journalist James Fallows provides an excellent description of the purpose of economic life in the Anglo-American and Asian models.* The purpose of economic life in the Anglo-American model is to raise the individual consumer's standard of living, whereas the Asian model places priority on increasing national strength by making the state more independent and self-sufficient. In terms of power, the Asian model seeks to concentrate power to serve the common good, and the Anglo-American model seeks to break up any concentrated power. From this perspective, economic development "means that people have more choice" and a greater number of opportunities to pursue personal wealth. In the Asian capitalist system, the primary goal is to "develop the productive base of the country" by

supporting the industries at home and those abroad that are owned by your citizens around the world. This also means using government resources to support efforts at securing both markets and strategic resources essential for economic growth. This state capitalist view suggests that the consumer's welfare and interests are less important than the corporation that is producing goods and services for the welfare of the state. Not surprisingly, then, China is considered an economic superpower by most of the world's leading economists.

The Obama administration pressured China to address a number of issues, including the value of its currency, its use of subsidies, and its failure to address issues related to the protection of intellectual property rights. In 2015, the Obama administration considered imposing sanctions against China for the purported cybertheft of US trade secrets and

Chinese workers sew clothes to be exported to the United States and Europe at a garment factory in Huaibei City in East China's Anhui province.

*James Fallows, *Looking at the Sun: The Rise of the New East Asian Economic and Political System* (New York: Vintage Books, 1995).

Contending Views of Capitalism *continued*

allegedly hacking into the Office of Personnel Management and stealing the personal data of nearly 21.5 million people. The Trump administration is very difficult to read in terms of US economic policy priorities. The administration is fixated on trade deficits and blames China for most of the problems in the United States. President Trump has recently called both China and Russia "revisionist powers" who are trying to rewrite global rules. The Trump administration believes these powers are trying to make the global economy less free and less fair.

The Chinese government generally dismisses international criticism as unwarranted finger pointing. China had a $594.5 billion trade surplus with the world in 2015, and its exports to the United States outpace imports by a four-to-one margin. Evidence is mounting that China is following a three-pronged strategy to maintain its economic growth. First, it uses the WTO to fight protectionism among its trade partners. China has filed more cases with the WTO's trade tribunals in Geneva than any other country. Second, China is holding down the

value of its currency, and since 2007, it has also suppressed a series of IMF reports that document the undervaluation of its currency. The third strategy involves what Chinese president Xi Jinping called the "project of the century," or the Belt and Road Forum for International Cooperation. As we discussed in the introduction to this chapter, China will provide more than $100 billion in financing for this project, which will involve nation-states in three continents.

Historically, every rising power has used the resources of the state to help key economic players grow. After World War II, Marshall Plan funds combined with other public investments to rebuild European industries and create thriving welfare states. Many nation-states still own or have major control over key industries such as energy, telecommunications, financial services, and manufacturing. So is China the only culprit here, or are we witnessing a shift from Anglo-American liberal capitalism to a state capitalist system? Will the current economic crisis force many states to take over key economic sectors to

provide employment, secure key resources, and protect the interests of their citizens?

For Discussion

1. A January 2012 issue of *The Economist* included a special section on state capitalism called "The Visible Hand," which argued that the future of capitalism may mean more government control of the economy. What do you think about that idea? Should government play a more extensive role in our economic lives?

2. The neoliberal institutions that we expect to manage the global economy (e.g., the IMF) push for less government intervention in the economy. Will these institutions need to change their guidelines, or should they be replaced with new institutions based on new global realities?

3. Both China and India are members of the G20, and their economic and political power is on the rise. Is this the end of Western hegemony? What might a more pluralistic form of global governance look like?

Despite such challenges, the core capitalist states did not give up on the developing world. Recall that before the Soviet Union collapsed, the ideological battle with the US was both an economic and political battle for global influence. The United Nations has provided the foundation for the creation of important organizations aimed at encouraging economic growth in the developing world. Most notable is the UN Development Programme, which works in nearly 170 countries and territories helping to eradicate poverty and reduce inequalities and exclusion. And the UNCTAD, self-described as the Trade Union of the Poor, is responsible for dealing with development issues, particularly international trade—the main driver of development.

Global Trade and Finance Actors in a Globalizing Economy

Countless discussions of globalization have brought its economic aspects front and center. For example, the late Milton Friedman, a Nobel Prize–winning economist, remarked that it has become possible "to produce a product anywhere, using resources from anywhere, by a company located anywhere, to be sold anywhere" (cited in Naisbitt 1994, 19). Global governance bodies like the Bank for International Settlements, the Group of Eight (G8), the IMF, the Organisation for Economic Co-operation and Development (OECD), the UNCTAD, the WBG, and the WTO have all put economic globalization high on their agendas (see Table 8.1). Usually, these official circles have endorsed and

Are we headed for a recession? A trader at the New York Stock Exchange nervously looks at his screen. In August 2019, the yield on two-year Treasury bonds briefly fell below the yield on ten-year Treasury bonds. This phenomenon, called an inverted yield curve, worried investors and hurt financial markets across the world. The yield curve has inverted before every recession since 1955.

encouraged the trend, as have most national governments. Meanwhile, many social movements have focused their critiques of globalization on economic aspects of the process. Their analyses have depicted contemporary globalization of trade and finance as a major cause of higher unemployment, a general decline in working standards, increased inequality, greater poverty for some (see Chapter 9), recurrent financial crises, and large-scale environmental degradation (see Chapter 10). In their different ways, all of these assessments agree that economic globalization is a key development of contemporary history. True, the scale and impact of the trend are often exaggerated. However, it is just as wrong to argue, as some skeptics have done, that claims about a new globalizing economy rest on nothing but hype and myth. Instead, as in the case of most historical developments, economic globalization involves an intricate interplay of changes and continuities. Certainly, the economic crisis that began in 2008, and continues in parts of Europe and Asia, shows how interconnected and globalized the world's economy has become.

One key reason for disagreements over the extent and significance of economic globalization relates to the contrasting definitions that different analysts have applied to notions of what it means to be global. What, more precisely, is "global" about the global economy? The following paragraphs distinguish three contrasting ways the globalization of trade and finance has been broadly conceived—namely, in terms of (1) the crossing of borders, (2) the opening of borders, and (3) the transcendence of borders. Although the three conceptions overlap to some extent, they involve important differences of emphasis.

TABLE 8.1	**Major Public Global Governance Agencies for Trade and Finance**
Asian Infrastructure Investment Bank	Established in 2016, this bank is led by the Chinese. There are ninety-three members, and as of January 2019 the bank was sponsoring 34 projects, with 60 percent co-financed with other development banks, including the World Bank. It is clearly challenging the current "development regime" by focusing on infrastructure and fast approval of applications. This bank will help to extend Chinese political and economic influence.
Bank for International Settlements (BIS)	Established in 1930 with headquarters in Basel. The bank has sixty member shareholding central banks (2015), although many other public financial institutions also use BIS facilities. The bank promotes cooperation among central banks and provides various services for global financial operations.
Group of Eight (G8)	Established in 1975 as the G5 (France, Germany, Japan, the United Kingdom, and the United States); subsequently expanded as the G7 to include Canada and Italy and, since 1998, as the G8 to include the Russian Federation. The G8 conducts semiformal collaboration on world economic problems. Government leaders meet in annual G8 summits, while finance ministers and/or their leading officials periodically hold other consultations.
Group of Twenty (G20)	Established in 1999, this group is made up of finance ministers and central bank governors of nineteen countries (Argentina, Australia, Brazil, Canada, China, France, Germany, India, Indonesia, Italy, Japan, Mexico, Russia, Saudi Arabia, South Africa, South Korea, Turkey, the United Kingdom, and the United States) and the European Union. The G20 is an informal forum that was created after the financial crisis in the mid-1990s. The members discuss national policies, plans for international cooperation, and ideas for reforming institutions that manage the global economy.
General Agreement on Tariffs and Trade (GATT)	Established in 1947 with offices in Geneva. Membership had reached 122 states when it was absorbed into the WTO in 1995. The GATT coordinated eight rounds of multilateral negotiations to reduce state restrictions on cross-border merchandise trade.
International Monetary Fund (IMF)	Established in 1945 with headquarters in Washington, DC. Membership consists of 189 states (2015). The IMF monitors short-term cross-border payments and foreign exchange positions. When a country develops chronic imbalances in its external accounts, the IMF supports corrective policy reforms, often called "structural-adjustment programs." Since 1978, the IMF has undertaken comprehensive surveillance both of the economic performance of individual member states and of the world economy as a whole.
International Organization of Securities Commissions (IOSCO)	Established in 1983 with headquarters in Montreal; secretariat now in Madrid. Membership consists of 214 official securities regulators (2015), as well as (nonvoting) trade associations and other agencies. The IOSCO aims to promote high standards of regulation in stock and bond markets, to establish effective surveillance of transborder securities transactions, and to foster collaboration between securities markets in the detection and punishment of offenses.
New Development Bank BRICS (NDB BRICS)	Formerly referred to as the BRICS Development Bank, it is a multilateral development bank operated by the BRICS states (Brazil, Russia, India, China, and South Africa) as an alternative to the existing US-dominated World Bank and IMF.

Organisation for Economic Co-operation and Development (OECD)	Founded in 1962 with headquarters in Paris. Membership consists of thirty-five states with advanced industrial economies (2015). The OECD provides a forum for multilateral intergovernmental consultations on almost all policy issues except military affairs; measures have especially addressed environmental questions, taxation, and transborder corporations. At regular intervals, the OECD secretariat produces an assessment of the macroeconomic performance of each member, including suggestions for policy changes.
United Nations Conference on Trade and Development (UNCTAD)	Established in 1964 with offices in Geneva. Membership consists of 194 states (2015). The UNCTAD monitors the effects of world trade and investment on economic development, especially in the South.
World Bank Group (WBG)	A collection of five agencies, the first of which was established in 1945, with head offices in Washington, DC. The WBG promotes development in medium- and low-income countries with project loans, structural-adjustment programs, and various advisory services.
World Trade Organization (WTO)	Established in 1995 with headquarters in Geneva. Membership consists of 164 states (2015). The WTO is a permanent institution to replace the provisional GATT. It has a wider agenda covering services, intellectual property, and investment issues, as well as merchandise trade. The WTO also has greater powers of enforcement through its Dispute Settlement Mechanism. The organization's Trade Policy Review Body conducts surveillance of members' commercial measures.

Cross-Border Transactions

Skepticism about the significance of contemporary economic globalization has often arisen when analysts have conceived the process in terms of increased cross-border movements of people, goods, money, investments, messages, and ideas. From this perspective, globalization is seen as equivalent to internationalization. No significant distinction is drawn between global companies and international companies, between global trade and international trade, between global money and international money, or between global finance and international finance.

When conceived in this way, economic globalization is nothing particularly new. Commerce between different territorial-political units has transpired for centuries and in some cases even millennia. Trading between Arabia and China via South and Southeast Asia occurred with fair regularity more than a thousand years ago. Long-distance monies of the premodern Mediterranean world, such as the Byzantine solidus from the fifth century onward and the Muslim dinar from the eighth to the thirteenth centuries, circulated widely. Banks based in Italian city-states maintained (temporary) offices along long-distance trade routes as early as the twelfth century, and by the seventeenth century, companies based in Amsterdam, Copenhagen, London, and Paris operated overseas trading posts.

Indeed, on certain measures, cross-border economic activity reached similar levels in the late nineteenth century as it did a hundred years later. Relative to world population of the time, the magnitude of permanent migration was in fact considerably greater than today. When measured in relation to world output, cross-border investment in production facilities stood at roughly the same level on the

The trade war between China and the United States began in 2018 and continues today. Factory workers like the woman in the photo are the ones hurt by the tariffs that disrupt free trade between these two economic giants. The tariffs, some as high as 30 percent, have covered thousands of different products, ranging from manufacturing supplies and agricultural products to consumer goods—refrigerators in the photo. So who wins in these types of wars?

Interdependence A condition where states (or peoples) are affected by decisions taken by others. Interdependence can be symmetric (i.e., both sets of actors are affected equally) or asymmetric (i.e., the impact varies between actors).

Protectionism Not an economic policy but a variety of political actions taken to protect domestic industries from more efficient foreign producers. Usually, this means the use of tariffs, nontariff barriers, and subsidies to protect domestic interests.

eve of World War I as it did in the early 1990s. International markets in loans and securities also flourished during the heyday of the gold-sterling standard between 1870 and 1914. Under this regime, the British pound, fixed to a certain value in gold, served as a global currency and thereby greatly facilitated cross-border payments. Again citing proportional (rather than aggregate) statistics, several researchers (e.g., Zevin 1992) have argued that these years witnessed larger capital flows between countries than in the late twentieth century. Meanwhile, the volume of international trade grew at some 3.4 percent per annum in the period 1870–1913 until its value was equivalent to 33 percent of world output (Barraclough 1984, 256; Hirst and Thompson 1999, 21). By this particular calculation, cross-border trade was greater at the beginning than at the end of the twentieth century.

For the skeptics, then, the contemporary globalizing economy is nothing new. In their eyes, recent decades have merely experienced a phase of increased cross-border trade and finance. Moreover, they note, just as growth of international **interdependence** in the late nineteenth century was substantially reversed with a forty-year wave of **protectionism** after 1914, so economic globalization of the present day may prove to be temporary. Governments can block cross-border flows if they wish, and national interest may dictate that states once more tighten restrictions on international trade, travel, foreign exchange, and capital movements. According to skeptics, contemporary economic globalization gives little evidence of an impending demise of the state, a weakening of national loyalties, and an end of war. Skeptics point out that most so-called global companies still conduct the majority of their business in their country of origin, retain strong national character and allegiances, and remain heavily dependent on states for the success of their enterprises.

ENGAGING WITH THE WORLD

Delegation of the European Union to the United States, Washington, DC

This office promotes EU policies in the United States, which includes presenting and explaining EU actions to the US administration and Congress. By engaging with political actors, the media, academia, business, and civil society, we raise awareness of EU issues and concerns, and promote the importance of the EU–US relationship among the American public. We also analyze and report on the political, social, and economic situation in the United States to our headquarters in Brussels.

The European Union Delegation to the United States began in 1954 as a small two-person information office for the newly formed European Coal and Steel Community. Today, the EU Delegation employs approximately ninety staff members, about thirty of whom are EU diplomats. The European Union offers a number of internships in a variety of areas, including trade, development, and global issues.

For more information go to https://eeas.europa.eu.

Open-Border Transactions

In contrast to the skeptics, enthusiasts for contemporary globalization of trade and finance generally define these developments as part of the long-term evolution toward a global society. This conception of globalization entails not an extension of internationalization but the progressive removal of official restrictions on transfers of resources between countries. In the resultant world of open borders, global companies replace international companies, global trade replaces international trade, global money replaces international money, and global finance replaces international finance. This process results in markets that are much larger than regional arrangements like the European Union and the North American Free Trade Association (NAFTA). From this perspective, globalization is a function of liberalization—that is, the degree to which products, communications, financial instruments, fixed assets, and people can circulate throughout the world economy free from state-imposed controls.

The Obama administration supported the idea that a global economy and global economic growth were good things and that regional trade agreements were the way forward. Obama and his economic advisers worked hard to create the TPP, a multinational trade agreement between twelve Pacific Rim countries. The TPP was to be the largest regional trade agreement in history focusing on trade barriers, issues related to intellectual property, and labor and environmental standards. It took President Trump only three days to withdraw from the TPP negotiations due to his lack of faith in free trade and his support for more mercantilist policies that protect American workers and American industry.

While the United States withdrew from the free market TPP, the eleven remaining countries have agreed to move forward without the United States. Other trade deals are also moving forward without the United States. The European Union and Japan created a free trade area covering more than 25 percent of the world's economy, thus pushing against the Trump administration and other nation-states calling for more protectionist policies. This new trading area will be the size of the one created by NAFTA—a trade agreement also under attack by the Trump administration. Canada also has a free trade agreement with the European Union that includes a strategic partnership agreement that will promote cooperation in areas like security and climate change. It is hard not to wonder why the current US administration is so opposed to trade agreements that remove tariffs and seek to shape or manage globalization and create valuable strategic partners.

Globalization and "America First"

Protectionism and economic nationalism are beliefs and policies on the rise across the globe. These policies are not good for global trade. In April 2017, President Trump ordered the US Commerce Department to consider adding trade quotas or tariffs to protect US producers of aluminum. Not so long ago there were some thirty smelting factories in the United States; there are now just five. To produce aluminum that is used for cars, cans, military equipment, and numerous construction projects, it takes a significant amount of electricity.

The Trump administration tends to blame China and its subsidies and tariffs for the job losses in this sector. In 2016, only 10 percent of the aluminum that we used came from China. However, ALCOA, formerly the Aluminum Company of America, and Century Aluminum have opened factories in Iceland and closed factories in the United States due to the cost of electricity. At present, Iceland makes more aluminum than the United States, as do Norway and Canada, because of the availability of cheap hydropower. The electricity in Iceland costs about 30 percent less than in the United States. In Iceland, a country with only 335,000 people and wide-open spaces, the electric utility built five highland dams that capture water from melting glaciers. Yes, the United States has lost jobs, but ALCOA shareholders gain and US consumers get lower prices. Iceland gets jobs and tax

money and finds an alternative to its major fishing industry. Did Iceland purposely target this US industry, or is this industry's mobility an element of the process of globalization?

In his book *The Great Convergence* (2016), economist Richard Baldwin introduces the concepts of old globalization and new globalization. The first phase of globalization (1800s–1900s) lowered the cost of moving goods around the world. This generally benefited the wealthy Northern states as they exchanged manufactured goods, commodities, and even services. The second phase, or the new globalization, began in the late twentieth century and lowered the cost of moving ideas. This meant that information and communication technology made it possible to transfer production activities to distant lands. In this case, the expertise that was in the United States was transferred to Iceland. Obviously, this happened in every industry and every economic sector. So cheap transportation and information technology helped states in the developing world develop an extensive manufacturing sector. Baldwin's research shows that while many developing states benefited from this North-to-South flow of expertise, six developing countries seem to benefit the most: China, South Korea, India, Poland, Indonesia, and Thailand.

Baldwin also explores the characteristics of the new globalization. He suggests that the impact is more sudden

and less controllable. Further, it is difficult for leaders to accurately predict which industries may leave the wealthy states in the North for low-wage states in the South. Iceland is not looking to increase the number of smelters. Instead, it is now looking to sell its electricity to the United Kingdom.

Clearly, the problem is more complex than protectionist policies, and leaders must learn to manage the processes of globalization.

Sources

Binyamin Appelbaum, "America's Disappearing Smelters," *New York Times*, July 2, 2017.

Richard Baldwin, *The Great Convergence* (Cambridge, Mass.: Belknap-Harvard, 2016).

For Discussion

1. What do you think the next phase of globalization will look like? Will the advantage return to the wealthy North or will the developing South catch up in all economic sectors?

2. Do leaders have the skills and expertise to manage the processes of globalization to protect jobs in some areas and promote their growth in other areas?

3. If globalization continues in this same trajectory, what industries do you think will move from wealthy states to regions where costs are much lower?

Globalists regard the forty-year interlude of protectionism (c. 1910–1950) as a temporary detour from a longer historical trend toward the construction of a single integrated world economy. In their eyes, the tightening of border controls in the first half of the twentieth century was a major cause of economic depressions, authoritarian regimes, and international conflicts such as the world wars. In contrast, the emergent open world economy will yield prosperity, liberty, democracy, and peace for all humanity. From this perspective, often termed *neoliberalism*, contemporary economic globalization continues the universalizing project of modernity launched several centuries ago.

Recent history has indeed witnessed a considerable opening of borders in the world economy. Since 1948, a succession of interstate accords through the GATT has brought major reductions in customs duties, quotas, and other measures that previously inhibited cross-border movements of merchandise. Average tariffs on manufactures in countries of the North fell from more than 40 percent in the 1930s to less than 4 percent by 1999. The GATT's successor agency, the WTO, has greater competencies both to enforce existing trade agreements and to pursue new avenues of liberalization—for example, with respect to shipping, telecommunications, and investment flows. Meanwhile, regional frameworks like the European Union and NAFTA have removed (to varying degrees) official restrictions on trade between participating countries. Encouraged by such liberalization, cross-border trade expanded between 1950 and 1994 at an annual rate of just over 6 percent. Total international trade multiplied fourteen-fold in real terms over this period, and expansion of trade in manufactures was even greater, with a twenty-six-fold increase (World Trade Organization 1995).

Borders have also opened considerably to money flows since 1950. In 1959, the gold-dollar standard became fully operational through the IMF. Under this regime, major currencies—especially the US dollar—could circulate worldwide (though not in communist-ruled countries) and be converted to local monies at an official **fixed exchange rate**. The gold-dollar standard thereby broadly recreated the situation that prevailed under the gold-sterling standard in the late nineteenth century. Contrary to many expectations, the US government's termination of dollar-gold convertibility on demand in 1971 did not trigger new restrictions on cross-border payments. Instead, a regime of **floating exchange rates** developed. Moreover, from the mid-1970s onward, most states with developed economies reduced or eliminated restrictions on the import and export of national currencies. In these circumstances, the average volume of daily transactions on the world's wholesale foreign exchange markets burgeoned from $15 billion in 1973 to $1,900 billion in 2004.

Alongside the liberalization of trade and money movements between countries, recent decades have also witnessed the widespread opening of borders to investment flows. These

Fixed exchange rate The price a currency will earn in a hard currency. Here a government is committed to keep it at a specific value.

Floating exchange rate The market decides what the actual value of a currency is compared to other currencies.

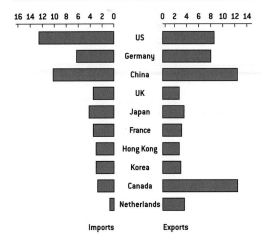

Imports   Exports

The Main Trading Nations.

These two graphs illustrate the top ten exporting and importing countries in terms of percentage share of world exports and imports. What patterns do you see in these graphs? What do these patterns suggest about global trade?

movements involve both direct investments (i.e., fixed assets like research facilities and factories) and portfolio investments (i.e., liquid assets like loans, bonds, and stocks). One result is that the 2008 global economic implosion began with the sale of securities of unwise mortgages made in the United States.

In general, states have welcomed FDI into their jurisdictions in contemporary history. Indeed, many governments have actively lured externally based business by lowering corporate tax rates, reducing restrictions on the repatriation of profits, and relaxing labor and environmental standards. Since 1960, there has been a proliferation of what are variously called international, multinational, transnational, or global corporations. The number of such companies grew from 3,500 in 1960 to nearly 80,000 in 2006. In 2018, global FDI inflows were $1.3 trillion (UN Conference on Trade and Development World Investment Report 2015, 2).

Deregulation The removal of all regulation so that market forces, not government policy, control economic developments.

Substantial liberalization has also occurred since the 1970s with respect to cross-border portfolio investments, which contributed to the 2008 economic recession and the continuing global crisis. For example, many states now permit nonresidents to hold bank accounts within their jurisdictions. Other processes of **deregulation** have removed legal restrictions on ownership and trading of stocks and bonds by nonresident investors. Further legislation has reduced controls on participation in a country's financial markets by externally based banks, brokers, and fund managers. As a result of such deregulation (e.g., the repeal of the Glass-Steagall Act in 1999), financial institutions from all over the world have converged on global cities like Hong Kong, New York, Paris, and Tokyo.

In sum, legal obstructions to economic transactions between countries have greatly diminished worldwide in contemporary history. At the same time, cross-border flows of merchandise, services, money, and investments have reached unprecedented levels, at least in aggregate terms. To this extent, enthusiasts for globalization as liberalization can argue against the skeptics that borders have opened more than ever. However, significant official restrictions on cross-border economic activity persist. They include countless trade restrictions and continuing **capital controls** in many countries. While states have overall welcomed FDI, as of yet there is no multilateral regime to liberalize investment flows comparable to the GATT/WTO with respect to trade or the IMF with respect to money. In addition, many governments have loosened visa and travel restrictions in recent times, but **immigration controls** in general are as tight as ever. To this extent, skeptics have grounds to affirm that international borders remain very much in place and can be opened or closed as states choose.

Capital controls The monetary policy device that a government uses to regulate the flows into and out of a country's capital account (i.e., the flows of investment-oriented money into and out of a country or currency).

Immigration controls A government's control of the number of people who may work, study, or relocate to its country. It may include quotas for certain national groups for immigration.

Transborder Transactions

As mentioned earlier, most debates concerning economic globalization have unfolded between skeptics, who regard the current situation as a limited and reversible expansion of cross-border transactions, and globalists, who see an inexorable trend toward an open world economy. However, these two positions do not exhaust the possible interpretations. Indeed, neither of these conventional perspectives requires a distinct concept of globalization. Both views resurrect arguments that were elaborated using other vocabulary long before the word *globalization* entered widespread circulation in the 1990s. In a third conception, human lives are increasingly played out in the world as a single place. In this usage, globalization refers to a transformation of geography that occurs when a host of social conditions becomes less tied to territorial spaces.

Along these lines, in a globalizing economy, patterns of production, exchange, and consumption become increasingly de-linked from a geography of territorial distances and territorial borders. *Global* economic activity—for industries and people linked to it—extends across widely dispersed terrestrial locations and moves between locations scattered across the planet, often in effectively no time. Although the patterns of *international* economic interdependence are strongly influenced by territorial distances and national divisions, patterns of *global* trade and finance often have little correspondence to distance and state boundaries. With air travel, satellite links, the internet, telecommunications, transnational organizations, global consciousness (i.e., a mindset that conceives of the planet as a single place), and more, much contemporary economic activity transcends borders. In this third sense, globalization involves the growth of a **transborder** (as opposed to cross-border or open-border) economy.

This rise of **supraterritoriality** (transcendence of territorial geography) is evidenced by, among other things, more transactions between countries. However, the geographic character of these global movements is different from the territorial framework that has traditionally defined international interdependence. This qualitative shift means that contemporary statistics on international trade, money, and investment can only be crudely compared with figures relating to earlier times. Moreover, economic statistics ignore or do not count activities that are not modern but are nonetheless vital in some societies—for example, a woman gathering firewood to cook the evening meal in a traditional society or a grandparent providing unpaid childcare in present-day New York City. Hence, the issue is not so much the amount of trade between countries but the way much of this commerce shapes transborder production processes and global marketing networks. The problem is not only the quantity of money that moves between countries but also the immediacy with which most funds are transferred. The question is not simply the number of international securities deals as much as the emergence of stock and bond issues that involve participants from multiple countries at the same time. In short, if one accepts this third conception of globalization, then both the skeptics and the enthusiasts are largely missing the crucial point of historical change.

Transborder Economic, political, social, or cultural activities crossing or extending across a border.

Supraterritoriality Social, economic, cultural, and political connections that transcend territorial geography.

▶ Global Trade

The distinctiveness of transborder, supraterritorial economic relations will become clearer with the help of illustrations of global trade given in this section. Others regarding global finance are discussed in the next section. In each case, their significance relates mainly to contemporary history (although the phenomena in question made some earlier appearances).

The rules of the global trading system are largely only those the countries themselves put on the firms that operate within their borders. Most of the world's trade takes place within the framework of the WTO; however, the organization is a multilateral discussion forum, not a global trade system. Member states of the WTO agree, among other things, to lower tariffs and to eliminate nontariff barriers to trade, but its member states must enforce the agreements. The principle that guides the WTO is that multilateral free trade pacts are better than bilateral deals. Another key principle is **most favored nation status**, whereby member states pledge not to discriminate against their trading partners.

Of course, disputes occur in the world's trading system, often to serve a domestic political purpose. Consider how both the US "America First" movement and the Brexit campaign served the interests of a particular socioeconomic group that demanded that jobs be protected. Other examples include disagreements from time to time between the United States and the European Union about bovine growth hormone in beef products grown in the United States, and the long-running dispute between the United States and China over trade-related aspects of intellectual property rights. To address such disagreements, the WTO has a dispute-resolution panel that keeps the process at the multilateral level so that members will not take unilateral action that could undermine the WTO's goals. Frequently, however, once a country begins the Dispute Settlement Body process, both parties settle the dispute before it reaches the full panel. Because of the risk of retaliation, members prefer to utilize the good offices and reconciliation and mediation services of the secretary-general, as provided for in Article 5 of the WTO covenant.

Transborder Production

Transborder production arises when a single process is spread across widely dispersed locations both within and between countries. Global coordination links research centers, design units, procurement offices, material-processing installations, fabrication plants, finishing points, assembly lines, quality-control operations, advertising and marketing divisions, data-processing offices, after-sales services, and so on.

Transborder production can be contrasted with territorially centered production. In the latter instance, all stages of a given production process—from initial research to after-sales service—occur within the same local or national unit. In global production, however, the stages are dispersed across different countries. Each of the various links in the transborder chain specializes in one or several functions, thereby creating economies of scale or exploiting cost differentials between locations. Through **global sourcing**, a company draws materials, components, machinery, finance, and services from anywhere in the world. Territorial distance and borders figure only secondarily, if at all, in determining the sites. Indeed, a firm may relocate certain stages of production several times in short succession in search of profit maximization.

Before the 1940s, such global factories were unknown. They did not gain major prominence until the 1960s, and most have spread since the 1970s.

Most favored nation status The status granted to most trading partners that says trade rules with that country will be the same as those given to their most favored trading partner.

Global sourcing Obtaining goods and services across geopolitical boundaries. Usually, the goal is to find the least expensive labor and raw material costs and the lowest taxes and tariffs.

Transborder production has developed primarily in the manufacture of textiles, garments, motor vehicles, leather goods, sports articles, toys, optical products, consumer electronics, semiconductors, airplanes, and construction equipment.

With the growth of global production, a large proportion of purportedly international transfers of goods and services have entailed **intrafirm trade** within transborder companies. When the intermediate inputs and finished goods pass from one country to another, they are officially counted as "international" commerce; yet they primarily involve movements within a global company rather than between national economies. Conventional statistics do not measure intrafirm transfers, but estimates of the share of such exchanges in total cross-border trade have ranged from 25 to more than 40 percent.

Much (though far from all) transborder production has taken advantage of what are variously called special economic zones, export processing zones, or free production zones. Within these enclaves, the ruling national or provincial government exempts assembly plants and other facilities for transborder production from the usual import and export duties. The authorities may also grant other tax reductions, subsidies, and waivers of certain labor and environmental regulations. The first such zone was established in 1954 in Ireland, but most were created after 1970, mainly in Asia, the Caribbean, and the *maquiladora* areas along the Mexican frontier with the United States. Several thousand export processing zones are now in place across more than one hundred countries. One distinguishing trait of these manufacturing centers is their frequent heavy reliance on female labor.

Intrafirm trade The international trade from one branch of a transnational corporation to an affiliate of the same company in a different country.

Global goods Products that are made for a global market and are available across the world.

Transborder Products

Much of the output of both transborder and country-based production has acquired a planet-spanning market in the contemporary globalizing economy. Hence, a considerable proportion of international trade now involves the distribution and sale of **global goods**, often under a transworld brand name. Consumers dispersed across many corners of the planet purchase the same articles at the same time. The country location of a potential customer for, say, a Samsung Galaxy smartphone, Beyoncé's latest album, or Kellogg's Corn Flakes is of secondary importance. Design, packaging, and advertising determine the market far more than territorial distances and borders.

Like other aspects of globalization, supraterritorial markets have a longer history than many contemporary observers appreciate. For example, Campbell Soup and Heinz began to become household names in widely dispersed locations across the world in the mid-1880s following the introduction of automatic canning. From the outset, Henry Ford regarded his first automobile, the Model T, as a world car. Coca-Cola was bottled in twenty-seven countries and sold in

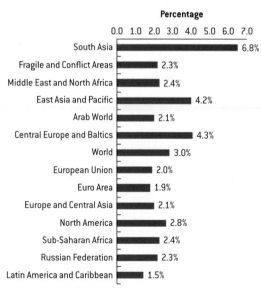

Percentage

South Asia	6.8%
Fragile and Conflict Areas	2.3%
Middle East and North Africa	2.4%
East Asia and Pacific	4.2%
Arab World	2.1%
Central Europe and Baltics	4.3%
World	3.0%
European Union	2.0%
Euro Area	1.9%
Europe and Central Asia	2.1%
North America	2.8%
Sub-Saharan Africa	2.4%
Russian Federation	2.3%
Latin America and Caribbean	1.5%

Real GDP Growth.
GDP real growth rate compares GDP growth on an annual basis adjusted for inflation and expressed as a percentage (2018 estimate in percentage).

High-tech products and services account for 18 percent of global exports. While Silicon Valley is considered by many to be the center of high-tech industries, Stockholm actually has the most billion-dollar startups per capita of any region in the world, including music streaming giant Spotify.

seventy-eight by 1929 (Pendergrast 1993, 174). Overall, however, the numbers of goods, customers, and countries involved in these earlier global markets were relatively small.

In contrast, global goods pervade the contemporary world economy. They encompass a host of food products (e.g., Dunkin' Donuts has over 3,100 stores in thirty countries); bottled beverages (Red Bull energy drink is available in more than 169 countries); printed publications (*The Hunger Games* trilogy was published in fifty-one languages and sold in fifty-six markets), and travel services (Airbnb has listings in over 34,000 cities in 190 countries). See Tables 8.2 and 8.3 for more insight into the pervasiveness of global goods. In all these sectors

TABLE 8.2	**Your Global Morning as a College Student**

With an 8 a.m. class, you rely on a good working alarm clock to wake up. You also rely on a global production and distribution system.

If you use an old-fashioned alarm clock rather than your smartphone, your alarm clock is a product of the Sony Corporation, a Japanese-based multinational corporation. The clock was assembled in a Sony plant in Brazil from components produced in Japan, Mexico, and Germany. It was shipped to the United States in a Greek-owned ship manufactured in Finland by a company owned by a South Korean firm, licensed in Panama, and staffed by a multinational crew including citizens of African and Asian states.

You do not have much to wear to class because you have not had time to do laundry.

You are wearing the international. Your shorts were made in Japan from cotton exported to Japan from the United States. Your socks were made in Vietnam using wool grown in Australia.

You have just enough time to stop at the dining hall for some breakfast.

Your stomach is full of the international. The bacon you ate was brought to you by the UPS Corporation, a multinational shipping company. The pig your bacon came from consumed grain that was grown in Canada. The bread you ate was Wonder Bread, a product of International Telephone and Telegraph, another multinational company. The technology that toasted your bread is a product from another multinational, General Electric. The butter that you put on your toast contains dried milk imported from Germany. Finally, the coffee you drank is a product of the Nestlé Corporation, a Swiss multinational.

You wonder when and if sports will return once the global pandemic is better controlled and how athletes will adjust to the new date for the Tokyo Olympics and whether the US Open tennis tournament with all the top international players will take place the so you take a look at the local newspaper.

Now you are reading the international. Much of the news on the front page that you skimmed is about events outside the United States and the role the United States plays as a global leader. The newspaper received much of its news from the British Broadcasting Corporation, Agence France-Presse, the Associated Press, and Reuters, all transnational information agencies. The major sports story today is about the economic impact of the loss of major sporting events all over the globe.

TABLE 8.3	An Example of a Global Product: Your Lenovo ThinkPad
Memory	Ten manufacturers worldwide, the largest in Korea
Case and keyboard	Made in Thailand
Wireless card	Intel, made in Malaysia
Battery	Made in Asia (various locations in the region possible)
Display screen	Two major screen makers are Samsung and LG Philips in South Korea.
Graphics controller chip	ATI, made in Canada, or TMSC, made in Taiwan
Microprocessor	Intel, made in the United States
Hard drive	Made in Thailand
Assembly	Mexico

and more, global products inject a touch of the familiar almost anywhere on Earth a person might visit.

Today, many stores carry transborder articles. Moreover, since the 1970s, a number of retail chains have gone global. Examples include Japan-based 7-Eleven, Sweden-based IKEA and H&M, UK-based Body Shop, and US-based Walmart. Owing largely to the various megabrands and transborder stores, shopping centers of the twenty-first century are in good part global emporia.

Other supraterritorial markets have developed since the 1990s through **electronic commerce**. Today's global consumer can—equipped with a credit card, telephone, or internet access—shop across the planet from home. Mail-order outlets and telesales units have undergone exponential growth, while e-commerce on the World Wide Web has expanded hugely.

> **Electronic commerce** The buying and selling of products and services over the telephone or internet. Amazon and eBay are examples of leaders in this area of commerce.

Through transborder production and transworld products, global trade has become an integral part of everyday life for a notable proportion of the world's firms and consumers. Indeed, these developments could help explain why the recessions of contemporary history have not provoked a wave of protectionism, despite frequently expressed fears of "trade wars." In previous prolonged periods of commercial instability and economic hardship (e.g., during the 1870s–1890s and 1920s–1930s), most states responded by imposing major protectionist restrictions on cross-border trade. Reactions to the recession that began in 2008 have been more complicated (see Milner 1988). Although many territorial interests have pressed for protectionism, global commercial interests have generally resisted it.

Global Finance

Finance has attracted some of the greatest attention in contemporary debates on globalization, especially following a string of crises in Latin America (1994–1995), Asia (1997–1998), Russia (1998), Brazil (1999), and Argentina (2001–2002), as well as the 2008 global financial collapse that is still being felt in some areas of the world. The rise of supraterritoriality has affected both the forms money takes and the ways it is deployed in banking, securities, derivatives, and (although not detailed here) insurance markets. As international cross-border activities, such dealings have quite a long history. However, as commerce that unfolds through telephone and computer networks that make the world a single place, global finance has experienced its greatest growth since the 1980s.

Global Money

The development of global production and the growth of global markets have each encouraged—and been facilitated by—the spread of global monies. It was noted earlier that the fixed and later floating exchange regimes operated through the IMF have allowed a number of national currencies to enter transnational or global use. Today, retail outlets in scores of countries deal in multiple currencies on demand.

No national denomination has been more global in this context than the US dollar. About as many dollars circulate outside as inside the United States. Indeed, in certain financial crises, this global money has displaced the locally issued currency in the everyday life of a national economy. Such "dollarization" has occurred in parts of Latin America and Eastern Europe. Since the 1970s, the German mark (now superseded by the euro), Japanese yen, Swiss franc, and other major currencies have also acquired a substantial global character. Hence, huge stocks of notionally "national" money are now used in countless transactions that never touch their home soil.

Foreign exchange dealing has become a thoroughly supraterritorial business and has no central meeting place. Many deals have nothing directly to do with the countries where the currencies involved are initially issued or eventually spent. Trading can also take place without distance. Transactions generally occur over the telephone and are confirmed by telex or email between buyers and sellers regardless of distance. Meanwhile, shifts in exchange rates are communicated instantly on video monitors across the main dealing rooms worldwide.

Transborder money also takes other forms besides certain national currencies. Gold has already circulated across the planet for several centuries, although it moves cumbersomely through territorial space rather than instantly through telecommunication lines. A more fully supraterritorial denomination is the SDR, issued through the IMF since 1969. SDRs

Venezuelan national militia members and supporters rally against the foreign blockade in August 2019. Inflation in Venezuela reached a staggering 10 million percent. Even if the country is able to restore order and get inflation back under control, it will lack power and influence in the region. Venezuela has lost millions of citizens who have fled the country, including the vast majority of its educated professional class.

reside only in computer memories and not in wallets for everyday transactions.

Other supraterritorial money has entered daily use in plastic form. Bank cards are used to extract local currency from automated teller machines (ATMs) worldwide. Additionally, several types of smart cards (e.g., Mondex, part of the MasterCard network) can simultaneously hold multiple currencies as digital cash on a microchip. Certain credit cards like Visa and MasterCard are accepted at millions of venues the world over to make purchases in whatever the local denomination is.

Through the spread of transborder currencies, distinctly supraterritorial denominations, digital purses, and global credit and debit cards, contemporary globalization has significantly altered the shape of money. No longer is money restricted to the national, state, or territorial form that prevailed from the nineteenth to the middle of the twentieth century.

Shanghai's financial district, Lujiazui. In the semi-annual Global Financial Centers Index released in September 2019, Shanghai was selected as the world's fourth most important financial center. While New York and London still top the list, six of the top ten are in East Asia. Do you think this global financial shift toward Asia is significant? How do you think it will impact future policy decisions in the West?

Global Banking

Globalization has touched banking mainly in terms of the growth of transborder deposits, the advent of transborder bank lending, the expansion of transborder branch networks, and the emergence of instantaneous transworld interbank fund transfers.

So-called eurocurrency deposits are bank assets denominated in a national money different from the official currency in the country where the funds are held. For instance, euroyen are Japanese yen deposited in, say, Canada. Eurocurrency accounts first appeared in the 1950s but mainly expanded after 1970, especially with the flood of petrodollars (money earned from the sale of oil) that followed major rises of oil prices in 1973–1974 and 1979–1980. Eurocurrencies are supraterritorial; they do not attach neatly to any country's money supply, nor are they systematically regulated by the national central bank that issued them.

Globalization has also entered the lending side of banking. Credit creation from eurocurrency deposits first occurred in 1957, when American dollars were borrowed through the British office of a Soviet bank. However, euroloans mainly proliferated after 1973 following the petrodollar deluge. Today, it is common for a loan to be issued in one country and denominated in the currency of a second country (or perhaps a basket of currencies of several countries) for a borrower in a third country by a bank or syndicate of banks in a fourth or additional countries.

Global banking takes place not only at age-old sites of world finance like London, New York, Tokyo, and Zurich but also through multiple **offshore finance centers**. Much like export processing zones in relation to manufacturing, offshore financial arrangements offer investors low levels of taxation and regulation. Although a few

Offshore finance centers The extraterritorial banks that investors use for a range of reasons, including the desire to avoid domestic taxes, regulations, and law enforcement agencies.

offshore finance centers, including Luxembourg and Jersey (a dependency of the United Kingdom that is part of the Channel Islands), predate World War II, most have emerged since 1960, and they are now found in over forty jurisdictions. For example, less than thirty years after passing relevant legislation in 1967, the Cayman Islands hosted more than five hundred offshore banks with total deposits of $442 billion (S. Roberts 1994; Bank for International Settlements 1996, 7).

The supraterritorial character of much contemporary banking also lies in the immediacy of interbank fund transfers. Electronic messages have largely replaced territorial transfers by check or draft—and cost far less. The largest conduit for such movements is the Society for Worldwide Interbank Financial Telecommunications (SWIFT). Launched in 1977, SWIFT connects more than 10,800 financial institutions in 208 countries. In 2016, over 6.5 billion electronic payments were sent, which equates to approximately 25.81 million messages per day.

Global Securities

Globalization has altered not only banking but also the shape of securities markets. A security is a tradable financial asset, such as stocks or bonds; securities markets, which are part of the greater financial market, are where securities can be bought and sold. Thanks to globalization, some bonds and stocks have become relatively detached from territorial space and many investor portfolios (groupings of financial assets) have acquired a transborder character. Electronic interlinkage of trading sites has created conditions that allow for securities dealing to take place anywhere and at any time. Each of these factors contributed to the 2008 economic collapse; subprime US home mortgages were sold in European markets and traded 24/7. A subprime mortgage is a loan with a higher interest rate attached that is intended for individuals with poor credit scores. When the housing market collapsed in the United States and more people failed to pay their mortgages, the mortgage bundles purchased by banks around the world lost their value. The US mortgage crisis certainly contributed to the current global crisis, which is more about sovereign debt and the lack of available credit from banks trying to recover from the previous crisis in 2007–2008.

Contemporary globalization has seen the emergence of several major securities instruments with a transborder character. These bonds and equities can involve issuers, currencies, brokers, and exchanges across multiple countries at the same time. For example, a so-called eurobond is denominated in a currency that is alien to a substantial proportion of the parties involved: the borrower who issues it, the underwriters who distribute it, the investors who hold it, or the exchange(s) that list it. This transborder financial instrument is thereby different from a foreign bond, which is handled in one country for an external borrower. Cross-border bonds of the latter type have existed for several hundred years, but eurobonds first appeared in 1963. In that year, the state highway authority in Italy issued bonds denominated in US dollars through managers in Belgium, Britain, Germany, and the Netherlands, with subsequent quotation on the London Stock Exchange.

On a similar pattern, a euroequity issue involves a transborder syndicate of brokers selling a new share release for simultaneous listing on stock exchanges in several countries. This supraterritorial process contrasts with an international offer, where a company based in one country issues **equity** in a second country. Like foreign bonds, international share quotations have existed almost as long as stock markets themselves. However, the first transborder equity issue occurred in 1984, when 15 percent of a privatization of British Telecommunications was offered on exchanges in Japan, North America, and Switzerland concurrently with the majority share release in the United Kingdom. Transworld placements of new shares have occurred less frequently than eurobond issues. However, it has become quite common for major transborder firms to list their equity on different stock exchanges across several time zones, particularly in Asia, Europe, and North America.

Not only various securities instruments but also many investor portfolios have acquired a transborder character in the context of contemporary financial globalization. For example, an investor in one country may leave assets with a fund manager in a second country who in turn places those sums on markets in

> **Equity** A number of equal portions in the nominal capital of a company; the shareholder thereby owns part of the enterprise; also called "stock" or "share."

CASE STUDY

Southern Debt in Global Finance

Background

The global character of much contemporary finance is well illustrated by the struggles that many middle- and low-income countries have had with large transborder debts. The problems developed in the 1970s, when a surge in oil prices generated huge export earnings of so-called petrodollars, which were largely placed in bank deposits. The banks in turn needed to lend the money, but demand for loans in the OECD countries was low at the time owing to recession. So instead, large bank loans went to countries of the South (in some cases, partly to help pay for the increased cost of oil imports). Often the lenders were insufficiently careful in extending these credits, and often the borrowers were reckless in spending the money. Starting with Mexico in August 1982, a string of borrowing governments in the South defaulted on their transborder loans.

The Case

The initial response to this situation of unsustainable debts was to implement short-term emergency rescue packages for each country as it ran into crisis. Payments were rescheduled, and additional loans were provided to cover unpaid interest charges. This piecemeal approach only tended to make things worse. From 1987 onward, a series of comprehensive plans for third world debt relief were promoted.

During the following decade, unsustainable commercial bank loans were gradually written off or converted into long-term bonds. Many bilateral loans from Northern governments to Southern borrowers were also canceled. However, in the mid-1990s, major problems persisted in regard to debts owed by low-income countries to multilateral lenders such as the IMF and the World Bank. A much-touted Highly Indebted Poor Countries (HIPCs) initiative, launched in 1996 and recast in 1999, brought slow and limited returns. In 2005, the G8 summit parties agreed to write off the debts of eighteen HIPCs to the multilateral agencies.

Outcome

Programs of debt relief for low-income countries have received major support from global citizen campaigns. Activists formed the first Debt Crisis Network in the mid-1980s and regional coalitions such as the European Network on Debt and Development emerged in the early 1990s. These efforts coalesced and broadened in the global Jubilee 2000 campaign of the late 1990s, which, among other things, assembled seventy thousand people in a "human chain" around the G8 summit in Birmingham, United Kingdom, in 1998. Most commentators agree that these global citizen mobilizations significantly increased, improved, and accelerated programs of debt relief.

Southern Debt in Global Finance *continued*

For Discussion

1. Why was it considered so important to pay off the debts of developing countries? Would a similar system work to help Greece today?
2. How much do you think colonialism and the Cold War contributed to the debt in developing countries?

3. The Jubilee movement was a transnational social movement that had some success. Why do you think we have not seen a similar movement in support of the Millennium Development Goals and subsequent Sustainable Development Goals?

a collection of third countries. Thus, even when individual securities have a territorial character, they can be combined in a supraterritorial investment package. Indeed, a number of pension funds, insurance companies, and unit trusts have created explicitly designated "global funds" whose component securities are drawn from multiple corners of the world. Many transborder institutional investors have furthermore registered offshore for tax and other cost advantages. For example, the Africa Emerging Markets Fund has its investments in Africa, its listing in Ireland, and its management office in the United States.

Finally, securities markets have gone global through the growing supraterritorial character of many exchanges since the 1970s. The open-outcry trading floors of old have largely given way to electronic transactions by telephone and computer networks. These telecommunications provide the infrastructure for distanceless deals (called "remote trading") in which brokers, in principle, can be located anywhere on Earth. Most major investment banks (Daiwa Securities, Dresdner Kleinwort, Fidelity, etc.) now coordinate offices across several time zones in around-the-clock, around-the-world trading of bonds and shares. The first computerized order-routing system became operational in 1976, connecting brokers across the United States instantly to the trading floor of the New York Stock Exchange. Since 1996, similar developments have linked brokers anywhere in the European Union directly to its main exchanges. For its part, the wholly computer-based National Association of Securities Dealers Automated Quotations system (NASDAQ) has, since its launch in 1971, had no central meeting place at all. This transborder cyberspatial network has become the world's largest stock market, listing around 3,300 companies with a combined market value of over $13 trillion as of 2019.

Global Derivatives

Futures Derivatives that oblige a buyer and seller to complete a transaction at a predetermined time in the future at a price agreed on today. Futures are also known as "forwards."

A fourth area of finance suffused with globalization—and a major villain in the drama of the 2008–2009 economic collapse—is the derivatives industry. A derivative product is a contract, the value of which depends on (hence, is "derived" from) the price of some underlying asset (e.g., a raw material or an equity) or a particular reference rate such as an interest level or stock market index. Derivatives connected to tangible assets like raw minerals and land date from the middle of the nineteenth century, and derivatives based on financial indicators have proliferated since their introduction in 1972.

Derivatives contracts take two principal forms. In the first type, called **futures** or "forwards," a buyer and seller are obligated to complete a transaction at a predetermined time in the future at a price agreed on today. In the second main type, called **options**, parties have a right (but without obligation) to buy or sell at a specified price for a stipulated period of time up to the contract's expiry date.

Additional technical details and the various rationales relating to derivatives need not detain us here; for our purposes, we will emphasize the magnitude of this financial industry. Public derivatives exchanges have proliferated worldwide since 1982 along with even larger over-the-counter (OTC) markets. The notional value of outstanding OTC financial derivatives contracts alone reached $544 trillion in July 2018 (Bank for International Settlements 2018, 2).

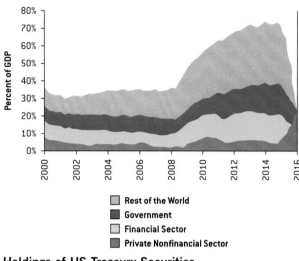

Rest of the World
Government
Financial Sector
Private Nonfinancial Sector

Holdings of US Treasury Securities.
What two groups own the most US Treasury securities?

Like banking and securities, much derivatives business has become relatively distanceless and borderless. For example, a number of the contracts relate to supraterritorial indicators, such as the world price of copper or the interest rate on euro–Swiss franc deposits. In addition, much derivatives trading is undertaken through global securities houses and transworld telecommunications links. A number of derivatives instruments are traded simultaneously on several exchanges around the world. For example, contracts related to three-month eurodollar interest rates have been traded concurrently on Euronext. LIFFE (a pan-European derivatives exchange), the New York Futures Exchange, the Sydney Futures Exchange, and the Singapore Exchange. Owing to these tight global interconnections, major losses in the derivatives markets can have immediate worldwide repercussions.

Options Derivatives that give parties a right (without obligation) to buy or sell at a specific price for a stipulated period of time up to the contract's expiration date.

Continuity and Change in Economic Globalization

Having now reviewed the development of a supraterritorial dimension in the contemporary world economy and emphasized its significance, we need to recognize continuities alongside these changes. One can appreciate the importance of globalization without slipping into globalism. In the following sections, we will discuss four factors of continuity: the unevenness of globalization, which we call irregular incidence; the enduring importance of territoriality; the role of the state in an era of globalization; and the persistence of nationalism and cultural diversity.

Irregular Incidence

Globalization has not been experienced everywhere and by everyone to the same extent. In general, transborder trade and finance have developed furthest in East Asia,

North America, and Western Europe; in urban areas relative to rural districts; and in wealthier and professional circles. At the same time, few people and places are today completely untouched by economic globalization.

Supraterritorial trade and finance have transpired disproportionately in the North and most especially in its cities. For instance, although McDonald's fast food is available in nearly thirty-six thousand establishments across more than one hundred countries, the vast majority of these meals are consumed in a handful of those lands. In contrast to currencies issued in the North, the national denominations of countries in Africa have had scarcely any mutual convertibility. More than three-quarters of FDI, credit card transactions, stock market capitalization, derivatives trade, and transborder loans flow within the North.

This marginalization of the South is far from complete, however. For instance, certain products originating in the South have figured significantly in global markets (e.g., wines from Chile and South Africa and vacation packages in the Caribbean). Electronic banking has even reached parts of rural China. A number of offshore finance centers and large sums of transborder bank debt are found in the South. Global portfolios have figured strongly in the development of new securities markets in major cities of Africa, Asia, Eastern Europe, and Latin America since the mid-1980s. The Singapore Exchange and the São Paulo–based Bolsa de Mercadorias & Futuros (BM&F) have played a part in the burgeoning derivatives markets of recent decades.

Indeed, involvement in global trade and finance is often as much a function of class as of the North–South divide. The vast majority of the world's population—including many in the North—have lacked the means to purchase most global products. Likewise, placing investments in global financial markets depends on wealth, the distribution of which does not always follow a North–South pattern. For example, elites in the oil-exporting countries of Africa, Latin America, and the Middle East have owned substantial amounts of petrodollars.

Transborder markets and investments can be shown to have contributed significantly to growing wealth gaps within countries, as well as between North and South (Scholte 2005, Chapter 10). For example, the global mobility of capital, in particular to low-wage production sites and offshore finance centers, has encouraged many countries, including the United States, to reduce upper tax brackets and to downgrade some social welfare provisions. Such steps have contributed to growing inequality across much of the contemporary world. Increasingly, poverty has become connected as much to supraterritorial class, gender, and race structures as to country of domicile.

The Persistence of Territory

The transcendence of territorial space in the contemporary world economy must not be overestimated. Evidence presented earlier in this chapter suggests that distance and borders have lost the determining influence on economic geography that they once had. However, this is not to say that the nation-state has lost all significance in the contemporary organization of production, exchange, and consumption.

On the contrary, after several decades of accelerated globalization, a great deal of commercial activity is still linked to specific countries and has only a secondary supraterritorial dimension. Although transborder manufacturing through global factories has affected a significant proportion of certain industries, many globally distributed products (such as Boeing jets and Ceylon teas) are prepared within a single country.

Many types of money, too, have remained restricted to a national or local domain. Likewise, the great bulk of retail banking has stayed territorial, as clients deal with their local branch offices. In spite of substantial growth since the 1980s, transborder share dealing remains a small fraction of total equity trading. Moreover, a large majority of turnover on most stock exchanges continues to involve shares of firms headquartered in the same country.

Most global commercial activity has not been wholly detached from territorial geography. Local circumstances have strongly influenced corporate decisions regarding the location of transborder production facilities. In the foreign exchange markets, dealers have mainly been clustered in half a dozen cities, even if their transactions are largely cyberspatial and can have immediate consequences anywhere in the world. It remains rare for a transborder company to issue a large proportion of its stock outside its country of origin.

Hence, the importance of globalization is that it has ended the monopoly of territoriality in defining the spatial character of the world economy. The global dimension of contemporary world commerce has grown alongside, and in complex relations with, its territorial aspects. Globalization has been reconfiguring economic, social, and political geography (along with concurrent processes of regionalization and localization), but it has by no means eliminated territoriality.

The Survival of the State

Similarly, globalization has repositioned the (territorial) state rather than signaled its demise. The expansion of transborder trade and finance has made claims of Westphalian sovereign statehood obsolete, but states themselves remain significant. Through both unilateral decisions and multilaterally coordinated policies, states have done much to facilitate economic globalization and influence its course.

As already mentioned, states have encouraged the globalization of commerce through various policies of liberalization and the creation of special economic zones and offshore finance centers. At the same time, some governments in the developing world have also slowed globalization within their jurisdiction by retaining certain restrictions on transborder activity. However, most states have eventually responded to strong pressures to liberalize. In any case, governments have often lacked effective means to fully enforce their territorially bound controls on globally mobile capital. With respect to immigration restrictions, states have largely sustained their borders against economic globalization, but even then, substantial traffic in unregistered migrants occurs.

Yet states are by no means powerless in the face of economic globalization. Even the common claim that global finance lies beyond the state requires qualification. After all, governments and central banks continue to exert a major influence on money supplies and interest rates, even if they no longer monopolize money creation and they lack tight control over the euromarkets. Likewise, particularly through cooperative action, states can significantly shift exchange rates, even if they have lost the capacity to fix the conversion ratios and are sometimes overridden by currency dealers. Governments have also pursued collective regulation of transborder banking to some effect via the Basel Committee on Banking Supervision, set up through the Bank for International Settlements in 1974. The survival of offshore finance centers, too, depends to a considerable extent on the goodwill of governments, both the host regime and external authorities. Recent years have seen increased intergovernmental consultations, particularly through the OECD, to obtain tighter official oversight of offshore finance. Similarly, national regulators of securities markets have collaborated since 1984 through the International Organization of Securities Commissions (IOSCO).

In short, there is little sign that global commerce and the state are antithetical, given that the two have shown considerable mutual dependency. States have provided much of the regulatory framework for global trade and finance, albeit sharing these competences with other regulatory agencies. Sadly, despite the potential for collective action, none of the measures countries undertook could stop the pace of the economic collapse in late 2008.

The Continuance of Nationalism and Cultural Diversity

Much evidence also confounds the common presumption that economic globalization is effecting cultural homogenization and a rise of cosmopolitan orientations over national **identities**. Identities are social and thus always formed in relationship to others. Constructivists generally hold that identities shape interests; we cannot know what we want unless we know who we are. But because identities are social and produced through interactions, identities can change. The growth of transborder production, the proliferation of global products, the multiplication of supraterritorial monies, and the expansion of transworld financial flows have shown little sign of heralding an end of cultural difference in the world economy.

It is true that global trade and finance are moved by much more than national loyalty. Consumers have repeatedly ignored exhortations to buy American and the like in favor of global products. (This is one reason US automakers Chrysler and General Motors had to beg for cash bailouts from the federal government in 2008–2009.) Shareholders and managers have rarely put national sentiments ahead of the profit margin. Foreign exchange dealers readily desert their national currency to reap financial gain.

However, in other respects, national identities and solidarities have survived—and sometimes thrived—in the contemporary globalizing economy. Most transborder companies have retained a readily recognized national affiliation. Most firms involved in global trade and finance have kept a mononational

Identity The understanding of the self in relationship to an "other." Identities are social and thus always formed in relationship to others. Constructivists generally hold that identities shape interests; we cannot know what we want unless we know who we are. But because identities are social and produced through interactions, identities can change.

board of directors, and the operations of many of these enterprises continue to reflect a national style of business practice connected with the country of origin. Different national conventions have persisted in global finance as well. For instance, since equities have traditionally held a smaller place in German finance, globalization in that country has mainly involved banks and the bond markets. Cultural diversity has also persisted in transborder marketing. Local peculiarities have often affected the way a global product is sold and used in different places. Advertising has often been adjusted to local tastes to be more effective.

Like globalization in general, its economic dimension has not had universal scope. Nor has the rise of global trade and finance marked the end of territorial space, the demise of the state, or full-scale cultural homogenization. However, recognition of these qualifications does not entail a rejection of notions of globalization on the lines of the skeptics noted earlier.

◗ Conclusion

Prior to the summer of 2008, the world's economy seemed to be gaining wealth. Aside from the historic high price for petroleum products, most economic sectors showed no sign of distress. Yet the seeds of the economic recession that began in 2008 were already planted. As you read in this chapter, the complex relationship of trade in goods and financial instruments was seemingly doomed to fail. Too much money was invested in arcane instruments like derivatives and mortgages disguised as secure investments. The globalized trade and finance sectors were largely unregulated by host countries. Governments tried financial methods that worked in past recessions and economic crises. Slowly, many of these reforms and interventions—both new and old—have worked to arrest the economic crisis and to help many countries stabilize their banking industries and their financial markets. The US economy is recovering, but partisan political disputes and the rising cost of health care and social security, without an increase in taxes and other revenues, may trigger another economic crisis in the United States that will create economic instability around the world. Europe's debt crisis is far from over and may result in slow growth in the rest of the world. In addition, several emerging economic leaders, such as India, China, and Brazil, are not growing as fast as they were before the crisis. The worst of the financial crisis might be past, but the pain of loss is still being felt in rich and poor states across the world.

Economic elites and political leaders come together every year at the World Economic Forum in Davos, Switzerland. Here, Cyril Ramaphosa, president of South Africa, and Paul Kagame, president of Rwanda, meet to discuss the future of their economies in Africa. Every year, thousands of politicians, journalists, businesspeople, economists, academics, and celebrities gather in Davos to explore ideas and develop strategies that could shape the future of the global economy.

Managing Global Political Risks

One thing globalization has done is challenge the principle of national sovereignty. It has also increased the number of political and economic actors with the capacity to make choices that have an impact on political and economic stability as well as the national security of any state. Former national security adviser and secretary of state Condoleezza Rice and her Stanford colleague, Amy Zegart, introduce readers to the content of their Stanford MBA course in their book *Political Risk: How Businesses and Organizations Can Anticipate Global Insecurity* (2018). The authors suggest that the political risk landscape has dramatically changed with new actors, issues, sources of uncertainty, and many situations presenting significant risks. The authors talk about ten types of political risk (90–91), including geopolitics, internal conflicts, laws and regulation, breaches of contract, corruption, extraterritorial reach such as unilateral sanctions, natural resources manipulation, social activism, terrorism, and cyberthreats. These risks originate from a variety of sources, including individuals, states, corporations, international organizations, and nonstate actors.

In Chapter 3, Rice and Zegart discuss megatrends in business and technology as well as key trends in politics after the Cold War. In addition to the rise of China and the aggressive behavior of Russia, they discuss "shocks to the international system." They argue that the most significant event was the terrorist attacks on the United States in 2001 (Rice was the US national security adviser at the time). The global financial crisis in 2008 represented a second major shock that had an impact on both rich and poor states. This crisis may have initiated demands for change in fragile states and in regions of instability. The Arab Spring was a movement demanding major reforms in authoritarian states and an opening up of corrupt and unfair economic markets. The final shock, according to the authors, was "great powers behaving badly" (73). This means Russia and China asserting their interests and challenging the liberal global political economy and US control of the dominant political and economic systems. Obviously, this challenges the interests of many global economic and political actors.

As this is a study with its origins in an MBA program at Stanford, Rice and Zegart present a framework for effective risk management that involves simple steps that help shape policy responses to challenges and the resulting risks.

CONTRIBUTORS TO CHAPTER 8: *Steven L. Lamy and John Masker*

KEY TERMS

Bretton Woods system, p. 312
Capital controls, p. 324
Deregulation, p. 324
Electronic commerce, p. 329
Equity, p. 333
Fixed exchange rate, p. 323
Floating exchange rate, p. 323
Foreign direct investment (FDI), p. 308

Free market, p. 315
Futures, p. 334
Global goods, p. 327
Global sourcing, p. 326
Great Depression, p. 310
Identity, p. 338
Immigration controls, p. 324
Interdependence, p. 320
Intrafirm trade, p. 327

Marshall Plan, p. 312
Most favored nation status, p. 326
New International Economic Order, p. 314
Offshore finance centers, p. 331
Options, p. 335
Poverty, p. 314

Protectionism, p. 320
Special Drawing Right (SDR), p. 312
Supraterritoriality, p. 325
Transborder, p. 325
World Bank Group (WBG), p. 312
World Trade Organization (WTO), p. 311

REVIEW QUESTIONS

1. In what ways did the Bretton Woods framework for the postwar economy try to avoid the economic problems of the interwar years?

2. What was the breakdown in the Bretton Woods system?

3. What are the three main conceptions of economic globalization?

4. To what extent is economic globalization new to contemporary history?

5. How does transborder production differ from territorial production?

6. What are some of the reasons that the economic crisis has gone global?

7. How has globalization of trade and finance affected state capacities for economic regulation?

8. How have global products altered ideas of cultural diversity?

9. To what extent can it be said that global capital carries no national flag?

10. Assess the relationship between globalization and income inequality.

11. In what ways might global commerce be reshaped to promote greater distributive justice?

 Learn more with this chapter's digital tools, including the Oxford Insight Study Guide, at **www.oup.com/he/lamy6e**.

THINKING ABOUT GLOBAL POLITICS

Globalization: Productive, Predatory, or Inconsequential?

INTRODUCTION

Globalization has become a buzzword that many pundits and scholars use to describe anything and everything happening in the world today. All the authors in this text share several definitions, and these suggest that globalization is more than just an economic process. But what makes this era of globalization different from previous eras? Is it a positive, negative, or marginal process? How do the various processes of globalization shape issues and events in the political, economic, social, and cultural worlds? This exercise will explore some of these questions.

DISCUSSION

1. Find a definition of globalization that makes the most sense to you. What are the different dimensions of globalization? What does *globalization from above and below* mean?

2. Globalization is said to cause *denationalization* or *delocalization*. What does that mean?

3. Is globalization a recent process? What makes this era different from previous periods of world trade and interdependence? Were the periods of colonialism and imperialism early phases of globalization?

4. What factors push globalization, making it faster, wider, and deeper?

5. Is the process of globalization taking power away from the state, or does it actually enhance the power of some states and weaken others? How?

FOLLOW-UP EXERCISE

What do we expect a state to do? In theory, we expect a state to provide services and resources in three areas:

1. *Defining activities*, which include supporting a means of exchange or marketplace, providing a system of law and order, and protecting the boundaries of the state.

2. *Accumulation-of-wealth activities*, such as building infrastructure.

3. *Redistribution activities*, such as providing health care and education.

Professor Manuel Castells (2005) has written that globalization has led to four crises within states: an *efficiency crisis*, a *legitimacy crisis*, an *identity crisis*, and an *equity crisis*. Is this just an academic claim, or are countries really suffering in these areas? Find at least two countries where one, several, or all of these crises are having a major impact on a state's capacity to provide for its citizens in the three basic areas listed. More precisely, how does globalization influence a state's ability to provide defining activities, accumulation-of-wealth activities, and redistribution activities?

9 Poverty, Development, and Hunger

Two men transporting used drums using a hand-pulled vehicle in Dhaka, Bangladesh. This is the eighth most populous country in the world, with 163 million people, and now it has been forced to take in some 250,000 Rohingya refugees who are fleeing the ethnic violence in Myanmar.

Progress is more plausibly judged by the reduction of deprivation than by the further enrichment of the opulent. We cannot really have an adequate understanding of the future without some view about how well the lives of the poor can be expected to go. Is there, then, any hope for the poor?

—AMARTYA SEN

Development is about transforming the lives of people, not just transforming economies.

—JOSEPH STIGLITZ

The first UN Sustainable Development Goal (SDG) is aimed at ending global poverty. The Bill and Melinda Gates Foundation has created the Goalkeepers (www.globalgoals.org) program and report. This data and action program will track progress on the seventeen Sustainable Development Goals and include a review of leaders, innovations, and practices (see Table 9.3). The foundation will publish the report every year until 2030 when the goals are to be met. This yearly report will be shared with all 193 UN members who adopted these goals and those states and civil-society actors committed to addressing poverty, disease, and climate issues. The Goalkeepers report will present best- and worst-case scenarios related to work in each goal and will alert governments considering cutting their support for programs. For example, if funding for HIV programs is cut by 10 percent, it may cost as many as 5.6 million lives.

The Gates Foundation hopes to motivate young leaders to get involved in programs aimed at meeting the SDGs. In their effort to increase the world's commitment to development, Bill and Melinda Gates emphasize the problem-solving possibilities in each of the goal areas with their plea for action:

> *Poverty and disease in poor countries are the clearest examples we know of solvable misery. It is a fact that this misery is solvable and we have it within our power to decide how much of it actually gets solved. Let's be ambitious. Let's lead to end extreme poverty, fight inequality and injustice and fix climate change.*

Since 1945, we have witnessed not only increasing individual and nongovernmental organization (NGO) advocacy but also unprecedented official development policies and impressive global economic growth. Yet global political and economic polarization is increasing, with the economic gap growing between rich and poor states and people. As we have

CHAPTER OUTLINE

Introduction 344

Poverty 346

Development 348

Hunger 362

Conclusion 369

FEATURES

THEORY IN PRACTICE The Terms of Development 357

CASE STUDY Life in Zimbabwe: Poverty, Hunger, Development, and Politics 360

WHAT'S TRENDING? Saving a Life 368

THINKING ABOUT GLOBAL POLITICS Development Assistance as Foreign Policy Statecraft 370

After reading and discussing this chapter, you should be able to:

Define the terms *poverty*, *development*, and *hunger* as they relate to global politics.

Explain international economic liberalism as a development model.

Explain why the orthodox development model did not provide for economic development in former European colonies.

Analyze development using the theories of realism, liberalism, Marxism, constructivism, and feminism.

Describe the Washington Consensus, and identify three of its effects on developing countries.

Explain why poverty, development, and hunger affect women and children more than men in developing societies.

Washington Consensus The belief of key opinion formers in Washington that global welfare would be maximized by the universal application of neoliberal economic policies that favor a minimalist state and an enhanced role for the market.

Global governance The regulation and coordination of transnational issue areas by nation-states, international and regional organizations, and private agencies through the establishment of international regimes. These regimes may focus on problem solving or the simple enforcement of rules and regulations.

seen in other issue areas in this book, people who work in the academic discipline of international relations have had different ways of thinking about this gap.

- Traditionally, realists have concentrated on issues relating to war and have seen national security and development economics as separate issue areas.
- Mainstream realist and liberal scholars have largely neglected the challenges that global underdevelopment presents to human security—freedom from fear, freedom from want, and the rule of law.
- Dependency theorists have been interested in persistent and deepening inequality and relations between North and South, but for decades they received little attention in the discipline.
- During the 1990s, debate flourished, and several subfields developed that touched on matters of poverty, development, and hunger, albeit tangentially (e.g., global environmental politics, gender, international political economy).
- The contributions of a range of theorists and scholars in recent years have significantly raised concerns about the persistence of global poverty, and these same scholars have introduced sophisticated research tools to understand the multidimensional elements of poverty. Certainly the focus on the impact of globalization has increased both critical and mainstream research about human security and development.

Now in the twenty-first century, the discipline is better placed to engage with the interrelated issues of poverty, development, and hunger by influencing the diplomatic world, where interest in these issues is growing, spurred on by fears of terrorist threats and recognition of the uneven impact of globalization (Thomas and Wilkin 2004).

Introduction

Despite the trend toward increased activism, poverty, hunger, and disease remain widespread, and women and girls continue to make up the majority of the world's poorest people. Since the 1980s and 1990s, the worldwide promotion of neoliberal economic policies (the so-called **Washington Consensus**) by **global governance** institutions has been accompanied by increasing inequalities within and among states. During this period, the second world countries of the former Eastern bloc were incorporated into the third world grouping of states, and millions of people previously cushioned by their governments were thrown into poverty. As a result, the developing world is characterized by rising social inequalities, and, within the third world countries, the adverse impact of globalization has been felt acutely. Countries have been forced to adopt free market policies as a condition of debt rescheduling and in the hope of attracting new investment to spur development. The global picture is very mixed, with other factors such as gender, class, race, and ethnicity contributing to local outcomes (Buvinic 1997, 39).

In 2000, the United Nations recognized the enormity of the current challenges with the acceptance of the Millennium Development Goals (MDGs). These set time-limited, quantifiable targets across eight areas, including poverty, health, gender, education, environment, and development. The first goal was the eradication of extreme poverty and hunger, with the target of halving the proportion of people living on less than $1.25 a day by 2015. The results of the MDG process were mixed, but in general, the process was successful. For example, the number of people in extreme poverty decreased from 1.926 billion in 1990 to 836 million in 2015. From 1990 to 2015, the number of people with access to primary education and clean water has also increased. The share of the world's population living in extreme poverty fell to 10 percent in 2015. Thus, these goals provided a useful framework for development. In the final MDGs report in 2015, UN secretary-general Ban Ki-moon suggested that there was still significant work to be done as UN members adopted the SDGs, which build on the success of the MDGs, in September 2015:

> *Yet for all the remarkable gains, I am keenly aware that inequalities persist and that progress has been uneven. The world's poor remain overwhelmingly concentrated in some parts of the world. In 2011, nearly 60 per cent of the world's one billion extremely poor people lived in just five countries. Too many women continue to die during pregnancy or from childbirth-related complications. Progress tends to bypass women and those who are lowest on the economic ladder or are disadvantaged because of their age, disability or ethnicity. Disparities between rural and urban areas remain pronounced.*

The attempts of the majority of governments, international NGOs, and NGOs since 1945 to address global hunger and poverty can be categorized into two very broad types depending on the explanations they provide for the existence of these problems and the respective solutions they prescribe. These can be identified as the dominant mainstream, or orthodox, approach, which provides and values a particular body of developmental knowledge, and a critical alternative approach, which incorporates other more marginalized understandings of the development challenge and process (see Table 9.1). Most of this chapter will be devoted to an examination of the differences between the mainstream/orthodox approach and the critical alternative approach in view of the

The multidimensional poverty index includes one dimension of poverty, standard of living, that consists of sanitation, drinking water, electricity, and housing. In this photo, people in Northern India live in shelters without many of these essential services. The lack of adequate housing is a problem in both rich and poor states.

TABLE 9.1	Mainstream and Alternative Conceptions of Poverty, Development, and Hunger		
	Poverty	**Development**	**Hunger**
Mainstream Approach	Unfulfilled material needs	Linear path—traditional to modern	Not enough food to go around
Critical Alternative Approach	Unfulfilled material and nonmaterial needs	Diverse paths, locally driven	There is enough food; the problem is distribution and entitlement

three related topics of poverty, development, and hunger, with particular emphasis placed on development. The chapter concludes with an assessment of whether the desperate conditions in which so many of the world's citizens find themselves today are likely to improve.

After reading and discussing this chapter, you will have a better sense of the factors that cause poverty and the status of efforts aimed at addressing global poverty. You will also know about the global institutions that are dedicated to addressing the problems of development.

ENGAGING WITH THE WORLD

Oxfam International

In 1942, a group of Oxford students, Quakers, and social activists created the Oxford Committee for Famine Relief with the aim of pressuring the British government into allowing food aid through the Allied blockade so it could reach starving people in occupied Greece. Today Oxfam has grown into an international confederation of twenty NGOs working with partners in ninety countries to end poverty. The organization offers internships that provide a challenging professional development experience aimed at combatting global poverty and injustice. Check out www.oxfam.org/en/countries/volunteer-us.

▶ Poverty

Poverty According to the United Nations, poverty is a denial of choices and opportunities, a violation of human dignity. It means lack of basic capacity provided by material possessions or money to participate effectively in society.

Different conceptions of poverty underpin the mainstream and alternative views of development. There is basic agreement on the material aspects of poverty, such as lack of food, clean water, and sanitation, but disagreement on the importance of nonmaterial aspects. Also, key differences emerge in regard to how material needs should be met and, hence, about the goal of development.

Most governments, international organizations (e.g., the International Monetary Fund [IMF] and World Bank), and citizens in the West and elsewhere adhere to the orthodox conception of **poverty**, which refers to a situation where people do not have the money to buy adequate food or satisfy other basic needs and are often classified as un- or underemployed.

Since 1945, this mainstream understanding of poverty based on money has come about as a result of the globalization of Western culture and the attendant expansion of the free market economy. Thus, a community that provides for itself outside monetized cash transactions and wage labor, such as a hunter-gatherer group, is regarded as poor. This meaning of poverty has been almost universalized. Poverty is seen as an economic condition dependent on cash transactions in the marketplace for its eradication. These transactions in turn depend on development defined as economic growth. The same economic yard-stick is used to measure all societies and to judge if they merit development assistance.

A more comprehensive or multidimensional view of poverty is the Global Multidimensional Poverty Index (MPI), which is the basis of poverty research being conducted by the Oxford Poverty and Human Development Initiative (https://ophi.org.uk). The index was developed with the UN Development Pro-gramme (UNDP) for its 2010 development report. The MPI is described as a mea-sure of "acute multidimensional poverty in over 100 developing countries." It certainly adds to the traditional economic indicators by adding three dimensions of poverty: health, education, and living standards. Within these categories the index focuses on ten indicators to build a *personal profile of deprivation* or dimen-sions of poverty in which a person is deprived of human necessities. The ten indi-cators are nutrition and child mortality (in the health dimension), years of schooling and school attendance (in the education dimension), and cooking fuel, sanitation, drinking water, electricity, housing, and assets (in the standard of living dimen-sion). This index focuses on poverty at the level of an individual. If someone is considered deprived in one-third or more of these ten indicators, the index will identify the individual as *MPI poor.*

Poverty has widely been regarded as a characteristic of the third world, and it has a gendered face that realist and liberal perspectives often ignore. By the mid-1990s, an approach had developed whereby it was seen as incumbent on the developed countries to help the third world eradicate poverty. As studies show that women and children are the most severely impacted by the conse-quences of poverty, development economists are paying more attention to female poverty and women's roles in economic development. The solution ad-vocated to overcome global poverty is the further integration of the global econ-omy (C. Thomas 2000) and of women into this process (Pearson 2000; H. Weber 2002). Increasingly, however, as globalization has intensified, pov-erty defined in such economic terms has come to characterize significant sec-tors of the population in advanced developed countries such as the United States (see Bello 1994).

But for some, poverty cannot be measured in terms of cash. Critical alterna-tive views of poverty place the emphasis not only on money but also on spiritual values, community ties, and the availability of common resources. In traditional

Survival In this context, it is the survival of the person by the provision of adequate food, clean water, clothing, shelter, medical care, and protection from violence and crime.

Community A human association in which members share common symbols and wish to cooperate to realize common objectives.

subsistence methods, a common strategy for **survival** is provision for oneself and one's family via **community**-regulated access to common water, land, and food. The work of the UNDP since the early 1990s is significant here for distinguishing between income poverty (a material condition) and human poverty (encompassing human dignity, opportunity, and choices).

The issue of poverty and the challenge of poverty alleviation moved up the global political agenda at the close of the twentieth century, as evidenced by the MDGs. World Bank figures for the 1990s showed a global improvement in reducing the number of people living on less than $1 a day (its orthodox measurement of extreme poverty, changed to $1.90 in 2011). Despite this improvement, the picture was uneven. In sub-Saharan Africa, the situation deteriorated, and elsewhere, such as the Russian Federation, the Commonwealth of Independent States, Latin America and the Caribbean, and some non–oil-producing Middle Eastern states, the picture remained bleak. In 2005, the World Bank stated that almost half the world—more than 3 billion people—lived below the poverty line. On a positive note, though, the world met the MDG target of halving global poverty. The number of people living on less than $1.25 has been reduced from 1.9 billion in 1990 to 836 million in 2015. However, the target of halving the proportion of people suffering from hunger was missed. Another narrow miss was the goal of achieving universal primary education: School enrollment increased from 83 percent in 2000 to 91 percent in 2015.

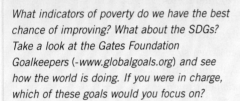

WHAT'S YOUR WORLDVIEW?

What indicators of poverty do we have the best chance of improving? What about the SDGs? Take a look at the Gates Foundation Goalkeepers (-www.globalgoals.org) and see how the world is doing. If you were in charge, which of these goals would you focus on?

 # Development

Development In the orthodox view, top-down; reliance on "expert knowledge," usually Western and definitely external; large capital investments in large projects; advanced technology; expansion of the private sphere. In the alternative view, bottom-up; participatory; reliance on appropriate (often local) knowledge and technology; small investments in small-scale projects; protection of the commons.

Modernization theory A theory that considers development synonymous with economic growth within the context of a free market international economy.

Having considered the orthodox and critical alternative views of poverty, we now turn to an examination of the important topic of development. This examination will be conducted in three main parts. The first part starts by examining the orthodox view of development and then proceeds to an assessment of its effect on postwar development in the third world. The second part examines the critical alternative view of development and its application to subjects such as empowerment and democracy. In the third part, we consider the ways the orthodox approach to development has responded to some of the criticisms made of it by the critical alternative approach.

When we consider the topic of **development**, it is important to realize that all conceptions of development necessarily reflect a particular set of social and political values. Since World War II, the dominant understanding—favored by the majority of governments and multilateral lending agencies—has been **modernization theory**, a theory that considers development synonymous with economic growth within the context of a free market international economy. Economic growth is identified as necessary for combating poverty, defined as the inability of people to meet their basic material needs through cash transactions. This is reflected in the influential reports of the World Bank, where countries are categorized according to their income. Countries that have lower national incomes per capita are regarded as less developed than those with higher incomes, and they are perceived as being in need of increased integration into the global marketplace.

As the wave of decolonization swept the world in the 1960s and early 1970s, an alternative view of development has emerged from a few governments, UN agencies, grassroots movements, NGOs, and some academics. Their concerns have centered broadly on entitlement and distribution. Poverty is identified as the inability to provide for the material needs of oneself and one's family by subsistence or cash transactions and by the absence of an environment conducive to human well-being, broadly conceived in spiritual and community terms. These voices of opposition are growing significantly louder as ideas polarize following the apparent universal triumph of economic liberalism at the end of the Cold War. The language of opposition is changing to incorporate matters of democracy such as political empowerment, participation, meaningful self-determination for the majority, protection of the commons, and an emphasis on growth that benefits the poor. The fundamental differences between the orthodox and the alternative views of development can be seen in Table 9.2 In the following two sections, we will examine how the orthodox view of development has been applied at a global level and assess what measure of success it has achieved.

TABLE 9.2 Development: A Contested Concept

The Orthodox View	The Alternative View
Poverty: A situation suffered by people who do not have the *money to buy food* and satisfy other *basic material needs*	**Poverty:** A situation suffered by people who are not able to meet their *material and nonmaterial needs* through their own effort
Purpose: Transformation of traditional subsistence economies (defined as "backward") into industrial, commodified economies (defined as "modern"). Production of surplus. Individuals sell their labor for money rather than producing to meet their family's needs.	**Purpose:** Creation of human well-being through sustainable societies in social, cultural, political, and economic terms
Core ideas and assumptions: The possibility of unlimited economic growth in a free market system. Economies would reach a "takeoff" point, and thereafter, wealth would trickle down to those at the bottom. Superiority of the Western model and knowledge. Belief that the process would ultimately benefit everyone. Domination, exploitation of nature.	**Core ideas and assumptions:** Sufficiency. The inherent value of nature, cultural diversity, and the community-controlled commons (water, land, air, forest). Human activity in balance with nature. Self-reliance. Democratic inclusion, participation: for example, a voice for marginalized groups such as women and indigenous groups. Local control.
Measurement: Economic growth; gross domestic product (GDP) per capita; industrialization, including of agriculture	**Measurement:** Fulfillment of basic material and nonmaterial human needs of everyone; condition of the natural environment; political empowerment of marginalized
Process: Top-down; reliance on "expert knowledge," usually Western and definitely external; large capital investments in large projects; advanced technology; expansion of the private sphere	**Process:** Bottom-up; participatory; reliance on appropriate (often local) knowledge and technology; small investments in small-scale projects; protection of the commons

Post-1945 International Economic Liberalism and the Orthodox Development Model

During World War II, there was a strong belief among the Allied powers that the protectionist trade policies of the 1930s had contributed significantly to the outbreak of the war. As we learned in Chapter 8, even before World War II had ended, the United States and the United Kingdom drew up plans for the creation of a stable postwar international order. Providing the institutional bases were the United Nations, its affiliates the IMF and the World Bank Group, plus the General Agreement on Tariffs and Trade (GATT). The latter three provided the foundations of a liberal international economic order based on the pursuit of free trade but allowing an appropriate role for state intervention in the market in support of national security and national and global stability (Rapley 1996). This has been called **embedded liberalism**. Because the decision-making procedures of these international economic institutions favored a small group of developed Western states, their relationship with the United Nations, which in the General Assembly has more democratic procedures, has not always been an easy one.

Embedded liberalism A liberal international economic order based on the pursuit of free trade but allowing an appropriate role for state intervention in the market in support of national security and national and global stability.

In the early postwar years, reconstruction of previously developed states took priority over assisting developing states. This reconstruction process really took off in the context of the Cold War, with the transfer of huge sums of money from the United States to Europe in the form of bilateral aid from the Marshall Plan of 1947. In the 1950s and 1960s, as decolonization progressed and developing countries gained power in the UN General Assembly, the focus of the World Bank and the UN system generally shifted to the perceived needs of developing countries. The United States was heavily involved as the most important funder of the World Bank and the United Nations and also in a bilateral capacity.

In the developed Western countries, among the managers of the major multilateral institutions, and throughout the UN system there was a widespread belief that third world states were economically backward and needed to be "developed." Western-educated elites in those countries believed this process would require intervention in their economies. In the context of independence movements, the development imperative came to be shared by many citizens in the third world. The underlying assumption was that the Western lifestyle and mode of economic organization were superior and should be universally aspired to.

The Cold War provided a context in which there was a competition between the West and the Eastern bloc to win markets in the third world. The United States believed that the path of liberal economic growth would result in development and that development would result in a global capitalist system, which favors the United States. The USSR, by contrast, attempted to sell its centralized economic system as the most rapid means for the newly independent states to achieve industrialization and development. Unfortunately for the Soviet government, because of its own food-supply and consumer-goods production problems, the country's material foreign assistance was usually limited to military equipment.

The majority of third world states were born into and accepted a place within the Western, capitalist orbit, primarily because of preexisting economic ties with their former colonial occupiers. However, a few, by either choice or lack of options, ended up in the socialist camp. Yet in the early postwar and postcolonial decades, all newly independent states favored an important role for the state in development.

With the ending of the Cold War and the collapse of the Eastern bloc after 1989, this neoliberal economic and political philosophy came to dominate development thinking across the globe. The championing of unadulterated liberal economic values played an important role in accelerating the globalization process, representing an important ideological shift. The embedded liberalism of the early postwar decades gave way to the neoclassical economic policies that favored a minimalist state and an enhanced role for the market: the Washington Consensus. The belief was that global welfare would be maximized by the **liberalization** of trade, finance, and investment and by the restructuring of national economies to provide an enabling environment for capital. Such policies would also ideally ensure the repayment of debt. The former Eastern bloc countries were now seen to be in transition from centrally planned to market economies, and throughout the third world, the role of government was reduced and the market was given the role of major engine of growth and associated development. This approach was presented as common sense, with the attendant idea that "There Is No Alternative" (C. Thomas 2000). It informed the strategies of the IMF and World Bank, and, importantly, through the Uruguay Round of trade discussions carried out under the auspices of GATT, it shaped the World Trade Organization.

By the end of the 1990s, the G7 (later the G8, when Russia joined in 1996) and associated international financial institutions were championing a slightly modified version of the neoliberal economic orthodoxy, labeled the **post–Washington Consensus**, which stressed growth benefiting the poor and poverty reduction based on institutional strength, continued domestic policy reform, and growth through trade liberalization. Henceforth, locally owned national poverty-reduction strategy (PRS) papers would be the focus for funding (Cammack 2002). These papers quickly became the litmus test for funding from an increasingly integrated lineup of global financial institutions and donors.

The Post-1945 International Economic Order: Results

There has been an explosive widening of the gap between the rich and the poor since 1945 compared with previous history. Nevertheless, there have been major gains for developing countries since 1945 as measured by the orthodox criteria of

Liberalization Government policies that reduce the role of the state in the economy, such as the dismantling of trade tariffs and barriers, the deregulation and opening of the financial sector to foreign investors, and the privatization of state enterprises.

Post–Washington Consensus A slightly modified version of the Washington Consensus promoting economic growth through trade liberalization coupled with pro-poor growth and poverty-reduction policies.

WHAT'S YOUR WORLDVIEW?

Some scholars have suggested that the Cold War was about whose rule book would govern the world—the Soviet view of socialism or the US brand of capitalism. Capitalism won, but it does not seem to be working for many who live in the developing world. If there is only one economic option—capitalism—how do you sell it to those who are still in poverty? Are there other brands of capitalism that might work better (for example, state capitalism promoted by China or Nordic capitalism practiced in Finland, Norway, or Sweden)?

Regional diversity Each region of the world has experienced economic development differently based on traditions, culture, historical development, and even geographic location.

economic growth, GDP per capita, and industrialization. A striking feature of both is the marked **regional diversity**. The East Asian experience has been generally positive throughout this period, but not so for Africa. China has been strong since the early 1980s, and India has fared better since the late 1980s.

In the 1990s, the picture was far from positive. The UNDP reports "no fewer than 100 countries—all developing or in transition—have experienced serious economic decline over the past three decades. As a result, per capita income in these 100 countries is lower than it was 10, 20, even 30 years ago" (UN Development Programme 1998, 37). Moreover, the 1990s saw twenty-one countries experience decade-long declines in social and economic indicators, compared with only four in the 1980s (UN Development Programme 2003). Financial crises spread across the globe and indicated marked reversals in Mexico, the East Asian states, Brazil, and Russia. The African continent looked increasingly excluded from any economic benefits of globalization, and thirty-three countries there ended the 1990s more heavily indebted than they had been two decades earlier (Easterly 2002). By the end of the century, not a single former second or third world country had joined the ranks of the first world in a solid sense. Significant growth occurred in a handful of countries, such as China, India, and Mexico—the new globalizers—but the benefits were not well distributed within those countries. Despite significant improvements in global social indicators like adult literacy, access to safe water, and infant mortality rates, global deprivation continues. This is illustrated vividly in Figure 9.1.

Having outlined the broad development achievements and failures of the postwar international economic order, we will now evaluate these from two different development perspectives: a mainstream orthodox view and a critical alternative view.

Economic Development: Orthodox and Alternative Evaluations

The orthodox liberal assessment of the past sixty years of development suggests states that have integrated most deeply into the global economy through trade liberalization have grown the fastest, and it praises these "new globalizers." It acknowledges that neoliberal economic policy has resulted in greater inequalities within and between states but regards inequality positively as a spur to competition and the entrepreneurial spirit.

It was clear at least from the late 1970s that "trickle-down" (the idea that overall economic growth as measured by increases in the GDP would automatically bring benefits for the poorer classes) had not worked. Despite impressive rates of growth in GDP per capita enjoyed by some developing countries, this success was not reflected in their societies at large, and while a minority became substantially wealthier, the mass of the population saw no significant change. For some bankers in multilateral organizations and conservative politicians in rich countries, the even greater polarization in wealth evident in recent decades is not regarded as a

Goals and Targets	Africa		Asia				Oceania	Latin America and the Caribbean	Caucasus and Central Asia
	Northern	Sub-Saharan	Eastern	South-Eastern	Southern	Western			

GOAL 1 | Eradicate extreme poverty and hunger

Reduce extreme poverty by half	low poverty	very high poverty	low poverty	moderate poverty	high poverty	low poverty	—	low poverty	low poverty
Productive and decent employment	large deficit	very large deficit	moderate deficit	large deficit	large deficit	large deficit	very large deficit	moderate deficit	small deficit
Reduce hunger by half	low hunger	high hunger	moderate hunger	moderate hunger	high hunger	moderate hunger	moderate hunger	moderate hunger	moderate hunger

GOAL 2 | Achieve universal primary education

Universal primary schooling	high enrolment	moderate enrolment	high enrolment	high enrolment	high enrolment	high enrolment	high enrolment	high enrolment	high enrolment

GOAL 3 | Promote gender equality and empower women

Equal girls' enrolment in primary school	close to parity	close to parity	parity	parity	parity	close to parity	close to parity	parity	parity
Women's share of paid employment	low share	medium share	high share	medium share	low share	low share	medium share	high share	high share
Women's equal representation in national parliaments	moderate representation	moderate representation	moderate representation	low representation	low representation	low representation	very low representation	moderate representation	low representation

GOAL 4 | Reduce child mortality

Reduce mortality of under-five-year-olds by two thirds	low mortality	high mortality	low mortality	low mortality	moderate mortality	low mortality	moderate mortality	low mortality	low mortality

GOAL 5 | Improve maternal health

Reduce maternal mortality by three quarters	low mortality	high mortality	low mortality	moderate mortality	moderate mortality	low mortality	moderate mortality	low mortality	low mortality
Access to reproductive health	moderate access	low access	high access	moderate access	moderate access	moderate access	low access	high access	moderate access

GOAL 6 | Combat HIV/AIDS, malaria and other diseases

Halt and begin to reverse the spread of HIV/AIDS	low incidence	high incidence	low incidence	low incidence	low incidence	low incidence	low incidence	low incidence	low incidence
Halt and reverse the spread of tuberculosis	low mortality	high mortality	low mortality	moderate mortality	moderate mortality	low mortality	moderate mortality	low mortality	moderate mortality

GOAL 7 | Ensure environmental sustainability

Halve proportion of population without improved drinking water	high coverage	low coverage	high coverage	high coverage	high coverage	high coverage	low coverage	high coverage	moderate coverage
Halve proportion of population without sanitation	moderate coverage	very low coverage	moderate coverage	low coverage	very low coverage	high coverage	very low coverage	moderate coverage	high coverage
Improve the lives of slum-dwellers	low proportion of slum-dwellers	very high proportion of slum-dwellers	moderate proportion of slum-dwellers	moderate proportion of slum-dwellers	moderate proportion of slum-dwellers	moderate proportion of slum-dwellers	moderate proportion of slum-dwellers	moderate proportion of slum-dwellers	—

GOAL 8 | Develop a global partnership for development

Internet users	moderate usage	low usage	high usage	moderate usage	low usage	high usage	low usage	high usage	high usage

The progress chart operates on two levels. The text in each box indicates the present level of development. The colours show progress made towards the target according to the legend below:

- Target met or excellent progress.
- Good progress.
- Fair progress.
- Poor progress or deterioration.
- Missing or insufficient data.

For the regional groupings and country data, see *mdgs.un.org*. Country experiences in each region may differ significantly from the regional average. Due to new data and revised methodologies, this Progress Chart is not comparable with previous versions.

Sources: United Nations, based on data and estimates provided by: Food and Agriculture Organization of the United Nations; Inter-Parliamentary Union; International Labour Organization; International Telecommunication Union; UNAIDS; UNESCO; UN-Habitat; UNICEF; UN Population Division; World Bank; World Health Organization - based on statistics available as of June 2015.

Compiled by the Statistics Division, Department of Economic and Social Affairs, United Nations.

Figure 9.1 **2015 Progress Chart for UN Millennium Development Goals.**

problem as long as the social and political discontent the inequality creates is not so extensive as to potentially derail implementation of the liberalization project itself. This discontent will be alleviated by the development of national PRSs, which, it is claimed, put countries and their peoples in the driver's seat of development policy, thus empowering the local community and ensuring a better distribution of benefits.

Advocates of a critical alternative approach emphasize the pattern of distribution of gains within global society and within individual states rather than growth. They believe that the economic liberalism that underpins the process of globalization has resulted, and continues to result, in growing economic differentiation between and within countries and that this is problematic. Moreover, they note that this trend has been evident during the very period when key global actors have been committed to promoting development worldwide and, indeed, when there were fairly continuous world economic growth rates and positive rates of GDP growth per capita (Brown and Kane 1995; see Table 9.3).

Dependency theorists such as Andre Gunder Frank (1967) regard the increasing gap between rich and poor as inevitable and undesirable. These theorists stressed how the periphery, or third world, was actively underdeveloped by activities that promoted the growth in wealth of the core Western countries and of elites in the periphery.

At the beginning of the twenty-first century, however, exponents of a critical alternative—in contrast to their orthodox colleagues—began to question the value of national PRSs, arguing that while a new focus on issues such as health and education is important, the more fundamental issue of possible links between Washington Consensus policies and poverty creation is being ignored.

The orthodox and alternative evaluations are based on different values, and they are measuring different things. Glyn Roberts's words are pertinent: "GNP growth statistics might mean a good deal to an economist or to a maharajah, but they do not tell us a thing about the quality of life in a Third World fishing village" (1984, 6).

A Critical Alternative View of Development

Since the early 1970s, there have been numerous efforts to stimulate debate about development and to highlight its contested nature. Critical alternative ideas have been put forward that we can synthesize into an alternative approach. These have originated with various NGOs, grassroots development organizations, individuals, UN organizations, and private foundations. The Nobel Prize committee recognized the alternative approach when in 2006 it gave the Peace Prize to Muhammad Yunus and the microcredit loan institution Grameen Bank, which he founded in Bangladesh. The Grameen Bank provides credit (in the form of small loans) to the poor without requiring collateral. Disparate **social movements** not directly related to the development agenda have contributed to the flourishing of the alternative viewpoints—for example, the women's

Social movement A mode of collective action that challenges ways of life, thinking, dominant norms, and moral codes; seeks answers to global problems; and promotes reform or transformation in political and economic institutions.

movement, the peace movement, movements for democracy, and green movements (C. Thomas 2000). In 1975, the Dag Hammarskjöld Foundation published the noteworthy *What Now? Another Development?*, which argued that the process of development should be

- need oriented (material and nonmaterial);
- endogenous (coming from within a society);
- self-reliant (in terms of human, natural, and cultural resources);
- ecologically sound; and
- based on structural transformations (of economy, society, gender, and power relations).

Since then, various NGOs, such as the World Development Movement, have campaigned for a form of development that incorporates aspects of this alternative approach. Grassroots movements have often grown up around specific issues, such as dams (e.g., on the Narmada River in India) or access to common resources (the rubber tappers of the Brazilian Amazon; the Chipko movement, which began as a women's movement to secure trees in the Himalayas). Such campaigns received a great impetus in the 1980s with the growth of the green movement worldwide. The two-year preparatory process before the 1992 UN Conference on Environment and Development in Rio de Janeiro, Brazil, gave indigenous groups, women, children, and other previously voiceless groups a chance to express their views. This momentum has continued, and it has become the norm to hold alternative NGO forums parallel to all major UN conferences.

Democracy, Empowerment, and Development

Democracy is at the heart of the alternative conception of development. Grassroots movements play an important role in challenging entrenched structures of power in formal democratic societies. In the face of increasing globalization, with the further erosion of local community control over daily life and the further extension of the power of the market and **transnational corporations**, people are standing up for their rights as they define them. They are making a case for local control and local empowerment as the heart of development. They are protecting what they identify as the immediate source of their survival—water, forest, and land. They are rejecting the dominant agenda of private and public (government-controlled) spheres and setting an alternative one. Examples include the Chiapas uprising in Mexico (which attempted to bring attention to the needs of indigenous people after the North American Free Trade Agreement [NAFTA] went into effect) and Indian peasant protests against foreign-owned seed factories. Protests at the annual meetings of the World Trade Organization and protests of the IMF and World Bank have become routine since the late 1990s and are indicative of an increasingly widespread discontent with the process of globalization and the distribution of its benefits.

Transnational corporation A company or business that has affiliates in different countries.

Development has left many behind. Here a child sits on the sidewalk where she lives with her family in Buenos Aires, Argentina. The two-year-old runs down the sidewalk, dodging cardboard boxes, a worn-out sofa, and a broken refrigerator without noticing the cars zooming dangerously close to her and others. These are the risks of living on the streets, and this is a major global problem. How should we respond?

Such protests symbolize the struggle for substantive democracy that communities across the world are working for. In this context, development is about facilitating a community's participation and lead role in deciding what sort of development is appropriate for it; it is not about assuming the desirability of the Western model and its associated values. This alternative conception of development therefore values diversity above universality and is based on a different conception of rights.

For some commentators, national PRSs offer the opportunity—albeit as yet unrealized—for greater community participation in making development policy in the South. If all parties operate in the spirit that was intended, the PRS process could enhance representation and voice for states and peoples in the South, and it offers the best hope available for expanding national ownership of economic policy.

Now that we have looked at the critical alternative view of development, we will look at the way the orthodox view has attempted to respond to the criticisms from the alternative view.

The Orthodoxy Incorporates Criticisms

Sustainable development
Development that meets the needs of the present without compromising the ability of future generations to meet their own needs.

In the mainstream debate, the focus has shifted from growth to sustainable development. The concept was championed in the late 1980s by the influential Brundtland Commission (officially entitled the World Commission on Environment and Development; see Brundtland et al. 1987) and supported in the 1990s by a series of UN global conferences. Central to the concept of **sustainable development** is the idea that the pursuit of development by the present generation should not be at the expense of future generations. Similarly, when faced with critical NGO voices, the World Bank in 1994 came up with its Operational Policy 4.20 on gender. The latter aimed to "reduce gender disparities and enhance women particularly in the economic development of their countries by integrating gender considerations in its country assistance programs" (www.worldbank.org).

Most recently, incorporating the language of poverty reduction into World Bank and IMF policies includes phrases like "growth with equity" and "pro-poor growth," which some would argue are nothing more than buzzwords because they underlie macroeconomic policy that remains unchanged. An examination of the contribution of the development orthodoxy to increasing global inequality is not on the agenda. The gendered outcomes of macroeconomic policies are largely ignored.

The Terms of Development

Can any theory of international relations explain the problems of economic underdevelopment? International relations specialists even have trouble deciding what to call the countries of the world once held in European colonial bondage. *Third world* made sense at one time. The term originated with Alfred Sauvy, a French demographer, who in 1952 compared the economic and political conditions of European colonies with those endured by the Third Estate in France prior to the revolution. The typology was a simple one: First world countries had capitalist free market economies, second world countries in the Soviet bloc and China had centrally planned economies, and third world countries lacked industrial bases and provided raw materials for export. With the end of the Cold War, this tripartite typology made less sense. Until 1989, *third world* provided a less demeaning alternative to terms often found in the political science literature on Africa, Asia, Oceania, and Latin America: *underdeveloped* or *less developed country*, sometimes called *least developed country*. A brief look at a map reveals another problem. The *global South* is another term often used to indicate the former European colonies in Africa, Asia, and Latin America; the other side of this dyad is the *global North*, meant to describe the former colonial occupiers. But not all countries in the global South are poor, and not all countries that were once colonial occupiers—Portugal and Spain, for instance—are rich. Instead, there

are pockets of wealth and poverty in both the South and the North.

There is another problem for theorists: What do we mean by the term *development* itself? The term might mean industrial output and its related exchange of goods and services. If that is the case, then the term implies that industrialization is a proper goal. But the problem of global climate change suggests that industrialization, as it has been practiced, is not a good thing (see Chapter 10). Moreover, the term, according to some gender theorists, only considers transactions that can be counted or that rely on an amount calculated in a currency. This method of accounting can overlook transactions that take place in a barter market or economic activities traditionally done by women: raising crops for household consumption, cutting firewood, caring for children. In a capitalist economy, in Western Europe or the United States, such activities could have a dollar amount attached. For example, the US tax code gives a deduction for the cost of childcare.

The realist perspective looks at the problems of economic and political underdevelopment, using the standard definitions found in scholarly books: Countries are poor because they are poor. Since international politics is a constant struggle for power in conditions of anarchy, then some countries must lose in that struggle. This perspective can help explain the series of internal and transborder wars in central Africa since the late 1980s. Short on their own resources, the neighbors of the Democratic Republic of the Congo

tried to destabilize that country to gain access to mineral wealth.

Radical perspectives like Marxism once offered hope for a restructured global system. However, whatever comfort the doctrine once promised, the demise of the Soviet Union ended it. What was left was a theory that outlined the causes and results of political and economic exploitation but proposed an apparently bankrupt solution.

For analysts in the liberal tradition, the policy prescription does not offer much hope either. This tradition tends to recommend that the former colonies integrate themselves into the global economy, perhaps by planting a cash crop for export or by using untapped resources. As we have seen in this chapter, however, countries that borrow money from international financial institutions can get caught in a debt trap if the price for the export commodity declines. This can leave the country economically worse off.

Unfortunately, no matter what they are called—the third world, the global South, the less developed countries—for many countries, poverty and hunger prevail.

For Discussion

1. Instead of disagreeing about terminology, should leaders work on comprehensive plans to help the poor of the world?

2. Are there alternative views of development that might challenge the orthodox position?

3. What does a state-centric focus (on states as the primary actor in global politics) overlook?

Despite promises of new funding at the UN Monterrey Conference on Financing for Development in 2002, new transfers of finance from developed to developing countries have been slow in coming; meanwhile, most expected new promises to be made by the G8 during their summit in 2009. In addition to new finance, that summit saw commitments to write off $40 billion of debt owed by the heavily indebted poor countries. However, the commitment was not implemented with immediate effect and did not cover all needy countries. The North–South agenda has changed little in the years since the Rio Summit, when sustainable development hit the headlines.

In September 2015, the assembled members of the United Nations adopted a new sustainable development agenda that continues the efforts around the MDGs. These seventeen SDGs (see Table 9.3) are to be realized by 2030 and will require global cooperation across public, private, and civil-society organizations. Agenda 2030 repeats the call for the eradication of poverty but also includes climate-change mitigation as an element of sustainable development.

It is important to note that some parts of the UN family have been genuinely responsive to criticisms of mainstream development. The UNDP is noteworthy for its advocacy of the measurement of development based on life expectancy, adult literacy, and average local purchasing power—the Human Development Index (HDI). The HDI results in a very different assessment of countries' achievements than does the traditional measurement of development based on per capita GDP (A. Thomas et al. 1994, 22). For example, China, Sri Lanka, Poland, and Cuba fare much better under HDI assessments than they do under more orthodox assessments, whereas Saudi Arabia and Kuwait fare much worse.

An Appraisal of the Responses of the Orthodox Approach to Its Critics

In 2000, a series of official "+ 5" mini-conferences were held, such as Rio + 5, Copenhagen + 5, and Beijing + 5, to assess progress in specific areas since the major UN conferences five years earlier. The assessments suggested that the international community had fallen short in its efforts to operationalize conference action plans and to mainstream these concerns in global politics.

Voices of criticism are growing in number and range. Even among supporters of the mainstream approach, voices of disquiet are heard, as increasingly the maldistribution of the benefits of economic liberalism are seen as a threat to local, national, regional, and even global order. Moreover, some regard the social protest that accompanies economic globalization as a potential obstacle to the neoliberal project. Thus, supporters of globalization are keen to temper its most unpopular effects by modifying neoliberal policies. Small but nevertheless important changes are taking place. For example, the World Bank has produced guidelines on the treatment of indigenous peoples, resettlement, the environmental impact of its projects, gender, and disclosure of information. It is implementing social safety nets when pursuing structural-adjustment policies, and it

TABLE 9.3	**Sustainable Development Goals**

	Goal	Description
	Goal 1	End poverty in all its forms everywhere.
	Goal 2	End hunger, achieve food security and improved nutrition, and promote sustainable agriculture.
	Goal 3	Ensure healthy lives and promote well-being for all at all ages.
	Goal 4	Ensure inclusive and quality education for all and promote lifelong learning.
	Goal 5	Achieve gender equality and empower all women and girls.
	Goal 6	Ensure access to water and sanitation for all.
	Goal 7	Ensure access to affordable, reliable, sustainable, and modern energy for all.
	Goal 8	Promote inclusive and sustainable economic growth, employment, and decent work for all.
	Goal 9	Build resilient infrastructure, promote sustainable industrialization, and foster innovation.
	Goal 10	Reduce inequality within and among countries.
	Goal 11	Make cities inclusive, safe, resilient, and sustainable.
	Goal 12	Ensure sustainable consumption and production patterns.
	Goal 13	Take urgent action to combat climate change and its impacts.
	Goal 14	Conserve and sustainably use the oceans, seas, and marine resources.
	Goal 15	Sustainably manage forests, combat desertification, halt and reverse land degradation, halt biodiversity loss.
	Goal 16	Promote just, peaceful, and inclusive societies.
	Goal 17	Revitalize the global partnership for sustainable development.

Source: United Nations Development Programme 2016.

Life in Zimbabwe: Poverty, Hunger, Development, and Politics

Background

It is possible the average person in Zimbabwe was not aware of the global economic downturn of 2009. If people in the southern African country did know about the collapse of banks and, according to the IMF, the loss of perhaps 51 million jobs worldwide, this knowledge would not have changed their lives very much. With a 2008 per capita GDP of $200, things could not have gotten much worse. Zimbabwe was once the breadbasket of sub-Saharan Africa, and although much of the world has recovered from the 2009 crisis, in 2017, Zimbabwe's economy imploded. Fuel queues and shortages of food and key commodities are now back in the picture.

The Case

The previous year had seen an array of problems that few developing countries had seen recently. First, a series of bad harvests had pushed more people than usual to rely on food aid provided mainly by foreign aid agencies, such as the UN's World Food Programme, and some EU countries. In power since 1980, President Robert Mugabe's government had banned aid from Britain because the former colonial power had sought to have Zimbabwe suspended from the

In Zimbabwe, a corrupt and inept government tried to reduce prices on basic commodities and left markets with nothing. Will this change with the resignation of Robert Mugabe?

Commonwealth, an organization of now-independent former British colonies. Critics of Mugabe's government blame the famine not just on low rainfall but, even more, on the badly planned land reform effort that took land away from the most prosperous farmers and gave it to landless Zimbabweans. Although the Mugabe government called the reform program "Zimbabwe for Zimbabweans," not only people of European descent lost land but also people who were not members of President Mugabe's ethnic group. Resistance to land reform led to riots, as government paramilitary units forced people from their farms and into illegal squatter camps.

The famine exacerbated preexisting economic problems. Zimbabwe had little to offer for export earnings beyond the agricultural sector, which provided more than 400,000 jobs. When the land reform began, unemployment increased, as did the inflation rate, because the government printed more money to cover its operating expenses. The CIA's *World Factbook* estimates that prior to the currency reform of January 2009, Zimbabwe's annual inflation rate was 11.2 million percent. With the formation of a new government in 2009, the Zimbabwean economy has been on the rebound. GDP grew by more than 5 percent in 2009 and 2011. International and regional banks have released favorable investment reports. However, the amount of resources for public services is very low. This internal economic debacle coincided with the rapid price rise for a barrel of oil. Like many other developing countries, Zimbabwe does not have domestic sources of petroleum products and must import what it needs. In 2016, Robert Mugabe was in charge for his thirty-sixth year, and economic experts suggested that his policies would be as destructive as ever. Those with resources were likely to leave or be looking for an exit.

Many analysts of African affairs say that bad harvests, bad weather, and high oil prices are not to blame for Zimbabwe's troubles. Rather, they assert, President Mugabe himself is to blame for the current situation. Left alone by Great Britain and other countries, the president established his personalist regime that favored his family and other members of his ethnic group and intimidated other ethnic groups in Zimbabwean society. Anyone who wanted to advance in the country had to be a member of Mugabe's political party, the Zimbabwe African National Union–Popular Front (ZANU–PF). Like other parties in the country but unlike political parties in most liberal democracies, it is linked to an ethnic group, but membership in the party was not guaranteed. Parliamentary elections in March 2008 sparked another crisis. When the Movement for Democratic Change (MDC) won more seats than ZANU–PF and Mugabe came in second to MDC's leader Morgan Tsvangirai in the presidential election, people knew that trouble was ahead. Mugabe's supporters violently harassed MDC members, an action that caused Tsvangirai to withdraw from the race. Years later, the economic and political situation may not change much with the new government. The new leader is Emmerson Mnangagwa, who served under Mugabe for thirty-seven years and whose new government is filled with many former officials who have been accused of corruption and human rights abuses.

Outcome

Given this string of unfortunate internal events, an average Zimbabwean can be forgiven if the failure of banks in Iceland, New York, and London was not a cause for great alarm. If workers at Macy's, Home Depot, or Merrill Lynch lost their jobs, this was not news for a resident of Harare. The subprime mortgage crisis in the United States must sound otherworldly to a person who lives in a galvanized metal shack in a shantytown on the outskirts of Bulawayo. The real news is that economic growth fell from 1.4 percent in 2015 to 0.07 percent in 2016.

For Discussion

1. In times of global economic stress, should states with developed economies increase their assistance to states like Zimbabwe?
2. To what extent are Zimbabwe's problems the result of European colonization?
3. Do states have an obligation to help other states even if authoritarian leaders lead those states?

is promoting microcredit as a way to empower women. With the IMF, it developed an initiative for heavily indebted poor countries to reduce the debt burden of the poorest states. What is important, however, is whether these guidelines and concerns really inform policy and whether these new policies and facilities result in practical outcomes that have an impact on the fundamental causes of poverty.

The bank has acknowledged that such changes have been incorporated largely due to the efforts of NGOs, which have monitored its work closely and undertaken vigorous international campaigns to change its general operational processes and the way it funds projects. These campaigns continue. The Bretton Woods Campaign, Fifty Years Is Enough, Jubilee 2000, and, most recently, the Make Poverty History campaign have been particularly significant in calling for open, transparent, and accountable decision making by global economic institutions, for local involvement in project planning and implementation, and for debt write-off. The U2 singer Bono and his One Campaign have been very active in advocating for change and supporting all efforts to end poverty. In addition to the NGO pressure for change, pressure is building within the institutional champions of the neoliberal development orthodoxy.

There is a tremendously long way to go in terms of gaining credence for the core values of the alternative model of development in the corridors of power nationally and internationally. Nevertheless, the alternative view has had some noteworthy successes in modifying orthodox development. These may be significant for those whose destinies have until now been largely determined by the attempted universal application of a selective set of local, essentially Western, values.

 Hunger

In addressing the topic of global hunger, it is necessary to examine a paradox. Although "the production of food to meet the needs of a burgeoning population has been one of the outstanding global achievements of the post-war period" (International Commission on Peace and Food 1994, 104, 106), in 2015 nearly 815 million people—one in nine—around the world did not have enough food (World Food Programme 2018). Poor nutrition is the cause of death for nearly 3.1 million children each year. The current depth of hunger across different world regions is shown in Map 9.1. Famines may be exceptional phenomena, but why is hunger an ongoing problem?

We would be remiss if we did not report that there has been some success in the effort to reduce poverty and hunger. Government aid organizations, the United Nations, regional organizations, and NGOs have been working to end hunger. In 2015, the UN Food and Agricultural Organization reported that since 1990, the number of people suffering from hunger has been reduced by some 216 million people. Unfortunately, according to Max Roser and his "Our World in Data" website, some 795 million people are still undernourished.

The Orthodox, Nature-Focused Explanation of Hunger

The orthodox explanation of hunger, first espoused by Thomas Robert Malthus in his *Essay on the Principle of Population* in 1798, focuses on the relationship between human population growth and the food supply. It asserts that population growth naturally outstrips the growth in food production so that a decrease in the per capita availability of food is inevitable. Eventually, a point is reached at which starvation, or some other disaster, drastically reduces the human population to a level that can be sustained by the available food supply. This approach places great stress on human overpopulation as the cause of the problem and seeks ways to reduce the fertility of the human race or, rather, that part of the human race that seems to reproduce faster than the rest—the poor of the third world. Supporters of this approach, such as Paul Ehrlich and Dennis and Donella Meadows (1972), argue that there are natural limits to population growth—principally that of the carrying capacity of the land—and that when these limits are exceeded, disaster is inevitable.

The available data on the growth of the global human population indicate that it has quintupled since the early 1800s and is expected to grow from 7.5 billion in 2017 to 9.8 billion in 2050. More than 50 percent of this increase is expected to occur in seven countries: Bangladesh, Brazil, China, India, Indonesia, Nigeria, and Pakistan.

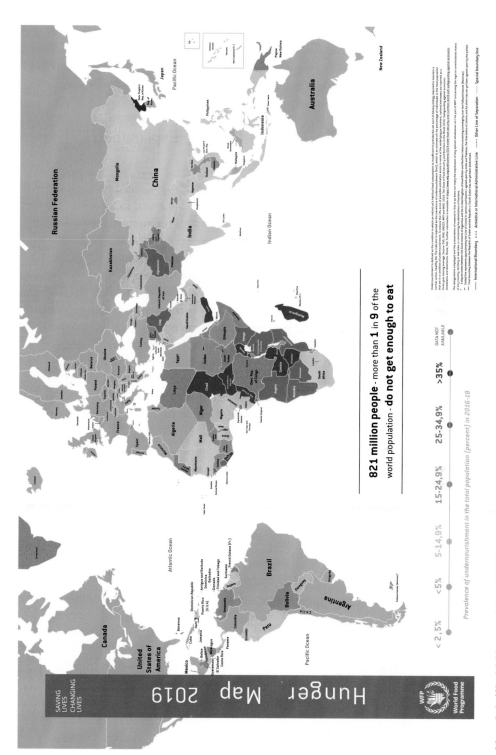

821 million people - more than **1 in 9** of the world population - **do not get enough to eat**

Prevalence of undernourishment in the total population (percent) in 2016-18

< 2,5%   <5%   5-14,9%   15-24,9%   25-34,9%   >35%   DATA NOT AVAILABLE

Map 9.1 World Hunger Map, 2019.

What patterns of hunger do you see around the world? Why does hunger persist? With climate change and weather extremes is hunger likely to increase around the world?

Source: World Food Programme 2019.

Table 9.4 lists the most populous countries—almost all of which are located in the third world. Figures like these have convinced many adherents of the orthodox approach to hunger that it is essential for third world countries to adhere to strict family-planning policies that one way or another limit their population growth rates. Indeed, in the case of the World Bank, most women-related efforts until very recently were in the area of family planning.

The Entitlement, Society-Focused Explanation of Hunger

Critics of the orthodox approach to hunger and its associated implications argue that it is too simplistic in its analysis and ignores the vital factor of food distribution. It fails to account for the paradox that despite the enormous increase in food production per capita that has occurred over the postwar period (largely due to the development of high-yielding seeds and industrial agricultural techniques), little impact has been made to reduce the huge numbers of people in the world who experience chronic hunger. For example, the UN Food and Agricultural Organization estimates that although there is enough grain alone to provide everyone in the world with 3,600 calories a day (i.e., 1,200 more than the UN's recommended minimum daily intake), there are still nearly 795 million hungry people.

Furthermore, critics note that the third world, where the majority of malnourished people are found, produces much of the world's food, whereas those who consume most of it are in the Western world. Meat consumption tends to rise with household wealth, and a third of the world's grain is used to fatten

TABLE 9.4 **World Population, 2018 and 2050 (Projected)**

Most Populous Countries, 2018			Most Populous Countries, 2050		
Rank	Country	Population (millions)	Rank	Country	Population (millions)
1	China	1,389	1	India	1,708
2	India	1,311	2	China	1,344
3	United States	331	3	United States	398
4	Indonesia	265	4	Nigeria	398
5	Brazil	210	5	Indonesia	360
6	Pakistan	210	6	Pakistan	344
7	Nigeria	208	7	Brazil	226
8	Bangladesh	161	8	Bangladesh	202
9	Russia	141	9	Democratic Republic of Congo	214
10	Mexico	127	10	Ethiopia	165

Source: Population Reference Bureau.

animals. A worrying recent trend is the use of corn grown in the United States to produce green fuel, thus reducing what is available to feed the hungry people overseas. Such evidence leads opponents of the orthodox approach to argue that we need to look much more closely at the social, political, and economic factors that determine how food is distributed and why access to food is achieved by some and denied to others.

A convincing alternative to the orthodox explanation of hunger was set forward in Amartya Sen's pioneering book *Poverty and Famines: An Essay on Entitlement and Deprivation* (1981). From the results of his empirical research work on the causes of famines, Sen concluded that hunger is due to people not having enough to eat rather than there not being enough to eat. He discovered that famines have frequently occurred when there has been no significant reduction in the level of per capita food availability and, furthermore, that some famines have occurred during years of peak food availability. For example, the Bangladesh famine of 1974 occurred in a year of peak food availability, yet because floods wiped out the normal employment opportunities of rural laborers, the latter were left with no money to purchase the food that was readily available, and many of them starved.

Therefore, what determines whether people starve or eat is not so much the amount of food available to them but whether or not they can establish an entitlement to that food. If there is plenty of food available in the stores but a family does not have the money to purchase that food and does not have the means of growing their own food, then they are likely to starve. With the globalization of the market and the associated curtailing of subsistence agriculture, the predominant method of establishing an entitlement to food has become the exercise of purchasing power, and consequently, those without purchasing power will go hungry amid a world of plenty (Sen 1981, 1983).

Sen's focus on entitlement enables him to identify two groups that are particularly at risk of losing their access to food: landless rural laborers, such as in South Asia and Latin America, and pastoralists, such as in sub-Saharan Africa. The landless rural laborers are especially at risk because no arrangements are in place to protect their access to food. In the traditional peasant economy, there is some **security** of land ownership, and therefore, rural laborers have the possibility of growing their own food. However, this possibility is lost in the early

WHAT'S YOUR WORLDVIEW?

There are many NGOs like Oxfam, Save the Children, and CARE that have worked hard to end global poverty and hunger. Do you think that groups like this can end hunger and poverty without radically changing the global economy? Simply put, is it possible to eradicate poverty without transforming the global capitalist system?

Security The measures taken by states to ensure the safety of their citizens, the protection of their way of life, and the survival of their nation-state. Security can also mean the ownership of property that gives an individual the ability to secure the enjoyment or enforcement of a right or a basic human need.

In this photo, a Nigerian boy stands in front of graffiti reading, "Trust No Body," a reference, local residents say, to oil company officials who fail to fulfill their promises to the people living in the oil-rich delta region of Nigeria. Why are the people so poor in this area teeming with oil and natural gas riches? Someone is getting rich, and why are these people left behind? These same questions are being asked all over the world.

stages of the transition to capitalist agriculture, when the laborers are obliged to sell their land and join the wage-based economy. Unlike in the developed countries of the West, no social security arrangements are in place to ensure that their access to food is maintained. In this context, it is important to note that the IMF/World Bank austerity policies of the 1980s ensured that any welfare arrangements previously enjoyed by vulnerable groups in developing countries were largely removed; therefore, these policies directly contributed to a higher risk of hunger in the third world.

Building on the work of Sen, researcher Susan George in *The Hunger Machine* (Bennett and George 1987, 1–10) details how different groups of people experience unequal levels of access to food. She identifies six factors that are important in determining who goes hungry:

1. The North–South divide between developed and developing countries
2. National policies on how wealth is shared
3. The rural–urban bias
4. Social class
5. Gender
6. Age

One could add to the list two other very important, and often neglected, factors: race and disability. Consequently, a person is more likely to experience hunger if he or she is disabled rather than able-bodied, black rather than white, a child rather than an adult, poor rather than wealthy, a rural dweller rather than a town dweller, and an inhabitant of a developing country rather than an inhabitant of a developed country.

Globalization and Hunger

It is possible to explain the contemporary occurrence of hunger by reference to the process of globalization. Globalization means that events occurring in one part of the globe can affect, and can be affected by, events occurring in other, distant parts of the globe. Often, as individuals, we remain unaware of our role in this process and its ramifications. When those of us in developed countries drink a cup of tea or coffee or eat imported fruit and vegetables, we tend not to think about the site of production of these cash crops in the developing world. In their book *Refashioning Nature: Food, Ecology, and Culture* (1991), David Goodman and Michael Redclift looked at the effects that the global system of food production have had (as opposed to a local, national, or regional system), and the closing part of this discussion on hunger is based largely on their findings.

Since 1945, a global food regime has been established, and now in the twenty-first century, we are witnessing an increasingly global organization of food provision and of access to food, with transnational corporations playing the major role. Local subsistence producers, who traditionally have produced to meet the needs of their family and community, may now be involved in cash-crop production for a distant market. Alternatively, they may have left the land and become involved in the process of industrialization. The most important actor in the development and expansion of this global food regime has been the United States, which, at the end of World War II, was producing large food surpluses. These surpluses became cheap food exports and initially were welcomed by the war-ravaged countries of Europe. Many developing countries also welcomed them because the then-prevalent model of development depended on the creation of a pool of cheap wage labor to serve the industrialization process. Hence, to encourage people to move off the land and away from subsistence production, the incentive to produce for oneself and one's family had to be removed. Cheap imported food provided this incentive, while the resulting low prices that were paid for domestic subsistence crops made them unattractive to grow; indeed, for those who continued to produce for the local market, such as in Sudan, the consequence has been the production of food at a loss (Bennett and George 1987, 78). Not surprisingly, the production of subsistence crops for local consumption drastically declined in the postwar period in the developing world.

The postwar, US-dominated, global food regime has therefore had a number of unforeseen consequences. First, the domestic production of food staples in developing countries was disrupted. Second, consumer preferences in the importing countries changed in line with the cheap imports, and export markets for American-produced food were created. This created a dependency on food aid (Goodman and Redclift 1991, 123). Third, there has been a stress on cash-crop production. The result has been the drive toward export-oriented, large-scale, intensively mechanized agriculture in the South. Technical progress resulted in the green revolution, with massively increased yields produced from high-yield seeds and industrialized agricultural practices. In some respects, this has been an important achievement. However, the cost has been millions of peasants thrown off the land because their labor was no longer required; the greater concentration of land was in a smaller number of hands; and there was environmental damage from pesticides, fertilizers, and inappropriate irrigation techniques.

In this photo, an internally displaced woman prepares a meal. The current US war in Afghanistan began in 2001 and although peace talks with the Taliban have begun, US troops are still serving as advisors and the country is far from stable. In 2017, absolute poverty was increasing, with 39 percent of the Afghans now in that category. That means one in three citizens is unable to satisfy their basic human needs. Most Afghan children still don't attend school and face the prospect of a life of poverty no different from their parents. Prospects for girls are bleaker: In rural areas 90 percent of women and 63 percent of men are illiterate. How might poverty contribute to extremist movements and ongoing conflict?

Since the early 1980s, the reform of national economies via structural-adjustment policies has further undermined the national organization of agriculture and given a further boost to the activities of agribusiness. The aggressive pursuit of unilateralist trade policies by the United States, such as the invocation of

One of the poorest countries in the world is North Korea, yet its government continues to spend vast sums of money on weapons and military forces. In this 2019 photo, North Korean farmers replant rice seedlings in a field, hoping that an ongoing drought will end soon. Meanwhile, South Korea vowed to move quickly on its plans to provide $8 million worth of humanitarian aid to North Korea, and it is also considering sending food to its northern neighbor. Why would a government continue to allow its citizens to starve and spend all of its money on weapons?

free trade to legitimize opening the Korean agricultural market, has added to this. Global trade liberalization, especially the Uruguay Round's Agreement on Agriculture (the original text of which was drafted by the multinational Cargill's vice president Dan Amstutz; Oxfam 2003, 23), is further eroding local food security and throwing peasant producers and their families off the land. This has fueled resentment in the South about the global rules governing agriculture. In India, disputes over intellectual property rights regarding high-yielding crop seeds have resulted in violent protests by peasant farmers at foreign-owned seed factories. In the North, NGOs have campaigned against the double standards displayed by their governments in expecting Southern countries to liberalize their food markets while the Northern countries continue to heavily subsidize and protect their own.

WHAT'S TRENDING?

Saving a Life

What do you do about a problem like global poverty? Can you actually play a role in reducing this problem? Deciding how you can participate to make this world a little better is something that we rarely talk about in our textbooks.

Princeton professor of bioethics Peter Singer makes a plea for action and presents a number of ideas in his book *The Life You Can Save: Acting Now to End World Poverty* (2009). Simply put, he asks us to make a choice to save a child from hunger and the many diseases that could be cured if the parents had money to pay for medical attention. He asks us to consider giving 5 percent of what we earn to organizations that are addressing global poverty:

If you and other well-off people in affluent nations were all to give, say, 5% of your income for the fight against global poverty, it would probably not reduce your happiness at all. (169)

How many of us could live without bottled water when our tap water is fine? How about one less $5 coffee each

day or even one less each week? As a student worker, you may not make very much money, but if you make $200 a week, your commitment is only $10.

Singer's basic argument is based on more than our moral intuitions (15–16):

First Premise: Suffering and death from lack of food, shelter, and medical care are bad.

Second Premise: If it is in your power to prevent something bad from happening, without sacrificing anything nearly as important, it is wrong not to do so.

Conclusion: If you do not donate to aid agencies, you are doing something wrong.

In the final chapter, Singer created a seven-point plan that, if followed, makes those who embrace it part of the solution to world poverty (thelifeyoucansave.org). In 2008, 27,000 children died each day because of poverty, and if you decide to participate, you may help reduce these numbers.

Conclusion

In this chapter, we have seen how poverty, development, and hunger are more than merely domestic political issues. Academic theories of international relations tended to ignore these problems until the mid-1980s, when the third world debt crisis threatened to undermine key parts of the global financial system. Political leaders in the rich countries of the North—and, in many cases, the South—acted the way realism predicted: to protect the interests of their own states.

CONTRIBUTORS TO CHAPTER 9: *Caroline Thomas, Steven L. Lamy, and John Masker*

KEY TERMS

Community, p. 348
Development, p. 348
Embedded
  liberalism, p. 350
Global governance, p. 344
Liberalization, p. 351

Modernization
  theory, p. 348
Post–Washington Consensus, p. 351
Poverty, p. 346
Regional diversity, p. 352

Security, p. 365
Social movement, p. 354
Survival, p. 348
Sustainable
  development, p. 356

Transnational
  corporation, p. 355
Washington
  Consensus, p. 344

REVIEW QUESTIONS

1. What does poverty mean?
2. Explain the orthodox approach to development and outline the criteria by which it measures development.
3. Assess the critical alternative model of development.
4. How effectively has the orthodox model of development neutralized the critical alternative view?
5. Compare and contrast the orthodox and alternative explanations of hunger.
6. What are the pros and cons of the global food regime established since World War II?

7. Account for the growing gap between rich and poor states and people after fifty years of official development policies.
8. Use a gendered lens to explore the nature of poverty.
9. Is the recent World Bank focus on poverty reduction evidence of a change of direction by the bank?
10. Which development pathway—the traditional or the alternative—do you regard as more likely to contribute to global peace in the twenty-first century?
11. Are national poverty-reduction strategies contributing to national ownership of development policies in the third world?

Learn more with this chapter's digital tools, including the Oxford Insight Study Guide, at **www.oup.com/he/lamy6e**.

Development Assistance as Foreign Policy Statecraft

Expectations

You will be asked to evaluate contending arguments for aid (official development assistance, or ODA) and then make a case supporting ODA and a case against ODA for developing states.

Procedure

Step One

Participants will be divided into three groups and asked to evaluate proposals requesting development assistance with a specific worldview in mind. The groups and their designated worldview are:

1. Western Security Organization: realists who have a competitive view of international relations.
2. European Social Democrats: liberal internationalists favoring multilateral cooperation.
3. World Federalists: modern-day utopians or radical liberals who seek to create a world government based on human-centric values and world law.

Step Two

Your task is to make recommendations on how much and what kind of aid or development assistance should be allocated. You may recommend the following:

A. **Project Aid:** funds for specific activities such as the construction of roads and irrigation systems.
B. **Program Aid:** funds that are lent to correct problems in a country's capital flow. The funds are used to correct balance-of-payment problems or to enable the country to increase its supply of capital in the form of either savings or foreign currency.
C. **Technical Assistance:** this includes experts and advisers, training or educational programs, and the supply of equipment for projects.
D. **Food Aid:** food, medicine, and equipment sent to countries to feed the starving or increase the available stocks of food.
E. **Specific Aid:** to deal with emergency situations (e.g., drought relief, natural disasters).
F. **Military Assistance:** to maintain order and make certain the country is stable and the government is not at risk because of extreme poverty or radical movements.

Step Three

You must decide on ODA allocations for the following countries:

Country 1 has requested $100 million in aid from the developed donor countries. The country is governed by a weak democratic system. A Marxist party is strong but holds few government positions. The party currently in power was always pro–United States and now is an active participant in US-led multilateral activities. The economy depends heavily on the export of one crop and one mineral. There is little industry. The aid money will be used to improve and extend the road system, improve the dock and port facilities in the country's only port city, and fund agricultural extension projects.

Country 2 has requested $50 million in aid. The country is governed by a socialist party and has strong ties with Europe's more social democratic states. The president of the country often participates in meetings of heads of state of nonaligned nations, and the country's leaders are very active in multilateral organizations. This country has a diversified economy that exports agricultural products, some minerals, and light manufactured goods. The requested aid will be used to improve the national university, send students abroad for advanced college degrees in business management and science, import farm machinery, and purchase high-tech equipment to develop manufacturing in computers and technology related to the environment.

Country 3 has requested $150 million in aid. The country is totally dependent on outside support. It has suffered from a severe drought, and three tribal groups continue to challenge the military government. The country's only resources are uranium and an abundance of cheap labor. Most aid has ended up in the hands of the elites and has not been used to improve the quality of life of most of the population. Recently, the leaders have begun to discuss a

continued

possible alliance with Syria and Iran. The aid will be used to develop a comprehensive education system, develop facilities in rural areas, and build a national highway and rail system.

Based on the assumptions of your group's worldview:

1. Rank the three countries in terms of aid priority.
2. Select an appropriate program (e.g., military assistance and drought relief for Country X).
3. Be prepared to defend your choices. Each group will have an opportunity to decide on its priorities and then present them. Each group should also be prepared to critically review the allocations made by the other groups.

Step Four

As you debate your group's position on these requests, consider the following questions. You may want to ask the other groups to justify their positions by responding to these questions. As you finish the exercise, these three questions may provide a useful debriefing or evaluation of your debate:

- What is the strongest argument for giving or not giving some form of aid to each country?
- What assumptions about each country and the international system defined your allocation priorities?
- Discuss the relative strengths and weaknesses of bilateral and multilateral aid programs. Would you agree with the statement that suggests the complexity of world development problems requires multilateral responses?

10 Environmental Issues

The night sky glows from the light of wildfires in Portugal in late 2017. Massive fires on an unprecedented scale have occurred with greater frequency around the world—for example in Australia, where bushfires burned out of control for months. Climate and weather experts say changing rainfall patterns because of human activity are to blame for the conflagrations. What can be done if we continue to deny the effects of climate change?

Whether our world is to be saved from everything that threatens it today depends above all on whether human beings come to their senses, whether they understand the degree of their responsibility and discover a new relationship to the very miracle of being. The world is in the hands of us all.

—VACLAV HAVEL

If you act like there is no possibility for change, you guarantee that there will be no change.

—NOAM CHOMSKY

Citizens in every part of the world face an existential threat that we can do something about if we act now. That threat is climate change, and it has already begun to impact quality of life around the world. Some of the effects are far away, but even those distant effects are shaped by our decisions. For example, Dirk Notz, a scientist at the Max Planck Institute for Meteorology in Hamburg, Germany, has conducted research that shows that for every metric ton of CO_2 released in the air, three square meters of Arctic ice disappears. The typical American is melting fifty square meters of frozen ice every year. Why does this matter? Climate scientists have been telling us for years that CO_2 acts as a greenhouse gas that traps heat and melts ice. Melting ice accelerates global warming because ice reflects sunlight and the ocean absorbs it. A warming ocean creates a number of weather events that indicate a warming climate. Unfortunately for all of us, the problem goes beyond ice in distant lands. Furthermore, many political leaders choose to ignore and deny the scientific evidence that is right before our eyes. Some analysts have been calling this a "war on science" seemingly driven by narrow, selfish economic goals. For example, before he was elected president of the United States, Donald Trump wrote on Twitter:

> *The concept of global warming was created by and for the Chinese in order to make the US manufacturing noncompetitive.*

This modern era of global warming began in the 1970s, and climate scientists state that 2019 was the hottest year on record. More recently, people around the world have experienced fires, floods, droughts, and severe storms and other unusual weather patterns. The uneven impacts of

CHAPTER OUTLINE

Introduction 375

Environmental Issues on the International Agenda: A Brief History 376

The Environment and International Relations Theory 385

The Functions of International Environmental Cooperation 390

Climate Change 399

Conclusion 405

FEATURES

GLOBAL PERSPECTIVE The "Doomsday" Seed Vault 388

THEORY IN PRACTICE Regime Theory and the Montreal Protocol 389

CASE STUDY Common But Differentiated Responsibilities? 404

WHAT'S TRENDING? Is the Human Game Coming to an End? 406

THINKING ABOUT GLOBAL POLITICS The Environment: Images and Options 407

these events raise concerns about environmental justice and questions about who are the victims as climate change shapes our future.

Any discussion about climate change and the historical 2015–2016 Paris Agreement has been polarized by politics and competing interests that create and promote their own version of science and scientific evidence. Thus, the Paris conference that produced this voluntary agreement came as a relief to those most affected by environmental tragedies, because nearly two hundred nation-states reached consensus on the need to cut greenhouse gas emissions. The United States was part of the original agreement, but the Trump administration has announced a deadline for withdrawing from the agreement. More important, the Trump administration has rolled back many of the Obama administration's greenhouse gas regulations, which will make it impossible for the United States to meet its promise to lower emissions by at least 26 percent below 2005 levels by 2025. As a nation, we are out of the Paris climate agreement, but several states and cities and a significant number of corporations have created an alliance to work to achieve the promises made in Paris. But when the US secretary of state asserts that rapid warming of the Arctic regions represents a land of "opportunity and abundance" for development, what can concerned local and global citizens do?

Without a doubt, the world's environmental problems have only gotten worse since 1987, when the Brundtland Commission released its UN-sponsored report on the global environment, *Our Common Future*. The report provided the foundation for the 1992 Earth Summit and introduced concepts like sustainable development and foresight capacity that urged leaders and citizens alike to consider the well-being of future generations and the Earth when making economic and political decisions.

Despite leadership from current and former political personalities such as Nobel Prize winner Al Gore and strong grassroots efforts in some industrial countries to "reduce, reuse, and recycle" and to "think globally, act locally," why are other international leaders and many other citizens unwilling to change their lifestyles to respond to urgent existential challenges like climate change, air and water pollution, and resource scarcity? Why is it so hard to reach agreement when scientific reports clearly confirm the severity of environmental degradation across the globe? Why are some leaders of political and economic organizations rejecting climate science? Although there are no easy answers to these global environmental problems, such questions can at least be understood more clearly with a careful examination of the facts, along with some perspective afforded us by considering the history and theory of international cooperation involving environmental issues.

Introduction

Although humankind as a whole now appears to be living well above Earth's carrying capacity, the **ecological footprints** of individual states vary to an extraordinary extent. See Map 10.1, which illustrates the size of countries in proportion to their carbon emissions. If everyone were to enjoy the current lifestyle of the developed countries, more than three additional planets would be required.

Maybe it is time for the children to lead? Speaking at the World Economic Forum in Davos in January 2019, Swedish teen Greta Thunberg challenged the assembled business and political leaders, saying: "I don't want you to be hopeful. I want you to panic. I want you to feel the fear I feel every day. And then I want you to act." Other globally active teens brought that message to 110 countries when over 1,300 "climate strikes" happened during May and June 2019.

This situation is rendered all the more unsustainable by the process of globalization, even though the precise relationship between environmental degradation and the overuse of resources, on the one hand, and globalization, on the other, is complex and sometimes contradictory. Globalization has stimulated the relocation of industry to the global South, caused urbanization as people move away from rural areas, and contributed to ever-rising levels of consumption, along with associated emissions of effluents and waste gases. While often generating greater income for poorer countries exporting basic goods to developed-country markets, ever-freer trade can also have adverse environmental consequences by disrupting local **ecologies** (communities of plants and animals), cultural habits, and livelihoods.

However, some analysts believe there is little evidence that globalization has stimulated a "race to the bottom" in environmental standards, and some even argue that growing levels of affluence have brought about local environmental improvements, just as birth rates tend to fall as populations become wealthier. Economists claim that globalization's opening up of markets can increase efficiency and reduce pollution, provided the environmental and social damage associated with production of a good is properly factored into its market price. Similarly, as we will see in this chapter, globalization has promoted the sharing of knowledge and the influential presence of nongovernmental organizations (NGOs) in global environmental politics. Whatever the ecological balance sheet of globalization, the resources on which human beings depend for survival, such as fresh water, a clean atmosphere, and a stable climate, are now under serious threat.

Global problems may need global solutions and pose a fundamental requirement for **global environmental governance**. Yet the history of environmental cooperation demonstrates that local or regional action remains a vital aspect of responses to many problems. One of the defining characteristics of environmental politics is

Ecological footprint A measure that demonstrates the load placed on Earth's carrying capacity by individuals or nations. It does this by estimating the area of productive land and water system required to sustain a population at its specified standard of living.

Ecologies The communities of plants and animals that supply raw materials for all living things.

Global environmental governance The performance of global environmental regulative funßctions, often in the absence of a central government authority. It usually refers to the structure of international agreements and organizations but can also involve governance by the private sector or NGOs.

School books at Inchope primary school in Inchope, Mozambique, drying in the sun after the school was damaged by Cyclone Idai, March 25, 2019. Across Malawi, Zimbabwe, and Mozambique more than 1,200 people died as a result of this massive storm and over 100,000 were left homeless.

the awareness of such interconnections and of the need to "think globally, act locally." NGOs have been very active in this respect, as we saw in Chapter 5.

Despite the global dimensions of environmental change, an effective response still must depend on a fragmented international political system of 195 sovereign states. Global environmental governance consequently involves bringing to bear interstate relations, international law, and transnational organizations in addressing shared environmental problems. Using the term *governance*—as distinct from *government*—implies that regulation and control need to be exercised in the absence of a central government, delivering the kinds of service that a world government would provide if it were to exist. In this chapter, we will briefly explore essential concepts employed in regime analysis, which is commonly applied in the study of international governance.

Environmental Issues on the International Agenda: A Brief History

Before the era of globalization, there were two traditional environmental concerns: conservation of natural resources and damage caused by pollution. No forms of pollution respect international boundaries, and action to mitigate or avert environmental harm sometimes had to involve more than one state. Early international agreements were designed to conserve specific resources, such as fisheries (1867 convention between France and Great Britain) or fur seals (1891, 1892, 1911 conventions between Great Britain, the United States, and Russia). In 1935, the Trail Smelter case demonstrated that reducing transboundary pollution required joint effort and could be accomplished peacefully. In this landmark case, pollutants from a mineral smelter in Canada drifted south and contaminated portions of Washington state. The resulting treaty between the two countries asserted the legal principle that countries are liable for damage that their citizens cause in another country.

There were also numerous, mostly unsuccessful, attempts to regulate exploitation of maritime resources lying beyond national jurisdiction, including several multilateral fisheries commissions. The development of the 1946 International Convention for the Regulation of Whaling (and its International Whaling Commission) marked a move away from the goal of the late nineteenth-century fur seal conventions, which entailed conserving an industry by regulating catches, toward the preservation of the great whales by declaring an international

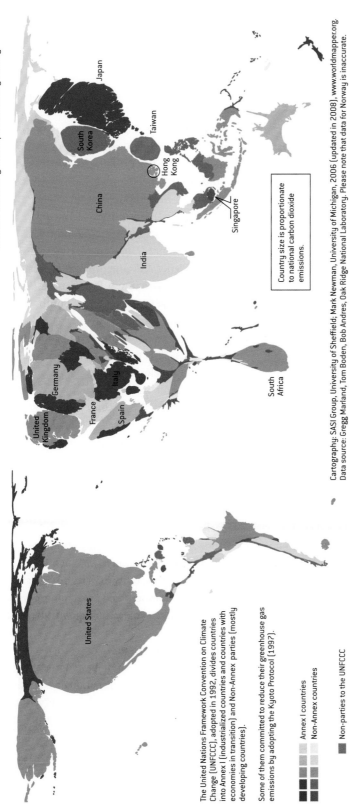

Total CO₂ emissions

form fossil-fuel burning, cement production and gas flaring

Country size is proportionate to national carbon dioxide emissions.

Japan

South Korea

Taiwan

Hong Kong

China

Singapore

India

Germany

United Kingdom

France

Spain

Italy

South Africa

United States

The United Nations Framework Convention on Climate Change (UNFCCC), adopted in 1992, divides countries into Annex I (industrialized countries and countries with economies in transition) and Non-Annex parties (mostly developing countries).

Some of them committed to reduce their greenhouse gas emissions by adopting the Kyoto Protocol (1997).

Annex I countries
Non-Annex countries

Non-parties to the UNFCCC

Map 10.1 World Carbon Emissions.

What patterns of CO₂ emission do you see around the world? Does a nation-state's responsibility toward ending global climate change increase if its CO₂ emissions are higher?

Cartography: SASI Group, University of Sheffield; Mark Newman, University of Michigan, 2006 (updated in 2008), www.worldmapper.org. Data source: Gregg Marland, Tom Boden, Bob Andres, Oak Ridge National Laboratory. Please note that data for Norway is inaccurate.

moratorium on whaling. This shift still generates bitter confrontation between NGOs, most International Whaling Commission members, and the small number of nations—Japan, Norway, and Iceland—that wish to resume commercial whaling and kill what they call "research whales."

After World War II, global economic recovery resulted in damaging pollution to the atmosphere, watercourses, and the sea, notably the Mediterranean, leading to international agreements in the 1950s and 1960s regarding matters such as discharges from oil tankers. These efforts, though, were not the stuff of great-power politics. Such "apolitical" matters were the domain of new UN **specialized agencies**, like the Food and Agriculture Organization, but were hardly central to diplomacy at the UN General Assembly in New York.

However, the salience of environmental issues grew in the 1960s, and in 1968, the UN General Assembly accepted a Swedish proposal for what became the 1972 UN Conference on the Human Environment "to focus governments' attention and public opinion on the importance and urgency of the question." The conference led to the creation of the UN Environment Programme (UNEP; see Table 10.1). Yet it was already clear that for the countries of the South, which constituted the majority in the UN General Assembly, environmental questions could not be separated from their demands for development, aid, and the restructuring of international economic relations. This political context surrounded the emergence of the concept of **sustainable development** (development that meets the needs of the present without compromising future ability to meet needs). Before the Brundtland Commission formulated this concept in 1987, however, the environment was pushed to the periphery of the international agenda by the global economic downturn of the 1970s and then the onset of the second Cold War, or the end of détente.

Environmental degradation continued nonetheless. Awareness of new forms of transnational pollution, such as sulfur dioxide ("acid") rain, joined existing concerns over point-source pollution (when the pollutant comes from a definite source), followed by a dawning scientific realization that some environmental problems—the thinning of the stratospheric ozone layer and the possibility of climate change—were truly global in scale. The attendant popular concern over such issues and the relaxation of East–West tension created the opportunity for a second great UN conference, where the connection between environment and development was explicitly drawn. Although this conference was subject to many subsequent interpretations, its political essence was an accommodation of the environmental concerns of developed states and the development demands of the South.

The 1992 UN Conference on Environment and Development, or Earth Summit, raised the profile of the environment as an international issue while concluding international conventions on climate change and the preservation of biodiversity. The event's underlying politics were evidenced in its title: It was a conference on "environment and development," where the most serious arguments concerned aid pledges to finance environmental improvements. The United Nations created a process to review the implementation of the Earth Summit

Specialized agencies
International institutions that have a special relationship with the central system of the United Nations but are constitutionally independent, having their own assessed budgets, executive heads and committees, and assemblies of the representatives of all state members.

Sustainable development
Development that meets the needs of the present without compromising the ability of future generations to meet their own needs.

TABLE 10.1	**Recent Global Environmental Actions**
1987	Release of the Brundtland Commission report, *Our Common Future*
	Montreal Protocol on Substances That Deplete the Ozone Layer
1988	Establishment of the Intergovernmental Panel on Climate Change (IPCC)
1989	Basel Convention on the Control of Transboundary Movements of Hazardous Wastes and Their Disposal
1992	UN Conference on Environment and Development (UNCED) results in the Rio Declaration on Environment and Development and Agenda 21
	UN Framework Convention on Climate Change (UNFCCC)
	Convention on Biological Diversity
	Commission on Sustainable Development
1997	Kyoto Protocol
2002	World Summit on Sustainable Development
2008	First Commitment Period of Kyoto begins
2009	Copenhagen Accord
2010	Cancun Agreements
2012	Rio+20 UN Conference on Sustainable Development
2015	UN Conference on Climate Change
2016	Paris Climate Accord
2020	Paris Accord enters into force

agreements, including meetings of the new Commission on Sustainable Development and convening a special session of the UN General Assembly in 1997.

On the tenth anniversary of the UN Conference on Environment and Development in 2002, the World Summit on Sustainable Development was held in Johannesburg, South Africa. The change of wording indicated how conceptions of environment and development had shifted since the 1970s. Now discussion was embedded in recognition of the importance of globalization and of the dire state of the African continent. Poverty eradication was clearly emphasized along with practical progress in providing clean water, sanitation, and agricultural improvements. One controversial element, however, was what role private–public partnerships would play in such provision.

These UN conferences marked the stages by which the environment entered the international political mainstream, but they also reflected underlying changes in the scope and perception of environmental problems. As scientific understanding expanded, it became common, by the 1980s, to speak in terms of global environmental change. This was represented most graphically by the discovery of the ozone hole and the creeping realization that human activities might be dangerously altering the global climate.

Alongside environmental degradation and advances in scientific knowledge, the international politics of the environment has responded to the issue-attention cycle in developed countries, peaking at certain moments and then declining. The causes are complex, and during the 1960s, they reflected the countercultural and radical movements of the time along with wider public reactions to a series of trends and events. The most influential of these was the publication of Rachel Carson's book *Silent Spring* (1962), which powerfully conjoined the conservationist and antipollution agendas by bringing to light the damage inflicted on bird life by industrial pesticides like DDT. Well-publicized environmental disasters, such as the 1959 mercury poisoning at Minamata in Japan and the 1967 wreck of the *Torrey Canyon* oil tanker close to beaches in southwestern England, fed public concern. The failure of established political parties to respond effectively to these issues encouraged the birth of several new high-profile NGOs—Friends of the Earth, Greenpeace, and the World Wildlife Fund for Nature—alongside more established pressure groups such as the US Sierra Club and the British Royal Society for the Protection of Birds. The interest in international environmental action, and most of the NGOs exerting pressure to this end, represented an almost exclusively developed-world phenomenon.

In recent years, public alarm over the impact of climate change has propelled environmental issues up the political agenda again. Environmental activists and the public demand international action and governance, but what exactly does this mean?

In seeking natural explanations for the occurrence of natural catastrophes, geologists and other scientists look to the history of Earth, which they divide into two periods. The Holocene period, or the recent ten thousand years of Earth, is considered a period of weather and temperature stability. This is when humans began building civilizations. In the current geologic era, the Anthropocene, the world has been remade by human behavior. The biggest change is the emission of CO_2, which traps heat near the planet and creates more energy in the atmosphere. Climate scientists predict that rising temperatures will have serious side effects, such as deeper droughts, more floods, more moisture in the air, and potentially more

Bleached corals in Sekisei Lagoon, the largest coral reef area in Japan. According to the Environment Ministry, almost 75 percent of the country's largest coral reef has died, due to rising sea temperatures. Experts have said that the bleaching has spread to approximately 90 percent of the Sekisei reef. The death of coral reefs globally will have a disastrous result for biodiversity and food supplies.

serious storms like hurricanes and tornadoes. These conditions are what some now call a period of *weather panic* or global *weather weirding*. According to climate scientists, 2016 was the hottest year globally in recorded history. The more heat there is, the more problems we can expect with the weather. Scientific research shows that the past five years were collectively the warmest years on record.

Oxfam reported that the number of natural disasters increased from 133 a year in the 1980s to more than 350 a year now. Skeptics argue that there have always been periods of weird weather and extreme events, but scientists argue that these events are becoming severer and more frequent. The scientific community has asked world political leaders to make hard choices and support action in response.

Although in 2009 the UN Framework Convention on Climate Change (UNFCCC) Conference of Parties failed to replace or extend the **Kyoto Protocol**, which set targets for reducing environmentally harmful gas emissions, it did result in the Copenhagen Accord. The Copenhagen Accord included a list of national pledges on greenhouse gas reductions (and a pledge for China and India to make improvements in energy efficiency rather than reductions). It was also acknowledged that there was a need to keep temperature rises below 2°C, a need to set up a climate fund to assist developing countries, and a need to work on halting deforestation. These arrangements did not amount to a renewal of the Kyoto Protocol or a new comprehensive climate agreement, but the governments did commit themselves to producing such an agreement by 2015.

Kyoto Protocol A global environmental treaty passed in 1997 that set binding targets for thirty-seven industrialized countries and the European community for reducing greenhouse gas emissions.

The Paris Climate Summit 2015 and 2016

In late 2015, world leaders gathered in Paris for the UN Conference on Climate Change. At the forefront of the discussions was the topic of greenhouse gas emissions from human activities and that increasingly high levels are driving climate change. (See Figure 10.1) Climate change has the greatest impact on the poor and most vulnerable people. Equity plays a central role in the entire climate regime, and the climate policies discussed in Paris focused on strategies geared toward poverty alleviation and sustainable development. This latest gathering demonstrated that climate change is truly a global challenge that requires collaboration and coordination at the international level.

All 195 participating states and the European Union at the Paris meeting of the UNFCCC reached agreement in December 2015. The agreement or accord was signed in April 2016

Researchers have confirmed that a record heat wave in Europe during 2019 corresponded with a record loss of ice from Greenland's frozen cover. Warmer winters in the Northern Hemisphere have also resulted in far less snowfall in Greenland, the Alps, and the Himalayas. Billions of people in Asia depend upon meltwater from the latter for their water supply. What will they do when it all dries up? What will the world do as the ocean depth rises due to ice melt?

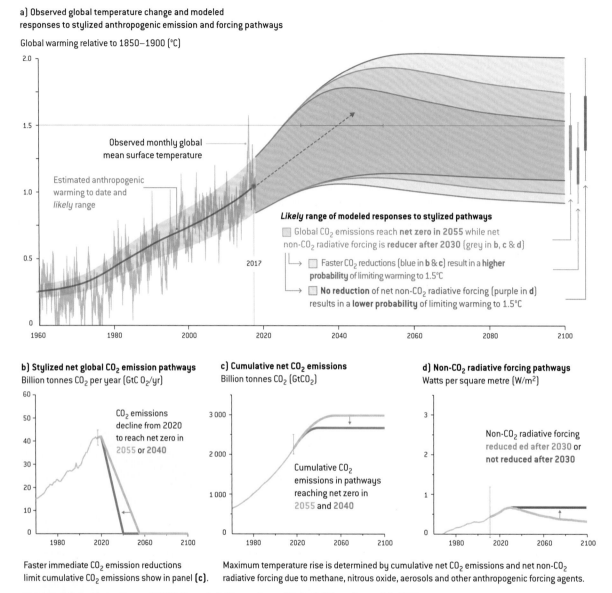

a) Observed global temperature change and modeled responses to stylized anthropogenic emission and forcing pathways

Global warming relative to 1850–1900 (°C)

Observed monthly global mean surface temperature

Estimated anthropogenic warming to date and *likely* range

2017

Likely **range of modeled responses to stylized pathways**

Global CO_2 emissions reach **net zero in 2055** while net non-CO_2 radiative forcing is **reducer after 2030** (grey in **b**, **c** & **d**)

Faster CO_2 reductions (blue in **b** & **c**) result in a **higher probability** of limiting warming to 1.5°C

No reduction of net non-CO_2 radiative forcing (purple in **d**) results in a **lower probability** of limiting warming to 1.5°C

b) Stylized net global CO_2 emission pathways
Billion tonnes CO_2 per year (GtC O_2/yr)

CO_2 emissions decline from 2020 to reach net zero in **2055** or **2040**

Faster immediate CO_2 emission reductions limit cumulative CO_2 emissions show in panel **(c)**.

c) Cumulative net CO_2 emissions
Billion tonnes CO_2 (GtCO_2)

Cumulative CO_2 emissions in pathways reaching net zero in **2055** and **2040**

Maximum temperature rise is determined by cumulative net CO_2 emissions and net non-CO_2 radiative forcing due to methane, nitrous oxide, aerosols and other anthropogenic forcing agents.

d) Non-CO_2 radiative forcing pathways
Watts per square metre (W/m²)

Non-CO_2 radiative forcing **reduced ed after 2030** or **not reduced after 2030**

Figure 10.1 Data from IPCC Special Report on Global Warming of 1.5°C.
Source: https://www.ipcc.ch/sr15/

and went into effect in November 2016. This was the twenty-first UNFCCC Conference of the Parties, or COP 21, and it accomplished the following:

- It reaffirmed the goal of limiting temperature increase to well below 2°C, while urging all parties to try to limit the increase to 1.5°C.
- The accords established binding commitments by all parties to make nationally determined contributions (NDCs) and to create domestic policies to achieve these commitments.

- All parties are committed to reporting on the progress with the NDCs and to report regularly on their emissions. All of these efforts and reports are also subject to international review.
- New NDCs are to be developed every five years and these should be aimed at achieving greater goals than previous NDCs.
- The accords reaffirmed the obligations of wealthier developed states to support the efforts of developing states. The developing states were also encouraged to make some contributions to these efforts.
- The agreement continued the goal of mobilizing $100 billion a year in support by 2020. A higher goal will be set for 2025.
- Parties agreed to explore ways to address "loss and damage" from climate change.

Paris was a remarkable event for several reasons. The agreement lays out a long-term plan for dealing with greenhouse gases, and although some of the goals were reduced in the negotiations, the results suggest the beginning of a low-carbon future. Paris was a starting point, but most of the participants recognized the need for greater cuts in emissions to stop global average temperatures from warming more than 2°C over preindustrial levels (see Table 10.2).

Unfortunately, the UNEP 2018 Emissions Gap Report shows that industrial emissions have been steady for the past four years but are projected to rise. Not one of the industrial states is on course to hit its goals. China has increased coal burning, and the Trump administration's emphasis on fossil fuels may actually slow down the process of reducing global emissions. To achieve the temperature goals of the Paris Agreement, countries need to strengthen the ambition of NDCs and increase the effectiveness of domestic policy. Domestic policies translate mitigation ambition into action and send an important signal to commit to mitigation and ensure long-term decarbonization.

| TABLE 10.2 | **Climate Change Facts from the Intergovernmental Panel on Climate Change (IPCC) Special Report on 1.5°C** |

1. Human activities have caused a global temperature rise of 1.0°C above pre-industrial levels, and will likely reach 1.5°C between 2030 and 2052 if it continues at the current rate.
2. Global temperature rise of 1.5°C will pose great risks to health, livelihoods, food security, water supply, human security, and economic growth, and will become more severe with warming of 2°C.
3. Estimates of the outcome of global emission reduction goals under the Paris Agreement would not limit global temperature rise to 1.5°C.
4. To limit temperature rise to 1.5°C with no or limited overshoot will require rapid and far-reaching transitions in energy, land, infrastructure, and industrial systems. These transitions are unprecedented in terms of scale, but not in terms of speed, and would need to be across all sectors, with increased investments in several mitigation options.
5. Adaptation strategies, catered in specific national contexts, will benefit sustainable development and poverty reduction with global warming of 1.5°C.

Source: Climate Change Facts from the Intergovernmental Panel on Climate Change (IPCC) and the United Nations (www.ipcc.ch/sr15/).

From Bonn 2017 to Madrid 2019

In 2017, the parties to the Paris Agreement met in Bonn, Germany, to begin developing rules and regulations for implementing the Paris Agreement. The United States sent two delegations: a low-level delegation from the US government and an alliance of representatives from states, cities, universities, and major corporations. The Bonn meeting focused on how to speed up reductions in greenhouse gas emissions and to hold participants to their emission targets. A second issue was how to collect more money for the Green Climate Fund to help developing states with their climate action. At the September 2018 Bangkok meeting, parties sought ways to increase participation in the fund, for as of that session only $3.5 billion had actually been committed out of the $10.3 billion target.

The US unofficial alliance was led by former New York City mayor Michael Bloomberg, California governor Jerry Brown, and others representing cities, states, the private sector, and civil society. They made it clear that the American people were staying in the agreement and made everyone understand that they had some clout in this process. This unofficial group formed the core of what became known as the C40 network that connects 94 megacities in which approximately 700 million people reside and a quarter of the global economy activity takes place.

About the same time as the Bonn Conference, the US State Department and the Interior Department sent high-level political officials to participate in a conference in Texas sponsored by the Heartland Institute. This organization rejects the scientific fact-based consensus on the cause and impact of climate change. Further, representatives from this organization have made claims that CO_2 is not a pollutant and is not the driver of global warming.

Later in December 2018 at Katowice, Poland, the parties met once again. The selection of that particular city highlighted the tensions between domestic and the global environmental movement , for Katowice is a center of the Polish coal industry. Highlighting that connection, Polish president Andrzej Duda asserted, "There is no plan today to fully give up on coal." For advocates of an aggressive implementation of the Paris Agreement, the meeting at Katowice was a failure. Parties to the agreement managed to keep Paris Accord alive, but just barely. The final statement provided for the following:

1. A uniform set of standards that every country would follow for measuring its emissions and tracking its climate policies;
2. Promises from countries to increase their plans to cut emissions ahead of talks in 2020;
3. Agreements by richer countries to provide better records of the aid they intend to give to poorer nations so they can install more clean energy and build infrastructure to protect against natural disasters; and
4. A process for helping countries that are struggling to meet their emission goals to get back on track.

The Environment and International Relations Theory

Academics who study the international relations of the environment try to understand the circumstances under which potentially effective international cooperation can occur. Most scholars have used the concept of regime as the basis for their understanding. Note, for instance, how the defining characteristics of regimes—principles, norms, rules, and decision-making procedures—can be applied to the environmental cases mentioned in this chapter. Those who try to explain the record of environmental regimes tend to adopt a liberal-institutionalist stance, stressing as a key motivating factor the joint gains arising from cooperative solutions to the problem of providing public goods such as a clean atmosphere (see Chapter 3). One significant addition to the regime literature made by scholars of environmental politics points out the importance of scientific knowledge and the roles of NGOs in this area. Whereas orthodox regime approaches assume that behavior is based on the pursuit of power or interest, analysts of international environmental cooperation have noted the independent role played by changes in knowledge (particularly, scientific understanding). This cognitive approach appears in studies of the ways that transnationally organized groups of scientists and policymakers—often referred to as *epistemic communities*—have influenced the development of environmental regimes.

Liberal-institutionalist analysis of regime creation may still be the predominant approach to global environmental change, but it is not the only one. It makes the important assumption that the problem to solve is how to obtain global governance in a fragmented system of sovereign states. Marxist writers would reject this formulation (see Chapter 3). For them, the **state system** is part of the problem rather than the solution, and the proper object of study is the way global capitalism produces relationships that are profoundly damaging to the environment. The global spread of neoliberal policies accelerates those features of globalization—consumerism, the relocation of production to the South, and the thoughtless squandering of resources—that are driving the global ecological crisis (see Chapter 8). Proponents of this view also highlight the incapacity of the state to do anything other than assist such processes. It follows that the international cooperation efforts described here at worst legitimize this state of affairs and at best provide some marginal improvements to the devastation wrought by global capitalism. For example, proponents would point to how free market concepts are now routinely embedded in discussions of sustainable development and how the World Trade Organization (WTO) rules tend to subordinate attempts to provide environmental regulation of genetically modified organisms (GMOs). This argument is part of a broader debate among political theorists concerning whether the state can ever be "greened." The opposing view suggests that when coping with a threat as large and immediate as climate change, cooperation between states and international cooperation remain the only plausible mechanisms for providing the

State system The regular patterns of interaction between states but without implying any shared values between them. This is distinguished from the view of a "society" of states.

TABLE 10.3	The Antarctic Treaty Regime
1959	Antarctic Treaty
1972	Convention for the Conservation of Antarctic Seals
1980	Convention on the Conservation of Antarctic Marine Living Resources
1988	Convention on the Regulation of Antarctic Mineral Resource Activities
1991	Protocol on Environmental Protection to the Antarctic Treaty (Madrid Protocol)

Desertification The extreme deterioration of land in arid and dry subhumid areas due to loss of vegetation and soil moisture; it results chiefly from human activities and is influenced by climatic variations. This condition is principally caused by overgrazing, overdrafting of groundwater, and diversion of water from rivers for human consumption and industrial use; all of these processes are fundamentally driven by overpopulation.

Ecosystem A system of interdependent living organisms that share the same habitat, functioning together with all of the physical factors of the environment.

necessary global governance, and we simply need to do the best we can with existing state and international organizational structures.

With the end of the Cold War, some realist international relations specialists began to apply their ideas about anarchy and war to the study of environmental politics. As a result, they contended that conflict, not cooperation, shaped the issue, and they sought proof of this hypothesis. Largely ignoring examples of cooperation like the Antarctic Treaty system (see Table 10.3), they argued that environmental change contributes to the incidence of both internal conflict and interstate war, even though the causal connections are complex and involve many factors. It is already evident that **desertification** (the extreme deterioration of land due to loss of vegetation and soil moisture) and the degradation of other vital resources are intimately connected with cycles of poverty, destitution, and war in Africa. But these factors can also be attributed to the effects of European colonization of the continent. However, if we consider such predicted consequences of climate change as mass migrations of populations across international boundaries and acute scarcity of water and other resources, the outlines of potential future conflicts come into sharper focus.

Thus, the more immediate *and* persistent consequence of warfare may be the destruction of **ecosystems** (systems of organisms sharing a habitat) that such conflict causes. For example, during World War I, artillery shelling devastated farmland along the trench lines in northern France and Belgium, creating eerie moonscapes for years after the war. Similarly, in Vietnam, the detrimental environmental effects of US weapons, including the use of the herbicide Agent Orange (a form of the carcinogenic compound dioxin) and the carpet-bombing of wide swaths of jungle and rice paddies, remain visible today. More recently, tank-training exercises in the Mojave Desert of California have increased erosion of the fragile landscape. During both Gulf Wars, fires set at oil wells sent carcinogenic materials aloft to be carried downwind, where people who breathed the air became sick. The oil also leached into the already-threated groundwater systems. In addition, the depleted-uranium antitank bullets fired during those wars put radioactive material into the air and soil. Even the less obvious effects of warfare can have unforeseen, negative impacts. A recent lawsuit filed in the US federal courts charged that US Navy sonar-training exercises can hurt the hearing of migrating whales, causing them to become disoriented. The Navy was ordered to stop the sonar training by July 2016.

Recent research suggests that climate change and environmental degradation might be the source of major violence against specific ethnic communities. The violence in Rwanda between Hutus and Tutsis may have been a fight over productive farmland, and the killing of African tribesmen in Darfur by Northern Arabs may have been about access to water and other resources. Therefore, existing ethnic tensions may be accentuated by weather events and climate change.

Left out of most discussions about international relations theory and the environment is the **ecotopian** perspective. The **deep ecology** movement, or the **ecocentric** view, represents a radical or transformational perspective. Deep ecologists are purists rejecting the idea of inherent human superiority and giving equal moral weight to all elements of nature. Many of the utopians who seek system transformation have called for an alliance between red (socialist) and green (environmentalist) organizations to address the two overarching political issues of our time: human inequality and environmental destruction.

Deep ecologists lack faith in capitalist systems that are technologically dependent, prone to move toward large centralized corporate control, and protected by undemocratic, elitist political institutions. Strongly opposed to materialism and consumerism, they argue that our throwaway, shop-till-you-drop consumer culture should be replaced by an emphasis on meeting basic human needs. Otherwise, they fear, the environment will be devastated. Ecological and natural laws should help shape morality in human affairs, and the costs of environmental degradation must be considered when policy choices are made. Following their recommendations would certainly require a significant transformation in our political and economic thinking and in our policy priorities.

Ecofeminism is also underrepresented in most international relations theory discussions. As we saw in Chapter 3, by the 1980s feminist theories began to have a greater impact on the field. Ecofeminists see a connection between the exploitation of the environment and the exploitation of women. As study after study has indicated, because of their living conditions in developing states, women will suffer from the effects of climate change more than men will.

This academic-level environmental theory discourse is largely about what is called "instrumental versus intrinsic" debate. The question is simple: Do we protect the environment because humans can use it or because the environment has its own inherent value? We saw this earlier in this chapter when we briefly surveyed the key international environmental agreements. For instance, do we save fur seals, birds, and whales because humans use them, or because those animals are parts of a complex, connected ecosystem? The so-called **anthropocentric** reply to this question is simple—humans are at the top of the "food chain" and therefore have the right to exploit the biomass on the Earth to the benefit of humans. As you might imagine, there is considerable debate within the academic community about the ethics and practicality of this anthropocentric position.

Ecotopian Someone who believes in protecting and preserving the environment and promotes progressive political goals that promote environmental sustainability, social justice, and economic well-being.

Deep ecology Often identified with the Norwegian philosopher Arne Naess, the core belief is that the living environment has a right to live and flourish. The "deep" refers to the need to think deeply about the impact of human life on the environment.

Ecocentric Having a nature- or ecology-centered rather than a human-centered set of values.

Anthropocentric An ethical standpoint that views humans as the central factor in considerations of right and wrong action in and toward nature.

How do theoretical approaches like constructivism, radical-liberal, ecotopian, and some feminist theories of international relations help us understand environmental problems in ways that traditional theories like realism and liberalism do not?

Clearly, the environmental degradation caused by wars and the devices of war is impossible to dismiss yet even more difficult to address; by its very nature, warfare involves a breakdown of international cooperation. However, when states are not at war and cooperation *is* a viable option, what does it look like and how does it function? Now that we have explored some of the theories surrounding international environmental cooperation, in the next section we will further discuss global mechanisms—or how states and transnational actors attempt to solve environmental issues through formal agreements and cooperative actions.

GLOBAL PERSPECTIVE

The "Doomsday" Seed Vault

Background

One day in February 2008, like a scene out of a postapocalyptic science fiction movie, more than two hundred invited guests hunkered inside puffy parkas at the official opening of the Svalbard Global Seed Vault. Unfortunately dubbed in news media the "Doomsday Vault," the facility is located on an island not far from the North Pole. There, at the end of a four-hundred-foot tunnel carved into a mountain and isolated from the outside by a series of air locks, governments store as many as 2 billion seeds representing almost 4.5 million species of food plants. It is intended to be the storehouse of last resort for the world's plants.

The entrance to the Svalbard Global Seed Vault is located near Longyearbyen on Spitsbergen, Norway.

The Case

The seed vault is the idea of an NGO based in Rome called the Global Crop Diversity Trust. An affiliate of the UN's Food and Agriculture Organization, the trust administers the facility, which cost more than $9 million. The vault is one response to fears about the long-term effects global warming might have on biodiversity and crop output. It is a repository for samples of food seeds in the event that a temperature increase causes plant extinctions. The location of the tunnel is one sign that the host Norwegian government, which covered the entire cost of construction, and Global Crop Diversity Trust believe the threat of global warming is very real. It is far above the current high-tide mark and well above where mean high tide will be if the Arctic, Antarctic, and Greenland ice sheets continue to melt at present rates. Beginning in 2016 and continuing each summer after, the tunnels of

the vault have been flooded with meltwater from the surrounding snow and melting permafrost.

Billing itself as "A Foundation for Food Security," the Global Crop Diversity Trust gives grants to support food-plant research and to maintain gene banks in accordance with the goals of the 1983 International Treaty on Plant Genetic Resources for Food and Agriculture and the 1993 Biodiversity Convention. It is a physical manifestation of the ideas of ecotopianism and the precautionary principle of international law. In practical terms, the trust seeks to maintain vital food products eaten in the developing world such as bananas, sorghum, barley, cassava, lentils, and several varieties of beans.

There seems to be little not to like about the Svalbard Global Seed Vault, aside from the imminent threat of the highly negative effects of global warming. However, the FAQ section of the Global Crop Diversity Trust's website (www.croptrust.org) provides some hints about one possible controversy. The site says that national governments will deposit seeds and that each government will retain ownership of its seeds. A look at the donors section of the website suggests an explanation for this statement of seed ownership. There among the list of donors, such as EU governments, the US Agency for International Development (USAID), the Rockefeller Foundation, and the Bill and Melinda Gates Foundation, are the names of two giants of the agribusiness chemical industry: DuPont and Syngenta AG. Prior to changing its name to Syngenta AG in 2001, the chemical firm was known by several names, including Ciba. Ciba invented both DDT and 2,4-D. DDT was the villain in Rachel Carson's *Silent Spring*; 2,4-D is better known as a component of Agent Orange, an herbicide that US forces sprayed in uncounted millions of gallons on Vietnam during the 1960s and early 1970s.

Outcome

As we have seen so far in this book, perspective matters when seeking to understand international politics. Some environmental activists resent the fact that anthropocentric agribusiness interests seem to be trying to exploit global warming by supporting the Global Crop Diversity Trust, especially because the chemical industry bears some of the guilt for causing the greenhouse gas problem in the first place. However, as Syngenta AG's website indicates, the company is trying to do its best to save biodiversity. Which side is correct? The answer may be buried under a mountain in the permafrost zone at the end of a tunnel six hundred miles from the North Pole.

For Discussion

1. If the goal of the Global Seed Vault is good, does it matter who the donors are?
2. Should the concept of national sovereignty extend to control of the world's seeds?
3. Our reliance on technology and plants resistant to all sorts of natural enemies has increased our vulnerability. Does it make sense for us to return to more natural or organic ways of agriculture?

Regime Theory and the Montreal Protocol

THE CHALLENGE

Academic advocates of international regime theory discussed in this chapter contend that four factors—context, knowledge, interest, and power—can explain why and when countries decide to create a formal commitment in a given issue area. The same four factors also help explain what kinds of restraints countries permit on their behaviors. The evolution of international cooperation to protect the ozone layer provides an excellent case to test this hypothesis. In brief, if there are significant disagreements about the scientific evidence and one or more countries want to limit cooperation, then it is unlikely that other countries will be able to establish an effective international regime.

OPTIONS

The consequences of the thinning of the stratospheric ozone layer include excessive exposure to UVB radiation, resulting in increased rates of skin cancer for human beings and damage to immune systems. Stratospheric ozone depletion arose from a previously unsuspected source—artificial chemicals containing fluorine, chlorine, and bromine that were involved in chemical reactions with ozone molecules at high altitudes. Most significant were the chlorofluorocarbons (CFCs), which had been developed in the 1920s as "safe" inert industrial gases and had been widely produced and used over the next fifty years for a variety of purposes, from refrigeration and air conditioning to propellants for hair spray. Despite growing scientific knowledge, there was no universal agreement on the dangers

Regime Theory and the Montreal Protocol *continued*

posed by these chemicals, and production and use continued—except, significantly, where the US Congress decided to ban some nonessential uses. This meant that the US chemical industry found itself under a costly obligation to find alternatives. Until a US-based chemical company developed an alternative to the harmful CFC compound, US diplomats blocked serious discussions at the international level. As evidence on the problem began to mount, the UNEP acted to convene an international conference in Vienna. It produced a relatively weak "framework convention"—the 1985 Vienna Convention for the Protection of the Ozone Layer—agreeing that international action might be required and that the parties should continue to communicate and to develop and exchange scientific findings. These findings proved to be very persuasive, particularly with the added public impetus provided by the dramatic discovery of the Antarctic ozone hole.

APPLICATION

Within two years, the Montreal Protocol was negotiated. Some analysts point to a change in the US negotiating stance as the reason for the rapid passage of the protocol. Why did this change occur? An American chemical giant found a replacement compound

for the ozone-depleting CFCs, seemingly confirming part of the regime-creation hypothesis. In the Montreal Protocol, parties agreed to a regime under which the production and trading of CFCs and other ozone-depleting substances would be progressively phased out. The developed countries achieved this for CFCs by 1996, and Meetings of the Parties have continued to work on the elimination of other substances since that time. There was some initial resistance from European chemical producers, but the US side had a real incentive to ensure international agreement because otherwise its chemical industry would remain at a commercial disadvantage.

The other problem faced by the negotiators involved the developing countries, which themselves were manufacturing CFC products. As the Indian delegate stated, it was the developed countries' mess and their responsibility to clear it up! Why should developing countries be forced to change over to higher-cost CFC alternatives? There were two responses. The first was an article in the protocol giving the developing countries a grace period. The second was a fund, set up in 1990, to finance the provision of alternative non-CFC technologies for the developing world.

Illegal production and smuggling of CFCs were evident in the 1990s. This tested the monitoring and compliance systems of the protocol (which included the possible use of trade sanctions against offenders). Nonetheless, the regime has generally proved to be effective and has continually widened its scope of activities to deal with further classes of ozone-depleting chemicals. The damage to the ozone layer will not be repaired until the latter part of the twenty-first century, given the long atmospheric lifetimes of the chemicals involved. However, human behavior has been significantly altered to the extent that the scientific subsidiary body of the Montreal Protocol has been able to report a measurable reduction in the atmospheric concentration of CFCs. Therefore, it seems that the context, knowledge, interest, and power hypothesis is correct.

For Discussion

1. How might the alternative theories we have studied explain the case of CFCs and regime creation?
2. Can you think of examples in hich a leader in one environmental issue is a laggard in another?
3. Given the apparent pace of climate change in the polar regions, is the regime-creation process too slow to solve Earth's problems?

The Functions of International Environmental Cooperation

Because environmental issues, such as pollution control, often involve more than one country—or region, or hemisphere—states must establish international governance regimes to regulate these transboundary environmental problems and sustain the global commons. Yet these regimes encompass more than formal agreements between states, although such agreements are very important. Moreover, there are other functions and consequences of international cooperation beyond regime formation, which we will learn about in the following sections.

Transboundary Trade and Pollution Control

When animals, fish, water, or pollution cross national frontiers, the need for international cooperation arises. The regulation of transboundary environmental problems is a long-established function of international cooperation, reflected in hundreds of multilateral, regional, and bilateral agreements providing for joint efforts to manage resources and control pollution.

An important example is the 1979 Convention on Long-Range Transboundary Air Pollution and its various protocols. They responded to the growing problem of acidification and acid rain by providing mechanisms to study atmospheric pollution problems in Europe and North America and securing commitments by the states involved to control and reduce their emissions. Another set of multilateral environmental agreements regulates the transboundary movement of hazardous wastes and chemicals in the interest of protecting human health and the environment. These agreements require that when hazardous chemicals and pesticides are traded, the government from whose territory the exports originate shall obtain the "prior informed consent" of the importing country (see Table 10.4).

Controlling, taxing, and even promoting trade have always been some of the more important functions of the state, and trade restrictions can also be used as an instrument for nature conservation. The 1973 Convention on International Trade in Endangered Species does this by attempting to monitor, control, or prohibit international trade in species (or products derived from them) whose continued survival might be put at risk by the effects of such trade. Species at risk are "listed" in three appendixes to the convention. Some six hundred animal and three hundred plant species currently receive the highest level of protection (a trade ban) through listing in Appendix I. However, decisions on the "up-listing" and "down-listing" of species are sometimes controversial, as in the case of the African elephant or the northern spotted owl, bald eagle, and gray wolf in the United States.

The use of trade penalties and restrictions by multilateral environmental agreements has been a thorny issue whenever the objective of environmental protection has come into conflict with the rules of the General Agreement on Tariffs and Trade (GATT)/WTO trade regime (see Chapters 5 and 8). Such a problem arose when the international community attempted to address the controversial question of new biotechnology and GMOs. The claims of (primarily American) biotechnology corporations, which had made huge investments in developing GMO seed, pharmaceuticals, and food products, that these innovations had positive environmental and development potential (through reducing pesticide use and increasing crop yields) were met with much resistance. European publics,

TABLE 10.4	**Some Environmental Treaties with Weight in International Environmental Law**
Atmospheric Pollution	
1985	Convention on Long-Range Transboundary Air Pollution
1988	Protocol Concerning the Control of Emissions of Nitrogen Oxides
1988	Protocol on the Reduction of Sulfur Emissions or Their Transboundary Fluxes
Stratospheric Ozone Layer	
1985	Vienna Convention for the Protection of the Ozone Layer
1987	Montreal Protocol on Substances That Deplete the Ozone Layer
Hazardous Wastes	
1989	Basel Convention on the Control of Transboundary Movements of Hazardous Wastes and Their Disposal
1991	Bamako Convention on the Ban of the Import Into Africa and the Control of Transboundary Movement and Management Within Africa of Hazardous Wastes
2001	The Stockholm Convention on Persistent Organic Pollutants
2013	Minamata Convention on Mercury
Marine Pollution	
1969	International Convention on Civil Liability for Oil Pollution Damage
1971	Brussels Convention Relating to Civil Liability in the Field of Maritime Carriage of Nuclear Material
1973–1978	International Convention for the Prevention of Pollution From Ships (MARPOL)
1992	London Convention on the Prevention of Marine Pollution by Dumping Wastes and Other Matter
Wildlife	
1971	Ramsar Convention on Wetlands of International Importance Especially as Waterfowl Habitat
1973	International Convention for the Regulation of Whaling
1973	Convention on International Trade in Endangered Species (CITES)
1979	Bonn Convention on the Conservation of Migratory Species of Wild Animals
2018	Ban on Commercial Fishing in the Arctic (Arctic Council)

supermarkets, and some developing countries were very wary of GMO technologies on safety and other grounds, which led to pressure for controls on their transboundary movement and to the negotiation of the Biosafety Protocol to the Convention on Biological Diversity in 1992. Signed in 2000, the resulting

Cartagena Protocol established a procedure for obtaining agreements in advance when GMOs are transferred across frontiers for ultimate release into the environment. The criteria to guide decisions on blocking imports reflected a precautionary approach rather than insistence on conclusive scientific evidence of harmfulness. Much of the argument in negotiating the Cartagena Protocol concerned the relationship of these new environmental rules to the requirements of the trade regime and arose from the concern of the United States, and other potential GMO exporters, that the protocol would permit a disguised form of trade protectionism. Whether the WTO trade rules should take precedence over the emerging biosafety rules was debated at length until the parties agreed to avoid the issue by providing that the two sets of rules should be mutually supportive.

A polar bear in the Canadian Arctic walks over sea ice. Polar bears were the first species to be declared endangered due to climate change. They rely on the rapidly disappearing ice sheets for survival. Polar bears are one of many animals threatened by the "Era of Biological Annihilation," the contemporary period in which species are becoming extinct at one hundred times the previous natural rate. Is it possible to slow this process down?

The Green Belt Movement

This is an environmental organization that empowers communities, particularly women, to conserve the environment and improve livelihoods of those on the margins. It was founded in 1977 by Wangari Maathai, the first African woman and environmentalist to win the Nobel Peace Prize. She was awarded the prize for her contributions to sustainable development, democracy, and peace. The Green Belt Movement acts in four main areas of activity: (1) tree planting and water harvesting, (2) climate change, (3) mainstream advocacy, and (4) gender livelihood and advocacy. The organization has planted over 51 million trees since 1978, with an average survival rate of 70 percent. Internship and volunteer opportunities available. Think about applying: www.greenbeltmovement.org/.

Norm Creation

The development of international environmental law and associated norms of acceptable behavior has been both rapid and innovative over the last thirty years. Some of the norms mentioned earlier are in the form of technical policy concepts that have been widely disseminated and adopted as a result of international discussion. The precautionary principle has gained increasing, but not uncritical, currency, as have concepts like sustainable development, polluter pays, preventive action, and common differentiated responsibility. Coined by German policymakers, the precautionary principle states that where there is a likelihood of environmental damage, banning an activity should not require full and definitive scientific proof. As we saw in the earlier example of GMOs, the latter has tended to be the requirement in trade law. The norm of "prior informed consent" has also been promoted alongside that of "the polluter pays." In the longer term, one of the key effects of the climate-change regime (dealt with in detail later) may be the dissemination of new approaches to pollution control, such as emissions trading and joint implementation.

The UN Earth Summits were important in establishing environmental norms. The 1972 Stockholm Conference produced its Principle 21, which combines sovereignty over the use of national resources with states' responsibility for ensuring that activities within their jurisdiction do not cause external pollution. This should not be confused with Agenda 21, issued by the 1992 Earth Summit. Agenda 21 was a complex, voluntary action plan for sustainable development put forth by the United Nations. Agenda 21 was frequently derided, not least because of its nonbinding character, but this internationally agreed-upon compendium of environmental "best practice" subsequently had a wide impact and remains a point of reference. For example, many local authorities have produced their own Agenda 21s. Under the Aarhus Convention (1998), North American and European governments agreed to guarantee to their publics a number of environmental rights, including the right to obtain environmental information held by governments, to participate in policy decisions, and to have access to judicial processes.

Technology transfer The process of sharing skills, knowledge, technologies, methods of manufacturing, and facilities among governments and private actors (e.g., corporations) to ensure that scientific and technological developments are accessible to a wider range of users for application in new products, processes, materials, or services.

Children clean plastic out of the filthy waterways of Dhaka, Bangladesh. Pollution remains a major problem in every society and our waste continues to contaminate water, land, and the atmosphere. Plastic waste often ends up in the Pacific Ocean, with the largest collection, the Pacific Garbage Patch, covering an area larger than Texas. Do you have a recycling program in your community that will diminish our levels of harmful waste?

Aid and Capacity Building

Although not a specific norm of the type dealt with earlier, sustainable development provides a normative framework built on an underlying deal between developed and developing worlds. Frequent North–South arguments about the levels of aid and **technology transfer** that would allow developing countries to achieve sustainable development have ended in disappointment and unfulfilled pledges. In 1991, the UNEP, UN Development Programme, and World Bank created the Global Environmental Facility as an international mechanism specifically for funding environmental projects in developing countries. Since 1992, the Global Environmental Facility has provided $17 billion in grants and organized $88 billion in additional financing for nearly four thousand projects in 170 countries. Funds are replenished every four years, and for 2014–2018, 30 countries pledged a record $4.43 billion.

Most environmental conventions now aim at **capacity building** through arrangements for the transfer of funds, technology, and expertise because most of their member states lack the resources to participate fully in international agreements. The stratospheric-ozone and climate-change regimes aim to build capacity and could not exist in their current form without providing for this function.

Capacity building The provision of funds and technical training to allow developing countries to participate in global environmental governance.

Scientific Understanding

International environmental cooperation relies on shared scientific understanding, as evidenced by the form of some important contemporary environmental regimes. An initial framework convention will signal concern and establish mechanisms for developing and sharing new scientific data, thereby providing the basis for taking action in a control protocol. Generating and sharing scientific information have long been functions of international cooperation in public bodies such as the World Meteorological Organization and myriad academic organizations such as the International Council for the Exploration of the Seas and the International Union for the Conservation of Nature. Disseminating scientific information on an international basis makes sense, but it needs funding from governments because, except in areas like pharmaceutical research, the private sector has no incentive to do the work. International environmental regimes usually have standing scientific committees and subsidiary bodies to support their work. Perhaps the greatest international effort to generate new and authoritative scientific knowledge has been in the area of **climate change** through the Intergovernmental Panel on Climate Change (IPCC).

Climate change A change in the statistical distribution of weather over periods that range from decades to millions of years. It can be a change in the average weather or a change in the distribution of weather events.

Set up in 1988 under the auspices of the World Meteorological Organization and UNEP, the IPCC brings together the majority of the world's climate-change scientists in three working groups: on climate science, impacts, and economic and social dimensions. They have produced assessment reports in 1990, 1995, 2001, 2007, and 2014, which are regarded as the authoritative scientific statements on climate change. The reports are drafted carefully and cautiously with the involvement of government representatives and represent a consensus view.

The Fourth Assessment Report, published in February 2007, concluded that "warming of the climate system is unequivocal, as is now evident from observations of increases in global average air and ocean temperatures, widespread melting of snow and ice and rising global sea level" (IPCC 2007, 4). Most of the temperature

India has the dubious distinction of having seven of the ten most polluted cities in the world. The World Health Organization estimates that 7 million people worldwide die every year due to air pollution. If the country is to continue its march to economic development, what must it do to protect its citizens?

increase "is *very likely* due to the observed increase in anthropogenic greenhouse gas concentrations" (IPCC 2007, 8; original italics). The use of words is significant here, for the IPCC defines *very likely* as more than 90 percent certain. This represents a change from the previous report, which had only estimated that human activity was *likely*, or more than 66 percent certain, to be responsible for temperature increases.

In 2008, the IPCC agreed to prepare the most recent available IPCC report, published in 2014 (AR5), which stated, "Each of the last three decades has been successively warmer at the Earth's surface than any preceding decade since 1850" (IPCC 2014, 9). The report also concluded that it is "very likely that the Arctic sea ice cover will continue to shrink and thin and that Northern Hemisphere spring snow cover will decrease during the 21st century as global mean surface temperature rises," which means that the global glacier volume will continue to decrease (IPCC 2014, 13).

Like many recent scientific reports on climate change, the AR5 report also points out that "Human influence on the climate system is clear. This is evident from the increasing greenhouse gas concentrations in the atmosphere, positive radiative forcing, observed warming, and understanding of the climate system" (IPCC 2014, 19). These warnings continued with the October 2018 Special Report that stated unequivocally, "Human activities have caused a global temperature rise of 1.0°C above pre-industrial levels, and will likely reach 1.5°C between 2030 and 2052 if it continues at the current rate."

Governing the Commons

Global commons The areas and resources not under national sovereignty that belong to no single country and are the responsibility of the entire world. The oceans beyond the two-hundred-mile limit, outer space, and Antarctica are global commons areas.

The **global commons** are usually understood as areas and resources not under sovereign jurisdiction—that is, not owned by anybody. The high seas and the deep ocean floor come within this category (beyond the two-hundred-nautical-mile exclusive economic zone that states could claim under the 1992 UN Convention on the Law of the Sea), as does Antarctica (based on the 1959 Antarctic Treaty). Outer space is another highly important commons area, with use vital to modern telecommunications, broadcasting, navigation, and surveillance. Finally, there is the global atmosphere.

The global commons have an environmental dimension not only as resources but also as a kind of garbage dump for waste products from cities and industry. The fish and whale stocks of the high seas have been relentlessly overexploited to the point where some species have been wiped out and long-term protein sources for human beings are imperiled. The ocean environment has been polluted by land-based effluent and oil and other discharges from ships. It has been a struggle to maintain the unique wilderness of the Antarctic in the face of increasing pressure from human beings, and even outer space now faces an environmental problem in the form of increasing orbital debris left by decades of satellite launches. Similarly, the global atmosphere has been degraded

WHAT'S YOUR WORLDVIEW?

We now live in a world where people seem to select their own narrative and the facts that are associated with that narrative. Thus, they select their own truth, and this means they often reject scientific data that account for climate change. How do you convince the climate deniers that this is real?

in a number of highly threatening ways, through damage to the stratospheric ozone layer and, most important, by the enhanced **greenhouse effect** now firmly associated with changes to Earth's climate. This is often characterized as a "tragedy of the commons." Where there is unrestricted access to a resource owned by no one, there will be an incentive for individuals to grab as much as they can, and if the resource is finite, there will come a time when it is ruined by overexploitation as the short-term interests of individual users overwhelm the longer-term collective interest in sustaining the resource.

> **Greenhouse effect** The trapping of the sun's warmth in Earth's lower atmosphere due to gases that act like the glass of a greenhouse.

The Arctic is often described by environmentalists and some governments as a global commons region, as is the Amazon region. These areas are *shared resource areas*. In the case of the Arctic region there are eight nation-states that have sovereignty over Arctic territory and the various oceans and seas in the region. For the world, this region is seen as critical for the global health of the planet, but for the Arctic states this is home, and they have a responsibility to provide jobs, housing, healthcare, education, and both domestic and international security. The Arctic Council is a regional organization that includes indigenous communities from the region, and it has developed policies and strategies for dealing with common problems in the region. Perhaps the eight countries that control different parts of the Amazon might create a policy regime like the Arctic Council to encourage cooperation among those states to deal with environmental challenges.

Environmental Regimes

Within the jurisdiction of governments, it may be possible to solve the problem of the "tragedy of the commons" by turning the global commons into private property or nationalizing them, but such a solution is, by definition, unavailable. Therefore, the function of international cooperation in this context is to provide a substitute for world government to ensure that global commons are not misused and subject to tragic collapse. Regimes have been created that have enjoyed varying degrees of effectiveness. Many of the functions that have been discussed can be found in these global commons regimes, but their central contribution is a framework of rules to ensure mutual agreement between users about acceptable standards of behavior and levels of exploitation consistent with sustaining commons ecology.

Enforcement poses difficult challenges due to the incentives for users to "free ride" by taking more than a fair share or refusing to be bound by the collective arrangements. Free riding can potentially destroy regimes because other parties

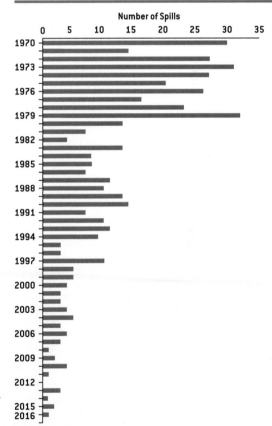

Number of Oil Spills, 1970–2018.
The fight against maritime pollution has had some successes. More aggressive law enforcement and better ship design have combined with an understanding in the industry that pollution harms us all. Could this be a way out of the "tragedy of the commons"?

will then see no reason to restrain themselves either. In local commons regimes, inquisitive neighbors might deter rule breaking, and NGOs can play a similar role at the international level. However, it is very difficult to enforce compliance by sovereign states; this is a fundamental difficulty for international law and hardly unique to environmental regimes. Mechanisms have been developed to cope with the problem, but how effective they, and the environmental regimes to which they apply, can be is hard to judge; this involves determining the extent to which governments are in legal and technical compliance with their international obligations. Moreover, it involves estimating the extent to which state behavior has been changed as a result of the international regime concerned. Naturally, the ultimate and most demanding test of the effectiveness of global commons regimes is whether or not the resources or ecologies concerned are sustained or even improved.

Some of the first and least successful global commons regimes were the various fisheries commissions for the Atlantic and elsewhere, which sought agreement on limiting catches to preserve stocks. Pollution from ships has been controlled by MARPOL (the 1973 international marine environmental convention—short for "marine pollution"), and there is a patchwork of other treaties to manage such issues as the dumping of radioactive waste at sea. For the Antarctic, a remarkably well-developed set of rules designed to preserve the ecological integrity of this last great wilderness has been devised within the framework of the 1959 Antarctic Treaty. The Antarctic regime is a rather exclusive club: The treaty's "Consultative Parties" include the states that had originally claimed sovereignty over parts of the area, and new members of the club must demonstrate their involvement in scientific research on the frozen continent. There is a comprehensive agreement on conserving the marine ecosystem around the continent, and in the late 1980s, preparations for regulated mineral mining were defeated by a new 1988 Protocol on Environmental Protection, which included a fifty-year mining ban. The success of a restricted group of countries, with only a minimal level of formal organization, in governing this crucial laboratory for understanding global environmental change demonstrates what can be achieved by international action.

Antarctic science was crucial to the discovery of a problem that resulted in what is perhaps the best example of effective international action to govern the commons. In 1985, a British Antarctic Survey balloon provided definitive evidence of serious thinning of the stratospheric ozone layer (see this chapter's Theory in

The number of extreme weather events has increased due to climate change; so too has the number of refugees from these dangerous weather conditions. One research organization estimates that since 2008 roughly 24 million people have been displaced each year. Which countries will become the havens for these environmental refugees? Is this climate-forced migration sustainable?

Practice box for more information). A diminishing ozone layer is a global problem par excellence because the ozone layer protects Earth and its inhabitants from the damaging effects of the sun's ultraviolet radiation. The problem's causes were isolated, international support was mobilized, and a set of rules and procedures was developed that proved to be effective, at least in reducing the concentration of the offending chemicals in the atmosphere, if not yet fully restoring the stratospheric ozone layer.

In a speech at the December 2019 Conference of Parties 25 meetings in Madrid, Michael Bloomberg makes the case that the United States is still in the talks and that, if not the federal government, states, cities, some corporations, and citizens still care and support action.

Climate Change

Unlike the ozone-layer problem, which was clearly the result of damage caused when people used CFCs, climate change and the enhanced greenhouse effect had long been debated among scientists. Only in the late 1980s did sufficient international scientific and political consensus emerge to stimulate action—a clear case of the development and influence of an epistemic community. There were still serious disagreements, however, over the likelihood that human-induced changes in mean temperatures were altering the global climate system.

Naturally occurring greenhouse gases in the atmosphere insulate Earth's surface by trapping solar radiation. Before the Industrial Revolution, carbon dioxide concentrations in the atmosphere were around 280 parts per million (ppm). They have since grown significantly. In 2007, they were measured at 379 ppm; in 2015, they surpassed 400 ppm. For instance, the May 2019 average at Mauna Loa Observatory in Hawaii (NOAA) is 414.66 ppm. This rising concentration is due to burning fossil fuels and reductions in some of the "sinks" for carbon dioxide (anything that absorbs more carbon dioxide than it releases), notably forests. Methane emissions have also risen with the growth of agriculture (Intergovernmental Panel on Climate Change 2007, 11).

The best predictions of the IPCC are that if nothing is done to curb intensive fossil-fuel emissions, there will likely be a rise in mean temperatures on the order of 4.3–11.5°F (2.4–6.4°C) by 2099. The exact consequences of this are difficult to predict based on current climate modeling, but sea-level rises and turbulent weather are generally expected. While at Copenhagen the 2°C target had been agreed, by 2015 there was international agreement in Paris that to avoid dangerous climate change, temperature increases should be held well below 2°C and efforts should be made to limit increases to 1.5°C. In the first decade of the twenty-first century, unusual weather patterns, storm events, and the melting of polar ice sheets added a dimension of public concern to the fears expressed by the scientific community.

As a common problem, climate change is on a quite different scale from anything that the international system has previously encountered. Climate change is not a normal international environmental problem; it threatens huge changes in living conditions and challenges existing patterns of energy use and security. There is almost no dimension of international relations that climate change does not actually or potentially affect, and it has already become the subject of "high politics," discussed at G8 summits and in high-level meetings between political leaders.

One way of examining the dimensions of the problem and the steps taken at the international level to respond to the threat of climate change is to make a comparison to the stratospheric-ozone problem discussed in the previous section. There are, of course, some similarities. CFCs are in themselves greenhouse gases, and the international legal texts on climate change make it clear that controlling them is the responsibility of the Montreal Protocol. The experience with stratospheric-ozone and other recent conventions has clearly influenced efforts to build a climate-change regime. At the very start of climate discussions, the same approach was adopted: a framework convention followed by protocols.

The UNFCCC was signed at the 1992 Earth Summit in Rio de Janeiro, Brazil. It envisaged the reduction of greenhouse gas emissions and their removal by carbon sequestration, a process through which carbon-based gases are injected into the ground or into peat bogs. The signatories hoped that including a commitment from the developed nations to cut their emissions back to 1990 levels by 2000 would be a start. In a US election year, this proved to be impossible, and the parties to the convention had to be content with a nonbinding declaration that an attempt would be made. There was a binding commitment, however, for parties to draw up national inventories of emissions sources and sinks. As this included the developing nations, many of whom were ill equipped to fulfill this obligation, there was also funding for capacity building. Most important, the convention locked the signatories into holding a continuing series of annual Conferences of Parties to consider possible actions and review the adequacy of existing commitments, supported by regular meetings of the subsidiary scientific and implementation bodies. By 1997, the parties agreed on a "control" measure—the Kyoto Protocol, which set targets for emissions reductions by developed countries.

The problem faced by the framers of the Kyoto Protocol was vastly more complex and demanding than that which their counterparts at Montreal had confronted so successfully in 1987. Instead of controlling a single set of industrial gases for which substitutes were available, reducing greenhouse gas emissions would involve major changes in energy production, transportation, and agriculture—the fundamentals of life in modern societies.

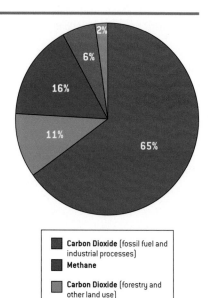

Global Greenhouse Gas Emissions by Type of Gas.

The key greenhouse gases in the atmosphere are carbon dioxide, methane, nitrous oxide, and fluorinated gases (F-gases). Do some research to determine what sorts of human activities are responsible for emitting these types of gases.

Legend:
- Carbon Dioxide (fossil fuel and industrial processes)
- Methane
- Carbon Dioxide (forestry and other land use)
- Nitrous Oxide
- F-gases

Reducing greenhouse gas emissions challenges the whole idea of sustainable development. Doing so would involve real sacrifices in living standards and create tough political choices for governments, although there are potential economic benefits from cutting emissions through the development of alternative-energy technologies. Another option is to change what we eat. For instance, the cattle industry is a significant cause of non-point-source methane and other environmental impacts. As a UNEP report indicates, "Agriculture, particularly meat and dairy products, accounts for 70% of global freshwater consumption, 38% of the total land use and 19% of the world's greenhouse gas emissions" (source: www.unep.fr/shared/publications/pdf/dtix1262xpa-priority-productsandmaterials_report.pdf).

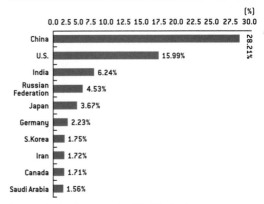

Largest Producers of CO_2 Emissions Worldwide, 2016.

Since the Industrial Revolution, carbon dioxide concentrations have grown significantly. If nothing is done to curb intensive fossil-fuel emissions, what will happen to the average global temperature? What effects might that have?

The Kyoto Protocol to the Climate Convention entered into force in 2005. It committed developed countries to make an average 5.2 percent cut in their greenhouse gas emissions from a 1990 baseline. Within this range, different national targets were negotiated: 8 percent for the European Union, 6 percent for Japan, and 7 percent for the United States. Unfortunately, the United States, representing one of the worst greenhouse gas–offending countries by several indicators, eventually refused to participate because its economic competitors, China and India, were not required to make similar cuts. These targets were to be achieved by the first commitment period, 2008–2012. To achieve these targets, three mechanisms were agreed on.

The first was **emissions trading**, which provided that rights to emit carbon could be bought and sold. The European Union established its own emissions-trading system, and carbon markets began to grow up elsewhere. The second and third offset mechanisms, **Joint Implementation** and the **Clean Development Mechanism**, allowed countries to meet their own national targets by investing in carbon-reduction projects elsewhere in the world. There has been extensive use of the Clean Development Mechanism, especially in China.

Even with what appeared to be a flexible framework and some useful reduction mechanisms built into the Kyoto Protocol, there was much disagreement and international posturing. One reason for dissent was that, despite an unprecedented international scientific effort in support of the IPCC to establish the causes and consequences of global warming, there was not the kind of scientific consensus that had promoted agreement on CFCs—at least not in 1997. At the time, there was disagreement over the significance of human activities and over projections of future change (a gap that has since

Emissions trading A system that provides that the rights to emit carbon can be bought and sold.

Joint Implementation A system that allows a developed country to receive credits against its own emissions-reduction target by financing projects in another developed country, the argument being that money is best spent where it can achieve the greatest reduction in world emissions of greenhouse gases.

WHAT'S YOUR WORLDVIEW?

The UN's Sustainable Development Goals, adopted in September 2015, are aimed at ending poverty, fighting inequality and injustice, and managing climate change by 2030. What factors work against success with climate-change goals? Are there any factors that suggest the global community might succeed?

Clean Development Mechanism A system that allows a developed country to receive credits against its own emissions-reduction target by financing projects in a developing country, the argument being that money is best spent where it can achieve the greatest reduction in world emissions of greenhouse gases.

narrowed dramatically). There were those who had an economic interest in denying or misrepresenting the science, including fossil-fuel interests and oil-producing countries, such as Saudi Arabia. At the other end of the spectrum, the Alliance of Small Island States, some of whose members' territory would disappear under projected sea-level rises, were desperately concerned that such projections be taken seriously.

Even though the effects of climate change are not fully understood, there is enough evidence for some nations to calculate that there might be benefits to them from climatic alterations. Regions of Russia, for example, might become more temperate with rises in mean temperature and thus more suitable for agricultural production (although one could argue equally well the extremely damaging effects of melting permafrost in Siberia). In North America, variations in rainfall patterns have already begun to disrupt agriculture that relies on irrigation. Snowfall patterns in the major mountain ranges are changing, and some species of frogs and insects—especially honeybees necessary for crop pollination—are slowly disappearing. One generalization that can be made with certainty is that the developing nations, with limited infrastructure and major populations located at sea level, are most vulnerable. In recognition of this and on the understanding that a certain level of warming is now inevitable, international attention has begun to shift toward the problem of adapting to the effects of climate change, as well as mitigating its causes.

At the heart of the international politics of climate change as a global environmental problem is the structural divide between North and South (see Chapters 8 and 9). One of the most significant principles set out in the UNFCCC was that of common but differentiated responsibilities. That is to say, although climate change was the common concern of all, it had been produced as a consequence of the development of the old industrialized nations, and it was their responsibility to take the lead in cutting emissions.

The Kyoto Protocol, in its first phase, accomplished relatively little, and much more greenhouse gas reduction occurred under the Montreal Protocol in the same period, for CFCs are also powerful greenhouse gases. Given the fact that by 2005 developing countries were responsible for the majority of current emissions, and that in 2007 China overtook the United States as the primary emitter, it became increasingly clear that an effective climate agreement would have to include all the Parties to the Convention. This continues to be very difficult to achieve because of the legitimate claims to development and climate justice made by

When it began operation in September 2018, the Walney windfarm off the Cumbria coast of the United Kingdom was the largest in the world and a central component of the UK's goal to decarbonize power generation by 2030. Energy produced from wind and solar sources must increase if we are to meet the emissions reductions promised as part of the Paris Accord. Is a change to new energy forms possible when the fossil-fuel industries are so politically powerful in most developed countries?

Southern countries and, of course, because many of the emissions from a country like China have been displaced by the globalization of production from Europe and America. It is also true that developed countries, suffering from the world economic crisis of 2008, were not prepared to take risks with their economies. In 2007, it was agreed that there would be two negotiation tracks, one on the future of Kyoto and the other on the future of the UNFCCC. The United States was prepared to participate in the latter because it avoided Kyoto "targets and timetables."

In 2009, the UNFCCC met in Copenhagen but failed to produce a new legally binding and comprehensive agreement on climate change. Instead, the United States and the BASIC countries (a coalition of large emerging economies [Brazil, South Africa, India, and China]) struck a deal known as the Copenhagen Accord. Unlike Kyoto, this agreement provided for countries to offer their "contributions" to emissions reductions that they regarded as appropriate. All countries would participate, breaking down the strict divide between developed and developing countries, but the principle of common but differentiated responsibilities would remain. How strictly contributions will be assessed and how far they will be legally binding remains to be seen.

The contributions offered under the Copenhagen Accord were not sufficient to put the world on a pathway that would avoid breaching the 2°C threshold. The Paris talks were an opportunity to lock in climate action commitments at the national level. The European Union pledged to cut its emissions by 40 percent, while the United States stated that it would cut its emissions by 26 to 28 percent by 2025. China agreed to cut its emissions as well.

The goal of limiting warming by 1.5°C set in Paris is better than the goal of 2°C that was set in Copenhagen, but it is a meaningless one if states do not take essential measures. How can they be encouraged to do so? One important way is to make sure that there is "transparent" reporting of national actions so that it will be clear whether governments are living up to their promises. Who will make certain countries meet their goals? The following is a list of outcomes from the Paris talks:

WHAT'S YOUR WORLDVIEW?

Few political leaders fail to recognize the current environmental challenges. However, when it comes to environmental issues, some nation-states are incrementalists (they want to work slowly toward environmental policy action) and others are postponers (they want to delay any action); a third group of leaders deny the very existence of major environmental challenges. With these different perspectives shaping policy debates, do you think the world will ever get its act together and effectively address some of these global issues?

- **Pledges to curb emissions** Before the conference began, some 180 countries had submitted plans or *intended nationally defined contributions* (INDCs) to cut their emissions. Nationally determined contributions are part of the agreement but are not legally binding. The aspects of the agreement that are binding cover procedures for reporting, transparency, and analysis. INDCs are part of the agreement but are not legally binding. It must be noted that existing INDCs are not sufficient to prevent global temperatures from rising beyond 2°C.

- **Long-term global goal for net zero emissions** Participants promised to reduce global emissions as soon as possible.

Common But Differentiated Responsibilities?

A key principle of the climate-change regime, written into the 1992 UNFCCC, was the notion of "common but differentiated responsibilities." This, in effect, meant that although all nations had to accept responsibility for the world's changing climate, it was developed nations that were immediately responsible because they had benefited from the industrialization generally regarded as the source of the excess carbon dioxide emissions (see Map 10.1).

Consider the relationship between national carbon dioxide emissions and share of global population. The United States emits around 15 to 16 percent of the global total but has only 4.5 percent of the global population. China is the world's biggest emitter of carbon dioxide, producing approximately 28 percent of the global total, and has nearly 20 percent of the world's population. On the other hand, the thirty-five least developed nations emit less than 1 percent and account for more than 10 percent of the world's population.

Accordingly, the developed countries were listed in Annex I of the convention, and it was agreed that they, rather than developing countries, would have to lead the way in making emissions reductions.

This approach was followed in the Kyoto Protocol, where only developed-country parties are committed to make reductions. Even before the protocol was agreed upon, the US Senate passed the Byrd-Hagel Resolution making it clear that it would not ratify any agreement where developing nations, who were now economic competitors of the United States, did not also need to make emissions reductions.

However, in 2004, the International Energy Agency published projections that underlined how globalization was radically changing the pattern of energy-related carbon dioxide emissions; it estimated that emissions would rise by 62 percent by 2030 but, most significantly, that at some point in the 2020s, developing-world emissions would overtake those of the developed Organisation for Economic Co-operation and Development (OECD)

countries. It therefore became clear that to have any chance of success, the future climate-change regime would have to include emissions reductions by countries such as China and India but that they in turn would not even consider reductions if the United States remained outside the Kyoto system.

The fundamental question is thus: *On what basis should countries be asked to reduce their emissions?* The most radical and equitable answer might be to give each individual a fixed carbon allowance, probably allowing rich people to maintain something of their lifestyle by buying the allowances of the poor. A more likely alternative is to find ways of creating and then raising a global carbon price so that alternatives to fossil fuel become economically attractive. Which approach would you support? Why? What alternatives can you imagine?

For Discussion

1. Why is climate change such a politically charged issue?
2. Developing states want a chance to develop like the rich countries of the global North. What is the argument against their development? Should they care about the environment?
3. Economic interests and environmental concerns are often in conflict. As states develop, do they have a responsibility to prevent further environmental degradation?

Sources

"Global CO_2 Emissions Are Set to Stall in 2015," *The Economist*, December 8, 2015, www.economist.com/ blogs/graphicdetail/2015/12/climate-change.

"The Largest Producers of CO_2 Emissions Worldwide in 2015, Based on Their Share of Global CO_2 Emissions," *Statista*, accessed February 2, 2016, www.statista. com/statistics/271748/the-largest-emitters-of-co2-in-the-world/.

The goal is to reach net zero emissions between 2050 and 2100. The UN climate science panel has stated that net zero emissions must happen by 2070 to avoid major environmental problems.

• **Take stock every five years** The agreement includes a review mechanism aimed at checking on the national pledges every five years. In some cases, they will ask countries to ramp up their pledges to stay under 2°C. The first review will be in 2023.

- **Loss and damage** This is a mechanism for providing funds for countries that face major losses from extreme weather events. To get this accepted, the United States was protected from financial claims from vulnerable countries.
- **Money** Funds need to be provided to developing countries so that they can adapt to climate change and find alternatives to fossil fuels. Developed states will provide $100 billion a year beyond 2020. The agreement states that by 2025, the amount of the fund will be reassessed and will likely increase.

The increase of urban green spaces can help reduce heat and deal with air pollution. In Frankfurt, Germany, a growing number of businesses and private homes now have "green roofs," which help to clean the air of carbon dioxide and decrease water runoff. How are you "acting locally"?

Parties to the Paris conference will achieve a great deal if they work in a multilateral fashion toward goals related to climate change, economic development, and other social and political issues. Cooperation is critical for success, as is sacrifice and setting aside national interests for the good of global and common interests.

As we reported earlier in this chapter, the Katowice Conference of 2018 was an opportunity for the participants to firm up the commitments made at the Paris Conference by each country to cut carbon emissions and to figure out a way to measure progress toward both national and global goals. Participants also needed to address the need for funds to help developing countries meet their obligations and remain economically stable. Unfortunately, the conference resulted in what many analysts saw as inadequate, halfway measures.

The real puzzle is this: What will the United States do? The Trump administration sent a delegation to Bonn, but President Trump has announced that the United States would abandon the Paris climate agreement in 2020. In a possible balancing alternative, an American alliance of states, cities, corporations, and civil society participated and said they will work toward the goals of the Paris Agreement even if the federal government is not honoring it. The leader in this group is California, which has the fifth largest economy in the world.

Conclusion

In this chapter, we have seen that cooperation to protect the global environment, though sometimes difficult to achieve, is possible. The determinants of successful cooperation can be found in international-regime theory, beginning with the acceptance of proper norms of behavior because the costs of not cooperating are

Is the Human Game Coming to an End?

Bill McKibben is the founder of 350.org, one of the leading environmental organizations concerned with climate change. In his 2019 book *Falter: Has the Human Game Begun to Play Itself Out?* McKibben suggests that we are ill prepared to address the environmental challenges we now face. He makes the case that our problems involve more than climate change "Put simply, between ecological destruction and technological hubris, the human experiment is now in question" (1).

This is not an uplifting book, and when you consider the implications of climate change and the meager global response, the message should not be an optimistic one. We have made a case in this book that stories or narratives matter and often shape how we see the world. McKibben shares a story about turtle nests on the beach near NASA facilities and how humans have worked to protect those beaches so that life continues for those turtles. From his experience on those beaches, he draws two lessons that tell us much about his life, concerns, and accomplishments as a well-respected and knowledgeable environmental activist. The first lesson is that "we really do live on an unbearably beautiful planet" (254). The second lesson presents a dilemma. McKibben states that with all of the life on this planet, we humans are the only ones who can destroy the world as we know it—but we can also decide to save it. Changing our way of life and refraining from practices that increase global warming are options for us, but McKibben is not optimistic. In his view, humans are faltering and the human game is playing itself out.

Why is change so difficult when the scientific evidence tells us we must act? Are we incapable of embracing change? According to McKibben, the game may be playing itself out because of what he calls *leverage*. He never clearly defines leverage, but it seems to be related to the power and influence of wealthy oil and gas industry leaders. McKibben mentions the Koch brothers, Exxon, and other major industry players as those who seem to control our political system and thus have great influence over our policy choices. These actors use their leverage to prevent any meaningful policy responses to climate challenges.

McKibben points out that this continues even though climate change costs the US economy about $240 billion a year and the global loss is about $1.2 trillion a year. McKibben traces the excessive leverage given to the energy industry back to the Reagan administration, who successfully criticized President Carter as weak and ignorant of the strength of the US economy for his emphasis on solar energy and alternatives to fossil fuels. Carter created the US Department of Energy in 1977. Carter also directed his administration to make a one-year study on the future of the environment. Maybe things would have been different if the oil and gas corporations had not used their leverage to elect Reagan.

potentially too great. Indeed, the environmental issues we are faced with today—global climate change, desertification, and other environmental degradation—can become more severe and less manageable for future generations, as we have seen in our own brief history of the twentieth and early twenty-first century. Solving these issues now requires new perspectives and unprecedented cooperation on a global scale. In terms of climate change, the most significant environmental challenge, scientists suggest there is still hope to put the world on the pathway that avoids breaching the 1.5°C threshold. The December 2019 UN Conference on Climate Change is the twenty-fifth Conference of the Parties, but it will also be one of the most important ones as there is a great need for the parties to come up with solutions, and to do so fast, if we want to slow down the global warming process.

CONTRIBUTORS TO CHAPTER 10: *John Vogler, Steven L. Lamy, and John Masker*

KEY TERMS

Anthropocentric p. 387
Capacity building, p.395
Clean Development
 Mechanism, p. 401
Climate change, p. 395
Deep ecology, p. 389

Desertification, p. 386
Ecocentric, p. 387
Ecological footprint, p. 375
Ecologies, p. 375
Ecosystem, p. 386
Ecotopian, p. 387

Emissions trading, p. 401
Global commons, p. 396
Global environmental
 governance, p. 375
Greenhouse effect, p. 397
Joint Implementation, p. 401

Kyoto Protocol, p. 381
Specialized agencies, p. 378
State system, p. 385
Sustainable development,
 p. 378
Technology transfer, p. 394

REVIEW QUESTIONS

1. What are the possible connections, both negative and positive, between globalization and environmental change?

2. Why did environmental issues appear on the international agenda, and what were the key turning points?

3. Summarize the consequences of the 1972 UN Conference on the Human Environment and the 1992 UN Conference on Environment and Development.

4. How would you interpret the meaning of *sustainable development*?

5. How can regime concepts be applied to the study of international environmental cooperation?

6. Can international trade and environmental protection ever be compatible?

7. Why did the framework convention/control protocol prove useful in the cases of stratospheric-ozone depletion and climate change?

8. How does the "tragedy of the commons" story help illustrate the need for governance of the global commons?

9. Describe the free rider problem in relation to the climate-change regime.

10. Consider the possible security implications of the climate predictions made by the Intergovernmental Panel on Climate Change.

Learn more with this chapter's digital tools, including the Oxford Insight Study Guide, at **www.oup.com/he/lamy6e**.

The Environment: Images and Options

Introduction

This exercise asks students to evaluate different and contending images of the future. These images of the future consider environmental, political, economic, and sociocultural factors.

 Reluctantly, many citizens are now coming to the realization that there are real environmental costs associated with humankind's goal to achieve "the good life." Citizens and leaders alike are also now recognizing the potential challenges posed by continuing policies that abuse the delicate ecological balance. In this exercise you will explore these challenges to economic and political security and the good life.

THINKING ABOUT GLOBAL POLITICS   *continued*

Procedure

Before beginning to explore the four alternative futures, read and review journal articles or texts that explore environmental problems associated with the contending images. Here are some suggested readings:

- The World Commission on Environment and Development, *Our Common Future* (New York: Oxford University Press, 1987)
- Barry Hughes, *World Futures: A Critical Analysis of Alternatives* (Baltimore: Johns Hopkins University Press, 1985)
- Robert Woyach, "Global Resources and Growth," in S. Lamy (ed.), *Contemporary International Issues* (Boulder, CO: Lynne Rienner, 1988)

   Second, review the different elements of the four possible futures. What are the fundamental similarities and differences among these images? Consider which future you feel would be most beneficial to you and your family.

Would this future create a world society in which all people could benefit? Why or why not? Which future would result in the following conditions?

1. Full employment
2. Less air pollution
3. More time for recreational activities
4. Less government
5. Greater equality
6. More citizen participation
7. Exploration and use of alternative energy sources
8. A world economy that encourages equitable and balanced growth
9. A reduction of waste and overconsumption
10. Less spending on military
11. More economic opportunities
12. Increased conflict

Debriefing Questions

1. What image of the future is challenged by a more balanced ecological view?
2. Do these images of the future correspond in any way with the different theories in Chapter 3?
3. Why are environmental issues becoming so significant in international politics?
4. Is a sustainable development strategy a possibility for the future? (Sustainable development is usually defined as a process of development that meets the needs of the present without compromising the ability of future generations to meet their own needs.)

The Four Possible Futures

	Future One	Future Two	Future Three	Future Four
Society	A society that provides the necessities for all while encouraging equal opportunities for self-development.	A free-enterprise society in which major economic growth provides economic benefits for all.	A society in which people recognize the limits to uncontrolled growth; people limit personal wealth, build communities that are in harmony with nature, and encourage reduction of waste.	A society in which independent people are given opportunities to develop themselves without harming the environment.

THINKING ABOUT GLOBAL POLITICS *continued*

	Future One	Future Two	Future Three	Future Four
	As well as being individuals, most people live in social groups. People need support from one another to grow and be happy.	People benefit most when there is equal opportunity for all people to seek their own best interest. Government must not tell them what to do or what not to do.	People must cooperate, not compete. They must blend their own self-interest into that of the greater good.	Well-informed individuals can exercise freedom of choice to satisfy their own interest. This will contribute to creative problem solving and increased well-being for all.
Environment	The world around us is to be used. New inventions will make some resources (e.g., the sun and wind) useful before or after others (coal and gas) are used up.	The land and sea around us are full of riches. They should be used to the fullest in making us happy and prosperous.	It is important to preserve the balance between ourselves and the land and sea around us. They belong both to us and to those who come after us.	By inventing new ways of using our resources, we can prosper without harming our natural riches.
Government	Central government should be strong and guarantee a job for all with equal pay for equal work. It must also allow people to develop private businesses.	Central government should play a very limited role in our lives. Its main jobs are to keep peace at home and protect us from attack.	Attention should be turned away from central government and toward local community government. Local government aids social and natural harmony.	Central government should give some support to its citizens. It should provide education and information and protect our natural resources.
Economics	Maximum effort will be made to cut our dependency on foreign resources. The government will pay for basic human services such as healthcare and education.	Large-scale industry can best use the natural resources of our land and oceans. They are most fit to lead development and make the most money in a world eager to buy our goods.	Local economies promote doing more with less in the design of all systems and question the ever-growing demand for consumer goods. Industries favor reuse or recycling of materials.	New industries with advanced equipment and the invention of new technologies should be encouraged. All new industries must be responsible for using our resources with care.

GLOSSARY

Absolute gains The notion that all states seek to have more power and influence in the system to secure their national interests. Offensive neorealists are also concerned with increasing power relative to other states. One must have enough power to secure interests and more power than any other state in the system—friend or foe.

Acquiescent strategy A foreign policy strategy in which a state defers to the interests of a major power.

Adaptation strategies Changes in foreign policy behavior in reaction to changes in the international system or international events and adjusting national goals to conform to the effects of events external to that state.

African Union (AU) Created in 2002 and consisting of fifty-five member states, this union was formed as a successor to the Organization of African Unity. It maintains fourteen goals primarily centered on African unity and security, human rights, peace security and stability, economy, sustainable development, and equality.

Al Qaeda Most commonly associated with Osama bin Laden, "The Base" (its meaning in Arabic) is a religious-based group whose fighters swear an oath of fealty to the leadership that succeeded bin Laden.

Anarchic system A realist description of the international system that suggests there is no common power or central governing structure.

Anarchy A system operating in the absence of any central government. It does not imply chaos but, in realist theory, the absence of political authority.

Anthropocentric An ethical standpoint that views humans as the central factor in considerations of right and wrong action in and toward nature.

Appeasement A policy of making concessions to a territorially acquisitive state in the hope that settlement of more modest claims will assuage that state's expansionist appetites.

Arab Spring Protests and revolutionary uprisings that began in Tunisia in 2010 and spread across Egypt, Libya, Syria, Yemen, Bahrain, Saudi Arabia, and Jordan in 2011. At their core was a desire for more democratic and transparent political systems and more open and equitable economic systems.

Armistice A cease-fire agreement between enemies in wartime. In the case of World War I, the armistice began at 11 a.m. on November 11, 1918.

Arms embargo Similar to economic sanctions, an arms embargo stops the flow of arms from one country to another.

Arms race A central concept in realist thought. As states build up their military to address real or perceived threats to their national security, they may create insecurity in other states. These states in turn develop their military capacities and thus begin an arms race. This never-ending pursuit of security creates the condition we know as a security dilemma.

Association of Southeast Asian Nations (ASEAN) A geopolitical and economic organization of several countries located in Southeast Asia. Initially formed as a display of solidarity against communism, it has since redefined and broadened its aims to include the acceleration of economic growth and the promotion of regional peace.

Asymmetric conflicts In symmetric warfare, armies with comparable weapons, tactics, and organizational structures do battle. Wars are fought on near-equal terms. When stakes are high and those actors in conflict are not equal in terms of weapons and technology, the weaker side adopts asymmetric tactics such as guerrilla warfare, roadside bombs, attacks on civilians, and other terrorist tactics.

Balance of power In the international system, a state of affairs in which there is parity and stability among competing forces, and no one state is sufficiently strong to dominate all the others. Realists believe that a balance of power among great powers is the only way to provide global stability.

Bipolar order or bipolarity An international political order in which two states dominate all others. It is often used to describe the nature of the international system when the two superpowers, the Soviet Union and the United States, were dominant powers during the Cold War.

Blitzkrieg The German term for "lightning war." This was an offensive strategy that used the combination of mechanized forces—especially tanks—and aircraft as mobile artillery to exploit breaches in an enemy's front line.

Bretton Woods system A system of economic and financial accords that created the International Monetary Fund, the World Bank, and the General Agreement on Tariffs and Trade/World Trade Organization following World War II. It is named after the hamlet in northern New Hampshire where leaders from forty-four countries met in 1944.

Capacity building The provision of funds and technical training to allow developing countries to participate in global environmental governance.

Capital controls The monetary policy device that a government uses to regulate the flows into and out of a country's capital account (i.e., the flows of investment-oriented money into and out of a country or currency).

Capitalism A system of production in which human labor and its products are commodities that are bought and sold in the marketplace.

Charter rights Civil liberties guaranteed in a written document such as a constitution.

Civic nationalism The idea that an association of people can identify themselves as belonging to the nation and have equal and shared political rights and allegiance to similar political procedures.

Civil society The totality of all individuals and groups in a society who are not acting as participants in any government institutions or acting in the interests of commercial companies.

Clandestine or "sleeper" cell Usually, a group of people sent by an intelligence organization or terrorist network that remains dormant in a target country until activated by a message to carry out a mission, which could include prearranged attacks.

Class A social group that in Marxism is identified by its relationship with the means of production and the distribution of societal resources. Thus, we have the bourgeoisie (the owners or upper classes) and the proletariat (the workers).

Classical realism The belief that it is fundamentally the nature of people and the state to act in a way that places interests over ideologies. The drive for power and the will to dominate are held to be fundamental aspects of human nature.

Clean Development Mechanism A system that allows a developed country to receive credits against its own emissions-reduction target by financing projects in a developing country, the argument being that money is best spent where it can achieve the greatest reduction in world emissions of greenhouse gases.

Climate change A change in the statistical distribution of weather over periods that range from decades to millions of years. It can be a change in the average weather or a change in the distribution of weather events.

Coercive diplomacy The use of diplomatic and military methods that force a state to concede to another state. These methods may include the threat of force and the mobilization of the military to gradually "turn the screw" but exclude the actual use of force. The implication is that war is the next step if diplomacy fails.

Cold War The period from 1946 to 1991 defined by ideological conflict and rivalry between the United States and the Soviet Union. This was a global struggle for the hearts and minds of citizens around the world that was characterized by political conflict, military competition, proxy wars, and economic competition.

Collective security An arrangement where "each state in the system accepts that the security of one is the concern of all, and agrees to join in a collective response to aggression" (Roberts and Kingsbury 1993, 30).

Common security At times called "cooperative security," it stresses noncompetitive approaches and cooperative approaches through which states—both friends and foes—can achieve security. It is the belief that no one is secure until all people are secure from threats of war.

Community A human association in which members share common symbols and wish to cooperate to realize common objectives.

Comparative advantage A theory developed by David Ricardo stating that two countries will both gain from trade if, in the absence of trade, they have different relative costs for producing the same goods. Even if one country is more efficient in the production of all goods than the other (absolute advantage), both countries will still gain by trading with each other as long as they have different relative efficiencies.

Concert of Europe An informal institution created in 1815 by the five great powers of Europe (Austria, Britain, France, Prussia, and Russia), whereby they agreed on controlling revolutionary forces, managing the balance of power, and accepting interventions to keep current leaders in power. This system kept the peace in Europe from 1815 until World War I.

Congress of Vienna A meeting of major European leaders (1814–1815) that redrew the political map of Europe after the Napoleonic Wars. The congress was an attempt to restore a conservative political order in the continent.

Constructivism An approach to international politics that concerns itself with the centrality of ideas and human consciousness. As constructivists have examined global politics, they have been broadly interested in how the structure constructs the actors' identities and interests, how their interactions are organized and constrained by that structure, and how their very interaction serves to either reproduce or transform that structure.

Containment An American political strategy for resisting perceived Soviet expansion.

Cosmopolitan culture A pattern of relations within which people share the same goals and aspirations, generally to improve that culture for all members.

Cosmopolitan democracy A condition in which international organizations, transnational corporations, and global markets are accountable to the peoples of the world.

Critical theory Theories that are critical of the status quo and reject the idea that things can be fixed under the present system. These theories challenge core assumptions of the dominant paradigm and argue for transformation and not just reform.

Deep ecology Often identified with the Norwegian philosopher Arne Naess, the core belief is that the living environment has a right to live and flourish. The "deep" refers to the need to think deeply about the impact of human life on the environment.

Defensive realism A structural theory of realism that views states as security maximizers—more concerned with absolute power as opposed to relative power. According to this view, it is unwise for states to try to maximize their share of power and seek hegemony.

Democratic deficit Leaders have created many policy-making institutions at the global, regional, and national levels with policymaking power led by individuals who are appointed and not elected. Thus, policy decisions are not subject to review by citizens.

Democratic peace thesis A central plank of liberal-internationalist thought, the democratic peace thesis makes two claims: first, liberal polities exhibit restraint in their relations with other liberal polities (the so-called separate peace), but second, they are imprudent in relations with authoritarian states. The validity of the democratic peace thesis has been fiercely debated in the international relations literature.

Deregulation The removal of all regulation so that market forces, not government policy, control economic developments.

Desertification The extreme deterioration of land in arid and dry subhumid areas due to loss of vegetation and soil moisture; it results chiefly from human activities and is influenced by climatic variations. This condition is principally caused by overgrazing, overdrafting of groundwater, and diversion of water from rivers for human consumption and industrial use; all of these processes are fundamentally driven by overpopulation.

Détente The relaxation of tension between East and West; Soviet-American détente lasted from the late 1960s to the late 1970s and was characterized by negotiations and nuclear arms control agreements.

Development In the orthodox view, development is a top-down process that relies on "expert knowledge," usually Western and definitely external, and involves large capital investments in large projects, advanced technology, and expansion of the private sphere. In the alternative view, development is a bottom-up process that is participatory, relies on appropriate (often local) knowledge and technology, and involves small investments in small-scale projects and protection of the commons.

Diplomacy The process by which international actors communicate as they seek to resolve conflicts without going to war and find solutions to complex global problems.

Doctrine A stated principle of government policy, mainly in foreign or military affairs, or the set of beliefs held and taught by an individual or political group.

Domestic Sources or National Attributes Factors at this level include a state's history, traditions, and political, economic, cultural, and social structures, as well as military power, economic wealth, and demographics, and more permanent elements like geographic location and resource base.

Ecocentric Having a nature- or ecology-centered rather than a human-centered set of values.

Ecological footprint A measure that demonstrates the load placed on Earth's carrying capacity by individuals or nations. It does this by estimating the area of productive land and water system required to sustain a population at its specified standard of living.

Ecologies The communities of plants and animals that supply raw materials for all living things.

Economic base For Marxists, the substructure of the society is the relationship between owners and workers. Capitalists own the means of production and control technology and resources. The workers are employed by the capitalists, and they are alienated, exploited, and estranged from their work and their society.

Economic sanctions A tool of statecraft that seeks to get a state to behave by coercion of a monetary kind—for example, freezing banking assets, cutting aid programs, or banning trade.

Ecosystem A system of interdependent living organisms that share the same habitat, functioning together with all of the physical factors of the environment.

Ecotopian Someone who believes in protecting and preserving the environment and promotes progressive political goals such as environmental sustainability, social justice, and economic well-being.

Electronic commerce The buying and selling of products and services over the telephone or internet. Amazon and eBay are examples of leaders in this area of commerce.

Embedded liberalism A liberal international economic order based on the pursuit of free trade but allowing an appropriate role for state intervention in the market in support of national security and national and global stability.

Emissions trading A system that provides that the rights to emit carbon can be bought and sold.

Empire A distinct type of political entity, which may or may not be a state, possessing both a home territory and foreign territories. This may include conquered nations and colonies.

Enlightenment A movement associated with rationalist thinkers of the eighteenth century. Key ideas (which some would argue remain mottoes for our age) include secularism, progress, reason, science, knowledge, and freedom. The motto of the Enlightenment is *"Sapere aude!"* (Have courage to know!) (Kant 1991, 54).

Equity A number of equal portions in the nominal capital of a company; the shareholder thereby owns part of the enterprise; also called "stock" or "share."

Ethic of responsibility For realists, it represents the limits of ethics in international politics; it involves the weighing up of consequences and the realization that positive outcomes may result from amoral actions.

Ethics Ethical studies in international relations and foreign policy include the identification, illumination, and application of relevant moral norms to the conduct of foreign policy and assessing the moral architecture of the international system.

Ethnonationalism A strain of nationalism marked by the desire of an ethnic community to have absolute authority over its own political, economic, and social affairs. Loyalty and identity shift from the state to an ethnic community that seeks to create its own state.

European Union (EU) The union formally created in 1992 following the signing of the Maastricht Treaty. The origins of the European Union can be traced back to 1951 and the creation of the European Coal and Steel Community, followed in 1957 with a broader customs union (the Treaty of Rome, 1958). Originally a grouping of six countries in 1957, "Europe" grew by adding new members in 1973, 1981, and 1986. Since the fall of the planned economies in Eastern Europe in 1989, Europe has grown and now includes twenty-eight member states.

Failed or collapsed state A state that fails to provide basic services for its citizens. Such a state cannot protect its boundaries, provide a system of law and order, or maintain a functioning marketplace and means of exchange.

Feminism A political project to understand and to end women's inequality and oppression. Feminist theories tend to be critical of the biases of the discipline. Many feminists focus their research on the areas where women are excluded from the analysis of major international issues and concerns.

Fixed exchange rate The price a currency will earn in a hard currency. Here a government is committed to keep it at a specific value.

Floating exchange rate The market decides what the actual value of a currency is compared to other currencies.

Foreign direct investment (FDI) The capital speculation by citizens or organizations of one country into markets or industries in another country.

Foreign policy style Often shaped by a state's political culture, history, and traditions, this describes how a country deals with other states and how it approaches any decision-making situation. For example, does it act unilaterally or multilaterally? Does it seek consensus on an agreement or does it go with majority rule?

Foreign policy tradition A tradition that includes national beliefs about how the world works and a list of national interests and priorities based on these beliefs. It also refers to past actions or significant historical events that act as analogs and give guidance to leaders about what strategy would best secure their national interests.

Foreign policy The articulation of national interests and the means chosen to secure those interests, both material and ideational, in the international arena.

Fourteen Points President Woodrow Wilson's vision of international society, first articulated in January 1918, included the principle of self-determination, the conduct of diplomacy on an open (not secret) basis, and the establishment of an association of nation-states to provide guarantees of independence and territorial integrity (League of Nations).

Fragile state A state that has not yet failed but whose leaders lack the will or capacity to perform core state functions.

Free market A market ruled by the forces of supply and demand, where all buying and selling is not constrained by government regulations or interventions.

Free trade An essential element of capitalism that argues for no barriers or minimal barriers to the exchange of goods, services, and investments among states.

Functionalism An idea formulated by early proponents of European integration that suggests cooperation should begin with efforts aimed at resolving specific regional or transnational problems. It is assumed that resolution of these problems will lead to cooperation, or spillover, in other policy areas.

Futures Derivatives that oblige a buyer and seller to complete a transaction at a predetermined time in the future at a price agreed on today. Futures are also known as "forwards."

G20, or Group of Twenty An assembly of governments and leaders from twenty of the world's largest economies: Argentina, Australia, Brazil, Canada, China, France, Germany, India, Indonesia, Italy, Japan, Mexico, Republic of Korea, Russian Federation, Saudi Arabia, South Africa, Turkey, United Kingdom, United States, and the European Union.

Genocide The deliberate and systematic extermination of an ethnic, national, tribal, or religious group.

Glasnost A policy of greater openness pursued by Soviet leader Mikhail Gorbachev from 1985, involving more toleration of internal dissent and criticism.

Global commons The areas and resources not under national sovereignty that belong to no single country and are the responsibility of the entire world. The oceans beyond the two-hundred-mile limit, outer space, and Antarctica are global commons areas.

Global environmental governance The performance of global environmental regulative functions, often in the absence of a central government authority. It usually refers to the structure of international agreements and organizations but can also involve governance by the private sector or nongovernmental organizations.

Global factors Lorem ipsum dolor sit amet, usu indoctum accommodare ad, latine copiosae consulatu mel at, eum ex principes gubergren mediocritatem. Vis commodo utroque sensibus ea, inani accumsan consequuntur ea vix, te prompta interesset per.

Global goods Products that are made for a global market and are available across the world.

Global governance The regulation and coordination of transnational issue areas by nation-states, international and regional organizations, and private agencies through the establishment of international regimes. These regimes may focus on problem solving or the simple enforcement of rules and regulations.

Global politics The politics of global social relations in which the pursuit of power, interests, order, and justice transcends regions and continents.

Global polity The collective structures and processes by which "interests are articulated and aggregated, decisions are made, values allocated and policies conducted through international or transnational political processes" (Ougaard 2004, 5).

Global sourcing Obtaining goods and services across geopolitical boundaries. Usually, the goal is to find the least expensive labor and raw material costs and the lowest taxes and tariffs.

Globalization A historical process involving a fundamental shift or transformation in the spatial scale of human social organization that links distant communities and expands the reach of power relations across regions and continents.

Government The people and agencies that have the power and legitimate authority to determine who gets what, when, where, and how within a given territory.

Great Depression The global economic collapse that ensued following the Wall Street stock market crash in October 1929. Economic shock waves rippled around a world already densely interconnected by webs of trade and foreign direct investment.

Great power A state that has the political, economic, and military resources to shape the world beyond its borders. In most cases, such a state has the will and capacity to define the rules of the international system.

Greenhouse effect The trapping of the sun's warmth in Earth's lower atmosphere due to gases that act like the glass of a greenhouse.

Gross domestic product (GDP) The sum of all economic activity that takes place within a country.

Grotian tradition A liberal tradition in international relations theory named for Hugo Grotius that emphasizes the rule of law and multilateral cooperation. Grotians believe the international system is not anarchic, but interdependent: A society of states is created in part by international law, treaties, alliances, and diplomacy, which states are bound by and ought to uphold.

Hard power The material threats and inducements leaders employ to achieve the goals of their state.

Hegemony A system regulated by a dominant leader, or political (and/or economic) domination of a region. It also means power and control exercised by a leading state over other states.

Holocaust The attempts by the Nazis to murder the Jewish population of Europe. Some 6 million Jewish people were killed in concentration camps, along with a further million that included Soviet prisoners, Roma, Poles, communists, homosexuals, and the physically or mentally disabled.

Human development The notion that it is possible to improve the lives of people. Basically, it is about increasing the number of choices people have. These may include living a long and healthy life, access to education, and a better standard of living.

Human rights The inalienable rights such as life, liberty, and the pursuit of happiness that one is entitled to because one is human.

Human security The security of people, including their physical safety, their economic and social well-being, respect for their dignity, and the protection of their human rights.

Humanitarian intervention The use of military force by external actors to end a threat to people within a sovereign state.

Hyperpower The situation of the United States after the Cold War ended. With the Soviet Union's military might greatly diminished and China having primarily only regional power-projecting capability, the United States was unchallenged in the world.

Idealism Referred to by realists as utopianism since it underestimates the logic of power politics and the constraints this imposes on political action. Idealism as a substantive theory of international relations is generally associated with the claim that it is possible to create a world of peace based on the rule of law.

Ideational/ideal interest The psychological, moral, and ethical goals of a state as it sets foreign and domestic policy.

Identity The understanding of the self in relationship to an "other." Identities are social and thus always formed in relationship to others. Constructivists generally hold that identities shape interests; we cannot know what we want unless we know who we are. But because identities are social and produced through interactions, identities can change.

Immigration controls A government's control of the number of people who may work, study, or relocate to its country. It may include quotas for certain national groups for immigration.

Imperialism The practice of foreign conquest and rule in the context of global relations of hierarchy and subordination. It can lead to the establishment of an empire.

Individual/Human Dimension This level of analysis explores the range of variables that can affect leaders' policy choices and implementation strategies. Belief systems, personality factors, and other psychological factors often influence decision-making.

Integration A process of ever-closer union between states in a regional or international context. The process often begins with cooperation to solve technical problems.

Intercontinental ballistic missiles (ICBMs) Weapons system the United States and Soviet Union developed to threaten each other with destruction. The thirty- to forty-minute flight times of the missiles created a situation that is sometimes called "mutually assured destruction" (MAD) or "the balance of terror."

Interdependence A condition where states (or peoples) are affected by decisions taken by others. Interdependence can be symmetric (i.e., both sets of actors are affected equally) or asymmetric (i.e., the impact varies between actors).

International Court of Justice (ICJ) The main judicial organ of the United Nations consisting of fifteen judges elected jointly by the General Assembly and Security Council. The ICJ handles disputes between states, not individuals and states, and although a state does not have to participate in a case, if it elects to do so it must obey the decision.

International institutions Complexes of norms, rules, and practices that prescribe behavioral roles, constrain activity, and shape expectations.

International law The formal rules of conduct that states acknowledge or contract between themselves.

International nongovernmental organization (INGO) A formal nongovernmental organization with members from at least three countries.

International organization Any institution with formal procedures and formal membership from three or more countries. The minimum number of countries is set at three, rather than two, because multilateral relationships have significantly greater complexity than bilateral relationships.

International relations The study of the interactions of states (countries) and other actors in the international system.

Interparadigm debate The debate between the main theoretical approaches in the field of global politics.

Intersectionality A way of understanding and analyzing the complexity in the world, in people, and in human experiences. The events and conditions of social and political life and the self can seldom be understood as shaped by one factor. They are generally shaped by many factors in diverse and mutually influencing ways.

Intervention The direct involvement within a state by an outside actor to achieve an outcome preferred by the intervening agency without the consent of the host state.

Intrafirm trade The international trade from one branch of a transnational corporation to an affiliate of the same company in a different country.

Intransigent foreign policy A foreign policy that challenges the rules established by the great powers or rule-making states.

Jihad In Arabic, *jihad* means "struggle." Jihad can refer to a purely internal struggle to be a better Muslim or a struggle to make society more closely align with the teachings of the Koran.

Joint Implementation A system that allows a developed country to receive credits against its own emissions-reduction target by financing projects in another developed country, the argument being that money is best spent where it can achieve the greatest reduction in world emissions of greenhouse gases.

Kantian tradition A revolutionary tradition in international relations theory named for Immanuel Kant that emphasizes human interests over state interests.

Kyoto Protocol A global environmental treaty passed in 1997 that set binding targets for thirty-seven industrialized countries and the European community for reducing greenhouse gas emissions.

League of Nations The first permanent collective international security organization aimed at preventing future wars and resolving global problems. The League failed due to the unwillingness of the United States to join and the inability of its members to commit to a real international community.

Legitimacy An authority that is respected and recognized by those it rules and by rulers or leaders of other states. The source of legitimacy can be laws or a constitution and the support of the society.

Levels of analysis Analysts of global politics may examine factors at various levels—such as individual, domestic, systemic, and global—to explain actions and events. Each level provides possible explanations on a different scale.

Liberal account of rights The belief that humans have inherent rights that the state has a responsibility to protect.

Liberal democracy A state with democratic or representative government and a capitalist economy that promotes multilateralism and free trade. Domestic interests, values, and institutions shape foreign policy. Liberal democracies champion freedom of the individual, constitutional civil and political rights, and laissez-faire economic arrangements.

Liberal feminism A position that advocates equal rights for women but also supports a more progressive policy agenda, including social justice, peace, economic well-being, and ecological balance.

Liberal internationalism A perspective that seeks to transform international relations to emphasize peace, individual freedom, and prosperity and to replicate domestic models of liberal democracy at the international level.

Liberalism of privilege The perspective that developed democratic states have a responsibility to spread liberal values for the benefit of all peoples of Earth.

Liberalism A theoretical approach that argues for human rights, parliamentary democracy, and free trade—while also maintaining that all such goals must begin *within a state*.

Liberalization Government policies that reduce the role of the state in the economy, such as the dismantling of trade tariffs and barriers, the deregulation and opening of the financial sector to foreign investors, and the privatization of state enterprises.

Machiavellian tradition A tradition in international relations theory named for Niccolò Machiavelli that characterizes the international system as anarchic; states are constantly in conflict and pursue their own interests as they see fit.

Market democracies See *liberal democracy*.

Marshall Plan Officially known as the European Recovery Program, it was a program of financial and other economic aid for Europe after World War II. Proposed by Secretary of State George Marshall in 1948, it was offered to all European states, including the Soviet Union.

Marxism A theory critical of the status quo, or dominant capitalist paradigm. It is a critique of the capitalist political economy from the view of the revolutionary proletariat, or workers. Marxists' ideal is a stateless and classless society.

Material interest The physical goals of state officials as they set foreign and domestic policy.

Material structure An arrangement based on economic, political, and military resources.

Material Things we can see, measure, consume, and use, such as military forces, oil, and currency.

Materialism In this context, it is the spreading of a global consumer culture and popular-culture artifacts like music, books, and movies. Christopher Lasch called this the "ceaseless translation of luxuries into necessities." These elements are seen as undermining traditional cultural values and norms.

Middle powers These states, because of their position and past roles in international affairs, have very distinctive interests in world order. Middle powers are activists in international and regional forums, and they are confirmed multilateralists in most issue areas.

Military-industrial complex The power and influence of the defense industries and their special relationship with the military. Both have tremendous influence over elected officials.

Modern state A political unit within which citizens identify with the state and see the state as legitimate. This state has a monopoly over the use of force and is able to provide citizens with key services.

Modernization theory A theory that considers development synonymous with economic growth within the context of a free market international economy.

Most-favored-nation status The status granted to most trading partners that says trade rules with that country will be the same as those given to their most favored trading partner.

Multilateral diplomacy Cooperation among three or more states based on, or with a view to formulating, reciprocally binding rules of conduct.

Multilateralism The process by which states work together to solve a common problem.

Multinational corporation or enterprise (MNC/ MNE) A business or firm with administration, production, distribution, and marketing located in countries around the world. Such a business moves money, goods, services, and technology around the world depending on where the firm can make the most profit.

Munich Agreement of 1938 An agreement negotiated after a conference held in Munich between Germany and the United Kingdom and other major powers of Europe along with Czechoslovakia. It permitted Nazi Germany's annexation of Czechoslovakia's Sudetenland, an area along the Czech border that was inhabited primarily by ethnic Germans.

Nation A community of people who share a common sense of identity, which may be derived from language, culture, or ethnicity; this community may be a minority within a single country or live in more than one country.

National interest The material and ideational goals of a nation-state.

National security A fundamental value in the foreign policy of states secured by a variety of tools of statecraft, including military actions, diplomacy, economic resources, and international agreements and alliances. It also depends on a stable and productive domestic society.

National self-determination The right or desire of distinct national groups to become states and to rule themselves.

Nationalism The idea that the world is divided into nations that provide the overriding focus of political identity and loyalty, which in turn should be the basis for defining the population of states. Nationalism also can refer to this idea in the form of a strong sense of identity (*sentiment*) or organizations and movements seeking to realize this idea (*politics*).

Nation-state A political community in which the state claims legitimacy on the grounds that it represents all citizens, including those who may identify as a separate community or nation.

Natural law The idea that humans have an essential nature, which dictates that certain kinds of human goods are always and everywhere desired; because of this, there are common moral standards that govern all human relations, and these common standards can be discerned by the application of reason to human affairs.

Neoclassical realism A version of realism that combines both structural factors such as the distribution of power and unit-level factors such as the interests of states.

Neoliberalism Theory shaped by the ideas of commercial, republican, sociological, and institutional liberalism. Neoliberals see the international system as anarchic but believe relations can be managed by the establishment of international regimes and institutions. Neoliberals think actors with common interests will try to maximize absolute gains.

New International Economic Order (NIEO) A declaration adopted by the UN General Assembly calling for a restructuring of the international order toward greater equity for developing countries, particularly in reference to a wide range of issues related to trade, finance, commodities, and debt.

"New" terrorism See Postmodern or "new" terrorism.

New wars Wars of identity between different ethnic communities or nations, and wars that are caused by the collapse of states or the fragmentation of multiethnic states. Most of these new wars are internal or civil wars.

Niche diplomacy Every state has its national interests and its areas of comparative advantage over other international actors. This is its area of expertise and where it has the greatest interest. Hence, this is where the state concentrates its foreign policy resources.

Noncompliance The failure of states or other actors to abide by treaties or rules supported by international regimes.

Nongovernmental organization (NGO) An organization, usually a grassroots one, that has policy goals but is not governmental in its makeup. An NGO is any group of people relating to each other regularly in some formal manner and engaging in collective action, provided the activities are noncommercial and nonviolent and are not conducted on behalf of a government.

Nonintervention The principle that external powers should not intervene in the domestic affairs of sovereign states.

Non–nuclear weapon states (NNWS) A state that is party to the Treaty on the Non-Proliferation of

Nuclear Weapons, meaning that it does not possess nuclear weapons.

Nonpolar world A world in which there are many power centers, and many of them are not nation-states. Power is diffused and in many hands in many policy areas.

Nonpolar An international system in which power is not concentrated in a few states but is diffused among a variety of state and nonstate actors.

Nonstate actor Any participant in global politics that is neither acting in the name of government nor created and served by government. Nongovernmental organizations, terrorist networks, global crime syndicates, and multinational corporations are examples.

Normative orientation In foreign policy, promoting certain norms and values and being prescriptive in one's foreign policy goals.

Normative theory The systematic analyses of the ethical, moral, and political principles that either govern or ought to govern the organization or conduct of global politics; the belief that theories should be concerned with what ought to be rather than merely diagnosing what is.

Norms These specify general standards of behavior and identify the rights and obligations of states. Together, norms and principles define the essential character of a regime, and these cannot be changed without transforming the nature of the regime.

North Atlantic Treaty Organization (NATO) Organization established by treaty in April 1949 including twelve (later sixteen) countries from Western Europe and North America. The most important aspect of the NATO alliance was the US commitment to defend Western Europe. Today NATO has twenty-eight member states.

Nuclear deterrence Explicit, credible threats to use nuclear weapons in retaliation to deter an adversary from attacking with nuclear weapons.

Nuclear terrorism The use of or threat to use nuclear weapons or nuclear materials to achieve the goals of rogue states or revolutionary or radical organizations.

Offensive realism A structural theory of realism that views states as power maximizers.

Offshore finance centers The extraterritorial banks that investors use for a range of reasons, including the desire to avoid domestic taxes, regulations, and law enforcement agencies.

Oligarchs A term from ancient Greece to describe members of a small group that controls a state.

Options Derivatives that give parties a right (without obligation) to buy or sell at a specific price for a stipulated period of time up to the contract's expiration date.

Organization of African Unity (OAU) A regional organization founded in 1963 as a way to foster solidarity among African countries, promote African independence, and throw off the vestiges of colonial rule. The OAU had a policy of noninterference in member states, and it had no means for intervening in conflicts; as a result, this organization could be only a passive bystander in many violent conflicts.

Organization of American States (OAS) A regional international organization composed of thirty-five member states. It is the world's oldest regional organization, founded in 1890 as the International Union of American Republics; in 1948 it changed its name to the OAS. Its goals are to create "an order of peace and justice, to promote their solidarity, to strengthen their collaboration, and to defend their sovereignty, their territorial integrity, and their independence."

Ostpolitik The West German government's "Eastern Policy" of the mid- to late 1960s, designed to develop relations between West Germany and members of the Warsaw Pact.

Paradigm A model or example. In the case of international relations theory, the term is a rough synonym for "academic perspective." A paradigm provides the basis for a theory, describing what is real and significant in a given area so that we can select appropriate research questions.

Paradox A seemingly absurd or self-contradictory statement that, when investigated or explained, may prove to be well founded or true.

Peace enforcement An action designed to bring hostile parties to agreement; it may occur without the consent of the parties.

Peace of Utrecht (1713) The agreement that ended the War of the Spanish Succession and helped to consolidate the link between sovereign authority and territorial boundaries in Europe. This treaty refined the territorial scope of sovereign rights of states.

Peace of Westphalia (1648) A series of treaties that ended the Thirty Years' War and was crucial in delimiting the political rights and authority of European monarchs.

Peacekeeping The interposition of third-party military personnel to keep warring parties apart.

Peacemaking Active diplomatic efforts to seek a resolution to an international dispute that has already escalated.

Perestroika Gorbachev's policy of restructuring, pursued in tandem with glasnost and intended to modernize the Soviet political and economic system.

Pluralism A political theory holding that political power and influence in society do not belong just to the citizens nor only to elite groups in various sectors of society but are distributed among a wide number of groups in the society. It can also mean a recognition of ethnic, racial, and cultural diversity.

Positivists Analysts who use the scientific method to structure their research.

Postconflict peacebuilding Activities launched after a conflict has ended that seek to end the condition that caused the conflict.

Postmodern or "new" terrorism Groups and individuals subscribing to millennial and apocalyptic ideologies and system-level goals. Most value destruction for its own sake, unlike most terrorists in the past, who had specific goals, usually tied to a territory.

Postmodern state A political unit within which citizens are less nationalistic and more cosmopolitan in their outlook on both domestic and foreign policy.

Postmodernity An international system where domestic and international affairs are intertwined, national borders are permeable, and states have rejected the use of force for resolving conflict. The European Union is an example of the evolution of the state-centric system (Cooper 2003).

Post–Washington Consensus A slightly modified version of the Washington Consensus promoting economic growth through trade liberalization coupled with poverty-reduction policies.

Poverty According to the United Nations, poverty is a denial of choices and opportunities, a violation of human dignity. It means lack of basic capacity provided by material possessions or money to participate effectively in society.

Power This is a contested concept. Many political scientists believe that power is the capacity to do things and, in social and political situations, to affect others to get the outcome one wants. Sources of power include material or tangible resources and control over meaning or ideas.

Premodern state A state within which the primary identity of citizens or subjects is to national, religious, or ethnic communities.

Prescription Recommendations for state survival in the international system based on international relations traditions.

Preservative strategy A foreign policy aimed at preserving power and status in the international system.

Preventive diplomacy Measures that states take to keep a disagreement from escalating.

Problem-solving theory Realism and liberalism are problem-solving theories that address issues and questions within the dominant paradigm or the present system. How can we fix capitalism? How can we make a society more democratic? These are problem-solving questions that assume nothing is wrong with the core elements of the system.

Promotive foreign policy A foreign policy that promotes the values and interests of a state and seeks to create an international system based on these values.

Protectionism Not an economic policy but a variety of political actions taken to protect domestic industries from more efficient foreign producers. Usually, this means the use of tariffs, nontariff barriers, and subsidies to protect domestic interests.

Protectionist An economic policy of restraining trade between states through methods such as tariffs on imported goods, restrictive quotas, and a variety of other government regulations designed to allow "fair competition" among imports and goods and services produced domestically.

Protestant Reformation A social and political movement begun in 1517 in reaction to the widespread perception that the Catholic Church had become corrupt and had lost its moral compass.

Public diplomacy The use of media, the internet, and other cultural outlets to communicate the message of a state.

Radical liberalism The utopian side of liberalism best exemplified by the academic community called the

World Order Models Project. These scholars advocate a world in which states promote values like social justice, economic well-being, peace, and ecological balance. The scholars see the liberal order as predatory and clearly in need of transformation.

Rapprochement The re-establishment of more friendly relations between the People's Republic of China and the United States in the early 1970s.

Realism A theoretical approach that analyzes all international relations as the relation of states engaged in the pursuit of power. Realists see the international system as anarchic, or without a common power, and they believe conflict is endemic in the international system.

Realpolitik First used to describe the foreign policy of Bismarck in Prussia, it describes the practice of diplomacy based on the assessment of power, territory, and material interests, with little concern for ethical realities.

Reciprocity A form of statecraft that employs a retaliatory strategy, cooperating only if others do likewise.

Regime A set of implicit or explicit principles, norms, rules, and decision-making procedures around which actors' expectations converge in a given area of international relations. Often simply defined as a governing arrangement in a regional or global policy area.

Regional diversity Each region of the world has experienced economic development differently based on traditions, culture, historical development, and even geographic location.

Relative gains One of the factors that realists argue constrain the willingness of states to cooperate. States are less concerned about whether everyone benefits (absolute gains) and more concerned about whether someone may benefit more than someone else.

Responsibility to Protect Resolution (R2P) Resolution supported by the United Nations in 2005 to determine the international community's responsibility in preventing mass atrocities, reacting to crises, protecting citizens, rebuilding, and preventing future problems.

Revolution in Military Affairs (RMA) The effect generated by the marriage of advanced communications and information processing with state-of-the-art weapons and delivery systems. It is a means of overcoming the uncertainty and confusion that are part of any battle in war.

Risk culture A pattern of relations within which people share the same perils.

Security The measures taken by states to ensure the safety of their citizens, the protection of their way of life, and the survival of their nation-state. Security can also mean the ownership of property that gives an individual the ability to secure the enjoyment or enforcement of a right or a basic human need.

Security community A regional group of countries that have the same guiding philosophical ideals—usually liberal-democratic principles, norms, values, and traditions—and tend to have the same style of political systems.

Security dilemma In an anarchic international system (one with no common central power), when one state seeks to improve its security, it creates insecurity in other states.

Self-help In realist theory, in an anarchic system, states cannot assume other states will come to their defense even if they are allies. Each state must take care of itself.

Skyjackings The takeover of a commercial airplane for the purpose of taking hostages and using them to bargain for a particular political or economic goal.

Social movement A mode of collective action that challenges ways of life, thinking, dominant norms, and moral codes; seeks answers to global problems; and promotes reform or transformation in political and economic institutions.

Social structure An arrangement based on ideas, norms, values, and shared beliefs. According to constructivists, the social domain does not exist in nature but is constructed through processes of interaction and the sharing of meaning.

Society of states An association of sovereign states based on their common interests, values, and norms.

Soft power The influence and authority deriving from the attraction that a country's political, social, and economic ideas, beliefs, and practices have for people living in other countries.

Sovereign equality The idea that all countries have the same rights, including the right of noninterference in their internal affairs.

Sovereignty The condition of a state having control and authority over its own territory and being free from any higher legal authority. It is related to, but distinct from, the condition of a government being free from any external political constraints.

Special Drawing Right (SDR) Members of the International Monetary Fund (IMF) have the right to borrow this asset from the organization up to the amount that the country has invested in the IMF. The SDR is based on the value of a "basket" of the world's leading currencies: British pound, euro, Japanese yen, and US dollar.

Standard operating procedures (SOPs) The prepared-response patterns that organizations create to react to general categories of events, crises, and actions.

Standards of civilization A nineteenth-century, European discourse about which values and norms made a country civilized or barbaric and uncivilized. The conclusion was that civilized countries should colonize barbaric regions for the latter's benefit.

State sovereignty The concept that all countries are equal under international law and that they are protected from outside interference; this is the basis on which the United Nations and other international and regional organizations operate.

State system The regular patterns of interaction between states but without implying any shared values between them. This is distinguished from the view of a "society" of states.

State A legal territorial entity composed of a stable population and a government; it possesses a monopoly over the legitimate use of force; its sovereignty is recognized by other states in the international system.

Statecraft The methods and tools that national leaders use to achieve the national interests of a state.

Strategic Arms Reductions Treaty (START) Negotiations between the United States and Soviet Union over limiting nuclear arsenals began in 1982 and progressed at a very slow pace over eight years. The eventual treaty in 1991 broke new ground because it called for a reduction of nuclear arms rather than just a limit on the growth of these weapons.

Strategic Defense Initiative (SDI) A controversial strategic policy advocated by the Reagan administration and nuclear physicists such as Edward Teller, who helped create the hydrogen bomb. The plan, which was often derisively nicknamed "Star Wars," called for a defensive missile shield that would make Soviet offensive missiles ineffective by destroying them in flight.

Structural realism (neorealism) A theory of realism that maintains that the international system and the condition of anarchy or no common power push states and individuals to act in a way that places interests over ideologies. This condition creates a self-help system. The international system is seen as a structure acting on the state with individuals below the level of the state acting as agency on the state as a whole.

Superpower A state with a dominant position in the international system. It has the will and the means to influence the actions of other states in favor of its own interests, and it projects its power on a global scale to secure its national interests.

Superstructure The government or political structure that is controlled by those who own the means of production.

Supranational global organization An authoritative international organization that operates above the nation-state.

Supraterritoriality Social, economic, cultural, and political connections that transcend territorial geography.

Survival In this context, it is the survival of the person by the provision of adequate food, clean water, clothing, shelter, medical care, and protection from violence and crime.

Sustainable development Development that meets the needs of the present without compromising the ability of future generations to meet their own needs.

Systemic factors To most realists, the anarchic nature of international relations may be the most important factor at this level. However, the individual and collective actions states have taken to cope with anarchy via treaties, alliances, and trade conventions—formal contracts created by states in an attempt to provide order—also constitute significant systemic facto.

Tactics The conduct and management of military capabilities in or near the battle area.

Technology transfer The process of sharing skills, knowledge, technologies, methods of manufacturing, and facilities among governments and private actors (e.g., corporations) to ensure that scientific and technological developments are accessible to a wider range of users for application in new products, processes, materials, or services.

Terrorism The use of violence by nonstate groups or, in some cases, states to inspire fear by attacking civilians and/or symbolic targets and eliminating opposition groups. This is done for purposes such as drawing widespread attention to a grievance, provoking a severe response, or wearing down an opponent's moral resolve to effect political change.

Theocracy A state based on religion.

Theory A proposed explanation of an event or behavior of an actor in the real world. Definitions range from "an unproven assumption" to "a working hypothesis that proposes an explanation for an action or behavior." In international relations, we have intuitive theories, empirical theories, and normative theories.

Thirty Years' War (1618–1648) The last of the great wars in Europe fought nominally for religion.

Tradition In international relations, a way of thinking that describes the nature of international politics. Such traditions include Machiavellian, Grotian, Kantian, and Marxism as a critical theory.

Transborder Economic, political, social, or cultural activities crossing or extending across a border.

Transnational actor Any nongovernmental actor, such as a multinational corporation or a global religious humanitarian organization, that has dealings with any actor from another country or with an international organization.

Transnational advocacy network (TAN) A network of activists—often, a coalition of nongovernmental organizations—distinguishable largely by the centrality of principled ideas or values in motivating its formation.

Transnational corporation A company or business that has affiliates in different countries.

Transnational nonstate actor Any nonstate or nongovernmental actor from one country that has relations with any actor from another country or with an international organization.

Treaty of Versailles, 1919 The agreement that formally ended World War I (1914–1918).

Trench warfare Combat in which armies dug elaborate defensive fortifications in the ground, as both sides did in World War I. Because of the power of weapons like machine guns and rapid-fire cannons, trenches often gave the advantage in battle to the defenders.

Truman Doctrine A statement made by President Harry Truman in March 1947 that it "must be the policy of the United States to support free people who are resisting attempted subjugation by armed minorities or by outside pressures."

United Nations Founded in 1945 following World War II, it is an international organization composed of 193 member states dedicated to addressing issues related to peace and security, development, human rights, humanitarian affairs, and international law.

United Nations Charter (1945) The legal regime that created the United Nations. The charter defines the structure of the United Nations, the powers of its constitutive agencies, and the rights and obligations of sovereign states party to the charter.

United Nations Economic and Social Council (ECOSOC) This council is intended to coordinate the economic and social work of the United Nations and the UN family organizations. The ECOSOC has a direct link to civil society through communications with nongovernmental organizations.

United Nations General Assembly Often referred to as a "parliament of nations," it is composed of all member states, which meet to consider the world's most pressing problems. Each state has one vote, and a two-thirds majority in the General Assembly is required for decisions on key issues. Decisions reached by the General Assembly only have the status of recommendations and are not binding.

United Nations Secretariat The Secretariat carries out the administrative work of the United Nations as directed by the General Assembly, Security Council, and other organs. The Secretariat is led by the secretary-general, who provides overall administrative guidance.

United Nations Security Council The council made up of five permanent member states (sometimes called the P5)—namely, Great Britain, China, France, Russia, and the United States—and ten nonpermanent members. The P5 all have a veto power over all Security Council decisions.

United Nations Trusteeship Council Upon creation of the United Nations, this council was established to provide international supervision for eleven Trust Territories administered by seven member states in an effort to prepare them for self-government or independence. By 1994, all Trust Territories had attained self-government or independence, and the council now meets on an ad hoc basis.

Universal Declaration of Human Rights The principal normative document on human rights, adopted by the UN General Assembly in 1948 and accepted as authoritative by most states and other international actors.

Venture philanthropy The practice of supporting philanthropists or social entrepreneurs by providing them with networking and leveraging opportunities.

Veto power The right of the five permanent members of the Security Council (United States, Russia, China, France, and Great Britain) to forbid any action by the United Nations.

Warsaw Pact An agreement of mutual defense and military aid signed in May 1955 in response to West Germany's rearmament and entry into NATO. It comprised the USSR and seven communist states (though Albania withdrew support in 1961). The pact was officially dissolved in July 1991.

Washington Consensus The belief of key opinion formers in Washington that global welfare would be maximized by the universal application of neoliberal economic policies that favor a minimalist state and an enhanced role for the market.

Weapons of mass destruction (WMDs) A category defined by the United Nations in 1948 to include "atomic explosive weapons, radioactive material weapons, lethal chemical and biological weapons, and any weapons developed in the future which have characteristics comparable in destructive effects to those of the atomic bomb or other weapons mentioned above."

Widening school of international security Sometimes called the Copenhagen school, these are authors who extend the definition of security to include economic, political, societal, and environmental policy areas.

World Bank Group (WBG) A collection of five agencies, the first established in 1945, with head offices in Washington, DC. The WBG promotes development in medium- and low-income countries with project loans, structural-adjustment programs, and various advisory services.

World Trade Organization (WTO) A permanent institution established in 1995 to replace the provisional General Agreement on Tariffs and Trade (GATT). It has greater powers of enforcement and a wider agenda, covering services, intellectual property, and investment issues, as well as merchandise trade.

REFERENCES

Acharya, A. (2004), "A Holistic Paradigm," *Security Dialogue* 35: 355–356.

Acharya, A. (2007), *Promoting Human Security: Ethical, Normative and Educational Frameworks in South East Asia* (Paris: United Nations Educational, Scientific, and Cultural Organization).

Addams, J. (1922), *Peace and Bread in Time of War*, with introduction by Katherine Joslin (Urbana: University of Illinois Press, 2002 [reprint]).

Adler, E. (1992), "The Emergence of Cooperation: National Epistemic Communities and the International Evolution of the Idea of Nuclear Arms Control," *International Organization* 46: 101–145.

Allison, G. (1971), *Essence of Decision; Explaining the Cuban Missile Crisis* (Boston: Little, Brown).

Allison, G. (2000), "The Impact of Globalization on National and International Security." In J. S. Nye and J. D. Donahue (eds.), *Governance in a Globalizing World*, 72–85 (Washington, DC: Brookings Institution).

Andrew, H. (2002), "Norms and Ethics in International Relations." In W. Carlnaes, T. Risse, and B. Simmons (eds.), *Handbook of International Relations* (Thousand Oaks, CA: Sage).

Anheier, H., Glasius, M., and Kaldor, M. (eds.) (2004), *Global Civil Society Yearbook 2004* (London: Sage).

Armstrong, D. (1993), *Revolution and World Order: The Revolutionary State in International Society* (Oxford: Clarendon Press).

Aron, R. (1966), *The Century of Total War* (Garden City, NY: Doubleday).

Axworthy, L. (2003), *Navigating a New World* (Toronto: Alfred A. Knopf Canada).

Bacevich, A. (2008), "Introduction." In R. Niebuhr, *The Irony of American History* (Chicago: University of Chicago Press).

Bakker, E. (2006), *Jihadi Terrorists in Europe, Their Characteristics and the Circumstances in Which They Joined the Jihad: An Exploratory Study* (Clingendael: Netherlands Institute of International Relations).

Bank for International Settlements (1996), *International Banking and Financial Market Developments* (Basel: Bank for International Settlements).

Bank for International Settlements (2006), Semiannual OTC Derivatives Statistics at End-June 2006. www.bis.org/statistics (accessed June 25, 2007).

Bank for International Settlements (2015), Statistical Release: OTC Derivatives Statistics at End-June 2015. www.bis.org/publ/otc_hy1511.pdf (accessed February 12, 2016).

Barnett, M. (2011), "Social Constructivism." In J. Baylis, S. Smith, and P. Owens, *The Globalization of World Politics* (Oxford: Oxford University Press).

Barraclough, G. (ed.) (1984), *The Times Atlas of World History* (London: Times Books).

BBC News (2016), "Migrant Crisis: Migration to Europe Explained in Seven Charts." *BBC News*, March 4, www.bbc.com/news/world-europe-34131911 (accessed March 8, 2016).

Beitz, C. (1979), *Political Theory and International Relations* (Princeton, NJ: Princeton University Press).

Bellamy, A. J. (2002), *Kosovo and International Society* (Basingstoke, UK: Palgrave).

Bello, W. (1994), *Dark Victory: The United States, Structural Adjustment, and Global Poverty* (London: Pluto Press).

Bennett, J., and George, S. (1987), *The Hunger Machine* (Cambridge, UK: Polity Press).

Bethell, L. (1970), *The Abolition of the Brazilian Slave Trade: Britain, Brazil, and the Slave Trade Question 1807–1869* (Cambridge, UK: Cambridge University Press).

Bloom, M. (2005), *Dying to Win: The Allure of Suicide Terror* (New York: Columbia University Press).

Bloomberg News (2016), "China Trade Surplus Swells as Exports Rise in Boost for Yuan." *Bloomberg News*, January 12, www.bloomberg.com/news/articles/2016-01-13/china-s-exports-unexpectedly-rebound-as-yuan-weakness-kicks-in (accessed February 12, 2016).

Booth, K. (1999), "Three Tyrannies." In T. Dunne and N. J. Wheeler (eds.), *Human Rights in Global Politics* (Cambridge, UK: Cambridge University Press).

Booth, K. (ed.) (2004), *Critical Security Studies in World Politics* (Boulder, CO: Lynne Rienner).

Booth, K., and Dunne, T. (1999), "Learning Beyond Frontiers." In T. Dunne and N. J. Wheeler (eds.), *Human Rights in Global Politics*, 303–328 (Cambridge, UK: Cambridge University Press).

Braun, L. (1987), *Selected Writings on Feminism and Socialism* (Bloomington: Indiana University Press).

Breman, J. G. (2001), "The Ears of the Hippopotamus: Manifestations, Determinants, and Estimates of the Malaria Burden." *American Journal of Tropical*

Medicine and Hygiene 64(1/2): 1–11. www.ajtmh.org/ cgi/reprint/64/1_suppl/1-c (accessed June 25, 2007).

Brewer, A. (1990), *Marxist Theories of Imperialism: A Critical Survey*, 2nd ed. (London: Routledge).

Brittan, A. (1989), *Masculinity and Power* (Oxford: Basil Blackwell).

Brocklehurst, H. (2007), "Children and War." In A. Collins (ed.), *Contemporary Security Studies*, 367–382 (Oxford: Oxford University Press).

Brodie, B. (ed.) (1946), *The Absolute Weapon: Atomic Power and World Order* (New York: Harcourt Brace).

Brown, D. (2006), "Study Claims Iraq's 'Excess' Death Toll Has Reached 655,000." *Washington Post*, October 11, A12.

Brown, L. R., and Kane, H. (1995), *Full House: Reassessing the Earth's Population Carrying Capacity* (London: Earthscan).

Brundtland, G. H., et al. (1987), *Our Common Future: Report of the World Commission on Environment and Development* (The Brundtland Report) (Oxford: Oxford University Press).

Bull, H. (1977), *The Anarchical Society: A Study of Order in World Politics* (London: Macmillan).

Bureau of Investigative Journalism (2016), *Get the Data: Drone Wars* (London: Bureau of Investigative Journalism). www.thebureauinvestigates.com/ category/projects/drones/drones-graphs (accessed February 24, 2016).

Buvinic, M. (1997), "Women in Poverty: A New Global Underclass," *Foreign Policy* 108: 38–53.

Buzan, B. (1991), *People, State & Fear: An Agenda for International Security Studies in the Post–Cold War Era*, 2nd ed. (Hertfordshire, UK: Harvester Wheatsheaf; first published in 1983).

Calleo, D. (1982), *The Imperious Economy* (Cambridge, MA: Harvard University Press).

Cammack, P. (2002), "The Mother of All Governments: The World Bank's Matrix for Global Governance." In R. Wilkinson and S. Hughes (eds.), *Global Governance: Critical Perspectives* (London: Routledge).

Carver, T. (1996), *Gender Is Not a Synonym for Women* (Boulder, CO: Lynne Rienner).

Castells, M. (2005), "Global Governance and Global Politics," *Political Science and Politics* 38(1): 9–16.

Centers for Disease Control (2005), Fact Sheet: Tuberculosis in the United States, March 17. www.cdc.gov/tb/pubs/ TBfactsheets.htm (accessed June 25, 2007).

Chalk, P. (1996), *West European Terrorism and Counter-Terrorism: The Evolving Dynamic* (New York: St. Martin's Press).

Ching, F. (1999), "Social Impact of the Regional Financial Crisis." In L. Y. C. Lim, F. Ching, and B. M. Villegas (eds.), *The Asian Economic Crisis: Policy Choices, Social Consequences and the Philippine Case* (New York: Asia Society). www.asiasociety.org/publications/update_ crisis_ching.html (accessed June 25, 2007).

Christensen, T., Jørgensen, K. E., and Wiener, A. (eds.) (2001), *The Social Construction of Europe* (London: Sage).

Clark, I. (1980), *Reform and Resistance in the International Order* (Cambridge, UK: Cambridge University Press).

Clark, I. (1989), *The Hierarchy of States: Reform and Resistance in the International Order* (Cambridge, UK: Cambridge University Press).

Coglianese, C. (2000), "Globalization and the Design of International Institutions." In J. S. Nye and D. Donahue (eds.), *Governance in a Globalizing World*, 297–318 (Washington, DC: Brookings Institution Press).

Cohn, C. (1987), "Sex and Death in the Rational World of Defense Intellectuals," *Signs* 12(4): 687–718.

Collier, P. (2018), *The Future of Capitalism: Facing The New Anxieties* (New York: Harper Collins).

Collins, P., and Bilge, S. (2016), *Intersectionality* (Malden, MA: Polity Press)

Connell, R. W. (1995), *Masculinities* (London: Routledge).

Cooper, A., Higgott, R., and Nossal, K. R. (1993), *Relocating Middle Powers* (Vancouver: University of British Columbia Press).

Cooper, R. (2000), *The Breaking of Nations: Order and Chaos in the 21st Century* (New York: Atlantic Monthly Press).

Council on Foreign Relations (2016), *Global Conflict Tracker* (New York: Council on Foreign Relations). www.cfr .org/global/global-conflict-tracker/p32137#!/conflict/ civil-war-in-syria (accessed February 8, 2016).

Cox, R. (1981), "Social Forces, States and World Orders: Beyond International Relations Theory," *Millennium Journal of International Studies* 10(2): 126–155.

Cox, R. (1989), "Middlepowermanship, Japan, and the Future World Order," *International Journal* 44(4): 823–862.

Crenshaw, M. (ed.) (1983), *Terrorism, Legitimacy, and Power* (Middletown, CT: Wesleyan University Press).

Cronin, A. K. (2002–2003), "Behind the Curve: Globalization and International Terrorism," *International Security* 27(3): 30–58.

Davis, Z. S., and Frankel, B. (eds.) (1993), *The Proliferation Puzzle: Why Nuclear Weapons Spread and What Results* (London: Frank Cass).

Department for International Development (2005), *Fighting Poverty to Build a Safer World* (London: HMSO). www .dfid.gov.uk/pubs/files/securityforall.pdf (accessed June 25, 2007).

Department for International Development (2006), *Eliminating World Poverty: Making Governance Work for the Poor*, Cm 6876 (London: HMSO). www.dfid .gov.uk/pubs/files/whitepaper2006/wp2006section3 .pdf, (accessed June 25, 2007).

Dower, J. W. (2017), *The Violent American Century* (Chicago: Haymarket Books)

Doyle, M. W. (1986), "Liberalism and World Politics," *American Political Science Review* 80(4): 1151–1169.

Doyle, M. W. (1995a), "Liberalism and World Politics Revisited." In C. W. Kegley (ed.), *Controversies in International Relations Theory: Realism and the Neoliberal Challenge*, 83–105 (New York: St. Martin's Press).

Doyle, M. W. (1995b), "On Democratic Peace," *International Security* 19(4): 164–184.

Doyle, M. W. (1997), *Ways of War and Peace: Realism, Liberalism, and Socialism* (New York: W. W. Norton).

Easterly, W. (2002), "How Did Heavily Indebted Poor Countries Become Heavily Indebted? Reviewing Two Decades of Debt Relief," *World Development* 30(10): 1677–1696.

The Economist. (2015), "From Cold War to Hot War," *The Economist*, February 12, 19–22.

Ekins, P. (1992), *A New World Order: Grassroots Movements for Global Change* (London: Routledge).

Elshtain, J. B. (1987), *Women and War* (New York: Basic Books).

Elshtain, J. B., and Tobias, S. (eds.) (1990), *Women, Militarism, and War: Essays in History, Politics, and Social Theory* (Totowa, NJ: Rowman & Littlefield).

Enloe, C. (1989), *Bananas, Beaches and Bases: Making Feminist Sense of International Politics* (London: Pandora Books).

Enloe, C. (1993), *The Morning After: Sexual Politics at the End of the Cold War* (Berkeley: University of California Press).

Enloe, C. (2000), *Maneuvers: The International Politics of Militarizing Women's Lives* (Berkeley: University of California Press).

Environmental Degradation and Conflict in Darfur: *A Workshop Organized by the University of Peace of the United Nations and the Peace Research Institute*, University of Khartoum, December 15–16, 2004.

Falk, R. (1995a), "Liberalism at the Global Level: The Last of the Independent Commissions," *Millennium Special Issue: The Globalization of Liberalism?* 24(3): 563–576.

Falk, R. (1995b), *On Humane Governance: Toward a New Global Politics* (Cambridge, UK: Polity Press).

Falk, R. (2016), *Power Shift: On the New Global Order* (London: Zed Books).

Fanon, F. (1990), *The Wretched of the Earth* (Harmondsworth, UK: Penguin).

Fausto-Sterling, A. (1992), *Myths of Gender: Biological Theories About Women and Men* (New York: Basic Books).

Fausto-Sterling, A. (2000), *Sexing the Body: Gender Politics and the Construction of Sexuality* (New York: Basic Books).

Finnemore, M. (1996a), "Norms, Culture, and World Politics: Insights from Sociology's Institutionalism," *International Organization* 50(2): 325–347.

Finnemore, M. (1996b), *National Interests in International Society* (Ithaca, NY: Cornell University Press).

Finnemore, M., and Sikkink, K. (October 1998), "International Norm Dynamics and Political Change," *International Organization* 52: 887–918.

Finnis, J. (1980), *Natural Law and Natural Rights* (Oxford: Clarendon Press).

Forsythe, D. P. (1988), "The United Nations and Human Rights." In L. S. Finkelstein (ed.), *Politics in the United Nations System* (Durham, NC, and London: Duke University Press).

Fox-Keller, E. (1985), *Reflections on Gender and Science* (New Haven, CT: Yale University Press).

Frank, A. G. (1967), *Capitalism and Underdevelopment in Latin America* (New York: Monthly Review Press).

Freedman, L. (2017), *The Future of War: A History* (New York: Public Affairs).

Friedman, J. (ed.) (2003), *Globalization, the State and Violence* (Oxford: AltaMira Press).

Friedman, T. (2005), *The World Is Flat: A Brief History of the 21st Century* (New York: Farrar, Straus, Giroux).

Fukuyama, F. (1989), "The End of History," *The National Interest* 16 (Summer): 3–18.

Gaddis, J. L. (2004), *Surprise, Security and the American Experience* (Cambridge, MA: Harvard University Press).

Gardner, G. T. (1994), *Nuclear Nonproliferation: A Primer* (London and Boulder, CO: Lynne Rienner).

Gendering Human Security: *From Marginalisation to the Integration of Women in Peace-Building* (Oslo: Norwegian Institute of International Affairs and Fafo Forum on Gender Relations in Post-Conflict Transitions, 2001). www.fafo.no/pub/rapp/352/352.pdf (accessed June 25, 2007).

George, A. (1991), *Forceful Persuasion* (Washington, DC: USIP).

Giddens, A. (2000), *Runaway World: How Globalization Is Shaping Our Lives* (London: Routledge).

Gioseffi, D. (ed.) (2003), *Women on War: An International Anthology of Women's Writings from Antiquity to the Present*, 2nd ed. (New York: Feminist Press at the City University of New York).

Glendon, M. A. (2002), *A World Made New: Eleanor Roosevelt and the Universal Declaration of Human Rights* (New York: Random House).

Goel, V., and Wingfield, N. (2015), "Mark Zuckerberg Vows to Donate 99% of His Facebook Shares for Charity," *New York Times*, December 1, www.nytimes.com/2015/12/02/technology/mark-zuckerberg-facebook-charity.html?_r=1 (accessed February 26, 2016).

Goldstein, J., and Keohane, R. (eds.) (1993), *Ideas and Foreign Policy: Beliefs, Institutions, and Political Change* (Ithaca, NY: Cornell University Press).

Gong, G. W. (1984), *The Standard of "Civilization" in International Society* (Oxford: Clarendon Press).

Goodman, D., and Redclift, M. (1991), *Refashioning Nature: Food, Ecology, and Culture* (London: Routledge).

Gottlieb, R. S. (ed.) (1989), *An Anthology of Western Marxism: From Lukacs and Gramsci to Socialist-Feminism* (Oxford: Oxford University Press).

Gowa, J. (1983), *Closing the Cold Window: Domestic Politics and the End of Bretton Woods* (Ithaca, NY: Cornell University Press).

Grace, C. S. (1994), *Nuclear Weapons: Principles, Effects and Survivability* (London: Brassey's).

Gray, C. S. (1996), "The Second Nuclear Age: Insecurity, Proliferation, and the Control of Arms." In W. Murray (ed.), *The Brassey's Mershon American Defense Annual, 1995–1996: The United States and The Emerging Strategic Environment*, 135–154 (Washington, DC: Brassey's).

Gray, C. S. (1999), "Clausewitz Rules, OK? The Future Is the Past—with GPS," *Review of International Studies* 25: 161–182.

Green, D. (1995), *Silent Revolution: The Rise of Market Economics in Latin America* (London: Latin America Bureau).

Greenwood, B. M., Bojang, K., Whitty, C. J., and Targett, G. A. (2005), "Malaria," *Lancet* 365(9469): 1487–1498.

Gunaratna, R. (2002), *Inside Al Qaeda: Global Network of Terror* (New York: Columbia University Press).

Haass, R. (2008), "The Age of Nonpolarity," *Foreign Affairs* 87(3): 44–56.

Haraway, D. (1989), *Primate Visions: Gender, Race, and Nature in the World of Modern Science* (New York: Routledge).

Haraway, D. (1991), *Symians, Cyborgs, and Women: The Re-Invention of Nature* (New York: Routledge).

Harrington, M. (1989), *Socialism Past and Future* (New York: Arcade Publishing).

Hartsock, N. (1998), *The Feminist Standpoint Revisited and Other Essays* (Boulder, CO: Westview Press).

Hebron, L., and Stack, J. F. (2011), *Globalization* (Boston: Longman).

Held, D. (1993), "Democracy: From City-States to a Cosmopolitan Order?" In D. Held (ed.), *Prospects for Democracy: North, South, East, West*, 13–52 (Cambridge, UK: Polity Press).

Held, D. (1995), *Democracy and the Global Order: From the Modern State to Cosmopolitan Governance* (Cambridge, UK: Polity Press).

Held, D., and McGrew, A. (2002), *Globalization/Anti-Globalization* (Cambridge, UK: Polity Press; 2nd ed., 2007).

Henderson, J., Jackson, K., and Kennaway, R. (eds.) (1980), *Beyond New Zealand: The Foreign Policy of a Small State* (Auckland, New Zealand: Methuen).

Hennessy, R., and Ingraham, C. (eds.) (1997), *Materialist Feminism: A Reader in Class, Difference, and Women's Lives* (London: Routledge).

Hettne, B. (1999), "Globalization and the New Regionalism: The Second Great Transformation." In B. Hettne, A. Intoai, and O. Sunkel (eds.), *Globalism and the New Regionalism* (Basingstoke, UK: Macmillan).

Higgins, R. (1994), *Problems and Process: International Law and How We Use It* (Oxford: Oxford University Press).

Hill, C. (2003), *The Changing Politics of Foreign Policy* (Basingstoke, UK: Palgrave Macmillan).

Hirst, P., and Thompson, G. (1999), *Globalization in Question: The International Economy and the Possibilities of Governance* (Cambridge, UK: Polity Press).

Hoffman, B. (2016), "ISIS Is Here: Return of the Jihadi," *The National Interest* (January–February, digital edition).

Hoffman, S. (1981), *Duties Beyond Borders: On the Limits and Possibilities of Ethical International Politics* (Syracuse, NY: Syracuse University Press).

Holbraad, C. (1984), *Middle Powers in International Politics* (London: Macmillan).

Holsti, K. (1991), *Peace and War: Armed Conflicts and International Order 1648–1989* (Cambridge, UK: Cambridge University Press).

Homer-Dixon, T. (1991), "On the Threshold: Environmental Changes as Causes of Acute Conflict," *International Security* 16: 76–116.

Homer-Dixon, T. (1994), "Environmental Scarcities and Violent Conflict: Evidence from Cases," *International Security* 19(1): 5–40.

Huckerby, J. (2015), "When Women Become Terrorists," *New York Times*, January 21, www.nytimes.com/2015/01/22/opinion/when-women-become-terrorists.html (accessed February 8, 2016).

Hudson, J. (2014), "Congress Approves Arming of Syrian Rebels," *Foreign Policy*. http://foreignpolicy.com/2014/09/18/congress-approves-arming-of-syrian-rebels/ (accessed February 17, 2016).

Hudson, V. (2007), *Foreign Policy Analysis: Classic and Contemporary Theory* (Lanham, MD: Rowman and Littlefield).

Hudson, V., and Leidl, P. (2015), *The Hillary Doctrine: Sex and American Foreign Policy* (New York: Columbia).

Human Rights Watch (2015), *World Report 2015: China: Events of 2014* (New York: Human Rights Watch).

Human Security Report Project (2012), *Human Security Report 2012: Sexual Violence, Education, and War:*

Beyond the Mainstream Narrative (Vancouver: Human Security Press).

Humphreys, M., and Varshney, A. (2004), *"Violent Conflict and the Millennium Development Goals: Diagnosis and Recommendations,"* CGSD Working Paper No. 19 (New York: Center on Globalization and Sustainable Development, The Earth Institute at Columbia University). www.earthinstitute.columbia.edu/cgsd/documents/humphreys_conflict_and_MDG.pdf (accessed June 25, 2007).

Huntington, S. (1993), "The Clash of Civilizations," *Foreign Affairs* 72(3): 22–49.

Huntington, S. (1996), *The Clash of Civilizations and the Remaking of the World Order* (New York: Simon & Schuster).

Hurrell, A., and Woods, N. (1995), "Globalization and Inequality," *Millennium* 24(3): 447–470.

Hymans, J. E. (2006). *The Psychology of Nuclear Proliferation* (Cambridge, UK: Cambridge University Press).

Ikenberry, G. J. (1999), "Liberal Hegemony and the Future of American Post-War Order." In T. V. Paul and J. A. Hall (eds.), *International Order and the Future of World Politics*, 123–145 (Cambridge, UK: Cambridge University Press).

Ingebritsen, C., Neumann, I., Gstohl, S., and Beyer, J. (2006), *Small States in International Relations* (Seattle: University of Washington Press).

Intergovernmental Panel on Climate Change (IPCC) (2007), *Climate Change 2007: The Physical Science BASIS*, Contribution of Working Group 1 to the Fourth Assessment Report of the Intergovernmental Panel on Climate Change. www.ipcc.ch.

International Commission on Intervention and Sovereignty (2001), *The Responsibility to Protect* (Ottawa, Canada: International Development Research Centre).

International Commission on Peace and Food (ICPF) (1994), *Uncommon Opportunities: An Agenda for Peace and Equitable Development* (London: Zed).

Jolly, R., and Ray, D. B. (2006), *National Human Development Reports and the Human Security Framework: A Review of Analysis and Experience* (Brighton: Institute of Development Studies).

Junaid, S. (2005), *Terrorism and Global Power Systems* (Oxford: Oxford University Press).

Kant, I. (1991), *Political Writings*, H. Reiss (ed.) (Cambridge, UK: Cambridge University Press).

Karp, A. (1995), *Ballistic Missile Proliferation: The Politics and Technics* (Oxford: Oxford University Press for Stockholm International Peace Research Institute).

Keck, M., and Sikkink, K. (1998), *Activists Beyond Borders: Transnational Advocacy Networks in International Politics* (Ithaca, NY: Cornell University Press).

Keohane, R. (1984), *After Hegemony: Cooperation and Discord in the World Political Economy* (Princeton, NJ: Princeton University Press).

Keohane, R. (ed.) (1989a), *International Institutions and State Power: Essays in International Relations Theory* (Boulder, CO: Westview Press).

Keohane, R. (1989b), "Theory of World Politics: Structural Realism and Beyond." In R. Keohane (ed.), *International Institutions and State Power: Essays in International Relations Theory* (Boulder, CO: Westview Press).

Keohane, R. (2002a), "The Globalization of Informal Violence, Theories of World Politics, and the 'Liberalism of Fear.'" In R. Keohane (ed.), *Power and Governance in a Partially Globalized World*, 272–287 (London: Routledge).

Keohane, R. (2002b), "The Public Delegitimation of Terrorism and Coalitional Politics." In K. Booth and T. Dunne (eds.), *Worlds in Collision: Terror and the Future of Global Order*, 141–151 (London: Palgrave Macmillan).

Keohane, R., and Nye, J. (eds.) (1972), *Transnational Relations and World Politics* (Cambridge, MA: Harvard University Press).

Kinsella, H. M. (2003), "For a Careful Reading: The Conservativism of Gender Constructivism," *International Studies Review* 5: 294–297.

Kinsella, H. M. (2005a), "Discourses of Difference: Civilians, Combatants, and Compliance with the Laws of War," *Review of International Studies* (Special Issue): 163–185.

Kinsella, H. M. (2005b), "Securing the Civilian: Sex and Gender and Laws of War." In M. Barnett and R. Duvall (eds.), *Power in Global Governance*, 249–272 (Cambridge, UK: Cambridge University Press).

Kinsella, H. M. (2006), "Gendering Grotius: Sex and Sex Difference in the Laws of War," *Political Theory* 34(2): 161–191.

Kirkpatrick, J. (1979), "Dictatorships and Double Standards," *Commentary* 68(5): 34–45.

Kissinger, H. A. (1977), *American Foreign Policy*, 3rd ed. (New York: W. W. Norton).

Knutsen, T. (1997), *A History of International Relations* (Manchester: Manchester University Press).

Koehler, S. (February 7, 2007), "Professor Explains Continuous Threat from Land Mines," *Ozarks Local News.* www.banminesusa.org (accessed June 25, 2007).

Krause, K., and Williams, M. C. (eds.) (1997), *Critical Security Studies: Concepts and Cases* (London: UCL Press).

Laqueur, W. (1996), "Post-Modern Terrorism," *Foreign Affairs* 75(5): 24–37.

Lavoy, P. (1995), "The Strategic Consequences of Nuclear Proliferation: A Review Essay," *Security Studies* 4(4): 695–753.

Leventhal, P., and Alexander, Y. (eds.) (1987), *Preventing Nuclear Terrorism* (Lexington, MA, and Toronto: Lexington Books).

Lind, W. S., et al. (1989), "The Changing Face of War: Into the Fourth Generation," *Marine Corps Gazette* (October): 22–26.

Little, R. (1996), "The Growing Relevance of Pluralism?" In S. Smith, K. Booth, and M. Zalewski (eds.), *International Theory: Positivism and Beyond*, 66–86 (Cambridge, UK: Cambridge University Press).

Longino, H. E. (1990), *Science as Social Knowledge: Values and Objectivity in Scientific Inquiry* (Princeton, NJ: Princeton University Press).

Luard, E. (ed.) (1992), *Basic Texts in International Relations* (London: Macmillan).

MacFarlane, N., and Khong, Y. F. (2006), *Human Security and the UN: A Critical History* (Bloomington: Indiana University Press).

Mackinnon, C. (1993), "Crimes of War, Crimes of Peace." In S. Shute and S. Hurley (eds.), *On Human Rights* (New York: Basic Books).

Mandelbaum, M. (2019), *The Rise and Fall of Peace on Earth* (New York: Oxford).

Marx, K. (1888), "Theses on Feuerbach." In *Selected Works*, K. Marx and F. Engels, 28–30 (London: Lawrence and Wishart, 1968).

Marx, K. (1992), *Capital* (student edition), C. J. Arthur (ed.) (London: Lawrence & Wishart; first published 1867).

Marx, K., and Engels, F. (1848), *The Communist Manifesto*, intr. by E. Hobsbawm (London: Verso, 1998).

Mathews, J. (1997), "Power Shift," *Foreign Affairs* 76(1): 50–66.

McKibben, B. (2019), *Falter: Has the Human Game Begun to Play Itself Out?* (New York: Henry Holt).

Mead, W. R. (2001), *Special Providence: American Foreign Policy and How It Changed the World* (New York: Knopf).

Meadows, D. H., Meadows, D. L., and Randers, J. (1972), *The Limits to Growth* (London: Earth Island).

Mearsheimer, J. (1994–1995), "The False Promise of International Institutions," *International Security* 19(3): 5–49.

Mearsheimer, J. (2001), *The Tragedy of Great Power Politics* (New York: W. W. Norton).

Mearsheimer, J. (2018), *The Great Delusion: Liberal Dreams and International Realities* (New Haven, CT: Yale).

Metz, S. (2004), *Armed Conflict in the 21st Century: The Information Revolution and Post Modern Warfare* (Honolulu: University Press of the Pacific).

Meyer, S. M. (1984), *The Dynamics of Nuclear Proliferation* (Chicago: University of Chicago Press).

Milner, H. V. (1988), *Resisting Protectionism: Global Industries and the Politics of International Trade* (Princeton, NJ: Princeton University Press).

Mingst, K. (2004), *Essentials of International Relations* (New York: W. W. Norton).

Mitrany, D. (1943), *A Working Peace System* (London: RIIA).

Morgenthau, H. J. ([1948], 1955, 1962, 1978), *Politics Among Nations: The Struggle for Power and Peace*, 2nd ed. (New York: Alfred A. Knopf).

Morgenthau, H. J. (1952), *American Foreign Policy: A Critical Examination* (also published as *In Defence of the National Interest*) (London: Methuen).

Morgenthau, H. J. (1960), *Politics Among Nations* (New York: Alfred A. Knopf).

Morgenthau, H. J. (1985), *Politics Among Nations*, 6th ed. (New York: McGraw-Hill).

Mousseau, F., and Mittal, A. (October 26, 2006), Free Market Famine: Foreign Policy in Focus Commentary. www.fpif.org/pdf/gac/0610famine.pdf (accessed June 25, 2007).

Muldoon, J. (2004), *The Architecture of Global Governance: An Introduction to the Study of International Organizations* (Boulder, CO: Westview Press).

Naisbitt, J. (1994), *Global Paradox: The Bigger the World-Economy, the More Powerful Its Smallest Players* (London: Brealey).

Nardelli, A. (2015), "Germany Receives Nearly Half of All Syrian Asylum Applicants." *The Guardian*, November 5, www.theguardian.com/world/2015/nov/05/asylum-applications-to-germany-see-160-rise (accessed February 8, 2016).

Nardin, T. (1983), *Law, Morality and the Relations of States* (Princeton, NJ: Princeton University Press).

National Consortium for the Study of Terrorism and Responses to Terrorism (2015), *Mass-Fatality, Coordinated Attacks Worldwide, and Terrorism in France.* www.start.umd.edu/pubs/START_ParisMassCasualtyCoordinatedAttack_Nov2015.pdf (accessed February 8, 2016).

National Counter Terrorism Center (2005), NCTC Fact Sheet and Observations Related to 2005 Terrorist Incidents. www.NCTC.gov (accessed June 25, 2007).

National Security Strategy (2001, 2002). *National Security Strategy of the United States of America* (Washington, DC: US Government Printing Office).

Norchi, C. (2004), "Human Rights: A Global Common Interest." In Jean Krasno (ed.), *The United Nations: Confronting the Challenges of a Global Society* (Boulder, CO: Lynne Rienner Publishers).

Nussbaum, M. (1996), *For Love of Country: Debating the Limits of Patriotism* (Boston: Beacon Press).

Nye, J. S. (2004), *Soft Power* (New York: Public Affairs).

O'Brien, R. (1992), *Global Financial Integration: The End of Geography* (London: Pinter).

Nye, J. (2020), *Do Morals Matter? Presidents and Foreign Policy From FDR to Trump* (New York: Oxford).

Office of the Director of National Intelligence (2005), Letter from Al-Zawahiri to Al-Zarqawi, October 11.

Ogilvie-White, T. (1996), "Is There a Theory of Nuclear Proliferation?" *The Nonproliferation Review* 4(1): 43–60.

Ogilvie-White, T., and Simpson, J. (2003), "The NPT and Its Prepcom Session: A Regime in Need of Intensive Care," *The Nonproliferation Review* 10(1): 40–58.

Olson, J. S. (ed.) (1988), *Dictionary of the Vietnam War* (New York: Greenwood Press).

Onwudiwe, I. D. (2001), *The Globalization of Terror* (Burlington, VT: Ashgate).

Ougaard, M. (2004), *Political Globalization—State, Power, and Social Forces* (London: Palgrave).

Owens, P. (2007), *Between War and Politics: International Relations and the Thought of Hannah Arendt* (Oxford: Oxford University Press).

Oxfam (2003). "Boxing Match in Agricultural Trade," Briefing Paper No. 32. www.oxfam.org (accessed June 25, 2007).

Oxfam (2006), Grounds for Change: Creating a Voice for Small Farmers and Farm Workers with Next International Coffee Agreement. www.oxfam.org/en/policy/briefingnotes/bn0604_coffee_groundsforchange (accessed June 25, 2007).

Palme Commission (1982), *Common Security: A Programme for Disarmament. The Report of the Palme Commission* (London: Pan Books).

Panofsky, W. K. H. (1998), "Dismantling the Concept of 'Weapons of Mass Destruction,'" *Arms Control Today* 28(3): 3–8.

Pape, R. (2006), *Dying to Win: The Strategic Logic of Suicide Terrorism* (New York: Random House).

Pastor, R. (1999), *A Century's Journey: How the Great Powers Shape the World* (New York: Basic Books).

Pearson, R. (2000), "Rethinking Gender Matters in Development." In T. Allen and A. Thomas (eds.), *Poverty and Development into the Twenty-First Century*, 383–402 (Oxford: Oxford University Press).

Pendergrast, M. (1993), *For God, Country, and Coca-Cola: The Unauthorized History of the Great American Soft Drink and the Company That Makes It* (London: Weidenfeld & Nicolson).

Peters, J. S., and Wolper, A. (eds.) (1995), *Women's Rights, Human Rights: International Feminist Perspectives* (New York: Routledge).

Petzold-Bradley, E., Carius, A., and Vincze, A. (eds.) (2001), *Responding to Environmental Conflicts: Implications for Theory and Practice* (Dordrecht, the Netherlands: Kluwer Academic).

Piketty, T. (2014), *Capital in the Twenty-First Century* (Cambridge, MA: Belknap Press of Harvard University).

Pogge, T. (2002), *World Poverty and Human Rights: Cosmopolitan Responsibilities and Reforms* (Cambridge, UK: Polity Press).

Power and Interest News Report (2006), "Asia's Coming Water Wars," August 22. www.pinr.com (accessed June 25, 2007).

Price, R. (1998), "Reversing the Gun Sights: Transnational Civil Society Targets Land Mines," *International Organization* 52(3): 613–644.

Price, R., and Tannenwald, N. (1996), "Norms and Deterrence: The Nuclear and Chemical Weapons Taboos." In P. J. Katzenstein (ed.), *The Culture of National Security: Norms and Identity in World Politics*, 114–152 (New York: Columbia University Press).

Pugh, M. (2001), "Peacekeeping and Humanitarian Intervention." In B. White, R. Little, and M. Smith (eds.), *Issues in World Politics*, 2nd ed. (London: Palgrave).

Rabasa, A., Chalk, P., et al. (2006), *Beyond al-Qaeda: Part 2, The Outer Rings of the Terrorist Universe* (Santa Monica, CA: RAND).

Rapley, J. (1996), *Understanding Development* (Boulder, CO: Lynne Rienner).

Rehn, E., and Sirleaf, E. J. (2002), Women, War, Peace: The Independent Experts' Assessment on the Impact of Armed Conflict on Women and Women's Role in Peace-Building. www.unifem.org/resources/item_detail.php?ProductID=17 (accessed June 25, 2007).

Reus-Smit, C. (1999), *The Moral Purpose of the State* (Princeton, NJ: Princeton University Press).

Reus-Smit, C. (2001), "The Strange Death of Liberal International Theory," *European Journal of International Law* 12(3): 573–593.

Rhodes, E. (2003), "The Imperial Logic of Bush's Liberal Agenda," *Survival* 45: 131–154.

Rice, S. (2006), "The Threat of Global Poverty," *The National Interest* 83: 76–82.

Richardson, J. L. (1997), "Contending Liberalisms: Past and Present," *European Journal of International Relations* 3(1): 5–33.

Rischard, J. F. (2002), *High Noon: Twenty Global Problems, Twenty Years to Solve Them* (New York: Basic Books).

Roberts, A. (1996), "The United Nations: Variants of Collective Security." In N. Woods (ed.), *Explaining International Relations Since 1945, 309–336* (Oxford: Oxford University Press).

Roberts, A., and Kingsbury, B. (1993), "Introduction: The UN's Roles in International Society Since 1945." In A. Roberts and B. Kingsbury (eds.), *United Nations, Divided World* (Oxford: Clarendon Press).

Roberts, G. (1984), *Questioning Development* (London: Returned Volunteer Action).

Roberts, S. (1994), "Fictitious Capital, Fictitious Spaces: The Geography of Offshore Financial Flows." In S. Corbridge et al. (eds.), *Money, Power and Space* (Oxford: Blackwell).

Roche, D. (1986), "Balance Out of Kilter in Arms/Society Needs," *Financial Post*, January 18, 8.

Rodrik, D. (1999), *The New Global Economy and Developing Countries: Making Openness Work* (Washington, DC: Overseas Development Council, 148).

Rorty, R. (1993), "Sentimentality and Human Rights." In S. Shute and S. Hurley (eds.), *On Human Rights* (New York: Basic Books).

Rosamond, B. (2000), *Theories of European Integration* (Basingstoke, UK: Macmillan).

Rose, G. (1998), "Neoclassical Realism and Theories of Foreign Policy," *World Politics* 51(1): 144–172.

Rosenau, J. (1981), *The Study of Political Adaptation* (London: Pinter Publishers).

Sagan, S. D., and Waltz, K. N. (1995), *The Spread of Nuclear Weapons: A Debate* (New York and London: W. W. Norton; 2nd ed., 2003).

Sageman, M. (2004), *Understanding Terror Networks* (Philadelphia: University of Pennsylvania Press).

Sargent, L. (ed.) (1981), *Women and Revolution: A Discussion of the Unhappy Marriage of Marxism and Feminism* (Boston: South End).

Scholte, J. A. (2005), *Globalization: A Critical Introduction* (Basingstoke, UK: Macmillan; 2nd ed., 2005).

Schwarz, A. (1999), *A Nation in Waiting: Indonesia's Search for Stability* (Sydney, Australia: Allen & Unwin).

Schweller, R. L. (1996), "Neo-Realism's Status-Quo Bias: What Security Dilemma?" *Security Studies* 5: 90–121.

Schweller, R. L. (1998), *Deadly Imbalances: Tripolarity and Hitler's Strategy of World Conquest* (New York: Columbia University Press).

Seidler, V. (1989), *Rediscovering Masculinity: Reason, Language, and Sexuality* (London: Routledge).

Sen, A. (1981), *Poverty and Famines* (Oxford: Clarendon Press).

Sen, A. (1983), "The Food Problem: Theory and Policy." In A. Gauhar (ed.), *South-South Strategy* (London: Zed).

Sen, A. (1999), *Development as Freedom* (Oxford: Oxford University Press).

Shue, H. (1996), *Basic Rights*, 2nd ed. (Princeton, NJ: Princeton University Press).

Simon Fraser University, Human Security Research Group (2011), Human Security Report 2009–2010.

www.hsrgroup.org/human-security-reports/20092010/text.aspx

Singer, P. W., and Friedman, A. (2014), *Cybersecurity and Cyberwar* (New York: Oxford Press)

Slaughter, A-M. (2017), *The Chess Board and the Web: Strategies of Connection in a Networked World* (New Haven, CT: Yale University Press).

Smith, K. E., and Light, M. (eds.) (2001), *Ethics and Foreign Policy* (Cambridge, UK: Cambridge University Press).

Smith, M. J. (1986), *Realist Thought from Weber to Kissinger* (Baton Rouge: Louisiana State University Press).

Smith, M. J. (2002), "On Thin Ice: First Steps for the Ballistic Missile Code of Conduct," *Arms Control Today* 32(6): 9–13.

Smith, S. (1999), "The Increasing Insecurity of Security Studies: Conceptualising Security in the Last Twenty Years," *Contemporary Security Policy* 20(3): 72–101.

Spivak, G. C. (1988), "Can the Subaltern Speak?" In C. Nelson and L. Grossberg (eds.), *Marxism and the Interpretation of Culture* (Basingstoke, UK: Macmillan).

Steans, J. (1998), *Gender and International Relations: An Introduction* (Cambridge, UK: Polity Press).

Stiglitz, J. E. (2018), *Globalization and Its Discontents. Anti-Globalization in the Era of Trump* (New York: Norton)

Suganami, H. (1989), *The Domestic Analogy and World Order Proposals* (Cambridge, UK: Cambridge University Press).

Suhrke, A. (2004), "A Stalled Initiative," *Security Dialogue* 35(3): 365.

Tang, J. H. (ed.) (1994), *Human Rights and International Relations in the Asia-Pacific Region* (London: Pinter).

Tasch, B. (2015), "The 23 Poorest Countries in the World," *Business Insider*, July 13, www.businessinsider.com/the-23-poorest-countries-in-the-world-2015-7 (accessed February 26, 2016).

Thomas, A., et al. (1994), *Third World Atlas*, 2nd ed. (Milton Keynes: Open University Press).

Thomas, C. (2000), *Global Governance, Development, and Human Security* (London: Pluto).

Thomas, C., and Wilkin, P. (2004), "Still Waiting After All These Years: The Third World on the Periphery of International Relations," *British Journal of Politics and International Relations* 6: 223–240.

Thucydides ([1954], 1972), *The Peloponnesian War*, R. Warner (trans.) (London: Penguin).

Tickner, J. A. (1992), *Gender in International Relations: Feminist Perspectives on Achieving Global Security* (New York: Columbia University Press).

Tickner, J. A. (2014), *A Feminist Voyage Through International Relations* (New York: Oxford University Press).

Tow, W. T., and Trood, R. (2000), "Linkages Between Traditional Security and Human Security."

In W. T. Tow, R. Thakur, and In-Taek Hyun (eds.), *Asia's Emerging Regional Order* (New York: United Nations University Press).

UN Conference on Trade and Development, Division on Transnational Corporations and Investment (1996), *Transnational Corporations and World Development* (London: International Thomson Business Press).

UN Conference on Trade and Development (2006a), *Trade and Development Report* (Geneva: United Nations Conference on Trade and Development).

UN Conference on Trade and Development (2006b), *World Investment Report 2006* (Geneva: United Nations Conference on Trade and Development).

UN Conference on Trade and Development (2015), *World Investment Report 2015: Reforming International Investment Governance* (Geneva: United Nations Conference on Trade and Development).

UN Development Programme (1994), *United Nations Human Development Report* (New York: Oxford University Press).

UN Development Programme (1997), *United Nations Human Development Report 1997* (New York: United Nations Development Programme).

UN Development Programme (1998), *United Nations Human Development Report 1998* (Oxford: Oxford University Press).

UN Development Programme (2003), *United Nations Human Development Report* (New York: United Nations Development Programme).

UN Development Programme (2005), *Human Development Report 2005: International Cooperation at a Crossroads* (New York: United Nations Development Programme).

UN Development Programme (2015), *Human Development Report 2015: Work for Human Development* (New York: United Nations Development Programme).

United Nations (2002), *Women, Peace, and Security: Study Submitted by the Secretary-General Pursuant to Security Council Resolution 1325 (2000)* (New York: United Nations). www.un.org/womenwatch/feature/wps (accessed June 25, 2007).

United Nations (2004), *A More Secure World*. UN Secretary-General's High-Level Panel on Threats, Challenges, and Change. www.un.org/secureworld

United Nations (March 2005), *In Larger Freedom: Towards Development, Security and Human Rights for All: Report of the Secretary-General*.

United Nations Framework Convention on Climate Change (2015), *Paris Agreement* (Paris: Conference of the Parties, Twenty-first session).

United Nations High Commissioner for Refugees (2015), *2015 UNHCR Country Operations Profile—Sudan* (New York: United Nations). www.unhcr.org/pages/49e483b76.html (accessed February 8, 2016).

United Nations Inter-Agency Committee on Women and Gender Equality (December 7–8, 1999), *Final Communiqué, Women's Empowerment in the Context of Human Security* (Bangkok: ESCAP). www.un.org/womenwatch/ianwge/collaboration/finalcomm1999.htm (accessed June 25, 2007).

United Nations Peacekeeping (2016), *Peacekeeping Fact Sheet* (New York: United Nations). www.un.org/en/peacekeeping/resources/statistics/factsheet.shtml (accessed February 26, 2016).

University of British Columbia, Human Security Center (2005), *Human Security Report 2005: War and Peace in the 21st Century* (New York: Oxford University Press).

University of British Columbia, Human Security Center (2006), *The Human Security Brief 2006*. www.humansecuritybrief.info (accessed June 25, 2007).

Uppsala Conflict Data Program (UCDP), *Uppsala University, Uppsala, Sweden/Human Security Report Project, School for International Studies*, Simon Fraser University, Vancouver, Canada.

U.S. Department of State (March 31, 2003), *Country Reports on Human Rights Practices, Burma*. www.state.gov/g/drl/rls/hrrpt/2002/18237.htm (accessed June 25, 2007).

Vincent, R. J. (1974), *Nonintervention and International Order* (Princeton, NJ: Princeton University Press).

von Grebmer, K., et al. (2013). "2013 Global Hunger Index—The Challenge of Hunger: Building Resilience to Achieve Food and Nutrition Security. 'Global Hunger Index Scores by Severity' Map" (Bonn, Germany: Welthungerhilfe; Washington, DC: International Food Policy Research Institute; Dublin, Ireland: Concern Worldwide).

Wallace-Wells, D. (2019), *The Uninhabitable Earth: Life After Warming* (New York: Tim Duggan Books).

Wallerstein, I. (1979), *The Capitalist World-Economy* (Cambridge, UK: Cambridge University Press).

Walt, S. (2002), "The Enduring Relevance of the Realist Tradition." In I. Katznelson and H. V. Milner (eds.), *Political Science: The State of the Discipline* (New York: W. W. Norton).

Waltz, K. (1959), *Man, the State and War* (New York: Columbia University Press).

Waltz, K. (1979), *Theory of International Politics* (Reading, MA: Addison-Wesley).

Waltz, K. (1989), "The Origins of War in Neorealist Theory." In R. I. Rotberg and T. K. Rabb (eds.), *The Origin and Prevention of Major Wars*, 39–52 (Cambridge, UK: Cambridge University Press).

Walzer, M. (1977), *Just and Unjust Wars: A Moral Argument with Historical Illustration* (Harmondsworth, UK: Penguin and New York: Basic Books).

Walzer, M. (1994), *Thick and Thin: Moral Argument at Home and Abroad* (Notre Dame, IN: University of Notre Dame Press).

Walzer, M. (1995), "The Politics of Rescue," *Dissent* (Winter): 35–40.

Weaver, O., Buzan, B., Kelstrup, M., and Lemaitre, P. (1993), *Identity, Migration and the New Security Agenda in Europe* (London: Pinter).

Weber, H. (2002), "Global Governance and Poverty Reduction." In S. Hughes and R. Wilkinson (eds.), *Global Governance: Critical Perspectives* (London: Palgrave).

Weber, M. (1949), *The Methodology of the Social Sciences*, E. Shils and H. Finch (eds.) (New York: Free Press).

Weiss, T. G. (2004), "The Sunset of Humanitarian Intervention? The Responsibility to Protect in a Unipolar Era," *Security Dialogue* 35(2): 135–153.

Wendt, A. (1992), "Anarchy Is What States Make of It: The Social Construction of Power Politics," *International Organisation* 46(2): 391–425.

Wendt, A. (1995), "Constructing International Politics," *International Security* 20(1): 71–81.

Wendt, A. (1999), *Social Theory of International Politics* (Cambridge, UK: Cambridge University Press).

Wessel, I., and Wimhofer, G. (eds.) (2001), *Violence in Indonesia* (Hamburg: Abera-Verlag).

Weston, B. H., Falk, R., and D'Amato, A. (1990), *Basic Documents in International Law*, 2nd ed. (St. Paul, MN: West Publishing).

Wheeler, N. J., and Booth, K. (1992), "The Security Dilemma." In J. Baylis and N. J. Rengger (eds.), *Dilemmas of World Politics: International Issues in a Changing World* (Oxford: Oxford University Press).

Wiener, A., and Diez, T. (eds.) (2004), *European Integration Theory* (Oxford: Oxford University Press).

Wilkinson, P. (2003), "Implications of the Attacks of 9/11 for the Future of Terrorism." In M. Buckley and R. Fawn (eds.), *Global Responses to Terrorism* (London: Routledge).

Wood, B. (1998), *The Middle Powers and the General Interest* (Ottawa: North-South Institute).

World Food Programme (2016), *Hunger Statistics* (Rome: World Food Programme). www.wfp.org/hunger/stats (accessed January 28, 2016).

World Health Organization (n.d.), *Roll Back Malaria: The Economic Costs of Malaria* (Geneva: WHO). www.rbm .who.int/cmc_upload/0/000/015/363/ RBMInfosheet_10.htm (accessed June 25, 2007).

World Health Organization (February 2006), Avian Influenza ("Bird Flu")—Fact Sheet. www.who.int/ mediacentre/factsheets/avian_influenza/en (accessed June 25, 2007).

World Trade Organization (1995), *International Trade: Trends and Statistics* (Geneva: WTO).

World Trade Organization (2013), *9th WTO Ministerial Conference, Bali, 2013, Briefing Note: Regional Trade Agreements* (Geneva: WTO).

Wright, R. (1986), *Sacred Rage: The Wrath of Militant Islam* (New York: Simon & Schuster).

Yale University Cambodian Genocide Program. www.yale .edu/cgp

Zakaria, F. (1998), *From Wealth to Power: The Unusual Origins of America's World Role* (Princeton, NJ: Princeton University Press).

Zalewski, M. (1993), "Feminist Standpoint Theory Meets International Relations Theory: A Feminist Version of David and Goliath," *Fletcher Forum of World Affairs* 17: 13–32.

Zalewski, M., and Parpart, J. (eds.) (1998), *The "Man" Question in International Relations* (Boulder, CO: Westview Press).

Zengerle, P., and Lawder, D. (2014), "U.S. Congress Approves Arming Syrian Rebels, Funding Government," *Reuters*. www.reuters.com/article/us-iraq-crisis-congress-vote-idUSKBN0HD2P820140919 (accessed February 17, 2016).

Zevin, R. (1992), "Are World Financial Markets More Open? If So, Why and with What Effects?" In T. Banuri and J. B. Schor (eds.), *Financial Openness and National Autonomy: Opportunities and Constraints* (Oxford: Clarendon Press).

CREDITS

435

FIGURES/MAPS

Chapter 2
Pg. 40: Cartography © Philip's; pg. 44: Cartography © Philip's; pg. 45: Source: The New Humanitarian (https://www.thenewhumanitarian.org/maps-and-graphics/2017/04/04/updated-mapped-world-war); pg. 54: Source: Federation of American Scientists (https://fas.org/issues/nuclear-weapons/status-world-nuclear-forces)

Chapter 5
Pg. 179: "The United Nations System" © United Nations Department of Public Information, 2007; pg. 180: © United Nations; pg. 205: Union of International Associations; pg. 211: *2012 Global Go To Think Tanks Report and Policy Advic. FINAL UNITED NATIONS UNIVERSITY EDITION, JANUARY 28, 2013. Think Tanks and Civil Societies Program © 2012, University of Pennsylvania, International Relations Program*

Chapter 6
Pg. 230: Source: Conventional Arms Transfers to Developing Nations, 2008-2015, PAGE 25.; Pg. 233: Source: Conventional Arms Transfers to Developing Nations, 2008-2015, page 21.; pg. 242: Federation of American Scientists; Nuclear Threat Initiative; pg. 260: New York Times

Chapter 7
Pg. 284: Freedom in the World 2018: Democratic Breakthroughs in the Balance. Selected Data from Freedom House's Annual Survey of Political Rights and Civil Liberties. Freedom House: https://freedomhouse.org/report/freedom-world/freedom-world-2019; pg. 294: UCDP/PRIO

Chapter 8
Pg. 323: Source: Australian Trade Commission and the World Trade Organization, 2015; pg. 327: Source: World Bank; pg. 335: Source: Federal Reserve Bank of St. Louis

Chapter 9
Pg. 353: United Nations, based on data and estimates provided by: Food and Agriculture Organization of the United Nations, Inter-Parliamentary Union, International Labour Organization, International Telecommunication Union, UNAIDS, UNESCO, UN-Habitat, UNICEF, UN Population Division, World Bank, and World Health Organization—based on statistics available as of June 2015. Compiled by Statistics Division, Department of Economic and Social Affairs, United Nations; pg. 359: United Nations Development Programme 2016; pg. 363: ©World Food Programme 2019; pg. 364: Population Reference Bureau

Chapter 10
Pg. 377: Cartography: SASI Group, University of Sheffield; Mark Newman, University of Michigan, 2006 (updated 2008), www.worldmapper.org / Data source: Gregg Marland, Tom Boden, Bob Andres, Oak Ridge National Laboratory. Please note that data for Norway is inaccurate.; pg. 382: Source: Climate Change Facts from the Intergovernmental Panel on Climate Change (IPCC) and the United Nations (https://www.ipcc.ch/sr15/); pg. 397: The International Tanker Owners Pollution Federation Limited; pg. 400: Source: IPCC (2014); Exit EPA Disclaimer based on global emissions from 2010. Details about the sources included in these estimates can be found in the Contribution of Working Group III to the Fifth Assessment Report of the Intergovernmental Panel on Climate Change; pg. 401: https://www.carbonbrief.org/analysis-fossil-fuel-emissions-in-2018-increasing-at-fastest-rate-for-seven-years

INDEX

Page numbers followed by f, m, and t refer to figures, maps, and tables, respectively.

Aarhus Convention, 394
Abe, Shinzō, 10, 195
abortion, 79, 152, 161
absolute gains, 226
Academi (PMF), 236
accountability politics, 208
Acheson, Dean, 48
acid rain, 378, 391
acquiescent strategies, 156
adaptation strategies, 157
Addams, Jane, 116
AEI. *See* American Enterprise
    Institute
AfDB. *See* African Development Bank
Afghanistan
    Al-Qaeda in, 70
    asymmetric conflicts in, 234
    COIN strategy and, 70, 234–235
    as failed state, 129t
    NATO in, 71, 148, 235, 239–240, 265
    poverty and, 367
    Soviet Union and, 49t, 60, 255
    Taliban in, 60, 70, 219, 255
    US forces in, 234
    war on terrorism and, 60, 69
Afghanistan War
    destabilization, 5
    drone warfare in, 238
    neoliberalism and, 99
    Obama and, 60
    Pakistan and, 71
    treatment of prisoners, 147
    US and, 8, 70, 189, 234, 250
    in war on terrorism, 70, 71
Africa. *See also specific countries*
    decolonization in, 43–46, 188,
        274, 276
    desertification, 386
    environmental issues, 379
Africa Emerging Markets Fund, 334
African Climate Conference, 124
African Development Bank
    (AfDB), 313
African Union (AU), 12, 197, 222
Aga Khan International Scholarship
    Foundation, 154, 211

Agenda 21, 394
An Agenda for Peace (Boutros-Ghali), 184
Agent Orange, 386, 389
Age of Discovery, 89
Ahmadinejad, Mahmoud, 247
AI. *See* Amnesty International (AI)
AIIB. *See* Asian Infrastructure
    Investment Bank
air pollution. *See* atmospheric
    pollution
al-Baghdadi, Abu Bakr, 252
Albania, 202
al-Bashir, Omar, 287
Albright, Madeleine, 57, 100
Al Jazeera, 6, 262
Alliance of Small Island States, 402
Allison, Graham, 98, 136, 139
Al-Qaeda
    in Afghanistan, 70
    defined, 253
    drone attacks on, 238
    extremist affiliates of, 254t
    ISIS and, 8, 259–260
    Islamic Caliphate seven-stage
        strategy, 259
    liberalism and, 100
    media communication, 262
    military force against, 265
    9/11 and, 69–70, 250, 253
    religion and, 73
    social media use, 232
    Taliban refuge for, 70
    terrorism by, 8, 253, 259–260
Al-Qaeda Associated Movement
    (AQAM), 253, 254t
Al-Qaeda in the Arabian Peninsula
    (AQAP), 254t
Al-Qaeda in the Indian Subcontinent,
    254t
Al-Qaeda in the Islamic Maghreb
    (AQIM), 254t
Al-Shabaab, 219, 254t
alternative theories. *See* critical
    theories
Amazon region, 68, 397
American Civil War, 38

American Enterprise Institute (AEI), 143t
American exceptionalism, 127
American Revolution, 37
Amnesty International (AI), 14, 104,
    169, 206, 278, 301
Amstutz, Dan, 368
anarchic system, 83, 84, 95, 139
anarchy, 56, 59, 87, 93, 115, 139
Angola, 45, 49t, 52
Annan, Kofi, 187, 298, 302–303
Antarctica, 396
Antarctic Treaty, 386, 386t, 396, 398
anthropocentric view, 387
apartheid, 150
appeasement, 42, 43
Apple, 26
AQAM. *See* Al-Qaeda Associated
    Movement
AQAP. *See* Al-Qaeda in the Arabian
    Peninsula
AQIM. *See* Al-Qaeda in the Islamic
    Maghreb
Arab-Israeli War, 49t, 51
Arab Spring, 9, 24, 60, 130, 283, 295
Arctic Council, 124–125, 397
Argentina, 329, 356
armistice, 41
arms deliveries worldwide, 230f
arms embargo, 150
arms race, 50, 221, 267
arms transfer agreements, 233f
articulation phase of foreign policy,
    142–144, 145f
ASEAN. *See* Association of Southeast
    Asian Nations
Asia. *See also specific regions and
    countries*
    capitalism, 309, 315–316
    decolonization, 43–46, 188,
        274, 276
    economic crisis (1997), 158, 283,
        329
    human rights, 288–289
Asian Development Bank, 152, 313
Asian Infrastructure Investment
    Bank (AIIB), 198, 313, 318t

Asian values, 288–289
asymmetric conflicts, 234, 250
atmospheric pollution, 378, 391, 391, 395, 405. *See also* carbon dioxide emissions; ozone depletion
attractive power, 155
AU. *See* African Union
autocracy, 73
Axworthy, Lloyd, 133, 301
Azerbaijan, 63

Bacevich, Andrew, 123, 235
"Back to the Future" (Mearsheimer), 225
balance of power, 36–39, 84
Baldwin, Richard, 322
Baltic region, 63, 64, 88
Bangkok Declaration, 289
Bangladesh, 394
Bank for International Settlements (BIS), 98, 317, 318*t*, 338
Ban Ki-moon, 176, 345
banks
    bailouts, 310
    foreign policy and, 134, 140
    global economic crisis (2008), 10
    global governance by, 169
    globalization, 312–313, 331–332, 337–338
    investment, 334
    regional development, 313
Barnett, Michael, 19
bartering, 89
Bartholomew (ecumenical patriarch), 124
Basel Committee on Banking Supervision, 338
Beck, Susan, 213
beggar thy neighbor trade policies, 313
Beijing Consensus, 101, 315
Beitz, Charles, 186
Belarus, 63
Belgium, 45, 79
belief systems, as explanation for behavior, 137
Belt and Road project, 130, 306, 307–308, 316
Bentham, Jeremy, 93, 94–95, 273
Berggruen Institute, 143*t*
Berlin blockade, 48, 49*t*
Berlin crisis, 49*t*, 50
Berlin Wall, 55
Bharti Foundation, 211
Biafran Civil War, 203

Biegun, Stephen, 234
bilateral agreements, 152, 195, 308–309, 326
bilateral diplomacy, 95
Bilge, Sirma, 114
Bill and Melinda Gates Foundation, 152, 211, 343, 389
BINGOs. *See* business and industry INGOs
bin Laden, Osama, 60, 69, 72, 115, 250
biodiversity, 203, 392–393
bipolar structure, of Cold War, 46, 55, 177, 248
BIS. *See* Bank for International Settlements
Bismarck, Otto von, 39
Black September, 252
Blackwater (PMF), 236–237
Blair, Dennis, 310
Blair, Tony, 72, 287
blitzkrieg, 42, 43
Bloomberg, Michael, 384, 399
Boko Haram, 219, 220, 222, 254*t*, 277
Bolsonaro, Jair, 68
Bolton, John, 168, 188, 244
Bonn Conference, 384
Bono, 152, 198, 208, 361
"boomerang effect," 260
Booth, Ken, 83
Bosnia, 207
The Bottom Billion (Collier), 118
bounded rationality, 19*t*
Boutros-Ghali, Boutros, 184
Brandt, Willy, 51
Branson, Richard, 210
Brazil, 68, 190, 329
Brazil, Russia, India, China, and South Africa (BRICS countries), 68, 69, 198, 313, 318*t*
Brent Spar incident, 207
Bretton Woods system, 91, 158, 310, 312
Brexit
    agreement, 94
    division over, 61–62, 145
    economic nationalism and, 3, 6, 10, 61–62, 196–197
    globalization and, 7, 81, 127
    Johnson election and, 8
    as nationalist movement, 196–197
    protests, 8, 192
BRICS countries. *See* Brazil, Russia, India, China, and South Africa
Bright, John, 274

Britain. *See* Great Britain
British Royal Society for the Protection of Birds, 380
Brookings Institution, 143*t*, 198
Brown, Gordon, 100, 287
Brown, Jerry, 384
Brundtland Commission, 282, 356, 374
Brussels Convention (1890), 274
Bull, Hedley, 90*t*
Burundi, 174
Bush, George H. W., 54, 55, 58, 137, 154, 208, 285
Bush, George W.
    constructivist language of, 114
    Darfur genocide and, 287
    global war on terror and, 58, 145, 213
    ICBMs support, 148
    Iraq invasion and, 72, 144, 227
    liberalist language of, 94, 100
    neoconservatism and, 188
    9/11 attack reaction, 69, 250
    Predator drone attacks and, 238
    unilateralism and preemptive war, 68
    USAID goals, 152
business and industry INGOs (BINGOs), 205
Buzan, Barry, 136, 223
Byrd-Hagel Resolution, 404

C40, 13
CACM. *See* Central American Common Market
Calleo, David, 311
Cambodia, 49*t*, 65
Cameroon, 220
Canada, 123, 303, 321–322
capacity building, 395
capital controls, 324
capitalism
    in Asia, 309, 315–316
    China and, 66–67, 105, 311, 315–316
    defined, 46
    free trade and, 95, 315–316
    globalization and, 24–25, 351
    imperialism and, 108
    liberal, 27
    Marxism and, 18, 105*t*, 109, 230, 271*t*
    MNCs and, 201
    morality and, 118
    in New World Order, 59
    promotion by US, 58
    terrorism as reaction to, 256

carbon dioxide (CO$_2$) emissions, 373, 377*m*, 399, 401*f*, 404
Carlos the Jackal, 253
Carnegie Endowment for International Peace (CEIP), 143*t*
Carr, E. H., 41, 167
Carson, Rachel, 380, 389
Cartagena Protocol (2000), 392–393
Carter, Jimmy, 52, 53, 406
Carter Doctrine, 52
Castells, Manuel, 13–14
catalysts, middle powers as, 159
CBD. *See* Convention on Biological Diversity
CBRN. *See* chemical, biological, radiological, and nuclear capabilities
CDM. *See* Clean Development Mechanism
CEDAW. *See* Convention on the Elimination of All Forms of Discrimination Against Women
CEIP. *See* Carnegie Endowment for International Peace
celebrity diplomacy, 208–210
cell phones, 26. *See also* social media
Center for American Progress, 143*t*
Center for Strategic and International Studies (CSIS), 152
Central African Republic, 129*t*, 185, 185*t*
Central America, 46, 53, 146. *See also specific countries*
Central American Common Market (CACM), 146
Central American Court of Justice, 146
Central American Integration System (SICA), 146
Central American Peace Conference, 146
CFCs. *See* chlorofluorocarbons
Chad, 129*t*
Chan Zuckerberg Initiative, 210
Charter, UN. *See* UN Charter
Charter of Fundamental Rights, of EU, 275
charter rights, 272
Chávez, Hugo, 68
Chechnya insurgency, 63
chemical, biological, radiological, and nuclear capabilities (CBRN), 150, 243, 247, 276
Chemical Weapons Convention, 276
Cheney, Dick, 70

The Chessboard and the Web: Strategies of Connection in a Networked World (Slaughter), 303
children
    advocacy for, 204, 208–209
    Global March Against Child Labor, 278
    global poverty and starvation, 229, 368
    rights of, 268
    Save the Children, 151, 169, 203, 301
    sex trafficking and violence against, 185
    as soldiers in war, 296
    UNICEF, 301
China. *See also* Belt and Road project
    arms transfers, 233*f*
    as BRICS country, 68, 318*t*
    capitalism and, 66–67, 105, 311, 315–316
    carbon dioxide emissions by, 402–403, 404
    civil war in, 48
    Cold War and, 49*t*, 51
    Communist Party, 65, 105
    cyberwarfare, 149, 315
    economy, 27, 66–67
    expansion into South China Sea, 65, 78
    gray zone tactics of, 236
    human rights, 117, 143–144, 208
    human rights violations, 308
    hybrid war strategy, 236
    influence of, 306
    intellectual property rights disputes, 326
    manufacturing in, 26
    military spending and strength, 17, 66
    nationalism in, 73
    new silk road, 80
    North Korea and, 244
    nuclear weapons, 50, 67, 246
    as P5 member, 103, 178
    power and influence, 57, 66–67, 198
    rejection of liberal order, 77
    Shanghai financial district, 331
    Soviet relations with, 46, 51
    Sudan and, 288
    terrorism and, 255
    trade war with US, 10, 309, 320
    US relations with, 51, 67

    as world leader, 3, 58
    WTO and, 316
chlorofluorocarbons (CFCs), 389–390, 400
Chomsky, Noam, 373
Chrétien, Jean, 301
Christchurch, New Zealand, mass shooting, 9, 24
CITES. *See* Convention on International Trade in Endangered Species
civic nationalism, 127
Civil and Political Rights, Covenant on, 174, 277, 291
civilian casualties, 295–296
civil society, 81, 198–200
civil war
    American, 38
    Biafran, 203
    in China, 48
    in DRC, 219–220, 295
    in Syria, 5, 60, 64, 70, 219, 260, 260*t*, 281
    in ungoverned regions, 266
    in Yemen, 60, 229
clandestine (sleeper) cells, 262
class, 106–107
classical realism, 85*t*, 86–87
Clausewitz, Carl von, 231–232
Clean Development Mechanism (CDM), 401, 402
climate change, 399–406. *See also* Paris Accords
    activism, 375
    defined, 395
    endangered species due to, 393
    ethic tensions due to, 387
    foreign policy, 124–125, 135, 155
    geologic history of, 380–381
    as global factor, 21–22, 124, 161, 378, 380–381, 406
    Intergovernmental Panel on Climate Change, 382*f*, 383*t*, 395–396, 399
    responsibilities for, 404
    threat of, 282, 373–374
    US opposition to action, 10
    wildfires and, 372
Clinton, Hillary, 155, 162–163
Clinton, William "Bill," 58, 94, 208, 285, 288
Clooney, Amal, 300
Clooney, George, 142
CNN effect, 285

CNN Freedom project, 206
CO$_2$ emissions. *See* carbon dioxide emissions
Cobden, Richard, 90*t*, 95, 274
Coca-Cola, 202
coercive diplomacy, 154
Coglianese, Cary, 169
Cohn, Carol, 229
COIN. *See* counterinsurgency strategy
Cold War, 46–54
    acquiescent strategy in, 156
    arms spending after, 55–56
    balance of power, 84
    bipolar structure, 46, 55, 177, 248
    China and, 49*t*, 51
    collective security system and, 97
    conflict, confrontation, and compromise, 49–51
    constructivist view, 114
    crises, 49*t*, 50
    decolonization and, 43–46
    détente and, 51–54
    effect on global politics, 35
    end of, 4, 11, 47, 157, 221, 228
    in Europe, 47–48, 65
    Germany division during, 48
    global politics during, 73
    hegemony in, 46
    human rights violations, 291
    intelligence organizations growth, 50
    MAD and, 245
    Mearsheimer on, 225
    North Korea and, 49*t*, 65
    nuclear war prevention, 47, 53, 54, 245
    onset of, 47–49
    second, 52–54
    structural realism and, 225
    third world markets, 350
    US hegemony evolution, 58
    war on terrorism and, 54–56, 263
collapsed states. *See* failed states
Collected Works (Marx), 105
collective security, 96–97, 177
Collier, Paul, 118
Collins, Patricia Hill, 114
Colombia, 202, 263, 292
colonialism. *See* decolonization
commerce, globalization of, 262–263
Commission on Sustainable Development (CSD), 379
common security, 282
communication. *See also* social media

globalization and, 9, 23, 24
    by terrorist groups, 262
communism
    in Asia, 45–46, 48–49, 65
    collapse of, 55, 59
    domino theory, 48
    in Latin America, 67–68
    Marx on, 107
    Reagan Doctrine and, 162
    terrorism and, 249, 255
The Communist Manifesto (Marx & Engels), 107
Communist Party
    in China, 67, 105
    in Soviet Union, 54, 109, 228
community
    defined, 224, 348
    epistemic, 199
    security, 224, 227, 280
    survival and, 348
comparative advantage, 84, 85
competitive imperialism, 44*m*
Concert of Europe, 37–38, 84
Conference of Parties (CoP), 381, 382–383, 399, 400, 406
Conference on Security and Co-operation in Europe (CSCE), 294
conflicts, by type, 294*f*
Congress of Vienna (1815), 38, 274
conservation of natural resources, 376–378
constitutional institutions, 173*t*
Constitutional Treaty, 195
constructivists and constructivism, 114–117
    defined, 18
    foreign policy and, 133
    global security view, 227–228
    identity, 338
    international institutions and, 115
    international relations and, 22–23, 105*t*
containment, 48
Contribution to the Critique of Political Economy (Marx), 106
Control Room documentary, 232
Convention Against Torture and Other Cruel, Inhuman or Degrading Treatment or Punishment (1984), 278
Convention Concerning Forced or Compulsory Labor (1930), 274
Convention on Biological Diversity, 392

Convention on International Trade in Endangered Species (CITES), 391
Convention on Long-Range Transboundary Air Pollution, 391
Convention on the Elimination of All Forms of Discrimination Against Women (CEDAW), 277–278, 287
Convention on the Prohibition of the Use, Stockpiling, Production, and Transfer of Anti-Personnel Mines and on Their Destruction. *See* Ottawa Convention
Convention on the Rights of the Child (1989), 209
Cooper, Andrew, 208
Cooper, Robert, 128
Copenhagen Accord, 381, 399, 403
CoPs. *See* Conference of Parties
cosmopolitan culture, 24
cosmopolitan democracy, 27, 103
Costa Rica, 146
Council of Ministers (EU), 194*t*
Council on Foreign Relations, 143*t*
counterinsurgency (COIN) strategy, 70, 234–235
counterterrorism (CT) policy, 235, 263–265
Country Strategy Notes (UN), 191
Court of Auditors (EU), 194*t*
Covenant on Civil and Political Rights, 174, 277, 291
Covenant on Economic, Social and Cultural Rights, 292
COVID-19, 129
Cox, Robert W., 77, 108, 160
Crimea, 78, 148
crimes against humanity, 189, 286, 287–288, 300, 302
criminal and terrorist networks, 212–213
crises. *See also* economic crises; refugees
    Cold War, 49*t*, 50
    COVID-19, 129
    Cuban Missile Crisis, 47, 50, 139
    of globalization, 14
    Suez crisis, 184
critical security, 228–229
critical theories, 104–117, 105*t*
    characteristics of, 109
    constructivism, 114–117

defined, 108
on development, 349*t*, 354–356
feminist theory, 110–114
of global politics, 118
on hunger, 346*t*, 364–366
Marxism, 105–110
on poverty, 346*t*, 347–348
Cronin, Audrey Kurth, 249
cross-border transactions, 319–320
CSCE. *See* Conference on Security and
Co-operation in Europe
CSD. *See* Commission on Sustainable
Development
CSIS. *See* Center for Strategic and
International Studies
CT. *See* counterterrorism policy
Cuba, 67–68, 94, 157
Cuban Missile Crisis, 47, 49*t*, 50, 139
cultural diversity, 73, 97, 338–339
cultural globalization, 7
currency, 323, 330–331
Cyber Quest, 76
cyberwarfare. *See also* hybrid warfare
China and, 315
global security and, 76, 133, 149,
161, 266
incidents, 237*f*
key players, 236*t*
Russia and, 63, 64, 65
Cyprus, 184, 185*t*
Czechoslovakia, 42

DAC. *See* Development Assistance
Committee
Dag Hammarskjöld Foundation, 355
Dalai Lama, 198
Dallaire, Romeo, 269
Darfur
genocide, 135, 287–288, 387
NGOs and, 142
R2P policy and, 303
refugees, 131
UN peacekeeping operations, 185*t*
data governance, 10
Davies, David, 17
decision-making process, 10, 19*t*,
173*t*, 191, 203, 212
Declaration of Principles of
Indigenous Rights, 287
Declaration of the Rights of Man and
of the Citizen, 273
Declaration on the Establishment of a
New International Economic
Order, 314

decolonization
in Asia and Africa, 43–46, 188,
274, 276
Cold War and, 43–46
development and, 349, 350
in Europe, 43
human rights and, 186, 270
Marxism and, 105
process of, 43–46
terrorism and, 249
UN and, 191
deep ecology movement, 387
defensive realism, 88
democracy. *See also* liberal democracy
cosmopolitan, 27, 103
development and, 349, 355–356
human rights and, 100
liberal internationalism and, 91, 93
market, 55
parliamentary, 89, 92
promotion by, 288
security communities and, 227
terrorism and, 255
wars and, 227
in the world, 8, 284*m*
democratic deficit, 103
democratic peace thesis, 94, 227
Democratic Republic of the Congo (DRC),
129*t*, 185*t*, 219–220, 224, 295
Deng Xiaoping, 315
Denmark, 123
dependency theory, 344, 354
DEPP skills, 79–80
deregulation, 324, 351
derivatives, global, 334–335
describe, explain, predict, and
prescribe (DEPP skills), 79–80
desertification, 386
détente, 51–54
development, 348–362. *See also*
orthodox development model;
sustainable development
aid for, 370–371
comparison of approaches, 349*t*
critical alternative approach to,
346*t*, 354–356
Dag Hammarskjöld Foundation on,
355
defined, 348
democracy and, 349, 355–356
failures, 356
human, 280
international economic liberalism,
350–352, 356–362

liberalization and, 323
liberal view, 344
mainstream approach to, 346*t*
modernization theory, 348
protests about, 354–356
realist view, 344
regional diversity, 352
social movements, 354–355
terminology of, 357
TNCs and, 355
Development Assistance Committee
(DAC), 160
Diana (princess), 208
DiCaprio, Leonardo, 210
diffusion of power, 33
diplomacy
bilateral, 95
celebrity, 208–210
coercive, 154
counterterrorist technique, 264
defined, 153
media messaging, 153–154
multilateral, 172
niche, 159–160
nuclear weapons and, 245
preventive, 184, 295
public, 153–154
disarmament, 54, 231, 242, 280
disaster assistance, 151
Dispute Settlement Body process
(WTO), 326
diversity
biodiversity, 203, 392–393
cultural, 73, 97,
338–339
regional, 352
Doctors Without Borders. *See*
Médicins Sans Frontières
Dodge Line, 312
dollarization, 330
domestic attributes, in levels of
analysis, 21, 137–139, 138*t*
domino theory of communism, 48
Doomsday Vault, 388
Douglas, Michael, 210
Doyle, Michael, 94
DRC. *See* Democratic Republic of the
Congo
drones. *See* unmanned aerial vehicles
(UAVs)
drought, 368
drug cartels, 27
Duda, Andrzej, 384
Dunant, Jean Henri, 203

Earth Summits, UN, 378–380, 394, 400

East Asia, 64–67

EBRD. *See* European Bank for Reconstruction and Development

ecocentric view, 387

ecofeminism, 387

ecological footprint, 375

ecologies, 375, 402

Economic, Social and Cultural Rights, Covenant on, 292

economic base, 106

economic crises
  Asia (1997), 158, 283
  in Europe, 5–6
  global crisis (2008–2009), 9–10, 310, 315, 317, 339–340
  globalization and, 4–5, 9–10, 140, 158, 196
  in Greece, 5–6, 61
  in Japan, 57
  in Russia, 62
  as security challenge for US, 310

economic globalization, 5–7, 23, 311–312, 335–339

economic liberalism, 310, 350–352

economic liberalization, 102

economic nationalism, 34

economic rights, 291–293

economic sanctions
  against Britain, 50
  against CFC smugglers and illegal producers, 390
  against China, 308–309, 315
  against Cuba, 68
  defined, 150, 180
  as foreign policy stick, 148, 340
  as gray zone tactic, 76, 266
  against Iran, 60, 150, 244
  against Iraq, 154
  against Japan, 42
  by League of Nations, 96
  against Nicaragua, 68
  against Sudan, 288
  against Turkey, 150
  UN imposition, 150, 168, 180
  US imposition, 50, 60, 148, 150, 154, 188, 243–244, 248, 315
  against Venezuela, 68

economic security, 124, 279

economy. *See also specific countries*
  East Asia, 65–66
  global, 41

human rights aspects, 271t

international peace/security and, 190

Latin America, 329

terrorism and, 256–257

ECOSOC. *See* UN Economic and Social Council

ecosystems, 386

ecotopian tradition, 117, 387, 388

EDF. *See* Environmental Defense Fund

efficiency, crisis of, 14

Egypt
  Arab Spring, 24
  Britain and, 50
  Cold War and, 49t
  influence of, 306
  Israel and, 51
  Muslim Brotherhood in, 60, 61
  Suez crisis, 184

Ehrlich, Paul, 362

Eisenhower, Dwight, 50, 188, 230

electronic commerce, 329

El Paso, Texas, mass shooting, 9, 24

El Salvador, 49t, 146

El-Sisi, Abdel-Fattah, 306

embedded liberalism, 350, 351

emissions trading, 401

empires, 95

endangered species, 391, 393

Engels, Friedrich, 104, 107

enlargement, 59

Enlightenment, 93

Enloe, Cynthia, 112–113

entitlement, 364–366

environment. *See also* climate change; *specific pollution types*
  alternative futures, 407–409
  degradation of, 376–381, 386, 388
  history of, 376–384
  human rights aspects, 272t
  international cooperation and, 390–399
  international relations theory and, 385–388
  specialized agencies for, 378

Environmental Defense Fund (EDF), 91

environmental justice, 15

environmental rights, 394

environmental security, 279

environmental treaties, 391–393, 392t

epistemic communities, 199, 385

EPZs. *See* export processing zones

equity

crisis of, 14

financial, 333

Erdogan, Recep Tayyip, 131

Essay on the Principle of Population (Malthus), 362

Essence of Decision (Allison), 136, 139

ETA. *See* Euzkadi Ta Askatasuna

ethic of responsibility, 82

ethnic cleansing
  cultural explanations of, 253
  environmental impetus for, 387
  human security and, 283
  INGO activism against, 207
  memorials, 273
  NATO actions against, 189, 240
  Nazi death camps, 39
  new wars and, 239
  as R2P crime, 302
  Rohingya ethnic group, 282

ethnic wars in former Yugoslavia, 57, 59

ethnonationalism, 127

ethnonationalist/separatist terrorism, 249

EU. *See* European Union

Europe. *See also specific countries*
  Cold War in, 47–48, 65
  colonialism in, 43–46
  economic crisis in, 5–6
  imperialism and, 45, 73
  Marshall Plan in, 48
  in New World Order, 59–62
  post-Cold War, 57

European Atomic Energy Community, 193

European Bank for Reconstruction and Development (EBRD), 313

European Central Bank, 194t

European Coal and Steel Community, 193

European Commission, 194t

European Commission on Human Rights, 291

European Common Market, 61, 311

European Council, 194t

European Court of Human Rights, 291

European Court of Justice, 194t

European Economic Community, 193

European Parliament, 194t

European Union (EU), 193–197
  aid for refugees, 132
  Brexit and, 61–62, 192
  challenges facing, 61–62

Charter of Fundamental
Rights, 275
defined, 193
as diplomatic leader, 244
as economic leader, 196
for economic prosperity, 34
free trade agreements, 321–322
globalization and, 10
Global Seed Vault and, 388
growth of, 59
institutions of, 194t, 226
integration of, 193–197
Iran nuclear deal and, 243–244
Latin America and, 146
military investment by, 240
as nonstate actor, 12
postmodern states and, 128–129, 230
regional governance and, 160,
193–197
societal security and, 222
Sustainable Development Goals
and, 309
US tariffs on, 150
Euzkadi Ta Askatasuna (ETA), 252
evaluation phase, of foreign policy,
145f, 145–147
Evans, Gareth, 159, 301
exceptionalism, 127
export processing zones (EPZs), 327

Facebook. See social media
facilitators, middle powers as, 159
failed (collapsed) states, 5, 15, 128, 129t,
224, 237–239
fake news, 76
Falk, Richard, 102, 215
Fallows, James, 315
*Falter: Has the Human Game Begun to
Play Itself Out?* (McKibben), 406
family planning, 79, 151–152, 364
famine, 207, 360, 362, 365
FAO. See UN Food and Agriculture
Organization
Farrow, Mia, 117
FDI. See foreign direct investment
Federal Republic of Central America, 146
Feinstein, Dianne, 147
feminism, 110–114
as critical theory, 18, 105t
development perspective, 357
ecofeminism, 387
global security views, 228–230
human rights and, 298–299
realism reformulated, 111t

FFP. See Fund for Peace
FIFA Women's World Cup, 2019, 154
finance. See also economic crises;
global finance
CT control strategy, 264
globalization of, 5–7, 10, 317
money and, 323, 330–331
financial controls, 264
Finland, 123
Fischer, Fritz, 39
Five Star Movement, 7
fixed exchange rates, 323
floating exchange rates, 323
food regime, 366–367
food security, 279, 388
Ford, Henry, 327
Ford Foundation, 211
foreign assistance, 150–152, 151f
foreign direct investment (FDI),
308, 324
foreign exchange, 330
foreign policy, 122–165
acquiescent strategies, 156
adaptation strategies, 157
banks and, 140
climate change, 124–125, 135, 155
constructivism and, 133
definition of, 125, 126–134
diplomatic messaging and media,
153–154
economic welfare, 130
evaluation phase of, 145–147
expectations from, 135–136
foreign assistance, 150–152, 151f
formulation phase of, 144–145
global factors for, 140–141
great-power, 157–159
hard and soft power in, 154–155
Hillary Doctrine, 162–163
humanitarian, 215
implementation phase of, 145
individual/human dimension
factors for, 137
initiation/articulation phase of,
142–144
intransigent, 157
levels of analysis in, 136–141, 137f
makers of, 134
middle-power, 159–160
military and economic tools in,
148–150
national factors for, 137–139
NGOs and, 134
peace and stability, 130

perspectives on, 130–134
phases of, 134, 142–147, 145f
preservative strategy, 156
prestige and, 130
process, 141–147, 145t
promotive, 156
security, 130
small-state, 160–162
states, nationalism, and national
interests in, 126–130
strategies and tools, 147–155
styles, 156–162
systemic factors for,
139–140
territory and resources expansion,
130
think tanks, 142, 211f, 211–212
traditions, 156–162
formulation phase of foreign policy,
144–145, 145f
foundations (organizations), 152, 199,
206, 209, 211, 354–355. *See also
specific foundations*
Fourteen Points speech, of Wilson, 41,
95, 116
FPZs. See free production zones
fragile states, 5, 128, 129t, 224,
237–239
France
colonization by, 45
division of Germany and, 46
in EU, 34
liberalism, 89
Munich Agreement, 42
nuclear weapons and, 50
as P5 member, 103, 178
revolution, 37–38
Rwanda and, 285–286
Suez crisis, 184
Francis (pope), 124, 282
Francis (saint), 215
Franco-Prussian War (1870–1871), 39
Frank, Andre Gunder, 354
Freedman, Lawrence, 231, 266
free production zones (FPZs), 327
free trade
Central American agreements, 146
China and, 10, 315–316
definition, 95
liberalism on, 95, 99–100
neoliberalism on, 98–99
prior informed consent, 391, 394
radical liberalism on, 103
US opposition to G20 action, 10

French Revolution, 37–38
Friedman, Jonathan, 224
Friedman, Milton, 317
Friedman, Thomas, 3, 56
Friends of the Earth, 380
Fuerzas Armadas Revolucionarias de Colombia, 263
functionalism, 97
fundamental institutions, 173t
Fund for Peace (FFP), 241
The Future of War (Freedman), 231, 266
futures, 334, 335

G7. *See* Group of Seven
G8. *See* Group of Eight
G20. *See* Group of Twenty
gains, relative vs. absolute, 226
Galeano, Eduardo, 33
Gandhi, Mahatma, 110, 115
Gates, Bill, 152, 198, 208, 343
Gates, Melinda, 208, 343
GATT. *See* General Agreement on Tariffs and Trade
GDP. *See* gross domestic product
GEF. *See* Global Environmental Facility
Geldof, Bob, 207
gender
     development and, 356, 357
     feminist theory on, 112
     human rights and, 298–299
General Agreement on Tariffs and Trade (GATT), 311, 313–314, 318t, 323, 350, 393. *See also* World Trade Organization
genetically modified organisms (GMOs), 368, 385, 391–393, 394
Geneva Conventions (1926), 274, 294
genocide
     in Darfur, 135, 287–288
     defined, 44
     Holocaust, 39, 42, 43
     as R2P crime, 302
     in Rwanda, 253, 273, 285–286, 387
Genocide Convention (1948), 290
George, Susan, 366
Georgia, 63
Germany
     counterterrorism exercises, 235
     division of, 48
     economic crisis and, 5–6
     as emerging European leader, 3
     EU and, 34, 196
     Green Party, 117

inflation, during Great Depression, 41
refugees and, 6, 132, 145, 280
reunification, 59, 65
Russian energy and, 63
Versailles Treaty violations, 90
World War I and, 39–41, 95
World War II and, 41–42, 43, 83
Germany's Aims in the First World War (Fischer), 39
Ghana, 44
Gillard, Julia, 307
Gladstone, William, 274–275
glasnost, 54
global banking, 312–313, 331–332, 337–338
global campaign politics, 208
global commons, 396–397
Global Crop Diversity Trust, 388
global culture, 24
global economic system, 34, 41, 311–312, 324–325
Global Emergency Response Coalition, 142
Global Environmental Facility (GEF), 202, 394–395
global environmental governance, 375–376
global factors in levels of analysis, 21–22, 138t, 140–141
global finance
     banking, 312–313, 331–332, 337–338
     derivatives, 334–335
     money, 330–331
     securities, 332–335, 335f
     Southern debt, 333–334
Global Fund to Fight AIDS, Tuberculosis and Malaria, 152
global gag rule, 79, 161
global goods, 327–329, 328t, 329t
global governance, 167–217
     about, 167–170
     celebrity diplomacy in, 208–210
     civil society and, 198–200
     criminal/terrorist networks and, 212–213
     defined, 27, 169, 344
     environmental, 375–376
     financial institutions, 317, 318–319t
     by foundations and think tanks, 211–212
     globalization and, 27
     humanitarian foreign policy and, 215

international law, 170–176
     by international nongovernmental organizations, 203–208
     for multinational corporations, 200–202
     peace and security as goal of, 183–190
     regional organizations and, 193–198
     three pillars of, 214
     trade institutions, 317, 318–319t
     uncertainty concerning, 78
     United Nations and, 176–193
global information networks (GINs), 217
globalization
     America First and, 322
     capitalism, 24–25, 351
     of commerce, 262–263
     cosmopolitan culture and, 24
     defined, 4, 223, 341
     dimensions of, 23–28
     drug cartels and, 27
     economic, 4–5
     economic crisis and, 9, 140, 158, 196, 339
     environment and, 375
     foreign policy and, 126
     global culture, 24
     hunger and, 366–368
     hyperglobalists, 7, 56
     interdependence and, 104
     international order and, 56–68
     iPhone and, 26
     Marxist view, 104, 107
     of nationalism, 9
     new wars and, 237–239
     9/11 and, 29
     redefinition of world politics, 303
     risk culture and, 24
     state influenced by, 158
     terrorism and, 28–29
     terrorism as reaction to, 256
     Western imperialism, 25
globalized system, nation-state goals, 33
Global March Against Child Labor, 278
global money, 330–331
global North, 357, 368. *See also* North-South divide
global politics
     defined, 11
     globalization and, 23–24
     international relations and, 11–14

levels of analysis for, 20–22, 22f
research of, 19–23
theories of, 15–20
trends shaping, 8–11
global polity, 24
global securities, 332–335, 335f
Global Seed Vault (Doomsday Vault), 388
global sourcing, 326
global South. *See also* North-South divide
debt, 333–334
environmental issues, 357, 378, 385
food security, 368
marginalization in global economy, 336
terminology, 357
global trade
cross-border transactions, 319–320
liberalization, 368
main trading nations, 323f
major global agencies, 318–319t
monetary system and, 312–316
most-favored nation status, 326
open-border transactions, 321–324
transborder transactions, 324–329
WTO and, 326
Global Trends: Paradox of Progress, 8
Global Trends 2030: Alternative Worlds, 33
global war on terrorism (GWOT), 69–74
challenges to human rights and security, 290, 294
congressional support, 145
counterterrorism and, 235
economic sanctions, 150
enemy in, 253
launch of, 8, 35, 58
law enforcement and, 264
Obama and, 60
positive/negative analysis of, 252f
progress, 249
realist-theory perspective, 250
Global Zero, 245
GMOs. *See* genetically modified organisms
GNP. *See* gross national product
Goalkeepers program and report, 343
gold-dollar standard, 323
Goodall, Jane, 210
Goodman, David, 366
Gorbachev, Mikhail, 54, 228
Gore, Al, 374

government regulated and initiated INGOs (GRINGOs), 205
governments, 11
Grameen Bank, 354
Grandi, Filippo, 159
gray zone tactics. *See* cyberwarfare; hybrid warfare
Great Britain. *See also* Brexit
in Cold War crises, 49t
Concert of Europe and, 38, 84
Egypt and, 50
Iraq War and, 72
liberalism and, 89
nuclear weapons and, 50
as P5 member, 103, 178
Suez crisis, 50, 184
terrorism in, 8
World War I and, 39–41, 95
The Great Convergence (Baldwin), 322
Great Depression, 41, 310
great powers
Concert of Europe, 37, 39
foreign policy and, 157–159
increasing tensions among, 78–79
League of Nations and, 41
P5 members, 178–180
peace among, 73
Greece, 5–6, 61
Green Belt Movement, 393
Green Climate Fund, 384
greenhouse effect, 397
greenhouse gas emissions
in atmosphere, 400f
climate change and, 373–374, 396, 399–403
global, 377m
producers, 401f
reduction targets, 381–384
Green parties, 117
Greenpeace International, 14, 147, 207, 380
Grenada, 53
Grenzschutzgruppe-9, 263
GRINGOs. *See* government regulated and initiated INGOs
gross domestic product (GDP)
defined, 66
development and, 352
growth, 327f
security and, 219
gross national product (GNP), 160
Grotian tradition, 16–18, 133
Grotius, Hugo, 16, 90t, 269
Group of Eight (G8)

activism and, 206
climate change and, 400
description of, 318t
development and, 358
economic globalization and, 317
as great powers, 157
HIPC debt, 333
Group of Seven (G7), 351
Group of Twenty (G20)
defined, 10
description of, 318t
as great powers, 32, 157
India as leader, 128
meetings, 2
Guaidó, Juan, 158
Guantánamo Bay, 83, 250
Guatemala, 146
Guinea, 129t
Gulf War (1990–1991), 99, 225, 285, 386
Guterres, Antonio, 122, 123, 181, 185
GWOT. *See* global war on terrorism

Hague Convention for the Suppression of Unlawful Seizure of Aircraft (1970), 263
Hague Conventions (1907), 274
Haiti, 129t
Haley, Nikki, 168
Hamas, 254t
hard power, 154–155
Harrington, Michael, 104
Havel, Vaclav, 373
HDI. *See* Human Development Index
health security, 279
Heartland Institute, 384
Hedges, Chris, 219
hegemony
contemporary Marxism on, 108
defined, 46
free trade and, 95
great powers and, 157
influence and, 82
liberal, 100–103
Mearsheimer on, 88
military, 148
Soviet, 46
US, 46, 61, 68, 100–102, 164, 188
Held, David, 27, 103
Heritage Foundation, 143t
Heston, Charlton, 210
Hezbollah, 60, 186
Hidalgo, Anne, 13

High-Level Pledging Event for the Humanitarian Crisis in Yemen, 122

Highly Indebted Poor Countries (HIPCs) initiative, 333, 358, 361

High Noon: Twenty Global Problems, Twenty Years to Solve Them (Rischard), 216

Hillary Doctrine, 162–163

Hines, Andrew, 200

HIPCs. *See* Highly Indebted Poor Countries initiative

Hiroshima atomic bomb, 43, 243

historians, global politics and, 20

Hitler, Adolf, 41–42, 96

Hobbes, Thomas, 81

Hoffmann, Bruce, 260

Holocaust, 42, 43

Holy Roman Empire, 36

home-grown terrorism, 9

homogeneity of thought, 24

homosexual rights, 297

Honduras, 146

Hudson, Valerie, 138, 162

Hudson Institute, 143t

human development, 280

Human Development Index (HDI), 358

Human Development Reports, 100, 279, 280, 296

humanitarian activism, history of, 283–291

humanitarian assistance, 151

humanitarian intervention
in 1990s, 284–286
Asian values, 288–289
challenges to universalism and, 286–291
defined, 283
failed, 287–288

human rights. *See also* international human rights legislation
Asia and, 288–289
China and, 208
Cold War violations, 291
during conflict, 293–299
cosmopolitan democracy perspective, 103–104
defined, 272
democracy and, 100
economic consequences, 271t
environment, 272t
foreign policy, 123–124
gender and, 296–299
gendered perspective on, 298–299

Hillary Doctrine, 163
human security and, 268–305
implications of, 271t
international law, 174–175
legislation protecting, 278
national security, 271t
networks, 303
nonintervention and, 174, 274
state sovereignty and, 274–275
UN Security Council and, 175
war on terrorism and, 294
women's rights, 114
worldview comparisons, 271–272t

Human Rights Watch
on children's rights, 209
China's domestic reforms and, 143
on Darfur refugee camps, 288
on ethnic violence, 220
foreign policy evaluation by, 147, 206
as NGO, 97
radical liberalism and, 104

human security
common security, 282
during conflict, 293–299
defined, 186, 279
economic rights and, 291–293
family planning and, 79
feminist views on, 229
human development and, 280
human rights and, 268–305
international community role, 299–303
national security and, 305
NGOs and, 301
origin of concept, 279–280
political rights and, 291–293
refugees and, 131–132, 280–282
United Nations and, 97, 186
war and, 103

Human Security Center, 294

Human Security Report (2009/2010), 295

human trafficking, 206, 212, 213, 297

hunger, 362–368
critical alternative approach to, 346t, 364–366
famine and, 207, 352, 360, 365
food regime, 366–367
global hunger index (2019), 363m
globalization and, 366–368
orthodox approach to, 346t, 362–364
security and, 365–366

The Hunger Machine (George), 366

Huntington, Samuel, 71

Hurd, Douglas, 226

Hussein, Saddam, 54–55, 72, 285, 294

hybrid warfare. *See also* cyberwarfare
avoidance of major war, 266
description of, 148
as four block war, 231
global security and, 76
as new type of warfare, 220, 236
political stability and, 221
Russia and, 227
technology and, 265

hyperglobalists, 7, 56

hyperinflation, 42

hyperpower, 57–58

IAEA. *See* International Atomic Energy Agency

IBFAN. *See* International Baby Food Action Network

IBRD. *See* International Bank for Reconstruction and Development

ICBMs. *See* intercontinental ballistic missiles

ICC. *See* International Criminal Court

Iceland, 232

ICES. *See* International Council for the Exploration of the Seas

ICISS. *See* International Commission on Intervention and State Sovereignty

ICJ. *See* International Court of Justice

ICRC. *See* International Committee of the Red Cross

IDA. *See* International Development Association

IDB. *See* Inter-American Development Bank

idealism, 17

ideational/ideal interests, 117, 126

identity
crisis of, 14
cultural, 256
defined, 256, 338
foreign policy and, 138
human security and, 296–299
national, 338

IFC. *See* International Finance Corporation

IFG. *See* International Forum on Globalization

IGOs. *See* international governmental organizations

IJM. *See* International Justice Mission

Ikenberry, G. John, 99, 198

ILO. *See* International Labor Organization

IMF. *See* International Monetary Fund

immigration controls, 324

imperialism, 43–46, 44*m*
    capitalism and, 108–110
    defined, 93, 256
    economic, 256
    Europe and, 45, 73
    globalization as, 25
    human rights violations, 290
    World War II and, 43

The Imperious Economy (Calleo), 311

implementation phase of foreign policy, 145, 145*f*

INDCs. *See* intended nationally defined contributions

India
    air pollution in, 395
    arms race and, 221
    as BRICS country, 68, 318*t*
    development-related protests in, 355
    economic success of, 27, 201–202
    as emerging economic player, 3
    G20 and, 316
    IJM and, 206
    intellectual property rights disputes, 368
    military spending, 67
    MNC issues in, 201–202
    as modern state, 128
    Nonaligned Movement and, 157
    nuclear weapons, 50, 57, 67, 71, 240–241
    Pakistan rivalry with, 57, 71, 221, 240–241
    poverty, 345
    power and influence, 67, 190, 197
    Russian weapon purchases by, 83
    SCO and, 255
    UN peacekeeping in, 185*t*
    war on terror and, 69

indigenous rights, 287

individual/human dimension, of levels of analysis, 21, 137, 138*t*

Indonesia, 157

INF. *See* Intermediate-Range Nuclear Forces Treaty

Infant Formula Action Coalition, 204

inflation, 41–42, 330

information politics, 206–207

Ingebritsen, Christine, 151, 161

INGOs. *See* international nongovernmental organizations

initiation phase, of foreign policy, 142–144, 145*f*

In Larger Freedom (UN report), 300

Institute for Economics and Peace, 219

institutional theory, 98

integration
    in Central America, 146
    defined, 97
    of EU, 193–197

intellectual property rights
    China-US disputes, 315, 326
    global war on, 212
    India disputes, 368
    TPP and, 321
    trade negotiations on, 158
    USMCA, 68
    WTO enforcement, 311, 319

intelligence organizations, 50, 265

intended nationally defined contributions (INDCs), 403

Inter-American Development Bank (IDB), 202, 313

intercontinental ballistic missiles (ICBMs), 52–54, 148

interdependence
    defined, 97, 320
    globalization and, 5–7, 31, 104, 325

intergovernmental approach in foreign and security policy, 193, 195

intergovernmental organizations, 197, 205, 232, 289

Intergovernmental Panel on Climate Change (IPCC), 382*f*, 383*t*, 395–396, 399

Intermediate-Range Nuclear Forces (INF) Treaty, 54, 99, 245–246

internally displaced persons, 131, 281, 297

International Atomic Energy Agency (IAEA), 78, 244, 247–248

International Baby Food Action Network (IBFAN), 204

International Bank for Reconstruction and Development (IBRD), 312

International Campaign to Ban Landmines, 208, 296

International Centre for Settlement of Investment Disputes, 313

International Civil Aviation Organization, 263

International Commission on Intervention and State Sovereignty (ICISS), 301–302

International Committee of the Red Cross (ICRC)
    foreign policy role, 147
    Geneva Convention of 1864, 175
    human security mission, 301
    as INGO, 203, 205
    Nobel Peace Prize recipient, 203, 207
    Yemen humanitarian crisis and, 123

international community, role in human security, 299–303

International Conference on the Relationship Between Disarmament and Development, 280

International Convention for the Regulation of Whaling, 376

International Convention for the Suppression of the Financing of Terrorism, 264

International Council for the Exploration of the Seas (ICES), 395

International Court of Justice (ICJ), 53, 178, 182–183

International Covenant on Civil and Political Rights, 174, 277, 291

International Criminal Court (ICC), 299–300
    challenges to, 174
    children's rights and, 209
    Darfur genocide, 287
    deterrent effects of, 295
    establishment of, 123, 160
    human rights and, 303
    war crimes and, 175

International Crisis Group, 147, 301

International Day for the Elimination of Violence Against Women (2018), 114

International Development Association (IDA), 312

international economic liberalism, 350–352

International Energy Agency, 404

international environmental cooperation functions, 390–399
    aid and capacity building, 394–395
    environmental regimes, 397–399
    global commons, 396–397
    norm creation, 393–394
    scientific understanding, 395–396
    transboundary trade and pollution control, 391–393

International Finance Corporation (IFC), 312–313

International Forum on Globalization, 15

international governmental organizations (IGOs), 91

international human rights legislation, 275–278
CEDAW, 277–278
Convention Against Torture and Other Cruel, Inhuman or Degrading Treatment or Punishment, 278
enforcement of, 278
International Covenant on Civil and Political Rights, 277
Universal Declaration of Human Rights, 102, 174, 275–277, 278

international institutions, role of, 171–173, 173*t*

International Justice Mission (IJM), 206

International Labor Organization (ILO), 176, 274

international law, 170–176
criticisms of, 174–175
defined, 170
Grotian tradition, 16
history of, 37, 38
human rights and, 174–175
international institutions and organizations, 171–173
reciprocity and, 21, 139
supranational law and, 175–176
violations of, 53
Western bias, 174

International Monetary Fund (IMF)
Asian economic crisis (1997), 158
bilateral agreements through, 152
Bretton Woods system and, 310, 312
China currency valuation, 316
on China-US trade war, 309
currency and, 330
extremist calls for reform of, 58
as global finance actor, 317, 318*t*
globalization and, 10
HIPC initiative, 361
on income inequality, 100
international economic liberalism and, 350
as neoliberal-institutional organization, 98
open-border transactions and, 323
poverty and, 346–347
SDRs, 312, 330–331
as supranational global organization, 176

international nongovernmental organizations (INGOs), 203–208
accountability politics, 208
defined, 198
forms of power, 206–208
global campaign politics, 208
global governance and, 213–214
global hunger and poverty addressed by, 345
growth of, 205*f*
information politics, 206–207
leverage politics, 207
sources of power, 205–206
symbolic politics, 207
transnational advocacy networks and, 199
types of, 205

International Organization of Securities Commissions (IOSCO), 318*t*, 338

international organizations, role of, 171–173, 173*t*

International Partnership against Impunity for the Use of Chemical Weapons, 276

international peace and security maintenance, 183–190

international relations. *See also specific theories*
constructivism and, 22–23, 105*t*
defined, 11
global politics and, 11–14
history of, 35
realism and liberalism with, 250
theories on, 15, 16–17, 79–80

international security, 222–230
climate change and, 124
constructivist views, 227–228
feminist views, 228–230
League of Nations and, 41, 177–178
liberal institutionalist views, 226–227
Marxist views, 230
new challenges, 161
radical liberal views, 230
realist views, 225–226
utopian views, 230
widening school of, 222

International Security Assistance Force (ISAF), 70, 71

International Service for Human Rights (ISHR), 64

International Task Force on Prevention of Nuclear Terrorism, 246–247

International Trade Organization (ITO), 310

International Union for the Conservation of Nature (IUCN), 395

International Whaling Commission (IWC), 376–378

Internet. *See also* social media
terrorism and, 8, 9, 29, 261–262

interparadigm debate, 18

Interpol, 263

intersectionality, 114

Inter-Services Intelligence (ISI), 71

intervention. *See also* humanitarian intervention; nonintervention
defined, 187
NATO mixed motives for, 286
within states, 187–190

intrafirm trade, 327

intransigent foreign policy, 157

InvenSense, 26

IOSCO. *See* International Organization of Securities Commissions

IPCC. *See* Intergovernmental Panel on Climate Change

iPhone, 26

IRA. *See* Irish Republican Army

Iran
after 9/11, 69–70
hybrid war strategy, 236
IAEA and, 78, 244, 247–248
loss as Western ally, 52
nationalism, 73
noncompliance and, 247–248
nuclear weapons of, 60, 78, 99, 150, 157, 221, 241, 243–244, 247
Stuxnet cyber attack on, 149
Syria and, 5
war on terrorism and, 69

Iraq
asymmetric conflicts in, 234
G. W. Bush and invasion of, 144, 227
ISIS in, 8, 60, 258
Kuwait invasion by, 54–55, 97, 137
military technology and, 233
nuclear program, 247–248
PMF role in US-led invasion, 237
post-war violence, 295
war on terrorism and, 69–70

Iraq-Iran War, 184

Iraq War
Britain and, 72
consequences of, 5, 70, 295
drone warfare in, 238

liberalism language for, 100
neoliberal view, 99
9/11 and, 69–70
prisoners, treatment of, 147
US and, 8, 60, 144
Irish Republican Army (IRA), 252
irregular incidence, in economic
globalization, 335–336
ISAF. *See* International Security
Assistance Force
ISHR. *See* International Service for
Human Rights
ISI. *See* Inter-Services Intelligence
ISIS. *See* Islamic State of Iraq and Syria
Islamic Caliphate, 259
Islamic fundamentalism, 60, 69
Islamic State of Iraq and Syria (ISIS),
258–260
attacks blamed on, 8–9, 219, 260m
defeat of, 252
drone warfare against, 238
in Mosul, 258
Obama and, 60
realism vs. liberalism, 78
religion and, 73
social media use, 8, 140, 232, 251
Syrian conflict and, 5, 145
in war on terrorism, 70
women recruits, 297
Israel
Arab-Israeli War, 49t, 51
détente and, 72
Jerusalem as capital, 60
Stuxnet cyber attack by, 149
Suez crisis, 50, 184
UN peacekeeping in, 186
Italy, 7, 42
ITO. *See* International Trade
Organization
IUCN. *See* International Union for the
Conservation of Nature
IWC. *See* International Whaling
Commission

Japan
economic crisis in, 57
economic sanctions for, 42
free trade area with EU, 321
as G20 member, 10
as middle power, 124
NPT and, 66
nuclear attacks on, 243
reconstruction, 312
response to terrorist attacks, 265
Russia and, 65

Tokyo underground attack, 247
Versailles Treaty violations, 90
World War I and, 40
World War II and, 42–43, 91
Jean, Wyclef, 208
Jemaah Islamiyah, 254t
Jenkins, Brian Michael, 248, 252
jihad, 73, 257–258
Johnson, Boris, 8, 94, 196, 276
Joint Comprehensive Plan of Action,
241, 243–244
Joint Implementation, 401
Jolie, Angelina, 208
Jordan, 49t
Juncker, Jean-Claude, 94
"just" war, 249

Kabila, Joseph, 224
Kagame, Paul, 339
Kahn, Herman, 143t
Kaldor, Mary, 237
Kang Kyung-wha, 234
Kant, Immanuel, 16, 22, 90t, 93–94
Kantian tradition, 15, 16–18, 79
Katowice Conference, 384, 405
Kazakhstan, 255
Kennedy, Edward, 204
Kennedy, Paul, 190
Kenya, 57, 301, 303
Keohane, Robert, 97, 98
Keynes, John Maynard, 310
Khrushchev, Nikita, 50
Kim Jong Un, 79, 150, 168, 244
Kirkpatrick, Jeanne, 162
Kissinger, Henry, 4, 51, 82, 215
kleptocracy, 130
knockout blow in war, 266
Knutsen, Torbjørn, 37
Korean War, 48–49, 49t
Kosovo, 185t, 189, 284, 286
Krause, Keith, 228
Kristof, Nicholas, 155
Krulak, Charles, 231
Kuhn, Thomas, 18
Kurds, 5
Kuwait, 54, 97, 137, 233
Kyoto Protocol, 381, 400–403, 404
Kyrgyzstan, 255

landmines, 208, 296, 300, 303
Land O'Lakes, 202
Lashkar-e-Taiba (LeT), 254t
Latin America. *See also specific countries*
baby milk advocacy network, 204
economic crisis of 1994–1995, 329

EU and, 146
globalization and, 67–68
MNCs in, 202
US relations with, 67–68
*Laudato Si: On Care for Our Common
Home* (Pope Francis), 124, 282
law enforcement, 264
LBGTQ rights, 297
LDCs. *See* less developed countries
League of Nations
collapse of, 96
collective security and, 95–96
creation, 41
defined, 41, 177
human rights and, 275
liberalism and, 89
peacekeeping by, 96
purpose, 40
realism and, 90
United States and, 95–96
as UN predecessor, 177
Wilson and, 149
Lebanon, 185t, 186
Le Drian, Jean-Yves, 276
Le Duc Tho, 51
left-wing terrorism, 249
legitimacy, 14, 117
Leidl, Patricia, 162
less developed countries (LDCs), 357
LeT (Lashkar-e-Taiba), 254t
levels of analysis, 20–22
domestic factors, 21, 137–139, 138t
in foreign policy, 136–141, 137f
global factors, 21–22, 138t, 140–141
for global politics, 20–22, 22f
individual/human dimension, 21,
137, 138t
national factors, 21, 137–139
systemic factors, 21, 138t, 139–140
leverage politics, 207
Leviathan (Hobbes), 81
liberal account of rights, 273–274
liberal capitalism, 27
liberal democracy, 18, 41, 42, 50, 62,
99
liberal feminism, 105t, 112
liberal institutionalism, 98–99,
226–227, 385
liberal international economic order
(LIEO), 311
liberal internationalism, 57, 77–78, 91,
93, 100
liberalism, 89–104
core assumptions of, 102t
defined, 18, 89, 92–93

liberalism (*continued*)
democracy and, 18, 41, 42, 50, 62, 99
development perspective, 344, 357
embedded, 350, 351
essential elements of, 93–98
foreign policy and, 133
free trade and, 99
Grotian tradition, 16
history of, 89–91
human rights view, 271–272t
on MNCs, 201
national security view, 223t
neoliberalism, 98–99, 323, 350–352
perspective of, 118
philosophical inadequacies of, 273
of privilege, 99
radical, 100–104
taxonomy of, 90t
universal rights and, 273–274
liberalization, 323, 351, 352, 368
Liberation Tigers of Tamil Eelam, 261, 297
Libya, 24, 53, 239–240, 249, 303
LIEO. *See* liberal international economic order
The Life You Can Save: Acting Now to End World Poverty (Singer), 368
Lim, Darren, 198
Lin, Patrick, 238
Lisbon Treaty, 196
Lithuania, 64, 88
Locke, John, 90t
Loevin, Isabella, 122
Looking at the Sun: The Rise of the New East Asian Economic and Political System (Fallows), 315
Luther, Martin, 36

Maastricht Treaty, 193
Maathi, Wangari, 393
MacArthur Foundation, 211
Machiavelli, Niccolò, 16, 82, 85t, 86
Machiavellian tradition, 16–17, 82
Macron, Emmanuel, 2, 10, 152, 154
MAD. *See* mutually assured destruction
Maduro, Nicolás, 68, 158
Magna Carta (1215), 272
mainstream approach. *See also* orthodox development model
to hunger, 346t, 362–364
to poverty, 346t, 346–347

Malaysia, 45
Mali, 185t
Malthus, Thomas Robert, 362
Man, the State and War (Waltz), 84
managers, middle powers as, 159
Manchester, England, 8
Mandelbaum, Michael, 73, 123
Mao Zedong, 48, 110
marine pollution, 10, 394, 396, 397t, 398
maritime resources, 376–378
market democracies, 55. *See also* liberal democracy
MARPOL, 398
Marshall Plan, 48, 312, 316, 350
Marx, Karl, 33, 104–107, 273
Marxism, 105–110
capitalism and, 18, 105, 109, 230, 271t
class in, 106–107
contemporary, 108
as critical theory, 104
as critical tradition, 16
development perspective, 357
economic base, 106
environmental regime views, 385
on foreign policy, 134
global security view, 230
human rights view, 271t
on MNCs, 201
national security view, 223t
revolutionary, in Asia, 45–46
material interests, 117, 126
materialism, 253
material structure, 227, 228
Mattis, Jim, 70, 231
McKibben, Bill, 406
MDGs. *See* Millennium Development Goals
Meadows, Dennis and Donella, 362
Mearsheimer, John, 85t, 87–88, 157, 159, 225
MEAs. *See* multilateral environmental agreements
media. *See also* social media
as foreign policy tool, 153–154
Médicins Sans Frontières (Doctors Without Borders), 203, 206, 207, 301
megatrends in global politics, 33–34
Melian dialogue (Thucydides), 87, 120
mercantilist approach to economic decision-making process, 310
Merkel, Angela, 2, 132, 195

Mexican Commission for Refugee Assistance, 281
Mexico, 94, 281
Middle East. *See specific countries*
middle powers, 123–124, 159–160
MIGA. *See* Multilateral Investment Guarantee Agency
militarization, 113
military aid, 151
military and economic tools in foreign policy, 148–150, 149f
military force, as CT strategy, 264
military hegemony, 148
military-industrial complex, 230
Millennium Development Goals (MDGs), 190, 191, 209, 345, 348, 353f
Milošević, Slobodan, 286
Mitrany, David, 90t
Mittal, Sunil, 211
Mitterrand, François, 285
MNCs. *See* multinational corporations
mobility, terrorism and, 262–263
modernization theory, 348
modern state, 128–130
Monroe Doctrine, 67, 162
Montenegro, 59, 64
Montreal Protocol, 389–390, 400
morality
capitalism and, 118
ethics and, 83
liberalism and, 89, 255
realism and, 250
A More Secure World: Our Shared Responsibility (UN report), 187, 300
Morgenthau, Hans, 77, 82, 85t, 86, 111t, 130, 132
Morsi, Mohammed, 61
Moses, Marlene, 124
most-favored nation status, 326
Movement for Democratic Change (Zimbabwe), 361
Mugabe, Robert, 360–361
Multidimensional Poverty Index (MPI), 100, 345, 347
multilateral diplomacy, 172
multilateral environmental agreements (MEAs), 391
Multilateral Investment Guarantee Agency (MIGA), 313
multilateralists and multilateralism, 60, 91, 100, 169

multinational corporations (MNCs), 12, 200–202, 206, 314
Munich Agreement (1938), 42
Murad, Nadia, 300
Muslim Brotherhood, 60, 61, 254*t*
mutually assured destruction (MAD), 245
Myanmar. *See* Rohingya ethnic group

Naess, Arne, 387
NAFTA. *See* North American Free Trade Agreement
Nagasaki atomic bomb, 43, 243
Naim, Moises, 212
NAM. *See* Nonaligned Movement
Nansen, Fridtjof, 131
Napoleonic Wars, 37–38
Nardin, Terry, 186
NASDAQ. *See* National Association of Securities Dealers Automated Quotations
Nasser, Gamal Abdel, 50
nation, defined, 12, 13
National Association of Securities Dealers Automated Quotations (NASDAQ), 334
National Consortium for the Study of Terrorism and Responses to Terrorism, 296
national factors in levels of analysis, 21, 137–139
national interests, 80, 125–127, 130–136
nationalism
    current rise of, 77–78
    defined, 127
    economic, 201
    ethnonationalism, 248
    foreign policy and, 127–129
    globalization of, 9, 338–339
    liberal internationalism and, 91, 93
    Marxism and, 45–46
    on MNCs, 201
    in Russia, 62–63
    security competition and, 73
    Trump and, 99
National Military Strategic Plan for the War on Terrorism, 253
national security
    climate change, 124
    concept of, 279
    defined, 222
    humanitarian intervention and, 283
    human rights aspects, 271*t*

human security and, 305
hybrid warfare, 76
nationalism and, 73
nonintervention and, 82
realism and, 132, 188, 222, 223*t*, 225–226
Trump administration, 308–309
worldviews on, 223*t*, 271*t*
national self-determination, 37, 43, 47, 50, 59, 127
nation-states, 12–13, 33, 35, 125
NATO. *See* North Atlantic Treaty Organization
natural disasters, 380–381*t*
natural law, 272
natural resources conservation, 376–378
Nature Conservancy, 202
Nauru, 124
Nazi party, 42
NDB BRICS. *See* New Development Bank BRICS
Nebenzia, Vassily, 166
Nelson Mandela Foundation, 211
neoclassical realists and neoclassical realism, 85*t*, 88–89, 130
neoconservatives and neoconservatism, 69, 70, 72, 188, 255
neoliberal institutionalism, 98
neoliberalism, 98–99, 323, 350–352
neorealism. *See* structural realism
Nestlé, 202, 204
Netanyahu, Benjamin, 243
Netherlands, 79, 116
New America (organization), 143*t*
New Development Bank BRICS (NDB BRICS), 198, 313, 318*t*
New International Economic Order (NIEO), 314
New Start Treaty, 246
new terrorism (postmodern), 213
    defined, 257
    emergence of, 57–58
    jihad, 73
    new wars, 237–239
    religion and, 257–258
new wars concept, 237–239
New World Order, 55, 59–62
NGOs. *See* nongovernmental organizations
Nicaragua, 49*t*, 53, 68, 146
niche diplomacy, 159–160

niches in international system, 156
NIEO. *See* New International Economic Order
Nigeria, 6, 203, 222, 277, 365
9/11 terrorist attacks
    Al-Qaeda role in, 69–70, 250, 253
    bin Laden and, 69
    CBRN capability concerns and, 247
    globalization and, 9, 29
    global war on terrorism and, 58, 69
    Iraq War and, 72
    national security and, 294
    NATO action and, 239
    realist-theory perspective on, 250
    UN Security Council on, 187
Nixon, Richard, 51
Nkrumah, Kwame, 44, 110
NNWS. *See* non-nuclear weapon states
Nobel Peace Prize recipients
    Addams, 116
    Brandt, 51
    Doctors Without Borders, 207
    Friedman, 317
    Gore, 374
    International Campaign to Ban Landmines, 207
    International Red Cross, 203, 207
    Kissinger, 51
    Maathai, 393
    Murad, 300
    Ostrom, 169
    Stiglitz, 309
    Yunus, 354
Nonaligned Movement (NAM), 157
noncompliance, 247
nongovernmental organizations (NGOs), 203–208, 213–214. *See also* international nongovernmental organization
    children's rights and, 209
    defined, 11, 203
    environment and, 375–376, 380
    eradication of hunger and poverty, 365
    foreign policy and, 134
    global hunger and poverty addressed by, 345
    global problem solving, 216–217
    human security and, 301
    initiation/articulation of foreign policy, 142
    mobilization CT strategy, 264
    as nonstate actors, 97

nonintervention
Britain on, 37
defined, 274
human rights and, 274
international law and, 174
realist view on, 82
UN and, 187–190
Universal Declaration of Human
Rights and, 276
non-nuclear weapon states (NNWS),
242, 247
nonpolar world, 155, 161
nonstate actors
aid programs, 152
celebrity diplomacy and, 208–210
civil society and, 198–199
criminal and terrorist networks as,
69, 212–213
defined, 12, 169
foundations as, 152, 199, 206, 209,
211, 354–355
global governance by, 169
INGOs as, 198–199, 203–208,
205*f*, 214
international law and, 175–176
terrorist groups, 251
think tanks as, 142, 211*f*,
211–212
normative orientation, 160
normative theory, 17
norms, 228, 393–394
North American Free Trade
Agreement (NAFTA), 68, 145,
321, 323, 355
North Atlantic Treaty Organization
(NATO)
in Afghanistan, 71, 149, 235,
239–240, 265
aid for refugees, 132
in Baltic states, 88
in Cold War crises, 49*t*
creation, 48
defined, 49, 226
global security and, 226–227
growth of, 59
in Iraq, 149
ISAF mission, 70, 71
Kosovo intervention by, 283, 286
limited area of activities, 59
new roles for, 239–240
nuclear weapons and, 50, 52–54
Resolute Support Mission, 71,
239–240
Russian views of, 64

Northern Ireland, 61
North Korea
Cold War and, 49*t*, 65
Communist Party, 65
hunger in, 368
IAEA and, 78
nuclear weapons of, 65, 78, 79, 136,
141, 148, 150, 157, 168–169, 221,
234, 241, 244, 250
realist view, 250
United States and, 244
UN Security Council sanctions, 150
North-South divide, 336, 344, 366, 402
Norway, 123, 147–148, 303
Notz, Dirk, 373
Nous Toutes collective, 114
NPT. *See* Nuclear Nonproliferation
Treaty
Nuclear Nonproliferation Treaty
(NPT), 50, 66, 240, 246
nuclear proliferation and
nonproliferation, 240–248, 242*m*
nuclear terrorism, 246–247
nuclear war, Cold War prevention of, 47
nuclear weapons
2017 estimated number of, 54*f*
Britain, 50
China, 50, 244, 246
diplomacy and, 241, 245
effects of, 243–244
France, 50
Gorbachev on, 54
increasing, 67
India, 50, 57, 71, 240–241
Iran, 60, 78, 150, 157, 221, 241,
243–244
NATO and, 50, 52–53
North Korea, 65, 78, 79, 136, 141,
148, 150, 157, 168–169, 221, 234,
241, 244, 250
Obama on, 245
Pakistan, 50, 57, 67, 71, 240–241
Reagan on, 52–53, 54
realist view, 245
Russia, 245–246
war and, 266
Nusra Front, 254*t*
Nye, Joseph, 97, 155, 180
Nyerere, Julius, 110

OAS. *See* Organization of American
States
OAU. *See* Organization of African Unity
Obama, Barack

on China economy, 315
Cuba relations with, 68
Hillary Doctrine and, 163
ICBMs and, 148
ISIS and, 145
liberalist language, 94
multilateralism of, 60
on nuclear weapons, 245
open-border transactions and, 321
Predator drone attacks and,
60, 238
public diplomacy of, 153
rules of engagement under, 235
ODECA. *See* Organization of Central
American States
OECD. *See* Organisation of Economic
Co-operation and Development
offensive realism, 87
offshore finance centers, 331
oil spills, 380, 397*t*
oligarchs, 62–63
Olympic games
1972, in Germany, 252
2008, in China, 117
2016, in Brazil, 68
One Campaign, 208
Onuf, Nick, 19
OPEC. *See* Organization of the
Petroleum Exporting Countries
open-border transactions, 321–324
Open Society Foundation, 211
Operational Policy 4.20 on gender, 356
Operation Iraqi Freedom, 100
options (financial markets), 335
Organisation of Economic
Co-operation and Development
(OECD), 160, 317, 318*t*, 319*t*, 338,
404
Organization for Security and
Co-operation in Europe (OSCE),
226, 294
Organization of African Unity (OAU),
197
Organization of American States
(OAS), 12, 197
Organization of Central American
States (ODECA), 146
Organization of the Petroleum
Exporting Countries
(OPEC), 314
Origins of the Second World War
(Taylor), 42
orthodox development model
alternative view vs., 346*t*, 349*t*

criticisms, 356–362
economic development evaluations, 352–354
international economic liberalism, 350–352
responses to critics, 358–362
sustainable development, 356
OSCE. *See* Organization for Security and Co-operation in Europe
Ostpolitik, 51
Ostrom, Elinor, 169
OTC. *See* over-the-counter
Ottawa Convention (1997), 171, 172, 296, 299–300
Ottoman Empire, 37, 275
Our Common Future (UN report), 374
Our World in Data website, 362
outsourcing, 26, 236–237
over-the-counter (OTC) markets, 335
Oxfam International
children's rights and, 209
description of, 346
funding, 151, 206
on natural disasters, 381
as NGO, 97
as nonstate actor, 169
poverty eradication, 365
ozone depletion, 378, 389–390, 396–397, 398–399

P5 (permanent members of UN Security Council), 178–180. *See also* veto power
Pacific Garbage Patch, 394
Pacific Small Island Developing States, 124
Pakistan
Cold War and, 49*t*
drone warfare in, 238
India rivalry with, 57, 71, 221, 240–241
Nonaligned Movement and, 157
nuclear weapons, 50, 67, 71, 240–241
sales tax regime protest, 176
SCO and, 255
UN peacekeeping in, 185*t*
US alliance with, 71
war on terrorism and, 69, 70–71
Palme Commission, 282
Panama, 287
Panetta, Leon, 238
paradigms, 18, 19
paradox, 27–28, 29

Paris Accords, 9–10, 124–125, 156, 244, 374, 381–384, 403–406
Paris Peace Conference (1919), 39, 41
parliamentary democracy, 89, 92
The Parliament of Man (Kennedy), 190
parliaments, women in, 113*t*
Pastor, Robert, 133
patron-client relationships, 67, 156
Pax Americana, 307, 311
peacebuilding, 184, 300. *See also* United Nations
peace enforcement, 184
Peace in Parts (Nye), 180
peacekeeping
in Darfur, 287
defined, 184
in DRC, 220, 224
humanitarian assistance with, 151
human security and, 300
by League of Nations, 96
operations, 185*t*
sexual violence and, 185, 269, 299
UN Security Council and, 166, 180, 287
peacemaking, 184
Peace of Utrecht (1713), 36
Peace of Westphalia (1648), 13, 35, 36–37, 73, 80
peace thesis, democratic, 227
Peloponnesian War, 87, 120
perestroika, 54
permanent members (P5) of UN Security Council, 178–180. *See also* veto power
permanent structured cooperation (PESCO), 240
persistence of territory, 336–337
personality type, as explanation for behavior, 137
personal security, 279
Peru, 261
PESCO. *See* permanent structured cooperation
Pillar, Paul, 263
Pitt, Brad, 208
Plato, 219
Ploumen, Lilianne, 79
pluralism, 72, 73, 97
PMFs. *See* privatized military firms
Poland, Nazi invasion of, 43
polar bears, 393
polarity, 84*f*
poliheuristic theory, 19*t*
political globalization, 7

political nature of war, 232
political realism, 111*t*
political rights, security and, 291–293
Political Risk: How Businesses and Organizations Can Anticipate Global Insecurity (Rice & Zegart), 340
political security, 280
pollution, 376–381. *See also specific types of pollution*
Pompeo, Mike, 124
population, world, 364, 364*t*
Portugal, 45, 372
positivists, 140–141, 144
postconflict peace building, 184
postmodernity, 230
postmodern state, 128–130, 230–231
postmodern terrorism. *See* new terrorism
postmodern war, 236–237
post-Washington Consensus, 351
Potsdam conference, 48
poverty
community and, 347–348
critical alternative approach to, 346*t*, 347–348
defined, 346
global security and, 161
human rights and, 293
inequality and, 345
mainstream approach to, 346*t*, 346–347
persistence of, 314, 344
of third world and women, 345, 347
Poverty and Famines: An Essay on Entitlement and Deprivation (Sen), 365
poverty-reduction strategy (PRS), 351, 354, 356
Powell, Colin, 70, 287
power(s). *See also* great powers; veto power of P5
attractive, 155
balance of, 36–39, 84
China as, 57, 66–67
concept of, 80
defined, 80
diffusion of, 33
in global politics, 118
hard and soft, 66, 125, 154–155
India as, 67
League of Nations, 95–96
middle, 159–160
nation-states shift in, 35

power(s) (*continued*)
polarity, 84*f*
realism and, 80–82
soft, 66
Soviet Union as, 46
superpowers, 43, 44, 156
United States as, 38–39, 46
Power Shift: On the New Global Order
(Falk), 215
precautionary principle, 393–394
premodern state, 128
prescriptions for state survival, 16
preservative strategy, 156
preventive diplomacy, 184, 295
The Prince (Machiavelli), 82
Principle 21, 394
prior informed consent, 391, 394
privatized military firms (PMFs),
236–237
Proactiva Open Arms, 203
problem-solving theory, 108
program aid, 151
project aid, 150
promotive foreign policy, 156
propaganda, 43, 154, 232, 261. *See also*
hybrid warfare
proselytizing, 261–262
prospect theory, 19*t*
protectionism, 10, 84, 86, 320, 320,
322–323, 393
Protestant Reformation, 36
Protocol on Environmental Protection,
398
Proust, Marcel, 3
proxy wars, 46–47, 49*t*. *See also* hybrid
warfare
PRS. *See* poverty-reduction strategy
public diplomacy, 153–154
Public Safety and Terrorism
Sub-Directorate (Interpol), 263
Putin, Vladimir, 63–64, 65, 130, 306

Qaddafi, Muammar, 239, 240, 303
quasi-INGOs (QUANGOs), 205

R2P. *See* Responsibility to Protect
Resolution
radical extremism, 254*t*, 266, 298–299
radical Islamism, 57, 69, 70, 71, 219
radical liberalism, 100–104, 102*t*
deep ecology, 387
on human rights, 271–272*t*
on human security, 79

idealism as, 16, 17
on security, 230
Radiohead, 208
RAM. *See* rational-actor model
Ramaphosa, Cyril, 339
RAND Corporation, 143*t*
rapprochement, 51
rational-actor model (RAM), 136,
142–147, 145*t*, 162
rational choice theory, 19, 19*t*
Reagan, Ronald, 52–54, 63, 79, 94, 406
Reagan Doctrine, 162
realism, 80–89. *See also* structural
realism
assumptions, 79, 80
classical, 85*t*, 86–87
core assumptions of, 102*t*
current rise of, 77–78
defensive, 88
defined, 17, 80
development perspective, 344, 357
environmental regime views, 386
essential elements of, 81–85
foreign policy and, 130–133
global security view, 225–226
human rights view, 271–272*t*
on international law, 173
national security view, 132, 188,
222, 223*t*
neoclassical, 85*t*, 88–89
nuclear arsenal views, 246
offensive, 87
perspective of, 78, 118
political, 111*t*
on power, 81–82
rise of, 17–18
self-help, 83–85
statism, 81–82
survival, 82–83
taxonomy of, 85*t*
types of, 85–89
war on terrorism and, 250
realpolitik, 228
reciprocity, 139, 144
Redclift, Michael, 366
*Refashioning Nature: Food, Ecology, and
Culture* (Goodman & Redclift),
366
refugee camps, 288
refugees
constructivist view, 115
Darfur, 288
Germany and, 6, 145, 280
human security and, 280–282

plight of, 131–132
Syria crisis, 5, 281
UN response, 168
regimes
defined, 170
environmental, 397–399
food, 366–367
international institutions level, 173*t*
regional development banks, 313
regional diversity, 352
regional governance, 160, 193–198, 321
regionalism, 170, 193, 214
regional trade agreements (RTAs), 170,
323
relative gains, 98, 226
religion
gendered perspective on human
rights, 298–299
Muslim clothing ban, 298
new terrorism and, 257–258
religious groups INGOs (RINGOs),
205
religious terrorism, 249
Resolute Support Mission, of NATO,
71, 239–240
Responsibility to Prevent (R2P), 302
Responsibility to Protect Resolution
(R2P), 176–177, 190, 239, 278,
299, 301–303
revolutionary wars, 37–39
revolution in military affairs (RMA),
232–236
Rice, Condoleezza, 188, 250, 340
rice farming, 368
right-wing terrorism, 249
RINGOs. *See* religious groups INGOs
Rischard, J. F., 216–217
The Rise and Fall of Peace on Earth
(Mandelbaum), 73
risk culture, 24
RMA. *See* revolution in military affairs
Rockefeller Foundation, 211, 389
Rohingya ethnic group, 159, 168, 282,
342
Roosevelt, Franklin, 42
Roosevelt, Theodore, 38–39, 67
Rorty, Richard, 290
Rosenau, James, 156
Roser, Max, 362
Rothkopf, David, 266
Rousseau, Jean-Jacques, 84, 85*t*
Rousteing, Olivier, 152
RPF. *See* Rwandan Patriotic Front
RTAs. *See* regional trade agreements

Rugby World Cup (2019), 265
Russia. *See also* Soviet Union
  annexation of Crimea, 78
  arms transfers, 233*f*
  Baltic states and, 64, 65, 88
  as BRICS country, 68, 318*t*
  Chechnya insurgency, 63
  Crimea and, 148
  cyberwarfare, 148
  economic crisis of 1998, 329
  gray zone tactics of, 236
  history, post-Cold War, 62–64
  hybrid war strategy, 236
  influence of, 306
  interference in elections, 64, 65,
    144, 149
  Japan and, 65
  landmines and, 171
  military strength of, 17
  nationalism, 73, 127–128
  North Korea and, 244
  nuclear weapons, 245–246
  as P5 member, 103
  rejection of liberal order, 77
  Syria and, 5, 64
  Ukraine and, 148, 227
  United States and, 63–64, 70
  weapons sales by, 83
  as world leader, 3, 58
Russian Revolution (1917), 47
Russo-Japanese War, 39
Rwandan genocide, 253, 273, 285–286,
  387
Rwandan Patriotic Front (RPF), 285

sabotage. *See* hybrid warfare
sacred terrorism, 249
Sadat, Anwar, 60
Sagan, Scott, 169, 241, 246
Sahnoun, Mohamed, 301
SALT. *See* Strategic Arms Limitation
  Talks
same-sex couples, 297
Samsung, 26
Sánchez, Ilich Ramírez (Carlos the
  Jackal), 253
sanctions, economic. *See* economic
  sanctions
Satellite Sentinel Project, 288
Saudi Arabia
  Afghanistan War and, 49*t*
  Arab Spring, 283
  in G20, 10, 32
  human rights and, 277

Islamic fundamentalism in, 60
  MNCs and, 202
  objections to Universal Declaration
    of Human Rights, 277
  terrorism and, 69
  Yemen civil war and, 122, 124, 229
Saudi Aramco, 202
Sauvy, Alfred, 357
Save the Children, 151, 169, 203, 301
Schengen Agreement, 262
Schwarzenegger, Arnold, 13
Schweller, Randall, 88
scientific understanding of
  environmental issues, 395–396
SCO. *See* Shanghai Cooperation
  Organization
Scotland, 61
SDGs. *See* Sustainable Development
  Goals
SDI. *See* Strategic Defense Initiative
SDRs. *See* Special Drawing Rights
Second Cold War, 52–54
security, 222–230. *See also* human
  security; international security;
  national security
  approaches to, 224–230
  collective, 96–97, 177
  common, 282
  defined, 222, 365
  foreign policy and, 130
  hunger and, 365–366
  of terrorist organizations, 262
  ungoverned territory and, 220
  wealth and, 256
security aid, 151
security community, 224, 227
security dilemma, 83–84, 159, 246
Seleka rebels, 220
self-help, 83–85
Sen, Amartya, 293, 343, 365
September 11, 2001 terrorist attacks.
  See 9/11 terrorist attacks
Serbia, 233, 286
"Sex and Death in the Rational World
  of Defense Intellectuals"
  (Cohn), 229
sexual violence
  as crime against humanity, 297
  peacekeepers and, 185, 269
  in war, 269, 297, 300
SEZs. *See* special economic zones
Shanghai Convention on Combating
  Terrorism, Separatism, and
  Extremism, 255

Shanghai Cooperation Organization
  (SCO), 12, 17, 255–256
shared resource areas, 397
Shaw, George Bernard, 33
She Decides global movement, 79
SICA. *See* Central American
  Integration System
Sierra Club, 380
Silent Spring (Carson), 380, 389
Singer, Peter, 238, 368
skeptics on globalization, 7, 56, 158,
  319–320
SK Hynix, 26
skyjackings, 251
Slaughter, Ann Marie, 303
Slavery Convention (1926), 274
sleeper cells, 262
small-state foreign policy, 160–162
Smith, Adam, 95, 310
"Social Forces, States, and World
  Orders: Beyond International
  Relations Theory" (Cox), 108
socialism, 104, 108–110, 310
social issues and international peace/
  security, 190
social justice, 15
social media
  Arab Spring and, 9
  celebrity diplomacy and, 210
  feminism and, 114
  globalization and, 9, 23, 24
  initiation/articulation of foreign
    policy, 142
  ISIS use of, 8, 140
  Russian interference with US
    elections, 144
  terrorists' use of, 8, 9, 29, 232,
    261–262
  Trump's use of Twitter, 24, 153
social movements, 199, 354–355
social nature of war, 232
social science, 20–22
social structure, 227
Society for Worldwide Interbank
  Financial Telecommunications
  (SWIFT), 332
society of states, 36
soft power, 66, 68, 125, 155
Somalia, 6, 58, 129*t*, 184, 284–285
SOPs. *See* standard operating
  procedures
Soros, George, 198, 307
South Africa
  apartheid, 44, 162

South Africa (*continued*)
as BRICS country, 68
economic boycott of, 150
ICC withdrawal, 174
nuclear weapons, 50–51
objections to Universal Declaration of Human Rights, 276–277
South China Sea, 65, 78
Southeast Asia, 65, 289
South Korea, 26, 49*t*
South Sudan, 6, 129*t*, 185*t*
sovereign equality, 36
sovereignty. *See also* state sovereignty
concept of, 13–14
defined, 13, 82
human rights and, 274–275
Peace of Westphalia and, 36
realist theory and, 79
statism and, 80–82
Soviet Union. *See also* Cold War; Russia
Afghanistan and, 49*t*, 60, 255
Berlin blockade by, 48
in Cold War crises, 49*t*
collapse of, 60
Communist Party of, 109
fragmentation of, 221–222
as global power, 46
objections to Universal Declaration of Human Rights, 277
socialism and, 104
third world and, 52
in World War II, 42
Special Drawing Rights (SDRs), 312, 330–331
special economic zones (SEZs), 327
specialized agencies, 378
sports, 154. *See also* Olympic games
Srebrenica syndrome, 286
Sri Lanka, 80, 249, 261
standard operating procedures (SOPs), 139
standards of civilization, 275
START. *See* Strategic Arms Reductions Treaty
startups, 328
Star Wars (Strategic Defense Initiative), 53
statecraft, 125, 370
state(s)
attention to conditions within, 185–187
concept of, 13
defined, 12, 125

failed, 15, 128, 129*t*, 237–239
fragile, 128, 129*t*
globalization effect on, 158
intervention within, 187–190
modern, 128–130
postmodern, 128–130, 230–231
premodern, 128
society of, 36
survival of, 16, 337–338
types of, 128–130
state sovereignty, 176, 189, 225, 274–275, 293, 301–302
state system, 385
statism, 80–82
Stein, Arthur A., 167
Stiglitz, Joseph, 309, 343
Stockholm Agreement, 123
stock markets, 334, 335
Strait of Hormuz, 58
Strategic Arms Limitation Talks (SALT), 52
Strategic Arms Reductions Treaty (START), 54
Strategic Defense Initiative (SDI), 53
structural realism, 85*t*, 87–89, 225–226
Stuxnet, 148
subversion. *See* hybrid warfare
Sudan, 6, 129*t*, 168, 185*t*. *See also* Darfur
Suez Canal, 50, 184, 218
suicide bombers, 71
Summit of Non-Aligned Nations, 314
superpowers, 43, 44, 57–58, 156
superstructure, 106
supranational global organizations, 176, 195
supranational law, 175–176
supraterritoriality, 325
survival
community and, 348
defined, 348
realism element, 82–83
of the state, in global finance, 337–338
of states, 16
sustainable development
common security and, 282
defined, 356, 378
goals, 9, 358, 359*t*
in mainstream debate, 356–358
NGOs and, 301
UN Peacebuilding Commission and, 300

Sustainable Development Goals (SDGs)
children's rights, 209
country-level actions, 191
EU and, 309
Goalkeepers program, 343
list, 401
response to global problems, 9, 100
as third-generation rights, 275
2030 Sustainable Development Agenda, 191
Svalbard Global Seed Vault, 388–389
Sweden, 79, 122, 123, 161
SWIFT. *See* Society for Worldwide Interbank Financial Telecommunications
Switzerland, 14
symbolic politics, 207
Syria
asymmetric conflicts in, 234
chemical weapons in, 276
civil war, 5, 60, 64, 70–71, 219, 260, 260*t*, 281
Cold War and, 49*t*
drone warfare in, 238
as failed state, 129*t*
refugee crisis, 5, 281
Russia and, 5, 64
UN peacekeeping in, 185*t*
US and EU sanctions, 150
systemic factors in levels of analysis, 21, 138*t*, 139

tactics. *See also* cyberwarfare; hybrid warfare
defined, 232
RMA emphasis on, 233
Taiwan Semiconductor Manufacturing Company, 26
Taiwan Strait, 49*t*
Taliban
in Afghanistan, 257, 265
Al-Qaeda and, 70
in former communist bloc, 255
global security and, 219
liberalist language against, 100
peace talks with, 60, 367
resurgence, 71
TANs. *See* transnational advocacy networks
Tanzania, bombing of US embassy in, 57
Taylor, A. J. P., 41
technical assistance, 151

technology. *See also* cyberwarfare;
intellectual property rights;
social media
initiation/articulation of foreign
policy, 142
military and, 43, 233
technology transfer, 394
terrorism. *See also* Al-Qaeda; global
war on terrorism; Islamic State
of Iraq and Syria; new
terrorism; 9/11 terrorist attacks;
Taliban
civilian casualties, 296
communication and, 262
defined, 57, 224
ethnonationalist/separatist, 249
fragile states as incubators of, 5
globalization and, 28–29, 253–260
home-grown, 9, 24
Internet use and, 8, 9, 29, 261–262
left-wing, 249
mobility, 262–263
nuclear, 246–247
propaganda materials, 261–262
protests against, 257
response to attacks, 265
right-wing, 249
sacred, 249
Sri Lanka attack, 249
Tokyo underground attack, 247
transnational terrorism, 251–258
UN security agenda and, 187
terrorist networks, 212–213
terrorist organizations, security of, 262
Tet offensive, 46
Thatcher, Margaret, 54, 63, 137
theocracy, 72, 73
theory. *See also* critical theories; *specific
theories*
defined, 15–16, 79
global politics, 15–20
international relations, 15, 16–17,
79–80
Theory of International Politics (Waltz),
83
think tanks, 134, 142, 143t, 211f,
211–212
third world
Cold War and, 350–351
common security, 282
debt crisis, 333, 369
development, 348, 350–352
globalization and, 344–345
human security, 294

hunger, 362–364, 366
neoliberalism, 101
population, 364t
poverty, 347
socialism, 108–110
Soviet Union and, 52
terminology, 357
Third World Action Group, 204
Thirty Years' War (1618–1648), 13, 35,
36–37
Thorsson, Inga, 280
Thucydides, 22, 85t, 87, 120
Thunberg, Greta, 375
Tickner, J. Ann, 111t, 229
Tigers of Asia, 27–28
Tito, Marshal, 48
TNCs. *See* transnational corporations
Toshiba, 26
TPP. *See* Trans-Pacific Partnership
trade wars
China-US, 10, 26, 309, 320
fear of, 329
as leverage builder, 150
traditions
defined, 16
ecotopian, 117, 387, 388
foreign policy, 156–162
international relations theory, 16–18,
79, 82, 133
tragedy of the commons, 397
Trail Smelter case, 376
transborder, defined, 325
transborder transactions, 324–329
transboundary pollution, 376, 378,
391–393
transnational actors, 11, 97, 134
transnational advocacy networks
(TANs), 199
transnational corporations (TNCs),
314, 355
transnational social movement
organizations (TSMOs), 199
transnational terrorism, 251–258
cultural explanations, 253–256
economic explanations, 256–257
horrific acts of violence, 265
religion and, 257–258
Trans-Pacific Partnership (TPP), 308,
321
Traub, James, 208
Treaty of Portsmouth, New Hampshire
(1905), 38
Treaty of Versailles (1919), 41, 89,
90, 96

Treaty on European Union, 193
trench warfare, 40, 41
trickle-down theory, 352
Trudeau, Justin, 2
Truman, Harry, 47–48, 188
Truman Doctrine, 48
Trump, Donald
on Afghanistan, 60
America First policies, 8, 127, 309,
322
on climate change, 373
economic nationalism and, 7
election of, 6, 7, 10, 62, 127
foreign aid policy, 79
foreign policy, 99, 145
Iran nuclear deal opposition, 241,
244
on Jerusalem as capital of Israel, 60
Kim Jong Un meetings, 150, 168,
244
NAFTA and, 68
National Security Strategy,
308–309
NATO and, 240
North Korea and, 79, 244
on nuclear weapons, 245–246
Paris Accords withdrawal,
124, 405
rules of engagement under, 235
trade with China, 316
Trans-Pacific Partnership
opposition, 308, 321
Twitter use of, 24, 153
on US-Russia relations,
63–64
war on terrorism and, 70–71
Trusteeship Council, UN, 182
TSMOs. *See* transnational social
movement organizations
Tsvangirai, Morgan, 361
Tunisia, 24, 60
Tupac Amaru Revolutionary
Movement, 261
Turkey, 5, 83, 131
Turkmenistan, 63
Twitter. *See* social media
2030 Sustainable Development
Agenda, 190

UAVs. *See* unmanned aerial vehicles
Ukraine, 63, 78, 148, 227
ul Haq, Mahbub, 280
ultimatum, 154
UN. *See* United Nations

UNCED. *See* UN Conference on Environment and Development
UN Charter (1945)
  defined, 177, 181
  economic sanctions, 180
  on human rights, 175, 189, 275
  negotiation of, 172
  on peacekeeping, 183–184
  rights contained in, 178*t*
  signing of, 191
UN Children's Fund (UNICEF), 151, 176, 182, 301
UN Commission for Conventional Armaments, 243
UN Commission on Human Rights, 278
UN Commission on Sustainable Development, 379
UN Conference on Climate Change. *See* Paris Accords
UN Conference on Environment and Development (UNCED), 355, 378–380
UN Conference on Trade and Development (UNCTAD), 308, 316, 317, 319*t*
underdeveloped countries, 357
UN Development Fund for Women (UNIFEM), 301
UN Development Programme (UNDP)
  creation of, 176
  Global Environmental Facility, 394
  Human Development Reports, 100, 279, 280
  on human security, 300–301
  on income and human poverty, 100, 348
  MPI, 347
  on post-1945 economic decline, 352
  post-Cold War role, 311, 316
UN Economic and Social Council (ECOSOC), 97, 181, 192–193
UN Environment Programme (UNEP), 378, 383, 390, 394, 395, 401
UN Food and Agriculture Organization (FAO), 362, 364, 378
UN Framework Convention on Climate Change (UNFCCC), 381–382, 400, 404
UN General Assembly, 180–181
  defined, 177
  environmental issues, 378
  on humanitarian intervention, 276
  New International Economic Order, 314

Responsibility to Protect Resolution, 176
Universal Declaration on Human Rights, 276
ungoverned regions, 5, 220
UN High Commissioner for Refugees (UNHCR)
  on definition of refugee, 131
  on demographics of refugees, 297
  human security and, 268, 280–282, 301
  on Rohingya crisis, 159, 168
  on Syrian crisis, 168
UNICEF. *See* UN Children's Fund
UNIFEM. *See* UN Development Fund for Women
UN Inter-Agency Committee on Women and Gender Equality, 296–297
UN International Court of Justice (ICJ), 53, 182–183
Union Carbide, in India, 202
United Kingdom. *See* Great Britain
United Nations (UN), 176–193. *See also* peacekeeping; Sustainable Development Goals; *specific agencies, commissions, and conventions*
  aid for refugees from, 132
  collective security of, 177
  creation and structure of, 91, 178–183, 179*f*
  crisis response, 167–168
  Declaration on the Establishment of NIEO, 314
  economic sanctions imposed by, 150, 168, 180
  extremist calls for reform of, 58
  as global actor, 12
  High-Level Pledging Event for the Humanitarian Crisis in Yemen, 122
  history of, 177–178
  international economic liberalism and, 350
  membership growth, 180*f*
  neoconservatism and, 188
  preventive diplomacy, 295
  reform of, 103, 190–193
  role of, 214
  security missions, 232
  on sexual violence, 269
  on state sovereignty, 187

United States (US). *See also specific presidents*
  Afghanistan War and, 5, 70–71, 189, 234, 238
  arms transfers, 233*f*
  China-US relations, 51, 67, 320
  in Cold War crises, 49*t*
  economic sanctions imposed by, 50, 60, 148, 150, 154, 188, 243–244, 248, 315
  entry into World War I, 40
  EU Delegation to, 320–321
  gray zone tactics of, 236
  hegemony, 46, 61, 68, 100–102, 164, 188
  as hyperpower, 57–58
  Iraq War and, 144, 227, 238
  Latin America relations with, 67–68
  League of Nations and, 95–96
  liberalism in, 89
  North Korea and, 244
  as P5 member, 103
  Pakistan and, 71
  Pax Americana and, 307, 311
  refugee crisis and, 281
  Russia and, 64, 65
  securities issued by, 335*f*
  as world power, 38–39, 46
Universal Declaration of Human Rights, 102, 174, 275–277, 278
universalism, 286–291
universities, 134
unmanned aerial vehicles (UAVs), 60, 70, 220, 238
UN Monterrey Conference on Financing for Development, 358
UN Peacebuilding Commission, 187
UN Secretariat, 181
UN Security Council, 178–180
  on 9/11, 187
  on humanitarian intervention, 300
  human rights and, 175
  on nuclear noncompliance, 247
  P5 of, 178–180
  peacekeeping and, 166, 180, 287
  R2P authorizations, 302–303
  reforms, 191–192
  role, 103
  sanction imposition, 150
  veto power, 96, 103, 178, 180, 192
  Western powers and, 174

UN Trusteeship Council, 182
Uruguay Round, 351, 368
US, Mexico and Canada Agreement (USMCA), 68
US Agency for International Development (USAID), 145, 151–152, 163, 202, 389
US Fulbright Program, 154
US Information Agency, 154
US National Intelligence Council, 8, 33
utopianism. *See* radical liberalism

Vedrine, Hubert, 57
Venezuela, 68, 158, 292, 330
venture philanthropy, 210
veto power of P5, 96, 103, 178, 180, 192
Victims Resource Center, 213
Vienna Declaration on Human Rights (1993), 289
Vietnam, 46, 49t, 65, 124, 209, 386
Vietnam War, 46, 51, 97
violence, 265, 295, 297. *See also* sexual violence; terrorism; war

Wales, 61
Walt, Stephen, 88
Waltz, Kenneth, 82, 83, 84, 85t, 87, 88, 140, 241
Walzer, Michael, 186, 290
war. *See also specific wars*
    changing character of, 230–240
    civilian casualties, 295–296
    democracy and, 227
    ecosystems impacted by, 386
    environmental degradation from, 386, 388
    as historical change agent, 232
    "just," 249
    nature of, 231–233
    outsourcing of, 236
    post-Cold War, 73
    postmodern, 236–237
    proxy, 47, 49t
    reasons for going to, 39–40
    RMA and, 233–236
    social and political behavior of, 232
    types of, 294f
    UAV use in, 238
    world, 39–43, 40m, 45m
war crimes, 175, 207, 287, 295, 300, 302
war on terrorism. *See* global war on terrorism

War on Want, 204
Warsaw Pact, 49
Washington Consensus, 101, 315, 344, 351
WBG. *See* World Bank Group
weapons of mass destruction (WMD), 231, 243, 247
weather panic, 381
weather weirding, 381
Weber, Max, 81, 115, 132
Wehrmacht, 43
Weimar Republic, 42
Weiss, Thomas, 284
Wendt, Alexander, 115
Western bias, in international law, 174
Western European Union (WEU), 226
Westoxification, 9
Westphalian system, 56, 126
whaling, 376–378
Wheeler, Nick, 83
White, Harry Dexter, 310
WHO. *See* World Health Organization
widening school of international security, 222
Wight, Martin, 16
wildfires, 68, 372
William J. Clinton Foundation, 211
Williams, Michael C., 228
WILPF. *See* Women's International League for Peace and Freedom
Wilson, Woodrow, 40–41, 90t, 95, 116, 149
WMD. *See* weapons of mass destruction
WMO. *See* World Meteorological Organization
Wolfowitz, Paul, 188
women. *See also* feminism; human trafficking; sexual violence
    as actors in conflicts, 297
    effects of war on, 269
    family planning, 79, 151–152, 364
    Hillary Doctrine, 163
    hunger and, 364
    in parliaments, 113t
    in peacekeeping missions, 297–299
    poverty of, 347
Women in the World Summit, 2017, 155
Women's International League for Peace and Freedom (WILPF), 116

Women's Peace Party (WPP), 116
WOMP. *See* World Order Models Project
Wonder, Stevie, 210
World Bank
    bilateral agreements and, 152
    Bretton Woods system and, 310
    economic sanctions, 150
    extremist calls for reform of, 58
    family planning policies, 364
    Global Environmental Facility, 394
    globalization and, 10
    HIPC initiative, 361
    as neoliberal-institutional organization, 98
    Operational Policy 4.02 on gender, 356
    poverty and, 346–348
    as supranational global organization, 176
World Bank Group (WBG), 312–313, 317, 319t, 350
World Commission on Environment and Development, 282
World Council of Indigenous Peoples, 287
World Cup (Brazil 2014), 68
World Development Movement, 355
World Economic Forum, 339, 375
World Food Programme (WFP), 168
World Health Organization (WHO), 160, 168, 176, 204, 300–301, 311
World Meteorological Organization (WMO), 395
World Order (Kissinger), 4, 215
World Order Models Project (WOMP), 134, 164–165, 215
world population, 364, 364t
World Summit on Sustainable Development (WSSD), 379
World Trade Center, 57, 247
World Trade Organization (WTO)
    China and, 316
    defined, 311
    description of, 319t
    dispute settlement by, 314, 326
    economic globalization and, 317
    extremist calls for reform of, 58
    on GMOs, 385, 391–393
    organizational structure of, 172
    RTAs and, 170
    as supranational global organization, 176

World Vision, 206
World War I
    Britain and, 39–41
    civilian casualties, 295
    Germany and, 39–41
    idealism after, 17
    interdependent economies
        and, 95
    refugees after, 131
    trench warfare, 40
World War II
    civilian casualties, 295
    Germany and, 41–42, 43
    imperialism and, 43
    Japan and, 42–43, 91, 243, 312
    refugees after, 131
world wars, 39–43, 40*m*, 45*m*
World Wildlife Fund for Nature, 380
WPP. *See* Women's Peace Party

WSSD. *See* World Summit on
    Sustainable Development
WTO. *See* World Trade Organization

Xe Services LLC, 236
Xi Jinping, 130, 306, 316

Yalta conference, 48
Yeltsin, Boris, 62–63
Yemen
    civil war, 60, 229, 281
    drone warfare in, 238
    as failed state, 129*t*
    humanitarian crisis, 6, 103, 229
    humanitarian crisis relief, 122, 123
    refugees, 281
    as ungoverned region, 5
Yousafzai, Malala, 277
Yugoslavia (former)

asymmetric conflicts in, 234
ethnic cleansing in, 253
ethnic wars in, 57, 59
fragmentation of, 221–222, 225
independence from Moscow, 48
NATO intervention in, 286
peacekeeping in, 184, 189
refugees from, 132
war crimes in, 175, 207
Yunnus, Mohammad, 354

Zakaria, Fareed, 85*t*
Zegart, Amy, 340
Zimbabwe, 129*t*,
    360–361
Zimbabwe African National Union-
    Popular Front (ZANU-PF),
    360–361
Zuckerberg, Mark, 210